Organizational Behavior and Administration

CASES, CONCEPTS, AND RESEARCH FINDINGS

BY

PAUL R. LAWRENCE, M.B.A., D.C.S. & JOHN A. SEILER, M.B.A., D.B.A.
Professor of Organizational Behavior   *Lecturer on Business Administration*

IN COLLABORATION WITH

JOSEPH C. BAILEY, PH.D., A.M. (hon.)   JAMES V. CLARK, M.B.A., D.B.A.
Professor of Human Relations   *Associate Professor of Business Administration, University of California, Los Angeles*

ROBERT L. KATZ, M.B.A., D.C.S.   LOUIS B. BARNES, M.B.A., D.B.A.
Lecturer on Business Administration, Stanford University   *Associate Professor of Organizational Behavior*

CHARLES D. ORTH, 3rd, M.B.A.   ARTHUR N. TURNER, M.B.A., PH.D.
Lecturer, Assistant Dean and Director of Alumni Programs   *Associate Professor of Business Administration*

EXCEPT AS NOTED, ALL OF
THE GRADUATE SCHOOL OF BUSINESS ADMINISTRATION,
HARVARD UNIVERSITY

1965 · REVISED EDITION

RICHARD D. IRWIN, Inc. and THE DORSEY PRESS

HOMEWOOD, ILLINOIS

REVISED EDITION

First Printing, May, 1965

Second Printing, November, 1965

Third Printing, September, 1966

Fourth Printing, May, 1967

Fifth Printing, November, 1967

Sixth Printing, May, 1968

Seventh Printing, September, 1968

Eighth Printing, June, 1969

Ninth Printing, December, 1969

Tenth Printing, February, 1970

Eleventh Printing, June, 1970

Twelfth Printing, September, 1970

Thirteenth Printing, June, 1971

Fourteenth Printing, June, 1972

Fifteenth Printing, January, 1973

Library of Congress Catalog Card No. 65–17684

PRINTED IN THE UNITED STATES OF AMERICA

To the Original Teachers of Administrative Practices

Professors Learned, Roethlisberger, Hower, Lombard, and Glover

NOTE

The cases presented in this book were prepared to provide a basis for discussion and were not designed as illustrations of either correct or incorrect handling of administrative problems. Every case in this book is based on actual events. All names in the cases have been disguised.

Preface

THIS BOOK is about the way people actually behave in business organizations. It is addressed to those who intend to assume positions of leadership in business organization, in line or staff, at top, bottom, or middle levels of management—all practitioners of the art and science of business management. The book is concerned with helping these people improve their own personal competency in understanding and dealing with the many human problems that arise in complex organizations.

How can we account for some of the stubborn human problems that prevail in many modern organizations? Why are some employees hostile, others apathetic? Why do some people restrict their output? Why are some groups enthused about their work experiences and others completely indifferent? Why are some supervisors so harassed? Why do sales, production, engineering, and other groups often get into persistent costly feuds with each other? Why do superiors so often get "unintended consequences" from issuing some "simple" directions? Why do misunderstandings so often develop betweeen field forces and home office? Under what conditions are you more apt to find collaborative relations between different parts of an organization? In order to find better answers to questions of this kind, this book primarily focuses on the *social* and *organizational* aspects of human behavior. The new section in this revised edition on Individual Behavior and Development has been added to introduce this theme without shifting the book's emphasis on *social* and *organizational* behavior.

What kinds of material are in the book? In the first place the book presents a considerable number of case descriptions of the actual behavior of people in organizations. Many of these cases are new ones that have been prepared since the first edition was published. These cases were not written to demonstrate some point about how people are supposed to act. They were written, instead, with careful attention to reproducing what was actually going on in the situation, no matter how confusing or contradictory some of the facts and events might seem. Of course, these cases do not and could not contain all the relevant facts. But the point is still valid that conscious care was taken to avoid writing them to "prove" some theory of human behavior.

On the other hand, these cases are not presented as if each one were a

vii

completely unique problem to be analyzed *de novo,* with no relation to other cases and the existing knowledge about human behavior. They have been grouped into clusters and given a particular ordering in this book, to help students accumulate and build the simulated experience that the discussion of cases can provide. One case can be used to build on another in a rough but effective kind of inductive learning.

Most of the sections in the book contain cases of several general types: cases that are richly *descriptive* of a pattern of behavior that is commonly seen in industrial organizations in our culture, cases that are designed for *drill* in the use of a conceptual scheme, cases that are fairly complete reports of systematic *research,* cases that present simply the fragmentary symptoms of a problem as it might initially come to the attention of an administrator responsible for taking *action.* Cases of all these types, if carefully analyzed, can provide means both for the accumulation of organizational knowledge and for the acquisition of increasing skill in diagnosing both the general and the unique about every case.

This book also contains what is usually called text material, but of a somewhat unusual kind. Most texts set out to survey all the more widely accepted theories and relevant research in the area. This book deliberately does not do this. Instead it presents a very few conceptual schemes and a limited sample of the findings of research in the field. The several reasons for this policy are important for an understanding of how the book can best be used.

The chief reason arises from the present state of knowledge and theory building in the field of organizational behavior. This field is relatively new as a field of systematic study, and the number of propositions about behavior that have been satisfactorily verified by research is quite small. The importance of the field, however, has attracted many serious investigators who have developed a considerable number of concepts and theories to help explain the behavior they observe. As yet, these theories have not been subject to very vigorous testing. Undoubtedly, in time many of them will prove useful for further research, some will be verified, and some will be disproved. In the meanwhile, what, of all of this, is useful for the individual who is interested in becoming a practitioner, a business manager and not a researcher? The answer that this book provides is to select from the many available conceptual schemes those few that seem particularly helpful to us as guides to the seeing-thinking process used by practitioners in analyzing specific problems. This is done because of our commitment to the assumption that it is more useful to practice using one scheme until it becomes an internalized part of one's seeing-thinking equipment than to acquire a speaking acquaintance with many schemes.

The second major reason will help account for why this book presents only a rough sample of the systematic research on organizational behavior with little attempt at an integrated theoretical interpretation of the various findings. In presenting research abstracts, the aim of the book is not so much to acquaint students with what is now known as it is to illustrate how future administrators can make use of systematic research as guides to their own behavior. It is fairly safe to say that there will be much more useful research in this field in the lifetime of the current generation of college students than there has been in all of history so far. This is why it is more important to learn how to usefully tap into the future flow of research in the field than it is to get completely up to date now. For this reason most of the studies are presented in an abbreviated form; it is left up to the student to spot their uniformities and their contradictions and to begin his own process of trying to find a theory that can account for the many findings. By this process the student can see for himself some of the practical values and limitations of systematic research. As he struggles with understanding cases he will see the utility of a soundly based explanatory theory and also the difficulty of achieving one.

Finally, all the material in the book—cases, concepts, and research findings—was selected to help nurture students' faith that there is order in the human universe; that man's behavior is not a chaotic chance affair; that, within limits, it is predictable; that intelligence can usefully supplement intuition in the conduct of important human affairs; and that knowledge and skillful diagnosis of human behavior, our own as well as others, can help liberate us from slavish conformity and from narrow moralistic judgments, and can help us to become more realistic, more understanding, and, in the deepest sense of the word, more productive.

P. R. L.	C. D. O.
J. A. S.	J. V. C.
J. C. B.	L. B. B.
R. L. K.	A. N. T.

BOSTON, MASSACHUSETTS
April, 1965

Acknowledgments

THE AUTHORS wish to acknowledge their indebtedness to the following men who, as staff members at the Harvard Business School, played a major role in preparing some of the cases in this book: John D. Donnell, Charles Hampden-Turner, J. B. Kassarjian, Gerald C. Leader, Laurent Picard, Andre Priem, Harold Spear, Melvin Steckler, James Stratton, and Peter Vaill. Contributions to preparation of some of the earlier cases were also made by Harold F. Craig, R. Stanley Laing, Harriet R. Lynton, and David N. Ulrich.

We are also indebted to many of our faculty colleagues, present and past, for various valuable direct contributions they have made to the materials in this book, and, even more importantly, the indirect contributions they have made over the years to the development of the basic ideas underlying the Administrative Practices course here at the Harvard Business School. We are especially grateful to Douglas R. Bunker, Gene W. Dalton, John D. Glover, Ralph M. Hower, Edmund P. Learned, George F. F. Lombard, Jay W. Lorsch, David Moment, Fritz J. Roethlisberger, and James R. Surface.

We thank the many publishers and authors who have granted us permission to quote copyright material. The source of each of these quotations is indicated in the appropriate place. With only a few exceptions all cases in this book have been individually copyrighted by the President and Fellows of Harvard College. They are reprinted here by special permission and may not be reproduced in whole or in part without written permission.

Finally, we wish very much to acknowledge the considerable help we have received in the preparation of the manuscript from Mrs. Nina Frank and Miss Mary Hourihan.

Even though we gladly acknowledge the many contributions of others to this book, we, the authors, are fully responsible for the book and accept any and all of its faults.

P. R. L.	C. D. O.
J. A. S.	J. V. C.
J. C. B.	L. B. B.
R. L. K.	A. N. T.

BOSTON, MASSACHUSETTS
April, 1965

Table of Contents

PAGE

Section I. The Human Problems of Administration

Introduction   3

Cases

1. Harkness Machinery Company (A)   10
2. Harkness Machinery Company (B)   15
3. Dashman Company   16
4. Al Ruskin   18
5. Jim McFee (A)   25
6. Jim McFee (B)   29
7. Daycomb Company   30
8. Beacon Publishing Company   32

Concepts and Research Findings

1. The Functional Point of View, by Alexander H. Leighton . .   41

Section II. Work Group Behavior

Introduction   47

Cases

1. Metropolitan Steel Company   51
2. Excelsior Bakeries, Inc.   66
3. Betty Randall   73
4. The Slade Company   76
5. The Times-Herald   89
6. Markham Instrument Company 114
7. The Case of the Changing Cage, Parts 1–5 . 124, 126, 127, 129, 130
8. Superior Slate Quarry, Parts 1–4 . . . . . 132, 135, 136, 138
9. Maynard Aircraft, Parts 1–2 . . . . 140, 142
10. Kilkenny Lumber Company, Parts 1–4 . . . 144, 147, 148, 150
11. The White Company, Parts 1–2 . . . . 151, 153

Concepts and Research Findings

1. A Conceptual Scheme for Describing Work Group Behavior . . 154
2. The Relay Assembly Test Room Experiments 165
3. The Bank Wiring Observation Room 175
4. Conveyor Work, Interaction Potential, and Worker Satisfaction 184
5. Worker Satisfaction in English Automobile Plants 185
6. Group Membership, Satisfaction, and Productivity 187
7. Work Group Behavior in Restaurants 189
8. Productivity and Social Behavior in a Selling Group . . . 191
9. Group Cohesiveness, Anxiety, and Productivity 193
10. Sociometrically Selected Work Teams, Productivity, and Turn-
    over 195

PAGE

11. Experimental Reorganizations in an Indian Textile Plant . . 196
12. Organizational Systems and Engineering Groups: A Comparative
    Study of Two Technical Groups in Industry 199
13. The Comparative Effectiveness of Groups and Individuals in
    Solving Problems, by D. R. Bunker and G. W. Dalton . . . 202

Section III.   Individual Behavior and Development

Introduction   209
Cases

    1. Anderson Manufacturing and Development Company . . . 211
    2. Arthur Walton   229
    3. Ben Reed 238
    4. Norse Electronics (A)   241
    5. Norse Electronics (B)   243
    6. Excellent Insurance Company (A)   245
    7. Excellent Insurance Company (B)   252
    8. Walt Rogers   255
    9. Gillen Radio Corporation 259
   10. Cleveland Junior Chamber of Commerce 263

Concepts and Research Findings

    1. Defenses and the Need to Know, by Roger Harrison 266
    2. Personality Formation—The Determinants, by Clyde Kluckhohn
       and Henry A. Murray 273
    3. The Process of Natural Growth, by Robert W. White . . . 284
    4. Motivation, Role Behavior, and Development, by David Moment 302
    5. Modes of Resolving Role Conflict 305
    6. A Tentative Formulation of a General Law of Interpersonal Rela-
       tionships, by Carl R. Rogers 308

Section IV.   Supervisory Behavior and Remedial Action

Introduction   317
Cases

    1. The Electronics Stock Control Group,
       Parts 1 to 5 . . . . 320, 323, 324, 326, 327
    2. Battleship "Y" 328
    3. American Radiatronics Corporation 345
    4. Allied Food Company 377
    5. The Stiles Corporation   383
    6. Merrill Manufacturing Company,
       Parts 1 to 5 . . . . 388, 391, 394, 396, 398
    7. Work Group Ownership of an Improved Tool 405
    8. The Crown Fastener Company   411
    9. Claremont Instrument Company 415

Concepts and Research Findings

    1. Productivity and Leadership in an Insurance Company . . . 423
    2. Some Effects of Close and Punitive Styles of Supervision . . 425

3. Conditions Influencing the Effects of Leadership Styles on Group Performance 427
4. First-Line Supervisors, Upward Influence, and Work Group Satisfaction 430
5. Supervisory Identification with Management and/or Workers . 431
6. The Foreman: Master and Victim of Double Talk, by Fritz J. Roethlisberger 434
7. Engineering Supervisors in the Middle, by Louis B. Barnes . . 439
8. Results of a Supervisory Training Program 443
9. The Need Hierarchy: A Theory of Motivation 446
10. Motivation in Work Groups: A Tentative View, by James V. Clark 451

Section V. Intergroup Behavior

Introduction 471
Cases
1. United Diesel Corporation 473
2. American Magnolite Company 482
3. Haig Chemical Company 503
4. The Thermophysics Research Group 523
5. Fort Worth Pharmaceutical and Chemical Corporation . . . 528
6. Perkins Component Company 541
7. Belmont-White Company 549
8. Grayson Company 552

Concepts and Research Findings
1. A Systematic Way of Thinking About Intergroup Behavior . . 558
2. The Role of the Norm of Reciprocity in Social Stabilization . . 565
3. A Sociotechnical Conceptual Scheme 569
4. Organizational Structure and Scientific Transfer 578
5. Diagnosing Interdepartmental Conflict 582
6. Reduction of Intergroup Conflict 598
7. Top Management Collaboration and Conflict 602

Section VI. Behavior in the Total Organization

Introduction 607
Cases
1. Twin City Trust Co. 610
2. The Gordon Company 623
3. The Hampton Shipyard 631
4. Marshall Company (A) 640
5. Marshall Company (B) 650
6. Marshall Company (C) 660
7. Marshall Company (D) 667
8. Marshall Company (E) 671
9. Marshall Company (F) 678
10. Marshall Company (G) 682

PAGE

11. Lewis Equipment Company 686
12. Empire Glass Company 700
13. Higgins Equipment Company (A) 728
14. Higgins Equipment Company (B) 743

Concepts and Research Findings

1. "Classical" Organization Theory 757
2. Staff-Line Relationships, by Douglas McGregor 761
3. Two Concepts of Authority, by Walter B. Miller 766
4. Two Views of Japanese Industrial Organization 776
5. The Influence of Technical Change on Organization Structure . 782
6. The Sears Roebuck Study 788
7. Experiments in Structural Design 790
8. Management by Integration and Self-Control, by Arthur H. Kuriloff 792

Section VII.   Organizational Change

Introduction 807

Cases

1. Alpha Company (A) 810
2. Alpha Company (B) 822
3. Dan Weber 831
4. Supra Oil Company 848
5. The Yoker Company 855
6. Tidewater Manufacturing Company 859
7. Randley Stores, Inc. (A) 870
8. Randley Stores, Inc. (B) 885
9. Denver Transportation Company 900
10. Dallas Chemical Corporation 909

Concepts and Research Findings

1. Criteria for Planning Organizational Change, by Gene W. Dalton 914
2. Resistance to Change, by Paul R. Lawrence 928
3. Participation in Decision Making and Work Group Productivity 931
4. The Effect of Group Decision on Subsequent Behavior . . . 933
5. An Experimental Change of Decision Levels and Effects on
   Productivity and Satisfaction 937
6. A Study of Organization Development, by Robert R. Blake,
   Jane S. Mouton; Louis B. Barnes, and Larry E. Greiner . . . 939
7. Changes in Institutions and the Role of the Change Agent, by
   Kenneth D. Benne 952
8. A President's Experience with Democratic Management, by
   James E. Richard 960

Indexes

Index to Cases 977
Index to Concepts and Research Findings 980

SECTION I

The Human Problems of Administration

Introduction

ON THE BALANCE BETWEEN SKILL AND KNOWLEDGE

"Education is the acquisition of the utilization of knowledge. This is an art very difficult to impart."
—Aims of Education
ALFRED NORTH WHITEHEAD

IT MAY not be readily apparent from Professor Whitehead's concise language that his aphorism applies with especial force to training for the professions. Yet consider, for example, its applicability to law and medicine. One point, in schools devoted to the latter subject, on which agreement is nearly universal among medical educators is that: "The most we can hope to do while we have a student is to get him to think like a doctor." An equal unanimity of view exists, I understand, in the better law schools just as it does with us, where we desire students to take a professional attitude toward their careers in business. Clearly, it is impossible to teach them all there is to know about the extravagantly diverse world of business; yet if we can help them to acquire the art of the utilization of knowledge someday to be needed, we have been helpful in a way that should last a lifetime.

A teaching goal that aspires to such an aim may inspire great efforts and sustained dedication. It leads, however, into repeated failures, unforeseeable frustration, and to never-ending change and experimentation with all the materials and methods we use in trying to impart the art that is the key to the education Whitehead writes of. Out of our collective experience, we consider nothing more important or more useful than to try to point out in this introduction, as quickly and as clearly as possible, to colleagues who may use this book in their pursuit of kindred aims, the nature of the recurrent failures and the reasons behind the frustrations we have encountered. Our hope is that if we do so we can reduce for others the failures and frustrations that may be inherent or, if not that, then at least forewarn, and thereby forearm.

Basically what we have learned is the necessity of teaching administration as a skill (i.e., "art") linked inseparably to knowledge. Knowl-

3

edge, without the skill to use it, is inert and surplus baggage to the practitioner. Skill without the continual infusion of new knowledge leaves its possessor practicing in the grip of unmodified routines, subject to boredom, and, in the end, certain of seeing the skill he uses outmoded by men able to alter, elaborate, and extend their skill with new knowledge. Therefore, in imparting this art, we have learned the hard way, that our most difficult task is the struggle to keep skill linked to knowledge in delicate balance, so that they will reinforce, and not nullify, each other. They must be acquired hand in hand or in linked sequence, because that is the way they must be used or else the art of the utilization of knowledge has not been gained.

Our course has illustrated, in the phases of its development at the School, both the difficulty and the necessity of maintaining the balance between skill AND knowledge. Its history, in essence, is an account of getting-out-of balance followed by the effort to gain a new equilibrium. Sometimes skill was given overemphasis at the expense of knowledge. Then, in subsequent reaction, skill became subordinated to knowledge. An effort to re-establish balance, in every instance thus far, has asserted itself. It does so because annually, in our student product, it becomes painfully clear to us that overemphasis on either skill OR knowledge fails equally to impart to students the art we know they need.

Men overdosed with knowledge discourse with prolix glibness on what is wrong in the cases before them and what is needed to set matters straight again. They are then generally unable to exhibit any of the practitioners' skill as to how to resolve the problems they had analyzed verbally, and, what is equally discouraging, they clearly feel no responsibility for doing so—no responsibility, in short, for utilizing their knowledge. Many such students, indeed, show disdain for trying to practice in an elementary way what is the unavoidable daily skill of an operating executive. Such students climb high into an untroubled ivory tower where they cannot, and do not, feel any challenge in trying to exercise the fascinating art of utilizing their knowledge.

Men are as easily, and as dangerously, misled by an overemphasis on skill. When this occurs, which is understandably less frequent in an academic setting where most tendencies favor knowledge, theory, erudition, students may acquire a surprising deftness for untangling separate problems, but the distressing result is their inability to discern any uniformities from case to case, and a reluctance to try to pry out recurrent phenomena. They feel it is unfair, "longhaired," to require them to seek a few limited generalities, to articulate a simple, useful way of thinking about all the phenomena in front of them. No ivory tower for them. They're "operators," "practical men"; period! This overemphasis on skill prevents their acquiring some simple scheme wherewith to organize and to conceptualize their learning so that they can articulate and transmit their experience to others. Such men cannot cumulate and contribute to the stream of conscious knowledge. They are not prepared to pass on the torch of increasing skill and knowledge from hand to hand.

Partisans for stressing either skill *or* knowledge have to experience these results of lack of balance before they "believe" in the necessity of linking both. Both must be achieved if the teacher is to realize his golden opportunity of multiplying his efforts endlessly through others. He is quite without comfort in learning that overemphasis on skill leads directly to the same cul-de-sac as overemphasis on knowledge.

Why have we been plagued with these pendulum swings from side to side? Why is one overemphasis succeeded by another? Is it we, or is it something inherent in the task we've set ourselves? The causes for these oscillations are more numerous than we can cover here. There are probably some we fail to see, but we shall point out a few that are important.

It is primarily in professional graduate schools that instructors feel a continual pressure to "make men think like doctors" (lawyers, administrators, etc.). Gifted teachers in nongraduate schools often do this in their subjects brilliantly, yet for their students it comes as a windfall, a memorable extra. In professional schools it is a must. As a consequence, the problem of balanced training is a pressing one only in the smallest fraction of our educational system.

A further reason why emphasis oscillates between skill and knowledge arises from the constant circulation of personnel within a teaching group. New members bring with them new interests and personal insights—sufficient reasons in themselves to plan for circulation. The new interests customarily spring from newly accomplished research work which, for young men, realistically represents the main highway to academic advancement. Furthermore, as men with intellectual gifts they are keenly alert to all the news and rumors about similar work by their colleagues and competitors everywhere. From the ferment generated by this enthusiasm for research (i.e., knowledge) it is easy for them to suppose students will be equally excited and, if an instructor's enthusiasm is contagious, they are. And, off they all march, ever deeper in minutiae, up into an ivory tower! Earliest it dawns on the instructor where they all have come to rest, and his surprise is paralleled by a genuine dismay, because he usually shares the conviction of the teaching group as to the inutility of skill without knowledge, and vice versa. What had happened to him was simply his first personal experience with how unintentionally, imperceptibly, insensibly, the required balance between skill and knowledge is lost. This is a lesson that must be learned at first hand, for it cannot be grasped—believed—from the experience of others at second hand. While he, and others, too, are learning thus how delicate is the balance sought, the course emphasis, perforce, has shifted and, when acknowledged, must be again redressed. Nonetheless, the healthy and inevitable fact of circulation of personnel accounts for some of the oscillation.

A factor related to the foregoing two plays a part of indeterminable importance. This factor relates to erudition, or what Whitehead terms inert knowledge, which to outward appearances, can be transferred in large doses daily. Impressive amounts can be recalled for testing at the close of each semester. This is familiar academic terrain. The skill required to do this is less taxing than the one Whitehead had in mind. The standards here are conventionalized; understandable to students and teachers and to deans, all habituated to them. It is a measurable input-output operation far less trying on the nervous system than to be reaching for intangibles which need to be put in doubtful phrases such as a frame of mind, an attitude, an outlook, or "getting a man to think like a doctor."

When such intangibles are sought, even when some small, observable accomplishment seems attained, the instructor unavoidably feels less sure of *his* accomplishment, of the value of his contribution. Years must pass, not semesters, before the gains will be clear to either student or instructor. And, in the best cases, when either student or instructor, or both, do have a conviction of accomplishment, it often seems to the latter a frail and untrustworthy outcome for so much effort. It can require years for a teacher not merely to have faith, but to truly *know,* that even a small difference in a man's way of thinking and perceiving can make a very large difference in all he does thereafter. Instructors who adopt our aim must have time to discover for themselves the lifelong chain reaction which is set off, once skill-plus-knowledge are linked together indissolubly in a student's mind. Until this truth is validated for each instructor, their continuing uncertainties also will contribute to the oscillations of the course.

The reasons given so far for the difficulties we have encountered in trying to transmit skill AND knowledge in a balanced relationship, and which we believe to be essential to the art of the utilization of knowledge, all stem from the problems of the teacher and his teaching group.

There are still other reasons, and serious ones, too, that make impartation of Whitehead's art difficult. These will be ignored here, because it is about those given that teachers can do the most—if they choose—now. Today.

The reasons given, in substance, amount to saying that teachers, too, must learn their art—an art, by Whitehead's definition, that takes at least as long to learn as to learn to do recognized first-rate research. The rewards of teaching are as uncertain and as remote as those of research work; and they are accompanied by equally long periods of frustration and doubt. These facts generally come as a shock to brilliant young men who have won advanced degrees with distinction yet have had no warning that success in pedagogy may easily require of them an effort as strenuous and protracted as the one they have so recently completed.

So still another force bears on the oscillations experienced. The actual time and effort required, from men who are *willing* to shoulder the risks inherent in making skill AND knowledge, linked and balanced, their goal in teaching, is quite considerable. For each new man, or each group of new men, must be allowed to explore what the limitations on his efforts are, must be encouraged to probe for short cuts, to question existing practices and their premises, while he learns how he, as an individual, can make his most effective contribution to the goal of teaching men "to think like administrators." This is a lonely task to which others can contribute but little beyond support and encouragement.

Taking a wider view, the art of the utilization of knowledge strikes us as the inner key to most of the momentous issues confronting the people and the nations of the world today. Knowledge, especially scientific and technical knowledge (and belatedly, social and psychological knowledge), is accumulating at geometric rates while the art of its utilization falls further and further behind. Sufficient evidence of this widening gap appears daily in the news from underdeveloped countries, where political instability and technological helplessness underscores a simple proposition: knowledge without the skill to utilize it is no better than no knowledge at all. Skill to utilize knowledge must coexist in balance with knowledge, or the results are frustration and futility.

The most critical problem that lurks behind the looming crises of our century is how to break the bottleneck between the current accumulations of knowledge AND the skill to utilize them. This art must now reach vastly greater numbers of people than ever before. Until it does, our complex, interdependent, industrially based culture has not become adaptive to the environment it has created, and may not survive.

Historically, the pedagogical tool upon which we have put our principal reliance in facing the challenging dilemmas and difficulties outlined here has been the case method. That method is surely not the only pedagogy that fosters the welding of skill AND knowledge. Out of the present ferment about education we pray that others will emerge to equal or surpass it, for the need of pedagogical creation and invention is acute. Yet, it is one that we know invites the welding of skill AND knowledge and, when rightly used, compels it. Since the problems of its use and misuse have been presented elsewhere[1] no more need be said here than to point out that some implements do exist for attacking the key problems of our day.

To those then, who embark with this course book, on the endless adventure of teaching organization and administration, we fervently hope that at times of discouragement their spirits will be renewed by remembering that they are playing for stakes that involve the destiny of a civilization. They are battling to breach the massive walls that everywhere retard mankind's ability to utilize knowledge, already available and able to deliver our species from illiteracy, hunger, and perhaps even from the self-destructive compulsions that erupt periodically in war. Such a goal is distant, but is attainable and must be striven for. There is no longer any evasion of the problem of learning how to transmit skill-plus-knowledge to the generation that faces us. Even now we are runners in that race H. G. Wells foresaw for our century—"the race between education and catastrophe." May awareness of the issues at stake be a tonic to us—to all of us, students and learners, still striving for the never-ending education Whitehead summoned us to seek.

.   .   .   .

The opening section of this course book has been devised to illustrate the need for a balanced development of both knowledge and skill in relation to small group behavior, the position of the supervisor, intergroup relationships, and total organizational behavior, i.e., to the full range of organizational situations which shall be separately studied in subsequent sections of the book. Through discussion of the many variables to be discovered in these cases, students begin to see the need to utilize common knowledge more systematically and more skillfully and to see the importance of distinguishing sharply between what is now known and what is not yet known and should be searched for.

---

[1] Kenneth R. Andrews (ed.), *The Case Method of Teaching Human Relations and Administration* (Cambridge, Massachusetts: Harvard University Press, 1953). F. J. Roethlisberger, *et al., Training for Human Relations, An Interim Report of a Program for Advanced Training and Research in Human Relations, 1951–1954* (Boston: Harvard University, Division of Research, Graduate School of Business Administration, 1954).

An administrator confronted with discouragingly complex human and social situations is repeatedly tempted to single out one piece of behavior as responsible for the desirable or undesirable consequences he must cope with. To guard him against this fallible but fatal human tendency to "find the villian," the emphasis in this course will be to examine each element of behavior, whether of an individual, a small group, or a large organization, as a responsive part of a system of *interrelated* and *interdependent* parts. Every element performs a function in relation to the whole. This is "the functional point of view" (that opposes and displaces the "find-the-villian" point of view) which is a key concept for this book and for the course it offers. The excerpt from Alexander Leighton's book, *Human Relations in a Changing World,* presents this important concept. We urge you to read the excerpt and thereafter apply the concept to every case we take up and study for discussion, for it is central to the understanding of a system.

J. C. B.

Cases

1. HARKNESS MACHINERY COMPANY (A)[1]

THE HARKNESS MACHINERY COMPANY was organized in four divisions. The stamping division of the company was located on the first floor of the central plant. Functionally, it was an integral part of the main company but its payroll and corporate affairs were separately administered. The employees of the other divisions of the company were members of an AFL union, but the employees of the stamping division were members of a CIO union. The local of this CIO union had a reputation for being a tough, fighting organization and the employees of the stamping division reflected this attitude in their relations with the employees of the other divisions of the company.

Frank Boland, personnel manager of the stamping division, received a phone call from the division nurse one afternoon. She reported that there was a power press operator in her office whom she believed Mr. Boland should see. She summarized the situation briefly. The worker, Jan Dabrowski, had come to her office complaining of a head cold. He had insisted he was unable to continue work for the afternoon, so the nurse had written him a sick pass. As he was about to leave her office he had commented, "I guess I will have to quit my job now." She was surprised by this remark since the company had a rather liberal sick-leave policy. When she asked him what he meant, he simply said that it had little to do with his sickness, but he could no longer continue working with the men in his department. She suggested that he might want to take the matter up with Mr. Boland, and Mr. Dabrowski had assented. The nurse added in her comments to Boland that the worker was extremely agitated and had apparently suffered some kind of mistreatment. The personnel manager suggested that she have Dabrowski come to his office right away.

Mr. Boland took out Dabrowski's personnel file and was reminded by it that this employee had a rather unusual background for a power press operator. When Dabrowski arrived at his office, Boland asked him to be seated and then questioned him on why he felt he would have to quit his

---

[1] This is a two-part case. Your instructor may wish to have you discuss Part A before reading Part B.

job. Dabrowski spoke emotionally, explaining that the men downstairs knew that he was susceptible to colds. He said that these men purposely opened windows near him so that he was working in a draft. He said that this was their way of tormenting him and that when he complained about it, they laughed at him and opened other windows as soon as he had shut the ones which had been opened previously. While referring to the other workers in this section, Dabrowski used the terms "mean, bad, evil people." His speech was halting and he had a slight accent. Several times during the discussion, emotion caused tears to well in his eyes and, temporarily, he was unable to continue. A sample of the conversation was as follows:

> BOLAND: Do you feel that they open the windows near you on purpose?
> DABROWSKI: Yes they do. They are mean, bad people. They make fun of me because I was not born here. I am a displaced person and they know that. They ask me why don't I go back to where I come from. I like it here very much, but do they think that I gave up my country because I wanted to?

During the conversation, Dabrowski told Boland much of his personal history and many things about his family. He had been a judge of the criminal courts of Poland, as his father had been before him. The Dabrowski family had been well known and were highly respected members of the landed class. During the Nazi invasion they lost everything, and Jan and his family were shipped to Germany where he was put into a forced labor camp. During the ensuing period Dabrowski narrowly escaped death on several occasions, but he managed to survive until the American Army arrived. Because of his lack of knowledge of the English language, the only job he could get with the American Army was that of a kitchen helper. As his knowledge of English increased, he was able to obtain jobs requiring greater skill. For example, he mentioned working as a bookkeeper in a PX where he had devised new systems of records. The last job that he had performed before coming to the United States was that of a legal adviser to the military government. He mentioned letters of recommendation which he had received from the military government and several times he expressed the desire to show these letters to Mr. Boland at some future date, when he would have them with him.

Jan spoke proudly of his family. He was particularly proud of his children. He said that his daughter was attending a fine secretarial school. He thought that she would have no trouble in finding a position because girls with secretarial training were scarce at that time. He was especially proud of his son, who, although he had been in America for only two years, got 95 in English and was listed on the honor roll at his high school. Jan said, regarding the subject of his son's future training, that since the boy showed promise in the technical subjects, he would like to send him to an engineering school, even though his father and his grandfather had chosen law as a career. In any case, Jan said that this idea of future training for his son was largely a dream because, at the present time, he was earning only enough money to support the family.

Though the conversation had originally been initiated by Dabrowski's "I guess I will have to quit my job now," the only other reference he made to quitting was that if he did quit the result would be a severe financial hardship to his family. He felt that, because of his handicaps, in terms of age and language difficulties, he would find it difficult to get another job. Nevertheless, he felt that he could not take the persecution any longer. During the discussion, he talked a great deal about his work situation. He referred to one man as "my worst enemy" and then added that he oftentimes had to work close to or even with this man. In such cases, he said that he always attempted to avoid conflict. The conversation continued as follows:

DABROWSKI: Even so, I like my job here. When I worked on the night shift everything was o.k. Then they shut down the night shift. The foreman, he was no good, and the men did not work very hard. Of all the men on the shift, I was the only one transferred to the day shift. I appreciate this very much. The works manager knows about my case. He is a very kind person, and he and Morris, the foreman, have treated me very well. I appreciate what they do for me. I work hard. Already today I have done 2,100 operations which would be a good day's record and it is only 1 o'clock. But they tell me to slow down. They ask me why do I work so hard. One man there is the worst. Already I know that this man has been called in to Morris for not doing enough work. He is always after me to slow down. He doesn't want me to turn in too much work so that he will look bad, but I get paid a good wage, and I want to feel that I am earning what I get paid.

I try to turn in a good day's work. I am treated very well and I try hard to do my work. All the time that I am here, I have only missed five or six days' work. The records will show this. But the men there, they do not work hard. They are bad people. When I came to this country, I thought that persecution and intolerance were left behind me, but I find that there are this kind of people here too. They tell me to go back to where I came from. They want me to leave. Don't they realize that I am just trying to earn enough bread to keep my family going? They tell me that since I went to college, I have no business down there. They do not understand my position.

But I try to avoid any trouble always. I do not want to fight or argue with them, even though they make fun of me and try to hurt me. I don't even go into the locker room with them at quitting time, but I wait until they are all out and then I go in there and change. When I go in there they make crude, dirty remarks, so I wait until they have all gone out, even though it makes me later going home.

BOLAND: Have you mentioned this situation to Morris?

DABROWSKI: No. Once I told Bob, Morris' assistant, about the windows, and asked him to shut them, but they opened other ones on me later. I don't tell Morris or Bob about the way things are there because then the men will make it that much worse for me. I know that this can happen.[2]

At this point Boland suggested that Dabrowski go home for the afternoon, as he had planned, and take care of his cold. Meantime, he, Boland, would look into the situation and talk with Dabrowski further the next morning.

After Dabrowski left, Boland called the foreman of the power press department. The latter expressed some annoyance at the manner in which Dabrowski had left the department without notifying him. In response to a description of Dabrowski's complaint of mistreatment, the foreman disclaimed any knowledge of the situation, although, he said, trouble with the windows was very common and, during cold weather, was a constant source of disagreement. He suspected that Dabrowski was exaggerating this problem by imagining that the other men were purposely opening the windows to discomfort him. The foreman reported that Dabrowski was an excellent worker, one he would not want to lose. He doubted, however, that the man would actually quit. On direct questioning the foreman admitted that Dabrowski's problem could exist as had been described without the foreman's knowledge. He said he would keep his eyes open, but even if the men gave signs of persecuting Dabrowski, it would be difficult to prove and even more difficult to do anything about.

On reflection, Boland believed that the situation Dabrowski described could actually exist in the department and that management, as things stood at the time, would be largely unable to correct it. This being the

---

[2] Boland suspected that Dabrowski was referring to a recent incident in which some of the men had been picking on a fellow worker who had a hunchback. This situation resulted in a brawl in the shop and the resultant firing of the two men caught fighting, even though management knew that many more of the workers were involved, although not actually fighting. In this case, the men had made the deformed man's life miserable, leading him to a rage that manifested itself in the fight. The quiet campaign had been going on for some time previous to the fight.

case, he considered the possibility of transferring Dabrowski. He knew that the personnel manager of the downtown plant of the company had been looking for a receiving clerk unsuccessfully for several months. The atmosphere of the downtown plant was considerably different from that of the stamping division, and there would be less union problem in making such a transfer than in placing Dabrowski elsewhere in the division. This solution seemed a happy one, but Boland determined to give it more thought overnight.

2. HARKNESS MACHINERY COMPANY (B)

EARLY THE morning after his discussion with Jan Dabrowski [see Harkness Machinery Company (A)], Frank Boland, personnel manager of the stamping division, called the personnel manager of the downtown plant, Ralph Connor. He told Connor about the Dabrowski case and asked him if he would be willing to interview the man. Connor agreed to do so.

When Dabrowski arrived, Boland offered him the chance of applying to Connor for transfer, stressing that the decision was Connor's. Dabrowski jumped at the opportunity, profusely thanking Boland for this opportunity.

Later that morning Connor called Boland to say that he had hired Dabrowski as a receiving clerk and that he looked like just the man he wanted. He thanked Boland for making the referral.

Three days later, in discussing the situation over the phone with Connor, Boland was informed that Dabrowski's first two days were entirely successful and that he showed great promise for the future. Connor claimed that Dabrowski's willingness to work and the way he had pitched in had caused some of the younger men to rise to greater efforts on their jobs.

3. DASHMAN COMPANY

THE DASHMAN Company was a large concern making many types of equipment for the armed forces of the United States. It had over twenty plants, located in the central part of the country, whose purchasing procedures had never been completely co-ordinated. In fact, the head office of the company had encouraged the plant managers to operate with their staffs as separate, independent units in most matters. Late in 1940, when it began to appear that the company would face increasing difficulty in securing certain essential raw materials, Mr. Manson, the company's president, appointed an experienced purchasing executive, Mr. Post, as vice president in charge of purchasing, a position especially created for him. Manson gave Post wide latitude in organizing his job, and he assigned Mr. Larson as Post's assistant. Larson had served the company in a variety of capacities for many years, and knew most of the plant executives personally. Post's appointment was announced through the formal channels usual in the company, including a notice in the house organ which was published monthly by the Dashman Company.

One of Post's first decisions was to begin immediately to centralize the company's purchasing procedure. As a first step, he decided that he would require each of the executives who handled purchasing in the individual plants to clear with the head office all purchase contracts which they made in excess of $10,000. He felt that if the head office was to do any co-ordinating in a way that would be helpful to each plant and to the company as a whole, he must be notified that the contracts were being prepared at least a week before they were to be signed. He talked his proposal over with Manson, who presented it to the board of directors. They approved the plan.

Although the company made purchases throughout the year, the beginning of its peak buying season was only three weeks away at the time this new plan was adopted. Post prepared a letter to be sent to the twenty purchasing executives of the company. The letter follows:

Dear ——:

The board of directors of our company has recently authorized a change in our purchasing procedures. Hereafter, each of the purchasing executives in the several plants of the company will notify the vice president in charge of purchasing of all contracts in excess of $10,000 which they are negotiating, at least a week in advance of the date on which they are to be signed.

I am sure you will understand that this step is necessary to co-ordinate the purchasing requirements of the company in these times when we are facing increasing difficulty in securing essential supplies. This procedure should give us in the central office the information we need to see that each plant secures the optimum supply of materials. In this way the interests of each plant and of the company as a whole will best be served.

Yours very truly,

Post showed the letter to Larson and invited his comments. Larson thought the letter an excellent one, but suggested that since Post had not met more than a few of the purchasing executives, he might like to visit all of them and take the matter up with each of them personally. Post dismissed the idea at once because, as he said, he had so many things to do at the head office that he could not get away for a trip. Consequently, he had the letters sent out over his signature.

During the two following weeks, replies came in from all except a few plants. Although a few executives wrote at greater length, the following reply was typical:

DEAR MR. POST:

Your recent communication in regard to notifying the head office a week in advance of our intention to sign contracts has been received. This suggestion seems a most practical one. We want to assure you that you can count on our co-operation.

Yours very truly,

During the next six weeks the head office received no notices from any plant that contracts were being negotiated. Executives in other departments, who made frequent trips to the plants, reported that the plants were busy, and the usual routines for that time of year were being followed.

4. AL RUSKIN

IN THE late spring of 1955, Al Ruskin dropped in to see one of his professors at the Harvard Business School. Ruskin had graduated from the school three years earlier.

After a few pleasantries about families and friends, Ruskin began to talk about his current job situation. With the professsor interjecting an occasional question and expression of interest, Ruskin proceeded to tell the following story:

AL RUSKIN: I guess you know I'm still working for Amalgamated Industries.

PROFESSOR: Well, I wasn't sure.

RUSKIN: I've been in their sales department ever since I left the school. As you know, we have a huge sales organization. I've had two or three different jobs; but right now, I'm working in the market research division, and there are about thirty of us in that outfit. The work of the division is broken down into four different sections, and then there is another group of clerical people who do the actual figure calculations and help get out the analytical reports of the division. I'm working in one of these four sections as an analyst. There are about six of us doing that kind of work in the section I'm in. We report to our section chief, and then the division has a couple of assistant managers and a manager of the division who reports to a vice president.

PROFESSOR: What kind of work do you do?

RUSKIN: Well, I'm an analyst, and we work on different management problems that are sent down to us. There's always more than enough work to do. Right now, I'm pretty discouraged about the setup. The trouble is with the supervision up the line. Some of them either don't know about the problems or just don't face up to what's going on. As far as I can see, all of them are trying to act like superanalysts instead of like supervisors. For a while on this job, I was able to look at what was going on in a detached way, and it didn't bother me very much. Sometimes, another fellow who graduated from Harvard Business School and myself get together and discuss these problems and enjoy talking about them. But in the last few weeks, it's been getting under my skin.

Let me give you an instance of what is bothering me. Let me tell you about the first big report I worked on. I got really excited about that job. It involved an issue as to whether or not the company should continue

18

with a certain product line. They had about decided to discontinue it when I started digging into some of the figures, and it seemed to me that the figures indicated they might come out with a different answer. I worked very hard on it. I spent a number of nights working on it and got quite excited about the project.

When I had finished my report, I let my section chief know, and he came right over to my desk. He held out his hand for the report, and I gave it to him; he turned around and walked out of the office and went to see the vice president.

The other two analysts who were in the office with me had been watching this. As soon as the door was closed, they looked over at me, and one of them said: "Well, how does it feel, Al? Do you like the way it feels?" Then they laughed and said: "Don't worry, Al; after that's happened to you about half a dozen times, you'll get sort of used to the way it feels, and it won't be quite so tough."

PROFESSOR: Did you ever hear anything more about the report?

RUSKIN: Well, a couple of days later, the chief mentioned to me that he had taken it upstairs, and the people there weren't too impressed with the potential profits that could be realized with my proposal. Of course, I don't think my chief or the people he was talking with really understood what I was proposing. But that was the end of it. I think he was a little let down that they didn't get more excited about it. I know I certainly was. You see, part of the problem is that our supervisors have the notion that they have to do their own analysis job on all the reports we turn in to them. They think they have to have all the answers at their fingertips when they go to talk to the people up the line that the reports are being prepared for.

PROFESSOR: Are most of your reports prepared for the top management group?

RUSKIN: Yeah, we work them up for them. For instance, some fellow at the top of the organization will think of a question he would like to get an answer on. He will wonder what the profit picture is or is going to be on some particular product. He will ask the question, and then it filters down to our group, and we have to go out and dig up or develop all the data and prepare the report for him. I don't think the people at the top often realize how much work is going into those reports, and I don't think we analysts always realize just what problem the executive is really concerned with.

These requests affect our district offices, too. You see, for six months before I got into this headquarters group, I was working as a field analyst in one of our district offices. The three analysts there spent their time running around getting data requested by headquarters. None of them had time to be of help to the local sales force. I was sent out on temporary duty, so I did have time to help the local people on a couple of the studies they were interested in. They really appreciated the help. Those field men impressed me as being "on the ball" and very desirous of hav-ing the help of good analytical stuff. They knew what they wanted and used the figures in directing their sales efforts when they got them; but they couldn't get much help from their own analysts because they were so busy doing work for headquarters.

The fellow I was working for out there asked me if I would like to go to work for him on a permanent basis and painted a good picture of the job. I told him I would be interested if it could be arranged. I really en-joyed that kind of work. You felt that you had some notion of what you were accomplishing by your efforts. But there's quite a story on why I didn't get that job.

PROFESSOR: I'd be interested to hear something about it.

RUSKIN: Well, apparently that fellow at the district office really went to bat to try to get my services. What it involved was getting a transfer for me. He went to headquarters with the request and got the approval of the fellow who's head of market research. I didn't learn all this until after the request had finally been turned down. The trouble came up when the division head checked with one of the assistant man-agers who knew me and my work. Apparently, the assistant manager told the manager that he would like to keep me in this organization. That stopped the transfer. No one asked me about it. I don't doubt the assistant manager who did it thought he was doing it not only for the good of our local section but probably also for my good. But it isn't ex-actly the way I'd go about doing that kind of thing. I don't think it even occurred to him to check with me on it.

PROFESSOR: How do you account for that?

RUSKIN: Well, I'm not sure just how to account for it. The problem seems to go quite a way up. They tell me that even the vice president we report to sits down and adds up the figures again on any report or study brought to him. I guess when the rest of the supervisors see him doing that, they figure they've got to sit down and recheck everything and add up all the figures before they pass a report on. They've got a lot of peo-ple working for them, but they never think of themselves as doing a supervising job.

Every job that comes along in this division is handled as a crisis. I thought that the job that was hot when I first arrived was an unusual thing—that this was a rush job and that things would quiet down shortly. They never have quieted down. Every job is a crisis. You are always working against extremely tight deadlines, and you always have to do a sort of halfway job. You never know exactly what it is you're supposed to be doing, so you just grind it out as best you can. It seems as if you always make a few mistakes when you're doing it that way.

People in this organization seem to delight in finding the mistakes of others. For instance, our group turns out a periodic letter on commercial operations; and apparently, almost everybody else in the department immediately reads this letter to see if he can find any mistakes in it. Within a matter of a few minutes after the letter is released, we start getting phone calls from people who have spotted things that are wrong. I don't mean by this that they find matters of real significance, but rather such things as a misspelling or a figure that is slightly in error.

It seems as if all the supervisors up the line feel they are in direct competition with one another. They are all concentrating on trying to impress their immediate bosses as being particularly keen analysts. They never seem to have time to look at what is going on in their own groups. You can imagine what that does to the state of mind of the fellows who are at the bottom of the organization. It isn't so bad on me and the other fellow from Harvard Business School, because we have the feeling, rightly or wrongly, that we can leave this company and get good jobs in other companies. We don't feel tied to this organization for our career. But that isn't true of most of the fellows in the department. Most of them do not know of any other place they can work. They feel they have to make the best of the situation for their career. After they have worked around here for a while, most of them seem to get pretty bitter.

The senior analyst I work with is still a pretty young man, but he's amazingly cynical and bitter about the organization. I try to be careful not to be too influenced by his views because, pretty clearly, he is seeing the worst side of things. But that's apt to happen to people after they've been around for a while. However, I think most of the people who have no choice but to stay don't really dare to take a close look at what is going on in the organization and face up to whether or not it is worth while. They seem to get used to the constant state of tension and crisis around the place and sort of resign themselves to it.

Let me see if I can give you some examples of the kind of problems that keep coming up. Just a few weeks ago, I got caught in the bind on a situation typical of the sort of thing that is apt to happen. In order to get a report out in time to meet a deadline, I needed the help and co-operation of a group of the clerical people who were handling the figures. Several people in that group were involved. I had the feeling that there was some confusion about what was needed and when it was needed.

On several occasions, I went to my boss and asked him if he would call a meeting for me with the supervisors concerned with helping me on the job. I thought we needed it in order to get a clear understanding of who was to do what, and when. Each time, he said that I was making too much of a fuss about it and that he didn't see any reason why we needed to get together to get the job done. He said it was perfectly evident that the other people had the responsibility for doing their part of it, and it was up to them to do it.

You see, I didn't think it was a matter of their being willing to do it; I thought it was a matter of some confusion about just what was needed. But as I feared, the jobs I needed them to do for me did not get done as they should have been done and at the right time. I talked to them about it personally, but they still were not getting done on time. So at the last minute, I felt I had to go to my boss and tell him that the work of the other group was not being done properly and on time. He went over to the boss of these people and told the story, and then they were called on the carpet by their boss for not keeping up with our schedule. Of course, they think now that I'm a real s.o.b. for having done this to them.

I guess it's not quite that bad. I think we understand each other pretty well; but it was a messy situation, and I could see it coming and could see no way of avoiding it. I couldn't seem to get the point across to my boss that we needed to get together to make sure that everybody understood what was being done.

I could give you a couple of other instances of the way my particular boss works with me. For example, a while back, he passed me in the hall and, just as a passing remark, said that I'd be getting a raise in my next check. Nothing more was said. I suppose that's the way a lot of people handle an announcement of that kind, but it's not my idea of how to let a fellow know he's got a raise. I muttered, "Thank you," and that was the extent of the conversation. If I were giving a person a raise, I'd use the occasion to sit down and tell him about the things he's doing well and maybe point out some things he's not doing too well.

On another occasion, my boss asked me to get out a fairly simple little statement about some distribution figures. He and the senior analyst and I were sitting around the desk with the reports in front of us, and he asked me simply to draw out and restate in summary form certain figures that were on a piece of paper. He took his pencil and pointed to the items on the list he wanted me to make a summary of. I didn't know anything about what the job was for and simply did as he told me. I took out the particular items and sent in the report.

Well, it turned out to be wrong. We forgot to include some item that should have been included; and because the mistake wasn't caught until some time later, a good deal of work had to be redone in another part of the office. When the mistake was found, my boss called me in and said he was taking responsibility for the error. Then he proceeded for the next fifteen minutes to tell me, in effect, that I'd better be careful not to make mistakes of that kind again.

Well, what can you do when something like that happens to you?

I don't blame him too much. It's just that he and a bunch of other fellows are caught in this system of trying to be perfect and not admit any mistakes. It's funny, too; but in that kind of organization, I think all of us make more mistakes than we normally would. Everything is done at such a hectic pace, and there are so many changes being made at the last minute when you're trying to get out a report. You always seem to be making very simple little mistakes. These turn up later on, to everybody's embarrassment. As I said before, they say that the vice president still gets out his pencil and checks questionable figures; and the awful part of it is, he finds mistakes that weren't caught coming all the way up the line.

You know, I really like the analytical work I'm doing, but I'm getting terribly discouraged with the job. Part of the trouble is that you never know just what's being done with the reports and studies you turn out. Sometimes, I wonder if I have a tendency to exaggerate these problems; but then, some new incident comes along and convinces me that this is the way things are, the way they're probably going to stay.

Lately, I've been doing a little outside job for a small company on some of my week-end time. I'm helping the owner to use available market information in planning his operations and distribution setup. It's a funny thing, but I've been getting more fun out of doing that in my spare time than I ever get out of my regular job. You really feel you're accomplishing something when you do a job for an outfit like that.

I just don't know whether or not it's worth while to stay with Amalgamated Industries. I really believe I have a fairly decent chance to move up in the organization. I think if I stuck around another five or ten years, I would be getting up the line. Maybe I'm kidding myself; but I think, without any false modesty, that my prospects are pretty good. But I'm not at all sure it's worth the effort. I'm not at all sure I'd be able to do anything that would really help the situation very much.

PROFESSOR: You don't see any way you can contribute and change this pattern.

RUSKIN: Well, I really don't, from my level of the organization. I think you could if you were higher up the line. I don't know if it would be too easy even then. You see, it takes a lot of courage to say what should be said in order to get these things straightened out. I guess by the time they get up that way, most of the fellows are so worried about their jobs that they don't dare say some of the things they think ought to be said, even if they know what needs to be done. At my level, right now, I don't know just what you could do. I try to talk to my boss about some of these things, but it doesn't seem to make much difference. My senior analyst tells me he's written a number of reports and recommendations suggesting some changes he thinks would begin to get at some of these problems. He has always submitted them to his boss, and nothing more has ever happened to them. As least as far as he knows, nothing has happened at all, and his boss hasn't really explained to him why he hasn't done anything with them. I suppose over a lifetime in this organization, you could really make a little headway; but I don't know, I'm beginning to think life's too short to spend all your time bucking that kind of situation.

5. JIM McFEE (A)

I HAVE BEEN asked by one of the professors of the Harvard Business School to write up some of my experiences on a job in a Detroit automobile plant during a recent summer vacation.

At the time I took the Detroit job I was 24 years old. It was my first job as a worker in a large industrial plant. I had been brought up in a middle-class family, and my father was a successful businessman and banker in a medium-size community. I was graduated from college in 1943 and had spent three years in the Navy. At the time of my discharge in July of 1946 I completed plans to enter the Harvard Business School that fall and decided it would be helpful and instructive to spend part of the summer working in a large factory. I therefore left my home, secured a temporary room in Detroit, and through the United States Employment Service obtained a job in an automobile plant.

At the employment office of the automobile plant I was given a routine interview and physical examination, and was told to report for work the next morning. In approaching my new job I was determined to find out as much as I could about industrial life from the workman's point of view.

I reported to work at the plant at 6:45 A.M. With five or six other people I stood around in the entrance passage for about ten minutes until a large uniformed plant guard walked up and asked, "Are all of you men starting work here?" We nodded and he motioned us over to a window cage. As our names were called out we stepped up to receive a plant badge with a six-digit number on it. Then the guard motioned us through a door into the factory area.

There the first thing that impressed me was the noise of the shop. In order to speak to another person it was necessary to shout into his ear. The group gathered along the wall just inside the door and waited for further instructions. I noticed two middle-aged men with open vests and rolled-up shirt sleeves looking us over and talking to one another. One of these men beckoned to a man standing near me, and they walked off together. Finally the other man signaled to me to follow him.

We wound our way through a maze of machines until we stopped before a small machine which seemed to be a sort of modified drill press. Without comment he picked up one of several metal plates stacked along side of the machine and placed it on the machine table. He then

25

proceeded to lower a revolving tool by means of a hand-operated wheel control and performed what looked like a chamfering operation on the center hole of the metal plate. He then turned with the plate and hung it on a hook on a conveyor line which moved overhead. After repeating this operation about six times, while I watched and tried to remember the operations, he stepped back and motioned to me to take his place. I started to perform the work as best I could while my "instructor" stood by and watched.

Evidently I started by gripping the metal plate the wrong way, as my instructor interrupted me to demonstrate again the proper grip. After I had finished the first piece of metal he shouted to me, "Spin this into position," pointing to the side operating control wheel. When I hung it on the conveyor, he immediately grabbed it and turned it around on the hook. Gesturing, he indicated that the plates with yellow paint daubed on them should be hung on yellow hooks, red plates on red hooks, and unpainted plates were to be matched with unpainted hooks. He also showed me that the plates were to be hung with the concave side out. Within ten minutes I made three mistakes in hanging up the plates, which he immediately corrected without comment.

After spending about 15 minutes with me, he left. As I worked along I felt extremely clumsy and did not seem to be able to get much rhythm into my work. There were a number of questions I wanted to ask somebody about my job, but my machine was isolated from the others, and I would have had to leave my work in order to speak to another worker. In about 15 minutes my "instructor" returned and shouted to me, "You have to keep that conveyor line filled up." At this point I tried to tell him that I had not brought my lunch with me and asked him where I could eat at noon. He pointed to an opposite corner of the shop and promptly left.

I tried to work a little faster, but I was becoming painfully aware that my hands were getting badly scratched and cut from handling the rough metal plates. After a half hour or so of this a strange workman came up and motioned me away from the machine. He took my place, lined up a big stack of rough plates, and started working on them at a terrific rate of speed. He filled up the conveyor line while I watched. He then turned and walked away. I was sure that he was sent over to show me up, since I couldn't begin to match his rate of speed. I plodded along the best I could. After a couple of hours I wanted to go to the toilet but did not know where it was, and I thought I might be fired if I wandered off looking for it. My "instructor" stopped by two or three times to urge me to speed up my work, and the unknown workman also took over my job several times. Neither gave me an opportunity to initiate a conversation with them.

Somehow I managed to stay at my machine for what seemed an endless time and until a gong sounded, when everyone started rushing off in one direction. Deciding it must be lunch time, I followed the crowd to one end of the shop and found them forming a line behind a counter where I was able to buy sandwiches and milk. I wiped my hands on my pants and ate lunch. I was unable to find anyone from my department to whom I could talk about the shop. The half-hour lunch period was soon over, and I returned to my machine.

During the afternoon I often thought I would be unable to keep my arms moving, and several times I was sure that my watch had stopped. When the workday was finally over I was convinced that my work assignment was impossible and my "instructor" a slavedriver. I returned to my room about 4:30 in the afternoon and without bothering to eat dinner slept straight through until the next morning.

The next day I was assigned a new job. Although I later found out that I was switched because the regular man on my first job had returned from a one-day absence, at the time I thought it was because I had failed on my assignment. On my new assignment as a member of a line assembly team, I was able to talk to the other team members. The assembly team was supervised directly by a relief man or working foreman who received a slightly higher wage than the rest of the crew but who was a member of the union and was not considered a part of management by the rest of the crew. During my second day at the plant this working foreman secured a pair of gloves and a handwiping rag for me and informed me that he would relieve me so that I could take a 10 minute rest in the morning and another in the afternoon.

This working foreman also made most of the individual work assignments on the team job. He started me working on the toughest job of tightening down nuts. In the process of teaching me the job, he pointed out several minor techniques that would make the work easier. Whenever I fell behind the team in production, he would come over and work beside me to help me catch up or transfer me temporarily to an easier job. By the end of the first week I had learned to pace myself with the work speed of the team without undue effort. During the three weeks I was on the team assembly job, three new men were brought into the team and each in turn were assigned the toughest job while the rest of us were shifted to easier work.

While on this job I found out that my first "instructor" was, of course, our department foreman but nobody seemed to know his name.

Within two weeks I joined the union on my own initiative, and the first meeting I attended was held primarily for shop committeemen. As I entered the meeting, the committeeman from my department recognized me.

"Isn't your name McFee?"

"Yes, I work in the brake department."

"I thought I recognized you. Just joined the union, didn't you? My name is Bradley. I'm your shop committeeman. This meeting tonight is primarily for shop committeemen, but we are glad to have a new member here in order to get acquainted with him. I would like to have you meet some of these men."

Bradley then proceeded to introduce me to a number of the men attending the meeting. During the course of our conversation, he said, "Say, McFee, weren't you an officer in the Navy?"

"I was, but I'm surprised you knew."

"I could tell by the Navy serial number you put down on your union application. We need young fellows like you with leadership training in the union. You've probably found conditions pretty tough over in the plant. We don't like the way things are, but we are working to make them better. I hope we can count on your help."

I came to know Bradley quite well during the next few weeks and he became the best friend I had in the shop.

After three weeks on the assembly line job, I was shifted to a new job on which the production method had just been changed from line assembly to complete individual assembly. Shortly after I started on this new job, one of my fellow workers told me that no one was going to produce more than 25 units an hour, even though we had been told by the department foreman that the new standard production rate on the job was 35 units per hour. I had no feelings of guilt about complying with this work restriction because it seemed unreasonable to expect anyone to produce 35 units per hour. The foreman asked every worker each hour how many units he had produced in the preceding hour and it was the custom to report no more than 25 units completed, even if more had been finished. A few days later, without any explanation, the foreman notified us that the standard production rate had been reduced to 30 units per hour. All of the working group felt that this reduction proved the usefulness of work restriction.

6. JIM McFEE (B)

WHILE I was still working in the automobile plant I read several articles in the *New York Times* which expressed some of the management's published opinions on industrial problems at this time. One relating to the automobile industry was of particular interest to me, as follows:

New York Times, September 8, 1946
Lax Productivity Charged to Labor
RUSSELL PORTER

. . . Making liberal allowances for the reconversion needs for nonproduction workers, Mr. Wilson, [president of General Motors] estimated that General Motors worker efficiency averages only about 80% of prewar standards. . . .

The present decrease in efficiency is attributed by manufacturers largely to a widespread postwar "restlessness" and indifference resulting in a rate of absenteeism three times the prewar and a general lack of interest in work, a high labor turnover, and a disposition on the part of some veterans and displaced war workers to accept government unemployment doles instead of going back to work. This "wrong attitude" as Mr. Wilson calls it has been accelerated, many think, by a hangover from the prewar union organizing campaigns in the mass production industries. . . .

7. DAYCOMB COMPANY

ON JANUARY 1, 1942, Henry Carlow was promoted from district sales manager to one of the eight new merchandise manager positions created by the executives of the Daycomb Company. After graduating from college in 1928 and a business school in 1930, he had entered the employ of the Daycomb Company as a salesman and had gradually worked up to the position of district sales manager. In this capacity he had shown considerable initiative, and late in 1941, the officers of the company decided to promote him to a merchandise manager's position in the head office.

The Daycomb Company had a general sales manager, Mr. Benson, who supervised the marketing of its wide line of products. The eight merchandise managers under him had charge of either a specialized commodity line or a particular marketing channel. Mr. Benson, who was relatively new in the concern, had been instrumental in the promotion of Mr. Carlow, although he knew Mr. Carlow mainly from his record as district sales manager.

Mr. Carlow's first assignment, upon his arrival at the head office of the company, was to complete within three months a survey of his product line and his markets, and to file with Mr. Benson a report which was based on that survey. On March 20, 1942, Mr. Carlow's report was ready. Since he had traveled widely over the United States in obtaining data for his report, he had had little opportunity to become well acquainted with Mr. Benson. Moreover, he had made no effort to determine Mr. Benson's working habits or the manner in which Mr. Benson wanted reports prepared. The report was about three fourths of an inch thick and had no introductory summary. It contained recommendations for immediate action, raised questions of general policy for the future, and included all the supporting data upon which these recommendations and proposed policies were based.

Mr. Carlow was surprised when his report did not receive immediate consideration from Mr. Benson, and after three weeks he tried to make an appointment with him to discuss it. Mr. Benson's secretary stated that the sales manager was too busy to discuss the report at that time. Mr. Carlow then took a trip into the field for about three weeks, during which time he interviewed various district sales managers of the company and some of the leading customers. Upon his return, he saw Mr.

Benson in his outer office and questioned him. Mr. Benson admitted that he had not had time to read the report. He stated that it was the first order of business on his docket and that he would give Mr. Carlow a ring as soon as he was ready.

Mr. Carlow was much disturbed by the reception given what he considered a good report, and he was especially distraught because certain of his recommendations required immediate action. Action on other proposals, on the contrary, could be delayed for a period of from three to six months.

8. BEACON PUBLISHING COMPANY

THE BEACON Publishing Company of Philadelphia, publisher of a weekly newspaper, enjoyed a large commercial business in the production of advertising newspapers, circulars, and "throwaways" of newspaper type and size. It employed about seventy-five persons. The mechanical employees were all members of the various printing trade unions. Though the company had no signed agreement with any of them, it operated according to the agreements in effect with the owners of the city's other newspapers and was privileged to display the union label on its work. The unions were an important factor in the industry and had been successful in building up a strong loyalty on the part of their members.

Late in 1934, Roger Clark became mechanical superintendent and production manager of the company. Clark, then 25, had graduated from the University of Michigan in 1931 with the degree of Bachelor of Arts. Originally a student in the College of Engineering of the university, he had transferred to the College of Literature, Science, and the Arts at the end of the first semester of his junior year. His major interest was economics, and his courses included several in accounting and other subjects related to business. Subsequent to his graduation, Clark had been employed as a statistician by a large distributor of petroleum products in Buffalo, New York, and later in the production department of the Beacon Publishing Company's largest customer. In the latter company, he had under his direction the sixty employees in its mechanical departments.

James F. Kennedy, manager of the Beacon Publishing Company, on the first day of Clark's employment, explained to him that his duties were to:

1. Keep the customers satisfied.
2. Act as buffer between Kennedy and the mechanical employees.
3. Improve quality and service.
4. Reduce costs.

Kennedy then called in the heads of the four mechanical departments (composing, photoengraving, stereotyping, and pressroom), all of whom reported to him and all of whom Clark knew. Kennedy explained to them that they should now report to Clark, that Clark was

32

expected to co-ordinate their efforts, and that he (Kennedy) expected 100 per cent co-operation from all of them. There was visible displeasure on the part of the foremen, whose ages were about 55, 50, 45, and 62; but all shook hands with Clark, and the meeting was dismissed.

At the time of Clark's employment the Beacon Publishing Company was erecting a new plant. The rapidly expanding "throwaway" business had outgrown much of the old equipment, especially the presses. Customers had been clamoring for a more varied type of product, additional colors, shorter production time, and lower prices. Previously, the company had enjoyed a virtual monopoly in this type of business in the Philadelphia area; it was able to charge prices that covered its costs and netted a substantial profit. Its prices, however, had often been compared unfavorably with prices charged for similar work in other cities. The company decided to expend some $180,000 for a building and new equipment, principally a high-speed, superduty press of the type employed by metropolitan newspapers. Its design incorporated a number of modern automatic or semiautomatic features to reduce the chance that errors in judgment in the operating crew would affect the quality of the printing. This press, in addition to being fitted for printing in four colors and for any size newspaper from two to sixty-four pages, was expected to increase production by at least 50 per cent.

As soon as Clark was hired, Kennedy turned over most of the detail of installation and erection of the new equipment to him. Decisions in regard to layout and the hundreds of minor problems that arose in working with architects, suppliers of equipment, electricians, and others occupied most of Clark's days through December and January, so that he had little time to devote to problems of current production. It was his impression, however, that things were proceeding smoothly; at least, no serious problems were brought to his attention. His few contacts with customers were pleasant and mainly anticipatory of the "new era" of costs and service that would shortly follow the opening of the new plant.

About January 10 a sling, which was being used to lower into place one of the cylinders of the new presses, broke during the operation. The two-ton part fell a distance of about nine feet, springing one of its journals and damaging the frame of the press. Clark insisted that repairs be made with the greatest care and that new parts be supplied where necessary, because of the important bearing of accurate alignment upon quality production. This accident delayed the completion of the installation by about two weeks.

About February 1, when the press was nearing completion, Bill

Murphy, runner of No. 1 press at the old plant,[1] came into the new pressroom. Murphy was about 33 years of age. He had been a football star at a Philadelphia high school in earlier years and had afterward played semiprofessional football. Something of a local hero, he was

Exhibit 1

BEACON PUBLISHING COMPANY

PRESSROOM ORGANIZATION, OLD PLANT

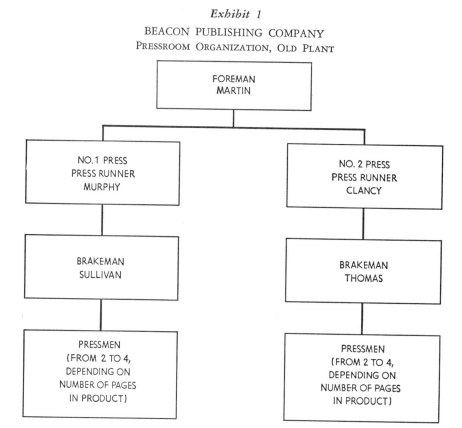

good-looking and cordial to his fellow workers. He was the leader of a clique of three or four Beacon pressmen who maintained their seniority standing at the Philadelphia *Tribune,* one of the large city papers, in whose pressroom the pace of work was generally considered easygoing, by working there at least once each week.[2] Most of the other Beacon pressmen had seniority standing at the *Daily Courier,* another large pa-

---

[1] See Exhibits 1 and 2.

[2] Arrangements such as this were not uncommon in the printing trades. A pressman who had trained at one of the large papers might be able to transfer to a more responsible position at a smaller paper and at the same time retain his seniority at the larger one by agreeing to substitute for one of its pressmen on the latter's day off. The pressman who had transferred would then have to provide a substitute for himself at his regular job, but he could usually arrange for this through the union without difficulty.

Exhibit 2
BEACON PUBLISHING COMPANY
PRESSROOM ORGANIZATION, NEW PLANT

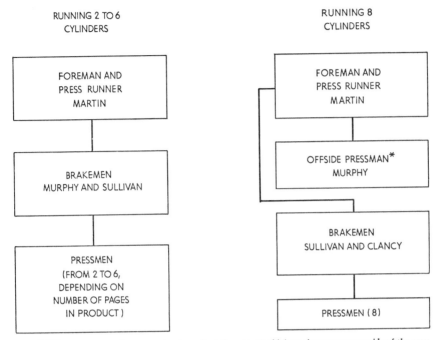

RUNNING 2 TO 6
CYLINDERS

RUNNING 8
CYLINDERS

FOREMAN AND
PRESS RUNNER
MARTIN

BRAKEMEN
MURPHY AND SULLIVAN

PRESSMEN
(FROM 2 TO 6,
DEPENDING ON
NUMBER OF PAGES
IN PRODUCT)

FOREMAN AND
PRESS RUNNER
MARTIN

OFFSIDE PRESSMAN*
MURPHY

BRAKEMEN
SULLIVAN AND CLANCY

PRESSMEN (8)

* Offside pressman merely to cut color, i.e., adjust the amount of ink on the pages on one side of the press.

per well known for its modern, efficient methods. Rivalry between the *Tribune* and the *Courier* was keen. Murphy was a capable workman, but had been warned several times about drinking on the job. He nodded to Clark, spent some fifteen minutes looking over the machine and its appurtenances, then sauntered over to where Clark was talking to the erection foreman and the salesman for the press manufacturer.

ROGER CLARK: What do you think of her, Bill?

BILL MURPHY: Some tub. She's like No. 16 at the *Tribune*.

CLARK: Not exactly; this one has staggered roller bearings, shorter leads, and is some three tons heavier.[3] She's built for 80,000 papers per hour; No. 16 is built for 72,000.

MURPHY: Ha! No. 16 never did better than 35,000.

SALESMAN: No. 16 at the *Tribune* is one of the best machines in this city. The production is there, if the pressman would allow the press to produce.

MURPHY: Yeah? All the pressmen in Philadelphia couldn't keep the sheets up[4] on that tub. What do you expect to get out of this one, Clark?

[3] All features leading to improved quality

[4] Paper properly threaded.

CLARK (*enthusiastically*): Of course, we won't run it much above 75,000. That should give us a net of 50,000 papers up to sixteen pages.

MURPHY: With that bum cylinder and the cracked side frame? You'll be lucky to get 30,000. I'll make a bet right now that you never do any better than we do with those two old coffee mills we are running now.

The two machines used in the old plant were single-width machines, capable of producing two 12-page papers or one 24-page paper with each revolution. Most runs were of 12 pages; the usual number of men working was thirteen, including the foreman. Orders were given by the foreman directly to the press runners, who either carried them out personally or relayed them to the brakemen and pressmen. Observance of this formality was very rigid; for example, if the foreman wanted more tension[5] on the sheets in No. 1 press, he would hold up a clenched fist to Murphy, who in turn would clench his fist to Sullivan (sign language was often used for communication because of the noise of the press).

That night, at home, Clark recalled the conversation with Murphy and considered again the expectation of increased production with the new machine. The damage to the press during its erection he discounted, because of the guaranty of the manufacturer that the machine would be placed in perfect condition. The factors that should yield increased production he set down as follows:

	Old Machines	New Machine
1. Faster cylinder speed:		
Number of papers each revolution	2	1
Revolutions per minute	200	667
Papers per minute	400	667
Two machines (old setup): double width (new setup)	2	2
Total papers per minute	800	1,334

2. Fewer stoppages to change rolls of paper.
Old machines (single width)—78 rolls (77 stoppages) per run of 300,000 12-page papers.
New machine (double width)—39 rolls (38 stoppages) per run of 300,000 12-page papers.

3. Improved working conditions, laborsaving devices:
   a) In the new pressroom, rolls were to be stored on their bilges, or sides, so that they could be easily rolled to a dolly and thence to the press. In the old pressroom, rolls were stored two high, on end, and had to be turned on their sides and rolled by hand across a bumpy floor.
   b) Electric hoists were provided to lift the rolls into the new machine. In the old plant, rolls had to be hoisted by hand with chainfalls.
   c) The new machine provided 100 per cent safe, fully automatic controls.
   d) The new pressroom was clean and well lighted; it provided better ventilation, toilet, and locker facilities.

---

[5] Securing even tension on the paper being printed was one of the most critical problems of press design and operation, since the web of paper was so easily torn. The tension had to be equal across the width of the web and throughout its length while the press was running at high speeds and also during starting and stopping, when it was changing speeds rapidly.

Clark therefore concluded that attainment of 50 per cent greater production would be relatively simple; in fact, even 60 per cent could be anticipated.

On February 15, 1935, the new plant was placed in operation, and the old plant was sold. The new press was operated only one shift per day, plus overtime as required. It was the only press in the plant used for the production of advertising newspapers and other promotional material of that sort.

There were countless "bugs" in the new equipment; and for the next month, Clark was satisfied to get the work out at all, without worrying too much about hourly production. The weekly summaries, however, showed that the per hour production in the pressroom was averaging slightly more than 30,000, no better than in the old plant. Wage rates, which were paid on an hourly basis, had not been changed; nor had the company planned to alter them, inasmuch as the management was certain that the company would receive enough additional work on the basis of lower prices and better quality to maintain the employees' hours of work and therefore their "take-home" pay. In fact, they believed the new press would result in an increase of overtime work, paid for at the rate of time and a half.

At the end of March, Kennedy called this production deficiency to Clark's attention and emphasized that customers were pressing for reduced prices. He ordered Clark to investigate the causes of the deficiency and to make every effort to increase production at once. Accordingly, Clark devoted most of his time to the pressroom. He spent many hours in conversation with John W. Martin, foreman of the Beacon pressroom.

Martin was about 45 years of age. He had been a first sergeant of artillery in World War I, and was sometimes familiarly addressed as Sarge. He had been made foreman about seven years previously, largely on a seniority basis, when the man who was foreman at that time had concluded that the work was too strenuous for his advanced years. Martin's education had stopped at about grade eight, but he had been much impressed by mathematics when he came into contact with "logrithums" during his artillery service. He liked to carry a micrometer caliper, which he could not read, and to talk of surface speeds, pitch lines, and other technical terms he had picked up in his twenty-five years around pressrooms. Kennedy had at one time been much impressed by Martin; but, Kennedy told Clark, Martin had given him so many "bum steers" that he had lost confidence in him. He said Martin was a conscientious worker, who was good on quality and had apparently gotten all the production possible out of the presses in the old plant.

Martin maintained seniority at the *Daily Courier* and considered that shop the acme of perfection. Martin was disliked by some of the foremen and men in other departments, particularly because he had, during the period in which he had impressed Kennedy, forced them to "cut their goods to fit his cloth." They said he was a confirmed buck passer. The doggerel quoted below, which appeared on the pressroom bulletin board and which was generally attributed to the stereotype foreman, had created quite a stir just prior to Clark's arrival.

MARTIN'S LAMENT

It must be the paper, it must be the ink,
It must be the plates or something, I think.
For it can't be the press, and it can't be me,
For I've been thirty years in the business, you see.

Clark summarized Martin's reasons for the production showing as follows:

1. Poor paper.
2. The cylinder that had been dropped during erection.
3. Poor printing plates.
4. "You'll have to get me a whip to get any more out of these men."

Clark knew that the criticism of the paper was unfounded. He had the alignment of the dropped cylinder checked by an impartial machinist, who found it to be perfect. Furthermore, production did not improve when the cylinder was idle. There was some justification for the criticism of the plates; consequently, the stereotype machinery was overhauled, and the foreman of that department was closely supervised in all his operations. With the improved plates, a gain of 1,500 papers per hour was obtained.

Martin's fourth point, "You'll have to get me a whip to get any more out of these men," was the one which most interested Kennedy when, in the course of a conversation with Clark, he learned of the four points. A hardheaded former real estate operator, Kennedy was opposed to unions, particularly the pressmen's union, with whose members he had had several arguments. Referring to the fourth point, he said to Clark: "Those fellows go out too much. The other night when I stopped in on my way home from the theater, only five men of a crew of nine were in the room. And I'll bet that the others were half drunk when they came back. Post a notice forbidding them to go out except during the regular lunch periods."

The notice was posted. Production dropped to below 30,000 per hour, and two of the better pressmen did not show up for work. Further, the going-out did not stop. Kennedy called in the president of the pressmen's union, who said he would "speak to the boys." Although their going-out did not stop, production crept up to 35,000 per hour.

Clark spent more and more time in the pressroom. Pressure for reduced prices was becoming acute, and there were rumors that competitors were starting in business. Clark's observation was that the press in general ran well, but that there were too many web breaks[6] and that too much time was consumed in changing rolls. He recommended that the roll stands be altered to accommodate larger rolls and that automatic tension devices be installed. These changes were made at a cost of $3,000. Production remained the same. Occasionally, he offered suggestions to Martin, who always had at least a dozen reasons why they would not work.

One day, Clark entered the pressroom by a seldom-used door and overheard Martin telling the men: "I've been twenty-five years in this business, and along comes a guy smoking a cigarette and tells me what to do."

Shortly after that incident, Martin's wife died. Clark, who had come to dislike Martin thoroughly, nevertheless immediately called him on the telephone, offered his condolences, and inquired whether there was anything that he or the company might do. Martin seemed grateful. The next night, Clark attended the wake. He was ushered into the kitchen of Martin's home and seated with the president of the pressman's union, the chairman of its board of trustees, several Beacon pressmen, and pressmen from other shops. Upon leaving, he was asked to join the union officials and several of the pressmen in a drink. He accepted.

During Martin's absence from the shop for about a week, Murphy, because of his senior position, acted as foreman. Production rose to 40,-000 papers per hour. Upon Martin's return, production dropped to 38,000; but to Clark, it seemed that it required more effort on Martin's part to get 38,000 than it did on Murphy's part to get 40,000.

Clark thought that Martin's attitude, however, was better. From time

---

[6] Exact responsibility for web breaks was difficult to assign. Factors caused by press design had been largely eliminated from the presses in use at the Beacon Publishing Company. Some were undoubtedly caused by any slight unevenness in the quality of the paper. Careful make-ready and running of the press by a crew always kept web breaks at a minimum.

to time, he did accept suggestions. Clark then began to invite him to his home occasionally, and on several evenings assisted Martin's son, who was having trouble with his high school algebra.

Production all the while was slowly improving. By November, it had reached 42,000. Martin constantly complained "off the record" to Clark about Murphy. He could not, he said, make charges against him, because they were both members of the pressman's union, whose bylaws prevented one member bringing charges against another; but he asserted that Murphy was "a bad influence." Martin said Murphy was always discovering at the last minute some fault or defect that would delay production. With Murphy "out of there," Martin felt that 50,000 or 55,000 papers per hour could be attained.

During the rush of Christmas business and overtime employment, Murphy several times appeared to have all the work he could handle. Clark was aware that the other pressmen, not of Murphy's clique, took every opportunity to place him in a position where he would be drawn unfavorably to Clark's attention. About the middle of January, during a run, a change of plates had to be made. On this particular run, it was not Murphy's job as offside pressman to plate up; but inasmuch as the pressman whose job it was had gone out, Murphy made the change. During the process of locking on the new plates, he was interrupted by Martin. When the press was started, two of the plates he had put on came off, doing some damage to the plate clips and impression blankets. Martin immediately sent Murphy home and reported the incident to Clark.

Concepts and Research Findings

1. THE FUNCTIONAL POINT OF VIEW*

Alexander H. Leighton

THE CONCEPT of function has been borrowed by certain social scientists from physiology. In the latter field it has to do with asking such questions as, What is the role (function) of the heart or a gland in relation to the whole body? As applied to anthropology, Radcliffe-Brown puts it this way:

> The concept of function . . . involves the notion of a *structure* consisting of a *set of relations* among *unit entities,* the *continuity* of the structure being maintained by a *life-process* made up of the *activities* of the constituent units.

If, with these concepts in mind, we set out on a systematic investigation of the nature of human society and of social life, we find presented to us three sets of problems. First, the problems of social morphology—what kinds of social structures are there, what are their similarities and differences, how are they to be classified? Second, the problems of social physiology—how do social structures function? Third, the problems of development—how do new types of social structure come into existence?

By the definition here offered "function" is the contribution which a partial activity makes to the total activity of which it is a part. The function of a particular social usage is the contribution it makes to the total social life as the functioning of the total social system. Such a view implies that a social system (the total social structure of a society together with the totality of social usages, in which that structure appears and on which it depends for its continued existence) has a certain kind of unity, which we may speak of as a functional unity. We may define it as a condition in which all parts of the social system work together with a sufficient degree of harmony or internal consistency, i.e., without producing persistent conflicts which can neither be resolved nor regulated.

Opposition, i.e., organized and regulated antagonism is, of course, an essential feature of every social system.[1]

---

* Alexander H. Leighton, *Human Relations in a Changing World* (New York: E. P. Dutton & Co., Inc., 1949), pp. 156–61.

[1] A. R. Radcliffe-Brown, "Concept of Function in Social Science," *American Anthropologist,* Vol. XXXVII, July–September, 1935.

Bronislaw Malinowski says: "The primary concern of functional anthropology is the function of institutions, customs, implements and ideas. It holds that the cultural process is subject to laws and that the laws are to be found in the function of the real elements of culture."[2]

Since this matter is difficult to realize on the basis of abstract terms alone, three illustrations are offered: the first is from animal ecology, the second from entomology and the third from medicine. Although drawn from non-social science fields because less entangled, they are nevertheless relevant.

Suppose that a naturalist is studying a wilderness area for purposes of conservation. He finds that the various plants and animals as they go through their life cycles of growth and reproduction exist in a state of complex interdependence. His attention is directed toward mountain sheep that are diminishing in number and also to the presence of wolves. Were he a sportsman or rancher, he would be likely to assume that the wolves were *the cause* of the reduction in sheep and to maintain this view with no little heat. The naturalist, however, does not stop with such a single idea. He observes, theorizes and tests his theories with further observations. He finds that the wolves kill the sheep but that they also kill numbers of other animals that are in competition with the sheep for the same food. He discovers that the sheep suffer from scarcity of food, from the washing out of certain chemicals from the soil due to erosion, from diseases and from the winter killing of lambs. In the end, the naturalist may find that the wolves are one of a number of serious threats to the sheep and that their reduction would help the sheep population. Or, he may find that the balance of nature is such in this particular case that the wolves aid the sheep more than harming them, by keeping down the number of animals that eat the same food. In either event, the naturalist sees multiple forces at work in a state of interdependence, rather than a single cause that fits like a key into a lock. Moreover, he does not take sides with sheep, wolves or other animals in such a way as to blind his understanding of how they are interdependent.

Suppose another naturalist is studying insects purely from an interest in advancing knowledge. If he turns his attention to bees he will find that complex interrelationship of individuals to make a hive that has often been described. There are the workers, the drones and the

---

[2] "Culture," in *Encyclopedia of the Social Sciences* (New York: Macmillan Co., copyright 1931), Vol. IV.

A mathematically oriented discussion of functional dependence may be found in Eliot Dismore Chapple and Carleton Stevens Coon, *Principles of Anthropology* (New York: Henry Holt & Co., 1942).

queen, each with patterns of behavior that aid the continued existence of the colony with a striking disregard for the well-being of any one individual. The drones are starved, mutilated and thrown out when their functions have been performed. Workers that arrive home with frayed wings or begin to fail in their productive capacity receive the same treatment. Even the queen, ordinarily surrounded by attendants who minister to her needs, is destroyed when infirmities begin to creep upon her. The naturalist will observe further that all this behavior does function with considerable efficiency to perpetuate individual hives and bees as a whole. He will make these discoveries in a spirit of finding out how it all works and without pronouncing judgments on the bees, without calling the drones "useless" or the destruction of damaged workers "wicked."

For the third picture, suppose a doctor is carrying out research on the cause of tuberculosis. His first goal is to understand the process, and he finds before long that he cannot regard the tubercle bacillus as *the cause* of the disease. It becomes evident that millions of people harbor the germ without developing any signs or symptoms of tuberculosis. The research physician must, therefore, study the reactions and interactions of glands, nerves, blood vessels, lymphatic system, and other organs and functions of the body in relation to the whole, to the tubercle bacillus and to other germs that might have a predisposing or immunizing effect. Nor is the list exhausted here, for it is also necessary to look into such matters as diet, light, nature of work and the possible presence of hereditary and psychological factors. The germ, it turns out, is only one of a number of conditions that must be present before tuberculosis occurs. At no time does the doctor get wound up in hating the germ and in weaving patterns of revenge into his research. He keeps his mind on the central aim of finding out what is going on so that remedial change can be introduced.

In these illustrations at least two common elements are evident. The first is an attempt to understand any item as part of a larger whole, as the product of multiple, interacting forces, rather than the result of a single cause that can be ferreted out like a detective uncovering a murderer. The second is that the forces are regarded as natural rather than good or bad. One's own hopes, fears, and ideas of what *should be* are set aside in favor of discovering what *is*. Whether the naturalist likes or dislikes wolves is not relevant to understanding their relationship to the sheep. The man who studies the bees may be himself a believer in democracy, fascism, or communism, but this must not be allowed to intrude itself into his reports about their social life and how it works for them. The physician does not permit belief in the wickedness of the tubercle bacillus to lead him into underestimating or overestimating its power, nor to neglecting all the other matters that are equally important in understanding and controlling tuberculosis.

Few people will quarrel with all this as long as it is confined to the natural sciences, but many difficulties arise as soon as these few and simple points are transferred to the study of human behavior and an effort is made to view society as the naturalist looks at the animal kingdom, the physician the functions of the body and the astronomer the stars. In place of such a view the policy maker, like most other people, has it ingrained in him from his early years to measure human affairs in terms of good and evil. Starkly simple explanations are sought to the neglect of deeper understanding and hence opportunity for control.

.   .   .   .

This kind of thinking recurs continuously in all sorts of contexts. If war is threatened, if an economic depression descends, if unemployment appears, if Congress fails to pass the Fair Employment Practice Bill, if a strike takes place, if patients in a mental hospital are mistreated, if a child is found neglected, we always give far more attention to discussing the rights and the wrongs of the situation, in deciding who is to blame and in taking sides, than to understanding the forces that have brought it about and deciding what can be done to control them. If we can make somebody suffer for it, we are likely to go away satisfied, leaving the situation no better than before.

We are always looking for the villain instead of human beings going through the business of living as best they can, some helpfully and some destructively in their actions toward the welfare of others. Preoccupation with the search for the villain blinds us to the constellation of events past and present that gave rise to him. From the functional point of view, "what gives rise" is the question. Can we, through understanding the forces that produce villains, alter situations so that there will be less ground on which they can flourish?

Must we be forever content with trapping rats? Cannot we also stop up their holes and rid ourselves of the places that breed them? The world is getting too small for the luxury of villains and there is a widespread need for the physician's obsession with getting at causes and not tinkering with symptoms only.

These, then, are the implications of the functional view. By and large, they enter only a little into most of the thinking that gives rise to policy.

SECTION II

Work Group Behavior

Introduction

THE SIX cases of Section I depict the breadth and depth of behavioral issues with which this course book is designed to help the student deal, and the ideas in the functional point of view reading are basic to the kind of analysis needed to begin to cope with issues of this type. With this introductory sense of the scope of the book in mind, we begin study in earnest by giving our attention first to the behavior of people who are working as members of groups.

Why is the subject of work group behavior important to study, and why does it come first rather than at some later place in the course? Primarily because most of the time, most of the people with whom any of us work or upon whom we depend at work are in fact behaving not as isolated individuals, but as members of small groups. Since group membership is almost inescapable throughout every modern organization, most behavior in organizations, of managers and workers alike, can best be understood and predicted through analysis of relationships between people who share group membership at work.

Furthermore, the meaning of the group to its members is very frequently a more direct influence on behavior than any other single set of factors. Yet, the influence of social forces is frequently ignored or thought of as less interesting or fruitful a sphere of study than, say, personality. In fact, however, we know considerably more of practical significance to the administrator about the functioning of groups than we do about personality, on the one hand, or larger organizations, on the other. Since work groups at every level of the business organization are a core element of organizational behavior, we seek first to understand how and why they function as they do.

The first few cases in this section illustrate some of the puzzling ways in which people in work groups are likely to behave. Metropolitan Steel Company presents a colorful picture of "work restriction" by incentive operators, an explanation of which raises important questions about group process and structure. In the Excelsior Bakeries, Inc., and Betty Randall cases, the small group's influence upon individual behavior is demonstrated in a way which uncovers problems of conflicting group loyalties and management policy. The Slade Company illustrates a group behavior pattern which meets many of management's needs but violates formal rules of the organization. All these cases indicate that in order to interpret the work group's adaptation to its environment, it is necessary to understand in some detail the pattern and functions of the group's internal behavior and the relationships which emerge between its members.

The Times-Herald and Markham Instrument Company cases take us off the production floor into professional and management group settings. Here the behavior we are confronted with is more complex than what we have seen before, both because the members of these groups must respond to more subtle cues about what is expected of them and because they are composed of representatives of other groups, each with its own values and special competence. Nevertheless, the basic processes of small groups are as apparent in these higher-status groups as they are in those composed of blue-collar workers.

The remaining five cases in the section differ from those referred to above by the fact that they are each composed of several parts. The Case of the Changing Cage, Superior Slate Quarry, Maynard Aircraft, Kilkenny Lumber Company, and the White Company are divided in several ways. Some of these cases are divided into succeeding time periods to make possible the prediction of events from one time period to the next. Other parts share information about one period of time in such a way that predictions about behavior can be made from limited information about conditions and some of these cases are divided in both of these ways. In any of these cases, analysis, prediction, and recommendations for action must precede becoming informed about what is in succeeding parts. Therefore, the student should not read beyond Part I before being told to do so by his instructor. Since these cases are designed to give practice in analysis and prediction—a kind of test of one's own ability to comprehend work group behavior—it is important that this sequence be followed. The last three of these cases include specific questions to be answered before going on to the next part and follow-up assessments of predictive accuracy.

The adequacy of the "predictions" which you are asked to make in the sequential cases described above, and the quality of the analyses of all the cases in this section depend on your having a reasonably systematic way of relating the various elements of each situation to one another and of seeing the function of each element in its relation to the situation as a whole. The paper, "A Conceptual Scheme for Describing Work Group Behavior" (Reading 1), presents a particular set of conceptual ideas which are useful in analyzing and predicting the behavior of members of work groups, as influenced by such "given" factors as the nature of the task, the technology, and management's policy and practice. In short, here is a way of thinking which can greatly increase the understanding and skill with which work groups can be administered. But like any conceptual scheme, it must be practiced before it can be useful.

The adequacy of our predictions and quality of our analyses also depend on the extent of our knowledge about work group behavior. For this reason, you will find a number of abstracted research readings at the end of the section. These abstracts attempt to summarize a sample of the more significant research that has been done on small work groups in industry. Included are both older studies that have been landmarks in the development of knowledge on this subject, and newer studies that have special significance for administrators. They represent approaches to the subject from different schools of thought, using different concepts and research methods. In general, the abstracts present only those findings from each study which could be stated concisely. The abstracts do not attempt to describe in any detail the methodology and theoretical framework of the various studies, and they necessarily omit important qualifications and illustrations in the original data. They are presented as an introduction to the growing body of systematic research in this field of which an administrator should be aware. And they provide each student with the opportunity to develop a set of propositions about group behavior which integrate and explain the findings in a way he believes will be useful to him.

We think of the concepts and research findings in this section, as in every other, to be a means of *improving the probability* that our understanding of what is going on and our predictions of what will happen next are accurate. It would be folly, indeed, for us to begin to think that we are dealing in certainties. Far from it, we aspire to reducing the chance of error from a potential 100 per cent to something better than 50–50. During your lifetime, a great deal more will be discovered to reduce the chance of error even further. It seems unlikely, now, that perfect understanding and, certainly, perfect predictability will ever be realized in the complex arena of human behavior in organizations. It is hoped, however, that practice in using some of the knowledge and some of the concepts we now possess will give you such a sense of improved administrative capacity that you will want to update yourself continuously in the many years of practice which lie ahead.

While working through all this material, it has proven helpful to read one or two detailed researches in which the behavior of a particular work group is described and analyzed in considerably greater detail than is possible in any one research abstract or teaching case. One study which our students have found especially useful for this purpose—and have enjoyed reading—is Zaleznik's case study of work and social behavior in a factory group.[1] The readings included in this section will provide references to additional work group researches which can profitably be explored in greater detail.

---

[1] A. Zaleznik, *Worker Satisfaction and Development* (Boston: Division of Research, Harvard Business School, 1956). See also, George F. F. Lombard, *Behavior in a Selling Group* (Boston: Division of Research, Harvard Business School, 1955).

Cases

1. METROPOLITAN STEEL COMPANY*

IN SEPTEMBER, 1945, Donald Roy obtained a job as a radial drill press operator in a machine shop of the Metropolitan Steel Company. About that time, Roy had a conversation with a friend, Orvis Collins, who was employed as a production worker in a nearby factory. Roy and Collins exchanged reports of their early work experiences. When they found that both their jobs were paid on a piecework basis, Collins told Roy about his introduction to piecework when he first started work:

> ORVIS COLLINS: The shop superintendent told me that he considered it important to get in with the right people at the beginning and drew a folder out of his desk from which he read a poem about thinking. The title of the poem was something like "If We Only Think." The thesis of the poem was that if we give thought to each of our daily actions, we get along better with other people.
>
> He then read an essay, "The Crooked Stick," which appeared to have been clipped from some advertising matter. The point of the essay was that there are crooked sticks in every woodpile, and that they are more trouble than they are worth. He said he thought it would be a good thing if we could find some way to make those people who are troublemakers see that being troublemakers is not to their own advantage.
>
> He *then* explained the incentive system and said that it was a fair system because each man was paid with regard to the amount of work he did, and not simply for being on the job. He said if I worked hard, in a couple of months I would be earning $1.50 an hour. He added, however, that some people are not interested in giving their best to the company and therefore do not earn as much as some of the more unselfish ones.

Collins then related to Roy a conversation he had had soon afterward with Bob, one of the workers at the factory:

---

* The data reported in this case have been secured with permission from the following published sources: Donald Roy, "Quota Restriction and Goldbricking in a Machine Shop," *American Journal of Sociology*, Vol. LVII, No. 5 (1952), pp. 427–42; Orvis Collins, Melville Dalton, and Donald Roy, "Restriction of Output and Social Cleavage in Industry," *Applied Anthropology*, Vol. V, No. 3 (1946), pp. 1–14; William F. Whyte *et al.*, *Money and Motivation* (New York: Harper & Bros., 1955), pp. 11–38.

BOB: Well, I suppose you've been up to see Heinzer [the superintendent]. Gosh, I remember when I went up to see him.

COLLINS: What did you talk about?

BOB: It was a hot August afternoon, and we all sat around there in a big circle. Heinzer did the talking. He just went on and on about the company, and what a good place the company is to work at, and how democratic it is here, and how everybody can talk to anybody he pleases about any gripe, and how he wanted to hear about it if there was anything we didn't like. He just went on and on.

COLLINS: What else?

BOB: He told us about how the piecework system was set up so that nobody could hang on anybody else's shirttail. He said it was every man for himself. He said: "You've got your friends, sure; but you're not going to give them anything unless they give you something in the way of a bargain in return."

He went on this way: "Now, say that you want to buy a suit, and you have a friend who is in the clothing business; you might go in and say: 'Look here, Ted, I'm looking for a suit, and I want to pay about $25 for it. What have you got?' Ted shows you what he has in stock, and you're pretty well satisfied with one for $30. You say: 'I'll come in Monday with the money, Ted,' and you go out. But while you're walking down the street, you see this other suit in the window. Just the same suit Ted offered you for $30, but this outfit only wants $25. All right, young man, which suit do you buy?"

Heinzer looked right at me, and I knew what he was getting at. So I thought for a minute and said: "I'd buy the $30 suit and lose the extra $5.00 if I could help a friend."

Heinzer didn't know what to say. He took off his straw hat and wiped his forehead with his handkerchief. Then he said: "But that isn't good business, young man."

I said: "When it comes to buying a suit from a friend or from some other fellow, I'll buy from a friend, and I don't care about business." (We knew we were both talking about piecework.)

Heinzer thought for a long time; then he said: "But that's not the way the world is run. Now, what would you do if you were walking down the street with your wife and met another fellow? And this friend was wearing a suit identical with the one you had on, and your wife was with you and his wife was with him, and your wife said to this fellow: 'Why, that's just like Bob's suit. How much did you pay for it?' And the fellow said: 'I paid $25 for it at such and such a store and bought my wife a new hat with the $5.00 I saved by not trading at our mutual friend's store.'" (He had fancy names for all these people worked out and everything, and you could tell he had been working up this story for a long time; but I'll bet this was the first time he had to use it this way.)

I said to Heinzer: "Whoa, just a minute; my wife wouldn't say such a thing. My wife isn't selfish. She would want me to do the right thing by my friend." That ended Heinzer's talk.

He just said: "I guess that'll be all for today, boys." As we walked out, he said to me: "That's all right, son. I like a man who can give a straight answer." Like heck he does. That was just some more psychology stuff. He took a course over at ———— University on psychology, and now everything is psychology to him. He thinks that this psychology bunk he learned is giving him a big advantage over guys who don't know it. Always trying to get the best of the other guy! They can take all the psychology in the world, and you know what they can do with it as far as I'm concerned, because there's nothing that can beat good, old-fashioned honesty.

Roy found that his own experiences were somewhat similar to Collins'. When Roy was hired, a personnel department clerk assured him that the radial drill operators were averaging $1.25 an hour on piecework. Since Roy had had no previous machine-shop experience, and since a machine would not be available for a few days, he was advised to spend some time watching Jack Starkey, a radial drillman with a great deal of seniority and skill.

One of Starkey's first questions was: "What have you been doing?" When Roy said he had worked in a Pacific Coast shipyard at a rate of pay over $1.00 an hour, Starkey exclaimed: "Then what are you doing in this place?" When Roy replied that averaging $1.25 an hour wasn't bad, Starkey exploded.

JACK STARKEY: Averaging, you say! Averaging?

DONALD ROY: Yeah, on the average. I'm an average guy, so I ought to make my buck and a quarter, that is, after I get on to it.

STARKEY (*angrily*): Don't you know that $1.25 an hour is the *most* we can make, even when we *can* make more? And most of the time, we can't even make that. Have you ever worked on piecework before?

ROY: No.

STARKEY: I can see that! Well, what do you suppose would happen if I turned in $1.50 an hour on these pump bodies?

ROY: Turned in? You mean if you actually did the work?

STARKEY: I mean if I actually did the work and turned it in.

ROY: They'd have to pay you, wouldn't they? Isn't that the agreement?

STARKEY: Yes! They'd pay me—once. Don't you know that if I

turned in $1.50 an hour on these pump bodies tonight, the whole damn methods department would be down here tomorrow? And they'd retime this job so quick it would make your head swim! And when they retimed it, they'd cut the price in half, and I'd be working for 85 cents an hour instead of $1.25!

It took a while for Roy to find out exactly what Starkey was talking about, but he learned a little more about what Starkey meant from Joe Mucha, the day man on his machine. Mucha shared Roy's job repertoire and kept a close eye on Roy's production. On November 14, the day after Roy first attained quota, Mucha advised: "Don't let it go over $1.25 an hour, or the time-study man will be right down here! And they don't waste time, either. They watch the records like hawks. I got ahead, so I took it easy for a couple of hours."

Mucha told Roy that he had noticed that Roy had made $10.01 the day before and warned him not to go over $1.25 an hour. He told Roy to figure the setups and the time on each operation very carefully so that he would definitely not total over $10.25 in any one day.

Starkey spoke to Roy after Mucha left. "What's the matter? Are you trying to upset the apple cart?" He explained in a friendly manner that $10.50, for example, would be too much to turn in, even on an old job. "The turret-lathe men can turn in $1.35," he said, "but their base rate is 90 cents, and ours is 85 cents."

Starkey warned Roy that the methods department could lower prices on any job, old or new, by changing the fixture slightly or changing the size of drill. According to Starkey, a couple of operators (first and second shift on the same drill) got to competing with each other to see how much they could make. They got up to $1.65 an hour, and the price was cut in half. From then on, they had to run that job themselves, as none of the other operators would accept it.

According to Starkey, it would be all right for drill pressmen to turn in $1.28 or $1.29 an hour, when it figured out that way, but it was not all right to turn in $1.30 an hour.

Several weeks after Roy started working, two operators staged the following conversation for his benefit:

ED: That guy (*pointing across the room*) is the greatest rate buster in the shop. Give him a job he can make a nickel on, and he'll break his back for the company.

MIKE: That's no lie. He's ruined every job on that machine. They've cut him down to the point where he has to do twice the work for half the pay. A few more like him would ruin this shop. [Roy later learned from the timekeeper that this "rate buster" had a very high "take-home."]

ED: It's guys like that who spoil the shop for the rest of us. Some-body ought to take a piece of Babbitt and pound some sense into his thick skull. That's the only kind of treatment a guy like that understands.

MIKE: We're handling him the best way as it is. The only way to handle those bastards is not to have a thing to do with them. That guy hasn't got a friend in the place, and he knows it. You can bet your life he thinks about that every time he comes to work.

Roy noticed that, with one exception, all the men who seemed to be called "rate busters" ate lunch apart from the work group and from each other. (When Collins attempted to strike up a friendship by "hanging around" a rate buster's machine, he was told: "Why the hell don't you get out of here and let a man work? There's enough guys around here who've got enough in their pockets so they can afford to spend their time and the company's gassing with you. I can't. I'm a poor man.")

The one rate buster who did eat with the rest of the men was John. Aggressive in his dealing with his fellow workers, John was at any time prepared to defend his views. For this reason, he was often the center of heated arguments. These arguments were usually political in nature, and on such subjects as whether Russia had any part in winning the war, whether Roosevelt planned to become a dictator, or whether work-men had the right to strike. In the behavior of the group, there was often noticeable an attempt to draw John out, to bait him. John often became wildly excited in the course of these discussions, to the amuse-ment of the group. Following is an example of one of these discussions:

SWEDE: Not all unions are rackets.

JOHN: The guys who run them all are racketeers. I don't need any-body walking around telling me where I'm going to work and why.

SWEDE: Without a union, the boss tells you where you're going to work; and if you don't like it, you can't open your mouth.

JOHN: If you don't like it, you can get out. Put yourself in the posi-tion of the employer. Do you want somebody coming and telling you whom you can hire and whom you can't?

SWEDE: The point is, I'm not an employer. I'm an operator, and I want to get just as much as I can out of it.

JOHN: That's just it. The union is for the guy who doesn't want to work. The guy who wants to work doesn't have any trouble. My grand-father worked without union protection, and I can work without union protection.

HANK: Where did he work? Down on the farm? (*Laughter from the group.*)

JOHN: You guys make me sick! The way you loaf around here, you're stealing just as much as if you walked up to F. E. Berrett[1] and stuck a gun in his ribs.

BILL: The trouble with a gun, John, is that they can run you in for it.

Roy found that, unlike the rate busters, most of the other operators seemed to have time to "burn." One evening, Ed Sokolsky, one-time second-shift operator on Starkey's drill, commented on a job the latter was running:

ED SOKOLSKY: That's a gravy job. I worked on those, and I could turn out nine an hour. I timed myself at six minutes.

ROY: Really? At 35 cents apiece, that's over $3.00 an hour!

SOKOLSKY: And I got ten hours;[2] I used to make out in four hours and fool around the rest of the night.

Sokolsky claimed he could also make over $3.00 an hour on the two machines he was presently running, but he could turn in only $1.40 an hour or, occasionally, $1.45 or $1.50 for the two machines together. He said that he always "made out" for a ten-hour shift by 11:00 o'clock, that he had nothing to do from 11:00 to 3:00, and had even left early, getting someone to punch his timecard for him.

"That's the advantage of working nights," said Sokolsky. "You can make out in a hurry and sit around, and nobody says anything. But you can't get away with it on day shift with all the big shots around. Jack has to take it easy on these housings to make them last eight hours, and that must be tough."

Old Pete, another old-timer, confided to Roy: "Once, when they had timed me on some connecting rods, I could have made $20 a day easy. I had to run them at the lowest speed on the machine to keep from making too much. I had a lot of trouble once when I was being timed, and they gave me $35 a hundred. Later, they cut it to $19.50 a hundred, and I still make $9.50 a day."

Roy's own first "spare time" came on November 18. That day, he made out with such ease on the pedestals that he had an hour to spare. To cover the hour, he had to poke along on the last operation, taking twice as much time to do forty-three pieces as he ordinarily would. A few days later in the washroom, before Roy started work, Willie commented on Roy's "gravy" job, the pedestals:

---

[1] President of Metropolitan Steel Company.

[2] During this period, some workers were working a ten-hour shift, some an eight-hour shift.

WILLIE: The methods department is going to lower the price on the pedestals; there was some talk today about it.

ROY: I hope they don't cut it too much. I suppose they'll make some change in the jigs?

WILLIE: They'll change the tooling in some way. Don't worry, when they make up their minds to lower a price, they'll find a way to do it.

However, in March, Roy experienced a sudden increase in skill and found himself capable of making out early on jobs other than the pedestals. With this increase of skill, Roy found the pedestals quickly fading as the supreme contributors of "gravy." For example, on March 22, Roy stalled along, turning out only 89 casings, which he added to his kitty of 40 for a turn-in of 129. Mucha had a kitty of 13, and Roy figured that the 116 pieces left would just do Mucha tomorrow. Although the shift did not end until 11:00, Roy finished his last piece about 9:30 and started cleaning the machine about 10:00 o'clock. Roy noticed that Tony, who worked beside him, was also through early, standing around his machine. "This is the earliest you've made out, isn't it?" Tony asked. "That's the kind of job I like. Then I can go at it and enjoy it."

On April 7, Roy was able to enjoy four hours of "free time." He turned out 43 connecting rods in the four hours from 3:00 to 7:00, averaging nearly 11 an hour. At 7:00 o'clock, there were only 23 pieces left in the lot, and he knew there would be no point in building up a kitty for Monday if Mucha punched off the job before Roy got to work. Roy could not go ahead with the next order (also a load of connecting rods) because the rules made presentation of a work order to the stock chaser necessary before material could be brought up. So he was stymied and could do nothing the rest of the day. He had 43 pieces and added 11 from yesterday's kitty to turn in for a total 54. He sat around the rest of the evening, and none of the bosses seemed to mind.

Roy also found, about this time, that he was receiving quite a bit of unasked-for "help." For example, one night, he had just started work on a new job, calling for outside hex cuts on a housing ring. The layout department had laid out the cuts, each equidistant from the others. Jake said to Roy: "I'll let you in on a little secret. You put on your smooth jaw vise, and I'll show you how to cut those babies in no time." Jake had made a plug which slipped inside the housing. He set the cutter and took the cuts off the finished surface of the plug. By eliminating the surface gauge, he had cut the job down so that Roy was making well over $4.00 an hour. Roy turned in the job for $1.10 after loafing 5.3 hours. (Since he was a new man, $1.10 was "tops" for him on this job.) Jake was very secretive about the plug and made Roy return it to him as soon as he had finished. He stowed it in his tool locker, saying: "Forget you ever saw this thing until you need it again." After that, Roy found that each group had a collection of special cutting tools, jigs, and fixtures which were carefully concealed from members of the incentive department. These tools were usually made on company time. Through the use of such devices, many operations could be performed in a fraction of the time allowed for them.

Another night, when Roy came to the cage to punch off rework, the time-cage girl said: "You don't want to punch off rework yet, do you?" and suggested that he should get a start on the next job before punching off rework. On still another occasion, Art, the foreman, was at the time cage when Roy punched off the day work of rereaming and on to the piecework of drilling. Art came around to Roy's machine shortly after. "Say," he said, "when you punch off day work onto piecework, you ought to have your piecework already started. Run a few, then punch off the day work, and you'll have a good start. You've got to chisel a little around here to make money."

Roy once accidentally turned in a job for twice his "rate" as set by the group. The foreman caught the job ticket before the timekeeper had punched it and called it to the attention of one of the setup men, who returned it to Roy with the admonition to be more careful. Roy altered the card so that he was paid his "usual rate."

Roy was repeatedly warned to watch out for time-study men. Gus told him that a girl hand-mill operator had been discharged a year ago when a time-study man caught her running one job while punched in on another. The time-study man came over to the girl's machine to time a job, only to find the job completed and the girl running another.

Time-study men were a favorite topic of conversation. One day, Roy was present when Starkey was giving some detailed advice to Tennessee, another relatively inexperienced man, in ways of coping with the time-study man:

> STARKEY: If you expect to get any kind of a price, you got to out-wit that s.o.b.! You got to use your noodle while you're working, and think your work out ahead as you go along. You got to add movements you know you ain't going to make when you're running the job. Remember, if you don't screw them, they're going to screw you! Every movement counts!
>
> Another thing, you were running that job too damn fast before they timed you on it. I was watching you yesterday. If you don't run a job slow before you get timed, you won't get a good price. They'll look at

the record of what you do before they come around and compare it with the timing speed. Those time-study men are sharp!

TENNESSEE: I wasn't going very fast yesterday. Hell, I was going as slow as I could without wearing myself out slowing down.

STARKEY: Well, maybe it just looked fast because you were going so steady at it.

TENNESSEE: I don't see how I could run it any slower, I stood there like I was practically paralyzed!

STARKEY: Remember those guys are paid to screw you, and that's all they got to think about. They'll stay up half the night figuring out how to beat you out of a dime. They figure you're going to try to fool them, so they make allowances for that. They set the prices low enough to allow for what you do.

TENNESSEE: Well, then, what chance have I got?

STARKEY: It's up to you to figure out how to fool them more than they allow for.

TENNESSEE: The trouble with me is, I get nervous with that guy standing in back of me, and I can't think.

STARKEY: You just haven't had enough experience yet. Wait until you have been here a couple of years, and you'll do your best thinking when those guys are standing behind you. I was timed once on some levers like the ones you're running. I got a price of $4.00 a hundred, and I could make about $2.00 an hour. But I didn't run them the way they were timed. When the time-study man came around, I set the speed at 180. I knew damn well he would ask me to push it up, so I started low enough. He finally pushed me up to 445, and I ran the job later at 610. If I'd started out at 445, they'd have timed it as 610.

Then I got him on the reaming, too. I ran the reamer for him at 130 speed and .025 feed. He asked me if I couldn't run the reamer any faster than that, and I told him I had to run the reamer slow to keep the hole size. I showed him two pieces with oversize holes that the day man ran. I picked them out for the occasion. But later on, I ran the reamer at 610 speed and .018 feed, same as the drill, so I didn't have to change gears.

Then, there was a burring operation on the job, too. For the time-study man, I burred each piece after I drilled and reamed, and I ran the burring tool by automatic feed. But afterwards, I let the burring go till I drilled 25 pieces or so, and I just touched them up a little by holding them under the burring tool. I used to make out in five hours, easy, on that job.

Always keep in mind the fact that you can't make money if you run the job the way it's timed. They time jobs just to give you your base rate if you kill yourself trying to make it, no more. You've got to get the job timed below the speeds and feeds you can use later. Whenever a piece is timed at maximum speeds and feeds, there's no hope! You have as much chance as a snowball in hell!

TENNESSEE: Yeah, but what if they make you speed it up to maximum speed? What are you going to do then?

STARKEY: You got to be tough with them. Remember, those guys don't know their ass from a hole in the ground as far as these machines are concerned. When they tell me to speed up to about what I figure I can run the job, I start to take my apron off and tell them: "All right, if you think it can be run that fast, you run it!" They usually come around. You should have seen Ray Ward when he was working on the drill presses. Ray knew his drills. He'd burn up a drill every four or five pieces when they were timing him, and say the speed was too high for the tough stuff he was running. Tough stuff, my ass! They'd lower the speed and feed to where he wasn't burning up the drills; then afterwards, he'd speed up and cut through that tough stuff like cheese.

TENNESSEE: What I want to know is, how in hell could Ward burn up the drills like that? You can't just burn up a drill when you feel like it.

STARKEY: It's in the way you grind the drill. Ray used to grind his own drills, and he'd touch them up before they timed him. The wrong kind of a grind will burn up a drill at a lower speed than the drill can take if it's ground right for the job. There are all sorts of ways to skin a cat, and Ray knew 'em all. He could start with the head or the tail or any one of the four feet. Ray knew all the tricks!

I used to have to laugh at the way he got up a sweat when they were timing him. He'd jump around the machine like a monkey on a string, with the sweat just pouring off him. His shirt used to get soaking wet, and he'd have to wring it out afterwards. And when they finished timing him, he'd stagger away from the machine a little, like he'd given everything he had in him. But of course, it got to a point where he wasn't fooling anybody any more, except maybe some new time-study man who came along, and the time-study department would have him tipped off about Ray.

I never did see Ray sweat a drop when he was actually running a job; he was always about forty pounds overweight, the laziest guy I ever did see. He'd move a box up to the machine and putter around all day like he was making mud pies or something.

Roy noticed, however, that with all this elaborate strategy, even the canniest operators often gave their best in a timing duel, only to get "hopeless" prices for their pains. These jobs were usually called "stinkers" by the men. From the day Roy first came to the shop, he heard a lot of talk about these stinker jobs. Al McCann (the man who probably made quota most often) said he gave a new job a trial; if it was no good, he took his time. After that, Roy noticed that whenever McCann worked on the chucks, he apparently made little effort to make out.

Mucha said of a certain job: "I did just one more than you did. If they don't like it, they can do it themselves. To hell with them. I'm not going to break my back on stuff like this. I could have made out, but why kill myself for day rate?"

Old Pete, the multiple man, said: "I ran some pieces for twenty-five minutes to see how many I could turn out. I turned out twenty at 1.5 cents apiece [72 cents an hour]. So I smoke and take it easy. I can't make out."

Roy noticed that when Sokolsky, one of the better operators on the line, was working on an operation on which he could not make out, he did not go at his task with much vigor. He either poked around or left his machine for long periods of time; and Paul, the setup man, seemed always to be looking for him. Steve, the superintendent, was constantly bellowing: "Where in hell is Ed?" or "Come on, Ed, let's have some production around here!" One night, Roy heard him admonishing Sokolsky: "Now, I want you to work at that machine till 3:00 o'clock. Do you understand?"

Roy watched with real interest when Starkey and the men who worked his machine on the other shifts were assigned a major job they regarded as poorly priced—an item called a hinge base. Roy observed them working on the hinge bases off and on for over nine months. During the period, three men worked second shift on Starkey's machine, in the following sequences: Sokolsky, Dooley, and McCann. When Starkey and Sokolsky first started working on hinge bases in December, Roy noticed that they did not seem to be doing very well. Sokolsky cursed intermittently and left his machine for long periods of time. The foreman would find the machine idle and would bellow about it. Sokolsky began to call the piece a "stinker."

Sokolsky seemed to have continual trouble with his jig, a revolving piece attached to the side of the table. Two disks seemed to stick together, and he was always (every day or so) using the crane to dismantle the jig (a very heavy one). He sanded the discs and oiled them, taking several hours for the cleaning operation. Steve did not seem to like it. Whenever Paul found the jig torn down and Sokolsky away somewhere, he would yell: "Where the hell's Ed?" in a provoked manner.

In February, Roy was told by Sokolsky that he and Starkey were turning out about twenty-four pieces in a ten-hour period, that the job had been timed several times, but no raise in price had been given. The two men were asking for a price of 38 cents. Sokolsky said they could turn out three an hour; but until they got a decent price, they would turn out two an hour. Toward the end of that evening, Roy noticed that Sokolsky was sitting on a box doing nothing, his machine idle.

ROY: What's the matter? Did they stop the job on you?
SOKOLSKY: I stopped it. I don't feel like running it.

In March, Dooley took over the night shift on Starkey's machine. One night, while he was working on hinge bases, Dooley admitted he could barely make out on the job, but "Why knock myself out for day rate? We're doing three an hour or less until we get a better price!"

In August, after McCann started working on the hinge bases, he told Roy they had gotten a price raise on the hinge bases, from 23 to 28 cents, and another to 31 cents.

AL McCANN: But it's still not high enough. As it is now, we can make exactly 94 cents an hour. We're trying to get 35 cents. We can turn out one piece in exactly sixteen minutes. That's not four an hour. We've been giving them three an hour.

One night, Gil, the foreman, sat or stood behind McCann for at least an hour, and Roy could see McCann did not like it. He worked steadily but with deliberate slowness, and did not look at Gil or speak to him.

But one night late in August, McCann told Roy that he (McCann) was making out on the hinge bases, that he had gotten disgusted Friday, speeded up the tools, and turned in thirty-one pieces for earnings of $9.60 on an eight-hour shift.

McCANN: It was easy, just as easy as the frames. Now, I'm kicking myself all over for not doing it before. All I did was to change the speed from 95 to 130. I was sick of stalling around all evening, and I got mad and decided to make out and let the tools burn up. But they made it all right, for eight hours. What's the use of turning in 94 cents an hour when you can turn in $1.25 just as easy? They'd never raise a price you could make 94 cents on, anyhow. Now, maybe they'll cut it back.

After Roy had been on the job for several months, he noticed that while he didn't mind the work, he did find that when he was doing a job on which he wasn't trying to make out, the time seemed to drag. Roy found himself struggling to attain quota "for the hell of it" because it was a "little game" and kept him from getting bored. In addition to escaping the monotony of factory labor by playing a game, Roy found that fast, rhythmical work seemed less tiring.

Dooley watched Roy set up for the frames one night and remarked: "You can make out on that if you want to break your neck." "Breaking his neck" was a welcome relief from the monotony of carefully pacing his work. Roy was so sleepy he could hardly keep his eyes open before he started on the frames; but at 11:00 o'clock, he felt bright and wide awake.

Slow jobs seemed to wear Roy out far more than the fast ones. Roy mentioned this to John, one of the other operators, who said: "That's the way with me. I've got to keep my mind occupied, or I get bored; it wears me out. I can't stand around, either. When I am going hell-bent for election on a good piecework job, the evening passes very swiftly, and I don't realize that I am tired until it is all over. On those day work jobs, I get so bored I could stand in the aisle and yell."

In his conversations with the men in the shop, Roy found that rate cutting was the most frequent subject of conversation. In spite of the fact that both union and management had made strong guaranties that rates would not be cut, the workers were unconvinced. Leonard Bricker, an old-timer in the shop, maintained that management, once bent on slashing a piecework price, would stop at nothing.

LEONARD BRICKER: Take these $1.25 jobs. One guy will turn in $1.30 an hour one day. Another fellow will turn in, say, $1.31 or $1.32. Then the first fellow will go up to $1.35. First thing you know, they'll be up to $1.50, and bang! They'll tear a machine to pieces to change something to cut a price.

SWEDE: Pay it by the hour, or pay it by the job, that little man in the straw hat won't pay you any more than he has to.

MIKE: They won't cut the rate on this job, but what's to prevent them from changing the casting a little and giving it another number? Then it's a different job, and they'll set a lower rate on it. Piecework is like leading a goat around with a carrot. You give the goat a nibble, but you never let him have a real bite.

Roy noticed, however, that he had never heard any of the men mention any specific examples of either direct or indirect rate cutting. On one occasion, a worker spoke about management plans to "put the screws" on certain jobs and claimed that there had been several recent instances of rate cutting. Roy asked which jobs had been cut. When the worker could not name one, the steward standing nearby said: "Shut up, you make me sick—always crying before you are hurt."

After Roy had worked at the shop for a little over ten months, he decided to take a look at what he had done in that time. Each day, he had jotted down some notes about his production and earnings. When he added it all up, he found that he had worked 1,851 hours, 1,351 of which were "production piecework" hours. The remaining 500 hours were taken up with time study, rework, and setup. In 670 (50 per cent) of the production piecework hours, he had made out. That is, he produced enough pieces of work to "earn," at the piece rates for the kind of work done, the 85-cent per hour "base rate" which he was guaranteed for every hour spent on the job.

Roy's hourly earnings on production piecework varied from $0.09 to $1.66. Exhibits 1 and 2 show the spread of hourly earnings for the

Exhibit 1

METROPOLITAN STEEL COMPANY
PRODUCTION PIECEWORK HOURS WORKED,
BY TEN-CENT EARNINGS INTERVALS

	Period I November through February		Period II March through August		Total November through August	
Earnings per Hour (in Cents)	Hours Worked	Per Cent	Hours Worked	Per Cent	Hours Worked	Per Cent
Unknown*............66.4	11.4	37.5	4.9	103.9	7.7
5– 14................. 3.0	0.5	...	...	3.0	0.2
15– 24.................13.5	2.3	37.5	4.9	51.0	3.8
25– 34.................37.8	6.5	12.0	1.6	49.8	3.7
35– 44.................93.0	16.0	57.1	7.4	150.1	11.0
45– 54.................74.0	12.8	70.5	9.1	144.5	10.6
55– 64.................43.1	7.4	14.6	1.9	57.7	4.3
65– 74.................36.8	6.3	27.0	3.5	63.8	4.7
75– 84.................49.0	8.5	8.7	1.1	57.7	4.4
Total under 85 cents......416.6	71.7	264.9	34.4	681.5	50.4
85– 94.................39.1	6.7	12.1	1.6	52.1	3.8
95–104................. 9.7	1.7	9.8	1.2	19.5	1.5
105–114................. 3.8	0.7	14.1	1.8	17.9	1.3
115–124.................18.0	3.1	65.0	8.4	83.0	6.1
125–134.................93.2	16.1	403.1	52.3	496.4	36.7
135–174................. ...	...	1.5	0.3	1.5	0.2
Total 85 cents or over.....163.8	28.3	505.6	65.6	670.4	49.6
Total................580.4	100.0	770.5	100.0	1,351.9	100.0

* All "unknown" hourly earnings fell below the base rate level of 85 cents per hour.

various jobs. Roy divided the ten months into two periods in order to separate out the initial learning period from the period when he had attained a little higher level of skill.

Although he did not keep a complete record of the hourly earnings of Mucha on the radial drill, Roy frequently jotted down Mucha's output for the day, and found that Mucha's figures ran fairly close to his own. Furthermore, it was Roy's opinion that his record during the second period was not out of line with that of other operators in the

Exhibit 2

METROPOLITAN STEEL COMPANY

PRODUCTION PIECEWORK HOURS WORKED,
BY TEN-CENT EARNINGS INTERVALS

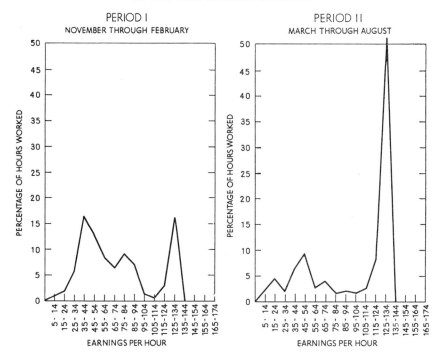

shop. Of the men on the same shift with Roy, doing the same kind of work, McCann, Starkey, Koszyk, and Sokolsky could all turn out greater volume than Roy and, in his opinion, were his betters in all-around skills. Seven were below him in these respects, but only three of them (Smith, Rinky, and Dooley) had worked long enough to be much a part of the group. Roy thought he was about average in both skill and work assigned to him.

During the last two months of the period (July and August), Roy estimated that he had "goofed off" an average of over two hours on the days when he made out. Since these make-out days represented 46 per cent of all days he worked, he figured that if he had wanted to be a rate buster, he could have made on the average an extra $1.58 a day.

2. EXCELSIOR BAKERIES, INC.[1]

UPON COMPLETING my junior year in college in early June, I returned to my home town, Pottersville, New York. The next day I went to see Roger Farnum, the plant superintendent of the local branch of Excelsior Bakeries, Inc., to find out when I should report for work. I had worked at the Excelsior plant the previous summer as a general helper on the slicing and wrapping crew for hamburger and hot dog rolls. Since I was a union member and had spoken to Farnum during spring vacation about a job for this summer, I was positive of being rehired.

When I walked into the office, Farnum said jokingly: "Hi, George! Ready to go to work for a change after all that book learning?" I was rather surprised to see Farnum so jovial and cordial. I remembered him as always having a long face and never saying more than two words at a time. I finally answered: "Yes, sir, any time you say and as soon as possible."

"Well, on the recommendation of Murphy, you're going to run the hamburger and hot dog machine this summer. Murphy wants to work on the ovens; and since we don't want to change a regular worker over to the wrapper just for a couple of months, we figured you would accept the added responsibility and could handle the job."

Phil Murphy, a regular employee of the plant, had run the wrapping machine last summer and had been leader of a crew of three other summer workers and me. I had visited Murphy at the plant during spring vacation, and he had told me he was going to work on the ovens this year because it was day work and paid more. I had casually mentioned to him at that time to try to get me the wrapping machine job, but I hadn't thought of it again, since it had always been assigned to a regular worker.

I was extremely pleased to accept the job, for I knew it meant 6 cents more an hour, and it would entail some leadership responsibility. I thought to myself: "Now I will be part of management and not just another worker."

---

[1] During the winter following the events described in this case, the writer submitted it as a report for a course in administration he was taking in a graduate school of business.

66

Farnum told me to report for work that following Sunday, a week earlier than I had expected, so I could familiarize myself with the machine before the "rush season" started.

Excelsior Bakeries, Inc., was a large firm with many plants spread across the entire United States. The Pottersville branch produced mainly white, rye, whole wheat, and French bread, but supplemented these major lines with hamburger and hot dog rolls, dinner rolls, doughnuts, and other bakery products. It also distributed, in its area of operation, pies, cakes, crackers, and other specialities produced in the Boston plant.

Pottersville was located in a region noted for its many summer resorts, camps, and hotels, which are open from June until September. During the summer season, production and sales of the local Excelsior plant increased tremendously as the summer population swelled the normal demand. This seasonal rise was especially significant in hot dog and hamburger rolls, whose sales increased over the winter months by approximately 100–150 per cent in June, 150–250 per cent in July, and 250–300 per cent in August. Because of this great seasonal increase, the company had to hire about fifteen employees just for the three summer months. Five of the "extra help" were needed on the wrapping crew for hot dog and hamburger rolls. These workers were usually drawn from college students on vacation, employment agencies, and transients. In the past several years the extra help had been predominantly college students, because they were more dependable and willing to remain on the job right up to Labor Day.

After I reported to work, I spent the first week with the regular employees. Ed Dugan, a past operator of the wrapping machine, worked with me, teaching me all the techniques of operating the machine efficiently. The machine was rather old and had to be tended carefully at all times, so that the cellophane wrapping paper would not jump off the rollers. The wrapping paper was expensive, and Joe McGuire, the night foreman, "blew his top" whenever a lot of paper was wasted.

Exhibit 1 shows the working area and the positions of each operator on the slicing and wrapping crew. Worker No. 1 took the pans of rolls from the racks and fed the rolls out on a conveyor, which carried them into the slicing machine. Worker No. 2 stacked the sliced rolls into two rows, one on top of the other, making groups of eight or one dozen. Worker No. 3 slid the groups of rolls down the table to worker No. 4, who fed them into the wrapping machine. Worker No. 5, the wrapping machine operator and crew leader, placed the wrapped packages in a box, keeping count of the actual number packaged. The work was rather routine and extremely monotonous and boring. Workers No. 1 through No. 4 continually exchanged positions in order to break the monotony.

The plant employees worked on a five-day week—working on Sun-

Exhibit 1

EXCELSIOR BAKERIES, INC.
WRAPPING MACHINE LAYOUT

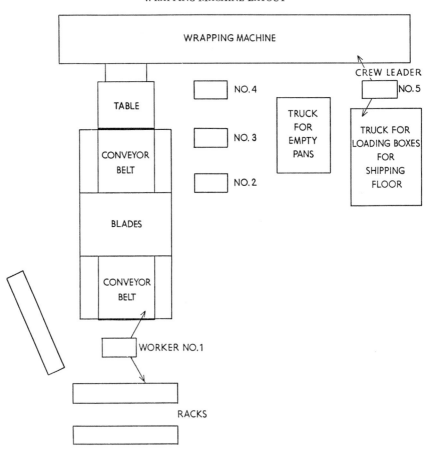

day and Monday; off on Tuesday; working Wednesday, Thursday, and Friday; and off again on Saturday. Production was on daily orders from the various sales routes. The salesmen left the plant early in the morning with their loaded trucks and, after making their deliveries, returned in the afternoon with the orders for the next day. The volume varied from day to day, and the rolls were ready for wrapping at varying times. Therefore, the wrappers generally reported for work at a different time each day, being notified by the plant superintendent. Usually, the crew began about 6:00 to 8:00 P.M. and worked until all the orders were filled for that night. The number of hours worked ranged from seven to fifteen or even more. All time over eight hours was overtime and paid for as time and a half. If a worker was a union member, the company had to guarantee him seven hours' pay for any night on which they called him in. If there were not seven hours of slicing and wrapping, the foreman found something else for the men to do, such as thoroughly cleaning the machines, greasing the pans, or doing other odd jobs. If a man wished, though, he could ask to punch out before seven hours were up, thereby forfeiting the guaranteed seven hours' pay for that night and receiving pay only for the hours he had worked.

Four different types of packages were wrapped on the machine: hamburger and hot dog dozen-roll packages, and hamburger and hot dog packages of eight rolls. A different size and type of paper was used for each package. Different-sized plates had to be used in the machine also. On an average night a complete change-over of the machine had to be made about six times, each alteration taking about ten minutes. In addition, it took about five minutes to replace a roll of paper when it ran out, and two to three minutes to replace the labels and seals. During these change-overs and replacements, which were made by the machine operator, the rest of the crew smoked cigarettes out on the shipping dock or else folded boxes for the operator if he needed them. I never asked anyone to make boxes if he wanted to have a cigarette or wanted to get a drink of water. But if a man was just sitting around or "goofing off," I would ask him to fold boxes, as the crew is supposed to do during these breaks. McGuire hated to see anyone sit around, but he never begrudged anyone a cigarette.

With the start of my second week, orders rose, and the rest of the summer help was called in. I was very pleased when three of my close friends were assigned to my crew. Art Dunn, a student at Williams, had worked on the wrapping crew with me the previous summer, as had Jack Dorsey, a student at the University of Vermont. Bill Regan, a Fordham student, had not worked for Excelsior the previous summer; but he had lived next door to me, and we had grown up together. The four of us had been close friends during high school days and since graduation, even though we went to different colleges. Harry Hart, the fourth man, was also new to the wrapping crew. Hart had graduated from high school a year before the rest of us and was attending the University of Massachusetts. We old-timers were already union members. The new men joined soon after they began work.

With the help of Dunn and Dorsey, I was able to train Regan and Hart quickly; and within a couple of nights, they were thoroughly proficient in all four positions. During these first two nights, Dunn and Dorsey thoroughly indoctrinated Regan and Hart into the "code" of the wrapping crew.

Excelsior Bakeries offered college students an excellent opportunity to make a considerable amount of money during the summer, paying an hourly rate of $1.63 and providing plenty of overtime. The code of the wrapping crew was a concerted group action to set the number of hours to be worked on a certain night. At the beginning of the night's work, the crew could fairly well estimate from the production orders just how long it should take to put the work out. If it was estimated to take about eight hours, the crew would purposely slow down to stretch it to nine or nine and a half hours, so they could get overtime pay. On almost any night the work could be stretched out by an hour or so. Only on big nights of 12 or more hours did the crew work at normal speed. As an indication of the effectiveness of this slowdown, there were several occasions when a seven- or eight-hour night was estimated, but the crew "pushed the stuff through" and finished in six hours in order to have a few beers before the local bar closed at 3:00 A.M.

As a member of this crew the previous summer, I was one of the strong advocates of this code. If a new worker or a temporary replacement from somewhere else in the plant appeared on the crew, he had to conform, or the group gave him much verbal abuse or the even worse "silent treatment." These were unbearable conditions, and the new man always accepted the code.

Murphy, the previous year's leader, although a regular employee of the plant, had co-operated with the group and never complained. He used to say: "After all, I want the overtime, too!"

After the first few nights of work, I noticed the code had begun to operate. I had never stopped to think of the effects this slowdown had on management and the operations of the plant. It raised labor production costs, delayed the salesmen in leaving for their routes, and raised other problems as well. At first, I was rather confused as to whether I should allow this practice to continue or, as "part of management," put my foot down and take action to stop it. Because I could not think of any satisfactory course of action which would satisfy everyone, I allowed the code to operate. I rationalized myself into believing: "Well, if management isn't going to do anything about it, why the hell should I worry about it?"

The first couple of weeks went smoothly. The only problems I had to face were minor arguments among the crew and the usual horseplay and "goofing off" in the middle hours of the morning.

McGuire, the night foreman, occasionally would say to me, smiling: "Took you guys a pretty long time to get those rolls out tonight, didn't it?" or, on a really short night: "You can really shove those rolls through when you feel like having a few brews!" McGuire could not see us working from his office, as the line of racks blocked his view, but he regularly walked over to check on us. When he appeared, the man feeding the slicing machine would place the rolls on the conveyor belt "back to back" with no space in between, the maximum rate at which the crew could operate. When he was in his office or "up front," a space of about six to twelve inches was allowed between rolls, thereby reducing the speed of production by 10 to 15 per cent.

Occasionally, a "little war" would break out between the wrapping crew and two doughnut men across the aisle from the wrapping machine; the members of each group would throw doughnuts or hot dog and hamburger rolls at the others. One night, one of these battles was beginning to get out of hand to the point where the boys had stopped work. I reprimanded them and told them to "knock it off" and get back to work. Regan called me a "company man," and Dunn said something about the "lieutenant with the gold-plated bars."

I was trying to ignore the comments when suddenly I heard the paper snap. I stopped the machine and adjusted it; but even after the machine had been adjusted, package after package kept coming through unwrapped or "crippled." I tried everything I knew to find the cause of the trouble; but just when I thought I had the machine running properly, something else would go wrong. By this time, I was ready to give up and call McGuire for his advice.

Then I noticed the four crewmen having a good laugh for themselves. I had been so concerned about trying to change the adjustments on the machine that I had not noticed Regan tinkering with the machine at the other end. He was also feeding the hot dog rolls improperly, breaking them before putting them in the machine so they would slide off and get caught, thereby drawing unevenly on the paper. I lost my temper completely and was in the process of a real argument with Regan and the rest of the crew when McGuire came down to see why the machine was shut down. When he asked, I stuttered: "Hell, Joe, these—ah—this damn machine isn't drawing right. I've tried everything, but I think I've finally found the real reason. Let's try it now, fellas!"

That night, when I was making my final count with McGuire and the shipping foreman, I was considerably short on hot dog rolls, because of the many losses caused by Regan's tampering with the machine. McGuire gave me quite a reprimand and said I'd better "watch it."

The next night, when I came to work, Farnum stopped me and asked why I had lost so much paper the night before. I told him it was a breakdown in the machine. He gave me orders to weigh each roll of paper before we started wrapping each night and to weigh it again when we finished. I was to record the weights on tabulation control sheets kept in his office.

That night, before starting work, I told the crew what had happened and what McGuire and Farnum had said to me. I told them that I was being held responsible for paper and production control, and that I would tolerate no more "horsing around," especially tampering with the machine. I emphasized that I would not go "on the carpet" again for *anyone*.

Relations between me and the crew, with the exception of Hart, were rather strained for a couple of nights. None of them said very much to me. Also, I did not go swimming or play golf with them for a couple of days, as we usually did every afternoon. However, I had no more incidents of this sort, and the crew continued to meet the output schedule as they had previously. Gradually, the incident was forgotten, and relations among us became what they had been before.

During the latter part of August, the annual Excelsior clambake was held. In the late afternoon, McGuire called me over to the bar to have a drink: Mr. Farnum and Mr. Sommers, the plant general manager, were with him. McGuire threw his arm around me and said to Farnum: "George did a great job this summer on the wrapper, didn't he, Rog?"

"Best season we've had so far, Joe."

3. BETTY RANDALL

ON MARCH 15, 1949, Betty Randall came in to see Mr. Robbins, the plant personnel director, to talk over a problem she said was troubling her. Betty was a hand assembly production worker in a modern 600-employee branch plant located in a large eastern city. After Betty told Mr. Robbins her story, he asked her to write out a description of the situation. Her statement is reproduced below.

I consider this case not unusual nor typical, but as having happened to me and to a few others. As I am not equipped to do the work, it offers little or no solution to the problem at hand. I wouldn't be writing this report if I had not remembered the advice given by Mr. Robbins of personnel. He told a group that should we have a problem, to please consult him before walking out. However, I will mention here that I have seen a few very conscientious workers walk out without "fighting the case."

When I was first hired, Mr. Lipton, the foreman, introduced me to the young lady who taught me the process of soldering lead wires. I asked her how much production I would be expected to turn in daily, and she secured this information for me from the other girls. This seemed at the moment like a fantastic sum, but she assured me that after a few days I would become quite efficient, which I soon did. I'm not one to "bite the hand that feeds me," so I began working and finally developed the system into sort of a game.

A few weeks later, one of the girls asked me how I was doing, and I told her that I was doing fine. She looked at my production sheet and swore. She was astonished to see how much I was producing each hour. She bitterly reminded me that girls that had been here for several months or even years were not producing what I had accomplished in a few weeks. I laughed that off as somewhat of a compliment. That was my big mistake as far as co-operating with the company or satisfying my gregarious tendencies was concerned. I was immediately and severely ostracized.

During the weeks that ensued, I noticed I was not completely alone; there were a few others who were also "friendless." However, it was soon apparent that ostracism was not satisfying the desires of their fiendish little plan. Threats were to follow, and follow they did. Having worked in the "violent ward" of a psychopathic hospital, I was not the least bit nervous because of these threats, but others were. I noticed a few things about the character, temperament, and education of those who were apparently "bossing." They were usually the old-timers and loafers —girls with a great deal of confidence and little reason for it. Sometimes, their reasons for fighting the enormous business organization, which represents their security, were quite convincing: "Your work is never appreciated." "They'll always want more and more," "You haven't got a chance to get a merit wage increase unless you go out with the boss. . . ." After this general talking-to, the poor girls began to wonder; some of them stayed a few days and then didn't turn up for work. The clique had scored again.

I sat and wondered as I worked. What to do? I was assured I had the bosses on my side, but then. . . . The long, dead silence and the vulgar, stupid remarks of the other girls soon began to get under my skin. I worked quite a while at the psychopathic hospital, and "they" never bothered me; but these stupid little people and their moronic remarks soon began to annoy me something terrible. Because my production was high, I was asked to work Saturdays. This brought a violent counter-thrust from the rebels.

Soon, their campaign began to affect me exactly as they had planned. (Or am I giving them too much credit?) My production was dropping. The assistant foreman, Bert, asked me if I was ill. When I told him my troubles, he advised me to see Mr. Lipton, which I did. Mr. Lipton listened attentively and asked the names of the rebels, which I readily gave, not feeling at all like an informer. He then assured me, though stammering, that justice would prevail. I noticed little change.

The little minds had other desires than to keep their jobs secure; they wanted to jeopardize the position of their immediate superiors. Bert, who had advised me to talk to Mr. Lipton, commonly held the reputation of being a communist, nailed on him by "my rebels." I have always maintained in my philosophy that if one cannot become great by one's own methods of accomplishment, then one will probably pull everyone else down below him, until by comparison he is above the mob, hence great. This is commonly known as scapegoatism. These girls carry this farther than I ever dreamed would be done. Scapegoating is a common activity of the uneducated. Education of the population, while not the solution, will greatly aid in the eventual solution of this problem.

However, back to the practical aspects of the problem at hand. I had convinced myself that most of the girls were not the kind I would care to associate with, anyway, so my scope of activity was not ruptured too severely. As they ignored me, I ignored them. As they cursed me, I ignored them. However, something happened that I had not counted on. I became physically ill from the entire situation. Having had a few lectures on psychosomatic diseases, I knew I had not incorrectly diagnosed the case.

My relief came in the form of a temporary transfer to another department. I knew it would take some time before the girls would become acquainted with my case, and the rest was welcome. I was shocked to find that no one was interested in my "reputation." I was further shocked when I began to notice that harmony, tranquility, and co-operation prevailed in this department. It is my opinion that part of the cause for such co-operation in this department may be attributed to the fact of one boss—and a capable, understanding man, at that.

Then, I was told to return to my former department, where I was greeted by my boss with: "Enjoy your vacation?" This does not strike me as being very complimentary to one who has been conscientious from the beginning.

I had been taught to report all inferior-grade materials, and this particular morning I found the wire defective. After reeling yards of red tape from a few of my bosses, I finally was sent to Mr. Lipton. Again, Mr. Lipton was glad to see me. "I want you to get back to your machine, sit down, and mind your own business. Your production is failing. Why?" This I was told before I had a chance to speak. Here, I explained about the strain I was under and about the inferior materials. He then told me to work as best I could with the inferior materials, as he didn't want to send any of the girls home. I then told him I had thought of leaving. He sarcastically mentioned that perhaps it was for the best. This shock drove me to Mr. Robbins of personnel, and to standing here in my living room dictating this to my husband, the typist of the family.

4. THE SLADE COMPANY

RALPH PORTER, production manager of the Slade Company, was concerned by reports of dishonesty among some employees in the plating department. From reliable sources, he had learned that a few men were punching the timecards of a number of their workmates who had left early. Porter had only recently joined the Slade organization. He judged from conversations with the previous production manager and other fellow managers that they were, in general, pleased with the over-all performance of the plating department.

The Slade Company was a prosperous manufacturer of metal products designed for industrial application. Its manufacturing plant, located in central Michigan, employed nearly five hundred workers, who were engaged in producing a large variety of clamps, inserts, knobs, and similar items. Orders for these products were usually large and on a recurrent basis. The volume of orders fluctuated in response to business conditions in the primary industries which the company served. At the time of this case, sales volume had been high for over a year. The bases upon which the Slade Company secured orders, in rank of importance, were quality, delivery, and reasonable price.

The organization of manufacturing operations at the Slade plant is shown in Exhibit 1. The departments listed there are, from left to right, approximately in the order in which material flowed through the plant. The diemaking and setup operations required the greatest degree of skill, supplied by highly paid, long-service craftsmen. The finishing departments, divided operationally and geographically between plating and painting, attracted less highly trained but relatively skilled workers, some of whom had been employed by the company for many years. The remaining operations were largely unskilled in nature and were characterized by relatively low pay and high rate of turnover of personnel.

The plating room was the sole occupant of the top floor of the plant. Exhibit 2 shows the floor plan, the disposition of workers, and the flow of work throughout the department. Thirty-eight men and women worked in the department, plating or oxidizing the metal parts or preparing parts for the application of paint at another location in the plant. The department's work occurred in response to orders communicated by production schedules, which were revised daily. Schedule revisions, caused by last-minute order increases or rush requests from customers, resulted in short-term volume fluctuations, particularly in the plating, painting, and shipping departments. Exhibit 3 outlines the activities of the various jobs, their interrelationships, and the type of work in which each specialized. Exhibit 4 rates the various types of jobs in terms of the technical skill, physical effort, discomfort, and training time associated with their performance.

Exhibit 1

THE SLADE COMPANY

MANUFACTURING ORGANIZATION

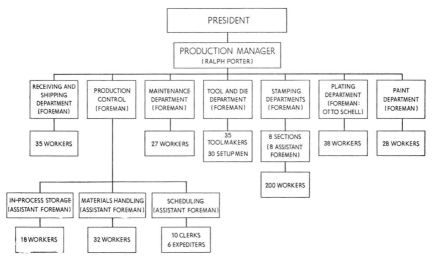

The activities which took place in the plating room were of three main types:

1. Acid dipping, in which parts were etched by being placed in baskets which were manually immersed and agitated in an acid solution.
2. Barrel tumbling, in which parts were roughened or smoothed by being loaded into machine-powered revolving drums containing abrasive, caustic, or corrosive solutions.
3. Plating—either manual, in which parts were loaded on racks and were immersed by hand through the plating sequence; or automatic, in which racks or baskets were manually loaded with parts which were then carried by a conveyor system through the plating sequence.

Within these main divisions, there were a number of variables, such as cycle times, chemical formulas, abrasive mixtures, and so forth, which distinguished particular jobs as they have been categorized in Exhibit 3.

The work of the plating room was received in batch lots whose size averaged a thousand pieces. The clerk moved each batch, which was accompanied by a routing slip, to its first operation. This routing slip

Exhibit 2

THE SLADE COMPANY

PLATING ROOM LAYOUT

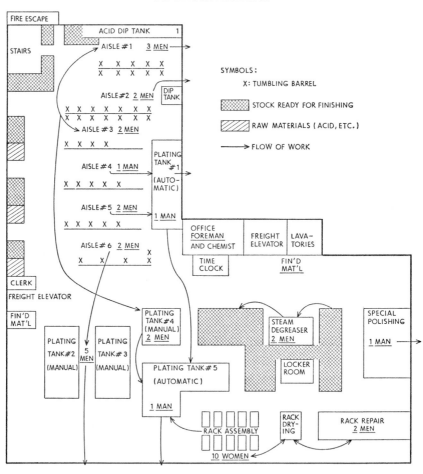

indicated the operations to be performed and when each major operation on the batch was scheduled to be completed, so that the finished product could be shipped on time. From the accumulation of orders before him, each man was to organize his own work schedule so as to make optimal use of equipment, materials, and time. Upon completion

Exhibit 3

THE SLADE COMPANY

OUTLINE OF WORK FLOW, PLATING ROOM

AISLE 1.   Worked closely with Aisle 3 in preparation of parts by barrel tumbling and acid dipping for high-quality* plating in Tanks 4 and 5. Also did a considerable quantity of highly specialized, high-quality acid-etching work not requiring further processing.

AISLE 2:   Tumbled items of regular quality and design in preparation for painting. Less frequently, did oxidation dipping work of regular quality, but sometimes of special design, not requiring further processing.

AISLE 3:   Worked closely with Aisle 1 on high-quality tumbling work for Tanks 4 and 5.

AISLES 4 AND 5:   Produced regular tumbling work for Tank 1.

AISLE 6:   Did high-quality tumbling work for special products plated in Tanks 2 and 3.

TANK 1:   Worked on standard, automated plating of regular quality not further processed in plating room, and regular work further processed in Tank 5.

TANKS 2 AND 3:   Produced special, high-quality plating work not requiring further processing.

TANK 4:   Did special, high-quality plating work further plated in Tank 5.

TANK 5:   Automated production of high- and regular-quality, special- and regular-design plated parts sent directly to shipping.

RACK ASSEMBLY: Placed parts to be plated in Tank 5 on racks.

RACK REPAIR: Performed routine replacement and repair of racks used in Tank 5.

POLISHING: Processed, by manual or semimanual methods, odd-lot special orders which were sent directly to shipping. Also, sorted and reclaimed parts rejected by inspectors in the shipping department.

DEGREASING: Took incoming raw stock, processed it through caustic solution, and placed clean stock in storage ready for processing elsewhere in the plating room.

---

* Definition of terms: *High or regular quality:* The quality of finishes could broadly be distinguished by the thickness of plate and/or care in preparation. *Regular or special work:* The complexity of work depended on the routine or special character of design and finish specifications.

of an order, each man moved the lot to its next work position or to the finished material location near the freight elevator.

The plating room was under the direct supervision of the foreman, Otto Schell, who worked a regular 8:00-to-5:00 day, five days a week. The foreman spent a good deal of his working time attending to maintenance and repair of equipment, procuring supplies, handling late schedule changes, and seeing that his people were at their proper work locations.

Working conditions in the plating room varied considerably. That part of the department containing the tumbling barrels and the plating machines was constantly awash, alternately with cold water, steaming acid, or caustic soda. Men working in this part of the room wore knee boots, long rubber aprons, and high-gauntlet rubber gloves. This uniform, consistent with the general atmosphere of the "wet" part

Exhibit 4

THE SLADE COMPANY

SKILL INDICES BY JOB GROUP*

Jobs	Technical Skill Required	Physical Effort Required	Degree of Discomfort Involved	Degree of Training Required†
Aisle 1	1	1	1	1
Tanks 2–4	3	2	1	2
Aisles 2–6	5	1	1	5
Tank 5	1	5	7	2
Tank 1	8	5	5	7
Degreasing	9	3	7	10
Polishing	6	9	9	7
Rack assembly and repair	10	10	10	10

* Rated on scales of 1 (the greatest) to 10 (the least) in each category.
† The amount of experience required to assume complete responsibility for the job.

of the room, was hot in summer, cold in winter. In contrast, the remainder of the room was dry, was relatively odor-free, and provided reasonably stable temperature and humidity conditions for those who worked there.

The men and women employed in the plating room are listed in Exhibit 5. This exhibit provides certain personal data on each department member, including a productivity-skill rating (based on subjective and objective appraisals of potential performance), as reported by the members of the department.

The pay scale implied by Exhibit 5 was low for the central Michigan area. The average starting wage for factory work in the community was about $1.25. However, working hours for the plating room were long (from 60 hours to a possible and frequently available 76 hours per week). The first 60 hours (the normal five-day week) were paid for on straight-time rates. Saturday work was paid for at time and one half; Sunday pay was calculated on a double-time basis.

Exhibit 5

THE SLADE COMPANY

PLATING ROOM PERSONNEL

Location	Name	Age	Marital Status	Company Seniority	Department Seniority	Pay	Education	Familial Relationships	Productivity-Skill Rating*
Aisle 1	Tony Sarto	30	M	13 yrs.	13 yrs.	$1.50	High school	Louis Patrici, uncle Pete Facelli, cousin	1
	Pete Facelli	26	M	8 yrs.	8 yrs.	1.30	High school	Louis Patrici, uncle Tony Sarto, cousin	2
	Joe Iambi	31	M	5 yrs.	5 yrs.	1.20	2 yrs. high school		2
Aisle 2	Herman Schell	48	S	26 yrs.	26 yrs.	1.45	Grade school	Otto Schell, brother	8
	Philip Kirk	23	M	1 yr.	1 yr.	0.90	College		.†
Aisle 3	Dom Pantaleoni	31	M	10 yrs.	10 yrs.	1.30	1 yr. high school		2
	Sal Maletta	32	M	12 yrs.	12 yrs.	1.30	3 yrs. high school		3
Aisle 4	Bob Pearson	22	S	4 yrs.	4 yrs.	1.15	High school	Father in tool and die dept.	1
Aisle 5	Charlie Malone	44	M	22 yrs.	8 yrs.	1.25	Grade school		7
	John Lacey	41	S	9 yrs.	5 yrs.	1.20	1 yr. high school	Brother in paint dept.	7
Aisle 6	Jim Martin	30	S	7 yrs.	7 yrs.	1.25	High school		4
	Bill Mensch	41	M	6 yrs.	2 yrs.	1.10	Grade school		4

*On a potential scale of 1 (top) to 10 (bottom), as evaluated by the men in the department.
†Kirk was the source of data for this case and, as such, was in a biased position to report accurately perceptions about himself.

Exhibit 5—Continued

Location	Name	Age	Marital Status	Company Seniority	Department Seniority	Pay	Education	Familial Relationships	Productivity-Skill Rating
Tank 1	Henry La Forte	38	M	14 yrs.	6 yrs.	$1.25	High school		6
Tanks 2–3	Ralph Parker	25	S	7 yrs.	7 yrs.	1.20	High school		4
	Ed Harding	27	S	8 yrs.	8 yrs.	1.20	High school		4
	George Flood	22	S	5 yrs.	5 yrs.	1.15	High school		5
	Harry Clark	29	M	8 yrs.	8 yrs.	1.20	High school		3
	Tom Bond	25	S	6 yrs.	6 yrs.	1.20	High school		4
Tank 4	Frank Bonzani	27	M	9 yrs.	9 yrs.	1.25	High school	Tony Sarto, nephew	2
	Al Bartolo	24	M	6 yrs.	6 yrs.	1.25	High school	Pete Facelli, nephew	3
Tank 5	Louis Patrici	47	S	14 yrs.	14 yrs.	1.45	2 yrs. college		1
Rack Assembly	10 women	30–40	9M, 1S	10 yrs. (av.)	10 yrs. (av.)	1.05	Grade school (av.)	6 with husbands in company	4 (av.)
Rack Maintenance	Will Partridge	57	M	14 yrs.	2 yrs.	1.20	Grade school		7
	Lloyd Swan	62	M	3 yrs.	3 yrs.	1.10	Grade school		7
Degreasing	Dave Susi	45	S	1 yr.	1 yr.	1.05	High school		5
	Mike Maher	41	M	4 yrs.	4 yrs.	1.05	Grade school		6
Polishing	Russ Perkins	49	M	12 yrs.	2 yrs.	1.20	High school		4
Foreman	Otto Schell	56	M	35 yrs.	35 yrs.	(Not available)	High school	Herman Schell, brother	3
Clerk	Bill Pierce	32	M	10 yrs.	4 yrs.	1.15	High school		4
Chemist	Frank Rutlage	24	S	2 yrs.	2 yrs.	(Not available)	2 yrs. college		6

As Exhibit 5 indicates, Philip Kirk, a worker in Aisle 2, provided the data for this case. After he had been a member of the department for several months, Kirk noted that certain members of the department tended to seek each other out during free time on and off the job. He then observed that these informal associations were enduring, built upon common activities and shared ideas about what was and what was not legitimate behavior in the department. His estimate of the pattern of these associations is diagrammed in Exhibit 6.

The Sarto group, so named because Tony Sarto was its most respected

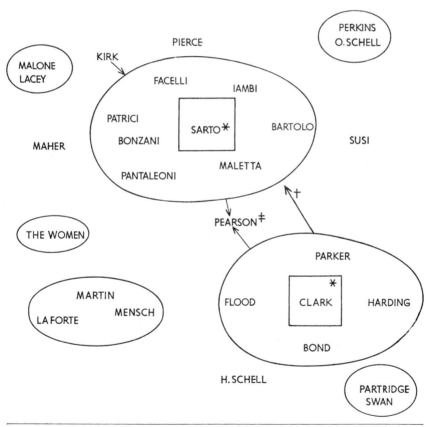

Exhibit 6

THE SLADE COMPANY

INFORMAL GROUPINGS IN THE PLATING ROOM

---

* The boxes indicate those men who clearly demonstrated leadership behavior (most closely personified the values shared by their groups, were most often sought for help and arbitration, and so forth).

† While the two- and three-man groupings had little informal contact outside their own boundaries, the five-man group did seek to join the largest group in extraplant social affairs. These were relatively infrequent.

‡ Though not an active member of any group, Bob Pearson was regarded with affection by the two large groups.

member and the one who acted as arbiter between the other members, was the largest in the department. The group, except for Louis Patrici, Al Bartolo, and Frank Bonzani (who spelled each other during break periods), invariably ate lunch together on the fire escape near Aisle 1. On those Saturdays and Sundays when overtime work was required, the Sarto group operated as a team, regardless of weekday work assignments, to get overtime work completed as quickly as possible. (Few department members not affiliated with either the Sarto or the Clark groups worked on week ends.) Off the job, Sarto group members often joined in parties or week-end trips. Sarto's summer camp was a frequent rendezvous.

Sarto's group was also the most cohesive one in the department in terms of its organized punch-in and punch-out system. Since the men were regularly scheduled to work from 7:00 A.M. to 7:00 P.M. weekdays, and since all supervision was removed at 5:00 P.M., it was possible almost every day to finish a "day's work" by 5:30 and leave the plant. What is more, if one man were to stay until 7:00 P.M., he could punch the time cards of a number of men and help them gain free time without pay loss. (This system operated on week ends, also, at which times members of supervision were present, if at all, only for short periods.) In Sarto's group the duty of staying late rotated, so that no man did so more than once a week. In addition, the group members would punch a man in in the morning if he were unavoidably delayed. However, such a practice never occurred without prior notice from the man who expected to be late and never if the tardiness was expected to last beyond 8:00 A.M., the start of the day for the foreman.

Sarto explained the logic behind the system to Kirk:

> You know that our hourly pay rate is quite low, compared to other companies. What makes this the best place to work is the feeling of security you get. No one ever gets laid off in this department. With all the hours in the week, all the company ever has to do is shorten the work week when orders fall off. We have to tighten our belts, but we can all get along. When things are going well, as they are now, the company is only interested in getting out the work. It doesn't help to get it out faster than it's really needed—so we go home a little early whenever we can. Of course, some guys abuse this sort of thing—like Herman—but others work even harder, and it averages out.
>
> Whenever an extra order has to be pushed through, naturally I work until 7:00. So do a lot of the others. I believe that if I stay until my work is caught up and my equipment is in good shape, that's all the company wants of me. They leave us alone and expect us to produce— and we do.

When Kirk asked Sarto if he would not rather work shorter hours at higher pay in a union shop (Slade employees were not organized), he just laughed and said: "It wouldn't come close to an even trade."

The members of Sarto's group were explicit about what constituted a fair day's work. Customarily, they cited Herman Schell, Kirk's work partner and the foremen's brother, as a man who consistently produced below that level. Kirk received an informal orientation from Herman during his first days on the job. As Herman put it:

> I've worked at this job for a good many years, and I expect to stay here a good many more. You're just starting out, and you don't know which end is up yet. We spend a lot of time in here; and no matter how hard we work, the pile of work never goes down. There's always more to take its place. And I think you've found out by now that this isn't light work. You can wear yourself out fast if you're not smart. Look at Pearson up in Aisle 4. There's a kid who's just going to burn himself out. He won't last long. If he thinks he's going to get somewhere working like that, he's nuts. They'll give him all the work he can take. He makes it tough on everybody else and on himself, too.

Kirk reported further on his observations of the department:

> As nearly as I could tell, two things seemed to determine whether or not Sarto's group or any others came in for week-end work on Saturday or Sunday. It seemed usually to be caused by rush orders that were received late in the week, although I suspect it was sometimes caused by the men having spent insufficient time on the job during the previous week.
>
> Tony and his group couldn't understand Herman. While Herman arrived late, Tony was always half an hour early. If there was a push to get out an extra amount of work, almost everyone but Herman would work that much harder. Herman never worked overtime on week ends, while Tony's group and the men on the manual tanks almost always did. When the first, exploratory time study of the department was made, no one in the aisles slowed down, except Herman, with the possible exception, to a lesser degree, of Charlie Malone. I did hear that the men in the dry end of the room slowed down so much you could hardly see them move; but we had little to do with them, anyway. While the men I knew best seemed to find a rather full life in their work, Herman never really got involved. No wonder they couldn't understand each other.
>
> There was quite a different feeling about Bobby Pearson. Without the slightest doubt, Bob worked harder than anyone else in the room. Because of the tremendous variety of work produced, it was hard to make output comparisons, but I'm sure I wouldn't be far wrong in saying that Bob put out twice as much as Herman and 50 per cent more than al-

most anyone else in the aisles. No one but Herman and a few old-timers at the dry end ever criticized Bobby for his efforts. Tony and his group seemed to feel a distant affection for Bob, but the only contact they or anyone else had with him consisted of brief greetings.

To the men in Tony's group the most severe penalty that could be inflicted on a man was exclusion. This they did to both Pearson and Herman. Pearson, however, was tolerated; Herman was not. Evidently, Herman felt his exclusion keenly, though he answered it with derision and aggression. Herman kept up a steady stream of stories concerning his attempts to gain acceptance outside the company. He wrote popular music which was always rejected by publishers. He attempted to join several social and athletic clubs, mostly without success. His favorite pastime was fishing. He told me that fishermen were friendly, and he enjoyed meeting new people whenever he went fishing. But he was particularly quick to explain that he preferred to keep his distance from the men in the department.

Tony's group emphasized more than just quantity in judging a man's work. Among them had grown a confidence that they could master and even improve upon any known finishing technique. Tony himself symbolized this skill. Before him, Tony's father had operated Aisle 1 and had trained Tony to take his place. Tony in his turn was training his cousin Pete. When a new finishing problem arose from a change in customer specifications, the foreman, the department chemist, or any of the men directly involved would come to Tony for help, and Tony would give it willingly. For example, when a part with a special plastic embossing was designed, Tony was the only one who could discover how to treat the metal without damaging the plastic. To a lesser degree, the other members of the group were also inventive about the problems which arose in their own sections.

Herman, for his part, talked incessantly about his feats in design and finish creations. As far as I could tell during the year I worked in the department, the objects of these stories were obsolete or of minor importance. What's more, I never saw any department member seek Herman's help.

Willingness to be of help was a trait Sarto's group prized. The most valued help of all was of a personal kind, though work help was also important. The members of Sarto's group were constantly lending and borrowing money, cars, clothing, and tools among themselves and, less frequently, with other members of the department. Their daily lunch bag procedure typified the "common property" feeling among them. Everyone's lunch was opened and added to a common pile, from which each member of the group chose his meal.

On the other hand, Herman refused to help others in any way. He never left his aisle to aid those near him who were in the midst of a rush of work or a machine failure, though this was customary throughout most of the department. I can distinctly recall the picture of Herman leaning on the hot and cold water faucets which were located directly above each tumbling barrel. He would stand gazing into the tumbling pieces for hours. To the passing, casual visitor, he looked busy; and as he told me, that's just what he wanted. He, of course, expected me to act this same way, and it was this enforced boredom that I found virtually intolerable.

More than this, Herman took no responsibility for breaking in his assigned helpers as they first entered the department, or thereafter. He had had four helpers in the space of little more than a year. Each had asked for a transfer to another department, publicly citing the work as cause, privately blaming Herman. Tony was the one who taught me the ropes when I first entered the department.

The men who congregated around Harry Clark tended to talk like and copy the behavior of the Sarto group, though they never approached the degree of inventive skill or the amount of helping activities that Tony's group did. They sought outside social contact with the Sarto group; and several times a year, the two groups went "on the town" together. Clark's group did maintain a high level of performance in the volume of work they turned out.

The remainder of the people in the department stayed pretty much to themselves or associated in pairs or triplets. None of these people were as inventive, as helpful, or as productive as Sarto's or Clark's groups, but most of them gave verbal support to the same values as those groups held.

The distinction between the two organized groups and the rest of the department was clearest in the punching-out routine. The women could not work past 3:00 P.M., so they were not involved. Malone and Lacey, Partridge and Swan, and Martin, La Forte, and Mensch arranged within their small groups for punch-outs, or they remained beyond 5:00 and slept or read when they finished their work. Perkins and Pierce went home when the foreman did. Herman Schell, Susi, and Maher had no punch-out organization to rely upon. Susi and Maher invariably stayed in the department until 7:00 P.M. Herman was reported to have established an arrangement with Partridge whereby the latter punched Herman out for a fee. Such a practice was unthinkable from the point of view of Sarto's group. It evidently did not occur often because Herman usually went to sleep behind piles of work when his brother left or, particularly during the fishing season, punched himself out early. He constantly railed against the dishonesty of other men in the department, yet urged me to punch him out on several "emergency occasions."

Just before I left the Slade Company to return to school after fourteen months on the job, I had a casual conversation with Mr. Porter, the production manager, in which he asked me how I had enjoyed my experience with the organization. During the conversation, I learned that he knew of the punch-out system in the plating department. What's more, he told me, he was wondering if he ought to "blow the lid off the whole mess."

5. THE TIMES-HERALD[1]

The Times-Herald, one of the major daily newspapers in a large middle-western city, published afternoon and evening editions, six days a week as well as a single Sunday edition. The paper was founded in the late nineteenth century by Samuel B. Fischer and was managed by his descendents in 1962. Its stated publishing policy was to remain impartial in political disputes and to report news in an objective manner avoiding sensational issues.

As Exhibit 1 indicates, the editorial department of *The Times-Herald* was under the direct supervision of Bob Smith,[2] managing editor. While assistant managing editors and the associate editor supervised the news reporters, feature reporters and columnists, the rewriting and editing functions were the direct responsibility of the city editor and the news editor. Joe O'Malley, the city editor, managed the city desk which directed the daily reporting of local news and the writing of stories. Thus, while the assistant managing editor assigned reporters to major events or "beats" for coverage, the city editor directed the daily gathering of news. Stories were either written by reporters or telephoned by them to rewite men who converted the news items into finished stories. National and foreign news was gathered predominantly by one of the several wire services which *The Times-Herald* subscribed to, although *The Times-Herald* occasionally sent senior reporters to cover world events of particular interest to readers. The wire-service copy and the local stories from the city desk were all routed through the news desk, which was supervised by Fred Dugan, news editor.[3] Fred and the copy editors on the news desk (desk men) edited the copy and decided which stories would be included in the paper. Exhibits 2 and 3 provide a floor plan of the city room and the news desk, respectively.

After the news had been processed by the men on the news desk, the copy which was to be included in the paper was dropped through a chute (see Exhibits 2 and 3) to the composing room two floors below. Here the make-up editor, Gene Little (a member of the news desk, who spent

---

[1] All names have been disguised.

[2] All editorial department personnel, including the managing editor, were referred to by their first names.

[3] While this case deals with the day news desk there was also a smaller desk ("the lobster desk") of four men who worked from midnight to 8:00 A.M. preparing news for the early editions. This group was also the responsibility of Fred Dugan.

Exhibit 1

THE TIMES-HERALD

ORGANIZATION OF EDITORIAL DEPARTMENT*

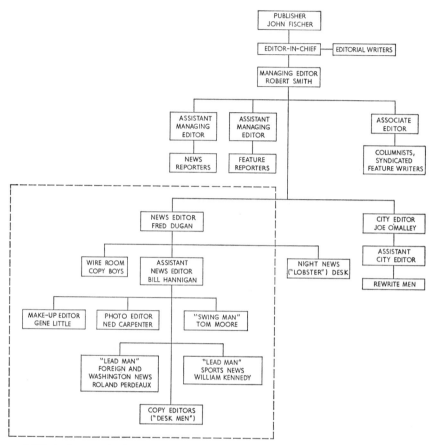

* This is the casewriter's conception of the organization since no formal chart existed. Dotted line encloses news desk positions.

most of his time in the composing room), laid out the front page. Gene also helped composing room personnel solve any layout problems as they fitted news into spaces not occupied by previously laid out advertising copy on the inside pages. After the layout had been completed, the edition was ready for printing.

In addition to the news editor and the make-up editor there were several other supervisory positions on the news desk. The assistant news editor, William Hannigan, referred to in newspaper parlance as the "slot man," assigned the stories to the various desk men and reviewed the edited results before sending them to the composing room. As

Exhibit 2

THE TIMES-HERALD

THE CITY ROOM OF *The Times-Herald**

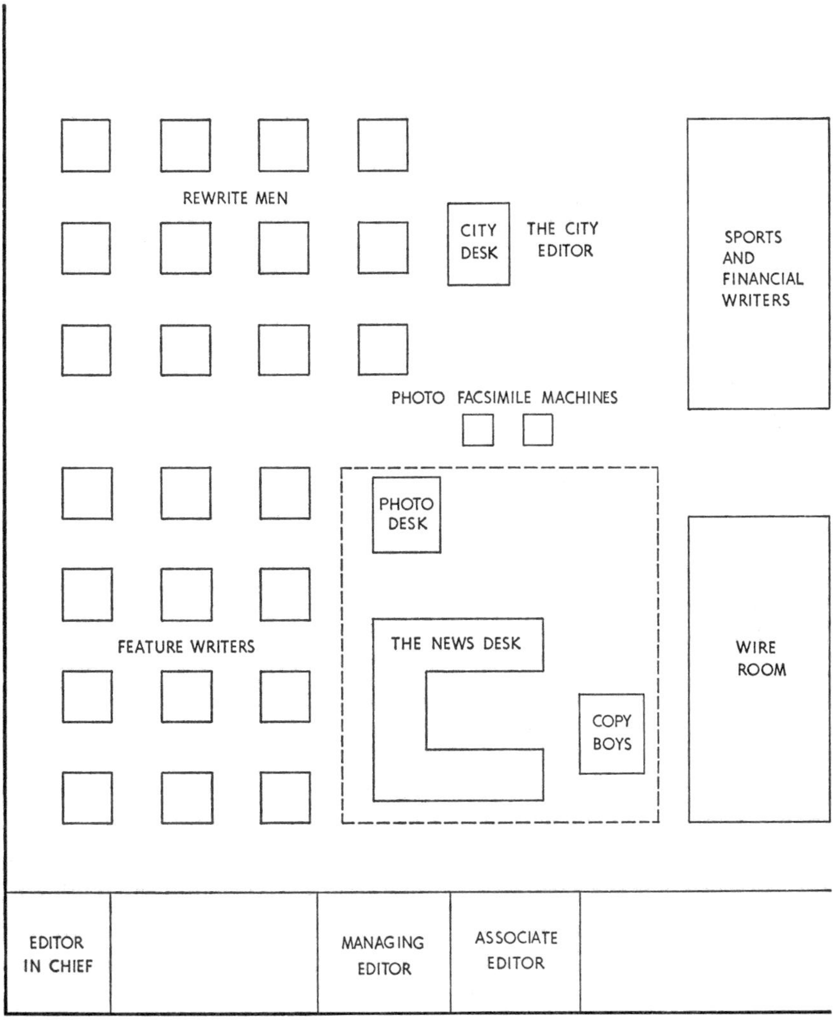

* Dotted line encloses all news desk positions except for make-up editor who worked in composing room.

Exhibit 3 indicates, the news desk was divided into three sections, one for local and national (other than Washington, D.C.) news, one for foreign and Washington news, and one for sports. The slot man made assignments directly to the desk men working on local news, but for other news worked through "lead men," Rolly Perdeaux for Washington and foreign news and Will Kennedy for sports news. These lead

Exhibit 3

THE TIMES-HERALD

The Times-Herald NEWS DESK*

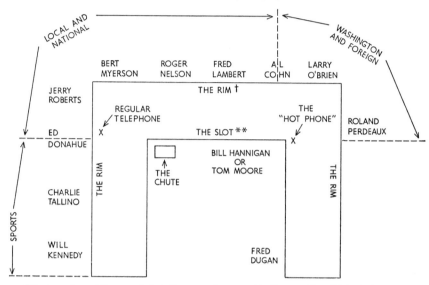

* Two members of the news desk staff are not shown on this diagram. Gene Little (make-up editor) and Ned Carpenter (photo editor) held jobs requiring them to work away from the desk (see Exhibit 2). Although the desk men rotated seats, this figure represents a typical seating chart. Ed Donahue substituted for Charlie Tallino and Will Kennedy on their days off and Al Cohn sometimes worked on local news.

† The news desk of *The Times-Herald,* as at most newspapers, was arranged in a horseshoe shape. The outer edge was referred to as "the rim" and the inner edge as "the slot." Thus since the assistant news editor always occupied the center he was traditionally called the "slot man."

men supervised one or two desk men in editing their particular category of copy. Another supervisory position on the desk was the "swing man," Thomas Moore, who, as his title implies, substituted for supervisory and other personnel on their days off. The news desk operated on a six-day week, but the desk men worked only five of the six. According to Fred Dugan, the job of swing man required a high degree of skill and flexibility, since Tom had periodically to perform the work of the assistant news editor, the make-up editor, and the photo editor, as well as the work of lead men and some of the regular copy editors.

Although the photo editor's desk was slightly removed from the news desk, he worked for the news editor and with other desk personnel in selecting photographs to accompany various stories and in writing captions for them.

The Men on the Desk

As Exhibit 4 indicates most of the copy editors had long journalistic careers behind them. By tradition, the desk at *The Times-Herald,* as at

Exhibit 4

THE TIMES-HERALD

Desk Personnel

Name	Position	Age*	Service at The Times-Herald	Service on News Desk†	Prior Journalistic Experience
Fred Dugan	News editor	48	32	28	Copy boy, copy editor on *The Times-Herald*
Bill Hannigan	Asst. news editor (slot man)	52	33	22	Copy boy, reporter, copy editor on *The Times-Herald*
Tom Moore	Swing man	42	20	16*	Copy boy, reporter, copy editor on *The Times-Herald*
Gene Little	Make-up editor	48	27	16	Copy boy, reporter, copy editor on *The Times-Herald*
Ned Carpenter	Photo editor	55	20	20	Several positions on small-town newspapers
Roland Perdeaux	Lead man, foreign and Washington	58	33	33	Reporter on a small-town newspaper; copy editor on *The Times-Herald*
Will Kennedy	Lead man—sports	40	22	10	Copy boy, sports writer, copy editor on *The Times-Herald*
Fred Lambert	Desk man—sports	56	13	13	Reporter, copy editor on another metropolitan newspaper
Roger Nelson	Desk man—local	55	28	28	Reporter on small-town newspaper
Al Cohn	Desk man—local or foreign	62	34	34*	Reporter on another metropolitan newspaper
Ed Donahue	Desk man—local or sports	36	6	6	Copy boy and reporter on another metropolitan newspaper
Jerry Roberts	Desk man—local	72	20	20	District manager for wire-service, wire-service reporter
Bert Myerson	Desk man—local	32	2	2	Reporter on another metropolitan daily
Larry O'Brien	Desk man—foreign	50	4	4	Reporter and copy editor on metropolitan daily
Charlie Tallino	Desk man—sports and local	38	2	2*	Several positions on a neighborhood weekly newspaper

* *The Times-Herald* had no regular retirement age. Personnel worked until they felt they wanted to retire.
† Asterisk indicates service on lobster desk as well as day desk. Al Cohn and Tom Moore had been on day desk about one year while Charlie Tallino had been on day desk six months.

most newspapers, had been staffed with senior men who, because of age or family responsibility, no longer desired to work the long and irregular hours required of reporters, and who displayed a skill at, and an interest in, copy editing. Recently, however, Fred Dugan had become concerned that there were not enough younger men on the desk to provide a balanced appraisal of news copy and to provide continuity as the older men retired. He also believed that younger men were needed to provide long-range replacements for the executive positions on the desk. He therefore arranged to have several younger men assigned to the desk. While they had less experience than their seniors, these newcomers came to the copy desk after several years of experience in various phases of reporting and editorial work, either with the *The Times-Herald,* or with other papers. In order to make room for these younger men Bob Smith had transferred copy editors who indicated suitable interest and competence to the position of chief editor of a feature department or to senior writer's jobs in these departments. In the spring of 1962, Fred Dugan was attempting to evaluate the effects of this change in the complexion of the copy editor's position on the operation of the desk.

Fred spoke about the use of younger men on the desk:

> There is a feeling among many newspapermen that the copy desk is the end of the line. The feeling in the trade is that older people end up on the desk, but you can't put out a successful paper on that basis. At the present time in the newspaper business obtaining good copy editors is the most pressing employment problem. If you were to look at smaller papers, the old age of the desk men might be a striking feature, but on a big paper such as ours things are too fast moving to operate this way. We have to continue to try to bring younger men in as copy editors.

When a man came to work for the desk from outside *The Times-Herald,* he sometimes worked as a part-timer before being given a permanent desk position. For example, this was the way Bert Myerson, one of the newer desk men, was originally brought to *The Times-Herald* from another local paper. As Fred Dugan explained, "We wanted him on a part-time basis to see if we liked him and he liked us. He worked out well, so we put him on full time. He is one of our promising younger men now."

Many of the desk men had initially become interested in a journalistic career while working on school newspapers, beginning work at *The Times-Herald* as copy boys in the evening or during the summer while they were going to college. Roger Nelson was one of these. "Rog" went to work for a small-city newspaper during a summer vacation from the University of Chicago, where he was majoring in fine arts. After graduation he returned to this paper and a few years later joined *The Times-*

Herald as a copy editor. A few men like Will Kennedy, whose father had been a well-known sports cartoonist, had become interested in working for *The Times-Herald* because of family connections.

Bert Myerson spoke of his attitudes about work on the desk:

> The desk used to be a dead end. Now it appears that this may not be so. The progression used to be reporter, rewrite, desk. Now that some of the other fellows [former copy writers] have moved on as feature and editorial writers, I'm hopeful it means you can move from the desk to other things. On the desk you are learning newspaper technology, but you don't have an opportunity to learn about any one area in depth. Yet the work on the desk is interesting, because we see such a variety of stuff.

"Rolly" Perdeaux, who was the lead man on foreign and Washington news exemplified the attitude of the senior desk men:

> My wife says I'm like a fireman. I can't wait to get to work. I think the thing that makes us like this business so much is the opportunity for creativity. Everybody feels that they have a part in putting out the paper. If you ask the reporters, pressmen, or the mailmen, they'll also say, just like we do, that without them the paper wouldn't go out.
>
> But working on the desk is particularly interesting, because it is the nerve center of the paper. We are extremely important as a last outpost between the public and the news sources.

The desk men were concerned about maintaining journalistic standards in editing the news. Comments such as these were typical:

> A speech by Khrushchev is a tough one to handle. You don't want to make it too big, yet it is news. If you let them get too much propaganda out of it by giving them a big headline, you can panic the public. You are doing a disservice to the public and your country.

. . . .

> We have a responsibility to the public. I'm proud to work for *The Times-Herald,* because we make an effort not to be jingoistic, or warmongers. We take time to make a "head" accurate and not misleading, but still to make it appealing to the public.
>
> We want the story to be fair, and we don't want it to be offensive. When we know one of the competitors is going to break a story, we want to get it in and beat them to it.

. . . .

> When the [wire-service] describes the color of somebody's beard or what he was wearing, it is O.K., but when it is what somebody says, they are usually wrong, so I don't like to use their stuff.

. . . .

The casewriter observed that these standards were not only valued by the desk men, but were also reflected in comments by employees in other parts of *The Times-Herald* and in the paper's editorial policy. Bill Hannigan, the slot man, explained:

> It may be difficult to recognize our rules, because they are not written down, but we do have them. By the time a man gets to the news desk he has learned *The Times-Herald* way of doing things. We don't go for sensationalism. We are straight down the line politically and we try to be fair to all sides. Since everybody knows these things, they get done quietly and unobtrusively. By the time something gets past the rewrite men, the city editor, past the men over there [pointing to the desk men on the rim] and past me, it should agree with *The Times-Herald* policies. I check things over to make sure they are right. However, the boys in the composing room will often catch something and call me to see if it got by us, and it often did. They don't have any technical responsibility for this down there, but they help us.

Assignments of men to the various positions on the desk were based on three criteria: availability of openings, ability of the men, and, particularly, their interest. Will Kennedy and Charlie Tallino, who edited sports copy, discussed the assignment process:

> WILL: Take for example Perdeaux. Washington and foreign news is his job. He's a good man for it—lecturer and world traveler. He teaches at [a local university]. He used to lecture a lot about foreign affairs. He has traveled to the Holy Land and Rome in the last few years.
> CHARLIE: Right, you get into an area because you have an interest in it and like it.
> WILL: It wouldn't do to have someone on our job who knows nothing about sports.

Will Kennedy also explained how Tom Moore had been assigned the job of swing man.

> Tom came over from the lobster desk and was jumped over some of the others. Lam and Roger didn't want to run around that much, so Fred gave it to the younger man. It depends somewhat on what people want. None of the other guys would want to be on sports.

While permanent assignments were made on this basis, the fact that the desk operated on a six-day week made it necessary for several of the men in addition to the swing man to rotate between various positions. It was usually the newer men on the desk who moved from one position to another, while the senior men generally remained at a regular position. One exception to this was Al Cohn, who rotated between working on foreign and Washington news and local news whenever he wanted. Fred Dugan explained Al's almost daily shifts in assignments:

I don't really care where Al lands, as long as all the seats are occupied. He is one of our senior citizens, and we let him work wherever he feels like sitting down when he comes in each morning.

Supervisory personnel on the desk were usually selected from among desk personnel or from persons working in other parts of the paper with prior experience on the desk. Comments such as this one by Will Kennedy were typical of the sentiments the men expressed about the supervisors.

> Fred [Dugan] is really creative. He is not satisfied to let the front page remain the same through many editions. He really works to make it the best possible.[4]

Al Cohn, who had recently transferred from the lobster desk, expressed a similar view:

> On the lobster desk I was brass, here I am just one of the boys. I transferred over though because my wife had been ill and also because I saw it as a chance to work with Fred, who is really a bright guy. I've watched him ever since he started as a copy boy. As far as we are concerned, he's a case of the right man on the right job.

A Day on the News Desk

The city room was in full operation from 6:30 A.M. to 5:00 P.M. each day. The period between midnight and 8:00 was referred to as the "lobster shift" and was manned by a skeleton crew which stood by in case of a sudden important news development and also processed routine incoming news for use in the early, "bulldog," edition. The men on the day news desk began to arrive at 6:00 A.M. The first to arrive was usually Larry O'Brien, the "early man." He sorted copy from the lobster shift and began making rough selections about what copy was suitable for inclusion in the first edition. At about 7:00 Fred Dugan and Bill Hannigan arrived and familiarized themselves with the important stories by talking with Larry O'Brien. The following exchange might be typical:

> LARRY: Well, we've got a revolution going in Burma this morning. The new man's name is Lee Win. That should fit any headline.

---

[4] The day news desk was responsible for putting out six editions which went to press at the following times: 9:20 A.M., 11:50 A.M., 1:00 P.M., 3:10 P.M., 3:50 P.M. Copy for each edition had to be sent to the composing room at least forty-five minutes before these press times. How much variation there was between editions was a function of the news developments on a particular day. Generally, however, there would be some changes between each edition, so that the final edition would have little resemblance to the early edition. It was not uncommon to have the entire front page remade in the course of one or two editions.

BILL (*laughs*): "Lee Win—Wins," huh? Well, I guess we'll want to use that unless something better breaks. What else have you got . . . ?

By 7:30 most of the other desk men had arrived and begun work. As each man came in, he stopped by the locker room and removed his street wear and suit coat, since everyone including the editor-in-chief worked in his shirt sleeves. At the desk, each man brushed off the area in front of his chair and made certain that the copy boys had filled the paste pots and supplied him with paper pads. If there were no work immediately available the men began to thumb through the last edition from the evening before.

If there were any late arrivals, they might be greeted like Rolly Perdeaux welcomed Al Cohn when the latter arrived ten minutes late one morning:

AL: Morning boys.
ROLLY: Well, are you the early man for tomorrow?
AL: You're confused. I'm not the early man, I'm the late man.

Fred Dugan was informed each morning by the business office how much space he would have available for news copy in that day's editions. The amount of news space was determined by the amount of advertising sold and the size newspaper which could be sold profitably with this amount of advertising. Thus, it was necessary when heavy news days coincided with light advertising to eliminate news copy which would ordinarily warrant inclusion in the paper. The casewriter noticed that the copy editors were all concerned when such a "tight paper" occurred and frequently complained about not being able to include important stories. Fred Dugan was responsible for allocating news space within the paper to local and national, Washington and foreign, and sports news. When news space was limited, Fred usually first cut the size of the sports page before eliminating important stories from the regular news pages.

Once the size of the paper was determined and the work at the desk gained momentum, Bill Hannigan reviewed stories as they came in from the city desk and the wire services. Sports and Washington and foreign news was passed on to the respective lead man, but Bill himself made the decision as to what local and national news items were to be included in the edition. If he wanted it to go in, the copy was given to one of the desk men on the rim who edited it for accuracy, grammatical correctness, style, and length, and then wrote the headline. Basically, the same procedure was followed by Will Kennedy and Rolly Perdeaux in their sections, although they also worked directly on some of the copy themselves, usually the major stories. The length of the story and the size of type for the headline were specified by Bill Hannigan, for local and national news as well as major foreign and Washington stories, although Will Kennedy made his own decisions about the sports page, since he was also responsible for its layout.

When a copy editor had finished a particular story he pasted the parts of the story to a sheet of paper on which he had written the headline, the page the story was to run on (although this was only specified for the major stories), and the edition it should run in, and handed all this back to Bill Hannigan or his lead man. After a check to see if the story had come out the way he had expected, the supervisor dropped it into the chute leading to the composing room.

Tom Moore explained the philosophy of the supervisors at the desk with regard to reviewing stories.

> We believe in a little checking up, but generally the people are mature enough to take care of their own jobs. We usually just give the story a quick once over because the men know how to handle them. With a new man or a major story we might take more time.

Al Cohn and Lam Lambert discussed the way most of the men felt about having their work reviewed:

> AL: You'll never find another desk like this. Nobody's afraid of anyone else, including the boss. If someone makes a mistake we let him know about it. We expect some mistakes. We recognize, because of the time pressures, that people will make mistakes.
>
> LAM: If somebody makes a mistake we explain what's wrong so it won't happen again, instead of firing him like they do on some other papers.
>
> AL: Yes, *The Times-Herald* has a much calmer, better work atmosphere than the other papers in town.

The casewriter observed that while most of the desk men showed no concern about supervisory review of completed stories, Charlie Tallino was an exception. On several occasions the casewriter noticed Charlie watching nervously as Bill Hannigan looked over his work on local news stories. When Bill dropped the story into the chute without comment, Charlie gave an audible sigh of relief. On a particular morning Charlie was working on an important story on the death of prize fighter Bennie Paret which was to appear on the front page. Charlie gave the story to Tom Moore, who was working in the slot that day, and watched carefully as Tom read it. Fred Dugan stopped and looked over Tom's shoulder at the story and then picked it up and brought it back to Charlie saying, "I don't like the head too well. Can't we do better than this?"

Charlie replied, "I'll get it," and again worked on the headline for several minutes, after which Fred returned and they discussed it further. Fred finally suggested a word which Charlie said, "was just the one I was looking for," and the story was dropped to the composing room. Charlie told the casewriter, after this incident, "Fred really has a gift for finding the right 'head' for a story. He makes it seem easy."

The front page was the particular domain of Fred Dugan himself. He determined the major part of its content and sometimes wrote the lead headline and edited the lead story, although these tasks were often assigned to Bert Myerson, Roger Nelson, Al Cohn, or Fred Lambert who performed them with little supervision. Bill Hannigan, Rolly Perdeaux, and Will Kennedy kept Fred informed of major stories which might deserve front page attention. In Fred's absence, Bill Hannigan made decisions on front page content, as well as performing Fred's other duties.

The desk men continued working on stories as long as there was copy available. When there was a slack period, which might occur several times during the day, they spent most of their time either reading earlier editions of *The Times-Herald,* looking for "typos" (typographical errors) or reading competitive newspapers to see how they were handling stories that *The Times-Herald* had run in earlier editions. The desk man who found a "typo" would cut the article out, paste it to a sheet of paper and mark it with the appropriate proofreader's symbols. He would then drop it down the chute. The casewriter observed on several occasions that the more experienced desk men would be assigned stories which kept them at work for long periods, while at the same time, Ed, Charlie, and Bert were reading newspapers or chatting.

While the men worked they discussed current stories, political and world events, or family and personal problems. Frequently they asked each other for help on a particular story or headline. For example, Rog Nelson asked Al Cohn and Larry O'Brien for help in the phrasing of a headline on the nuclear test-ban negotiations:

> ROG: Should we use "No-Give on Part of Russians" in the headline?
> AL: I don't think you've got the right meaning there.
> LARRY: You are inventing the word and really using a verb as a noun. It sounds awkward to me. Why don't you try "Russians Won't Give."
> ROG: Let me see how that works.

There was also a great deal of joking between the men on the desk. For example, one day early in March as Ed Donahue was ordering coffee from the cafeteria, he asked Al Cohn if he would like anything, and the following exchange occurred:

AL: What's the special for today?

ED: I'm not sure, but they are going to have Kelley green matzoh balls for St. Patrick's Day.

AL: Is that so? Passover isn't for a couple of weeks yet, but get me a green bagel with my coffee.

ED: You want sour cream with it?

AL: No, that's high on cholesterol.

On another occasion Ed Donahue and Will Kennedy spent most of a morning joking with Charlie Tallino about the latter's having crashed a St. Patrick's Day open house by wearing a green tie.

One morning Al Cohn was sitting alongside Bert Myerson carrying on a one-sided conversation with him, while Bert was working. Ed Donahue removed a small piece of cotton from his desk drawer and took it to Bert with the whispered suggestion that he stuff it in his ear, "to stop Al from banging on it." Bert smiled and winked in response. This was done so quietly that neither Al nor the other desk men were aware of the incident. After Al had left for lunch, Ed recounted the incident to several of the other desk men who appeared to find it amusing and exchanged several jokes about Al's tendency to "bang on your ear." This conversation ended abruptly when Bill Hannigan looked up from a story he was reading and said, "Come on, Ed."

Humorous exchanges were not confined to the perimeter of the news desk. For example, a former desk man, now a financial writer, often engaged in humorous banter with the desk men as he dropped stories into the chute. One morning he approached the chute with a story which he stuck under Will Kennedy's nose:

WILL: I wondered what you guys had been doing in that cubbyhole of yours all these years.

FINANCIAL WRITER: This is the treasury balance. You guys may not know it but you can't put out the paper without the treasury balance. (*Laughter from the desk men.*)

WILL: As far as I can tell you are just like the feature writers—you don't know what live news is any more. . . .

During the period the casewriter was at *The Times-Herald* the desk men joined with the reporters and rewrite men in joking about a new glass-enclosed booth for the telephone operators which was being constructed near the city desk. The booth was designated as "the communal shower bath," "the sidewalk toilet," and by Al Cohn as "an isolation booth for noisy desk men."

The desk men sometimes found themselves the target of jokes. Charlie Tallino was checking a list of returning servicemen which had been prepared by a rewrite man when he found on the list the name of "Herschel Harshbarger," a pseudonym used on hotel registers by one of the star *Times-Herald* reporters. After Charlie disclosed his discovery to the other copy editors they all watched with amusement as he went over to "straighten out" the rewrite man.

The desk men also spent time discussing how *The Times-Herald* news coverage compared to that of competitive papers. For example, one morning Will Kennedy noted that a story carried by other local papers was not appearing in *The Times-Herald*. After a flurry of activity as several men tried to determine why this had happened, Bill Hannigan discovered that, "the story came in late yesterday and the lobster shift should have handled it." This precipitated a general discussion of how the lobster desk failed to pass on stories, with everyone stopping work to join in the criticism of the lobster desk. The casewriter noticed that although several of the desk men had at one time or another worked the lobster desk, they all frequently criticized it as the cause of mistakes which occurred during the day. This often happened even when it appeared to the casewriter that one of the day desk men might have been expected to catch the error. On another occasion the casewriter observed one of the feature writers come to the desk and ask to borrow a type-writer. Ed Donahue nodded his assent. Several hours later Will Kennedy wanted to use the typewriter and asked where it was. Ed and Charlie Tallino informed him that, "The damn features boys stole it again." Ed and Charlie then went off, cursing, to find the machine, and bring it back "where it belongs!"

Fred Dugan did not usually take an active part in the joking and conversation, but he often joined in the laughter and occasionally made a contribution. While Bill Hannigan was a frequent participant in all the exchanges around the desk, the casewriter noticed that Tom Moore did not contribute to the conversations and often showed no reaction to the joking.

Exhibit 5 provides a summary of all these contacts. It is based on approximately eighteen hours of observation over a six-day period.

This pattern of working and socializing continued throughout the morning with only occasional interruptions. The first of these came between 9:30 and 10:00 each morning when Bill Hannigan or Jerry Roberts would suggest that it was time for coffee. Usually without being asked, Charlie Tallino would make up the coffee list, asking each man what he wanted, even though this usually involved hunting for Fred Dugan and Ned Carpenter, the photo editor, who often were in some far corner of the city room. The only member of the desk who did not order

Exhibit 5

THE TIMES-HERALD

Nonrequired Interactions

RECIPIENTS	INITIATORS	SPORTS — KENNEDY	DONAHUE	TALLINO	LOCAL — LAMBERT	ROBERTS	MYERSON	NELSON	COHN	FOREIGN — O'BRIEN	PERDEAUX	EXECUTIVES — LITTLE	CARPENTER	MOORE	HANNIGAN	DUGAN	OUTSIDE PERSONNEL†	TOTAL RECEIVED
SPORTS — KENNEDY		X	6	10							1				3	2	8	30
DONAHUE		5	X		1			1						1	2	1	1	12
TALLINO		2	1	X	1										1			5
LOCAL — LAMBERT		3	3	1	X	3	1		2	1					1		7	22
ROBERTS		1	3	1		X			1						2			8
MYERSON		1	3		2	3	X	1	2						2	1		15
NELSON		1			2	1	2	X	1						2	1		10
COHN			2	1	4	2	1		X	3		1	1		1	1		17
FOREIGN — O'BRIEN					1				2	X	2							5
PERDEAUX		1	1		1				1	4	X			2	3	5	3	21
EXECUTIVES — LITTLE			1	1	1							X				2		5
CARPENTER				4						1		1	X		1	1		7
MOORE			1	1										X		3	1	6
HANNIGAN		4	3	1		1		1	1	1	5	1		3	X	2	3	26
DUGAN											2	4	5	4	2	X	6	23
TOTAL INITIATED		18	24	20	11	12	4	3	10	9	10	7	6	10	19	20	29	212
SURPLUS OF RECEIPTS (DEFICIT OF RECEIPTS)*		12	(12)	(15)	11	(4)	11	7	7	(4)	11	(2)	1	(4)	7	3	X	
WORKED ON MAJOR STORIES OR SUPERVISOR		YES	NO	NO	YES	NO	YES	YES	YES	NO	YES	YES	YES	YES	YES	YES		

* This represents the difference in interactions received and initiated. A surplus indicates more receipts than initiations and a deficit the opposite condition.

† Outsider refers to interactions received from personnel other than news desk personnel.

coffee with them was Gene Little, make-up editor, who was working in the composing room. The list would then be given to a copy boy who would bring the order back from the cafeteria. While Charlie prepared the list most of the time, there were occasions when Ed Donahue and Bert Myerson would perform this task. One morning Bert Myerson suggested humorously to Al Cohn that he make up the coffee list. Al ignored his entreaties until Lam Lambert said, "Come on Al, are you buying?" Al then made up the list.

Another interruption in the work routine occurred at 10:30 when Gene Little, who spent 90 per cent of his time in the composing room, brought up copies of the first edition to the desk men. This was the signal, if the work load permitted, for everybody to take a few minutes and scan the paper. A few minutes later a copy boy would appear with copies of the same edition for all city room personnel, including the men at the news desk.

Gene Little described this early edition as "our first and our worst. We get better as the day goes along, but we don't have time to catch everything on this early one." While Gene was in the composing room most of the day, he was in constant contact with Bill Hannigan and Fred Dugan over "the hot phone" which provided a direct link between the news desk and the composing room. The casewriter observed that while the hot phone was in easy reach of most of the men on "the rim," only the slot man or news editor answered it. If the persons occupying these positions were away from the desk Rolly Perdeaux would answer the telephone after it had rung several times. There was another telephone near the sports men which was used for routine calls. This was usually answered by Charlie Tallino.

Another interruption in work activity might occur when the publisher's secretary arrived to take up a collection for a retirement or engagement gift, or to set the time for an office party celebrating such events. On one such occasion she came to tell the copy editors that a retirement party was set for 3:00 that afternoon. When Charlie Tallino heard this he became quite upset, because he had not made a contribution when the collection was made a few days earlier on his day off. He offered to contribute to the gift, but the secretary said she had already purchased it, and invited Charlie to the party anyway. Charlie continued to insist that he wanted to give something, until Jerry Roberts said, "That's O.K. Charlie, we've got the money we need. We all miss giving once in a while."

About 11:30 the desk men began to leave for lunch. Because of the necessity of continually staffing the desk, only two or three men could be absent simultaneously. Each man obtained permission from the slot man before going to eat. For the most part the men ate in the company cafeteria. Whom they ate with seemed to the casewriter to depend upon when they and others were free to leave the desk. When two desk men left together, they would usually sit together in the cafeteria, joining friends from other parts of the paper. If a desk man went to lunch alone, he would either join other desk men who were already in the cafeteria, or friends from other parts of the paper, depending upon where seats were vacant.

Fred Dugan, Tom Moore, and Bill Hannigan always went to lunch at different times. Fred usually ate with the assistant managing editor or with other senior personnel. Bill Hannigan usually brought his lunch and ate in a lounge adjoining the cafeteria, reading a competitive newspaper as he ate. Tom Moore also brought his lunch and ate alone in the sports room, which was vacant at that time of day. As he ate, Tom read the *New York Times.*

Activities in the afternoon continued in a fashion similar to those of the morning, although the desk men might seek other diversions if there were a light work load. Will Kennedy and Ed Donahue often worked crossword puzzles. Al Cohn sometimes occupied himself by writing poems, which he then gave Lam Lambert to read. Lam and Al might then spend several minutes discussing possible rhymes and meters.

The general conversation around the desk often shifted to other subjects. On one day it might be Jerry Roberts recounting the retirement party for the 90-year-old church editor who had retired the week before. According to Jerry, "She had been prevailed upon to retire because she had been getting a bit cantankerous in her dealing with the ministers." Another day the conversation might focus on a "think piece" Rolly Perdeaux had written for the Sunday edition on the Algerian problem.[5] Rolly would be the center of attention as he answered questions about the situation and received compliments about the article.

At several points during the day, telephone calls from the general public were received over the regular telephone asking for information about baseball scores or how long it had taken Colonel Glenn to complete one orbit around the earth. The copy editors individually and as a group went to great lengths to attempt to find answers to these questions. Charlie Tallino delighted in telling stories about how he and Will Kennedy had settled barroom brawls over the telephone by providing answers to various queries about sports statistics.

When news was light, a group of former desk men would often congregate around the chute after they had dropped in a feature article or other copy discussing current issues or gossiping about mutual acquaintances with the men on the desk. These sessions were usually characterized by the same humorous banter that prevailed among the copy editors.

---

[5] The managing editor occasionally asked qualified desk men to write an article on this nature. They were given extra compensation for this work.

Frequently, often as much as once an hour, Joe O'Malley, the city editor, would bring an important breaking story to the news desk himself, usually with a shout explaining the story to everyone within earshot, "There's been a murder in the west end. . . ." "A school bus accident out in [a suburb]. Nobody's seriously hurt, as far as we know. We've got a man on the way out there." Joe would often stop alongside the news desk and chat with the desk men about the local political situation or an important local trial. From time to time he would register a complaint with Fred Dugan, Bill Hannigan, or other desk personnel about the manner in which one of the local stories had been handled. Typical of these complaints was one Joe brought to Ned Carpenter, photo editor:

> JOE: Hey, Ned, the caption on the picture of that building that burnt down on the south side isn't right. My man out there said the building was worth $150,000, not $100,000, like you said in the caption. The trouble is the photographer took the picture of the short side of the building. It runs for a block on the other side.

Before Ned could reply, Bill Hannigan, who was seated at the news desk several yards from Ned and Joe, interrupted.

> BILL: Joe, what do you guys think they made in that shack, ten dollar bills?

Joe laughed at Bill's rebuttal and began talking to him about a political scandal which was being covered in that day's paper. No other mention was made of the caption.

Each of these trips by Joe to the news desk made the casewriter especially aware of the contrast between the two sides of the city room. The men at the news desk spent almost the entire day at their positions, working and talking in quiet conversational tones, even when they were joking with each other. Stories were brought to them by copy boys, rewrite men, and O'Malley. The only other interruptions were the occasional visits of feature writers and other personnel who dropped stories in the chute and chatted quietly. Around the news desk a calm, businesslike atmosphere prevailed. In contrast the city desk always seemed to be at a high level of motion and noise. Joe O'Malley would be shouting instructions to rewrite men and to reporters across the room; telephones would be ringing interminably; reporters would be standing in a group laughing and talking loudly—all of which contributed to the general din.

On heavy news days the pressure of deadlines became more apparent to the casewriter and he noticed that casual conversation around the news desk became less prevalent. For example, on the day that Colonel John Glenn was welcomed by a huge crowd in New York City, there was also a major airplane disaster. This made it necessary to revise the front page in a matter of less than an hour to give major prominence to the airline accident. Activity around the desk became intense, and unnecessary conversation subsided. The men worked together calmly without outward signs of tension. When the changes had finally been made, Joe O'Malley passed by the desk and remarked, "Well, we took the heat off Glenn by having an airplane crash." This was greeted by laughter as Will Kennedy said, "You've got to be kind of cold-blooded to be a city editor."

The desk men were conscious of working under pressure. Al Cohn recalled his experiences during the Army-McCarthy hearings:

> I had to condense thirty columns of copy into sixteen columns each night for thirty nights. The tension got so terrific I had a skin eruption and had to be out for a month. You can't keep going night after night from midnight to 8 A.M. without let up. Someone else would have had a coronary.

Bill Hannigan indicated that the copy editors worked under more pressure than men on other parts of the paper:

> Different parts of the paper are different. In the business office they have more of a routine. Here and over there (*pointing to the city desk*) we have to worry about the clock, six deadlines a day. With us it is a little more difficult than with them [the city desk] since we make the final decision on whether a story goes in or not. After all this time we get used to the pressure and it doesn't bother us much.

Several men explained that co-operation among desk men was important. Rolly put it this way:

> There is a real spirit of co-operation to get the best results. Everyone knows that three heads are better than one. Teamwork is very important to deal with the semantic problems we work on. If someone's ideas are better than the ones you have, you are glad to accept them. Of course, we all are human and sometimes you are unhappy at a change. I got mad once [30 years ago] when they changed my headline. I'd only been here a few years then.

Larry O'Brien expressed a similar view:

> I've noticed that there seems to be more teamwork on a news desk or city desk than with a comparable business operation. There seems to be an *ésprit de corps*. You may not like some of the people you work with, but I have noticed that here and on other papers we work together.

The casewriter seldom saw persons around the news desk show anger openly. However, on one occasion, one of the feature editors stormed around the news desk, asking why a certain story had not been included in an early edition. The desk men continued their work and seemed not to notice the outburst. After the feature editor had left, Lam Lambert explained, "We just ignore people who do that." Several weeks later Jerry Roberts and Al Cohn became involved in a discussion about working conditions on other newspapers and an argument resulted. As the two began to argue heatedly, Ed Donahue broke in:

> ED: You two want to put on the gloves?
> LAM: They argue like a bunch of Unitarians. Being the only Unitarian here, I can speak with authority.
> ED: And the only damn Republican.
> LAM: Keep your evaluations to yourself.

Ed and Lam exchanged winks, as Jerry and Al changed the topic of conversation and began to reminisce about mutual friends who had retired from *The Times-Herald.*

The desk men frequently discussed the performance of former desk men who had left the desk for various reasons. While these appraisals were usually favorable, a journalism instructor at a local college who had worked on the desk temporarily one summer often came in for critical comment. According to the men on the desk, "He might have been able to teach the stuff, but he sure couldn't do it. . . ." "He was always banging on your ears about his house or about some such thing. He made so much noise sometimes we couldn't get the work out. We thought he would drive us crazy."

In addition to regular news activities, one of the copy editors was assigned each month to maintain the "rack." This was a backlog file of short news items with no time limitations which could be inserted in the paper as filler whenever they were needed. Fred Dugan made this assignment without keeping any formal record of who had performed it in past months. During the period the casewriter was at *The Times-Herald,* Bert Myerson had spent slightly more than a month working on the rack. One afternoon Fred Dugan noticed him working on a stack of material from the rack and said, "Well, I guess I'll have to spring you pretty soon. How long have you been on it? It's been over a month hasn't it?" Bert replied, "Just about."

Two days later, on Bert's day off, Bill Hannigan asked Larry O'Brien to work on the rack for the day. Larry communicated with facial expressions that he was not pleased at the assignment and finally said, "Can't you get someone else, Bill?" Bill nodded his assent and assigned Larry to work on foreign news instead. Several minutes later, when Ed Donahue arrived, he was assigned to the rack for that day. A few days later Fred assigned Lam Lambert to take over the rack from Bert. Shortly after this change was made the following conversation occurred between Gene Little and Bill Hannigan. Gene had been looking over the rack material stored in the composing room.

GENE: Lam can ease up on the rack. We have loads of material down there.

BILL: O.K. I'll tell him. (*He turned to Lam.*) I think you can lay off that stuff for awhile. Gene thinks we have plenty.

Fred Dugan explained the men's attitude toward the rack:

They consider the rack job onerous, because the rack stuff isn't breaking and exciting, like other news on the desk. They seem to feel the same way about it a reader does when he sees it in the paper. It is filler which can be skipped.

During the course of the day the desk men often made suggestions about handling various stories. The casewriter noticed that when the suggestions were made by Rolly, Lam, Roger, Al, Larry, Jerry, or Will, Fred Dugan and Bill Hannigan listened carefully and often adopted the suggestions. When the suggestions were made by Bert or Ed, Fred and Bill always listened attentively, but never seemed to act on them. Charlie Tallino was not observed making any suggestions, but carried out his work according to original instructions.

At about 3:00 the desk men began to wind up their work, and the men who had arrived earliest put their pencils and equipment into drawers and leisurely got ready to leave. They often stopped to chat with reporters or rewrite men or stayed at the desk reading the paper. By 4:00 the desk men all had gone for the day.

Other Social Activities

In addition to regular contacts at work, the desk men saw each other outside on several social occasions. They and former copy editors had formed a social club known as the GADS (Gourmets' and Drinkers' Society). Each member contributed fifty cents a month; the proceeds used to finance two social gatherings for members and their wives, one in the spring and one in the fall. Although responsibility for the planning of these functions was rotated among members, there was one officer, the president-treasurer, Lam Lambert.

The men who worked on the desk also joined other *Times-Herald* editorial department employees for occasional parties. A recent party was organized by several reporters in honor of "Herschel Harshbarger," the mythical character mentioned earlier. Jerry Roberts explained why these parties were held. "We had such a good time at retirement and engagement parties that we decided to get together more often." Since desk personnel lived in different parts of the metropolitan area, they did not see each other frequently except for these organized social events.

Executives' Evaluation of the Desk's Performance

Both Bob Smith, managing editor, and Fred Dugan told the case-writer that the performance of the desk was satisfactory to them both in terms of the quality of stories and headlines and in terms of the desk's ability to meet deadlines. Fred Dugan explained it this way:

I think we have a good organization now. Many of the men have been well trained in several positions, so their ability isn't limited and they are able to adjust to any situation which may arise. Beside a knowledge of his position a desk man must be well rounded, must be able to work quickly, and must have the poise to work under stress. Our men have these qualities; they couldn't be on the desk unless they did.

While reporting and writing may decide the quality of a newspaper, it is the appearance and presentation of these things which attracts the reader. A paper without all of these things is missing 50 per cent of its opportunity. Our goal on the desk is to try to make our 50 per cent of the task [presentation and appearance] as effective as possible. I believe we now do a good job at these things, but we are always striving to improve.

In the past and on other newspapers the desk is an old man's job, but we can't operate that way on this paper, because the news is moving too quickly for the older men to handle. We have gotten some younger men on the desk, and it is beginning to work well. But finding qualified young men is a problem. There are men around the paper who have worked on the desk during vacations and have done a good job, but they aren't temperamentally suited to desk work. They find the work too confining for them, and therefore I know having them on the desk wouldn't be mutually satisfactory. These men have the ability but not the desire. They would rather be moving, traveling, writing, and seeing their names on by-lines instead of accepting the more confining anonymous life of the copy editor. Of course the copy editor has the advantage of regular hours and no out-of-town assignments as well as a good group of fellows to work with.

Appendix A

TECHNICAL NOTE ON THE ROLE OF COPY EDITORS

Below are excerpts from *Headlines and Deadlines, A Manual for Copy Editors* by Robert E. Garst and Theodore M. Bernstein, both assistant managing editors of the *New York Times,* which help to explain the position of a copy editor (desk man) in the technology of the newspaper and in the journalism profession, as well as the skills required for this position.[1]

.   .   .   .

FROM THE PREFACE

Copy editing is one field in which the demand for workers usually exceeds the supply. This is likely to be permanently so because in an ideal sense there will never be a copy editor who knows enough to fill the requirements of his job thoroughly. The ideal copy editor would not only have a complete mastery over the technical phases of his work, such as the editing of copy and the writing of headlines, but would possess sound and swift judgment, would be an expert rhetorician and grammarian and would be thoroughly versed in government, politics, astrophysics, home gardening, shoes, ships, sealing wax and all subjects that find or are likely to find a place in the kaleidoscopic enterprise that is the modern newspaper.

.   .   .   .

FROM CHAPTER 1, "NEWSPAPER ORGANIZATION"

The emphasis in newspaper work has long—too long, perhaps—been put upon the reporter. While there is no wish to take from him credit for his many superb contributions to the excellence of the modern newspaper, it ought to be realized that there is a man who stands between him and his critical public—the copy editor. The sparkling, swift, entertaining story, signed by John Jones of *The Daily Star,* draws comment and approbation, but it is not often recognized by even his fellows that the copy editor's share in the creation of the gem may be as great if not greater than that of John Jones, Reporter.

It is not seldom that the wit, ingenuity and craftsmanship of the copy editor rescue from the limbo of unread newspaper stories the uninspired work of John Jones. It is the editorial pencil as much as the reportorial typewriter that puts before the public daily the readable information of the world's happenings. It is the copy editor who is essentially the guardian of what gets into the newspaper and how it looks when it gets there. He detects the errors, corrects the English, cuts out the dead wood of verbiage, tones the story up to its proper pitch or down to the level required by good taste or the libel laws.

The appeal of the reporter's work is great; the activity, the contact with the world, with its great men and with its ideas, make the stimulation of the job unparalleled in any profession. But the copy editor is closer to the heart of the newspaper's power; he is indeed its heart. Under his pencil flow the accounts of all important happenings anywhere. This sense of closeness to vital things, plus the capacity to shape information about them so that their importance will be shown in true perspective make the copy desk job second to none.

FROM CHAPTER 2, "THE COPY EDITOR"

Errors creep into newspaper copy from many sources. News passes through many hands; it is garbled in transmission; it is written and rewritten by men

---

[1] Robert E. Garst and Theodore M. Bernstein, *Headlines and Deadlines, A Manual for Copy Editors* (New York: Columbia University Press, 1961).

of varied ages, education and temperament; it is read and edited under similar conditions. Wrong perspective or partisanship, too much enthusiasm or too little, may handicap a story. The very speed with which newspapers must be printed permits mistakes to slip by the many persons who handle news in its course through the news machine. The continuous struggle of the newspaper is to eliminate errors. Many checks have been set up against them and the chief of these is the copy editor.

The copy editor is virtually the last man between his newspaper and the public. The copy may have been read several times before it reaches him, but its ultimate form, phraseology and spirit rest in his hands. Mistakes or poor writing that pass him are almost certain to reach the reader in print. They may be detected in the office in time to be corrected, but many such blunders are never discovered except by the newspaper reader.

The greatest weapon of the copy editor in his efforts to eliminate errors is an alertness that challenges every fact, every name, virtually every word. Every fact should be checked. Those that appear incorrect and cannot be verified must be eliminated. Statements that are absurd or dangerous are deleted without question. Likewise the facts should be weighed against one another to insure consistency.

The function of the copy editor is critical, not creative. In no circumstances should he rewrite a story completely. If it cannot be saved except by being rewritten, that work should be done by a rewrite man or by the reporter who wrote the original story. The desk man must cope with the material that is given him and make the most of it by recasting, striking out superfluous words, substituting active or colorful words for dead ones, expressing a phrase in a word and by other similar means.

. . . .

With a unanimity that is somewhat disconcerting to the copy editor, reporters profess to regard him as a mutilator of good copy and there is some ground for this opinion. There are some desk men temperamentally unfitted to make the most of another man's writing; their conception of what a story should be is so strong that virtual rewriting is the only course they can follow. Such men must be restrained and if they remain copy editors, trained to the viewpoint of the editorial pencil rather than to that of the reportorial typewriter. The general aim of the copy desk is to preserve as far as possible the words of the reporter, if they express what he desires to convey, and to retain the spirit imparted by him, if it is proper. As the final link in a long and expensive process, the copy editor can destroy the honest work of many reporters.

The business of writing and editing news is a cooperative undertaking, demanding the best of many brains. There is no place for pride of authorship. The desk man should recognize and retain the merits of the story given to him to edit, the reporter should recognize that the copy editor often saves him from grave mistakes and generally improves his work.

. . . .

The education, experience and knowledge of the copy editor cannot be too broad. The more he has learned, seen or knows, the greater his value to the newspaper. He should have a wide knowledge of names, places and events; he must be well-informed in the arts, sciences and social trends; he should know history and literature and be familiar with the machinery of government and laws.

It is imperative that he be acquainted with his own city, if he is an editor of local copy. He must know its geography, its people, its government, its officials, its buildings. If he is an editor of national copy he must have a wide knowledge of national politics, movements, figures and events. Copy editors dealing with legislation in the national or in state capitals should have detailed information about the machinery of legislatures. If the editor is dealing with foreign copy he must know much about the politics, economics and government of the countries concerned and of their recent history at the least. Finally, the copy editor must have common sense. The logic he uses to test the reasonableness of assertions in news stories is the same logic he applies in everyday affairs.

6. MARKHAM INSTRUMENT COMPANY

IN THE SPRING of 1959, the management of the Markham Instrument Company was confronted with an impasse in pricing the latest addition to its line of scientific measuring instruments. Markham had two basic product groups, instruments for use in scientific laboratories (Laboratory Products), and industrial instruments for use in manufacturing processes (Industrial Products). The present problem centered around the Dual Sensitivity Level Instrument (DSL) which was intended for the more specialized scientific laboratory market.

History of Development of the Laboratory Product Line

The line of scientific measuring devices which the Markham company introduced in 1924 was adversely affected by the business decline of the 1930's. In 1935, however, the potential for reversing this trend appeared in the form of a major product innovation. A company salesman discovered a young inventor who had developed an electronically controlled measuring device. Markham officials found from comparative tests with their own instrument that the "shoe box" (a name derived from the new instrument's dramatically reduced size) was superior in performance, and they purchased the rights to develop it.

No one at Markham understood the new machine sufficiently to complete its development. Just at this time, however, Alfred Reece (Markham's director of research in 1959) approached the company seeking part-time employment to support his doctoral studies. When he demonstrated a thorough understanding of vacuum tube technology, he was immediately hired. Working with Roger Finlay (representing sales and engineering) and Caleb Webster (mechanical engineering) he redesigned the shoe box until it met scientific and commercial standards.

Several competitors had already introduced comparable electronic devices to the scientific market, but they met considerable customer resistance. Dr. Markham pointed out in retrospect, "The change from electrical controls to a vacuum tube amplifier was a big one for Markham. Scientists and technicians were against it. We had advertised the electrically controlled version as the only reliable standard regulator, and this had become the general consensus among our customers. Radio types on the market had been widely criticized and we needed strong evidence to justify our change in attitude."

While Markham management believed their shoe box to be superior to competitors' electronic machines, they did not rely on this to overcome customer resistance. Instead they appealed to the customers' conservatism, which had been the major factor in blocking acceptance of competitors' machines. The new machine was designed to look and operate as much like the old machine as possible, even to the extent of compromising a few of the advantages of the electronic design. As Finlay said later, "Our customers distrusted the electronic devices which were already on the market, so there was nothing else to do but make ours look and act like the electrical one they were familiar with."

This strategy was successful. Dollar sales volume in 1936 doubled that of 1935, while the number of units actually tripled. Consistent with its past success, however, Markham continued to rely heavily on conscientious customer service to enhance its position in the scientific measurement field. Field sales offices and branch service agencies were set up throughout the country. Company salesmen, continuing their traditional practices, carried customer service to the extremes of repairing competitors' equipment, extending liberal credit and trade-in terms, and offering rapid emergency replacement service.

The next major change in these products occurred in 1946 when the company developed a chemical-sensitive paper, which among other improvements, eliminated the inconvenient use of recording inks. This development gave Markham a competitive advantage and simultaneously, due to sole control of the paper supply, provided an increase in profit margins. During this period a portable measuring device, long sought by scientific field workers, was also developed. Although these innovations gave Markham a technical lead, the company still depended on customer service for the basic maintenance of its market position.

During the early 1950's competitors began work on a machine which gave the scientist the option of measuring either of two sensitivity levels simply by throwing a switch. In 1957, the competitors' development work reached fruition, and these Dual Sensitivity Level (DSL) machines were introduced commercially. Markham was not disturbed by this new feature on competitive instruments, since potential applications for the additional sensitivity level were extremely limited. Furthermore, management's attention was diverted from this development by the addition to its own line of a transistorized portable, 40 per cent lighter than any then available. This machine's compactness was expected to attract scientists engaged in field experiments, while its price, flexibility, and reliability were expected to make it also a replacement for most applications of the standard model.

Markham elected to push the transistorized model at the expense of the older, larger instrument, basing its decision on a prediction that customers would prefer the smaller machine. In adopting this strategy, management was confident that its ability to take the customers' viewpoint, a company strength over the years, still enabled it to judge what the scientists wanted. Markham had historically been able to lag in technological innovation with little risk, because when their new products were finally introduced, they surpassed competition in meeting customer needs. Markham managers believe that this intimate relationship with the market was as strong as ever.

Company executives were quite pleased when sales of the transistorized model surpassed expectations. They were surprised, however, by two trends. First, sales of the older machine did not decline as had been expected. Secondly, Markham salesmen began asking for DSL instruments such as competition was offering.

To determine the feasibility of producing a DSL while maintaining the basic strategy of promoting the transistorized instrument, exploration was begun on the redesign of the transistorized model. By the end of 1957, a tentative DSL design was developed, although two stubborn technical problems, peculiar to a transistorized DSL remained unresolved. Before devoting more time to the solution of these difficulties, top management decided to review the entire issue of producing a DSL machine. After some deliberation the DSL was dropped as being a short-lived fad rather than a long-term trend. It was felt that the difficulties in overcoming the remaining technical problems would not be worth the effort, in view of the limited applications the customers had for the DSL feature.

During 1958, requests from the field for a DSL became more frequent, and Herb Olson (sales vice president) began pressing for a reversal of a decision not to produce such a device. He pointed out that salesmen were becoming increasingly embarrassed by customer insistence on DSL features. In view of these increasing requests, Roger Finlay (president) became convinced in the fall of 1958 that Markham should add a DSL to its line, if only to satisfy the "gadget" appeal of such an innovation. Since the older standard machines were continuing to sell, and since the development of a transistorized DSL was still problematical, it was decided to proceed with a DSL redesign of the older machine.

Shortly after making the decision to go ahead with a DSL, Roger Finlay met with Herb Olson (vice president, sales), Alfred "Doc" Reece (director of R&D), Caleb Webster (in charge of mechanical design of the DSL) and Bill Reynolds, (responsible for electronic design of the DSL). Finlay told the three R&D men that while he was anxious to get the new machine into production as quickly as possible, the company's reputation was also involved, so that it would be necessary to do the usual careful job. Reece asked if all the same features that were in the standard would be included in the DSL. Finlay replied that while the DSL was to be patterned after the standard model, he wanted all the latest features included. Herb Olson explained that although the DSL was to be offered at approximately the same price as the standard model, they would still have to maintain the traditional external appearance and features on the DSL. In response to a question from Doc Reece, Olson pointed out that they were not too concerned with the weight of the DSL, since it was not to be a portable. As the meeting ended, Reece indicated that they would have to do some careful planning to keep costs down, but he was sure it could be done. Webster and Reynolds agreed, stating that they thought the design could be completed by the end of the year.

In spite of this optimistic appraisal the members of the research and development department did not greet the decision to redesign the older machine with unrestrained enthusiasm. In the first place, they felt that completing the redesign of the transistorized machine would be ultimately feasible and would be more stimulating technically. Secondly, they had several other challenging ideas which they believed would place the company in the growing space and missile field. The redesign of the standard machine would cause them to put aside these more exciting projects for several months.

In spite of these reservations, design work went ahead on the DSL. Meanwhile, inquiries and complaints from the field about the delay in offering a DSL continued to come into the home office. While many sales personnel blamed R&D for the delay, Herb Olson explained the problem differently, "All these problems that the laboratory salesmen are having aren't just the fault of engineering. Top management simply didn't think the DSL was important. Well, this was a mistake. Of course, when this happens the people out in the field get to feeling sore and they come ask us why we don't have the equipment."

Ed Greene expressed a similar view, "Sollie (a formerly influential but now deceased member of R&D) was screaming four years ago for a DSL, but top management could see no need for it. Now all the machines on the market have this feature and we are breaking our neck trying to catch up."

Pricing Meeting, March 6, 1959

The development work on the DSL machine was completed by the end of 1958 and late in January 1959, production received the information it needed to establish production methods and estimate costs. By early March, cost estimates had been completed by the production department, and a meeting was arranged for the morning of March 6, to discuss the DSL selling price. The ten executives named in the seating chart, Exhibit 1, were all present when the meeting started, except Mr. Webster who arrived later.

Willard Tierney, acting as chairman, opened the meeting by asking Ed Greene to present his cost estimates. Greene's initial position (which he maintained throughout the meeting) was that the DSL was more expensive than had been expected. He concluded his presentation by

Exhibit 1

MARKHAM INSTRUMENT COMPANY

SEATING ARRANGEMENT—PRICING MEETING, MARCH 6, 1959

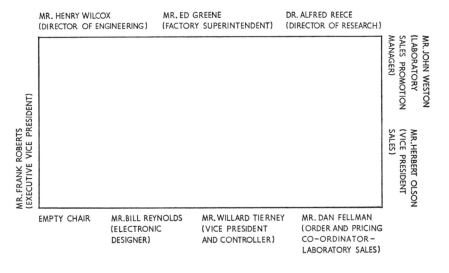

saying, "You are going to have to sell this machine for a lot more than you thought. I think these figures are sound. If anything, we have been too loose in our estimates and the figures are too low. We can't lower them any more."

Herb Olson took a different position, maintaining that something had to be done to lower costs so the new machine could be sold at a realistic price. Representative of his remarks is the following statement: "The fact that the figures are sound isn't going to help us meet competition. The way you [others at the meeting] are talking we would have to sell this machine for $1,000. If we did that our volume would go to hell in a hand basket."

Olson was not alone in finding the costs higher than expected. Caleb Webster remarked, "I am really surprised at these estimates. I didn't think they would be that high." Doc Reece also felt the estimates were higher than he had thought they would be. Bill Reynolds, on the other hand, found the estimates realistic as far as the electronic parts were concerned, "I'm not at all surprised at Ed's figures, because I knew what they would be from my design work."

Confronted with this impasse, Tierney summarized the situation at the end of the meeting, "I didn't think we could arrive at a decision today, and it doesn't look like we will, so why don't we adjourn and meet again next week? In the meanwhile Ed (Greene), Dan (Fellman), and Doc (Reece) can check over these costs to see if we can reduce them."

As the meeting broke up, Olson remarked, "If we can't do something about these costs, you guys can take it (the DSL) out in the field and give it to the salesmen yourselves. I won't do it."

Pricing Meeting, March 13, 1959

During the next week, Reece, Greene, and Fellman reviewed the cost estimates, and on March 13, a second meeting was held. The participants arranged themselves around the conference table as shown in Exhibit 2. Willard Tierney again served as chairman, opening the meeting by explaining that Doc Reece, Ed Greene, and Dan Fellman had agreed to certain minor changes in the DSL and that they now felt that it could be produced at $110 more than the standard. (This figure represented a decrease of $35 from the highest figure quoted at the previous meeting.) On this basis Tierney proposed that the DSL be priced at $875, $90 more than the standard. After he completed his remarks there was a full minute of silence which Caleb Webster interrupted.

> MR. WEBSTER: I still don't understand it. I'd like to know where the big differences lie because I didn't think it would be that much.
> MR. TIERNEY: Doc [Reece], can you itemize these so we will all know what they are in detail?

Reece and Greene then spent several minutes explaining the costs of various components, as well as the basis for their estimate of assembly costs. Webster, however, remained unconvinced. Tierney suggested that he and Greene work together to discover if further cost savings were possible. Greene replied.

> MR. GREENE: I don't think there are many big changes we can make. It has been cut to the bone already.

Exhibit 2

MARKHAM INSTRUMENT COMPANY

Seating Arrangement—Pricing Meeting, March 13, 1959

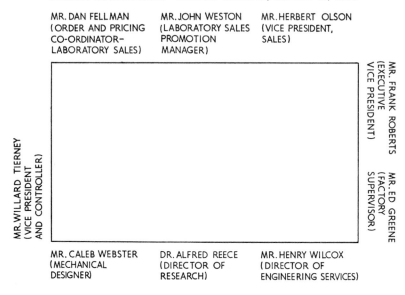

MR. DAN FELLMAN
(ORDER AND PRICING
CO-ORDINATOR–
LABORATORY SALES)

MR. JOHN WESTON
(LABORATORY SALES
PROMOTION
MANAGER)

MR. HERBERT OLSON
(VICE PRESIDENT,
SALES)

MR. WILLARD TIERNEY
(VICE PRESIDENT
AND CONTROLLER)

MR. FRANK ROBERTS
(EXECUTIVE
VICE PRESIDENT)

MR. ED GREENE
(FACTORY
SUPERVISOR)

MR. CALEB WEBSTER
(MECHANICAL
DESIGNER)

DR. ALFRED REECE
(DIRECTOR OF
RESEARCH)

MR. HENRY WILCOX
(DIRECTOR OF
ENGINEERING SERVICES)

ABSENT: MR. BILL REYNOLDS (ELECTRONIC DESIGNER)

MR. OLSON: Well, for example, look at that little trap door. It costs a lot of money.

Several minutes were devoted to the costs of the door which Roger Finlay had suggested to improve appearance and operating access. No one suggested changing the door, and the discussion then centered on the differences between the two models. Doc Reece concluded his explanation of the major causes for the difference.

DR. REECE: Look, there is twice as much shop time for parts on the DSL as there is on the old one. That is a big part of the difference. (*Pauses*) Sitting around the table here we aren't going to remove Caleb's [Webster] doubts about the reasons for this big difference. He thought it would be less than $25 and it turns out to be between $90 and $120.

The meeting then divided into several conversations. Herb Olson and Frank Roberts talked together with John Weston listening; Doc Reece and Ed Greene carried on a conversation with Henry Wilcox listening. The others waited. After several minutes Roberts addressed the entire group.

MR. ROBERTS: It appears to me that you aren't going to change the spots on the leopard. We have to fix a realistic price. You have all the estimates you can get.

In spite of this statement, discussion about cost differences continued with Reece and Greene furnishing more details about the costs of subassemblies to Webster. Roberts interrupted this discussion.

MR. ROBERTS: We haven't heard from Herb [Olson]. He's probably got a lot to say.

Mr. Olson joked with the group, and then began to discuss the competitive aspects of the situation.

MR. OLSON: We have to consider the selling price of this machine in comparison to competition. Competitors are selling their machines at between $440 and $460 to the dealers, which means they are about $800 at retail. Measuretech [a competitor] retails at $785, and their machine does everything ours does. Of course, they, like everyone else, offer discounts. Whatever we do, we have to be in the ball park on the initial list price. Perhaps controlling trade-ins will help some.
MR. ROBERTS: What do you think this price should be?
MR. OLSON: Oh, I suppose about $795, that's only $10 above the Standard Model.

Roberts, Wilcox, and Tierney then discussed the minimum DSL selling price. They agreed that using estimated costs, it would be necessary to price it at $875 to obtain the normal margin. Wilcox proposed that they set a target for cutting costs through redesigning the machine, because he thought cabinet and purchase part costs could be reduced in this manner. Olson supported this proposal, but Tierney disagreed.

MR. TIERNEY: I don't know what we can find. Ed [Greene] has made a careful estimate and there is still a $110 difference.
MR. ROBERTS: Well, maybe it is just being hopeful, but I think we should do what Henry [Wilcox] suggests.
DR. REECE: All Ed can control is the shop costs, shop time and assembly time. I don't think there is much fat in any of these figures.
MR. WEBSTER: I still can't see why the machine should be that high. The mechanical costs should be much less.
MR. GREENE: Let him [Webster] go somewhere to figure and add them up. Then he'll see. Damned if I'll give him any of my figures.
MR. TIERNEY: You know, I still would feel more comfortable pricing it at $875. Otherwise I think we might be cutting it too close.

MR. OLSON: Competition is rough in this line, Will; $850 sounds much better than $875. Even at $850 we will have to work like hell to beat Asprey and some of the others.

MR. GREENE: I'll tell you this, I'd still rather build that Asprey machine than ours.

The relative merits of competitors' machines were then discussed. The consensus was that competition was making the same machine, selling it at about $75 less than the $875 figure which had been suggested for the DSL. Olson suggested that Webster be allowed to restudy the design to see if he could reduce the cost so that the DSL could be priced at $850. Tierney replied.

MR. TIERNEY: All right, maybe we should call this meeting off, and give Caleb [Webster] a chance to satisfy himself.

MR. ROBERTS: That's just a waste of time. Let's get this settled.

Greene and Wilcox also objected to further study and Tierney withdrew his proposal.

MR. TIERNEY: You're right. After all, we have never priced any instrument with as much information as we have on this one.

MR. OLSON: That really doesn't make any difference. We still have to get the price down where we can sell it.

Tierney then continued the discussion of competitors' machines and prices. There was general agreement that the Simpson Company had, at $785, the best DSL presently on the market. Olson expressed particular concern about the advantage competitors had because of the light weight of their machines.

MR: OLSON: Look at these competitors' weights. Simpson's only weighs 20 pounds, while ours will be 34. Even Asprey's is 10 pounds less than ours. This is an important selling point and we can't ignore it.

DR. REECE: Damn it, don't start talking weights at this point. We were told from the start that they weren't important.

MR. TIERNEY: Herb [Olson], what do you think the end user pays for an Asprey?

MR. OLSON: Anywhere from $650 up. It depends entirely upon the deal and the trade-in. I was just wondering, though, if maybe we haven't got too many features on this machine. After all it is supposed to be sold as a general purpose machine.

DR. REECE: We designed it according to what Sales wanted. We have to go by what you fellows need. The trouble is that around here everybody wants everything with frosting on it.

MR. OLSON: Right, and then we price ourselves out of the market.

Exhibit 3

MARKHAM INSTRUMENT COMPANY
ORGANIZATION CHART—1959

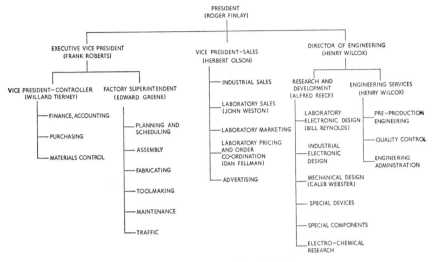

NOTE: Names are furnished only for persons mentioned in this case.

MR. TIERNEY: It seems to me that we had better change our whole official attitude if this is the way our market and our competition are acting.

MR. GREENE: O.K. Then we ought to start with an estimate of the market and the price and then design within that.

MR. OLSON: That's exactly what got us into this mess. The district managers are really going to be unhappy about this one. Finlay told them the DSL would be available at $800, and now you are talking about a minimum of $50 or $75 more than this. They aren't going to be happy about pushing this one. I still would like to see Caleb [Webster] take another crack at cutting the cost.

MR. ROBERTS: Doc, can you and the mechanic [Webster] take another shot at redesign after we get it into production? Maybe we can reduce costs then.

MR. TIERNEY: I think that is wishful thinking. We have to resolve this on the basis of the information we have.

7. THE CASE OF THE CHANGING CAGE*

Part 1[1]

THE VOUCHER-CHECK filing unit was a work unit in the home office of the Atlantic Insurance Company. The assigned task of the unit was to file checks and vouchers written by the company as they were cashed and returned. This filing was the necessary foundation for the main function of the unit: locating any particular check for examination upon demand. There were usually eight to ten requests for specific checks from as many different departments during the day. One of the most frequent reasons checks were requested from the unit was to determine whether checks in payment of claims against the company had been cashed. Thus, efficiency in the unit directly affected customer satisfaction with the company. Complaints or inquiries about payments could not be answered with the accuracy and speed conducive to client satisfaction unless the unit could supply the necessary documents immediately.

Toward the end of 1952, nine workers manned this unit. There was an assistant (a position equivalent to a foreman in a factory) named Miss Dunn, five other full-time employees, and three part-time workers.

The work area of the unit was well defined. Walls bounded the unit on three sides. The one exterior wall was pierced by light-admitting north windows. The west interior partition was blank. A door opening into a corridor pierced the south interior partition. The east side of the work area was enclosed by a steel mesh reaching from wall to wall and floor to ceiling. This open metal barrier gave rise to the customary name of the unit—"the voucher cage." A sliding door through this mesh gave access from the unit's territory to the work area of the rest of the company's agency audit division, of which it was a part, located on the same floor.

The unit's territory was kept inviolate by locks on both doors, fas-

---

* Data for the following case were taken from "Topography and Culture: The Case of the Changing Cage," *Human Organization*, Vol. XVI, No. 1 (1957), by Cara E. Richards and Henry F. Dobyns, with permission of authors and publisher.

[1] This is a sequential case. Your instructor may wish to have you discuss Part 1 of the case before reading subsequent parts

124

tened at all times. No one not working within the cage was permitted inside unless his name appeared on a special list in the custody of Miss Dunn. The door through the steel mesh was used generally for departmental business. Messengers and runners from other departments usually came to the corridor door and pressed a buzzer for service.

The steel mesh front was reinforced by a rank of metal filing cases where checks were filed. Lined up just inside the barrier, they hid the unit's workers from the view of workers outside their territory, including the section head responsible for over-all supervision of this unit according to the company's formal plan of operation.

THE CASE OF THE CHANGING CAGE

Part 2

ON TOP of the cabinets which were backed against the steel mesh, one of the male employees in the unit neatly stacked pasteboard boxes in which checks were transported to the cage. They were later reused to hold older checks sent into storage. His intention was less getting these boxes out of the way than increasing the effective height of the sight barrier so the section head could not see into the cage "even when he stood up."

The girls stood at the door of the cage which led into the corridor and talked to the messenger boys. Out this door also the workers slipped unnoticed to bring in their customary afternoon snack. Inside the cage the workers sometimes engaged in a good-natured game of rubber-band "sniping."

Workers in the cage possessed good capacity to work together consistently, and workers outside the cage often expressed envy of those in it because of the "nice people" and friendly atmosphere there. The unit had no apparent difficulty keeping up with its work load.

THE CASE OF THE CHANGING CAGE

Part 3

FOR SOME time prior to 1952 the controller's department of the company had not been able to meet its own standards of efficient service to clients. Company officials felt the primary cause to be spatial. Various divisions of the controller's department were scattered over the entire twenty-two-story company building. Communication between them required phone calls, messengers, or personal visits, all costing time. The spatial separation had not seemed very important when the company's business volume was smaller prior to World War II. But business had grown tremendously since then, and spatial separation appeared increasingly inefficient.

Finally, in November of 1952, company officials began to consolidate the controller's department by relocating two divisions together on one floor. One was the agency audit division, which included the voucher-check filing unit. As soon as the decision to move was made, lower level supervisors were called in to help with planning. Line workers were not consulted, but were kept informed by the assistants of planning progress. Company officials were concerned about the problem of transporting many tons of equipment and some two hundred workers from two locations to another single location without disrupting work flow. So the move was planned to occur over a single week end, using the most efficient resources available. Assistants were kept busy planning positions for files and desks in the new location.

Desks, files, chairs, and even wastebaskets were numbered prior to the move, and relocated according to a master chart checked on the spot by the assistant. Employees were briefed as to where the new location was and which elevators they should take to reach it. The company successfully transported the paraphernalia of the voucher-check filing unit from one floor to another over one week end. Workers in the cage quit Friday afternoon at the old stand, reported back Monday at the new.

The exterior boundaries of the new cage were still three building walls and the steel mesh, but the new cage possessed only one door—the sliding door through the steel mesh into the work area of the rest of the agency audit division. The territory of the cage had also been reduced in size. An entire bank of filing cabinets had to be left behind in the old location to be taken over by the unit moving there. The new cage was arranged so that there was no longer a row of metal filing cabinets lined up inside the steel mesh obstructing the view into the cage.

THE CASE OF THE CHANGING CAGE

Part 4

WHEN THE workers in the cage inquired about the removal of the filing cabinets from along the steel mesh fencing, they found that Mr. Burke had insisted that these cabinets be rearranged so his view into the cage would not be obstructed by them. Miss Dunn had tried to retain the cabinets in their prior position, but her efforts had been overridden.

Burke disapproved of conversation. Since he could see workers conversing in the new cage, he "requested" Miss Dunn to put a stop to all unnecessary talk. Attempts by female clerks to talk to messenger boys brought the wrath of her superior down on Miss Dunn, who was then forced to reprimand the girls.

Burke also disapproved of an untidy working area, and any boxes or papers which were in sight were a source of annoyance to him. He did not exert supervision directly, but would "request" Miss Dunn to "do something about those boxes." In the new cage, desks had to be completely cleared at the end of the day, in contrast to the work-in-progress piles left out in the old cage. Boxes could not accumulate on top of filing cases.

The custom of afternoon snacking also ran into trouble. Lacking a corridor door, the food bringers had to venture forth and pack back their snack trays through the work area of the rest of their section, bringing this hitherto unique custom to the attention of workers outside the cage. The latter promptly recognized the desirability of afternoon snacks and began agitation for the same privilege. This annoyed the section head, who forbade workers in the cage to continue this custom.

THE CASE OF THE CHANGING CAGE

Part 5

BURKE LATER made a rule which permitted one worker to leave the new cage at a set time every afternoon to bring up food for the rest. This rigidity irked cage personnel, accustomed to a snack when the mood struck, or none at all. Having made his concession to the cage force, Burke was unable to prevent workers outside the cage from doing the same thing. What had once been unique to the workers in the cage was now common practice in the section.

Although Miss Dunn never outwardly expressed anything but compliance and approval of superior directives, she exhibited definite signs of anxiety. All the cage workers reacted against Burke's increased domination. When he imposed his decisions upon the voucher-check filing unit, he became "Old Grandma" to its personnel. The cage workers sneered at him and ridiculed him behind his back. Workers who formerly had obeyed company policy as a matter of course began to find reasons for loafing and obstructing work in the new cage. One of the changes that took place in the behavior of the workers had to do with their game of rubber-band sniping. All knew Burke would disapprove of this game. It became highly clandestine and fraught with dangers. Yet, shooting rubber bands *increased*.

Newly arrived checks were put out of sight as soon as possible, filed or not. Workers hid unfiled checks, generally stuffing them into desk drawers or unused file drawers. Since boxes were forbidden, there were fewer unused file drawers than there had been in the old cage. So the day's work was sometimes undone when several clerks hastily shoved vouchers and checks indiscriminately into the same file drawer at the end of the day.

Before a worker in the cage filed incoming checks, she measured with her ruler the thickness in inches of each bundle she filed. At the end of each day she totaled her input and reported it to Miss Dunn. All incoming checks were measured upon arrival. Thus, Miss Dunn had a rough estimate of unit intake compared with file input. Theoretically, she was able to tell at any time how much unfiled material she had on hand and how well the unit was keeping up with its task. Despite this running check, when the annual inventory of unfiled checks on hand in the cage was taken at the beginning of the calendar year 1953, a seriously large backlog of unfiled checks was found. To the surprise and dismay of Miss Dunn, the inventory showed the unit to be far behind schedule, filing much more slowly than before the relocation of the cage.

8. SUPERIOR SLATE QUARRY

Part 1[1]

THE SUPERIOR Slate Quarry in the 1920's was one of the largest and oldest in the Vermont–New York slate belt. It had always enjoyed a good reputation, not only for the product it turned out, but also for its treatment of employees. It had recently been sold to Thomas North, who had formerly owned a minor interest in it. Although North had never directly operated slate quarries, his family had for two generations owned slate properties, and he was well regarded in the town of Gorham, a community of about 2,500 persons, where he lived. The population of Gorham was about one half Yankee, one fourth Irish, and one fourth Welsh.

Gorham's principal industry was slate quarrying and slate milling. The quarries where slate roofing was produced were located at the edges of the town. These slate quarries were open pits in which quarrymen drilled holes in the bedrock and blasted pieces of it loose. The large blocks were then hoisted on overhead cables from the quarry pit to the top and there lowered onto small cars on rails, which workers known as rockmen pushed to the nearby splitting shanties. The blocks were dumped off in front of the shanties, which were cheaply constructed wooden frame buildings about 10 by 10 feet in size. They were placed in rows along the track that ran from the quarry top.

Two slate splitters and one trimmer worked in each shanty; and at Superior Slate Quarry, there were eight such shanties. The splitters and trimmers were paid by the hour. The splitters worked on opposite sides of the shanty door while the trimmer at his foot-pedal trimming machine stood at the back. Although they were equipped with coal stoves, the shanties were usually cold in winter; and they were hot in summer. After a rockman had dumped his large block, which was always irregular in shape and size, the splitters marked it to guide them in breaking it up into sizes for the final splitting. This operation on the large block required a knowledge of the grain of the rock, for the block had to be broken along this grain. When the grain was determined, one

---

[1] This is a sequential case. Your instructor may wish to have you discuss Part 1 of the case before reading subsequent parts.

132

splitter had to steady the block on its edge while the other splitter struck the block a blow with a large wooden mallet, called a "beetle." It usually required only one blow before the block fell apart along the grain line. When the block was reduced to three or four smaller blocks, the splitters carried them into the shanty.

Here, each took a block, turned it on its side, and proceeded with chisel and mallet to split it along the grain into thinner and thinner pieces. When the blocks were reduced to pieces about three sixteenths of an inch in thickness, the pieces were placed on a low table between the two splitters and in back of the trimmer. The trimmer took each piece from the table, placed it along the cutting bar of the trimming machine, and proceeded to make it into as large a rectangle as he could get out of the piece. After it was trimmed, an operation which usually took only four cuts of the trimming blade, he placed it in a pile according to size. The trimmer was also expected to keep the waste chips of slate cleared away from his machine. When the day's work was done, these piles of shingles were removed from the shanties and placed outside in long rows.

The slate mills were within the town, along the river from which they derived their power. In these mills, structural slate products such as flooring, tile, billiard table tops, and other articles were finished. Because of the scraping and cutting of the planers and saws, millwork was noisy and dusty. Millwork in general required less skill and experience than slate splitting. Pay for millwork was lower by about a third than for slate splitting.

Exhibit 1 provides a further description of the technology of slate splitting.

The splitters and trimmers employed at the Superior Slate Quarry were all Welsh, while the slate mill employees were primarily Irish. The Welsh were all born in Wales; in contrast, the Irish were mostly first generation, born in this country. The Welsh workmen were men past middle age, and few of their children were old enough to work at the quarries, and those who did were not skilled in slate splitting. Many of the Welsh became citizens; and although they could speak English, they preferred to use their native tongue. They were more thrifty than the Irish, and many owned their homes.

Exhibit 1

SUPERIOR SLATE QUARRY

PART 1*

. . . An intimate knowledge of the physical properties of slate is essential in properly breaking and splitting the blocks. A skilled slate worker will drive a wedge, or plug, into a plug hole until a strain is placed on the rock, and he then procures a straight break by striking a blow at a particular point on the rock with a wooden sledge. Thus he can within certain limits force a fracture where desired. The slate is split on the grain into masses about 14 to 24 inches wide, and these masses are then broken across into the desired sizes for splitting into roofing slates. Various methods are used to subdivide the slate masses across the grain. Where they do not break readily or where the surfaces are very uneven when broken, they may be placed on a saw bed and cut across with a circular saw. If this method is used the blocks as they come from the quarry are sawed across and are later scalloped in the grain. Sawed blocks present smooth even ends that facilitate rapid splitting.

Some slates, however, break very readily and give a smooth uniform surface. Under such conditions breaking by hand is considered more economical than sawing. At one quarry observed the block is notched on two corners with a chisel and a cut made in the bottom of each notch with a small saw. The block is then turned and the opposite edge is cut smooth with a chisel. It is then struck one or two heavy blows with a large wooden mallet at a point exactly opposite the notches, with the result that a smooth even break is obtained. To cushion the blow and thus preserve the slate from damage, a thin flake of slate or a handful of fine slate rubbish is usually placed on the rock surface at the point where the mallet strikes. At one quarry where the rock breaks readily the corners are not notched but are cut with a small handsaw. The surface is then simply marked with a chisel which is struck repeated blows with a hand hammer. The slab is then turned over and sledged with a wooden mallet, or "beetle," on the opposite edge in the usual fashion.

. . . The trimmer takes the slabs from the splitter and cuts them to a rectangular shape. The most common trimming equipment in Pennsylvania is a straight blade about three feet in length run by a foot treadle. The outer end of the blade is attached to an overhead spring pole so that the blade strikes repeated blows when once set in motion with the treadle. The use of manpower machines undoubtedly diverts much of the energy that could be used in handling the slates, and obviously mechanical cutting blades would result in a considerably greater production of slate per man with a much smaller expenditure of human energy. The operators in the soft-vein slate belt of Pennsylvania are aware of the increased production that might result from the use of mechanical trimmers, but attempts to introduce them have been unsuccessful. This lack of success is said to be due to inability to increase or decrease the speed of the trimmer for different grades of slate. With the foot-treadle machine the trimmer runs the machine at a slower speed for the weaker slates. The mechanically driven machines, running at constant speed, so greatly increased the percentage of slate breakage that they were abandoned in favor of the foot-treadle machines.

---

* Excerpts from *The Technology of Slate*, by Oliver Bowles (Washington, D.C.: U.S. Government Printing Office, 1922), pp. 64–66.

SUPERIOR SLATE QUARRY

Part 2

THE WELSH kept to themselves socially and maintained their traditional clannish customs, habits, and beliefs. They mingled little with either Irish or Yankee. It was generally recognized that the Welsh and the Irish did not get along well together.

The Welsh were without exception men who took great pride in the product of their hands; they had been accustomed for generations to working together in small groups. They looked down on work in mills as dusty, noisy, "unhealthy" places where "unskilled" Irishmen worked. They loved the rock and took great pride in working it by hand at every stage from quarry to yard. They often said: "Machines, no matter how well built, can never tell the grain. They leave marks which often mar the beauty of the finished stone."

The three men in a shanty helped each other with the work. Often, when the pieces to be trimmed were piling up, one of the splitters stopped his own work to clear away the waste chips which fell from the trimming machine. Likewise, when the trimmer was ahead of the splitters, he brought them fresh water from the spring or helped them carry their blocks. When the whistle blew for lunch, they all sat down together to share their food. Each night, as the men picked up their lunch boxes to leave, they viewed with pride the work of their hands. As they passed by their neighbors' shanties, they looked in at the neat piles and exclaimed at the number of squares others had finished. Then, talking in their native tongue, they moved on slowly toward their homes.

The superintendent at the Superior quarry was Mr. Williams, called "Jack" by the men. He was Welsh, and a leader among them in Gorham. His office was in a one-room building a short distance from the quarry. Here, he kept records on production, inventory, and hours of labor. He spent much of the day going from shanty to shanty talking in Welsh to the splitters. At other times, he visited the pit and checked with the quarry foreman on the rock.

SUPERIOR SLATE QUARRY

Part 3

FOUR YEARS after he purchased the Superior Slate Quarry, North was faced with the problem of deciding whether or not to invest a considerable amount of money to erect a large mill to house his slate splitters and trimmers. At this time the slate-roofing industry was receiving stiff competition from manufacturers of composition shingles. Although its competitors were able to benefit from technological improvements, the slate industry in Vermont, because of the nature of the rock, could use few new inventions. The slate rock still had to be split by hand, and the industry as a whole remained at the handicraft level. The Federal Bureau of Mines, however, had made an intensive study of this problem and had sent materials on its findings to all slate quarry operators.[2]

North, after looking over the government's suggestions for improving quarry methods, decided to draw up plans for a large mill to house the slate splitters and trimmers who worked at his quarry. He postponed the decision on whether or not to erect it until he had seen final plans. He talked over the matter with Williams, and together they drew up the plans. The new mill would eliminate many operations which the splitters customarily did. The blocks, as they came from the quarry, were to be brought into the mill by an overhead mechanical crane and lowered by electric lifts onto two saw beds, one at each end of the mill. Here, they were to be sawed up into correct sizes for splitting. The operation would not only relieve the splitters of breaking up the blocks, but would also leave the blocks with one or more squared sides and would thus help the trimmers to eliminate waste.

Blocks would then be carried from the saw bed by an unskilled, low-paid worker to the splitters, whose only job would be to split the blocks. They would place the pieces which they split on a car, which was to be pushed over rails to another part of the mill where the trimmers would be lined up in a row at power-driven trimming machines. The trimmers were to be relieved of removing waste chips by another low-paid man. The finished shingles would be removed by motor trucks to the yard.

---

[2] Examples of these materials can be found in Exhibit 1, Part 1, and Exhibit 3, Part 4.

Exhibit 2
SUPERIOR SLATE QUARRY, PLAN OF NEW MILL
PART 3

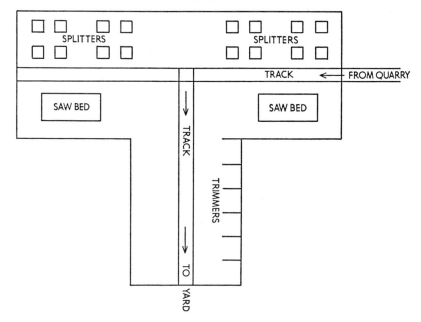

North designed the new mill to be more comfortable in winter than the shanties by installing a hot-water heating system. In summer the mill would be cooler than the shanties, since the ceiling would be high and the mill well ventilated. The saws, of course, would be noisy and would raise some dust; yet, it would not be harmful, nor would it compare with that in the mills in town.

By streamlining the flow of material, and by operating with the new machines and equipment, the superintendent and the owner expected production to improve substantially. The same number of splitters and trimmers were to be employed. The only new men to be hired would be the two sawyers, who were to be Welsh, and the two low-paid workers, who were to be Irish.

SUPERIOR SLATE QUARRY

Part 4

WHEN THE plans of the new mill had been completed and North had made additional estimates of costs and production, he decided to erect the mill. When it was first completed and put into use, the men were enthusiastic about the change and expressed their satisfaction to Williams. After a month, however, they had less and less to say about the new setup. Some of the splitters even suggested that it was too dusty. They were not intent on their splitting work and often looked around as if to see what their neighbors, now more numerous than before, were doing. Some complained of the noise; and when the whistle blew at night, they wasted little time in leaving for home.

Fewer and fewer of the men passed "the time of day" with Williams when he came into the mill; and he, too, became less communicative. At first, he planned and carried out many changes which he thought would improve the efficiency of the operation. Later, he came less often to the mill and spent more time in his office going over figures in the production ledger. A typical series of figures for the months after the new mill opened was as follows: 1,248; 1,260; 1,250; and later, 1,175; 1,150.

After eight months of operation in the new mill, Williams advised North to raise pay rates 5 cents an hour. This increase brought the splitters' pay to 72 cents an hour and the trimmers' to 67 cents, higher rates than any paid in the slate district. Production did not increase.

Exhibit 3

SUPERIOR SLATE QUARRY

PART 4*

One of the most efficiently planned slate mills observed is that of the Auld & Conger Co., between Poultney, Vt., and Granville, N.Y. The plan of the mill is shown in [the figure below], which represents but three of the 10 units of the plant. The blocks are unloaded beside the track *A,* where they are reduced to proper size for the slate splitters. One skilled operator marks the position of drill holes on the blocks and supervises drilling and wedging, which may, therefore, be done by relatively unskilled men. The slabs when prepared for the splitters are piled on the arms of rotating racks, *D,* which occupy spaces in the wall of

---

* Excerpts from *The Technology of Slate,* by Oliver Bowles (Washington, D.C.: U.S. Government Printing Office, 1922), pp. 66–68.

the closed shed. In cold weather cold-air currents through the spaces thus opened in the wall may be shut out by means of canvas flaps. The splitter working at E in the closed shed rotates the rack until the loaded arms are inside the shed within convenient reach. While he is occupied in splitting, a further supply of slabs is being prepared and loaded on the outer arms. The split slates are likewise placed on the arms of the rotating rack F, and by a half revolution they are brought within convenient reach of the trimmer at G. One great advantage of the rotating rack is that the trimmer is freed from the danger of accident to his fingers, a danger which is ever present where the splitter is throwing slates on the pile from which the trimmer is taking them. Belt conveyors H beneath the floor carry the waste from trimmers and splitters to dump carts on a depressed roadway at the side of the mill. Finished slates are piled on rack cars. In the morning the loaded cars are run out to the yards, and empty cars back to the trimmers for their day's work.

A roofing-slate unit may consist of two men, a trimmer and splitter, who prepare their own slabs from the larger blocks. At most plants the slabs are prepared for the splitters so that splitting and trimming are uninterrupted. Skilled slate workers having the slabs prepared for them may finish a maximum of a square an hour, though six to eight squares a day is an average accomplishment. A square is the amount of slate required to cover 100 square feet of roof.

PLAN OF AULD & CONGER CO. ROOFING SLATE MILL

A, Track for Bringing Blocks of Slate; B, Compressed-Air Line; C, Space for Block Makers; D, Rotating Racks for Slate Blocks; E, Splitters; F, Rotating Racks for Split Roofing; G, Trimmers; H, Belt Conveyor for Waste.

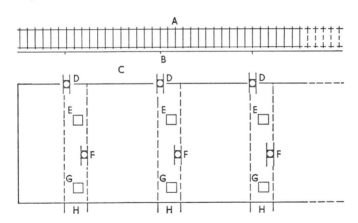

9. MAYNARD AIRCRAFT

Part 1[1]

THE INSTRUMENTATION department of Maynard Aircraft played an important role in the development of new aircraft. The department at Plant 7 consisted of ten engineers and eighty technicians who worked on individual airplanes. Thus, a particular aircraft might at any one time have from one to four instrumentation engineers working on it and from one to six technicians who carried out the orders issued by the engineers.

Before a job could be started, the engineers had to submit a written work order to the instrumentation foreman, who approved it and passed it on to the lead man. The lead man, in turn, assigned the work to one or more of the technicians who happened to be available from the eighty-man group and gave each of these technicians a written order with the technician's name on it. At the end of the job an inspector examined the work and put his approval stamp on the back of the work order. The order was then returned to the foreman and was stamped and logged by the foreman in a workbook. The engineers officially had no direct control over the technicians, but since their written work orders were seldom blocked by the instrumentation foreman, the engineer had little trouble obtaining his work requests.

The nature of the work was such that skill and knowledge in working with electrical parts was definitely desirable. Most technicians had previously been in electronics companies as assembly workers, so that operations such as soldering wires and plugs presented no difficulty for them. However, more often than not, the particular job to be done involved working inside the airplane itself, which was full of test equipment and very limited in free space. Since several crews of men were working on the same plane, often it was necessary to work in a cramped, poorly lit section of the plane where other workers were engaged in a job. Thus, what would ordinarily be an easy and routine operation, might take much longer than normal to carry out due to the inaccessibility of the location or the fact that other men were in the technician's way. Another drawback of the technician's job was the unevenness of the work flow. Often one man would be given a number of work orders which he could

---

[1] This is a sequential case. Your instructor may want you to discuss Part 1 before reading Part 2 or to answer the questions at the end of Part 1 and then go right on to Part 2.

not possibly complete in the specified time. When this happened, the engineers had to wait for the work to be done. At other times, however, a technician might go for one or two days without receiving a work order and consequently have nothing to do. This would happen when most of the planes were out on test flights or when the lead man was particularly concerned with some other job and had not had the time to make his usual rounds.

The technicians were paid on an hourly basis, and periodically were given small raises, so that wages were determined on the basis of seniority. The starting rates were about $2.25 per hour, while the highest rate paid to a technician was $3.50. The majority of technicians worked the eight-hour normal day shift, but several men would always be assigned to work on the night shift. Every two months this assignment would be shifted to others in the department so that the benefits or inconvenience of this night work were equally distributed to all of the technicians. (Some men enjoyed "working nights" as there were very few other workers around and no instrumentation foremen or lead men.)

During the day, the men could take smoking breaks outside in the halls whenever they wished and were, for the most part, loosely supervised. The lead man was a very easygoing person who walked from plane to plane handing out new work orders and collecting those which had been stamped by the inspector. He always spent extra time chatting with the men and was well liked by everyone.

PREDICTIONS

MAYNARD AIRCRAFT

PART 1

From what I know of the operations of the instrumentation department described in Part 1, I would predict that:

a) Productivity of the technicians in terms of *i*) quantity, and *ii*) quality would be (high) (standard) (below standard). Explain the reasons for your predictions.

b) Technicians would be (highly) (moderately) (dis-) satisfied with their job. Explain why.

c) Social interaction between technicians would be (high) (medium) (low) *i*) during working hours, *ii*) outside the plant. Explain the reasons for your predictions concerning both *i*) and *ii*).

d) Relations between technicians and engineers would be (cordial) (neutral) (strained). Explain why.

MAYNARD AIRCRAFT

Part 2

MANY OF the technicians saw much of each other off the job, either through company sponsored sports such as bowling or through activities of their own arranging. A typical technician also spent considerable time talking to other technicians during the day. He might go into the halls between the hangars and enter into a group conversation with four or five other technicians (especially prevalent during coffee breaks) or might seek out a friend working on another plane and coax him into taking a "break." During lunch periods the technicians usually ate in their cars, either by themselves or in pairs. Those who had tool benches in the hangar ate there, but there was little communication on the whole, at this time. The men either ate, read their newspapers, or attempted to sleep.

The engineers rarely spent any free time with the technicians and had their own office where they remained whenever they were not working on a plane.

The technicians felt that the engineers were no smarter than they, and that much of the work assigned by the engineers was needless and poorly thought out. They were reluctant to do a job quickly and efficiently since they felt that they would only be presented with harder work that much faster. They employed many stalling techniques, such as taking a long "break" while they were supposed to be procuring a part from the stock room, or going to borrow a tool, which they claimed not to own.

The engineers, in an effort to expedite matters, would stand close by during a particular job, hoping to speed up the work, but rarely if at all did this achieve their purpose.

The friction between the engineers and technicians had, over the last few years, steadily increased to the point where work assigned by the engineers to the technicians rarely was completed in a manner satisfactory to the engineers, either in terms of time spent on the job or the quality of the work performed. The technicians felt that their opinion on matters relating to jobs at hand was rarely given any weight. The work had lost all interest for them and every day was only another eight hours.

The foreman of the instrumentation department was somewhat sympathetic to the problems of his men but felt relatively powerless, as far as changing the orders given to him by the engineers.

The plant superintendent had recently become very concerned with the situation existing in the instrumentation department as it was greatly hampering flight testing operations which were crucial in the development of new aircraft. He felt immediate action had to be taken to clear up this situation.

POSTPREDICTION ANALYSIS

Refer to your predictions at the end of Part 1. How closely do they match the information above? Do inaccuracies in your predictions reflect inadequate analysis? If so, explain the analytical failure. If not, what additional information would you have needed in Part 1 to improve your predictive accuracy and how would you have used that information?

10. KILKENNY LUMBER COMPANY

Part 1[1]

THE KILKENNY LUMBER COMPANY owned and managed a large tract of forest in the northeastern United States. The company employed a number of men to maintain the tract according to modern forestry practice. In rotation, various areas of the tract were annually harvested by removing mature trees. Each winter, in preparation for harvesting and when other forestry tasks were at a standstill, a timber-marking crew composed of eight to ten regular company employees traveled through a selected area designating the trees to be cut and estimating the usable volume of lumber. In the spring, contractors moved over the area removing the marked trees.

Tree marking required considerable timbering knowledge and judgment. Once a tree was designated as mature and economical for harvest, height and diameter were calculated, defects estimated, and volume calculated. This volume was recorded along with a number code for the tree and was subsequently used as a basis for payment from the contractor. The code number was painted on the tree itself, as an indication of permission for cutting by the contract crew.

Tree-marking errors were costly. Missed trees or improper postponement of cutting meant lost sales and poor contractor relations, the latter depending on the maximum density of mature trees for his profit. Incorrect volume calculations meant lost money to Kilkenny or costly arbitration with the contractor. Designation of immature trees for cutting also cost Kilkenny money, particularly since the harvesting cycle was extremely long.

Several procedures had been adopted to reduce the chance of marking errors. The crew formed a moving line, each man fifty feet away from the men on either side. A man's place in the line was set by informal crew decision. The line was to keep within a predetermined strip of forest and the men kept in proper relation to each other by periodic shouts to determine relative positions and by supervisory observation. Supervisors also spent considerable time, particularly at the beginning of

---

[1] This is a sequential case. Your instructor may want you to discuss Part 1 before you read succeeding parts, or he may want you to answer the questions provided and then continue on through the case.

the winter, training the crew members to make judgments and measurements. Supervisors checked each man's work periodically to make sure it met standards. If not, additional training was given. If it still did not meet standards, the man was assigned to other work if it were available. Although there were no production quotas, the men were expected to keep up with the moving line and mark approximately the same number of trees. Despite occasional variations in terrain, disparity of work loads was not an issue.

Working conditions were arduous. Temperatures often fell below $0°F$. Snow was heavy and often fell during working hours. The terrain

Exhibit 1

KILKENNY LUMBER COMPANY

TIMBER-MARKING CREW, 1962

Title	Rank*	Pay Grade	Seniority	Age	Education
Leader.................Professional forester		9	3 years	25	College degree
Assistant leader.........Subprofessional forester		7	30 years	55	College, 1 year
Crewman†..............Professional forester		7	6 years	28	College degree
Crewman†..............Professional forester		7	4 years	26	College degree
Crewman†..............Professional forester		5	3 years	25	College degree
Crewman...............Subprofessional forester		5	15 years	38	High school diploma
Crewman...............Subprofessional forester		5	1 year	22	College, 2 years
Crewman...............Subprofessional forester		3	4 years	45	High school diploma

* Rank was attained by formal education, examination and experience. Professional foresters normally were responsible for maintenance of forest districts, often supervising crews of subprofessional foresters and other lower-ranking woodsmen.

† These three men had been assigned to this crew from a distant and organizationally separate district of Kilkenny's land. They were assigned to the crew because of lack of other work and were expected to gain new practical experience from the marking assignment. They customarily worked together in their home district. Unlike the rest of the crew, which lived near the district being marked, these men lived away from home on a subsistence and transportation allowance during the week.

was uneven and the men had to carry food and supplies on their backs. Generally the men had no opportunity to dry out or warm up during the twelve hours of daylight in which they worked.

The crew which began work in December, 1962 (see Exhibit 1), had received timber-marking training, though, as usual, all the men worked at other tasks during the rest of the year. A brief period of further training had been carried out by the leader and his assistant before the crew began regular work. Past timber-marking experience indicated that a crew like this could easily mark timber with the desired accuracy and speed.

The crew leader and his assistant were considered by Kilkenny management to be excellent foresters and teachers. In woodsman tradition, crew leaders were expected to carry out supervisory tasks and at the same time, turn out more individual marking than any one of their men. The leaders of this crew were able to live up to this tradition. Both leaders tended to allow the men privileges not strictly according to regulation, such as long lunch hours before a fire, early departures for home, and frequent work breaks, particularly when the weather was severe.

PREDICTIONS

KILKENNY LUMBER COMPANY

PART 1

From what I know of the tree-marking operation described in Part 1, I would predict that:

a) Productivity of the crew would be (high) (standard) (below standard). Explain the reasons for your prediction.

b) Crewmen would be (highly) (moderately) (dis-) satisfied with their job. Explain why.

c) Group members would (get along well with each other) (get along with some but not others) (not get along well with each other). Explain why. If you predict the second alternative, state who you would predict would get along well and who would not.

d) Crewmen will, in terms of the given job description, (do what they are supposed to do, no more or less) (do about what they are supposed to do and some other things as well) (not do many things they are supposed to do but will do other things). Explain your prediction. If you predict the second or third alternative, briefly describe "other things."

e) The group (or subgroups of the group) will have and/or develop the following beliefs and informal standards or norms about crew behavior. Explain why, taking care to identify the group or subgroup to which you refer in each instance.

KILKENNY LUMBER COMPANY

Part 2

THE TIMBER-MARKING CREW split into two informal groups soon after work in the forest began. One group was composed of the three professional foresters who had been assigned to the crew from a distant district. They constantly complained about the weather, the inadequacy of equipment, and their leaders. They found the leader to be a taskmaster who worked them too hard, his assistant a busybody who was too fussy about quality. The quantity of work performed by these three ranged between one third and one half of that attained by the other crewmen who were considered to be performing at a normal pace. Efforts at retraining produced no change. Absences among the three were high and excuses, though plentiful, often proved to be fabricated. The three men kept to themselves, building their separate fire at lunch time.

The rest of the crew tended to stick together. Although some of these men lacked the skill and training possessed by professional foresters, the men helped each other and production and quality were high. The leaders, feeling rejected by the three professional foresters, ate with the subprofessionals.

The leaders were angered by the three recalcitrant crewmen. They interpreted the latter's behavior as an attempt to be reassigned to a more pleasant job. Since no other positions were open and because the leaders disliked the thought of giving in to what they considered a play for preferential treatment, they told the three men they would have to stay out in the cold, work or not. Conditions did not improve.

POSTPREDICTION ANALYSIS

Refer to your predictions at the end of Part 1. How closely do they match the information above? Do inaccuracies in your predictions reflect inadequate analysis? If so, explain the analytical failure. If not, what additional information would you have needed in Part 1 to improve your predictive accuracy and how would you have used that information?

KILKENNY LUMBER COMPANY

Part 3

AFTER SEVERAL WEEKS, the leaders decided on two alternative strategies to increase the productivity of the professional foresters. First, the three men would be dispersed along the line and placed near the leader and his assistant instead of congregating at the far end of the line and trailing off as they had chosen to do (see Exhibit 2).

Exhibit 2

KILKENNY LUMBER COMPANY

POSITIONS IN LINE OF MARCH

A. BEFORE CONTEMPLATED CHANGE: *

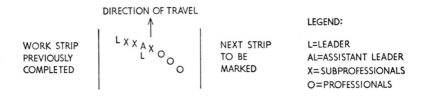

WORK STRIP	DIRECTION OF TRAVEL	NEXT STRIP	LEGEND:
PREVIOUSLY		TO BE	L=LEADER
COMPLETED		MARKED	AL=ASSISTANT LEADER
			X=SUBPROFESSIONALS
			O=PROFESSIONALS

B: CONTEMPLATED CHANGE:

WORK COMPLETED | TRAVEL | WORK YET TO BE DONE

* The unevenness of the line was compensated for by stopping forward progress before the end of the day and bringing the tail end of the line up to par with the leading edge.

If this strategy failed, the leader would assume responsibility for the professionals as a separate group away from the rest of the crew and hope to increase their production by close supervision.

PREDICTIONS

KILKENNY LUMBER COMPANY

PART 3

From Part 3 of the case, I would predict that:

a) The first strategy will be (successful) (partly successful) (unsuccessful). Explain why.

b) The second strategy (will) (will not) be attempted. If you predict the first alternative, the second strategy will be (successful) (partly successful) (unsuccessful). Explain why.

c) Some other strategy (will) (will not) be necessary. If you predict the first alternative, explain what that strategy should be, and why you expect it to succeed.

KILKENNY LUMBER COMPANY

Part 4

INSERTING the professionals between other crew members served to slow the entire work line. Although quality did not suffer, productivity for the whole crew dropped off to a total figure lower than that previously achieved. Consequently, the second strategy was attempted. However, while the subprofessional crew resumed their former pace, the professionals moved even slower than they had under the initial arrangement. The leaders were at a loss to find a way to attain the productivity which they felt certain the crew members were capable of achieving.

POSTPREDICTION ANALYSIS

Refer to your predictions at the end of Part 3. How closely do they match the information above? Do inaccuracies in your predictions reflect inadequate analysis? If so, explain the analytical failure. If not, what additional information would you have needed in Part 1 to improve your predictive accuracy and how would you have used that information?

11. THE WHITE COMPANY[1]

Part 1[2]

THE WHITE COMPANY is one of some eighty electroplating plants in the city of Detroit, which applied nickel and chrome plating to automobile parts. Price competition among these eighty plants was very intense.

The company had a nonunion work force which fluctuated between fifteen and fifty, depending on orders from the auto manufacturers. Few personnel records were kept. There was a standard policy of firing anyone who showed any interest in unionism. Hiring and training practices were not formalized, and the number of workers varied widely from day to day, depending upon immediate contracts. There was practically no job training. No more than a few minutes were spent in pointing out workers' duties and in introductions to co-workers.

The work was mostly unskilled, and the company employed many manual work methods instead of the semiautomatic equipment found in other companies. It used a number of practices designed to cut costs:

(1) Repairs were neglected and workers were expected to make up for this mechanical ineffectiveness, (2) personal (work) equipment was not quickly replaced . . . , (3) many safety practices were neglected . . . , (4) hiring and training were fitted with a situation of high turnover, so that new workers were given little training, and fired if they did not quickly learn to turn out a standard amount of production . . . , (5) over-all wages were so low that the most highly paid workers received only average union wages for the industry and the workers did not receive the usual union fringe concessions.

The workers in the plant could be categorized into two main groups: high-turnover personnel, and long-service employees. The backgrounds of the workers in the plant were quite different for longer-service people as compared to high-turnover workers. High-turnover personnel tended to be either part-time workers, such as students or relatives and friends of long-service workers; experienced workers who were on strike else-

---

[1] Information for this case was taken from W. F. Goode and Irving Fowler, "Incentive Factors in a Low Morale Plant," *American Sociological Review*, Vol. XIV, No. 5 (1949).

[2] This is a sequential case. Your instructor may want you to discuss Part 1 before reading Part 2 or to answer the questions at the end of Part 1 and then go right on to Part 2.

where or temporarily laid off; or finally, young newcomers to the labor market. The five longer-service personnel were different in many respects but had in common a quite desperate need for a job, either because they had physical handicaps which would make them unemployable in many places or, in the case of women, because they had to support dependent husbands. Some of the long-service workers had been with the plant since its beginnings. Almost all of them could perform nearly every task and could substitute for an absent worker.

PREDICTIONS
THE WHITE COMPANY
PART 1

From what I know about the White Company, I would predict that:

a) Worker productivity would be (high) (moderate) (low). Explain the reasons for your prediction.

b) Satisfaction in the plant would be (high) (moderate) (low). Explain the reasons for your prediction.

THE WHITE COMPANY

Part 2

THE LONG-SERVICE EMPLOYEES under pressure from management initiated a work pace which the high-turnover group had to follow. Those who did not follow such a pace were exposed to reprimand by word, gesture or look from the long-service workers. If they continued this lack of cooperation, informal pressures on the foremen by the key workers would eventually cause their discharge. Because of the timing aspects of electroplating, frequent bottlenecks occurred. However, these bottlenecks did not necessarily mean delays in production. They rather meant that at such times the key workers would attack the bottleneck with increased energy and, with the spontaneously induced help of the high-turnover personnel, would erase the difficulty. If this in turn produced a piling up of units at a later phase of the plating process, then the key personnel utilized the same practices and again the bottleneck was relieved. According to an expert in the industry, the White Company's level of worker productivity was running only 12 to 14 per cent below those firms that had invested in semiautomatic equipment. The company was "financially successful against strong competition."

Morale in the plant was low. "Workers exhibited considerable animosity toward the owners as well as the production manager," and "among the workers themselves."

POSTPREDICTION ANALYSIS
Refer to your predictions at the end of Part 1. How closely do they match the information above? Do inaccuracies in your predictions reflect inadequate analysis? If so, explain the analytical failure. If not, what additional information would you have needed in Part 1 to improve your predictive accuracy and how would you have used that information?

Concepts and Research Findings

1. A CONCEPTUAL SCHEME FOR DESCRIBING WORK GROUP BEHAVIOR*

As IS indicated by the following sample of work group studies (Readings 2–13) researchers in this area have used a wide variety of methodologies and approaches. What follows is an effort to spell out one terminology and system of concepts for describing the behavior of small groups of people at work. This particular "conceptual scheme" is based primarily on the work of Professor George C. Homans.[1]

Required and Emergent Group Behavior

It is a matter of common experience, as well as a finding of repeated small group research studies, that when people work together, they soon develop ways of thinking and behaving that are different from, or in addition to, the behavior which is required to perform the job. For example, they may do more or less work than they are supposed to, do it in a different manner than is prescribed, or engage in purely social activity. Sometimes, this "emergent" behavior in fact assists in the more effective performance of the assigned task; and at other times, it hinders it. In any case, for many people, it seems to be unpredictable and not well understood. We need a scheme for describing and understanding the ways people in work groups actually behave. A useful theory of work group behavior will emphasize the difference, and also the *interrelatedness,* of:

1. That behavior with which the group starts, so to speak, i.e., what is *given* and what is *required* by external forces and conditions in order that the assigned task of the group may be performed; *and*
2. That behavior which develops internally, or *emerges* over and above that which is given or required.

This is not to say that it is necessary or even possible to determine whether any observed behavior or attitude on the part of group members is given or required, on the one hand, or emergent, on the other.

[1] See G. C. Homans, *The Human Group* (New York: Harcourt, Brace & Co., Inc., 1950); H. W. Riecken and G. C. Homans, "Psychological Aspects of Social Structure," in Gardner Lindzey (ed.), *Handbook of Social Psychology* (Cambridge: Addison-Wesley Publishing Co., Inc., 1954), Vol. II, pp. 786–832.

Often, such distinctions are very difficult to make, and they are not always useful. Nevertheless, the observer, or student, or leader of any
group will find it easier to understand and predict how the members of a
group are likely to behave (for example, how they will probably react to changing circumstances) if he keeps in mind that much of the
behavior that will eventually emerge is *separate* from but *related* to
the ways of thinking and behaving which people bring with them to
the group plus the behavior required by the job. *Some* kind of behavior other than the bare minimum required by the job will inevitably
emerge, and this behavior will not be random but will have a pattern
and an understandable relationship with that which was given and required. Furthermore, this relationship will eventually work in both
directions, i.e., what emerges will in turn influence (feed back on) what
is required and given. (For example, if restriction of output at a certain
level emerges, this fact, once recognized, will affect future management
decisions which will, in turn, have new influences on the formal job
requirements, and thereby either modify or reinforce the original
emergent behavior.) With greater understanding of this relationship
between the given and emergent aspects of a group's behavior, management is less likely to be surprised at what emerges.

The Elements of Group Behavior

In order to achieve such understanding, it is helpful to look separately at the different elements of group (or any human) behavior, and
to study how these elements are related to each other. The conceptual
scheme we are describing uses three major elements: *activities, interactions,* and *sentiments.* In describing behavior which is required by the
nature of the task or by the necessity for the organization to survive in
its environment, or which the members bring with them to the group
as an outcome of their life outside it, we speak of *required* or *given* or
external activity, interaction, and sentiment. Thus, we conceive of an
external system for every group, consisting of the following elements
and the relationships between them: *required activity, required interaction, required sentiment,* and *given sentiment.* In addition, we use the
term *values* to refer to one particular category of given sentiments. In
describing behavior which is not required or given but which is elaborated by the group beyond the demands of the external system, we use
the term *emergent.* The emergent elements and their relationships
comprise the group's *internal system.* In addition, the scheme pays
particular attention to one category of emergent sentiments, namely,
the *norms* which develop in the group. In short, the basic vocabulary of

this scheme consists of the following seven terms: *external, internal, activity, interaction, sentiment, value,* and *norm.*

Other words for describing group behavior could have been chosen, but these terms are useful ones *if* there is some consensus about their meaning. As used here, these terms can be defined as follows:

Activity: What a person does (e.g., talks, runs, calculates, manipulates machinery, falls asleep, makes the quota, engages in horseplay, and so forth.)

Interaction: A communication or contact between two persons such that the activity of one responds to the activity of the other. Every conversation is an interaction (or a series of interactions), but there are also many nonverbal communications or contacts which are equally valid as interactions as here defined (and in some talking, no real interaction is taking place). In observing interactions, it is usually important to note by whom they are *initiated* and whether two or more people are simultaneously involved. (Some interactions in work groups are not initiated by anyone, but rather there is a joint response to the demands of the evolving situation or work process.[2])

Sentiment: An idea, belief, or feeling, for instance, about the work and others involved in it. This is obviously a very large category, capable of much more detailed analysis.[3] Note that, unlike activities and interactions, sentiments are not directly observable. Sentiments such as "This room is too hot for me to feel like working," or "My boss is a great guy," can be inferred from observed activity and interaction, or from expressed responses to specific questions, but not observed at first hand.

Required Sentiment: A belief or feeling which an employee must have in order to be willing to perform the task as assigned.

Given Sentiment and Value: A belief or feeling which a member brings with him into a group because of his life outside it and his personal background. When given sentiments pertain to ideals and aspirations which are desirable but impossible to realize absolutely, they are called values. Thus, "[a] *value* is an unlimited idea of what is desirable," such as a belief in fair treatment, good pay, or "freedom" from "being pushed around."[4] The degree to which an individual lives up to or represents the values that are most important to others is important in determining his "external status" in their eyes. Thus, for any group, certain values from

---

[2] F. B. Miller, " 'Situational' Interactions—A Worthwhile Concept?" *Human Organization,* Vol. XVII, No. 4 (Winter, 1958–59), pp. 37–47.

[3] The definitions given here of the terms *sentiment* and *value* are quite different from Homans' recent formulation. See G. C. Homans, *Social Behavior: Its Elementary Forms* (New York: Harcourt, Brace & Co., Inc., 1961), esp. pp. 30–50.

[4] A. Zaleznik, C. R. Christensen, and F. J. Roethlisberger, *The Motivation, Productivity, and Satisfaction of Workers: A Prediction Study* (Boston: Division of Research, Harvard Business School, 1958), p. 44.

the outside culture define the relative status of different members; men may be accorded higher status than women, one ethnic background more respect than another, and so forth.

Norm: A certain kind of emergent sentiment, namely, an idea or belief about what the sentiments, activities, or interactions in a particular group *should* be. In contrast to a value, "a norm is a limited idea of what is desirable; it can be fully realized."[5] Norms develop in any group, with greater or less degree of consensus; and they serve to define how, as a member in good standing, one should behave in relation to outsiders, other members, the job, and the emergent nonwork activities. The extent to which a group member upholds such norms helps define his "internal rank" or social standing in the group. Thus, internal rank is related to norms in much the same way as external status is related to values. For example, if a particular sentiment about productivity is a norm, the degree to which each member shares this sentiment and acts to uphold it will influence his standing in the group (and/or vice versa, his standing in the group, as established in other ways, is likely to influence the extent to which he shares this norm). Strictly speaking, the term *norm* applies not to a general ideal but rather to a standard of behavior which can be violated only at the risk of punishment from other members of the group.

So far, we have emphasized that group behavior *emerges* which is different from that which is given or required by the work, and we have defined the meaning of the terms by which the basic elements of this behavior can be described. In doing so, we have started to point to some of the more important relationships which exist between these elements, as well as between the given and emergent aspects of group behavior. To understand how this scheme can be useful, we should describe and illustrate some important hypotheses concerning the relationships between emergent activity, interaction, sentiment, and norms. However, first let us confine attention to the "external system," considering especially where required and given behavior comes from and how it is likely to be significantly different in various kinds of groups.

Background Factors Determining Required and Given Behavior (2)[6]

It is obvious that any job requires certain activities for its successful performance, and that the nature of these activities varies according to the particular technology and job design. There are also significant variations in the extent to which the precise nature of the activities required to perform the job are specified, that is, in the amount of individual variation in activity that is permissible in accomplishing the

---

[5] *Ibid.*

[6] Numbers in parentheses refer to the influences represented in Exhibit 1.

work. Required activities depend not only upon the job design and technology, but also upon management policies and practices and upon the assumptions and behavior of the immediate supervisor. In other words, two identical jobs within the same technology can result in a somewhat different set of required activities because of different assumptions by management concerning how much individuals should be allowed to contribute to determining precisely how the work should be performed. Required activities also are influenced by the individual characteristics and backgrounds of the people performing the job

Exhibit 1

WORK GROUP BEHAVIOR

RELATIONS BETWEEN ELEMENTS OF EXTERNAL AND INTERNAL SYSTEMS

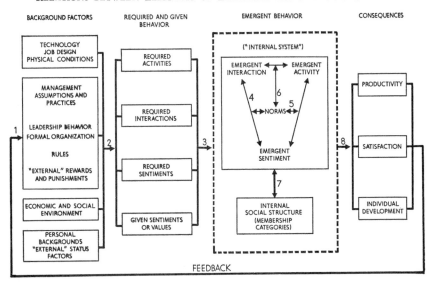

(variations in aptitude, training, and so forth). Different outside social and economic influences will also affect required activities, primarily through their influence on management policy and the particular system of rewards and punishment used in an organization.

This same set of influences—technology, job design, management policy and practice, leadership behavior, personal backgrounds, and economic and social environment—also define the particular required interactions that will obtain between the members of any work group. The nature of the job, management's behavior, and so forth will require that certain people interact with certain other people; whereas, between other members, no interaction may be required.

It is not so obvious, but equally true, that the same set of background factors which determine required activities and interactions also establish certain "required sentiments." There are always certain beliefs about himself, work, other people, and so forth which an individual must have in order to perform the job in the manner in which he is supposed to. The technology, the management, the environment, and the individual's own background all help determine which sentiments must be present in a group, at least to some extent, before the members will be willing to perform the task assigned them. However, the different determinants of required sentiments can be in conflict with each other, for example, some technologies require a higher degree of willingness to exercise individual initiative than is appropriate according to management's assumptions about what sentiments workers are supposed to have.

In addition, there may be some conflict between the sentiments required by the technology, for example, and the "given sentiments." These, it will be remembered, are beliefs and values which individuals bring with them to work, and are determined by their previous personal backgrounds and experiences in the outside environment. The values shared by members of a work group, as a result of their backgrounds and previous work experiences, will obviously be an important influence on their approach to the job, on their ideas about status, and on their developing relationships with each other.

All the behavior considered so far, namely, the required activities, interactions, and sentiments, and the given sentiments, then, are theoretically determined by a set of "background factors" over which members of the group have little or no control, namely, their own personal characteristics and backgrounds, external economic and social influences, management policies and practices, the supervisor's behavior, the technology, and job design. The first two columns of Exhibit 1 attempt to represent the more important influences existing between these background factors and the required and given elements of behavior. Note that one of the most important influences on management policy is the "feedback" received from the eventually emerging productivity, satisfaction, and individual development of the members of the group (1). Among the results of this feedback, for example, may be a management decision to modify the technology.

Conflicts are possible between some of these required and given elements; but if this were all there was to group life, predicting group behavior would be relatively easy and uninteresting. (It would also be a pretty dull business for the members.)

Emergent Behavior

Unfortunately or fortunately, depending upon one's point of view, in considering what is "given" and "required," we have looked only at a bare minimum of group behavior. The *actual* behavior of almost any group is far more complicated and interesting. However, enough small groups have been systematically studied under a wide enough variety of circumstances to develop a number of useful general propositions concerning the emergence of the various elements of behavior (sentiments, interactions, activities, and norms) and the relationships between these emergent elements.

It is important to emphasize that these propositions are "useful" but not universally reliable. They all assume that a host of other variables which in any concrete situation influence behavior are temporarily inactive. In spite of the unreality of this assumption, however, the propositions do provide a helpful beginning for understanding emergent small group behavior; and often, they can be used in making reasonably accurate predictions concerning the particular behavior which is *likely* to emerge in a given group under certain circumstances. Some of these propositions will appear obvious, and others will appear far-fetched. A more valid criterion for judging them is their usefulness in understanding and predicting concrete behavior—and in this respect, several different kinds of research have shown them to stand up remarkably well, considering the present early stage of development in behavioral science. (In the following discussion, *some* of these propositions will be presented in simplified form, although to be understandable, brief, and at the same time fair to the conceptual scheme will be difficult, if not impossible. The theory from which the following propositions are derived, like any good theory, consists essentially of a system of *interrelated* hypotheses, no part of which makes much sense without an understanding of the whole.)

Given Sentiments and Emergent Behavior (3)

A careful analysis of the values which members bring to a group will obviously aid prediction about the activities, interactions, sentiments, and norms that are likely to emerge. Values are, by definition, closely related to norms, and the relationship between values and the other elements is also fairly easy to predict. For example, more frequent than usual interaction, and more favorable sentiments, can be expected to emerge between members whose given sentiments are similar. High "status" derived from the external social system is likely to be related—

initially, at least—to emergent interpersonal sentiment and "rank" in the internal social structure.

Required and Emergent Behavior (3)

Obviously, all the required elements establish at least the starting place from which the emergent elements develop. Emergent interaction is more likely between members who are required to interact, between those whose jobs (required activities) place them near each other, and so forth. Emergent behavior is likely to be related to (or to compensate for) the demands of the technology, including such conditions as heat, noise, lighting, and so forth, as well as the degree of repetitiveness and mechanical pacing required by the job. The extent to which certain sentiments are required, such as identification with the total process or willingness to innovate or take responsibility, will have more or less obvious influences on emergent sentiment, interaction, and activity. It is always important to remember that, barring outside restraints, what is required *is* only the beginning. Members of almost any group seem to have a strong need to complicate their life together by developing interactions, activities, and sentiments which are *not* required; and this development *can* lead to behavior which is not only different from but in actual conflict with the original requirements.

Interaction and Sentiment (4)

The above two paragraphs were concerned with relations between the external and internal systems. Now, we confine our attention to the internal system by presenting hypotheses about how the different *emergent* elements of behavior are related to each other. A basic hypothesis concerning emergent behavior is that interaction and interpersonal sentiment are closely related. More specifically, the hypothesis states that, in the absence of contrary influences, favorable sentiments emerge between members who interact frequently and, vice versa, frequent interaction emerges between members who like each other. Under certain circumstances, increasing interaction may be associated with *less* favorable sentiments; but the notion that *other things being equal,* members who like one another will interact more frequently than those who do not, is in a sense the key hypothesis concerning the emergent elements of the "internal system."

Activities, Sentiments, and Norms (5)

Unfavorable sentiments will be directed against members who do not share or who violate the norms generally accepted in the group.

Furthermore, these unfavorable sentiments frequently lead to the emergence of further activities which have the function of punishing the violators of the norms and which may well lead to further defensive or aggressive activities by the violators. Thus, a circular situation is likely to arise in which both the violators and the upholders of the group's norms each have their sentiments about the others reinforced by the others' activities.

Activities, Norms, and Interactions (6)

The quantity and quality of interaction between two members, A and B, is related not only to the sentiment between them, but also to the extent to which A perceives B's activities as violating the norms of the group. In other words, when a member violates a norm, interaction toward him will initially *increase* as efforts are made to "bring him into line." However, if these efforts fail and he persists in violating the norm, he will be the recipient of increasingly unfavorable sentiments and consequently *decreasing* interaction. Thus, the punishment for persistent norm violation is isolation from regular membership, and only those willing to pay this price will persist in such activity. Since, in work groups, important norms almost inevitably emerge concerning output, it follows that "slackers" or "rate busters" can expect hostility followed by low interaction with other members (although they may form a subgroup with others who share their values).

Social Structure and Membership Categories (7)

It can be seen that starting with a relatively simple set of required behaviors, a complex pattern of activity, interaction, and sentiment between the members is likely to emerge which will have as a vital function preserving the norms and protecting the group against outside pressures perceived as threats to the behavior pattern that the group finds relatively satisfying. Emergent interactions, when observed, can be used to map out the probable pattern of interpersonal sentiment, or vice versa. Recipients of favorable sentiment are likely to be frequent interactors, and their activities will be likely to conform closely with the group's norms. Thus, there usually emerges in a work group a core of "regular members," which will include the informal leader or leaders of the group. In general, social standing in the group will depend upon faithfulness to its norms. The informal leaders, in particular, will tend to be frequent *initiators* of interaction involving more than two people. They will be especially careful to live up to the group's norms, since they have the most to lose by violating them.

At the other extreme from the "regulars," there will usually be several "isolates" whose interaction with other members is infrequent; they will have adapted to this situation and will express little interest in more regular membership or in observing the group's norms. In between these two extremes will be members at various degrees of "regularity." Among them may be some "deviants" whose interaction rate among themselves and even with the regulars is relatively frequent, but who are denied regular membership because of unwillingness or inability to accept the dominant norms and values.

In spite of the wide variations in the nature of the social structure which emerges from group to group, the above rough classification of membership categories (regular, deviant, isolate) is often useful in interpreting behavior of individual members. And from what has been said of the interrelationships between emergent interaction, activity, and sentiment, and the function of this behavior as a defense against outside influences, it can be seen why these categories, once established, tend to reinforce themselves.

Consequences (8)

In fact, the reinforcing dynamic of these interrelated elements of behavior is their most significant characteristic. The patterns which emerge tend to persist. The social structure helps to preserve the norms which develop concerning activity and interaction. The resulting influence on the group's *productivity* is likely to be strong and persistent, since in almost any group, norms emerge which specify quite precisely the quantity and quality of work expected of a member in good standing, and the pressures to conform to these norms are not easy to resist. Any increase in the perceived external threat to the group's emergent behavior is likely to increase the extent to which the norms and social structure control the members' activity.

The relationships and nonwork activities which emerge in a group will strongly influence the *satisfactions* which group members derive from their work experience. Where there is relatively frequent interaction and members like one another, where the social structure is relatively stable and well understood, satisfaction is usually relatively high. This can be true whether productivity is high or low; thus, the relationship between productivity and satisfaction is more complex than is sometimes assumed.

Another "consequence" of work group behavior, in addition to productivity and satisfaction, may be called *individual development*. Groups vary greatly in the extent to which they encourage or limit their members' needs to learn, grow, and develop as individual human beings. In any work group, there emerges a pattern of interaction, sentiment, and activity, a set of norms which define the extent to which members are able to fulfill their own potentialities, to achieve the personal goals and rewards important to them. Without a certain level of satisfaction, individual development is severely limited; but in many industrial work groups, satisfaction (from friendly relations with other members, for example) can be high while opportunities for the individual to learn and grow are severely limited. In the same way, individual development may be facilitated by high productivity, but only under certain conditions, as, for example, where a strong sense of individual contribution to the task is not in conflict with required sentiments or group norms.

Unfortunately, the conditions surrounding many industrial work groups are such that opportunities for individual development are often thwarted, and satisfaction derives almost entirely from activity not related to accomplishment of the formal task. Much of the emergent behavior may become largely defensive against perceived threats from the outside. While satisfying members' needs for social stability, such groups do little to satisfy needs for self-esteem and personal development. A more adequate understanding of why this is so, a more perceptive interpretation of the observable consequences of work group behavior, will make it possible to structure more intelligently those background factors which management can directly influence.

2. THE RELAY ASSEMBLY TEST ROOM
EXPERIMENTS

ONE OF the first, and still the most extensive, studies of the behavior and attitudes of workers in an industrial organization was carried out at the Hawthorne (Chicago) Works of the Western Electric Company between 1927 and 1932.[1] The general progress of this research can be summarized in terms of four phases, the last three of which each developed as an attempt to answer questions which were raised by the previous phase:

1. Preliminary experiments on the effects of changes in illumination, conducted between 1924 and 1927.
2. Experiments on the effects of changes in hours and other conditions of work, including rest pauses, of which the relay assembly test room study is the best known.[2]
3. Development of a plantwide interviewing program and analysis of employee attitudes.[3]
4. Analysis of social organization at work, particularly through detailed study of the bank wiring observation room.[4]

The following summary of the relay assembly test room experiments is taken from the report of a Committee on Work in Industry of the National Research Council, which was appointed in December, 1937. The report was written by George C. Homans, the secretary of the committee.[5]

---

[1] The two most comprehensive accounts of this research are T. N. Whitehead, *The Industrial Worker* (2 vols.; Cambridge: Harvard University Press, 1938); and F. J. Roethlisberger and W. J. Dickson, *Management and the Worker* (Cambridge: Harvard University Press, 1939). Many summaries and evaluations of the work have since been published by other authors. For a recent critique, see H. A. Landsberger, *Hawthorne Revisited* (Ithaca: Cornell University, Studies in Industrial and Labor Relations, Vol. 9, 1958).

[2] Roethlisberger and Dickson, *op. cit.,* Part I, "Working Conditions and Employee Efficiency."

[3] *Ibid.,* Part II, "A Plan for the Improvement of Employee Efficiency"; and Part III, "A Conceptual Scheme for the Understanding of Employee Complaints."

[4] *Ibid.,* Part IV, "Social Organization of Employees."

[5] Committee on Work in Industry, National Research Council, *Fatigue of Workers: Its Relation to Industrial Production* (New York: Reinhold Publishing Corp., 1941), pp. 56–66. Reproduced by permission of author and publisher.

The program of research which will be described grew out of a study conducted at Hawthorne by the Western Electric Company in collaboration with the National Research Council, the aim of which was to determine the relation between intensity of illumination and efficiency of workers, measured in output. One of the experiments made was the following: Two groups of employees doing similar work under similar conditions were chosen, and records of output were kept for each group. The intensity of the light under which one group worked was varied, while that under which the other group worked was held constant. By this method the investigators hoped to isolate from the effect of other variables the effect of changes in the intensity of illumination on the rate of output.

In this hope they were disappointed. The experiment failed to show any simple relation between experimental changes in the intensity of illumination and observed changes in the rate of output. The investigators concluded that this result was obtained, not because such a relation did not exist, but because it was in fact impossible to isolate it from the other variables entering into any determination of productive efficiency. This kind of difficulty, of course, has been encountered in experimental work in many fields. Furthermore, the investigators were in agreement as to the character of some of these other variables. They were convinced that one of the major factors which prevented their securing a satisfactory result was psychological. The employees being tested were reacting to changes in light intensity in the way in which they assumed that they were expected to react. That is, when light intensity was increased they were expected to produce more; when it was decreased they were expected to produce less. A further experiment was devised to demonstrate this point. The light bulbs were changed as they had been changed before, and the workers were allowed to assume that as a result there would be more light. They commented favorably on the increased illumination. As a matter of fact, the bulbs had been replaced with others of just the same power. Other experiments of the sort were made, and in each case the results could be explained as a "psychological" reaction rather than as a "physiological" one.

This discovery seemed to be important. It suggested that the relations between other physical conditions and the efficiency of workers might be obscured by similar psychological reactions. Nevertheless the investigators were determined to continue in their course. They recognized the existence of the psychological factors, but they thought of them only as disturbing influences. They were not yet ready to turn their attention to the psychological factors themselves. Instead, they were concerned with devising a better way of eliminating them from the experiments, and the experiments they wanted to try by no means ended with illumination. For instance, there was the question of what was called "fatigue." Little information existed about the effect on efficiency of changes in the hours of work and the introduction of rest pauses. The investigators finally came to the conclusion that if a small group of workers was isolated in a separate room and asked to co-operate, the psychological reaction would in time disappear, and they would work exactly as they felt. That is, changes in their rate of output would be the direct result of changes in their physical conditions of work and nothing else.

The decision to organize such a group was in fact taken. A small number of workers was to be selected and placed in a separate room where experiments were to be made with different kinds of working conditions in order to see if more exact information could be secured. Six questions were asked by those setting up the experiment. They were the following:

1. Do employees actually get tired out?
2. Are rest pauses desirable?
3. Is a shorter working day desirable?
4. What is the attitude of employees toward their work and toward the company?
5. What is the effect of changing the type of working equipment?
6. Why does production fall off in the afternoon?

It is obvious that several of these questions could be answered only indirectly by the proposed experiment, and several of them touched upon the "psychological" rather than the "physiological" factors involved. Nevertheless, all of them arose out of the bewilderment of men of experience faced with the problem of dealing with fellow human beings in a large industrial organization. In fact, one of the executives of the company saw the purpose of the experiment in even simpler and more general terms. He said that the experiment grew out of a desire on the part of the management to "know more about our workers." In this way began the experiment which is referred to as the Relay Assembly Test Room. With this experiment and the others that followed, members of the Department of Industrial Research of the Graduate School of Business Administration, Harvard University, came to be closely associated.

In April 1927, six girls were selected from a large shop department of the Hawthorne works. They were chosen as average workers, neither inexperienced nor expert, and their work consisted of the assembling of telephone relays. A coil, armature, contact springs, and insulators were put together on a fixture and secured in position by means of four machine screws. The operation at that time was being completed at the rate of about five relays in six minutes. This particular operation was chosen for the experiment because the relays were being assembled often enough so that even slight changes in output rate would show themselves at once on the output record. Five of the girls were to do the actual assembly work; the duty of the sixth was to keep the others supplied with parts.

The test room itself was an area divided from the main department by a wooden partition eight feet high. The girls sat in a row on one side of a long workbench. The bench and assembly equipment were identical with those used in the regular department, except in one respect. At the right of each girl's place was a hole in the bench, and into this hole she dropped completed relays. It was the entrance to a chute, in which there was a flapper gate opened by the relay in its passage downward. The opening of the gate closed an electrical circuit which controlled a perforating device, and this in turn recorded the completion of the relay by punching a hole in a tape. The tape moved at the rate of one-quarter of an inch a minute and had space for a separate row of holes for each operator. When punched, it thus constituted a complete output record for each girl for each instant of the day. Such records were kept for five years.

In this experiment, then, as in the earlier illumination experiments, great emphasis was laid on the rate of output. A word of caution is needed here. The Western Electric Company was not immediately interested in increasing output. The experiments were not designed for that purpose. On the other hand, output is easily measured, i.e., it yields precise quantitative data, and experience suggested that it was sensitive to at least some of the conditions under which the employees worked. Output was treated as an index. In short, the nature of the experimental conditions made the emphasis on output inevitable.

From their experience in the illumination experiments, the investigators were well aware that factors other than those experimentally varied might affect the output rate. Therefore arrangements were made that a number of other records should be kept. Unsuitable parts supplied by the firm were noted down, as were assemblies rejected for any reason upon inspection. In this way the type of defect could be known and related to the time of day at which it occurred. Records were kept of weather conditions in general and of temperature and humidity in the test room. Every six weeks each operator was given a medical examination by the company doctor. Every day she was asked to tell how many hours she had spent in bed the night before and, during a part of the experiment, what food she had eaten. Besides all these records, which concerned the physical condition of the operators, a log was kept in which were recorded the principal events in the test room hour by hour, including among the entries snatches of conversation between the workers. At first these entries related largely to the physical condition of the operators; how they felt as they worked. Later the ground they covered somewhat widened, and the log ultimately became one of the most important of the test room records. Finally when the so-called Interviewing Program was instituted at Hawthorne, each of the operators was interviewed several times by an experienced interviewer.

The girls had no supervisor in the ordinary sense, such as they would have had in a regular shop department, but a "test room observer" was placed in the room, whose duty it was to maintain the records, arrange the work, and secure a co-operative spirit on the part of the girls. Later, when the complexity of his work increased, several assistants were assigned to help him.

When the arrangements had been made for the test room, the operators who had been chosen to take part were called in for an interview in the office of the superintendent of the Inspection Branch, who was in general charge of the experiment and of the researches which grew out of it. The superintendent described this interview as follows: "The nature of the test was carefully explained to these girls and they readily consented to take part in it, although they were very shy at the first conference. An invitation to six shop girls to come up to a superintendent's office was naturally rather startling. They were assured that the object of the test was to determine the effect of certain changes in working conditions, such as rest periods, midmorning lunches, and shorter working hours. They were expressly cautioned to work at a comfortable pace, and under no circumstances to try and make a race out of the test." This conference was only the first of many. Whenever any experimental change was planned, the girls were called in, the purpose of the change was explained to them, and their comments were requested. Certain suggested changes which did not meet with their approval were abandoned. They were repeatedly asked, as they were asked in the first interview, not to strain but to work "as they felt."

The experiment was now ready to begin. Put in its simplest terms, the idea of those directing the experiment was that if an output curve was studied for a long enough time under various changes in working conditions, it would be possible to determine which conditions were the most satisfactory. Accordingly, a number of so-called "experimental periods" were arranged. For two weeks before the operators were placed in the test room, a record was kept of the production of each one without her knowledge. In this way the investigators secured a measure of her productive ability while working in the regular department under the usual conditions. This constituted the first experimental period. And for five weeks after the girls entered the test room no change was made in working conditions. Hours remained what they had been before. The investigators felt that this period would be long enough to reveal any changes in output incidental merely to the transfer. This constituted the second experimental period.

The third period involved a change in the method of payment. In the regular department the girls had been paid according to a scheme of group piecework, the group consisting of a hundred or more employees. Under these circumstances, variations in an individual's total output would not be immediately reflected in her pay, since such variations tended to cancel one another in such a large group. In the test room, the six operators were made a group by themselves. In this way each girl received an amount more nearly in proportion to her individual effort, and her interests became more closely centered on the experiment. Eight weeks later the directly experimental changes began. An outline will reveal their general character: Period IV: two rest pauses, each five minutes in length, were established, one occurring in midmorning and the other in the early afternoon. Period V: these rest pauses were lengthened to ten minutes each. Period VI: six five-minute rests were established. Period VII: the company provided each member of the group with a light lunch in the midmorning and another in the midafternoon, accompanied by rest pauses. This arrangement became standard for subsequent Periods VIII through XI. Period VIII: work stopped a half-hour earlier every day at 4:30 P.M. Period IX: work stopped at 4 P.M. Period X: conditions returned to what they were in Period VII. Period XI: a five-day work week was established. Each of these experimental periods lasted several weeks.

Period XI ran through the summer of 1928, a year after the beginning of the experiment. Already the results were not what had been expected. The output curve, which had risen on the whole slowly and steadily throughout the year, was obviously reflecting something other than the responses of the group to the imposed experimental conditions. Even when the total weekly output had fallen off, as it could hardly fail to do in such a period as Period XI, when the group was working only five days a week, daily output continued to rise. Therefore, in accordance with a sound experimental procedure, as a control on what had been done, it was agreed with the consent of the operators that in experimental Period XII a return should be made to the original conditions of work, with no rest pauses, no special lunches, and a full-length working week. This period lasted for twelve weeks. Both daily and weekly output rose to a higher point than ever before: the working day and the working week were both longer. The hourly output rate declined somewhat but it did not approach the level of Period III, when similar conditions were in effect.

The conclusions reached after Period XII may be expressed in terms of another observation. Identical conditions of work were repeated in three different experimental periods: Periods VII, X, and XIII. If the assumptions on which the study was based had been correct, that is to say, if the output rate were directly related to the physical conditions of work, the expectation would be that in these three experimental periods there would be some similarity in output. Such was not the case. The only apparent uniformity was that in each experimental period output was higher than in the preceding one. In the Relay Assembly Test Room, as in the previous illumination experiments, something was happening which could not be explained by the experimentally controlled conditions of work.

There is no need here to go into the later history of the test room experiment, which came to an end in 1933. It is enough to say that the output of the group continued to rise until it established itself on a high plateau from which there was no descent until the time of discouragement and deepening economic depression which preceded the end of the test. The rough conclusions reached at the end of experimental Period XII were confirmed and sharpened by later research. T. N. Whitehead, Associate Professor of Business in the Graduate School of Business Administration, Harvard University, has made a careful statistical analysis of the output records. He shows that the changes which took place in the output of the group have no simple correlation with the experimental changes in working conditions. Nor can they be correlated with changes in other physical conditions of which records were kept, such as temperature, humidity, hours of rest, and changes of relay type. Even when the girls themselves complained of mugginess or heat, these conditions were not apparently affecting their output. This statement, of course, does not mean that there is never any relation between output rate and these physical conditions. There is such a thing as heat prostration. It means only that, within the limits in which these conditions were varying in the test room, they apparently did not affect the rate of work.

The question remains: With what facts, if any, can the changes in the output rate of the operators in the test room be correlated? Here the statements of the girls themselves are of the first importance. Each girl knew that she was producing more in the test room than she ever had in the regular department, and each said that the increase had come about without any conscious effort on her part. It seemed easier to produce at the faster rate in the test room than at the slower rate in the regular department. When questioned further, each girl stated her reasons in slightly different words, but there was uniformity in the answers in two respects. First, the girls liked to work in the test room; "it was fun." Secondly, the new supervisory relation or, as they put it, the absence of the old supervisory control, made it possible for them to work freely without anxiety.

For instance, there was the matter of conversation. In the regular department, conversation was in principle not allowed. In practice it was tolerated if it was carried on in a low tone and did not interfere with work. In the test room an effort was made in the beginning to discourage conversation, though it was soon abandoned. The observer in charge of the experiment was afraid of losing the cooperation of the girls if he insisted too strongly on this point. Talk became common and was often loud and general. Indeed, the conversation of the operators came to occupy an important place in the log. T. N. Whitehead has pointed out that the girls in the test room were far more thoroughly supervised than they ever had been in the regular department. They were watched by an observer of their own, an interested management, and outside experts. The point is that the character and purpose of the supervision were different and were felt to be so.

The operators knew that they were taking part in what was considered an important and interesting experiment. They knew that their work was expected to produce results—they were not sure what results—which would lead to the improvement of the working conditions of their fellow employees. They knew that the eyes of the company were upon them. Whitehead has further pointed out that although the experimental changes might turn out to have no physical significance, their social significance was always favorable. They showed that the management of the company was still interested, that the girls were still part of a valuable piece of research. In the regular department, the girls, like the other employees, were in the position of responding to changes the source and purpose of which were beyond their knowledge. In the test room, they had frequent interviews with the superintendent, a high officer of the company. The reasons for the contemplated experimental changes were explained to them. Their views were consulted and in some instances they were allowed to veto what had been proposed. Professor Mayo has argued that it is idle to speak of an experimental period like Period XII as being in any sense what it purported to be—a return to the original conditions of work. In the meantime, the entire industrial situation of the girls had been reconstructed.

Another factor in what occurred can only be spoken of as the social development of the group itself. When the girls went for the first time to be given a physical examination by the company doctor, someone suggested as a joke that ice cream and cake ought to be served. The company provided them at the next examination, and the custom was kept up for the duration of the experiment. When one of the girls had a birthday, each of the others would bring her a present, and she would respond by offering the group a box of chocolates. Often one of the girls would have some good reason for feeling tired. Then the others would "carry" her. That is, they would agree to work especially fast to make up for the low output expected from her. It is doubtful whether this "carrying" did have any effect, but the important point is the existence of the practice, not its effectiveness. The girls made friends in the test room and went together socially after hours. One of the interesting facts which has appeared from Whitehead's analysis of the output records is that there were times when variations in the output rates of two friends were correlated to a high degree. Their rates varied simultaneously and in the same direction—something, of course, which the girls were not aware of and could not have planned. Also, these correlations were destroyed by such apparently trivial events as a change in the order in which the girls sat at the workbench.

Finally, the group developed leadership and common purpose. The leader, self-appointed, was an ambitious young Italian girl who entered the test room as a replacement after two of the original members had left. She saw in the experiment a chance for personal distinction and advancement. The common purpose was an increase in the output rate. The girls had been told in the beginning and repeatedly thereafter that they were to work without straining, without trying to make a race of the test, and all the evidence shows that they kept this rule. In fact, they felt that they were working under less pressure than in the regular department. Nevertheless, they knew that the output record was considered the most important of the records of the experiment and was always closely scrutinized. Before long they had committed themselves to a continuous increase in production. In the long run, of course, this ideal was an impossible one, and when the girls found out that it was, the realization was an important element of the change of tone which was noticeable in the second half of the experiment. But for a time they felt that they could achieve the impossible. In brief, the increase in the output rate of the girls in the Relay Assembly Test Room could not be related to any changes in their physical conditions of work, whether experimentally induced or not. It could, however, be related to what can only be spoken of as the development of an organized social group in a peculiar and effective relation with its supervisors.

Many of these conclusions were not worked out in detail until long after the investigators at Hawthorne had lost interest in the Relay Assembly Test Room, but the general meaning of the experiment was clear at least as early as Period XII. A continuous increase in productivity had taken place irrespective of changing physical conditions of work. In the words of a company report made in January 1931, on all the research which had been done up to that date: "Upon analysis, only one thing seemed to show a continuous relationship with this improved output. This was the mental attitude of the operators. From their conversations with each other and their comments to the test observers, it was not only clear that their attitudes were improving but it was evident that this area of employee reactions and feelings was a fruitful field for industrial research."

At this point the attention of the investigators turned sharply from the test room to the regular shop department from which the girls had come. Why was the mental attitude of the girls different in the test room from what it had been in the department? In their conversations with one another and in their comments to the observers, the girls were full of comparisons between the test room and the department, very much to the disadvantage of the latter. They felt relief from some form of constraint, particularly the constraint of supervision. They were exceedingly disparaging about the supervisors in the department, although management felt that the department had particularly good supervisory personnel. These facts suggested that the management of the company really knew very little about the attitudes which employees took toward conditions in the plant and very little also about what constituted good supervisory methods. Such was the atmosphere in which the so-called Interviewing Program, the third phase of the work at Hawthorne, was planned. So far the interests of the investigators had been centered on the question of what were good physical conditions of work. Now they shifted definitely in the direction of a study of human relations.

3. THE BANK WIRING OBSERVATION ROOM

THE FOURTH major phase of the Western Electric research on workers' attitudes and behavior was the bank wiring observation room study.[1] The following summary is taken from the report of the Committee on Work in Industry of the National Research Council. The report was written by George C. Homans and published in 1941.[2]

In order to . . . make a more detailed investigation of social relations in a working group, and to supplement interview material with direct observation of the behavior of employees, the Division of Industrial Research decided to set up a new test room. But the investigators remembered what happened in the former test room and tried to devise an experiment which would not be radically altered by the process of experimentation itself. They chose a group of men—nine wiremen, three soldermen, and two inspectors—engaged in the assembly of terminal banks for use in telephone exchanges, took them out of their regular department and placed them in a special room. Otherwise no change was made in their conditions of work, except that an investigator was installed in the room, whose duty was simply to observe the behavior of the men. In the Relay Assembly Test Room a log had been kept of the principal events of the test. At the beginning it consisted largely of comments made by the workers in answer to questions about their physical condition. Later it came to include a much wider range of entries, which were found to be extremely useful in interpreting the changes in the output rate of the different workers. The work of the observer in the new test room was in effect an expansion of the work of keeping the log in the old one. Finally, an interviewer was assigned to the test room; he was not, however, one of the population of the room but remained outside and interviewed the employees from time to time in the usual manner. No effort was made to get output records other than the ones ordinarily kept in the department from which the group came, since the investigators felt that such a procedure would introduce too large a change from a regular shop situation. In this way the experiment was set up which is referred to as the Bank Wiring Observation Room. It was in existence seven months, from November 1931, to May 1932.

The method of payment is the first aspect of this group which must be

---

[1] See "The Relay Assembly Test Room Experiments," pp. 168–177.

[2] Committee on Work in Industry, National Research Council, *Fatigue of Workers: Its Relation to Industrial Production* (New York: Reinhold Publishing Corp., 1941), pp. 77–86. Reproduced by permission of author and publisher.

described. It was a complicated form of group piecework. The department of which the workers in the observation room were a part was credited with a fixed sum for every unit of equipment it assembled. The amount thus earned on paper by the department every week made up the sum out of which the wages of all the men in the department were paid. Each individual was then assigned an hourly rate of pay, and he was guaranteed this amount in case he did not make at least as much on a piecework basis. The rate was based on a number of factors, including the nature of the job a worker was doing, his efficiency, and his length of service with the company. Records of the output of every worker were kept, and every six months there was a rate revision, the purpose of which was to make the hourly rates of the different workers correspond to their relative efficiency.

The hourly rate of a given employee, multiplied by the number of hours worked by him during the week, was spoken of as the daywork value of the work done by the employee. The daywork values of the work done by all the employees in the department were then added together, and the total thus obtained was subtracted from the total earnings credited to the department for the number of units of equipment assembled. The surplus, divided by the total daywork value, was expressed as a percentage. Each individual's hourly rate was then increased by this percentage, and the resulting hourly earnings figure, multiplied by the number of hours worked, constituted that person's weekly earnings.

Another feature of the system should be mentioned here. Sometimes a stoppage which was beyond the control of the workers took place in the work. For such stoppages the workers were entitled to claim time out, being paid at their regular hourly rates for this time. This was called the "daywork allowance claim." The reason why the employees were paid their hourly rate for such time and not their average hourly wages was a simple one. The system was supposed to prevent stalling. The employees could earn more by working than they could by taking time out. As a matter of fact, there was no good definition of what constituted a stoppage which was beyond the control of the workers. All stoppages were more or less within their control. But this circumstance was supposed to make no difference in the working of the system, since the assumption was that in any case the workers, pursuing their economic interests, would be anxious to keep stoppages at a minimum.

This system of payment was a complicated one, but it is obvious that there was a good logical reason for every one of its features. An individual's earnings would be affected by changes in his rate or in his output and by changes in the output of the group as a whole. The only way in which the group as a whole could increase its earnings was by increasing its total output. It is obvious also that the experts who designed the system made certain implicit assumptions about the behavior of human beings, or at least the behavior of workers in a large American factory. They assumed that every employee would pursue his economic interest by trying to increase not only his own output but the output of every other person in the group. The group as a whole would act to prevent slacking by any of its members. One possibility, for instance, was that by a few weeks' hard work an employee could establish a high rate for himself. Then he could slack up and be paid out of all proportion with the amount he actually contributed to the wages of the group. Under these circumstances, the other employees were expected to bring pressure to bear to make him work harder.

Such was the way in which the wage incentive scheme ought to have worked. The next question is how it actually did work. At first the workers were naturally suspicious of the observer, but when they got used to him and found that nothing out of the ordinary happened as a result of his presence in the room, they came to take him for granted. The best evidence that the employees were not distrustful of the observer is that they were willing to talk freely to him about what they were doing, even when what they were doing was not strictly in accord with what the company expected. Conversation would die down when the group chief entered the room, and when the foreman or the assistant foreman entered everyone became serious. But no embarrassment was felt at the presence of the observer. To avoid misunderstanding, it is important to point out that the observer was in no sense a spy. The employees were deliberately and obviously separated from their regular department. The observer did not, and could not, pass himself off as one of them. And if only from the fact that a special interviewer was assigned to them, the members of the group knew they were under investigation.

The findings reached by the observer were more detailed but in general character the same as those which had emerged from the early interviews of other groups. Among the employees in the observation room there was a notion of a proper day's work. They felt that if they had wired two equipments a day they had done about the right amount. Most of the work was done in the morning. As soon as the employees felt sure of being able to finish what they considered enough for the day, they slacked off. This slacking off was naturally more marked among the faster than among the slower workmen.

As a result, the output graph from week to week tended to be a straight line. The employees resorted to two further practices in order to make sure that it should remain so. They reported more or less output than they performed and they claimed more daywork allowances than they were entitled to. At the end of the day, the observer would make an actual count of the number of connections wired—something which was not done by the supervisors—and he found that the men would report to the group chief sometimes more and sometimes less work than they actually had accomplished. At the end of the period of observation, two men had completed more than they ever had reported, but on the whole the error was in the opposite direction. The theory of the employees was that excess work produced on one day should be saved and applied to a deficiency on another day. The other way of keeping the output steady was to claim excessive daywork allowance. The employees saw that the more daywork they were allowed the less output they would have to maintain in order to keep the average hourly output rate steady. The claims for daywork allowance were reported by the men to their group chief, and he, as will be seen, was in no position to make any check. These practices had two results. In the first place, the departmental efficiency records did not represent true efficiency, and therefore decisions as to grading were subject to errors of considerable importance. In the second place, the group chief was placed in a distinctly awkward position.

The findings of the observer were confirmed by tests which were made as a part of the investigation. Tests of intelligence, finger dexterity, and other skills were given to the workers in the room, and the results of the tests were studied in order to discover whether there was any correlation between output on the one hand and earnings, intelligence, or finger dexterity on the other. The studies showed that there was not. The output was apparently not reflecting the native intelligence or dexterity of the members of the group.

Obviously the wage incentive scheme was not working in the way it was expected to work. The next question is why it was not working. In this connection, the observer reported that the group had developed an informal social organization, such as had been revealed by earlier investigations. The foreman who selected the employees taking part in the Bank Wiring Observation Room was co-operative and had worked with the investigators before. They asked him to produce a normal group. The men he chose all came out of the same regular shop department, but they had not been closely associated in their work there. Nevertheless, as soon as they were thrown together in the observation room, friendships sprang up and soon two well-defined cliques were formed. The division into cliques showed itself in a number of ways: in mutual exclusiveness, in differences in the games played during off-hours, and so forth.

What is important here is not what divided the men in the observation room but what they had in common. They shared a common body of sentiments. A person should not turn out too much work. If he did, he was a "rate-buster." The theory was that if an excessive amount of work was turned out, the management would lower the piecework rate so that the employees would be in the position of doing more work for approximately the same pay. On the other hand, a person should not turn out too little work. If he did, he was a "chiseler"; that is, he was getting paid for work he did not do. A person should say nothing which would injure a fellow member of the group. If he did, he was a "squealer." Finally, no member of the group should act officiously.

The working group had also developed methods of enforcing respect for its attitudes. The experts who devised the wage incentive scheme assumed that the group would bring pressure to bear upon the slower workers to make them work faster and so increase the earnings of the group. In point of fact, something like the opposite occurred. The employees brought pressure to bear not upon the slower workers but upon the faster ones, the very ones who contributed most to the earnings of the group. The pressure was brought to bear in various ways. One of them was "binging." If one of the employees did something which was not considered quite proper, one of his fellow workers had the right to "bing" him. Binging consisted of hitting him a stiff blow on the upper arm. The person who was struck usually took the blow without protest and did not strike back. Obviously the virtue of binging as punishment did not lie in the physical hurt given to the worker but in the mental hurt that came from knowing that the group disapproved of what he had done. Other practices which naturally served the same end were sarcasm and the use of invectives. If a person turned out too much work, he was called names, such as "Speed King" or "The Slave."

It is worth while pointing out that the output of the group was not considered low. If it had been, some action might have been taken, but in point of fact it was perfectly satisfactory to the management. It was simply not so high as it would have been if fatigue and skill had been the only limiting factors.

In the matter of wage incentives, the actual situation was quite different from the assumptions made by the experts. Other activities were out of line in the same way. The wiremen and the soldermen did not stick to their jobs; they frequently traded them. This was forbidden, on the theory that each employee ought to do his own work because he was more skilled in that work. There was also much informal helping of one man by others. In fact, the observation of this practice was one means of determining the cliques into which the group was divided. A great many things, in short, were going on in the observation room which ought not to have been going on. For this reason it was important that no one should "squeal" on the men.

A group chief was in immediate charge of the employees. He had to see that they were supplied with parts and that they conformed to the rules and standards of the work. He could reprimand them for misbehavior or poor performance. He transmitted orders to the men and brought their requests before the proper authorities. He was also responsible for reporting to the foreman all facts which ought to come to his attention. The behavior of the employees put him in an awkward position. He was perfectly well aware of the devices by which they maintained their production at a constant level. But he was able to do very little to bring about a change. For instance, there was the matter of claims for daywork allowance. Such claims were supposed to be based on stoppages beyond the control of the workers, but there was no good definition of what constituted such stoppages. The men had a number of possible excuses for claiming daywork allowance: defective materials, poor and slow work on the part of other employees, and so forth. If the group chief checked up on one type of claim, the workers could shift to another. In order to decide whether or not a particular claim was justified, he would have to stand over the group all day with a stop watch. He did not have time to do that, and in any case refusal to honor the employees' claims would imply doubt of their integrity and would arouse their hostility. The group chief was a representative of management and was supposed to look after its interests. He ought to have put a stop to these practices and reported them to the foreman. But if he did so, he would, to use the words of a short account of the observation room by Roethlisberger and Dickson, "lose sympathetic control of his men, and his duties as supervisor would become much more difficult."[3] He had to associate with the employees from day to day and from hour to hour. His task would become impossible if he had to fight a running fight with them. Placed in this situation, he chose to side with the men and report unchanged their claims for daywork. In fact there was very little else he could do, even if he wished. Moreover he was in a position to protect himself in case of trouble. The employees always had to give him a reason for any daywork claims they might make, and he entered the claims in a private record book. If anyone ever asked why so much daywork was being claimed, he could throw the blame wherever he wished. He could assert that materials had been defective or he could blame the inspectors, who were members of an outside organization. In still another respect, then, the Bank Wiring Observation Room group was not behaving as the logic of management assumed that it would behave.

Restriction of output is a common phenomenon of industrial plants. It is usually explained as a highly logical reaction of the workers. They have increased their output, whereupon their wage rates for piecework have been reduced. They are doing more work for the same pay. They restrict their output in order to avoid a repetition of this experience. Perhaps this explanation holds good in some cases, but the findings of the Bank Wiring Observation Room suggest that it is too simple. The workers in the room were obsessed with the idea that they ought to hold their production level "even" from week to week, but they were vague as to

---

[3] F. J. Roethlisberger and W. J. Dickson, *Management and the Worker,* Business Research Studies, No. 9 (a monograph) (Boston: Division of Research, Harvard Business School, 1934). All quotations relating to the Western Electric researches are from this study as well as from the book of the same title by the same authors.

what would happen if they did not. They said that "someone" would "get them." If they turned out an unusually high output one week, that record would be taken thereafter as an example of what they could do if they tried, and they would be "bawled out" if they did not keep up to it. As a matter of fact, none of the men in the room had ever experienced a reduction of wage rates. What is more, as Roethlisberger and Dickson point out, "changes in piece rates occur most frequently where there is a change in manufacturing process, and changes in manufacturing process are made by engineers whose chief function is to reduce unit cost wherever the saving will justify the change. In some instances, changes occur irrespective of direct labor cost. Moreover, where labor is a substantial element, reduction of output tends to increase unit costs and instead of warding off a change in the piece rate may actually induce one."

What happened in the observation room could not be described as a logical reaction of the employees to the experience of rate reduction. They had in fact had no such experience. On the other hand, the investigators found that it could be described as a conflict between the technical organization of the plant and its social organization. By technical organization the investigators meant the plan, written or unwritten, according to which the Hawthorne plant was supposed to operate, and the agencies which gave effect to that plan. The plan included explicit rules as to how the men were to be paid, how they were to do their work, what their relations with their supervisors ought to be. It included also implicit assumptions on which the rules were based, one of the assumptions being that men working in the plant would on the whole act so as to further their economic interests. It is worthwhile pointing out that this assumption was in fact implicit, that the experts who devised the technical organization acted upon the assumption without ever stating it in so many words.

There existed also an actual social situation within the plant: groups of men, who were associated with one another, held common sentiments and had certain relations with other groups and other men. To some extent this social organization was identical with the technical plan and to some extent it was not. For instance, the employees were paid according to group payment plans, but the groups concerned did not behave as the planners expected them to behave.

The investigators considered the relations between the technical organization and the social. A certain type of behavior is expected of the higher levels of management. Their success is dependent on their being able to devise and institute rapid changes. Roethlisberger and Dickson describe what happens in the following terms: "Management is constantly making mechanical improvements and instituting changes designed to reduce costs or improve the quality of the product. It is constantly seeking new ways and new combinations for increasing efficiency, whether in designing a new machine, instituting a new method of control, or logically organizing itself in a new way." The assumption has often been made that these changes are designed to force the employee to do more work for less money. As a matter of fact, many of them have just the opposite purpose: to improve the conditions of work and enable the employee to earn higher wages. The important point here, however, is not the purpose of the changes but the way in which they are carried out and accepted.

Once the responsible officer has decided that a certain change ought to be made, he gives an order, and this order is transmitted "down the line," appropriate action being taken at every level. The question in which the investigatiors were interested was this: What happens when the order reaches the men who are actually doing the manual work? Roethlisberger and Dickson make the following observations: "The worker occupies a unique position in the social organization. He is at the bottom of a highly stratified organization. He is always in the position of having to accommodate himself to changes which he does not originate. Although he participates least in the technical organization, he bears the brunt of most of its activities." It is he, more than anyone, who is affected by the decisions of management, yet in the nature of things he is unable to share management's preoccupations, and management does little to convince him that what he considers important is being treated as important at the top—a fact which is not surprising, since there is no adequate way of transmitting to management an understanding of the considerations which seem important at the work level. There is something like a failure of communication in both directions—upward and downward.

The worker is not only "asked to accommodate himself to changes which he does not initiate, but also many of the changes deprive him of those very things which give meaning and significance to his work." The modern industrial worker is not the handicraftsman of the medieval guild. Nevertheless, the two have much in common. The industrial worker develops his own ways of doing his job, his own traditions of skill, his own satisfactions in living up to his standards. The spirit in which he adopts his own innovations is quite different from that in which he adopts those of management. Furthermore, he does not do his work as an isolated human being, but always as a member of a group, united either through actual co-operation on the job or through association in friendship. One of the most important general findings of the Western Electric researches is the fact that such groups are continually being formed among industrial workers, and that the groups develop codes and loyalties which govern the relations of the members to one another. Though these codes can be quickly destroyed, they are not formed in a moment. They are the product of continued, routine interaction between men. "Constant interference with such codes is bound to lead to feelings of frustration, to an irrational exasperation with technical change in any form, and ultimately to the formation of a type of employee organization such as we have described —a system of practices and beliefs in opposition to the technical organization."

The Bank Wiring Observation Room seemed to show that action taken in accordance with the technical organization tended to break up, through continual change, the routines and human associations which gave work its value. The behavior of the employees could be described as an effort to protect themselves against such changes, to give management the least possible opportunity of interfering with them. When they said that if they increased their output, "something" was likely to happen, a process of this sort was going on in their minds. But the process was not a conscious one. It is important to point out that the protective function of informal organization was not a product of deliberate planning. It was more in the nature of an automatic response. The curious thing is that, as Professor Mayo pointed out to the committee, these informal organizations much resembled formally organized labor unions, although the employees would not have recognized the fact.

Roethlisberger and Dickson summarize as follows the results of the intensive study of small groups of employees: "According to our analysis the uniformity of behavior manifested by these groups was the outcome of a disparity in the rates of change possible in the technical organization, on the one hand, and in the social organization, on the other. The social sentiments and customs of work of the employees were unable to accommodate themselves to the rapid technical innovations introduced. The result was to incite a blind resistance to all innovations and to provoke the formation of a social organization at a lower level in opposition to the technical organization."

4. CONVEYOR WORK, INTERACTION POTENTIAL, AND WORKER SATISFACTION

As A part of the Yale Studies in Technology and Industrial Relations, 202 automobile assembly line workers were interviewed for their views of talking on the job.[1] These men were all doing assembly line work that typically limited interaction in several important ways:

1. A man was required to stay in his work position, with very limited exceptions.
2. His work (while not skilled) required a steady attentiveness to co-ordinate eye and hand movements—so-called "surface mental attention."
3. His work was technologically isolated and independent of that of his adjacent fellow workers.
4. The "group" of men who were close enough for any one worker to talk to was strictly a geographical group only and was a different "group" for every man on the line.
5. Supervision generally frowned on talking and in some cases punished offenders.

These factors limited interaction primarily to the use of sign language and short shouted phrases.

The interviews indicated that the repetitiveness of the work made it all the more desirable to the workers to talk "to break the monotony." All of the 202 men interviewed had been "on the line" for at least twelve years. Even after this time, nearly 80 per cent said they liked to talk on the job; and most of them said that if all interaction was abolished, the work would become intolerable. The interviews indicated that the men resented not being able to follow conventional conversation patterns: looking at the listener, being able to pause for conversation, and completing the "talk."

The study found that the desire to talk at work correlated significantly with the attitudes (1) that the job was uninteresting and (2) that the company was not doing what it could for the workers. It also found that workers who desired to talk tended to have a better over-all work adjustment (as judged by the researchers on the basis of studying each interview as a whole) with an increase in the number of people with whom they could interact.

---

[1] Frank J. Jasinski, "Technological Delimitation of Reciprocal Relationships: A Study of Interaction Patterns in Industry," *Human Organization,* Vol. XV, No. 2 (1956).

5. WORKER SATISFACTION IN ENGLISH AUTOMOBILE PLANTS

IN 1946 and 1947, extensive interviews were conducted with employees of two English automobile factories and one steel mill.[1] Among many other factors, these studies gave evidence on the relation between

Exhibit 1*

FACTORIES A AND B

RELATION BETWEEN SATISFACTION AND TYPE OF WORK

Assessments of Satisfaction	Conveyor Operations				Nonconveyor Operations							
					Line Work				Individual Work			
	A		B		A		B		A		B	
	No. of Men	Per Cent	No. of Men	Per Cent	No. of Men	Per Cent	No. of Men	Per Cent	No. of Men	Per Cent	No. of Men	Per Cent
++	8	18.6	33	19.5	55	28.2	9	30.0	32	31.4	6	33.3
+	15	34.9	58	34.3	85	43.6	13	43.3	44	43.1	9	50.0
0	13	30.2	54	32.0	41	21.0	7	23.3	17	16.7	3	16.7
−	6	14.0	21	12.4	13	6.7	1	3.3	8	7.8	0	0.0
− −	1	2.3	3	1.8	1	0.5	0	0.0	1	1.0	0	0.0
All categories....	43	100.0	169	100.0	195	100.0	30	99.9	102	100.0	18	100.0
Index of satisfaction.....	0.53		0.57		0.92		1.00		0.96		1.17	

* S. Wyatt and R. Marriott, *A Study of Attitudes to Factory Work* (London: Medical Research Council, 1956), p. 12.

Exhibit 2*

FACTORIES A AND B

NUMBER AND PERCENTAGE OF MEN ON CONVEYOR AND NONCONVEYOR OPERATIONS WHO SPOKE ABOUT INTEREST AND MONOTONY

Subject	Conveyor Operations				Nonconveyor Operations							
					Line Work				Individual Work			
	A (43 Men)		B (169 Men)		A (195 Men)		B (30 Men)		A (102 Men)		B (18 Men)	
	No.	Per Cent	No.	Per Cent	No.	Per Cent	No.	Per Cent	No.	Per Cent	No.	Per Cent
Interest..............	15	34.9	58	34.3	109	55.9	17	56.7	68	66.7	17	94.4
Monotony............	23	53.5	93	55.0	82	42.1	11	36.7	40	39.2	5	27.8

* S. Wyatt and R. Marriott, *A Study of Attitudes to Factory Work* (London: Medical Research Council, 1956)' p. 20.

[1] S. Wyatt and R. Marriott, *A Study of Attitudes to Factory Work* (London: Medical Research Council, 1956).

185

conveyor work and worker satisfaction. Exhibit 1 shows the over-all satisfaction scores for conveyor and nonconveyor work in the two automobile plants. Exhibit 2 indicates the workers who specifically talked about either the intrinsic interest of the job or the monotony of the job. Exhibit 3 shows the effect on satisfaction in one factory of longer job cycle times for the conveyorized work of body fitting.

Exhibit 3*

FACTORY B

RELATION BETWEEN CYCLE TIME AND SATISFACTION WITH THE
OPERATION (BODY FITTING)

Cycle Time of Operation (Minutes)	Number of Men Performing Operation	Number of Men Giving Each Assessment					Index of Satisfaction
		++	+	0	−	− −	
10 or less.....	17	1	5	8	2	1	0.18
11–20.........	20	5	4	4	5	2	0.25
21–30.........	21	3	6	8	4	0	0.38
31–40.........	18	1	7	9	1	0	0.44
41–50.........	6	3	1	2	0	0	1.17

* S. Wyatt and R. Marriott, *A Study of Attitudes to Factory Work* (London: Medical Research Council, 1956), p. 23.

6. GROUP MEMBERSHIP, SATISFACTION, AND PRODUCTIVITY

AN INTENSIVE study of a department of some fifty workers in a small to medium-sized manufacturing company in 1954–55 explored the relationships between organizational environment, personal characteristics, types of group membership, satisfaction, and productivity.[1] Satisfaction and productivity were primarily determined by position in the informal social organization, which in turn was mainly related to *status* (the degree to which an individual's activities and characteristics realized the group's norms and values) and *status congruence* (the extent to which the various components of status were "in line" with each other).

The members of the department were men and women of different ages, lengths of service, pay categories, and ethnic backgrounds, engaged in light machining and assembly of two product lines. The department foreman was regarded as friendly, fair, and helpful; he did not violate the values and informal leadership patterns which existed within the department. Although little interaction or group activity was required by the work itself, there were many nonjob activities which were related to the existing social organization, such as coffee groupings, card games, savings clubs, and pools.

The research design required formulation and testing of a number of hypotheses concerning relationships between job-related and nonjob-related interaction and activity, social and personal background, group membership and leadership, satisfaction, and productivity. When the predicted relationships were found not to exist, revised hypotheses were formulated for more systematic testing in further research.

Some of the relationships between the variables studied which appeared in this department and which might be found to exist also in other similar work groups were as follows:

A. Determinants of group membership
    1. The higher the total status and the higher the status congruence, the more likely was an individual to be a regular group member

---

[1] A. Zaleznik, C. R. Christensen, and F. J. Roethlisberger, *The Motivation, Productivity, and Satisfaction of Workers: A Prediction Study* (Boston: Division of Research, Harvard Business School, 1958).

(i.e., member of a subgroup with high prestige which shares the values of the larger group).

2. The lower the total status, regardless of the status congruence, the more likely was an individual to be a deviant group member (i.e., member of a subgroup with low prestige which violates the values of the larger group).

3. The higher the total status and the lower the status congruence, the more likely was an individual to be an isolate.

4. Individuals who were identified with the (dominant) in-group value(s) (in this case, Irish ethnicity) were likely to become regular group members.

5. Individuals with high status and high status congruence who were members of work groups with high status and high status congruence tended to become informal leaders.

B. Determinants of productivity and satisfaction

1. Productivity and satisfaction were related to group membership; they were not related to the rewards (pay and job status) an individual received from management.

2. Regular group members tended to be satisfied and to conform to the group norms of productivity and to management's expectations; they were "on the line" producers.

3. Nonregular group members (deviants and isolates) tended to be less satisfied and not to conform to the group's norms.

4. Nonregulars whose personal background and aspirations led them to identify positively with the group tended to produce below the group's norms.

5. Nonregulars whose personal background and aspirations led them to identify negatively with the group tended to produce above the group's norms.

7. WORK GROUP BEHAVIOR IN RESTAURANTS

A FIELD study of organizational behavior in large urban restaurants was conducted in 1944–45.[1] Twelve restaurants were studied intensively; interviews were conducted in thirteen others.

Perhaps the most important single finding was that people working in a restaurant did in fact form a social organization and that existing relationships and the standing of individuals in this organization had a very important bearing on customer service and efficiency, satisfaction, and morale of both workers and supervisors.

It was discovered, for instance, that where the required activities and interactions placed low-status workers (waitresses, runners) in a position of initiating action on higher status workers (countermen, cooks), the almost inevitable result was conflict, resistance, and poor service. Examples of this were countermen who resented being rushed by waitresses (as opposed to waiters) or cooks who resented being told that the serving pantry needed a particular item when the person telling them this happened to be a bus boy sent down from the pantry with the message.

The development of social groups, Whyte found, was a primary need of restaurant employees. Where well-integrated social cliques existed, and where supervisors recognized the need of employees to be members of such cliques, absenteeism and turnover were minimized. These cliques tended to form around members of the same age, sex, and outside interests; and employees who were older than the average or who did not identify with the interests of the majority often found themselves isolated and eventually left to seek employment elsewhere.

Whyte also noted that "the worker's job performance, the incentives he has for working and his relations with fellow workers and with management are all influenced by his status and the direction of his mobility." For instance, "a young girl from a lower class city or rural home who goes to work in a restaurant of high social standing" has increased her status and thus may be termed "upward mobile." Her status in the social system of the restaurant, however, is relatively low (young, no experience, no seniority); and while the job may be a "good one" to her in terms of her previous background, she will still be responded to

---

[1] William F. Whyte, *Human Relations in the Restaurant Industry* (New York: McGraw-Hill Book Co., Inc., 1948).

by other workers and supervisors in terms consistent with her low status in the social organization. If this response is not friendly, and if at the same time her relationship with customers is not a good one, the combined pressures are apt to be too much for her, and she will be subject to crying fits or will quit.

8. PRODUCTIVITY AND SOCIAL BEHAVIOR IN A SELLING GROUP

A STUDY was made over a period of four years of a group of salesmen in a large retail furniture store that catered primarily to lower class customers.[1] The study focused on the emergent structure of the group, the outside reference groups that salesmen identified with, and the sales volume of the different salesmen.

The 22 men in the group were paid a base weekly salary and in addition a 3 per cent commission on all sales made after they had met a monthly sales quota. The annual pay of the 22 men ranged from $6,000 to $10,000. When the 22 men were ranked according to their sales volume over a full year, there was no apparent difference between the top-producing 11 and the bottom 11 in terms of age, job seniority, formal education, or liking for the job. All of the men saw the job as a "dead end" in regard to promotion, and all but two gave "money" as the chief advantage of selling as a career.

The group had developed norms against salesmen engaging in a variety of practices to make sales at the expense of other salesmen, and against "snitching" to management. For the most part, all the salesmen (including the high producers) indicated in interviews that high production was achieved by violating these norms. The researcher's next problem was to discover why so many salesmen were able persistently to violate the norms in spite of the group's hostility and ostracism. To address this question, the salesmen were asked to give the name and occupation of outside friends. Eight salesmen named friends of higher status than themselves. Seven of these eight men were among the top eight producers, and the eighth was ranked twenty-first. It was expected that if these eight were violators of the group norms, they would be rejected and disliked by the group. In fact, these eight were observed to be objects of hostility for 39 persons, while the other 14 were rejected by only six persons. The same pattern held for responses to the question of selecting "best-liked" and "least-liked" people. The eight were named as best liked only seven times, while the other 14 received 61 choices. The eight were named "least liked" 38 times and the other 14 only 14 times.

---

[1] C. J. French, "Correlates of Success in Retail Selling," *American Journal of Sociology*, Vol. LXVI, No. 2 (1960).

The author concludes:

By all measures used, then, these eight men who named friends more highly placed than themselves were the most rejected, and rejecting, members of the sales group. If naming highly placed friends indicated that they had taken as a reference group people placed higher than their present occupation (and consequently higher than their present work group), then the reference group was the factor most highly associated with production. Since high production depended upon one's willingness to violate norms, and those whose reference group was higher than salesmen felt the least obliged to observe the norms of their fellow workers, whom they probably looked upon as inferior, they had, as it were, an advantage.

The salesman's position in the informal structure and his productivity were both closely related to conformity. Efforts on the part of the sales group to compel conformity were ineffective in the case of persons who could resist informal pressures. The informal controls could not expel the violator, and the norm against "snitching" prevented the group from invoking the formal controls of the management. In fact, efforts at social control seemed to make the situation worse. The effectiveness of the informal controls depended upon the individual's identifying himself with the sales group but, the more he encountered hostility and rejection, the less likely was he to acquire identification. Unethical practice—as the group defined it—then became easier for him, and his sales productivity increased.

9. GROUP COHESIVENESS, ANXIETY, AND PRODUCTIVITY

IN 1950 a study was conducted in a heavy machinery company of the relation between work group cohesiveness (defined as attraction to the group or resistance to leaving it) and various measures of anxiety and productivity.[1] The employees involved were 93 per cent male, varied in age, mostly married, and relatively well educated. Pencil-and-paper questionnaire responses were analyzed for 228 work groups with a total of 5,871 members.

For each group an "index of cohesiveness" was constructed, based on members' responses to the following questions:

Do you feel that you are really a part of your work group?

If you had a chance to do the same kind of work for the same pay, in another work group, how would you feel about moving?

How does your work group compare with other work groups . . . on each of the following points: the way the men get along together, the way the men stick together, the way the men help each other out on the job?

This measure of group cohesiveness was then correlated with measures of productivity, of work-related anxiety, of factors hypothesized to facilitate cohesiveness, and of feelings of "supportiveness" by the company (e.g., the degree of favorable attitude toward the company as a place to work and the perceived extent of the foreman's interest in his men). The major findings follow.

Work-Related Anxiety

Members of high cohesive groups were significantly less likely than members of low cohesive groups to report (1) feeling "jumpy" or "nervous"; (2) feeling under pressure for higher production (except that for groups with *low* actual productivity, feelings of pressure *increased* with high cohesiveness); (3) feeling lack of "supportiveness" by the company; (4) feeling unable to "get along" when too old to work. Relationships between cohesiveness and other measures of anxiety were also in the predicted direction, although less significant.

---

[1] S. F. Seashore, *Group Cohesiveness in the Industrial Work Group* (Ann Arbor: Survey Research Center, University of Michigan, 1954).

193

Productivity Standards

There was less variability in actual productivity *within* high cohesive groups than within low cohesive groups. There was greater variability in actual productivity *between* high cohesive groups than between low cohesive groups. Among groups which scored high in "company supportiveness," greater cohesiveness was associated with a higher perceived reasonable level of productivity (the group's idea of "a fair day's work.") Among groups with less favorable attitudes toward foreman and company, greater cohesiveness was associated with a lower perceived reasonable level of productivity. The same relationship between cohesiveness, company support, and productivity standards was obtained in the case of the *actual* level of productivity, although in this case the relationship was most significant when "company supportiveness" was measured by attitudes toward the union. (A favorable attitude toward the union was assumed to indicate a lack of "company support.") In other words, high cohesive groups tended toward higher than average actual productivity when attitudes toward the union were unfavorable, and toward lower than average productivity when attitudes toward the union were favorable.

Conditions Facilitating Group Cohesiveness

Cohesiveness was positively related to perceived job prestige; e.g., the higher the group's cohesiveness, the more likely were its members to report that their jobs ranked "better than most" in the plant. Cohesiveness was positively related to length of service; high cohesive groups had more members with over three years' service than low cohesive groups. There was a significant relationship between cohesiveness and group size; cohesiveness generally decreased as size increased up to about twenty-five members. (There was no significant relationship between cohesiveness and similarity in age and educational level.)

The author's major conclusion was that greater group cohesiveness is associated with less anxiety, with higher productivity when confidence in management is high, and with lower productivity when this confidence is lacking.

10. SOCIOMETRICALLY SELECTED WORK TEAMS, PRODUCTIVITY, AND TURNOVER

Two groups of carpenters and bricklayers composed of 38 and 36 members were experimentally given a chance to express their first three preferences for a work partner.[1] The work assignments of the men were then rearranged to conform to these preferences—first into mutual-choice teams of two; then, when technically necessary, these pairs were combined into larger work teams. Twenty-two workers received their first choice as partners, 28 their second, and 16 their third. The eight remaining isolates (nonchosen) were paired. A few adjustments in team assignments were made during the course of the experiment, mostly initiated by workers, and mostly made in the first two months. The results in terms of costs and turnover are summarized in Exhibit 1.

Exhibit 1

Variable	Mean	Standard Deviation	Critical Ratio
1. *Turnover:*			3.69
a) Before experimental period (9 months)...	3.11	1.03	
b) During experimental period (20 months)..	0.27	0.23	
2. *Labor cost index—per row of housing units:*			27.75
a) Engineers' prior estimate...............	37.20		
b) Before experimental period (9 months)...	36.66	0.52	
c) During experimental period (20 months)..	32.22	0.67	
3. *Materials cost index—per row of housing units:*			13.16
a) Engineers' prior estimate...............	33.50		
b) Before experimental period.............	33.00	0.57	
c) After experimental period.............	31.00	0.56	

The author reported he could find no other changes that could in any way account for the changes in performance.

[1] R. H. Van Zelst, "Sociometrically Selected Work Teams Increase Productivity," *Personnel Psychology*, Vol. V, No. 3 (1952).

11. EXPERIMENTAL REORGANIZATIONS IN AN INDIAN TEXTILE PLANT

DURING 1953 and 1954, two major experimental reorganizations were carried out in two different weaving rooms, one using automatic looms and the other nonautomatic looms, of the Ahmedabad Manufacturing and Calico Printing Company with the consulting assistance of personnel from the Tavistock Institute of Human Relations, London, England. The purpose was to improve over-all results along such lines as costs, quality, worker earnings, satisfaction, etc.

The first experiment[1] involved the recombination of several different jobs on a group of 224 automatic looms. The pre-experimental arrangement called for each weaver to handle 24 to 32 looms; each battery filler, 40 to 50 looms; each smash hand, 60 to 80 looms; each jobber, gater, etc., 112 looms; and each bobbin carrier, oiler, etc., 224 looms. The experimental reorganized arrangement combined twelve jobs into three jobs and set up seven-man teams to perform these jobs for a group of 64 looms. The ratio of looms per worker was increased from 7.7 to 9.1.

In the second reorganization[2] the pre-experimental arrangement was for one weaver to handle almost all of the operations required to run two nonautomatic looms. Management was particularly interested in improving the quality of the product. The experiment introduced eleven-man teams containing five different job classifications that operated a group of forty looms.

In terms only of job assignment and work organization, the two experiments might seem to be moving in different directions: less division of labor in automatic weaving and more division of labor on the nonautomatic looms. However, for the researcher a single set of propositions about worker behavior guided both experimental changes. These propositions, which emphasized the desirability of conceiving of workers not as separate individuals but as members of small work groups, were summarized by Rice as follows:

> 1. Irrespective of wages and working conditions, a work group will derive satisfaction from the efficient organization and performance

---

[1] A. K. Rice, "Productivity and Social Organization in an Indian Weaving Shed," *Human Relations,* Vol. VI, No. 4 (1953).

[2] *Idem,* "The Experimental Reorganization of Non-Automatic Weaving in an Indian Mill," *Human Relations,* Vol. VIII, No. 3 (1955).

of the task for which it has been organized, and an inefficient organization or performance will diminish the chances of satisfaction. A work group should therefore have neither more nor fewer members than can efficiently complete a given task.

2. Since task completion is believed to be an important source of satisfaction, a work group should be of such a size that its members can experience, so far as is practicable, the completion of a "whole" task.

3. When individual tasks performed by members of a work group are interdependent, the relationships between those performing the tasks will have important effects on productivity. A work group should therefore provide its members with satisfactory interpersonal relationships.

4. Since practical self-government can provide satisfaction for group members, a work group should have control over its own day-to-day work and organization; that is, its "governing system" should be internally structured.

5. The coincidence of obvious physical and activity boundaries enables a work group to identify itself with its own "territory"; and as a corollary, groups of workers "owning their territory" are more likely to form internally structured, stable, and cohesive group relationships than those in indeterminate or overlapping territories.

6. The range of skills required of group members should be such that all of them can comprehend all the skills and, without necessarily having or wanting to have these skills, could all aspire toward their acquisition.

7. The fewer differences there are in work group status (and pay) consistent with offering opportunities for promotion, the more likely is the internal structure of a group to stabilize itself, and the more likely are its members to accept internal leadership.

8. When individual members of small work groups become disaffected to the extent that they can no longer fit into their work group, they need, if group stability is to be maintained, to be able to move to other small work groups engaged on similar tasks.

Both experiments changed not only the division of labor, but also involved the simplification and clarification of the formal structure of supervision, the adoption of more "permissive and collaborative relationships" between the workers and management, and changes in the payment system.

Both experiments were judged highly successful by management. In the first experiment, loom efficiency moved from an average of 79.8 to 95 per cent, and the cloth damage rate fell from 31.8 to 19.9 per cent. In the second experiment, while worker earnings increased 90 per cent, the labor cost index only moved from 100 to 117, while the production index moved from 100 to 121. The quality change was difficult to measure, but there was general agreement that quality was significantly improved.[3]

---

[3] For a follow-up study of the first experiment, see A. K. Rice, "Productivity and Social Organization in an Indian Weaving Mill: II," *Human Relations.* Vol. VIII, No. 1 (1955). Both experiments, and related changes in management organization, are described in detail in *idem, Productivity and Social Organization: The Ahmedabad Experiment* (London: Tavistock Publications, Ltd., 1958).

12. ORGANIZATIONAL SYSTEMS AND ENGINEERING GROUPS: A COMPARATIVE STUDY OF TWO TECHNICAL GROUPS IN INDUSTRY

THE RESEARCH reported by Barnes[1] compares two engineering groups in two different industrial organizations. Each group was an engineering department in a fairly large manufacturing company. The two departments are referred to as Departments A and B and their organizations as Companies A and B. Companies A and B formed the organizational systems within which Departments A and B functioned.

The research consisted of identifying and describing the organizational system for each department, then in exploring and comparing the relationship between each system and the backgrounds, behavior, performance, and satisfaction of each group's members. To aid in this task, the author proposed certain hypotheses and predictions to be tested with data from each department.

The research began in Company A. Its organizational system, within which Department A members worked, is described as a *relatively closed* system because Company A's management, including Supervisor A, tended to stress management controls and (1) relatively low member autonomy, (2) low opportunities for interaction, and (3) low upward influence. Addressing this relatively closed system, the author framed an initial hypothesis proposing that individual members would behave according to the values and norms of their dominant value system or reference group. It was predicted that individuals who identified themselves with either (1) their profession (Professionals), (2) the organization (Organizationals), or (3) familial-religious values (Socials) would behave according to that particular reference group's values and norms. Consequently, the hypothesis states that *an individual behaves in accord with the values and norms of his dominant reference group.* The predictions proposed that:

1. Professionals tend toward relatively low nonwork activities, low interactions, and low mutual friendships as they strive to attain the values of science, e.g., truth and knowledge.
2. Organizationals tend toward relatively high nonwork activities, high interactions, and high mutual friendships as they strive to

---

[1] L. B. Barnes, *Organizational Systems and Engineering Groups: A Comparative Study of Two Technical Groups in Industry* (Boston: Division of Research, Harvard Business School, Harvard University, 1960).

attain the values of the organization, e.g., promotion, organizational prestige, and social acceptance.

3. Socials tend toward relatively high nonwork activities, high interactions, and low mutual friendships as they strive to attain the values of good group membership, e.g., popularity and acceptance by higher status groups.

The Department A findings showed that Professionals tended to rank low on nonwork activities, interactions, and mutual friendships. Organizationals ranked high. Socials (mostly technicians) tended to behave more according to age level than according to reference group affiliation. Younger Socials tended to behave more like Organizationals. Older Socials tended to behave more like Professionals.

Beyond these initial predictions, Professionals tended toward highest engineering performance and toward lowest satisfaction. Organizationals tended toward highest satisfaction, though ranking lower in job performance than Professionals. Socials tended toward higher satisfaction than Professionals, though their job performance was ranked lowest in the department, since most were technicians.

At this time the research moved beyond Department A hypothesis testing and toward more divergent explorations with several intriguing questions. These were:

1. What other factors besides an organizational system and its leadership help to explain Department A's polarized reference groups and social structure?

2. What would an engineering group look like in a more open organizational system? What hypotheses and predictions could be formulated for comparing relatively open and closed systems?

To answer the first question, the author explored the relationships between a department member's status characteristics and his reference group and social structure positions. To answer the second question, the author sought and found in Company B "a company which seemed to offer a more open organizational system. As we have noted already, it cannot be rigorously compared with Company A, but in this imperfect world, Company B was the closest we came to finding both a relatively open system and a roughly comparable organizational situation."

Before Company B was selected, however, six hypotheses were proposed comparing relatively open and relatively closed organizational systems. These hypotheses were each accompanied by specific predictions. The hypotheses read:

1. Dissimilar value emphases in a group are more apt to lead to polarization of reference group identification and accompanying be-

havior patterns in relatively closed than in relatively open organizational systems.

2. Job and social status positions are more apt to govern or dominate a person's behavior and job performance levels in relatively closed than in relatively open organizational systems.
3. The nature of an organizational system (i.e., relatively closed or relatively open) affects a group's social structure.
4. The nature of an organizational system affects a group's interaction patterns.
5. The nature of an organizational system affects the perceived job opportunities, job challenges, and satisfactions of group members.
6. Social structure position is less highly related to performance in relatively open than in relatively closed organizational systems.

These hypotheses and their accompanying predictions were designed to test some causes and consequences of a more open organizational system. Department B existed within an organizational system whose management and supervisor actively encouraged high autonomy, interactions beyond those required by the job, and *mutual* influence between status levels. At the same time, the company's vice president of manufacturing noted that:

> Department B does an excellent job of getting its work out. . . . I suppose that if there is any single group in the company that is working over their own heads, beyond their own capacities, it would be those people. That isn't bad either, of course, because they are in a position where they are reaching out for something, always trying to do a little more and a little better than their capabilities permit. It is the only way they can grow.

The research findings in Department B generally supported the hypotheses and predictions. The relatively open system apparently helped create a less rigid social structure, less status consciousness, and higher satisfaction. Though productivity patterns could not be compared with any real accuracy, management and customer productivity expectations were better met in Department B than in Department A.

In the final chapters of the book, the research explores other differences that emerged between Departments A and B. To begin with, formal education as a status factor differed in importance in the two departments. In addition, the research showed different degrees of status congruence in Departments A and B. Finally, the two organizational structures affected the ways in which individuals behaved and worked in each department. In all three cases, these factors tended to reinforce each department's organizational system.

13. THE COMPARATIVE EFFECTIVENESS OF GROUPS AND INDIVIDUALS IN SOLVING PROBLEMS

Douglas R. Bunker and Gene W. Dalton

FOR A NUMBER of years various researchers have been studying the problem-solving effectiveness of groups as compared with individuals working by themselves. A review of this literature suggests the carefully qualified conclusion that certain kinds of groups can be more effective than individuals in solving certain kinds of problems. This quibbling statement is derived from both the variety of substantive findings reported and a recognition of some of the methodological limitations of these studies in providing generalizable conclusions which apply to natural groups dealing with "real" problems.

The Task as a Variable

It is characteristic of research on group-versus-individual problem solving for the experimenter to impose a task with clearly defined work rules and a standard, quantifiable criterion of success. The nature of the task is critical to the type of research results obtained. If its performance requires merely the pooling of additive bits of information until some fixed quantity is achieved, then groups will routinely do "better" than individuals. If, conversely, the task requires a division of labor in which the performances of all group members are linked in series, then the group can do no better than the performance of its poorest member— the weak-link phenomenon. Both types of studies are reported in the literature, but neither directly represents the work of a group *qua* group.

One early experiment reported by Thorndike[1] illustrates both the methods and typical results from research focusing on task differences. The principal hypothesis tested in this study was that greater group superiority will be associated with tasks which require a greater range of responses. This tended to be confirmed across a series of different tests in which it was indicated that the superiority of groups increased as you moved from a task involving the choice of a response from among several given alternatives to task requiring production of a free response to fit fixed criteria. One of Thorndike's tasks which did not directly fit

---

[1] R. L. Thorndike, "On What Type of Task Will a Group Do Well," *Journal of Abnormal and Social Psychology*, Vol. 33 (1938), pp. 409–13.

with his other results confirming the hypothesis is independently illuminating. He found that groups were superior to individuals in *solving* a crossword puzzle, but that individuals were more efficient in *constructing* a crossword puzzle. In solving a puzzle, success is facilitated by the production of a profusion of alternative responses, for they can be immediately and objectively tested for fit, and while incorrect responses are sifted out, correct responses accumulate toward a complete solution. In constructing a puzzle, however, clear-cut, simple criteria of success are not available. Responses cannot simply accumulate toward a successful solution by a process of gradual confirmation. The task is more complex, requiring that many things be kept simultaneously in mind and developed as an integrated whole. The group product, Thorndike reports, "frequently amounted to nothing but the best individual performance of a member of the group, turned in for the group."

In making the point that the efficiency of groups for problem solving depends somewhat on the task, let us keep in mind that the types of tasks for which individual and group performance differences have been explored cover only a limited range of the types of work requirements which groups must meet in organizational settings. In experimental studies the group goal is generally given, while in real-life situations goal formation is an important and demanding aspect of group work. Continuing work groups also frame policy, develop strategies, solve technical problems, and devise tactics for the implementation of group decisions. Such work is qualitatively different from the purely intellectual process involved in solving or constructing crossword puzzles.

Group Superiority—Majority Rule or Discussion

In a more recent experimental study Barnlund[2] not only compared the problem-solving abilities of individuals compared with groups, but also developed a number of clues as to what tends to enable experimental groups to secure superior results. Is it because the superior individual supplies the correct answer to the group, because the simple majority of the answers of individuals working alone provides a superior answer, or is it because of the problem-solving qualities of an open discussion within the group? To explore these questions, Barnlund used a complex intellectual task involving the ability to draw logical conclusions from given arguments. Individuals receiving similar scores when working alone on the first half of the test were assigned to the same experimental groups so that the factor on individual differences in ability would be reduced to a minimum. The experimental group then, using discussion,

---

[2] Dean C. Barnlund, "A Comparative Study of Individual, Majority, and Group Judgment," *Journal of Abnormal and Social Psychology*, Vol. 58, No. 1 (January, 1959).

worked out the second half of the test in the same amount of time allowed for the first half. This procedure allowed comparisons between three problem-solving methods, (1) individual work, (2) "group" results determined by mathematically tallying the majority decision of each experimental group's members working alone, and (3) group results under discussion conditions. The results indicated that:

1. Majority decisions, when deadlocks are evenly divided between right and wrong answers, are not significantly different from those made by the average individual and are inferior to those of the best member of the group working alone.
2. Group decisions, reached through cooperative deliberation, are significantly superior to decisions made by individual members working alone and to majority rule.

In order to throw additional light on these findings some of the group discussion sessions were recorded and analyzed for clues to the psychological factors affecting the high level of group performance. Barnlund reported that the following factors were contributing to group success:

Membership in the experimental groups produced a higher level of interest in the successful completion of the task. Members concentrated more intently on the assigned problems after being appointed to a group than they did when solving the problems individually. Group members found themselves more and more deeply involved as they proposed, and were forced to defend, their ideas. Participants identified with their own groups to such a degree that when some members became fatigued, others urged them to continue working.

Membership in the experimental groups had an inhibiting as well as facilitating effect. Knowledge that one's opinions were to be shared publicly made group members more cautious and deliberate in their own thinking. The necessity of explaining a conclusion forced many students to be more self-critical. Errors that might have been committed privately were checked before they were communicated to others.

Groups had greater critical resources than did individuals working alone. In spite of the uniform level of ability, group members saw different issues and a larger number of issues than did a single person working alone. A greater number of viewpoints increased the group's chances of selecting a valid one. Even the poorest members contributed significantly to the quality of the group product. Remarks that went no deeper than "I don't understand" or "That's absurd" often saved the group from error by forcing others to justify their opinions and in so doing disprove their own conclusions.

A more objective view of the problem resulted from competition between the private prejudices of group members. The test arguments were stated in loaded terms designed to make the choices between conclusions as difficult as possible. Each individual, however, brought a different set of values to his group. When arguments were stated so they appealed to persons of one persuasion, those in opposition were anxious to detect their error. In this way, liberals counteracted conservatives, Republicans offset Democrats, and "independents" guarded against critical lapses on the part of fraternity members. Groups were forced to become more objective, and this, of course, increased their chances of drawing valid conclusions. The significance of this one factor alone would be hard to overestimate.

Discussion of the test items also prevented other incidental mistakes from occurring. Some groups had to check their instructions several times because members had different interpretations of them. Discussion often led to a clarification of terms used in the test, and, where logical fallacies spring from ambiguous terms, this may account for some of the gains. A number of groups formulated general principles as they went along to help them avoid repeating errors in later problems.

What, then, prevented experimental groups from attaining even higher scores than they did? Analysis of the transcripts revealed two factors that together accounted for a majority of the group errors. The first was that group members agreed immediately and unanimously upon the wrong answer to a problem. Further study of the issue was then considered unnecessary and wasteful. . . . The virtue of disagreement and the possible function of a "No-Man" in group deliberations, needs further testing.

The second factor was that groups, when they reached a deadlock, were unable to use their differences of opinion for their own advantage. When conflicts became intense they were resolved by surrender of the less aggressive members or by compromising on a third solution which was almost always incorrect but served to protect the egos of the parties to the controversy. Apparently disagreement stimulates thought up to a point; beyond that point, groups may lack the patience and skill to exploit it.

Effective Groups—Experimental vs. Natural

The generalized issue of groups versus individuals as problem solvers must also include the point that groups differ in their capacity to deal effectively with problems. One important factor, of course, is the "life span" of the group.[3] Experimental groups are usually contrived, short-lived collectivities in stark contrast to working groups which have continuity and meaningful identity as a group. While the experimental

---

[3] R. F. Bales and F. L. Strodtbeck, "Phases in Group Problem-Solving," in D. Cartwright and A. Zander, *Group Dynamics, Research and Theory* (Evanston, Ill.: Row Peterson, 1960).

group does have the advantage of several disparate points of view, it does not have the necessary accompaniment of a set of relationships and mutually understood decision-making mechanisms to enable the members to utilize efficiently their varied resources.

But long-lived groups also vary greatly in their effectiveness. Shared experience, alone, is no guarantee of high performance. From the various studies of long-lived experimental groups and natural work groups, a number of attempts have been made to formulate those features which are characteristic of effective problem-solving groups.[4] Although the orientations of the investigators have varied, there are a few features which tend to be common to these formulations.

Central among these is the idea that effective problem-solving groups have worked out some mechanisms for (*a*) sharing and building on another's information and ideas, and (*b*) examining and resolving differences.

They are conscious of their own operations. For example, at some point there is an open discussion of the objective or task of the group until it is formulated in such a way that it is well understood and accepted by the members. Likewise, a balance is maintained between the task and emotional needs of the members of the group.

There is an open confrontation of differences. Disagreements are not suppressed or smoothed over before they are examined and understood. Criticism and attempts to influence are both overt and legitimate.

Decisions are made in some way which facilitates the examination and comparison of differences and alternatives. Some kind of consensus is reached which goes beyond simple majority voting or steam-rolling.

Finally, supportive relationships are established which provide a context in which differences can be confronted and new ideas tested. The members listen to one another. Divergent ideas are given a hearing. Ridicule is not utilized to suppress extreme ideas. Respect is shown for the point of view of others both in the way contributions are made and received.

---

[4] For examples, see Rensis Likert, *New Patterns of Management* (New York: McGraw-Hill Book Co., Inc., 1961); and D. Kretch, R. Crutchfield, and E. L. Ballachey, *Individual in Society* (New York: McGraw-Hill Book Co., Inc., 1962).

SECTION III

Individual Behavior and Development

Introduction

As soon as one begins to study human behavior in organizations somewhat systematically, as we have done in the first two sections of this book, he is confronted by the difficult task of generalizing about the behavior of people despite the fact that each person is a unique individual. This section of the book is an attempt to raise some of the questions about the way in which individuals influence and are influenced by the work systems in which we find them. It is also an attempt to answer, or at least give a way of thinking about, these questions.

The first two cases in the section concern the personal development of managers as they face critical career decisions. In order to understand these decision points, we are given certain information about the backgrounds of these men, particularly how they have reached their present managerial positions.

The next three cases—Ben Reed, Norse Electronics, and Excellent Insurance—describe incidents in which the assumptions of people at work are strong determinants of how they behave and how effective they are. Some of these assumptions seem to be unique to the particular individual, but others appear to come from sources common to large numbers of people who share some background characteristics.

In Walt Rogers, as in other cases in this section, but here in more specific detail, we have a chance to develop a fairly thorough picture of how the world and the man himself (and, particularly, the relationship between the two) look from inside an individual. We may find it useful to try to gain this kind of picture of each person whose behavior we are trying to understand, since his behavior will only make substantial sense to us as we see how he, himself, makes sense of it. This interview also gives us an idea of how two people can work together to gain a greater understanding of each other. Gillen Radio Corporation and Cleveland Junior Chamber of Commerce describe situations which require just such an understanding. In Gillen we have an opportunity to look at two people talking with each other and to see in detail how clearly or ambiguously they are communicating with each other. The Cleveland case gives us a chance to role-play, actually or through discussions, and to learn how two people whose points of view we know can work out their differences.

The readings represent several statements about how people's behavior is shaped, how human beings develop, and what is involved in their behavior in work situations. Defenses and the Need to Know is a simple statement straightforwardly alerting us to two apparently antithetical but actually complementary characteristics in all human beings. The two papers by Kluckhohn and Murray and by White offer basic concepts for understanding individual development. The following two readings bring us to the man-on-the-job and to the concept of role and its relation to individual development. Finally, the reading by Carl Rogers suggests some basic dynamics in successful and unsuccessful interpersonal relationships.

This section of the book requires careful consideration of some fundamental concepts for understanding individual behavior, where it comes from and how the development of people plays itself out on the job. We are asked in this section to try to understand individual human beings and to think of ways in which we, as potential managers, could most effectively relate to them in a work situation.

Cases

1. ANDERSON MANUFACTURING AND DEVELOPMENT CO.*

"HAM" WILSON looked at the public relations man across his desk with irritation. Then, with his characteristic self-control in dealing with company colonels, he suppressed the quick words that were on his tongue.

It had been a rough morning—a morning of hard, disciplined argument over promotional copy for the new compacting machine. While Ham had become visibly upset and impatient to end the session, the PR man kept smiling, stubbornly fighting it out one point at a time. Ham disliked him intensely.

Although Anderson Manufacturing and Development had not had a PR man long, this guy was surely making up for lost time. Little by little he had taken under his wing everything that had anything to do with business development and promotion. He was young—somewhere in his early thirties, maybe four or five years older than Ham himself—and in spite of his smiling, driving assurance, technically ignorant. He didn't even understand what was basically new in the compactor, Ham thought with resentment.

Ham was proud of his compactor. He had directed its development from the beginning. The original concept had been tossed to him as a kind of challenge by his boss, the chief engineer, and Ham had given it long hours of exploratory thought and work on his own. And then he had become excited about it, sold it hard, and management had bought it. They had given him a tight budget and time schedule and he had made it. He felt damn good about that machine.

"You keep approaching this copy in the wrong way, Ham," the PR man was saying.

---

* This case was prepared by Walter Milne under the direction of Professors A. H. Rubinstein and H. A. Shepard for courses in management of research and development conducted at the School of Industrial Management, Massachusetts Institute of Technology, Cambridge, Massachusetts, and is used with the latter's permission.

211

"This is aimed at the guys who are holding the money bags and you keep criticizing everything as though we were writing a technical report. I don't want to misrepresent your baby, believe me, but I'm trying to sell it. We've put a lot of money into its development and we're going to put a lot more into its promotion. Now we've got to sell it. I need good copy. Everybody upstairs wants good copy."

Ham was tempted to tell him what everybody upstairs could do, but checked himself again. He stared blankly at the copy, convinced that he was still right: it stunk. Worse, it seemed to border on dishonesty in some of its implications.

"What I would like to do," Ham finally said to PR, "is to have a chance to talk to the boss before we make a final decision on this. I don't want to let it go through as it stands on my own say-so."

"O.K., Ham," said PR, "but remember that I have to get final copy to the printer by the end of the week. I think what we've got right now is all right," he added, "and I certainly wouldn't want to see it watered down anymore."

PR left as he had come—smiling, self-sufficient, and with hearty good words.

What a joker, Ham thought to himself. He wondered how a guy like that could live with himself, how he could do Anderson Manufacturing any real good. Apparently he did—at any rate he sat upstairs in a big room in executive row.

By way of contrast, Ham looked around his own little cubby. His battered desk and chair, and one visitor's chair, all but filled it. "The Conference Room," the boys called it. He laughed, and then lost his laugh when a knock at the door reminded him that he had asked Holden to see him as soon as PR had left.

Bill Holden came in, easy and relaxed as always, and slouched into the chair at Ham's desk. He was a bright, young D.Sc. whom Ham himself had hired. But there were times when he wished he hadn't—and this was one of the times.

"Bill," Ham began, "I've just had a rough time with PR and I'm not going to beat around the bush. When your test results weren't in last Friday, you promised me—quite literally promised me—that we'd have 'em first thing this morning. And we don't have 'em. We practically rescheduled the whole program so that you could do some additional work with the physics group, and now you haven't made the new schedule. What are we going to do about it?"

"I know I promised to have them today, Ham," said Holden, "and believe me, I was shooting for it. The physics group work just took more time than I had expected. We're on some pretty fundamental stuff, and Dr. Maul asked me to do some library work on it. The whole thing just ran beyond our original expectations."

"Bill," snapped Ham, "your attitude confuses me; honestly, it does. I don't doubt that the physics group is doing important work, but you knew damn well that you were assigned part-time to my B project. And you know that when I juggled the schedule I was doing it to give you a break—you, personally. I never should have done it, but you practically pleaded with me and promised that you would come through on schedule. What do you think we're doing here anyway?"

Ham was flushed and angry, but Holden let it roll off easily.

"I suppose we're doing a lot of different things," Holden said in a tone that seemed half apology, half challenge. "The Chief was talking to me just the other day about the importance of the physics group work and about what a vital part I could play in it. You know it's pretty fundamental stuff, and frankly, that's why it appealed to me. It's well related to my previous experience—some of my doctoral work. I thought that's why you rearranged the schedule."

"Bill," said Ham, "you're talking nonsense and you know it. If all my men felt the way you do about the job, about fitting their work into the pattern, why the whole lab would fall apart."

"Well the whole thing seemed reasonable to me," said Holden. "After all, we're working for the same boss and good results in one place ought to be just as good as good results in another."

"Bill," said Ham in a rising voice, "you know damn well that's not so. Honestly, you're talking as though you were still a schoolboy and it didn't matter what you did—as though you didn't have responsibility to anyone else."

"But I've done good work," said Holden.

"I know it, and everybody knows it," interrupted Ham. "You've been here what—two, three years? During that time you've had more good ideas than anybody else on the lot. You're a good man, and the Chief has given you a pretty free rein. That's why I can't understand this. You try to run your affairs like a one-man band, but this lab is not being run the way you think it is."

Holden just kept looking at Ham.

"Everybody seems to think I've been doing O.K," Holden repeated defensively. "I've always tried to do my best."

"Sure you have," said Ham, "but you run around this place as though we were subsidized like the Royal Academy. You know we're not subsidized by anybody—we're organized to make money, and in order to make money we've got to push the stuff out the door. It matters a hell of a lot to me whether we do or not, because if we don't, it means my neck."

Ham looked at Holden and Holden looked at the floor and there was a long silence.

Ham liked Holden, but he was also a little envious of him, for Holden had the *big* degree. He also had brains. In fact, he had been good for the lab, Ham had to admit, even though he never worried much about meeting a schedule.

But hell, he said to himself as Holden looked up, I have to worry about a schedule even if Bill would rather be doing other things. Sometimes, he thought, I'd rather be doing other things myself.

"Bill," said Ham, finally cutting into the long silence, "I'm sorry I lost my temper. I've never blown my stack like this before. I was wrong in doing it now."

"I'm sorry too, Ham," said Holden. "You make me feel as though I've let you down personally. You've been very decent with me and I certainly didn't mean to let you down. If you want me to finish off the test runs. . . ."

"No, no need," interrupted Ham, a little wearily.

"When I didn't have the final figures this morning, I took what you'd already done and passed it on to Porter. He's got one of his boys finishing it out. The Chief expected a report before this, but he hasn't been pressing me for it."

Ham doodled for a minute on his scratch pad, and then went on:

"This is no life and death matter as you well know, Bill, and I'm sorry I acted as though it were. The point is not so much that you fouled up this schedule, but that you've fouled up for still another time. Anybody can understand missing once in a while, but it never seems to bother you that you have a reputation for never worrying about time. It would bother me. Every time I miss a schedule it bothers me."

Ham doodled again.

"You certainly know the things I've been saying are right, Bill," he said. "I think we should forget it for now, but let's understand that something's got to be done. I'll speak to the Chief as soon as I can, and we'll see what's to be done."

Holden backed out awkwardly, muttering apologies. As soon as he had left, Ham picked up the phone and called the Chief. The conversation was brief: Ham had a couple of problems he'd like to talk about; could he see the Chief sometime soon? "Sure" was the response—in about an hour, for lunch. Fine; done.

At lunch, the Chief characteristically opened right up with a hearty, "What's on your mind, Ham?" He asked it with a smile—a big, genuine, ready smile.

"Well, Chief, I had kind of a bad morning."

"I heard about it," said the Chief.

Ham didn't conceal his surprise. So PR had run to see the Chief, Ham thought. PR had tried to load the dice. That was a lousy trick.

"From PR?" Ham asked.

"No," said the Chief, looking hard at Ham, "from Bill Holden. He was in to see me right after he left your office. He told me the whole story. And as a matter of fact, Ham, there's a part of the story you don't know: Holden's being assigned to Doc Maul's group as part of a general reorganization that's been approved by the board."

Ham started, and he listened uneasily as the Chief began to explain. The reorganization was to involve the whole works. The lab was to be split into three groups. The Chief was to have over-all charge, but the company was going to appoint an assistant chief engineer who would be responsible for some forty engineers and as many nonprofessionals. Doc Maul was going to direct a smaller group on some of the more fundamental work. This was going to be a low-pressure group.

"Maul's group may not work out at all," the Chief went on, "but we're going to give it a try. It won't be much different from the way the physics group has operated anyway.

"This is where Holden fits in. He's to be a research associate—which, as you know, is a new title with us—Maul's right-hand man. Holden knows about this and he's happy about it. I think one of the reasons he stopped into my office today was to check on whether you knew it, and of course, you didn't.

"What happened was that Maul jumped the gun in telling Holden what his duties were to be, and Holden jumped the gun in acting like a research associate. He realizes that and he's sorry."

The Chief looked at Ham with an apologetic smile.

"I was going to tell you all this at the end of the week, Ham, after the executive committee had formally approved our plans. But let's forget Holden and get right down to brass tacks. Let's see what this is going to mean on our side of things."

Ham's uneasiness increased as the Chief went over things in more detail.

Maul was to become head scientist, he said. The Chief himself was to pick up two assistants. One of the two was to have the title assistant chief engineer. He would work in parallel with the Chief and have charge of about a third of the groups. The other new appointment was to be assistant to the chief engineer—a kind of leg man for the Chief.

"Now how do you fit into all this, Ham?" the Chief asked rhetorically. Ham took a big bite of pie and gestured his curiosity.

"We have discussed this whole thing pretty thoroughly," the Chief went on, "and we've looked at all the men we've got and we've talked to some from outside in an exploratory way. After looking and talking, we're well decided we want you to be assistant chief engineer."

Ham grinned. This felt good. Here he'd been working his fanny off and up to now, he thought, there hadn't been any gold stars on his report card. This really felt good.

"Actually, Ham," the Chief was saying, "you've been doing a big part of this job already. You know our procedures and you've proved you can keep on top of things. Whatever may have happened this morning I'd read as just a bad day. The record shows you work well with the men and keep them happy and push the stuff out."

Ham thought to himself that this was right. He had been doing part of this job all along. It had started nearly two years ago when Maul was out sick and the Chief began to dump things in his lap. And when Maul came back, the lab started to grow and the Chief kept handing him things. There was no formal pattern—it was one of those things that had just developed.

Still, there had been plenty of time to participate in project work, too. Ham thought of the compactor. He had lived with that thing night and day. And that had been a good part of the setup as it was. Whenever something had come along that he had wanted to jump into, the Chief had always said to go ahead. And he had jumped into the compactor with both feet. That's the only way to do, Ham thought, when you really want to get something done.

The Chief was now talking specifics about the new job.

It would mean a substantial raise—about 15 per cent. Better still, it would mean participation in the bonus plan. It would mean a big new office. And it would mean a lot of little things: a private secretary, a membership in the executive's club, office expenses for journals and magazines—a whole new potful of the niceties of life.

Ham had an impulse to jump up and shake the Chief's hand and to rush out and call his wife, who had taken the youngsters on a two weeks' trip to her mother's. But the impulse was only a quick flash. It passed and was replaced by something like fear. This wasn't something Ham wanted to jump into—not just like that anyway.

As the Chief went through the slow, deliberate ritual of filling and lighting his pipe, Ham expressed his thanks for being considered for the position. But while he said the right things fully and fluently, he thought of reasons for delaying his decision.

He thought of the reports, the judgments, the budgets, the people. He thought of sweating out one project while you were worrying about the next. And strangely enough, he thought of PR.

He thought of PR because there was a guy he never wanted to be, a guy who was a kind of Mr. Management Merry-go-round in person. He wondered briefly if some day PR would wake up and realize he'd been running his whole life without ever catching up to anything. He wondered if some day after it was too late PR would wish he hadn't run so hard and so fast.

There was a pause during which the Chief looked searchingly at Ham.

"You're thinking this is a pretty big decision, Ham?" the Chief asked.

Ham nodded. "A very big decision," he said with emphasis.

"I agree," said the Chief, "and naturally no one wants you to make a snap judgment about it. The vice president told me to tell you to take your time. Personally, I want you to take a good hard look at it.

"We both know," the Chief added, "that you did a whale of a fine job with the compactor, and it may be that that's the kind of thing you ought to stick with, that that's the kind of thing you really want. You've got to balance that equation for yourself, Ham. I emphasize this because if you do take the new appointment—and it's got a lot to offer—you ought to realize that you'll be completely away from the bench.

"When you sold me on the compactor," the Chief went on, "we arranged things so that you could see it through yourself. That wouldn't be likely to happen again. Of course, you'll sit on top of these things and you'll take pride in these accomplishments, but in a different way—an entirely different way."

The Chief stopped talking and scratched a match to relight his pipe. Ham stirred his second cup of coffee.

"I understand what you're saying all right," said Ham, "and, believe me, I have very mixed feelings about it. I'm tempted by the new job—naturally—and I feel very flattered by the offer. But I do know that I like the purely technical side of things. And I know that if I took the new job I'd want to keep up in my field."

The Chief smiled at Ham as he waited for him to go on.

"I've enjoyed the courses I've been taking at the Institute." Ham continued, "and I'm satisfied that they've done me a lot of good. If I took this appointment, I'd keep working for my degree—just as I have been—one course at a time. And I'd probably sit in on some seminars. In fact I'd try to keep up technically in every way I could."

The Chief smiled again and then spoke quickly and earnestly:

"You can sell yourself on that line of argument pretty easily, Ham," said the Chief, "because it makes so much good sense on the face of it. But I'll give you long odds that it won't work that way. I don't want to be discouraging, but the older you get the harder it gets. It's hard to find the time—even harder to find the energy.

"Believe me," added the Chief with a wry smile, "I know. I went through it myself."

Ham thought about this. He thought of how little he really knew about the Chief. He did know he had been a top turbine man. And he knew the Chief had once won the Stalworthy medal "for outstanding contributions to turbine development." Not much of a medal, maybe, Ham thought, but still a medal—a symbol of achievement and recognition. Yet the Chief had traded this away for a stock-bonus deal with the Anderson company. Ham wondered if he had any regrets. He wished he knew.

"The fact is," Ham heard himself saying a little apologetically, "I'd rather thought that this year I might have a go at the degree on a half-time basis. You remember that we talked about this last year and you said then that the company would sponsor me."

"I did say that, Ham," replied the Chief, "and I'm sure that we can still do it if that's what you want."

"Well, I'm not sure at all," said Ham, "but I have a tentative program worked out and I've lined up a thesis."

"If this is what you want, Ham," returned the Chief, "I'd be the first to say Godspeed. My only advice would be to encourage you to pick a good thesis project. There are a lot of awfully facile theses written in that department, and I wouldn't want to see you fall into that kind of trap."

"As a matter of fact," Ham answered quickly, "I've got a pretty exciting project in prospect. Werner wants me to work with him, and you know his work. This could mean a lot for me professionally. There's no denying I would like that. I think anybody would."

"Ham," said the Chief quietly, "I understand your feelings perfectly, and I won't try to dissuade you if that's what you really want. You've got some good projects under your belt here, and a good job with Werner would never hurt you."

The Chief paused and brushed a few tobacco crumbs from the table-cloth to the floor.

"If I decide to finish up the degree on a half-time basis," Ham asked, "will I prejudice my chances here at the lab?"

"Ham, you know better than that, I hope," replied the Chief. "I'm with you either way. And as far as the people upstairs go, forget it. There's no problem there."

The Chief brushed at a last elusive crumb of tobacco.

"No, you won't prejudice your future, Ham," he added, "but it will be a different kind of future."

The Chief looked at Ham for a minute. Then he knocked his pipe on the ashtray and looked at his watch. The lunch was over.

· · · · · · · · · · · · · ·

When Ham returned to his desk he sat down with the uneasy feeling that he hadn't been demonstrative enough in thanking the Chief for the opportunity he'd been offered. But he was interrupted by an unexpected call from Jack Masters, an old classmate and a fraternity brother of Ham's at the Institute. Jack was in town on business and their brief, hearty conversation quickly closed with arrangements for dinner at Ham's club.

As Ham cradled the phone, he let his mind savor past memories. He was glad Jack was in town, he decided. Jack was a real solid citizen. It would be good to see him.

During the next two hours, Ham tried to put some final changes into his annual report, which was due next week. It was not until long past midafternoon that he became aware that only his hands were busy with the papers in front of him. His mind was still churning with confusion over the decision that lay ahead. With a gesture of disgust, he pushed the papers to the back of his desk and left the office. Without real purpose, he walked the length of A wing until he stopped at the cell where George Porter was finishing up the tests that Holden should have done. Porter and one of his technicians were running things with a quiet, easy competency. Ham liked George—everybody did.

"How are things going?" Ham called. Porter grinned and held up a finger asking him to wait a minute. Ham waved an O.K.

Ham never thought about George Porter much, but he thought about him now as he waited. He thought about him, because he suddenly realized that Porter wasn't so very much different from him. Of course, he was twenty years older, but he had the same kind of background, the same kind of education. And Porter, Ham thought to himself, was a guy in a well-worn groove. For the first time, this realization worried him.

Back before the war, George Porter and one of the founders of the Anderson company had run a little one-horse shop. And there Porter had helped develop one of the basic patents that had brought Anderson Manufacturing into being. But Porter had never grown away from the first project. Not that he didn't keep improving it, for he did. Just last month, for instance, he had finished making changes that would let it be tied in with a computer-controlled line. A new series of Air Force contract orders had already come in on that development. That's the way Porter's baby was: high quality and custom-built, and the military kept it well fed.

"Just about winding up, Ham," said Porter, coming out of the open cell. "It all went very easily, no troubles at all. The data look good."

Ham took the clipboard and scanned the data, plotting them mentally against the earlier runs. "They do look good," he said.

Porter, pleased, turned back to his technician. "They look good, Al," he shouted, and the technician grinned.

Ham thrust his hands into his pockets and leaned back against the wall as Porter and the technician kept feeding in the adjustments on the last run. Ham thought about Porter some more. He thought about how helpful Porter had been to him when he first joined the lab. Ham had been in Porter's group then, and they had been quite close for a while.

Ham recalled his first visit to Porter's home. Porter lived in the country, and he farmed a little. It wasn't much of a farm, Ham supposed: a couple of hundred chickens, a cow, a small garden. He remembered how impressed he'd been that first night that everything they'd eaten—from the very tasty salad to the peach dessert—had been grown right there. Ham hadn't seen much of the Porters recently, for Ham's wife ran their social life, and she didn't care for the Porters. He was sorry, for he rather liked George and his rawboned, easygoing wife.

Porter came out of the test cell and took the clipboard from Ham to record the data on the final run.

Funny, Porter's doing this job himself, Ham thought. After all, the tests were routine enough and a couple of technicians could have handled the job if company policy hadn't required that an engineer be present. But Porter could have covered this requisite by having one of his young engineers do the job. Yet he didn't, for that's the way Porter was—he never passed anything on to anybody else. He would worry, he once told Ham, that it wasn't being done right if he wasn't out there on the job. As Ham thought about this, he concluded that any worries Porter had were mighty little worries.

When the last run was completed, Ham took the clipboard again and looked at the final readings. They were right on the button.

"We'll all get the Anderson A of Approval for this one," Ham said, and Porter and the technician laughed at this reference to a standing company joke. Ham surprised himself by laughing, too.

"Flip you fellows for a coke," he said. "Odd man pays." Porter laughed again.

"You know, Ham," he said, "that's probably the thousandth time you've tried to match me for a coke, and I've never taken you up on it. Not today, either."

Ham smiled, threw back a friendly insult, and then added that the cokes were on him. While Ham was getting them, Porter and the technician shut down the machine. Then they all lounged back on the bench beside the test cell, drank their cokes, and talked. They talked trivia, and Ham didn't say much. But Porter and the technician talked easily, sharing a rough kind of camaraderie.

Ham finished his bottle first, exchanged pleasantries with the two men, and walked on down the wing. As he turned the corner to his office, he looked back to see Porter and the technician closing down for the day. Although he couldn't tell for sure, he thought Porter was whistling. Ham watched him for a minute, and then almost imperceptibly shrugged his shoulders and walked slowly back to his office.

. . . .

Ham met Jack Masters that evening in the lobby of the Engineer's Club. They exchanged quick greetings and went directly to the bar. It was a solid, comfortable bar, a good place to talk.

Over the first drink, Masters carried the conversation. He renewed old times, talked about new prospects. Masters was a good talker, and Ham enjoyed listening to him. He hadn't changed much, Ham thought, except that he was a little heavier, a little less volatile.

Masters was with National Company and had been in their New York office for nearly two years. He talked objectively and happily about his job. It seemed like a good deal, and Ham said so two or three times.

"Believe me, Ham," Masters kept saying in self-deprecation, "I'm nobody in the company."

Over the second drink, Ham edged the talk around to his own prospects. Masters was immediately interested. He asked the right questions and drew out the right details. He understood Ham's doubts quickly enough and as quickly dismissed them.

"Hell, Ham," he said, as they went in to dinner, "you don't have a problem, you have an opportunity. You've been doing part of this job already and you like it well enough—that ought to be all you need. I had to cut a lot of bait before I got this kind of bite."

"What do you mean, you 'had to cut bait'?" Ham asked. He was curious. And he was more than curious, for he was searching eagerly for any patterns of experience he might be able to match against his own.

Masters explained that after he'd been in National's Dallas operation for nearly three years, he began to have an almost panicky fear that he was stagnating. His jobs had become routine, and so had his raises. Masters had decided right then, as he put it, to fight his way out of the corner he was in. He did it by broadening himself technically. He did it by very deliberately avoiding getting stuck in the same kind of job too many times. He did it by smelling out every opportunity that was in the wind.

The break had come when his boss, an assistant to the chief engineer, went overseas to set up a new production facility in the Near East. This man's going left a kind of administrative vacuum which the company decided not to fill. But Masters flew into it and picked up every responsibility he could. He made himself a kind of communications center. And when the assistant's leave was extended, Masters was appointed acting assistant in Dallas. Then, before the first man returned, he was transferred to Jersey and then to New York.

"Well, your story's something like mine in some ways," said Ham, "only I didn't consciously try to bring anything off the way you did."

"That may be," said Masters, "but I think we all do this kind of thinking, whether it's conscious or not. Personally, I like to plan things out quite deliberately, for then you have more control over them. That just seems like a matter of good sense to me."

"What you're saying," said Ham with a laugh, "makes me feel a little like a country boy who's somehow getting along only because he's luckier than he ought to be. You're arguing that a guy has to be an opportunist to get ahead."

"Nothing opportunistic about it at all," Masters interrupted. "It's rather a question of creating opportunity, and certainly a question of taking opportunity whenever it comes along. Take this new job of yours—if you don't take it, somebody else will. That's the way I look at things."

"Maybe I'm just quibbling," said Ham, "so let's say I'm ready to buy your argument. This is not what really bothers me anyway. What bothers me is how do you know you ought to get out of technical work; how do you convince yourself that you ought to throw it all away?"

Masters explained it very readily in terms of money and status. He told Ham that he had analyzed National Company as thoroughly as though he were going to invest a couple of million dollars in it. This was only good sense, he said, for there he was, investing his whole life in it. And his analysis showed that all the glory in National Company went to the guys in the management seats—all the glory, all the money, and all the status. He also discovered that more than half the top men in National had come up out of research and development in the first place, and so he decided that the odds were all in favor of his trying the same thing.

"Right now," Masters said, as though clinching the argument, "I'm making half again as much as the guys who came into the lab with me and stayed there. And I'm more flexible," he added. "I can do more things and I'm worth more to the company."

Ham bristled a bit at this. The implication was that the man on the bench was some inferior kind of character, and he found himself resenting it. The argument was also clearly something of a personal challenge.

"All this may have been pretty clear-cut in your case, Jack," said Ham, "but I don't think it is in mine. You're with a big outfit—maybe that's where I should be, but I'm not—and I've got to look at my own situation. You fellows at National talk about millions the way we talk about thousands.

"Let's say I look at this thing pragmatically," Ham went on, "and I would agree with you that maybe this has been in my thinking all along. From a practical standpoint, I would say that you can afford to be secure and happy about your choice because your company is fat. If I were with National, I might feel the same way. You don't have to worry about finding your next job."

"You don't mean that," said Masters. "You know darn well that if I didn't do my job today, I'd be out on my can tomorrow. We're not running a philanthropy any more than you are."

"No, that's not what I mean," Ham rejoined. "What I mean is that you're insulated from all the wear and tear that affects a guy like me. You're not going to mess your job and you're not going out on your can. But I might."

Ham was wound up now.

"When the Chief talked to me today, Jack," he said, "he quoted a lot of figures about the progress of the company. But I'll be frank with you—we run on government contracts—we couldn't keep our shop open six months without the military."

Ham disclosed that one of his own projects had had a prospective government contract cut right out from under it and some of the engineers had been let go. Ham worried that this might happen to the whole kit and caboodle. Then what would happen to the little guy low down on the management ladder, he asked?

"Would I go to you, to National Company, and say won't you please take me on? Would I say I'm a helluva good man even though I haven't any patents to prove it. Would I say I'm loyal and I need the work and if you take me on you'll never regret it?"

Ham was talking at Masters now rather than to him. He wasn't stopping for answers.

"The way I see it," he argued, "if I stick to the technical part of R&E, I've got money in the bank. I'm negotiable. I can go to anybody in the industry, and I can say here's what I've got and here's what I've done, and they can see it right away."

Ham stopped to sign the dinner checks and to order a second cup of coffee. He looked across at Masters again and apologized for his rush of words. He slowed himself down.

Maybe some of these arguments were pretty tenuous, he agreed, but there were other things. There was the plain and simple joy of accomplishment in good project work, for instance.

Ham had written Masters about the compactor, and now he was speaking feelingly about it. That was the kind of thing a guy had to immerse himself in and that was one of the joys he was talking about. If you went into administration full time, you kissed that sort of thing good-by. And you lost something pretty substantial.

Ham let Masters chew over this point while they finished their coffee. Then they went out to the reading room, where they sat in a couple of comfortable chairs and flicked their cigarette ashes into the fireplace.

After a while Ham said: "Jack, I've been thinking pretty seriously about going back for my doctorate on a half-time basis. The company will sponsor me and Professor Werner wants me to do my thesis under him."

"Well," said Masters, "I remember that you wrote me about a year ago to say that you were thinking about it. I wrote back and urged you to forget it, and I thought you had given it up."

Masters blew a few smoke rings and thoughtfully watched them flatten out and lose their shape.

"If you do go back on a half-time schedule, will you use your compactor for a thesis?" he asked Ham.

"No, I can't," said Ham, "the machine isn't really mine. I guess I didn't tell you that."

Ham explained that a friend of Bill Holden's—a local man—had come up with the basic concept. Holden had brought him around to see the Chief as a kind of personal favor.

"But believe me," Ham added quickly, "there was plenty wrong with that machine when we first saw it. The inventor didn't have a sound idea of the basic processes involved. In fact, the odds on this thing's paying off looked so slim that nobody really wanted to touch it. But then I came up with a process that made it look better, and we worked like hell on it, and now we've got something that's really good."

Masters took a last drag on his cigarette and flipped it into the fireplace.

"Suppose you do go back for this degree of yours on a half-time basis," he asked Ham, "what's going to become of it?"

"Why, just what I've been saying," said Ham. "In the first place I think it's a good move, just from a practical point of view."

"I don't," Masters countered. "I think you're kidding yourself. Look at this guy Holden, for example. He's already *at* where you're only going to be. And all the time you're sweating out the earn-while-you-learn routine, he'll be jogging along piling up points. And then when you come back full-time and give it the old college try to catch up, you'll find that all the heroes have already been made."

"Well, maybe you're right," laughed Ham, "but why couldn't I look around just the way you did, only from an R&D point of view? I might just look around for the spot where the R&D man is well off, and then I'd aim for that and try to hit it."

"You won't find it," said Masters with emphasis. "I laugh at this because I think of our annual report in which we say solemn things about basic R&D being the prime mover of everything that comes down the pike, and we publicly pat its little head and sing hymns of praise. And I'm telling you—off the record and as a friend—that all of this is hypocritical as hell. It's like a bad scenario with half the lines stolen from 'The Life of Louis Pasteur.' I don't know who we think we're kidding—unless it's all the sweet old ladies who own most of our stock."

"That's pretty typical of some high-powered wheel in public relations," Ham laughed. And he laughed again recalling his morning meeting with PR over the promotional piece on the compactor.

"And maybe," Ham added with a smile, "this is a pretty good 'for instance' for my argument that by and large you'll find more honest substance in lab work than anywhere else on the lot."

"I won't argue that you won't find muttonheads in management," said Masters, "but you know darn well that you find them in the lab, too."

Ham nodded his agreement.

"You take the guys on the bench," Masters went on, "and you can pick among them qualitatively. And you know that on any team you've got a few with damn good brains. But you know also that you've got some other good brains seeing things through. It's not just the turn of the wheel that sends one group up and another group down. There are guys seeing things through all along the line. And some of them take plenty of risks."

Ham thought that this was right, too. He had bought a risk, he thought, when he had sold the Chief on the compactor. They had looked at him and said, "O.K., it's your baby." It was a money down, win or lose proposition; luckily he'd won.

In contrast, Ham thought of Holden and Holden's new appointment. This was a different kind of deal. The company would carry Holden as a kind of overhead. It was like a sweeps ticket; maybe they'd get their money back and maybe they wouldn't. The whole psychology of the thing was different.

Ham also thought of the pleasure he'd found in "seeing things through" for some of the men and some of the projects the Chief had assigned to him. There was a sense of accomplishment in this, too, he thought.

"Jack," Ham finally said, "I haven't been trying to give you an argument to deny what you might call the joys of management. I've tasted some of them, and I've found that I liked them. It's just that I have very mixed feelings, and I've been trying to see it from all sides.

"And you know," he added after a pause, "I honestly feel that I'm almost ready to decide to take the job."

Masters looked at Ham and smiled broadly with sheer delight.

"Ham," he said, "that's the most sensible thing your befuddled old brain has produced tonight. Let's have a nightcap on it before you lose it."

As they had their nightcap, they talked about their families and they made vague arrangements about getting together again "soon." When they had finished, Ham drove Masters back to his hotel. They were tired and they rode most of the way in silence. It was not until Masters shook hands on leaving that he returned again to Ham's decision.

"Ham," he said, "maybe I've got more faith in your company than you have, but I think it's a comer. And I think in this new job you've got a helluva fine opportunity to grow with it. Frankly, I think you'd be a sucker to do anything else. Do yourself a favor and take the job."

"Jack, I'm almost ready to think I will," said Ham, as he waved good-by. And maybe I will, he thought, as he drove the long fifteen miles to Cooperstown. He was glad he had seen Jack, he decided as he turned into his drive. It had been good to talk with him.

The next morning at the plant Ham sat for a long time with his annual report again. And again he stared idly at the pages, thinking and worrying, especially worrying. He wished that he could avoid the decision altogether, that the Chief or somebody else would come up with some inevitabilities as to why it could go only one way or another.

As Ham sat worrying, his mail arrived. It provided something of a diversion, and he was grateful for its coming. He spotted among the usual run of internal mail a letter from the Society. He read it with mounting disbelief, and then read it again to make sure. There was no mistaking what it said: his paper on the compactor had won the Society's annual George Peabody Award for the best paper of the year by a young engineer. In stiff, formal phrases the letter sent congratulations from the president of the Society and outlined the Awards Night program at which the Peabody Medal would be presented.

Ham grinned, and the grin grew into a big bubble of elation. Quickly he tucked the letter in his pocket and hurried down the wing to see the Chief. The Chief was in, and he shared Ham's delight as he offered hearty congratulations. He also called the vice president with the news while Ham was still in the office. Ham could hear the vice president's voice gather enthusiasm and begin to dominate the conversation. He couldn't make out the words, but the sounds were friendly.

"He says that you're to make the Society's schedule," said the Chief as he hung up, "and that your wife is to go with you if she can. And he wants you to take any extra time you may need on either side of the meeting—all at company expense, of course."

Ham felt good. It was nice to have these guys in your corner.

"You're not to let the new job make the slightest bit of difference in planning your schedule around this award," the Chief added.

Ham's bubble burst. There was no escaping the thing.

"He also says," the Chief went on, "that he would like to have an answer by the twenty-seventh, if possible. Now that they've made up their minds to move on this, they want to go ahead as quickly as possible."

Ham felt a sudden emptiness in his stomach. "Sure, Chief," he said, "by the twenty-seventh. I ought to have an answer all right, I've already given it a lot of thought."

"And Ham," said the Chief, smiling, "one last thing: be sure to get in touch with PR on this award so that we can exploit it as fully as possible for the company."

Ham nodded and said he would. He added a few words of personal thanks to the Chief and left. He wanted to get back to his office as quickly as possible. He wanted to come to grips with this thing. He wanted to get it settled.

As he hurried past the physics lab, he saw Holden—cup of coffee in hand—sitting at one of the tables, talking animatedly with Dr. Maul. As Ham neared his own cubby, he saw Porter lounging near the door, waiting for him with the formal report on yesterday's run. And as Ham drew nearer, he could hear that Porter was whistling.

2. ARTHUR WALTON

ART WALTON left the meeting in something of a daze. It was hard to believe that he was going to lose control of the key engineering group around which he had so painstakingly built his department. He'd have nothing left but a scattering of service groups, now. It wasn't that this loss would hurt him financially or damage his chances for promotion. It had nothing to do with him, really. He knew he had a well-established reputation for running the best department of its kind in the company. It was just one of the battles in the war between R&D and production, just part of the struggle for survival that Art's latest boss was going through. As much as Art could understand that his production engineering group had to be transferred to the production department during this period of crisis when development contracts for the division were dwindling away, it still left him with no real job. Now, Art couldn't continue ignoring that conscience of his which had been nagging him for some months, insisting that he leave the Ribble Company and get back on the track of the career he had always wanted for himself.

Art Walton—the Early Years

Art Walton was a Vermonter by birth and upbringing. His father had represented a large company in the northern New England region until the early stages of the depression, when he was asked to return to New York City for assignment. He refused the offer, preferring to resign, in spite of the scarcity of jobs, rather than leave the small-city Vermont life which he and his family had come to love. The Walton's were forced to live quite simply thenceforward, but Art never felt they were "poor." In fact, he recalled his childhood with great enjoyment. His family was a close unit, sharing together—mother, father, and two sons—household and athletic activities, particularly ice skating. Art's father found more time than most fathers to be with his family.

Art had to admit, when his friends kidded him about it, that the stereotypical image of the Vermonter, the "Green Mountain Boy," was one he cherished. He wanted to be resourceful and independent as his father had been and as, it seemed to Art, most of the important adults in his childhood were. Too, he wanted to feel that he was being true to the basic, even earthy, values which were so often associated with Vermont.

Art considered himself an adequate student in high school. He got B's most of the time. He enjoyed school as an integral part of an enjoyable growing up, though he never considered himself a prime student. More important to his life were extracurricular school activities, social functions and athletics, most particularly skating. In his senior year of high school, he won membership on the Olympic hockey team. During the year after high school, he worked in a small industrial plant to get money for college, trained for the Olympics, and won hockey scholarships at several northeastern colleges. Then, just before he was to leave for the Olympics, he had a serious skating accident which resulted in a permanently disabling spine injury.

For a year he recuperated. As he thought back on the incidents of this period, he could not recall undergoing serious shock,

> . . . a breast-beating type of thing that you see in the movies. There were temporary unsettling thoughts and reflections, but I never felt a terrible loss. I guess I simply took it as a fact that I wouldn't be able to do all the things I had always done. I got pretty good at living in a brace. I don't skate nearly so well as I used to, but I can get around. I did a fair amount of traveling around for a while, helping other people get used to orthopedic difficulties.

Higher Education

Even before his personal association with the profession, Art had wanted to be an orthopedic surgeon.

> Then some teacher told me I was so punk in Latin I would not make premed requirements. I've since found that is no longer true and it makes me mad. Anyway, I decided on engineering.

Several of his college scholarships were honored, despite Art's inability to skate competitively.

> Being a year older than my classmates and still not too ambulatory, I ground away and got straight A's, each term getting more boring than the one before. Then I heard about a program at another university, a joint affair between the business and engineering schools leading to a Masters in engineering and management. This seemed to me to be just what I wanted, and I was accepted. I wanted to be more technical than business people I'd known in Vermont, but even more I wanted to do things on my own, to manage something. I guess that was why I was so attracted to surgery; you were on your own but with good technical training behind you. Shortly before I was to start this combined program, it was discontinued, so I went through with the regular engineering program and got my M.S.

After graduation, Art married a Vermont girl and immediately matriculated in the M.B.A. degree program in the same university in which he had taken his M.S. In his application Art described his ambition

> . . . to be the largest frog in a small, well-run puddle. I hope to work for a larger firm or firms for a few years, in positions of liaison between businessmen and scientists. There is a real need for more mutuality of knowledge and sympathy between the two.

He went on to declare that he planned, after gaining this experience, to manage the affairs of a small company, preferably one in a rural setting with substantial opportunity for outdoor activity.

Art's business education experience was both intensive and just what he had been aiming for.

> I loved the small-business course; did well in production, which was a natural with my background; had a great deal of trouble in finance; enjoyed the course for sales managers and did well in it; the course in human behavior was interesting and I did so-so in it. I was pretty much a slightly above-average student.

Art's Job History

When graduation from business school came, along with the Walton's first child (he was to have three more over the next few years), Art decided to short-cut his original job plans and go right into a small business.

> In seven years I had taken only two summers off from studying. I'd gotten pretty sick of it and the late hours. I wanted autonomy and the good life of Vermont, or some place like it. Small business was my main drive; getting away from the hard-driving, cosmopolitan life was second.

Before school ended, Art heard of a small food-processing company which was looking for a manager.

> I spent a month looking at that opportunity but turned it down. Instead I went back to Vermont and joined a small-business consulting company which had just been formed. The consulting was kind of interesting as an interim thing, but I think all of us in the company were trying to find the perfect opening in the perfect little company. The job was satisfying in many ways. It was frustrating in one respect. You never saw anything through to completion. Your best-laid plans were lodged in someone else's hands, and they too often misfired.

Through a friend, Art learned of a small machine tool company in New Hampshire.

A fellow a little older than I had just bought it and wanted a second in command. I came in as vice president, and while he acted as salesman, I stayed home and ran the place. For awhile we did quite well, building up from fifteen to forty employees. We sold a limited line of tools to textile companies. Then came the Australian wool embargo, and our regular business just disappeared. We staved off failure for awhile by getting small subcontracts. Every Friday afternoon, pay time, we'd meet the mail train, hoping customers we had phoned the day before, begging for our money, would have put their checks in the mail. Sometimes we made the payroll, sometimes we didn't. This was a wearing experience, but in many ways it was very gratifying.

Eventually the banks foreclosed us. Maybe if both of us had had five years' more experience we'd have seen further ahead, used our imagination more and developed some market possibilities. It would have taken real genius with what we had to work with—practically no capital and run-down machinery, but maybe somehow we could have gotten around our problems. But we were blinded by our optimism.

Art's next opportunity brought him back to the city, where he was offered a business manager's post in a small, new, manufacturing subsidiary established by an engineering consulting firm to carry on a government contract. He and a design engineer

> . . . set up the facility in a small industrial town near the city, built our own buildings, a half-dozen or so, hired and trained some of our own people, and did all our own development and manufacturing work. I guess I just plain react to power. I enjoyed having a certain amount of power over the destinies of our several work groups. We lost the contract, I think, because we kept ourselves too insular technically. We tried to do it all ourselves without getting any development consultation. I didn't really understand that for a long time, neither did my partner. He has remained one of my closest friends, by the way.

For a time Art thought of going into the consulting part of the firm's business.

> With them behind me I thought I could get farther into the doing of things without having to bid adieu to my ideas once I'd thought of them. But, then a golden opportunity, at a 70 per cent salary increase, came along to manage a young company, a specialty sheet metal forming outfit.

Art's new firm was owned by a few retired executives who turned operations over to Art. The major stockholder,

> . . . an elderly gentleman, took a good look over my shoulder, but he was always a great help, never an impediment. He died and none of the other stockholders took such constructive interest in what I was doing. I didn't

realize what a loss this was until later. When I stepped in, it was a roaring business. Volume varied tremendously from month to month but on three-fourths of a million dollars annual sales, we usually netted between ten and fifteen thousand dollars a month. The profit was fantastic. Then sales went to pot when two prime contractors of ours lost their contracts. Each week I had to lay off more people. I got to the point of staying full time on sales trips myself, doing anything to buttress our reps and drum up business when I should have been home some of the time, at least, looking after operations.

That was when I began to miss the old man. He would have made me cut back sooner, held back my youthful optimism and that of the other directors, and kept us from needlessly spending money holding onto people. It bothered the devil out of me laying off people who'd been there ten years and I'd only been there a year and a half.

Then I got into disagreement with another senior stockholder. He wanted us to get into things I felt and feel were ridiculous, and which would simply have eaten away what few assets we had left. And he wouldn't back us in a joint venture with a complementing firm which I and the other directors felt held promise. It was a tough industry. We had a few unique production tricks, but there were others who could do much the same as we could. We did drive most of our local competitors to the wall before we went there. It does my ego good to know that the people who are running it now, under a recapitalization, aren't doing any better, and I am still credited, I hear, with having developed the only two profitable lines the company has.

It was the biggest shock of my life when I got kicked out. I should have seen it coming. I was the highest salaried person in the place, so my leaving would make the biggest saving. And this old stockholder kept asking me if one of my subordinates was ready for more responsibility. I just didn't pay any attention. I felt I was putting my all into it and, no matter what, in spite of all the layoffs, I wouldn't be let go. If we went under, we'd go under, but they wouldn't can the manager, as they do in baseball. I *was* the company. But, I was canned. It set me back for awhile.

I think my trouble, my failure on that job, was I just wasn't such a hot salesman. I hated to go in and approach some pipsqueak buyer. I used to stew about it. And I hated to go through those evenings out in Cleveland or someplace with some buyer and his wife whom I was obviously doing my best to bribe nicely. I despised it and didn't do it well. I was just too young to be hard-nosed and flint-hearted about it.

As I look back on it, I like to think now that I'd have sense enough not to break my back over every single buyer but say the hell with it, so-and-so just isn't worth this or send someone else to take him out on the town or send him a bottle next Christmas. Or, if I just had to do it, do it without all the zeal and yet repugnance behind the zeal. I think I could discriminate better now. I think if I had really decided one buyer was critical, I could have been more comfortable with the uncomfortable part of it. I'm afraid I just let fires come at me, and I fought them all as though they were all alike.

At this point I joined one of those so-called miracle electronic outfits, Solon Electronics. I went into Solon saying, "The hell with it, I shall not try another small company." I'm ashamed to think how long I just existed in that job, not putting anything in or getting anything out. I just didn't really give a damn.

Solon was run by a charming guy. He welcomed me as the white-haired lad he's been waiting for to be his number two man. It took me a month to discover that that's what he'd told three others. Each, like me, lasted as the golden boy for six months, and then we got shunted off and just hung around. Toward the end I picked up a bit. I became co-director of engineering, and then I started up a production engineering function. I was looking around for opportunities in other companies when Solon closed its doors.

The Ribble Company

During the year and a half at Solon, while he "convalesced" from so unceremoniously being fired, Art slightly modified his career aspirations. He still wanted a small-business management opportunity. But he hoped to find it within a larger, more stable institution, looking for an opportunity not vastly different from the management of the consulting firm subsidiary which he had so greatly enjoyed.

> About the time I was thinking of getting on my feet and moving out of Solon, there was a lot of talk about the Ribble Company acquiring small firms and leaving them in at least a semiautonomous state. Ribble figured they could beat competition by buying up a small outfit with a unique idea, pour in a heavy investment from a central research group but in all other ways leave it pretty much autonomous. I figured what I needed to do was get into a job at Ribble that would give me the kind of background they would want for a manager of one of these small companies. I thought production engineering would do just that. I wanted a job that would be the bridge between research and manufacturing so I could say that I knew the big-company system, and that I knew how to manage this tension-member between the developers and the producers. Then I'd be the logical choice to run a smaller part of the company.

Art was hired as manager of the engineering section in one of Ribble's more advanced development divisions. The Ribble Company's annual sales were in the several hundred million dollar range. Art's division dealt almost exclusively in government contracts, each of which amounted to several millions of dollars revenue. As the division developed, so did the extent of Art's jurisdiction, until, by 1962, he had built what he considered to be an integrated production engineering liaison unit effectively operating between basic research and manufacturing.

A lot of graduates from the business school I'd gone to were in it at that time. They were trying to get more people with such training to bolster their technical people. One of them helped me get the job. A lot of them have left since. I think lack of direction in the company has driven them to find some company which seemed to have a straighter aim. But, at the time, the company seemed to me to have the stability I was looking for. A lot has happened in the past four years to convince me otherwise, at least partly. Direction is terribly quixotic. Divisions come and go and so do presidents. The people are handled kindly. It's kind of a welfare state. A man loses his job overnight, but they always find another spot for him where he can't do any harm, and without a loss in pay. It makes people think it really doesn't matter what they do, they'll always be taken care of somehow. Not a very healthy situation for the company.

I started out with two production engineering supervisors reporting to me. Then when my superior, the development department head, left, I applied for and got his job and that added several more sections: components and material engineers, publications prototype shops and procurement. Then our outfit merged with another lab, and I got several more sections, which gave me all of engineering for our division, except for purely design groups. My lack of electronic system engineering training keeps me from wanting or getting the latter.

There were a lot of political shenanigans going on during all of this. In each case, at least two departments could logically have made a case for getting hold of the sections I got. We each would sell various parties on what we had to offer. The Machiavelli's in this process tended to lose out. The winning tactic, at least the one I always used, was to put up the logic as I saw it and let the logic do my fighting for me. It always worked for me.

In some other places this idea has gotten me in trouble. I tend to my knitting, do the job, and let that pull me through. It has worked for me at Ribble in spite of the fact that I have been somewhat insensitive to some of the political maneuverings which have gone on around me. I'm just one level below where all the chaotic shifts tend to take place—I've had seven bosses since I came here.

I guess I've been rather single-minded about running my own operation and letting the rest of the corporate world go into all kinds of gyrations around me without it getting to me. I get my kicks out of meeting and wrestling with the day-to-day things. As I've added groups to my jurisdiction, each has presented problems. My attention has focused on each of them successively until they became integrated and were working well. When that job is over, I step back two or three steps and look for another trouble spot. Of course, we spend a lot of time on long-range planning meetings. In fact, it is the plans we made there which have been so shaken by the most recent loss of our most central unit, production engineering.

The last trouble spot left in the department was the publications group. I guess I'm pretty paternalistic. Unless someone who works for me has his affairs running pretty smoothly, I tend to get pretty much into his business, mostly by sweet talk. I worked with the publications head for a long time on this basis. I tried to find a way we could help each other. I wanted him to let me get him some people to help get some facts together that would help make sense of his problem. In this case he just wouldn't accept my help. I felt he needed to replace two of his people or reorganize their units and get them some help. He flatly refused. It was only then that I had to agree with the rest of my staff people that nothing more could be done. Finally, I backed off and simply told him that if those two people failed, it would be his neck which was out, not theirs. They failed and I had to replace him. This has been my usual way of operating. So long as we can work out a way to help each other, I'll stick with him. But if he refuses the help, then that is his decision and he's got to live by it. If his decision is wrong and he can't keep up, then he is going to forfeit something and maybe it's his job.

Now I just don't have any fires left to fight. We've won the respect of the design engineers. I have a very loyal group of men loyal to me and to the way the department is being run, who work extremely well together —they seem to sense what needs to be done before anyone brings it up overtly. And my last real trouble section has been getting straightened out in the last few months.

Art had been singled out by divisional and corporate management on a number of occasions for managing the most effective product support engineering department in the Ribble Company. His salary level reflected the confidence of his superiors. However, the Ribble Company, shortly after Art joined it, abandoned its policy of purchasing and maintaining the autonomy of small manufacturers. Art's expectation to head one of these subsidiaries, thus, disappeared. Still, while there were production engineering fires to be fought, he thought little of moving on to a situation which would provide the small-company satisfactions he still so deeply desired.

To some extent the short run obscures the long. The fires come up, you deal with them and move on to the next. It's like surgery, a kind of sport, a challenge from the immediate environment. Either you win or you lose, but then the game is over and you go on to the next game, next week.

I have never really understood myself well enough to know whether I was being cowardly in not going back into the small-business fray, or whether I was misguided in thinking that that's where I should be just because it was across the brow of the hill. I think I've gotten too much of a kick out of doing a good job totally within my limited responsibility. I've got very much fun out of that, and I have paid too little attention to the world around me, just hoping that this kind of record will open up other vistas if the larger environment fails around me. Which is a kind of naive hope.

The Loss of Production Engineering

The sudden news that the production engineering section was to be withdrawn from his department brought Art up short as he was driving home from the meeting that night.

That production engineering section is the core of my department. I created it. My 300 people revolve around that section. Without it I will have a lot of people reporting to me, a great variety of functions, but I won't and the department won't have the real driving interest. With our contracts slipping away, overhead has to be cut, and we and production have been duplicating a lot of functions. We can't continue to exist separately. I had hoped we could take over the two smaller groups in production which do our kind of work. More of that infighting I've been trying to steer clear of. This isn't important to a lot of people but it's major to me. If it goes through, as I guess it will, I'll get so frustrated I don't see how I can avoid making a major job change for myself.

I can't kid myself any longer that I've really got anything here—I know I'm doing wrong by myself to stay on—it's just been so much fun. I can't see anything at Ribble for me once I set aside those day-to-day challenges. And now that I've been able to get the pieces of the department working well together, I can't say I haven't fulfilled my responsibility for developing my department. Of course, even with the loss of the production engineering group there will still be day-to-day challenges but not a long-term challenge to be worked through and solved. Is it enough to say, at my age (39), that I have a smoothly running department filled with people who are loyal to me and to the concepts we've developed? Wouldn't I rather be able to say I've run an organization of some size, some scope and done it competently, imaginatively, with drive?

Am I just kidding myself and that's why I've been holding back and haven't done anything? Am I just temporarily frustrated with large business and the politics? But, in a smaller outfit, at least you deal directly with everyone who influences you and what you're doing. It's more than just reporting to a different level. Is that what I want then, another chance in a smaller business? Then again, maybe after the shock of this disappointment wears off in a few days, I'll see it just a little differently.

3. BEN REED*

BEN REED, 27, graduated from State University in June 1959, with a B.A. degree in psychology.

Shortly after graduation he took a job as assistant office manager with the Acme Medical Association, a group health insurance organization. His salary was $5,000 per year. As assistant office manager he was responsible for supervising approximately forty female office employees who performed sorting, totaling, and recording operations concerning medical claims charged against Acme.

The office workers were situated at several rows of desks in a large open room. As assistant manager, Ben Reed had a desk in the same room but off to one side of the desks of the girls. His immediate supervisor, Mr. Charles Grayson, the office manager, had been with Acme for twenty years and had risen to his present position from a beginning job as a clerical assistant. During his career at Acme, he had watched the company grow and progress, and often referred to the increase in employees under his supervision with a great deal of pride.

According to Ben Reed, his work at Acme was not especially challenging. In describing his job, he stated that his main duties were to check the timecards of the office workers each morning, to make sure that everything was in order, and to answer questions concerning claims that the girls might bring to him. In addition, he did special statistical studies at the request of the controller's office or Mr. Grayson. These studies were infrequent, and during his first four months with Acme, Ben participated in only two such studies. He estimated that on the average he actually "worked" no more than one or two hours a day.

Partially because of some courses he had taken at the University, Ben Reed had some strong convictions concerning the supervision of the office employees. He was concerned about the situation at Acme for two reasons: (a) the high turnover of office employees—which averaged about 48 per cent per year and, (b) the apathy of many of the girls toward their work. He realized that he was new in the organization but nevertheless felt obligated to make some suggestions which he felt would improve the situation with regard to the office force. Mr. Grayson, his immediate superior, often did not agree with these suggestions.

* From *Human Elements of Administration*, by H. R. Knudson, Jr., copyright © 1963, Holt, Rinehart and Winston, Inc. Reprinted with the permission of the publishers.

For example, in order to utilize partially his unproductive time, Ben suggested that as he had had several courses in physiology as a premed student before transferring to psychology, it might be helpful if he could spend an hour or two a week in instructing the office staff in some of the basic fundamentals of physiology. The nature of the work was such that knowledge of the various functions and systems of the body would, he felt, be helpful in speeding up the sorting and processing of claims that came in. Ben suggested to Mr. Grayson that he would be happy to conduct these informal classes as a part of his regular duties. Mr. Grayson, however, did not feel this was a good suggestion and did not permit Ben to go through with his idea.

Ben also had a disagreement with Mr. Grayson over the handling of the case of Doris Martin. Doris, a clerk-typist, approached Ben one day while Mr. Grayson was out of the office to report that she was sick and desired to go home. Ben made the necessary arrangements for her to have the rest of the day off. When Mr. Grayson heard of this incident he was very upset. He told Ben that he did not have the authority to make these kinds of decisions and that he, Mr. Grayson, would make all such decisions in the future. Although Ben felt that, because of his position as assistant office manager, because Mr. Grayson was not in the office at the time the situation occurred, and because Doris Martin was obviously sick, he had made a good decision, he let the matter drop.

On December 10, 1959, Mr. Robert Colvin, Controller of Acme Medical Association, called Ben into his office to discuss plans for a new electronic data processing installation that the company was considering putting in to speed up the processing of claims. He spent about two and one-half hours with Ben explaining the proposed system and concluded the interview by stating that he felt that as new men often had good ideas for improvement, he would welcome any thoughts that Ben might have.

Ben was enthusiastic about Mr. Colvin's approaching him, and spent several hours that night at home working out a plan that would permit the new process to be installed in his area with a minimum of difficulty. He submitted his ideas to Mr. Colvin the next morning.

Mr. Colvin was very much impressed with Ben's ideas and immediately called a meeting of several of the officials of Acme, including Mr. Grayson, to review Ben's plan. This meeting was held during the early afternoon of December 11. About 3:00 P.M., Mr. Grayson entered the area in which the girls' and Ben's desks were located, approached Ben's desk, and slammed the folder containing Ben's plans down on the desk, exclaiming, "What in the hell is this?" Before Ben could reply, Mr.

Grayson commenced in a loud voice to lecture on the necessity of going through channels when submitting reports, ideas, and suggestions. His remarks attracted the attention of the office girls, most of whom stopped work to watch the disturbance. Ben Reed interrupted Mr. Grayson to suggest that they might continue their discussion in Mr. Grayson's office which was glass-enclosed and out of earshot of the girls. Mr. Grayson snatched the folder from Ben's desk and stalked into his office, Ben following.

The discussion in Mr. Grayson's office consisted mainly of a continuation of Mr. Grayson's remarks. After he had concluded his remarks, Ben stated that he had not been satisfied with his relationship with Acme and intended to submit his resignation in the very near future. He then left Mr. Grayson's office.

The next day, December 12, Mr. Grayson asked Ben to step into his office for a few minutes. He apologized to Ben for his conduct of the previous day, remarking that he had had several things on his mind which had upset him and that he certainly had full confidence in Ben's abilities. Ben accepted this apology, remarking that he might have flown off the handle a little bit himself. The meeting ended on a cordial note.

On December 13, Ben Reed submitted his resignation and subsequently left the Acme Company on December 24, 1959.

4. NORSE ELECTRONICS (A)

THE NORSE ELECTRONICS COMPANY was a young, rapidly expanding Boston firm which manufactured and sold specialized electronic instrumentation systems used in industrial processing. The company had established a reputation for high-quality instruments of advanced design. The heaviest concentration of Norse customers lay in the northeastern quadrant of the United States, although an increasing number of sales were being secured from companies in California and in several southwestern states.

The Houston office, manned by one sales engineer and an electronics technician, had been established three years ago to exploit the mushrooming industrial firms which had sprung up in Texas and surrounding states. The decision to open the Houston office had been made largely on reliable reports that several small Texas firms which made competitive or complementary instrumentation were enjoying rapid growth from local sales. Norse's southwestern sales volume in the subsequent three years, however, had not grown to expectations.

Norse Electronics' vice president of sales, Philip Sims, was becoming increasingly concerned over the disappointing sales reports from Houston. He believed that this poor record was at least partially due to the high turnover rate of sales engineers through the Houston office. In the past three years, three of Norse's most promising sales engineers had been sent to Houston. Two had resigned from Norse when their requests for transfer from Houston had been denied. Mr. Sims had just received a request for transfer from the third salesman, Nick Randolph, after he had been in Houston only ten months.

Nick was twenty-eight years old, born in Boston, an electrical engineering graduate from M.I.T. He had been employed by Norse for six years, four of them as a sales engineer covering part of the New York territory. He was considered by Norse management to be a quick-witted, technically competent, and highly personable salesman. In Mr. Sims's opinion, Nick was the most likely to succeed in Houston, though his background was much like that of his predecessors.

On request from his superior, Nick reported the reasons for his transfer application. Nick had been happy about his move to Texas. He liked Houston and quickly made many friends there. However, he soon grew to dislike the way his job was turning out. He could not seem to make the usual headway with potential customers. Because of the large investment represented by his products, he usually dealt with top executives. He said he could not seem to get his ideas across to these men. This bewildered him because he had, in prior assignments, developed a highly successful technique in dealing with busy executives. He meticulously prepared his sales presentation in advance so that as little time as possible was required in getting the "Norse facts" across. His New York customers had often complimented him on this direct, brief, lucid presentation.

When he went into a Texas manufacturer's office, ready to present a concise, customer-oriented description of his products, he ran into a "stone wall." The customer would glance at Nick's material, then lapse into general conversation. In between stories about deep-sea fishing trips, deer hunting, Texas ranch life, or some other discussion far afield from processing instruments, Nick would try to bring the conversation back to the issue at hand—the benefits of a Norse installation. Only after considerable effort on Nick's part would the customer give his attention to the presentation. By that time, it seemed to Nick that the presentation was an anticlimax of little interest to the customer, and too often the interview was terminated with little hope of a follow-up sale.

Nick concluded that the Houston businessmen he had seen were either pitifully unaware of the potential applications of Norse equipment to their manufacturing processes or they were simply giving him a polite but unmistakable "brush-off." He had heard from one of his predecessors in the Houston office that "You can't do business with Texas businessmen," but he had discounted this opinion as a sign of incompetence. Now he believed it.

5. NORSE ELECTRONICS (B)

AFTER MR. SIMS heard Nick's account of his misadventures in Houston, he began to wonder whether Nick wasn't right, that Norse's potential customers in Texas, so far from the seat of much innovation in the East, were naive in thinking about instrumentation applications in their manufacturing processes. But, if that were true, why were Texas electronic firms having such success?

His faith in Nick's analysis seemed confirmed by a chance conversation Mr. Sims had with a Texas manufacturer he met at a party several weeks later. Stimulated by the conviviality of the occasion, Mr. Sims and the Texan began to josh each other about the virtues of their respective regions. Part of the conversation went like this:

TEXAN: One thing a Texan really knows—that's how to live. How you people stand this jostling around I've had since I got here I'll never understand.

SIMS: It's just that we don't have all that oil land to fall back on up here. We've got to keep moving—use our wits to keep ahead of you birds. If we don't move fast, you'll overrun us and we'll all get sleepy.

TEXAN: You've been listening to too much of that cow music. We sleep when it's sleeping time—move when it's moving time—enjoy each other when it's enjoying time—and we can tell the difference between one and another. We get just as much done—more maybe—but we don't let getting things done take over. I've seen it in some of you boys who come to work at home. It takes a year to slow them down before they can look around and see where they are. After that they start acting like human beings instead of machines.

SIMS: I still say without all that oil—and maybe some of that grazing land—you wouldn't have time for that so-called good life you lead.

TEXAN: I'm not going to apologize for our God-given resources—they've helped make Texas great. But, you ought to spend some time with us. That isn't "frontier town" down there anymore. Like Khrushchev says, only we'll really do it, we're going to overwhelm you—at your own game. But, I pray it'll never be at the expense of some basic virtues. I hope we'll never forget that men come together as friends first, businessmen second. When the day comes that the men I do business with don't accept me as a friend, I stop doing business. And when I hold out my hand in friendship to them and they turn away and meet me only in commerce, I stop doing business then, too. I've seen what happens to people who live up here. They can't even see the hand being held out to them. They've lost sight of those things. They live a rude, crude kind of life. My friend, come down to big country where everybody's got room to be a human being. And. have another drink to hold you over until you get there.

6. EXCELLENT INSURANCE COMPANY (A)

THROUGHOUT THE winter of 1952–53, Robert Jennings, a research worker from the Harvard Business School, spent several weeks studying the industrial department of the home office of the Excellent Insurance Company in Cleveland, Ohio. The home office of the company employed more than 4,000 people, 500 in the industrial department. The company had an extensive business in industrial, group, and ordinary life insurance. With more than 100 branch offices and 4,000 agents, the company had contracts for industrial insurance with more than 4,000,000 policyholders. The holders of industrial policies paid small weekly premiums as low as 10 cents. Annual dividends on these policies ranged from five to ten times the weekly premium.

The service functions of the home office were organized in several departments. Three, called policy departments, handled the service transactions on existing policies, such as paying dividends and processing the transactions involved in the issue of new policies and the surrender of existing ones.

John Warner, manager of the industrial department, was responsible to Calvin Bunbury, vice president in charge of all three policy departments.[1]

In the dividend division of the industrial department were kept the company's records of the annual dividends on each industrial policy.[2] The clerks in this division checked these records for accuracy and filed them. On the average, the division processed the records of 4,000,000 separate dividends a year, an average of about 15,000 each working day. Thirty-five clerks were in the division. The work was being converted from manual operations to a new punched-card accounting system. Jennings was studying the introduction and administration of the new system, the installation of which was nearly complete by April. From his discussions with a number of managers, Jennings became interested in some events which were only loosely related to the new accounting system. This case is a result of that interest.

On the morning of April 16, Jennings talked with Norman Homans,

---

[1] For a partial organization chart, see Exhibit 1.

[2] A partial organization chart of the department is shown also in Exhibit 1.

Exhibit 1

EXCELLENT INSURANCE COMPANY

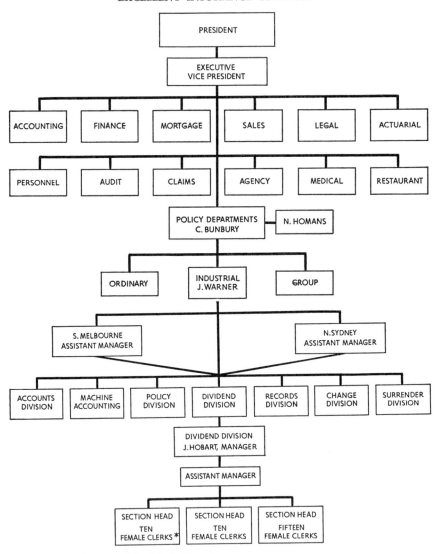

* Kathy O'Toole was one of the clerks in this section.

an administrative assistant to Bunbury. Jennings had talked to Homans on a number of previous occasions. Homans had been assigned to introduce Jennings to other members of the management of the policy departments. During the conversation, Homans mentioned a problem he had regarding Kathy O'Toole. Excerpts from the conversation follow:

NORMAN HOMANS: It all started one time when I was up having lunch with one of the personnel directors. He told me that a waitress in the executive dining room was interested in improving her position in life by getting a job as a clerk.

The girl he referred to was Kathy O'Toole. I know Kathy O'Toole quite well. She often waited on our table, and I was impressed with her efficiency, energy, and general attitude toward life. She is a married woman of about 42 who came back to work at the company after her family grew up.

Anyhow, she went to the personnel department and asked them if they had any openings in the clerical line because she didn't want to be a waitress all her life. I knew she was going to school at night studying secretarial work with a view of one day fulfilling her ambition to become a secretary, and I also knew that she was interested in getting a job in the clerical area prior to an opportunity coming up where she could use her secretarial training.

I said to the personnel director: "I may be able to do something about it. I'll look into whether we have a slot in one of the policy departments in which we could use her." I knew that we had plenty of room in the policy departments for good clerks, and I thought that here was a chance to get a good clerk—someone a bit above the average. You know that we are short of good clerks. We have been for some time.

That afternoon, I talked to Mr. Melbourne. He said that we could use more help in the dividend division and that there was an opening there. We arranged a transfer for Kathy from the job as waitress to a job as clerk in the dividend division. Then the next thing I heard was that she didn't want to be transferred until after Christmas because she wanted to get her share of the Christmas tips. We thought this was reasonable, so we transferred her in January.

There were repercussions. Quite a number of the fellows around the office here knew Kathy because she is a bright and breezy type of girl and seems to know everyone, particularly those on whom she had waited at the table. When they passed her in the corridor, they would ask her: "How is it going, Kathy? How do you like your new job?" We felt that she might have a bit of a problem in terms of transferring from waitress to clerk. We thought that perhaps some of the girls might say, "She's only a waitress," so we picked out the industrial department. We thought there was less chance of any problems there because they do more working and less talking in the industrial department than they do in some of the others, and we thought that they would get on with their work and not bother about whether she was a waitress or what she was. Anyhow, these boys asked her how things were going and how she liked it; and her report was that she hated the job, didn't like it a bit, and wanted to get out of it. Kathy continued that she didn't have enough work to do and that it was an awful job.

Then I heard that she tried to get a transfer from this department. I heard various stories about how she went about it. One was that she knew Bill Field quite well. She used to wait on his table, too, and he works in the ordinary department. According to his story, Kathy went over to see Bill and asked whether he had any vacancies in his area. He said yes, he had plenty of opportunities in his area. He needed girls in some of the accounting work where they were short of clerical help in the statistical record section, and he talked to her about an opportunity available there.

After this, Kathy went to the personnel department and wanted to know if she could be transferred to the ordinary department. The interviewer that handled this job—her name is Miss Avon—talked to Kathy and later talked to Joe Main, the assistant personnel manager, asking him what they should do about the situation. Apparently, they thought that this wasn't the way things should be done; they didn't like clerks to make their own transfer arrangements.

While all this was going on, I heard from different people that things were happening. For example, the manager of the dividend division, Mr. Hobart, heard about her making arrangements for a transfer and got annoyed about it. He said he didn't care for this type of thing going on; that she wasn't much of a clerk, anyhow; and that she wouldn't sit down and get on with her job. He said she was always hopping up and making phone calls and walking out here and there, and her general behavior wasn't good enough for him. When Kathy was asked about this, her reaction was that she never had enough work to do and she didn't know what to do with herself.

Now, I don't know who is right. If she doesn't have enough to do, there is something wrong with the way Hobart administers his division. On the other hand, it is her job to get on with her work and not to be making phone calls and behaving in that manner. You see, there is a bit of a problem, in a way, because she knows so many of the people from the executive dining room on a friendly basis that she is inclined to be presumptuous.

As a matter of fact, I've got myself in a spot now because I feel I've got to justify my own action. This feeling of mine is increased by the fact that Melbourne warned us that he had heard from the grapevine that this girl liked things her own way and was inclined to put on a performance if things didn't get done the way she considered was right. It is amazing what Melbourne hears on his grapevine; and it has been my experience that when he hears something, it is pretty accurate. He seems to know—I don't know how—but he just seems to find out about people. In fact, I've got to the situation now where I take his opinion against mine any time.

Anyhow, the next thing that happened on this matter was when Miss Avon talked to Bill Field. He apparently said that he didn't have an opening available. It seems that he thought about the matter in the light of some comments he heard about Kathy—such comments as the fact that she wasn't a very good clerk—and Miss Avon reported to me that he wasn't so sure he did have an opening available for her. Miss Avon told me that she thought it would be better if we didn't let Kathy make her own transfer arrangements. Miss Avon said that she had talked to Joe Main and that she had decided to tell Kathy that there was no vacancy in the ordinary department, but that there was an opening in the accounting department, and that Kathy could take a look at the job over there and, if she liked it, she could have it. Incidentally, Kathy had threatened to leave the company and said that if she had to stay in the dividend division, she would do so.

In her interview with Miss Avon, Kathy said that she was sold on the company, but she wasn't going to put up with working in the dividend division.

At the next interview, Miss Avon told Kathy that she couldn't have the job in the ordinary department but that she could have a job in the accounting department. Kathy had a look at the job in the accounting department and went back to Miss Avon and said, no, that wasn't the type of job she wanted. Kathy said: "If I can't have the job in the ordinary department, I don't know what I will do, but I won't stay in the dividend division."

Next, Kathy turned up at the medical clinic, saying that she had a bad headache. She had never been in the clinic before. Following her visit, we got a call from the medical people, who said that Kathy was in a highly nervous state and that if we didn't do something about her problems, we would end up with a group insurance case on our hands and she would be out, with us paying her for some time.

We thought that it was a little silly that we should be getting ourselves into the position of having a group insurance case just for not letting the girl transfer where she wanted to, and I thought that the personnel people had really not used the right approach when they limited her transfer. I told them that it was wrong for them to be subjective about a problem and to limit this transfer just because they thought this girl was expecting too much. I thought that if there was a transfer available to the ordinary department, and the ordinary department was prepared to have her, they should let her go. After all, the ordinary policy department is under Mr. Bunbury's jurisdiction, too, and we can keep an eye on the situation. At the same time, I thought it should be made clear to her that if this job didn't suit her, she would have no complaints.

The personnel people have asked me to talk to Kathy about it; if they do arrange the transfer, they want me to tell her that this is the last time she will get any special consideration. As far as I am concerned, all I want is to be done with it. I wish I had never taken it on; and yet, she seemed like a good bet in terms of getting a good clerk.

When Jennings left Homans' office that morning, he recalled some of his impressions of the dividend division. He had spent several days in the division and had heard a number of opinions regarding the new system. Hobart, the manager, thought that the new system would be much better than the old. He remarked that it should make it easier to handle the fluctuations in the volume of work which occurred from period to period. These fluctuations, on occasion, left the girls with very little to do; while on other occasions, the volume required the inventorying of work which could not be done by the normal work force. A company policy of speedy service discouraged the inventorying of work on daily transactions, and Hobart did not like to be in the position of admitting that his division could not meet its deadlines. Consequently, he was reluctant to reduce his regular work force during periods when the load was light because he anticipated difficulty in handling peak loads which he knew would occur from time to time.

Many of the comments Jennings heard about the new punched-card system were very favorable. Several of the girls who worked in the dividend division liked the new system much better. Nevertheless, some of them commented that the fluctuating volumes of work did create slow periods and periods when the pressure was really on.

Some of the fluctuations in volume were caused through errors made by agents. The work of the dividend clerks was so organized that most of it was standardized and simplified. It was only when the agents made errors that the job of the clerks became complicated. When an error occurred, the clerks had to ascertain its cause and fill out a form to notify the agent and give him the reason. When no errors were made, a clerk could process a thousand dividends in less time than was required for a hundred dividends in an agency where errors occurred. Consequently, the work load of the dividend division corresponded closely with the degree of accuracy maintained by the several thousand agents operating throughout forty-eight states.

The section of the division to which Kathy was assigned serviced about one hundred district offices. Shortly before Kathy was assigned to the section, 12 girl clerks were doing this work. In April, 1953, the new system made it possible for the work of one section to be done by 10 girls. Two of the senior ones were transferred to more skilled work in other divisions of the department. Even then, the work in the section was not sufficient to keep the girls occupied all the time. Consequently, whenever he was in need of temporary assistance in other divisions of the department, Melbourne, the assistant manager, would transfer a few of the girls from the dividend section. Some of the girls, Jennings knew, did not like being transferred temporarily to assist other divisions. They felt that the harder they worked to get their own work finished, the more chance they had of being assigned to assist somewhere else. Consequently, the girls were inclined to stretch out the job during slack periods and make a special effort to look busy whenever Melbourne was about.

7. EXCELLENT INSURANCE COMPANY (B)

WHEN JENNINGS came into the division the afternoon following his conversation with Homans, he continued his usual procedure of asking the girls to tell him about their work and what they thought of the new punched-card system. He stopped at Kathy's desk during his conversations and asked her to tell him about her work.

KATHY O'TOOLE: I don't think I'm a very good one for you to talk with because I haven't been here very long and I'm going to be transferred soon.

ROBERT JENNINGS: Why are you being transferred?

KATHY: Well, I don't like the work here. It is too quiet. You don't have enough to do. The time really drags. I like to have some work to do so that I can keep busy and the clock will move along. Sitting here with nothing to do just drives me crazy. I don't mind sorting these things that I've got to do now because it is something to fill in time, but there are times when I could just go to sleep, and I'm not like that. Some of these young girls just seem to like to walk around very slowly and gradually get the job done. They are like my own daughter. I often tell her that she doesn't move and that she doesn't get things done, and she tells me that she gets just as far in the long run, but I can't understand these kids these days. They seem to be prepared to sit and let things go by. They just walk around very casual-like. See that one walking down there now? My goodness! I would be around there and back again in no time.

JENNINGS: Do you like to keep busy?

KATHY: Yes, I do. I think that is why I don't like the work here. It is just not enough for me. It depends upon what your view is, but I can't change myself at this stage. I'm too old. I'm 42, and I've always been busy doing things. I want something that is challenging and interesting. When I first started here, they said: "You know, Kathy, this needs to be done; and Kathy, that needs to be done." After I had been told a couple of times, I'd ask why, and they just wouldn't bother to tell me why. They don't tell me anything. I said to our section head: "I want to know what happens here. Why do these things come in here? I would then be a little more interested, knowing where these things go and why I am doing this." So he explained it to me. But most of these kids that come in here are prepared to sit down; and when they are told things, they do them and are not interested in why or anything else. When I came here, I didn't think anything was going to be like this, and I am just not satisfied to stay.

JENNINGS: You don't like this system of work, then?

KATHY: The system is all right. It is good. As a matter of fact, I think it does things pretty well. The only thing is that there is an awful waste in all the time spent here, everybody checking and sending things backwards and forwards when someone makes a silly mistake in the agency. It seems to me that it would be a good thing if they had that sort of thing checked out in the agency. Then a lot of those things could be caught before they come in here.

JENNINGS: They would need an extra girl in the agency to do that sort of thing, wouldn't they?

KATHY: Yes, they would, I suppose. But they could check a number of these things, and you'd think the agents could make them out a little better and correct these mistakes. Perhaps I am a little silly there; the more mistakes they make, the more clerks they need here in the office, and I could talk myself out of a job. But the point is that I am not interested in sitting here doing nothing all the time. I have to be up and doing. I've always been busy all my life, and I can't understand some of the younger people these days. They just don't want to do things. They seem to sit around. The way they dress—they come in with bobby socks and curling pins. I just can't understand it. I think it is indicative of your way of working—the way you dress. For instance, if you came in here with a pair of loafers and a sport shirt, you wouldn't give the right impression, would you? Well, I think we should look after ourselves and dress on the job, just the same as a man. We should do things properly.

JENNINGS: Do you think the job to which you are going to be transferred will be better?

KATHY: Well, I don't know exactly where I am going to be transferred. It seems to take quite a lot to get transferred around this place; but if I am transferred where I want to go to, the work will be much better. There is more opportunity there and a chance to get ahead if you show yourself. The thing is that in this division, all the jobs are much the same. No matter how a girl works and tries, she can't get ahead here; there is nowhere to go. All they do is routine work, and that is not enough.

JENNINGS: What sort of work do you like?

KATHY: I'd like any work that is interesting and where there is plenty to do and you are doing different things. It is a long story, and I'll tell you how I happened to come here in the first place.

You see, my two children are grown up. My daughter is at the university now. She wanted to do clerical work at one stage, and we let her do clerical work; and then she found that she hated clerical work and wanted to go to college, so her father said: "Well, you started in doing clerical work. You can stick it out for the rest of the year and go to college next year." Anyhow, we let her go to college this year, and she is very happy there now. She is living away from home, and I think it is the best thing she could have done. I always told her what to do at home; and at least, she makes decisions for herself now, and I think she is better off for it. She is at college. My boy is grown up. He is in the Marines. Now that the children aren't at home, the place is just empty.

I like the conditions of work here, and the managers in this company are wonderful. The only thing is that I'd like to work where I can do something interesting. You know, some of these girls here are prepared to put up with anything. They just don't know any better. But I know so many of the executives that I met in the dining room that I wouldn't meet otherwise, and I know them pretty well, and I feel that I'm in a position to know better than to just put up with this type of thing here.

JENNINGS: Is the actual work, when you are doing it, uninteresting?

KATHY: No, that part of the work is all right. As a matter of fact, I don't mind it when I've got the work to do. It is quite interesting and quite good, but you don't seem to be kept occupied. Anyhow, I just don't want to stay on this type of work. I have ambition. I want to be an executive's secretary. One of these days, I'm going to be. You know, I've got no reason to rush from here like some of these other girls who are just putting in time until they get married. I like it here, and I don't see any reason why I shouldn't make a career of it. I've got plenty of years ahead of me; and I might work here until I retire, if they give me something interesting. My husband picks me up at night and drives me in in the morning; our working hours coincide very conveniently. I can handle the home without any trouble now that the children are away; and instead of just sitting at home without anything to do, I'd rather come here and work. I don't come here for the money, you know. I'm only interested in something to do. My husband wouldn't let me work for a long while. For instance, when the children were small, he wouldn't even have considered it; but nowadays, I'd just be sitting around an empty house. I just couldn't stand it. I'd much rather come here.

The following morning, Homans told Jennings that he was to talk with Kathy that afternoon.

HOMANS: This is an interesting problem. I've got Kathy coming in to see me at 3:00 o'clock this afternoon, and I've got to know what to say to her then. I'm not sure what I'm going to do. I know one thing: I want to get something fixed and be done with it, so I'll have to think pretty carefully about what I say to her.

8. WALT ROGERS

MR. WARNER was district superintendent for one of the departments of a large corporation operating on a state-wide basis. He was responsible for the direction and over-all supervision of a group of 125 employees, predominantly men. The size of Warner's district and the nature of the work had made it more efficient and economical to locate subsidiary offices at strategic points throughout the territory, rather than to have the entire force operate out of the district headquarters.

As part of his supervisory activities, Mr. Warner customarily visited each of the suboffice locations at least once a week. During a regular visit to one office he noticed that Walt Rogers, one of the employees, seemed very much depressed and showed little interest in his job and less in the people around him. As a matter of fact, Mr. Warner tried to engage him in conversation, but to no avail, since Rogers did not even reply to his greeting. Later, Mr. Warner asked the foreman of the group what was troubling Rogers, and he replied, "Oh, he's been like that ever since he flunked the test."

The test in question was a prescribed examination given by a federal agency to those who wanted to qualify for mobile radio repair work, which was one of the newer but fast-growing fields in which the company operated. Qualification for the license would have enabled Rogers to progress to a better assignment than his then present position of equipment repairman.

Mr. Rogers was thirty-six years old, was married, and had several children. He had had sixteen years' service with the company. During the war he had been granted a three-year military leave of absence, during which period he became interested in radio work. After his return to duty and despite his interest in this field, three years elapsed before he requested the opportunity to take a five-week training course given by the company to prepare employees with the necessary aptitudes for this type of work.

Mr. Rogers' request had been forwarded through organization lines to Mr. Warner, who considered the application very carefully before he approved it. Rogers had been under his supervision for five years, and the district superintendent felt that he knew him quite well. He was aware of the fact that Rogers was not too friendly with his co-workers, and was rated by them as being sarcastic, snobbish, and a "griper." From close observation, Mr. Warner was inclined to agree with the tag placed on Rogers by his fellow workers, and on several occasions had discussed Rogers' shortcomings with him. In each instance Rogers admitted the correctness of the charges but said he couldn't do anything about it.

Despite these factors, Mr. Warner felt that Rogers had the ability to do the specialized work, and upon the local foreman's recommendation, had approved the request. Rogers had attended the next regularly scheduled training course, during which time he had performed satisfactorily.

Normally, Mr. Warner's method of approach was very direct. During all his thirty-five years of service he had worked with men, and felt that men wanted a "spade called a spade," and he acted accordingly. Some of his men liked, and some resented, these methods of Mr. Warner. For his knowledge of the job, his fairness and ability, however, all who had any dealings with him respected him.

Since Warner did not have all the facts about Rogers, and since he knew that he would be seeing Rogers probably within the next week, Mr. Warner took no further action at the time on the situation brought so forcibly to his attention by Rogers' behavior. Within the next several days after the incident mentioned, however, Mr. Warner secured all the facts he needed. The following week when Rogers came to the district office for some special equipment, Mr. Warner took the opportunity to discuss the outcome of the course and examination with Rogers, as follows:

WARNER: Come in, Walt. Sit down. What are you so gloomy about this morning?

ROGERS: I'm not gloomy.

WARNER: I guess that's right. You always look that way.

ROGERS: What do you want me to do, walk around with a silly grin on all the time?

WARNER: Not unless you feel like it, Walt, but does a grin necessarily have to be silly?

ROGERS: I guess not, but these people who walk around, always cheerful, give me a pain.

WARNER: Why not be cheerful? Who do you like best to do business with—a cheerful man or a fellow with a chip on his shoulder?

ROGERS: Oh, I suppose a fellow who is good-natured is easier to get along with. . . . (Pause.) Well?

WARNER: Well, what?

ROGERS: You wanted to see me, didn't you?

WARNER: Yes, I thought we ought to talk over a couple of things.

ROGERS: I've got nothing to talk about.

WARNER: The hell you haven't. When a man sulks around like you've been, there's something bothering him.

ROGERS: What's bothering me is my business. I'll do my job, and that's all I'm getting paid for.

WARNER: That's what you think. Now look, junior, everybody around here has to get along with everybody else. We have to meet the public; we have to give them service; and we have an obligation to do it graciously and leave a good taste in their mouths.

ROGERS: Ain't I doing all right? What have I done wrong now?

WARNER: I didn't say you had done anything wrong, but, as long as you've asked the question, we've had a couple of complaints from customers that they would rather we send somebody else to their places to work.

ROGERS: I'd like to know who it was. I've been doing all right. Who was it anyhow? I'll go down there and see them.

WARNER: You aren't going anywhere to see anybody. Now, you come down to earth. The whole trouble with you is you're a good winner and a poor loser. You're cocky as all hell, but you've fumbled one and you can't take it.

ROGERS: I thought you'd hold that one against me. I shouldn't have taken that course anyway. That's a job for a more experienced man. I don't get paid that much money.

WARNER: Well, in the first place you asked for the chance. Nobody made you take it. In the second place, you're not done yet. You're going back for a refresher and another try, and to get your chin up out of your boot tops. A man who can't take the bumps when they're coming to him has no right to the good times when they come along. I know that job isn't easy, but other fellows have made the grade, and you thought you could do it. Heck, I should think it would have been duck soup for you. You've already got a third-class license. The other men had to start from scratch.

ROGERS: It was a lot harder than I thought it would be. You say I've got to try again?

WARNER: Certainly, you've got to try it again. We've spent money on you now. Unless you want to admit you're licked, then we'll have to try someone else.

ROGERS: Don't you think I can make it?

WARNER: I don't have any ideas at all. You missed the first try, and now you act like you're licked. You tell me whether you can do it.

ROGERS: I don't see why I can't if the other men did. They're no smarter than I am. Something just seemed to go wrong on that course. I had seen a lot of it before, but I seemed to have trouble with it. It wasn't the "math," and the formulas seemed to make sense in the classroom, but in the hall they asked a lot of questions I hadn't heard before.

WARNER: Wasn't it a matter of applying principles you'd learned to a new situation? You know, Newton learned about gravity by watching an apple fall, but he had sense enough to apply that to a book, a chair, or anything else that was left unsupported.

ROGERS: That probably sort of describes it, I guess; you know, I believe I could try again and find it a little easier this time.

WARNER: It's up to you. I believe we could put Bill Martin through it if you don't want to try again.

ROGERS: Oh, cripes! Not that guy! Let me go back again, I know I'll get it this time.

WARNER: That's what you said before, but you didn't do it.

ROGERS: I know, but I will this time. I'll study the book through again before I go back to school. I know I can do it.

WARNER: That's better, and remember this, Walt, I think you can do it. If you fail, I won't hold it against you. Anybody is liable to fail. Hell, I'd hate to tell you how many times I've been set back on my heels, but a man will always get up and take another swing. It's no disgrace to lose, but it is a disgrace not to try.

ROGERS: Oh, I wasn't licked. I'm not used to being beaten, and I guess it kind of hurt, that's all. If it's all right with you, I'd like to go back again. I like that work, and I'd like to stay on it.

WARNER: O.K. That's what I brought you in here for. Good luck to you and go to it.

ROGERS: Huh! Wise guy, eh! But you win, and thanks.

9. GILLEN RADIO CORPORATION

THE GILLEN RADIO CORPORATION maintained, as part of its personnel program, a centrally located training school. This school gave courses of instruction in various branches of radio work, including the installation and maintenance of private radio systems, to employees who were sent in by their supervisors. The school was under the direction of a training supervisor by the name of Philip Stone, and reporting to him were a number of instructors, all of whom were classified as part of the management of the business.

Ben Mason, the instructor in charge of the class in the installation and maintenance of private radio systems, had formerly been a workman who was made a management employee for the purpose of conducting radio classes in early 1948. Mason had had long experience in radio, having been a "ham" for many years, and he had built many sets. He was considered to be very expert. He had also received extensive training on television maintenance.

In March, 1948, one of the radio repair classes had been in session for seven days when Mason advised Philip Stone that it would be necessary to remove Jim Roberts, one of the students, from his class. Mason reported that Roberts was making very poor progress in the theory phases of the training and was holding up the class. Roberts seemed to be highly nervous in class and appeared to be thoroughly confused. On one occasion he said, when Roberts was out of matches, Mason had offered him a cigarette lighter instead, and when Roberts could not light it, he shoved it back with an exclamation that he couldn't even make that work, so how could he do radio repairs? The instructor also learned that Roberts had lost his appetite and was not sleeping well at night.

Mason himself was somewhat upset at the thought of having to drop the student as he had had several failures in some previous classes. Although he did not have any part in selecting the students, he was fully aware of their background and training. Sometimes, in order to establish rapport in the group, he was in the habit of having each man describe his background to the rest of the class.

Stone felt that he should talk with Jim Roberts before taking any action on Mason's suggestion. Before the interview he reviewed Roberts' entire history and talked with his supervisor at his home location. During this investigation the following facts developed: Jim Roberts had been an employee of the company for one-and-a-half years, having been employed directly after his discharge from military service. He was a high school graduate. He had been sent to the school on two previous occasions, the first time for instruction in electrical installation work. The instructor at that time reported, "He lacked self-confidence; however, he retained and applied major details of all subjects taught, had good analytical ability, but needed experience on the job."

Later Roberts took a slightly more advanced electrical course, at which time the instructor reported, "Very good progress and with experience will develop further." Stone also reviewed the student's employment test scores, and found that he had above-average ability. In his contact with Roberts' foreman, who had been Roberts' supervisor for only two months, he found that Jim Roberts was the only employee available at the location who could be given radio training. He also found that Roberts was making good progress on his regular work assignment.

After Stone, the training supervisor, had gathered these facts, he arranged to make a visit to the school to see the class in session. While at the school, Stone took advantage of an opportunity to speak to Roberts privately and started a conversation with him.

STONE: Hello, you're Jim Roberts aren't you? I don't know if you remember me, but I'm Philip Stone. I interviewed you when you were first thinking about coming to work for the company.

ROBERTS: Certainly, I remember you, Mr. Stone.

STONE: I don't think I've been back to Berwick since I was there on that recruiting trip. What has been going on in town? (Roberts and Stone exchange several comments about Roberts' home town.) How is the job working out for you?

ROBERTS: I've been very happy at it. The customers I've done work for are mostly people I've known around town and I've enjoyed the work.

STONE: I'm glad to hear that.

ROBERTS: Say, some of the customers have been asking me when we're going to be able to catch up on all the back orders we haven't been able to fill yet. Do you know when that will be? (Stone offered to get the answer to this question for Roberts.)

I don't know if you heard that I've got one of the new trucks to work with. It really is a nice one. There is a place for all the tools and supplies so you know just where things are. I sure hope the man who is filling in for me won't mess up the truck while I'm gone. (Pause) My job means a lot to me; that's why I'm so worried about this course.

STONE: You're worried about this course?

ROBERTS: Yes. You see, I thought I had been making out pretty well on my job back home, but this classroom study isn't going so good. The instructor hasn't said anything to indicate that I'm not going to pass, but I can tell from the way the other men answer questions that they have learned much more about radio than I have.

STONE: You think they are getting more out of the training than you?

ROBERTS: You see, I didn't have any previous notice of the course. I had no time to study up, and from day-to-day it seems the training is getting farther over my head. The other fellows talk about technical things such as wave guides, shapes of the modulated frequencies, and so on, and sometimes I don't even know what the terms mean. The situation is getting almost hopeless.

STONE: Just what do you feel is expected of you after completion of this course?

ROBERTS: From what the instructor has told me, we will be expected to locate minor troubles, such as faulty tubes and other items that can be fixed on the job.

STONE: How about major troubles?

ROBERTS: We expect to have spare units, and our present procedure is to replace the entire unit and send the defective one back to the repair shop. The instructor has already given us several troubles to clear.

STONE: Shooting trouble already? Tell me about that.

ROBERTS: I'm not very good. The other boys seem to find the troubles quickly and are able to explain in great detail just how the failure caused the radio to do what it did. That makes me feel that I won't be able to hold my end up after I finish the course. Those fellows sure are on the beam.

STONE: So they're pretty hot radio men already?

ROBERTS: Well, a couple of them have radio licenses, and practically all of them have worked at radio on the side, or while they were in the service. They are a swell bunch of fellows, and they're all very much interested in radio. Take Joe, for instance; he was a "ham" even before he went into the service, and didn't do anything but work on radio during his three and a half years in the Navy. But the others are almost as good on trouble as he is. Boy! Can they talk radio and shoot trouble.

STONE: On the sample troubles you were telling me about, have you had need for the technical training and terms that the other men have discussed in the classroom?

ROBERTS: No, I guess not, so far, but frankly, it bothers me a lot when they seem to talk so freely about things that I do not even understand, when it really does apply to the course.

STONE: Much of this technical background is helpful, but it's well beyond the intended scope of the course. Don't you feel that you can do the things you have been trained on so far?

ROBERTS: I can do them, after a fashion, but what has me worried is the ease with which the other fellows cleared the troubles. But I guess I'd have to be a superman to do as well as the others with only seven days' training on radio.

STONE: I see what you mean!

ROBERTS: By the way, if I get by all right in this course, do you suppose that I can qualify for a G.I. radio course out-of-hours?

Stone explained how he could make application for this training.

10. CLEVELAND JUNIOR CHAMBER OF COMMERCE[1]

The Junior Chamber of Commerce of Cleveland was a voluntary organization of young businessmen in the community. The two principal objectives of the organization were to provide civic service and an opportunity for leadership training for its members. The organization sponsored a number of community service activities, and its members had a chance to exercise leadership in the organization and execution of these different types of service activities. For example, the organization might sponsor a Christmas party for underprivileged children, or a community festival, or a summer day camp, or perhaps a local automobile safety campaign.

In the fall of 1954, Peter Trapper, the president of the Cleveland Junior Chamber of Commerce, made a luncheon date to talk over a Jaycee problem with William Joslin, the chairman of the committee sponsoring a spring clean-up campaign. For some time, Trapper had been concerned with the way Joslin was handling his committee responsibilities. He scheduled the lunch to talk to him about this matter.

The following is a summarized statement of how Trapper saw the situation:

> Bill Joslin joined our group about a year ago, a short time before I took over as president. Right from the beginning I was impressed with the competency of Bill. He had some good ideas in our general membership meetings. He has got a good reputation here in the community. He is the head of his own small and highly successful business. I understand he is involved in quite a few community organizations. Late last spring he evidenced some interest in the talk we were having about the possibility of staging a big spring clean-up campaign for the downtown area. He seemed to me to have a lot of interest and drive on the matter, so with the approval of our other executive officers, we named him chairman of this committee. Because this was the first time we had undertaken this kind of a project, we picked some of our very best members to work with him on this committee. They were all fellows who had served on different committees and had really shown that they were willing to put in some time and effort. You see, that's one of the problems we have in our kind of

---

[1] All names and places have been changed for disguise purposes.

organization. Not all our members are willing to take the time to really work at our organizational projects. Most of the officers of our organization are quite aware of this and have worked at developing different devices for lifting the enthusiasm and support of our membership in our different projects. Of course, being new, Bill didn't have too much experience with our organization. But he has had a lot of experience in business, so I wasn't too worried about the way he was going to handle this assignment. As far as I was concerned, he had got off to a good start. He sent out a notice to all the committee members of the first committee meeting. When I saw a copy of the notice he sent out, I was a little concerned as to the turnout he was going to get at the meeting. The notice didn't say much, except the time and place of the meeting, and I wasn't sure that it was going to capture the interest of all the members, but he had an excellent group and got a good turnout at that first committee meeting. I wasn't there but it was reported to me by a couple of the members that they had an excellent session and that a number of good ideas were introduced as to how to conduct the spring campaign and get things organized. Bill then called a second committee meeting just three or four weeks after that and they made quite a bit of further progress in developing their plans.

Then, all of a sudden everything seemed to stop. Six weeks went by and I heard nothing further about the activities of this committee. At that point I got somewhat concerned, but I didn't do anything right at the time. Two more weeks went by and still nothing had happened, so I put in a phone call to Bill. I couldn't get him, so I left word with his secretary asking him to call me back. He didn't call me back. I put in a couple more calls and again I couldn't get him. After a few more days without a return call, I was becoming quite concerned. In particular, I had to find out just what the committee's plans were for dates for their spring campaign, so that we didn't have a conflict in our schedule with another project. At that point I sent Bill a letter and I didn't get a reply. I couldn't understand this. I sent him another letter and still I got no answer. Right now I've decided that I must have been wrong in my original judgment of Bill. I thought he was really interested in this project and in our whole Jaycee organization. It now looks to me like he is one of the hangers-on who is enthusiastic one day and then forgets all about it from then on. It looks like I'm going to have to keep pushing him and pushing him to try to get this spring clean-up campaign rolling along as it should. Yesterday he finally called me back in response to my last letter. He gave me some lame excuse of how busy he had been in his business for the last couple of months. At that point I made this appointment with him to get together today to talk over the whole matter.

One of the reasons I am most concerned about this is that in the last few weeks I have run into a few of Bill's committee members. They haven't heard any word from him during the past three months as to what is going on. The members I talked to were getting pretty discouraged about it. They had been all enthusiastic about the project when they had their first committee meeting, but it has been so long now since something has happened that Bill is really losing the support of the committee. No matter what he does now, I think he is going to have a lot of trouble getting them to work for him. When I see him this noon, I am really going to have to get him moving on this whole thing or we'll be in an awful jam.

The following is a summarized statement of how William Joslin viewed the situation:

When I first joined the Jaycees a year ago, it seemed to me like a very good organization. It was a good bunch of live-wire fellows who were interested in doing some useful things around town here and in learning something for themselves in the process. It's just the kind of group I like to get in and really do something with, but right now I'm sort of "fed to the teeth" with the whole organization. That president of theirs seems to think he has to treat people like children. He ought to be thankful that I undertook that job of running the spring clean-up campaign. He ought to know that when I take on an assignment of that kind I do it and I see it through to the end. He seems to be going on the assumption that he has to do it for me and keeps bothering me about it all the time. We got our committee off to a good start early in the summer, and we've still got plenty of time before next spring to work out our final plans. Of course, if I hadn't been so busy this summer, I would have had another meeting or two, but how was I to know that my business would get me so tied up for the whole summer. I barely had time enough to see my family, much less to get any work done for the Jaycees. But it isn't as if I haven't been doing something. I've got two or three really red-hot ideas about this spring campaign that came to me this summer that I think will really pay off, but I'm not at all sure I want to do anything more with it now. I believe that if I'm given an assignment I should be given the right to go ahead and do it my own way. I'm sick and tired of the petty needling, all the phone calls and letters I've been getting from that guy. If he keeps trying to tell me how to run that job, I'm just going to resign and get out of the organization. There are plenty of other places where you can do some useful things without having to put up with that kind of treatment. When I see him at lunch today, if he gives me any more of those snide remarks, I'm going to quit on the spot and see how he likes that.

Concepts and Research Findings

1. DEFENSES AND THE NEED TO KNOW*

Roger Harrison

THE PURPOSE of this paper is to discuss the ways we have of protecting our views of ourselves and others.[1] Specifically, it is intended to rescue the concept of "defensive behavior" from the ostracism in which it is usually held, to restore it to its rightful place as a major tool of man in adapting to a changing world, and to consider how defenses may help and hinder us in profiting from a learning situation.

Let us consider how we understand the world we live in, and particularly those parts of it concerning ourselves and our relations with other people. First of all, we organize the world according to *concepts,* or categories. We say that things are warm or cold; good or bad; simple or complex. Each of these concepts may be considered a dimension along which we can place events in the world—some closer to one end of the dimension, some closer to the other.

Actually, we can't really think without using these categories or dimensions to organize our thoughts. Any time we consider the qualities of ourselves, other persons, or events in the inanimate world, we have to use categories to do it. We are dependent for our understanding of the world on the concepts and categories we have for organizing our experiences. If we lack a concept for something which occurs in the world, we either have to invent one or we cannot respond to the event in an organized fashion. How, for example, would a person explain his own and others' behavior without the concept of love and hate? Think how much behavior would simply puzzle or confuse him or, perhaps, just go on by without really being perceived at all, for lack of this one dimension.

Concepts do not exist in isolation; they are connected to one another by a network of relationships. Taken all together, the concepts we use to

* Taken from "Defenses and the Need to Know," by Roger Harrison, *Human Relations Training News,* Vol. 6, No. 4 (Winter 1962–63). With permission of the author, minor changes have been made in the original article to adapt it to a more diverse audience than that for which it was first intended.

[1] This paper was stimulated by a lecture by Harrington Ingham and a paper by Abraham Maslow.

understand a situation, plus the relationships among the concepts, are called a *conceptual system.* For example, we may say, "People who are warm and friendly are usually trusting, and hence, they are often deceived by others." Here we have a conceptual system linking the concepts of *friendly warmth, trust in others,* and *ease of deception.* Because concepts are linked one to another, the location of an event on one concept usually implies something about where the event is located on each of a whole network of concepts. It is thus almost impossible to take in a small bit of information about a characteristic of a person or event without its having a whole host of implications about other characteristics.

Images and stereotypes operate this way: when we discover that a person is a Negro, or a company president, a social scientist, or a husband, the information on these concepts immediately calls up a whole network of expectations about other characteristics of the person. In the case of stereotypes, these expectations may even be so strong that we do not check to find out whether our conceptual system worked accurately this time, but may even go to the other extreme of ignoring or distorting information which doesn't fit the conceptual system, so that the system may remain quite unaffected by disconfirming experiences.

The study of defenses, like the study of stereotypes, is the study of the processes that protect the organization of conceptual systems in the face of information and experiences which, if accurately perceived, would tend to break down or change the relationships among concepts in the system.

Why should conceptual systems be resistant to change? Actually, if they were simply intellectual exercises, they probably would not. In real life, conceptual systems come to have *value* attached to them. The values seem to be of two kinds: one kind I will call *competence value.* By the competence value of a conceptual system I mean its value for helping us to be effective in the world. After all, the conceptual systems we have were developed because we needed some way of making sense of the world; of predicting what kinds of results would follow from what kinds of causes; of planning what kinds of actions we needed to take in order to accomplish some desired result.

People have the conceptual systems they have because in some important situations the systems proved *adaptive* for them; by seeing the world in just this way they were able to get along better, to be more effective, to prepare better for what was coming next. For human beings conceptual systems are, in a very real sense, very nearly the most important survival equipment we have. Animals have instinctual patterns of response:

complex systems of behavior that are set off without thinking in response to fairly fixed patterns of stimulation. Human beings have to do it the hard way, by developing systems of concepts that make sense of the world and then using these systems to make decisions as to what to do in each situation. Those conceptual systems that pay off over and over again tend to become parts of our permanent equipment for understanding the world and for deciding what to do in it. If we were to lose these systems we would become like ships without rudders; we would have lost our control systems and, with them, our chances of acting in an organized, intelligent fashion to meet our needs. This is what I mean by the *competence value* of conceptual systems.

Unfortunately, no conceptual system fits the world perfectly. In the interests of economy we simplify and leave things out as being unimportant: for example, we act as though relationships which are *statistical* (they are only true most of the time) are *necessary,* and hence true all of the time. On the rare occasions when the relationships don't hold, we tend to overlook it, rather than trying to understand why things didn't go as expected. We may, for example, conceptualize the qualities of decisiveness, aggressiveness, and masculinity as incompatible with a ready ability to express affection. This conceptual system may not change even when we are faced with the clear expression of affection on the part of a man about whose decisiveness and masculinity we have had ample evidence in the past. We simply pass it off as, "He's not himself," or, "He's not really showing affection," or even, "Deep down inside he isn't so decisive and masculine as he appears to be." We go through a lot of mental gymnastics to avoid seriously questioning a conceptual system which has proved useful in the past. So, frequently, the *last* alternative explanation we consider is, "It is perfectly possible for a man to express deep affection readily and still be decisive, aggressive, and masculine." Such an alternative would mean the significant alteration of a conceptual system.

The trouble is, you can't just alter one little conceptual system at will, and let it go at that. Concepts are too closely and complexly linked to change one or two relationships in isolation. One change leads to another, and pretty soon a major reorganization is going on. It may be, of course, that the reorganization may lead to substantial improvement in the person's understanding and effectiveness in the world, but in the meantime there may be considerable turmoil and confusion as the person questions relationships that once seemed solidly established and before new ways of seeing the world have been adequately tested and confirmed.

Of course, the more important the particular conceptual system in question is in making it possible for the person to meet his needs, the more strain and upset is involved in changing it. For example, one might believe that heavy objects fall more rapidly than light ones. The disconfirmation that would follow upon learning that all objects fall at the same rate would perhaps be uncomfortable, but only moderately so. Consider, on the other hand, the anxiety and stress which could be produced by the discovery that complying with another's demands does not always make the other like you and may, indeed, have the opposite effect. For a person who has put much reliance in his interpersonal relations on the techniques associated with such a conceptual system, its disconfirmation may have the dimensions of a major crisis in life.

So, much of the time we hang on to our not-so-accurate conceptual systems because they work for us most of the time, and to give them up would plunge us into mild or severe confusion without any real promise of eventually attaining a more accurate, effective reorganization. The picture does not look so good for improvement, and before I finish, it will look even bleaker.

There is another kind of valuing that goes on in placing events into conceptual systems, and I will call it *evaluation*. This is the well-known process of saying that some states of affairs are better and some are worse. For most conceptual systems, there is an element of evaluation; most concepts have a good end and a bad end, and we would rather see events come out on the good ends than on the bad.

Again, it is less important to see events come out well in some areas than in others. The closer we get to conceptual systems that are concerned with our *self-perceptions* and our important relationships with others, the more important evaluation becomes, and the more uncomfortably responsible we feel when events don't fall on the valued ends of the concepts. Thus, if we value love as against hate, and intelligence against stupidity, it becomes important to protect conceptual systems that organize the events so that we can see ourselves as brilliant and loving. People may desperately protect quite maladaptive, ineffective conceptual systems in order to maintain a favorable perception of self or others.

Sometimes *competence value* and *evaluation* compete for influence in the conceptual system. For example, some persons have led such difficult childhoods that it is only by seeing themselves as bad, worthless people that they can seem to make sense out of the awful things that people they trusted have done to them; at the same time, they have normal needs for self-esteem, and for seeing themselves at the valued ends of concepts. These people may experience considerable conflict between these two motivational influences on their conceptual systems.

These, then, are the "defenses." They serve to keep us from becoming confused, upset, and rudderless every time something happens contrary to our expectations. Frequently, they protect our liking for ourselves and others when we and they fail to live up to our ideals. Defenses give life more stability and continuity than could ever be justified by reference to the contingency and complexity of real events alone. Defenses keep our relations with others more pleasant and satisfying, protecting us from our own and others' anger, and helping us to go on loving people who are usually less than perfect and sometimes less than human.

At the same time, these same defenses block our learning, often dooming us to make the same mistakes over and over again. They make us blind to faults of our own we could correct, as well as those we can do nothing about. Sometimes they make us turn the other cheek when a good clout in the nose would clear the air and establish a new and firmer footing for an honest relationship. They can, in extreme cases, make so many kinds of information dangerous to our conceptual systems that we narrow and constrict our experiences, our feelings, and our thoughts, becoming virtual prisoners of our own protection.

I believe there is in each of us a kind of counterforce which operates in the service of learning. Let's call it a *need to know,* or a drive toward competence. We are used to thinking about physiological needs, and we recognize there are probably social needs, such as needs for love; but we often overlook the need for competence and knowledge. Yet it is in operation all around us. We see it in the baby when he begins to explore as soon as he can crawl; we see it again in the "battle of the spoon," where the child actually gives up the certainty of getting the food into his mouth for the less effective but exciting experiment of "doing it himself." We see this need again as the adolescent struggles to carve out for himself a life that is uniquely his own; and we see it reflected in continuing efforts to understand and master the world as adults. People who read history for pleasure, who have creative hobbies, or who voluntarily continue their education are all manifesting this drive toward competence and knowledge.

The need to know is the enemy of comfort, stability, and a placid existence. For its sake we may risk the discomfort of examining and revising our assumptions about groups and people; we may expose ourselves to the anxiety-provoking experience of "personal feedback," in which we often learn that others do not see us quite as we see ourselves; we place ourselves in groups where we know in advance we will be confused, challenged, and occasionally scared. Some of us expose ourselves to such situations more than once; to me, there could be no more convincing proof that the need to know is frequently stronger than the desire to maintain the comfort and stability of accustomed conceptual systems.

The discussion group thus frequently becomes a battleground between our desires to increase our competence and understanding, and to bolster our defenses. In this battle, we tend to take the side of the need to know and, like partisans everywhere, we malign, attack, and propagandize against the other side. Sometimes we forget that both sides are parts of a person, and that if either side destroys the other the person loses a valuable part of himself. This is particularly true in the case of defenses. We know from clinical practice and, I think, from personal experience and logic, that when a person's first line of defense becomes untenable, he drops back to another one, a sort of "second string" defense. Unfortunately, since we usually put our best and most adaptive defenses out in front, the second string is apt to be even less effective and reality-oriented than the first. To put it strongly, the destruction of defenses does not serve learning; instead, it increases the anxiety of the person that he will lose the more or less effective conceptual systems he has with which to understand and relate to the world, and he drops back to an even more desperate and perhaps unrealistic defense than the one destroyed. Though it may seem paradoxical, we cannot increase learning by destroying the defenses which block it.

What we can do is to create situations where people will not need to stay behind their defenses all the time. We can make it safe to sally forth from behind the moat, so to speak, secure in the knowledge that while we are exploring the countryside no one will sneak in and burn the castle.

People need their defenses most when they are most under threat and pressure. To make a mistake or become confused or admit to oneself that the world, ourselves, and others are not quite what we thought they were means that while we are revising or building new conceptual systems we will not be able to cope so well as before with the "slings and arrows" of a difficult situation. If we need every bit of competence we possess, we simply can't afford to give up conceptual systems which are tried but not perfect, in favor of exciting new ways of looking at things that are untested.

It is for this reason that I believe we cannot really begin to learn deeply from one another in a discussion group until we create relationships of mutual support, respect, and trust.

When we know that others will not place us in situations where we need every bit of our competence to cope with what is going on; when we know they will respect our own personal rate of growth and learning; when we know we have friends to help if we get into difficulties exploring new relationships, understandings, and behavior—then we can begin to look hard at the inadequacies in our ways of making sense of the world. We can examine those "exceptions to the rule" that we've always half expected might prove the rule inadequate; we can afford to really explore why ways of behaving that used to work fine are for some reason not producing satisfactions for us the way they used to, or why they seem to work with some people but not others; and we can really listen to the things people say that indicate they don't see us quite the way we see ourselves.

Out of this kind of exploration can come new and more effective conceptual systems, new ways of behaving that go along with them, and the excitement and pride that accompany increases in competence and knowledge. And when the excitement is over, and the new ways have been tested and integrated and have become habitual ways of seeing and behaving, I hope we will not be surprised to find that under conditions of stress we defend them against new learning just as strongly as we did the old. For these two partners go hand in hand: the need to explore and learn and the need to defend against disconfirmation and confusion. The challenge is to know how we can create conditions under which we can suspend one to enhance the other.

2. PERSONALITY FORMATION—THE DETERMINANTS*

EVERY MAN is in certain respects
a) like all other men,
b) like some other men,
c) like no other man.

He is like all other men because . . . there are common features in the biological endowments of all men, in the physical environments they inhabit, and in the societies and cultures in which they develop. . . . Every man experiences birth and must learn to move about and explore his environment, to protect himself against extremes of temperature and to avoid serious injuries; every man experiences sexual tensions and other importunate needs and must learn to find ways of appeasing them; every man grows in stature, matures, and dies; and he does all this and much more, from first to last, as a member of a society. . . .

All men are born helpless into an inanimate and impersonal world which presents countless threats to survival; the human species would die out if social life were abandoned. Human adaptation to the external environment depends upon the mutual support which is social life; and, in addition, it depends upon culture. . . . Culture is a great storehouse of ready-made solutions to problems which human animals are wont to encounter. This storehouse is man's substitute for instinct. It is filled not merely with the pooled learning of the living members of the society, but also with the learning of men long dead and of men belonging to other societies.

In certain features of personality, most men are "like some other men." . . . The statistical prediction can safely be made that a hundred Americans, for example, will display certain defined characteristics more frequently than will a hundred Englishmen comparably distributed as to age, sex, social class, and vocation.

But being "like some men" is by no means limited to members of social units like nations, tribes, and classes. Seafaring people, regardless

* Copyright 1948, 1953 by Alfred A. Knopf, Inc. Adapted from *Personality in Nature, Society and Culture,* Second Edition, Revised and Enlarged, edited by Clyde K. Kluckhohn and Henry A. Murray, by permission of Alfred A. Knopf, Inc., and the authors.

This paper represents a complete revision of an earlier scheme published by C. Kluckhohn and O. H. Mowrer, "Culture and Personality: A Conceptual Scheme," *American Anthropologist,* Vol. 46 (1944), pp. 1–29. The present writers gratefully acknowledge their indebtedness to Dr. Mowrer.

of the communities from which they come, tend to manifest similar qualities. The same may be said for desert folk. Intellectuals and athletes the world over have something in common; so have those who were born to wealth or poverty. Persons who have exercised authority over large groups for many years develop parallel reaction systems, in spite of culturally tailored differences in the details of their behaviors. . . .

Finally, there is the inescapable fact that a man is in many respects like no other man. . . . The ultimate uniqueness of each personality is the product of countless and successive interactions between the maturing constitution and different environing situations from birth onward. . . . Although the personalities of children who have experienced a trauma of the same type will often resemble each other in certain respects, the differences between them may be even more apparent, partly because the traumatic situation in each case had certain unique features, and partly because at the time of the trauma the personality of each child, being already unique, responded in a unique manner. Thus there is uniqueness in each inheritance and uniqueness in each environment, but, more particularly, uniqueness in the number, kinds, and temporal order of critically determining situations encountered in the course of life.

The writers suggest that clear and orderly thinking about personality formation will be facilitated if four classes of determinants (and their interactions) are distinguished: constitutional, group-membership, role and situational. These will help us to understand in what ways every man is "like all other men," "like some other men," "like no other man."

1. Constitutional Determinants

The old problem of "heredity or environment" is essentially meaningless. The two sets of determinants can rarely be completely disentangled once the environment has begun to operate. The only pertinent questions therefore are: (1) which of the various genetic potentialities will be actualized as a consequence of a particular series of life-events in a given physical, social, and cultural environment? and (2) what limits to the development of this personality are set by genetic constitution? . . . There are substantial reasons for believing that different genetic structures carry with them varying potentialities for learning, for reaction time, for energy level, for frustration tolerance. Different people appear to have different biological rhythms: of growth, of menstrual cycle, of activity, of depression and exaltation. The various biologically inherited malfunctions certainly have implications for personality development, though there are wide variations among those who share the same physical handicap (deafness, for example).

Sex and age must be regarded as among the more striking constitutional determinants of personality. Personality is also shaped through such traits of physique as stature, pigmentation, strength, conformity of features to the culturally fashionable type, etc. Such characteristics influence a man's needs and expectations. The kind of world he finds about him is to a considerable extent determined by the way other people react to his appearance and physical capacities. Occasionally a physically weak youth, such as Theodore Roosevelt was, may be driven to achieve feats of physical prowess as a form of over-compensation, but usually a man will learn to accept the fact that his physical make-up excludes him from certain types of vocational and social activities, although some concealed resentment may remain as an appreciable ingredient of his total personality. Conversely, special physical fitnesses make certain other types of adjustment particularly congenial.

2. Group-Membership Determinants

. . . Some of the personality traits which tend to distinguish the members of a given group from humanity as a whole derive from a distinctive biological heritage. Persons who live together are more likely to have the same genes than are persons who live far apart. If the physical vitality is typically low for one group as contrasted with other groups, or if certain types of endocrine imbalance are unusually frequent, the personalities of the members of that group will probably have distinctive qualities.

In the greater number of cases, however, the similarities of character within a group are traceable less to constitutional factors than to formative influences of the environment to which all members of the group have been subjected. Of these group-membership determinants, culture is with little doubt the most significant. . . . Those who have been trained in childhood along traditional lines, and even those who have as adults adopted some new design for living, will be apt to behave predictably in many contexts because of a prevailing tendency to conform to group standards.

Not only the action patterns but also the motivational systems of individuals are influenced by culture. Certain needs are biologically given, but many others are not. All human beings get hungry, but no gene in any chromosome predisposes a person to work for a radio or a new car or a shell necklace or "success." Sometimes biologically-given drives, such as sex, are for longer or shorter periods subordinated to culturally acquired drives, such as the pursuit of money or religious ascetism. And the means by which needs are satisfied are ordinarily defined by cultural habits and fashions. Most Americans would go hungry rather than eat a snake, but this is not true of tribes that consider snake meat a delicacy.

Those aspects of the personality that are not inherited but learned all have—at least in their more superficial and peripheral aspects—a cultural tinge. The skills that are acquired, the factual knowledge, the basic assumptions, the values, and the tastes, are largely determined by culture. Culture likewise structures the conditions under which each kind of learning takes place: whether transmitted by parents or parental substitutes, or by brothers and sisters, or by the learner's own age mates; whether gradually or quickly; whether renunciations are harshly imposed or reassuringly rewarded.

Of course we are speaking here of general tendencies rather than invariable facts. Deviation from cultural norms is inevitable and endless, for variability appears to be a property of all biological organisms. But variation is also perpetuated because those who have learned later become teachers. Even the most conventional teachers will give culture a certain personal flavor in accord with their constitution and peculiar life-experiences.

Some types of variation, however, are more predictable. For example, certain differences in the personalities of Americans are referable to the fact that they have grown up in various sub-cultures. Jones is not only an American: he is also a member of the middle class, an Easterner, and has lived all his life in a small Vermont community. This kind of variation falls within the framework of the group determinants.

The component elements of a culture must, up to a point, be either logically consistent or meaningfully congruous. Otherwise the culture carriers feel uncomfortably adrift in a capricious, chaotic world. In a personality system, behavior must be reasonably regular or predictable, or the individual will not get expectable and needed responses from others because they will feel that they cannot "depend" on him. In other words, a social life and living in a social world both require standards "within" the individual and standards roughly agreed upon by individuals who live and work together in a group. There can be no personal security and no stability of social organization unless random carelessness, irresponsibility, and purely impulsive behavior are restrained in terms of private and group codes.

Culture is not the only influence that bears with approximate constancy upon all the members of a relatively stable, organized group. But we know almost nothing of the effects upon personality of the continued press of the impersonal environment. Does living in a constantly rainy climate tend to make people glum and passive, living in a sunny arid country tend to make them cheerful and lively? What are the differential effects of dwelling in a walled-in mountain valley, on a flat plain, or upon a high plateau studded with wide-sculptured red buttes? Thus far we can only speculate, for we lack adequate data. The effects of climate and even of scenery and topography may be greater than is generally supposed.

Membership in a group also carries with it exposure to a social environment. Although the social and cultural are inextricably intermingled in an individual's observable behavior, there is a social dimension to group membership that is not culturally defined. The individual must adjust to the presence or absence of other human beings in specified numbers and of specified age and sex. The size of a society, the density of its population, its age and sex ratio are not entirely culturally prescribed, although often conditioned by the interaction between the technological level of the culture and the exigencies of the physical environment. The quality and type of social interaction that is determined by this social dimension of group membership has, likewise, its consequences for personality formation.

Before leaving the group-membership determinants, we must remind the reader . . . that . . . the individual personality is never directly affected by the group as a physical totality. Rather, his personality is molded by the particular members of the group with whom he has personal contact and by his conceptions of the group as a whole. Concretely, not the group but group agents with their own peculiar traits determine personality formation. Of these group agents, the most important are parents and other members of the individual's family. They, we repeat, act as individuals, as members of a group, and as members of a sub-group with special characteristics. . . .

3. Role Determinants

The culture defines how the different functions, or roles, necessary to group life are to be performed—such roles, for example, as those assigned on the basis of sex and age, or on the basis of membership in a caste, class, or occupational group. In a sense, the role determinants of personality are a special class of group-membership determinants; they apply to a strata that cross-cut most kinds of group membership. The long-continued playing of a distinctive role, however, appears to be so potent in differentiating personalities within a group that it is useful to treat these determinants separately.

Moreover, if one is aware of the role determinants, one will less often be misled in interpreting various manifestations of personality. In this connection it is worth recalling that, in early Latin, *persona* means "a mask"—dramatis personae are the masks which actors wear in a play, that is, the characters that are represented. Etymologically and historically, then, the personality is the character that is manifested in public. In modern psychology and sociology this corresponds rather closely to the role behavior of a differentiated person. From one point of view, this constitutes a disguise. Just as the outer body shields the viscera from view, and clothing the genitals, so the public personality shields the private personality from the curious and censorious world. It also operates to conceal underlying motivations from the individual's own consciousness. The person who has painfully achieved some sort of integration, and who knows what is expected of him in a particular social situation, will usually produce the appropriate responses with only a little personal coloring. This explains, in part, why the attitudes and action patterns produced by the group-membership and role determinants constitute a screen which, in the case of normal individuals, can be penetrated only by the intensive, lengthy, and oblique procedures of depth psychology.

The disposition to accept a person's behavior in a given situation as representative of his total personality is almost universal. Very often he is merely conforming, very acceptably, to the cultural definition of his role. One visits a doctor in his office, and his behavior fits the stereotype of the physician so perfectly that one says, often mistakenly, "There indeed is a well-adjusted person." But a scientist must train himself to get behind a man's cultivated surface, because he will not be able to understand much if he limits his data to the action patterns perfected through the repeated performance of the roles as physician, as middle-aged man, as physician dealing with an older male patient, etc.

4. Situational Determinants

Besides the constitutional determinants and the forces which will more or less inevitably confront individuals who live in the same physical environment, who are members of a society of a certain size and of a certain culture, and who play the same roles, there are things which "just happen" to people. A student, say, who is undecided as to his career, or who is about equally drawn to several different vocations, happens to sit down in a railroad car next to a journalist who is an engaging and persuasive advocate of his profession. This event does not, of course, immediately and directly change the young man's personality, but it may set in motion a chain of events which puts him into situations that are decisive in molding his personality.

The situational determinants include things that happen a thousand times as well as those that happen only once—provided they are not standard for a whole group. For example, it is generally agreed that the family constellation in which a person grows up is a primary source of personality styling. These domestic influences are conditioned by the cultural prescriptions for the roles of parents and children. But a divorce, a father who is much older than the mother, a father whose occupation keeps him away from home much of the time, the fact of being an only child or the eldest or youngest in a series—these are situational determinants.

5. Interdependence of the Determinants

A balanced consideration of "personality in nature, society, and culture" must be carried on within the framework of a complex conceptual scheme which explicitly recognizes, instead of tacitly excluding, a number of types of determinants.

For example, we may instance a network of cultural, role, and constitutional determinants. In every society the child is differently socialized according to sex. Also, in every society different behavior is expected of individuals in different age groups, although each culture makes its own prescriptions as to where these lines are drawn and what behavioral variations are to be anticipated. Thus, the personalities of men and women, of the old and the young, are differentiated, in part, by the experience of playing these various roles in conformity with cultural standards. But since age and sex are biological facts, they also operate through life as constitutional determinants of personality. A woman's motivation and action patterns are modified by the facts of her physique as a woman.

Some factors that one is likely to pigeonhole all too complacently as biological often turn out, on careful examination, to be the product of complicated interactions. Illness may result from group as well as from individual constitutional factors. And illness, in turn, may be considered a situational determinant. The illness—with all of its effects upon personality formation—is an "accident" in that one could predict only that the betting odds were relatively high that this individual would fall victim to this illness. However, when the person does become a patient one can see that both a constitutional predisposition and membership in a caste or class group where sanitation and medical care were substandard are causative factors in this "accidental" event. Similarly, a constitutional tendency towards corpulence certainly has implications for personality when it is characteristic of a group as well as when it distinguishes an individual within a group. But the resources of the physical environment as exploited by the culturally-transmitted technology are major determinants in the production and utilization of nutritional substances of various sorts and these have patent consequences for corpulence, stature, and energy potential. Tuberculosis or pellagra may be endemic. If hookworm is endemic in a population, one will hardly expect vigor to be a striking feature of the majority of people. Yet hookworm is not an unavoidable "given," either constitutionally or environmentally: the prevalence and effects of hookworm are dependent upon culturally enjoined types of sanitary control.

Complicated interrelations of the same sort may be noted between the environmental and cultural forces which constitute the group membership determinants. On the one hand, the physical environment imposes certain limitations upon the cultural forms which man creates, or it constrains toward change and readjustment in the culture he brings into an ecological area. There is always a large portion of the impersonal environment to which men can adjust but not control; there is another portion which is man-made and cultural. Most cultures provide technologies which permit some alterations in the physical world (for example, methods of cutting irrigation ditches or of terracing hillsides). There are also those artifacts (houses, furniture, tools, vehicles) which serve as instruments for the gratification of needs, and, not infrequently, for their incitement and frustration. Most important of all, perhaps culture directs and often distorts man's perceptions of the external world. What effects social suggestion may have in setting frames of reference for perception has been shown experimentally. Culture acts as a set of blinders, or series of lenses, through which men view their environments.

Among group-membership determinants, the social and cultural factors are interdependent, yet analytically distinct. The fact that human beings are mammals and reproduce bi-sexually creates a basic predisposition toward at least the rudiments of social living. And the prolonged helplessness of human infants conduces to the formation of a family group. Also, certain universal social processes (such as conflict, competition, and accommodation) are given distinct forms through cultural transmission. Thus, while the physically strong tend to dominate the weak, this tendency may be checked and even to some extent reversed by a tradition which rewards chivalry, compassion, and humility. Attitudes towards women, towards infants, towards the old, towards the weak will be affected by the age and sex ratios and the birth and death rates prevalent at a particular time.

The social and cultural press likewise interlock with the situational determinants. There are many forces involved in social interaction which influence personality formation and yet are in no sense culturally prescribed. All children (unless multiple births) are born at different points in their parents' careers, which means that they have, psychologically speaking, somewhat different parents. Likewise, whether a child is wanted or unwanted and whether it is of the desired sex will make a difference in the ways in which it will be treated, even though the culture says that all children are wanted and defines the two sexes as of equal value.

A final example will link the constitutional with both the group-membership and situational determinants. Even though identical twins may differ remarkably little from a biological standpoint, and participate in group activities which are apparently similar, a situational factor may intrude as a result of which their experiences in social interaction will be quite different. If, for instance, one twin is injured in an automobile accident and the other is not, and if the injured twin has to spend a year in bed, as the special object of his mother's solicitations, noticeable personality differences will probably develop. The extent to which these differences endure will depend surely upon many other factors, but it is unlikely that they will be entirely counteracted. The variations in treatment which a bed-ridden child receives is partly determined by culture (the extent to which the ideal patterns permit a sick child to be petted, etc.) and partly by extra-cultural factors, (the mother's need for nurturance, the father's idiomatic performance of his culturally patterned role in these circumstances, etc.).

6. Similarities and Differences in Personality

In conclusion, let us return for a moment to the observed fact that every man is "like all other men, like some other men, like no other man." In the beginning there is (1) the organism and (2) the environment. Using this division as the starting point in thinking about personality formation, one might say that the differences observed in the personalities of human beings are due to variations in their biological equipment and in the total environment to which they must adjust, while the similarities are ascribable to biological and environmental regularities. Although the organism and the environment have a kind of wholeness in the concrete behavioral world which the student loses sight of at his peril, this generalization is substantially correct. However, the formulation can be put more neatly in terms of field. There is (1) the organism moving through a field which is (2) structured both by culture and by the physical and social world in a relatively uniform manner, but which is (3) subject to endless variation within the general patterning due to the organism's constitutionally-determined peculiarities of reaction and to the occurrence of special situations.

In certain circumstances, one reacts to men and women, not as unique organizations of experience, but as representatives of a group. In other circumstances, one reacts to men and women primarily as fulfilling certain roles. If one is unfamiliar with the Chinese, one is likely to react to them first as Chinese rather than as individuals. When one meets new people at a social gathering, one is often able to predict correctly: "That man is a doctor." "That man certainly isn't a businessman, he acts like a professor." "That fellow over there looks like a government official, surely not an artist, a writer, or an actor." Similarities in personality created by the role and group-membership determinants are genuine enough. A man is likely to resemble other men from his home town, other members of his vocation, other members of his class, as well as the majority of his countrymen as contrasted to foreigners.

But the variations are equally common. Smith is stubborn in his office as well as at home and on the golf course. Probably he would have been stubborn in all social contexts if he had been taken to England from America at an early age and his socialization had been completed there. The playing of roles is always tinged by the uniqueness of the personality. Such differences may be distinguished by saying, "Yes, Brown and Jones are both forty-five-year-old Americans, both small-businessmen with about the same responsibilities, family ties, and prestige—but somehow they are different." Such dissimilarities may be traced to the interactions of the constitutional and situational determinants, which have been different for each man, with the common group-membership and role determinants to which both have been subjected.

Another type of resemblance between personalities cuts across the boundaries of groups and roles but is equally understandable within this framework of thinking about personality formation. In general, one observes quite different personality manifestations in Hopi Indians and in white Americans—save for those common to all humanity. But occasionally one meets a Hopi whose behavior, as a whole or in part, reminds one very strongly of a certain type of white man. Such parallels can arise from similar constitutional or situational determinants or a combination of these. A Hopi and a white man might both have an unusual endocrine condition. Or both Hopi and white might both have had several long childhood illnesses which brought them an exceptional amount of maternal care. While an over-abundance of motherly devotion would have had somewhat different effects upon the two personalities, a striking segmental resemblance might have been produced which persisted throughout life.

In most cases the observed similarities, as well as the difference between groups of people are largely attributable to fairly uniform social and cultural processes. When one says, "Smith reminds me of Brown," a biologically inherited determinant may be completely responsible for the observed resemblance. But when one notes that American businessmen, for example, have certain typical characteristics which identify them as a group and distinguish them from American farmers and teachers it can hardly be a question of genetic constitution. Likewise, the similarities of personality between Americans in general as contrasted with Germans in general must be traced primarily to common press which produces resemblances in spite of wide variations in individual constitutions.

To summarize the content of this chapter in other terms: The personality of an individual is the product of inherited disposition and environmental experiences. These experiences occur within the field of his physical, biological, and social environment, all of which are modified by the culture of his group. Similarities of life experiences and heredity will tend to produce similar personality characteristics in different individuals, whether in the same society or in different societies.

3. THE PROCESS OF NATURAL GROWTH*

OUR FINDINGS fully confirm the value of a threefold approach to the understanding of lives. Our three subjects (described in previous chapters) would have been strangely misinterpreted if we had failed to consider the shaping influence of the culture, social class, group experiences, and occupational and other roles. They would have been strangely disembodied if we had omitted all reference to drive, the learning process, temperament, and the nature of their abilities. They would have been peculiarly depersonalized if we had left out the special impact of their parents and the details of their struggle to master anxiety and find outlets for their interests. . . .

Although our insight has been greatly benefited by a combined social, biological, and psychodynamic approach, we have also experienced certain enduring frustrations. . . . general concepts such as social class and occupation, drive and motive, psychosexual stage and parental attitude, have required many qualifications in order to fit the individual case. . . . general concepts did not help us to understand process or change. . . . so many forces operate at once in a given personality, producing an elaborate lattice of interconnected events rather than a simple model of cause and effect. But perhaps our most recurrent difficulty has been that of accounting for natural growth. It seems imperative to devote more thought to what happens when *lives are in progress.*

. . . .

Toward a Positive Conception of Natural Growth

. . . We must take serious account of the following points: (1) that the person undergoes more or less *continuous change;* (2) that the person is acted upon by a multiplicity of influences to which he necessarily makes a *selective response;* and (3) that the person not only receives influences but takes *action on the environment.* Man is not static, nor is he passive and helpless. It will also be necessary, because our examples of growth include the years of young adulthood, to consider seriously (4) the *nature of the reality* in which adult development occurs.

---

* Selected by permission from the final chapter of *Lives in Progress,* by Robert W. White (New York: Holt, Rinehart & Winston, 1952), pp. 327–66. The deletions which have been made in this chapter mostly concern references to subjects more fully described in earlier chapters. Although the following can be read independently with value, the reader may also wish to refer to the complete volume.

1. . . . normal growth signifies unblocked learning, a process of *continuous change.* The personality is a system that normally undergoes continuous reorganization with the passage of time.

2. Each individual is acted upon by a great multiplicity of influences. . . . (But this fact cannot justify the) generalization: that personality can be understood as a direct reflection of its shaping forces. . . . A person is a nexus of competing and conflicting influences to which he must *respond selectively,* creating for himself a workable synthesis. He is inevitably the scene of frustration and conflict, and he can avoid hopeless confusion only by becoming an active transformer of his experience.

3. No one doubts the general principle that there is a constant interaction between the person and his environment. This implies both that the environment acts on the person and that the person *acts on the environment.* Scientific workers, however, have been loathe to examine the second part of the transaction, preferring to regard the person as the thing to be explained and the environment as the thing that explained him. . . . The fact is that people very definitely affect their environments, even in childhood, and that what happens next in their development is often determined by these effects. . . .

4. The *nature of the reality* in which adult development takes place can be specified only in the most general terms. . . . The question of reality must be raised, however, because there is a tendency to make unwitting assumptions which seriously misrepresent the conditions of adult life. Mental health is often identified with being flexible and adaptable, ready for anything, an all-around person with versatile skills and interests. . . . One might say that it depicts the life of a traveling salesman who constantly meets new people in new territories and who shifts from company to company so that he has to keep learning the merits of new goods. . . but it certainly does not cover all the conditions of adult life. . . . Sometimes there is very little demand for quick change in an adult's life. What is needed is a capacity for steady growth within a relatively constant framework of activities and relationships. . . . Some features of life call for the broadening of experience; others require its deepening. . . .

Having taken these preliminary steps toward a positive conception of natural growth, we shall proceed to set forth certain ideas concerning growth trends.

Growth Trends: 1. The Stabilizing of Ego Identity

Ego identity refers to the self or the person one feels oneself to be. In infancy the sense of identity is little developed, but progressive experience brings sharper outline and clearer definition. As we have seen, ego identity is never entirely a social product. It is partly constructed from within, having perhaps its first basis in what is experienced as "I" and "me" in contrast to what is "not me." Gradually the sense of identity becomes a fuller and richer establishment, compounded of bodily sensations, feelings, images of one's body, the sound of one's name, the continuity of one's memories, and an increasing number of social judgments delivered through the words and behavior of others. During adolescence there is a time when ego identity becomes heavily dependent on the judgments of one's peers. "The danger of this stage," says Erikson, "is role diffusion. It is primarily the inability to settle on an occupational identity which disturbs young people. To keep themselves together they temporarily overidentify, to the point of apparent complete loss of identity, with the heroes of cliques and crowds."[1] Once this difficult period has been traversed, however, ego identity can continue its development along less diffuse channels.

Direction of Growth.   There are many vicissitudes in the development of ego identity, but the overall trend is toward an increase of stability. When one takes a long enough span of time, continuing well into adulthood, ego identity can be seen to become not only more sharp and clear but also more consistent and free from transient influences. . . . To be called a coward by a kindergarten playmate may be an extremely upsetting experience; one is not sure to what extent the epithet may be deserved. To be called a coward at the age of thirty is quite another matter. It may be upsetting if the person feels that others have discovered a weakness he was trying to hide, but it will not be upsetting at all if the person knows that it is not true. The point is that at thirty a person pretty much knows whether or not he is a coward; he can make a self-judgment on the basis of his accumulated experience, and he knows that this judgment is sounder than the one arriving from outside. Even praise is not accepted when inner judgment cannot agree that it was deserved. . . . Accumulated experience, organized as an increasingly stable set of self-feelings and self-estimates, more and more outweighs the impact of new events.

It is not an objection to this way of looking at the matter to say that with some people ego identity does not seem to grow more stable over the years. Any theory about growth makes the allowance that fixation and regression can occur. It makes the further allowance that conditions may not always be favorable for extensive growth. In giving the *stabiliz-*

---

[1] E. H. Erikson, *Childhood and Society* (New York: W. W. Norton & Co., 1950), p. 228.

ing of ego identity its status as a growth trend, we are suggesting that change in this direction represents an increasingly full realization of capacities for development. It results, moreover, in a greater capacity to exert an influence on the surrounding world. . . . The more sure he becomes about his own nature and peculiarities, the more solid is the nucleus from which his activity proceeds.

. . . .

Process of Growth. When we turn from the *direction* of change to the *process* of change, our focus of attention shifts to the single steps that cumulatively make up a growth trend. . . . Although we speak of continuous change and cumulative development, it would certainly be arbitrary to interpret these expressions literally as meaning an unbroken growth through time. Growth trends occur through specific incidents which are sometimes well-separated in time. Some incidents, moreover, are much more important than others, even to the extent of producing an astonishing transformation. . . .

One type of event that often contributes to the stabilizing of ego identity is placement in an occupational status or in some other socially recognized position. Social roles provide us with a means of establishing identity. They also provide us with opportunities for action whereby we further define and stabilize ourselves. . . . As a person shapes his behavior into his occupational role, his marital role, and his parental role, for example, his experience begins to accumulate more and more selectively. The stored-up sources of his stability come increasingly out of behavior within roles. Under stable social conditions much strength can thus be borrowed from the environment through consistent playing of consistently defined roles.

It is not possible, however, to understand the stabilizing process without taking into account the interest and initiative that a person brings to any proffered role. . . .

It must be remembered, furthermore, that social roles do not define individual identities in a precise or sufficient sense. If a person's sense of identity consisted of nothing except that he was a doctor it could hardly be called well-stabilized. Within any one social role there is room for a great deal of individuality. Three vice-presidents in a bank, for example, might bring very different skills and very different personal interests into the company, each making his own special contribution to the enterprise. . . .

Consideration of the part played by social roles thus leads us to perceive the types of experience that are most conducive to stabilizing one's ego identity. Stated schematically, any episode has this effect which serves to heighten the efficacy of accumulated personal experience as against new outside judgments, fresh experiences of success and failure, or new objects of possible identification. This heightened efficacy results most readily from a situation of choice in which there are immediate pressures on either side. Decision necessarily turns on becoming more aware of personal preference and of the things for which one really wants one's life to stand. . . . we believe in general that learning takes place most readily in connection with reward. But it is an essential part of our concept that a stable identity is not overthrown by single experiences of failure. . . . Failure and frustration can contribute a great deal to the stabilizing of ego identity when they are not so overwhelming as to destroy the basis of confidence. The person one feels oneself to be becomes stably established only through discarding a number of persons one gradually feels oneself not to be. These discards make it possible to throw much more energy along the main line, so that identity comes to be increasingly founded on one's better potentialities.

Obviously no single growth trend can do justice to everything that happens in the ego system. The trend we have described in this section resembles in certain respects, though not entirely, McClelland's concept of a trend toward *self-consistency,* a trend that has been given central importance in Lecky's theory of personality.[2] Two somewhat different aspects of growth have been described by Allport under the headings *extension of the self* and *self-objectification.* Extension of the self signifies that a person has "a variety of autonomous interests," that he devotes himself to friends, family, children, cultural interests, work, and so forth, all of which have objective value beyond his immediate pleasure or satisfaction. Self-objectification refers to "that peculiar detachment of the mature person when he surveys his own pretensions in relation to his abilities, his present objectives in relation to possible objectives for himself, his own equipment in comparison with the equipment of others, and his opinion of himself in relation to the opinions others hold of him."[3] . . . The stabilizing of ego identity is but one of several ways in which the ego system proceeds toward full development.

Growth Trends: 2. The Freeing of Personal Relationships

. . . Like many other aspects of human behavior, personal relationships are deeply colored by their childhood history. They start very early

[2] D. W. McClelland, *Personality* (New York: William Sloane Associates, 1951), pp. 542–59; P. Lecky, *Self-Consistency: A Theory of Personality* (New York: Island Press, 1945).

[3] G. W. Allport, *Personality: A Psychological Interpretation* (New York: Henry Holt & Co., 1937), Chap. 8.

under circumstances that are not altogether auspicious. The infant's first relationships are with people upon whom he is dependent for all the comforts and necessities of life. Never again will the situation be so one-sided, yet it is here, with basic security always at stake, that the infant lays down his first patterns of human interaction. . . . When a child first moves out into the world, he starts to use an already practiced repertory of social behavior. He treats the nursery-school teacher as if she were his mother, the other children as if they were brothers and sisters. He does not, as we sometimes put it, respond to them fully in their own right as new individuals; as a result, his responses are often poorly fitted to the new circumstances.

Responding to people in their own right as new individuals is not easy even for the most socially seasoned adult. . . . Our social learning is forever lagging behind the demands put upon it, and our most alert and sensitive responses are apt to reveal bits of inappropriate historical coloring. To some extent this lag results from the inherent difficulties that attend learning in a social situation. When we learn something like the multiplication table, or the way an internal combustion motor is put together, we can at least concentrate on what we are trying to learn. In a social situation, on the other hand, several things are likely to be going on at once. Social interactions have a content as well as an emotional undertone. . . . When someone talks about a trip he has taken, for instance, we respond simultaneously to the contents of his description and to the attitude he displays toward us. Perhaps a very "subjective" listener will respond wholly to the attitude, searching the narrator's manner and tone of voice for proof of affection, condescension, or distaste, and recalling nothing about the geography of the trip. Perhaps a very "objective" listener will come away with a full knowledge of the itinerary but no impression whatever of the person who took the trip. These extremes serve to point up the dilemma of social learning. Most of our social interacting is learned under conditions of high distraction. We do not fully perceive either the other person or ourselves, and this circumstance tends to favor the persistence of old attitudes rather than the learning of new ones.

In view of this weakness in the typical learning situation, and in view of the high emotional stakes that are often involved, it is no wonder that personal relationships are easily injured by anxiety and defenses. Anxiety adds to the distraction; defenses freeze the repertory of safe social behavior and block the attempting of new responses. Suppose that a person has learned to cover social discomfort by fast, superficial chattering, thus avoiding both the silences that would make him anxious and the serious discussions that would challenge his competence. His discomfort forbids him to stop chattering; thus he never learns how people would respond to him, or how he would respond to them, in any other kind of interaction. Social learning is peculiarly vulnerable to the workings of anxiety and defense. . . .

Social Growth in Psychotherapy. When we conceive of neurosis as being based on a defensive block in the learning process, psychotherapy falls into focus as a matter of removing defensive blocks so that learning can be resumed. The growth that goes on during and after a period of psychotherapy is therefore no different in principle from the normal course of development when important blocks have not been present. The essence of psychotherapy is to provide a situation in which the patient will feel progressively less anxious, less defensive, more able to put out new feelers in social behavior and thus to enlarge his capacity for personal relationships. . . .

The central feature of the therapeutic situation is the attitude taken by the therapist. This attitude is best described as *permissive.* The therapist accepts with composure and interest whatever the patient has to say. He shows that he considers it important, and he receives it without disapproval, criticism, or censure. He encourages the patient to talk freely even about embarrassing and frightening things, which he does not treat as if they betokened inferiority or wickedness. This is new and surprising; probably the patient has never before encountered such tolerance for his personal problems. As a result he becomes able to talk of more and more things, including experiences long forgotten and feelings long banished from his awareness. To be able to talk this way creates a new kind of human relationship. Because he receives such consistently permissive responses, the patient dares to increase the range of his feelings toward both the therapist and the other people in his life.

As time advances, however, the situation undergoes something of a change. The patient learns to relax a great many of his defenses, but this leads him to experience with renewed vividness the feelings that prevailed before his development became blocked. Let us suppose that his difficulties have lain chiefly in relationships with competitive people and that his development with respect to such people became blocked in childhood because of anxieties that sprang from trying to compete with a brother. After a while the patient finds himself feeling highly competitive toward the therapist, perhaps also extremely anxious about it. This is the *transference,* a reanimation of the crucial feelings that surrounded the earlier conflict. These feelings, whether of love, dependence, jealousy, hate or fear, are often experienced with great vividness and intensity. This time, however, they find a new reception. The therapist may point them out and interpret them, thus exposing their inappropriateness in the current situation, but he does not receive them in such a way as to create new cause for anxiety. Instead of being choked down again by fear, the feelings are named and brought under rational control so that they can contribute to a whole chain of new learnings. The process of therapy is a slow one, but its individual steps can all be conceived as acts of social learning. The permissiveness of the therapist's behavior makes it possible for the patient to try out an increasing range of formerly "dangerous" acts and feelings, until eventually he has reappraised even the original dangers that long ago blocked his development.

The process of cure does not take place, however, entirely during the therapeutic hours. The patient's improvement would indeed be fragile if it depended upon a permissiveness of response that is almost never found elsewhere in life. As he begins to feel greater freedom in his personal relationship with the therapist, the patient tries out his new behavior on other people and becomes able to increase his range even when the reception is not permissive. Except for the fact that the therapist stands ready to offer encouragement when these experiments receive a setback, the outside learning that accompanies psychotherapy is simply a natural course of growth. The patient belatedly makes the kind of growth that would have gone on through childhood and young adulthood if anxiety and defense had not effected a block. The therapist has provided the rare permissive atmosphere necessary to break the block, but the really vital learning must eventually be accomplished in the patient's own social orbit.

Direction of Growth.   The second of our growth trends moves in a direction which we shall now describe as the freeing of personal relationships. Under reasonably favorable circumstances the natural growth of personality moves in the direction of human relationships that are less anxious, less defensive, less burdened by inappropriate past reactions, more friendly, more spontaneous, more warm, and more respectful. Social interaction becomes more free not only from neurotic trends but also from the impulsive inconsiderateness and egocentricity of youth. The person learns not to be so immersed in his own behavior, so intent on the impression he is making or the point he is trying to put across, that he fails to perceive the people around him. He becomes increasingly able to interact, responding in a way that is related to their responses. As he moves in this direction he develops a greater range and flexibility of responses. He notices more things in the people with whom he interacts and becomes more ready to make a place for their characteristics in his own behavior. In this way he comes to interact more fully with other people, making more points of contact with them. Common interests emerge more quickly in new relationships, develop more lastingly in old ones. The person moves in the direction of increased capacity to live in real relationship with the people immediately around him.

In studying the trend toward the freeing of personal relationships we should concentrate primarily on the people who are important in a given life, those with whom there is frequent and significant interaction. Meeting new people and taking part in gatherings of acquaintances contribute to this growth trend but do not constitute its central events. We should notice also that the trend does not typically consist of a flat generalized increase of capacity to interact with every kind of person. The development proceeds partly by selection and concentration. Friendships are pursued when there are congenial similarities of interest and outlook, but people with whom interaction proves difficult are dropped out of the orbit. With subjects in the age range of those described in this book it is instructive to begin with the growth of their relationship to parents. Then come their spouses or potential spouses, their children, their intimate friends, their colleagues at work, and the people they frequently meet in their neighborhood and community. With some people there is a lasting desire for novelty in human relationships, and it is important to study their growth in their own chosen direction. . . .

Process of Growth. In general, the situation that is most conducive to change is one in which the other person responds unexpectedly, thus disrupting one's own habituated way of behaving. Children learn that other children are not mere assistants in their games when the assistants rebel and prove to have desires of their own. Children learn that other children are not enemies when the supposed enemies show friendly interest and kindness. Similarly, in the course of psychotherapy the patient learns to be unafraid because his behavior is greeted with boundless permissiveness and understanding. When faced with such surprises one learns to observe the other person, to understand and respect him, and one becomes more aware of one's own action. The next attempt at interaction will be a little different, and differences may accumulate in such a way as to constitute a decided trend toward the freeing of personal relationships.

. . . .

If a person's social behavior is not too heavily bound by defenses against anxiety, it tends to become more varied as experience accumulates. Each occasion on which the other person's behavior has to be observed adds an increment of knowledge about human diversity. It also adds an increment of variation to the repertory of social behavior. . . .

There are times, however, when a growth trend moves ahead by sudden jumps. Such occasions correspond to the "learning by insight" first emphasized by the Gestalt school of psychologists.[4] The other person is perceived first in one way, then in an entirely different way, the change representing a sudden reorganization of the perceptual field. . . . In a study of nursery-school children Lois Murphy showed that empathy was very much influenced by personal past experience. A child who had once had a broken arm, for instance, would display special solicitude when another child arrived with an arm in a sling.[5] The capacity to produce new behavior in social situations is thus favorably affected by having a large *empathic range,* a rich store of experiences which can be used as a basis for understanding the meaning of another person's behavior. Sometimes a person can use the tragedies in his own life as a means of understanding other people's tragedies.

The two growth trends thus far described prove to be not unrelated. One of the things that contributes to the freeing of personal relationships is the stabilizing of ego identity. . . . Interactions between parents and children rarely change as fast as would be warranted by the children's growth. A period of absence is therefore often of great benefit in putting things on a new footing. As the children become adults and stabilize their own identities they are apt to view their parents more objectively, with a more dispassionate criticism, and at the same time with a warmer and more empathic appreciation.

Growth Trends: 3. The Deepening of Interests

Interests play a curiously small part in current thinking about personality. They have often been crudely "measured" for purposes of vocational guidance, but little attempt has been made to formulate their place in the growth of personality. Interests do not present themselves as clinical problems, and they are hard to describe in a systematic way. Perhaps they have also suffered from our frequent habit of describing personality at a fixed point in time. Interests are not static; it is of their very essence that they constantly move forward and almost never reach final goals. Thus it happens that the scientist, typically a person of the strongest interests, has found few ways to study this elusive topic. Yet interests are often of tremendous importance in the personal economy of

---

[4] W. Kohler, *The Mentality of Apes* (New York: Harcourt, Brace & Co., 1927).

[5] L. B. Murphy, *Social Behavior and Child Personality* (New York: Columbia University Press, 1937), Chap. 9.

happiness. The loss of opportunities to pursue them can sometimes be an irreparable catastrophe.

.   .   .   .

The nature of interests was well set forth in one of John Dewey's notable contributions to education. An interest, he said, was always connected with an activity which engaged a person in a whole-hearted fashion.

> Interest is not some one thing; it is a name for the fact that a course of action, an occupation or pursuit absorbs the powers of an individual in a thorough-going way. But an activity cannot go on in a void. It requires material, subject-matter, conditions upon which to operate. On the other hand, it requires certain tendencies, habits, powers on the part of self. Wherever there is genuine interest, there is an identification of these two things. The person acting finds his own well-being bound up with the development of an object to its own issue. If the activity goes a certain way, then a subject-matter is carried to a certain result, and a person achieves a certain satisfaction.[6]

Direction of Growth. The growth trend with which we are now concerned may be said to take a direction toward the state of affairs described by Dewey. It is a trend toward increasing absorption in the object of interest, increasing identification of one's tendencies with "development of an object to its own issue." The absorption of a scientist in his experiments, an artist in his painting, a musician in his composition, a craftsman in his work, all serve to illustrate advanced points in this development. It is a common experience with creative people that they lose themselves in their work. Even the creatures of their fancy, such as the characters in a novel or the themes in a musical composition, acquire an almost autonomous existence, refusing at times to come out right, so that their creator must pace the floor or walk across the fields while waiting for them to assume a satisfactory shape. Similarly, the solution of a mathematical problem is often experienced as having to work itself out. Such instances are extreme, but they highlight the nature of an important trend in growth. Under reasonably favorable circumstances a person becomes increasingly capable of having his energies absorbed in the needs and properties of the objects with which he is working.

In speaking of a trend toward the *deepening* of interests we have in mind this increased capacity for absorption. Interests often enough grow broader as well as deeper, but our concern here is with one particular

---

[6] J. Dewey, *Interest and Effort in Education* (Boston: Houghton Mifflin Co., 1913), p. 65.

quality rather than with quantity or extensiveness. We are also not referring to the amount of time a person devotes to his interests; a trend toward deepening does not imply that he spends more and more of his hours in a state of absorption until at last everything else is excluded. The trend we have in mind is away from a state in which interests are casual, quickly dropped, pursued only from motives that do not become identified with advancement of the object. It is toward a state in which the sense of reward comes from doing something for its own sake. Our examples need not be so extreme as the artist or scientist. We can think instead of a man who allows himself to be nominated for the water board in a small town. At first he is motivated by a desire to participate in a necessary public service, to see his name in the town report, and to feel that he has the esteem of the citizens. Ten years later he may have become greatly interested in precipitation and watersheds, location of reservoirs, piping and pumping systems, filters and purifiers, and the economic side of a water supply. He has built up a store of knowledge and expertness. He is interested in making the town water system a better water system, and he might not care too much if through a printer's error his name was left out of the town report.

.   .   .   .

Process of Growth. There are no doubt many circumstances that favor the deepening of interests. . . . the encouraging interest of an older person seemed to give them (adolescents) needed assurance to pursue activities requiring detachment from the daily round of life. Adolescence is a period of intense loyalty to groups, intense conformity to the prevailing youth culture. Anyone who chooses to pursue an individual interest might therefore be expected to feel a need for special outside support. It seems likely, however, that something more is involved. . . .

Another of our subjects, not reported in this book, made the matter (even) clearer both through his behavior and through his responses on the Thematic Apperception Test. He indicated that creative interest always suffered when he felt competitive, hostile, or under the necessity to prove that he was not inferior. When the self was threatened and required defense, there was no energy left over to be expended on creative tasks. This man also responded very well to the interest of one of his teachers. Apparently the teacher's acceptance of him as a promising equal released him from the necessity of defense and allowed him to let his energies flow forth in new directions. We are entitled to suggest that the deepening of interests is favored by circumstances that abrogate anxiety and cancel expensive defenses. The peace of mind that goes with security and the rewards that come from encouragement are important aids to constructive growth.

The process of deepening occurs through satisfying transactions with objects of interest. It is characteristic of interesting objects that they offer an endless series of problems and challenges. One can never exhaust the things to be learned in a field of science or the obstacles to be overcome in research. One can never run through the possibilities of enjoyment or expression in art, literature, or music. People whose hobbies have grown to well-nigh professional proportions give ample testimony to the inexhaustibility of interesting things. Thus it is possible for satisfying transactions to go on and on, and this tends to build up funds of knowledge and expertness that make the person equal to still more difficult transactions. Just as growth in personal relationships makes one increasingly responsive to the characteristics of individual people, so growth in interests makes one increasingly alert to the properties of individual objects. Interests grow deeper through the cumulative effects of learning.

Occasionally the deepening of an interest occurs quite suddenly. In a way that almost resembles a religious conversion, a person "discovers his field" and goes forward with exuberant enthusiasm. . . . We can offer the guess that these sudden bursts of interest occur when several separate lines of previous interest become merged in a new unified activity, or when frustrated lines find their first real opportunity for free development. Our material provides these guesses, however, with only a small underpinning of facts.

The deepening of interests has a great deal to do with effectiveness and happiness in one's occupation. A person may want to become a doctor for many reasons: prestige, social status, money, identification with the white-coated heroes of the moving picture screen, a zeal to banish suffering, perhaps even a private mission to conquer the disease that has prematurely taken away a beloved relative. These can be powerful motives, but in themselves they do not make a good doctor. Granted a sufficient level of ability, the crucial thing is the possibility of becoming more and more deeply interested in the detailed subject-matter and daily activities of medicine. Whatever the initial motives, they will not produce a good doctor unless they can be channeled to support a deepening interest in the details of a doctor's arduous life. . . .

Ann Roe has made studies of artists, physicists, biologists, and several other groups of professional workers. If one examines the findings of psychological tests there proves to be a good deal of variation within each professional group and only a small number of marked differences between groups. The distinctive thing about these people seems to be that quite early in life they got interested in the subject-matter they later pursued as a vocation. The cumulative deepening of interest was the thing that guided them to their careers and that largely determined their success.[7]

Growth Trends: 4. The Humanizing of Values

In earlier times it was not infrequently assumed that moral conscience was an innate human faculty. It is more in line with a scientific approach to assume that this "faculty" has a traceable history and that its development depends upon lawful processes of learning. Freud's doctrine of the superego reflected a searching attempt to uncover the childhood roots of what in later life would be called conscience and a system of values. Freud exposed the irrational origins of what we would like to consider one of the most rational features of our adult lives. Piaget's studies of moral judgments in children added greatly to the picture of early irrationality. The young child's understanding cannot fully grasp the meaning of moral values, which are therefore interpreted in a literal fashion that often departs widely from adult intentions. All in all, values get a bad start in early life. They are accepted under a certain duress, they are misunderstood, they are taken over wholesale by identification, they are rejected wholesale in a phase of negativism, and they may well become a bone of contention in contests between parents and children. Out of such beginnings must we fashion the moral conscience which Kant considered to be one of the strongest proofs of the greatness of God.

Direction of Growth. In choosing to call our fourth growth trend the humanizing of values we are somewhat guided by Piaget's notable studies.[8] Piaget traced the evolution of the child's moral judgment between the seventh and fifteenth years. He demonstrated a trend from a literal belief in rules, almost as if they had an independent physical existence, to an attitude of relativity, in which precepts were perceived in relation to the social purposes they were designed to serve. Younger children did not grasp the fact that the rules for a game of marbles depended on mutual agreement and were adopted to make the game interesting and fair. They considered the rules to have an absolute

---

[7] A. Roe, "Artists and Their Work," *Journal of Personality,* Vol. 15 (1946), pp. 1–40. And also "Psychological Examinations of Eminent Biologists," *Journal of Consulting Psychology,* Vol. 13 (1949), pp. 225–46; "Personality and Vocation," *Transactions of the New York Academy of Science,* Vol. 9 (1947), pp. 257–67.

[8] J. Piaget, *The Moral Judgment of the Child* (New York: Harcourt, Brace & Co., 1932).

existence which precluded any kind of alteration. Older children conceived the rules of a game much as adults would conceive them, but they were not always lucid about the meaning of more complex values. Piaget pointed out that the growth trend could not be conceived simply as a maturing of intellectual capacity. It depended upon experience in social interaction whereby the child came to perceive for himself the consequences of precepts and their violation.

The growth trend observed in the study of somewhat older subjects is in a sense a continuation of Piaget's trend toward relativism. We prefer to call it a *humanizing* of values in order to emphasize the following facts: (1) the person increasingly discovers the human meaning of values and their relation to the achievement of social purposes, and (2) he increasingly brings to bear his own experiences and his own motives in affirming and promoting a value system. The overall trend, starting from childhood, might be described as a trend from absolute received values to a personally wrought value system. This does not mean that the person creates his value system without benefit of historical tradition. It does not necessarily mean that he substantially changes the content of his received values. The growth trend implies that his values, whatever their content, become increasingly his own, increasingly a reflection of his own experiences and purposes.

. . . .

Process of Growth. The general situation that leads to the humanizing of values is one in which existing values become an occasion for conflict. Perhaps a value that has been automatically accepted is challenged by a competing value. The person then faces the choice of espousing the new value or affirming the old one, and even if he chooses the latter course, . . . his affirming represents a new perception of what is involved and a new enlisting of motives that are really his own. Sometimes in such a conflict the person finds that the new value captures his personal loyalty. He then shifts to it, realizing more clearly than before what is implied both by the new value and by the old one. . . . Sometimes growth comes about when a person in the course of acting upon his usual values produces an unexpected and unwelcome result. Intending to be upright he finds that he has been cruel, or supposing that he is friendly and obliging he learns that he has been taken for a financial ride. . . .

In the humanizing of values, as in the freeing of personal relationships, an important place is occupied by the concept of *empathic range.* Often a marked growth occurs through sudden empathic identification with some new aspect of a value conflict. The process can best be illustrated by drawing an unusually clear example from our case files. A young woman in college was the younger of two children in a business family of highly conservative outlook. She felt that her brother was very much the favorite child and that she had been treated quite unfairly at home. During the wartime shortage of hospital personnel she spent a summer as a volunteer aide in a community hospital near her home. She was astonished and outraged when she realized that patients in private rooms were given far more care and attention than the patients in the wards. Nurses sprang to answer the private-room bell calls while ward patients might be kept waiting for half an hour. She suddenly began to question an economic system which produced so much unfairness in ministering to the common needs of the sick. It was clear that this challenging of received values became possible for her because of a powerful empathic response toward the ward patients. As a victim of domestic unfairness she burned with wrath at the plight of the less favored sick people. Empathy is often of crucial significance in breaking the hold of an unexamined value system. It enlarges one's personal outlook and makes it possible to see the conflicting human claims that offer the real challenge to any value system.

The trend toward the humanizing of values does not take account of everything that happens in the growth of value systems. It needs to be supplemented by another trend, one that has been described by Allport as moving toward a *unifying philosophy of life.* Allport comments as follows on the nature of this philosophy:

> Such a philosophy is not necessarily articulate, at least not always articulate in words. The preacher, by virtue of his training, is usually more articulate than the busy country doctor, the poet more so than the engineer, but any of these personalities, if actually mature, participates and reflects, lives and laughs, according to some embracing philosophy of life developed to his own satisfaction and representing to himself his place in the scheme of things.[9]

The trend we have been describing here does not carry any implication about a unified result. It often happens, in fact that when a person begins to use his own experience to humanize a well-knit system of received values his philosophy for a time becomes much less unified. This was the case with our hospital aide; she violently rejected the economic philosophy of her parents when she perceived one of its unfair consequences, but the job of thinking out her own economic philosophy proved slow and disturbing, so that for a time her views were neither stable nor

---

[9] G. W. Allport, *Personality, op. cit.,* Chap. 8.

consistent. Allport's remarks on a unified philosophy call attention to another aspect of development, one in which the person tries to make his humanized values work together in a common cause. . . .

The importance of analyzing a person's implicit philosophy is shown in a recent study by Smith, Bruner, and White on the relationship of opinions to other features of personality.[10] To some extent, opinions reflect external influences, but close scrutiny shows that individual experience comes in at certain points to give them a definite personal coloring. It is important to distinguish between opinions that are passively borrowed and those that represent humanized values. Any attempt to predict the future course of a person's opinions must take full account of this distinction.

. . . .

In Conclusion

It is a tragic fact of our time that we have become afraid both of our society and of human nature. The march of events has created this fear. The optimism of the nineteenth century, with its vision of unending progress through invention and business enterprise, has given place to a confused apprehension that the world order is falling to pieces and that civilization may soon be shaken to its foundations. Living in a crowded and impersonal society, barraged with information about facts far and near over which we have no control, each of us today is made relentlessly aware of his smallness and helplessness. We have become painfully conscious of the frequency of emotional strains and breakdowns under pressure of today's stressful conditions. We have had terrifying wars and seen many other ways in which man exhibits an inability to deal with his nature and manage his technical inventions.

Thus far the scientific study of man has unwittingly contributed to the trend toward apprehension and uncertainty. All three views of man—the social, the biological, and the psychodynamic—display that one-sided determinism which selectively views the person as the hapless product of forces and which shuns the corresponding study of the person taking action to change these forces. And we have insisted in this book that these approaches are sound; they reveal truth, and they therefore properly warn us not to face the future with blind optimism and a buoyant disregard for the difficult nature of the human undertaking. But equally we have insisted that some attempt should be made to examine the gap in the scientific account so that natural growth and the activity of

---

[10] M. B. Smith, J. S. Bruner, and R. W. White, *Opinions and Personality* (New York: J. C. Wiley & Son, 1956).

the person can be put back into the story. This gap should be filled in the interest of full knowledge, but there is all the more reason to urge filling it when we reflect that precisely here lie the very facts about human nature that offer man the hope of influencing his own destiny. Lewis Mumford calls man "the unfinished animal" and says, "Unlike other organisms, the final stage of his growth is not determined by his biological past: it rests with himself and is partly determined by his own plans for the future."[11] Even though he be a nexus of biological, psychodynamic, social and cultural forces, a person serves to some extent as a transforming and redistributing center, responding selectively to create a new synthesis. Under reasonably favorable circumstances personality tends to continue its growth, strengthen its individuality, and assert its power to change the surrounding world. Man is capable of natural growth, and no fact about him is more important for his ultimate welfare.

The hopeful thing about the scientific study of shaping forces is that man will use his knowledge to prevent himself from being excessively shaped. The more he learns about the silent imperatives of culture and social class, the tyrannies of group expectation and social roles, the demandingness of drives, the subtle slanting of behavior by natural temperament and ability, the heavy impress of childhood training and parental attitudes, the crippling action of anxiety and primitive defense—the more he can perceive and weigh these forces that mold him, the less does he need to be their slave. And he is certainly justified in going a step further and studying the positive side of his capacity for constructive change.

---

[11] L. Mumford, *The Conduct of Life* (New York: Harcourt, Brace & Co., 1951), p. 36.

4. MOTIVATION, ROLE BEHAVIOR, AND DEVELOPMENT*

THIS STUDY found and attempted to explain differences in the motivations, behaviors, and stages of personal development of the participants in four experimental problem-solving discussion groups. The participants in these groups were persons employed in business organizations. Their positions ranged from technical assistant through president and their ages ranged from under twenty-six to over fifty-five years. Two of the groups were drawn intact from their organizations while the participants in the other two groups were strangers to each other prior to the experiments.

A role typology was constructed from the participants' perceptions and evaluations of each others' performances in the group discussions. The typology was based on the number of choices received by each person from the other participants on two performance criterion questions:

1. [Who do you think] presented the best ideas . . . ?
2. [Who do you think] added most to the *congeniality* and *friendliness* of the discussion?

The titles and derivation of the role types were as follows:

Title	Choices Received on	
	Ideas	*Congeniality*
Stars............................	High	High
Technical Specialists................	High	Low
Social Specialists...................	Low	High
Low Chosen Participants............	Low	Low

Participants were also asked to evaluate fellow participants on the criterion of leadership. The Stars were the type most likely to receive choices as leaders, the Technical Specialists ranked second, while the Low Chosen Participants and Social Specialists were the types least likely to be perceived as leaders.

The Technical and Social Specialist types were considered to be representative of the extremes of role differentiation found in previous small

---

* This is the summary of a doctoral dissertation submitted at the Harvard Business School in March, 1961, by David Moment.

group studies. The Stars were expected to integrate both kinds of specialization in their performances. The Low Chosen Participants were a residual type whose behavior pattern was to be determined empirically.

It was found that the four role types behaved differently from each other in clearly distinguishable manners. The Stars, who were perceived as having *good ideas and being congenial,* tended to participate more than the others and tended to talk with others in a more personal manner, but were mixed in their production of other kinds of behaviors. They did some of everything that every one else did, but tended to avoid extremes. The Technical Specialists, who were perceived as having *good ideas but not being congenial,* tended to hold themselves back, avoid sociable behaviors, and relate themselves to the others by joking. The Social Specialists, who were perceived as being *congenial but not having good ideas,* tended to avoid conflict, support others, and behave in emotionally reactive and expressive manners. The Low Chosen Participants tended to behave more aggressively and competitively and were more negatively critical than were the others.

The four role types tended to be associated with different stages and conditions of personal development. The Stars tended to be older and more successful in their careers. The Technical Specialists tended to be younger and more highly educated than the others. The Social Specialists and the Low Chosen Participants had been less successful in their careers in relation to their ages.

Differences were also found in the patterns of scores produced by the role types on paper and pencil tests designed to measure motivational predispositions. The scores were derived from the Thematic Apperception Test and the Executive Preference Study. The patterns were as follows:

Role Type	Achievement Imagery on T.A.T.	Expressed Preference for Intrinsic Task Activities	Affiliation Imagery on T.A.T.	Expressed Preference for Social Activities
Stars	High	Low	Mixed	High
Technical Specialists	High	High	Low	Mixed
Social Specialists	Low	High	Mixed	High
Low Chosen Participants	Low	Mixed	High	Low

The Stars tended to be oriented toward *achievement and persons,* the Technical Specialists tended to be oriented toward *achievement and concrete tasks,* and the Social Specialists tended to be oriented toward *persons and concrete tasks.* The Low Chosen Participants tended to indicate concern with affiliation but not with achievement in their T.A.T. stories, but tended to indicate conscious rejection of social relationships on the Executive Preference Study.

The combination of age, salary, and education level were found to be the strongest predictors of role types. These attributes were measures of both historical experiences and current social statuses. The motivational predispositions and the behavior patterns associated with each role type were interpreted as resultants of the participants' opportunities to experience different kinds of role relationships and the rewards and deprivations which had accompanied their previous performances in social situations.

These findings and theoretical interpretations imply that individuals might to some degree contribute toward the development of their own competences and the competences of others by selectively exposing themselves and others to a variety of social situations involving a range of different role relationships. As part of their adventures in various role situations, they may consciously attempt to identify their own intentions, both overt and latent, try to identify their own behavior styles, and try to identify the consequences of their behaviors. These processes comprise a kind of social experimentation which is dynamically similar to both the experiential learning processes which lead to more mature personality development and to the experimental process for obtaining scientific knowledge.

5. MODES OF RESOLVING ROLE CONFLICT*

MOST OF the school superintendents studied in this research felt that such groups as teachers, politicians, church groups, parents, taxpayers' associations, etc., disagreed about the position the superintendent should take with respect to recommending increases in teachers' salaries. (The condition in which a person in a recognized social role feels that others' expectations of him are incompatible was called a condition of *role conflict* by the researchers.) The superintendents felt that some of these expectations were the legitimate, justifiable positions of the groups which held them, while the expectations of other groups were not rightfully those of members of such groups. The superintendents' judgment of the legitimacy of a group's expectations was one discussion used to study the conflicted role of the superintendents.

Another aspect of this role conflict situation accounted for by the researchers was the amount of economic or social power the superintendent felt each group had available with which to sanction his behavior. The researchers believed that both the superintendent's perception of the legitimacy of each group's expectations and the perception of the power of each group to reward or punish him would play a part in influencing how the superintendent dealt, in this case, with the teacher salary issue.

The researchers hypothesized that three different types of superintendents (the *moral,* the *expedients,* and the *moral-expedients*) would respond differently to similar combinations of perceived legitimacy and perceived power. Superintendents were classified from data gathered independently from that related to the decisions studied in the research. The *moral* orientation was defined as that in which the superintendent emphasized the legitimacy of an expectation. The *expedient* orientation was defined as that in which the superintendent was most concerned with the rewards and punishments which could be exercised as a result of his conformity or nonconformity to expectations. The *moral-expedient* orientation was defined as the one in which the superintendent took both legitimacy and power into account, acting in accord with his perception of the "net balance."

---

* This summary was prepared from the paper, "Role Conflict and Its Resolutions" by Neal Gross, Alexander W. McEachern, and Ward S. Mason, as published in E. E. Maccoby, T. M. Newcomb, and E. L. Hartley (eds.), *Readings in Social Psychology* (New York: Henry Holt & Co., 1958).

A fourth variable considered by the researchers was the actual decision reached by the superintendents when confronted with the choice
between recommending maximum increases in teacher's salaries or recommending minimum increases. The outcomes were codified as (*a*)
conformity to expectation *A* (highest salary increases), (*b*) conformity
to expectation *B* (lowest salary increases), (*c*) compromise, and (*d*)
avoidance of a position.

Exhibit 1

PREDICTIVE BEHAVIORS OF THREE ORIENTATION TYPES UNDER SIXTEEN
CONDITIONS OF ROLE CONFLICT

| | *Type of Role Conflict:* *Superintendent's Perception of:* | | | | *Predicted Behavior** | | |
| | *Expectation A* | | *Expectation B* | | | | |
	Is It Legitimate?	*Sanctions for Non-conformity?*	*Is It Legitimate?*	*Sanctions for Non-conformity?*	*Moralist*	*Expedient*	*Moral-Expedient*
1.	Yes	Yes	Yes	Yes	c	c	c
2.	Yes	No	Yes	Yes	c	b	b
3.	Yes	Yes	Yes	No	c	a	a
4.	Yes	No	Yes	No	c	c	c
5.	Yes	Yes	No	Yes	a	c	a
6.	Yes	No	No	Yes	a	b	c
7.	Yes	Yes	No	No	a	a	a
8.	Yes	No	No	No	a	a	a
9.	No	Yes	Yes	Yes	b	c	b
10.	No	No	Yes	Yes	b	b	b
11.	No	Yes	Yes	No	b	a	c
12.	No	No	Yes	No	b	b	b
13.	No	Yes	No	Yes	d	c	c
14.	No	No	No	Yes	d	b	b
15.	No	Yes	No	No	d	a	a
16.	No	No	No	No	d	d	d

* Abbreviations for superintendent behavior:
a = conformity to Expectation A
b = conformity to Expectation B
c = compromise
d = avoidance

For each of the sixteen possible combinations of perceptions concerning the legitimacy and sanction power associated with high and low
salary increases, the researchers predicted what action each of the three
types of superintendents would recommend. These predictions are
shown in Exhibit 1. As an aid to interpreting the exhibit, condition
six, for example, means: the superintendent perceives that those who
hold expectation *A* have a legitimate position but those loyal to *B*
expectation do not. *B* adherants, however, possess sanctions for nonconformity while those in the *A* group do not. The predictions are that a

superintendent with a Moralist orientation will conform to expectation *A,* one with an Expedient orientation will conform to *B,* while one with a Moral-Expedient orientation will recommend salary increases somewhere between the *A* and *B* positions.

The final results were that for the Moralists, 18/19 (95 per cent) of the researchers' predictions were correct; for the Expedients 21/23 (91 per cent) of the predictions were correct; for the Moral-Expedients, 38/43 (88 per cent) of the predictions were correct. Since for many of the combinations of role conflict conditions the orientation type did not make a difference as to predicted outcome, the cases where the orientation theoretically did make a difference (see combinations 2, 3, 5, 6, 9, 11, 13, 14, 15) were examined separately. In all cases of this kind the theoretical prediction was correct.

6. A TENTATIVE FORMULATION OF A GENERAL LAW OF INTERPERSONAL RELATIONSHIPS *

I HAVE many times asked myself how our learnings in the field of psychotherapy apply to human relationships in general. During recent years I have thought much about this issue and attempted to state a theory of interpersonal relationships as a part of the larger structure of theory in client-centered therapy. This present document undertakes to spell out, in a somewhat different way, one of the aspects of that theory. It endeavors to look at a perceived underlying orderliness in all human relationships, an order which determines whether the relationship will make for the growth, enhancement, openness, and development of both individuals or whether it will make for inhibition of psychological growth, for defensiveness and blockage in both parties.

The Concept of Congruence

Fundamental to much of what I wish to say is the term "congruence." This construct has been developed to cover a group of phenomena which seem important to therapy and to all interpersonal interaction. I would like to try to define it.

Congruence is the term we have used to indicate an accurate matching of experiencing and awareness. It may be still further extended to cover a matching of experience, awareness, and communication. Perhaps the simplest example is an infant. If he is experiencing hunger at the physiological and visceral level, then his awareness appears to match this experience, and his communication is also congruent with his experience. He is hungry and dissatisfied, and this is true of him at all levels. He is at this moment integrated or unified in being hungry. On the other hand if he is satiated and content this too is a unified congruence, similar at the visceral level, the level of awareness, and the level of communication. He is one unified person all the way through, whether we tap his experience at the visceral level, the level of his awareness, or the level of communication. Probably one of the reasons why most people respond to infants is that they are so completely genuine, integrated, or congruent. If an infant expresses affection or anger or contentment or fear there is no doubt in our minds that he *is* this experience, all the way through. He is transparently fearful or loving or hungry or whatever.

For an example of incongruence we must turn to someone beyond the stage of infancy. To pick an easily recognizable example take the man who becomes angrily involved in a group discussion. His face flushes, his tone communicates anger, he shakes his finger at his opponent. Yet when a friend says, "Well, let's not get angry about this," he replies, with evident sincerity and surprise, "I'm not angry! I don't have any *feeling* about this at all! I was just pointing out the logical facts." The other men in the group break out in laughter at this statement.

What is happening here? It seems clear that at a physiological level he is experiencing anger. This is not matched by his awareness. Consciously he is *not* experiencing anger, nor is he communicating this (so far as he is consciously aware). There is a real incongruence between experience and awareness, and between experience and communication.

Another point to be noted here is that his communication is actually ambiguous and unclear. In its words it is a setting forth of logic and fact. In its tone, and in the accompanying gestures, it is carrying a very different message—"I am angry at you." I believe this ambiguity or contradictoriness of communication is always present when a person who is at that moment incongruent endeavors to communicate.

Still another facet of the concept in incongruence is illustrated by this example. The individual himself is not a sound judge of his own degree of congruence. Thus the laughter of the group indicates a clear consensual judgment that the man is *experiencing* anger, whether or not he thinks so. Yet in his own awareness this is not true. In other words it appears that the degree of congruence cannot be evaluated by the person himself at that moment. We may make progress in learning to measure it from an external frame of reference. We have also learned much about incongruence from the person's own ability to recognize incongruence in himself in the past. Thus if the man of our example were in therapy, he might look back on this incident in the acceptant safety of the therapeutic hour and say, "I realize now I was terribly angry at him, even though at the time I thought I was not." He has, we say, come to recognize that his defensiveness at that moment kept him from being aware of his anger.

One more example will portray another aspect of incongruence. Mrs. Brown, who has been stifling yawns and looking at her watch for hours, says to her hostess on departing, "I enjoyed this evening *so* much. It was a delightful party." Here the incongruence is not between experience and awareness. Mrs. Brown is well aware that she is bored. The incongruence is between awareness and communication. Thus it might be noted that when there is an incongruence between experience and awareness, it is usually spoken of as defensiveness, or denial to awareness. When the incongruence is between awareness and communication it is usually thought of as falseness or deceit.

There is an important corollary of the construct of congruence which is not at all obvious. It may be stated in this way. If an individual is at this moment entirely congruent, his actual physiological experience being accurately represented in his awareness, and his communication being accurately congruent with his awareness then his communication could never contain an expression of an external fact. If he was congruent he could not say, "That rock is hard"; "He is stupid"; "You are bad"; or "She is intelligent." The reasons for this is that we never *experience* such "facts." Accurate awareness of *experience* would always be expressed as feelings, perceptions, meanings from an internal frame of reference. I never *know* that he is stupid or you are bad. I can only perceive that you seem this way to me. Likewise, strictly speaking I do not *know* that the rock is hard, even though I may be very sure that I *experience* it as hard if I fall down on it. (And even then I can permit the physicist to perceive it as a very permeable mass of high-speed atoms and molecules.) If the person is thoroughly congruent then it is clear that all of his communication would necessarily be put in a context of personal perception. This has very important implications.

As an aside it might be mentioned that for a person always to speak from a context of personal perception does not necessarily imply congruence, since any mode of expression *may* be used as a type of defensiveness. Thus the person in a moment of congruence would necessarily communicate his perceptions and feelings as being these, and not as being *facts* about another person or the outside world. The reverse does not necessarily hold, however.

Perhaps I have said enough to indicate that this concept of congruence is a somewhat complex concept with a number of characteristics and implications. It is not easily defined in operational terms, though some studies have been completed and others are in process which do provide crude operational indicators of what is being experienced, as distinct from the awareness of that experience. It is believed that further refinements are possible.

To conclude our definition of this construct in a much more common-sense way, I believe all of us tend to recognize congruence or incongruence in individuals with whom we deal. With some individuals we realize that in most areas this person not only consciously means exactly what he says, but that his deepest feelings also match what he is expressing, whether it is anger or competitiveness or affection or cooperativeness. We feel that "we know exactly where he stands." With another individual we recognize that what he is saying is almost certainly a front, a façade. We wonder what he *really* feels. We wonder if *he* knows what he feels. We tend to be wary and cautious with such an individual.

Obviously, then, different individuals differ in their degree of congruence, and the same individual differs at different moments in degree of congruence, depending on what he is experiencing and whether he can accept this experience in his awareness, or must defend himself against it.

Relating Congruence to Communication in Interpersonal Relationships

Perhaps the significance of this concept for interpersonal interaction can be recognized if we make a few statements about a hypothetical Smith and Jones.

1. Any communication of Smith to Jones is marked by some degree of congruence in Smith. This is obvious from the above.

2. The greater the congruence of experience, awareness, and communication in Smith, the more it is likely that Jones will experience it as a *clear* communication. I believe this has been adequately covered. If all the cues from speech, tone, and gesture are unified because they spring from a congruence and unity in Smith, then there is much less likelihood that these cues will have an ambiguous or unclear meaning to Jones.

3. Consequently, the more clear the communication from Smith, the more Jones responds with clarity. This is simply saying that even though Jones might be quite *in*congruent in his experiencing of the topic under discussion, nevertheless his response will have *more* clarity and congruence in it than if he had experienced Smith's communication as ambiguous.

4. The more that Smith is congruent in the topic about which they are communicating, the less he has to defend himself against in this area, and the more able he is to listen accurately to Jones' response. Putting it in other terms, Smith has expressed what he genuinely feels. He is therefore more free to listen. The less he is presenting a façade to be defended, the more he can listen accurately to what Jones is communicating.

5. But to this degree, then, Jones feels emphatically understood. He feels that insofar as he has expressed himself, (and whether this is defensively or congruently) Smith has understood him pretty much as he sees himself, and as he perceives the topic under consideration.

6. For Jones to feel understood is for him to experience positive regard for Smith. To feel that one is understood is to feel that one has made some kind of a positive difference in the experience of another, in this case of Smith.

7. But to the degree that Jones (*a*) experiences Smith as congruent or integrated in this relationship; (*b*) experiences Smith as having positive regard for him; (*c*) experiences Smith as being emphatically understanding; to that degree the conditions of a therapeutic relationship are established. I have tried in another paper to describe the conditions which our experience has led us to believe are necessary and sufficient for therapy, and will not repeat that description here.

8. To the extent that Jones is experiencing these characteristics of a therapeutic relationship, he finds himself experiencing fewer barriers to communication. Hence he tends to communicate himself more as he is, more congruently. Little by little his defensiveness decreases.

9. Having communicated himself more freely, with less defensiveness, Jones is now more able to listen accurately, without a need for defensive distortion, to Smith's further communication. This is a repetition of step 4, but now in terms of Jones.

10. To the degree that Jones is able to listen, Smith now feels emphatically understood (as in step 5 for Jones); experiences Jones' positive regard (a parallel to step 6); and finds himself experiencing the relationship as therapeutic (in a way parallel to step 7). Thus Smith and Jones have to some degree become reciprocally therapeutic for each other.

11. This means that to some degree the process of therapy occurs in each and that the outcomes of therapy will to that same degree occur in each; change in personality in the direction of greater unity and integration; less conflict and more energy utilizable for effective living; change in behavior in the direction of greater maturity.

12. The limiting element in this chain of events appears to be the introduction of threatening material. Thus if Jones in step 3 includes in his more congruent response new material which is outside of the realm of Smith's congruence, touching an area in which Smith is *in*congruent, then Smith may not be able to listen accurately, he defends himself against hearing what Jones is communicating, he responds with communication which is ambiguous, and the whole process described in these steps begins to occur in reverse.

A Tentative Statement of a General Law

Taking all of the above into account, it seems possible to state it far more parsimoniously as a generalized principle. Here is such an attempt.

Assuming (*a*) a minimal willingness on the part of two people to be in contact; (b) an ability and minimal willingness on the part of each to receive communication from the other; and (c) assuming the contact to continue over a period of time—then the following relationship is hypothesized to hold true:

> The greater the congruence of experience, awareness, and communication on the part of one individual, the more the ensuing relationship will involve: a tendency toward reciprocal communication with a quality of increasing congruence; a tendency toward more mutually accurate understanding of the communications; improved psychological adjustment and functioning in both parties; mutual satisfaction in the relationship.
>
> Conversely the greater the communicated *incongruence* of experience and awareness, the more the ensuing relationship will involve: further communication with the same quality; disintegration of accurate understanding, less adequate psychological adjustment and functioning in both parties; and mutual dissatisfaction in the relationship.

With probably even greater formal accuracy this general law could be stated in a way which recognizes that it is the perception of the *receiver* of communication which is crucial. Thus the hypothesized law could be put in these terms, assuming the same preconditions as before as to willingness to be in contact, etc.:

> The more that Y experiences the communication of X as a congruence of experience, awareness, and communication, the more the ensuing relationship will involve: (etc. as stated above.)

Stated in this way this "law" becomes an hypothesis which it should be possible to put to test, since Y's *perception* of X's communication should not be too difficult to measure.

The Existential Choice

Very tentatively indeed I would like to set forth one further aspect of this whole matter, an aspect which is frequently very real in the therapeutic relationship, and also in other relationships, though perhaps less sharply noted.

In the actual relationship both the client and the therapist are frequently faced with the existential choice, "Do I dare to communicate the full degree of congruence which I feel? Do I dare match my experience, and my awareness of that experience, with my communication? Do I dare to communicate myself as I am or must my communication be somewhat less than or different from this?" The sharpness of this issue lies in the often vividly foreseen possibility of threat or rejection. To communicate one's full awareness of the relevant experience is a risk in interpersonal relationships. It seems to me that it is the taking or not taking of this risk which determines whether a given relationship becomes more and more mutually therapeutic or whether it leads in a disintegrative direction.

To put it another way. I cannot choose whether my awareness will be congruent with my experience. This is answered by my need for defense, and of this I am not aware. But there is a continuing existential choice as to whether my communication will be congruent with the awareness I *do* have of what I am experiencing. In this moment-by-moment choice in a relationship may lie the answer as to whether the movement is in one direction or the other in terms of this hypothesized law.

SECTION IV

Supervisory Behavior and Remedial Action

Introduction

IN SECTION II we examined some of the behavioral patterns found in industrial work groups. We also examined some of the determinants and consequences of these patterns. Technological framework, management values, and group member backgrounds provided a catalytic context for the ongoing consequences of social structure, performance, and satisfaction. But even more important, these consequences of a particular time setting became partial determinants of behavior in succeeding time periods. In effect, each technical-social system, once born, continued to elaborate and change. Original determinants led to emergent behavior, which in turn helped to determine future behavioral consequences.

In Section III our focus was on individual behavior. We saw how behavior in the organizational present is so strongly influenced by the past conditioning of the individuals concerned. We saw how this unfolded in the developmental history of persons in the cases. But we also found that even small changes in the behavior of individuals in working interactions with one another can make a difference in outcomes.

Both Sections II and III are directly relevant to the concern of this section. Formal leadership is clearly an important variable in influencing group behavior, and leaders as individuals have their own unique needs and predispositions. In this section we shall examine leaders both as individuals and as influences in organization life. More specifically, we shall be concerned with a formal leader and his face-to-face job relationships with his immediate subordinates, with his superiors, and with others in the organization with whom he interacts directly.

Every formal leader, at every level of the organization, is a man in the middle of varying and complex pressures. It is a well-documented fact that the modern-day supervisor is expected to play different roles for different people. He is expected to be a "good boss" to his subordinates, not all of whom could agree on what they mean by that expression. His family expects him to be a "good husband and father"; and his superiors probably expect him to be a "good company man," among other things. Society expects that he will be a "good citizen," and his peers expect him to be a "good guy."

These conflicting external expectations might be met successfully but for two reasons. First of all, the different role demands placed upon each man in the middle confront him more often simultaneously than they do separately. They usually cannot be sealed off from one another, but instead encounter each other in conflict. Secondly, as we learned in our study of Section III, each man in the middle seeks to maintain an inner self-concept. He cherishes his own assumptions of what is "good" behavior on his part. These assumptions, built up over the individual's life experience, often trace their roots back to childhood, and they change slowly, if at all, when subjected to on-the-job pressures. The fact that these external pressures conflict with each other makes it even easier to understand why so many men in the middle retreat into a "play-it-safe" role pattern. They find it impossible to play a role which resolves the conflicts both inside and outside. In seeking to maintain the multiple dimensions of their own self-concept, they encounter too many other individuals engaged in the same quest who make role demands they cannot meet. Thus, the man in the middle finds it almost impossible to be a "good boss," a "good company man," and a "good guy" at the same time. He can choose to identify with one of these role patterns or the other, or—and let us not underestimate the difficulty—he can strive to achieve some more complex balance. This section will allow us to study a variety of supervisors at work to enlarge our understanding of this aspect of organizational life.

Of course the supervisor is not solely reactive to the many pressures of his immediate environment. He can also adopt a positive, proactive posture and take steps to influence his work life. He can diagnose chronic problem situations and take steps to remedy them. And since this is not a course to train researchers but rather "firing line" administrators we will, in our classroom discussions, want to move beyond the diagnostic stage and into the proposing of remedial action. The cases in this section are organized to allow both an initial emphasis on diagnosis and later on remedial action.

The first four cases in this section (Electronics Stock Control Group, Battleship Y, American Radiatronics Corporation, and Allied Food Company) are especially selected to provide a picture of four supervisors at work in widely divergent circumstances. They are supervising different kinds of tasks, different types of people, and at different levels of organization. All four of these supervisors are not only responding to events, they are by their behavior also actively helping to shape events. This action on their part induces us to emphasize a diagnostic approach to the cases. The results they achieve can usefully be compared to the research findings that relate different styles of leadership to different consequences (especially Readings 1–5). In the remaining five cases

(Stiles Corporation, Merrill Manufacturing Company, Work Group Ownership of an Improved Tool, The Crown Fastener Company, Claremont Instrument Company) we can see supervisors who, rightly or wrongly, seem less confident about what they are doing. Things seem to be getting out of hand. Under these circumstances we are naturally more strongly induced to develop our own proposals for remedial action.

Perhaps the most valuable tools for evaluating such situations are the ways of thinking about behavior in work groups we have already developed: the notion of a social system, the inputs, the outputs, and equilibriums. This section will give us the opportunity to use these ideas in relation to real-life problems.

The final two readings in this section (The Need Hierarchy and Motivation in Work Groups) provide a theory about the behavior of people in work groups that may be a useful guide to your thinking in regard to the cases. We need to be reminded, however, that even our best theories in this area are not thoroughly tested and need to be applied with considerable caution.

Cases

1. THE ELECTRONICS STOCK CONTROL GROUP

Part 1

THIS CASE concerns a group of approximately twenty-three Civil Service workers employed in an office environment at an inventory control point for military electronics material. Each worker was personally responsible for controlling world-wide stocks of a range of 300–3,000 repair parts. The workers were known as stock control analysts, and for each repair part in her category each analyst had a "stock status" sheet housed in a "tub file" alongside her desk. On the basis of reports received daily from field stocking depots, these stock status sheets were updated weekly by a Univac computer. The analysts were responsible for reviewing the computer recommendations concerning the necessity for additional procurement, redistribution of assets between stock points, or interservice transfer of excess material. This manual review of the computer's work was necessary because the computer operation had not been in effect long enough to validate its accuracy, and because management felt that the price and military essentiality of the items in question warranted a selective human judgment review.

The employees were split into the following work groups: ten electron tube analysts, four nonelectron tube analysts, six service section clerks, and two secretaries. As shown in Exhibit 1, the physical layout of the office isolated the work groups in question from other workers on the first floor of the building. The work area was compact, and as a result the workers were generally aware of what their neighbors were doing and of what was going on around their supervisor's desk.

There was a fairly strong sentiment among the workers that the job of electron tube analyst was more glamorous than any of the other jobs in the section. The fact that electron tubes were in general very high-cost items and had wide application in "exotic" military equipments, no doubt accounted for this feeling.

The nontube analysts performed identical work and were paid the

320

same salary given to the tube analysts, but the commodities they handled were not in themselves glamorous.

In general, there were more working problems related to electron tube than to nontube items; this was because of the technical complexity, price, and military essentiality of the tubes. As a consequence, the supervisor and his assistant had to spend more time working with the tube analysts than with other people in the section.

Service section clerks maintained files which contained historical logistic data related to the repair parts controlled by the section. The

Exhibit 1

DIAGRAM OF OFFICE LAYOUT

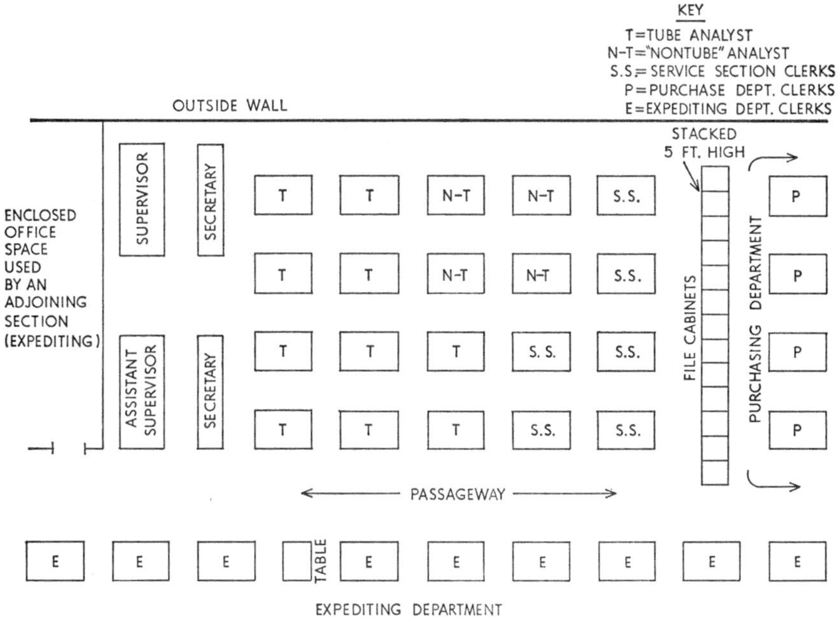

KEY

T = TUBE ANALYST
N-T = "NONTUBE" ANALYST
S.S = SERVICE SECTION CLERKS
P = PURCHASE DEPT. CLERKS
E = EXPEDITING DEPT. CLERKS

workers in this section performed research for the analysts and made available historical data as requested by the analysts. The salary of the service section personnel was about three fourths of an analyst's salary.

Each analyst worked independently, and was solely responsible for the complete control of a specific range of repair parts. The only required interaction between analysts was in the nature of temporary assistance to a fellow worker whenever the work load became unbalanced, as it sometimes did. Such assistance was inside the lines of the separate work groups, (i.e., tube analysts assisted only other tube analysts, nontube analysts assisted each other, and service section personnel likewise assisted only other service section personnel).

The technology of the situation required that each worker exercise sound judgment and be particularly conscientious. An error on the part of any individual worker would normally not be detected for days or weeks after it happened, but could have rather serious consequences. The group was quite mixed with regard to sex, age, ethnic background, and education.

PREDICTIONS

THE ELECTRONICS STOCK CONTROL GROUP

PART 1

From what I know of the stock control operations described in Part 1, I would predict that:

a) Productivity of the workers would be (high) (standard) (below standard).

b) Workers would be (highly) (moderately) (dis-) satisfied with their job.

c) Social structure would be (group oriented) (subgroup oriented) (both group and subgroup oriented).

d) Relations between workers and their supervisors would be (cordial) (neutral) (strained).

THE ELECTRONICS STOCK CONTROL GROUP

Part 2

IN GENERAL, the workers were conscientious and co-operative. They felt they were doing an important job, were co-operative with management and its goals, and valued their membership in the total working group. The fast workers often volunteered to help the slower ones, and when the work load was unbalanced, they assisted each other willingly. During lunch hours and breaks, the total group did things together voluntarily, but two major subgroups formed within the large group; the tube analysts were one subgroup and all the other workers formed the second subgroup. Occasionally the nontube people expressed the feeling that management and the immediate supervisors were too interested in the problems of the tube analysts and ignored the problems of other workers. On the other hand the tube analysts often said that they worked harder and shouldered more responsibility than did the other workers in the section. Usually these feelings were expressed in a joking manner.

POSTPREDICTION ANALYSIS

Refer to your predictions at the end of Part 1. How closely do they match the information above? Do inaccuracies in your predictions reflect inadequate analysis? If so, explain the analytical failure. If not, what additional information would you have needed in Part 1 to improve your predictive accuracy and how would you have used that information?

THE ELECTRONICS STOCK CONTROL GROUP

Part 3

THE PHYSICAL LAYOUT depicted in Exhibit 1 had been in effect for several years and the group in question had escaped the "desk shuffling" common in other parts of the building as the organization grew and responsibilities and work loads were realigned. However, the recent expansion of the purchase department finally made it necessary to relocate the stock control section at the other end of the building. Exhibit 2 shows the new layout after the move.

Exhibit 2

DIAGRAM OF THE REVISED OFFICE LAYOUT

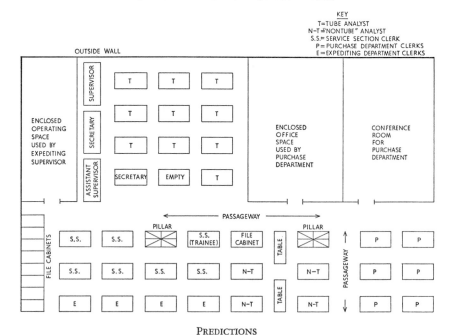

PREDICTIONS

THE ELECTRONICS STOCK CONTROL GROUP

PART 3

From what I know of the stock control operations and the change described in Part 3, I would predict that:

a) Productivity of the workers would (increase) (remain about the same) (decrease).

b) Job satisfaction of the workers would (increase) (remain about the same) (decrease).

c) Social group structure would (remain the same) (change).

d) Relations between workers and their supervisors would (improve) (remain about the same) (deteriorate).

THE ELECTRONICS STOCK CONTROL GROUP

Part 4

WITHIN A FEW DAYS after the move, things began to change. Production of the nontube workers began to decline, and absenteeism in this subgroup rose. Errors occurred more frequently, and a common excuse was that the mistake never would have happened if the supervisors had spent a little time with the nontube group. The joking between the tube and nontube workers turned to sarcasm and intersubgroup contacts during lunch and break periods virtually ceased. Although the production of the tube analysts did not change, errors occurred more frequently, and when detected were often blamed on late, inaccurate, or incomplete information from the service section.

The group supervisor had originally fought the relocation of the stock control group, and when the problems described above persisted, he attempted to have the group moved back to its original location or to another comparable location. However, the move of one group necessarily caused the move of another group of similar size, and management would not approve another shift.

Although the frequency and complexity of the day-to-day operational problems did not warrant it, the supervisor began to devote more time to the nontube group and less to the tube analysts.

POSTPREDICTION ANALYSIS

Refer to your predictions at the end of Part 3. How closely do they match the information above? Do inaccuracies in your predictions reflect inadequate analysis? If so, explain the analytical failure. If not, what additional information would you have needed in Part 3 to improve your predictive accuracy and how would you have used that information?

What do you think of the change in the supervisor's behavior? Will it tend to bring out any changes in the performance or satisfaction of any of the subgroups, or the groups' relations to each other?

THE ELECTRONICS STOCK CONTROL GROUP

Part 5

As THE SUPERVISOR devoted more time to the nontube people, he found that they really did not have many operational problems which required his help, but whenever he decreased the amount of time he spent in their work area, they would manufacture problems to draw him back.

After several weeks, production of the nontube workers improved and errors occurred less frequently. However, conditions were not as good as they had been prior to the relocation of the stock control group. The tube analysts were making less errors, but they failed to return to the high premove standards. The two subgroups continued to take lunch and break periods separately.

On several occasions, the stock control group supervisor was embarrassed in conferences with his supervisors because he was unable to recite from personal knowledge current facts surrounding certain perpetual problem tubes controlled by his analysts. Prior to spending more time with the nontube workers, he had been able to keep abreast of recent changes regarding the status of those tubes.

POSTPREDICTION ANALYSIS

Refer to your predictions at the end of Part 4. How closely do they match the information above? Do inaccuracies in your predictions reflect inadequate analysis? If so, explain the analytical failure. If not, what additional information would you have needed in Part 4 to improve your predictive accuracy and how would you have used that information?

2. BATTLESHIP "Y"

BATTLESHIP "Y" was commissioned on the East Coast in the fall of 1942, and after taking its shakedown cruise to the West Indies, arrived at the forward area in the Pacific war in January, 1943. During this time no unusual events had affected either ship or crew, with the possible exception that this ship granted more than the average amount of leave and liberty to its personnel. The ship carried about 2,700 men, of whom about 550 were assigned to the engineering department.

The problems of machinery operation and personnel indoctrination and training had been complicated during the precommissioning detail and the shakedown cruise by the lack of experienced personnel. This handicap was particularly noticeable in the engineering department, where the absence of experienced junior officers and enlisted men had increased the difficulties of maintaining proper machinery operation, machinery repair, and watch-standing procedure. The senior officers of the department had relied heavily on a few experienced commissioned officers and chief petty officers for whom the work load had been unusually heavy during these first few months.

The organization of the engineering department was functional below the chief and assistant engineering officers who ran the department. In each of four divisions, namely, boiler, main engine, electrical, and auxiliary, there was a division officer in charge, assisted by junior officers, warrant officers, and chief petty officers. Exhibit 1 indicates the organization of the engineering department and the details of the B Division, (Boiler Division) organization. The latter was organized to maintain and operate four firerooms, each containing two boilers and considerable auxiliary machinery. This auxiliary machinery in each fireroom consisted of approximately twenty pumps, one large deaerating feed tank, air compressors, and certain other small pieces of machinery. This arrangement of equipment on Battleship "Y" was radically different from that on former United States warships, which carried this auxiliary machinery in the engine rooms, whereas the firerooms contained little but the boilers. Machinist-mate ratings operated and maintained the auxiliary machinery, while water tender and boilermaker ratings had similar responsibility over the boilers.

Normally the crew stood one four-hour watch in three (four hours on, eight hours off). The following stations were manned in operating a

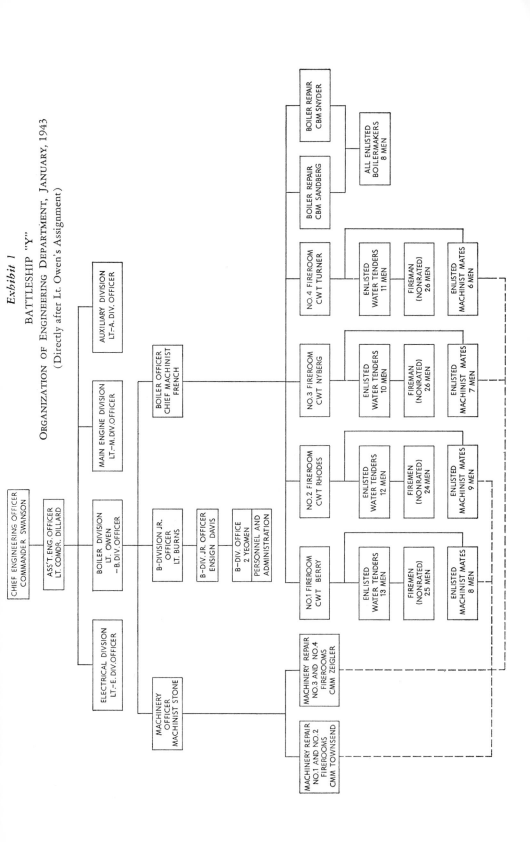

Exhibit 1

BATTLESHIP "Y"

ORGANIZATION of ENGINEERING DEPARTMENT, JANUARY, 1943

(Directly after Lt. Owen's Assignment)

fireroom: a first-class water tender was in charge of the entire fireroom and in charge of one boiler; another first-class water tender was in charge of the other boiler if both boilers were steaming; each steaming boiler required a first- or second-class water tender to "check" water (to insure that water was fed to the boiler); each steaming boiler required two firemen to tend the oil burners; a fireman was assigned to tend the deaerating feed tank; and a fireman was usually assigned as a messenger. On the lower or machinery level, a first-class machinist mate was in charge, assisted by a second-class machinist mate assigned to the feed pumps, a second- or third-class machinist mate assigned to the booster and condensate pumps, and a fireman assigned to the fuel oil pumps. Each watch consisted of eight or nine men, if one boiler was steaming, and twelve or thirteen men, if both boilers were steaming. It was usual to conduct routine cleaning and minor repairs while on watch, in addition to tending the operating machinery.

A chief water tender was in charge of each fireroom, two chief machinist mates were responsible for all machinery repair in the division, and two chief boilermakers were charged with boiler maintenance. Two warrant officers were assigned to the division; one supervised all boiler operation and repair, and the other all machinery operation maintenance. The division junior officers functioned under the division officer principally to administer the personnel of the division and conduct the division office work.

The B Division had always presented the most difficult problem in regard to personnel training, both because it was the largest division aboard ship (195 men) and because its function involved the most technical operations and required the most skilled and experienced personnel. The division was fortunate in having capable and experienced warrant officers and chief petty officers plus a backbone of high-grade rated men, but the majority of the crew were young reserves with little training or mechanical background.

Lt. Owen joined Battleship "Y" in January, 1943, and was assigned duties as the B Division officer by Commander Swanson, the chief engineer. Lt. Owen had obtained his commission in the Naval Reserve in June, 1940, after completion of the Reserve Officer Training Course at Yale University, where he had also studied mechanical engineering. Before reporting to Battleship "Y" he had served as chief engineer of two destroyers and had been graduated from a Navy engineering course at Massachusetts Institute of Technology. In both his destroyer engineering duties and in his recent course he had become familiar with the kind of equipment installed on Battleship "Y."

In introducing Lt. Owen to his future job, Commander Swanson said:

> Owen, I'm assigning you as B Division officer because we have a problem there. We are pretty well set in the other three divisions, but ever since leaving the States, we've had more and more trouble with B Division. Burns, who has it now, is doing the best he can, but he just doesn't have the background to handle it, and I feel that the division is getting out of hand. You've got two mighty good warrant officers in French and Stone, especially the former, and I think you've had enough experience to whip the division into shape. You'll have to keep an eye on your chief petty officers. Most of them are capable enough, but lately some of them, particularly Berry and Nyberg, have been giving Burns a bit of trouble. As you know, on this ship most of our operating difficulty is bound to come from the firerooms, because most of the pumps and auxiliaries are there, so it's mightly important that we get the situation squared away. At present, frankly, I'm not at all satisfied with the results turned in by B Division, and I think it's due to the way Burns is running it. He just hasn't got his men and officers organized properly, and he doesn't know enough engineering to lead them. I'd suggest that you get together with French and Stone and try to get a picture of the problem I'm trying to indicate to you. Mr. Dillard, the assistant engineer, and I will help you wherever possible.

Lt. Owen began at once to become acquainted with the personnel in the engineering department and in his division, with the organization and operation of the division, and with the problems which Commander Swanson had called to his attention. In his first few weeks as division officer, Lt. Owen became acquainted with the officers of the department and with his own division junior officers, warrant officers, chief petty officers, and leading enlisted men and was able to make a preliminary evaluation of the part each was playing in the organization.

The chief engineer, Commander Swanson, was a graduate of the United States Naval Academy in the class of 1928, and in Lt. Owen's opinion was a capable engineer with a keen mind and an energetic sense of responsibility. Lt. Owen discovered, however, that Commander Swanson was confident of his own engineering knowledge and ability to operate the engineering plant, and was not particularly receptive to suggestions from his subordinates. He rarely acted on the advice of anyone, with the exception of Mr. Dillard, who had reached the point where he offered advice and suggestions only when necessary. Commander Swanson was respected among the officers and men but shared none of the popularity of Mr. Dillard.

The assistant engineering officer, Lt. Commander Dillard, was an ex-enlisted man with an exceptional Naval record, as evidenced by his rise to the rank of lieutenant commander. Mr. Dillard was popular throughout the ship and admired by both men and officers for his knowledge and skill with machinery, his friendly understanding of the problems of the crew, and his continual efforts in behalf of the ship and crew in numerous activities outside of the engineering department, such as ship's parties, smokers, newspaper, and ship's welfare. The chief petty officers almost never questioned his judgment or advice, and this situation was rare in the Navy where chiefs sometimes tend to criticize the decisions of officers. Mr. Dillard's decisions on operation and maintenance of machinery were always received as the final word.

Two junior officers, Lt. Burns and Ensign Davis, were attached to the B Division. Neither had a great deal of experience, and neither had been successful in organizing either the men or the division work; the office records and routine, consequently, had been suffering. In several instances the division had been mentioned over the ship's loud-speaker for failure to comply with some aspect of ship's routine. This public chastisement had resulted in lowered divisional morale, as shown by the talk and attitude of the men after such an occurrence.

The two warrant officers, French and Stone, had had many years' experience in boiler and machinery repair work. French had nearly thirty years in the Navy and was thorough in his work and conscientious in his duties. Lt. Owen came almost immediately to rely heavily on French. French was recognized by Commander Swanson and Lt. Commander Dillard, by the CPO's, and by the men as an exceptionally capable warrant. Lt. Owen recognized his ability within a few days and was glad to trust him with much important work. French made a habit of keeping Lt. Owen informed on the status of the firerooms, as the latter had requested. Stone, although a younger man, was capable and thorough, but lately had been very much upset about his failure to secure control of his machinist mates and to obtain a definite statement of responsibility from his senior officers. He expressed himself to Lt. Owen, however, as willing and anxious to do anything necessary to bring about the desired results.

After about a week of observation, Lt. Owen became convinced that the trouble in B Division centered at the chief petty officer level. A breakdown at this level was particularly undesirable because it was upon these men that the division officer relied for the immediate supervision of machinery and personnel. All his chief petty officers, Owen discovered, were men who had from six to eighteen years of service, and all but one were in the regular Navy. As a group, he considered them above average in experience and capabilities, and their naval records substantiated this opinion.

Chief machinist French gave Lt. Owen his opinion of the chiefs by saying,

> Stone and I have been having a lot of trouble with some of the chiefs, particularly in the last month or so. They have become difficult to handle and are certainly not carrying their share of the load. They seem reluctant to help out either in properly operating the plant or in taking care of their men. It's hard to understand, too, because they did such a wonderful job before commissioning and on the shakedown. Now, however, they try to spend as much time as possible in the chiefs' quarters, and we have to be after them continually. Stone and I don't like it, and the men don't like it either. Personally, I think we'll have to clear up the situation soon because several incidents have occurred lately where we nearly had serious engineering casualties. The men aren't on their toes, discipline is poor, and I think it's the chiefs' attitude that's causing the sloppy operation. It won't take you long, Mr. Owen, to discover that these chiefs have any number of complaints about the ship; about the engineering department; the division; and most of the officers, including Mr. Burns, Stone, and myself.

Lt. Owen went out of his way to try to get acquainted with his chief petty officers and observed that nearly all of them, as individuals, were what he considered "good sailors," with Naval records indicating a high degree of proficiency in their professional as well as military duties.

CWT Berry, in charge of one fireroom, who impressed Lt. Owen as the ringleader of the group had sixteen years of service, mostly on destroyers. He was experienced and capable, both in fireroom operation and in machinery repairs, and was trusted and highly regarded by the two warrant officers. He was, in addition, a naturally likeable man with few or no enemies among the men and officers. His good humor and jovial, round-faced appearance, however, often disguised his harsh tongue and manner of criticizing other chiefs and officers. Lt. Owen was able almost immediately to have long, friendly talks with Berry, and discovered that Berry had many complaints, both personal and general, against the present organization. In addition, during the past few months, Berry had made numerous suggestions to responsible officers relative to more efficient and economical ways of operating the plant and division, but action on them had not been forthcoming.

CWT Turner, who had been promoted to chief petty officer in December, 1942, was in charge of a fireroom where he was having little success either in machinery operation or in securing results from his men. There was continual disciplinary trouble in his fireroom as well as occasional machinery breakdown due to personnel. He orally blamed the present divisional trouble as the cause of his own shortcomings. The warrant officers expressed to Lt. Owen their opinion that Turner had not been ready for promotion to chief petty officer and that he was not qualified or trustworthy in machinery repairs.

CWT Rhodes and CWT Nyberg, who were average, or slightly above average, in service and experience, were in charge of the other two firerooms. The former was quiet and would normally have been expected to do thorough although not spectacular work. He seemed to be carried along in the existing difficulty by the pressure of the other chiefs. Nyberg was a more energetic type, talked a great deal, was not as well informed technically as Berry or Rhodes, but could, when he desired, produce results. During this difficulty he was the most outspoken of the chiefs in their attitude of resentment and defiance.

Chief machinist mates Zeigler and Townsend were in charge of all machinery maintenance in the division, each caring for two firerooms. They were both experienced men with a number of years in the Navy, but were at an initial disadvantage aboard the Battleship "Y" because they had been assigned to a boiler division. This procedure had never been customary in the Navy, but was necessary on this ship because of the design, which placed all the auxiliary machinery in the firerooms instead of the engine rooms. The customary arrangement placed all machinist-mate ratings together either in the engine rooms or with the auxiliary division, and all water tender and boilermaker ratings together in the firerooms. Usually, therefore, there was no jurisdictional dispute between machinist mates and water tenders because their duties did not overlap. On the Battleship "Y," however, the fact that both machinist mates and water tenders were assigned to operate and maintain firerooms brought them into conflicts of responsibilities.

The principal complaint made by Zeigler and Townsend was of continual bickering with the chief water tenders in charge of the firerooms and the warrant officer in charge of boilers (French) in regard to the administration of the machinist-mate ratings, who were assigned to a fireroom under a chief water tender but who were required to work on machinery under a chief machinist mate. Even the two warrant officers agreed that this had been a serious point of contention and that there was still constant conflict as to which chief had authority over the machinist mates. An instance of this confusion was brought to Lt. Owen's attention shortly after he became the division officer when CMM Zeigler and CWT Nyberg came to see him in the B Division office.

CMM ZEIGLER: Sir, I can't possibly get that job on the main feed pump in Number 3 fireroom finished by tomorrow night if I can't use the men in Number 3 for the job. Mr. Stone told me you wanted the job completed by then, and I'd just broken the coupling and pulled the pump casing when Nyberg, here, took three of the men off the job to help him clean firesides in his Number 6 boiler. I've got all the carbon packing to fit and the journal to polish, and I've got to have those men. They are machinist mates anyhow and aren't supposed to work in that boiler.

CWT NYBERG: Two of those men aren't even rated machinist mates; they're only "strikers" (firemen going up for machinist-mate rating), they're attached to my fireroom, and I rate using them where I need them. I've got a lot of work to do in that boiler, and I can't do it without men. Zeigler's got more machinist mates than he needs for that feed-pump job, and he can work straight through on that while I can't work all night in that boiler. I'm getting mighty tired of having to argue with Zeigler every time I try to use my own men the way I want. Mr. French told me to put ten men in that boiler and I have to use those strikers to do it.

Of the two boilermakers, Snyder and Sandberg, only the former was a regular with sufficient experience for the repair work required. The latter was a reserve, who was conscientious and energetic but who had very limited boiler experience. Snyder was quiet and hard-working, and did not appear troubled by the disturbance in the division except that he made it clear to Lt. Owen by his remarks that he resented having a second chief boilermaker involved in his work. He had shown himself capable of handling the job alone because actually he received little help from Sandberg.

After Lt. Owen had been B Division officer for about three weeks, had listened carefully to all aspects of the disturbing internal problems in his division, and had made careful observations of men, officers, and organization, he took time to summarize the problem. He concluded that the following were the underlying causes of the difficulty:

A. The chief petty officers as a group felt that they had been unjustly treated.
   1. They had been deprived of normal leave during precommissioning because of the urgent need for their presence aboard ship to prepare crew and equipment for sea duty. At this time they were promised extra leave and liberty privileges before leaving the States. These promises by the chief engineer were generally not fulfilled.
   2. The ship itself had failed to establish certain extra privileges and marks of distinction to which the chiefs, particularly the old-timers,

felt they were entitled. Notable among these were special movies for CPO's (similar to those for officers), a private CPO ladder from the main deck down to their quarters, special CPO liberty privileges, and a reconsideration of the CPO duty watch procedure.

B. Many of the chiefs as individuals felt that they had been discriminated against, ignored, and mistreated.

   1. Turner contended, as did Nyberg also, that the former B Division officer had failed to distribute the members of the crew of the division equally among the firerooms, either in number or in talent, and consequently they were having difficulty in maintaining their firerooms on a par with the other two.

   2. Several of the chiefs, notably Berry, were discouraged by the fact that their carefully considered suggestions for the good of the division and the department had been ignored. They felt pride in their knowledge of the engineering plant, and resented being excluded from the administration of it.

   3. Nearly all the chiefs felt that in the present organization they were not permitted to carry the responsibility for men and machinery to which their positions entitled them. They were often by-passed in both administrative and operational questions, and the officers and warrant officers dealt directly with the men. In many cases also, enlisted men were promoted either without their knowledge or against their recommendation.

C. The lack of a definite policy by responsible officers on the question of the administration of the machinist mates was a source of continual friction. It had reached the point where it involved the two warrant officers and had divided the division into two factions which were constantly antagonistic.

D. There was a decided need in the division for an established chain of responsibility, by which the division officer could issue directives and then be assured by his subordinates that they had been carried out. It was vital to the operation of the ship to keep responsible officers advised at all times of the status of machinery. Prior to the time Lt. Owen reported as B Division officer, there had been no attempt on the part of the CPO's or warrants to keep the division officer constantly informed. As a result, there had been several embarrassing occasions on which Commander Swanson and even the ship's executive officer had spoken to Lt. Burns about casualties or machinery derangements in his division about which he knew nothing.

E. It was necessary to re-establish the customary forms of military discipline throughout the division. At the present time such discipline was nearly entirely lacking at all levels. Lt. Owen felt that it was vital to assure his chiefs and petty officers of his assistance in their efforts to obtain obedience from their subordinates. Most of the divisional petty officers who, with the chiefs, should have been the backbone of discipline felt unwilling to attempt to exact obedience as long as the divisional officers failed to give them constant support.

F. The divisional administrative organization, as centered in the division office under the division junior officers, was ineffective and a contributing factor to the uncertainty felt by the entire division.

G. Much remained for him to accomplish in developing a spirit of divisional pride among men and officers as well as in restoring to key individuals a sense of confidence in their own function in the organization.

With the foregoing analysis in mind, Lt. Owen realized that there was more than sufficient talent available in the division, but that an extensive reorganization and rebuilding job lay ahead in order to achieve smooth-functioning operation and to avoid the serious material casualties which he considered inevitable under the existing setup. Lt. Owen therefore took the steps described in the following pages.

1. He effected the transfer of both Lt. Burns and Ensign Davis. The former was sent to another ship, the latter to a new department. To replace them, he acquired another ensign, new to the ship, with little experience but with a good education, a quick mind, an energetic spirit, and a sense of responsibility which compelled him to see his assignments through to a conclusion. Lt. Owen placed Ensign Zane in charge of the office, indoctrinated him with the plans he had in mind for the reorganization of the division, and set him to work immediately on the administrative and personnel problems of the division. Charts were soon published indicating advancement and training status and progress, duty, watch requirements and assignments, and liberty and transfer schedules. Messing and bathing changes improving the crew's living conditions were instituted. A redistribution of personnel among firerooms was put into effect, insuring equal distribution, as far as number and talent were concerned.

2. He assigned Chief boilermaker Sandberg to assist Ensign Zane with the office duties. This move placed Chief boilermaker Snyder completely in charge of all boiler repairs under Chief machinist French. Sandberg proved valuable in the office work and conscientiously attacked the problems found in administering the personnel and in assuring that the division complied with the often very exacting ship's routine. The division, as a consequence, did not receive the frequent "calling down" it had been subjected to previously. Results in the office were encouraging, and the interest and spirit of the crew improved markedly.

Two older enlisted men, Miller and Russell, who had been suffering physical discomforts in the hot firerooms primarily because of their age, were assigned as master-at-arms and police petty officer, respectively, for the division. The two men were popular among the crew and functioned in their new assignments principally in insuring that the established routines of messing, berthing, working parties, liberty and recreation parties, and other crews' functions were carried out smoothly. They relieved Lt. Owen and Ensign Zane of many of the routine duties of the division, and furnished a liaison between the crew and the division office. Lt. Owen felt strongly the importance of assigning reliable men as master-at-arms and police petty officer. The previous division policy had been to assign a man to such duty as a disciplinary measure, and as a result the division troublemakers frequently became responsible for carrying out the routines of the division. By reversing this policy and appointing Miller and Russell to these positions, Lt. Owen increased his ability to control the personnel of the division and to keep informed of the troubles and feelings of the crew. As Miller and Russell became familiar with their duties, Lt. Owen, Ensign Zane, and the warrant officers were able to turn over many routine duties to these two enlisted men. Miller, in particular, was respected by the entire division and had the knack of persuading members of the crew to carry out their routine duties. In addition, when some condition was troubling the crew, Miller came to Lt. Owen with a description of the situation and frequently offered suggestions as to the most favorable solution.

3. Lt. Owen held several consultations from time to time with Ensign Zane, French, and Stone, in which he outlined certain proposed changes to be enacted. The two warrants contributed numerous suggestions, especially as to machinery upkeep procedure. A definite policy was agreed upon for each point in question.

4. With his plans for the reorganization of the division outlined, Lt. Owen called a meeting of all his chief petty officers in the CPO quarters and over a cup of coffee presented the program to them. He brought to the meeting a written list of all the proposals and suggestions each chief had made to him and discussed plans with regard to each. He assured them that he intended to safeguard their interests in regard to leaves and privileges; he commended them for their services in putting the ship in commission; and he concretely outlined the responsibility each was to have, making clear his intention to require frequent reports on the status of machinery and personnel. Lt. Owen was gratified with the results of the meeting, and felt that if he was able to take positive progressive steps, he would receive the support of the CPO's.

5. Soon afterwards the new division officer set in motion his plan for

solving the machinist-mate jurisdictional problem and for fixing definite responsibility on each of his chiefs and warrants. It was made clear
to all hands through a written published division order that each CWT
in charge of a fireroom was directly responsible, through the warrant
officers, to the division officer for the entire fireroom including operation, maintenance, and personnel. In fact, this order made the CWT
directly responsible for machinist mates and machinery repair, and made
the fireroom one unit controlled by one chief. The two chief machinist
mates, Zeigler and Townsend, now operated to maintain in repair all the
machinery units but were required to consult with the CWT involved as
to time and priority of repair, and personnel required. The two warrant
officers were to supervise this function and assist in repair scheduling.
Any disputes were to be referred to the division officer for decision.

Although this arrangement of CPO's appeared to place the CWT's
over the CMM's (and officially the CMM's were senior to the CWT's),
this seniority was never an issue. The vital question was jurisdiction
over the machinist mates. As it actually worked out, Lt. Owen consulted
both the CWT and the CMM involved in a case of machinery breakdown or repairs. The fact remained, however, that he held each CWT
responsible for the over-all operation of his fireroom. The CWT could
call on the CMM to supervise the machinist mates in repairs. Lt. Owen
held the CMM responsible for the maintenance and repair of all auxiliary equipment also.

The final delegation of responsibility among the chief petty officers
was as follows:

a) Each CWT was to be in charge of a fireroom, with full responsibility
   for all functions of fireroom and personnel.

b) CBM Snyder was to be responsible to French and Lt. Owen for all
   boiler repairs required by each fireroom. He was to consult on work
   with CWT involved.

c) CMM Zeigler and Townsend were to be responsible to Stone and Lt.
   Owen for all machinery repairs required by a fireroom as requested by
   CWT.

d) CBM Sandberg, assistant to Ensign Zane in the office, was to be responsible to Lt. Owen and Ensign Zane.

The organization as revised above was put to test soon after its
inauguration when the ship began preparations for an extensive fleet
operation against the enemy. To prepare the firerooms for prolonged
steaming, Lt. Owen requested that warrant officers French and Stone
confer with the chief petty officers and submit a list of recommended
repairs and routine maintenance to be accomplished in the ten-day

availability period. After the work lists had been prepared but before the overhaul period had started, Berry and Townsend asked permission to see Lt. Owen about the repair lists.

CWT BERRY: We don't seem to be getting off to a good start in Number 1 fireroom because Townsend here claims he can't accomplish all the machinery repairs on the list in ten days without help. And I've got two boilers to clean and can't spare him any men.

After calling in French and Stone and locating the work list for Number 1 fireroom, Lt. Owen said:

There may be more items on that list than we can accomplish, so we'll put a priority number on each item. You have forty-two men assigned to the fireroom now, of which six are on divisional duties (mess cooks, police petty officers, and like duties), so you can count on thirty-six men. We are steaming only one boiler so you'll require eight men per watch. On a watch-in-three basis that will take twenty-four men and leave you twelve men for a "turn-to" gang. The cleaning of Number 1 boiler both firesides and watersides, will take about eight men.

Berry interrupted, "But we can't work those men straight through on that boiler."

LT. OWEN: No, but you can use the men in your off-duty watch sections during the day and use your "turn-to" gang during the night. We'll have to work practically straight through to finish Number 1 boiler and do the firesides only of Number 2 boiler in ten days. So start on that basis and we'll see what progress we make.

Now, Townsend, your first job is to overhaul Number 1 fire and flushing pump and install a new thrust bearing; so start on that at once. Use the off-duty watch machinist mates and strikers during the day and take your four best repair men off watch both to supervise the job and to work at least part of the night. Work 'till you've completed that job. After that continue to use the same gang on the other items in this order: Number 1 main condensate pump, Number 3 main feed pump, Number 1 fuel oil service pump, Number 2 main feed booster pump, and finally install the gland drain on Number 5 forced draft blower.

Now, Berry, it's up to you to keep your eye on the progress of all these jobs, to keep me posted on the progress of each and tell me of any delays that hold you up. If you think you aren't going to finish, let me know and we'll assign men from another fireroom if necessary. If the arrangement we've outlined doesn't work, we'll change it, but your job is to see that those two boilers are cleaned and the flushing pump is completed, and then that we get as much of the other work done as time permits.

Townsend, you'd better let Berry know if you haven't enough men or if you can spare him any strikers.

French, you and Stone can let me know if you think we'll have to revise the schedule on the work list. I've no objection to any shifts you make in personnel between work gangs, but I want to know as each item progresses and is ready for final inspection.

6. In order to increase the quality of military discipline in the division, Lt. Owen began a program of military drills and inspections during daily quarters for the crew. On a battleship, even in wartime, quarters for the crew were held several times per week and inspections by the captain irregularly. Lt. Owen had noticed that the B Division was notoriously sloppy in these formations and inspections, particularly in regard to uniform, discipline, and the fundamental evolutions such as "hand salute," "right dress," "about face," "uncover," "cover," etc. It was on these basic deficiencies that he placed his emphasis. The B Division formed in a conspicuous place on the main deck aft. Because of its size it took a large area and any irregularities were noticeable as far forward as the bridge. Lt. Owen's objective was not military precision, but a respectable-looking division with a knowledge of how to act on formal occasions.

Lt. Owen personally supervised this program but required each CPO to assist with his own men. No one in the division, man or officer, was excused, and although the program was unpopular at the outset, mostly because the majority of the men had received very little such training and appeared awkward, the division began to have considerably more "snap" and to make a far more commendable showing than previously at ship inspections. All the officers of the division were encouraged by Lt. Owen to follow up their orders and to support any petty officer in exerting his authority. Effort was made to keep orders and requests to the proper channels and to insure that the chief petty officers were never by-passed in dealing with the crew.

7. Lt. Owen presented several organized proposals to the chief engineer, with the support and approval of Lt. Commander Dillard, the assistant engineer, in the interests of a better functioning plant and in the interests of smoother repair procedure. Most of these proposals had originated with the chiefs, and when Lt. Owen was able in several instances to have the proposals accepted and adopted, the chiefs and warrant officers were openly pleased.

An example was the question of boiler superheat control, which had troubled each of the chief water tenders ever since the ship had been in commission. Commander Swanson had always insisted that the superheat be carried at 850°F. despite the fact that extra fuel oil was required to produce this temperature and despite the fact that additional burners were required on the superheat side of the boiler. Such operation was contrary to the manufacturer's recommendations, the operating procedure proposed by the United States Navy Boiler and Turbine Laboratories, and the experience of the chief water tenders. When Lt. Owen had first discussed boiler operation in the firerooms with the chief water tenders, they had brought the subject to his attention. Berry, in particular, was outspoken in his criticism of the existing operating procedure. While he and Lt. Owen stood in front of a steaming boiler in Number 1 fireroom he said,

> Mr. Owen, aren't you afraid we may damage these superheaters using three burners on that side now, for instance, and only two on the saturated side?
>
> LT. OWEN: No, Berry, at this steaming rate there's enough steam flow to avoid overheating, but it's a bad habit to allow the men to develop because at low rates it may be dangerous. I understand that the Commander carries the superheat at 850°F. at all times to increase turbine efficiency and insure high superheat to the turbines. I personally am convinced, however, that the gain in turbine efficiency is more than offset by the reduction in boiler efficiency and increased fuel consumption, if it requires an extra burner.
>
> CWT BERRY: Well, Mr. Owen, we all know that it's bad practice; I personally asked the Commander and Mr. Dillard about it and offered to run a test to prove I'm right, but I just can't convince the Commander. I think Mr. Dillard agrees, but nothing has ever been done about it. With these new boilers the factory representatives told us definitely never to use more burners on the superheat side than on the saturated side; the boiler school taught all our men the same thing, and yet we operate all the time doing exactly what we've been taught not to do. It's not only that I'm afraid of overheating the superheater tubes, but I know I can steam with less oil by letting the superheat seek its own level between 750°–850° F. I'd like to operate my fireroom for a day my way, and see how it compares in fuel consumption with the others operated as they are now. Do you think you could talk to the Commander about it?

Lt. Owen followed Berry's suggestion and obtained permission to run comparative tests. Armed with the results of the tests, as well as with the support of Mr. Dillard, and with the results of his own experience and instruction, Lt. Owen convinced Commander Swanson that the superheat should be allowed to seek its own level when using an equal number of burners in each side of the boiler. The chief water tenders as well as the enlisted men appeared to Lt. Owen to heave a sigh of relief when the revised operation order was issued.

In various other ways Lt. Owen was able to give the chiefs a larger responsibility in running their plant. For example, they were allowed greater freedom in training trusted rated men as top fireroom watch standers and in removing certain top watch standers from the watch list to assist the chiefs in their supervisory duties. Lt. Owen required the chief petty officers to hold practical instruction for their fireroom crews during the long periods when the ship was at battle stations. In addition, he required each chief to be present in his fireroom during periods when the ship was getting under way, coming to anchor, or when vital repairs or operations were in progress.

8. After a period of five or six weeks had elapsed, it became evident to Lt. Owen that CWT Turner was demonstrating only slight improvement. His fireroom in appearance and operation was inferior to the other three, and he failed to adjust his organization to the new setup. Lt. Owen informed him that his work had not been satisfactory, and through the chief engineer, Owen arranged to transfer Turner to another ship. A young but capable first-class water tender was rated chief and given the responsibility of the fireroom. This event had a decided effect on the other chiefs, principally because the type of transfer given Turner was far from desirable. The appearance of the firerooms began to improve, the operational casualties began to decrease, and the CPO's devoted more and more of their time to their firerooms and their men.

9. For the benefit of his personnel and in an effort to improve their morale, Lt. Owen assisted by his other officers instituted several changes affecting the crew:

a) A system of rotation in watch-standing assignments plus an organized blackboard class which he personally conducted was adopted in an effort to insure a more adequate supply of trained personnel.

b) The old policy of transferring the least capable and most troublesome men, when orders were received requiring men to be sent to the States for leave, school, and reassignment, was reversed so that those men whose efforts had justified such an opportunity were now selected on the basis of sea duty, years of service, marital status, and service to the division. The adoption of this basis of transfer was made known to the crew and was warmly received.

c) All personnel advancement requirements were published for the crew, and all recommendations for advancement for enlisted personnel were now to be submitted by the CPO concerned and to be approved by the warrant officers before consideration by the division officer. Lt. Owen made it a policy rarely to alter the CPO recommendation list. In this manner, no man was elevated in rate unless the CPO's and warrants felt him qualified.

With these steps undertaken, Lt. Owen was confident that his divisional organization was prepared to handle the problems forced upon it. He felt sure that in time the personal talent and ability of the men in the division would produce the necessary results and that a divisional spirit and pride would result.

3. AMERICAN RADIATRONICS CORPORATION

THE AMERICAN Radiatronics Corporation was one of the leading producers and an early pioneer in the nuclear electronics industry. The company manufactured a line of nuclear instrumentation specialties and other electronic devices for nuclear applications. This case reports the results of a study of the nuclear tube assembly room, one of the production rooms of the Baltimore, Maryland, plant of the company. In this room the company's regular line of electronic tubes was assembled, tested, and prepared for shipment.

The casewriter's attention was initially called to the nuclear tube assembly room in a conversation he had with Ralph Langley, general foreman of the process department. In expressing his views about the various problems and plans he had in connection with each segment of the several production units in this department, Langley described the tube room group as the most successful and, from certain standpoints, the most interesting.

The casewriter followed up this lead by securing some additional background facts on the tube room. He found that, prior to Langley's assuming leadership of the department, some 24 months earlier, the girls in the room had acquired the reputation of being agitators, hotheads, and persistent troublemakers. Production was down, costs had gotten out of hand, and deliveries had become very unpredictable. Some thought had been given to eliminating the entire operation.

A report describing the existing problem, prepared by the director of industrial relations at the time, is presented in Exhibit 1. Some data on labor efficiency during the subsequent 24 months are presented in Exhibit 2. During the most recent three-month period the tube room's direct and allocated[1] monthly costs had averaged $12,350, while the actual sales value of the room's monthly production for the same three months averaged $35,800.

A recent special management report presented some additional figures of interest. Between January of the previous year and March of

---

[1] Indirect costs were allocated to the department at the rate of 425 per cent of direct labor dollars.

Exhibit 1

AMERICAN RADIATRONICS CORPORATION

INDUSTRIAL RELATIONS DIRECTOR'S REPORT

MEMORANDUM

RE: Process Department—Nuclear Tube Operation, July 10*
To: T. Bishop,† R. Langley
FROM: S. K. Lowe‡

I. *SUMMARY*

A brief summary of history, data from supervisors (various levels), employees, and exit interviews would indicate the following:

A. This section has always had a reputation for being a "problem department." It is less well organized than other sections (work flow, safety, basic processes, equipment, housekeeping, etc.). Group behavior gives evidence of intense frustration, personal differences, rumor mongering, and concern over operations. Misunderstandings regarding wages have been reflected by new employees; discouragement about "getting ahead" is reflected by them after a few short weeks of work, after "talking with the older girls in the department."

B. Productionwise, the section has had a history of not meeting delivery dates or production quotas—with a high rate of product rejects.

II. *ANALYSIS*

From examination, it would seem that problems may result from the following:

A. *Operations—Basic Product Difficulty.* The products (fairly diverse and delicate) have not been "beaten down." Quality is dependent upon process, thus requiring a different *kind* of standardizing. Certain tube reactions are still technically unexplained. Is it a problem of basic design?

B. *Instability of Product.* Product results, therefore, have been unstable and/or unpredictable.

C. *Work Flow.* Organization of the work flow, methods used, and work steps does not appear as well defined as other operations, largely due, it would seem, to basic unresolved technical problems.

D. *Work Standards and Conditions.* Standards of cleanliness, observing eating, smoking, etc., restrictions (directly affecting operations), have not been rigidly observed.

E. *Equipment.* Equipment failure and repair have, until recently, been a subject of complaint.

F. *Co-ordination.* There is evidence of need for better liaison with sales, scheduling, planning, and meeting promise dates.

---

* Ralph Langley took over the nuclear tube room department on June 15.
† Factory manager.
‡ Director of industrial relations.

III. *ATTITUDES*

A. *Top Management.* With a myriad of pressures (merger, new plant, move, etc.), perhaps this small department did not have adequate recognition of its fundamental technical dilemmas, or it did not know how to deal with the basic technical problems—thus unraveling the other tangled department threads. Perhaps, in the pressure of bigger problems, it received stepchild treatment.

B. *Supervisors.* To most management personnel concerned with its operation, the nuclear tube section was not only a headache, but a bewilderment. Had they been able to solve the basic technical difficulties, it would not have operated on a crisis basis, nor reflected the high degree of frustration which characterized their attitudes.

For the supervision level nearest the employees, the same pattern has existed over a period of time—inability to organize due to basic technical product difficulties, poor equipment, little attention or inadequate understanding *and solution* of basic technical problems.

C. *Employees.* Employees reflect a high degree of frustration and worry, for several reasons. They tend, naturally, to reflect the attitudes of their supervision. As a work group, they are older than average, tending to seek satisfaction from a well-ordered operation. This, by reason of product process, has not existed.

Employees are hourly and are used, from past employment, to more routine, less variable operations. They do not understand the *still experimental* technical "debugging" factors which must be resolved before operations run smoothly. It is not yet a traditional *production* department, although we tab it thus; it is still in a certain developmental stage.

Employees are distinctly upset by variations in tube results—not knowing "reasons why," feeling they should be getting more consistent results. The high number of rejects on items produced is hardly a source of job satisfaction *unless recognized and understood* as part of the stage of product development.

Employees may be confused by the variety and types of things on which they work—upset by poor scheduling and crisis upon crisis, coupled with hazy steps or unanalyzed process.

the current year, the group had shown a 53 per cent improvement in the dollar output of product per man-hour of work, direct labor efficiency had increased approximately 23 to 25 per cent, and there had been about 11 to 12 per cent improvement in the raw material utilization on tubes produced. During this same period, they operated at 81 per cent of their expense budget. In other words, they had used some $4,000 less on miscellaneous expenses than had been budgeted for such items. During this time period the hourly wages of the girls working

Exhibit 2

AMERICAN RADIATRONICS CORPORATION
NUCLEAR TUBE ROOM LABOR EFFICIENCY[1]
THREE MONTHS' MOVING AVERAGE[2]

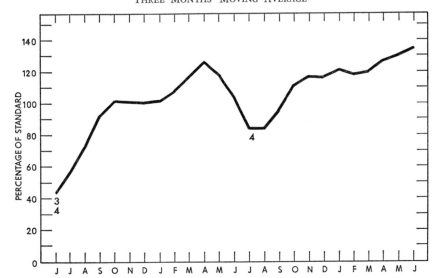

[1] Standard hours produced divided by hours on rated jobs (approximately 90 per cent of time is spent on rated jobs).

[2] All percentages are calculated on new standards.

[3] Prior to this period, labor efficiency figures are not available; however, the best estimates attainable indicate that efficiencies were averaging between 40 and 50 per cent of standard.

[4] Somewhat lower labor efficiencies are expected during the hot summer months than during the remainder of the year.

in the room had risen from an average of $1.45 per hour to $1.75 per hour.

In summary, the profit position for tube manufacturing operations as a whole was now one of the best in the company, where previously the activity had been operating at a loss. This record of progress had been widely recognized throughout the company.

In commenting about the group, Langley said:

> The more or less unique or different aspect of this performance was that it was accomplished by the group itself—not so much by any tangible thing that I or management had done. These people, who had previously been considered a problem group, are now performing in an efficient and profitable way; and they have a very active interest in seeing not only the group in which they were engaged, but the company as a whole, progress and make profits. It seems to me that this is quite an impressive thing for them to have accomplished by their own efforts.

As a result of this conversation with Langley and the other information he had obtained, the casewriter decided he would like to learn more about the tube room and how it operated. He arranged, therefore, on his next visit to the plant, to ask the company president, Frank Halbert, for permission to study the department.

In approving the study, Halbert said, in part: "I hope you find what you are looking for. It would be tremendously important for the whole economy to bust through this 'least work for the most pay' idea workers in this country have." Later, he said: "Do you really think there is any substitute for fear as a motivator? I doubt it. All of these fringe benefits and things won't do it; we've certainly learned that."

About Langley and operations in the tube room, Halbert commented approximately as follows:

> I don't want to downgrade Ralph Langley or anything like that—I think he has been extremely successful in what he is doing—but it should be kept in mind that that tube room is not such a tough place to handle. We have some real trouble spots in other parts of the company. The tube room, after all, because of the kind of work done there, lends itself to the girls' seeing the connection between what they do and the final product. The work has challenge; it's interesting. There are opportunities there for satisfaction in the work itself that you couldn't begin to find in these other places.

Background Facts about the Company and Its Products

In the course of his investigation, the casewriter learned a number of background facts about American Radiatronics Corporation and the conditions under which its tube manufacturing activities were conducted. The history of the company epitomized the pattern of development followed by many young companies that had taken part in the postwar nuclear electronics boom. Starting in a small garage workshop on a back street in Baltimore, the company had been founded approximately ten years earlier by two young scientists convinced of the coming industrial applications for nuclear processes and instrumentation. After an early period of rapid growth and a later series of mergers, the company prospered and finally stabilized at a level of sales in the range of $14,000,000 annually. It remained at this volume for several years. In most recent years the company had been experiencing increasingly tightening competition from other young companies that had also grown to formidable strength of size and resources, and from older electronics firms that had more recently decided to enter the burgeoning nuclear field. The later history of the company was marked also by a number of shifts in the top managment structure; the present management team had been installed approximately two years earlier.

The Baltimore plant contained the main factory and home office headquarters for the company. Located in an industrial park area on Baltimore's outskirts, the plant employed approximately six hundred people, most of whom commuted to work from Baltimore and its outlying suburbs. Well over half the company's sales volume was derived from the Baltimore plant's operations.

The Nuclear Tube Assembly Room

The nuclear tube assembly room was one of several production units in the plant's process department. Under Langley's direction the depart-

Exhibit 3

AMERICAN RADIATRONICS CORPORATION

PARTIAL ORGANIZATION CHART

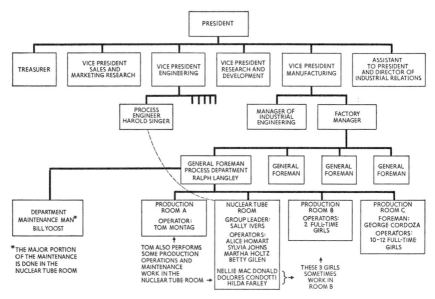

ment produced a variety of equipment parts, some of which went into larger equipment units manufactured by the company, while others were sold directly to customers. Exhibit 3 shows a partial organization chart of the company down to the level of this department's organization. Besides the nuclear tube assembly room, there were three other production units in the department, each housed in an adjacent separate room. The products and manufacturing processes for each of the production units were such that the work of one group was not linked to that of the others.

The nuclear tube assembly room produced all of the company's regular line of electronic tubes. These products varied considerably in size, shape, design, and materials. In appearance, they ranged from delicate glass vials three or four inches in length to massive steel chambers with bolted covers. Some were all-glass construction; still others consisted of all-metal assemblies, with numerous variations in the thickness and kind of metals employed. In all, approximately twenty-five different types of tubes were manufactured on a regular production basis, although not all styles were in production at the same time. A normal production month would call for eight to ten separate tube styles to be produced in quantities varying between three and five hundred per style. A number of miscellaneous small jobs consisting of repair, modifications, or experimental "mockup" of regular and/or experimental tubes were also assigned to the room each month. Out of the total number of tube types produced, four major tube styles accounted for approximately 80 to 84 per cent of the dollar value of the room's output.

The Production Process

The production process varied with each style of tube, depending upon the materials employed, the mechanical design of the tube, and the particular electronic properties called for by its function. The precise relationship between a given tube's design and its performance was not always clearly known. Certain tube designs were developed over the years by trial-and-error methods until a workable tube design was achieved, while others were developed from known formulations and in accordance with standard design procedures. For this reason, there was always an element of change in the air concerning details of the manufacturing process. For each tube a set of written standard operating procedures was developed by the company engineers to describe each assembly operation required; but from the viewpoint of production personnel, the history of modification and innovation that surrounded the evolution of many tube designs and production methods tended to imply that the process of developing ultimate designs was not yet at an end.

Most of the operations performed in the assembly process were of a handwork nature, in which a variety of jigs, small implements, heating torches, and special-purpose machines were employed. Customarily, the work was performed on a batch of parts at a time until a sufficient inventory of parts was accumulated to allow a number of tubes to be assembled in one operation.

The work of the tube room was roughly divided into (1) glasswork, which consisted of making tube shells and internal glass parts; (2)

metalwork, wherein internal metal springs, wires, grids, leads, etc., were made and prepared for use; (3) tube assembly, at which time the entire tube was put together; (4) vacuum testing and exhausting, where tubes were leak-tested, exhausted, and filled with special gases; and (5) electronic testing, where the tube was tested as a functioning unit. After final testing, tubes were labeled, recorded according to individual serial numbers, and packaged for shipment or inventory storage. At all stages of assembly, tubes were given visual and electrical tests to minimize defective parts or subassemblies finding their way to final assembly. All testing and quality control measures were performed by the production workers themselves, including the final test before packaging.

The Production Workers

The major part of the production work in the tube room was performed by eight women, one of whom served as group leader for the others. Each worker performed several kinds of operations, although each had, at the same time, one or more operations which she regarded as her particular specialty. These special jobs, which were part of the regular production process, had emerged over time as the most suitable work for a girl to do in view of her skills, her preferences, and the needs of the department. They were the most frequently recurring operations performed, accounting for roughly 50 per cent or more of her time, and were the chief identifying characteristic of each girl's job. In all, an almost infinite variety of combinations of worker and job were practiced in the room. It was not uncommon for several girls, each at different times, and occasionally at the same time, to perform the same operations. Not even the special jobs were necessarily exclusive, as usually at least two girls had the special skills required to do a given job; and in case of absences or emergencies, one would take over for the other.

The tube room production staff was augmented by two men, one of whom served as maintenance man for the whole department, while the other worked in the tube room part time assisting in various production operations. He did this when not busy in Room A, his normal work assignment, a single-man operation which did not keep him busy full time.

Some additional personal and job information about these people and the department general foreman, Langley, are given in Exhibit 4.

Pay Rates and Employee Evaluation

As shown in Exhibit 4, the employees of the tube room were paid on an hourly basis. Pay grades were established for each job classification by

Exhibit 4

AMERICAN RADIATRONICS CORPORATION

Job and Personal Information—Tube Room Personnel

Name	Job Classification	Pay	Age	Seniority with Company	Seniority in Tube Room	Education	Ethnicity	Marital Status
Ralph Langley	Department general foreman	Not available	41	3 yrs.	2 yrs.	MS in physics	Yankee	M
Bill Yoost	Maintenance mechanic	$2.20/hr.	39	3 yrs.	2 yrs.	High school and trade school	Yankee	M
Sally Ivers	Group leader, production worker AA	$2.17/hr.	43	12 yrs.	12 yrs.	High school	Yankee	S
Alice Homart	Production worker AA	$2.05/hr.	53	3 yrs.	3 yrs.	High school	Yankee	Widow
Nellie MacDonald	Production worker A	$1.85/hr.	46	5 yrs.	5 yrs.	College, 1 yr.	Yankee	M
Hilda Farley	Production worker A	$1.81/hr.	46	11 yrs.	1 yr.	Grammar school	Irish	S
Martha Holtz	Production worker A	$1.76/hr.	56	6 yrs.	4 yrs.	9 yrs. in Germany	German	M
Betty Gilen	Production worker A	$1.74/hr.	42	4 yrs.	4 yrs.	High school and art school (3 yrs.)	Yankee	W
Sylvia Johns	Production worker A	$1.71/hr.	42	1 yr.	1 yr.	Junior high school	Belgian	W
Tom Montag	Production worker B	$1.63/hr.	26	½ yr.	½ yr.	High school	French	M
Dolores Condotti	Production worker B	$1.61/hr.	31	3 yrs.	3 yrs.	Junior high school	Lithuanian	M

the industrial relations department according to an evaluation of the amount of skill and knowledge required of a worker in the job. Within each pay grade, there was an established range through which the hourly wage rate could progress. An employee's progression within range was determined by periodic merit reviews. At intervals of four months, each employee was rated by his department general foreman on evaluation forms designed to reveal his strengths and weaknesses. These evaluation forms were forwarded to the industrial relations department, where eligibility for pay increases was determined. The tube room workers were not unionized, although certain other manufacturing groups in the company had been organized some years previously by a large international trade union.

Work Standards and Output Records

Approximately 95 per cent of the tube assembly operations performed by the girls had been figured into standard hours by the company's industrial engineers. These standard hours were used in costing out direct labor costs for tube manufacturing operations by the accounting department, and they served as a standard of efficiency against which the room's actual performance was measured. Tube production for the total group was determined weekly when a physical inventory was taken of all finished and in-process tubes. Thus, labor invested in defective or destroyed tube parts or assemblies was "lost" to the group in figuring its net labor efficiencies. Monthly summaries of weekly efficiency figures were submitted to higher management for examination and review. Exhibit 2 presents these monthly efficiency figures for the previous twenty-four months.

All the labor efficiency figures in Exhibit 2 were based on revised standards put into effect three months prior to the study. The former standards, which had been set against the group's historical performance some years previously, had become inadequate in relation to the level of output then being achieved by the group. Consequently, Langley had initiated a review of all standards, "tube by tube, operation by operation," revising the allowed hours downward between 23 and 59 per cent on individual tubes to an average 34 per cent decrease on major tube types.

When Langley first took over supervision of the tube room group, the work force consisted of fourteen production workers. In the ensuing six months, improvements in the group's performance created a surplus of labor which, because of a relatively stable volume of operations, required a series of layoffs to be made. It was during this period that the original force was reduced to the present eight. The layoffs were made in two steps, with the girls selected for layoff primarily on the basis of seniority, with some secondary attention to the variety of work the girls could do, and the quantity and quality of their work. Langley commented:

> Those that stayed seemed to take it all right, even though none of them knew for sure whether she would be staying or not. They understood. One girl in the group I fired outright because of her attitude. She just couldn't and wouldn't fit in with the others. We had a long history of trouble with her.

During the twenty-four months since Langley took over the department, there were no major changes in the production facilities, manufacturing methods, or basic tube types in production. Much of the equipment in use was considered to be of antiquated and inefficient design. The improvements in group performance which were noted during this period were attributed primarily to improvements in labor efficiency and to informal production method innovations. Some minor alterations in tube design were made by the company's scientific personnel, and a number of such changes were initiated by members of the work group themselves; but as these changes were made, their laborsaving effects were largely incorporated into revised work standards.

How the Tube Room Group Operated

The most immediate and apparent feature of the room was its physical layout and the location of various work positions within it. The room itself was a large, gray, concrete-floored enclosure approximately 60 feet long by 50 feet across. Closely assembled rows of tables, workbenches, production machines, and test stands filled its central portions, while an ordered clutter of miscellaneous cabinets, shelves, benches, and additional production equipment banked its wall areas. A row of windows looked into Production Room C, immediately adjacent. A single door provided access and egress for the room.

Exhibit 5 shows some details of the room's layout and the locations at which various people worked during a one-week observation period. Movement throughout the room was frequent and widespread, and the occasions were very seldom in which at least one or two people were not in motion. The changing of settled work positions was likely to occur at any time during a day. Bantering, horseplay, and visiting were frequent occurrences; and at times, even periods of total inactivity, such as when a girl appeared to be daydreaming or silently contemplating her work, were observed. The pattern of activity did not appear to vary with the comings and goings of Sally Ivers, Langley, or any of the other supervisory personnel.

From the beginning of his study, the casewriter was interested in the social organization of the room. As a first approximation of his findings on this, Exhibit 6 summarizes the participation by individual workers in

Exhibit 5

AMERICAN RADIATRONICS CORPORATION

TUBE ROOM LAYOUT AND OBSERVED WORK POSITIONS DURING ONE-WEEK PERIOD

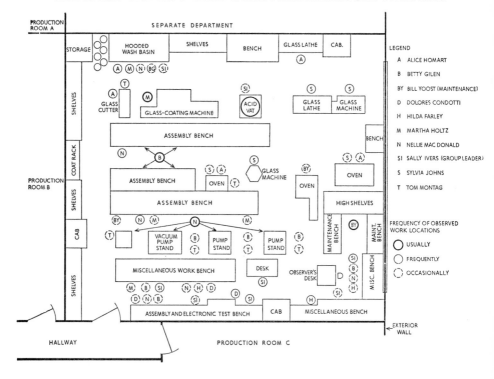

various nonwork activities. These activities were well established, and they occurred regularly. For the most part, they had been in existence for two years or more, dating back to the "premove" days at the old downtown Baltimore location. Although not participated in uniformly, they were well known to all, and were generally regarded as perfectly appropriate informal social devices of voluntary association.

Briefly, these activities were:

Coffee Breaks. Coffee breaks were allowed twice a day, at 10:00 o'clock in the morning and 3:00 o'clock in the afternoon. The official company position was that ten-minute breaks were allowed,[2] and they were to be taken at the work position. However, because of heat generated by certain machines in the production processes of the room, tube room workers were allowed to deviate from the rule by gathering elsewhere, in

Exhibit 6

AMERICAN RADIATRONICS CORPORATION

PARTICIPATION IN VARIOUS NONWORK ACTIVITIES

Name	Coffee Break, Alice	Lunch Table	Walks	Poor Box	Pool	Card Game	Coffee Break, Sally
Martha Holtz............	x			x			
Sylvia Johns.............	x	x		x	x		
Betty Gilen..............	x	x		x	x	x	
Alice Homart............	x	x		x	x	x	
Nellie MacDonald........	x	x	x	x	x		
Sally Ivers..............		x	x	x	x		x
Tom Montag............				x	x	x	x
Bill Yoost..............				x	x	x	x
Dolores Condotti.........				x	x		x
Hilda Farley............				x	x		x

cooler locations. The total group invariably broke up into two smaller groups at coffee time—one group gathering around Sally at her workbench-desk, and the other at the rear of the room near Alice Homart's customary work station (which, incidentally, was in one of the warmest areas in the room). The separate membership of these groups is given in Exhibit 6.

Lunch Table. This refers to the practice of several girls eating lunch together at a certain table in the company cafeteria. Although they did not need or use the whole table, the unoccupied places were never filled by other company personnel. The table usually filled, however, immediately after they left it. The girls ate quickly, usually finishing 10 or 15 minutes after they sat down, after which they dispersed to complete the 30-minute lunch hour in other activities. Members of the tube room group who did not join this table ate at various other tables in the cafeteria.

Card Game. These people met back in the tube room for a 10- to 15-minute card game before returning to work. The game was always played at Alice's work station.

Walks. Whenever the weather permitted, Sally and Nellie MacDonald took a stroll around the perimeter of the plant site and occasionally into the woods nearby. They had been known to persist in these walks even under conditions of light drizzle or when there was snow on the ground.

---

[2] In practice, these breaks were observed to vary in length.

The Pool. This consisted of a weekly drawing for high and low stakes of a pool made up of 50-cent contributions from active members. Names on discs were drawn from a tin can reserved for the purpose, with the high winner taking $5.00 and the low drawer taking the balance. Membership in this activity included a few people from outside the tube room. At one time the number of participants had been much larger, including all the production workers from Room C. They had at the time entered the pool after asking to join it. When they came in, three tube room girls dropped out—Alice, Nellie, and Martha Holtz (who at that time had been active). When Room C started its own pool, Alice and Nellie returned to their pool, saying: "As long as it stays in this department, we'll come back in." Martha never returned.

The "Poor Box." No one knew the origin of the term, but it referred to a weekly 10-cent collection—sometimes raised to a quarter when the "kitty" was low—used to finance special events such as going-away presents, wedding gifts, sickness and death remembrances, etc. A limited number of extradepartmental events could qualify; but usually, the poor box was reserved for tube room workers. Sally administered the funds; everyone joined in.

Work Assignments and Supervisory Practices

In performing their work, the girls customarily obtained their working instructions from Sally. This usually occurred first thing in the morning, when there was a short flurry of milling around, donning of work smocks, setting-up and adjustment of production equipment, and arrangement of parts, supplies, etc., preparatory to going to work. Throughout this, Sally would move from girl to girl, checking, answering questions, and discussing the day's work schedule. At times, this instruction giving would occur during the workday as a girl finished the batch of work she had been on. Often, the exchange would be phrased as: "O.K. if I go to so and so now?" and "Sure." Or if more detailed instructions were required, Sally and the other girl would go over to the appropriate work station and discuss the details together. On a number of occasions, changes in work position or kind of work being performed took place without any apparent prior consultation with Sally.

One of the most concrete features of work scheduling practices in the tube room was a monthly production schedule delivered to the group by the company's production planning department just before the first of each month. Sally spoke about this in the following manner:

SALLY IVERS: We get this production schedule sheet here on my desk the first of every month from production planning, showing the kinds and numbers of tubes we will have to produce for the month. Ralph Langley and I then look it over, and we make our plans for how we want to schedule the different jobs that need doing. We usually start with the toughest orders first—that is, the longest, or those we think we will have some trouble with—so that by the end of the month we will have just the smaller jobs to do.

CASEWRITER: How do you use the standard times shown on the sheet?

SALLY: We don't pay too much attention to them. They tell us what the standard time is for each of the tubes to be produced. If we make the standard time, that is good, and we usually do. In fact, very often we beat the standard time. You know, we have been doing a very good job here.

CASEWRITER: What if you don't make your schedule? That is, what if you don't make production for a month? Suppose you were near the end of a month and you saw that you were not going to make it, what would you do?

SALLY: We usually make it. If we don't, we don't get too upset because we can always make it up some other time; and besides, usually if we don't make it, there is a good reason for it.

Langley also commented about this same production sheet and how he and Sally used it in scheduling work.

RALPH LANGLEY: When the production sheet comes in to us, Sally and I look it over. Sometimes, we figure that they're asking for too many parts of one kind or not enough of another, so we change it. We look at the numbers on the sheet, then we check the stock, and then we sort of think about whether or not the figures look right.

CASEWRITER: What do you mean by "whether the figures look right?"

LANGLEY: Well, I mean sometimes the production planning people can make a mistake like anyone else. Sometimes, the company has so many tubes of one kind in stock that I just know they couldn't have wanted that many, so I will second-guess them. I keep an eye on the main company inventory, you know; it's in the room right over there down the hall. All I have to do is walk in and look around, and I can see how many of what kind of tubes are in stock there; and often, I happen to know how the sales are running on particular tubes.

You know, sometimes people from the sales department come down and ask questions about things—questions about tubes, how much they cost, whether we are having any particular difficulty with them. In fact, I have often spoken directly with customers. Of course, I am not supposed to do that, that is not right, but they will often refer a customer to me to talk about a particular tube; and in this way, I have a feeling of how the sales of different kinds of tubes are going.

With this information about sales, inventory, stock situation, and the general work load we are operating under here, I am able to make some pretty fair guesses about the figures that production planning has set up—that is, whether we should follow their figures or adjust them slightly. Sometimes, we miss, but not very often. Usually, it has worked out in the past that our estimates of what the best schedule should be are good. In fact, it has happened more than once that the people from production planning would come to me and ask for my opinion on how many tubes I think they should put on the production planning sheet.

One of the production girls, Betty Gilen, spoke about the production schedule in the following manner:

> BETTY GILEN: The day you'll see satisfaction written all over everyone's face is the last working day of the production month when we've met schedule. The last days before the end of the month, you'll see the girls walking to the production record over there, checking that, then checking the production schedule again on Sally's desk; and when they've made it, they really feel good. I know I do, and you'll see what I mean when you see the others acting that way, too.
>
> Now, this is provided they haven't been pushed. This is important, because we meet our own schedule. No one says anything to us, no one is breathing down our backs. We do it ourselves. It's really amazing the change that begins to come over people when they move into the last part of the month and see we're going to have to step it up in order to make our quota. Everyone works a little harder, everyone tries to get her part of the work out of the way a little faster and on to the next girl. We really start to work hard, hand in hand with one another. It's a wonderful thing to watch. This is what makes this department work together so well. It's the cement that binds us as a team, you might say. Everyone, and I would say there's not a single exception to this, is willing to co-operate; and we all feel the same way about meeting the schedule—as I said, as long as no one is pushing us, as long as we're doing it ourselves.

Attitudes toward the Work

In the course of his investigation, the casewriter held a number of conversations with other girls also about their work and how they felt about it. Here is the way several of them spoke during these conversations:

> MARTHA HOLTZ: Usually, I like to have smaller jobs to do to fill in with while the "coating" action is taking place here on my machine. But sometimes, like right now, when I'm all caught up on my smaller work, I just have to be patient and wait for the action to happen. . . .
>
> I like my job. It's a good job as far as jobs go. I'm very patient. I just sit here and do my work. I do other things around here, too, you know; but

right now, I'm doing mostly coating. I have done ceramic lining for Alice Homart over there, and fire polishing; and toward the end of the month, I even do testing. I can do a lot of jobs. I even used to work over in X department, you know. That's where I started to work for the company six years ago. . . .

One of the things I do is make the anodes for these tubes. We used to make them out of stainless steel, but now we always make them out of platinum. You know, that was funny. One day, about six months ago, while we were still making them out of stainless steel, I made a mistake and made them out of platinum instead, and I made up a whole batch of them that way before I realized it. When I finished, I told Sally Ivers about it and said: "I made a mistake. I made these anodes out of platinum instead of stainless steel." She said: "That's all right, Martha; let's test them out this way and see how they are." They tested out perfectly, so she told Ralph Langley about it; and the next time I made anodes for that tube, Sally told me to make them out of platinum again because they had tested out so well. Always before, we had trouble testing out a whole batch of them without having some bad ones; and you know, since we've been making them out of platinum, we have had hardly any bad ones at all. And to think, just because I'd made a mistake!

. . . .

ALICE HOMART (*referring to some tube stem assembles she is re-working from a batch made a few days earlier*): We've been having a lot of trouble with leaking stems lately, and we're trying to figure out where the trouble is by studying these stems from rejected tubes. I'm spending quite a bit of time right now trying to find the trouble.

CASEWRITER: How do you feel about spending your time examining these defective stems when it takes you away from regular production?

ALICE: I'm concerned about it. This is a headache, all the trouble we're having. That's why I'm spending so much of my time now trying to figure out what went wrong, so that we can get the production rate back up again. That makes sense, doesn't it? If I just ignored this trouble we're having and kept making stems, and if they were bad, we wouldn't really be getting any production out at all, would we?

CASEWRITER: I guess that's right. Does anyone ever say anything to you when you get behind on production?

ALICE: You bet they do. We hear about it, all right; and believe me, we hear about these leaky tubes, too. Nellie MacDonald shoots them right back at us when they don't make her leak test. That's what we're here for. No one stands over our shoulder counting what we do, but we know how many finished tubes we make and how many the production schedule calls for. Besides, it's always nicer when things are going along without any trouble. You know, we're not supposed to do this (*indicating the defective stem she is examining*); this is not our job.

CASEWRITER: Whose job is it?

ALICE: Well, no one's really, but we're not engineers. We're just production girls. We're not supposed to know the technical parts of this kind of work. The only thing is—there's no one else at the plant here who knows much more about this kind of work than we do. There's just us here in the room, so I guess it's up to Sylvia Johns and myself to figure out what goes wrong when we have trouble. Ralph Langley can help us sometimes, but he can't do everything. Besides, we're closer to the work.

. . . .

SYLVIA JOHNS: I'm a glass blower. I learned the business from my husband in Philadelphia, where we operated a neon sign glass company for 25 years before he died. I had to go back to work after he died, and that's why I'm here. I like my work here. It's a good job, but it wasn't easy for me to find the kind of work I like to do after my husband died. Actually, glass blowing is all I do here, and it's what I prefer doing, too. I never work much on tube assembly, although I guess I would if I had to. Glasswork is really my line. After all, 25 years—I know it. My husband taught me well before he died.

. . . .

CASEWRITER (*addressing Dolores Condotti at a work station where he has not seen her before*):   What are you doing here?

DOLORES CONDOTTI: Making springs.

CASEWRITER: What are "springs"? [They appeared to be small-diameter coil springs with long wire tails protruding from them at right angles.]

DOLORES (*after several attempts to describe the function of a spring in a tube*):   Oh, here, let me show you. (*Leading the casewriter over to a nearby cabinet, she opens it, removes a tube from a box, smashes the thin mica window in one end of it with a loud bang, and shows him the location of the spring.*)

CASEWRITER (*after they have returned to Dolores' work station*):   What was that tube you just smashed?

DOLORES: Oh, that was just an extra one. There's something wrong with it. That's why it was in that box in the cabinet. The other tubes in there were good ones for inventory. I make springs about twice a month. They say I'm the best spring maker here. I don't know if they really mean it or not, or if they're just trying to make me feel willing to make springs so no one else will have to do it.

. . . .

CASEWRITER (*standing beside Betty Gilen at her customary workbench*):   Could you tell me the name of this place here where you seem to be working most often?

BETTY: You could call this the heavy metal tube station. You see, I make all of the heavy tubes in here, and I guess I'm a sort of a specialist in it. But we're not making very many at the rate we're going now. I can only make tubes that the parts fit in, and these parts don't fit. You see this cover here? You see this container here? Well, these two parts are supposed to go together, and they don't. Somebody goofed. These covers are made in the machine shop, and the containers are made by a vendor, and you can see that the cover doesn't position right on the container, and that won't pass inspection. It holds on all right, but it's got to look real pretty. They're fussy about appearance, you know.

CASEWRITER: Does this delay affect you personally?

BETTY: Personally is right. It's driving me crazy. This is a big order, and we're 'way behind on it. We won't get them done—can't work on them at all. This means I haven't got anything to do. It means I've got to hunt jobs. It means the day is sixteen hours long for me these days. I fiddle here; I fiddle there; I don't really get anything done. I like to keep busy. It's really much better if you can just stay in one spot, have your work lined up, and go ahead and do it. You know, it's a lot harder to find work than it is to do the work itself.

CASEWRITER: Where else do you sometimes work?

BETTY: Oh, you'll find me over at the glass machine; you'll find me at the wash basin, and you've probably seen me quite a bit over at the pump stand there. You see, I do all the glass-welding. That is, I do all the glasswork in connecting tubes to the vacuum outlets. It's not that it takes any kind of particular genius to do it. It's not a matter of intelligence, but I'm kind of familiar with that type of work. As I say, I do all kinds of things. If you want to see where I'm working, you'd better look fast because I won't be there long.

Employee Attitudes toward Each Other

Here is how several of the girls talked and behaved with respect to their relations with one another:

ALICE: (*in response to a question about why there were two separate coffee groups*):   Why, I never thought about that until you mentioned it now. It's always been that way; I've never paid any attention to it. We've always had the two groups, but it doesn't mean anything. We're all friendly with one another. I guess we girls at this end of the room have always had our clique, as we usually call it, and the other girls have had theirs over there. Why, it was the same way before, when we were in Baltimore. The girls in the glass end would come to one end of the room to have their coffee together, and the other girls would have their coffee some place else. I can't imagine it being different. We glassworkers always kind of stuck together. After we came here, the three of us—Martha Holtz, Sylvia Johns, when she came to work for the company, and myself—would have coffee together, and Nellie MacDonald and Betty Gilen would join us. They have always joined us over here; but if any of us should happen to have our coffee over there, no one would say anything or think it unusual. We just don't.

CASEWRITER: How do you decide when to start and stop?

ALICE: Well, the company says we can have a break at 10:00 and 3:00, and we're supposed to have ten minutes; but Ralph Langley says it's up to us how long we take, just so we get our work out. So we don't go by the company rule. We just have our coffee, and then break up when we're through and go back to work.

CASEWRITER: How do you come to break up?

ALICE: I really don't know; we just stop. Sometimes, we take twenty minutes or so; sometimes, quite a bit less. At the end of the month, if we're rushed, we'll cut it pretty short; but no one ever says anything to us. Ralph has told us it's up to us girls, so we just gauge it by how busy we are.

. . . .

CASEWRITER (*addressing Betty one day at her workbench*): Are there any topics of conversation or things to talk about that you tend to avoid with one another as you visit, say, during coffee breaks, at lunch, or even during work?

BETTY: No, I don't think so. We'll talk about most anything. I know I feel perfectly free to talk about whatever I've got on my mind—our work schedule, things that happened at home on week ends, just about anything. One thing we do avoid is politics. That can get pretty hot, and we have had a few scrapes in the past, so we let that one alone entirely now. I guess there is another thing, too, in a general sort of way. If anyone is particularly bothered about anything, we will avoid that subject, whatever it is that she's bothered about. We don't want to hurt anyone or make her feel bad by rubbing salt in wounds. This is especially so if it is something connected with our work here. If there is something going on that someone is particularly upset about, we'll avoid talking about it as long as it is happening. Later, we will talk about it and laugh over it, but not at the time. We don't hurt anyone. We can't afford to. We get along by co-operating and being friendly with one another. That is how this department operates. When someone is in trouble, we help her. When someone is feeling bad, we try to make her feel better. We haven't got a single malcontent or troublemaker in the whole bunch.

Work Incidents

Following are two examples of work interactions witnessed by the casewriter which were fairly typical of the general patterns of work behavior he observed.

Incident No. 1. Nellie MacDonald needed a new valve installed on her vacuum pump machine, a maintenance service often performed by Montag when he was working in the tube room.

NELLIE MACDONALD: Hey, Tom, I need a valve put on.

TOM MONTAG: Yah, yah. [Tom was at the other end of the room, moving a heavy tank cylinder toward the pump stand.]

NELLIE: Well, come on, I'm in a hurry. If you'd stay in here where you belong instead of hiding away in Room A, you'd get these things done (*all this said in a lighthearted, jocular tone of voice*).

MONTAG (*approaching pump stand and Nellie with the heavy metal bottle*): Watch out; get out of the way, or you'll get this bottle on your toes!

NELLIE: You do that, and I'll lay you out flat.

MONTAG (*winking to other girls nearby*): She can do it, too.

Incident No. 2. One day, as the casewriter was working at his observation desk, he heard a loud pop and the sound of breaking glass. Looking up, he saw Betty standing at the finished tubes inventory cabinet, with the door open, and a tray of finished tubes in her hand. At her feet were the remains of a broken tube (retail value, about $45). Sally was standing about eight feet away, working at a bench, with her back to Betty. Nellie was at her pump stand about the same distance away. Sally did not look up, but continued steadily with her work. The noise was very audible and quite out of the ordinary of normal sounds in the room. Its point of origin, that is, from the direction of the finished tube cabinet, was also quite clear. Nellie, from her pump stand, looked over to Betty, shook her head slowly from side to side, and said, "Tsk, tsk, tsk," and then made a comment having something to do with what had caused the tube to fall out of the cabinet. Betty's elbow and tray were resting close to the shelf from which the broken tube had obviously fallen. Betty corrected her position and at the same time looked forlornly at the smashed tube. Nellie walked over to the other side of the room, obtained a broom and dustpan, and began to sweep up the mess, disposing of it in a trash can. Betty proceeded to the electronic test stand with the tray of tubes she had been carrying. It would have been very easy for Betty to put the tray down and clean up the broken glass herself. Throughout the incident, neither Betty nor Nellie glanced in Sally's direction, nor did Sally ever change the pace of her work or look up.

Ralph Langley's Behavior

The casewriter's own observations of Langley's behavior were that he had apparently developed relationships with the group in a way which allowed him to retain a high degree of involvement in the affairs of the room without extensive personal presence on his part. The casewriter had noticed over a two-week period of time the following general pattern of behavior on Langley's part: He would make a tour of the room each morning near the beginning of the workday, speaking briefly with nearly every one in the room when doing so (although usually in different order from day to day); and he would take part in various technical discussions that accompanied the start of a day's work. From then on, he would reappear at fairly regular intervals, two or three times during the day, or when some kind of unusual work event occurred.

During his periods of absence from the room, he visited the other rooms of his department, attended conferences and other scheduled meetings, paid informal visits to members of other departments in the company, or, as was more customary for extended periods of time, retired to his desk in one corner of Room B, next door to the tube room.

It was to this desk that members of the tube room group would come when they had a question or a problem. Any one of the girls or two men from the tube room were equally likely to visit Langley at his desk; and unless the situations prompting the visit were unusually complicated or pressing, he would respond with a few words of explanation, approval, or a promise to "do something about it." During a two-day period in which Langley once happened to spend nearly all his time at his desk, these visits averaged about six or seven per day. His characteristic demeanor during interactions with subordinates was grave and intently serious, although his face would often break into fleeting, eye-twinkling smiles. Seldom effusive, he nevertheless usually managed to convey by his bearing and verbal behavior an impression of friendliness and personal interest toward those with whom he happened to be dealing at any one time and an impression of calm, unhurried confidence in addressing the problems of his office.

Comments of the Girls about Langley

The occasions were very seldom during the conversations with members of the tube room work group that reference was not made at one time or another to Langley, the department general foreman. The comments made were almost universally approving.

> SALLY: If anything does go wrong around here, we first of all try to find out what the trouble is ourselves; and if that doesn't work, we go to get Ralph. Ralph always helps us out. Ralph always knows the answers.

> BETTY: Ralph is fair, and he knows what he is doing.

> MARTHA (*in connection with a rumor that Ralph Langley was being considered for promotion to a bigger job*): Ralph, he's the best. I don't know what we would do without him. He is always so fair, treats us all

alike. We're very proud of Ralph. We would miss him terribly if he left.

. . . .

NELLIE (*in response to a question concerning whether she could recall a recent event which had made her feel particularly good or bad*):   Well, I'm not sure what it is you are after with that question; but if you would like to know how I feel about Ralph's maybe being promoted, for one thing, I'll tell you. I would be very pleased for Ralph, very proud of him. We all would be. He deserves a promotion, and it's time he went on to bigger things. But as for me, it would mean I'd lost my purpose for working. It would never be the same again. I can't tell you exactly how I would feel; but when I first heard he might be leaving us, I was stunned. That guy made our work something it had never been before. I would never be able to feel the same way about George. [George Cordoza was also rumored to be Ralph's replacement.] George is all right. He's pleasant, and he's a nice guy, but I have a respect for Ralph I'd never be able to develop for George. And it's not only respect I feel for Ralph, but I have a very close relationship with him. Not outside of work at all; I mean here on the job. Ralph is my friend.

I always enjoy coming to work. I look forward to it every morning. We're a zany bunch in there—real screwballs—you couldn't find a bunch of people anywhere with more different personalities than we have. You've seen the way we horse around, the stunts we pull, and we don't feel the least bit embarrassed about it. We can get away with anything; but when it comes to our work, there's no one better than we are, either. My pump stand here, for instance, means everything in the world to me. There's a lot about it I don't understand, but I think about it all the time. I guess you'd say it's the biggest and most important thing in my life to me right now. I used to have a much bigger job in another company than the one I have right now. Believe it or not, I was once a floor lady during the war in a department that had 350 people in it, and many of them were men. That was a big job. Now, this is just a small department here, and I'm not over anyone, but I feel important. I feel there's a purpose in my life. I'm responsible for the pump stand, and it's a critical part of the operation in there. I can't describe to you really how I feel about it. It's a part of me, and I'm a part of it. I worry about how it's going. I'm checking it over all the time, and I'm turning out a lot of work on it.

But you see, it's not only the pump stand. It's how Ralph and people like him can make you feel about it. You know, Ralph is a very intelligent man. He has a great deal of technical knowledge, and he knows how to use it. But there are a lot of bright people around American Radiatronics and other companies like this one. There are only a few of them, though, that can use their knowledge to make a dumb person like me feel important. I know I'm not very bright, and it doesn't take much for anyone to make me feel really stupid, but Ralph has never done that. He's always made me feel that I am smart rather than dumb, that I've got ideas that are useful. Now, my knowledge about the pump stand is very limited, and I lean a great deal on Ralph to help me out of scrapes; but you know, every time I talk over a problem with him, I feel as though I'm learning something. And I *am* learning! It seems as though Ralph has a way of using his superior knowledge to help a person build up his own knowledge. He gives it to you—he doesn't use it on you. That's how I feel about Ralph as a friend, as the best boss I've ever had.

Then again, there's something else. Right now, we've run into a problem on the pump stand. There's something wrong in the exhaust manifold system. We're not getting the tubes clean enough. Sally and I have gone over and over the system, and we don't know what it is. We will wait for Ralph until he has time, and we know eventually he will help us out. Sure, we've got an engineer assigned to the department, that is, someone who is supposed to take care of these problems for us. We're not supposed to; we're just production girls, not supposed to know anything. And, brother, is he convinced of that! I'd walk out of the plant before I'd turn to him for help on my pump. In the first place, he doesn't really know much about them; and in the second place, with what little he does know, he can make you feel so darned stupid in such a short time that you could scream. We don't need him in here and don't want him. So you see, without Ralph, we would have no one. If he left us, we'd have really lost something, and we would know it.

Ralph Langley

The casewriter talked to Langley on a number of occasions about his perceptions of his job and his concepts of himself as an administrator. Following are excerpts from some of these conversations.

Conversation No. 1. How Langley talked about his relations with the tube room production girls.

LANGLEY (*speaking about what had been responsible for the marked improvement in the group's performance over the past two years*): I would say it was mostly a matter of treating the girls in there the way they wanted to be treated, the way they needed to be treated in order that they might feel as though they were part of American Radiatronics. When I first took over the department, one of the first things I told my girls was that as far as I was concerned, all I wanted them to do was to do the best job they could, to forget about standards, to forget about any kind of pressure or expectation other than just doing as well as they knew how.

I told them I felt they were working for American Radiatronics and not for me, that my job was to help them and not tell them what to do, that they were strictly on their own as far as getting out production was concerned, as far as scheduling their work was concerned, pacing themselves, watching their own waste, and so on. I stressed over and over again that they were to forget about standards, figuratively to throw the standards out, pretend they didn't even exist—if they didn't make standard, to forget about it, not worry about it—just to do the best job they knew how. If they got into trouble, they could ask me for help, and I would give it to them.

Above all, I told them, we were going to be interested in making a better tube and learning how to do our job better at all times. They didn't believe me at first, and some of them gave me a really rough time. But gradually, they learned I meant what I said, and things began to improve. Some of the girls who gave me the most trouble are now the most productive and helpful ones.

I have no supervisor in the room, as you know. I have Sally, who is group leader for the others. But each girl in the room is responsible for her own operation. If she gets into trouble, or if she has a question, she's free to come to me directly. I then work out her problems with her personally. I go in to them every now and then, just now and then, to keep an eye on things and to stay in touch. I check the production record to see how things are going, and I always speak to the girls. I try to be careful, whenever I come into the room, to see that I always talk to a different girl first each time. This way, each girl feels she is getting her fair share of attention. Now, these girls are not all the same. Some of them are pretty tough customers. Nellie MacDonald, in particular, has given me quite a lot of trouble in the past. So I'm extra careful in working with her.

I keep no secrets from the girls. They know as much about this operation, about what is going on in the top offices, as I do. I'm completely honest with them, and I ask that they be honest with me. And this has paid off, too, because none of my girls are afraid to admit their mistakes and they're always anxious to learn how to do something better. Of course, I may be exaggerating this a little bit. I have noticed lately that there is almost a tinge of neuroticism in the way several of the group have become so concerned about production and quality. It causes a little stir now and then. But anyway, most of the girls in there can perform any operation in the place, and they trade off. They know that as far as I'm concerned, it's up to them to decide how they want to distribute or organize their work.

Quite often, the department gets some extra work to do from one of the other departments, work that is not a part of the regular job in there. When we do get that, I just turn it over to one of the girls. She'll do it. The girls don't worry much about doing these extra jobs because they know that as far as I'm concerned, as long as they're doing their jobs the best they can, that's all I care about.

People have to be motivated. All people do. These girls are just the same as you and I. We like to feel we're important. We like to feel we're doing something worth while and that we're learning. We like to have a direction to be going in and know whether we are getting any place or standing still. I try to act this way with the girls. I'm always careful and insistent they're given full credit for everything they do. As far as I'm concerned, whatever is done in that room is their responsibility and their accomplishment. I keep out of their hair. When I talk with them, I talk with them about whatever is of interest to them. If it's about their families, fine; if it's about the work, fine.

Sometimes, when I see that things are not going so well—and they don't always go just right—I'm careful to avoid any distressing or threatening discussion. For instance, sometimes the production orders I bring in are downright staggering in the demands they represent for the girls. When I know I have a particularly tough one coming along, I'm careful to wait until the right time to tell the girls about it.

You know, I have a budget, but I don't use my budget to control my people. Rather, I use it as something which they themselves can get satisfaction out of. For instance, we have cut our operating expenses 'way down since I took over; but I didn't do it, my people did it. Our department maintenance man, Bill Yoost, administers our supplies expense budget himself. He does all his own ordering, and he does it in accordance with the amount of money he has available in his budget. These are supplies that are used not only by himself but by the girls in the department as well. Since they all know that it's up to them to control their expenses, they do it. If someone from another department comes and tries to borrow something which they know has been charged against their budget, they simply won't allow it. They'll say: "No, you'll run our expense budget over. You'll have to get it somewhere else."

I go over the budget with Bill once a month, whenever it comes out. We talk about it. From then on, it's up to him. I keep an eye on it every now and then just to see that he isn't running too far out on a limb; and if I see something wrong, I'll ask him about it. But if he tells me that he's making out all right, I let him go.

. . . .

Conversation No. 2. How Langley talked about the use of work standards.

LANGLEY: I believe in work standards as a broken yardstick of measurement that has no inherent validity but does have a practical value. To me, the function of the standards is to serve as a guidepost on the side of the road to tell us where we are today in relation to where we were yesterday and where we think we can go tomorrow. They provide management a means of determining in advance what they can sell their products for while being competitive and profitable.

I've indoctrinated my people not to take standards as having any intrinsic value in themselves, but rather to use them just as a guide. It isn't the standard that should determine how they work or pace themselves; instead, the energy, drive, and interest they put in their work should be determined by how they *feel* about their work. I tell my people: "Try to do the best you can comfortably and independent of what the standard says you should do. In other words, you should be taking your incentive from yourselves." But I also emphasize that it is of vital interest to the company, and therefore to themselves, that they make the operation as profitable as possible, because in a sense they are the company. Management is not the company; the stockholders are not the company; it's a combination. They, the workers, are just as meaningfully the company as management or the stockholders are, and in many ways even more so. I drive into them that they, as individuals and as a group, have a big stake in the company's profitability because one of the important satisfactions available to them is being engaged in a successful profitable activity. "After all," I tell them, "work is a way of life, and we've got to be getting something out of it as people. One of these things that can be important is the knowledge that we are connected with a successful operation that we helped make that way."

. . . .

Conversation No. 3. How Langley talked about the production schedule and other required features of his department's operation.

LANGLEY: Now, take the production schedule; that's sacred! That is a must. Under all circumstances, we must produce the schedule.

CASEWRITER: Is this because your superiors have imposed the schedule on you that same way, too?

LANGLEY: No, it's because I want it that way. This is what we're in business for. We want to get goods out the door. The way we go about doing that will, of course, make a difference in how successfully we accomplish the things not directly connected with production that are also real and important. But we want to keep the record straight. There is no wavering or compromise on the schedule. That will not be tolerated, and everyone knows it.

There are three things I am very firm on in the department. One of them is the production schedule. Another is the employee evaluation sheets. These sheets are absolutely required by management, and I can't get around them. I don't like them; I think they can do more harm than good at times; but they are there, and I have to go along with them.

The third thing is that I expect my people in this department to get along with one another. I say to the girls: "You must adjust to and with the group—become a part of it. At least, you must have a willingness to try to do this." I think they all know this; I've told them so directly, and I've talked about and around it repeatedly on every occasion I could. This doesn't mean I forbid people to have personal differences. That would be stupid. But I do require that they overcome whatever personal differences they might have to the extent of being able to function co-operatively with one another.

CASEWRITER: What would you do if someone did not live up to this requirement?

LANGLEY: Out she would go.

CASEWRITER: You mean you would fire her? Have you ever done so?

LANGLEY: I have. Two years ago, I had to get rid of one girl who just had to fight with everyone she worked with. I tried my best to help her, but it did no good. So I fired her; and everyone knew why, too.

. . . .

Conversation No. 4. How Langley talked about Bill Yoost and Tom Montag. This conversation took place one afternoon during the coffee break period. Langley was standing at one end of the room surveying the scene, especially the seating arrangement of the two coffee groups, when he commented:

LANGLEY: I think you will find this is the customary arrangement, except for Bill Yoost. You will find him spending more of his time in Room C now. You know, he is learning Room C operations. I think he has in mind stepping in there as a group leader if George Cordoza should move to a bigger job or need an assistant. That is why you will see him sticking pretty close to operations there and learning as much as he can about them. You won't see much of him in here any more.

CASEWRITER: What do you mean by that, Ralph? Is he free to decide where he wants to work and what he wants to do?

LANGLEY: Well, by that I mean you will find him staying more with that group in there than here. He has been working on Room C stuff for quite a while now and doing his maintenance work in here on and off when it needs doing. But he always used to come in here for his coffee break. Lately, the last several days or so, I notice he has started taking his break in there. I think he will keep doing that. He is trying to get acquainted with that group now. He wants that group leader job.

CASEWRITER: Does Tom Montag run around with any particular crowd here at American Radiatronics? [Montag was having coffee with Sally's group.]

LANGLEY: He used to when he was in Room A full time. But lately, he has started having all of his coffee breaks in here with the tube room group. I think you will find him spending more and more of his time in here. He has got Room A operations down now where he has more time to spend working into tube room operations. He is taking on more of Bill's maintenance work all the time. And there are a lot of other operations he is picking up, too. You will see Bill spending less and less of his time in here and Tom more and more.

CASEWRITER: It sounds as though Bill and Tom are free to decide pretty much what they want to do.

LANGLEY: Yes, in a way, they are. You know, there is the kind of work you get out of people when they are doing what is prescribed for them to do; and then, there is the bonus you get when they are doing what they want to do. I want Bill and Tom to figure out for themselves what they want to do, what they are happiest at, and let them do it as much as I can. That is my way of thinking.

Take Tom, for instance. Prior to Tom's going into Room A, which was about a year to a year and a half ago, 65 to 70 units a month of the work was considered to be a good production record. The man in there before Tom did manage to get it up to about 100 units a month. When Tom took over, he managed to get up to 100 to 110 units per month quite quickly without trying too hard. So I just let him alone, raised the standard up to that, and he kept pushing it ahead. Now, we are doing more work than ever in there—he has hit as much as 160 to 180 units a month; and yet, frequently, he is able to come in here and put in the equivalent of a full day's work in the tube room.

That is what I mean by the bonus you get for letting people do the kind of work they want to do. Tom is doing more than what was a full day's work in Room A previously; and at the same time, he is doing a lot in here besides. He wanted to do this, so he just figured out how he could get things done in there quicker in order to spend more time in here. I want him to find out what he likes to do best. Right now, I am kind of pushing him to take on the pump stand work, which he is doing besides picking up a lot of various maintenance work. No one knows at this time what he will end up liking best, but he is free to go in either direction without my telling him which one to take on. If it develops that he prefers the maintenance equipment kind of work, I'll ease off on the pump stand encouragement and let Nellie MacDonald take on more of that. It's up to Tom.

One thing, and this is important. I'm not trying to handle Tom. I'm not trying to get him to work harder. I don't think there is any possible way of giving him more work to do with him knowing I'm doing it and at the same time getting him to do it. Tom isn't trying to work harder, and I don't think I could make him work harder. The reason he is doing as well as he is, is because he hasn't been thinking in terms of getting more work done; he has been thinking about learning and about getting ahead. I know he would think I was taking advantage of him if all he heard from me was getting more work out. For instance, if instead of feeling the way I do, I felt that Tom wasn't getting enough work done out there in Room A, I wouldn't push him. I would let him alone to find his way. As it is now, he moves in, he learns more, he takes on more and more responsibility, and this is the way you grow. I changed his grade when I opened the door for him to go into the tube room. I jumped him up two grades. When I see he can take on more work yet, I'll jump him again.

. . . .

Conversation No. 5. How Langley talked about relations between groups at American Radiatronics Corporation. As Langley was standing in the tube room one day talking, a man wearing a white shirt and tie walked up to him.

WHITE SHIRT: Are you going to let us have Sally Ivers all right?

LANGLEY: Yeah, I think so. Let me talk to her first; then check back in a while, and you talk to her yourself.

WHITE SHIRT: Check back later, eh? O.K. I'll see you later, Ralph.

LANGLEY (*turning to the casewriter after the man has left*):   That was Ryerson from the research department. He wants to use Sally on some special work he needs to have done in the electronics lab. He likes to have her do it because it's very delicate work, and no one can do it as well as she can.

You know, we do this sort of thing back and forth all the time. We help them out, and they help us out, and there's a good relationship all around. If there's ever anything we need, all we have to do is ask for it, and they do the same thing with us.

I once spent close to four weeks almost full time helping them out on some equipment setup they were working on. There were four of us, three of them and myself. We formed a team, made our own designs, then put it together. It worked out very well. Their glass blower comes up here and does all our glass system repair work for us. If we ever need any stopcocks or other parts in a hurry, we just ask for them and get them without any questions. Now, if any other department should try to do this, they would be out of them. And you know, there has never been a piece of paper passed between us. They've never asked us to sign for anything or keep records. If we got three or four stopcocks from them—that's about $75 or so—they could, if they wanted to, write out a requisition, have us sign it, and get it transferred over to us. But they never do that. It just comes out of their budget, and the same with us.

You know, relations between different parts of an organization have to be built. They don't just happen. I started out in just small ways doing things for them; and as we began to build mutual trust and confidence, they started doing little things for us. Gradually, these exchanges got bigger. Now, I would say that they don't see any difference between us and them. We're just another part of their organization, and they're another part of ours. We don't distinguish between ourselves as far as things we can do together or for one another are concerned. It's a good feeling. This is an important problem at American Radiatronics—how to build relationships between different groups. Right now, relations are generally pretty poor, but I think they can be built up. It will be slow, and it'll be hard.

How an Outsider in the Company Saw the Nuclear Tube Room

One day the casewriter had an opportunity to visit briefly with someone from outside Langley's department who was at the same time familiar with the tube room activity and its customary mode of operation. The man was Harold Singer, a process engineer from the company's central engineering department. Singer was one of a group of men who served as technical specialists for various operating departments in the company and who also spent a considerable portion of their time on product development and long-range planning activities. A portion of Singer's remarks are reproduced below in the approximate form in which they were made:

HAROLD SINGER: I really can't understand how this operation makes money. The products are primitive in design, no changes have been made in years, and there's no engineering control of any kind. Everything is run on a casual, hit-or-miss basis. It shouldn't make money, but somehow it does. . . .

Dollarwise, they're doing a pretty good job in here, as far as it goes; but they've got one overriding weakness in the way they are presently set up. Do you realize the girls do all their own testing in here? The same girls that make the tubes test them. It just isn't logical. It's against human nature. You can't trust the same people who make something to test it also. It's not healthy. They'll always try to protect themselves. This group of test equipment over here should be operated by a distinctly separate group of people completely removed from the production and under different supervision. That's the only basis under which you can get reliable testing and guard against infiltration of loyalties back and forth between manufacture and testing. . . .

We've got plans in the works for taking on this place and really making it over. And when we do, we'll see to it that the testing operations are carried on in a separate department. We'll really whip this operation into shape. . . .

There's a tremendous potential in this kind of activity, but it's never been exploited. We've got designs on the board right now that would revolutionize the way of doing things around here if we could get them going. I'd like to make this a model show place for the company. Right now, it's the worst in the company. Look at all this dirt around and the disorganization. . . .

This place has never been under engineering control. That's the trouble with it. The products and processes here now are what they've traditionally been almost from the start. Most of the product design changes that have been made have been developed and put into practice by the production people themselves. That's not good. Too much can creep into an organization that way that isn't good for it. They design their own products, they alter and maintain their own production equipment and processes, and they are free to go off in all different directions at once.

The first thing we would do if we could get hold of this room would be to put every operation under close engineering surveillance. The whole setup needs to be revamped and overhauled from one end to the other. We'll do it, too. You won't recognize it two years from now. Some of the new products we have in mind will call for a level of sophistication in production methods, equipment design, and cleanliness that'll make this look sick. You've seen pictures of how some of these production departments look in other companies—cleanliness precautions that make them look like operating rooms, temperature and humidity controls, all white-painted walls and equipment. That's what we'll have here. Personnel is right now looking into available sources of production girls for us; and when we start getting them in here and training them properly, and install modern production methods with a true mass production setup, then you'll see what this department can do. . . .

I'd like to think time zero for this department's operations in this company's history will start three months from now. We've got all the preliminary design work and process system concepts worked out already; and in about three months, we'll begin to pick up some real speed. Two years from now, you won't know the place. In contrast, everything that will have gone on before will be nothing. Take a good look around at what you see in here right now; you'll never see it again. Before long, it will be like looking back at the covered wagon era.

4. ALLIED FOOD COMPANY

ON MARCH 10, 1955, Mr. Nelson Anders, general sales manager of the Allied Food Co., presided at an all-day meeting of sales executives from the company's Eastern sales region. The meeting was held in a hotel conference room in New York City. Exhibit 1 presents a partial organization chart of the Allied Food Co., and Exhibit 2 indicates the name, title, and seating place of the executives at the meeting. The March 10 meeting had been called by Mr. Anders to make some final detailed plans prior to the institution of a major reorganization of the Eastern sales region scheduled to start in less than a month.

The Allied Food Co. was a large national company that produced and purchased for resale a fairly complete line of food products. The company had been growing rapidly since World War II, and its sales in 1954 were well over $100,000,000. In the latter half of 1954, the top sales executives decided, after considerable study, to change the existing national sales organization from having a single sales force in a given sales territory to having a dual sales force. In other words, the company's products were to be split into two major groups, called groups A and B, and different salesmen were to sell each group of products. This change also called for a doubling of the number of people needed as territory sales managers (see Exhibit 3). It was decided to make this organizational change in the Eastern region first and, if it worked as expected, introduce it in time into the other sales regions. Prior to the March 10 meeting Mr. Anders had asked Mr. Butler, the Eastern regional sales manager, to request his district managers to nominate people for each of the newly created jobs of territory sales manager and to indicate how they would split their territorial sales forces. The resulting proposals for personnel changes in each district were available in advance in written form to all those attending the March 10 meeting.

The following account and excerpts of the March 10 meeting were prepared by a research man from the Harvard Business School who attended the meeting.

The discussion throughout the morning concerned such topics as the timing of the announcements of the new organizational plan, the problem of setting up appropriate sales quotas for the new sales territories, the problem of handling the customers who were now to be called on by two different representatives of the Allied Food Co., and several other problems related to the reorganization. Mr. Anders took an active part in these discussions. Mr. Butler was much less active and acted more as a moderator in calling on the different people who wanted to speak on the issue at hand. The problems that were raised seemed to be getting a very thorough discussion, and by and large, the group seemed to be agreeing on the ways that the different aspects of the change would be handled.

After lunch, by previous arrangement, Mr. Anders called the attention of the group to the problem of deciding on the specific people who would be given the new jobs of territorial sales managers and the question of making the related personnel shifts.

> ANDERS: We have to approach this problem this afternoon by going through one district at a time looking at the nominations that have been put up by the district managers. I suggest we start by looking at those districts where there are relatively few problems involved so that we can get some of these out of the way before we tackle the districts where it will probably be a little more difficult to find the answers.
>
> BUTLER: In that case, let's start with the Buffalo district.

The Buffalo district manager took about five minutes to explain the nominations he had made in the report he had prepared for the meeting. He had nominated one of his own men for each of the new jobs that were being created and spoke briefly of the qualities and personality attributes of the people he was proposing for those positions. After a couple of questions were asked him, everyone at the meeting seemed to agree with his proposals. Mr. Butler then asked the Baltimore district manager to present his report. The Baltimore manager also took about five or ten minutes to present his nominations, and these were very quickly accepted by the rest of the group.

The third district manager to report was Mr. Murdock from the New York district. He presented his nominations in much the same fashion as the previous two district managers. He then concluded his presentation:

> MURDOCK: I am down now to the final territory and that is our Newark territory. This territory presents a problem and I need some help on it. I don't feel that I have a qualified man in my district to nominate for that new job in Newark. We're up against some pretty rough competition there. We need a very competent man to take over that territory. What I feel we need is an older man who has had plenty of sales experience with our company and who has handled some tough assignments. He has to be able to make a very good appearance and to really know what he is doing in order to do a good job with that territory. As I've said, I think I've got some very good men in my territory. I've moved a number of them up to

take these new slots, and I think they'll do it well. But I don't feel I have another man who's ready to step into a job like this Newark one.

ANDERS: Does anyone have any suggestions for this problem?

EASTERN REGION SALES PERSONNEL MANAGER: I understand that the situation in our Boston district is somewhat related to the question that has been raised here about Newark. So why don't we take a look at the Boston picture and see if it doesn't help us settle this Newark problem in the New York district.

ANDERS: Fine, why don't you go ahead then.

Mr. Ranford, the Boston district manager, proceeded to give his proposed lineup for the new jobs as territory managers in the Boston district. After he had proceeded about halfway through this presentation he was interrupted.

ANDERS: I'm looking down here at the Hartford-Springfield territory [a territory in the Boston district]. I see you don't have a territory manager for Group B named there. How about this fellow Tompkins? Isn't he one of our senior salesmen in that territory?

RANFORD: Well—yes. We have considered Tompkins. We haven't recommended him for this job. All of the reports on him haven't been exactly good. I don't want to give the impression that he's not a good salesman because I think he is. Everybody says he's got a good record as a salesman, but the reports I get are that people aren't too sure he will work out as a territory manager, at least not right there in the Hartford-Springfield territory. I guess he's rubbed some people a little bit the wrong way, and I don't know if he would work out there. That's why we didn't put his name in as a nominee for a territory manager at this time. However, we do think he's a good man. I don't want you to think otherwise.

ANDERS: Well, what's the trouble, then?

MURDOCK: Maybe I'd better speak up here about the conversation I had with Ranford last night over cocktails. I was telling him about our problem down in Newark, and we came up with the idea that maybe this fellow Tompkins might be somebody we could move into this Newark job. I understand he's had some problems up there, but if we all have our eyes open on this, I'd be willing to take him for that Newark job.

ANDERS: Didn't I hear something about his having a pretty good-sized family?

RANFORD: That's right. I understand he has six kids.

ANDERS: And I thought I also heard he's recently bought himself a new home.

RANFORD: I think that's right. I think he did buy himself a home within the last few months.

ANDERS: Well, hadn't we better think about that? What's the move going to mean to him? If we push him into moving, is there a possibility we might lose him? It doesn't sound as if a move would be very easy for him.

EASTERN REGION SALES PERSONNEL MANAGER: I have had several chats with Tompkins about his personal situation and I might be able to add something here. Tompkins has been passed over twice for promotion to territory manager. This has upset him and if it happens again I predict that he will leave the company. But I don't think he wants to leave. And even though he stands to lose money on selling his house now, I think he would move to get a territory manager's job if he couldn't move up where he is.

Exhibit 1

ALLIED FOOD COMPANY

PARTIAL ORGANIZATION CHART—SALES DEPARTMENT

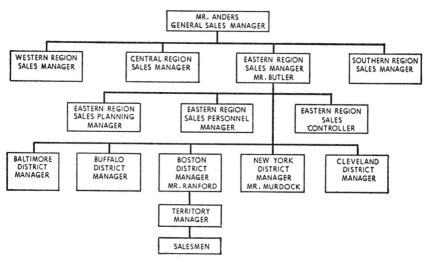

RANFORD: I was sort of hoping it wouldn't be necessary to bring all this up at this meeting, but maybe I'd better tell a little bit more about the story on Tompkins. It's a little complicated, but what it amounts to is that Tompkins has been going around talking to quite a few people in our organization about his difficulties in the Hartford-Springfield territory. He's got a good sales record but he's been talking to different people in our organization about his troubles, and mostly they add up to the fact that he's running down his current boss, John Clements [manager of the Hartford-Springfield territory]. Needless to say, it hasn't made Clements happy to have Tompkins running around undercutting his position. Clements isn't one of our strongest men, but he is perfectly okay as a territory manager. You'll see that we have Clements slated for a transfer to Providence. Well, Tompkins is really giving him a bad time—going outside channels to make things tough for him. It's things of that kind that made us think that it wouldn't be wise to move Tompkins up to the job of manager in that territory. This idea of moving him down to Newark seemed to be a pretty good way to handle the whole thing.

ANDERS: Maybe we ought to think about firing Tompkins. What would you say to that?

RANFORD (*pause*):   No, I wouldn't recommend that. He is certainly controversial, but on balance, I think he ought to be kept.

Exhibit 2

ALLIED FOOD COMPANY
SEATING ARRANGEMENT FOR MEETING, MARCH 10, 1955

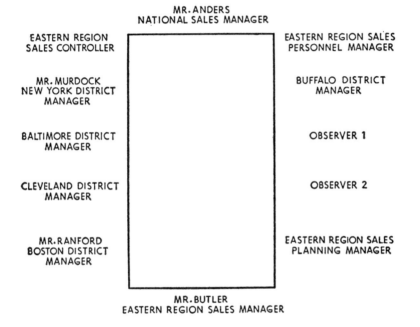

MR. ANDERS
NATIONAL SALES MANAGER

EASTERN REGION
SALES CONTROLLER

EASTERN REGION SALES
PERSONNEL MANAGER

MR. MURDOCK
NEW YORK DISTRICT
MANAGER

BUFFALO DISTRICT
MANAGER

BALTIMORE DISTRICT
MANAGER

OBSERVER 1

CLEVELAND DISTRICT
MANAGER

OBSERVER 2

MR. RANFORD
BOSTON DISTRICT
MANAGER

EASTERN REGION SALES
PLANNING MANAGER

MR. BUTLER
EASTERN REGION SALES MANAGER

ANDERS: Have you or have any of your subordinates called in Tompkins to tell him exactly what you think of his talking about his boss outside of channels?

RANFORD: I don't think that is the kind of thing that you necessarily have to tell a man. He ought to know better. It is all spelled out in our company policies. Besides, he could have caught on to how people felt about this from the cold shoulder he has been getting when he peddled his stories. We thought he would straighten himself out. I've been hearing stories about this for quite a while, but it has been hard to pin down. It's not easy to know just how to approach Tompkins on a matter of this kind. It's something that I've talked about a bit with Clements and some of the other men who have stopped by that territory and have had a chance to hear some of these things from Tompkins. But it always comes in little pieces and it's hard to know just what to do about it.

ANDERS: I take it, then, you haven't talked to Tompkins about this.

RANFORD: That's right.

ANDERS (*pause*): Do you have any serious objection to promoting Tompkins to be a manager of the Hartford-Springfield territory?

RANFORD (*pause*): No, I wouldn't say I could put up any serious objections to such a promotion.

ANDERS: Well, in that case, why don't we go ahead on that. Now let's go back to the New York problem. This doesn't help on the Newark vacancy, does it? (*Laughs.*)

Exhibit 3

ALLIED FOOD COMPANY
TYPICAL DISTRICT SALES ORGANIZATION CHART

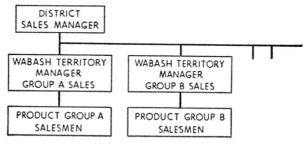

5. THE STILES CORPORATION

ONE PLANT of the Stiles Corporation had recently suffered an explosion in which several employees had been killed. Effective safety measures were eagerly being sought by top management. Shortly thereafter, in another Stiles plant which had had a relatively good safety record, a worker's skull was nearly crushed by an automatic die cast machine. The next day the plant manager and the factory manager told the factory superintendent to hold a meeting immediately with his general foremen and to report back whatever ideas the general foremen should propose for improving the plant's safety program. The superintendent called each of his general foremen personally to inform them of the meeting, but he did not tell them the meeting's purpose. He also asked the safety supervisor and two general foremen not in his jurisdiction to attend. See Exhibit 1 for a partial organization chart of the plant and Exhibit 2 for a seating chart of the meeting.

When the men were seated in the meeting room, the factory superintendent began speaking.

SUPERINTENDENT: We are not getting through to the people. It's showing up in our safety record. (*Here he cited the accident of the preceding night.*) This meeting is not for the purpose of criticizing. However, several months ago, we told you you had the right to shut down a job if you felt you had a safety hazard; you could send in a work order marked "safety," and it would get special priority in the maintenance department. However, you marked *all* your work orders safety. That wasn't right. We know that there must be other weak links in our safety setup too because, after this accident, a current foreman trainee said that exactly the same kind of an accident happened to him some time ago. He was wearing a baseball cap; he reached over and the die cast machine closed on the beak of his cap. Now, what I want to know is why we didn't know about this safety hazard before?

DEF.: What is the report on the accident now?

SAFETY: Well, we've been holding off an announcement. We don't like to make one without a report from the hospital.

SUPERINTENDENT: I have here with me some work orders, including one dated November 1, based on an idea advanced in a leadman's safety meeting on October 18. The only excuse I can get for this work order being delayed two weeks is that the minutes of the safety meeting were late.

SAFETY: Well, the minutes are late getting circulated from my office sometimes, but I won't admit that they are that late.

SUPERINTENDENT: You will have to get them out sooner and follow up on them.

SAFETY: That's true.

SUPERINTENDENT: If the minutes are two weeks late, people are no longer enthused about the ideas. In fact, they forget about them.

SHIP.: If it's this serious and needs to be fixed, why do you have to wait on any report?

Exhibit 1

THE STILES CORPORATION
PARTIAL ORGANIZATION CHART

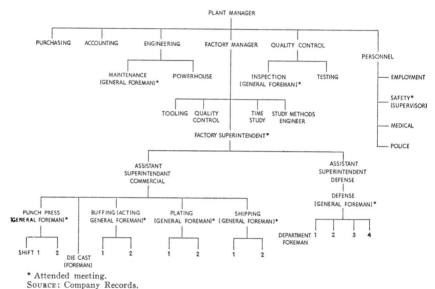

* Attended meeting.
SOURCE: Company Records.

SUPERINTENDENT: That's where your foremen should step in.

SAFETY: If we had as much interest around here in safety as we have in the production schedule, the situation would be different.

SUPERINTENDENT: The leadmen say that they don't get the five-minute monthly safety talk the foremen are supposed to give, and, if they do, it certainly isn't any safety talk.

DEF.: Why not talk about one thing at a time? Let's fix the responsibility for work orders. There ought to be a special color pad for "safety" work orders.

SUPERINTENDENT: Well, we have two men in maintenance doing nothing but working on these safety work orders now.

INSPECTION: When we wanted a guard on that new copper belt, you would have impressed the foremen had you waited and gotten it fixed right before you started production. Instead you started without any guard on the belt. And I can tell you why. Because I know. The reason was that parts started down the production line. This problem goes higher than the general foremen.

SAFETY: I say that safety comes first, and they say to me, "Hell, be honest. Safety doesn't come first."

Exhibit 2

THE STILES CORPORATION

SEATING CHART*

SUPERINTENDENT

| SECRETARY | SAFETY SUPER | VACANT | VACANT | VACANT | VACANT | MAINT. G.F. |

| PLATE G.F. | INSP.G.F. | | BUFF G.F. | | PUNCH G.F. | |

| SHIP G.F. | DEF. G.F. | VACANT | VACANT | VACANT | VACANT | VACANT |

* The meeting was held in a room with chairs arranged in rows, as shown.

SUPERINTENDENT: Well, the foreman should have hollered.

INSPECTION: Had he stopped the production, he would have been called a pantywaist, and the men would have been sent home.

SUPERINTENDENT: I don't agree.

INSPECTION: Don't kid me. I've been here for seventeen years.

SHIP.: Why is the foreman always responsible? Somehow, it's always back on him. Nothing here that happens isn't his fault. Someone else ought to do something around here.

MAINTENANCE: It was our oversight on the belt.

INSPECTION: Well, at least you are one man here that can give an honest answer.

SUPERINTENDENT: But the foreman should have taken action.

INSPECTION: I'm telling you that production comes first around this plant.

SUPERINTENDENT: No.

INSPECTION: Well, sometimes safety comes *second.*

SUPERINTENDENT: No.

SEVERAL GENERAL FOREMEN (*in a chorus*): Oh, yes. Oh, yes.

INSPECTION: The foremen don't believe you when you say safety comes first.

SUPERINTENDENT: They see we fix things if we get a work order.

INSPECTION: You had better start listening to their ideas and give them some better answers.

SUPERINTENDENT: I started this meeting off wondering if we were getting through to the operators. Then I started wondering if we were getting through to the foremen. Now I wonder if we are getting through to you general foremen.

SAFETY: We're hiring the bottom of the barrel. The men we get here are terrible. The type of people we are now hiring are nervous.

SUPERINTENDENT: No. I don't buy that. Even if a man is from the sticks, he doesn't want to get hurt. Now I don't want to get off the track here. I want suggestions.

MAINTENANCE: Well, do the same for safety as you do for production. If there is a safety hazard, call people into it until you get it fixed. Shut the machine down.

PLATE. (*to the superintendent*):   You assume that the foremen have no enthusiasm for safety. That just isn't so.

SUPERINTENDENT (*interrupting*):   Well, you'll have to keep after safety. That's what we need. Follow-up. Keep up your interest.

PLATE.:   This is all a matter of pressure. For example, the maintenance department has orders not to work anyone on safety maintenance this Saturday.

SUPERINTENDENT: If you'd let us know, we would do something about it. Approach us and drive it home but don't get mad about it. Now if you wanted to sell brushes and the lady said no, well, you would just have to keep selling. (*To the foreman of inspection*) Andy, do you have any ideas?

INSPECTION: I've said enough. You've got my answer.

MAINTENANCE: I say sell safety ahead of production.

SUPERINTENDENT: The only thing I get out of all of this is that we haven't sold ourselves on safety.

MAINTENANCE: You've got to show people—not talk it.

SUPERINTENDENT: Well, I want to tell you something right now. I'm going to make it a personal responsibility to call in the operators at random to check with them on their safety talks. What I'm convinced of is that we have to sell our supervision on safety. We do lots of talking but very little acting. Why, I was embarrassed when the personnel manager said, "Let's do something about safety," and he got out a letter about it. Why didn't we?

INSPECTION: After several months, we asked where the fans were that we had requested to lessen the danger of fainting and falls in some very hot departments, and one man said, "Well, let's just wait. The weather is about ready to change."

SUPERINTENDENT: Who said it?

INSPECTION: No personalities.

SUPERINTENDENT: Who?

INSPECTION: He sat there (*pointing to the chair customarily occupied by the factory manager*), and I'll tell you it left us cold.

SUPERINTENDENT: Well, he's busy. He can't see everything. We have to sell him too. I say sound off on your gripes.

INSPECTION: And have it in the minutes?

MAINTENANCE: I can't leave production work and go to safety jobs or I will be asked questions. Why do things get done around here? Why was that die job that had been hanging around for two months cleaned up in two hours? Because it was given priority by the top boss. That's what I'm trying to call attention to. You have to get the priority. You can't just talk to the people.

BUFF.:   We have to sell the people.

SHIP. (*interrupting*):   What's the purpose of this meeting?

SUPERINTENDENT: To improve safety.

SHIP.:   This man who was hurt, he was on that machine for seven months, wasn't he? The man we are making a foreman, the one who was nearly hurt, was on the machine for two years. Why didn't we get the safety idea across to him in two years? Answer that one. Why didn't he tell us that he had had a near accident?

PLATE.:   You have to ask them before they'll tell you. You have to say, "Have you had any close calls lately?" We're always talking about a five-minute safety talk. Why limit it to five minutes? Let the employee talk and cut out this clock watching.

BUFF.:   What we have to do is ask the men.

SUPERINTENDENT: Now, that's good. And it works too. That's exactly what I do in these leadmen meetings. I ask them for their ideas one by one.

PUNCH.:   That's exactly what I object to. You ask the leadmen each to give their ideas by name. So they withhold their safety suggestions from their foreman and save them up for your meeting, so they'll look good.

SHIP.:   The time to correct is when a mistake is being made. Teach them out on the floor. A thirty-minute speech won't help. At that meeting of the leadmen, the superintendent ought to write out a work order right on the spot instead of waiting until the general foreman writes it out.

SUPERINTENDENT: No. I can't do that. We can't bypass the foremen and the general foremen. Well, it's getting late so we will have to call this meeting to a halt. But I want you to know that I'm now going to ask the assistant superintendents to start checking with the men on the floor to see if they are getting their safety talks. The only way to get the foremen to give the talks is to check up on them. So I suggest that you start checking up on them yourself because we're going to. That's all for now.

6. MERRILL MANUFACTURING COMPANY*

Part 1

THE MERRILL MANUFACTURING COMPANY manufactures small products used in a variety of electrical equipment. For one product the company constitutes one of few sources of supply. Until the time of the difficulty recorded in this case, this article always went to customers with whom Merrill had established uniform specifications regarding types, sizes, and quality. The Carlton-Wheeler Company, a newcomer to the field, requested the Merrill Company to supply this item, but with quality specifications better than those generally required by the trade.

The Merrill management determined that the quality item required could be selected with careful inspection from regular production runs. A group of special inspectors, however, would have to be set up, each member to be instructed regarding the standards to be met. This posed the problem of additional expense. The cost problem for the extra inspection was submitted to Carlton-Wheeler executives. They readily agreed to meet the additional expenditures and their order was accepted.

Merrill thereupon prepared to put its program into operation. With the industry expanding, management foresaw that it might have to meet further problems involving "extra-quality specifications." If the program of the special inspectors proved successful, it might provide a method of flexible production adjustments. Management accordingly proceeded to plan carefully the organization of the special inspection group. Inspectors normally worked on inspection lines next to the production lines. The supervisor of inspection, John Brooks, demonstrated that the special inspectors could not continue their new work at their established locations without impeding the flow of regular work. Therefore, a "special inspection room" was outfitted, adjacent to the warehouse.

Mr. Brooks chose from among the regular inspectors thirty-six girls, twelve to a shift, for the special work. Since the isolated location would make regular supervision impracticable, he gave careful consideration to individual ability. Although the union contract provided for seniority,

* Reproduced from *Problems in Labor Relations* by Benjamin M. Selekman, Stephen H. Fuller, Thomas Kennedy, and John M. Baitsell (New York: McGraw-Hill Book Co., Inc., 1964), by permission of the Publisher and of the President and Fellows of Harvard College.

management conceived the proposed shifts as only temporary departmental assignments. Nonetheless, seniority was taken into consideration, and the selectees were girls of relatively long service. Fearful, however, that the older women might find transfers back and forth from regular to special work a more difficult adjustment to make, Mr. Brooks restricted his choices to the younger inspectors. The selections completed, each girl was interviewed by Mr. Brooks and the personnel manager, George Ashley. The following interview with Rose Townley, one of the special inspectors, was typical:

ASHLEY: Good morning, Rose. I thought it would be a good idea if we had a little talk before you went to the special inspection room, so you could understand exactly what we will all be trying to do.

ROSE: My friend, Cathie Grey, told me a little about it after she talked with you and Mr. Brooks.

ASHLEY: It's nice you and Cathie are being transferred together; Mr. Brooks told me you've always been friends. Of course, you understand the company didn't especially plan to transfer girls who were friends. You have all been selected on the basis of your ability, seniority, and aptitudes for moves from special to regular work, and back, as the new program demands.

ROSE: Oh yes, we understand that. We're all pretty good friends. After all, Centerville isn't like a big city. We know each other, most of us, outside of work too. Naturally I may like one person more than another.

ASHLEY: Of course. I know you've worked under Mr. Brooks long enough to understand that the inspection department always expects careful work. But in the special inspection room, you'll have to be even more careful. I'm sure Mr. Brooks has gone into this aspect of your transfer fully with you. He tells me each of you learned from him the four features of our product on which you must especially concentrate. There's no use in repeating these technical matters which he can give you more expertly. I want to talk with you about other aspects of your special work.

ROSE: Yes, Mr. Brooks explained all about the special inspection. He said we'd get a couple of days' training, too.

ASHLEY: Yes, that's right. We want to make sure that you all understand this transfer is a purely temporary arrangement. You'll be in the special room until this order is finished; then you go back to your former places on the regular inspection line.

ROSE: We won't lose on our department seniority, will we?

ASHLEY: Indeed, no! I want all you girls to understand you continue in every way as employees of our regular inspection department—on special temporary assignment. You continue to cumulate seniority; you get the same wage rates; you will share in any benefits the company may negotiate with the union. In the same way, you won't receive any special privileges as a result of your special work. You are quite clear about that, aren't you?

ROSE: Yes, we see that. We often watch for some special things in the regular runs too, when Mr. Brooks asks us.

ASHLEY: Exactly. It just seems more efficient to plan for special adjustments, now that the company may be getting new customers with new specifications. Of course, it's to the benefit of all of us to satisfy new customers just as we have always satisfied our old ones.

ROSE: I guess all of us want to get all the work we can.

ASHLEY: That's the spirit—and the company wants to give you all regular work at good wages. You know that! So we'll try to get the new orders and when they come, you girls will be ready to leave the regular inspection lines when necessary and do special inspection.

ROSE: Who will do *our* jobs on the regular lines while we're in the special room?

ASHLEY: We shall transfer girls from production, on the basis of seniority and ability. They'll hold the jobs until the special order is finished. Then you'll come back to your regular place, and they'll go back to production. Do you see how it will work?

ROSE: Yes, I do now, I guess.

MERRILL MANUFACTURING COMPANY

Part 2

THE SPECIAL ORDER took a little over six months. During that time the average monthly quit rate in the regular inspection department was 4.1; none of the special inspectors quit. Absenteeism at the regular inspection lines averaged 6.8 per cent; in the special inspection room, 2.3 per cent. Although Mr. Brooks was able to make only occasional supervisory visits, on each occasion he was impressed with the high morale among the special inspectors. They worked with gusto; he saw them coming and leaving in chatting, laughing groups. The Carlton-Wheeler Company expressed satisfaction with the product.

During the fifth month of this period, Mr. Ashley made a visit to the special inspection room shortly before the end of the first shift. A mild influenza epidemic had been felt in Centerville, and the employees had been circularized with a bulletin of precautionary measures. Mr. Ashley decided to take the occasion for a meeting with the special inspectors. Excerpts follow:

ASHLEY: I'm glad of this chance for a little talk together. I suppose you've heard that the company doctor thinks it very important for everyone to stay home at the first sign of a cold. A day home will protect you from real infection and safeguard others, too. So remember, even if a number have to be out, just stay home till the sniffles are over. We can send in a few substitutes from the regular inspectors if necessary. You girls can train them yourselves. It may not prove necessary to use them; yet it might be a wise precaution to prepare a few substitutes for emergency.

CATHERINE GREY: Oh no, Mr. Ashley, we wouldn't want that.

ROSE TOWNLEY: We don't want new girls sent in here.

SEVERAL VOICES TOGETHER: We'll make out. We don't need any substitutes. We'll get out the work!

ASHLEY (*surprised*): But it was just an idea for safeguarding you all.

ROSE TOWNLEY (*more quietly*): Well, we appreciate it, all right, but we're young and strong, and we'll manage.

BETTY BARTON: Some of us just have had to be absent before this, but we never let the work suffer.

ROSE TOWNLEY: You see, we always work out ways to meet things by ourselves—like when Anna Kowalski had to take her mother to the dispensary. Well, we didn't want Anna to lose time—they've had a lot of sickness—so we worked in the lunch hour. The eleven of us easily made enough to get Anna her day's wage.

ASHLEY: Well, I guess I didn't really hear that. You know the company cannot have you girls working during the lunch hour. I must order you not to do that again.

CATHERINE GREY: Well, Rose, you spilled the beans that time. But Mr. Ashley, really, it didn't hurt us a bit; in fact we all felt better for doing it.

ROSE TOWNLEY: Well, all right, next time we can ask permission, but it just goes to show you we can make out. We were off here by ourselves, and we didn't want Anna to lose money or the company to lose the work. We didn't think it would hurt anybody. But if a batch have to stay home now, why couldn't the rest of us come in Saturday?

ASHLEY (smiling): Well, there's a law about that, too. You'd have to get overtime.

ROSE: Even at that, I don't think the company would lose money. New people are never as fast as we can be. Anyway, if there's a flu epidemic, there might be other absences and you'd find it hard to get substitutes.

ASHLEY: Well, it was just a suggestion, and we wouldn't want to force anything on you. I guess you would make out, at that.

GRACE MILLER: Gee, that's swell! (Other approving exclamations rang through the room.)

ASHLEY (to Grace): Why, Grace, what are you doing here? Or am I wrong in believing you were second-shift inspection?

GRACE: You have a good memory, Mr. Ashley.

ROSE: Look at her blush! Well, I guess Mr. Ashley knows the shift on which we belong. Mr. Ashley, Grace is our first blushing bride of the special inspection room.

GRACE (laughing): Rose is ahead of the times, Mr. Ashley. I'm just engaged.

ASHLEY: Well, congratulations! And is the lucky man one of our Centerville boys?

CATHERINE GREY: We even claim him as a special inspection room romance. You see, Grace is engaged to Betty Barton's brother.

BETTY BARTON: And all the Bartons are glad too! It began at one of our theater parties. You see, we girls got to know each other pretty well these past months. And we've had lots of fun together outside—dances and theater parties and things like that. We all even spent a week end together once in New York. We really have awfully good times together.

ROSE TOWNLEY: That's how Grace came to change shifts. (Teasingly.) She needs time to doll up after work—and evenings for dates with the boy friend.

ROSE: So we got permission to change shifts from Mr. Brooks. We change shifts whenever something comes up. But Grace changed for good with Anna Kowalski. Now that Anna's mother is sick this gives Anna the morning to get her kid brothers and sisters off to school and clean the house.

ASHLEY: I can see you *have* made out, as you say.

MERRILL MANUFACTURING COMPANY

Part 3

SOME SIX WEEKS later the order for Carlton-Wheeler was completed. Mr. Ashley suggested that he and Mr. Brooks meet with the special inspectors. They read to them extracts from letters sent by the Carlton-Wheeler Company affirming Merrill's success in meeting the extra-quality specifications. Now, the executives informed the girls, they would be transferred back to their former positions on the regular inspection lines. But they could expect to receive a call to return to the special inspection room as further "special orders" came in.

About three weeks later, Mr. Brooks appeared in Mr. Ashley's office, obviously perturbed. The following conversation developed:

BROOKS: Well, here's a surprise for you! You won't believe it, but things seem to be going haywire with the special inspectors!

ASHLEY: Whatever in the world has happened? We seemed to have worked out just about the perfect setup there.

BROOKS: It gets me down that I learned of it through the union. Not that we don't get along with the union boys, but I pride myself about knowing what goes on in my department before they do.

Anyway, it seems Rose Townley finally went to Bill MacIntyre, the shop steward for the inspectors, with what she called "a grievance" for all the special inspectors. They all claim they should be on one regular inspection line. They persuaded Mac, too, apparently. If we want the right to move them between the regular lines and the special room, we owe them some privileges too; that's what Mac told me very seriously. They even feel they should have special seniority rights.

ASHLEY: But we made that clear right from the start. Every one of them agreed she'd have no special rights—that they'd go back to their old places. I suppose you told all that to Mac.

BROOKS: I did—and a lot more, too. I drew charts showing him how a special line for the special inspectors would disrupt the whole department. We placed those women on different lines according to their aptitudes on certain products, and we schedule the work that way. But Mac seemed impressed by the spiel the girls gave him; I gather Rose is quite active in the union and has a considerable following. But Mac's going to have trouble if we move those regular inspectors too. I warned him he'd better watch Mrs. McKenna and her side-kick, Mary Hammond.

ASHLEY: You mean McKenna will make trouble if she's "bumped" to make a place for the special inspectors?

BROOKS: Well, I wouldn't be a bit surprised. She is always crabbing —but she's a good inspector too, always 100 per cent. She thinks she's very good, too, and I know she's been pretty sour over not having been chosen as a special inspector. I was in a tight spot explaining we chose younger girls—McKenna's over forty. I've seen her and Townley having it out hot and heavy several times already. We're in for trouble, George, and I wonder what we should do next.

ASHLEY: At least we're absolutely solid in our position. We've planned this thing carefully; we explained matters at every step to the girls; we prepared them from the start that they simply couldn't ask for privileges. We're right, and they're wrong, and we'll just have to stand pat. The whole thing amazes me. Those girls seemed such a thoroughly fine lot—really square shooters. Whatever happened?

BROOKS: I wish I knew. Those girls are no fools—especially Rose Townley and Cathie Grey. They generally are pretty fair and square too; I suspect they went to Mac rather than me because they know I could hand them back their own statements about no special privileges. I just can't understand where things went wrong. We planned it all so carefully; everything seemed to be working out just as we wanted it.

ASHLEY: Well, we'll have to see about it, but don't give an inch on the main issue.

BROOKS: Mac told me those thirty-six girls were long-service employees and good union members. If the company couldn't grant such a simple request in return for their fine work, he said he would have to put the whole matter before their president, Lloyd Parsons.

ASHLEY: Well, why don't you ask Lloyd Parsons and Mac in for a talk—take the initiative. Parsons is usually a pretty level-headed fellow. Coming from the outside, he may see the whole problem with us.

MERRILL MANUFACTURING COMPANY

Part 4

MR. BROOKS arranged a meeting with Messrs. Parsons and MacIntyre for the same week. In the meantime, Mr. Ashley asked Mr. Brooks to get all the data that seemed relevant concerning Mrs. McKenna and Rose Townley. The record revealed the following:

Mrs. Agnes McKenna had been an inspector for fourteen years; she was now forty-four years old. She had been a member of the union since its entry; before then she had three times led protests against rate adjustments when new products had been added. Mrs. Mary Hammond, eight years with the company, had been placed opposite Mrs. McKenna when promoted to inspection and had remained Mrs. McKenna's "work partner." She was seconding Mrs. McKenna in the current disturbance, just as she did in most shop matters. Both women, but particularly Mrs. McKenna, were considered "money hungry" by the other employees. The husbands of both women had steady jobs.

Mrs. McKenna was known to be lazy except when there was an opportunity to make money. She and her husband lived in a one-room furnished apartment because, it was said, she refused to "slave" for anybody unless she got paid for it. Her personnel record showed she had lived for twelve years on a farm, acted as nurse to an invalid relative for four years, and had several jobs as a housemaid for well-to-do families during the next ten years.

Mrs. Hammond was seventeen at the time she was hired at Merrill. She had previous experience only as salesgirl in the five and ten, where she began working upon receiving her working papers at the age of fourteen. She had learned quickly at Merrill, had always carried a high efficiency rating, and had been promoted to inspection from assembly. She was married two years later, when she was nineteen, but continued to work to get a "start." At times she had intimated an intention of quitting. Her husband, classified 4F shortly after his induction into the armed services, had been discharged.

Rose Townley had come to Merrill upon graduation from high school. Like many of the younger employees, she entered the shop during war-production days; moreover, in the small town of Centerville, Merrill offered a large proportion of the jobs available to girls who had both to work and remain with their families. Rose was known to be devoted to her family, and proud of her gifted younger brother. Although engaged, she was determined to work to finance him through engineering school.

Not only in her own home, but in the shop and in the small-town circles, Rose was a person of many close ties. She was very "popular"; fellow workers of her own age turned to her when problems arose, and she proved resourceful in helping friends. She had considerable skill in planning "sociables" both in the shop and the union; many outings, parties, dances, and during the war, "relief" and similar activities seemed to originate with and be "managed" by her. Mr. Brooks considered her one of the department's best workers; her output records proved her both quick and accurate. She had seven years' service in the department.

MERRILL MANUFACTURING COMPANY

Part 5

WHEN THE UNION OFFICERS appeared for their scheduled appointment, Mr. Brooks had ready the seniority records of the department and other relevant data. When they left, he dictated the following summary of the discussion to present to Mr. Ashley:

BROOKS (*m*): I don't mind telling you, Lloyd, this whole thing surprises us. Management played fair and square with the girls, and every one of them agreed to go back to their regular places when the order was finished. We can't understand why the union backs them up on a thing like this. It doesn't seem right.

PARSONS (*u*): Just a moment, Mr. Brooks. I understand you expect to send them back to the special room any time you get an order requiring extra quality. It might be even worth your while to keep them together on a single line in the regular runs. That's all they ask; it's not much in return for what the company gets from the arrangement.

BROOKS (*m*): Well, maybe it doesn't seem so much, but we've thought this whole thing through from the start, and any such scheme would disrupt the whole department.

PARSONS (*u*): Well, how do you figure that? Rose Townley says all those girls are long-seniority employees. And you considered them able— you chose them. They have some rights in such a transfer. Rose feels it will really hurt things if their group is broken up.

BROOKS (*m*): But look here, Lloyd. If you bring up seniority, just remember that there was no obligation on us to consider seniority at all. There was nothing like a transfer. We were simply getting up a special arrangement to meet a special production problem. And certainly you recognize that the more orders the company can fill, the more steady work we have for our employees and your members.

PARSONS (*u*): You say you didn't have to consider seniority at all, but maybe you should have considered it—you'll certainly have to consider it now. If you *had* considered it, we wouldn't have this problem on our hands now. Seniority always means a lot to the union, and if you shift around our members you're going to hear about it. We put great store on seniority, and we can't permit our members to suffer any infringement on their job rights.

BROOKS (*m*): But, Lloyd, you're really on the wrong track there. This

398

was purely a production problem. You know the older women would find it harder to shift back and forth from regular to special, and back again.

PARSONS (*u*): Well, seems like the young inspectors aren't so flexible either.

BROOKS (*m*): I wish I knew what it really is. I'm sure it's not flexibility. Those girls, I don't mind telling you as we told them, did a fine job in the special room. And they have been doing their usual satisfactory work now on the regular runs. Nothing went wrong on our planning; the results show that. But somehow they feel entitled to special privileges, although they agreed at the start there would be nothing like that. That's what you've got to help us show them they just can't ask.

MACINTYRE (*u*): But the company must have taken seniority into some consideration. Rose tells me everyone of that special group is a long-service employee.

BROOKS (*m*): Surely the union isn't going to kick if we did more than the contract requires about taking seniority into account. Remember, this wasn't a question of promotion, or rehiring, or even transfer. It was just a production adjustment in one department.

PARSONS (*u*): Well, as soon as you considered seniority, the union had a right to be consulted. Maybe if you had called us in we could have helped avoid this trouble.

BROOKS (*m*): But look here, Lloyd; the very fact that older women aren't as adaptable shows we couldn't make seniority a controlling consideration.

PARSONS (*u*): Well, to the extent you did consider it, couldn't you give it equal weight in meeting the demand of these girls for a single inspection line? That would simply recognize them as a special inspection group. It isn't very much they're asking.

BROOKS (*m*): No, we couldn't—and for two reasons. As I told you, it would simply disrupt the whole department production-wise. Then, secondly, once we admit seniority in such rearrangements the girls would have to give way to many senior inspectors. The longest service employee among the special inspectors had eight years. In the regular group there are inspectors with nine years, ten years, and so on. Agnes McKenna has fourteen years, and she's already warned me she won't let anybody bump her.

MACINTYRE (*u*): Say, just between us, she's always griping.

BROOKS (*m*): I know just what you mean, Mac, and generally I too would be inclined to listen more to Rose Townley than to Agnes McKenna. But this time Agnes is right and Rose is wrong. In fact, I can't understand what got into Rose. I'm sure the other girls would follow her lead, and apparently she's been the one pressing this demand for them all. It just isn't like Rose to go back on her word—and that's what it is.

MacIntyre (*u*) (*quickly*): Well, Rose is just expressing what they all feel. They all want to work together in the regular room too. I know: they're after me all the time.

Brooks (*m*) (*smiling*): Oh, you needn't defend Rose to me, Mac. I like her too. But in this thing she's really all wrong. Look what we'd be up against. Every inspector on those regular lines has been chosen for her particular position. That department functions well, and naturally the inspectors develop aptitude by sheer experience in handling the products that come to them. Take twelve girls in each shift out of their places to put them together in a special line and there'd be chaos. You know how those things go; let us transfer some girls, and soon we'd be swamped by requests for transfers. Other girls would want to work next to their friends, or next to the door, or away from the windows. Everybody would find some good reason why she too should be somewhere else.

How would management decide? If we put it on seniority, those special inspectors could be bumped by the older women. Just study those seniority lists I've drawn up. And would you put it beyond Agnes McKenna to demand the right to "bump" one of those girls off the special line, if we set one up for them? You know Agnes. Why, you'd be in for trouble in the union, just as much as we would in the department.

MacIntyre (*u*): But why should we let Agnes. . . .

Parsons (*u*) (*interrupting*): Just a minute, Mac. Mr. Brooks has something there. I didn't realize the special inspectors had less seniority than the regular ones. The way Rose talked, I felt she was sure that seniority was on their side. And do you know I really think she believes that. Why don't we go back with these lists and talk some more to the special inspectors? These facts will show Rose that she's wrong.

Brooks (*m*): I'll be glad if you do. Rose should appreciate the facts once she sees them this way.

Parsons (*u*): I can't help saying once more, Mr. Brooks—and don't think I'm just rubbing it in—that if the company had called the union in, we could have warned you seniority would rise sooner or later. You'd have done better to choose on straight seniority; maybe those older women had a right to the special assignments.

Brooks (*m*): But remember it was purely a production problem, Lloyd—no promotion, no extra pay, no special privileges, no transfer out of the department, nothing like that. Flexibility was the main thing.

Parsons (*u*): Well, even if we had had these charts and what you've told us, we could have put Rose—and the others—straight when they first brought up their demand. If management only wouldn't be afraid to call in the union—at least for consultation.

Brooks (*m*): Well, Lloyd, we get along pretty well together; and you know management simply must keep its right to manage. We've got to be able to make the adjustments our schedules require. We'll be glad if you help us straighten this out.

PARSONS: (*u*):   It's a mess now; Rose is pretty convinced about the special group's rights in the matter. And with Agnes pulling on the other side—well, we just can't let ourselves in for a general "bumping" demand. I think you're right on that: to give those girls what they're asking might harm the whole department, and get into the union too. Well, the facts now are certainly clear, and we'll show these seniority lists to the girls.

Two days later, Mr. Parsons informed Mr. Brooks that he had been unable to persuade the special inspectors that their demand was unwarranted. Shortly thereafter, Bill MacIntyre came to see Mr. Brooks. He said things were getting "more tangled up" every day. Now the regular inspectors wanted "a showdown" to see just where they stood. Everybody was talking "seniority" to him. The two men agreed to arrange a conference at which spokesmen for each side would meet with Messrs. Brooks, Ashley, Parsons, and MacIntyre. When this conference convened three days later in Mr. Ashley's office, Rose Townley and Catherine Grey were present to speak for the "special" group; Agnes McKenna and Mary Hammond for the "regular" inspectors. The following discussion took place:

ASHLEY (*m*):   I'm glad we're all having this chance to talk this situation out. I'm sure we'll work things out together.

PARSONS (*u*):   Mr. Ashley, we're sure, too, that all of us here will be able to straighten this trouble out.

AGNES (*u*):   There'd never have been any trouble if some people's heads didn't get too big for their hats. I don't know why some people feel they're so much better than anybody else they have to work off by themselves.

ROSE (*u*):   Now, Agnes, let's not get personal. It's just a matter of our rights. I brought the union contract along and if you don't mind, I'd like to read the seniority clause so I can show you just how we girls look at it (*She reads from the contract.*):

1. Seniority is defined as the length of an employee's service in a department in respect to length of service with the company.
2. The purpose of seniority is to help establish, with ability, a jointly recognized policy of preference as to promotion, demotion, layoff, and rehiring.
3. In the event of such promotion, demotion, layoff, rehiring, the company and the union will take into consideration departmental seniority and ability, and when ability is relatively equal, seniority will prevail.
4. In the case of an employee-requested transfer, seniority shall be retained in the employee's regular department until six months'

service in the new department has elapsed, at which time accumulative service in the new department shall become effective and shall cancel seniority in the old department.

5. In the case of company-ordered transfers, seniority shall be effective as of hiring date.

6. An employee temporarily transferred to any department other than his regular department at the request of such other department shall continue to cumulate seniority in his regular department. When such employee is requested to return to his former regular department he may refuse such request without any penalty other than the loss of departmental seniority in his former regular department.

ROSE (*u*) (*looking up from the contract*): We girls feel we have very plain rights by these terms. We didn't ask to be transferred to the special room; the company transferred us. Now we were in the special room a little over six months. That means by Section 6 we can refuse to return to our regular department without any penalty except loss of seniority in that old department. But by Section 5 on a company transfer, we have seniority as of hiring date. So we have the right to demand that we be kept as a new department, with seniority in it as of our hiring dates. And that's all we ask.

BROOKS (*m*): Well I'm glad to get your ideas, Rose, and I will say you've built a plausible case. But those were not the terms of our bargain, were they? Didn't each of you agree that this was a temporary arrangement, and when the order was finished you'd return to your former places?

ROSE (*u*): Maybe we did, Mr. Brooks. But after all, none of us knew just how this thing would work out. And I'm sure the company wouldn't want us to give up our rights under the contract just because we didn't realize all that would be involved.

BROOKS (*m*): I don't think I quite understand. You still belonged to the inspection department, all the time.

ROSE (*u*): But that's just it, Mr. Brooks. We didn't. I mean maybe you'd call us only a subdivision of inspection, but we did become something new. We are not permanent on the regular runs; the company may have to send us back to the special room at any time.

CATHERINE GREY (*u*): We just feel as if we are a new department. That's why we want to stay together.

AGNES MCKENNA (*u*): Well, just a minute, if there's any new department formed, we have the right to bid for promotions under the seniority clause. I have fourteen years' seniority, and Mary here has eight.

MARY HAMMOND (*u*): That's what I say, too. I have more seniority than you, Rose, if there are any privileges. Agnes and I have always worked next to each other, and we could just move to the special line together.

PARSONS (*u*):   That's right, Rose. But it's not even quite like you say, Mary. Agnes has fourteen years all right, but there are girls with nine and ten years who have a right to bid before you, Mary.

ROSE (*u*):   But under Section 3, seniority prevails only if ability is equal. Now, we don't say we girls have more ability than any of the rest. But for these special assignments Mr. Brooks, and Mr. Ashley too, said the company needed girls who could be flexible. Flexibility then becomes a factor in ability under Section 3, and counts over seniority. And it's a company-ordered transfer, as defined in Sections 5 and 6.

BROOKS (*m*):   There's really no transfer. Transfers are from one department to another, but this concerns us all *in* inspection.

ROSE (*u*):   But it's a sort of new subdivision. You told us, Mr. Ashley, that we would make a group to whom special orders could be given. Well, we're going to have a regular inspection department and a special inspection department.

ASHLEY (*m*):   But we also explained, didn't we, that the program couldn't work unless you girls returned to your regular places? And if we transfer you, how could we refuse to transfer other girls for still other good reasons?

ROSE (*u*):   But we ask transfer for a good production reason. We're a special inspection group.

AGNES (*u*):   If you ask me, you're just a special bunch who got a notion you're better than the rest of us. You stick together all the time; I guess it's your dances and parties that are in your heads.

CATHERINE (*u*):   Agnes, you just are mean sometimes. What has dancing got to do with our work in inspection?

MARY (*u*):   Well, Agnes is right. You all look down on us who weren't able to go to high school like you.

ROSE (*u*):   Now, you're being silly, too, Mary. Why Anna Kowalski didn't go to high school, or Jean Holbrook, or Nancy Burke. Anyway, what has all this got to do with special inspection?

MACINTYRE (*u*):   Yes, let's stick to the issue.

AGNES (*u*):   Well, I have fourteen years' seniority, and no one is going to bump me, I can tell you. No one is going to push me around, whatever fine words you throw at us from the contract!

ROSE (*u*):   But the company defines what goes into ability in every situation, Agnes.

ASHLEY (*m*):   Exactly, Rose; and you agreed with us that the special work made no extra requirements.

ROSE (*u*):   But none of us knew how things would develop, Mr. Ashley. You said we did good work; you wanted flexibility; that was part of ability for this transfer. Anyway, it did turn out to be a real transfer; you will have to send us into the special inspection room when new orders come in. That's why we think it will work out for everybody's good if we're kept together on a special line.

PARSONS (*u*): Well, now that we have heard just how you girls cn both sides feel about it, maybe it would be a good idea for Mac and me to talk it over with management. (*The girls thereupon left.*)

BROOKS (*m*): Two stone walls for us, I guess.

PARSONS (*u*): Anything we do means trouble now. Rose worked up quite a case, didn't she?

BROOKS (*m*): She certainly did; there's a regular lawyer for the union, Lloyd. But she's just all haywire. I didn't want to argue it too much with her before Agnes and Mary, and put her in the wrong before them. There's friction enough already in the department, I'm afraid. I just can't understand how Rose can get things so twisted.

MACINTYRE (*u*): I don't blame Rose and the others if they don't like Agnes and her set. Agnes always tries to boss the younger girls. Maybe they are trying to get away from her tongue.

PARSONS (*u*): Maybe; but somehow I feel it's more than that. Agnes has a real case in this dispute. But where I part company with Mr. Ashley and you, Mr. Brooks, is that I think Rose has a real case now too. It sounds like my theme song, but I'm convinced you should have called the union in at the beginning. We would have urged you to give prime weight to seniority. And I can tell you right now, that we shall demand a stricter seniority clause in our next agreement.

BROOKS (*m*): Good Lord, you won't hamstring us more than we are already, will you? You know, I think if Mr. Ashley and I had a meeting just alone with the special inspectors, we might straighten things out. I didn't want to show up Rose's arguments before the others.

PARSONS (*u*): We showed her your seniority lists but that didn't budge her.

BROOKS (*m*): I'm afraid to let things go on this way. That department's fast getting demoralized. I think a meeting with the special girls might bring them around. I'd like to try it anyway.

PARSONS (*u*): Mr. Brooks, I really think this is union business now. Seniority is a strong union principle. Now that seniority has become the issue, it is we who have to straighten it out. We must make sure those girls all understand what's involved. And frankly we'll have to make sure the company gives the fullest possible weight to it.

ASHLEY (*m*): Well, Lloyd, the company has to insist likewise this is a production problem, not a seniority issue. If seniority safeguards job rights, our ability to bring in more orders safeguards jobs. I hope you'll see we're in this together. Well, let's all sleep on it tonight. Suppose you draw up a list of concrete, detailed suggestions on next steps—and we will too. Then we can come to a decision tomorrow.

7. WORK GROUP OWNERSHIP OF AN IMPROVED TOOL*

THE WHIRLWIND Aircraft Corporation was a leader in its field and especially noted for its development of the modern supercharger. Work in connection with the latter mechanism called for special skill and ability. Every detail of the supercharger had to be perfect to satisfy the exacting requirements of the aircraft industry.

In 1941 (before Pearl Harbor), Lathe Department 15–D was turning out three types of impeller, each contoured to within 0.002 inch and machined to a mirrorlike finish. The impellers were made from an aluminum alloy and finished on a cam-back lathe.

The work was carried on in four shifts, two men on each. The personnel in the finishing section were as follows:

1. *First Shift*—7 A.M. to 3 P.M.   Sunday and Monday off.
    a) Jean Latour, master mechanic, French Canadian, forty-five years of age. Latour had set up the job and trained the men who worked with him on the first shift.
    b) Pierre DuFresne, master mechanic, French Canadian, thirty-six years of age. Both these men had trained the workers needed for the other shifts.
2. *Second Shift*—3 P.M. to 11 P.M.   Friday and Saturday off.
    a) Albert Durand, master mechanic, French Canadian, thirty-two years of age; trained by Latour and using his lathe.
    b) Robert Benet, master mechanic, French Canadian, thirty-one years of age; trained by DuFresne and using his lathe.
3. *Third Shift*—11 P.M. to 7 A.M.   Tuesday and Wednesday off.
    a) Philippe Doret, master mechanic, French Canadian, thirty-one years of age; trained by Latour and using his lathe.
    b) Henri Barbet, master mechanic, French Canadian, thirty years of age; trained by DuFresne and using his lathe.
4. *Stagger Shift*—Monday, 7 A.M. to 3 P.M.; Tuesday, 11 P.M. to 7 A.M.; Wednesday, 11 P.M. to 7 A.M.; Thursday, off; Friday, 3 P.M. to 11 P.M.; Saturday, 3 P.M. to 11 P.M.; Sunday, off.

---

* The following case was reprinted with permission from *Personnel Administration: A Point of View and a Method,* by Paul Pigors and Charles A. Myers (New York: McGraw-Hill Book Co., Inc., 1956).

405

a) George MacNair, master mechanic, Scotch, thirty-two years of age; trained by Latour and using his lathe.

b) William Reader, master mechanic, English, thirty years of age; trained by DuFresne and using his lathe.

Owing to various factors (such as the small number of workers involved, the preponderance of one nationality, and the fact that Latour and DuFresne had trained the other workers) these eight men considered themselves as members of one work group. Such a feeling of solidarity is unusual among workers on different shifts, despite the fact that they use the same machines.

The men received a base rate of $1.03 an hour and worked on incentive. Each man usually turned out 22 units a shift, thus earning an average of $1.19 an hour. Management supplied Rex 95 High-Speed Tool-Bits, which workers ground to suit themselves. Two tools were used: one square bit with a slight radius for recess cutting, the other bit with a 45-degree angle for chamfering and smooth finish. When used, both tools were set close together, the worker adjusting the lathe from one operation to the other. The difficulty with this setup was that during the rotation of the lathe, the aluminum waste would melt and fuse between the two toolbits. Periodically the lathe had to be stopped so that the toolbits could be freed from the welded aluminum and reground.

At the request of the supervisor of Lathe Department 15–D, the methods department had been working on his tool problem. Up to the time of this case, no solution had been found. To make a firsthand study of the difficulty, the methods department had recently assigned one of their staff, Mr. MacBride, to investigate the problem in the lathe department itself. Mr. MacBride's working hours covered parts of both the first and second shifts. MacBride was a young man, twenty-six years of age, and a newcomer to the methods department. For the three months prior to this assignment, he had held the post of "suggestion man," a position which enabled newcomers to the methods department to familiarize themselves with the plant setup. The job consisted in collecting, from boxes in departments throughout the plant, suggestions submitted by employees and making a preliminary evaluation of these ideas. The current assignment of studying the tool situation in Lathe Department 15–D, with a view to cutting costs, was his first special task. He devoted himself to this problem with great zeal but did not succeed in winning the confidence of the workers. In pursuance of their usual philosophy: "Keep your mouth shut if you see anyone with a suit on," they volunteered no information and took the stand that, since the methods man had been given this assignment, it was up to him to carry it out.

While MacBride was working on this problem, Pierre DuFresne hit upon a solution. One day he successfully contrived a tool which combined the two bits into one. This eliminated the space between the two toolbits which in the past had caught the molten aluminum waste and allowed it to become welded to the cutting edges. The new toolbit had two advantages: it eliminated the frequent machine stoppage for cleaning and regrinding the old-type tools; and it enabled the operator to run the lathe at a higher speed. These advantages made it possible for the operator to increase his efficiency 50%.

DuFresne tried to make copies of the new tool, but was unable to do so. Apparently the new development had been a "lucky accident" during grinding which he could not duplicate. After several unsuccessful attempts, he took the new tool to his former teacher, Jean Latour. The latter succeeded in making a drawing and turning out duplicate toolbits on a small grinding wheel in the shop. At first the two men decided to keep the new tool to themselves. Later, however, they shared the improvement with their fellow workers on the second shift. Similarly it was passed on to the other shifts. But all these men kept the new development a closely guarded secret as far as "outsiders" were concerned. At the end of the shift, each locked the improved toolbit securely in his toolchest.

Both DuFresne, the originator of the new tool, and Latour, its draftsman and designer, decided not to submit the idea as a suggestion but to keep it as the property of their group. Why was this decision made? The answer lies partly in the suggestion system and partly in the attitude of Latour and DuFresne toward other features of company work life and toward their group.

According to an informational bulletin issued by the company, the purpose of the suggestion system was to "provide an orderly method of submitting and considering ideas and recommendations of employees to management; to provide a means for recognizing and rewarding individual ingenuity; and to promote cooperation." Awards for accepted suggestions were made in the following manner: "After checking the savings and expense involved in an adopted suggestion [the suggestion committee] determined the amount of the award to be paid, based upon the savings predicted upon a year's use of the suggestion." "It is the intention of the committee . . . to be liberal in the awards, which are expected to adequately compensate for the interest shown in presenting suggestions." In pursuance of this policy, it was customary to grant the suggestor an award equivalent to the savings of an entire month.

As a monetary return, both DuFresne and Latour considered an award based on one month's saving as inadequate. They also argued that such awards were really taken out of the worker's pockets. Their reasoning was as follows: All awards for adopted suggestions were paid out of undistributed profits. Since the company also had a profit-sharing plan, the money was taken from a fund that would be given to the workers anyway, which merely meant robbing Peter to pay Paul. In any case, the payment was not likely to be large and probably would be less than they could accumulate if increased incentive payments could be maintained over an extended period without discovery. Thus there was little in favor of submitting the new tool as a suggestion.

Latour and DuFresne also felt that there were definite hazards to the group if their secret were disclosed. They feared that once the tool became company property, its efficiency might lead to layoff of some members in their group, or at least make work less tolerable by leading to an increased quota at a lower price per unit. They also feared that there might be a change in scheduled work assignments. For instance, the lathe department worked on three different types of impeller. One type was a routine job and aside from the difficulty caused by the old-type tool, presented no problem. For certain technical reasons, the other two types were more difficult to make. Even Latour, an exceptionally skilled craftsman, had sometimes found it hard to make the expected quota before the new tool was developed. Unless the work-load was carefully balanced by scheduling easier and more difficult types, some of the operators were unable to make standard time.

The decision to keep the tool for their own group was in keeping with Latour's work philosophy. He had a strong feeling of loyalty to his own group and had demonstrated this in the past by offering for their use several improvements of his own. For example, he made available to all workers in his group a set of special gauge blocks which were used in aligning work on lathes. To protect himself in case mistakes were traced to these gauges, he wrote on them: "Personnel (*sic*) Property—Do not use. Jean Latour."

Through informal agreement with their fellow workers, Latour and DuFresne "pegged production" at an efficiency rate that in their opinion would not arouse management's suspicion or lead to a restudy of the job, with possible cutting of the rate. This enabled them to earn an extra 10% incentive earnings. The other 40% in additional efficiency was used as follows: The operators established a reputation for a high degree of accuracy and finish. They set a record for no spoilage and were able to apply the time gained on the easier type of impeller to work on the other types which required greater care and more expert workmanship.

The foreman of the lathe department learned about the new tool soon after it was put into use but was satisfied to let the men handle the situation in their own way. He reasoned that at little expense he was able to get out production of high quality. There was no defective work, and the men were contented.

Mr. MacBride was left in a very unsatisfactory position. He had not succeeded in working out a solution of his own. Like the foreman, he got wind of the fact that the men had devised a new tool. He urged them to submit a drawing of it through the suggestion system, but this advice was not taken, and the men made it plain that they did not care to discuss with him the reasons for this position.

Having no success in his direct contact with the workers, Mr. Mac-Bride appealed to the foreman, asking him to secure a copy of the new tool. The foreman replied that the men would certainly decline to give him a copy and would resent as an injustice any effort on his part to force them to submit a drawing. Instead he suggested that MacBride should persuade DuFresne to show him the tool. This MacBride attempted to do, but met with no success in his efforts to ingratiate himself with DuFresne. When he persisted in his attempts, DuFresne decided to throw him off the track. He left in his lathe a toolbit which was an unsuccessful copy of the original discovery. At shift change, MacBride was delighted to find what he supposed to be the improved tool. He hastily copied it and submitted a drawing to the tool department. When a tool was made up according to these specifications it naturally failed to do what was expected of it. The workers, when they heard of this through the "grapevine," were delighted. DuFresne did not hesitate to crow over MacBride, pointing out that his underhanded methods had met with their just reward.

The foreman did not take any official notice of the conflict between DuFresne and MacBride. Then MacBride complained to the foreman that DuFresne was openly boasting of his trick and ridiculing him before other workers. Thereupon, the foreman talked to DuFresne, but the latter insisted that his ruse had been justified as a means of self-protection.

When he was rebuffed by DuFresne, the foreman felt that he had lost control of the situation. He could no longer conceal from himself that he was confronted by a more complex situation than what initially he had defined as a "tool problem." His attention was drawn to the fact that the state of affairs in his department was a tangle of several interrelated problems. Each problem urgently called for decision that involved understanding and practical judgment. But having for so long failed to see the situation as a whole, he now found himself in a dilemma.

He wished to keep the good will of the work group, but he could not countenance the continued friction between DuFresne and MacBride. Certainly, he could not openly abet his operators in obstructing the work of a methods man. His superintendent would now certainly hear of it and would be displeased to learn that a foreman had failed to tell him of such an important technical improvement. Furthermore he knew that the aircraft industry was expanding at this time and that the demand for impellers had increased to such an extent that management was planning to set up an entire new plant unit devoted to this product.

8. THE CROWN FASTENER COMPANY

DURING THE summer between his junior and senior years at Dartmouth College, Edgar Hagan took a job as a student trainee with the Crown Fastener Company, a medium-sized manufacturer and distributor of nuts and bolts. The training program Hagan was placed in consisted of four weeks in the company warehouse, four weeks in the company factory, and two weeks in the company offices. There were five students in the program, all of whom had the understanding that they would receive jobs as salesmen with the company after two summers in the program.

On the first day of work, all five of the trainees met in the office of John Cusick, the superintendent of the warehouse. Cusick was a man in his middle thirties, a former decorated Navy veteran, and a graduate of Dartmouth College. After outlining the work program for the next four weeks and assigning each of the trainees to a specific department for the first two weeks, he offered this advice to them: "Fellows, I would be very careful in my relationships with the employees here if I were you. The majority of the people here are a pretty crude bunch. Their work is pretty much physical and routine in nature; as a result, we can afford to hire men of generally low intelligence. They're all either Italians, Poles, or Negroes from the slums, and they're tough customers. So watch out for your valuables, and don't start any trouble with them."

For the first two weeks, Hagan was assigned to the sixth floor, in the hexagon nut department, under the supervision of Guido Bovanni, a man who had been with the company since its inception twenty-two years before. Bovanni, a short but extremely powerful man, spoke in broken English and had quite a difficult time reading any material with which he was not previously familiar. When Cusick introduced Hagan to Bovanni, he said: "Guido, this is Edgar Hagan, a college trainee who'll be with us for the summer. I've decided to have him work here for the first two weeks, and I'd like you to teach him all you know about nuts. Give him all the odd jobs you have so he'll get experience with as many different types of nuts as possible. Well, good luck, Hagan. We'll get together again soon."

After Cusick had left, Bovanni said to Hagan: "A college boy, eh! I'll learn you about nuts, but I'll do it my way. Cusick thinks I can learn you in two weeks what I've learned in twenty years. Christ! Don't pay no attention to him. We'll start you helping the packers so you can work with the nuts we ship most of. You'll be lucky if you can learn them in two weeks. Then each day, I'll try to learn you a few of the nuts we don't see very often."

Hagan was amazed that each of the nine employees in the hexagon nut department quickly told him almost the same thing as soon as he was alone with them. Typical of these comments was this statement by Ted Grant, an elderly Negro packer: "If I were you, I'd stay on the good side of Guido. He's one hell of a good foreman and really knows his stuff. He can teach you more about nuts and bolts than any guy in this place. Work hard for him, and you'll get along swell here."

Hagan did his best to follow this advice and soon found that Bovanni was spending more and more time with him. He was very surprised when, on Friday, Bovanni said: "Grab your lunch, and let's go eat across the street." Bovanni regularly ate his lunch in a little bar across from the warehouse with a group of about seven other foremen. The conversation ranged from families to sports but soon settled on Cusick. Hagan was amazed at this because he, a newcomer, was there, and interpreted this to mean that Bovanni must have spoken to the men, saying that he was O.K. It was quickly obvious that Bovanni was the leader among this group; and when he summed up the conversation in the following manner, everyone seemed in complete agreement with him: "Cusick tries hard. He's tried to improve things here, but he hasn't had the experience. He must be able to handle Charley Crown,[1] though; look at the money he's got us for new equipment. But Christ, then he screws up and buys the wrong stuff. He just don't know what to do and won't listen when we tell him."

On Friday of Hagan's first week, Cusick issued a bulletin stating that all forms used in the routing of materials in the warehouse would be changed to a slightly more complicated type on which material locations could be designated more precisely. The bulletin was handed out to all warehouse employees with their pay envelopes at the close of work Friday. Included was a group of the new forms. The bulletin simply stated that the change was to be made and requested that each man familiarize himself with the new forms over the week end so that he could use them correctly on Monday. The men just took the material

---

[1] The president of the Crown Fastener Company.

and stuffed it into their pockets in their haste to catch their streetcars home.

On Monday morning, everyone in the hexagon nut department quickly went to work distributing the backlog of materials that had been delivered on Saturday, making a note of each shipment's ultimate location. As was the practice in this department, all of the department personnel met at Bovanni's desk at 10:30 A.M. to give this information to Bovanni so that he could copy it onto the formal forms which went to the office for inventory control. Bovanni claimed he used this procedure so that all the forms would be uniformly filled out and not mutilated by the men carrying them around as they worked. It was quite obvious, however, that his main purpose for insisting on this procedure was that he wanted to know where every shipment on his floor was located, so that when orders came through from the office, he could tell the men exactly where the material ordered was located, from memory. Hagan was constantly amazed by Bovanni's ability to remember exactly where, within each tier and row, a certain shipment was located. This ability had been built up over a period of years, and Bovanni was obviously quite proud of it.

At the Monday morning meeting, there was a considerable difference of opinion among the various department personnel as to how the locations should be entered on the new forms. Bovanni insisted that it should be done in the same manner as before, where the aisle and tier of each shipment were recorded, while most of the other men protested that additional information as to the exact location within each aisle and tier should be noted. Bovanni argued that this would provide unnecessary detail and would only confuse things. He was quite adamant about this, and the other men quickly acceded to his point of view.

The next morning, Cusick came up to the sixth floor and walked directly to Bovanni's desk. He said in quite a loud voice: "Guido, you're filling out the forms all wrong. Didn't you read the notice? You're still doing it the old way, and that's just what we're trying to get away from. Do you think we would go to all this trouble only to have things done in the same old way? Now you've really got the office all fouled up. We need new forms on all the materials you received yesterday. You'd better get at it right away so they can make orders out on some of that material."

Guido was sitting at his desk, looking up a catalogue number, while Cusick was talking to him. He was obviously getting madder and madder as Cusick spoke. Finally, he broke in.

GUIDO BOVANNI: Look, Mr. Cusick, this department never had no trouble with its locations before. We've been getting along fine. Why do you have to foul us by making us change everything? I've been running this department for one hell of a long time, and I guess to Christ I know as much about it as you do. Why don't you handle the top brass and let me handle my department? As long as I get the work done, what do you care how I do it? When those orders come through, I'll be able to find those kegs just like I always have.

JOHN CUSICK: That's the trouble with you, Guido; you only think of yourself. I've made this change in the entire warehouse. You're the only one bitching about it. From now on, the office wants a complete record of exactly where everything is. Now, dammit, as long as I'm running this warehouse, we're going to do it my way!

BOVANNI (*getting madder all the time*):   Listen, Cusick, you may run this warehouse, but I run this floor. Nobody really needs to know those locations except me, and you know it. The way we're doing things here works fine, and you know it. Why pick on me? Why don't you go climb on some of the other boys that don't get their work done? Why come nosing around here telling me how to do my job?

9. CLAREMONT INSTRUMENT COMPANY

ONE OF THE PROBLEMS facing the supervisory staff of the Claremont Instrument Company in the summer of 1948 was that of "horseplay" among employees in the glass department. For some time this question had troubled the management of the company. Efforts had been made to discourage employees from throwing water-soaked waste at each other and from engaging in water fights with buckets or fire hoses. Efforts to tighten up shop discipline had also resulted in orders to cut down on "visiting" with other employees. These efforts were made on the grounds that whatever took an employee away from his regular job would interfere with production or might cause injury to the employees or the plant machinery.

Production was a matter of some concern to the officials of the company, particularly since the war. In spite of a large backlog of unfilled orders, there were indications that domestic and foreign competition in the relatively near future might begin to cut into the company's business. Anything which could help to increase the salable output of the company was welcomed by the officers; at the same time, anything which might cut down overhead operating expenses, or improve the quality of the product, or cut down on manufacturing wastage was equally encouraged.

The Claremont Instrument Company had been located for many years in a community in western Massachusetts with a population of approximately 18,000. The company employed approximately 500 people. None of these people were organized in a union for collective bargaining purposes. The company produced a varied line of laboratory equipment and supplies. Many of its products were fabricated principally from glass, and over the years the company had built up a reputation for producing products of the highest quality. To a considerable extent this reputation for quality rested upon the company's ability to produce very delicate glass components to exacting quality standard. These glass components were produced from molten glass in the glass department. Exhibit 1 presents a partial organization chart of the company.

The entire glass department was located in one wing of the company's main factory. In this department the glass components such as tubes, bottles, decanters, and glass-measuring devices were made from molten

415

glass. Some of these glass parts were produced by hand-blowing operations, but most of them were produced on bottle-making machinery which in effect blew the molten glass into a mold. This operation of blowing the glass by hand or by machine was the most critical operation in the department and required a high degree of skill. Immediately following the blowing operation some of the parts were "punched." The

Exhibit 1

CLAREMONT INSTRUMENT COMPANY
PARTIAL ORGANIZATION CHART

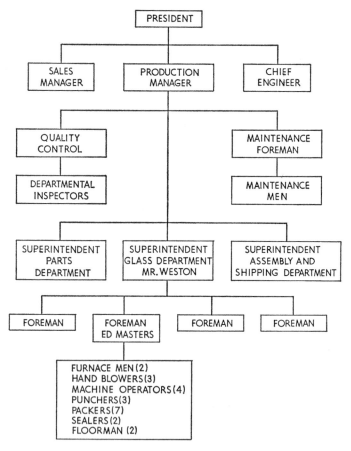

"puncher" was a mechanical apparatus into which the glass components were placed; as the machine revolved, a small gas flame melted the glass in a small area and blew a hole in the glass component. Next the parts were placed on a mechanical conveyor where they were annealed by an air-cooling process. Then the parts were picked off the conveyor by women known as packers whose duty was to inspect them for defects of many kinds and to give them temporary packaging in cardboard cartons for transit to other parts of the factory. The final operation in the department was performed by sealers whose job it was to seal these cardboard cartons and place them in stacks for temporary storage. Exhibit 2 is a floor plan of the glass department.

Exhibit 2

CLAREMONT INSTRUMENT COMPANY
FLOOR PLAN OF GLASS DEPARTMENT

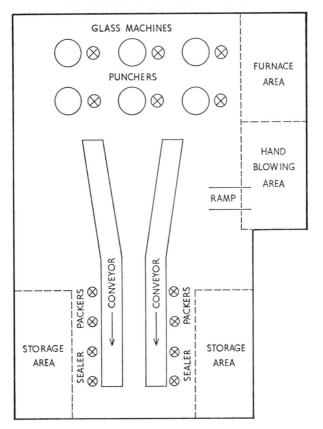

The glass department was operated on a continuous, twenty-four-hour, seven-day-a-week basis, because of the necessity of keeping the tanks of molten glass hot and operating all the time. Four complete shifts worked in the department. The different shifts rotated as to the hours of the day they worked. Roughly each shift spent two weeks at a time on the day shift, on the evening shift, and on the night shift. Each shift worked on the average five days a week, but their days off came at varying times throughout the week. The glass department was located in a separate wing of the plant and the employees of the department used a special entrance and a special time clock.

Each of the four shifts employed about twenty-three people. Each shift had its own foreman and assistant foreman and hourly workers as indicated in Exhibit 1. All these workers were men with the exception of the packers. The foreman was a full-time supervisor but the assistant foreman usually operated a glass machine and only substituted for the foreman in his absence. The furnace men prepared the molten glass for the glass blowers while the floormen cleaned up broken glass and other waste and filled in on odd jobs.

An inspector from the quality-control department and a maintenance man from the maintenance department were assigned on a full-time basis to each of the four shifts. The inspector worked with the packers and was responsible for the quality of all glass components. The maintenance man was responsible for the maintenance and satisfactory operation of all machinery in the department.

Several physical conditions made work in the glass department unique in the plant. The fact that the glass furnaces were located in this department meant that the department was always unusually hot. The glass-blowing machines were run principally by compressed air, and each movement of a machine part was accompanied by the hiss of escaping air. This noise combined with the occasional sound of breaking glass made it impossible for the members of the department to converse in a normal tone. An oil vapor was used to coat the inside of the molds on the glass machines, and when the hot glass poured into the mold, a smoke was given off that circulated throughout the department.

In the summer of 1948, Ralph Boynton, a student at the Harvard Business School, took a summer job as one of the floormen on one of the shifts working in the glass department. While on this job, he made the above observations about the Claremont Instrument Company in general and the glass department in particular. In the course of the summer, Ralph became particularly interested in the practice of engaging in horseplay, and the description that follows was based on his observations.

The foreman of Boynton's shift, Ed Masters, had worked a number of years in the glass department and had been promoted to foreman from the position of operator of one of the glass machines. In Ralph's opinion the foreman was generally liked by the shift employees. One of them commented to Ralph, "If everything is going okay, you don't see Ed around. If anything goes wrong, he's right there to try and fix it up."

Another one of them commented, "He pitches right in—gives us a hand—but he never says much." Frequently when a glass machine was producing glass components of unacceptable quality, Ralph noticed the foreman and the maintenance man working with a machine operator to get the machine in proper adjustment. On one occasion Ralph was assigned the job of substituting for one of the sealers. Shortly after Ralph had started his work Ed Masters came around and asked how he was doing. Ralph replied that he was doing fine and that it was quite a trick to toss the cartons into the proper positions on the stack. Ed replied, "You keep at it, and it won't be long before you get the hang of it. You'll be tired for a while, but you'll get used to it. I found I could do it and I am a 'ninety-seven-pound weakling.' "

Ralph also picked up a variety of comments from the employees about one another. The shift maintenance man, Bert, referred to the men on the shift as "a good bunch of guys." One of the packers referred with pride to one of the machine operators, "that guy can get out more good bottles than anybody else." On one occasion, when the glass components were coming off the end of the conveyor at a very slow rate, one of the packers went around to the glass machines to find out what the trouble was. When she came back she reported to the rest of the packers, "Ollie is having trouble with his machine. It's out of adjustment but he will get it fixed in a few minutes." Ralph noticed that a record was kept of the total daily output of each shift of packers. These women seemed anxious to reach a certain minimum output on each shift. When the components were coming through slowly, he heard such comments as, "This is a bad night." If the work had been coming slowly, the packers regularly started "robbing the conveyor" toward the end of the shift. This was the practice of reaching up along the conveyor and picking off components for packaging before they reached the packer's usual work position.

A short time after Ralph started to work, the company employed another new floorman for the shift. This new man quickly picked up the nickname of "Windy." The following were some of Windy's typical comments: "My objective is the paycheck and quitting time." "I love work so much I could lay down and go to sleep right beside it." "These guys are all dopes. If we had a union in here, we would get more money." "I hate this night work. I am quitting as soon as I get another job." Most of the other employees paid little attention to Windy. One of the sealers commented about him, "If bull were snow, Windy would be a blizzard." One night Windy commented to three of the men, "This is a lousy place. They wouldn't get away with this stuff if we had a union. Why don't the four of us start one right here?" None of the group replied to this comment.

Ralph had a number of opportunities to witness the horseplay that concerned the management. At least one horseplay episode seemed to occur on every eight-hour shift. For example, one night while Ralph stood watching Ollie, one of the machine operators, at his work, Ollie called Ralph's attention to the fact that Sam, the operator of the adjacent machine, was about to get soaked.

"Watch him now," Ollie said with a grin, "last night he got Bert and now Bert is laying for him. You watch now." Ralph caught sight of Bert warily circling behind the machines with an oil can in his hand. Sam had been sitting and quietly watching the bottles come off his machine. Suddenly Bert sprang out and fired six or seven shots of water at Sam. When the water hit him, Sam immediately jumped up and fired a ball of wet waste which he had concealed for this occasion. He threw it at Bert and hit him in the chest with it. It left a large wet patch on his shirt. Bert stood his ground squirting his can until Sam started to chase him. Then he ran off. Sam wiped his face and sat down again. Then he got up and came over to Ollie and Ralph. Sam shouted, "By Jesus, I am going to give him a good soaking." Ollie and Ralph nodded in agreement. Later Ollie commented to Ralph, "It may take as long as three hours for Sam to work up a good plan to get even, but Bert is going to get it good."

Sam was ready to get back at Bert as soon as he could be lured close enough to the machine. Sam pretended to watch his machine but kept his eye out for Bert. In a little while Bert walked jauntily by Sam's machine. They grinned at each other and shouted insults and challenges. Bert went over to a bench to fix something and Sam slipped around behind his machine, pulled down the fire hose and let Bert have a full blast chasing him up along the conveyor as Bert retreated. Sam then turned off the hose, reeled it back up and went back to his machine.

All the other employees on the scene had stopped to watch this episode and seemed to enjoy it. They commented that it was a good soaking. Bert came back to the machines after a while, grinning, and hurling insults while he stood by Sam's machine to dry off from the heat of the machine. The other operators kidded him some, and then everyone went back to work seriously.

A little later the foreman came through the department and noticed the large puddle of water on the floor. He instructed Bert to put some sawdust on the puddle to soak up the water. Ralph was told later that Ed Masters had told Bert, "I want more work and less of this horsing around." A few minutes later Ed Masters and Bert were discussing a small repair job that had to be done that evening.

On another occasion Ralph asked Ollie what he thought of the horseplay. Ollie commented, "It's something each guy has to make up his own mind about. Personally, I don't go in for it. I have got all the raises and merit increases that have come along, and I know Bert hasn't had a raise in over a year. Whenever something starts, I always look back at my machine so that I can be sure that nothing goes wrong while I am looking away. Personally, I just don't care—you have to have some fun, but personally, I don't go in for it."

Just at this point Al, one of the punchers, came down from the men's lavatory ready to take his turn on one of the punch machines. He was a moment or two early and stood talking to Sam. Ollie got up from where he had been talking to Ralph and started to holler, "Hey, Al—hey, Al." The other operators took up the chant, and all of them picked up pieces of wood or pipe and started drumming on the waste barrels near their machines. Al took up a long piece of pipe and joined in. After a minute or two, one of the operators stopped, and the drumming ended quickly. Al lit a cigarette and stepped up to take the machine for his turn.

Ralph later had an opportunity to ask Bert what he thought of the horseplay. Bert said, "You have to have some horseplay or you get rusty. You have to keep your hand in." Ralph noted that Bert's work kept him busy less than anyone else, since his duties were primarily to act as an emergency repairman and maintenance man. Ralph asked, "Why doesn't Ollie get into the horseplay?" Bert replied, "Ollie can't take it. He likes to get other people, but he can't take it when he gets it. You have got to be fair about this. If you get some guy, you are surer than hell you will get it back yourself. Now you take Sam and me. We've been playing like that for a long time. He don't lose his temper, and I don't lose mine. I knew I was going to get that hose the other night; that was why I was baiting him with a squirt gun." Ralph asked, "Does Ed Masters mind it very much?" Bert answered, "Hell, he's just like the rest of us. He knows you've got to have some of that stuff, only he gets bawled out by the superintendent if they see anything going on like that. That's why we don't play around much on the day shift. But on the night shift, that's when we have fun. The only reason we don't squirt the foreman is because he's the foreman. As far as we're concerned, he is no different from us. Besides he ain't my boss anyway. I'm maintenance. I don't care what he says."

About the middle of the summer, the superintendent of the glass department returned from his vacation and immediately thereafter an effort was made by him through the foremen to "tighten up" on shop discipline. The men on the machines and the punchers were forbidden to walk up to the other end of the conveyor to talk to the packers and sealers and vice versa. The foreman started making occasional comments like "keep moving" when he saw a small group together in conversation. On one occasion a small group stood watching some activity outside the plant. Ed came by and quite curtly said, "Break it up." Everyone seemed quite shocked at how abrupt he was.

About this same time, the word was passed around among the employees that a big push was on to step up the output of a certain product in order to make a tight delivery schedule. Everyone seemed to be putting a little extra effort into getting this job done. Ralph thought he noticed that the foreman was getting more and more "jumpy" at this time. On one occasion Ed commented to some of the employees, "I am bitter today." One of the machine operators asked him what the trouble was, and Ed made some comment about a foremen's meeting where the superintendent was telling them that the playing around and visiting would have to stop.

One night a short time later, Ralph saw that preparations were being made for an unusually elaborate trap for soaking Jim, one of the sealers who had recently begun to take part in the water fights. A full bucket of water was tied to the ceiling with a trip rope at the bottom in such a way that the entire contents would be emptied on Jim when he least suspected it. Many of the employees made a point of being on hand when the trap was sprung. It worked perfectly, and Jim was given a complete soaking. Ralph thought Jim took it in good spirit since he turned quickly to counterattack the people who had soaked him. Shortly after all the crew had gone back to work, Ruth, one of the packers, was coming down the ramp from the area where the hand-blowing operations were performed. She was carrying some of the glass components. Ruth slipped on some of the water that had been spilled during the recent fight and fell down. She was slightly burned by some of the hot glass she was carrying. Those who saw this happen rushed to her help. The burn, while not serious, required first-aid attention and the assistant foreman went with Ruth to the company dispensary for treatment. Ralph thought that the employees all felt rather sheepish about the accident. Ruth was one of the more popular girls in the department. The word went around among the employees that a report on the nature and cause of the accident would have to be made out and sent to higher management. Everyone was wondering what would happen.

Concepts and Research Findings

1. PRODUCTIVITY AND LEADERSHIP IN AN INSURANCE COMPANY

In the late 1940's a systematic study was made of female clerical groups in the Prudential Life Insurance Company.[1] The study was made of work groups that had high and low productivity records to learn what relation these differences had to various supervisory practices and attitudes. Both the employees and their supervisors were interviewed, and their responses were scored on a number of factors. The findings shown in Exhibit 1 were especially provocative.

Exhibit 1

Practices and Attitudes	Heads of High Productivity Sections	Heads of Low Productivity Sections
Close supervision.....................	6	11
General supervision..................	5	1
Not ascertained......................	1	0
Production centered...................	1	7
Employee centered....................	6	3
Not ascertained......................	5	2
Identified primarily with company......	2	8
Identified primarily with employees.....	9	4
Not ascertained......................	1	0

The researchers concluded, among other things, that:

The supervisors of the high-producing sections seem to think and act differently with respect to their supervisory functions than do the supervisors of the low-producing sections. They regard supervision as the most important part of their work and spend most of their time on it. Their

---

[1] Daniel Katz, N. Maccoby, and N. C. Morse, *Productivity, Supervision, and Morale in an Office Situation* (Ann Arbor: Institute for Social Research, University of Michigan, 1950), Part I.

methods of supervision appears to be one of setting up certain general conditions for their employees and then permitting their employees to work out the details of when and how the work will be handled. They do not seem to feel the need to get into the production process at every point to check on how things are going, to make changes, to reassign the work and, in other ways, to keep a close check on operations. Their attitudes toward the employees are consistent with this approach. They appear to look at the employees as people not essentially different from themselves, people capable of taking some responsibility, people with many different interests and needs.[2]

---

[2] *Ibid.,* p. 35.

2. SOME EFFECTS OF CLOSE AND PUNITIVE STYLES OF SUPERVISION

THE AUTHORS[1] conducted this study as a result of their review of previous studies in which widely varying degrees of relationship had been found between a close style of supervision and aggressive responses on the part of subordinates. The researchers hypothesized that since close supervision would seem to imply a deprecation of the subordinate's worth, certain subordinates, those with low self-esteem, would be more aroused by such an implication than those with high self-esteem. They expected that the arousal would take the form of aggressive feelings and action.

The researchers chose to compare subordinate response to three types of supervision. The first, general supervision, was defined as that in which the superior specified and checked up on subordinate behavior only enough to let subordinates know what they were supposed to do. The second, close supervision, structured worker behavior completely, both in preliminary specification and in follow-up. The third type of supervision, punitive, differed from the second in that it included intentional punishment as a method of gaining subordinate compliance. While the second type of supervision was expected to be frustrating, it was not to include the aggressive type of supervision behavior characteristic of the third type.

Four types of response were predicted to result more frequently with close and punitive supervisory styles than with the general style of supervision:

1. Verbal aggression toward the supervisor.
2. Low productivity (assumed to be a form of indirect aggression toward the supervisor).
3. Verbal aggression toward co-workers (assumed to be aggression toward the supervisor but displaced on peers).
4. Dissatisfaction with the work situation.

Separate predictions for close and punitive supervisory styles were not made because, it was postulated, both styles would be painful to subordinates, regardless of intention. Apparently, however, it was sus-

---

[1] Robert C. Day and Robert L. Hamblin, *American Journal of Sociology*, Vol. LXIX, No. 5 (March, 1964).

pected that the particular form of aggression resulting from the two styles might differ.

Data on self-esteem were gathered from subjects by responses to a ten-statement questionnaire dealing with feelings of confidence and inferiority. The subjects, ninety-six female college undergraduates divided into groups of four, performed identical assembly line tasks but under the three different styles of supervision. The responses to supervisory style were collected by observation and questionnaire.

Results

Close and punitive supervision produced the following response, as compared with responses from general supervision.

	Close	*Punitive*
More aggressive feelings toward supervisor	Yes	Yes
More aggressive feelings toward co-workers	Yes*	No
Greater dissatisfaction with task	No	No
More verbal aggression toward supervisor	No	Yes
More verbal aggression toward co-workers	No	No
More verbal dissatisfaction about task	No	No
Lower productivity	Yes†	Yes†

* Near significant.
† Close supervision reduced productivity by 25% and punitive by 23%, as compared to productivity under general supervision.

Discussing these results, the authors point out that under either style of supervision (frustrating or aggressing) feelings of aggression result. An indirect avenue of expression, reduced productivity, was used to express this aggression in both cases. Punitive supervision, however, apparently invited direct expression of aggression against the supervisor, while close supervision, whose hostility was not overt, restricted aggression to displacement on co-workers.

When self-esteem data were taken into account, it was found that those with low self-esteem were considerably more aggressive in their feelings toward the close supervisor than were those with high self-esteem. However, no such relationship obtained with respect to productivity, i.e., high and low self-esteem subordinates restricted productivity approximately equally. In the case of punitive supervision, self-esteem made no significant difference in subordinate responses either in terms of aggressive feelings or productivity. The authors did not attempt to explain their self-esteem findings.

3. CONDITIONS INFLUENCING THE EFFECT OF LEADERSHIP STYLES ON GROUP PERFORMANCE

FIEDLER has assembled and analyzed data from a number of sources in such a way as to relate leadership style to three measures of conditions favorable or unfavorable to the leader as a means of assessing the performance of work groups.[1] The measure of leadership style adopted is one which discriminates between supervisors who are perceived as permissive, considerate, fostering good interpersonal relations among group members (subsequently referred to here as Permissive) and supervisors who tend to be directive, controlling, more oriented toward task than toward people (subsequently referred to as Directive).

The various work situations were then measured by data classified under the following headings:

1. Affective leader-member relations (the leader is liked and accepted versus disliked and mistrusted).
2. Degree of task structure (highly structured and unambiguously prescribed tasks versus not prescribed, not clear or, not subject to single approaches or solutions).
3. Leadership-position power at his disposal (authority granted and supported by the organization either formally or informally versus rewards and sanctions usually not at his disposal).

Below are summarized the principal findings about the relationship among these variables to leadership style for a large number of task groups, such as bomber crews, tank crews, open hearth crews, management groups, service station managers, high school basketball teams, and the like. The data show a strong correlation between good task performance and a *Directive* style of leadership under conditions 1, 2, 3, and 8, and a strong correlation between good task performance and a *Permissive* style under conditions 4 and 5. Note that the list is ordered from the "most favorable conditions for the leader" to the "least favorable."

Perhaps the most striking indication of these findings is that for a

---

[1] Fred E. Fiedler, *A Contingency Model for the Prediction of Leadership Effectiveness* (Urbana, Illinois: Group Effectiveness Research Laboratory, Department of Psychology, University of Illinois, 1963).

number of fairly common situations a directive, controlling leader is likely to bring the work group to better results.

A part of Fiedler's explanation for these findings follows[2]

> In the very favorable conditions, where the leader has power, informal backing, and a structured task, the group is, as it were, ready to be directed on how to go about its task. Under the very unfavorable conditions the

Condition	Group Situation			Leadership Style Correlating with Productivity under Condition on Left
	Leader-Member Relations	Task Structure	Position Power	
1................Good		Structured	Strong	Directive
2................Good		Structured	Weak	Directive
3................Good		Unstructured	Strong	Directive
4................Good		Unstructured	Weak	Permissive
5................Mod. Poor		Structured	Strong	Permissive
6................Mod. Poor		Structured	Weak	No data
7................Mod. Poor		Unstructured	Strong	No relationship indicated
8................Mod. Poor		Unstructured	Weak	Directive

group is likely to fall apart, unless the leader's active intervention and control can keep the members focussed on the task. Under moderately favorable conditions, however, where the accepted leader faces an ambiguous task, a nondirective, permissive attitude may enable the group to participate more effectively, and to contribute a larger number of ideas which might lead to a good solution. A controlling leader may here be less effective because he may become too impatient, and he may inhibit original or off-beat suggestions. Where the sociometrically not too well accepted leader faces a structured task, the permissive, nondirective attitude might result in better performance since the members would not feel threatened by the leader, and since considerate leader behavior under these conditions is likely to mollify the members and induce them to cooperate.

It should again be pointed out that this classification system is designed primarily for the purpose of classifying the favorableness of the task-situation for the leader. While the classification treats the three dimensions as contributing equally to "favorableness," this is almost certainly an oversimplification. Thus, a leader might be so thoroughly resented that he could not operate effectively even under conditions in which the task is highly structured and his position enjoys high power. Similarly, a task may be so completely structured that any permissiveness on the part of the leader would be detrimental to performance. The present classification is a

---
[2] *Ibid.*, p. 14.

first approach which seems to apply to groups under a reasonably "normal range" of conditions.

In commenting on the implications of these findings, Fiedler says:[3]

The model indicates various strategies a leader might adopt in order to improve the effectiveness of his group. For example, a controlling, managing, and directive leader who is given a relatively unstructured task might first need to structure the task and to clarify the group's problem, to move his group from Condition 4 to Condition 1. Similarly, a [Directive] leader, whose group falls into Condition 8 (poor relations with group, weak leader position, and unstructured task) should concentrate on improving his interpersonal relations with his group members, thus moving his group into Condition 4 in which his leadership style would be conducive to good performance.

A different approach might apply for tasks which change their structure over time. It might here be possible to train a leader to modify his attitudes and behavior as the task progresses, or to utilize one type of leader during the unstructured planning and exploratory phases, and to substitute a different leader when the group task requires control and direction during its highly structured phases. Such a progression in task structure is, of course, quite common in research projects which tend to be ambiguous and unstructured during the planning phase and highly structured during the data gathering and data analysis phases. It is also well known (and consistent with the present model) that some business executives excel in organizing a company while others operate more effectively in the routine management phases.

---

[3] *Ibid.*, p. 18.

4. FIRST-LINE SUPERVISORS, UPWARD INFLUENCE, AND WORK GROUP SATISFACTION

THE STUDY reported here was begun in 1948 and published in 1952.[1] The researcher, D. C. Pelz, reported on relationships between a supervisor's influence with *his* superiors and the satisfaction of his subordinates. The research was conducted at the Detroit Edison Company. Some eight thousand nonsupervisory employees filled in a paper-and-pencil questionnaire. All supervisory and managerial personnel were interviewed.

The researchers tried, first of all, to relate supervisory behavior to employee satisfaction. No relationship was found, i.e., both high- and low-satisfaction groups had supervisors whose behavior was similar.

When each supervisor's perceived influence with superior was considered, though, the picture changed. Each first-line supervisor received an influence score based upon (1) his perceived influence with superior, (2) his freedom from supervisory control, and (3) his salary. These scores were related to two different measures of perceived supervisory behavior: (1) the degree to which the supervisor "takes sides with employees or management" and (2) the degree of his "social closeness" to employees.

The data showed that under "high upward influence" supervisors, a "siding with employees" was accompanied by a general rise in employee satisfaction. This was true for both "blue-collar" and "white-collar" work groups. Under "low upward influence" supervisors, the same behavior produced a slight drop in employee satisfaction. The findings were similar regarding influence and social closeness.

Apparently, a supervisor who sided with his employees or was socially close to them tended to supervise a highly satisfied group only if the supervisor had enough upward influence to make these behaviors pay off in terms of benefits for his employees.

[1] D. C. Pelz, "Influence: Key to Effective Leadership in the First Line Supervisor," *Personnel*, Vol. XXIX (1952), pp. 209–17.

5. SUPERVISORY IDENTIFICATION
WITH MANAGEMENT AND/OR WORKERS

A RESEARCH study in the Detroit Edison Company examined the independent evaluations of supervisors by superiors and subordinates. The study was done by members of the Institute for Social Research of the University of Michigan.[1] Data were gathered through written appraisals and employee interviews in the company's accounting department. Altogether, seventy-two supervisors were evaluated, each by four superiors. Six hundred and eighty-five subordinates (primarily "white collar") provided subordinate evaluations. While the explicit criteria used by superiors emphasized technical competence, the actual appraisal discussions and "write-ups" also stressed the supervisor's success in dealing with people. These management appraisals graded supervisors along a scale ranging from "immediately promotable" to "unsatisfactory."

Employee evaluations were derived from (1) employee expressions of feeling toward their supervisors and (2) employee descriptions of their supervisors' behavior.

Exhibit 1

RELATIONSHIP OF MANAGEMENT APPRAISAL RATING OF
SUPERVISORS TO EMPLOYEES' EVALUATION OF THE
SUPERVISORS' ABILITY WITH PEOPLE*

	Percentage of Employees Rating Supervisors as:				
Management Appraisal Rating	Excellent or Good	Average, or Poor	Percentage Not Answering	Number of Employees	Number of Supervisors
Immediately promotable (P+)..	71%	29%	...	28	5
Promotable (P).........	47 } 53%	53	...	49	5
Satisfactory plus (S+).....	55	44	1%	161	19
Satisfactory (S)..........	45	53	2	334	30
Questionable (Q).........	28 } 27%	72	...	92	10
Unsatisfactory (U)........	24	76	...	21	3
				685	72

* The relationships are statistically significant at the 5 per cent level or above.

[1] Floyd C. Mann and James K. Dent, "The Supervisor: Member of Two Organizational Families," *Harvard Business Review.* November–December, 1954, pp. 103–12.

Results from the study showed that superiors and subordinates were in closest agreement on the supervisors with the highest and lowest management appraisal ratings (see Exhibit 1). The majority of the subordinates of a supervisor rated high by his superiors said that:

1. They felt free to discuss important things about their job with him.[2]
2. They felt free to discuss personal problems with him.[2]
3. They knew what he thought of their work.[2, 3]
4. He "went to bat" for them when they had a complaint.[2]
5. He used general rather than close supervision.[2]
6. He frequently or often had group meetings where they could discuss things with him.[2]

So far, the data suggest that immediately promotable supervisors are seen by employees as members of their own work group. The supervisors create atmospheres of free discussion; they "go to bat" for subordinates; they let subordinates know where they stand; they discuss problems with the group, etc. However, another question showed the situation to be more complex than that. The researchers asked each subordinate: "For whom is your supervisor 'pulling?'" Exhibit 2 shows the responses to this question.

Exhibit 2 suggests that the supervisor who was seen by employees as a member and representative of *both* management and the working group was rated highest by management. Supervisors most often rated as pulling for the company were also apt to be rated low by management. Apparently, this management did not want its supervisors to pull for the company alone.

Finally, supervisors rated their own superiors. Eighty-three per cent of the 29 supervisors in the P+, P, and S+ categories rated their superior as excellent or good at handling people; 63 per cent of the S supervisors felt the same; 46 per cent of the Q and U supervisors felt likewise. All of the supervisors in the top three appraisal ratings were "very sure" they knew how they stood with their superiors. The same was true for 90 per cent of the S-appraised supervisors and 54 per cent of the Q- and U-appraised supervisors.[4] This was the case despite the fact that supervisors answered the question *after* their superiors had reviewed their appraisal ratings with them. Similarly, 72 per cent of the P+, P, and S+ supervisors reported that their superiors asked their

---

[2] Figures were statistically significant at a 5 per cent level or above.

[3] There were no formal employee rating procedures in these departments.

[4] It was necessary to combine the first three and last two evaluation groupings to get enough members to compute percentages and meet statistical tests.

Exhibit 2

EMPLOYEES' FEELINGS ABOUT SUPERVISORS' "MEMBERSHIP"*

PERCENTAGE WHO COMMENT ABOUT THEIR SUPERVISORS AS NOTED

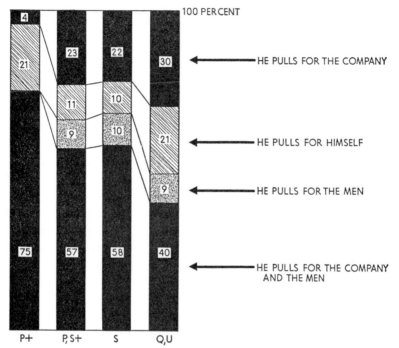

100 PERCENT

HE PULLS FOR THE COMPANY

HE PULLS FOR HIMSELF

HE PULLS FOR THE MEN

HE PULLS FOR THE COMPANY
AND THE MEN

P+   P,S+   S   Q,U

* The relationships are statistically significant at the 5 per cent level or above, except that the differences in the two categories "He pulls for himself" and "He pulls for the men" are too small to be meaningful. Symbols denote employee classifications according to management appraisal ratings of their supervisors; for meanings, see Exhibit 53.

opinion frequently, as opposed to 31 per cent of the Q and U supervisors. Over twice as many (79 per cent) of the high-rated supervisors as the low felt they participated or were allowed to make their own decisions when changes were to be made. The same proportions held for high versus low satisfaction (90 per cent versus 46 per cent) with the way they were brought into the decision-making process.

6. THE FOREMAN: MASTER AND VICTIM OF DOUBLE TALK*

Fritz J. Roethlisberger

The Position of the Foreman

NOWHERE IN the industrial structure more than at the foreman level is there so great a discrepancy between what a position ought to be and what a position is. This may account in part for the wide range of names which foremen have been called—shall we say "informally"?—and the equally great variety of definitions which have been applied to them in a more strictly formal and legal sense. Some managements have been eloquent in citing the foremen's importance with such phrases as: "arms of management," "grass-roots level of management," "key men in production," "front-line personnel men," and the like. Not so definite is the status of foremen under the National Labor Relations Act, since they can be included under the definitions given both for "employers" and "employees." To many foremen themselves they are merely the "go-betweeners," the "forgotten men," the "stepchildren" of industry. And what some employees call some foremen we shall leave to the reader's imagination.

But even without this diversity of names, it is clear that from the point of view of the individual foreman the discrepancy between what he should be and what he is cannot fail to be disconcerting. At times it is likely to influence adversely what he actually does or does not do, communicates or does not communicate to his superiors, his associates, and his subordinates. For this reason let us try to understand better the foreman's position in the modern industrial scene.

It is in his new streamlined social setting, far different from the "good old days," that we must learn to understand the modern foreman's anomalous position. The modern foreman has to get results—turn out production, maintain quality, hold costs down, keep his employees satisfied—under a set of technical conditions, social relations, and logical abstractions far different from those which existed 25 years ago.

* Excerpts from the article of the same name. Reprinted with permission of author and publisher from *Harvard Business Review*, Spring, 1945, pp. 283–98.

More Knowledge Required

For one thing, he has to "know" more than his old-time counterpart. Any cursory examination of modern foreman training programs will reveal that the modern foreman has to know (and understand) not only (1) the company's policies, rules, and regulations and (2) the company's cost system, payment system, manufacturing methods, and inspection regulations, in particular, but also frequently, (3) something about the theories of production control, cost control, quality control, and time and motion study, in general. He also has to know (4) the labor laws of the United States, (5) the labor laws of the state in which the company operates, and (6) the specific labor contract which exists between his company and the local union. He has to know (7) how to induct, instruct, and train new workers; (8) how to handle and, where possible, prevent grievances; (9) how to improve conditions of safety; (10) how to correct workers and maintain discipline; (11) how never to lose his temper and always be "fair"; (12) how to get and obtain cooperation from the wide assortment of people with whom he has to deal; and, especially, (13) how to get along with the shop steward. And in some companies he is supposed to know (14) how to do the jobs he supervises better than the employees themselves. Indeed, as some foreman training programs seem to conceive the foreman's job, he has to be a manager, a cost accountant, an engineer, a lawyer, a teacher, a leader, an inspector, a disciplinarian, a counselor, a friend, and, above all, an "example."

One might expect that this superior knowledge would tend to make the modern foreman feel more secure as well as to be more effective. Unfortunately some things do not work out the way they are intended. Quite naturally the foreman is bewildered by the many different roles and functions he is supposed to fulfill. He is worried in particular by what the boss will think if he takes the time to do the many things his many training courses tell him to do. And in 99 cases out of 100 what the boss thinks, or what the foreman thinks the boss thinks, will determine what the foreman does. As a result, the foreman gives lip service in his courses to things which in the concrete shop situation he feels it would be suicidal to practice. In the shop, for the most part, he does his best to perform by hook or by crook the one function clearly left him, the one function for which there is no definite staff counterpart, the one function for which the boss is sure to hold him responsible; namely, getting the workers to turn the work out on time. And about this function he feels his courses do not say enough—given the particular conditions, technical, human, and organizational, under which he has to operate.

Freedom of Action Restricted

Curiously enough, knowledge is not power for the modern foreman. Although he has to know a great deal about many things, he is no longer "the cock of the walk" he once was. Under modern conditions of operation, for example, there seems to be always somebody in the organization in a staff capacity who is supposed to know more than he does, and generally has more say, about almost every matter that comes up; somebody, in addition to his boss, with whom he is supposed to consult and sometimes to share responsibility; somebody by whom he is constantly advised and often even ordered.

To the foreman it seems as if he is being held responsible for functions over which he no longer has any real authority. For some time he has not been able to hire and fire and set production standards. And now he cannot even transfer employees, adjust the wage inequalities of his men, promote deserving men, develop better machines, methods, and processes, or plan the work of his department, with anything approaching complete freedom of action. All these matters for which he is completely or partially responsible have now become involved with other persons and groups, or they have become matters of company policy and union agreement. He is hedged in on all sides with cost standards, production standards, quality standards, standard methods and procedures, specifications, rules, regulations, policies, laws, contracts, and agreements; and most of them are formulated without his participation.

Far better than the old-timer of 25 years ago the modern foreman knows how much work should be done in what length of time; how much it is worth; what the best methods to be used are; what his material, labor, and burden costs should be; and what the tolerances are that his product should meet. But in the acquisition of all this untold wealth of knowledge, somehow something is missing. In some sense, not too clearly defined, he feels he has become less rather than more effective, less rather than more secure, less rather than more important, and has received less rather than more recognition.

Interactions with Many People

Let us explore further this feeling of the modern foreman. Not only does he have to know more than his old-time counterpart about the "logics" of management, but also he has to relate himself to a wider range of people. In any mass production industry the foreman each day is likely to be interacting (1) with his boss, the man to whom he formally reports in the line organization; (2) with certain staff specialists, varying from one to a dozen people depending on the size and kind of organization—production control men, inspectors, standards men, efficiency engineers, safety engineers, maintenance and repair men, methods men, personnel men, counselors; (3) with the heads of other departments to which his department relates; (4) with his subordinates

Exhibit 1

FORCES IMPINGING UPON THE FOREMAN

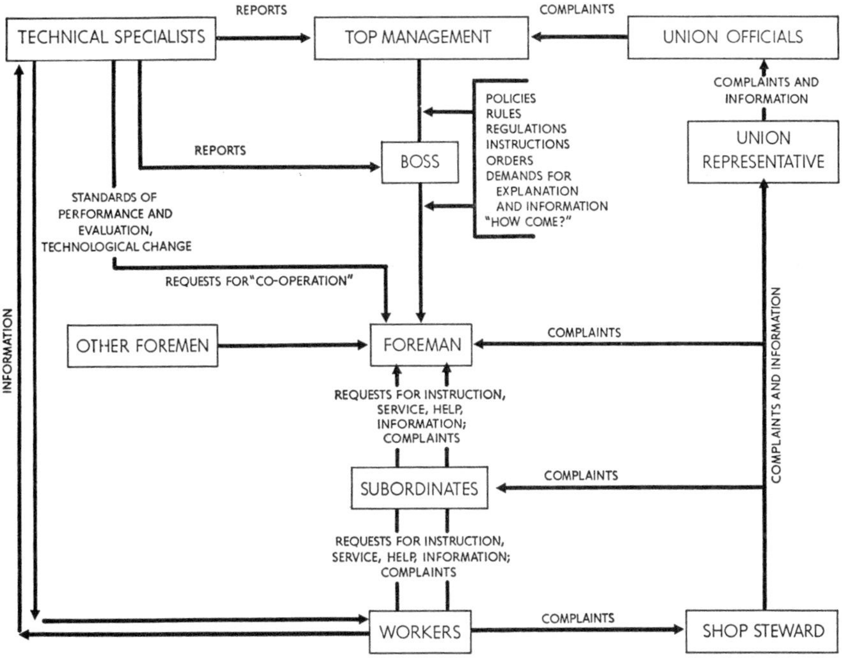

—subforemen, straw bosses, leadmen, group leaders, section chiefs; (5) with the workers directly, numbering anywhere from 10 to 300 people; and (6), in a union-organized plant, with the shop steward. Exploring the interdependence of each of these relationships as they impinge in toto upon the foreman makes it easier to understand how the modern foreman may feel in his everyday life. A diagram may help to make this clear (see Exhibit 1).

The Foreman's Situation Summarized

The salient features of the foreman's situation should now be clear. In very broad outline—tentatively and approximately formulated— the failure on the part of top management, in mass production industries in particular, to understand the social implications of its way of doing "business" has resulted in the development of certain rigidities which do not make for cooperation in the industrial structure.

(1) At the bottom of the organization there are people called *employees* who are in general merely supposed to *conform* to *changes* which they do not originate. Too often the attitude is that employees are merely supposed to do what they are told and get paid for it. Directing them there is—

(2) A group of *supervisors* who again are merely supposed to *uphold*—"administer" is the popular word—the standards of performance and policies determined by other groups, one of which is—

(3) A group of *technical specialists* who are supposed to *originate* better ways and better standards through which the economic purpose of the organization can be better secured and more effectively controlled by—

(4) A group of *top management* men who in their *evaluation* of the workers' behavior assume that the major inducement they can offer to people to cooperate is financial (i.e., that they are merely providing a livelihood, rather than a way of life); that informal organization is either "bad" or not "present"; and that authority comes from the top, so that no attention has to be given to that authority which is a matter of individual decision and comes from the bottom. This group's whole explicit theory of human cooperation—but not necessarily the practice of it—dates back to the eighteenth century: (*a*) society is composed of a rabble of unorganized individuals; (*b*) these individuals are only interested in the pursuit of profit and pleasure; and (*c*) in the pursuit of these ends the individual is essentially logical.[1]

In this environment the foreman stands—victim, not monarch, of all he surveys. And what does he survey? On the one hand, a monument of technical achievement such as no civilization has seen before, and, on the other hand, what Elton Mayo likes to refer to as "the seamy side of progress," a bleak and arid human scene scorched dry by the babel of words and logics which have long ceased to have any power to motivate or fill with renewed hope and vigor the hearts of men. Separated from management and separated from his men, dependent and insecure in his relation to his superiors and uncertain in his relations to his men, asked to give cooperation but in turn receiving none, expected to be friendly but provided with tools which only allow him to be "fair"—in this situation of social deprivation our modern foreman is asked to deliver the goods.

---

[1] These assumptions are taken from an unpublished paper written by Elton Mayo on "The Rabble Hypothesis," to be incorporated as a chapter in a book to be published shortly, *The Social Problems of an Industrial Civilization.*

7. ENGINEERING SUPERVISORS IN THE MIDDLE*

Louis B. Barnes

Department A's Organizational System Environment

The Chief Engineer

WE EARLIER described Company A as a large subsidiary of a still larger electronics firm. Company A's work was highly competitive. Not surprisingly, the company's general manager felt pressure both from the parent company and from competition to maintain low prices and high quality. Pressure upon the general manager affected his subordinates who felt the pressures and problems in their own areas. For example, engineering management believed that product quality was sacrificed to manufacturing schedules and demands for productivity.

. . . .

Perhaps we can summarize the chief engineer's point of view as follows, remembering that he represents management to the supervisor and members of Department A.

1. The company has a history of stressing productivity at the expense of quality and developmental work. Manufacturing dominates engineering.
2. Both I (the chief engineer) and Department A personnel feel that engineering is always in the position of compromising.
3. The company has confidence in Department A's employees as hard working and capable. Contributions and accomplishments are rewarded, as are seniority, informality, and the ability to work with other people.
4. I believe that Department A employees feel free to request changes and go to the top with complaints.
5. Only a very small portion of Department A's work is developmental work, though developmental work is badly needed and the department has a history of such work.
6. Talent for further product development work will probably come from the outside.
7. Department A engineers should spend more time in the factory

* Excerpt from Louis B. Barnes, *Organizational Systems and Engineering Groups: A Comparative Study of Two Technical Groups in Industry* (Boston: Division of Research, Harvard Business School, 1960), pp. 36–45. Reprinted with permission of author and publisher.

439

and be more practical in their specifications and recommendations. I (the chief engineer) have pushed Supervisor A very hard to get his engineers back into factory problems and practicality. This has resulted in some bitterness on his part.

Quite clearly, the chief engineer conveyed a science-engineering orientation to management and a management orientation to Department A. By the very nature of his position, the chief engineer played a man-in-the-middle role. He tried to communicate his subordinate's attitudes on science, research, and the importance of engineering to his

Exhibit 1

COMPANY A

THE CHIEF ENGINEER AND THE VALUES HE TRIED TO CONVEY TO MANAGEMENT AND SUPERVISOR A

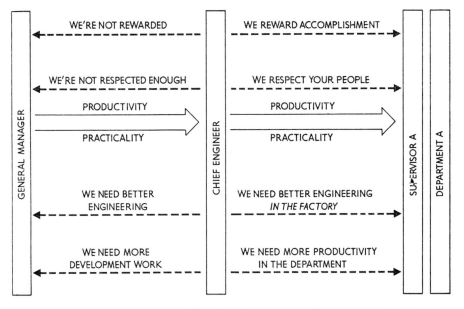

superiors in management. Likewise, he attempted to communicate his superior's concerns for productivity, practicality, and people to Department A and its supervisor. Inadvertently, he discouraged development work and encouraged factory relationships for Department A's engineers.

In effect, the chief engineer conveyed one set of values to management, another to Department A's supervisor. In his position as a man-in-the-middle, he was forced to play two roles, wear two hats, and be an engineer to management and a manager to engineers. His position and some of the values he tried to convey to management and Department A are shown in Exhibit 1.

Exhibit 1 also suggests that Supervisor A received pressure from the chief engineer, just as the chief engineer did from the general manager. How did Supervisor A respond to this situation?

Supervisor A

Supervisor A played the same man-in-the-middle role that the chief engineer did. Toward the chief engineer and management, Supervisor A pleaded the values of science and stressed the search for knowledge and its orderly development. Toward his subordinates Supervisor A displayed a dominant concern for productivity and practicality.

. . . .

As we did with the chief engineer, we can quickly summarize Supervisor A's major points.

1. I (Supervisor A) have a reputation and record of stressing the usefulness of scientific principles. Company experiences have proved me right.
2. Management and factory engineers tend to disregard scientific principles in favor of knob twisting, trial and error, and beliefs in "magic."
3. I have resisted moving into production-related work, but I am now insisting on it, nevertheless. We have much better technical background than do the factory engineers.
4. Management used to have confidence in me. They no longer do.
5. Some of my engineers resist the "quickie" assignments. I have to put pressure on them to get the work out, even though I don't like to do so.

Like the chief engineer, Supervisor A describes himself in a middleman position. On the one hand, he stresses scientific principles and deplores production engineering's knob twisting approach. On the other hand, he builds up subordinate resistance by asking them to turn out more "quickies," to get out into the factory, and to be less scientifically rigorous.

Exhibit 2 shows the apparent relationship between the general manager, the chief engineer, and Supervisor A. Each man stressed his own relative strength of position compared to that of the others. Each emphasized management and business values to his subordinates while defending engineering and science values before his superiors. Each apparently played the role required by his organizational position: an engineer to management, a manager to engineers. In playing these expected roles, each conflicted with superiors and subordinates

Exhibit 2

DEPARTMENT A

RELATIONSHIPS BETWEEN THE GENERAL MANAGER, THE CHIEF ENGINEER,
AND SUPERVISOR A, AS DESCRIBED BY EACH MAN

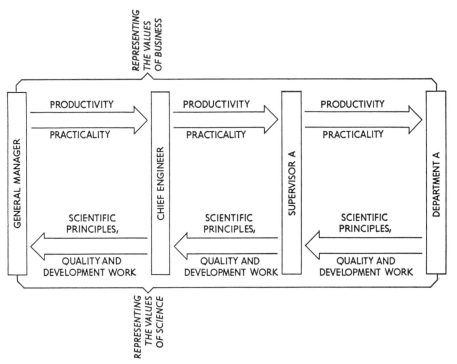

alike. Supervisor A's pleas for scientific rigor led the chief engineer to demand greater productivity and practicality. The pattern repeated at a higher level. The chief engineer stressed scientific principles, quality, and developmental work to his own superior. The general manager stressed productivity and practicality in response to management and competitive pressures.

8. RESULTS OF A SUPERVISORY TRAINING PROGRAM

A STUDY published in 1955 reports on the effects of an intensive two-week supervisory training program in industry. The research was supervised by the Personnel Research Board of Ohio State University with the co-operation of the International Harvester Company.[1]

The research involved three principal phases. The first pertained to learning which areas of supervisory leadership were important, along with developing reliable instruments for measuring these areas. The second phase used these instruments (questionnaires) to measure the extent and nature of changed attitudes as a result of the training experiences of 122 supervisors. (Similar questionnaires were given to the supervisor's superiors and subordinates to determine: [1] the leadership climate within which the supervisor worked and [2] the ways in which others perceived his behavior as a result of the training course.) The third phase related the different types of leadership to employee morale, general departmental efficiency, absenteeism, grievances, and turnover.

With respect to Phase 1, earlier Ohio State research on leader behavior disclosed two key leadership factors, independent of each other.[2] The first factor involved behavior indicating friendship, trust, and warmth between the leader and his subordinates. This factor was called *Consideration.* The second factor included leader behavior which defined relationships between leader and group member, prescribed channels of communication, defined roles for group members, and established ways of getting the job done. The factor was labeled *Initiating Structure.* The researchers tested their approaches extensively and developed what they felt was a scientifically reliable instrument.

Findings

The research team found, as they expected, a general increase in Consideration attitudes immediately following the training course. Initiating Structure attitudes decreased. The results were not surprising, since

---

[1] E. A. Fleishman, E. F. Harris, and H. E. Burtt, *Leadership and Supervision in Industry,* (Columbus: Personnel Research Board, Ohio State University, 1955).

[2] This independence was established after highly sophisticated statistical treatment, including response distributions to items, reliability estimates, and factor analyses.

the course had stressed human relations principles through role playing, visual aids, group discussions, lectures, and textbooks. However, the researchers were less prepared for the changes that occurred when supervisors went back to the job. From questionnaire data, it appeared that within two to ten months after training, supervisors ranked lower on Consideration behavior and attitudes than did nontrained supervisors. Moreover, the scores for Initiating Structure behavior and attitudes showed a tendency to increase among trained supervisors back at the plant. In other words, the immediate posttraining effect of increased Consideration attitudes did not last, nor was such behavior observed by subordinates after two months back on the job.

In order to explain this apparent learning reversal, the research team studied the plant leadership climate within which supervisors worked. The above-mentioned questionnaires were given to each supervisor's superior in management. The results showed that supervisors who operated under high Consideration leaders tended to rank significantly higher themselves in both Consideration attitudes and Consideration behavior. A boss who was considerate tended to have foremen who were that way. The same was true for Initiating Structure. Superiors who scored high on that dimension tended to have subordinate foremen with similar attitudes and behavior. The results suggest that supervisors were more responsive to their day-to-day relations with superiors than to a special training course with other supervisors.

The research team also measured the effects of training on leadership adequacy as seen by subordinates.[3] The results showed that employees liked working the most under trained supervisors who had returned from the course to leadership climates high in Consideration. In addition, worker morale was highest under supervisors who ranked high in Consideration.

It was impossible, during the research, to get actual production figures which would show the efficiency of each supervisor and his group. Instead, different management representatives rated the proficiency of each supervisor being studied. The results showed differences for production divisions and nonproduction divisions (e.g., stores, inspection, maintenance, etc.). In production divisions, supervisors with higher proficiency ratings tended to score higher on Initiation of Structure. In nonproduction divisions, higher proficiency ratings accompanied higher

---

[3] Individuals at different organizational levels filled out a questionnaire on how "an ideal foreman" would be expected to act. Workers favored more Consideration, less Initiation of Structure, and differed significantly from others in this respect. Supervisors were in between workers and higher level superiors, but closer to the latter in a tendency to favor higher Initiation of Structure.

Consideration scores. Apparently, those divisions under the greatest time pressures tended to have supervisors who were rewarded by management for high Initiation of Structure and low Consideration attitudes. In nonproduction divisions, the opposite was true.

Finally, the research showed that absenteeism was higher in groups whose supervisors were high in Initiation of Structure, lower in groups under high Consideration supervisors. Grievances were also higher under supervisors high in Initiation of Structure. Accidents and turnover had no appreciable relationship with either Consideration or Initiation of Structure.

In effect, employees liked to work under a supervisor whose leadership was considerate with low structuring. Under these conditions, absenteeism was low, while grievances were high when the supervisor initiated highly structured conditions. At the same time, proficiency ratings by management in production divisions tended to be higher for supervisors high in Initiation of Structure. Consequently, the production supervisor whose employees were high in morale, low in absenteeism, and had relatively few grievances tended to be less proficient in management's eyes.[4]

---

[4] These findings support an earlier Ohio State University study of leadership behavior and performance of airplane (B–29) commanders. Results indicated that the evaluation of the leader by subordinates was positively related to Consideration, while the evaluation by supervisors was related to Initiation of Structure. See A. W. Halpin, "The Leadership Behavior and Combat Performance of Airplane Commanders," *Journal of Abnormal and Social Psychology,* Vol. XLIX (1954), pp. 19–22

9. THE NEED HIERARCHY: A THEORY OF MOTIVATION

IN AN attempt to understand and account for human behavior, a number of theories of motivation have been advanced. A common approach has been to list the various "drives," wants, or needs which apparently motivate men. These attempts have often been criticized because the lists were long and unmanageable, because they failed sufficiently to take into account the nonphysiological needs, and because the needs often appeared contradictory.

A somewhat different way of thinking about man's needs has been suggested by Maslow.[1] He views man's needs in terms of a hierarchy, certain needs becoming operative only when other needs have been relatively satisfied. In an excellent summary of Maslow's scheme (originally prepared for a group of business executives), Professor Douglas McGregor of Massachusetts Institute of Technology describes the need hierarchy as follows:[2]

Physiological Needs

Man is a wanting animal—as soon as one of his needs is satisfied, another appears in its place. This process is unending. It continues from birth to death. Man continuously puts forth effort—works, if you please —to satisfy his needs.

Human needs are organized in a series of levels—a hierarchy of importance. At the lowest level, but pre-eminent in importance when they are thwarted, are his physiological needs. Man lives by bread alone, when there is no bread. Unless the circumstances are unusual, his needs for love, for status, for recognition are inoperative when his stomach has been empty for a while. But when he eats regularly and adequately, hunger ceases to be an important need. The sated man has hunger only in the sense that a full bottle has emptiness. The same is true of the other physiological needs of man—for rest, exercise, shelter, protection from the elements.

A satisfied need is not a motivator of behavior! This is a fact which is . . . ignored in the conventional approach to the management of

---

[1] A. H. Maslow, *Motivation and Personality* (New York: Harper & Bros., 1954).

[2] Douglas McGregor, *The Human Side of Enterprise* (New York: McGraw-Hill Book Co., Inc., 1960), pp. 36–39.

people. I shall return to it later. For the moment, an example will make the point. Consider your own need for air. Except as you are deprived of it, it has no appreciable motivating effect upon your behavior.

Safety Needs

When the physiological needs are reasonably satisfied, needs at the next higher level begin to dominate man's behavior—to motivate him. These are the safety needs, for protection against danger, threat, deprivation. Some people mistakenly refer to these as needs for security. However, unless man is in a dependent relationship where he fears arbitrary deprivation, he does not demand security. The need is for the "fairest possible break." When he is confident of this, he is more than willing to take risks. But when he feels threatened or dependent, his greatest need is for protection, for security.

The fact needs little emphasis that since every industrial employee is in at least a partially dependent relationship, safety needs may assume considerable importance. Arbitrary management actions, behavior which arouses uncertainty with respect to continued employment or which reflects favoritism or discrimination, unpredictable administration of policy—these can be powerful motivators of the safety needs in the employment relationship at *every level,* from worker to vice president. In addition, the safety needs of managers are often aroused by their dependence downward or laterally. This is a major reason for emphasis on management prerogatives and clear assignments of authority.

Social Needs

When man's physiological needs are satisfied and he is no longer fearful about his physical welfare, his social needs become important motivators of his behavior. These are such needs as those for belonging, for association, for acceptance by one's fellows, for giving and receiving friendship and love.

Management knows today of the existence of these needs, but it is often assumed quite wrongly that they represent a threat to the organization. Many studies have demonstrated that the tightly knit, cohesive work group may, under proper conditions, be far more effective than an equal number of separate individuals in achieving organizational goals. Yet management, fearing group hostility to its own objectives, often goes to considerable lengths to control and direct human efforts in ways that are inimical to the natural "groupiness" of human beings. When man's social needs—and perhaps his safety needs, too—are thus thwarted, he behaves in ways which tend to defeat organizational objectives. He becomes resistant, antagonistic, uncooperative. But this behavior is a consequence, not a cause.

Ego Needs

Above the social needs—in the sense that they do not become moti-vators until lower needs are reasonably satisfied—are the needs of greater significance to management and to man himself. They are the egoistic needs, and they are of two kinds:

1. Those needs that relate to one's self-esteem: needs for self-respect and self-confidence, for autonomy, for achievement, for compe-tence, for knowledge.
2. Those needs that relate to one's reputation: needs for status, for recognition, for appreciation, for the deserved respect of one's fellows.

Unlike the lower needs, these are rarely satisfied; man seeks indefi-nitely for more satisfaction of these needs once they have become im-portant to him. However, they do not usually appear in any significant way until physiological, safety, and social needs are reasonably satisfied. Exceptions to this generalization are to be observed, particularly under circumstances where, in addition to severe deprivation of physiological needs, human dignity is trampled upon. Political revolutions often grow out of thwarted social and ego, as well as physiological, needs.

The typical industrial organization offers only limited opportunities for the satisfaction of egoistic needs to people at lower levels in the hier-archy. The conventional methods of organizing work, particularly in mass production industries, give little heed to these aspects of human motivation. If the practices of "scientific management" were deliberately calculated to thwart these needs—which, of course, they are not—they could hardly accomplish this purpose better than they do.

Self-Fulfillment Needs

Finally—a capstone, as it were, on the hierarchy—there are the needs for self-fulfillment. These are the needs for realizing one's own poten-tialities, for continued self-development, for being creative in the broadest sense of that term.

The conditions of modern industrial life give only limited opportunity for these relatively dormant human needs to find expression. The depriva-tion most people experience with respect to other lower-level needs diverts their energies into the struggle to satisfy *those* needs, and the needs for self-fulfillment remain below the level of consciousness.

For purposes of initial explanation and simplicity, McGregor speaks in terms of separate steps or levels. Actually, Maslow suggests that these levels are interdependent and overlapping, each higher need level emerging before the lower needs have been satisfied completely. In our society, most people tend to be partially satisfied in each need area and partially unsatisfied. However, individuals tend to have higher satisfaction at the lower need levels than at higher need levels. Maslow helps to explain this by picturing the average citizen as (for illustrative purposes) 85 per cent satisfied in his physiological needs, 70 per cent satisfied in his safety needs, 50 per cent in his belonging needs, 40 per cent in his egoistic needs, and 10 per cent in his self-fulfillment needs.

Some writers have added to this original concept of hierarchy the idea of "elaboration at one level." They suggest that when the individual is blocked in his progression up the hierarchy ladder, he may begin endlessly to elaborate at one level of need satisfaction—for example, the endless pursuit of groups and friends for the emotional support they provide or the endless pursuit of more and more status symbols and the needs for recognition they satisfy.

A Modification of Maslow's Need Hierarchy Theory

In a study of engineering groups, Barnes implicitly assumed a modification of Maslow's need hierarchy theory.[3] Now, let us explicitly state this modification, since it has both teaching and research implications. Whereas Maslow arranged human needs in a hierarchy arrangement from low (physiological) to high (self-actualization) needs, Barnes proposed a more equal, but related, arrangement of man's higher need categories. Maslow postulated a hierarchy or ladder of four successive need categories following the physiological, i.e., safety, belonging, ego (self-esteem and other esteem), and self-actualization, each of which he believed must be relatively satisfied before the next need was really activated. Some observers question the hierarchy concept, however, and see difficulties in making concepts like self-actualization (i.e., to become everything that one is capable of becoming) operational.

Consequently, in his study of two engineering groups, Barnes set aside the category of self-actualization and viewed man's safety needs as overlapping the other higher needs. Whenever one of these was threatened, so was man's safety. This left a base of physiological needs and a higher need level consisting of self-esteem, esteem of others, and belonging, each in mutual relationship to the other. Barnes also related these needs to the three dimensions (autonomy, opportunity for interaction, and influence) which defined an organizational system in

[3] L. B. Barnes, *Organizational Systems and Engineering Groups: A Comparative Study of Two Technical Groups in Industry* (Boston: Division of Research, Harvard Business School, 1960), pp. 167–69.

his study. Consequently, an individual's self-esteem needs were met to the extent he had autonomy and freedom on the job. Other esteem needs related to the ways in which influence relationships were structured. Belonging needs were satisfied or frustrated according to the opportunities for interaction provided beyond those required by the job. Autonomy, interaction opportunity, and influence are not only crucial dimensions for a concept of organizational system, claims Barnes, they

Exhibit 1

A POSSIBLE RELATIONSHIP BETWEEN THE CONCEPTS OF
ORGANIZATIONAL SYSTEMS AND AN INDIVIDUAL'S NEEDS

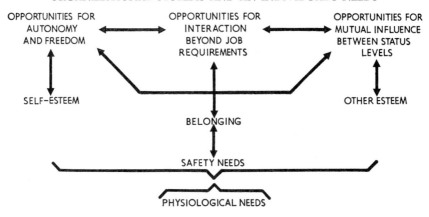

also relate to an individual's pluralistic needs, described by Maslow and other psychologists. The difference is that needs are now seen as interdependent variables, not as hierarchically dependent upon lower level satisfactions. From this point of view, whenever the safety of one need is threatened by external system structuring, all are threatened.

The reader can fit these relationships into this course book's earlier conceptual scheme on small groups by noting that autonomy, interaction opportunities, and influence are respectively related to the activities, interactions, and sentiment categories of George Homans' external system concepts. (See Exhibit 1.)

10. MOTIVATION IN WORK GROUPS: A TENTATIVE VIEW*

James V. Clark

THIS PAPER represents an attempt to examine a number of different researches in the field of organizational behavior and to see if their similarities can be highlighted and tentatively explained by the use of Maslow's need-hierarchy concept.[1]

A recent research experience of mine (so far published only in case form)[2] suggested for me that this process might be a useful way of generating new hypotheses and methods of measurement. The present paper is presented in the hope that others can be stimulated in the same way.

More specifically, this paper makes no claim that the answers concerning employee motivation and its determinants are all in. Neither does it claim that the questions generated by the examination of several researches from the point of view of the need-hierarchy concept are all presently researchable in a strict operational sense. Rather, the paper puts up what, for me, appears to be a potentially operational scheme for analyzing motivation and its organizational determinants. With such a scheme, it appears possible to study a number of different organizations comparatively, an effort which the field of organizational behavior needs.

I do believe, therefore, that the use of this theory puts us in a somewhat better position than that outlined in a recent research on worker motivation by Herzberg *et al.*

> This concept (Maslow's need hierarchy) has led many people to feel that the worker can never be satisfied with his job. How are you going to solve the dilemma of trying to motivate workers who have a continuously revolving set of needs? Since each individual may present at any one time a different scramble of his psychological need list, a systematic personnel

---

* Reprinted with permission from *Human Organization*, Vol. XIX, No. 4 (Winter, 1960–61), pp. 199–208. Footnotes adapted to style of present volume.

[1] A. H. Maslow, *Motivation and Personality* (New York: Harper & Bros., 1954).

[2] "Century Company (A–I)," Harvard Business School, EA–A 321–29.

practice hoping to cater to the most prepotent needs of its entire working force is defeated by the nature of the probabilities. Forgetting for a moment the individual "need hierarchies," it can be argued that there is sufficient homogeneity within various groups of employees to make for a relative similarity of "need hierarchies" within each group. Even so, the changes in prepotency for the group will occur, and personnel administration will have to keep up with them. For some who hold to this point of view personnel administration is reduced to the essential of labor-management bargaining. For others it means that personnel programs must be geared to be sensitive to the changes that are continually taking place in the needs of the employees. And since this can be done only by the supervisors, the training of supervisors in understanding human motivation, the factors underlying it, and the therapeutic or manipulative skills with which to cope with it is the most essential ingredient to any industrial-relations program.[3]

As this paper will show, I am not opposed to sensitive first-line administrators. However, other variables relating to satisfaction and productivity will be highlighted and in such a way as to suggest that the development of worker motivation is not a random scramble but is perhaps predictable, with only a modicum of sensitivity to employee needs.

.   .   .   .

Some Suggested Uniformities among Different Researches

Exhibit 1 shows how the need-hierarchy concept might be utilized to relate and explain the findings of a number of different studies. In other words, it takes McGregor's generalization of Maslow's theory, attempts to relate it to some existing studies, and concludes that workers under this or that combination of environmental conditions behave *as if* they were motivated in such-and-such a fashion.

Before we turn to this exhibit, however, a word of caution is in order. This way of relating and thinking about different organizational behavior researches is by no means perfect. First of all, the propositions which follow from the need-hierarchy theory are extremely difficult to test in a research sense. Secondly, the variety of environmental and internal-system factors affecting work group behavior cannot be categorized so as to make all known descriptions of work situations directly comparable from some one point of view. Finally, almost all researches leave out, or find uncontrollable, some variables that are necessary for

---

[3] Frederick Herzberg, Bernard Mausner, and Barbara B. Snyderman, *The Motivation to Work* (New York: John Wiley & Sons, Inc., 1959).

complete comparability. Nevertheless, some available researches suggest uniformities consistent with the need-hierarchy concept.

Exhibit 1 shows how a number of different "givens" in a work group's environment can prevent or frustrate an individual's opportunity for need satisfaction at different levels of the need hierarchy. The exhibit is based on the assumption that all individuals have a potential for activating all the needs on the need hierarchy. Likewise, the exhibit

Exhibit 1

SOME RELATIONS BETWEEN CONDITIONS IN THE WORK GROUP'S ENVIRONMENT, MOTIVATION, SATISFACTION, PRODUCTIVITY, AND TURNOVER-ABSENTEEISM

	(1)	(2)	(3)	(4)	(5)	(6)	(7)
							COMPANY PERCEIVED AS SUPPORTIVE
					LOW PERCEIVED CONTRIBUTION OPPORTUNITY	HIGH PERCEIVED CONTRIBUTION OPPORTUNITY	HIGH PERCEIVED CONTRIBUTION OPPORTUNITY
CONDITIONS IN THE WORK GROUP'S ENVIRONMENT				PRODUCTION-CENTERED LEADERSHIP	ACCOMMODATIVE LEADERSHIP	ACCOMMODATIVE LEADERSHIP	GROUP-CENTERED LEADERSHIP
			LOW STATUS CONGRUENCE	HIGH STATUS CONGRUENCE	HIGH STATUS CONGRUENCE	HIGH STATUS CONGRUENCE	HIGH STATUS CONGRUENCE
		LOW INTERACTION OPPORTUNITY	HIGH INTERACTION OPPORTUNITY	HIGH INTERACTION OPPORTUNITY	HIGH INTERACTION OPPORTUNITY	HIGH INTERACTION OPPORTUNITY	HIGH INTERACTION OPPORTUNITY
	LOW EMPLOYMENT SECURITY	HIGH EMPLOYMENT SECURITY	HIGH EMPLOYMENT SECURITY	HIGH EMPLOYMENT SECURITY	HIGH EMPLOYMENT SECURITY	HIGH EMPLOYMENT SECURITY	HIGH EMPLOYMENT SECURITY

(NEED ACTIVATION)

NEEDS							
SELF-ACTUALIZATION							
STATUS-PRESTIGE							
SELF-ESTEEM							
MEMBERSHIP							
SAFETY							

(EFFECTS ON PRODUCTIVITY AND TURNOVER-ABSENTEEISM)

	(1)	(2)	(3)	(4)	(5)	(6)	(7)
PRODUCTIVITY	HIGH	LOW	LOW?	LOW	MEETS MINIMUM REQUIREMENTS	HIGH	HIGH
TURNOVER-ABSENTEEISM	LOW	HIGH	HIGH	?	AVERAGE	LOW	LOW

KEY: [ ] NEED NOT ACTIVATED [▨] NEED ACTIVATED BUT RELATIVELY SATISFIED [▨] NEED ACTIVATED BUT RELATIVELY FRUSTRATED

assumes that an individual does not necessarily suspend or forget his unrealized needs during his hours on the job. Actually, in industrial situations, there are few data to support the first assumption, many data to support the second. Therefore, the exhibit can usefully be regarded as a tentative explanation of how and why most people, or an "average worker," would most typically react under different conditions at work.

The extreme left-hand scale of the middle block of graphs in Exhibit 1 represents the various levels of the need hierarchy (exclusive of the physiological needs). (In Maslow's description of his need hierarchy, the status-prestige need and the self-esteem need are placed side by side above the membership need. They are placed on top of each other here for graphic simplicity.)

The remaining columns of the middle block depict the pattern of an individual's need activation and satisfaction under a number of different external conditions. These patterns will be discussed in this paper in relation to certain researches. (It is not possible to show all possible combinations of external conditions; researches have not been conducted under such a wide variety of conditions.)

Across the bottom of the exhibit are two rows which show "productivity" and "turnover and absenteeism" for each column. These are by no means definitely established results, but the researches examined in this paper often suggested certain tendencies in regard to these variables which are shown. Consequently, by beginning with human needs, we can move to the relationship between the satisfaction of these needs, external conditions, and productivity and turnover-absenteeism.

Column 1 illustrates a situation in which employment security is extremely low. Such conditions might exist whenever alternative employment is unavailable (as in a depression) or is deemed by the workers to be not as desirable as present employment and where workers feel unprotected from a management which is perceived as arbitrary in its layoff and firing procedures.

Research by Goode and Fowler[4] in an automobile feeder plant illustrates this condition. In their study of a low-morale, nonunion plant a small group of high-service employees, for whom the job had become an absolute economic necessity, consistently produced according to management expectations. Turnover among other workers, for whom the job was less important, was high. They quit or were fired for not producing enough.

Interestingly enough, related situations were described some time ago, and were alluded to by Mitchell,[5] when he noted that the pace of work was slower in the flush times of 1900–1902 than it had been in the dull of times of 1894–96. He quoted a sample bit of testimony from the period. The superintendent of a company manufacturing electrical machinery said: ". . . Five years ago men did not restrict their output, union or non-union men, because they wanted to hold their jobs, and a man would do anything and all he was told to do. Now a

---

[4] W. F. Goode and Irving Fowler, "Incentive Factors in a Low Morale Plant," *American Sociological Review*, Vol. XIV, No. 5 (1949).

[5] W. C. Mitchell, *Business Cycles and Their Causes* (Berkeley: University of California Press, 1941).

man knows that all he has to do is to walk across the street and get another job at the same rate of pay. . . ."

Obviously, a group's productivity does not always increase in depression times. It fell off in the bank wiring room[6] shortly before the final layoffs. The suggestion being made here is that under employment conditions which an individual perceives as economically threatening *and* arbitrary (and such conditions probably exist most often in a depression), his higher needs cannot motivate. He is "stuck" on the safety level, and his behavior can only work toward the immediate goal of economic survival. Under conditions of this kind, financial rewards tend to be the primary incentives which motivate workers toward higher productivity.

Frustrated Membership Needs

Columns 2 through 4 all show situations in which membership needs are active, but frustrated. They are shown separately, because apparently they occur under different environmental conditions.

Column 2 shows a situation where workers are less concerned with employment security, because they have it, but where the job technology imposes physical or spatial requirements where interaction is impossible or severely restricted. This condition reflects and is labeled "low interaction opportunity." Such conditions and their effects on satisfaction were described in two automobile assembly plant studies.

Walker and Guest[7] rated jobs according to their "mass production characteristics" (noise, repetitiveness, restricted opportunity for movement, etc.). Workers holding such jobs often reported social isolation to be an important reason for job dissatisfaction. Moreover, absenteeism and turnover (extremely high throughout the automotive industry) were nearly twice as high for persons whose jobs exhibited "extreme mass production characteristics."

Another study of automobile assembly workers by Jasinski[8] showed that the men resented not being able to follow conventional conversation patterns: looking at the listener, being able to pause for conversation, and to complete the "talk." A correlation was found between an individual's desire to talk on the job and his attitude toward his job: The higher the desire to talk, the less interesting the job.

---

[6] F. J. Roethlisberger and W. J. Dickson, *Management and the Worker* (Cambridge: Harvard University Press, 1939).

[7] C. R. Walker and R. H. Guest, *The Man on the Assembly Line* (Cambridge: Harvard University Press, 1952).

[8] F. J. Jasinski, "Technological Delimitation of Reciprocal Relationships: A Study of Interaction Patterns in Industry," *Human Organization*, Vol. XV, No. 2 (1956).

It is possible that Van Zelst's study[9] of sociometrically restructured construction work groups may be illustrative of what happens when opportunities to interact are increased.

When men were allowed to work alongside others whom they themselves had chosen, turnover, labor cost and materials cost all dropped.

The inference can be drawn that these results occurred because membership level motivation was satisfied and higher needs became activated.

Another research, "The Case of the Changing Cage,"[10] suggests what happens to a work group's productivity and satisfaction when interaction opportunities are suddenly lowered. (In this case, however, interaction opportunity was decreased by a combination of physical changes and another variable we will discuss later—leadership behavior.)

Workers in a voucher-check filing unit in an insurance company worked together well, kept up with the work load, and expressed feelings of satisfaction. Their work area was inside a wire cage surrounded by filing cabinets and boxes through which the group's supervisor could not see. For efficiency purposes, the cage was moved to a new area in which the filing cabinets were arranged so that supervisors could see into the cage and restrict worker interaction. The workers could no longer engage in social activities which had been important to them (games, chatting, eating, etc.). Their output declined drastically, the amount of time spent in nonwork activities increased substantially, and the workers expressed considerable dissatisfaction with the new setup.

In short, it appears that if there are any major physical or spatial technological factors which restrict opportunities for interaction (under conditions where safety-level needs are not primary), membership needs will be frustrated and, consequently, any higher need levels will not be activated.

Column 3 illustrates a situation in which safety-level considerations are relatively unimportant because they are satisfied, interaction opportunities are high, but where workers are placed in low-status congruence work groups.

The need-hierarchy explanation of this situation would be as follows: Safety needs are not active, and membership needs are active but frustrated because social status differences among persons in the work

---

[9] R. H. Van Zelst, "Sociometrically Selected Work Teams Increase Productivity," *Personnel Psychology*, Vol. V, No. 3 (1952).

[10] Cara E. Richards and H. F. Dobyns, "Topography and Culture: The Case of the Changing Cage," *Human Organization*, Vol. XVI, No. 1 (1957).

group are too large for the group to deal with effectively. Therefore, no indications of higher level needs are present. As a consequence, people would not see their work as something to which they could or should contribute. But why should low- or high-status congruence affect membership motivation?

In Zaleznik, Christensen, and Roethlisberger's recent study, a "theory of social certitude" was advanced to explain this on an individual level:

> In the condition of social certitude, the individual may be high, middle, or low in total status. But at whatever level, his status factors are well established. As a social entity, therefore, he can place himself and be placed readily in the structure of a group. People relate to him in terms of common expectations of behavior toward a person well established at his particular level of status. In turn, the individual knows what to expect from others. These expectations may or may not be functional for the group or the individual—there may be a more productive role for an individual than his status, well established as it is, allows him to play. Nevertheless, in a condition of social certitude the individual becomes "structured" into a group. Whether he is structured into the group at a high rank or low rank will depend on the level of the individual's total status.
>
> The condition of ambiguity, where the individual's status factors are out of line, provides no readily apparent social position for him. As an ambiguous social entity, the group has no clear expectations regarding behavior from or toward such an individual. On the one hand, being high in one or more dimensions of status seems to require the form of behavior associated with a high status person. On the other hand, being simultaneously low in one or more dimensions of status seems to require behavior associated with a low status person. These mixed expectations create ambiguities and consequently anxiety in social relationships.[11]

This theory was advanced to explain why group members are attracted to or repelled by an *individual* whose status factors are out of line: some very high, some very low. Such an individual is ambiguous in relation to the group majority. The term "group-status congruence" refers to a collection of people who share similar status factors, even if the factors themselves may be out of line with one another for a given individual. In this kind of a situation, an individual who exhibits status factors different from the majority tends to be avoided by the majority even if his status factors are in line with one another. He is likely to be described by others as "not our class" or "not our kind of

---

[11] A. Zaleznik, C. R. Christensen, and F. J. Roethlisberger, *The Motivation, Productivity, and Satisfaction of Workers: A Prediction Study* (Boston: Division of Research, Harvard Business School, 1958).

person."[12] The four combinations between an individual and his group (high group-status congruence, high individual-status congruence; high group-status congruence, low individual-status congruence, etc.) have not been studied as such. At the present time, loosely stated, it appears that if, under most conditions, an individual has status factors to some extent different from the majority of people in the small group social structure to which he belongs, he will tend to be regarded as ambiguous by that majority, and hence will be regarded with anxiety.

Clark's supermarket research[13] was concerned with differences in group-status congruence between stores.

> He found that groups with high group-status congruence (which he called "high status factors in common" groups) exhibited low turnover and low absenteeism, both indications of membership-need level satisfaction. Moreover, he further found that stores which had high-status congruent groups in them also tended to have higher labor efficiency ratings. In addition, he found that members of these groups tended to speak of their work as more satisfying.

Adams' bomber crew study[14] was somewhat similar.

> He showed that crews with high group-status congruence tended to report feelings of satisfaction with group membership. However, Adams also showed that while crews with high-status congruence showed high technical performance up to a point, beyond that point, as group-status congruence increased, technical performance decreased.

Therefore, while Clark's and Adams' studies showed similar results in the relation between group-status congruence and membership satisfaction, their findings on group-status congruence and performance were less clear.[15] It is difficult to explain with confidence why Adams' highest technical performance groups were low-status congruent. Comparable data on social structure, motivation, satisfaction, and formal leadership might have provided clear explanations.

Not only the possible difference between these two studies, but the findings of other researches in the general area of status and how people

---

[12] J. V. Clark, *A Preliminary Investigation of Some Unconscious Assumptions Affecting Labor Efficiency in Eight Supermarkets* (unpublished DBA thesis, Harvard Business School, 1958).

[13] *Ibid.*

[14] Stuart Adams, "Status Congruency as a Variable in Small Group Performance," *Social Forces,* Vol. XXXII, No. 1 (1953).

[15] However, the two studies do not necessarily contradict each other on this point, since Clark studied no stores with status congruence measures as high as some of the bomber crews studied by Adams. Also, the two studies used different status factors and different ways to measure group-status congruence. Clark's research is continuing in an attempt to test for lower labor efficiency under conditions of higher group-status congruence.

react to it, all indicate that not enough is known yet about this subject to offer inclusive explanations for work group behavior. For example, Zaleznik's machine-shop workers[16] had developed a social structure which offered its members at least a minimal level of satisfaction. In comparison to other studies, his workers could be said to have exhibited low individual- and group-status congruence, although the congruence apparently was high enough for the group to form: It contained no Bolsheviks or Andaman Islanders. In short, the existing findings in this area suggest, but not conclusively, that under most industrial conditions a group will be more cohesive to the extent to which its members exhibit individual and/or group-status congruence. (An important exception will be discussed under Column 7 of Exhibit 1.)

The remaining columns, 4 through 7, show those situations where neither technological restrictions on interaction nor the given sentiments of workers (e.g., notions of member attraction stemming from status factors in common) are such as to prevent the formation of a satisfying social structure. Rather, the constrictions on group development portrayed here stem largely from the behavior of the formal leader of the work group.

Leadership Behavior

Since leadership is important here, it will be useful, before turning to the columns themselves, to describe roughly the leadership behavior under three different types.[17] The labels "accommodative," "production-centered," and "group-centered" will be briefly described, in that order.

The first, "accommodative," refers to situations where the leader's behavior neither challenges a group nor seriously violates its norms of how a leader should behave. The group's determination of its own work procedures is left alone. As a result, the formal leader does not seriously threaten the group's survival as a group.

This condition is a common one and was described in the following reports:

In the "Whirlwind Aircraft Corporation"[18] a group of workers developed an improved tool capable of increasing their productivity on a cer-

---

[16] A. Zaleznik, *Worker Satisfaction and Development* (Boston: Division of Research, Harvard Business School, 1956).

[17] It is beyond the scope of this article to evaluate these labels or to offer a different classification scheme.

[18] Paul Pigors and C. A. Myers, *Personnel Administration: A Point of View and a Method* (New York: McGraw-Hill Book Co., Inc., 1956), pp. 427–36.

tain item fifty percent. Actually, they increased productivity ten percent and used the remaining time to improve quality on some other products. A methods engineer was assigned to study the problem, but the group withheld information about the tool from him. For some time, the foreman was aware of this but was "satisfied to let the men handle it their own way." He reasoned that at little expense, he was able to get out production of high quality.

In Roy's research in a piecework machine shop,[19] workers had an elaborate set of restriction-of-output activities. The foreman instructed new men in parts of this system. To one man he said: "Say, when you punch off daywork onto piecework, you ought to have your piecework already started. Run a few, then punch off daywork, and you'll have a good start. You've got to chisel a little around here to make money."

In the Century Company,[20] workers in one area (B) reported that their foreman left them completely alone and had for several years. Prior to that time, he had supervised the men closely; but they had taught him not to, by telling him that they would refuse to work if he didn't let them alone.

Although the three situations above point to different degrees of foreman involvement in the group, the uniformity among them is that the leader has abdicated any influence in the setting of work procedures. The group determines its procedures. A variety of labels other than "accommodative" have been devised to describe such a foreman: "laissez-faire," "abdicratic," etc.

Other researches have pointed to the "production-centered" pattern of leadership behavior (and, moreover, suggested certain relations between such leadership and productivity).

In a study of productivity and leadership in an insurance company,[21] certain leaders were characterized as seeing their job primarily in terms of methods, procedures, and standards of production. Called production-centered leaders by the researchers, it was noted that such leaders headed seven out of ten low-producing sections.

In the Century Company (I) case,[22] one foreman said this about his idea of a good worker: "A good man is a man who is reasonable. . . .

---

[19] Donald Roy, "Efficiency and the Fix: Informal Intergroup Relations in a Piecework Machine Shop," *American Journal of Sociology*, Vol. LX, No. 3 (1954). See the Metropolitan Steel Company case in this volume.

[20] "Century Company (A–I)," *op. cit.*

[21] Daniel Katz, N. Maccoby, and N. C. Morse, *Productivity, Supervision, and Morale in an Office Situation* (Ann Arbor: Institute for Social Research, University of Michigan, 1950), Part I.

[22] "Century Company (A–I)," *op. cit.*

He does what the company tells him he should do. He does not try to do what he thinks he should do, but he does what he is told."

The people working for this foreman had these kinds of things to say about him: "Whenever my foreman sees a man sitting down, he comes up to him and gives him something to do. . . . I don't think he'll be happy until he sees everybody running around all the time. Our foreman shouldn't yell at a man in front of everybody or nail him down. . . . This makes friction and breaks down the group."

Borrowing the phrase from the above-mentioned insurance company research, the Century Company researchers labeled this foreman "production-centered."

This kind of leader is the direct opposite of the accommodative type, in that he allows the employees little or no influence in the setting-up of work procedures. Influence is supposed to move downward only, according to such a supervisor. Although we are calling such a leader production-centered, others have described him as "authoritarian," "autocratic," and "task-centered."

"Group-centered" leadership was indicated in the same two studies.

In the insurance company,[23] "employee-centered leadership" referred to supervisors who saw their job primarily in terms of the organization, training, and motivation of subordinates. Such supervisors headed six of seven high-producing sections. The researchers said that: "The supervisors of the high-producing sections . . . regard supervision as the most important part of their work. . . . Their method of supervision appears to be one of setting up certain general conditions for their employees and then permitting their employees to work out the details of when and how the work will be handled."

In the Century Company (I) case,[24] one foreman said this about his idea of a good worker: "In my estimation, a good furnace worker is a man who has confidence in himself. . . . A foreman should show confidence in his men, and this should be real confidence. I'm always ready to show confidence in a man, even though at first sight I might think he doesn't deserve it. What I do is give some directions to a man and then let him do his work without always being on his back. I want him to be free to do his work. . . . I realize that this requires a lot of talking on the part of the foreman. The men have to learn to trust their foreman. A foreman has to talk to his men to let himself be known by them. . . . Another thing, I like to tease the men, because it's one way for me to talk to them. It shows them I'm not dangerous."

---

[23] Katz, Maccoby, and Morse, *op. cit.*

[24] "Century Company (A–I)," *op. cit.*

The workers spoke about this foreman as follows: "Last week when ———was our foreman, we did not have any trouble. There were no complaints, no grievances, no beefs. It was hot, and he understood that we were having more difficulty working at this temperature than at other times. After all, a man needs encouragement. . . . He knows how to run the men. I wish we could keep him for a long time. . . . We're not the only ones who have noticed he is good. Everywhere he has been in the company, people have been glad to work for him."

The researchers classified this foreman as "group-centered."

This kind of leader has been described as "democratic," "group-centered," "employee-centered," etc. In this paper the group-centered label will be used. Regardless of the label, however, it can be seen that such a leader allows and encourages a *mutual* influence relationship with his men. Both the leader and his subordinates play a role in the setting-up of work procedures, and the mutuality is made legitimate and encouraged by this kind of leader.

Returning to . . . Exhibit 1 . . . , Column 4 shows the effects of the production-centered leadership condition in a situation where group formation potential is present. The behavior of a leader allowing low-influence opportunity, as described above, would tend to prevent a group from forming a satisfying relationship with each other and to its environment. Because workers are more conciously forced to attend to their work, their membership needs are frustrated.

The Century Company[25] cases showed two groups of furnace workers, both with equal numbers of high and low individually status-congruent people. Workers in furnace area "A" had a production-centered foreman and exhibited less social development, while workers in furnace area "B" had an accommodative foreman and showed more social development. The researchers made an attempt to assess motivation, also, and there was considerably lower indication of membership need activation in area A than in area B. Moreover, of those judged active at this need level in area A, the majority appeared frustrated.

This study shows an instance in which membership needs were frustrated by a production-centered foreman: By holding workers rigidly to their required activities, he never permitted the social group to form, even though it was potentially capable of so forming. Incidentally, while accurate productivity data were not available for the two particular shift crews studied, area A as a whole (all four shift crews together) was producing much less than area B.

---

[25] *Ibid.*

If production-centered leadership is introduced into a group that has already formed, however, there is some evidence to suggest that the group continues to function as a group: They unite around their hostility to management.

The "Case of the Changing Cage,"[26] alluded to before, illustrates this (although it contains no information about status congruence). The supervisor believed that he could better control output by looking into this cage and thereby reducing nonwork behavior. In the old cage, he could not see in but in the new cage he could. The result, however, was the nonwork activities actually increased (although they were less visible: the group went underground).

Whether or not such a situation is indicative of frustrated membership needs is difficult to say. Perhaps it can be said, though, that this group was simply elaborating its membership needs: Under this condition the nonwork behavior offered the only *possibility* for need satisfaction.

Columns 1 through 4 have all illustrated how environmental conditions can restrict the development of social structure in work groups. In addition, they also illustrated motivational consequences at lower need levels only. The remaining columns show situations in which there is indication that higher need levels can become activated. Since, in a formal organization, people activated at these higher need levels show a tendency to contribute their judgment and productiveness to the organization's task, the term "contributive motivation" may sometimes be a useful shorthand for all the need levels above the membership level. We shall use it occasionally in the rest of this paper.

Column 5 shows two changes in comparison to Column 4. One, the satisfaction of membership needs, comes from the accommodative leader who, by not threatening the group too much, allows it to form and perpetuate itself. The second change is the frustration of the esteem needs, due to the introduction of a condition which might be labeled "low perceived contribution opportunity." This refers to a worker's perception of a technological process as being predetermined for the most part. Here, except for the opportunity for an occasional change in setup, technology, etc., a member of a social group at work sees no continuing opportunity to contribute anything, to make a difference, to initiate, along with other members of this group, something useful on his environment. The Column 5 situation has often been described in organizational behavior research at the worker level because it is undoubtedly

---

[26] Richards and Dobyns, *op. cit.*

the most common. The self-esteem and status-prestige needs are released, because membership needs are relatively satisfied; but, since the workers' jobs prevent any satisfying feelings of group competence or mastery to emerge, and because the accommodative foreman has no concept of getting his group involved in setting up any of its own procedures, the esteem needs are frustrated. Typical comments of workers in such situations are:

A job is a job.
You have to work, so it might as well be here as anywhere.
This job isn't bad. It's a nice bunch of guys, but any moron could do the work, etc.

It appears as if the "regulars" in the Zaleznik, Christensen, Roethlisberger prediction study[27] and the famous bank wiring room workers[28] illustrate this column. Under such conditions, workers' productivity and satisfaction are determined mainly by their position in the social structure, since they are "stuck" on the membership level. Little, if any, opportunity for the satisfaction of contributive motivation exists.

Column 6 differs from Column 5 in that it shows the satisfied self-esteem need under conditions of a high perceived contribution opportunity, but a frustrated status-prestige need (frustrated by the lack of recognition on the part of an accommodative foreman) which the worker would feel was justified by his competence. The accommodative leader allows a group to develop simply by not being around or bothering to impede it. His *not* being around or *not* understanding the forces which motivate productiveness (i.e., self-esteem around job competence) make him less likely to reward the work with verbal or economic recognition of these perceived skills.

This motivational pattern and these environmental conditions were seen in the previously referred to Century Company case.[29] Workers in one furnace area (B) were glad their foreman was not around to interfere with their nonwork activities and their exercising of skill and judgment in their work. However, they resented the fact that he did not *understand* the extent of their technical competence and hence could not reward them adequately when it came time for him to evaluate them.

Before leaving Columns 1 through 6, which all illustrate one or another form of what Roethlisberger has called "frozen groups,"[30] an-

---

[27] Zaleznik, Christensen, and Roethlisberger, *op. cit.*

[28] Where there is a suggestion (untested) that social structure was determined by individual-status congruence. Cf. Roethlisberger and Dickson, *op. cit.*

[29] "Century Company (A–I)," *op. cit.*

[30] F. J. Roethlisberger, "Foreword," Zaleznik, *op. cit.*, pp. viii–xii.

other condition should be mentioned: "perception of company supportiveness." It has not been studied in enough situations to allow us to place it somewhere in Columns 1 through 6; however, two studies suggest its importance.

Seashore[31] found that high cohesive groups tended to produce significantly higher than average when they reported a high perception of company supportiveness and to produce significantly lower than average when they reported a low perception of company supportiveness.

In a piecework machine shop studied by Collins *et al.*,[32] a work group had an elaborate system of output restriction. The accommodative foreman knew about and actively supported the system. The general superintendent, however, exerted much effort in an attempt to break it up. He told workers they should not accept group pressure to conform and that they were foolish and dishonest if they did. The men saw the over-all company as being hostile toward them and went to considerable lengths to restrict output: They often finished their day's work in three or four hours, they had jigs and fixtures which increased their hourly productivity but which were unknown to management, etc.

Column 7 shows a condition that has only recently been analytically studied on a continuing basis in industry. However, studies concerning group participation in the process of instituting technological change (e.g., the well-known relay assembly test room[33] and the Coch and French[34] studies) might illustrate this situation for temporary periods where workers were involved in, and given recognition for, their ability to contribute to important organizational problems. Perhaps, too, the Lamson Company case[35] points to such a condition.

Skilled, experienced oil refinery workers were taken off their old job, given an extensive training course, and placed in a new tower. For several months, they worked alongside the engineers who were installing and "de-bugging" the new and complicated equipment. Their suggestions were encouraged and accepted by the engineers, and the men's behavior indicated they were highly satisfied with the experience.

Workers in such situations appear to be motivated at the higher need levels and to exist under maximal environmental conditions.

---

[31] S. F. Seashore, *Group Cohesiveness in the Industrial Work Group* (Ann Arbor: Survey Research Center, University of Michigan, 1954).

[32] Orvis Collins, Melville Dalton, and Donald Roy, "Restriction of Output and Social Cleavage in Industry," *Applied Anthropology*, Vol. V, No. 3 (1946).

[33] Roethlisberger and Dickson, *op. cit.*

[34] Lester Coch and J. R. P. French, Jr., "Overcoming Resistance to Change," *Human Relations*, Vol. I, No. 4 (1948).

[35] "Lamson Company," Harvard Business School, HP 318.

They have a high opportunity to interact, a task to which they see a high opportunity to contribute, and a leader who sets up a high opportunity for mutual influence between himself and his subordinates. Moreover, we can infer, too, that such workers would exist in an organizational environment which they saw as supportive. In addition, one study in an electronics factory (not yet published) suggests that the remaining environmental condition, high-status congruence, is a prerequisite for the motivation pattern seen in Column 7.

> However, in a recently published research by Barnes,[36] members of an engineering group exhibited low individual- and group-status congruence, yet had high opportunity to interact, high opportunity for mutual influence, and a high contribution opportunity. A few individuals, considered as a collection, had high group-status congruence, yet the social structure was not determined by this fact. Moreover, much of the group looked as if they might be exhibiting the need pattern seen in Column 7.

Barnes's research suggests, therefore, that when all other conditions are met, a group's social behavior is not "frozen" by the status factors its members brought with them. If one is interested in the growth and development of individuals in an organization, Barnes's study points to a hopeful situation.

Summary and Conclusion

By carefully examining Exhibit 1, we have attempted to describe factors which both release and constrain different motivations in members of industrial work groups. In addition, we have shown how, according to Maslow's theory, relative satisfaction of certain needs may release other needs which alter the picture. Roughly, Exhibit 2 illustrates this process, and is nothing more than a simplified restatement of Exhibit 1.

Incidentally, the similarity between Exhibit 2 and the small group conceptual scheme of Homans[37] is obvious. "Contribution opportunity" refers to the extent to which an individual's "required activities" are not so highly programmed that no room is left for the individual's contribution to them. "Interaction opportunity" refers to the extent to which an individual's "required interactions" do not limit him

---

[36] L. B. Barnes, *Organizational Systems and Engineering Groups: A Comparative Study of Two Technical Groups in Industry* (Boston: Division of Research, Harvard Business School, 1960).

[37] G. C. Homans, *The Human Group* (New York: Harcourt, Brace & Co., Inc., 1950).

from getting together, on a social as well as task basis, with others. "Influence opportunity," a function of leadership behavior, has an effect on an individual's motivation because of the kinds of "given sentiments" most of us appear to have about leadership. When we are closely controlled or highly programmed, this violates our expectations of a satisfying superior-subordinate behavior. "Status congruence" refers to another large body of "given sentiments" most people seem to have, ideas about status and class which are widespread in our culture.

Any emergent small group behavior feeds back on the "givens," however, as Homans and others have observed. And Exhibit 2 is oversimplified insofar as this feedback is not shown. Nevertheless, its

Exhibit 2

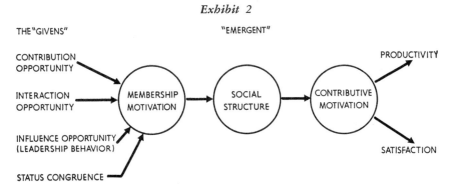

importance is obvious, particularly if one must understand and/or deal with a group through time. For example, a foreman of a work group which, for various reasons, was producing too little might change his leadership behavior from accommodative to production-centered, thus, perhaps, frustrating membership and self-esteem needs. Another example of such feedback might exist in a group under a group-centered leader who allowed mutual influence opportunities and whose members were active at the membership and contributive levels. Conceivably, these members would see continuous contribution opportunities in their jobs, thereby releasing further contributive motivation. Another example, and one which a number of my colleagues at the Harvard Business School and myself hope to test specifically in a current project, is the possibility that the structure of a group operating on higher need levels will be less determined by the status congruence of its members than it was at an earlier time, when it was operating more at the membership level.

In conclusion, the obvious fact remains to be emphasized that better techniques for the measurement of need activation in workers must be developed before this broad-stroke explanatory theory can be refined, altered, or rejected in the organizational behavior area. Only one of the studies cited—and that not yet published except in case form[38]—made an explicit attempt to assess motivation in Maslow's terms.

Research takes time, though, and those of us concerned directly with the immediate here-and-now problems of executives cannot always wait for our own and others' patient and time-consuming testing of intriguing notions of potential utility to practicing administrators. And, it seems to me, an administrator *can* use this general way of thinking to predict, at least on a gross basis, that certain consequences are quite likely to follow from the "givens" in any situation. Such a prediction might be economically valuable to him. He might, for example, behave differently during a technological or organizational change than he would have if he were not aware of the suggested effects of low interaction opportunity and contribution potential on motivation, social structure and productivity, and satisfaction. Conversely, if he were experiencing severe problems of dissatisfaction in his work force, he might seek to understand them in terms of this theory, and thereby highlight some "givens" which might be changed—interaction opportunity, for example. Such a change might cut down grievances, or even avert a strike.

Hopefully, this paper may serve to stimulate some better ways of testing the utility of Maslow's concepts for the study of organizational behavior. Certainly we are in need of integrative and operational concepts that both form the basis for replicable and comparative research and offer some utility to the practicing administrator.

---

[38] "Century Company (A–I)," *op. cit.*

SECTION V

Intergroup Behavior

Introduction

IN THE earlier sections of this book, we have examined cases and readings which primarily involve the behavior of individuals and groups. We have seen the persistent, recurring patterns which characterize the behavior of these people, and have examined some of the conditions which determine, in each situation, whether the patterns which emerge will conflict with or support organization, group, and individual objectives. We have viewed the difficult, ambiguous role of the first-line supervisor—"the man in the middle"—as he strives to maintain some balance between the demands of his superiors, the needs and values of his subordinates, and his own personal goals; and we have spent some effort in developing a framework for dealing with these small group supervisory situations.

In this section, we shall lean heavily on the concepts and skills developed earlier as we address problems of collaboration and conflict *between* groups and *among* supervisors and managers. Our data will depart in character from some of those data which have gone before, in that the simple, one-way authority relationships which have characterized many of the work group cases will not be so apparent among intergroup and intersupervisory relationships. While the image of management from a small group, or first-line, supervisory point of view has been a distant, amorphous one, it will now, in intergroup, intermanager perspective become highly differentiated and heterogeneous. The cases and readings in this section will deal with relationships at least one step above the small work group, with the interactions between small groups, as well as between departments, plants, divisions, and the formally or informally designated representatives of those groups at the management level.

As we shall see, each group in an organization is typified by behavior patterns which differentiate it from all other groups. These behavior patterns are governed by the rules or norms which each group has developed concerning what is and is not appropriate and commendable behavior. Yet, the successful functioning of the enterprise requires a high degree of co-ordination and co-operation among these differentiated groups. How does this take place? What are the elements which facilitate collaboration? What are the major determinants of conflict?

What can be done to encourage the one and lessen the other? These are the major questions with which we shall be concerned.

Intergroup behavior, because it includes in greater profusion everything which we have studied so far, represents a new level of complexity in our study of organizational behavior. To manage this new complexity, we need an enlarged, more encompassing set of conceptual ideas. Reading 1, "A Systematic Way of Thinking about Intergroup Behavior," presents an integrated scheme for analyzing intergroup situations. Enriching this diagnostic scheme are Readings 2–5, dealing with ideas of intergroup negotiation, the formal structure of intergroup relations, specialization and integration, and productive versus nonproductive intergroup conflict. The diagnostic help which these readings are designed to provide is especially suited to study of Cases 1–4. All of these cases are primarily diagnostic in character, although they do suggest issues for decision and action. United Diesel is a basic example of conflict between groups with opposing values. American Magnolite and Haig Chemical present problems of jurisdictional control. The Thermophysics Research Group is a prediction case of a department whose behavior deviates from the norms of the larger organization.

Of the remaining cases in the section, two, Fort Worth Pharmaceutical and Perkins Component, depict managers attempting to deal with intergroup problems in their day-to-day, routine activity. Belmont-White and Grayson, however, are open-ended, intergroup problem situations which require the utmost ingenuity for their effective resolution. All four of these cases are subject to the ideas in Readings 6 and 7 which, respectively, suggest methods of reducing nonproductive conflict and portray a top management group's methods for working together. In studying the last four cases in this section of the book, the student would also be well advised to review Readings 3, 4, and 5, since they contain a number of ideas for dealing with intergroup problems.

Cases

1. UNITED DIESEL CORPORATION

UNITED DIESEL Corporation was one of a few large-scale manufacturers of diesel engines for locomotives and other heavy equipment. For
many years, the heavy manufacturing investment required to break into
the industry had restricted the entry of new competition, while the rate
of market growth had kept prices at a level profitable for existing
manufacturers. More recently, however, competing forms of power
generation began to challenge the positions of the large diesel manufacturers. At the time of this case, price competition among diesel manufacturers had become severe.

United Diesel management was eagerly seeking ways to reduce manufacturing costs, delivery lead times, and customer maintenance problems. Because nearly every United Diesel engine was uniquely constructed to customer specifications, its engineering department had been
assigned projects which on the one hand would increase the degree of
engine standardization and on the other would simplify and increase the
efficiency of its engines.

The organization of the engineering department, including indications of work flow through the department, is diagrammed in Exhibit 1.
Typically, preliminary design and cost estimates were discussed by sales
engineers with customers (1).[1] As the prospect developed, sales called
in product design engineering (2) which acted throughout the project
as technical liaison between the customer and United Diesel (3). With
the help of specialist design groups (4), product design engineering
submitted a concrete proposal to the customer. If the proposal were
accepted, product design then administered the project by stimulating
the statement of firm requirements by specialist design groups (5)
[which worked directly with subelement draftsmen (6)], [as did product design (7)] by using specialist and subelement data to instruct the
work of general engine layout draftsmen (8) [who also worked directly
with their subelement colleagues (9)] and by consultation with mem-

---

[1] The numbers in parentheses correspond to numerical designations appearing in Exhibit 1. These numbers designate the sequence of relationships necessary to obtain and fulfill a customer contract.

bers of manufacturing planning (10) in which planning voiced its constraints and became informed of project development [much of this information flow passing directly between planners and draftsmen (11)]. As blueprints were completed, planning converted them into production instructions (12) by which production built the engines which were then custom installed in customer equipment (13). At any

Exhibit 1

UNITED DIESEL CORPORATION
ENGINEERING DEPARTMENT ORGANIZATION AND WORK FLOW

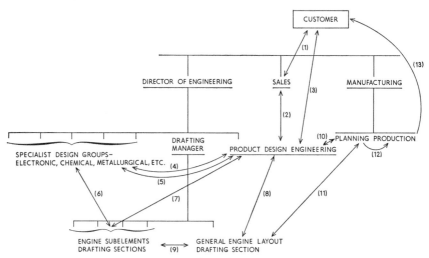

time in this work-flow cycle, product design engineering was on call to "shoot trouble" and, if necessary, initiate further negotiations with the customer.

A researcher from the Harvard Business School became interested in studying behavior in United Diesel's engineering department when he learned that United Diesel management was increasingly concerned by the mounting costs, diminishing speed, and apparent lack of creativity in its drafting rooms. Preliminary observations indicated that general engine layout drafting displayed behavior typical of other drafting sections and that the relationship between this section and product design engineering formed a kind of nerve center in the department. He secured permission to study these two groups and their relationship.

Product design engineering was composed of nine engineers and a manager. Two engineers specialized in customer liaison, two in manufacturing liaison, and five were assigned over-all responsibility for specific projects. All were graduate engineers. Three senior men were in their forties and had been with United Diesel for at least fifteen years.

The rest were in their late twenties or early thirties with no more than five years seniority. The senior engineers were all committed either to pure design activity or to a combination of design and engineering administration. The junior men tended to be somewhat less certain of their goals, which ranged from sales engineering to pure design to

Exhibit 2

UNITED DIESEL CORPORATION
GENERAL ENGINE LAYOUT DRAFTING SECTION ORGANIZATION

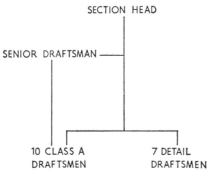

manufacturing engineering. The older men could remember when a national technical union had narrowly missed winning the right to represent United Diesel engineers.

General engine layout drafting's organization is shown in Exhibit 2. The section head assigned work to the men of his section. The senior draftsman was responsible for working through major design problems with engineers and for technical supervision of the Class A draftsmen. Each Class A draftsman was responsible for a project, though the youngest of these often worked under the supervision of those more senior. Detail draftsmen were assigned by the section head to make detailed working drawings from the master layout of a particular project or to work on routine changes in old drawings. All of these men except the section head were union members. One of the senior Class A draftsmen was president of the union local. Another was union steward for the section.

During the period of his orientation to these engineers and draftsmen, the researcher was busying himself studying company background material at a desk in the engineering office, when he overheard two engineers talking.

RALPH BURKE: Jim, one guy you want to steer clear of is Parker.[2] You know what he just did to me? I was in a meeting on that Crafts job. The customer's not happy, so Parker got everybody together who's been in

---

[2] Philip Parker was a sales executive in the company.

on it. He didn't like the design, and I admit he had some points. But do you know, he criticized engineering's judgment right in front of the drawing office people! Why couldn't he have talked with the engineers first so we could have headed the thing off before it got to a public demonstration? But no, he had to pull out our dirty linen right in front of a lot of drafting people. Parker's supposed to be interested in improving the communication line between the customer and the draftsman, but all he's doing is making the drawing office lose faith in engineering judgment. It was all I could do to sit there while he questioned my design ability, with those drafting people sitting back and taking it all in. We had to rush those Craft designs too much and I admit they were not red hot. But now Parker's got the draftsmen thinking I'm incompetent.

JIM PACKARD: Yeah, I know how you feel. One meeting like that can really set us back. We spend a hell of a lot of time figuring jobs in detail before passing them on to the drafting boys so they can trust our judgment that everything is going to fit together and work properly. Then some chump like Parker puts his foot in it, and the draftsmen don't know what's up. You and I both know how important it is to a draftsman to know just what's expected of him and how he's supposed to develop a design. This is what they need and want to know. But without some faith in us, they won't know where to turn. Someone ought to set Parker straight.

The researcher also had a number of opportunities to talk with draftsmen about their jobs and their working conditions, and especially about their relationships with the design engineers.

One old-time design draftsman, regarded by the engineers as "a plodder," told the researcher:

All the motivation to do good, creative designing has been lost around here. Take a chemist or a teacher. He doesn't care about money all the time; it's his work that he's interested in. It's what he can do. It used to be that way before, but not any more. Nowadays, nobody has any interest in what he's doing. They just tell you to draw some lines, and you draw them. In the old days, you would work on it with the engineer, you'd make your own layout, you would even do your own detailing, and you would work with the guys in the shop. Everything. In those days, you had responsibility for a whole job, for a whole engine; and you were interested in what you were doing, and you knew your work, and you were good at it. I could design a whole engine in the old days. There isn't a guy here in the whole department that could do that now.

I'm not surprised that nobody's got any incentive or wants any responsibility. In the old days, I would be so wrapped up in the job that I'd go out to the woods at night, my hands clenched so tight they bled, and scream with frustration because I couldn't figure something out on a design. Nowadays, it's all I can do to stay awake. I'm not interested any more. I could go to work any place. I'm a trained draftsman, not a line drawer. I'm a layout man. I could work in automatic machinery, electronics, or any place.

A little later, the researcher talked to Henry Nelson, a senior design draftsman who was respected by the other draftsmen. He said:

I came to United Diesel in 1923 with a background of six years of drafting experience with several concerns. Why had I chosen drafting? As a technical school student, I worked two summers in a drafting room and became quite impressed with the prestige the draftsmen enjoyed, so the die was cast.

Soon after starting with United, I had the opportunity to do more and more work of an engineering nature, so I did considerable home study to qualify for a transfer to engineering. It finally came at the end of six years and lasted about three years until the depression came, along with a new department manager. Because I had no college degree, I was transferred back to drafting.

This brings up the point that United has a barrier which cannot be passed by a draftsman unless he possesses a degree; whereas in the automobile plants and many other plants, a man can go as far as his abilities can take him.

Another point is the fact that if a man is exceptionally good at a given job, he finds himself pegged and often bypassed from promotion in favor of someone who may be less capable in the job he is holding. This means we have in some cases "eunuchs" who tell you what to do, even though they cannot do the job themselves.

The draftsman in United no longer enjoys the prestige of years past. Now he is considered a necessary evil or burden. While it is true that the draftsman is to a certain degree dependent on and guided by the engineer, he nevertheless has to interpret and execute the necessary working drawings for production of the design.

. . . A few years ago, I asked for a wage increase; and after six months or more, I was told that my name was on the list. In an interview with my supervisor, I was told that the reason the raise was delayed was that quite often I would design to suit myself rather than follow the engineer's wish. My reply was that I first followed the engineer's instructions; and then, to avoid sitting around thumb-twiddling, waiting for the engineer, I would try to work up other possible solutions. About six months later, I did get my increase, which actually was two years overdue.

The ironical part is that about one year later, "Value Analysis Seminars" were held for two large groups in two sessions of about five weeks' duration. One of the points stressed was that there was probably a better way of doing the job; consequently, all ideas should be studied, not immediately rejected, as is too often the case when they differ "from the way it has already been done for years."

A younger draftsman, regarded by the engineers as "something of a problem," explained: "A good draftsman is one who will take responsibility. Most of the men around here would do it if they only had more information. As it is now, nobody knows what's expected, so all he does is just exactly what is required."

Another old-timer designer at the next board, who was something of a social leader in the group, heard this last comment and chimed in:

> They always say the engineer doesn't know what we're doing, anyway, but he's got to act as though he does. So when you show him a drawing, he'll say, "Change this radius here," when the radius doesn't have any significance at all. They should respect our feeling for a problem and not always give an answer when they come in "cold" on something we know a lot about. Of course, they see a lot out in the field that leads them to infer that there are problems, but they shouldn't feel they always have to have an answer.

A middle-aged designer, about whose ability the engineers were sharply divided, joined the group. He said:

> Yeah, engineers always want to make changes in your designs. I don't have any trouble with Richardson (a senior design engineer). He always approves my work, but Burke has to play the game. He didn't use to check my work. Then, he make a stink over a new idea I put in, and now he does. He has to go over and over it and make suggestions; but nine times out of ten, he comes back to my original design.

And an older designer, evaluated by the engineers as "outstanding," added:

> The tendency of an engineer is to get unhappy when a designer puts his own ideas in and goes beyond the engineers. I've never felt I had anything extra to contribute from a design point of view. I give them what they want and express my own thoughts and ideas when I've got them, but not very forcefully. Mostly, the design ideas are a matter of detail (like wall thickness or contour or something). It's never a very big thing because we always work on about the same kind of designs. So what I have to offer is always going to be equal to whatever the engineer wants.

. . . .

Several days later the researcher posted himself in the drawing office, his eyes open for contacts between draftsmen and engineers. At 8:30 A.M., Henry Nelson, whose comments were quoted above, invited the researcher to join him in a visit with Ralph Burke[3] in the engineering

---

[3] Ralph Burke was one of the older junior men in product design. His work habits, level of competence, and outlook on life appeared to be typical of most engineers in his section.

office. As the two men walked the few hundred feet between offices, Nelson described the reason for his call on Burke.

Ralph came down to my drawing board a few days ago in a rush to get going on the packaging design[4] for the Proxmire job. I had already done a crude layout of the package over a month ago, but it had to be put aside because we didn't have the final "specs." I was just finishing another project when Ralph told me he had the Proxmire data, finally, and was most anxious to get under way. So I've been pushing hard to complete the job I had on my board, and now I'm free to go ahead with Burke.

It turned out that Burke was temporarily out of the office, so Nelson left him a note. Back at his drawing board, Nelson made further sketches, outlining his ideas for the Proxmire package. Whenever someone walked by his workplace, he glanced up, as if expecting Burke. On several occasions, Burke came into the drawing office to consult with other draftsmen, but he did not approach Nelson. The latter remarked to the researcher that he could not understand the delay, in view of Burke's previous insistence on getting the job started.

At 4:00 P.M. a clerk informed Nelson that Burke was ready to see him. Nelson gathered his sketches and, again accompanied by the researcher, walked to Burke's office. On Burke's desk was a copy of the preliminary package layout which Nelson had drawn. It became the focus of their conversation.

BURKE: Henry, you won't have to build the package as high as it's drawn here. The latest information indicates that a shorter package will allow sufficient maintenance access.

NELSON: All right. Do you know yet just how the package will connect with the customer's installation for it?

BURKE: Specific details on their installation aren't necessary for this job. If you keep the height to a minimum, there should be no problem of fitting the engine into the machine. Now, you'll want to use a corner radius of four inches on this size job.

NELSON: Four inches—just the radius for all the other jobs of this type.

BURKE: That's right. Just follow the ideas on previous layouts.

NELSON: What ideas did the customer give you about designing the package so it can be taken apart whenever repairs to the engine have to be made?

BURKE (after several minutes' silent study of the drawings):   I don't think any changes over what we knew before have been made in their "specs" on that aspect of the job.

NELSON: Well, we could handle the disassembly in a number of

---

[4] The housing in which the diesel would be enclosed.

different ways; and as I recall, no specific choice has been made up to now.

Burke sat back and again silently studied the drawing. After several minutes, Nelson assumed that Burke was not going to respond to his question. He pulled the sketch sheets he had been working on out of his pocket and spread them on top of the layout drawing.

NELSON: Here are some sketches I've been working on which seem to be flexible enough to take care of all possible repair contingencies, but I don't think the design would be so complex as to be uneconomical. You see, the panel on this end could be broken out to allow for this section of the engine to be removed without disassembling the whole package.

BURKE (*with a brief glance at Nelson's sketches*):   The chances are that if anything breaks down, it will be this section over here. That would require taking the whole package apart, anyway. Your end-panel idea would probably be used so seldom that it wouldn't be worth including. No, just design the package the way you've done similar ones.

NELSON: Well, if that's all, then, I'll get started on the final layout. What drawings should I look at to base this design on?

BURKE: It would be the XYZ job, but you'll have to look up the drawings. I wouldn't know which ones would be relevant. And you might as well take this layout drawing with you. I have no use for it.

NELSON: I'll get started on this as soon as I can.

.   .   .   .

After the meeting with Burke, the researcher asked Nelson what his reaction to it had been.

NELSON: Well, I was surprised that Ralph knew so little more than he had known before. I guess he's trying to keep things open so he can change his mind later. A lot of the engineers seem to work that way, particularly the young ones. They put up a front, as though they didn't have anything left to learn. They're afraid we'll find out how green they are. It hurts their pride to have a mere draftsman giving them answers or ideas. Well, I guess I can junk these sketches and do it his way. I won't bother him again with my ideas. My mistake was thinking that he wanted some help in the first place. For a guy who's been around here a long time, I can be pretty dumb sometimes.

Not long after the meeting between Nelson and Burke, the researcher found an opportunity to ask Burke what qualities in a draftsman he most highly valued.

BURKE: A draftsman should have good visual imagination and be able to create things. He should be able to give you what you want the first time you ask for it. Of course, that means you have to explain what you want and how you want it done, clearly and in detail. The trouble is that too many draftsmen spend valuable time putting extraneous ideas into the design. You have to keep a tight check on their work to make sure they haven't fouled up the machine. It's O.K. if they do something on their own *after* they've done what you've asked them to do.

Take Henry Nelson, for example. You were there the other day when we went over the Proxmire job. That's an important order, and we're way behind schedule on it. Henry knew it had to be completed quickly. And yet, he wanted to play around with some fancy ideas that weren't necessary and might well have weakened the over-all design. If he had spent the time he put into those sketches digging out background material from other jobs to build the basic design on, he'd be living up to my idea of how a good draftsman should behave.

· · · · · · · · · · · · · · · · · · · ·

A short time later the researcher talked with the director of engineering of United Diesel, Mr. Buckley. Buckley was responsible for all design and preproduction activities throughout the entire company. He said:

I don't understand it. Men just don't seem to want to work hard any more. Why, I can remember when we were smaller and I was a design engineer, we'd work till 2:00 or 3:00 o'clock in the morning, night after night, when we were trying to solve a difficult design problem. It was an enormous challenge to try to solve problems which we had no idea how to deal with. All of us had to learn a tremendous amount, and we thirsted for the knowledge and experience that would help us.

But today, all the men seem to be interested in is the money they make and their leisure time to enjoy it. They want job security, too—but the challenge of the job itself is gone. That's particularly true of the draftsmen. You know, those fellows like to think of themselves as sort of "engineers," and they get very sensitive about their status and prerogatives. But then they turn around and just barely work hard enough to get by. You have to keep after them all the time. Now, that's no way for a professional man to act. If they want recognition, why don't they earn it by hard, creative work?

2. AMERICAN MAGNOLITE COMPANY*

Part 1[1]

IN LATE November of a recent year a group of the top executives of the Midtown branch of the American Magnolite Company met to make some critical decisions in regard to a new product development. The product in question was a radically new type of ignition control tube that two industrial engineers, Fred Fisher and George Ames, had been developing since the previous August. The project had reached the point where Russ Keller, the head of industrial engineering, had asked for a meeting to decide primarily whether the project should remain with the industrial engineers who started it or be turned over to the plant's regular staff of development engineers.

The American Magnolite Company was a leading producer of all types of electrical and electronic equipment. It operated manufacturing plants in many parts of the country; and each plant specialized in the manufacture and, in many instances, the marketing, of a related group of products.

The Midtown branch plant produced and sold a family of electronic tubes and control devices. The plant had been established only a few years earlier and had always placed heavy emphasis on new product development. In fact, 150 of the plant's 550 employees were engaged in some way in development engineering work in comparison with a production force of 250 people. Exhibit 1 presents a partial organization chart of the plant, showing the key people involved.

The new ignition control tube—or the "Amicon" tube, as it came to be called—had started as an idea of Fisher's in August. He thought that by a radically new design approach, it might be possible to replace the ignition control tube the plant was currently producing with a new one that would be superior in quality and production cost. Fisher had been looking for some kind of special project that would interest him, and the Amicon tube idea met these needs. As he expressed it: "I was par-

---

*This case is based on material from the book *Administering Changes: A Case Study of Human Relations in a Factory*, by H. O. Ronken and P. R. Lawrence (Boston: Division of Research, Harvard Business School, 1952). Data reproduced by permission.

[1] This is a sequential case. Your instructor may wish to have you discuss Part 1 of the case before reading subsequent parts.

ticularly displeased with our department's general position in the company and felt we didn't really have a chance to show what we could do. Everything we tried, we got held up on; and I was dying to get hold of a project that I could really get my teeth into."

Fisher talked to his boss, Keller, about his ideas for a new tube; and Keller, in turn, sounded out Larry Barnes on the subject. As Keller recalled it: "I mentioned the idea to Larry Barnes, and he immediately got enthusiastic about it. He suggested that I see if we couldn't make up a few tubes to see if they would work."

Exhibit 1

AMERICAN MAGNOLITE COMPANY

PARTIAL ORGANIZATION CHART OF MIDTOWN PLANT

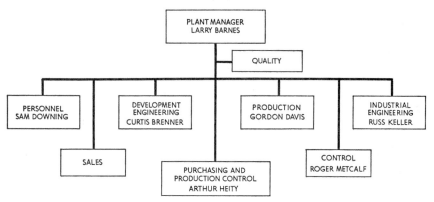

Fisher and Ames spent the months of September and October pretty well isolated in Fisher's office working on their ideas. Fisher gave an account of what they were doing and how they felt about the project:

Well, Ames and I got started working on it about last August. It really was a lot of fun. We used to try out every idea we got. We never assumed ahead of time that something wouldn't work until we tried it. We tried everything we could think of. For quite a while, we had this office set up as our experimental shop. We had a little engine lathe over there where we worked on the parts, and we had a test kit here where we tried them out. By starting from scratch on this problem, we learned a lot. A lot of the things we learned contradicted what everybody had previously thought about the problem.

Fisher went on to tell with enthusiasm how he enjoyed the work:

Those were great days! I never used to come to work later than 7 o'clock. A good many days, I would be working here so steadily that I wouldn't even notice it was time to quit until some time after 4:30. One day, I worked until 5:45 before I realized it was past quitting time. I always came in on Saturday and sometimes on Sunday. You know, I didn't get paid any overtime for those hours, either.

At the end of October, Fisher and Ames thought that their Amicon tube looked promising, and they were anxious to start making up more tubes for experimental purposes. The first thing they did in this direction was to secure approval for hiring two women to help them as experimental operators. During the first week in November, Sam Downing, the personnel director, hired two new employees, Claire Cochrane and Alice Nagle. These two girls went to work for Fisher and Ames, performing all the operations involved in making a limited quantity of experimental Amicon tubes.

During October and November the two men prepared specifications on the parts to be used in the new tube and on the processes to be used in producing and assembling these parts. These rough preliminary specifications were constantly being modified as the production experiments indicated improvements that could be made in design features and production operations.

Ames, with help from Fisher, converted an obsolete piece of equipment into an "envelope" machine to make the glass body cases for the new tube. This job took considerable time, since new parts had to be designed and built and then redesigned in order to get the "bugs" out of the machine. Ames always stood by this machine when it was in operation; and with many little adjustments and with the help of Claire and Alice, he could produce enough good-quality body cases in a few hours to keep the two girls supplied for several days.

Fisher and Ames also worked up some rough ideas for a semi-automatic machine for swaging the positive terminal. Karl Vronska, one of the industrial engineers' skilled machinists, was assigned the job of working out the design details and making the parts for this new piece of equipment. He spent considerable time conferring with the two men about the problems he was encountering in doing this job.

The results obtained from these activities were encouraging to the industrial engineers.

RUSS KELLER: In November, we started trying to put out these tubes on a regular basis, at least 20 or 30 a day. Fred and George were still making a lot of changes in the design of the tube and in the processes used. They were getting some very good results, though. The results were much better than what was being obtained on the old ignition control tube line.

One of the encouraging signs during this time was the relatively small number of Amicon tubes that proved to be defective. Only 200 Amicon tubes were assembled during November, but this was about what was expected. Of these 200 units, about 20 per cent were defective. This compared favorably with the regular ignition control tube; during the corresponding period, about one half of these tubes proved to be defective. In addition, it looked to the industrial engineers as if the Amicon tube could be produced with fewer operations and less labor than was needed for the production of the regular tube.

Barnes heard about these events through Keller, and he had some additional reasons of his own to be encouraged by these developments. As he commented later:

> Our ignition control business at the time amounted to about 10 per cent of the entire business of the plant. With the old ignition control tube, we knew we could never reach the potential market. That tube wasn't properly designed for low-cost mass production. The parts were too expensive, and they couldn't be assembled on automatic equipment. We tried one thing after another in an attempt to get the cost of that product down. I guess we spent about a year at it before it began to dawn on us that we weren't going to get much further with that type of design. We needed something quite radically new. Those were the conditions when we first started talking about the Amicon tube and thinking we might develop it as a substitute for the old tube.

In spite of these encouraging signs, Keller began to have some reservations about the way the project was developing. He commented: "I began to think we were getting in a little over our heads. What we were doing was really development engineering work, and that was supposed to be done by Brenner's people." Keller was not concerned with the ability of Fisher and Ames to master the technical problems. He was concerned with the organizational problems that might arise. Keller was also aware of the complication that Curt Brenner had only been with the company for two months. With these questions in mind, Keller went to Barnes, who suggested that he call a meeting of the key people involved to help decide on the proper handling of the project. In addition to Keller, Barnes invited Brenner, Gordon Davis, Roger Metcalf, and Art Heity to the meeting. While Barnes wanted the advice of all these men on the subject, he knew he would have to take responsibility for the consequences of the decision.

AMERICAN MAGNOLITE COMPANY

Part 2

At the management meeting on November 23,[2] it was decided to leave the Amicon tube project in the hands of the industrial engineers. Keller summarized the meeting by saying: "Even before Larry suggested it, Brenner volunteered the suggestion that I continue to work on the project. He said that he didn't have any men he could assign to it right away, and we had already made some progress and certainly had some good ideas and a lot of enthusiasm for the work. So we agreed to do it that way. I was glad to do it because we were all interested in trying to get it worked out." Art Heity commented: "Everyone agreed that the industrial engineers should go ahead with their work, even though this was a slightly irregular procedure. Brenner said that his development engineers would stay out of it unless the industrial engineers got into trouble—in that case, they would help out."

During the next seven months the project moved through several additional stages—Fisher, Ames, and their two girl assistants continued to make progress on the tube during December and January. In January the decision was made to put the product into regular production as of February 1. Keller and Fisher urged that this transfer be postponed, but their objections were overruled. Going into regular production meant bringing in a production supervisor and setting some specific output goals. Barnes set the goal of getting the product into full-scale, low-cost production by July. This meant getting up to an output of 100,000 units per month at per unit cost substantially below that of the old ignition control tube. In order to reach this goal, a number of complex steps needed to be taken. The most critical of these are listed below:

Product Design:
    Eliminate quality "bugs" in the design of the product.
Personnel:
    Train the new foreman in the technical ins and outs of the new product.
    Assemble and train a considerable work force: 20 to 30 people.

---

[2] See American Magnolite Company, Part 1, for further details.

EQUIPMENT AND SUPPLIES:

Finish designing and produce or purchase the equipment needed to
get production started: several test kits, an adequate envelope machine, a new etching device, an adequate swaging
machine, and several subassembly devices.

Design and produce supplementary jigs and fixtures to speed up the
production process: test kit holding fixtures, acid sinks, etc.

Lay out and set up a new production workplace.

Work the "bugs" out of the new equipment and fixtures.

Develop adequate sources of supply for a large volume of high-
quality, low-cost purchased parts.

Design and secure more fully automatic equipment for a later stage
of high-speed production: automatic envelope machine, etc.

The very nature of these jobs to be done required the co-operative efforts of many people from several functional groups, especially the
production people, the industrial engineers, and the development engineers. A number of episodes are described below that exemplify the
way these three key functional groups worked with each other in the
months that followed.

Industrial Engineers and Development Engineers

December. One of the design problems on the Amicon tube was
getting a good solder joint between the body case and the terminal.
Brenner suggested plating these parts prior to soldering to solve the
problem. He assigned one of his development engineers, Dick Gantos,
to trying out his idea. Gantos brought his plated parts to Fisher, who
tried assembling tubes with them but decided that they did not work
satisfactorily.

February. Another design problem involved the process for preparing the grids for the negative terminal assembly. Fisher and Ames had
been experimenting with a heat-treating process and felt encouraged by
the results. When Brenner heard about this, he felt this was a development engineering problem and assigned one of his men, Wally Parent,
to test the new heat-treating process on grids. On February 24, Brenner
reported the results of the test at one of the regular management meetings. He said that the test indicated that the heat-treated grids were not
so good as the grids processed in the routine fashion. Fisher began to say
something to the group about why he thought the test had turned out as
it did. Brenner precluded further discussion of the topic by saying that
in the future, all experiments and tests on grids should be conducted by

his group, in accordance with a memorandum to that effect issued by Barnes.

After the meeting, Fisher told how he felt about this entire incident:

> I was plenty sore when Parent had that report presented to the team about his poor results on the test with heat-treated grids. You know, you can utter a falsehood without actually telling a specific lie simply by leaving out a lot of pertinent information. He ran one test with heat-treated grids; and because it did not turn out well, he wrote a report that seemed to condemn the whole process. When he ran that test, I pointed out to him that in the process of working on the terminals, they had become corroded in some peculiar way that might give them trouble. He did not pay any attention to this. I reworked some of that same batch of heat-treated grids he was working on and got 25 perfect units out of it in 25 tries. It seems to me it would be more constructive to try to make a new idea work than to try to prove that it won't work by simply running one test.

March.   In spite of Fisher's negative report on plating prior to soldering, Brenner instructed Gantos to continue his experiments with the method on a part-time basis. During January and February, he ran different experiments in the development engineers' chemical laboratory on these soldering problems. By the third of March, Gantos had made some plated tube parts that he wanted to try soldering together on the regular testing kit set up on the production line. The following is the researcher's description of what happened when Gantos arrived at the production line to run his test:

> Dick Gantos brought some of his plated terminals over to the production line to see if Alice[3] could make a good solder joint with them while maintaining the proper electrical characteristics. He and Lou[4] stood by while Alice went to work with the new terminals. She first attached the grids to one batch of terminals. She etched the taper on the positive terminals and then sat down at her test kit and assembled three units in succession. Each of these units turned out to be defective, since in the process of soldering they lost the proper electrical readings. It seemed to the researcher that Alice was not handling the parts with her usual care. As she finished each unit, she handed it to Lou, who passed it without comment to Dick.
>
> Dick tried to explain the failures on the grounds that he had not been familiar with the method of etching the tapers. Lou replied that the method was written into the specifications.

---

[3] One of the original two girls on the project.

[4] Lou Corriveau, the production foreman assigned to the Amicon tube in February.

Dick made some comment about trying a cleaning operation, and then both he and Lou were called away for a moment. While they were gone, Fred Fisher walked up to where Alice was working. Alice said: "Take a look at these units I made with Gantos' parts. They all turned out bad."

It seemed to the researcher that she had a sort of "I-guess-we-told-them-so" tone in her voice as she told the story to Fred.

At this point, Dick came back, and he and Fred watched Alice assemble three more tubes with the plated parts. They, too, were defective. Gantos said he thought the trouble might be caused by the way Alice was applying the flux, but Fred denied it. Gantos then mentioned his doubts about the effect of the etching operation. Fred replied that the etching operation had never caused any trouble before. Dick finally walked away toward his laboratory, saying something about running some more experiments. Fred commented: "We tried to use those plated terminals before, and they didn't work. Gantos can't seem to get it through his head that we have to get good electrical readings on these units as well as good solder joints."

After this event, Gantos and Parent set up their own test kit in the laboratory in order to be independent of the regular line in doing their work on the Amicon tube. Gantos continued to work on the plating idea but never again asked the industrial engineers or production people to try out his ideas.

April–June. During these months, Parent and Gantos spent considerable time working on the project. Gantos, with help from Parent, continued to experiment in his laboratory with ways of improving the soldering of the Amicon tube. Parent, at specified time intervals, supervised the running of performance tests on samples of the tubes that were being produced, and he regularly reported the results of these tests at the team meetings. These two men ran a controlled experiment in April to test the relative usefulness of the industrial engineers' method of etching tapers and the regular method used for the old control tube. Parent periodically worked at keeping the design specifications on the Amicon tube up to date. These two men helped on the design of one part of the new etching equipment and experimented with new types of chemical solutions to be used in this process. In almost every instance, their evaluative reports indicated that the Amicon tube was not adequately meeting performance standards and that the industrial engineers' processes were inferior to other processes.

Meanwhile, the industrial engineers were performing a number of activities involving these same matters. In addition to working with Lou Corriveau on the production equipment, Fisher and Ames started again in April to experiment with new ways of securing a more satisfactory way of soldering the Amicon tube. They did most of the design work and supervised the construction of the new etching apparatus. When the etching apparatus was completed, they supervised its installation in the production line and worked to eliminate some of the "bugs" in the equipment and the process.

In spite of these overlapping activities, the two groups of engineers had virtually no face-to-face contact with each other during these months. From the first part of March until the middle of June the researchers neither observed directly nor heard of any occasion on which Fisher and Ames talked with Parent and Gantos outside of the regular meetings they were all required to attend. In June, Fisher said: "I get along with Gantos simply by leaving him alone."

During the December–June period the key members of the two engineering groups developed some strong negative feelings about each other and the state of the Amicon project, as indicated by the following comments to the researcher:

FRED FISHER: We haven't made any progress for the past month. It's certainly discouraging. They are still trying to make a good solder joint in the laboratory. I can't get it through Gantos' head that we don't just need a good solder joint, but we need electrical readings, too. . . . I have never been so close to exploding in my whole life. If they (the development engineers) are trying to kill our product, why don't they say so? That's what they're really doing, you know. You can always find something wrong with a product if you put it to extreme tests. There is nothing mechanical that you can't break if you try hard enough. You ought to see the performance tests they are running on the tubes. Ames was telling me something about them today. They're just trying to prove it won't work. . . . Things aren't coming at all well. We aren't getting anything done around here. We've got a couple of ideas for some equipment we want some day, but nothing much is getting done. We're still talking about the same things we were two months ago. We're still fighting the same old fights about plating or not plating.

I feel completely frustrated on this work now. It's terribly discouraging. I get blocked no matter what direction I go. By the time I have finished a day around here, I am all tied up in knots. My stomach feels like a lead weight. My wife notices it and asks me what's wrong when I get home. There are just too many people involved in this thing now—too many cooks—everybody has to get into the act. Everybody expresses his opinion, but nothing gets done.

DICK GANTOS: The Amicon tube project got started all wrong. We're going to have a hell of a time getting it straightened out. That product shouldn't have been turned over to the industrial engineers when it first started. Some Joe Doaks on the line gets an idea, so Barnes says to him go ahead and engineer the product. Joe can think and may get good ideas, but it is a different story to try and work out a finished product. That takes experience and engineering know-how. Even before we heard anything about the project, industrial engineering was getting it into production. When we saw what they had done, we knew they were going to have trouble. They just didn't listen to us.

WALLY PARENT: We resented having the industrial engineers doing the design work on the Amicon tube. It just wasn't right. It isn't so much the fact that they are doing it as the way they are doing it. The whole thing makes us look bad.

The industrial engineers and the development engineers accomplished very little together during this period. The one thing that these groups worked out jointly was the new etching apparatus, which was modestly successful. At no time, however, did they work out together any new design feature or process change that made an appreciable improvement in the product in terms of cost, quality, or output volume. This was in sharp contrast to the earlier design period, when new ideas for the product were being put into use at a rapid rate.

From February through June the development engineers also ran periodic performance tests of different kinds on the Amicon tubes. They tested both the final product and some of the production processes. In the latter part of June the development engineers tested a sample of the tubes that had been produced several months earlier. The results of this "life" test showed that a number of the tubes had "gone bad" electri-cally while in storage.

The statistical results of these tests were interpreted by the development engineers to mean that the product was essentially unsound.

GANTOS: They just aren't making the product right. Too much of their production fails when it is just sitting on a shelf for a couple of months.

Fisher gave these same statistics a different interpretation. He concluded from Parent's performance test reports that the development engineers were trying to prove the product no good by setting impossible standards. In late June, Fisher recognized that the product still had its shortcomings, but he believed they could be easily remedied.

FISHER: If the Amicon tube works, and we know it will work, then there are only a few problems to iron out, and they are mostly "manu-factured" problems. We made good Amicon tubes once; and we know they can be made again, if they will just let us iron out a few problems.

Industrial Engineers and Production

On February 1, Lou Corriveau, as the new foreman of the Amicon tube line, was given formal responsibility for production and made the supervisor of Alice and Claire, the two girls who had been helping Fisher and Ames. Corriveau was a relatively young supervisor who had been given a wide variety of production assignments. At the time he was given the Amicon tube job, he was told it was his "big chance." He expressed his reactions to the new job thus:

> You know, I have been transferred seven times in the last three years. I just get one operation started when they move me again. They've never really given me a chance to complete a job. They've sort of promised me if I get the Amicon tube rolling, I can count on it as a regular job. I certainly hope that's true, because I want to do a good job, and I want to see some results. I figure that if they give me a job like this, they must have some reasons for doing so. I told Davis if he thought I could do the job, he should give me enough time and a chance to do things my own way. If they don't give me a decent chance this time, I'll probably have to leave the company.

In the first few days after this transfer, Fisher went about his work on the project with no noticeable change. As he put it, he considered the formal transfer merely a "paper change." He continued to spend a high percentage of his time working with the two girls, Claire and Alice, on the little technical details of making tubes with their experimental equipment. He frequently sat down at the equipment to try his hand at making good tubes. He discussed with the girls all the details of the difficulties they were having.

Meanwhile, Corriveau was spending relatively little time around the Amicon tube work. He continued to spend most of his time in the lithotron section, where he still had some supervisory responsibilities. However, during these few days, he observed that he was being ignored by the industrial engineers in their work with the girls. He commented: "Fred and George are always stirring up the girls. Fred sits down with Claire, and they run all sorts of little experiments, changing things on the tubes and trying different ways of doing things without telling me what's going on."

Corriveau complained in this vein to Davis, and Davis apparently agreed with him, because a few days after the transfer Davis called Fisher into his office. The latter reported this incident to the researchers.

> FISHER: Davis called me into his office and told me, in effect, to stay away from the Amicon tube girls. He said it was all right for me to go

around and watch the work; but if I had any orders to give, I should talk to Lou, and no one but Lou should give any orders to the girls. I try; but you know, it's almost impossible to work that way.

A few days later, Fisher made statements about Corriveau that indicated his resentment about the way the latter was acting.

FISHER: Take this matter of Corriveau. He didn't know anything about making Amicon tubes when he was put in charge of producing them. Now he is having to learn everything over again, but the hard way. He goes right back through a lot of trial-and-error steps we've already been through. And he isn't too anxious to take our advice on these things.

Meanwhile, Corriveau was disturbed because the industrial engineers did not seem to be giving him adequate help on the matters he wanted help on. He went to Fisher with a request for a change in the job classification assigned to a key job in the new line, and he received a "book" answer as to why it could not be done. He kept experiencing one delay after another in getting delivery of the various pieces of production equipment that the industrial engineers were supposed to design and build for him. After a few days, Corriveau commented:

I'm not getting anywhere. I can't get anything done. We talk about everything, but no one does anything about it. When Davis tells me to do something by Friday, I have to have it done by Friday. He won't take Monday for an answer. But I can't get it through if I don't have the equipment. . . .

When I first came on this line, I had a meeting downstairs with Keller and Davis and some of those people. They promised me certain things in the way of equipment that they said were all ready to go. I was supposed to start production with them. I took over on Monday. At the end of the week, I still didn't have the equipment, so I wrote a report to Davis. How could I do what they asked me if I didn't have anything to work with? And if I didn't tell them I didn't have it, they would never know. It would look bad for me. Well, the industrial engineers talked as though I was attacking them or something.

After a few weeks, in the face of what seemed to him the engineers' indifference, Corriveau tried to force them to keep their promises.

CORRIVEAU: I don't like keeping after them, but it's the only way I can get anything done. Like Karl.[5] I have to check him in the morning, check him at noon, check him at night. I don't like that, either. At least, I am more tactful than they are. I don't just tell them to do something.

---

[5] Karl Vronska, a machinist who was working with Fisher and Ames, making some of the production equipment.

I have tried to go up and ask them if they need any help or anything. I'm going to start blasting if things don't move pretty soon.

Vronska, in turn, resented this pressure.

> KARL VRONSKA: I'm not worried about this die. I know that if I can just have enough time, sooner or later I'll find out what's causing the trouble; and my boss knows it, too. It's guys putting pressure on you all the time that make me mad. I get so sick of Lou. I'm going to push his teeth down his throat some day. I said to him one day: "You get out of here quick. When this is ready, I'll turn it over to you; but until then, it's none of your business. I'm going to do my work myself without any interference from you."

An incident that occurred around the envelope machine in mid-April exemplified the nature of the relationship. The envelope machine was an old piece of semiautomatic equipment that Fisher and Ames had salvaged and rebuilt to form the body cases for the tube. When the Amicon tube was put into production, this machine was working, but only sporadically. One of Ames's jobs was to keep it in running condition and to try to make it a dependable piece of equipment. This job involved Ames's spending many hours making adjustments on the machine and periodically redesigning and rebuilding parts of it. As time went on, Ames and the machinist Vronska, who occasionally helped him in this job, grew tired of the assignment. They wanted to turn all responsibility for the machine over to Corriveau. But whenever the machine got in trouble, Corriveau went to Ames to get it fixed. Everyone concerned began to get irritated and impatient. Ames accused Corriveau of not operating the machine properly, and the latter countered that the industrial engineers did not get it fixed right.

On the fourteenth of April, Ames and Vronska had spent the morning working on the envelope machine. About 11:00 o'clock, Corriveau joined the group and entered into their discussions. At the time the researcher appeared, the men had decided that the pins on which the parts were loaded were too long and were discussing how much to shorten them. Ames held several sample pins which he was measuring while Corriveau looked over his shoulder. Corriveau's gestures suggested that he was with difficulty refraining from taking the scaler and making the measurements himself. Before Ames spoke, Corriveau suggested cutting off $3/32$ of an inch, adding that the job could be done on a machine in the salvage section.

> VRONSKA: That machine isn't accurate enough.
> LOU CORRIVEAU: It's close enough.

VRONSKA (*standing up as if to leave*): Well, we're off. If you're going to run this, you don't need us.

CORRIVEAU: What do you mean? This hasn't anything to do with me. I didn't mean that.

VRONSKA: Go ahead and do it your way. It's all yours.

CORRIVEAU: Why, this machine isn't in production yet. When you can run a couple of hundred on it and have them O.K., I'll take it over.

VRONSKA: Well, if you want a machine that'll work, you've gotta have things the proper length. If something is supposed to be a certain size, it's gotta be exactly that size. Then you know what you're dealing with.

After considerable discussion, Ames suggested that each pin be cut to a length of $19\!/\!32$ of an inch. No further comment was made on where the cutting was to be done. Vronska remained standing where he was, measuring some bushings. Presently, he called Corriveau over and told him that they varied a good deal in length.

VRONSKA: You need some new bushings.

CORRIVEAU: Those are new. We just used them on the last two hundred envelopes we made.

VRONSKA: That makes no difference. They're different lengths. Some of them vary by almost .025.

CORRIVEAU: Karl, I can't throw them out. Do you know what they cost?

VRONSKA: It doesn't make any difference what they cost. We're only trying to see where the trouble comes from. If we reduce the tolerance in all these places where we know there is variation, we might be able to get it straightened out. I don't care how new these are. If they're different lengths, they're no good.

CORRIVEAU: You mean we have to throw out the bushings every time we make a couple of hundred envelopes?

VRONSKA: If you want good body cases, you'll have to.

CORRIVEAU: Why, Karl, these cost me $18 a hundred.

VRONSKA: So what? What's $18?

CORRIVEAU: I'm going to be over my budget. Do you know how much that die[6] cost me? Ninety dollars.

VRONSKA: You're not going to get that die, either.

CORRIVEAU: What do you mean?

VRONSKA: You can't make good terminals with it. Somebody told me you said that. If you can't make good terminals on it, I'm not going to give it to you. I'll fix it so you can't use it, if that's the way you feel about it.

---

[6] The die concerned was one that Vronska had built and was trying to perfect to do a delicate swaging operation on the positive terminal.

CORRIVEAU: Who told you that? Huh? Who told you I said that? Fred again!

VRONSKA: Just somebody told me you said it was no good.

CORRIVEAU: I didn't say that. I never said anything of the sort. The only thing I ever said was to ask a question about whether you could make good terminals with it. I wanted to know whether it was ready. If people go around stirring up trouble like that, no wonder we never get anywhere. You better go back to the person who told you that and ask him what I really said.

At that moment a bell rang, indicating that it was Vronska's lunch period, and he left without comment. Corriveau turned to Ames; his voice dropped; his shoulders sagged slightly.

CORRIVEAU: Well, if that is the way it's going to be, I'll just have to run the machine using only the heads that happen to be working. But I know one thing—they better make up their minds that they can forget about the production schedules. They're too idealistic.

GEORGE AMES: Well, I'll go see about cutting the pins.

CORRIVEAU: If you need any new pins, I have some. But you better not tell Karl about it; it might hurt his feelings.

During this period (February–June), the results secured by production and the industrial engineers on the Amicon tube fell far short of their February goals and were disappointing to all concerned.

In February, 198 Amicon tubes of acceptable quality were produced. In March, there were approximately 800 tubes produced as against an original schedule of 7,500. In April, approximately 2,500 tubes were produced as against an original (February) schedule of 20,000 and a revised schedule of 7,000. During May, production went up to about 5,000 tubes but dropped again in June to about 3,000. It will be recalled that the February plans called for production at the rate of 100,-000 tubes per month by the end of June.

During this time, relatively little progress was made toward securing and perfecting the production equipment. The envelope machine was improved but was still not completely dependable. Vronska's swaging die was not in shape to be used for production purposes. A new high-volume etching apparatus had been built but was not performing consistently. At no time had the industrial engineers and production collaborated on eliminating any of the design "bugs" in the product.

The people involved in the project recognized these poor results; and each, in his own way, expressed his disappointment:

FISHER: The tube is no further along than it was a couple of months ago. There has even been some retrogression. The readings, for instance, are not nearly so high on the units being produced now as they were on those we made early in the developmental stage.

.   .   .   .

AMES: That's right. Nobody seems to be interested in it now. Nobody cares whether school keeps or not. Sure, people still go to the team meetings, but then everybody goes away and forgets it, so that at the next meeting, they have to start all over again. This Amicon tube could have been in full production right now if this sort of thing wasn't happening all the time. They could have been saving $10,000 to $12,-000 a month. They could have turned out twice the production with half the number of girls working on the old control tube line.

.   .   .   .

CORRIVEAU: It's getting so you can't even ask a question around here without hurting someone's feelings. I'm getting tired of this. I try, but I don't get any co-operation. . . . I'm not getting anywhere. I can't get anything done. We talk about everything, but no one does anything about it.

.   .   .   .

The higher management of the Midtown plant was gravely concerned in late June with the state of the Amicon tube project. The top group concerned had experienced two important personnel changes in May. Barnes had left the company, and Metcalf had succeeded him as plant manager. Davis had been transferred; and Jim Hurtig, a general foreman, had taken over as production manager. These two men were joined by Keller, Brenner, and Heity in a meeting on July 1 to review the status of the Amicon tube project. Hurtig had instigated the meeting because he was upset with the poor production results. He was proposing that the tube be taken completely out of production and turned over to the development engineers for further basic engineering work. Keller felt this step was too drastic. Brenner doubted that the industrial engineers were technically competent to solve the tube's problems. Heity was discouraged about the entire project. Metcalf was simply anxious to come up with an answer that would make it possible to stop the losses and start making some profits on the Amicon tube.

AMERICAN MAGNOLITE COMPANY

Part 3

AT THE conclusion of the top management meeting on July 1, Metcalf made the following two decisions: (1) The Amicon tube section was to be taken out of a production status and put under the supervision of the development engineers until such time as the quality difficulties of the product were eliminated and the production processes and equipment were under control; (2) the industrial engineers were to have nothing to do with the design of the product.

AMERICAN MAGNOLITE COMPANY

Part 4

THE DEVELOPMENT engineers were pleased with the new arrangements set up by the July 1 meeting.

> PARENT: This is the sort of thing that should have been done a long time ago.

They went right to work on all aspects of the Amicon tube. By the first part of August, Parent reported that they were getting promising results in several ways.

> PARENT: Things look a lot better. It looks like we've got this soldering problem licked. . . . It's encouraging to be getting these things licked.

During July, Corriveau had his doubts about the benefits of the development engineers' work. He and the operators continued producing tubes on the line as they had before. Corriveau saw relatively little of the development engineers, who were doing most of their work in the laboratory. By the middle of August, however, he was attending short daily meetings with the development engineers to discuss their progress and the details of the day's work. The development engineers were beginning to introduce some innovations in the line that were helpful to Corriveau.

> CORRIVEAU: I'm getting better results from the changes the development engineers are introducing. They have reduced the number of defective units an awful lot.

Parent gave the researchers a description of the way he and the other development engineers worked with production on the day-to-day technical problems during this time.

> PARENT: We've got a good group working on this. The first thing every morning, all of us get together to discuss what we accomplished the previous day and what needs to be done the coming day. We take the problems one day at a time and work them out. We have a different man working on each aspect of the problem.

The results of the development engineers' program were so encouraging that they hoped to turn the production line back to a straight production status by the middle of September. As this date was approached, however, the development engineers found themselves with a new problem on their hands. The envelopes started cracking during the final soldering operation. No sooner had this problem been solved in October than they started having trouble with the leads coming off the negative terminals. During this time, both the development engineers and Corriveau became very discouraged with the project. For several weeks the production line was completely shut down. But throughout this difficult time, Corriveau was in daily contact with the development engineers, and they were always working on the hundreds of details involved in improving the product and getting it produced. Finally, in January, they were able to begin turning out tubes of fairly consistent high quality, and the production rate began to climb. There had been no dramatic changes in the basic design of the Amicon tube, but many little things were working better technically.

In the following months the Amicon tube work gradually shifted to a more routine production basis. The development engineers spent less and less of their time on the project. Corriveau put increasing emphasis on meeting his higher production quotas and on lowering his unit costs. The Amicon tubes were being sold as a premium-quality product at a premium price. In the late spring the Amicon tube project began to show a monthly operating profit for the first time; and from that date, it became a consistently profitable product.

The following excerpts from interviews with Parent and Fisher several months after the July 1 decision indicate the state of their relationship at the time.

> PARENT (*after explaining to the researcher some of the latest technical developments*): We're now getting into the second stage of operations. It's sort of an interim period between pilot production and full-scale production. For the next few months, we're going to have to co-ordinate more with the work that is being done by industrial engineering and production.
>
> RESEARCHER: Won't that be a rather critical stage?
>
> PARENT: Oh, I guess not any more than any other stage. Things can go wrong anywhere along the line. We're going to start tomorrow holding meetings to keep everything co-ordinated. People from industrial engineering and production will be coming to those meetings. Things will be going kind of slowly. It takes time.

RESEARCHER: You mean you'll have to be patient about getting re-sults?

PARENT: No, you can't be patient. I'm going to have to keep push-ing things along.

RESEARCHER: You'll be doing a lot of follow-up work, then?

PARENT: Yes, I'll be checking to see that we make headway. Then I'll be reporting to Brenner about how we're doing and keeping him informed. I'll be talking with him about the technical problems we're having and even some of the problems of personnel and our problems about getting along with production and things like that. Of course. these meetings will just be concerned with the immediate problems we're running into. We won't be discussing any big over-all plans, as we did in the old meetings. These meetings will be different.

Well, as I said, we're now getting into a rather critical stage of having to refine our production methods and reduce shrinkage. The in-dustrial engineers have just worked out a comprehensive program for getting in some good production equipment.

RESEARCHER: How do their plans look to you?

PARENT: I haven't had a chance to go over them in much detail; but it looks like a very good, vigorous program. It looks like the sort of thing we need. I'm glad to see them going at it this way. There has really been a big change in the way the industrial engineering group works around here. They're concentrating on production methods now and are willing to accept our design specifications. Of course, I don't want to give you the idea that I think the industrial engineers didn't make a big contribution to the Amicon tube. Actually, we wouldn't have had an Amicon tube if they hadn't done the work on it. They de-veloped a good mechanical design. They just ran into trouble because of the problems of chemistry and metallurgy involved. They really couldn't have been expected to solve those problems. You couldn't tell there was anything wrong with it by looking at it. You can sort of see how the whole thing happened.

This project has helped me a lot to understand the point of view of the industrial engineers and the production people. I used to think those people were just dumb, stupid, and no good. Now I can really under-stand their point of view. I think they have changed, too. You know, if you can't work in some way with the others on a project, then you just can't get anything done. Of course, I want you to understand, I don't entirely agree with everything that industrial engineers and production people believe in. I still don't see eye to eye with them. But now I can discuss problems with them without thinking they're dopes. I can under-stand their ideas, even if I don't agree with them.

Then Fisher has changed a lot, and we're working along with him fine now. Fred has been bringing his men down here and showing them what we're doing. I don't want to give you the impression that everything is rosy and that we're not going to have any more problems. It's going to take time to get this thing into full-scale production.

.   .   .   .

FISHER: Speaking of relationships, you know for a long time I was having a hard time with Lou. There has been a tremendous change just lately. Now we're getting along swell. It's no trouble at all. He's all the time coming to me for help and advice, and I try to do the best I can to help him. It's been a big change. . . .

I am terribly encouraged about the way things are going. Everything seems to be breaking at once. We have our program for the Amicon tubes all mapped out now. We have arranged to get in a lot of new equipment to do that job. That's working with the present specifications that were drawn up by the development engineers, too. We're sticking by our promise not to try and change those specifications. . . .

You know, I can understand now why the development engineers acted the way they did. They didn't like our doing their job. If I'd been in their shoes, I guess I would have acted the same way. . . .

You know, I think the way you have to get along in an organization is by being willing to give away your pet ideas and gain satisfactions from your job in other ways. . . .

I've decided that if I just concentrate my attention on getting along with other people around here that I work with, and on helping them out as much as possible, my own personal progress in the organization will probably come along automatically. It'll probably come along faster and better than it would if I worried about it directly. . . .

The situation has improved an awful lot in the last few months. Take the relations between our industrial engineering department and the development engineers. We really understand and appreciate what each group's function is, and we're beginning to go to each other for help instead of working at cross purposes. Roger Metcalf is helping a lot to work this thing out. I am perfectly aware it isn't enough to define responsibility on a piece of paper. You've got to clarify those responsibilities right in the heads of the people who are doing the work. They have to learn what their own job is in respect to the function of other engineers. I personally think it's quite amazing the way our relations with the development engineers have improved. We are closer right now than any other two groups in the plant. You will remember how bitter I was about that group a few months ago. I thought they were no good at all and couldn't find enough horrible names to call them. In a way, we sort of took the initiative by agreeing to stay out of their bailiwick. They've done an awful lot to help the situation, though.

3. HAIG CHEMICAL COMPANY

THE HAIG CHEMICAL COMPANY had been manufacturing fine chemicals since 1909 in a plant at Baltimore, Maryland. The company purchased raw materials and manufactured them into bulk chemicals for use by pharmaceutical and drug concerns, food and beverage manufacturers, industries, and the arts; and by physicians, dentists, and veterinarians. The principal function of the company was a factory processing of chemicals. The plant originally consisted of a single small building,

Exhibit 1

HAIG CHEMICAL COMPANY

Year	Total Net Sales
1929	$ 8,100,000
1930	*
1931	7,150,000
1932	6,210,000
1933	7,000,000
1934	7,550,000
1935	8,370,000
1936	9,450,000
1937	10,350,000
1938	9,700,000
1939	13,230,000
1940	15,660,000
1941	25,650,000
1942	28,100,000
1943	37,530,000
1944	37,440,000
1945	37,350,000

*Not Available

but by 1929 had grown into a large modern plant. The total net sales in 1929 were $8,100,000. Although sales dropped during the depression to $6,210,000 in 1932, by 1938 the figure had risen again to $9,700,-000. Exhibit 1 gives the sales record of the company. New product developments and the war quadrupled sales between 1938 and 1945.

Before 1933, all manufacturing had been organized under an operations department, which was responsible for experimentation and research, process and product development, production methods, and factory operation. All the technical personnel were administered by this department.

Organization of Research Department

The Haig Chemical Company in the early thirties had adopted a policy of expanding its research activities as a means of insuring its long-run growth and the maintenance of its position in the chemical industry. One of the first steps in this program was the organization of a separate research department reporting to the president of the company.

In 1933 the research department had been organized to provide modern facilities for research in organic chemistry, biochemistry, physical and inorganic chemistry, microbiology, process development, and chemical engineering. In the years between 1933 and the beginning of the war, large expenditures were made for the expansion of this research program; and modern laboratories were constructed with the latest equipment and manned by high-grade scientists, chemists, and technicians. The research activities of this department were closely coordinated with government, medical, educational, and scientific societies and agencies throughout the country to exchange ideas and to supplement the work of these various agencies; and the research department soon began to make a substantial contribution to the pure science of chemistry.

In the years following the foundation of the Haig research department, its chemists, engineers, and technicians pioneered in the discovery, development, production, and clinical evaluation of a number of new products which represented important advances in medicine, nutrition, and industrial chemistry. Because the demand for these products, especially during the war years, far exceeded the company's ability to produce them, facilities were expanded rapidly; and in 1945, these new products represented nearly 50 per cent of the total sales of the Haig Company, whereas in 1938, they had represented only about 1 per cent of sales. Largely as a result of the development and production of these new items, the sales of the Haig Company grew from $9,700,-000 in 1938 to $37,530,000 in 1943. Coincident with this growth in sales volume was a rapid and appreciable expansion both in plant facilities and in number of personnel. The research department had become a vital part of the Haig Company, contributing appreciably to the growth of the company in sales volume and in prestige.

The research department had originally been given the over-all responsibility for the development of new products and was in charge of a product from the time of its discovery until all the production difficulties had been overcome and the product had been turned over to the factory for manufacturing on a full scale.

The transition between the discovery of a new product by the research department and large-scale factory production of that item represented many steps involving long periods of experimentation, testing, processing, and designing. One executive characterized the number and variety of problems that arose during this period of transition as "absolutely incredible." In the early stages of development in the research department the product was analyzed and tested to determine possible industrial uses, medicinal application, toxicity, and curative powers, after which period production was finally accomplished in test-tube quantities. Before the product left the research laboratories, processes for larger scale production were formulated.

At this stage, also, the development division of the research department analyzed the product to determine the advisability of producing it on a large-scale factory basis. Considerations of cost, profit, availability of materials, need for the product by industry or medicine, suitability for plant production, and possible future developments were presented to the president and the management committee[1] by the research director with a recommended course of action.

The Haig Company operated on the principle that it was wise to "make all your mistakes on a small scale and your profits on a large scale." When decision to make a product had been reached and the research laboratories had decided on the most suitable manufacturing processes, the item was taken to the pilot plant where production was begun on a small scale. In the pilot plant the chemical engineers, aided by the chemists who had developed the product, designed and operated a small unit to test the processes for manufacturing the item. Here, the processes were revised to fit larger scale production; mechanical engineers were called in to design machinery and equipment for future factory production; industrial engineers began to lay plans for factory scheduling, layout, packaging, shipping, and flow of materials; and construction engineers made arrangements for any necessary expansion of plant facilities. Production in the pilot plant continued until the processes were satisfactory and the factory layout was ready for full-scale production. In some cases an item had been produced in the pilot plant

---

[1] The management committee (composed of Mr. Haig; Mr. Towne, the operations vice president; Mr. Ranyard, sales vice president; Mr. Nordly, the treasurer; Mr. Ferguson, the legal officer; and Mr. Richard Robinson, the secretary) was organized for the purpose of making company operating decisions.

for as long as two years because plant expansion had not been completed; the factory was therefore not ready for full-scale production, and yet there was an urgent need by the government, the armed forces, or civilian medicine for the product, even in quantities produced by the pilot plant.

With the shift of the production of the item from the pilot plant to the factory came a further period of redesign of equipment and change in process to fit the larger scale of manufacture. The chemical, mechanical, industrial, and construction engineers were all active during this period in efforts to iron out the wrinkles in the factory process. Even after the process was satisfactory and production completely turned over to the factory staff, research continued on the product and the process to discover other possible derivatives, by-products, substitute raw materials, faster or cheaper methods, and additional applications.

The organization of the research department is shown in Exhibit 2. The department was subdivided into seven divisions: Three were involved with pure scientific research; two were concerned with product and process development and chemical engineering; one was a records and information division; and one was a service group for the department.

The three pure research divisions engaged in organic and biochemical, microbiological, and physical and inorganic research involving investigation and experimentation in such fields as toxicology, pharmacology, chemotherapy, therapeutics, microanalysis, entomology, synthesis, nutrition, textile chemistry, and cereal chemistry. These divisions utilized the department's thoroughly equipped laboratories for their research. Each of the three groups was under the supervision of a director who was responsible to Dr. Alvin Dowell, the research director. Senior chemists in each group were in charge of various types of experimentation or of particular product analyses. These senior chemists were all men with college degrees in chemistry or physics; many of them had doctors' degrees, and some had taught the sciences in colleges.

Several top executives of the company characterized the chemists as follows: They were singularly devoted to pure science for science's sake, and research work represented a principal objective in their lives. As a group, also, they were disdainful of the money-making applications of science to production and engineering. These chemists were individualistic in their attitudes and in their working techniques; and yet, they tended to band together as a group of common interest and to set themselves apart in thinking as well in attitude from the other groups in the company. As individuals, they devoted long hours to the

Exhibit 2

HAIG CHEMICAL COMPANY
RESEARCH DEPARTMENT

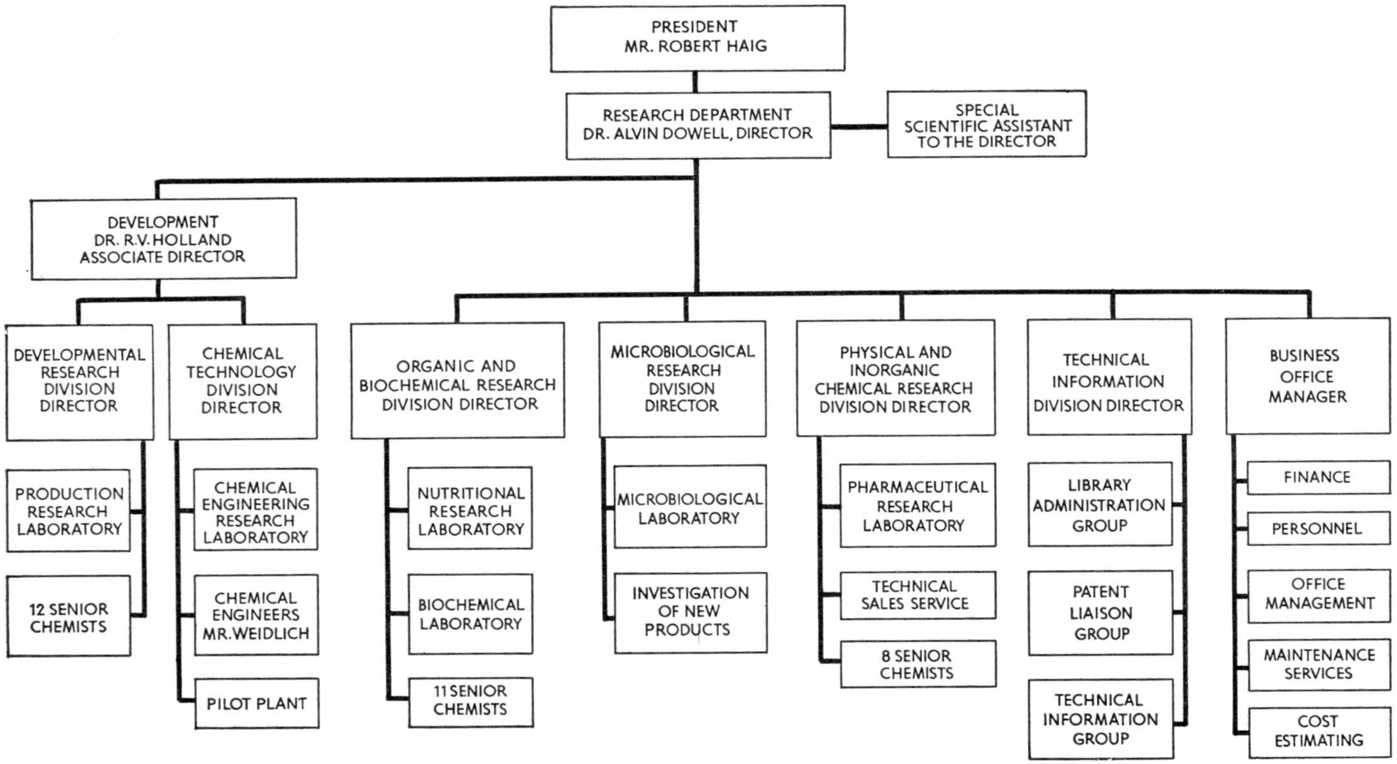

PRESIDENT
MR. ROBERT HAIG

SPECIAL SCIENTIFIC ASSISTANT TO THE DIRECTOR

RESEARCH DEPARTMENT
DR. ALVIN DOWELL, DIRECTOR

BUSINESS OFFICE MANAGER
- FINANCE
- PERSONNEL
- OFFICE MANAGEMENT
- MAINTENANCE SERVICES
- COST ESTIMATING

TECHNICAL INFORMATION DIVISION DIRECTOR
- LIBRARY ADMINISTRATION GROUP
- PATENT LIAISON GROUP
- TECHNICAL INFORMATION GROUP

PHYSICAL AND INORGANIC CHEMICAL RESEARCH DIVISION DIRECTOR
- PHARMACEUTICAL RESEARCH LABORATORY
- TECHNICAL SALES SERVICE
- 8 SENIOR CHEMISTS

MICROBIOLOGICAL RESEARCH DIVISION DIRECTOR
- MICROBIOLOGICAL LABORATORY
- INVESTIGATION OF NEW PRODUCTS

ORGANIC AND BIOCHEMICAL RESEARCH DIVISION DIRECTOR
- NUTRITIONAL RESEARCH LABORATORY
- BIOCHEMICAL LABORATORY
- 11 SENIOR CHEMISTS

DEVELOPMENT
DR. R.V. HOLLAND ASSOCIATE DIRECTOR

CHEMICAL TECHNOLOGY DIVISION DIRECTOR
- CHEMICAL ENGINEERING RESEARCH LABORATORY
- CHEMICAL ENGINEERS MR. WEIDLICH
- PILOT PLANT

DEVELOPMENTAL RESEARCH DIVISION DIRECTOR
- PRODUCTION RESEARCH LABORATORY
- 12 SENIOR CHEMISTS

laboratories and were conscientious and untiring in their investigations, becoming so absorbed in their work that they frequently were oblivious of surroundings and other people. A combination of imagination, inspiration, adequate background, and hard work was responsible for their success in research. The senior chemists were responsible to the director of their division, who was in each case a man of long experience, with interests and background similar to their own. He commanded their respect principally on the basis of his scientific skill and accomplishments. The research director, Dr. Dowell, was highly thought of by the senior chemists because of his prominence in pure scientific research and the manner in which he had organized the department to provide a high degree of scientific freedom to the chemists. He worked on the theory that the success of the research department could not be measured in daily output but must be considered in the light of months and years of results.

Of the two development divisions under the associate director of the research department, the developmental research division likewise was composed of senior chemists utilizing a laboratory for scientific process development, while the chemical technology division included the chemical engineers who were studying process application to pilot plant and factory operation. The chemists in the former division were men similar to those described in the pure research divisions except that their work involved investigation of process rather than product discovery and analysis. They were required to work rather closely with the chemical engineering group, which applied their processes to pilot plant and finally to full-scale production. There was a tie between the chemists and the chemical engineers based on the similarity of their work; but according to nontechnical executives, the chemists as a group felt that the pure scientific aspects of product and process development were of prime importance and that the chemical engineering and development work was of a less highly skilled and scientific nature.

The chemical engineers were men trained in college either in chemistry or in chemical engineering. Some had doctors' degrees, and all were fundamentally interested in applied chemistry and physics. The function of this group was to work in conjunction with the process chemists, to become familiar with the process, and to streamline it for pilot plant and factory use. Various features were considered by this group, including plant and equipment design, yield rates, rate of production, and scheduling of flow. It was evident to company executives that they respected the senior chemists in the department and were generally tolerant of the group scientific pride felt by the chemists.

In the laboratories, in addition to the senior chemists, were numerous younger chemists and technicians. Most of these were college graduates, who envisioned a future in chemistry similar to that enjoyed by the senior chemists. The attitude of devotion to science was prevalent throughout the laboratory groups.

The information and business office divisions were purely service functions for the department, established to provide an ample library, patent information, technical information, and various office and control services.

The research department had been established and developed with large expenditures by the Haig Company, and both the executives and the scientific men expressed their view that the facilities for both scientific work and comfortable office space were excellent. The laboratories were spacious, well lighted, well ventilated, and strictly modern; the offices and workrooms for chemists and engineers were large, comfortable, and well equipped; the service facilities were many; and the routine was conducive to uninterrupted study and investigation. The top management considered physical conditions for research to be nearly ideal, and the chemists and chemical engineers were obviously well satisfied with the arrangements.

The Engineering Groups

In developing a product from test-tube to full-scale factory production, the research department had the staff assistance of several groups of engineers. In addition to its own chemical engineers, it had the services of mechanical engineers, industrial engineers, and maintenance and construction engineers, as well as the factory production staff when needed. These engineers and the factory staff were under the line supervision of J. E. Towne, the operations vice president of the company.

The mechanical engineers were college-trained men for the most part, with degrees in mechanical engineering. This group was primarily concerned with the design of machinery and equipment for the pilot plant and factory. Upon specifications furnished by the chemical engineers and determined by observation and experiment, the mechanical engineers designed, procured, and installed such items as pumps, cylinders, piping, pressure chambers, heating units, refrigeration units, cranes, pulleys, and the hundreds of other pieces of equipment involved in chemical processing. These engineers were required to work in close conjunction with the chemical engineers who were charged with setting up the process in both pilot plant and factory. The chemical engineers as a group considered the mechanical engineers as a less highly skilled group performing a service function.

The industrial engineers were probably the most heterogeneous of all the engineering groups, largely because industrial engineering was one of the more recently developed and accepted engineering fields. In this group were men, mostly college graduates, who had been trained in mechanical, civil, or commercial engineering and in business or economics, as well as men trained only in night school classes. The men in this category were the least specialized, the least technical, and perhaps the least important engineering group in so far as new products were concerned. The functions of the industrial engineers consisted of scheduling production, planning flow of materials, providing packaging and shipping facilities, and making time and motion studies. The industrial engineers worked with the chemical engineers to determine the length and type of process, the skills involved, the safety precautions required, the packaging needed, and details for the time and motion study; contacted the mechanical engineers regarding layout of machinery, speed of operations, and operators required; and similarly worked with maintenance and construction engineers in the design and construction of plant facilities involving the flow of materials and the speed of operation. Company executives believed that the chemical engineers looked upon the industrial engineers as a nonscientific service group instrumental in the details of scheduling and planning. The mechanical and industrial engineers were closely related in background and general interest, and usually agreed readily on matters of machinery layout and operation.

The maintenance and construction engineers were a group of mechanical, civil, and electrical engineers, college trained for the most part, although some were noncollege men who had experience in contracting and construction work. The responsibility of this group was primarily the construction or alteration of plant facilities to accommodate new or revised processes and to maintain facilities throughout the plant. When a new process was scheduled for factory operation, the maintenance and construction group, in conjunction with the other engineering groups, and in accordance with specifications of the chemical and mechanical engineers, constructed the required machinery foundations, extended the factory, revised ceiling heights, and provided service piping. This engineering group had the lowest percentage of college-trained personnel and had a less vital part in new product procedure than the other groups, and was principally involved in plant maintenance, construction, and alteration in accordance with independent specifications. The chemical engineers, in particular, were not accustomed to working in close conjunction with this group.

The factory production staff was responsible for the actual operation of production processes. This group, composed of chemists and some chemical engineers, specialized in the problems of equipment operation and efficient production. They were strictly an operational group and did not assume responsibility for a product until the research department relinquished its control of the product's development and turned it over to the factory. In the initial establishment of a product in the factory, however, the factory staff assigned men to work with the chemical engineers as well as with the mechanical, industrial, and construction engineers, in instituting the process and in learning the details of the operation preparatory to assuming full control of the factory production. The viewpoint of the chemical engineers that chemical perfection in the product and process was essential sometimes proved to be at variance with the practical viewpoint taken by the factory engineers, who held that compromises had to be made to adapt the process to factory convenience and scheduling.

Organization of Engineering Departments

Before 1943, there had been no concerted effort to unify all the engineering functions within the company into a centralized engineering department. Each group of engineers, except those in the research department, had reported to the operations vice president. The industrial engineers were a separate group under T. B. Watson; and the mechanical, construction, and maintenance engineers were directed by R. A. Merrill. Each group had a particular function to perform. Each group usually exhibited a fractional point of view on new product development, and there was not so much intergroup understanding as might have been desirable. The management considered, however, that the organization was functioning tolerably well, in view of its rate of change and growth.

As the company grew rapidly and added new products and expanded its plant and personnel, the lack of engineering centralization became more and more noticeable. The increasing scale of operations, the problems of plant expansion, and new products increased the work of the operations vice president in co-ordination of factory activities. This, in turn, reduced the time he had for co-ordination of the work of the engineering groups at the very time when the volume of that work required not only more supervisory attention but possibly some further degree of specialization. The engineering groups continued to work together and with the research department on the informal basis of past practice. The results during the period of rapid expansion were as follows: many instances of duplication of effort, lack of co-ordination between engineering groups, inadequacies of data and statistics, and waste of time caused by conflicts of responsibility and authority between the engineering groups. Sometimes, engineers were assigned to a job for which they were less well qualified than other engineers. For instance, the research department frequently asked mechanical engineers to handle certain projects that might better have been handled by industrial engineers. There was no central control functioning effectively to determine responsibility and authority, to assign jobs, to avoid duplication, to gather data centrally, to centralize engineering facilities, to settle disputes, and to act as an expediting agent in carrying through proper action to conclusion.

An example of the duplication and inconvenience coincident with the noncentralization of engineering facilities was the drafting department. The engineering drafting department was located about one quarter of a mile from most of the engineering groups in the plant. Some of the groups did their own drafting, to avoid sending prints back and forth to the drafting department; other groups were forced to make it standard practice to send a girl on a bicycle at regular intervals to the drafting department to deliver or pick up drawings and blueprints. Although the inconvenience, annoyance, and loss of time to the engineers were obvious, no action had ever been taken to correct the situation.

An excellent example of the errors and inefficiencies occasioned by the lack of centralized control of engineering was illustrated at the time of the construction of a new plant near the existing plant in Baltimore. In the construction of the plant building the chemical engineers had required in their plans and estimates a 14-foot unobstructed overhead clearance. After the building had been constructed, however, it was discovered that service piping required for the floor above had to be placed below the ceiling; thus, the unobstructed height was reduced to 10 feet in some locations. This costly error was entirely due to the fact that no central control was placed on the engineering phases of the construction, to check such features and to insure that the chemical engineers and the construction engineers had co-ordinated their efforts on the design and erection of the building.

Top officials, in addition, referred to the existence of friction between the chemical engineers attached to the research department and the other engineering groups. This friction centered on the question as to which group was more qualified to handle a new product through the pilot plant and the factory. One of the chemical engineers expressed the reaction of the group when he said to one of the factory chemists:

Of course, it's a research department job to supervise a new product till the factory methods are straightened out and all the wrinkles are gone from the process. Dr. Dowell is responsible for it up to that point, and we belong to the research department; so we keep the job till it's completed, and then we turn it over to the factory. You factory people don't know anything about research, chemistry, chemical engineering, or the history of the discovery and development of this product. How can you be trusted to make it till we show you how?

The factory chemist countered by saying:

You research people should stick to your test tubes. Chemists and scientists have no business ever leaving the lab. You certainly don't understand factory operation, and that's why we are having so much trouble getting these new items produced. You keep thinking you are in a lab making 20 cc.'s instead of in the factory making thousands of pounds. We know the factory setup. All we need is the process; we'll do the rest!

In 1943 the company's management committee began discussions on the question of the consolidation of all engineering groups into a single engineering department. Mr. Towne, the operations vice president, was particularly active in promoting such a reorganization. He was able to convince the committee and Mr. Haig, on the basis of facts and figures which he presented, that the existing decentralized engineering organization was responsible for numerous duplications and inefficiencies. He suggested that in a $37,000,000 business, engaged primarily in technical production, it was essential that the engineering function be centralized under one leader and unified as to purpose, methods, and controls.

At Haig's request, Towne had a study made and a report prepared by several of the principal company engineers which indicated the prevailing weaknesses of the existing engineering organization and proposed changes needed to accomplish engineering unification. This report was submitted by Towne to Haig and to the management committee. It provided that all engineering, including chemical engineering now under the research department, should be centralized in a new engineering department under the operations vice president.

When the plan for the proposed engineering department became known throughout the plant, there was outspoken opposition from the chemical engineers and a rivalry among the other engineering groups as to which was to play the most prominent part in the proposed engineering department. Mr. Weidlich, head of the chemical engineering group, made his attitude known to Mr. Merrill, the head of the mechanical and construction engineers, when he said:

> We don't feel that we are nearly as much engineers as we are chemists. Our particular job is new products, and we work as closely as possible with research. By the time these products become factory problems for engineers, we are through with them. I can't understand how you figure we could be separated from the research department and still carry along these new products. It just doesn't make sense. I think the rest of the mechanical, industrial, and construction engineers might consolidate within your own department and call it an engineering section, if you want; but I'm certainly opposed to including all chemical engineers in that group because we just don't belong.

Dr. Dowell, director of research, when consulted on the issue by Mr. Haig, the president, expressed himself as opposed to the change involving the chemical engineers. Dowell explained his attitude when he said:

> I've consulted with Dr. Holland, my assistant, and we agree that it is undesirable from our viewpoint to divorce the chemical engineers from our organization as long as we are charged with new product responsibility from lab to factory and must depend so heavily on these engineers for the accomplishment of the job. It's inconceivable to me that such a program would secure results if I were forced to call on another, separately run department to accomplish the critical features of a job for which I'm held responsible.

In December, 1943, the Haig Company engaged the Garfield Company, management consultants, to study the management and organization problems occasioned by the rapid growth and expansion of the company. One of the first issues facing the consulting firm was the question of the proposed new engineering department. For several months the Garfield Company representatives familiarized themselves with the existing organization, the methods and procedures of research and production, and the inadequacies and deficiencies of the system. Finally, in June, 1944, the firm recommended to management that a consolidation of all engineering functions, including chemical engineering, be effected as soon as practical. The Garfield Company also recommended that an experienced engineer be brought in from the outside to assume the duties of chief engineer.

Although the report of the Garfield Company was similar in most respects to that submitted by Towne, the management felt that the investigation of the problem by the consultants had been of value. In the first place, management had been able to confirm its own decision on the issue, based on the report by company engineers; and in the second place, the presence of the Garfield Company as well-known consultants had given the question a position of importance throughout the plant and had done much toward convincing the research department and the chemical engineers that action was necessary. Although most of the chemical engineers still opposed the change, the recommendations made by the Garfield Company, as unbiased consultants, partially convinced them on the merit of the contemplated centralization of all the engineering functions.

Haig agreed to the recommendation that the company hire an outsider as chief engineer. He thought a new man would be able to work more co-operatively with Dowell, who had opposed the transfer of the chemical engineers. The new chief engineer required experience in chemical, mechanical, industrial, maintenance, and construction engineering, or a knowledge of how to use these types of engineers effectively. The growth of the company had created a need for a new type of technical chief. The management, not anticipating such rapid growth, had not given its various engineering heads a chance to acquire this broad experience, with the result that the top management doubted the possibilities of promotion from within to the new position. Given a new chief engineer with capacity for leadership, the management believed that any disappointment the old chiefs might feel would be offset in part by the fact that the expansion would give each of them greater responsibilities, a larger volume of work, and larger organizations to supervise. A new man, it was thought, might approach the question of division of responsibility between research and engineering with less bias than an insider.

Accordingly, in January, 1945, the Haig Company employed C. P. Ryan as chief engineer and charged him with the responsibility of organizing the engineering department, that is, centralizing all the company's engineering groups and functions, establishing the responsibilities of the engineering department in the company organization, and developing procedures for the satisfactory co-ordination of the engineering function with the other departments of the company, especially the research department. In accordance with its philosophy of management, the Haig Company allowed Ryan great flexibility and freedom of action in his efforts to establish this department. Haig instructed him in general on the results desired, but was neither prepared nor did he desire to give Ryan definite responsibilities and courses of action. Haig stated the company philosophy in a few words when he said: "We want to accomplish these changes by evolution rather than revolution. We want to let them develop gradually with as little heat from friction as possible. We can't be sure now of the ultimate goal, and to freeze a procedure or policy before it is seasoned would be bad business. We must crawl before we can walk."

Ryan was a man about 50 years of age who had been vice president of a small chemical manufacturing company in charge of engineering and manufacture. He had had nearly twenty-five years' experience in chemistry and chemical engineering, and was experienced in the techniques of chemical production. He was later described by Watson as "a hard-boiled sort of man who knows his job and who's not an easy man to talk down. He's reasonable and logical, but will never abandon a thing he believes in. He's exactly the man we've needed for this job, especially since there's been so much opposition to the plan."

Because he was convinced that one of the important steps in centralizing all engineers into a compact organization was to accomplish a physical consolidation of all engineering functions, Ryan laid plans for moving all Haig engineers, including the chemical engineers, into the same building. In June, 1945, the engineering department moved into the new building, which included desk and office space, drafting and blueprint facilities, an engineering records room for the collection of data and statistics, and a conference room.

There were minor problems of adjustment to the new space setup. Watson, who, as head of the industrial engineers, was in charge of planning and laying out the new engineering department office, had planned to avoid the use of cubicles for individual offices. Although the use of glassed-in cubicles was prevalent in the other company office buildings, Watson thought them a waste of limited space; in addition, he believed that more work could be accomplished in an engineering office without the obstacles to informal communication presented by glassed-in offices. Previously, the chemical engineers had enjoyed unusually good office space in the research buildings, and the loss of these physical comforts had been one of their objections to the move. The question of individual offices was under discussion for several weeks; Watson explained to Weidlich, the head chemical engineer, that the limited available floor space would not permit all the engineers to have enclosed offices. Ultimately, however, he decided, in order to promote harmony, to give the chemical engineers their offices, even though the remainder of the engineers would have none.

In planning the engineering department, Ryan adopted the organizational setup shown in Exhibit 3.

To accomplish this change, he had to break up the previous combination of the mechanical, construction, and maintenance engineers, who had all worked under Merrill. In the new organization, Merrill kept the construction and maintenance engineers; and his former assistant, Cody, took charge of the mechanical engineers. Merrill did not

Exhibit 3

HAIG CHEMICAL COMPANY

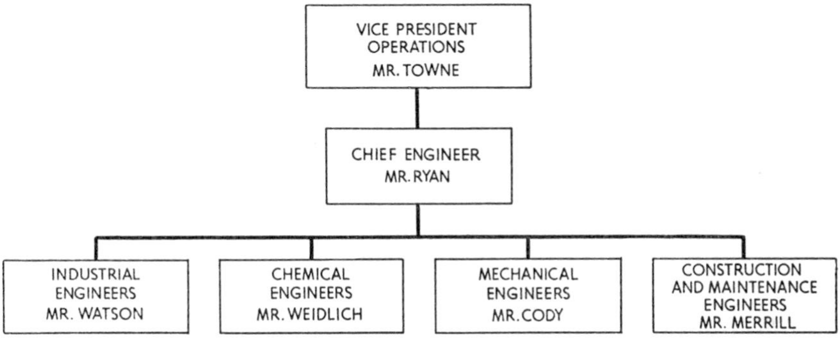

receive this step favorably. He had been with the Haig Company for nearly twenty years; he had actually hoped for the position of chief engineer; and he had been none too pleased with the introduction of Ryan as chief engineer. Merrill, a self-made man, with very little formal education, had shown himself very capable in his operation of the mechanical, construction, and maintenance groups. Towne and Haig had not selected him for the position of chief engineer primarily because his background was limited and included very little chemical or industrial engineering.

After Ryan had accomplished the physical consolidation of the engineers and had defined the departmental organization as shown in Exhibit 3, he set about to establish yardsticks for appraisal of results, to provide incentives for outstanding work, to institute informal channels of communication, and personally and forcefully to present the viewpoint of the combined engineering groups in any company discussions involving engineers. He held numerous dinner meetings at a Baltimore hotel, at which time the entire engineering force, under pleasant social surroundings, was able to discuss departmental engineering issues. Ryan made daily efforts to become familiar with his engineers, with the plant and its procedures, with key men in the research department and in the factory, and with the situations which caused confusion and conflict.

Ryan made a particular effort to reach close understanding with his four engineering group heads. He planned frequent conferences with Watson, Weidlich, Cody, and Merrill, in which they discussed in detail the problems that arose in their work, the areas which had formerly produced disagreement, the best procedures to follow, and other points involving the engineering department. In addition, Ryan dropped in to see these men at irregular intervals to discuss informally some phase of the department's operation. Ryan took the four men into his confidence on matters involving the department, particularly where departmental policy in regard to relations with other departments was concerned. In all these discussions, Ryan proved himself receptive to the ideas and opinions of the other engineers and was forceful in following up, outside the department, the decisions reached in conferences within the department. By giving wide distribution to any letters, publications, or memorandums involving the department, he hoped to develop interest by all engineers in departmental activities. He made it clear by memorandums that achievement by engineers would be recognized within the department and made the basis for promotion, salary raises, and company recognition. Through his group leaders, he attempted to establish yardsticks for appraisal of results by clarifying the particular functions of each group and the basis for satisfactory performance. The group leaders were to assign engineers to particular projects and to follow up their efforts in carrying out the details of the projects.

During this readjustment period, Ryan made special efforts to reach an understanding with Dowell on matters of responsibility, co-ordination, and authority between the two departments. The two men spent considerable time together in office meetings in the pilot plant and in the factory, discussing ways and means of placing new product development on a smooth functioning basis. At many of these discussions, Watson, Weidlich, Cody, Merrill, certain research department personnel, and various engineers were present. As problems arose that were difficult to settle on the spot, the engineers and chemists involved sometimes familiarized Dowell, Holland, and Ryan with the problem so that it might be settled by the formulation of a principle that would apply to other similar instances.

Dowell maintained responsibility for new products until they were being produced without difficulty in the factory. Ryan considered it the responsibility of his own department to provide all the functional services required by the research group. That is, the chemical engineers were to work in conjunction with the chemists on process and pilot plant operation; the mechanical engineers were to furnish all the machinery and equipment for pilot plant and factory operation; the industrial engineers were to take responsibility for all scheduling, time study, packaging, and shipping; the construction and maintenance engineers were to provide plant space and plant layout for the process; and finally, the engineering department was to co-ordinate these engineering functions to provide maximum control, minimum duplication, and the greatest possible effectiveness in aiding the research department to place a new item in quantity production.

Although Dowell held the responsibility for new products, Ryan, as chief engineer, possessed in effect a power of veto over any step in the process which he felt was inadvisable from an engineering point of view. For instance, if the research department decided to install a process involving equipment and machinery which did not meet with the chief engineer's approval, for reasons of design, cost, or availability, Ryan discussed his objection with Dowell, attempted to reach an agreement, and, if necessary, took the problem to the management committee for decision.

As time passed, it became evident that the engineers were all working together under one roof, were beginning to understand the attitudes of the other groups, and were answerable to one authority, Ryan, who was responsible for their promotions and recognition as well as for their activity. This caused a noticeable decrease in the friction which had formerly existed. The chemical engineers became accustomed to their new surroundings, although they continued to spend a considerable amount of time in the research department, particularly with the development chemists. They discovered that the move had not appreciably changed their relationships with the chemists and the research department. The chemical engineers developed individual friendships with men in the mechanical, industrial, and maintenance and construction groups, and found it easier to communicate informally with these groups. It became a common sight in the engineering office, as well as in the pilot plant and factory, to see members of several engineering groups discussing, informally, problems relating to certain features of a new product's development. Early in 1946, Weidlich, the head of the chemical engineers, who had so opposed the consolidation move, said to Merrill: "Bob, I'm actually surprised at how well this department is working out. It may be O.K., after all; and we are beginning to enjoy it here. There's no doubt that we are getting along better; and certainly, it's easy to see an improvement in the procedure on new products. Hope we didn't give too much trouble in the beginning."

At the same time, an increased smoothness was noticeable in the manner in which the groups carried out their functions in the pilot plant and in the factory. Weidlich and his chemical engineers became more familiar with the other engineering personnel and were better able to call on the right group for assistance and to explain what was required. The chemical engineers dominated the pilot plant because of their knowledge of the process, but came to rely on the mechanical engineers, particularly for consultation on machinery design. Although Dowell and the research department still held official responsibility for the product from beginning to end, the engineering groups actually took charge during the pilot plant and factory stages, and the research people began to serve mainly in an advisory capacity on the chemical aspects of the process.

Responsibility of Engineering and Research

By June, 1946, there had been no formal change in the responsibility of the research department for development of products from test-tube to full-scale factory production. The topic was being discussed, however, by engineers and by research personnel. Some of the engineers seemed to feel that the new engineering department should take over formally at the pilot plant stage, whereas the research men could see no reason why they should give up a responsibility that had been theirs since 1933 and without which they might not be fully capable of developing products and processes in accordance with their ideal standard. Since the volume of research work had increased so much and was of such great importance to the company, it was a moot question in the minds of many whether, once again, growth required a reshuffling of responsibilities. More specifically, the question was how responsibility for product development should be divided between research, engineering, and the factory production staff.

Under the operational scheme visualized by the engineers, the new product development would be generally as follows: When the research laboratory discovered a new product and had conducted sufficient preliminary research to justify study of the item and process from a production point of view, the chemical engineers would begin to work with research chemists and familiarize themselves with the process. When the decision was made to go ahead with production, the chemical engineers would make arrangements to institute the product in the pilot plant, and the mechanical and industrial engineers could assist where necessary. When the pilot plant operation was ready, the chemical engineers and chemists would jointly set the process in operation, but at this point the responsibility would shift because the major portion of the work load shifted from research to engineering. The chemists assigned by research to the project would continue to work with the chemical engineers. As the pilot plant operations became smooth and the product was prepared for the factory, the research chemists would have less and less to do and could be reassigned by the research department, with the understanding that they were available for consultation on any problems that might arise on the later development of the problem.

The foregoing viewpoint was not shared generally by the research department. The research department had felt the pressure by the engineering department ever since its organization, particularly as the engineering department increased in scope and effectiveness and bore more and more of the burden of carrying along the new product. Burnett, one of the research department division heads, explained his attitude by saying:

> It's my opinion that research on a product discovered and developed in our research labs and destined for production in our factory is not completed until all the kinks are taken out of the factory process. To say that research is over when the product leaves the lab is ridiculous. The only reason the item leaves the lab is that we feel better equipped to carry out the advanced stages of the research in the pilot plant and factory. Our job is more than the discovery of the product and the formula; it is, in addition, the discovery of the best means of processing it. That is a job for a trained chemist, especially for the chemist who did the primary research in the product.
>
> We recognize the contribution of the engineers to the production processes, but the building of machinery and equipment and the scheduling of work are only aids to the principal job of learning the most efficient way to produce the item. When we know these things, then it will be time for factory engineers to streamline their equipment and procedure for producing the item by the process that we've determined is most favorable. If, as is proposed, we turn a product over to the engineers when it leaves the test-tube stage in the lab, I'm afraid that research on the product will be cut short; and although the speed of putting the item into full production may be increased, the final product and the final

process will be inferior to what would be obtained if research were allowed to finish its job.

Ever since the chemical engineers were transferred from research to the engineering department, we have experienced difficulty in co-ordinating the various groups involved in the several phases of new product development under Dr. Dowell. For instance, there has been noticeable a tendency on the part of the factory chemists to resist late changes in process, as suggested by the research chemists, after the manufacturing processes have been designed. We in research feel that we must have the privilege of improving product and process at any time during their development, particularly until the actual factory yield reaches the theoretical yield. This company has a splendid reputation now for research and the development of fine chemicals and drugs; we are establishing our name for quality products; and we are making a substantial contribution to medicine, science, and industry. To continue this progress, we must insure that our products are as good as modern science can make them. That responsibility can be borne only by our research department and by our chemists and scientists. To deprive them of full responsibility for a new product until they are satisfied that it is as good as their facilities at present will make it would be to endanger the control over quality, which is the basis for our success.

4. THE THERMOPHYSICS RESEARCH GROUP

Part 1[1]

THE THERMOPHYSICS RESEARCH GROUP, a subunit of the aerophysics department which, in turn, was part of a large aircraft manufacturer's research facility, was recently organized to develop materials (pure metals, alloys, ceramics) and coatings (paints, finishes, chemical coatings) for these materials, to be used as special surfaces (usually the outside casing) of missiles and to conduct thermophysical research on metals and coatings in general.

The research facility employed approximately 300 technical people, most of whom had or were working toward advanced degrees. The organization of the research facility was well defined, and definite formal channels of information and direction flow had been established.

Each supervisor held an advanced degree, usually a doctoral degree in his specialty. Each supervisor and manager, on each level, maintained tight control over the work performed in his area.

All employees in research were status-conscious. The research facility, itself, was considered to represent high status in the company. All supervisors and managers, particularly on the departmental and managerial levels, were widely respected by their subordinates. Quite often they were feared, as well.

Everything an employee could or could not do was defined in various organization manuals and bulletins from "the top." Eight-twenty A.M. was the starting time for all employees; quitting time was 5:15. Forty-five minutes were allowed for lunch, usually taken in the company cafeteria. Such rules, in general, were closely adhered to.

Late working hours in research were considered a sign of "inefficiency" and "poor organization." The complete silence in the entire facility during working hours created an atmosphere analogous to that of a college library.

Dr. Philip Bartlett was designated as first head of the newly formed

---

[1] This is a prediction case. You should answer the questions at the end of Part 1 before continuing on to Part 2.

thermophysics research group. Dr. Bartlett age thirty-four, had been with the company for a little over one year in a separate research department, frequently referred to as the "rat race" or the "blood-and-guts" department of the company's research facility, due to the high degree of schedule pressure exerted on employees of the department.

Bartlett divided his group of twenty-one into three informal sections. The analytical section, six men, worked closely with other company departments (including the one from which Bartlett had come), responding to their needs concerning special materials requirements, materials and coatings applications, and techniques of handling these special surfaces.

The experimental section, consisting of eleven men, assisted the analytical section by conducting physics experiments, evaluating materials and coatings under simulated space conditions, and by providing "state-of-the-art" knowledge lacking in the smaller analytical section. The lab section also conducted any experiments or special projects given to them by Dr. Bartlett.

The data-reduction section, consisting of one man and three girls, assisted both the other sections in reducing data, computer programming, and in working long, complex, mathematical calculations.

The average age within the whole thermophysics research group was approximately twenty-six, and most held an advanced degree. The group had been formed by recruitment from other similar groups and from other departments.

Because a laboratory was required for the functioning of the thermophysics group, it was located in a building separate from the rest of the aerophysics department.

Dr. Bartlett's policies as head of the "T.P." group became clear soon after the group was organized. His first observation was, "This place is too goddam quiet for me." Concerning individual responsibility he remarked that, "When I give you a job to do, I don't expect to talk about it again until you've finished the project or the project has finished you." Further, "This area of research is in its infancy; consequently, there are few people in the nation that know more about the space environment and its effects on materials than any other group or individual in the nation."

Bartlett went on to point out that he wanted the group to be autonomous relative to the department, and preferred each section to operate as autonomously as possible. "This company is a jungle of red tape which strangles good research and impedes good exchange of findings. Leave the details to administrators. Don't allow yourself to get bogged down in forms and procedures. I'll answer for anything you do which the upper echelons consider out of line."

Bartlett let it be known from the beginning that he did not care when people came to work or when they left. "Just make sure your projects are completed within the scheduled time." T.P. members were free to eat lunch anytime and any place.

Bartlett's primary concern was being of assistance to the people who were responsible for development and fabrication of missile systems. Although the company produced many devices, Bartlett considered missiles to be its only important end product and felt that surface materials were of utmost importance in proper performance of missiles in space. He urged group members to distribute all findings to persons in all departments who might be interested. He also encouraged each individual to put his own name above Bartlett's on any letter or memo distributing such findings.

PREDICTIONS
THE THERMOPHYSICS RESEARCH GROUP
PART 1

1. Will the quality of work produced by the thermophysics research group under Dr. Bartlett be high, medium, or low? Explain your choice.

2. Will the quantity of work produced by Bartlett's thermophysics research group be high, medium, or low? Explain your choice.

3. Will there be a great deal of, a moderate amount of, or very little social activity in the thermophysics research group? Explain your choice.

4. Will social organization within the thermophysics research group be group-wide, in subgroup units, or fragmented? Explain your choice.

5. Will relations between members of the thermophysics research group and members of other units of the aerophysics department be cordial, neutral, or strained? Explain your choice.

6. Will relations between the thermophysics research group and men in superior management positions be cordial, neutral, or strained? Explain your choice.

7. Will individual satisfaction among members of the thermophysics research group be high, medium, or low? Explain your choice.

8. Will opportunities for individual learning and growth for members of the thermophysics research group be high, medium, or low? Explain your choice.

THE THERMOPHYSICS RESEARCH GROUP

Part 2

THE THERMOPHYSICS RESEARCH GROUP became well known within the company for the quality of information produced, the rapidity of replies to requests for help, and for its many publications. It also became well known for the behavior of its members. The data-reduction and analytical sections were famous for their "rubber-band" fights. Large crowds would gather in the lab amidst operating equipment for jokes and storytelling sessions. Many of the participants in these sessions were from other departments.

The entire group had lunch "outside" at least every two weeks. Any occasion, such as a birthday, was used as an excuse. These lunches usually lasted one and one-half hours. The experimental section had lunch "outside" every Friday as a ritual. Week-end parties or picnics were also very popular with the group.

Salaried employees in the thermophysics group seldom left work prior to 6:00 P.M. Dr. Bartlett and a few others would usually work until 7:00 P.M. Often individuals or small groups would work until 10:00 P.M. Each Saturday and Sunday would find at least one group member in the lab or in his office. Dr. Bartlett worked nearly every Saturday.

Dr. Bartlett's superior often asked him to quiet down and organize his group. Bartlett's usual rebuttal was a comparison of his group's performance to the performance of other groups and departments within Research.

POSTPREDICTION ANALYSIS

Refer to your predictions at the end of Part 1. How closely do they match the information above? Do inaccuracies in your predictions reflect inadequate analysis? If so, explain the analytical failure. If not, what additional information would you have needed in Part 1 to improve your predictive accuracy and how would you have used that information?

5. FORT WORTH PHARMACEUTICAL AND CHEMICAL CORPORATION[1]

IN THE SPRING of 1959, Wayne Malvern was spending many hours a day worrying about the difficulties involved in adding polyethylene to the list of profitable products manufactured by the Fort Worth Pharmaceutical and Chemical Corporation. Wayne knew that profitability depended upon the ability of all concerned to deal with serious technical problems which had emerged from the polyethylene process and was very much aware of his personal responsibility for initiating ideas and co-ordinating the efforts of those who might contribute to the solution of these problems.

Wayne was a staff member of the development division of Fort Worth's central research laboratories. The function of this division had been formally stated in a brochure circulated throughout the company as "first, to do the staff work needed by management to guide the company's chemical research and, second, to handle the process engineering and economic evaluation of chemical projects during their development stages." Or, as stated by Dr. Wynn Cote, one of the senior engineers on the development division staff "we are responsible for a process that makes a product of specified quality."

Fort Worth had been a major producer of pharmaceuticals in the United States for over forty years. After World War II, the company began to diversify into other phases of the chemical industry. Annual sales were about $750 million in 1958, with chemicals contributing a steadily growing percentage.

New product research and development and engineering of new plant facilities had been centralized in the central research laboratories since before World War II. Both pharmaceutical and chemical R&D were done at this laboratory, which was located in the suburbs of a large western city. As the chemical business increased, the size of the technical staff working on purely chemical R&D had increased proportionately until nearly 400 professional people were employed.

There were three major groups in the chemical R&D department: (1) the chemical research division, (2) the applications research division, and (3) the development division. All of these divisions possessed

---

[1] This case was made possible by a grant from the Industrial Research Institute.

laboratory facilities, although the chemical research laboratories were the most basic and extensive. Also housed in the central laboratories buildings was the engineering department, which planned, designed, and constructed plants for all product divisions of the parent company (see Exhibit 1). Intimately associated with the work of the chemical

Exhibit 1

FORT WORTH PHARMACEUTICAL AND CHEMICAL CORPORATION
PARTIAL ORGANIZATION CHART, CENTRAL RESEARCH LABORATORIES

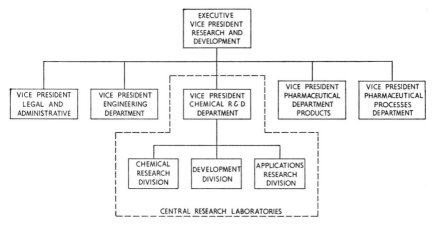

research and development divisions were the company's pilot plants and their associated laboratories, which were located many hundreds of miles from the central laboratories on the grounds of the company's major production facility.

The development division was staffed by twenty-five chemical engineers. These men were grouped rather informally under section heads according to areas of technical interest (see Exhibit 2 for details of the simple organization of the division). Wayne Malvern was, in 1959, a member of the specialty products section. He had a B.S. and M.S. from a large eastern university and had taken all the course work for his Ph.D. in chemical engineering before coming to work in the development division in 1955. By June of 1959, he was a staff engineer responsible for four products in polymer chemistry, of which only two were currently active. His work on one of these was nearly complete, since the commercial plant built to produce the product had commenced operations and had been evaluated as successful. His activities in connection with this product were therefore now confined to answering questions posed by people at the plant.

The other product, polyethylene, presented major technical problems and it is because of Wayne Malvern's attempts to deal with these problems that the present case came to the attention of Bob Handy, a case researcher.

Wayne's section head, Dr. Glen Side, had been associated with the division as staff member or head of various sections for eight years. He had just recently taken over the direction of the specialty products

Exhibit 2

FORT WORTH PHARMACEUTICAL AND CHEMICAL CORPORATION
ORGANIZATION OF DEVELOPMENT DIVISION

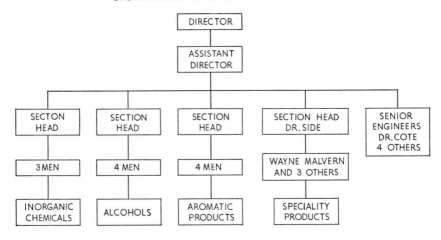

section and felt he was "still getting his feet on the ground" as far as his understanding of the problems presented by particular projects was concerned.

In addition to section heads and the staff members assigned to particular sections, the development division was served by five senior engineers. One of these senior engineers, for example, was Dr. Wynn Cote. Dr. Cote had about fifteen years' experience with the company, some in engineering design and some as a consultant to a commercial division. In common with the other four men bearing this title, he reported directly to the division directors. Describing his job, Dr. Cote said, "My job is almost the same as Wayne's, with the exception that I have very little supervision over me. Only on policy questions, such as decisions regarding the need for a project or the priority a project should receive, do I go to my superiors." The projects Dr. Cote worked on were similar to those assigned other staff members. Formally, he was free to do any work within the spectrum of the division's activities; informally, he usually received projects closely aligned to his background and interests. It was clear to Bob Handy that the senior engineers and chemists enjoyed considerable status in the chemical research and development laboratories. They all had private offices and walnut desks comparable to those of sections heads and while salary position was a well-guarded secret in this organization, it was an accepted fact that senior engineers' and chemists' salaries equaled and often surpassed those of section heads.

It had become increasingly clear to Handy, as he talked to members of the development division staff and observed their activities, that their major problem could be expressed as a need to get necessary experimental work done by researchers and engineers in other divisions. The development division had no authority to order this work, no money to finance it, nor any laboratory or experimental staff to do it themselves. At the same time, Handy realized that the laboratory divisions had responsibility for getting their own work done. All the development division staff had to work with were their technical skills and their ability to form good relationships with those who did have the necessary laboratory facilities and money to do the experimental work.

In explaining the polyethylene problem to Bob Handy, Wayne said: We have a commercial plant coming on line in four months. We can sell only 20 per cent of the plant's estimated capacity because of a product quality defect. Originally, the plant was planned for a lower capacity solely for internal consumption. Several large potential customers were quite pleased with the results of tests on small quantities; so we expanded the capacity several-fold. It wasn't until the plant was nearing completion that a quality defect was discovered in large batch testing. The applications people have determined that the catalyst residue is causing poor quality, and now I am involved in developing a process to reduce the residue. I will then have to recommend the process to engineering who will design a plant alteration and modify the polyethylene plant.

To design this process I need to have certain information on the catalyst's behavior. I classify this information into two types, "existing" and "unknown." Much of my job involves tracing down existing information. It can come from any one of many sources; to cite a few: past lab work, experience in the engineering and commercial divisions on this or related problems, consultants, or the literature. On this particular problem we're in a unique spot because this is the first project of this type in our company; so no commercial experience is available. Also, the past lab work contributes very little to our knowledge of catalyst activity since this was never a problem before. From what I've seen of the literature, that will not help too much either. We will, however, bring a consultant on polymer chemistry in to bring us up to date on this area of polyethylene chemistry.

As Wayne saw it, the situation as he had described it left him with two alternatives:

1. To design the process on the basis of an educated guess, or
2. To propose some experimental work designed to answer the questions on catalyst behavior.

On this project he did not believe there was much choice between these alternatives. He told Bob Handy, "You don't make guesses when the investment is $3 million and you know as little as we do. Educated guessing is for smaller projects where the results of a miss are not as disastrous and where the guess can really be educated."

As the situation appeared to Wayne, they not only had to design some experiments to get the information desired, but they also had to go out and sell one of the lab groups on doing the research. Before taking action and proposing his research program, Wayne reviewed in his mind the various pressures under which he had observed the laboratories operating.

He believed that the applications research group put a constant and very important pressure upon the other labs, especially those associated with the pilot plant, for the technical effort required to produce large amounts of material to be used in applications testing both at the central research labs and in the plants of potential consumers. As a result of this pressure, the labs and the pilot plant people tended to make the new product by using the original method of production and did very little experimentation in developing process information.

Counterbalancing this pressure was one applied by Wayne and his colleagues when they suggested experiments to provide the development division with process information. These were primarily data-gathering experiments, in contrast with the laboratories' own somewhat exploratory work, or applications research's demands for quantities of material.

The third external force exerted upon the labs came about when the engineering department requested detailed information which they required to design new plants. As a service to the chemical research labs, the development division channeled all of these latter requests through their department, because they could answer many questions without involving other central research personnel. Even when they did not have the needed data themselves, they knew which groups in the central laboratories would have it and could go directly to this group without bothering other researchers unnecessarily.

Wayne also recognized two patterns of pressure placed upon the research labs from within their own organization. First, laboratory management exerted a pressure on researchers to do broad exploratory work in specified areas. As Wayne commented, "The chemical research groups have a much more specific responsibility than engineering or applications. They are interested in maximizing the company's patent position in a minimum of time. They want to get the initial basic data and leave the detailed data collection to other groups."

The other major pressure was produced by the scientist's background, training, colleagues, and personal goals—all of which directed him to make a "real contribution." Obviously, there were many other pressures existing within the labs, both individual and group; however, those noted above were the major ones that Wayne and his colleagues recognized as being important in affecting suggestions for research work.

While thinking through the proposals he might make to the chemical research people on the polyethylene problem, Wayne believed it was important to take into account not only these obvious pressures upon lab personnel but also the reactions typical of the research chemists when faced with these pressures. Wayne knew that in the past two important reactions had affected his suggestions involving lab assistance. As Wayne put it: "Their first reaction is to minimize the amount of assistance they will provide depending on the degree of friendliness and obligation they feel toward the groups and the individuals involved, the scientific position of the person suggesting the work, and the importance of the question to be researched in light of their other work commitments." Bob Handy felt this statement was realistic because as he observed the interactions of Wayne and other development division staff members, he heard such comments as "We'll take this to the vice president if we have to"; "Inexperience and lack of reputation make it difficult to sell your ideas"; "I want to get to know the men at the pilot plant and establish a group like we had on the last job"; and, "I'm not recognized in polyethylene work yet."

The other reaction to pressure was the tendency of chemical research personnel to consider as second rate and unworthy of their effort tests involving engineering applications or process data collection. Wayne viewed this as a result of pressures from the scientific community to do only "substantial" work and noted that it was most evident in the tendency to view any preplanned program of research with alarm and to consider these as attempts to destroy a scientist's freedom to select his own problems of study. In his words: "It would be fallacious to go to the labs with a detailed program of what they should do and how they should do it. This turns the professional into a technician and blocks any possible two-way communication."

It was with this analysis of the pressures and reactions to them as a background, therefore, that Wayne began his analysis of the specific information he thought it important to obtain from the labs on the polyethylene problem.

During a week of continuous planning of a research proposal on the catalyst residue question, Wayne and Dr. Side were in close contact with the laboratories. Their first steps were directed toward finding what information was available from various sources, primarily from within the Fort Worth Corporation, but also from consultants. They also listed a series of questions which had to be answered before any of the proposed methods for catalyst residue removal could be recommended. Making every effort not to have their list seem to be a "how-to-do-it" program, they drew up a final list of information which had to be collected. Wayne said, "We go into quite a bit of detailed work at this point for two reasons; we have to be pretty selective about the questions we ask of the labs, since we don't have a budget. Also, we must have a clear picture of what we want and why we want it so we can do a good job of selling our program."

Dr. Side suggested at this juncture that Wayne take their version of the research proposal out to various persons familiar with the problem in the development division and have them criticize it and punch holes in it informally before presenting it formally to the group which might do the work.

In determining which group should receive the proposal, Wayne drew upon his knowledge of what all the groups were doing. He told Bob Handy, "We make it a point to get around and see the various lab groups and maintain good two-way communication with them. From this we know the status of the various groups as to work load, work interest, and degree of responsibility to and friendship with the development division. Thus we can base our recommendations on this inside information." For example, during the planning of the catalyst research, Dr. Side suggested that Wayne check both the central research groups and the pilot plant personnel to see what they were doing on the polyethylene catalyst problem and to determine whether or not they had made any informal arrangement as to how much future work they would do.

While they were preparing their research proposal, Wayne and Dr. Side decided that they were ready to push this proposal as far as necessary to obtain the information. Wayne said, "When we are working on a proposal we make some estimate as to how far and in what direction we should push it. It usually depends upon the importance of the work and the responsibilities of the groups involved. This is not a static process but rather a continuous one over the life of the proposal as the variables change. We certainly are selective in pushing projects very hard for we realize we don't have a blank check."

One day Wayne invited Bob Handy to take a trip with him over to the chemical research labs. He said, "I need some information on the amount of residue present during a part of the process that we believe to be critical before we make our research proposal. I'm going to try and talk one of the research chemists who is making polyethylene samples into making some residue measurements for me."

Wayne introduced Handy to Bill Narberth, a research chemist, and said, "How about making some residue measures on the next batch you make, Bill?"

> BILL: I'm willing but I've just recently made a batch and it looks as though it could be as long as a month before I make another.
>
> WAYNE: That's too long. I need it now. Could you make another batch sooner? You'll eventually need it.
>
> BILL: It would have to be pretty important for me to drop what I'm doing. You know my present job has about the same high priority as the catalyst residue problem. Why do you want it?

Wayne's explanation started a discussion on the validity of the question being asked, a discussion which another research chemist who came into Narberth's lab joined. Finally the problem of technical feasibility was settled.

> WAYNE: Then it's agreed. You'll give me a series of residue measures using the techniques you described on the next batch you make, but you can't see your way clear to making another batch solely for this test.
>
> BILL: That's right because of the importance of what I'm currently working on. I'll do the measure for you just as soon as I can. However, the next batch might be made a lot earlier than next month. Half of the last batch is used, and I made it only two days ago.
>
> WAYNE: Is there any possibility of getting some work done on the alpha method of catalyst removal? We need some information to complete our alpha study.
>
> BILL: That is one you'll have to ask Bob [Bill's section head]. As far as I know we have completed all the work that we are going to do on the alpha method. There are two or three men working on the beta method, and from what I hear the results look promising.
>
> WAYNE: Thanks for your time and help and when you get anything positive, let me know. Good-by.

On the way down the hall Wayne said to Bob Handy:

Let me fill you in on the background of how we work with the Laboratory Divisions on problems such as this. At intervals we hold a research meeting of all the men involved on a particular project to summarize what their progress has been and to hammer out some form of over-all agreement for future work. Once the future laboratory program has been agreed upon, new problems which arise unexpectedly must receive careful consideration before they can be given a higher priority and replace some other item on the program.

A good example of this is the alpha and beta methods of catalyst removal about which Bill and I were talking. Both alpha and beta methods were studied in the laboratory some time ago as possible methods of removing catalyst residues. The work on the beta method was more extensive, but even so, it was not pursued too vigorously, since at the time catalyst residue was not felt to be critical to product quality.

Recently, when catalyst residues suddenly appeared to be very important, we carried out an engineering study in the development division comparing the alpha and beta techniques. Our studies indicate that alpha looks more attractive economically, but would require considerably more process development work than the beta method. We plan to back the alpha technique in our memo proposing research, and I'm interested to see where the research people stand. In regard to my success in getting the residue measures, it was a compromise, just as many of our proposals end up. If I didn't like the agreement we reached, I could have done one of several things: taken the proposal one level higher in this division either formally or informally; taken it to another group or individual who could get the data; or, let the recommendation die. Most frequently the course of action is compromise or informally seeking help from the next level. This again depends upon the importance of the recommendation and the responsibilities of the individuals and groups involved. Compromise was fine on the residue measure because it wasn't that critical. However, on this alpha lab work I'm not satisfied with the way it has been going. Let's go see Bob Roslyn.

Wayne and Bob Handy proceeded to Bob Roslyn's office.

WAYNE: How are you doing? Looks as though you've acquired some new men since I saw you last.

BOB: Yes, we got several new men out of this year's quota of new graduates. I understand that you're staying awake nights on this polyethylene headache.

WAYNE: In fact, that's why I came to see you. We are interested in having some experiments run on catalyst removal by the alpha technique and were wondering if you could spare a man. (*Wayne then proceeded to explain to Bob Roslyn the problem on which Wayne was working and why he needed this data in order to solve the problem.*)

BOB: You know we have not done additional work on the alpha method, but we have several men working on the beta method and we are quite pleased with the results. Right now one of our men is just optimizing the variables in the method.

WAYNE: How about work on the alpha method?

BOB: We don't plan any additional work on the alpha method. The results of beta have been very encouraging, and there are too many problems in the alpha method. We think beta is the horse to back; so all our effort will go into that research.

WAYNE: Bob, I would be interested in knowing why you decided to concentrate on the beta method when our engineering and economic studies have pointed out the advantages of the alpha method?

BOB: We are familiar with your economic studies which show the advantages of alpha. However, because of the close timing involved in getting a suitable process for the commercial plant and our limited manpower, we decided it would be more desirable to develop the beta method. It will require considerably less effort and is the method on which we have the most previous experience. Sometime in the future we can do additional work on the alpha method so that, if successful, it could be used in future plant expansions or in new plants.

WAYNE: I can see your point Bob; however, I don't believe that the development work required would be nearly as extensive as you might think, and certainly the economic advantages are considerable. We are currently preparing a memorandum emphasizing the economic advantages and discussing the process development work that would be required on the alpha process. We still feel very strongly that the alpha process should be developed further. I think this may be a case where we should get all interested parties together in a meeting to discuss the pros and cons of both methods and be sure that everyone is in agreement that the beta method is the best solution after all factors are taken into consideration.

BOB: We certainly would be willing to discuss this with every one. Let me know when you would like such a meeting, and I'll see that our division is represented.

The discussion left the polyethylene problem and covered several other areas of mutual technical interest before it broke up. On the way back to his office, Wayne said, "It is time the development division took a stand on this problem. When we get back to the office I'll sit down and map out a strategy with Dr. Side for formally presenting our arguments for the alpha method."

During lunch that afternoon, Dr. Cote told Handy:

Depending upon the importance of a recommendation, the staff man of the development division would be willing to take the problem as high as the vice president to obtain a solution. Most of our problems are settled at the first or second level, usually by a compromise or by our success in selling a program to the lab. If we can't get a compromise, we take some formal action. This may merely be a memo stating what we want and why. Quite often this has the desirable results of forcing a lab group to do the work to absolve themselves of blame if anything happens because our proposal was not heeded. On other recommendations which are more important, our staff is willing to back it with all their weight. This usually means sending it up through the formal channels until agreement is reached at some level.

Wayne interjected:

You see it is very difficult to question another professional man directly without maligning his reputation. We avoid this because we don't want to disrupt our present relations with other divisions. It also takes a long time to go through the formal channels. Since such a step causes a lot of commotion, we are very selective about which suggestions we write a letter on and which ones we are vociferous about in other ways.

In talking with Wayne and other development division members, it became apparent to Bob Handy that certain activities played a prominent role in the division's job but were not directly related to their primary task of "providing a process and its economics." To Bob Handy it seemed that these were supportive roles which were directly improving the efficiency of the development division's interactions with outside personnel. In this instance Bob defined "improving efficiency" as maximizing the chances for acceptance of recommendations while minimizing the conflicts and disturbances created. He was certain that these activities were not carried on solely to improve division efficiency, and it was not apparent that efficiency was a conscious justification in any or all of these activities. However, Bob was sure that they were important to the division's success in its prime task.

For instance, all during the week that he was preparing the development division's formal proposal on the alpha method of catalyst research, Wayne was constantly being interrupted by people located in technical groups elsewhere in the laboratories asking him to answer questions or to provide information. Wayne commented:

As the central group in chemical R&D, we probably have the greatest density of information on any product in the development stage. The development division gains an early familiarity with a project and we make it a point to stress our information service. If we don't have the information, we usually do know the best place to procure it. This helps us quite a bit in our relations with the other divisions, for they feel obligated to us and are much more receptive to our suggestions. Having this information allows us to perform other services which also obligate the divisions and help improve our reception.

As another example, Wayne underlined the service the development division performed by channeling engineering's requests for information to the chemical research labs, since much of the desired information was already available there and men in the development division knew the location of it. They were thus in an excellent position to serve both engineering and research. If there were any requests for unknown information, Wayne appraised the request, developed a program to provide the answer, and suggested the program to the appropriate group. As an example he said, "When, or if, this polyethylene catalyst removal process ever gets to engineering for plant design and they run into a problem, I'll get the call. If I can't answer it from my own background, I'll know the right lab people to contact. The research labs instigated this program of using the development division as a buffer and seem to appreciate our efforts."

Wayne mentioned several other services the development division performed in their effort to maintain good relations with other divisions:

One of our big problems in this polyethylene work is that I have no established position of scientific prestige or reputation. In the past three years our top specialty products men have been transferred out to other parts of the company and with them went the prestige of the section. Dr. Side and I plan to develop our position by making some positive contributions on some other problems in polyethylene. This helps a lot when we have an idea to sell. In new areas such as this we will try to borrow prestige from persons already established. What we are trying to do is get the weight of informed scientific opinion on our side in this case. In fact, Dr. Side and I have a meeting scheduled with the man from engineering who designed the plant to get him to back our ideas on the alpha method.

Dr. Side commented:

While we are on the subject, we might as well mention the value of the project groups in our lab relations. Polyethylene is new and the group is not yet well established; in fact, that is one of Wayne's major tasks in the near future, the formation of a good communications network including every group or person intimately involved in the work. It is nothing formal; we had it on the last project and it worked fine, improved communications and relations with the labs. Wayne plans to spend some time with the pilot plant group working on establishing a mutual background on polyethylene. It works just as if we actually had a project group, except there is no red tape or supervision. Again Wayne's success depends a lot on his scientific position and friendship with the lab personnel.

As the date approached for the formal presentation of the research proposal on the alpha method, Wayne grew more nervous. He said, "Sometimes I wonder whether we have done all that is possible to gain an easy acceptance of our recommendations. At other times I think that a group such as the development division should have authority comparable with its responsibility." Bob Handy asked Wayne what he meant by "authority comparable with responsibility" and Wayne replied, "One can be all things to all men which in the long run is an impossible course of action because one must, at some time, take stands on particular issues. On the other side of the picture, you might take stands on everything. Quite often, nevertheless, what we need is an authoritative decision rather than a democratic discussion at lower levels. An authoritative decision causes no more discomfort than a democratic decision, and it takes much less time."

6. PERKINS COMPONENT COMPANY*

LATE IN THE MORNING of December 12, Ralph Franklin,[1] the foreman of the machine shop at Perkins Component Company, strode into the office of his immediate superior, Jerry Taylor, the factory manager.

> RALPH: I think any progress we've been making in our dealings with engineering has just gone up in smoke. Frank [Murtaugh] was just out in the machine shop and he was plenty upset about the tops for the "V" cabinets that we're just finishing. He said that we haven't followed the engineering drawings and that we're just going ahead with changes without even a "TA" (temporary authorization). I tried to explain to him the tops were made to the drawings but had to be reworked because the drawing was for the new-style top. You see, we had to rework them to match up with the old-style cabinets still being used in assembly. I didn't get very far in explaining how it actually happened, because Ted [Luther] came along and he and Frank got into a really hot argument. Frank got good and angry and walked out. I just wanted to be sure you knew about it. I know how you've tried to build up a good relation between engineering and ourselves.

This episode that Ralph Franklin brought to Jerry Taylor's attention was only the latest of a series of events that had influenced the relations between engineering and manufacturing at Perkins. The Perkins Component Company was a medium-sized (1,200 employees) producer of a line of highly technical industrial machinery. For a number of years an open and rather bitter struggle for status and influence had existed between manufacturing and engineering. The conflict often erupted in personal arguments between the vice president of engineering, Fred Burdett, and Ted Luther, the general manager of manufacturing. Both of these individuals were aggressive in attacking each other, particularly in managemnt meetings held by the president with all of his immediate subordinates. Burdett had often been successful in baiting and goading Luther into outbursts that tended to defeat Luther's purposes and frustrate him further.

This situation had been further complicated in the past six months by the fact that Tom Darrow, the chief industrial engineer, had initiated a

---

* This case was prepared by "Jerry Taylor" immediately after the events described. All names are disguised.

[1] See Exhibit 1 for an organization chart that depicts the formal relationship between all the people mentioned in the case.

series of radical changes in several old products, and was now pressing to make similar changes in a new product just released by engineering but not yet in production. Engineering had resisted these changes on the basis that they were being introduced in a haphazard manner with virtually no preliminary investigation and with some impairment of the quality of the product. Luther had repeatedly supported Darrow's posi-

Exhibit 1

PERKINS COMPONENT COMPANY

PARTIAL ORGANIZATION CHART

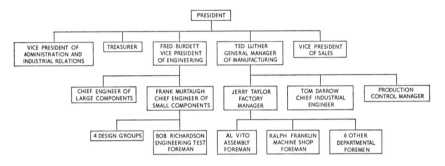

tion in the management committee meetings, claiming that these changes were within the prerogative of industrial engineering. He had further charged that engineering was resisting because they were afraid that manufacturing had taken the initiative on changes which engineering should have made earlier. Since Frank Murtaugh felt personally responsible for the engineering design of products Darrow was proposing to change, the situation had precipitated open hostility between Darrow and Murtaugh. When Darrow was unsuccessful in gaining formal engineering approval, he attempted to effect design changes informally by incorporating them in methods instructions which he urged the foremen to follow. Murtaugh was incensed by this behavior. Identifying Darrow as a manufacturing group representative, he became less disposed to co-operate with production people.

While the situation between manufacturing and engineering had gradually deteriorated, relations between the different units of the manufacturing organization were also conflicted. Feelings of win-lose competition were common between production control, industrial engineering, and the factory. The relations between the foremen of the several factory departments displayed similar characteristics—bickering and antagonism characterized their dealings with one another. All efforts to change this situation had been unsuccessful. Conflicts within manufacturing were often expressed in terms of the performance-evaluation system. Factory performance was measured by the comparison between the actual productivity of each factory department and estimated standards set by industrial engineering. The foremen and hourly workers constantly complained that the standards were unrealistic, that the methods on which they were based were incomplete and not capable of fulfilling the specified requirements, that the tools and fixtures provided were inadequate and of poor design, and that production schedules, based on these standards, were similarly unrealistic. The situation was further worsened by the fact that the accounting system did not allow cross charging. Both the work done for other sections of the factory and rework occasioned by engineering changes, poor quality materials, or incorrect purchased parts were charged against the department doing the work, even though it in no way was occasioned by their own mistakes. Industrial engineering insisted that the standards not only were adequate but actually generous and that the poor performance was a result of poor supervision and a generally recalcitrant work force. They advocated tighter controls with severe penalties for failure to achieve performance. There were also constant complaints from production control that factory supervision did not take production schedules seriously enough. Faced with the persistence of this apparent "indifference" to schedules, the production control people tried to do a more and more detailed scheduling job.

Approximately two months before the date of the case, the productivity report as a basis for judging factory performance was dropped, and a system was substituted which measured performance by how well the preplanned production schedules were met by each factory department, with an adjustment for over-all factory attainment of the dollar target for total shipments. This system placed primary emphasis on meeting departmental schedules with an extra premium on maximizing the combined factory performance. At the same time, the standards on each job, prescribed methods, and detailed scheduling were pushed into the background, and prime responsibility was clearly established as resting with the foremen for operating their departments effectively. In establishing the new procedures, Jerry Taylor, who had initiated the change, stressed the importance of mutual co-operation between department foremen without which accomplishment of the factory target would be impossible. The foremen were also urged to use the production control people as valuable aids to getting the materials in and out of their departments on time. Signs immediately began to appear that relations between factory groups and production control were improving. The first month's accomplishment under this scheme surpassed the targets for each department and for the factory as a whole.

Encouraged by these signs of progress within manufacturing, Jerry Taylor decided to see if he could improve the working relationships between manufacturing and engineering. As a first step in this direction, he made a firm commitment to engineering that the factory would adhere to engineering drawings and would make no changes or deviations from these specifications without engineering approval. It was agreed that the foremen and engineers should collaborate to seek design improvements and that engineering would incorporate all practical change requests in their designs in order to facilitate more efficient manufacturing practice. These agreements were clearly made known to industrial engineering, production control, and the factory foremen and had the specific approval of Ted Luther. By December 12, there was some evidence of more effective relations between the factory foremen and engineering personnel.

After Jerry Taylor had heard Ralph Franklin's initial account of the blowup with Frank Murtaugh, he continued the conversation:

JERRY: What brought this on? Did we really make them to the drawing?

RALPH: Well—yes, except we left out the operation of making the cutout for the screening on the request of Tom Darrow. Industrial engineering wanted to use the perforated material on this run instead of punching a cutout and spot welding the screening over the cutout. The job came through on a special work order. Darrow was supposed to get an ECO (engineering change order) or TA from engineering. After we were almost through, Tom came to me and said we would have to punch the four holes for the latches larger. The holes called for on the drawing are for a new-style latch which wouldn't match up with the cabinets which are already in assembly. We had to repunch the holes as rework.

JERRY: Actually, Ralph, these tops are not to print on two counts. First, the print did not call for the new perforated material, and second, the print does call for a new latching arrangement. These tops are not to the new print, and they are not to the print for the old style either—right?

RALPH: That's right!

JERRY: You realize, Ralph, that this whole business of making things to drawing is a very touchy matter with engineering. This ties into the war that's been going on between engineering and industrial engineering on who is responsible for design. Frank sees this as another example of Tom and Ted taking over engineering responsibility for design. Tom didn't try to get a TA because he won't admit that this is engineering's prerogative. This kind of bickering is making it damn difficult to get co-operative action between engineering and manufacturing. Regardless of whether

Tom likes it or not, we have agreed to stick to engineering specs and we must do it. Engineering has agreed that when we feel that there is good reason for deviating from the print they will co-operate—but we must let them know what we want to do and why—and we do this by asking for a TA. I'll talk to Frank and try to patch things up.

A short while later Bob Richardson, supervisor of engineering test, stopped Taylor and asked if he knew about the row between the machine shop and engineering:

BOB: I don't want to see anything happen that will break up what's beginning to develop between our groups, but Frank is real sore and he insists that, when the units hit final test, we must reject them if there are any unauthorized changes from the drawing. This puts me in the middle. If I don't reject them, Frank and Fred Burdett will nail me.

Why do our bosses have to be fighting all the time! You and I trust each other and our groups are co-operating and the quality is getting better all the time. This is good for the company. I'm sure that my people and your foremen can work together. But something like this happens and we are forced into foolish fighting.

This is some more of Tom Darrow's work, trying to bulldoze his way into things. He's always stirring up trouble. He hasn't got competence in his own job so he tries to take on everyone else's responsibility. Instead of helping the foremen do a better job, he keeps lousing things up to his own advantage. How can we respect anyone like that?

Burdett will make a big issue about this and it will get into the management committee meeting. I wish we could ease Frank on this thing and avoid a blowup. Do you think that if you talked with Frank you might get him to see that this situation is not of your making? I'm sure Frank realizes this but he can only take so much. Can't we get those guys [Luther and Darrow] out of the picture?

JERRY: I'm going to talk to Frank, Bob. I'm sure that this doesn't mean that engineering and manufacturing must fight. It's too bad this had to happen now, when we just started to make some progress on coming together. I appreciate your coming to tell me about this. I think you and your people have done a real job of working with Al Vito in equipment assembly. Al feels that he is making good progress, and from what you have been telling me lately, the quality is really a lot better.

BOB: It's damn good! We don't have to take our hat off to anyone for the quality of our machinery. Al is a good man to work with. The men on that line are a lot happier, too. They don't like to make junk either. Now that we have stopped the foolishness of trying to squeeze more speed at the expense of quality, things are a lot better—and I bet the productivity is a lot better, too. I don't get involved much with the machine shop, though. Luther has made some derogatory remarks in the management committee meeting about me spying on the shop, looking for things that will show them up. I have to admit that we did sharpshoot some in the past, but this was because our respective bosses were sharpshooting each other.

JERRY: I think it would be great if you'd get involved in the machine shop, Bob. I'm sure that you and your people could be of real help to Ralph. But, of course, it'll take time to build up the necessary trust. You'd have to make an effort to get to know Ralph better. I'm sure that he'll respond once he realizes that you want to help him.

BOB: Fine! How do we get started?

JERRY: Why don't we get together—the three of us—you, Ralph, and myself—and kind of chew over our objectives.

BOB: O.K. How about one o'clock tomorrow afternoon in your office?

JERRY: It's a date—one o'clock in my office. Thanks, Bob. I'm sure we'll make some progress.

After this conversation Jerry Taylor went to his office with the intention of getting in touch with Frank Murtaugh. He found Al Vito waiting for him with a problem that he was anxious to talk over. About ten minutes later, while Jerry and Al were still talking, Frank walked in. He started talking, without any preliminaries.

FRANK: I'm fed up! You know what happened this morning about the tops. Well, I've decided that if manufacturing wants to operate in a haphazard, irresponsible way, then I don't want anything to do with them. I'm through with industrial engineering—O.K., let them! When they louse things up, manufacturing can bail itself out, engineering won't help. I'm not going to make any more fuss about these tops. Actually, I don't disagree with the change to perforated stock. It's a good change—and the tops are O.K., but it was done in an irresponsible way. My people are going to concentrate on their development projects and to hell with manufacturing! It's the wrong way to work and it will cost the company money, but that's what they want and that's what they will get. (*He turned and started to leave.*)

JERRY: Wait a minute, Frank, you don't really mean that. You're angry now, but you know that you won't turn your back on your engineering responsibility regardless of how much it hurts. Manufacturing has fumbled the ball, but that doesn't mean they won't pick it up again. I told you that the shop will build things to print, and by God they will! We are wrong. When we knew a change in the tops was practical and desirable, we should have asked for a TA. In this instance the change is a good one, but another change which looked equally as good might turn out to be a damn costly mistake which would jeopardize the company's reputation. If we're going to operate effectively we have to follow the rules. A TA should have been requested, and a TA will be requested. This can be turned into a profitable mistake, Frank. It can bring home the importance of following through. I'm not afraid to admit we are wrong and neither are my foremen.

FRANK: Well, O.K., Jerry, thanks!

After Frank left, Jerry spent a few minutes filling Al in on what had happened and emphasized with him the importance of consistent follow-up on matters of this kind. He then went out to the machine shop to see Ralph Franklin.

JERRY: Ralph, I just got through talking with Frank. He is pretty sore but I think we can turn this whole thing into an advantage and close the gap between engineering and ourselves even more than it was before this happened. But it's going to take fast action on your part. Have you got a blank TA form?

RALPH: No, I don't make out TA requests. Industrial engineering is supposed to do that.

JERRY: Well, this is as good a time as any for you to start making them out. The responsibility for making the parts to print is yours. Before a deviation from print is allowed to pass, regardless of who requested it, it is your responsibility to be certain that the change will fulfill the intention of the design. And product design is primarily the responsibility of engineering. So the authorization must come from them. If you have to have an authorization, then you must have the right to ask for it. If you'll send out to final test, I'm sure Richardson will give you some forms. Fill one out and take it to Frank. Tell him you realize that it's your responsibility to follow through. I think you can pull this thing out of the fire.

About a half hour later, Taylor was sitting in his office when Frank walked in.

FRANK: Jerry, I want to apologize for my rude behavior. When Ralph came up to my office with the TA, I apologized to him. I behaved badly this morning. I want to work with you. I'm sure we can both do a lot to help each other. Thanks for not getting angry when I barged in on you.

JERRY: That's O.K., Frank, I'm glad we're together.

Later on Jerry Taylor saw Ted Luther and asked him what happened between Frank and himself that morning.

TED: That guy gives me a pain. He was griping to Ralph about the tops not being to print and I said, "So what?" He said that all changes should be covered by a TA. I said, "Why?" He said because some changes will affect the function of the design. I asked him when this had ever happened. He said on the RB 23 and some other product. I don't remember which one. I got mad and told him the engineering design on the RB 23 was no damn good in the first place, and that we had told them so when we first saw it. I said, "You and the rest of your stumble bums were too thick to listen." He said, "Oh, hell!" and turned on his heel and walked away.

JERRY: No wonder he was angry, Ted!

TED: Oh, I'm sick and tired of that guy. He isn't even a man, he's just a cry baby.

JERRY: He came in to see me and blew his stack. Ted, I agree with Frank and I intend to see that we do get TA's. I had Ralph make one out on this.

TED: Yeah, O.K. You're right. But I don't know how you've got the patience to put up with that guy.

JERRY: Ted, this may surprise you, but Frank was man enough to come back to my office and apologize for blowing up and what's more important he apologized to Ralph.

TED: Well, maybe you'll get some place with him, but I doubt it.

7. BELMONT-WHITE COMPANY

Two months ago, at an operating committee meeting, the president of the Belmont-White Company[1] asked Thornton Peet, the general sales manager, and Paul Robb, manager of the organization planning and procedures department, to get together and determine if better forecasts of sales and of inventory requirements could be made available in order to improve factory schedules, financial planning, and so on. Bert Kent and Charles Stevens, both of whom worked for Robb, and Robert Henry, Edwin Merrill, and David Spitz of the sales department, were assigned by Robb and Peet, respectively, to work on the problem. Stevens and Henry, being older and more experienced, and being regarded as rather senior men, immediately became the informal leaders of the work group. The five men worked out the technical problems to the satisfaction of both Stevens and Henry. The group attempted to consult with its immediate superiors as the work progressed.

After the study had been under way for some time, Henry told Stevens that he, Merrill, and Spitz seemed to be blocked by the opposition of the product division managers. Henry also told Stevens that he felt he "could not go over the division managers' heads" to Peet; and he asked Stevens to have his boss, Robb, inquire of the sales manager whether a conference might not be held to appraise the progress of the work. Stevens told Robb of Henry's request and the reason for it. Accordingly, Robb talked to Peet about the matter. Peet acquiesced, as he believed the problem ought to be solved as rapidly as possible. Peet invited the four product division managers, Robb, and the five-man working group to the conference and set the time for it. Peet told Henry to go ahead with Stevens and set up the presentation to be made at the conference.

As Henry and Stevens planned the conference, they decided that the group from the sales department—Henry, Merrill, and Spitz—were really on the spot. The three men all agreed that in order not to embarrass themselves or their bosses, the presentation of the joint conclusions of the working group ought to be made by Stevens.

---

[1] A partial organization chart of the company is shown in Exhibit 1.

At the meeting, Peet, the four product division managers, and the three men from sales who worked on the study were present, as were Robb of the organization planning and procedures department and his two assistants, Stevens and Kent. When Peet asked who was going to report progress, Henry suggested that Stevens was the best man to present their findings. Peet asked Robb if that was O.K. When the latter agreed, Stevens used half an hour to outline the concept of their work; he stated that both groups had agreed upon details and believed their recommendations would work; they were prepared to take personal responsibility for them. Both Merrill and Spitz asked

Exhibit 1

BELMONT-WHITE COMPANY

PARTIAL ORGANIZATION CHART

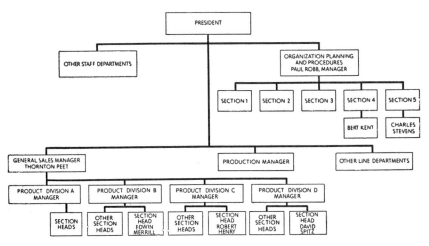

Henry to amplify certain points during the presentation. It seemed to Robb that they had in mind clarifying matters for their own bosses who might be opposed or might not understand.

Following Stevens' statement, the sales manager called upon his product division managers to give their reactions to the proposals. One of them gave the plan lukewarm support; the three others said it could not be accomplished. There was much discussion among the three who were opposed. Occasionally, Henry, Merrill, and Spitz tried to "get a word in edgewise," without much success. Once, Kent asked the Division B manager a question; the effect seemed to be mild anger at being interrupted.

Robb watched the whole proceeding with interest. He recalled that it had seemed to him that for the past two years, this same group of four product managers had opposed every step involving changes in methods or procedures. In his opinion, their "delaying tactics" had been costly to the company. Robb knew that the president expected him to break some of these bottlenecks. Robb was only a staff adviser, but he knew he "had the president's ear" whenever he needed it. He considered the sales manager to be progressive and thought Peet could not tolerate these conditions much longer. It seemed to Robb that Peet had line responsibility to get something done in this area. Robb liked these "old-line" product managers and did not want to hurt them if he could avoid it.

While Robb was in the midst of these musings, and after two hours of apparently fruitless discussion, Peet turned to him and said: "Robb, you have heard this whole discussion; what do you think we ought to do next?"

8. GRAYSON COMPANY

AN OLD established telephone company, the Grayson Company operated over a very wide geographical area. For the purpose of administration the operations were divided into several districts. Each district, in turn, was divided into five departments: commercial, traffic, engineering, construction, and maintenance, each headed by a district superintendent. The headquarters of the Jonesville district were in Jonesville, a city with a population of about 50,000. Jonesville was the only large urban community in the district, the rest of the district being primarily rural. Ralph Hall was the superintendent of maintenance for the Jonesville district. A partial organization chart of the Jonesville district is shown in Exhibit 1.

Exhibit 1

GRAYSON COMPANY

JONESVILLE DISTRICT PARTIAL ORGANIZATION CHART

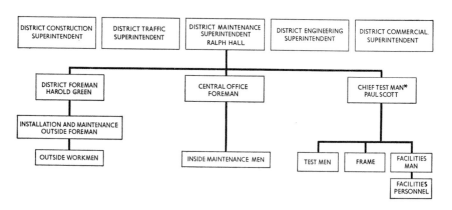

* Prior to 1943, Paul Scott's group had reported to Harold Green.

Hall was quite concerned about the test group supervised by Paul Scott, particularly since the group had a very important part in the over-all job of furnishing and maintaining service to the company's customers and was required to work very closely with all the other departments.

The commercial department, for example, accepted all customers' orders for telephone service and relayed them to the test group, which determined whether or not the necessary telephone facilities were available. If facilities were available, the test group assigned those to be used. After the assignments were completed, the test group sorted out the orders and assigned them to the outside workmen for completion. These workmen were supervised by outside foremen; but because the workmen were motorized and worked at scattered locations throughout the district, they saw their respective foremen only in the morning or in the evening at the garage or when their foremen made periodic visits to their jobs. On a routine job the test group determined which workman should handle the order and sent it along to him at the garage. Also, when a workman had no further work assigned or needed assistance, he called the test group; the test man to whom he talked in turn relayed the information to Scott. If it was a case of needing additional work, the test man, at Scott's direction, assigned him an order to complete. When a workman needed assistance, the question was referred to his outside foreman, if he was available; otherwise, Scott handled the situation. The test group also notified the outside installation and maintenance foremen of any special jobs so that material could be ordered and surveys made.

This test group also received all reports of telephone trouble relayed from customers and made tests to determine the nature and location of the trouble. If the trouble was in the central office, the group referred it to the inside maintenance men; and if it was outside the central office, the group gave it to outside workmen to clear up. The group also worked closely with the traffic department, notifying it when the outside workmen had completed a customer's order and service was ready for use, or when service was disconnected. The construction department employees also had many contacts with the test group in the course of making tests on new construction work and in effecting rearrangements of existing construction. In many ways the test group was directly responsible for the efficiency of the district.

Several groups of employees worked in the test group, namely, test men, frame men, and facilities personnel. The duties of the several groups varied. For example, the frame men worked in a different room from that of the test men and the facilities personnel. Their job was of a somewhat dirty and arduous nature, as they were required to work on rolling ladders to handle wire and to solder connections.

On the other hand, the test men were seated at a test board which ran along one side of the room. Most of these men had been outside workmen who had been promoted to test men, since technical experience was usually a prerequisite for this job. The work of the test men was generally considered to be quite desirable because it was felt to be almost a "white-collar" job. The test men spent most of their time talking to outside workmen over the telephone, making tests for them, and dispatching or completing orders.

The facilities personnel were in the same room, but were seated at desks some distance from the test board. In this group, all the personnel were women, with the exception of one facilities man. The facilities personnel assigned facilities to customers. Scott's desk was also located in this group.

The district organization as set up had been in effect since 1935, the only change being the removal in 1943 of Scott's group from the supervision of the district foreman, Harold Green, to the direct supervision of the district maintenance superintendent. Between 1935 and 1943 the test group had experienced considerable growth and expansion, as had the entire company.

Scott, the chief test man, was sent to Jonesville in 1935 and, when placed in his assignment, was given instructions, according to his own statement to Hall, "to clean the place up and put it on a working basis." On several occasions, he had remarked that when he took over the job, he felt that the group was inefficient, overcrowded, and overmanned, and that previous supervision had been loose and lackadaisical. Hall and others thought Scott was very well equipped with experience for his assignment, since he had supervised the facilities assignment for three years in another district and had been a workman in both the inside and the outside maintenance forces. He was 32 years old and had had thirteen years of service with the company when he was given this assignment. He entered the job with apparent enthusiasm and reorganized the test group, introducing efficient and modern methods. The operating data for the Jonesville district showed steady improvement and soon rated among the best in the company.

To Hall, Scott appeared as a rather quick-minded individual who, because of his knowledge and experience, was able to see through a problem very quickly and oftentimes became impatient with others because they could not understand the situation as speedily as he could. Scott was an only child; and according to his own statement, his father was the only person who had ever understood him. His wife was an employee of the commercial department.

During World War II the work in the test group was on an ordinary level, without much pressure. Shortly after V-J Day, however, a tremendous expansion in construction work was started by the Grayson Company in an attempt to supply customers on the waiting lists with service. This increase in construction jobs had its effect on the volume of work handled by the test group.

During the early part of this expansion program, Hall was appointed district maintenance superintendent. He was on the job only a short time when he began to hear complaints from various sources about the way the test group was being operated. He himself noticed, on his regular visits to the test group, that there appeared to be some unrest and undercurrents among the workers of the group. In talking with various employees, Hall got the impression that Scott ruled his men with an iron hand. Scott had designated one test man as an unofficial assistant. It seemed to Hall that Scott and this "assistant" were making too many of the decisions; he thought many of the decisions should be handled by the test men themselves. Hall believed that the other test men did not like this procedure and that they felt they should be permitted to assume authority and accept responsibility.

On the basis of further investigation, Hall deduced that shortly after the change in the personnel of the organization in 1939, some friction started to develop in the group. At that time, higher management decided to substitute women for men in the facilities work, with the exception of one facilities man who was retained to care for the more complicated problems.

It appeared to Hall that Scott resented the introduction of women into his group, and he—Hall—recalled several instances which seemed to bear out this belief. In one case a female employee who had been doing a good job became quite upset emotionally, lost considerable time, and finally asked for a transfer to another job, complaining of mistreatment. In another case a girl who was a very high-grade employee and eventually became the union representative for the group started to complain about Scott's treatment of the women in the group. In some cases, Hall concluded that she was distorting the facts. Again, when it was necessary to add employees, principally women, to cope with the increasing work load, Scott appeared to be reluctant to do so; he said that such a procedure would not do any good. He complained that he would just about get them trained when they would leave.

Several other occurrences also came to Hall's attention. On one occasion the general staff of the home office developed a plan to handle a maintenance problem and sent out instructions covering the details of the operation. Scott, however, did not agree with the method set up by the general staff and devised a plan of his own, which he put into operation, without approval of either the general staff or the district maintenance superintendent. Shortly thereafter, the outside foremen began to complain that their men were being used very inefficiently. Since Scott's program had been started, however, it seemed to Hall that it was impossible to make a change in the midst of it. From the sole viewpoint of the test group, Scott's method was the easiest way to do the job; but this fact was not, in the opinion of Hall and others, true of the other groups involved.

Hall also found other occasions when it seemed that Scott was not co-operating well with the outside foremen. When something went wrong, Scott always seemed to have the right answer and criticized the other foremen as being inefficient or not knowing their jobs. In any argument as to the correct practice to be followed, it seemed to Hall that Scott was usually correct. On various occasions the outside foremen complained that Scott countermanded orders they had given to their subordinates. For instance, one foreman had instructed a workman not to work overtime on a particular job; nevertheless, when the workman called the test group at the end of the day and reported that the job had not been finished, Scott ordered him to stay on the job and complete it before he left.

The construction department also complained that the test men were giving preference to the installation and maintenance men when they called in for tests, thus compelling the construction men to wait. When the construction department complained of this to Scott, his reply was that if the construction people would lay out their work, plan efficiently, and give him time to prepare, there would be no delay. Hall believed that everyone felt Scott knew his own job thoroughly but did not understand the problems of the outside groups because of lack of adequate field experience.

In talking to the man who had preceded him as district superintendent of maintenance, Hall learned that a number of years previously the outside foremen got together and called upon the man who was then superintendent to complain about Scott. That superintendent, however, was unsympathetic and dismissed them with the statement that Scott was doing the job the way it ought to be done and that he had full confidence in him.

Hall also talked to his own superior in the home office and found that he considered Scott to be one of the best chief test men in the company. Hall's supervisor felt that Scott had all the technical qualifications necessary for promotion; he recognized, however, that there was some friction in the group; he also believed that Scott had been in that particular assignment too long.

When the superintendent of maintenance for a small adjacent district was assigned temporarily to a different job, Hall thought it would be a good opportunity to observe Scott under a change of circumstances. He therefore arranged for Scott to take over the other job for three months, with the understanding that he would return to his old assignment as chief test man in the Jonesville district. During the period that Scott was in the temporary assignment, there was no indication of friction between him and others. In this assignment, Scott had under his supervision a central office maintenance force, an outside maintenance and installation force, and a test group.

In the meantime, Hall assigned one of the outside foremen to supervise Scott's group in Jonesville. During this time, things appeared to run smoothly in the group, and no complaints were heard from the other departments. After Scott returned from his temporary assignment, Hall overheard one of the outside foremen remark: "I wish Scotty had stayed on that temporary job. Now we'll have to put up with him again!"

Concepts and Research Findings

1. A SYSTEMATIC WAY OF THINKING ABOUT INTERGROUP BEHAVIOR*

EVERY COMPLEX organization is, by definition, made up of more than one of the small work groups upon which we focused our attention in Section II. It is a matter of common observation and of research evidence that these groups in organizations tend to develop some persisting patterns of behavior in their relations with each other. These relationships must, of course, meet at least the minimal needs for achieving the purpose of the total organization and the minimal needs of the separate groups for survival. Business managers often have the experience, however, of feeling blocked and frustrated in doing a better job of achieving various goals because of the nature of the existing patterns of intergroup relations. It is a common complaint, for instance, that the sales department is having a running feud or "cold war" with the production department, with occasional shots being fired by other entrenched groups. Of course, there is a great deal of variety in the particular form these relations take in different organizations. What is needed for the business practitioner, the professional manager, is a systematic way of thinking (a conceptual scheme) that he can use as a tool to help him analyze a particular intergroup problem and to help him build some tentative generalizations about these problems. The systematic study of intergroup relations in complex organizations is still in a rudimentary form, both in the development of theory and in empirical research. In spite of this fact, this paper is proceeding on the assumption that a crude tool is better than none and, therefore, that a conceptual scheme for analyzing intergroup behavior, even in rudimentary form, is well worth testing.

The small group conceptual scheme presented in Section II has been used as a model from which the analytical framework to be presented here has been developed. Furthermore, because the character of each small group in an intergroup relationship will influence the nature of that relationship, a few crucial components of the emergent small group system will play an integral part in intergroup analysis. We would be well-advised at this point, therefore, to review the description of that conceptual scheme.

In our small group analyses, a complex set of interdependent variables, called "givens" (including technology, leadership style, and social and economic environment), was conceived as producing certain requirements for activity, interaction, and sentiment. These "requireds," along with the other "givens" of cultural status relationships and individual backgrounds, were than described as producing the "emergent" system. At this point in our analysis, we were able to discuss the development of informal activities, interactions, values, and norms among the members of the small group. We could systematically describe the behavior occurring in the small group, see the rules and structure which governed that behavior, and deduce approximately, from earlier segments of the diagram, the interdependent factors which made that behavior, those rules, and that structure what they were. We found that these rules, structure, and behavior had certain consequences for the survival and growth potential of the organization, the small group, and the individual. These consequences, in turn, tended to "feed back" upon the "givens" and "requireds" (in the form of changes in formal and informal leadership behavior, in formal and informal procedures, in job design, etc.) in ways which were designed to result in behavior more functional for the organization, the group, the individual, or some combination of these.

This feedback mechanism and the interrelationship among the other factors symbolized by arrows in Exhibit 1, page 561, are of basic importance to our understanding of the small group conceptual scheme and the scheme to follow. Such interdependence is characteristic of all organic or organizational systems existing at any level of complexity; it parallels equilibrium in physical systems or homeostasis in organic systems.[1]

To construct an intergroup scheme, we are going to borrow these small group categories and adapt them for use in putting groups rather than individuals together in a comprehensible pattern. The intergroup pattern, instead of being a representation of a small group, will refer to a department, a plant, a division, a company, or even larger, more complex, organized institutions. The categories of the scheme will be

---

[1] The theory of equilibrium is taken from the natural sciences in its dynamic sense: a state of balance between the interdependent variables in a system such that the forces acting upon any one and all variables are equal. Homeostasis is a concept borrowed from physiology, indicating the tendency of organisms to maintain within themselves, by their own regulatory agencies, relatively stable conditions.

relevant to an "organizational world" which includes a number of "small group worlds."

One of our first assignments in constructing such a scheme is how to fit into it what we have already learned about small group behavior. We want to include those small group factors which are especially relevant for analyzing the pattern of intergroup behavior in any given organization. For this purpose, we shall focus primarily upon one class of small group data, presuming that we have well in mind the other classes with which this one is interdependently related. This class is composed of the values and norms which govern group members' expectations for behavior occurring within and outside the group. With some understanding of this facet of a small group in a particular situation, we can begin to see what it is like for a representative of a group to sally forth from his home base or to receive emissaries from other groups which have differing values. For example, we can begin to think of what it is like for a development engineer who believes strongly in systematic, disciplined, formally educated, logical thought processes to deal with a production foreman whose technical skill was developed on the job and remains largely intuitive, or with a sales representative whose experience tells him that logic is a poor second to personal acquaintance in closing a sales deal. Looking at the world from the internal frame of reference of a group member is a necessity for us because only then can we see the concept he has of himself as representing a group in his contacts with other groups, a concept which guides his judgment of the "outside" world's behavior toward him and his group and which influences his own behavior toward "outsiders."

Exhibit 1 is a diagram of the intergroup conceptual scheme, the first piece of which has just been described. The diagram shows crude representations of the small group conceptual scheme in the left margin, from which the first category of relevant intergroup background factors has been derived. In the exhibit, three small groups are represented, though, in any particular case, only two or more than three groups may be relating to each other.

Immediately below the comparison of small group norms and values box is a category of data abstracted directly from the culture which surrounds whatever organization we may be studying. That culture contains within it some more or less clear agreements about the relative status of particular personal backgrounds and, most particularly, of certain occupational categories (such as research scientist, salesman, and production worker). The people and groups within the organization will tend to be ranked internally according to this culturally determined

Exhibit 1

THE INTERGROUP CONCEPTUAL SCHEME

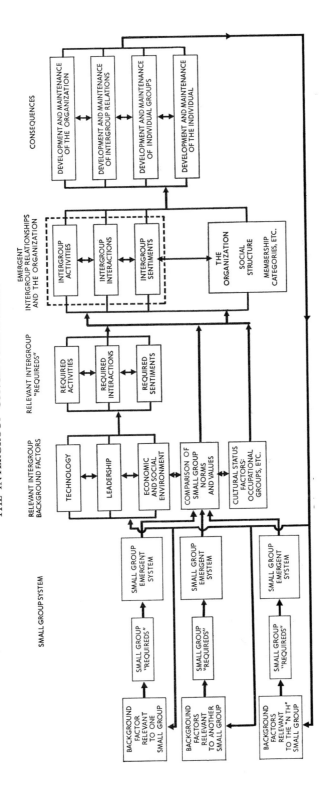

status hierarchy. And this ranking will influence the nature of the relationships between groups, just as will those groups' values and norms.

The other factors falling under the heading "Relevant Intergroup Background Factors" are already quite familiar. "Technology" refers to the nature of products, processes, plant, equipment, and other physical phenomena with which a particular organization is concerned. "Leadership" stands for the beliefs and behaviors of managers at all levels regarding the people and materials placed within their command. The "economic and social environment" box is the one in which we find those pressures which are exerted upon the organization to meet the needs and expectations of customers, government officials, vendors, the general public, and so on.

These three background factors—technology, leadership, and economic and social environment—tend to determine the nature of those phenomena listed under "Relevant Intergroup Requireds." What products or services the organization is to produce and under what physical circumstances, how its formal leaders conceive of their jobs, and what kinds of competitive and other environmental pressures are exerted upon the organization will tend to define, in broad terms, the required activities, interactions, and sentiments of a multigroup organization: which group will assume responsibility for what task, where that task will be performed, which group will pass on its product to what other group (or otherwise initiate activity for other groups), within what time limits the task must be completed and with what level of quality, and what physical equipment will be available to each group or cluster of interrelated groups for the performance of the task. Additionally, there will be some implicit or explicit stipulations of the attitudes (or sentiments) which are minimally required for performance of the organization's task.

The required factors form the framework within which the emergent system (in the third column of Exhibit 1) develops. But emergent intergroup behavior is likewise influenced by the two background factors we have already examined: the values and norms of each small group involved in interaction, and the culturally defined status rankings of those groups.

The emergent system of a multigroup organization is, indeed, very complex. Operationally, it is difficult to conceive, all at the same time, of the multitudinous interactions, activities, sentiments, and norms which characterize a total multigroup system. It is much easier, though by no means simple, to think of a pair of groups in interaction and to build up, through partial understandings, a picture of what we shall call the "organization." That is why the column titled "Emergent Intergroup Relationships and the Organization" is divided into two parts. The first segment, surrounded by a dotted line, refers to the relationships, shared activities, and common or divergent sentiments which exist between two groups out of the total number which make up the system. For example, we might give our full attention in a particular situation to the working relationship between a purchasing group and a production unit. They would likely have some contact together around the purchase of certain materials. In the course of that contact, we could specify the activities which brought them together and the sentiments which were aroused by that contact. Naturally, we want to keep in mind that these two groups' joint membership in a larger system would mean that they would likely share certain values and norms of that system, that they would be involved in certain activities and interactions which were part of the system's over-all pattern, and that they would each have a certain status and "membership position" within that larger system. The larger system is what we refer to in Exhibit 1 as the "organization."[2] The double-headed arrow between the intergroup and organization segments is an indication of the influence each pair of relationships, by virtue of being a part of the organization, has upon the total system and, in turn, the influence the total system (in its rules—norms—and values) has upon each pair relationship.

The organization can be thought of much in the same way that we have conceived of the small group. The organization, all the subgroups of a system together, can be observed in the performance of minimally required activities, as well as in the performance of activities over and above those required; the subgroups of the organization will be seen interacting with each other formally and informally; and there will be evidences in the organization of rules for behavior and sanctions for conformity and deviation and, thereby, classes of organization membership much like the regular, deviant, and isolate categories of the small group will be apparent.

---

[2] It should be pointed out that an organization designates a totality of relationships between subgroups, those relationships being more intense (i.e., more frequent and more significant) than relationships with other individuals or groups outside the organization. Thus, a production department, a manufacturing plant, a sales division, as well as an entire company, can be organizations, so long as there are distinguishable social and task subgroups within the organization which have a closer relation to each other than to other subgroups outside the organization. For example, a production department may be the organization for a number of interrelated fabrication and assembly units. But the production department itself will likely be a subgroup within a larger organization represented by a plant, a division, or a company.

Emergent behavior, just as in the small group scheme, produces consequences for the organization, for intergroup pairs, for individual groups, and for individuals within those groups. Any piece of behavior may be functional, dysfunctional, or both, for each one of these parts of the system and may have differing effects upon each one of them, depending upon whether we are looking at the impact of a piece of behavior upon the maintenance (preservation of the *status quo*) or development (growth) of any one of these parts of the total system or on the total system itself. For example, conflict between the sales and production departments over the scheduling of production may be dysfunctional for the maintenance of each group's belief that it is the more important of the two groups, but highly functional for maintenance of the organization, in that a schedule which adequately strikes a balance between customer demands and production costs is discovered as a result. It should not be difficult, in studying the cases in this section or in reviewing your own experience, to develop examples of other combinations of functionality and dysfunctionality along these several dimensions.

The "consequences" of emergent behavior tend, in a variety of ways, to feed back upon the "inputs" of the system, as they did in the small group scheme. This feedback causes changes to be made in the conditions underlying emergent behavior. The arrow on the chart (Exhibit 1) traveling from right to left is an indication of that feedback.

These, then, are the categories by which the facts about intergroup behavior can usefully be ordered, and these are the essential relationships between facts which can help us find out where the intergroup behavior we are observing came from and where it is leading. This conceptual scheme, of course, is only a beginning in our attempt to understand intergroup situations. Succeeding readings will deal with the special character of this level of organizational study and with some of the relevant uniformities in intergroup behavior which are now coming to light.

2. THE ROLE OF THE NORM OF RECIPROCITY IN SOCIAL STABILIZATION

ALVIN GOULDNER, in an article entitled "The Norm of Reciprocity: A Preliminary Statement,"[1] delineates the characteristics of social exchange between groups and individuals as a significant influence upon the stability of social systems in general. Although the utility of this concept is not restricted to analysis of intergroup behavior, it is particularly apropos of such diagnosis and is being included in this section of the book for that reason.

"There is no duty more indispensable than that of returning a kindness; . . . all men distrust one forgetful of a benefit." So Gouldner quotes Cicero, to begin his argument that a universal rule governs the social exchange[2] between men and groups of men in every culture on earth. Gouldner interprets reciprocity within the broader framework of sociological functionalism, quoting Merton: ". . . Analysis must begin with the identification of some problematic pattern of human behavior, some institution, role, or shared pattern of belief. 'The central orientation of functionalism is expressed in the practice of interpreting data by establishing their consequences for larger structures in which they are implicated.' "[3]

Gouldner holds that the concept of reciprocity is tacitly assumed as a basic component of functional analysis, since a foundation concept of functional analysis is the interdependence between social units. Often, the survival of a social unit (a production group, for example) is explained by the reasoning that that social unit's behavior is functional (provides a service) for the maintenance and development of other social units. Gouldner points out that such reasoning is sound only when the service provided by the one unit is, in fact, reciprocated and contingent upon service from other units. In other words, for one unit to survive and prosper because of the service it provides to others, those others must, by definition, be supplying a return service. However, such

---

[1] *American Sociological Review,* Vol. XXV, No. 2 (April, 1960), pp. 161–78.

[2] Social exchange, lest the reader suspect that reference is here being made only to transactions of tangible character, involves the widest assortment of goods. Love, friendship, help, advice, emotional support, and similar commodities are as relevant here as money or concrete goods.

[3] R. K. Merton, *Social Theory and Social Structure* (Revised and enlarged ed.; Glencoe, Ill.: Free Press, 1957), pp. 46–47.

a relationship does not imply that *equality* of exchange will always exist between social units. Power differences and unequal alternate sources of supply may well result in an imbalance in the social commodities which pass between groups or individuals. In such cases, Gouldner cites the existence of "compensatory arrangements that may provide means of controlling the resultant tensions, thereby enabling the problematic pattern to remain stable." He opens up the now value-laden concept of "exploitation" as a source of study for discovering the nature of these compensatory mechanisms. He points out, however, that the word *exploitation* is value laden because it represents violation of certain pervasive values, among them the *norm of reciprocal rights and duties.*

By reciprocity, Gouldner means that a right of A against B implies a duty of A to B and, similarly, that a duty of A to B implies a right of A against B. "In short, reciprocity connotes that *each* party has rights *and* duties" not just that "one's rights are another's obligations, and vice versa." Reciprocity he states as an empirical generalization, citing Malinowski, who observed "that people *owe obligations to each other* and that, therefore, conformity with norms is something they *give to each other.*" The rules for social exchange are governed, according to Malinowski, by a "presentiment of the consequences of reciprocity and of its breakdown."[4] Those rules, Gouldner points out, are based on a "higher level moral norm: you *should* give benefits to those who give you benefits." But, though obligations are closely linked to the intrinsic character of benefits exchanged, they "may vary with the status of the participants within a society." Nevertheless, the transaction in its totality, including, as part of the exchange, status and other factors which differentiate the interacting parties, is asserted to be "roughly equivalent."

Gouldner then turns to the function of the generalized norm of reciprocity as a stabilizer of social systems. First, he says, the norm acts as a force for social equilibrium because it accomplishes shared expectations of behavior among the members of the system. Further, "the norm of reciprocity . . . engenders motives for returning benefits even when power differences might invite exploitation." From Malinowski, again, comes the observation that social indebtedness tends to persist over time, "a time, then, when men are morally constrained to manifest their gratitude toward, or at least to maintain peace with, their benefactors." (Similar forces for stability are those obligations which have already been given compliance in the past.) Says Gouldner: "If this conclusion

---

[4] Bronislaw Malinowski, *Crime and Custom in Savage Society* (London: Paul, Trench, Trubner, 1932).

is correct, ... we should expect to find mechanisms which induce people to *remain* socially indebted to each other and which *inhibit* their complete repayment. This suggests a function performed by the requirement of only *rough* equivalence of repayment . . . , for it induces a certain amount of ambiguity as to whether indebtedness has been repaid and, over time, generates uncertainty about who is in whose debt."

Gouldner adds that the reciprocity norm is indeterminate rather than specific in its rules for conduct so that it "can be applied to countless ad hoc transactions, thus providing a flexible moral sanction for transactions which might not otherwise be regulated by specific status obligations. . . . Even when these are present and well established . . . the norm . . . provides a further source of motivation and an additional moral sanction for conforming with specific status obligations. . . . In this manner, the sentiment of gratitude joins forces with the sentiment of rectitude and adds a safety-margin in the motivation to conformity."

Gouldner makes the point, however, that as well as a "stabilizing mechanism," the norm of reciprocity may also be conceived as a "starting mechanism." As an example, he cites two individuals or groups which each have valuables sought by the other. Each feels that the other is motivated by self-gratification; and each, in turn, hopes to receive the other's valuables without relinquishing his own. Each suspects the other of precisely this intention and views the impending exchange as dangerous. Each takes the position, "You first!" "When internalized in both parties, the norm *obliges* the one who has first received a benefit to repay it at some time. . . . Consequently, there may be less hesitancy in being the first and a greater facility with which the exchange and the social relation can get underway."

In concluding, Gouldner emphasizes that he has limited his discussion to the functional aspects of the norm of reciprocity. He points out that it undoubtedly has dysfunctions around conflicts arising because of differences of judgment over the *ability* to repay and over the sufficiency of repayment. More important, the norm may be dysfunctional for human welfare in that it leads to the formation of relationships between parties who are able to repay, to the neglect of the needs of those unable to do so.

Gouldner's concept of the norm of reciprocity gives the observer of organizational behavior an opportunity to describe the relationships between groups in terms of the nature of the social transactions between them, the intergroup balance or imbalance of trade, and the compensatory mechanisms which arise to maintain stability among them. When one group violates the norm, the student can look for a breakdown in shared expectations, an exploitation of power, and a failure of self-starting relationships between groups. He can also expect to find significant social mechanisms which will come into existence to bring the violating group into conformity with the norm and which will also, in the meantime, work in the direction of providing stabilizing influences for the organizational system as a whole.[5]

---

[5] Sanctions imposed upon those who fail to reciprocate usually involve negative social goods such as hatred, enmity, ostracism, destructionism, and the like. In a very real sense, applying these sanctions tends to rebalance the relationship by meeting a failure to repay a favor with damage to the offender, damage in amount roughly commensurate with the value of the original favor.

3. A SOCIOTECHNICAL CONCEPTUAL SCHEME*

THIS ARTICLE explores the technical determinants of interaction between individuals and groups in work organizations. There are three major ways by which individuals and groups may be technically separated or brought together: by the way the work is divided among them; by the geographical distance between them; and by the period of time when they are at work. The nature of the task, however, requires that those individuals and groups which together are responsible for the completion of a task be able to communicate. If the interaction pattern imposed by the formal organization keeps these technically interdependent individuals and groups apart rather than bringing them together, consequences of social dissatisfaction, disintegration, conflict, and technical inefficiency will result. Consider, for example, the effectiveness of a surgical team whose members worked in different operating rooms, at different times of day and on totally separate aspects of the operation.

It will likely be apparent to the reader already that this kind of conceptual scheme would have been relevant and useful when we were considering some of the early small group cases. At that point, our common sense was usually sufficient to distinguish the nature of technical influences upon social organization and thus upon productivity. While we can ill afford to abandon common sense now, it is consistent with the additional complexities of intergroup behavior to try to master a systematic framework for thinking through the technical characteristics of intergroup behavior.

Miller's scheme involves those parts of the intergroup conceptual scheme labeled, among relevant intergroup background factors, *Technology;* among relevant intergroup requireds, *Activities, Interactions,* and *Sentiments;* all those factors listed under emergent intergroup relationships and the organization; and all of the consequences. What his conceptual framework adds to the intergroup conceptual scheme is a more substantial and detailed way of conceiving of how important interaction opportunities are for emergent group formation and satisfaction and, in turn, how influential compatible tasks and social structures are for effective job performance. His scheme is obviously partial in the

* An abstract of "Technology, Territory, and Time," by Eric J. Miller (*Human Relations,* Vol. XII, No. 3 [1959], pp. 243–72).

breadth of analysis it permits. Essentially, it allows us to assess only the effects of technology and formal organization upon intergroup behavior. Given the most functional structural framework, we still must take into account all of the other determinants of intergroup behavior which are outlined in the intergroup conceptual scheme. Even though technical factors are interdependently related to all other parts of the intergroup situation, and their more functional integration may facilitate intra- and intergroup collaboration, structural functionality alone cannot be thought of as the only relevant dimension for understanding intergroup behavior and doing something about it.[1]

The first part of Miller's paper is devoted to describing how an organization makes the transition from being a simple, small, face-to-face group to the more complex, multigroup organization with which we are most familiar. In the "simple system" (as Miller calls it), such as a service station or small retail store, there is usually no formal leader; or if there is, he spends most of his time working alongside his subordinates. As the simple group grows, so does the propensity for task specialization. Such specialization is functional for getting individual tasks done, but it is dysfunctional for the integrated performance of the whole task. Thus, more and more co-ordination is required until, eventually, at some critical point, an individual or subgroup is separated out and given responsibility for controlling and co-ordinating the work of the total group. At this point the organization moves from "simple system" to "complex system" status. Just what that point is differs among organizations; but it appears to depend upon size, technical complexity of the task, and "resilience" (i.e., "the capacity to withstand pressures—both external and internal—towards transformation into a complex system," that capacity being dependent upon those other factors in the intergroup scheme which influence the emergent social system).

Miller then introduces the three dimensions, mentioned above, upon which these subgroups will be technically differentiated: "It is postulated here that there are three possible bases for clustering of role-relationships and thus for the internal differentiation of a production system. These are technology, territory, and time. Whenever forces towards differentiation operate upon a simple production system, it is one *or more* of these dimensions that will form the boundaries of the emergent sub-systems and *will provide the basis for the internal solidarity of the groups associated with them.*"[2]

---

[1] The reader may find it useful to review this explanatory introduction after he has studied the exposition of Miller's conceptual scheme, which follows.

[2] Italics supplied.

Here, Miller is saying that however the subgroups are formally differentiated, that differentiation will be the basis for social organization, by virtue of the attendant facilitation or blockages to interaction, and that there is a requisite structure of task relationships inseparable "from the type of technology and specialization involved, from the geography of the territory in which the task is performed, and from the time scale of task performance—though within these limiting factors alternative structures may be possible" (and still be functional for task performance). However, other bases for grouping exist among people at work—their values, needs, sex, age, religion, race, and so on; and these groupings may, "by their coincidence with task-oriented groupings, accelerate differentiation; or, if they cut across these groupings, they may retard it." Once again, the significance of some of the other variables of the intergroup conceptual scheme comes into play.

Simple groups can resist becoming complex ones more easily (be more "resilient," in Miller's terms) if the members of subgroups move frequently from one subgroup to another. Similarly, the more the performance of one subgroup's task depends on the performance of all other subgroups (the more interdependent the subgroups are), the more likely it is that the simple system can do without external co-ordination (i.e., avoid becoming a complex system). In both cases, "equilibrium can be a substitute for a differentiated management function." Therefore, the more all the members of the system are familiar with all the tasks performed in the system, and the more they are confronted with the fact that all the subgroups depend on each other for completion of the over-all goal (see the concept of "superordinate goals" in "Reduction of Intergroup Conflict" [Reading 4]), the greater is the change that they can effectively co-ordinate themselves.

If simple systems are forced to become complex systems before they actually require external co-ordination, the cost of adding a co-ordinator is not met by a gain in increased efficiency. In fact, the collaborative relationships which have made external co-ordination unnecessary "are likely to be mobilized destructively against the imposed external management." However, postponing formal movement to a complex system beyond the group's natural capacity to deal with integration problems leads to a decline in efficiency because energy is diverted from production into holding the group together. The problems of co-ordinating the specialized subunits of a simple system are amplified by the fact that as subgroups are formed and grow in importance, subgroup members are internally conflicted between identification with the subgroup and identification with the total group. Not until the subgroups become explicit simple systems of their own, under the co-ordination of an external manager, can their members resolve this conflict and devote their energies once again to the primary task.

A complex system, then, would more likely operate efficiently if the timing from a simple to a complex form were opportune. However, timing is only one of the technical factors determining efficiency. Another which this article addresses is the choice of a basis for differentiating the subgroups or simple systems within the complex system. For example, a small machine shop which has grown to the point where external co-ordination is required may become differentiated by adding extra shifts (thus separating technologically identical subgroups by time) or by renting two more shops (thus separating the subgroups territorially). Further, if growth continues, perhaps both shift work and separate shops will be required, thus opening the choice of organizing predominantly along the time dimension *or* along the territorial dimension. Shall one man be put in charge of the same shift in all three shops, or shall he be put in charge of all three shifts in one shop? These choices are free ones only when time and territory are equally important in the technical process (e.g., when the units manufactured can as easily be moved for further processing between shops as from one shift to another within one shop, and so forth). The questions the owner of this machining company must ask himself are: "What are the task relationships inherent in my company? Do some subgroups have to work more closely together than they do with others to perform their respective tasks? Do the tool- and diemakers (for example) have to work most closely together, or do some of them work most naturally and regularly with a certain group of machine operators whose tool and die requirements have common characteristics?" As Miller points out:

Failure to differentiate on the appropriate basis will create stress in relationships, because the natural groupings inherent in the structure of task performance will run counter to the groupings dictated by the formal organization. Formal boundaries will cut through these natural groupings. This will inhibit development of solidarity in the formal units, with consequent lowering of work satisfaction and morale. In general, we can suggest that to the extent that the formal structuring deviates from the reality of the task situation, whether in the basis for differentiation or in the boundaries of the formal sub-units, to that extent will the management function itself have to multiply and become "top-heavy" in order to deal with the resultant dysphoria. Additional controls will have to be imposed.

If on the other hand a unit is appropriately sub-divided in relation to total task performance—if it is cut, so to speak, with the grain and not against it—both the internal management of the constituent sub-units and the overall integration of the total task are likely to require less effort.

As an organization grows, the need for adding more levels of co-ordination or for separating out previously combined subunits continues. Each successive change is influenced by the pattern implied by the changes which preceded it. For example, organizing a factory on functional lines (production, purchasing, receiving, shipping, planning and scheduling, and so forth) will foster social organization around those task orientations. If further expansion and technological innovation make some differentiation of subgroups by product rather than function more natural technically, the inertia of established social patterns will present obstacles in the way of such a reorganization.

Miller, at this point, sets about to outline the factors which may influence the choice of particular patterns of differentiation within the natural task structure he has described.

> Theoretically there are very many ways of differentiating a large organization. Depending on the size of commands and the amount of delegation, the number of levels can vary, and the basis of differentiation at each level offers many possible combinations. As we have seen, however, the inherent structure of the task imposes limitations on choice. It is now necessary to discuss in more detail some of the factors that make one choice more appropriate than others.

Throughput Time

In those cases in which a product moves slowly through the process, i.e., where the "throughput time" exceeds the duration of a shift (as in textile manufacture), there could not be a task-relevant grouping by time. The reason for this is that a shift manager responsible for all aspects of manufacture during his eight hours could not be expected to be fully accountable for his shift's performance. The command would first have to be narrowed down to groups of process (certain types of spinning, weaving, dyeing, and so forth), then to individual processes (specific spinning machines and so forth), and *then* to separate shift commands. In the other extreme, electricity generation is an example of very short throughput time in which time commands form a more coherent combination than grouping people performing one operation over different shifts. Therefore, long throughput emphasizes territorial and technological differentiations; short throughput emphasizes time differentiations.

Whole Tasks

Miller stresses the point that the organization be broken down so that each component has a "whole task." Depending on the nature of the task, this "wholeness" may be represented by time groupings (as with shifts in electricity generation), by technological groupings (weaving looms in a textile plant), by territorial groupings (track crews on a railroad), or by some combination of these. Thus, those in command have a realistic accountability, and those who work within the grouping derive satisfaction from identification with a recognizable goal. Miller points out that "[if] task relationships within a particular command are less intensive than relationships that cross the boundaries of the command, there is a strong indication that the command does not have a whole task."

Functional or Product Differentiations

Units may be differentiated technologically in different ways, such as by function (purchasing, assembly, fabrication, and so forth) or by product groups. The choice between one or the other of these differentiations rests largely upon whether there will be greater overlap between groups split functionally or by product. Does an assembly group have more intensive product relationships with other units outside of the assembly department than it has functional relationships with sister production units? If so, there may be grounds for forming a self-contained product unit composed of a number of subgroups currently organized functionally.

Equality of Subcommands

Management is easier if the sizes (not only in number of persons but in total responsibility for a part of the total task) of the units it directly co-ordinates are roughly equal. Under conditions of relatively equal power among subunits the manager can rely upon the self-regulation (or equilibrium), which is inherently more likely among peer groups than among groups of unequal value. The manager's co-ordinating role is by no means obviated by this equality, but it is usually facilitated by such a characteristic.

Intermediate Levels of Command

Whenever it appears that the number of units at one level in an organization has increased beyond the point of single command, inserting a new level of management may be considered. The difficulty is that there may be no "whole task" clustering possible at the intermediate level. For example, a production organization may have within it subgroups differentiated by the products each produces. The number of products, and thus subgroups, increases to the point where the production manager feels he is losing sufficient contact with those product groups. He wants to promote several product foremen, each to be in charge of several product groups, but each group is equally dependent upon or independent of all other groups. No combination of groups less than the total comprises a whole task differentiation. In such cases the creation of an intermediate co-ordination level may simply bring together "aggregates" rather than systems. In that event, Miller points out: "Interaction between individual units—or absence of interaction—is just as pronounced across the arbitrary territorial boundaries as it is within them. The intermediate managers will frequently be perceived by their superior as a barrier between himself and their subordinates, and by the subordinates as a barrier between themselves and their proper superior."

Differentiation by Territory

When productive units are separated by a considerable geographical distance (such as in completely decentralized production-sales units making and selling identical products in different territories), they are not likely to be interdependently related; and to that extent, they will require relatively less co-ordination. (Reliance upon a central supply of raw materials and/or a common consumer market, of course, would reduce this independence and thus would increase the importance of coordination among such spatially separated subsystems.) One problem which often occurs in the administration of such independent subunits results from the desire to place those units in a performance competition. The administrator may become so involved in resolving real or imagined incomparabilities between the systems that he neglects the primary task of the total system. And his subordinates are likely to become so engrossed in short-run competitive advantages that this behavior is dysfunctional for the long-term, effective operation of the total system.

Another problem arises out of the tendency for territorially differentiated units to take on a "distinctive competence," as Philip Selznick has called it. Though all units may be technologically identical, one may begin to specialize in a particular process or product. In the textile industry, where weaving machinery can be used to produce a large variety of products, such an occurrence is common. Not only do these "distinctive competences" result in additional planning complexities (for all their advantages in increased efficiency due to specialization), but they involve an incipient differentiation along technological lines. Such differentiation requires a different kind of management methodology. For example, competition between the subunits ceases to be an appropriate control mechanism when those units become heterogeneous technologically.

Differentiation by Technology

Subunits differentiated technologically derive their solidarity largely from distinctive competences. If integration is to be achieved, a balance must be struck between subunit solidarities and subunit recognition of the total task of the larger unit. Achievement of such a balance is not an easy chore. The production department which jealously guards its reputation for mechanical ability does not easily accede to demands that its opinion be subordinated to that of the sales department, even in favor of more effective production and sale of more competitive products.

Where technologically differentiated units are interdependently related (as are purchasing, fabrication, assembly, and so forth, in a single plant), co-ordination is facilitated where the units have clear territorial boundaries, where they have more intensive internal than external technological relationships, where their outputs are clearly measurable, where their power is roughly equal, and where the sequence of operations between units is unbroken. However, when the interdependence is sequential (e.g., where the purchasing group passes material to the fabricating group, then fabricating passes to assembly, and so forth), additional problems occur. The first group is characteristically independent of the others, and the last has no group which depends upon it. Because dependence always tends to give rise to conscious or unconscious hostility and resentment, each successive group can express its resentment by complaining directly about other groups or by passing on its resentment, through inferior work, to successor groups. The last group, lacking a dependent successor, may work out its frustrations on the total group by falling down in its task.

The primary management problem arising in those companies containing technologically differentiated and independent units (a common example being a concern which has purchased new enterprises for purposes of product diversification) is that the heads of those units have no natural basis for relating to each other. Furthermore, comparability between units is difficult except at abstract levels (such as profit percentage). Where these units are given independent company status, they seem more capable of exploiting their individual *expertise,* more flexible in responding to environmental change, and more likely to contribute to the task of the total unit than when arbitrarily centralized controls are imposed upon them.

Differentiation by Time

The major management problem in dealing with subunits which are differentiated by time alone relates to the throughput cycle, previously noted. Where units share a technology and territory but are separated by different work shifts, there tends to be a good deal of inevitable co-dependence. A number of accidental occurrences, such as machinery breakdowns, are likely to carry over from one shift to another. Of a more recurring character is the tendency for one shift to complete a certain amount of output and to pass on to the next shift a certain number of partially completed goods. The longer the throughput time, the higher the proportion of unfinished goods passed on to the next shift. Obviously, the property of self-containment is reduced under such circumstances, members of each shift have less sense of a whole task, and management's ability to measure a shift's performance is impaired. These problems are increasingly evident when shift work is devoted to maintaining equipment (a job whose prevalence increases with greater automation), since maintenance results are not likely to be confined to a time period as short as one shift. Miller suggests that managers often complicate these codependence problems by failing to think of each shift as a discrete unit and thereby unwittingly add to the factors which make for codependence. For example, scheduling procedures seldom are designed to maximize completion of the largest number of products on each shift. If managers were more aware of the nature of intrinsic task differentiation along the time dimension in their organization, they might find it desirable to try to avoid the circular dependence between shifts from becoming a deteriorating cycle. For example, assignment of responsibility for all three shifts to the first-shift supervisor is a common, often inadvertent way of increasing shift codependence at the price of shift self-containment.

Miller concludes this examination of some of the management problems associated with subunit differentiation by technology, territory, and time by noting that he has only touched "the fringe of all the possible variations." He emphasizes the fact, however, that considerations of such management problems, focusing upon the boundaries which separate units and the degree of dependence between them, may be relevant to the selection, training, and placement of managers.

4. ORGANIZATIONAL STRUCTURE AND SCIENTIFIC TRANSFER*

THE THEORETICAL FOCUS of this thesis is on the dual and apposing processes of the differentiation of functional departments (research, production, sales) in structure and orientation and of the integration of these departments into the task of the total system. The topical focus is on the process of product development and innovation (scientific transfer), which requires both a high degree of differentiation and likewise a high degree of integration if the organization is to compete effectively in a market which demands product innovation. The study was conducted in similar operations of two major diversified chemical companies.

The specialist groups involved in the different tasks connected with product innovation developed different points of view and tended to devise formal structures appropriate for their respective specialized activities but different from those of the other specialties. The major differences revealed can be briefly diagrammed along four dimensions as shown in Exhibit 1.

Exhibit 1

MEASURES OF DEPARTMENTAL DIFFERENTIATION

Dept.	Primary Environmental Orientation	Primary Time Orientation	Orientation Toward Co-Workers	Degree of Departmental Structure
Research	Science	Long	Permissive	Low
Sales	Market	Short	Permissive	Medium
Production	Plant	Short	Directive	High

The specialization of function and the differences which emerged were important for the effective operation of the separate sales, research, and production units, but they also tended to contribute to the misunderstandings and differences of opinion which inevitably arose around the innovation process. To meet the need for co-ordination and resolution of differences, each of the two companies studied by Lorsch established a

---

* This reading was largely taken from a teaching note prepared by Professor Ralph M. Hower of the Harvard Graduate School of Business Administration. It is an abstract of a doctoral thesis under the above title by Mr. Jay W. Lorsch, Harvard Graduate School of Business Administration, 1963, and of an article by Mr. Lorsch and Professor Paul R. Lawrence, "Organizing for Product Innovation," *Harvard Business Review,* January-February, 1965.

separate, "new product department," a formal device aimed at co-ordinating R&D, sales, and production. Each also made use of permanent cross-functional teams or committees to provide flow of information between the departments and to facilitate collaboration among them.

Despite apparent similarities in the formal co-ordinating departments there were subtle but important differences in the location and composition of the units in the two companies. There were likewise differences in the way they dealt with other departments and in the behavior of higher executives. Each of these elements—formal structure, interaction process, and supervisory behavior interacted and reinforced the other.

In Company A the differences between the three departments, as measured along the four dimensions shown in the above exhibit, tended to be more extreme than those in Company B, although similar in general configuration. The departments in Company A appeared to be more highly specialized and also to be better able to perform their specialized tasks. Because of the differences among them as to structure and orientation, however, one would be led to expect difficulty in their achieving the high degree of co-ordination needed.

This potential for greater difficulty in co-ordination in Company A was more than offset by certain structural and procedural differences which produced better over-all collaboration in A than existed in B. The new product department in Company A, in addition to its co-ordinating function, was involved in technical service and market development activities. In Company B the new product department, besides co-ordinating R&D, sales, and production, was directly involved in market planning and the co-ordination of sales activities. The result was that in Company A the new product department occupied a middle position, in structure and orientation, between the three departments it was to link—as close to any one as to any other, concerned about all three environments, and able to deal with both the short-range problems of sales and production as well as the long-range problems of research. In Company B, the new product department tended to be highly oriented toward the market and toward short-range time concerns. Thus it was not in an intermediate or balanced position between the three departments that it was supposed to coordinate. In Company A the executives perceived the co-ordinating department as being familiar with the problems, procedures, and ways of operating in the three departments it linked. In Company B there were complaints that the co-ordinating unit was too much involved in day-to-day detail relating to current sales and unable to develop long-range plans.

In each company certain interdepartmental disagreements were handled by a cross-functional co-ordinating committee, and here differences in interaction process and leadership behavior were apparent as well as a difference in the structural position of the committees. Company B operated with tighter spans of control, more specific rules, and a higher degree of structure. The level of decision for product innovation was higher in the organizational hierarchy of Company B than of Company A. In the latter the co-ordinating teams were mostly made up of first-line supervisors, men who had the detailed market and technical information necessary for decisions. They were the only ones who regularly attended meetings and they had the authority to make decisions. In Company B, by contrast, although the committee members were from a higher level in the hierarchy, they did not have the authority to make final decisions. They often brought to meetings both their superiors (executives with decision authority) and subordinates (men with the required technical and market knowledge.) There were two to three times as many participants in Company B's meetings as in those of Company A.

The established norms in Company B sanctioned withdrawal from disagreements and conflict. Thus many decisions were dropped, delayed, or referred "upstairs" for decision. The committee members in B appeared to lack the time and inclination to work through their differences. In Company A, on the other hand, the norm was to resolve differences at the committee level by fighting through disagreements constructively: "These things take several meetings to work out, but we are never really stalemated. We have decided in our committee that we won't be stalemated. There is more than one way to our ends. . . ." And this attitude in Company A's co-ordinating committees was reinforced by higher management. By its patience and its manifest expectation that the committee would achieve a working agreement, it kept decisions about innovation at relatively low operating levels. Company A's record clearly revealed more effective co-ordination and a significantly higher rate of product innovation than could be seen in Company B. The evidence strongly indicates that formal structure, the nature or process of co-ordination, and leadership style in Company A contributed to its greater success with scientific transfer.

In summary the findings of this study suggest the following conclusions:

1. The effectiveness of departments charged with responsibility for integrating other departments depends upon the degree to which the integrative unit is intermediate in structure and orientation among the departments it is to link.

2. The effectiveness of cross-departmental teams in achieving integration depends on the existence of norms for resolving conflicts at the level where those conflicts originate.
3. In the presence of the effectively operating integrative devices cited in 1 and 2, above, there is a tendency for individual departments to be more specialized, more expert, and more productive and for the organization as a whole to be more innovatively successful than in the absence of such effective integrative devices.

5. DIAGNOSING INTERDEPARTMENTAL CONFLICT*

Traditional Explanations

Why are some interdepartmental relationships successful and others not? Managers typically find themselves advancing one or the other of these explanations:

One popular opinion is the "personality clash" theory, which holds that stubborn prejudices and differences in ingrained personal styles (none of which are actuated by organizational influences) are behind nonproductive relations. As compelling as this explanation often seems to be, it fails to account for the fact that we seldom, if ever, encounter a group composed of people with identical or even closely similar personalities. Lacking evidence of such group identity, it is difficult to imagine an intergroup conflict between two "group personalities." This reasoning also fails to account for interdepartmental relations which are characterized by high productivity *and* some degree of personal antagonism. While personality differences undoubtedly play a part, they alone comprise an inadequate explanation of productive and nonproductive relations.

Another view holds that failure in interdepartmental relations is the result of "conflicting ideas." This theory asserts that nonproductive relations occur between groups whose respective memberships are so different in terms of skills, training, job activities, personal aspirations, and so on that they cannot possibly find a common area in which to communicate. While this explanation seems to apply to some nonproductive relations, it is not unheard of to find an advanced research group which works quite effectively with a nontechnical, highly consumer-oriented sales group. Seemingly, at least, groups can differ on many counts without a breakdown occurring in their relations. Furthermore, it is not unusual to find groups with remarkably similar points of view which seem to go out of their way to make trouble for each other. Something in addition to different points of view must be playing a part in forming the character of these relationships.

A third popular explanation for nonproductivity puts the blame on competition between groups for authority, power, and influence. Breakdowns occur because each department operates from an entrenched position which, if compromised, will bring the group nothing but defeat and loss of influence. Many nonproductive relationships seem to display char-

---

* This reading has been selected from an article of the above title by John A. Seiler, *Harvard Business Review*, September–October, 1963.

acteristics of this kind. But if this theory is to be sufficient unto itself, the only productive relationship would be one in which either or both of the groups had no desire or opportunity for influence over the other. Under these conditions, passivity would seem to be a requirement for productivity. Yet the most highly productive relations appear to take place between aggressive, confident, and high-achievement departments. Apparently other determinants, in addition to competition for prestige and power, must be operating to make interdepartmental relations successful or unsuccessful.

While no one of these theories is a sufficient explanation of why group relationships turn out the way they do, each has enough sense behind it to make it attractive. Consequently, what is needed is some way of pulling them together into a new and more useful way of thinking about interdepartmental conflicts. Let's begin this process by examining several actual cases of interdepartmental behavior.

I. Productive Focus on Task[1]

Company A developed and manufactured ethical pharmaceuticals. The activities required to transform a product idea into a marketable item were performed in sequence by subunits of the research, engineering, and production departments. An idea would first take form in a research department test tube. It would then be evaluated by research chemists and chemical engineers in the pilot plant. Next, new process equipment would be designed by mechanical engineers and job designs laid out around the equipment by industrial engineers. Actual plant construction and placement of equipment were accomplished by construction engineers, and, finally, production responsibility was assumed by production chemists. The members of these formal units agreed that research had the highest prestige of all the work groups and that the relative prestige of the other units declined in the order in which each became actively involved in the new product sequence.

The engineering and research departments were housed in their own buildings some distance from each other and from the plant. The chemical engineers worked most closely with the research chemists—sharing many ideas with them because of the similarity in their training, their work, and their aspirations. The chemical engineers also worked closely with the mechanical engineers in the pilot plant and in process equipment design. The chemical and mechanical groups shared a number of

---

[1] The cases cited in this article have been taken from the case and project research files of the Harvard Business School and are reproduced by permission of the President and Fellows of Harvard College.

ideas, though the mechanical engineers and research chemists thought quite differently about most things. The mechanical engineers worked closely with the industrial and construction engineers, who in turn were in close contact with factory personnel. These four latter groups shared similarities in background and in ideas.

Company A had an outstanding reputation for important production innovations and rapid development of ideas into mass-production items. Nevertheless, there was frequent argument among research, engineering, and production as to who should take responsibility for the product at what point in the development sequence. Engineering wanted control at the pilot plant. Production wanted control from the time the product entered its physical domain. Research wanted control, as one of its members put it, "until the actual factory yield reaches the theoretical yield."

The boundaries of control were actually somewhat difficult to pinpoint. Research was in command until factory problems seriously affecting quality were solved, except that research decisions were subject to engineering veto (in turn subject to top-management arbitration) anywhere beyond the pilot plant. In spite of continual argument about control jurisdiction, there were few engineering vetoes that ever reached arbitration.

The physical, mental, and emotional energies of these departments appeared to be devoted to the work at hand to a very high degree. While not absent from their relationships, conflicts took the form of tension between the inherently opposing values of quality and economy. The result was a competitive balance between the extremes of both. Why was conflict not destructive in this situation? There are basically three reasons:

1. Each of the three departments represented a social unit in which members could find not only satisfaction for their needs to belong, but also job interest, promotion opportunity, and so on. No one of these departments suffered from internal fragmentation.

2. At each point of significant interdepartmental contact, the members of the interacting groups agreed on certain important ideas as to how work should be accomplished. Wherever technical interdependence required intergroup contact, the groups tended to view each other and their common work with a markedly similar appreciation.

3. The hierarchy of authority among the departments was identical to the informally agreed-upon prestige hierarchy among these departments. This hierarchy was determined by the technical work limits set by one department for another, and by the initiation of activity by one depart-

ment for another. The work done by research, for example, limited what the chemical engineers could work on but, at the same time, was the impetus which set the chemical engineers to work on each new product. The same was true of relationships down through the development sequence.

Very simply, then, when a man (or a group) told another what to do and when to do it, he did so as a member of a group of superior prestige, as agreed on by both groups. We might say that the orders which passed from one group to another were "legitimate," since most workers feel that it is legitimate in our society for a person of higher prestige to direct the activities of someone with less prestige, while it is illegitimate for the opposite to occur.

Thus, in the Company A situation, departmental energies were not consumed by internal activities designed to make the department a socially satisfactory place to live nor by struggles to communicate across abysses of viewpoint differences. Because authority was being exerted by socially legitimate persons and groups, little if any energy was wasted in jockeying for prestige positions. There was an abundance of group energy left for work and for contest over the organizationally desirable balance of quality and economy. Furthermore, since the work itself was intrinsically rewarding and since supervisory practices encouraged work satisfactions, Company A's interdepartmental relations were highly productive, despite continual battles over quality versus economy.

The three elements—*internal social stability, external value sharing,* and *legitimate authority hierarchy*—comprise a triumvirate of measures which indicate the extent to which departmental energy will tend to be freed for productive work. These factors can be thought of as minimum requirements for interdepartmental effectiveness. For, in their absence, it is highly unlikely that either intrinsically interesting work or encouragement from supervision will achieve much in the way of productivity increases.

II. Wasteful Conflicts of Ideas

Company B designed, manufactured, and sold precision electronic instruments to scientific laboratories and industrial firms. The sales department was composed primarily of long-service, socially prestigious men (including the president) who had been instrumental in establishing what was referred to as a "family atmosphere" in the company. The sales department was the center of the dominant ideas in the company about how employees should behave.

During the manpower disruptions of World War II, the production department attracted a group of men who had started as workmen and had worked their way up the management ladder, often by transferring from one company to another. These men were perceived by the rest of the company (and even by themselves) as "rough diamonds." Their ideas about personal comportment were very different from those held dear in the sales department.

At the close of the war, certain irregularities in the behavior of top-level, old-line production management were laid bare by the rough diamonds. When the culprits were discharged, they left the rough diamonds in control of production.

At the same time, however, certain checks and balances—in reaction to the ease with which the wartime irregularities were committed—were built into the organization at the expense of production's jurisdiction over such functions as purchasing and stock control. These restrictions were highly resented by the new production regime which felt it was being punished by the "family" school, some of whose members (the discharged old-line production men) were the real culprits. This "injustice" widened an already considerable gap between sales' and production's views of "how things ought to be."

Sales and production came in contact primarily when the quarterly production schedule was being set and whenever sales initiated changes in the schedule within quarters. On these occasions tempers flared, walkouts occurred, and the services of the vice president–controller were required for mediation. Sales' concern for meeting customers' special desires was pitted against production's concern for uninterrupted runs of each instrument in the company's catalog.

Unlike the Company A situation where a balance was struck between quality and economy, in Company B the contest between customer satisfaction and economical production resulted in a breakdown of relations. Furthermore, the production department became an armed camp in which each junior member of the group was strictly warned against dealing with the sales department lest the latter influence production activities at less than the top hierarchical level of the department.

To make sure that sales could not infiltrate production, top production executives allowed the bulk of production's members little influence over internal production affairs. For its part, sales spent a great deal of time devising power plays to force production to deviate from set schedules. Top sales officials wasted hours personally exerting their authority in production offices to obtain schedule deviations. Retributions in the form of ultimatums and unprofitable scheduling "trades" of one instrument for another resulted. Sales' two subsections, scientific and industrial, vied with each other to see who could get the best production deal in the schedule, often at each other's and the company's expense.

In Company B, while the work itself was challenging and although supervision circumscribed that interest only to a modest degree (by removing purchasing and stock control from production's jurisdiction), relationships were relatively nonproductive between sales and production. Minimal standards of performance were met only by the intervention of a vice president in routine sales-production affairs. Energies were not absorbed in an effort to right an illegitimate authority sequence, for sales' commands were legitimated by sales' superior prestige, but in dealing with the breach of communication between two groups whose backgrounds and ideas were diametrically opposed in many important ways.

In turn, each department's internal relations, used as a means of combating the outgroup, absorbed a great deal of effort. Production kept a tight hold on its members, which caused subordinate frustrations, while sales was constantly patching the relations between its own two subgroups. Any work accomplished between the two groups was based on the question, "Will this effort strengthen our position in the battle with the other department?" Almost never could the two groups be said to agree that their combined efforts were satisfying to both, or even to one, of the parties.

The nonproductive conflict between these two departments can be viewed as the result of energies consumed by attempts to right an irreconcilably imbalanced trade.[2] By sales' values, sales' ideas should have dominated, tempered only by "practical" economic considerations. (In other words, production should have provided information on which sales could base its decisions.)

By production's values, however, production ideas received too little weight, if, indeed, they were accorded any weight at all. Production believed that sales' information should be added to production information and the decision should then be a cooperative one. For sales to achieve its idea of balance, production had to forfeit its idea of balance, and vice versa. So the conflict was irreconcilable. As the mathematicians put it, the two departments were playing a zero-sum game. One's gain was the other's loss, because their different ideas of what was "right" made it so.

---

[2] For further development of this concept, see Alvin Gouldner, "The Norm of Reciprocity: A Preliminary Statement," *American Sociological Review*, April, 1960, pp. 161–78.

III. Illegitimate Authority Conflicts

Company B's production department was engaged in another, but quite different, cross-departmental relationship of nonproductive character. The production engineering department (formally considered a peer of the production department) took research designs and translated them into parts lists, production drawings, and fabrication and assembly specifications, and in addition processed engineering change orders (ECOs). Much of production's work—both its content and its timing—depended on production engineering's efforts, since Company B's product designs were constantly changing.

Thus, production engineering was seen by production as telling production what to do and when to do it. On the other hand, production engineering was composed of men with skills no greater than, in fact, quite similar to, those possessed by production members. Production felt itself capable of performing not only production engineering's tasks but the more important tasks of job design and methods work which were within production's jurisdiction but outside production engineering's.

The two departments had almost no face-to-face contact. Communication between them was conducted through memos carried by lowly messengers. Production managers spent an inordinate amount of time checking for consistency among the various items produced by production engineering. When errors were discovered (as they seldom were), a cry of victory would ring out across the production office. A messenger would quickly be dispatched to carry the offending material back to production engineering, amply armed with a message elaborately outlining the stupidity which had produced such an error. The lack of direct contact between the two departments (other than this aggressive kind) made it impossible for technically desirable accommodations between the two departments to be made. The most common topic of production conversation centered about "those goddam ECOs," in spite of the fact that production originated as many ECOs (making changes for its own convenience) as did any other department.

In this case, energies were heavily focused on the impropriety of a low-prestige department like production engineering calling the tune for an equally prestigious or even superior department like production. Production devoted its energies to rebalancing trade between the two departments. In other words, production's prestige could be maintained only by calling more tunes than it danced. This rebalancing process had little to do with accomplishing any work. Yet it consumed vast amounts of production management time (particularly that of the factory superintendent who, of all people, checked every drawing); and, in the last analysis it failed its purpose, since the tide was too great to be stemmed, no matter how much energy was devoted to the effort.

IV. Value and Authority Clashes

Company C designed, manufactured, and distributed a large variety of electronic tubes of advanced design. One of its most rapidly selling tubes had a poor cost record—primarily, it was finally agreed, because of design inadequacies. In the process of trying to reduce costs through fabrication and assembly changes, the industrial engineering department had generated an idea for basic tube redesign. Several industrial engineers experimented informally with the new idea and achieved favorable results. When the matter was brought to the attention of the research department, it found its full schedule would not permit it to take over and develop the new idea. The industrial engineering inventors were given authority to continue development of the new tube. A development schedule was set and a development budget assigned to the industrial engineers.

For a time, progress was satisfactory. Then, when some metallurgical problems developed, the research department stepped in to make tests in an attempt to solve the problem. Conflict immediately developed. The industrial engineers maintained that the research department was unfair to the new tube because of the unrealistic way it conducted its tests. Research found it could get no cooperation in its desire to use industrial engineering equipment to conduct part of its investigation. Contact between the two groups dropped to zero, and investigations were conducted in parallel, though each group technically required the other's resources. Development schedules became a farce as one date after another passed without expected accomplishment.

The industrial engineers had become engaged in the project in the first place because, as one of its members put it, "I was particularly displeased with our department's general position in the company and felt we didn't really have a chance to show what we could do." One of the members of research mentioned that he thought of the industrial engineers as "just dumb, stupid, and no good." There was no meeting ground on the value which the two groups could bring to a common project. Nevertheless, there was general agreement that the research people possessed considerably greater prestige than did the industrial engineers.

In Company C, interdepartmental conflict became so energy-consuming that relationships were broken off entirely, to the detriment of the project at hand. Normally, research would have held the authority position—and legitimately so, according to its superior prestige. Pressured by scheduling circumstances and by the different points of view concerning what industrial engineering's role should be, the normal authority sequence was turned topsy-turvy. Industrial engineering did the prestige work of invention, directing research to carry out routine tests.

Suddenly, each group attempted to behave in such a way that its own view of a proper relationship would predominate. Research criticized industrial engineering's work and tried to force the industrial engineers back into the subordinate role of helping with tests. Industrial engineering, which always had been eager for a chance to get its "teeth into something," was enjoying the fruits of its initial invention (which, incidentally, later proved to be basically sound). Feeling that its desires were being violated, it tried to keep control of the prestige activities and went out of its way to "prove" that research was barking up the wrong tree.

None of these activities had any necessary relationship to developing a new tube. All energies were devoted to forcing one group's values on the other and maintaining what were believed to be legitimate prestige positions. The two departments were playing another zero-sum game in which what seemed positive trading for one was inevitably interpreted as negative trading by the other.

Varying Viewpoints

In each of these four cases, the forces siphoning energy away from productive work have been of a particular kind. In each instance, relationships within groups were at least socially satisfactory. (In Company B, the production group did enforce limits on member influence, but this discipline, because it was viewed as group defense, did not lessen cohesion within the department.) The work of the various groups was intrinsically interesting to group members. Supervision was relatively permissive in allowing group members to "complicate" their lives about the work itself. Obviously, these elements are not always present in organized situations. Equally obvious from our cases is the fact that these elements, by themselves, do not result in effective interdepartmental relations, though they may be considered to contribute to such relations if other conditions are also met.

Focal Points.   What the above cases focus on are the troubles caused by differences in point of view and legitimacy of authority. What these cases teach about group conflicts arising from these two trouble sources is just as true for our understanding of the interrelationships of individuals, for intergroup problems are only special cases of interpersonal issues. The only difference between them is the complexity of dealing with the problem, since the individual persons in our cases are representatives of social groups. Thus, their behavior cannot be modified by actions which are based on the assumption that groups respond exactly as do individuals. In short, the causes of conflict are similar, but the remedies are different.

Exhibit 1

DOMINANT INFLUENCES IN INTERDEPARTMENTAL RELATIONS

	WHERE POINTS OF VIEW ARE CLOSELY ALLIED	WHERE POINTS OF VIEW ARE IN CONFLICT
WHERE AUTHORITY* IS CONSISTENT WITH PRESTIGE DIFFERENCES	WE WILL TEND TO FIND.... ....COLLABORATION AND PRODUCTIVE CONFLICT.	WE WILL TEND TO FIND.... ....ENERGIES ABSORBED BY EFFORTS TO FORCE POINTS OF VIEW ON OTHER GROUPS. RELATIONS WILL BE FORMAL AND OFTEN ARBITRATED BY OUTSIDERS.
WHERE AUTHORITY IS INCONSISTENT WITH PRESTIGE DIFFERENCES	WE WILL TEND TO FIND.... ....ENERGIES DEVOTED TO REGAINING A "PROPER" AUTHORITY RELATIONSHIP. RELATIONS WILL USUALLY BE DISTANT AND BETWEEN LOW HIERARCHICAL LEVELS OF THE TWO GROUPS (e.g., messengers).	WE WILL TEND TO FIND.... ....ENERGIES INITIALLY EXPENDED ON FORCING POINTS OF VIEW AND RIGHTING AUTHORITY RELATIONS, BUT THE TASK WILL BE SO PATENTLY FRUITLESS THAT THE GROUPS WILL BREAK OFF CONTACT RATHER THAN EXPOSE THEMSELVES TO FURTHER THREAT.

* As indicated by work flow.

What happens when groups suffer from authority and viewpoint conflicts is summarized in Exhibit 1. Like any diagram dealing with a limited number of factors, Exhibit 1 runs the danger of implying that these cause-and-effect tendencies represent all that need be known about interdepartmental relations. Such an implication, were it intended, would, of course, be fatuous. Research in the area of interdepartmental problems has scarcely begun. Furthermore, we have already noted that other factors can be expected to intervene and render the exhibit's hypotheses as they should be called, inoperative. Three of these factors have been emphasized—group cohesion, job interest, and supervisory practices.

Once we allow for these mitigating factors, however, we will find it useful to conceive of interdepartmental relations as though they were subject to the dominant influences cited in the diagram. The manager can make this concept more relevant personally if he reviews his own observations of interdepartmental conflict to see how they compare with the kind of analysis described here.

Plan for Action

The question inevitably arises, "Suppose some sense can be made of interdepartmental difficulties by this kind of thinking; what then do we do with this understanding, even if it does prove to be accurate? How would we go about applying it to lessen interdepartmental conflicts in our company?" Let's look at some action ideas which stem from what has already been said.

Stop, Look, and Listen. As frustrating as it might seem, the first suggestion is to stop to see if action is required and, if it is, whether it is feasible. It often may be wise to heed the admonishment (in reverse of the usual form), "Don't just do something, stand there!" The basis for this wisdom lies in the fact that formal organizations often display some of the characteristics of a biological organism, particularly insofar as the latter has some capacity to heal itself. The administrator, if this contention be true, may find the role of the modern physician attractive. He attempts to control the environment so that natural healing processes can take place unhindered within the human body. Here are some examples of where such inaction might be appropriate:

Take the case of Company A. Should something be done to alter jurisdictions among Company A's departments? Or are the natural tensions between these departments, the energies to expand jurisdiction, operating in precisely the most beneficial way for the organization? The best advice in this case seems to be to keep an eye on that tension. Watch that it does not degenerate subtly into another Company C situation. If it moves too far in that direction, then action is required.

This example helps clarify an issue which we have been flirting with throughout this article: the problem of distinguishing productive from nonproductive conflicts. It may not suffice to say that conflict is productive if the parties to it end up satisfied and get there under their own steam. In any particular case, in the heat of a tight scheduling situation, many an administrator has interpreted *any* disagreement as nonproductive and has succumbed to the temptation to interfere. If schedules then have to be junked, the blame is thrown on the groups in disagreement. Had the administrator satisfied himself about the basic conditions within which the fighting groups were working, and listened carefully to see if the fights were *working* or *warring* arguments, he might have saved himself and his organization much trouble.

A case more dramatic than that cited above, and one where action seemed inappropriate, takes us back to the Company B organization. The production department, as might be suspected from what we already know about it, was striving to enlarge its domain to conform to its own ideas about production's importance. This striving provoked a potential clash with the research department when the frequency of special orders began to increase rapidly. Special orders required research design but not production engineering attention, the work of the latter group being devoted to mass-production items. Thus, research would naturally be required to deal directly with production in the case of special orders. Inevitably, production—as isolated historical instances had convinced research—would attempt to dominate these relationships whenever it could.

To avoid this eventuality, research developed a small production unit of its own, though production was fully capable of doing special work. This "organizational invention" of the research department, stepping into work for which it was neither intended nor formally responsible, eliminated the need for contact with production and sidestepped the inevitably non-productive conflict which would have resulted. The invention was costly in many ways, particularly in terms of valuable research time and space. But on balance it appeared to be the most adequate short-term resolution to a basic interdepartmental problem.

There are a host of other examples of this kind of self-regulation. Many of these measures are rather simple and expedient, if not conducive to removal of the basic causes of nonproductive conflict. Chief among these is the use of what may be called "expendable linkers" as go-betweens in conflicted interdepartmental relations. For example, a production department was observed to assign to its least important member the task of liaison between itself and other departments, where such expediting connoted the use of illegitimate authority. The expediter himself threatened no one, and adopted a most passive demeanor. Communication then took place not between main contenders who could only lose by such contact but through a neutral intermediary. The cursing went unheard by those for whom a damaging response would have been required.

Other examples involve the use of formal procedures or instruments such as the production schedule, fought over maybe once a quarter, but exerting independent authority between times and keeping sales and production away from each other's throats. None of these is an ideal solution to interdepartmental problems, but each is likely to emerge as a practical expedient in a difficult situation. The administrator may find his short-run problems solved if he is aware of the importance of these often unnoticed "inventions." Furthermore, if he wants to do away with these sometimes awkward mechanisms, he had better make sure he has something with which to replace them.

Types of Resolution

Our cases (and there are unlimited examples like them) have shown that some interdepartmental difficulties go beyond the capacity of the groups to resolve them at anything but a survival level, if that. That level may well be, and often is, intolerable for the organization as a whole. Let us look at the two alternative types of resolution.

First are the resolutions which arise in response to conflicts of authority. In such cases the work flow designed into the organization (e.g., the passage of blueprints from production engineering to production) violates the notions of the organization's members as to who legitimately should, by right of superior prestige, tell whom what to do. Although such problems are not restricted to particular hierarchical levels of the organization, they do tend to become more intense wherever prestige relations are ambiguous or under threat. The higher one goes in many organizations, the more these conditions tend to apply. There are several ways of resolving such problems:

1. An obvious solution is to take whatever steps are available to reduce prestige ambiguity and threat. For example, if Company B's management had realized how pertinent production's resentment at being rated "second class" was to the interdepartmental problems in which it was involved, investigation might have produced ways of clarifying production's status and of enriching its participation in important decisions. Instead, the factory superintendent was the last to be admitted to the executive council and was not accorded vice presidential rank, as were most other department managers. Management failed to take these steps because it feared domination by the superintendent. Yet more careful diagnosis might have revealed that the superintendent's striving for dominance was a result of his impression that management thought him unworthy of participation in decisions for which his expertise was, in fact, badly needed. The circle was vicious.

2. Another step in reducing the amount of nonproductivity in illegitimate authority relations is to reorganize subunits of the organization in such a way that authority and prestige become consistent. In Company B's production engineering and production relationship, such reorganization could have taken the form of incorporating production engineering into production's domain, much as was done in Company A, where the chemical engineers had been removed from research and placed in the engineering department. With production engineering subject to production's control, yet sharing many ideas with both research and production, a mingling of points of view could have been achieved and authority questions dealt with from within.

The very same kind of potential authority difficulty was avoided in Company B because scheduling was incorporated within production's jurisdiction. Another way of justifying such a resolution of conflict is to note that production's technical functions, as well as those of production engineering, were so closely allied and overlapping that to separate them was to form a barrier across which required contact was extremely difficult and at times impossible. Unfortunately, once again Company B's management so feared production dominance that its inclination was much more to reduce production's domain than to enlarge it.

3. Another extremely clear example of how structural reorganization can resolve not only the authority legitimacy problem, but also have side effects in bringing clashing points of view into sufficient harmony for communication to recommence, is contained in the actual resolution of the Company C difficulty reported above. The obvious solution was to take the research initiative away from the industrial engineers and put it back where prestige relations said it belonged, with research. The solution appeared obvious only because the breakdown between the two departments was so catastrophic.

Equally obvious before that breakdown was the apparently logical belief that the people who invent something should continue to develop it, both because the inventors would logically appear to be most expert in understanding the invention and because it is only fair that productive effort should be rewarded by continuing responsibility and credit. In fact, change was not instituted until the industrial engineers became so thoroughly frustrated by their continuing design failures that they could entertain the idea that their "baby" might be reorganized into more "proper" channels. Although costly in some ways and probably unconscious, management's decision to do nothing at first to set the interdepartmental relations back into the normal work pattern allowed industrial engineering to become receptive to such a change when it finally was made.

This crucial aspect of conflict resolution—receptivity to change—brings us to the second major strategy for helping departmental energies engage in constructive action instead of working against members of another department. This strategy involves what might be called intergroup counseling, therapy, or training. Conflicts in points of view are susceptible only to this strategy, short of complete personnel turnover in one or the other of the warring departments. And, because authority illegitimacy must inevitably engender conflict of viewpoint, it too can be mitigated, if only partially, by intergroup training. Several aspects of this strategy are worthy of attention, though the subject is a difficult and complex one.

Some studies show that intergroup conflict resolution hinges on a particular type of training which seeks an integration of viewpoints by making warring groups realize they are dependent on one another.[3] Such a strategy tends to work more readily when both groups fear some external threat to both of them. This idea is not greatly different from the idea contained in the observation that members of families may fight viciously with one another but when an outsider attacks one of the family, the family abandons its differences to fight together against the intruder. It seems obvious from the analysis presented in this article, however, that this strategy is operable only when prestige-authority issues are not present.

A number of researchers, teachers, and managers have begun to explore more direct methods for reducing point-of-view conflict. Some have pointed out that bringing group representatives together to explore their differences is usually doomed to failure since representatives, if they are to remain such, must be loyal to their respective groups.[4] Simple measures to increase contact also appear fruitless, because negative stereotypes end up simply becoming reinforced by the contact.

Other measures have proved more effective. Although they vary in form, almost all of these contain the following basic element: *the groups in conflict must be brought together as totalities under special conditions.*[5] The goal of all of these conditions is to reduce individual and group anxieties sufficiently so that a point of view can not only be made explicit but can be heard by those who do not share it. This procedure requires not only considerable candor between groups, but also candor within each group and within the individual himself. Naturally, sessions in which such training is supposed to take place can be extremely threatening and should be mediated by an external agent to keep threat within manageable bounds and help guide the groups into explorative rather than recriminative behavior.[6]

(EDITORS' NOTE: See Reading 4 in this section of the book for further development of these ideas for reducing conflict.)

Conclusion

Seldom, if ever, do problems of nonproductive conflict exist in isolation. It is extremely likely that wherever such conflict is found it has

---

[3] See *Intergroup Relations and Leadership*, edited by Muzafer Sherif (New York: John Wiley & Sons, Inc., 1962).

[4] See Robert Blake and Jane S. Mouton, *Group Dynamics—Key to Decision Making* (Houston, Texas: Gulf Publishing Co., 1961).

[5] See Herbert R. Shepard and Robert R. Blake, "Changing Behavior Through Cognitive Change," *Human Organization*, Summer, 1962, p. 88.

[6] See Chris Argyris, *Interpersonal Competence and Organizational Effectiveness* (Homewood, Illinois: Irwin–Dorsey Press, 1962).

been engendered by organizational and emotional maladjustments, each of which has fed upon the other. It would make sense, then, to attack interdepartmental problems while fully realizing that they may be spun into the warp and woof of the organization's fabric. Such an attack has far-reaching consequences for the organization. It means, for example, that the goals of the organization must be critically examined, since these tend to influence the way in which the work of the organization has been divided up and division of labor is at the core of interdepartmental problems.

Because goals, in turn, are heavily influenced by the organization's environment and by the way in which that environment is interpreted by executives and directors, the environment and the process by which it is interpreted also must come under scrutiny. Do those in control have a clear idea of their company's relation to its market? If not, why not? Have they made clear to the other members of the company the job to be done and what that job requires of each sub-element in the organization?[7]

These questions are fundamental to the building of an organization. Without answers to these questions, any attempt to resolve an illegitimate authority problem usually is a patch-up job, likely to create as many problems as it cures. Furthermore, without these answers, the members of the organization cannot avoid feeling that their relationships to each other are ambiguous—and aimless ambiguity is a breeding ground for insecurity, defensive behavior, and sapped energy.

Involving the members of an organization in the pursuit of clarifying the organization's goals—in establishing a meaningful identity for the firm—is, perhaps, the soundest process for tapping into the wells of productive energy.[8] Such a pursuit, carried on openly and sincerely, cannot help but raise issues of interdepartmental ambiguity, illegitimacy, and conflicting points of view to a level where they can be re-examined and dealt with. An easy process? No. But as "old wives' tales" have told us, no remedy is without pain.

[7] See Wilfred Brown, *Exploration in Management* (London: William Heinemann Ltd., 1960).

[8] Alfred Kenneth Rice, *The Enterprise and Its Environment* (London: Tavistock Publications, 1963).

6. REDUCTION OF INTERGROUP CONFLICT

THE DYNAMICS of intergroup conflict has been the subject of a number of macroscopic sociological and sociopsychological studies, primarily focusing upon the characteristics of racial and religious discrimination and stereotype. Very little systematic research has been accomplished at the microscopic level of interacting small groups within those smaller institutions with which we are most familiar, such as business, educational, philanthropic, or social organizations. Furthermore, very little experimentation designed to ascertain some of the conditions for reduction of intergroup conflict has been undertaken. This reading abstracts one of the few experiments of this type and summarizes, from another author's pragmatic experience, several strategies for increasing collaboration between groups.

In his article,[1] Sherif summarizes the results of an experimental study demonstrating the reduction of intergroup conflict by the introduction of superordinate goals. Superordinate goals are defined as those goals "compelling and highly appealing to members of two or more groups in conflict but which cannot be attained by the resources and energies of the groups separately."

Sherif explains that two groups were formed experimentally. At the end of this stage of formation, he concludes, "when individuals interact in a series of situations toward goals which appeal to all and which require that they co-ordinate their activities, group structures arise having hierarchical status arrangements and a set of norms regulating behavior in matters of consequence to the activities of the group."

The second stage of the experiment consisted of introducing situations in which one group could reach its goals only at the expense of the other. This resulted in the development of hostile attitudes and unfavorable stereotypes in each group for the other to the extent that interaction between them was minimized. At the same time, there was an increase in in-group solidarity and co-operation.

The introduction of superordinate goals in the third phase served to reduce this intergroup conflict. In sum, the groups did "co-operate in activities leading toward the common goal"; and over time, these joint activities reduced conflict between the groups.

---

[1] Muzafer Sherif, "Superordinate Goals in the Reduction of Intergroup Conflict," *American Journal of Sociology,* Vol. LXIII, No. 4 (January, 1958).

Sociometric measurements taken in the second stage showed no out-group friendship choices, while third-stage measurements showed a considerable number of cross-group friendship links. Likewise, a "decrease in the name-calling and derogation of the out-group, common during intergroup friction and in contact situations without superordinate goals" was manifested. "Stereotype ratings of the out-group changed significantly from largely unfavorable ratings to largely favorable ratings."

Sherif concludes by pointing out the consequences of attempts to reduce intergroup conflicts in the absence of superordinate goals: Communication between conflicting groups serves "as a media for further accusations and recriminations;" any favorable information about a disliked out-group is likely to be reinterpreted to fit the existing negative stereotypes; and the leader of a group is unable to take bold action toward reducing intergroup conflict, as his efforts are apt to be seen by his peers as going against the group's position.

"In short, various measures suggested for the reduction of intergroup conflict—disseminating information, increasing social contact, conferences of leaders—acquire new significance and effectiveness when they become part and parcel of interaction processes between groups oriented toward superordinate goals which have real and compelling value for all groups concerned."

. . . .

Blake[2] outlines five approaches to the reduction of intergroup tensions, building upon Sherif's concept of the importance of superordinate goals. These approaches are:

1. Negotiations by group members
2. Exchange of persons
3. Handing the conflict to judges
4. Common goals with crisscross panels
5. Intergroup therapy

Each of these is examined below.

1. Negotiations by Group Members

The critical limitation in seeking resolution through representative negotiation lies in the potentiality for conflicts of interest. For a representative to suffer defeat is to jeopardize his own membership status.

---

[2] Robert Blake, "Resolution of Differences through Interaction, Discussion and Decision" (an unpublished report).

To gain victory is to enhance his membership position. Victory or defeat are, therefore, likely measured by reference to the position embraced by the respective groups prior to negotiation. Where such conflict of interest occurs, loyalty overwhelms logic. Furthermore, since a chosen representative will likely be an informal group leader, he will be less free to negotiate than any other member of his group. Lower status members expect more from an associate in a leadership position than from any other member. Thus, the leader, in his negotiations, must behave in accordance with the strictest interpretation of his group's norms.

2. Exchange of Persons

The chances for successful increases in intergroup collaboration through exchanges of individual persons between groups is limited by two factors. People-to-people interaction across groups serves to make those whose attitudes initially are positive, more positive, and those whose attitudes initially are negative, more negative; therefore, only those who are initially neutral are susceptible to influence. And social, political, and economic attitudes, rather than being determined solely on an individual personality basis, are significantly anchored in reference group affiliations; the exchanged individual will resist influences which violate his group's norms. However, plans involving the exchanges of subgroups may create a favorable background for future intergroup conflict resolution. When individuals undergo new experiences *as a group*, attitudes anchored at the group level are themselves subject to modification.

3. Handing the Conflict to Judges

While a judge is not as subject to the "conflict of interest" problem, he is nearly as suspect by those whose position he defeats as is the representative who opposes his own group. Inherently, the judge's decision carries little force compared to the strength of the group's commitment to its position.

4. Common Goals with Crisscross Panels

Several conditions are necessary for enhancing the superordinate goal approach. Both sides must *desire* a genuine solution, and there must be a single problem definition agreed upon by both sides prior to a statement of preferred solutions. However, the superordinate goal approach is limited by the fact that it is difficult—if not, in some cases, impossible—for all members of competing groups to feel intimately involved in the drive toward attaining superordinate goals. Some system for choosing representatives is therefore necessary. The crisscross panel is one method of selection which minimizes status reductions that occur as a result of one representative opposing his group's position.

Each side develops a list of nominees whom they consider qualified to represent them with respect to one particular source of friction. Next, from the total list of nominees, all group members elect an equal number of representatives from each side as a common decision-making panel. The panel, then, contains members who represent their own group and simultaneously represent the other group as well. By such a method of selection, representatives are able to confront the problem relatively free of the "hero-traitor" dynamic which is characteristic of the usual unilateral group orientation.

5. Intergroup Therapy

Many problems, themselves subject to solution through the superordinate goal approach, cannot even be faced until deeper animosities *between* groups have been resolved or at least explored and neutralized. If emotion-laden negative attitudes and stereotypes are dealt with first, it becomes increasingly possible in a second phase to formulate and work toward the attainment of superordinate goals.

In private, each group discusses and seeks to agree on its perceptions and attitudes toward the other, and its perceptions of itself as well. Then, *representatives* of both groups talk together in the presence of all members from both sides, who are obligated to remain silent. During this phase, representatives are responsible for accurate communication of the picture that each group has constructed of the other and of itself. Representatives are used to maintain orderly communication and to increase the acceptance of responsibility for providing an accurate version of the situation. Members of both groups then discuss, *in private,* discrepancies in perception uncovered by their joint meeting. Finally, again working through representatives, each group helps the other to appreciate the bases of their differences, to correct invalid perceptions, and to consider alternative explanations of past behavior. The groups are now in an improved position to work toward superordinate goals.

7. TOP MANAGEMENT COLLABORATION AND CONFLICT

IN AN unpublished manuscript,[1] Katz reports on a unique study of the organizational behavior of the president and six vice presidents who comprised top management in a consumer products manufacturing and distributing company with sales in the $50–100,000,000 bracket. Katz intensively observed and interviewed these men at work over an extended period, in an attempt to ascertain the "elements which facilitated or impeded top management co-ordination on major policy problems affecting all departments." Although his best-known conclusion was a conceptual framework for evaluating administrative performance,[2] his findings regarding interdepartmental co-ordination at the top management level are especially relevant to this section of the course book.

In the company he studied, Katz identified the following elements as significant in facilitating collaboration among the top management, each of whom represented a particular function (e.g., production, sales, finance, etc.) or a particular product division:

1. *A Well-Defined Social Structure.* Long service in their present positions had given six of the seven members of top management considerable experience in working with one another. Each knew many of the strengths, weaknesses, and idiosyncrasies of the others. Roles and relative statuses had been clearly defined in practice. A substantial body of norms had been established and accepted.

2. *Shared Values.* Most of these "old-timers" shared a wide range of basic values regarding both corporate goals and organizational procedures. For example, five were "sales-oriented," giving that function primacy over all others. Six had a fairly common perception of where they felt the company ought to be going (regarding such basic items as quality, price, range of products, choice of markets and customers, corporate "image," etc.). Similarly, they shared beliefs that jurisdictional lines were unimportant, that each man should be the company's expert on something, that major innovations should be the province of the president only, etc.

---

[1] Robert L. Katz, *Executive Teamwork: Top Management Coordination in a Medium-Sized Company* (unpublished doctoral dissertation, Harvard Business School, 1956).

[2] *Idem.,* "Skills of an Effective Administrator," *Harvard Business Review,* January–February, 1955; also *Executive Skills: What Makes a Good Administrator?* (Hanover, N.H.: Amos Tuck School of Business Administration, Dartmouth College, 1954).

3. *Acknowledgement of Technical "Expertise."* Each of the seven top management men was acknowledged by the others as the most expert person in the company on specific problem areas. Rarely was anyone's judgment questioned on those aspects which lay wholly within his acknowledged area of *expertise.*

4. *Free Interchange.* An informal organizational structure existed, with little stress placed on titles or on job description. Widespread interaction was encouraged at all levels and between all units. Each man was expected to consult with any person in the company who could be of help in solving a particular problem, and each man expected to be consulted where his expert opinion was relevant. The physical layout of the headquarters office facilitated this free interchange by its relative absence of walls and partitions.

5. *Identification with the Company.* Each of the top executives felt that his personal reputation, both on the job and among his "outside" friends and acquaintances, was dependent upon the reputation and performance of the *company*—not simply of his own department.

6. *Penalties for Deviant Behavior.* Top management penalized one another, and men lower in the organization, by withdrawing support, realigning responsibilities, etc., for nonobservance of the norms of consultation, free interchange, and sublimation of personal and departmental interests to over-all company welfare.

7. *Organizational Structure Built around Individuals.* Each man performed those duties in which he was perceived as having greater ability than anyone else in the organization, in which he had interest, and in which he felt most comfortable. Advancement depended largely on ability to understand and utilize the system of informal interchange, and to establish one's own acknowledged area of competence. Meeting all aspects of specific *problems,* rather than performing discrete functions or compartmentalizing the problem by departments, provided the basis for organization structure.

8. *A Team with All Necessary Skills.* In the top management group, there existed adequate technical skill to cope with the company's most important recurring problems, sufficient human relations skill to maintain a high degree of interpersonal respect, and a well-defined "conceptual skill" (in the president) for visualizing the relationships of the various aspects to one another.

The operative norms and shared values legitimatized the president's being the primary integrator. He designated how functions *should* relate and "adroitly called forth the necessary experts and conceived the over-all master plan." Katz notes that this legitimatized behavior was the most essential element in the co-ordination of the efforts of this top management, but that it produced, in turn, a high degree of domination on the part of the president and dependency on the part of other management members.

Katz identified the major blocks to top management co-ordination in this company as:

1. *Self-Centered Behavior.* When a man (or a unit) felt he was not being accorded the respect and consideration he deemed due him, he often tended to react defensively and met his personal needs by "empire building," attempting to gain power at the expense of others, withholding information, doing only what was called for and no more, etc. Such behavior incurred circumscription by the other executives, which created still further defensiveness and insecurity.

2. *Variant Perceptions.* Even among earnest men of good will, differing values and experiences sometimes created difficulty in understanding or appreciating another person's point of view, feelings, or conclusions.

3. *Preconceptions.* Assumptions of "how things ought to be" from the wider culture and their experience led some members to place high value on certain procedures and outcomes, irrespective of the unique elements of the specific situation. When different members held conflicting beliefs as to desired outcomes, based largely on these extraorganizational mores, collaboration was thwarted. Similarly, and related to item 2, above, members seeking to define the problem without predisposition toward a specific outcome or course of action were sometimes perceived by those committed to specific outcomes as deviant and unworthy of trust.

Katz described this organization as being extraordinarily effective in maintaining its internal cohesiveness and in providing opportunities for social elaboration. But he cited numerous indications of organizational "frozenness" in developing new, creative, more appropriate behavior patterns and in relating quickly and effectively to changes in the market, sources of supply, competition, and general economic conditions. He claims that this unusually mature, well-developed company-wide social structure had turned most of its energies to reducing internal conflict and to building a high degree of collaboration, personal security, and feelings of individual importance. But in so doing, it had centered in one man (the president) the initiative for relating the organization to its environment, thus limiting the potential range and nature of the organization's response, as well as individual members' opportunities for new experiences from which to learn and develop.

SECTION VI

Behavior in the Total Organization

Introduction

THIS SECTION will offer an opportunity to look both backward, by consolidating into a broader framework the materials covered in earlier sections, and forward, toward a new focus on the patterns of behavior that cut across an entire organization, on higher top management behavior, and on organizational consequences.

This section does not present any new conceptual scheme for helping us understand organizational behavior, but it does present some detailed case descriptions of entire organizations or major parts of large organizations that allow us to use and test further the utility of all the schemes presented already. The scheme presented in the last section for analysis of intergroup behavior can prove especially useful as a guide to the analysis of the cases in this section. However, we expect that the emphasis in its use will shift from the relations between discrete groups to the analysis of the over-all emergent pattern of behavior in the entire organization. We shall be interested in both the forces that hold the system together and the forces that tend to disrupt it. We shall be observing the interdependence of the system—how changes in one part change the other parts and the whole. We shall be looking for the existence of norms that hold throughout an organization. We shall be interested in the various consequences of different over-all patterns. This focus on the over-all pattern in organizations clearly is closely tied to the behavior of those few individuals who hold the top leadership roles in any organization. This leads us to the second major theme of this section.

Our interest in top management behavior will especially stress the basic assumptions management makes about the nature of organization and the consequences of these assumptions throughout the organization. The particular assumptive framework top management adopts, wittingly or not, can have a major influence on the "tone" or "climate" that pervades the entire organization. These assumptions, in turn, are often rooted in the beliefs in the culture about such important matters as the nature of authority. It is in this way, and this way only, that this course will be dealing explicitly in any detail with the effect of the environment on the firm. In other words, we have chosen not to address directly the problem of assessing the outside economic, technical, legal, and institutional realities that influence the firm—not because these are unimportant fields for study but because not everything can be done here. But we shall, to repeat, be concerned with certain widespread beliefs in the culture and their effect on organizations via the beliefs and behavior of top management. These variables can be diagrammed within the framework we have used previously, as shown in Exhibit 1.

The cases and research reports that have been selected for this section are designed to contribute simultaneously to both of the themes of the

Exhibit 1

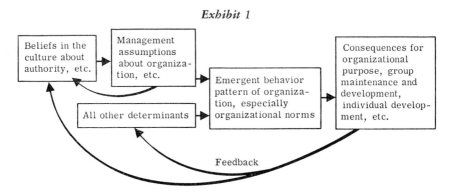

Feedback

section. Specifically, Reading 1 by March and Simon and Reading 2 by McGregor lift up different sets of widespread assumptions about organizations and the likely consequences of these assumptions. The March and Simon reading briefly reviews the classical organization theories, while McGregor contrasts the consequences for relations between line and staff people of operating on the basis of his now famous "Theory X and Theory Y" assumptions. The first three cases (Twin City Trust, The Gordon Company, and The Hampton Shipyard) provide opportunities to identify particular sets of management assumptions in quite different settings and to trace the complex network of consequences that flow from them. They also can serve as a drill in analyzing group and intergroup patterns and in relating them into an over-all pattern of behavior in each organization.

The Marshall Company series of cases presents a rather unique chance to examine in detail a single organization at all levels. These cases were prepared a number of years ago and have become something of a classic series. They can provide a vivid understanding of the interdependence of the parts of a social system and of the way in which behavior traits (whether functional or not from the point of view of organization purpose) reinforce one another to create a stability for the system. The Marshall cases do not seem to have any clear problem focus.

The key question here is the purely diagnostic one: How does this organization work? What are the norms, the unwritten ground rules, of this firm; and how do they relate to one another? How do decisions get made in this firm? This organization seems to be violating some of the common maxims about organizations. What are the consequences, and why? Is this a healthy organization? Will it be healthy in another decade? These are all difficult, thought-provoking questions that force a re-examination of some of our conventional beliefs about organization.

The next two readings (3 and 4) are also designed to push and stretch our customary assumptions about organizational life. Both of these papers dramatize the contrast between the way our Western society and other cultures, the Fox Indians and the Japanese, customarily think about authority and organization. The next three readings (5, 6, and 7) could well be read together, since they all focus on the formal structure of organizations and how it is related to the rate of technical change, the predispositions of top managers, and the nature of tasks. Again, remember that these studies are presented only as a sample of the systematic research that is becoming available on the firm as a total social system. The final reading describes a provocative experiment in organizational design being carried out by the Non-Linear Systems firm. This kind of organizational invention can serve to remind us that man has probably only begun to use his ingenuity in creating institutional forms that foster the performance of useful work.

The last four cases in this section (Lewis, Empire, Higgins [A], and Higgins [B]) describe companies struggling with some more familiar organizational problems. They call for careful, painstaking analysis of these over-all organizational problems to prepare the way for creative thinking about proposals for improvement. All of the concepts developed in the course so far can be brought to bear on these cases.

Cases

1. TWIN CITY TRUST CO.

DURING THE summer of 1956, John Smith, a casewriter from the Harvard Business School, approached officers of the Twin City Trust Co. and asked for permission to talk with people in the bank about the nature of the relationship between the main office and the branch offices. In granting this permission, Mr. Gordon, president of the bank, said: "I think you'll find that we are a decentralized operation."

Exhibit 1

TWIN CITY TRUST CO.

LOCATION OF TWIN CITY TRUST COMPANY'S OFFICES

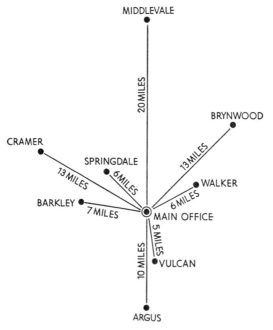

Twin City Trust Co., a commercial bank and a member of the Federal Reserve system, was located in a large eastern city and had assets of over $100,000,000. During its existence, more than fifty years, it had expanded by merging with smaller banks and by opening new offices until, by 1956, it operated eight branch offices in addition to its main office. These branches were located either in Twin City or in immediately adjacent communities. Exhibit 1 is a sketch showing the approximate geographical relationship of the offices. Exhibit 2 is a partial organization chart of the bank.

The Argus and Vulcan branches were located in industrial areas of Twin City, and each was headed by a vice president. Brynwood was a large residential suburb adjacent to Twin City, and the branch there was managed by a vice president. The Middlevale, Barkley, Springdale, and Cramer branches were located in residential suburbs; the first two were headed by assistant treasurers and the other two by branch managers. The Walker office was located in a "light commercial" area of Twin City, was managed by a branch manager, and had a drive-in window. In the bank the vice presidents and the treasurer were referred to as "senior officers," and assistant treasurers as "junior officers." When an assistant vice president was asked by Smith whether he would consider himself a junior or senior officer, he replied: "That's a good question. The four of us don't know whether we are considered junior or senior."

Visits to the Branches

Smith first visited the branch offices, where he talked in each instance with the manager and on some occasions with other officers. Following are excerpts from these interviews.

Comments by Vice Presidents

VICE PRESIDENT 1: Before Twin City bought this bank, we ran the whole show here. When they bought the bank, the president told me, "You continue to run your own show," and we pretty well have. George Davis at the main office is senior vice president, and he is supposed to act in an advisory capacity to us on loans. As you know, there are many large firms right here in this area who are customers of ours. Fortunately, they are good, sound firms; we handle their loans right here and keep the necessary records here in our office. Of course, that material is always available if someone at the main office would want to see it.

‘ . . . .

VP2: We were bought out by Twin City about ten years ago; and since then, they have let us keep on running things as we had been doing. There is not much friction between the branch and the main office. Oh, there are little things. For instance, I think the main office has too many forms. But on the whole, there are no problems. Our employees are better off since we came into Twin City. . . .

I have tried to become an expert in so-called "broker's" loans. There's not much industry around here; and since the 1920's, this bank has invested part of its funds in broker's loans. I have a relationship with several note brokers; and they will call me and say that they have a

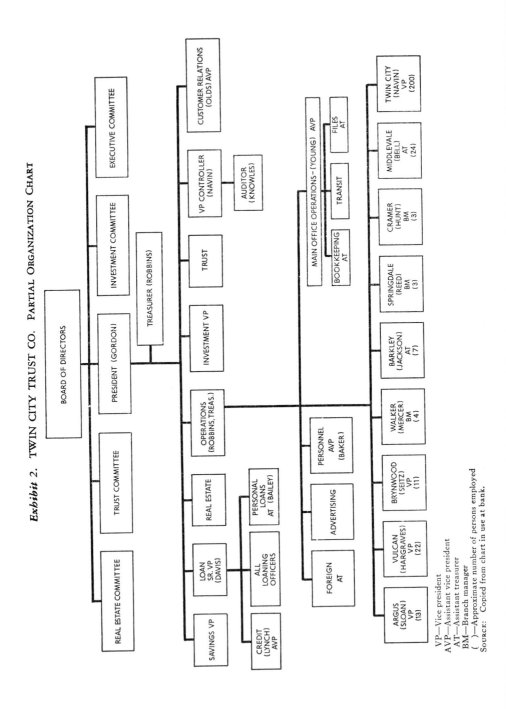

Exhibit 2. TWIN CITY TRUST CO. PARTIAL ORGANIZATION CHART

VP—Vice president
AVP—Assistant vice president
AT—Assistant treasurer
BM—Branch manager
( )—Approximate number of persons employed
SOURCE: Copied from chart in use at bank.

note for, say, $50,000, that is secured by, let's say, $80,000 worth of securities, some of which are probably listed stocks, some not. Well, I ask about the stocks; and if I'm satisfied of their value, then the matter becomes one of horse trading over the interest rate. Once we have made the loan, we have to watch the collateral to be sure to call for more margin in case the value of the securities drops below the legal requirements. All in all, we've had good experience with these kinds of loans, and I make them pretty much on my own.

.   .   .   .

VP3:   In my view the biggest problem the branches have is one of communication. The bank is doing much better about this, but there is still a way to go. By communication, I mean mainly getting word out to the branches about what's going on in the bank. I've been with the bank over thirty years, and it used to be that you found out that a new director was elected to the board by reading it in the newspaper. One time, I recommended one of my men for officership. I didn't hear anything about it until one day his phone rang; and since he was away from his desk and I was standing right there, I answered it. The guy at the other end was at the main office; and after I told him that my man was out for a while, he said: "I just called to congratulate him on being elected an officer." (*Pause.*) I realize that there are some things that you can't broadcast, but my feeling was that there were things which they could have told us that they did not tell us. However, with the formation of the senior officers' committee and the institution of officers' meetings, I think this has improved.

JOHN SMITH: In what ways do you pass information on to your subordinates?

VP3:   We try to have meetings to do that and to give the employees a chance to ask questions. The problem is finding suitable times for those meetings, and I think we fall down there. In other words, I think there is still a big communication problem between the officers and their subordinates. On the whole, I think the employees are still often in the dark about what's going on in the bank. . . .

Any branch manager can make any loan within the legal limit of the bank. We don't have any conflict with the main office about loans. Mr. Davis was at this office for quite a while, and he knows the area well. We invariably see eye to eye on the loans.

Comments by Assistant Treasurers

ASSISTANT TREASURER 1:   For the most part, my differences with the main office concern personnel. For instance, occasionally a person comes in here looking for a job. If we think the person has good prospects, we send him or her down to the main office. But if that person is hired, we frequently never see him again. Of course, I realize that they have nine offices to worry about, and I am not confident that I could staff this office on my own, but it does bother me when some of those people look like very good employees and then I can't get them back.

The other thing is that sometimes we disagree with the main office about raises. A while back, I had two women up for review. One of them, in my view, wasn't worth what she was getting, let alone deserving a raise; whereas the other, in my opinion, should have gotten more than the $2.00 raise that was being passed out. But the personnel officer said that both of them should be raised $2.00, which to me did not reflect the difference in their merit.

SMITH: How often do officers from the main offices visit you?

AT1: Not often enough. I think all of us would like to have them come out more often.

SMITH: What is your authority in making loans?

AT1: Our practice of decentralization means that the branch manager is pretty much on his own in making loans. There are no restrictions on how much I can loan. Of course, on a new account or a larger than usual request from an old account, I would check with someone at the main office. I have never been criticized about any loan I made.

One thing did burn me up once. There was a merchant who was asking for more money than his balance sheet warranted. I knew that, of course, but I was also impressed with the attractiveness of his store and the way he did business. And so I asked the senior loan officer to come out and go with me and meet the guy. But he preferred not to come out.

.   .   .   .

AT2: I'd say that there isn't much conflict between this branch and the main office. As a matter of fact, there isn't much chance for it. They set up the procedures, and it is up to us to follow them.

Comments by Other Branch Managers

As shown in Exhibit 1, the offices, which were managed by men who were not officers of the bank, were relatively small, usually having three or four employees, including the manager. When asked about what loans they made, these branch managers indicated that they did not have requests for large loans. They all indicated that in the case of instalment loans, they helped the applicant fill out the application, added any comment that they could make from personal knowledge of the applicant, and then sent it to the personal loan department for processing. In the event that a customer sought a real estate loan, the managers would help him fill out the application and then send him to the real estate department at the main office. These men indicated that most of the loans they made on their own were in the nature of unsecured, ninety-day notes of $500 or less.

BUSINESS MANAGER 1:   Our biggest problem here is getting good personnel. You see, in a small office like this, a teller has to know how to do a variety of different things. Therefore, we can't train a green man here very well.

SMITH: Who handles raises for your employees?

BM1:   Mr. Baker [assistant vice president in charge of personnel] handles all that.

SMITH: Who determines what hours you are open?

BM1:   Management. (*Pause.*) Of course, if I had an opinion about it, I'd state it.

. . . .

BM2 [on personnel matters]:   The two people I have here are experienced people. They know at the main office what their capabilities are. I don't have anything to do with their raises; in fact, I don't know how much they get paid.

SMITH: Do you have anything to say about whom they send to you?

BM2:   No, but I know that the main office wouldn't send out anyone who couldn't do the job. . . .

I think it would be better if the officers visited the branches more often. Mr. Gordon [the president] comes in once a year, but there aren't any who come regularly. I guess they're all too busy running the main office. You know, they just put in a new vice president; he's not a banker, he's a lawyer. Mr. Gordon's a lawyer. But I think this new vice president could do things like visit the branches.

SMITH: Why do you want this closer supervision?

BM2:   I don't know. It's just that you would like to have them know what you are doing. For instance, my correspondence. I write letters here; and so far as I know, no one at the main office has ever looked at a letter of mine to see what I write. Of course, if a customer complained about a letter from me, then I'd hear about it from the main office; but otherwise, they don't know what I am saying in the name of the bank. . . . I just think they ought to check up on what we're doing. Maybe they have ways of checking up.

SMITH: What do you mean?

BM2:   Well, for instance, earlier this afternoon, someone phoned and asked whether we were open. You can't tell, that might have been someone from the main office calling to see what I would say.

. . . .

BM3 [on personnel matters]:   Those problems are handled at the main office. As you probably know, employees are evaluated on the anniversary date of their employment and six months later. At those times, Mr. Baker calls me to get my opinion of the employee; and on the basis of that, plus his error record,[1] if he's a teller, Mr. Baker decides what to do.

SMITH: Do you tell the employee the outcome?

BM3: No, Mr. Baker does.

SMITH: Do the officers come here often?

BM3: We see Mr. Olds [assistant vice president in charge of customer relations] fairly often; and if we're lucky, Mr. Gordon gets here on his annual visit. The others we don't see. Of course, Mr. Baker comes out twice a month to pay.

SMITH: Do you visit the main office or other branches very often?

BM3: You must bear in mind that at branches like this one the manager can't very well leave. Both from the point of view of security and of having someone around who knows what to do, I can't leave this immediate business section while the bank is open.

Interviews with Personnel at the Main Office

After visiting the branches, Smith began interviews with officials at the main office, selecting those whose duties brought them into contact with the branches. Excerpts from some of those interviews follow.

MR. YOUNG [assistant vice president (in charge of main office operations)]: I think of three problems that come up around the branches. In the first place, there is the matter of getting everyone to follow standard procedures. You establish a rule for doing things a certain way; but if you don't keep alert and keep checking regularly, you will go out some time later and find that you can't even recognize your original rule. Everybody will be doing things a little bit differently.

The second kind of a problem really isn't too much of one, but it has to do with things like "insufficient funds" checks. Each day, I get a list of these checks, and I try to work through the branch managers on their customers. I usually ask the branch manager for his opinion on whether we ought to honor the check, write the customer about it, or what. I'll take the branch manager's recommendation unless experience has shown me that he doesn't have very good judgment about these matters. Some of them don't want to be as firm about these matters as we have to be. All in all, however, this is not much of a problem; it is more a procedure.

The third thing I had in mind is really the most serious problem, that is, the matter of communication. People in the branches complain that they would like to hear things firsthand instead of hearing it along the street somewhere. We are doing better about this than we used to, but

---

[1] Each month a report was circulated to officers and branch managers showing for each teller the number of errors made and how much the overage or shortage was.

we still have a way to go. In my opinion, this points up our need for a manager of branches, a man to whom all the branch managers would report.

SMITH: What would he do?

YOUNG: Of course, there would be this matter of taking care of communication. If someone here had a new instruction or something, instead of calling eight offices, he would just call the manager of branches and let him spread the word along. But I think the most important function would be to insure that we make the best use of our personnel. A manager of branches could accumulate data regularly on the efficiency of the branches. We have some branch managers who like to keep their offices understaffed because it makes it look as though they are making more money for the bank that way. Some others keep their branches overstaffed so that they always have a spare man in case something happens. If you understaff, you don't give the customers the service they deserve; if you overstaff, of course, you are hurting the bank's earnings. A manager of branches could visit the offices, and watch and see whether employees were being fully used and whether customers were getting the service they should get. He could see that the operations were efficiently arranged, that the premises were kept in good shape, etc.

For another thing, he [the manager of branches] would be the man that the branch managers could bring their problems to. When it came to matters of promotion or transfers, he should be in a position to recommend a man for the job or else to state why the man should not be promoted into the job.

SMITH: What are some of the procedures that cause difficulty?

YOUNG: Well, take our rule that we do not cash checks for persons who are not customers of the bank. That is a rule; but at the same time, we give tellers some leeway on it. They have to use good judgment about when to apply the rule. For instance, at our branches in the industrial areas, if a man comes in and wants to cash a check, the teller can explain the rule; and being a businessman, the chances are that he'll understand and take it O.K. But in the suburban banks, there are persons who would take this as a personal affront; they would think that we were doubting their honesty. In such instances the wise thing might be to go ahead and cash the check.

SMITH: How do you, on the one hand, publish a rule and, on the other hand, tell people to use their own judgment?

YOUNG (smiling):   It is difficult, but we do a lot of it through our meetings. We have four meetings a year, attended by the branch managers and the head tellers from each branch. At these, we explain any new procedures and give the men from the branches a chance to ask questions. Every once in a while, someone will say that when he turned a person down on cashing a check, that person said that another branch had cashed his check. When it comes up this way, we try to discuss why it might be advisable to ignore the rule on certain occasions or under certain conditions.

.   .   .   .

MR. KNOWLES [auditor]: As I understand it, you are interested in problems between the branches and the main office. I've got one right here. (*He produces a sheet of paper with the following heading: "HOW CAN A BANK, WITH NINE OFFICES, KEEP ITS CASH EXPOSURE DOWN TO A MINIMUM SO THAT IN CASE OF A HOLDUP THE LOSS WILL BE SMALL?"*) One of my men here is designated as "security officer" for the bank. As such, he is supposed to go around to each office every week to see that it is keeping its cash exposure down. We are working on the theory that if we can't prevent holdups, one thing that we can do is to keep the cash exposure down to the point where it won't be profitable for robbers to hold us up. One of our small branches was held up a while back, and the robbers got $28,000.

Now, it's ridiculous for them to have that much cash exposed. We have provided all tellers with five-minute delay safes. That means that you can't open the safe for five minutes. None of these holdup men are going to stay around for five minutes because they know that someone has probably pushed the alarm and that the police are probably on their way. These bank robbers figure on getting in and out in under three minutes; so, you see, if you have five-minute delay safes at each teller's window, the robbers are not going to get the money in those safes. These safes are fixed so that the teller can push packages of bills into the safe through a slot without opening the safe, and what we preach all the time to the tellers is that they should put any large amounts of money they receive right into that safe. It sure makes a difference because another one of our branches was "knocked over" after that $28,000 loss; and there, when the tellers kept their exposure down, the bandits got only $4,000. That makes a difference. These guys usually work in threes, and the risk of twenty-five years in the penitentiary against splitting $4,000 is not nearly as tempting as a deal like that $28,000 job.

But here's the problem, even though we tell them this story and put these safes in for them: The tellers, or at least some of them, don't keep their exposure down. They always have a hundred excuses for not being able to put their cash away. Sometimes, when the security officer goes around, he finds a teller who has cash stacked right up inside the window. Well, someone sees that and says to himself: "Gee, that would be an easy bank to stick up!"

The way things are now, everyone holds the security officer responsible for this situation. If a place is held up and they get a lot of money like they did that one time, the board of directors and the president and everybody blame it on the security officer. Now, I say that this should be the responsibility of the branch manager. At best, we can only check the tellers once a week, and that takes a lot of time; but the branch manager could check his own tellers every day to see to it that they were keeping their exposure down. As it is now, the branch managers just say that that is the responsibility of the security officer. I'll bet if they told the branch managers that they were going to be held responsible to see to it that cash exposure was kept down and that they would be fired if something happened like that $28,000 job, the exposure would go down. But as it is now, we can't get them [branch managers] to assume the responsibility.

.   .   .   .

MR. LYNCH [assistant vice president (credit manager)]:   As you probably know, any branch manager can loan up to the legal limit of the bank. As a matter of fact, we have a rule that any loan of over $100,000 should be signed by two senior officers; but legally, a branch manager has the power to loan the legal limit. In some cases, I don't think that the men out at the branches do the job they should be doing on collecting information on the loan and on making decisions. For one thing, we have been disappointed in the apparent lack of interest on the part of the younger men in the branches in learning more about loans.

For about three years now, we have had a series of meetings during the winter at which all loan officers, particularly the younger ones, were given a chance to learn more about making loans. For these, we made up some case histories about marginal loans we had made or considered making. We gave the men all the information we had at the time and asked them to study that material and to come to the meeting prepared to discuss the loan. Sometimes, we deliberately left out some important pieces of information, just to see whether they would ask for it. At first, these meetings seemed to go pretty well; but last year, they were a big flop. It seemed to me that these guys weren't even interested. I don't know what it was, but they didn't discuss the loans. They didn't ask some of the pertinent questions that should have been asked. In general, they just acted as if they didn't give a damn. I've been advocating more loan training around here for some time, and I was really discouraged about the lack of interest.

One aspect of this is our decentralization policy. We sort of give people their own head; and I think, at times, that we overdo it. For instance, sometimes one of the officers out in one of the branches doesn't give us the information we need on a loan he has already made. Anybody is liable to slip up once in a while, but some of them do it pretty often. When this happens, no one really lays down the law to that individual and says: "Look, when you make that kind of a loan, we want you to get such-and-such information *before* you make the loan!" Perhaps what we need most in this regard is a man who would be the manager of the branch managers, a guy who would crack down on them.

SMITH: Do the loaning officers at the branches check with you often on loans they are considering?

LYNCH: Not as often as I think they should. In general, however, the younger men at the branches tend to call me when they are in doubt. Of course, the senior officers would be more likely to check with Mr. Davis [senior vice president and loan officer].

.   .   .   .

MR. BAKER [assistant vice president (in charge of personnel)]: As you probably know, I visit the branch offices twice a month to pay. I have the payroll arranged now so that I can stop and talk with a branch manager who indicates that he has something he wants to talk about. We used to evaluate the performance of all employees in January and July. But recently, we started a system whereby we review an employee's performance six months after he comes with us and then semiannually on that anniversary. On paying visits, I try to check with the branch manager and get his opinion on any personnel whose review will be coming up soon.

SMITH: Who decides whether to give an employee a raise or not?

BAKER: Well, the branch manager and I talk it over, and we can almost always agree on what should be done. At some branches, they want to be what I consider too generous. I know that feeling because I was once a branch manager myself and I had people working for me who were wonderful. I took every chance to get them more money. But now, my job is to try to keep things pretty well in line throughout the bank. Of course, once in a while, I run into a situation where I think the branch is not generous enough, and I try to loosen them up.

SMITH: If you and the branch manager decide not to give an employee a raise, who tells him?

BAKER: If we are in agreement about it, then I have the branch manager tell him and explain why. Sometimes, I sit in on it. When it comes to firing, of course, they always ask me to do it. Nobody enjoys firing, but my answer is to go out to the branch and to sit down with the employee and the branch manager, and then the two of us explain why we are letting him go. Of course, in the case of dishonesty, we wouldn't fool around with the person.

SMITH: In your view, do the ambitious younger men resist being assigned to the branches?

BAKER: I don't know that they actually resist it; but I do know that whenever we bring a man back to the main office from a branch, he is usually delighted to come. A branch manager's job can be very frustrating. I opened up two branch offices, and it was fun at first. But once you get everything set up, it gets boring. For instance, in one office I opened, after I got things set up, I didn't have much to do but sit there. So I went out and called on the businesses in my area. Most of them were garages and small shops. Once I had done that, I couldn't very well turn around and visit them again right away. And so I'd usually be all finished by 3:00 o'clock and not know what to do with myself. It was frustrating, and I was delighted to come back here.

.   .   .   .

SMITH: How do you think the younger men look upon an assignment to one of the branches?

MR. NAVIN [vice president, controller, who had recently reached the bank's retirement age and was serving the bank in a part-time capacity]: I'm not sure, but they surely don't need to feel that they will be forgotten there. Since the branch office is small, a man has the opportunity to learn a greater variety of things than he would learn staying here. Look at Olds, and Lynch, and Baker; those men were all branch managers. They did a good job in the branches, and then they were brought back here into better jobs. This bank is still not so large that we can't keep an eye on young men out in the branches. I can think of eight or so young men out in the branches now whom top management has its eye on.

.   .   .   .

MR. DAVIS [senior vice president, loan officer]:   I suppose that the important difference between having branches and not having them, as far as my work is concerned, is simply that it gives me eight more loan officers to supervise and they are farther away. On the whole, however, we don't have much of a problem in control. As you probably know, we are a decentralized organization. There is another bank in this area which is comparable in size and in its branches; but there, a branch manager cannot make a loan of over $500 without concurrence from the main office. We don't work that way. We don't put any restrictions on the loan officers as to the amounts they can loan.

This all means, of course, that once in a while, one of the younger men makes a loan that I wouldn't make. When I see it, I try to talk to him about it and show him my point of view. As a matter of fact, there are occasions when it's a good thing to have one of the younger men make a bad loan. After he has done so and has sweat blood trying to work through the loan, he will be a much better loan officer. Naturally,

I wouldn't want anyone to make a bad loan of much size; but as I say, sometimes if a small one turns sour, it's worth a lot in terms of experience.

My major concern is that the younger men don't show much interest in learning more about loans. I'm within two years of retirement, and I regret the fact that I won't be able to keep on doing what I'm doing, because I love my work. But some of these younger branch managers don't seem to be interested in loaning. I tell them: "Look, some day when you're all cleaned up at your branch at about 3:00 o'clock, come on in here to the main office, and let's discuss any problems you have." But none of them ever do it. We have had a series of meetings, using actual case histories, but I was disappointed to see that the younger men didn't seem to be interested. In order for them to learn, we can only meet them half way.

.   .   .   .

MR. ROBBINS [treasurer]:   I have always operated these branches on the theory that you pick a trained man, put him out there, and say to him: "This is your branch; now, run it." We have followed this practice, but we've been disappointed. I don't know what the answer is, but the branch managers haven't shown much initiative.

SMITH: In what ways have they fallen down?

ROBBINS: Mainly in respect to getting out and securing new business. Their idea is that you open up the office, take care of the people who come in, and then close up. This usually means that they are all finished by about 3:00 P.M. They don't go out and seek new business.

SMITH: Have they been told what is expected?

ROBBINS: Of course; I think they should know this. As I say, when we send them out to a branch, we consider them qualified to run the branch and feel that we shouldn't have to keep after them all the time. The complaint we get from the branches is that they feel neglected. They say we ignore them.

2. THE GORDON COMPANY

UNTIL 1945, the Gordon Company, a small foundry, realized 90 per cent of its sales volume from one type of casting of a complex design that required unusual fabricating care and accuracy. The size, shape, weight, and structural strength of this major product required casting skills of a special kind, which Gordon employees had been able to develop to customers' satisfaction over many years. The remaining 10 per cent of the company's dollar volume was secured from a variety of special jobs which required a greater variety of fabricating skills. The nature of the postwar market caused the company's owners to decide to manufacture a wider line of products. A number of problems were encountered, however, in the attempt to do so.

The Pre-1945 Situation

The technical process for making castings began with the preparation of patterns and the conditioning of sand (see Exhibit 1 for foundry layout), both of which were used in making casting molds. The machinery used in mold making, modern in design though old in conception, was especially well suited to the company's traditional products. Molten metal was poured into the molds which, when cool, were broken apart, destroying the mold and releasing the rough casting. A separate division performed finishing operations in another part of the plant. The division of labor in the foundry was partly by function, partly by type of product (see Exhibit 2). There were three principal work groups (machine men, cupola gang, and job molders) and three subsidiary work groups (pattern room, core room, and extra men).

The machine men, so called because their molds were made by use of a special jolt rollover machine, worked solely on the company's principal product. One of the group conditioned the sand and operated the sand-handling equipment; four men operated the jolt rollover machines; another, the finisher, remedied mold defects and put the two mold halves together ready for pouring; and two shake-out men removed the completed castings from the molds. All the machine operators spent the last two hours of each shift pouring the molds they had made that day.

Machine molding, a highly repetitive process, did not require a high degree of skill or flexibility, though the machine operation required more experience than other jobs in the machine group. Speed, manual strength, and co-operation were important elements in the repertory of these men, and each displayed such abilities. All except the sand man, who was on hourly pay, received a group piece rate for acceptable castings. Shares were distributed among the men according to the type of job performed.

Exhibit 1

THE GORDON COMPANY
SCHEMATIC DIAGRAM OF FOUNDRY LAYOUT

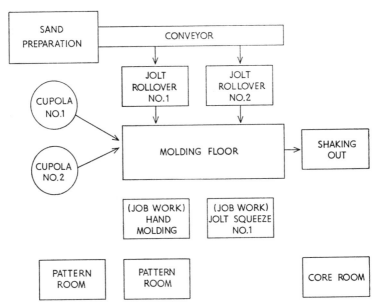

The second principal group was composed of the two job molders, one who operated the jolt squeeze machine (more flexible than the jolt rollovers) and the other who hand-built molds for orders not suitable for machine molding. Each man did all the operations involving his orders, from sand preparation to shaking out. Job molding required a greater variety of skills than machine molding, the job molders being older (over fifty) and possessing more seniority (about twenty years) than the machine men. They were paid individual piece rates for the acceptable castings they produced.

The third principal work group was the cupola gang which prepared the molten metal. The yard man prepared scrap iron for the chargers who put this and other raw materials into the cupola furnace in requisite proportions. The bottommen kept the furnace lining in repair and fired and tapped the furnace of its molten charge. The forehearth tender operated the small subsidiary furnace from which the molten metal was actually ladled. Charging and tapping were highly skilled jobs involving potential for extremely costly errors. Men in the cupola gang were paid by the hour.

The subsidiary groups provided service to one or another of these principal work gangs. One of the pattern makers concentrated on making and repairing machine patterns, while the other worked solely on

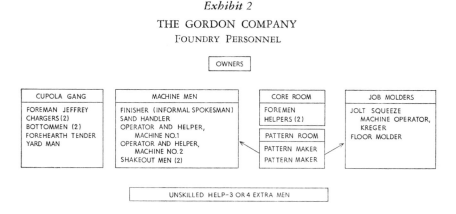

Exhibit 2

THE GORDON COMPANY

FOUNDRY PERSONNEL

OWNERS

CUPOLA GANG	MACHINE MEN	CORE ROOM	JOB MOLDERS
FOREMAN JEFFREY CHARGERS (2) BOTTOMMEN (2) FOREHEARTH TENDER YARD MAN	FINISHER (INFORMAL SPOKESMAN) SAND HANDLER OPERATOR AND HELPER, MACHINE NO.1 OPERATOR AND HELPER, MACHINE NO.2 SHAKEOUT MEN (2)	FOREMEN HELPERS (2) PATTERN ROOM PATTERN MAKER PATTERN MAKER	JOLT SQUEEZE MACHINE OPERATOR, KREGER FLOOR MOLDER

UNSKILLED HELP–3 OR 4 EXTRA MEN

job-molding patterns. They had greater contact with the men who used their patterns than with each other. The core-room men shaped and baked sand forms, which were placed in the molds to form irregular internal cavities. The three or four unskilled "extra" men performed odd jobs throughout the foundry.

Supervision of the foundry was rudimentary. Except for the cupola gang and the core men, the foundry workers had no direct formal supervision below the superintendent level. However, the cupola foreman, Jeffrey, who was seventy years old and possessed a lifetime of practical foundry experience, assumed a somewhat unique informal position. He was highly respected by all the foundry men, many of whom, regardless of job, deferred to his authority and to his "feel" for the work, which kept his cupolas operating successfully most of the time. This deference was especially apparent among the machine men.

A number of other informal supervisory relationships had grown up among the foundry groups. The core-room foreman, a man over fifty, assigned work to the job molders. The machine men received their schedules from the pattern maker who was directed by the factory superintendent. The machine men, however, looked to their finisher for leadership more than to anyone else, communicating with the superintendent through him. Internally, the machine group exercised sanctions on its own members, hazing too slow or too fast workers until they conformed to the group standard, transferred, or quit. The extra men received their orders from the machine men and from anyone else in the foundry.

The vagueness in division of responsibility and authority in the supervisory organization had never been a source of concern to company management, primarily because they and the workers had known and worked with each other for so long that expectations and responsibilities were well understood. The men largely worked on their own within a patterned routine. Only when a casting was found to be defective did a problem arise, since responsibility could not easily be traced. There was a tendency for each work group to blame another for the fault. Defective castings were sufficiently rare and, when they did occur, remelting was such a ready solution that no procedure had ever been established for assigning responsibility more closely.

The Postwar Change

As experimentation with new products began, the owners discovered that no one in the foundry possessed sufficient technical knowledge to deal with the new problems these products presented. None of the company's employees had had formal technical training. The owners and the superintendent agreed that it would be necessary to hire a technically trained foundry manager. The old superintendent was to assist the new man as the latter requested, but he was to concentrate his attention on changes which would be required in the finishing division. The owners tacitly assumed that these two men would be on an equal level, though that assumption was never made explicit.

After a thorough search for qualified candidates, the owners were most attracted to a Mr. Bass, a fifty-year-old chemical engineer. He came well recommended by the faculty of his undergraduate school and, in a personal interview, made a good impression on the owners by enthusiastically recounting his prior experiences and by his "fine personality." He was subsequently hired.

No formal announcement of Mr. Bass's election was planned prior to his arrival. In the interim the rumor spread that a new manager was coming and that he would bring his own people with him. When Kreger, the jolt squeeze operator, repeatedly explained to the owners what a good worker he was, despite his advanced age, a detailed explanation of Mr. Bass's coming was made. It was emphasized that the new manager would make no drastic changes.

When Mr. Bass arrived early in January, 1946, he brought with him a large library of metallurgical books and periodicals, and evidenced in many conversations, in which he took an active part, that he was familiar with modern developments in his field. When he expressed a desire to make no immediate changes but merely to become acquainted with his new job, the owners felt they had secured the man they needed.

Before Mr. Bass had been in the foundry a week, the machine men presented him with a demand for higher wages. He passed the matter over to the owners, who settled the issue directly with the men at a conference which Mr. Bass attended. The negotiations ended with the men receiving a small raise.

After Mr. Bass had been on the job for two months, the first contract for a new product was obtained. The item was in two parts, one suitable for the jolt rollover machines, the other for the jolt squeeze machine. Mr. Bass told the owners, and they agreed, that the job-molding group would have to be enlarged because Kreger would soon be outstripped by the machine men, particularly since the volume of miscellaneous job orders was increasing rapidly.

The first man hired, Maxwell, was an experienced molder and an old friend of Kreger's. He operated a new jolt squeeze machine placed next to Kreger's. Kreger's and Maxwell's production held to a steady rate of 75 to 80 molds apiece per day. Curtis, a young man, was subsequently hired by Mr. Bass to operate a third jolt squeeze machine. His machine was some distance from the other two. (See Exhibit 3 for layout changes and additions described in the remainder of this case.) After the first few days he put down 125 molds a day. Kreger's and Maxwell's production spurted up for ten days, thence dropped back to, and remained at, its previous level. Kreger and Maxwell studiously avoided Curtis. Kreger once again began to reassure the owners of his ability, stating that when he finished a mold they could count on its being good. Within the next month, three more jolt squeeze machines were delivered, and Mr. Bass selected three men from the machine group to operate them.

Mr. Bass, meanwhile, was beset by a number of problems. Although he instructed the pattern makers to keep up with the volume of new work, the molders were often delayed by lack of patterns. The new job molders, accustomed in other companies to having their sand conditioned for them, requested that a man be assigned to do that work. Accordingly, Mr. Bass instructed the extra men to add this job to their duties. They preferred, however, to pursue their old routines. Piece rates and the length of production runs also created problems. Mr. Bass was often not able to establish new rates before an order was placed in production, particularly in the case of rush business. The timekeeper then had to use hourly rates in computing earnings. Furthermore, the rush of business made it difficult to collect into one run a series of similar molds. Both of these limitations made it difficult for the men to estimate

Exhibit 3

THE GORDON COMPANY

SCHEMATIC DIAGRAM OF FOUNDRY LAYOUT INCLUDING CHANGES MADE DURING EXPANSION PROGRAM

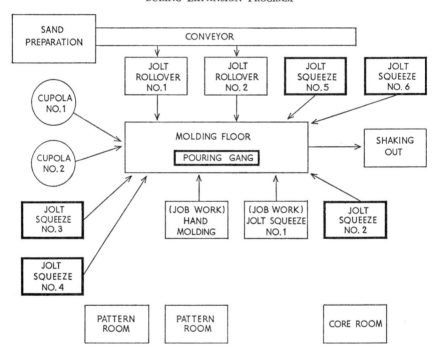

or feel satisfied with their earnings. Although Mr. Bass tried to keep ahead of these problems by solving them himself or assigning them to someone else for solution, neither procedure seemed effective. The men were busy on their accustomed routines, and Mr. Bass was faced with a multiplicity of both routine and new issues.

Between April and August a number of crises occurred. The molders, dissatisfied with their earnings, demanded a guaranteed minimum wage. Tempers flared among the men, resulting in time off being taken without notice. By August only Kreger remained of the original jolt squeeze machine men, the rest having left the company or transferred back to the jolt rollover group. Even some of the replacements had left and been replaced.

Meanwhile, the machine group, though less affected than the job molders, was also encountering difficulty. To increase machine molding capacity without adding machines and operators, Mr. Bass had employed a gang of Negroes, at whose head was an experienced worker, to do the pouring for the whole foundry. They were paid by the hour. At first the machine group's production jumped from 74 to 111 castings per man per day, then fell back to 97. Only when reassured by the owners that incentive rates would not be cut was the 111 rate resumed. The machine men criticized every move of the pouring gang, referring to them as "those coons." Defective castings rose from 3 per cent to 12 per cent of production. The machine men demanded that they not be penalized beyond the 3 per cent rate.

During this period the machine men dealt directly with the owners about their dissatisfaction, ignoring Mr. Bass. Finally, the owners instructed Mr. Bass to interfere with the machine group as little as possible. Few new evidences of dissatisfaction arose thereafter.

While the above problems were mounting, the cupola gang presented its own peculiar difficulties. Postwar demand in the scrap iron market created more than usual variations in the characteristics of material. Extra care had to be taken in charging the cupolas, and Mr. Bass insisted, in Jeffrey's presence, that the chargers "weigh it, boys." When a suitable mobile scale was obtained, the men persisted in moving the metal to the scale, rather than vice versa. The resultant delay caused the chargers to avoid weighing the charge, and Mr. Bass felt it necessary to add a man to the cupola gang. Mr. Bass was also concerned about control of the depth of the fuel bed in the cupolas and instructed Jeffrey to measure its depth accurately and frequently. Shortly after this instruction was given, Jeffrey lost the old bent rod he had used periodically to check his intuitive judgment of the bed's depth. The loss was not discovered until four months later when Jeffrey was confined by illness. Despite these apparent difficulties, the cupola gang had continued to produce a satisfactory quality of molten metal.

When Jeffrey fell ill, Mr. Bass assumed direction of the cupolas. Being unfamiliar with the cupolas' peculiarities, however, he had trouble producing good iron. When it became generally known that Mr. Bass was writing notes to Jeffrey asking him how to handle certain problems, the foundry men were convinced that Mr. Bass was incompetent. This evidence of weakness was constantly referred to, particularly by Jeffrey's close friend, the timekeeper.

As a result of all these events, by October Mr. Bass had become immersed in the details of running the cupolas and the job-molding group, in effect having become foreman of each group. His other duties had disappeared, however, since the men did not take their problems to him. Mr. Bass had not found the occasion to discuss his problems with the factory superintendent.

The foundry's first new contract was completed in October. While job order volume was increasing, the first contract was not renewed nor were any new contracts secured. Despite the fact that costs for many years had been more than satisfactory, the Gordon Company was now being consistently underbid.

3. THE HAMPTON SHIPYARD

THE HAMPTON Shipyard near Philadelphia, Pennsylvania, was situated on a landlocked harbor which connected with the sea through a channel deep enough to float the largest battleship. Covering an area of 120 acres, the shipyard had twelve building ways, or slips, the biggest of which would accommodate ships up to 1,000 feet in length and 150 feet in beam. Outfitting was carried out on five large piers built on water having an average depth of thirty feet below mean low-water level.

Established in 1890, the shipyard was well known for its output of naval and commercial vessels of every type and size. The naval vessels ranged in type and size from small naval vessels to battleships and aircraft carriers. The commercial vessels ranged in type and size from trawlers to luxury liners.

In 1954 the shipyard had about three thousand employees and was the largest employer in the surrounding locality. The shipyard workers were first unionized in 1938; and in 1946, they were organized by a national union. Prior to 1946, industrial relations were fairly harmonious; there was a low turnover of labor, and the apprentice school system led to many sons of old-time workers being employed. In 1946 the national union called a strike on a national issue which was not settled for five months.

The majority of employees of the shipyard were skilled tradesmen. The trades represented included welding, burning, ship fitting, drilling, chipping, pipe fitting, electrical, sheet metal, painting, carpentering, riveting, and rigging. Operations such as riveting and rigging were carried out by gangs, but most of the other operations were performed by individual tradesmen under the supervision of leading men.

In June, 1954, James Ambrose, the general superintendent of the shipyard, was reminded that, recently, layoffs in manpower, which had been made necessary by the decline in the volume of operation of the shipyard, had reduced the number of supervisors available for the daily "roving committee." Ambrose knew that on some days the roving committee had been reduced to two or three supervisors. He felt that he would have to rearrange the groups and reassign some supervisors or let the daily patrol of the roving committee expire.

631

The roving committee at the Hampton Shipyard was first instituted in August, 1949. At the time, Ambrose was dissatisfied with the behavior of employees; he felt that a number of men were ceasing work before the whistle sounded for lunch at 12:00 noon and for quitting time at 4:00 P.M. Ambrose was particularly dissatisfied with the lines which formed at the eight banks of timekeepers' clocks prior to the blowing of the whistle. (For the plant layout, see Exhibit 1.) Am-

Exhibit 1

THE HAMPTON SHIPYARD

PLANT LAYOUT

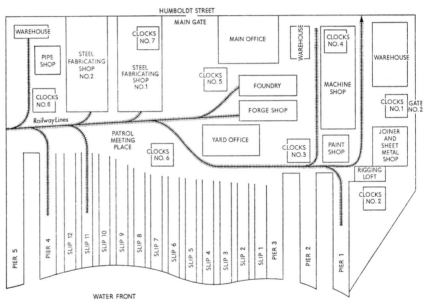

brose reasoned that the men would have to leave their jobs on the ships being built on the slips and being outfitted at the piers several minutes prior to the time when they lined up at the timekeepers' clocks; and he knew that at some shipyards, this practice had ballooned to the point where men stopped work half an hour and more before the whistle sounded.

To force the men to work full time, Ambrose formed a roving committee of divisional superintendents, foremen, and assistant foremen,[1] and required this committee to patrol specific areas of the yard daily at fifteen minutes prior to the sounding of the whistle. He set up a

---

[1] For the casewriter's concept of the formal relationships at the shipyard, see Exhibit 2.

fixed schedule and required the rotation of assigned areas so that all the areas of the yard were somewhat covered each day by the patrols. To enforce his wishes, Ambrose instructed the patrol to take badge numbers for subsequent issue of "chits" wherever offenses warranted such issue. Chits in books had been issued to supervisors previously and consisted of a notification in triplicate of the offense, together with the penalty for the offense. Exhibit 3 shows a chit.

The formation of the roving committee was designed to serve as an additional supervision of the men working on the ships. Ambrose

Exhibit 2

THE HAMPTON SHIPYARD

PARTIAL ORGANIZATION CHART*

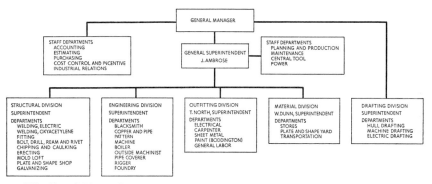

* The shipyard did not ordinarily make use of a formal organization chart. This chart is the casewriter's concept of the formal relationships.

NOTE: The supervisory force in each department of the five divisions consisted of a foreman, an assistant foreman, quartermen, and leading men. Quartermen supervised from five to 10 leading men. Leading men supervised from 10 to 15 men on the ships and as high as 35 men in the shops.

thought this additional supervision was necessary for a number of reasons. He knew, for instance, that supervisors below the rank of superintendent would never cross the departmental lines in order to question a man about the reason for his presence in any particular locality. Ambrose thought this questioning of individuals who had left their jobs on the ships without permission was necessary in order to tighten the discipline of working until the whistle sounded. The daily patrol of the roving committee was instructed to take the badge numbers of men not on jobs and to report these numbers through Ambrose's office to the foreman of the department concerned. The foreman was instructed to notify action taken on these reports; and if a man did not have a good reason for being away from his job, the foreman was to issue a chit.

Ambrose thought that the roving committee was successful in improving conditions at quitting time because he did not observe as many infractions of the rule after the patrol was instituted. After several weeks, he believed that conditions had improved considerably and that the patrol was no longer necessary, so he gave instructions for its discontinuance.

In June, 1950, a few months after the patrol had been discontinued, the work force of the shipyard had increased to 6,000 employees, and

Exhibit 3

THE HAMPTON SHIPYARD*

CHIT STUB		CHIT
Serial No. 23575		Employee's Name _____ Serial No. 23575
Badge No.		Employee's Badge No. _____
Name		1 ☐ Loafing
		2 ☐ Losing time
Hull No.		3 ☐ Leaving job early
		4 ☐ Arriving on job late without reason
		5 ☐ Off job without permission
Date		1 ☐ First offense—*warning*
		2 ☐ Second offense—*one week off*
		3 ☐ Third offense—*discharge*
Time		The infraction of some company rules and regulations will result in *immediate discharge*.
Offense	Offense No.	Some, but not all, of these rules are:
1 ☐	1 ☐	6 ☐ Employee found sleeping in the yard
2 ☐	2 ☐	6(*a*) ☐ Intoxicated
3 ☐	3 ☐	6(*b*) ☐ Gambling
4 ☐		6(*c*) ☐ Stealing
5 ☐		6(*d*) ☐ Defacing or destroying property
		6(*e*) ☐ Horseplay
		6(*f*) ☐ Other
		Hull _____ Date _____ Time _____
		_____
		Supervisor's Signature
Immediate Discharge Offenses		First copy to industrial relations department
6 ☐ 6(*d*) ☐		Second copy to employee
6(*a*) ☐ 6(*e*) ☐		Third copy to department office
6(*b*) ☐ 6(*f*) ☐		
6(*c*) ☐		

* The local of the national union "went along" with this chit system of issuing written warnings of offenses.

there were indications that the buildup would continue, although Ambrose did not envisage its reaching the proportions of the wartime force of 30,000 unless the United States became involved in another world war. In June, Ambrose had occasion to visit some other shipyards; and during those visits, he noticed a great deal of laxity regarding the enforcement of the rule of working until the whistle sounded. At his next weekly meeting with the foremen, Ambrose brought up the problem of men quitting early. He said that if they allowed laxity in enforcing this rule, they would soon find the men disregarding all rules. After some discussion, in which the foremen admitted that some men were inclined to quit early, Ambrose arranged for the timekeeping department to provide him with a list of all employees who punched out at 4:00, 4:01, and 4:02 P.M.

The timekeeping department kept a record of the men who punched out at these times for the next several weeks, and each foreman was notified of the badge numbers of the men in his department who appeared on this list of "early birds." Ambrose noticed that an excessive number of the men listed were employed by the paint department, so he questioned Mr. Boddington, the foreman of the paint department, about the reason for the excessive number of his men on the "early bird" list. Boddington defended his men and attributed the fact that they appeared on this list to the approved practice of allowing painters to leave their jobs on the ships five minutes before quitting time so that they could return brushes and pails to the paint shop. He pointed out that this approved practice was the only exception to the rule that all men should stay on the job until the whistle sounded, and he claimed that this accounted for the fact that his men were often first to clock out.

In July, 1950, Ambrose was dissatisfied with the record of "early birds," so he called a meeting with the officers of the Supervisors' Association.[2] At this meeting, Ambrose said that it was the responsibility of the immediate supervisors to keep the workmen on the job until quitting time. The officers agreed, and they went on to express their view that the supervisors could do a better job of keeping their men working until quitting time if management people of the foremen and superintendent level made it a habit to be present in the slipways and on the piers just before quitting time. They also suggested that the situation was not as bad as the general superintendent had reported, and they invited him to take a walk around any part of the yard he chose with representatives of the association to see for himself that the supervisors were on the job.

After some discussion, it was decided that a roving committee should be set up to patrol the yard daily from 11:45 to 12:00 noon and from 3:45 to 4:00 P.M. Ambrose requested the foremen of departments to

---

[2] The Supervisor's Association was a social organization of the supervisory personnel below the rank of assistant foreman. These supervisors were not organized for bargaining purposes; the traditional role of the association was social in nature, with the specific job of organizing social activities such as yearly picnics. From time to time, the general superintendent had used the officers of the association as a means of conveying information of a general nature concerning all members of the association; and in particular, the president of the Supervisors' Association often spent considerable time answering questions regarding the group bonus scheme of incentive payment for supervisors.

assign their supervisors to patrol on different days so that each patrol group contained ten supervisors from ten different departments. He decided to leave the assignment of foremen to the patrol at the discretion of the divisional superintendents because he felt that the foremen might have more important things to do around quitting time.

When the patrol was first instituted, Ambrose went with each patrol every day. Subsequently, when he found this assignment interfering with his other work, he assigned the divisional superintendents to take charge of the patrol each day, except that he himself took charge one day each week. From that time on, the patrol met each day at the head of Slip 9 and, fair weather or foul, patrolled portions of the yard each day. The portion of the yard to be patrolled was selected by the superintendent in charge of the patrol without notice. The supervisors accompanying the superintendent had no prior knowledge of the area to be patrolled on any particular day.

In October, 1951, when employment at the shipyard had decreased to approximately 4,000 employees, the groups of supervisors forming the patrols were rearranged to accommodate for some changes which had occurred in personnel. In 1953, when employment at the yard had increased to 6,000 employees, the groups were again rearranged; and at that time, Ambrose decided to reduce the patrol from ten to eight supervisors.

During the period in which this regular patrol operated, the supervisors were well aware that the men had set up some countermoves of their own. A very efficient warning system had been organized by the men to alert areas of the yard which were directly in the path of the patrol; and conversely, areas which apparently were not being covered on any one day were informed that they could relax. The men had named the patrol the "Gestapo" and often made unflattering comments about it to supervisors.[3] Most of the supervisors thought the patrol did assist in keeping men working until the whistle sounded. During this period a number of chits, averaging one per day, were issued. The threat of issue of a chit, however, was used much more often than actual issue. From August, 1949, to June, 1954, 1,601 chits were issued, 1,408 being first-offense, 161 second-offense, and 32 third-offense or immediate-discharge chits.

The pay system in force at the shipyard during this period was a complicated one. The company policy was to encourage the achievement of maximum production for the mutual benefit of the employees

---

[3] Excerpts from the union flier are shown in Exhibit 4.

and the company. In line with this policy the company had established, in addition to hourly base rates of pay, an incentive pay system based on standard piecework rates. On the average, about 60 per cent of the employees were employed from time to time on contract work offering this incentive pay. The contracts for work on the ships varied in size from one day's work to three or four weeks' work. The contracts were written by rate setters employed in the cost control and incentive department. Men working on the ships moved back and forth, sometimes employed on hourly pay and sometimes on incentive contract pay. According to observations of Ambrose and some other supervisors, men on incentive contract pay were just as prone to quit work before the whistle sounded as were men on hourly pay.

Exhibit 4

THE HAMPTON SHIPYARD

Excerpts from Two Union Fliers

GESTAPO

It is to be noted that Ambrose and his roving crew are still hard at work, checking on men off the job. It is my understanding that, starting Monday morning, they will check all men off the job at all times. *Well,* a word to the wise is sufficient.

. . . .

As you have noticed, leading men, supervisors, foremen, and high yard officials are cruising the yard before the lunch period and quitting time, checking up on employees who are not on their jobs. This is a function of management, and your union has nothing to do with it.

Many of the bosses dislike this job they have to do—acting as a police force. But they, too, have to take orders. So, boys, protect yourself; stay out of the toilets, and don't give them a chance to pass out chits.

During discussions about the patrol the supervisors admitted that they felt they needed some assistance in stopping men from quitting early, because often a supervisor, such as a leading man electrician, would be responsible for men working throughout an entire ship or even for men working on two different ships, and he could not possibly maintain a surveillance of his men all at once. The supervisors working on the ships often compared their problem of supervision with the easy task of supervision in the machine and fabricating shops, where men were under the immediate eye of their supervisors. Ambrose had also required his own staff assistants to form and man patrols near the gangways of ships tied up at the piers and to maintain a surveillance of areas near the time clocks, but he felt that these measures and the listing of badge numbers by the guard at the gangways of men leaving the ship fifteen minutes before quitting time were not sufficient to enforce the rule of working until the whistle sounded.

The supervisors, individually, did not like the job of going on the daily patrol, particularly on days when the weather was bad, and they did not like the unflattering comments which were made about the "Gestapo."

In June, 1954, employment at the Hampton Shipyard was at the low point of 3,000 employees. Many who remained were old-timers, and a number of the men had been supervisors at some previous time. Ambrose found some of the patrol groups of the roving committee reduced by layoffs and demotions to two or three supervisors.[4] He felt he would have to rearrange the groups once more or let the roving committee expire. He was not sure whether the patrol was still needed during this period of minimum manpower, and he knew that some people were critical of the usefulness of the patrol. However, he did not consider that the old-timers were immune to the temptation of quitting a few moments before the whistle sounded, though he did wonder whether the patrol served to keep them working on the job; and he was well aware of the unflattering references, such as the use of the name "Gestapo." One day, when he was discussing the patrol with some of his subordinates, Ambrose said: "I know that conditions at lunch time and quitting time in other shipyards are much worse than in this yard. I know also that the patrol is criticized, and perhaps it only keeps the fellows out of sight; but can you show me a better system? If anybody comes up with a better answer, I'll certainly give it a try."

On June 15, 1954, Joe Campbell, an engineer in the planning department, had occasion to accompany Mr. North, the superintendent of the outfitting division, on a trip to Trenton to a competing shipyard. North noticed, and commented to Ambrose later, that at Trenton there were at least 1,000 men gathered at the main gate which was 200 to 300 yards from the ships, five minutes before the whistle sounded. North remarked that Mr. Welch, the general superintendent of the Trenton shipyard, was with them when they encountered this crowd waiting at the main gate, and Welch thought nothing of it. He merely apologized to North because the crowd of men were blocking North's car from leaving by the main gate. North went on to say that in comparison, he thought the behavior of the men at the Hampton Shipyard regarding quitting early was remarkably good.

A few days after his visit to the Trenton yard, Campbell happened to stop in at a small stores department shack at the head of Slip 10, to get out of the rain. North was also present when the daily patrol, under

---

[4] Layoffs and demotions during slack periods were administered in order of seniority.

the supervision of Mr. Dunn, the superintendent of the material division, formed at the head of Slip 9 and proceeded toward Pier 5. As the direction in which the patrol was headed became apparent, Campbell heard Fred Cernot, the store man in charge of the shack, pick up the telephone and call another store man in a shack on Slip 11. Campbell distinctly heard Cernot say into the telephone: "Say, Ted, Dunn's got the 'Gestapo' today, and he's headed your way." Dunn was the superintendent of the material division, which included the stores department. Campbell was not certain, but he thought that North must have heard Cernot warning Ted that the "Gestapo" was headed in that direction. Campbell was sure that Cernot knew North was present, because North, who was well known to the men thoughout the yard, was standing right next to the telephone.

The general superintendent's office and those of his divisional superintendents were all situated on the second floor of the yard office. Ambrose and his divisional superintendents often contacted one another on matters of mutual interest when they were in their offices around quitting time. About quitting time on the day that North had heard Cernot warning the store man on Slip 11, he related the incident to Ambrose. "I was amused," said North, "to see their efficient warning system in action. That store man at the head of Slip 10 lost no time in warning the guy on Slip 11 that the 'Gestapo' was headed his way."

4. MARSHALL COMPANY (A)*

THE MARSHALL Company, one of the oldest papermaking companies in the United States, was producing a greater tonnage of paper in the summer of 1947 than ever before in its history. During the war years the demand had risen sharply for paper of the high quality for which this company was noted. To meet this increased demand, the management after the war had doubled the capacity of two of its papermaking machines and was in the process of rebuilding another. At the same time, in anticipation of increasing competition, it was rebuilding its steam plant and powerhouse for more economical operations. Because of undiscriminating demand, coupled with a shortage of materials during the war, the quality of the products had necessarily suffered; the company was now retraining its personnel to the higher paper standards that the management considered customers would soon demand. Sales, production, and quality control personnel were working closely together on the problems involved in making paper in large volume of a quality satisfactory to the customers.

Austin Brewster, the vice president in charge of production, was dealing largely with the stresses and strains created by these conditions. In certain lines, material shortages had become more acute; personnel problems took a large amount of his thought; he was considering certain revisions of the employees' pay system; supervisory problems were particularly important; and he was spending substantial time on the selection and training of management personnel to fill certain positions, including his own, that would ultimately open up as members of the company retired.

The Marshall Company enjoyed a high reputation for quality and reliability. It produced a wide variety of standard grades of paper used in high-quality book publishing and special grades requiring a specialized knowledge of paper chemistry as well as of manufacturing techniques. In 1947 the special grades comprised about a quarter of total output but accounted for a higher proportion of net profits. These grades had originally been developed to make use of equipment too old to turn out the standard grades in the large quantities that were necessary to make them profitable.

There were about fifteen mills in the United States producing varying grades of book paper. The Marshall Company employed about one half as many people as the largest mills and about twice as many as the smallest mills. There were, of course, many mills producing low-grade magazine and newsprint paper, but they did not compete with the Marshall Company.

The mill had provided the town in which it was located with a long history of economic security. Heavy investment in plant machinery and considerable know-how were necessary to operate a paper mill; profits depended in part on steady customer acceptance; customer contacts tended to become well established. For these reasons, it was not easy for a newcomer to enter the paper industry and threaten the positions of established companies. By observing progressive inventory and market-ing policies, and by spreading the work among its employees, the Mar-shall Company had done much to protect its employees from even such sharp economic downswings as that of 1932. During this depression period the mill operated at a loss but remained open five days a week.

In the summer of 1947, shortages of papermaking materials and limitations on productive capacity throughout the paper industry were still serious enough to make the volume fall short of customers' re-quirements. According to Brewster, customers seldom rejected a ship-ment and in general were not inclined to be too particular about quality requirements. The Marshall Company, however, anticipated that within a year, their customers' expectations regarding service and qual-ity would tighten up considerably.

Mill Location and Employee Relations

The mill had been located for more than ninety years in a small New England town with a population of 13,500. Although the town was only a few minutes from a nearby city, it was distinctly rural in atmosphere. The people were largely of French-Canadian and Yankee stock. Although some of the townspeople worked in a small shoe factory, the supervisors at the Marshall Company said that they had their pick of the town's labor supply. The mill provided the town's chief payroll and paid about half its taxes. About 2,600 people worked in the mill; of these, about 95 per cent lived in the town. The yearly labor turnover at the mill amounted to about 1 per cent. A large number of the employees had lived in the town for more than twenty-five years. Many families had had members in the mill for two or three generations.

The employees were paid on an hourly basis. In some departments, there was a bonus system based on output, with a deduction for waste. Supervisory personnel were paid according to a salary schedule determined by Brewster. For many years, it had been Brewster's policy to keep the mill "out in front" of other New England paper mills in wages paid the employees. Over the last fifteen years, general pay raises at the Marshall Company had regularly preceded pay raises at other mills.

The company management often said: "What helps the town, helps us." Many of the employees were able to buy their homes when the company guaranteed their loans at the bank and deducted the payments from the weekly wages. Workers often sought Brewster's advice on whether the house in which they were interested was a "good buy."

Brewster was interested in keeping personal contact with his employees. It was well known among the workers that any one of them could talk to Brewster whenever he wished. The problems which the help brought to him were frequently financial; they needed loans to pay for a new home, a new baby, or a divorce. Often, an employee raised questions relating to his position, his desire for transfer or promotion, or dissatisfaction with the way a supervisor had handled him. One of the employees remarked about Brewster: "He's a great guy. He ain't no different from us."

The mill was originally a family concern and, within the memory of many of the employees still at the mill, headed by a member of the Marshall family. Robert Mower, the president in 1947, whose office was located in a large eastern city at some distance from the mill, was known personally to many employees. Some years earlier, he had spent a period of time in the mill, working in each of the departments. It was not uncommon for workers to reminisce about "when Bob Mower had my job."

Various locals of the Congress of Industrial Organizations, the American Federation of Labor, and the United Mine Workers had made frequent efforts to organize the mill.

The Mill

The mill straddled a narrow river, from which it took a large volume of water for operations. It was located on the northern side of the town and covered 40 to 50 acres on both sides of the river. The mill gate, through which one entered the plant, was on the west side of the river near the main office of the company. Near the main office were the buildings that housed the largest papermaking machines. The men who worked on these machines habitually spoke of them as being "on this side of the river" and of those to the east of the river as being "on the other side." The soda pulp mill which produced part of the wood pulp used in the process was also "on this side of the river," as was the woodyard, where the cordwood was stored in a pile nearly 100 feet high until it was brought into the soda mill for processing. On the east side of the river, which ran alongside these buildings, was the coating department (where special finishes were added to the plain paper that was made on the paper machine); the machine shop and maintenance department; the power plant; and the finishing department (where the paper was cut into sheets or rolled, inspected, and packed according to the customers' specifications, and shipped). On the easternmost edge of the mill property was located a building housing the research department.

More than two thirds of the personnel of the mill were employed in the paper machine department, where the paper itself was made, and in the finishing department, where the final inspection of the paper took place. Joe Murray, a member of the Harvard Business School faculty, making an extended visit to the mill late in 1947, was particularly interested in these two departments and in the ways in which they were supervised, from the foremen up to Brewster himself. The material in this and the following cases was developed out of more than five years of contacts between the Marshall Company and the Harvard Business School, which culminated in the visit by Murray.

The Operation of the Mill

The logs, brought to the mill by railroad, were carried to the soda mill by conveyor, chipped, mixed with chemicals, "digested" by steam heat to form a pulp, and bleached. Economical operation of this department depended on the many recovery processes whereby the chemicals used in the process were reclaimed for further use. This department normally maintained a twenty-four-hour reserve of pulp supply for the paper machines.

Operations in the papermaking department proper began with the beater rooms, where the pulp was prepared for the paper machines. The purchased pulp in sheet form, soda pulp from the company's mill, paper waste recovered from the later stages of the operations, filling materials, dyes, water, and other ingredients were mixed together in the beaters according to specifications for each order of paper. From the beaters the prepared stock was pumped to the paper machines in adjoining rooms and buildings. Several hours' supply of pulp prepared for use by the paper machines was maintained in the beaters. Each of the two groups of machines was served by a beater room, and each machine was served by one or more separate beaters.

The paper machines varied in size. The largest was approximately seventy yards long and cost about a million dollars. At the end of the war the company had rebuilt two of its largest paper machines to combine the coating and papermaking processes and at the same time to increase their speed and capacity. The use of these combined machines was a major recent development in the industry. Another machine was being rebuilt in June, 1947, to enlarge its speed and capacity; it was not, however, to receive coating equipment. Furthermore, plans for rebuilding two more of the largest machines were in their final stages.

The operation at the paper machine was largely one of matting the fibers to form a continuous paper sheet. The stock was pumped into a head box at the beginning of the paper machine, from which it flowed onto an endless wire screen traveling rapidly. As it traveled, the "wire" moved from side to side with a vibrating motion which matted the fiber. Thus a wet, weak paper was formed. From this wire, much of the water which carried the fibers to the wire dropped through into a pit below. Most of the rest of the process on the paper machine was one of drying the paper. Near the end of the wire screen, the paper passed over suction boxes and a suction roll; then it went under press rolls which squeezed the water out; and finally, it passed along a series of steam-heated drying rolls. At the end of these drying rolls, it was passed through a vertical series of steel rolls, called calender rolls, where a smooth, hard finish was put on the paper.

As it left the calender stacks, the paper was wound on a reel. When this reel was full, it was moved to the winding equipment (the final section of the paper machines), where it was rewound as it was trimmed and cut into rolls of the required widths. This entire process, from the time the stock left the beaters until the paper was wound into rolls at the end of the paper machine, was continuous and on some machines reached speeds up to 750 feet per minute. The paper machines maintained a one- or two-day backlog of work for the coating and finishing departments.

From the paper machines the rolls might be sent in any one of four directions for further processing in the remainder of the mill. They might be sent to the coating department if the order required a certain kind of surface on the paper. There, a liquid coating would be applied, dried, and calendered to give a smooth surface. On the other hand, the paper might be sent to the supercalendering department, if a coated grade was not ordered, but a supercalendered finish was required. If the surface of the paper as it left the paper machines was as ordered, the rolls of paper might be sent directly to either the cutters or the rewinders, where the paper would either be cut into flat sheets of required size and inspected to remove defective sheets or be rewound and inspected for shipping as rolls. Sheet paper from the cutters was sent to another part of the finishing department, where it was sorted by grades, inspected again, packed in boxes or on skids made in the box shop, and prepared for shipment. The rolls were wrapped and sent to the shipping room.

Beginning with the beaters, the paper was manufactured under individual production orders sent out from the scheduling office. Many of these orders contained specifications for one of a large variety of standard grades. In the great majority of cases the orders included variations to suit individual customers' requirements. The few orders that were sent to the mill for purposes of building up inventory followed standard specifications exactly. A smaller proportion of the orders were for specialty items; these also involved numerous variations to suit the individual customer.

In scheduling production, the office had to take into account the wide variety of characteristics among the paper machines. The scheduling office, headed by Mr. Elcott, performed the complex job of assigning individual customers' orders, which were seldom exactly alike, to the machines that were best suited to handle them. Elcott was concerned with such matters as the width of the machine in relation to the order, the weight of paper the machine was designed to dry effectively, and the type and grades that he had been scheduling for the crews on particular machines in the past and with which they were therefore familiar. The orders were changed on nearly all machines at least once every two or three days and frequently several times a day. The scheduling personnel arranged the orders so as to utilize the width of the machines most efficiently and to minimize the variations in the furnish and in the machine adjustments that would be necessary in the mill. This personnel was skilled in achieving the maximum economical utilization of the paper machines.

The control room was located on the western side of the river in a building that spanned the river and served as a bridge between the two sides of the plant. Here, the first supervisory step was taken in the continuous inspection process of making high-quality paper. Although the hands on the paper machines inspected their own work and their foremen kept a close eye on the quality of the paper as it was being made, it was in this control room that the inspectors looked over the samples sent in hourly from each machine. The paper received two types of testing: mechanical and visual. Test girls carried on continuous testing of certain physical and chemical characteristics of the paper which were important in terms of the use for which the paper was intended, including basic weight, bulk, bursting strength, tearing strength, opacity, ash content, acidity, porosity, and certain other characteristics. The inspectors themselves looked every hour for such things as surface characteristics, fiber formation, dirt, color, and similar matters. All the supervisory personnel visited the control room periodically to look over the samples and test results and to exchange information. It was here that decisions were often reached and instructions issued for the most efficient handling of the orders in the later stages of the production process. For example, the specifications of an order might call for no further processing after it left the paper machines. Samples in the control room, however, might indicate that an inadequate finish was currently being put on the paper at the paper machine. The rolls of paper, therefore, would be sent to the supercalendering department to bring the finish up to standard.

These test results often indicated changes that could be made at the paper machine before the order was completed. The runners who brought the samples hourly from the machines also brought back to the machines the results of these control room tests. From this information the machine hands were often able to make adjustments that brought the paper within specifications for the order.

A similar control room was operated in the coating department to maintain the efficiency of the coating and calendering work done there. The supercalendering department also took regular samples of the paper being supercalendered for visual checks on the quality of its work.

From river water and wood pulp to the finished product, the work of producing paper that was satisfactory to the customer was highly complex. The characteristics of each of the ingredients—water, pulp, filler, sizing, color, and other materials—were never exactly predictable or controllable. The possible combinations of ingredients were numberless. From the pulp mill through the paper mill, an infinite number of combinations of mechanical adjustments were possible in order to get a limited range of desired results. The effects of some of these tended to conflict with each other or cancel out. Many of the adjustments to keep the paper within the tolerances specified by the established standard grades and by the customers had to be made while the paper was running through the machines. On the paper machines, more than one hundred of these adjustments were possible, and less than half a dozen automatic devices had been found useful in controlling them. The customers' specifications were exacting, since printing presses were often set to work to paper thicknesses controlled to the third decimal place, and the imprint of ink on paper had to be exactly controlled, both physically and chemically.

The Mill Organization

While the president, the treasurer, and the vice president in charge of sales had their offices in a large eastern city, Brewster, the vice president in charge of production, had his office at the mill (see Exhibit 1). Brewster carried on the internal administration of the mill without detailed supervision by the head office. He was responsible for deciding on capital expenditures, with the approval of the board of directors. He had full responsibility for labor relations. He was accountable to the president and board of directors for keeping costs down and production up. Brewster kept the amount of detail he handled at a minimum in order to have ample time to consider many external relationships of the mill, such as those with the state and federal governments and with the public, and many other long-range problems. Brewster was assisted by John Graham, the production manager; Richard Shaw, the chief engineer; a purchasing agent; a director of research; and a personnel manager.

Leverett Perrin, shown on the organization chart as reporting directly to the treasurer in the city office, spent all his time at the plant. He not only handled the accounting system and funds for the treasurer but also prepared accounting and statistical reports for Brewster. Perrin was assisted by a staff group which handled the accounting, cost, time-study, payroll, and bonus routines.

Graham, the production manager, was assisted by Paul Blanchard, a younger man who was responsible for the quality control of plain papers (i.e., uncoated papers), and the production and quality of all specialty papers (some of which were uncoated and therefore regarded as "plain" papers in addition to being called "specialties"). Blanchard was assisted by a group known as the specialty department, responsible for quality control of all specialty grades. Graham was assisted also by the staff groups in charge of scheduling, waste control, and testing. Mr. Fletcher, the chief inspector, who worked under Graham, was responsible for the quality of all plain papers produced, both those which were sold as plain paper and those which were later coated. He worked closely with Dave Nichols, superintendent of the paper mill, whose chief concern was production. Bill Phinney, superintendent of the pulp mill (including the woodyard); Mr. Prout, superintendent of the coating department; and Frank Goodwin, superintendent of the

Exhibit 1. MARSHALL COMPANY (A) PRODUCTION ORGANIZATION CHART*

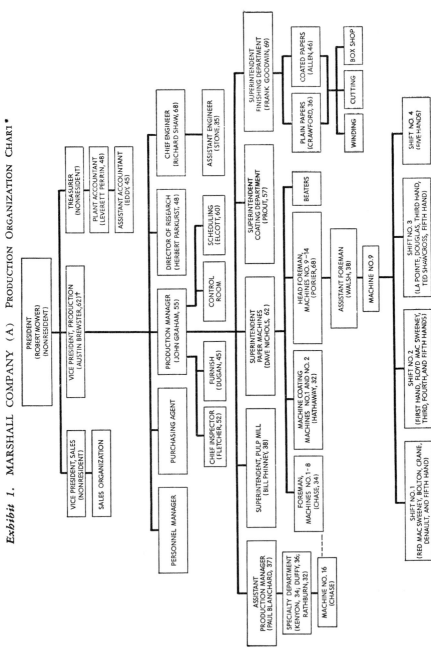

* This organization chart was developed by members of the Harvard Business School research staff for convenience in the use of case material. It is not an official or complete portrayal of the mill organization. The case material will show the actual relationships of the mill personnel, which the organization chart itself does not and cannot indicate.

† Figures represent approximate ages.

finishing department, as well as Nichols, superintendent of the paper mill, were men who had been with the company for many years and in whom the management felt a great deal of confidence. Each of the superintendents was assisted by one or more foremen directly supervising the machine hands.

Of particular significance in the Marshall Company were the close relationships between the sales office and the production group in the paper mill. All salesmen took a fifty-two-week training course in the mill. Telephone calls between the mill and the sales office concerning specific customer problems were extremely frequent. Salesmen visited the mill often to discuss research and quality control problems. The quality control personnel visited the customers from time to to time to help plan new uses for paper or to help solve technical difficulties. These activities played an informal but important part in the organization.

Shaw, the chief engineer, was in charge of the steam and power production, and the maintenance and construction work. He supervised a large and thoroughly trained staff. Brewster relied heavily on the ability of Shaw and his organization to keep the mill in running order and to make major changes from time to time in the production equipment.

The research staff, under the direction of Herbert Parkhurst, consisted of about twenty-five college-trained chemists who worked closely with the sales and production personnel in the development of new uses for paper in a wide variety of industrial and commercial fields, and in the improvement of existing paper and processes. They also made a wide variety of chemical analyses of raw materials received.

The functions of the personnel department were limited mostly to employment and plant safety.

In the present case, it may be noted that the above comments regarding the mill organization and the organization chart in Exhibit 1 were drawn up by Murray. For reasons that will become apparent, Murray found no organization charts in use at the mill.

5. MARSHALL COMPANY (B)

In 1946, when wartime restrictions had been relaxed, the management of the Marshall Company decided to rebuild some of its largest paper machines. The company had found this reconstruction necessary to keep up with the demands of customers, which had been increasing since 1943. The rebuilding of machine No. 9, the third to be undertaken, was completed in June, 1947.

Machine No. 9 had been rebuilt at a cost to the company of a quarter of a million dollars. In its present form, it was expected to be one of the biggest and fastest machines in the mill. The process of rebuilding, carried out by the engineering department of the mill in close collaboration with the company which had originally designed the machine, had required six weeks. During that time the regularly assigned papermaking crews of No. 9 had worked around the machine doing general cleanup and whatever other duties they could manage.

On the morning of Sunday, June 29, 1947, Joe Murray, a member of the Harvard Business School faculty, who had been studying the operations of the Marshall Company for several weeks, went into the mill to watch the starting up of machine No. 9 for the first time following its rebuilding.

The day before, Dave Nichols, the mill superintendent, had remarked to Murray that the machine crews would be glad to resume their regular work as papermakers. He was aware, however, that the changes on the machine involved serious problems for the men, and he was concerned about making the transition as easy as possible for them. An upset on the paper machines was a serious matter, since both management and the men regarded the machines as the point around which the work of all the other departments focused.

It was because of these considerations and because of general interest throughout the mill, that Murray wanted to be on hand when No. 9 was started up. Synchronizing the various parts of the machine was expected to be a painstaking job, probably requiring several days. In addition, many parts of the machine were new; in particular, the drying rolls had been enlarged, and considerable new automatic equipment had been added. Before the rebuilding the machine had run at an average of 420 feet a minute; when first started up again, it would have to move at only about 200 feet, gradually working up to an expected average of 750 feet a minute as the bearings loosened up and the crew learned to handle it at that rate. These changes meant that the crews not only had to learn to handle the new equipment, but also had to make a double adjustment in their own movements, first working more slowly than they had before and then developing greater speed than ever before as the machine worked up to its maximum. Nichols said that he expected maximum speed to be attained in about eight weeks.

The entire crew assisted in starting a run of paper through a machine. When the pulp had built up on the wire so that the fiber cohered and the wet paper was sufficiently strong to support its own weight for a few inches, the first hand turned on a vertical jet of water which cut the moving stock into two streams. The wider stream was allowed to fall off the wire into a pit. The narrower stream formed a moving strip about a foot wide. The first hand turned on a flow of compressed air which lifted this strip and carried it to the first felt. The felt was an endless conveyor, the same width as the wire, which carried the paper under the first press roll. The press roll squeezed much of the remaining water out of the paper.

These steps were repeated when the second hand fed the strip of paper from the first felt onto a second one, which also carried it under a press roll. From the second press roll the second hand fed the paper into the driers, large steam-heated rolls which dried the paper as it passed over them. Next in line after the driers, and about six feet apart, were two calender stacks, each a vertical series of rolls through which the paper was passed under pressure to give it a hard, smooth finish. From the calenders, it passed to a drum reel, on which it was wound into large rolls called reels.

After the narrow strip was passing properly through the whole machine, the first hand got the signal from one of the crew at the dry end. He then moved the vertical jet of water slowly across the wire at a right angle to the flow of paper. As described above, this jet had cut the paper into two moving streams, one narrow and one wide. As the jet moved across the paper, the narrow strip gradually widened. By the time the jet had reached the far side of the paper, what had originally been a narrow strip was now the entire width of the paper passing from the wire on through the rest of the paper machine. Sometimes, the first hand moved the jet across as soon as the paper was well started into the driers, but before it had reached the drum reel. Completed reels were moved to the winding equipment, located about ten feet behind the drum reel, where they were cut and rewound into rolls of specified widths.

Every point in the process at which the paper was handled manually was a potential trouble spot. One reason was that most of the hand operations occurred at points where there were gaps in the machinery over which the paper had to support its own weight. Another reason was that the speed at which the paper was fed into the appropriate roll had to be synchronized with the speed of the machinery or a break would occur. The crew members needed considerable skill, therefore, to handle the paper at these spots.

The crew had to be alert to control many adjustments at every stage in the operation. These adjustments were intended to control the texture of the paper, its thickness, finish, and to some extent its content; to prevent the paper from having cuts, wrinkles, holes, slime spots, and other defects; to regulate the speed, heat, and other factors in the operation of the machine, and in other ways to control the quality and speed of output.

To keep No. 9 running twenty-four hours a day required four shifts of five-man crews; throughout the mill the standard shift was six hours. The smooth operation of the machine required close co-operation among the members of the machine crew. Although there was a commonly accepted division of labor among the men on the crews, Murray knew that it was not rigidly adhered to. Roughly, the first hand (who was also known as the machine tender, runner, or papermaker) had over-all responsibility for the operation of the machine and sole responsibility for the "wet end," that section of the machine extending from the headbox to the driers. He controlled the flow of stock into the headbox and onto the wire and made changes in composition of the stock. He frequently consulted the foreman or the chief inspector before making such changes. He made numerous adjustments affecting the quality of the paper, and tested samples regularly at the desk at the "dry end" to check these adjustments. These tests included weighing and examining the samples.

More complicated tests were made in the control room on samples picked up once an hour. Results of all the tests were entered periodically in a machine data sheet kept at the desk of the machine, and the first and second hands examined these reports regularly. Many factors affecting quality which were controllable at the wet end showed up only when the paper was inspected at the dry end. The first hand relied on his second for this information. The first hand also watched at the wet end for trouble such as froth, dirt, lumps in the pulp, and holes in the wire. In addition to his work at the wet end, he handled much of the paper work at the desk. Although their duties were at the wet end except for the desk work, in practice many first hands spent a good deal of time at the dry end, relying on a mechanical signal (on No. 9 machine, this signal was a photoelectric cell) to warn them of breaks on the wet end.

The other four men on the crew worked at the dry end, that portion of the machine beginning with the drying rolls and extending through the winding equipment. The second hand was formally responsible for the dry end. He watched closely for defects in the paper coming off the driers. Many kinds of defects warned him that there was trouble in the machinery which required immediate action. In correcting certain kinds of defects, he worked very closely with the first hand. The second hand also took care of some of the tests and paper work. In addition to these duties, he supervised the work of the third, fourth, and fifth hands more closely than did the first hand, since their work was entirely at the dry end. For this reason, he was often described as the man who was "really responsible for the crew." The primary work of the third hand was on the winding equipment, cutting and winding the reels off the paper machine into rolls of the sizes specified by the order. In this work, he was assisted by the fourth and fifth hands, who also did the simple manual labor around the machine.

When Murray came into the mill on Sunday morning, he counted about forty men already working on the machine. Besides the machine crew and the wire crew, which were under the direction of Nichols, there were mechanics, carpenters, pipers, and others from the engineering department. Mr. Stone, assistant to Richard Shaw, the chief engineer, came in a little later and stayed several hours. During the day a number of workers also came into the room to watch operations. Men from machine No. 14, next door, the next machine scheduled for rebuilding, stood in the doorway whenever matters on their own machine did not demand their attention. Several people from the control room came in to watch for a while. Mr. Fletcher, the chief inspector, who was in charge of the routine operations of the mill this Sunday, spent as much time by No. 9 as his other work would permit. John Graham, production manager of the company, was there all day. Nichols periodically reported to him about recent developments and his plans for taking care of them. Graham would characteristically nod his head when Nichols was finished, but make no comment. Nichols, in talking to Murray about this, later said: "Mr. Graham doesn't often say much to me when I am starting up a machine. Later on, he will tell me some of the things he thought might have been improved—even some of the little things. But now, he won't bother me." Most of the men from the production office spent at least a couple of hours around No. 9. The three top men from the finishing department and some men from the pulp mill were also present for short visits. Machine No. 9 occupied a room by itself, which was filled most of the day with men observing the starting-up of the big new machine.

Murray particularly wanted to see the reactions of the men and the way those in charge handled the men. Soon after he arrived, he walked over and greeted Nichols, who was making some adjustments on the automatic gauges at the wet end.

"We'll get her rolling this afternoon," Nichols said, without preliminaries. "We're working on the gauges on the hydraulic rollers; the mechanics are working on them now. We can tell the pressure on the rolls from those gauges over on the wall panel. We've never had that before. If it works, we can tell how much pressure is being put on the paper. We'll try it before we start the run and see if it works. There are a lot of new things on this machine."

"There certainly are," Murray agreed. "Have you given the men any special instructions about the new equipment?"

"It's too early to give instructions yet," Nichols replied. "I have to see how it runs. It's new to me, too. Every machine is different, no matter if it is made by the same manufacturer to the same blueprint. You think when you've seen one machine, you've seen them all, but that's not true. I learn as I go along." He glanced around him. "Of course, the men are 'on nerves,' too," he added. "They don't know what to expect."

"They're all a little anxious," Murray observed.

"Yes, indeed," Nichols replied, "as anxious as I am myself. I expect some accidents. We always have some when we start up a new machine; somebody gets hurt." Nichols walked over and joined a group, including both machine crewmen and mechanics, who were installing a roller. Several men raised the heavy bar with their shoulders, while one of their number adjusted its position with a wrench. The latter handed his wrench to Nichols when he came up, and Nichols worked with it until he was satisfied. The job took about fifteen minutes.

In the meantime, Murray talked with Mr. Hunter, an engineer from the company which had originally built the machine. Murray had chatted with him occasionally during the rebuilding.

"What do you think of her now?" Murray asked.

"Well, I'm pretty jittery," Hunter said. "I'm always jittery when we start up a machine. There are so many parts that require nice adjustment. Each one has to be timed so that it will move a little faster than the one before."[1]

"That means a lot of points require careful judgment," Murray observed.

"It certainly does," Hunter said. "It's almost impossible to calculate them. You have to find out by trying, and sometimes you make mistakes."

Nichols had been working on No. 9 constantly since 7:00 A.M. About 11:00 o'clock, he gave instructions to start up the machine but to run no stock over it. After listening for a few minutes to the almost deafening noise from the hundreds of new bearings, Nichols went out to his own office for a smoke. Murray followed him.

> JOE MURRAY: How's it going?
> DAVE NICHOLS: Pretty well.
> MURRAY: Sounds as if it were running pretty heavy.
> NICHOLS: Sure is. She tightened up on me. She'll sound better after a couple of weeks—like a car, you know. You have to break her in easy. Of course, you know, the engine broke down about an hour ago, but I think we got it fixed temporarily. Just didn't have enough power to turn her over. They'll change the pulley on the engine tonight, to give it more of a hold. I'll run stock over her for a while this afternoon to see if she draws O.K.; then run her tonight to see if she will loosen up.

That afternoon, Nichols ordered the first hand to start stock through the headbox. It ran freely for eight or ten minutes, building up on the wire. Gradually, as the load on the engine increased, the wire began to slow up, and the stock thickened. The man nearest the switch stopped the machine, but the stock on the wire overflowed. In a moment pulp and water were running all over the floor. There were a number of hoses for washdowns and other purposes around the base of the machine. The men standing nearest the hoses, both machine hands and mechanics, immediately picked up hoses and started washing down the wire. Hunter commented to Murray: "If it ever dries on them, they'll have an awful time." One of the men brought out a supply of hip boots, and most of the men put them on. Nichols did not take time to do so; he was working with the men all the time. All of the spectators retreated out of the way of the running stock. One of the men washing down the wire was splashed by a man handling the hose on the opposite

---

[1] By maintaining a slightly higher speed at each subsequent unit of the machine, it was possible to keep a certain degree of tension on the moving paper.

side of the machine. He grinned and splashed back. The exchange lasted only a few seconds, and no one else paid any attention to it.

Nichols worked on the machine until about 4:30; by that time, nothing more could be done until the engineers made some further adjustments. The men were allowed to go home. After talking with the engineers and the night supervisor, who had just come in, Nichols also left.

On Monday morning the 6:00 o'clock shift again was occupied with trying to get No. 9 started. Murray noticed that several men from the night shifts who had not worked the night before, since only the engineers had been needed, came in to see how the machine was working. During the morning, Murray sat for a moment on the window sill beside two of the regular crewmen, Ernie Crane and Denault. "So you're going to be making paper again," Murray said.

Crane replied: "Oh, yeah; we've had a five weeks' vacation."

"How do you feel about all this?" Murray asked, nodding toward the machine.

"Oh, fine, it needed to be done," Crane replied. "It will take a while to get used to it, though."

"You mean all the new equipment?" Murray asked.

"Yes; and then, on the old machine, we knew where to step and where to put our hands and where everything was. It was just like walking—you didn't have to think about it. Now, it's all different," Denault explained.

"It makes you kind of jittery," Murray observed.

"A little nervous," Crane agreed. "You have to throw the paper on the pulleys at just the right speed so that it catches. There's quite a trick to it, but I'm not like some guys. They worry all the time: 'Will this go wrong? Can I do this?' When they feel like that, they have accidents. They get nervous and move a little faster than the machine. I used to be like that, but not any more."

"Oh, well, in five or six weeks, we'll get used to this machine, too," Denault joined in. "It's a lot faster now. This will do 750 feet a minute."

"Does that mean it's harder work to keep up with it?" Murray asked.

"Oh, no," the men replied. "The machine helps you. These gadgets were put on it to do things we had to do before. It's really easier to have them."

At that point the men moved over to the machine. On Sunday and so far on Monday the crew members had stood watching whenever they were not actually working on the machine or handling a trial run.

Sometimes, they approached the machine and appeared to be studying it. Other times, they stood back by the windows. Occasionally, they performed small mechanical tasks on the machine, such as helping to shift the rollers and adjust them. The first hand was in contact with Nichols or Jack Walsh, the assistant foreman, continually; and no special message to him was necessary when Nichols was ready to start the stock over the wire. When the first hand mounted the headbox to start the trial run, the other crew members stood ready. As soon as the first hand moved over to the wire, the rest of the crew came running to help start the paper through the machine. Al Bolton, the second hand, climbed up on the machine by the press rolls and started to feed the pulp onto the felts. It went fairly smoothly; but when he tried to feed the strip from the second felt into the drying roll, he ran into difficulty.

At this spot, accurate timing was essential. To perform the operation, the second hand stood balanced on foot rests placed several feet above the floor, straddling the walkway between the wet and dry ends. Facing the strip of paper coming off the press roll, he picked up the end of the strip, passed it into the air in a hand-over-hand motion until his timing was synchronized with the speed of the paper coming off the roll, then twisted his body to follow the motion of the paper and tossed it onto ropes which were to pick it up and guide it through the driers. If he passed the paper only a little too fast or too slowly, it broke. As Bolton got up on the foot rests, most of the men in the room gathered to watch. He tried half a dozen times, but each time the paper broke just as he got it into the ropes. After several minutes, Nichols, who was standing just behind him, put his hand on Bolton's leg without speaking. Bolton immediately got down; and the first hand, who had been standing in the walkway watching, climbed up. His second attempt was successful. Nichols said later, in referring to this incident: "Al's all right. He was just getting nervous."

The paper started several times; but each time, it broke within a few minutes; adjustments had to be made on the machine, and the stock was started again. Nichols once fed the paper into the driers himself. Once Poirier, the elderly foreman, made two attempts to feed the paper into the ropes but did not succeed. That time the stock was so thin that the pulp was not strong enough to support its own weight. Each time the paper was passed from the wet to the dry end, Nichols stood beside or behind the man doing it. He frequently offered suggestions. When trouble developed with the paper winding on the drum reel, Nichols went over and worked with the men. Even when there was no specific problem, he stood near the men, occasionally talking to them. The men, too, were constantly moving around the machine or standing where they could watch certain key points. Only occasionally did they sit in the windows for a moment to catch the little breeze that was coming in.

At one such moment, Bolton remarked to Murray: "I'll give you a tip on Dave Nichols. When he slaps that right foot down hard, that means he's nervous."

Murray noticed a number of times during the day that Nichols was "stomping," and it seemed to occur when something happened on the machine and he was not at the trouble spot. At the end of the day, Nichols remarked to Murray: "I always get worried and excited when we start up a new machine. You could see I was nervous, but it went pretty well."

During the next week, Nichols spent most of his time on No. 9, working along with the men, helping to make the final adjustments on the machine, and giving the men guidance in handling the problems that arose.

Murray also spent a good deal of time around No. 9 during this week and the following weeks; thus, he had opportunity to observe the crews in action and to talk to many of them. When the machine had been running about three weeks, Murray observed one day that the paper was breaking repeatedly after leaving the calender stacks. He had seen Red MacSweeney at the dry end talking with the crew and helping them make various adjustments, particularly in the amount of pressure on the calender stacks. The paper continued to break. The men finally agreed that to make an effective adjustment, they would have to shut down the machine, and this they were reluctant to do. Consequently, they sent for Nichols. A few minutes later, Nichols came into the room and went directly to the drum reel. He talked to Bolton for a moment, looked the situation over, and suggested that the difficulty might be handled by adjusting a spreader bar, which was designed to correct uneven tension in the moving paper. Nichols started to turn the adjusting screws at one end of the bar, calling directions to Bolton, who was working at the other end. After experimenting with various degrees of tension in several of the screws, they finally got the paper winding without a break. As soon as this was accomplished, Nichols walked away.

Murray had noticed that as the month advanced, Nichols took a less and less active part on the machine. When he was around, he gradually moved back toward the wall so that he could observe the men. He came near the machine only to make a specific suggestion or to work on a definite problem. By the end of the month the machine was running at a speed of 500 feet.

Murray also noticed that a great many of the actions of the men were dictated by some occurrence on the machine that demanded immediate attention. This was particularly true of the third, fourth, and fifth hands, and decreasingly so for the second and first. These two men had more time to move back and forth on the machine and to sit and talk with any of the hands who were free for the moment. Frequently, the men went behind the machine together for smokes. Asked about this latter practice, one hand told Murray that smoking around the machines was not allowed because of fire insurance regulations. "The company built a $10,000 rest room for us," he said, "but we don't like to be away from the machines long enough to go down there. If you are around the machine, you might be able to avoid trouble—like lots of times, you can catch wrinkles that would make bad paper if they went through."

On his way out, Murray passed one of the other machines scheduled for rebuilding in the near future. After some talk with the first hand about their interest in No. 9, Murray mentioned the changes planned in Farmer's machine. "Yeah," Farmer said, "I'm glad I won't be running it when it's rebuilt. Too much trouble, with the coating machinery they're going to add on."

"What about the rest of the crew?" Murray inquired.

"The second hand won't be on," Farmer replied. "He's not fast enough. He's been on this machine twenty-five years, and he's slowing down on some of the work. The third hand helps him with it. They wanted him to go on one of the slow machines two years ago, but he wouldn't do it."

After the rebuilt machine had been in operation for four weeks, Murray decided to appraise his observations. He felt that, clearly understood, what he had seen would help him to grasp the problems of Graham and Nichols in administering this part of the mill. Although the changes on No. 9 were less sweeping than those contemplated for some other parts of the mill, Murray believed that an understanding of the way the organization had adjusted to them would be helpful in following the development of the expansion program.

6. MARSHALL COMPANY (C)

FOR THE month following the starting-up of No. 9 paper machine, Joe Murray, a member of the Harvard Business School faculty studying the Marshall Company paper mill, spent a good deal of time around it. During this month, he found a number of things about the relations among the men that interested him.

Murray had already observed on machine No. 9, as on the other machines in the mill, that while the duties of the first hands were mainly at the wet end, most of them also spent much of their time at the dry end.[1] Since machine No. 9 had only a single calender stack prior to its rebuilding, the first hands on that machine were helping the second hands learn to manage the two stacks on the rebuilt machine. When there was a break, the first hands often jumped in with the other men; in case of a bad break, they even helped to pick up the waste paper or "broke." When everything was going well, the first hand often sat on the edge of the table after he finished making his samples and chatted with any hands not occupied at the moment. The first hands discussed with their second and third hands the problems of handling the machine and of running the various orders on which they were working. Frequently, they joined the other men at the back of the room for a smoke.

Aside from his contacts with the second hand, the first hand had comparatively little working contact with the rest of his crew. The second hand actually directed the others, trained them, answered their questions, and worked directly with them on many occasions such as changing the core on the drum reel or handling a break at the dry end. The third, fourth, and fifth hands worked more closely together, since they handled the winding equipment. They worked elsewhere on the machine only in changing the core on which the paper was rolled or in case of a break at the dry end, although they usually gathered to watch when there was a break at the wet end. When they were not actually working, they wandered around the machine watching the others and asking questions.

Murray was interested in watching the crews when there was a break

---

[1] See Marshall Company (B) for details about machine No. 9.

at the dry end. One day, for instance, he was near the machine while Red MacSweeney's crew was on. Suddenly he heard a shout, which he knew meant trouble. Ernie Crane, the third hand, had noticed a break between the drying rolls and the first calender stack. As he shouted to the rest of the crew, he stepped into the narrow walkway and started stripping off the narrow shred of paper coming from the rolls. The rest of the crew, with the exception of the first hand, who was occupied at the wet end, arrived at a run. There was very little space for the waste to pile up between the drying rolls and the calender stack. The fourth hand, next to arrive at the trouble spot, picked up a spike with which to separate a narrow strip of paper from the broken sheet. By holding this spike against the paper as it passed over the last drying roll, he split the paper into two widths, one wide and one narrow. Al Bolton, the second hand, attempted without success to feed the narrow strip between the calender rolls in the first stack. The fourth and fifth hands attempted to tramp down the waste, but it quickly piled up a foot or more deep in spite of their efforts. Grasping a narrow bar only inches from the hot drying rolls, they stood on the heap of waste paper and kicked it under the machine to get it out of the way.

Bolton finally succeeded in getting the narrow strip of paper moving properly between the calender rolls. While this strip went through the rolls, the remaining widths of the sheet continued to pile up before the rolls as waste. The third hand then ran across the machine through the heaped-up waste, drawing his spike across the paper coming over the last drying roll and thus widening the strip that Bolton had fed through the calender rolls. The paper kept breaking, and the procedure was repeated six or seven times. The men worked quickly, keeping out of one another's way in the narrow space. When the paper was going through again, the process was repeated at the second calender stack and again at the drum reel to start the paper winding. In each case the first man on the spot performed the first function necessary, no matter which hand he was.

Watching this operation, Murray was reminded of something Len Shawcross, one of the older first hands, had told him. Teddy Shawcross, his son, worked in another crew on No. 9. Len said that Teddy had been on his shift when he first began to work on a paper machine; but after he had made a good start, Shawcross said to him: "Son, it would be better for you if you were on someone else's crew. I'll jump on you quicker than anybody else on my crew. Besides, now you are working for the company and the crew, and for me, too. It would be more to your interest to be on a crew where you could work for the team without having to think about your father." Shawcross concluded: "Teddy thought it over; and after a while, he came around to my way of thinking. He is on the early shift now."

Talking with Bolton after the paper was again winding properly, Murray remarked: "I'm interested in the way you fellows jump to the breaks. You don't waste any time getting there, and the first fellow on the spot goes ahead."

"Oh, sure, you have to," Bolton said. "The thing is, you all have to work together. You can't just do your own job; you have to pull with the crew."

"I wonder if that explains what I saw this morning." Murray said. "There was a break on the wet end, and I noticed your third hand feeding the paper into the drying rolls." Bolton had let Crane, the third hand, manage the paper through the several steps between the wire and the driers. He had tried to show Crane how to use an air hose to get all the slack out of the paper and make it lie flat. Crane was unable to get the paper perfectly flat; and the result was that after a few minutes' run, it would break. Several times, Bolton let Crane manage all these steps, but it broke each time. Bolton then took care of the air hose while Crane fed the paper, and it went through without a break.

When Murray mentioned this incident to him, Bolton replied that he had been training Crane in second hand's work. Murray inquired about this, and Bolton explained that each man was technically responsible for training the man under him. However, since the second hand was "really the active boss of the men on the machine," he carried the main responsibility for training the younger men. The first hand trained the second to be a first hand; the second trained all the men under him. Murray asked whether Bolton "put the men through a regular course of sprouts." But Al replied: "Oh, no. You really just learn by doing. You master your own job, and then you watch the next fellow working, and do as much as you can. Of course, some of the guys think if you do your own job and then stop, that's what you get paid for. But you don't learn anything that way."

"Isn't there any feeling that you cut in on someone else's job by learning it?" Murray asked.

"Oh, no. You can do as much as you know how," Bolton said. "A good man will keep you busy answering his questions; and when he does that, you bring him along. Of course, the thing is, you've gotta keep learning so you know more than the other guys." Bolton paused and seemed for several seconds to be thinking intently. "There's one fellow," he said, hesitantly. "He's no good. He came over from the other side of the river during the war and worked up to be second hand. Now, guys are coming back from the service who know more than he does. Men under him are better than he is, but he gives orders and pretends to know more than anyone else. No one likes him."

Murray had a good guess as to whom Bolton meant. He had long been aware that there was a difference between crews, and one stood out in his mind as the least effective of the four shifts. This crew was headed by La Pointe, a man of about 60. La Pointe stayed strictly at the wet end and did not come near the dry end except to work at the desk or make his samples. Even these jobs he did quickly and hurried back to the wet end. Murray had seen him talk to the rest of his crew only once; on that occasion, La Pointe came down to the dry end, issued an order, and immediately returned to his post near the wire. Murray had a clear impression that La Pointe was afraid of the rebuilt machine. It had struck him early that La Pointe set the few automatic controls and then showed great reluctance to change anything unless there was a break or a change in the kind of paper to be run.

Kenneth Douglas, the second hand on La Pointe's crew, to whom Bolton referred, was a big man who looked younger than his 50 years. Murray had observed that Douglas yelled at the men a good deal but did not seem to get as quick results when trouble arose as did the other second hands. Although there seemed to be little small talk among the men on this crew, Murray found Douglas pleasant enough to talk with. He described one of his men as "a good Joe." "Everybody likes him," Douglas said; "he always has something to say that makes you laugh."

The third, fourth, and fifth hands on La Pointe's crew spent most of their time working on the winding equipment. They handled their equipment with less skill than the men on the other shifts, and they seemed to have a great many breaks in the winding. Murray knew that on all shifts the third, fourth, and fifth hands worked the most steadily; but on this crew alone, they worked continuously, almost never taking time to talk with the others or to duck out for a smoke.

Because of what Bolton had told him, Murray became interested in La Pointe's crew. Several days after his conversation with Bolton, he noticed a new man working on the crew. He mentioned it to James, a young college graduate who was "going through the mill" as part of his training for an administrative position. "Isn't Teddy ordinarily on Red MacSweeney's crew?" Murray asked.

"He used to be," James replied. "This crew has just been changed. It was the poorest crew, so Teddy was brought in to help even it up."

Murray wondered whether the men knew why the transfer had been made; and James replied: "Oh, I think so. The output figures are kept posted at the desk. If one crew is always 10,000 pounds behind and hasn't had breakdowns, you know there's something wrong."

"You mean everyone knows there is a difference between crews?" Murray ventured.

"Oh, sure," James responded. "For instance, Red MacSweeney's crew is as good as we have. This one, La Pointe's crew, is so excitable. The second hand is the most excitable guy I have ever seen. The minute something goes wrong, he's all up in the air, so the rest of them get excited and don't know what to do."

Murray wanted to know what had become of the man whom Teddy replaced. James did not know for sure but thought he had been sent to the beater room, where less skill was required.

That afternoon, Murray mentioned the change to Red MacSweeney, who was first hand on the crew from which Teddy had been taken, and whom Murray knew fairly well. MacSweeney replied that the fourth hand on La Pointe's crew had just been sent to work in the beater rooms because he had not done his job properly. "It wasn't really the boy's fault," MacSweeney added. Murray thought he showed a trace of bitterness. "The kid is a little slow to catch on, but he could have been trained all right by a good second hand. Douglas just didn't teach the kid what to do; so of course it looked to the bosses as though the boy wasn't doing his job. It was really Douglas's fault, but he blamed it on the boy. That's what happens when a guy won't take responsibility for his own mistakes."

"Couldn't La Pointe do anything for him?" Murray asked.

"Well," MacSweeney said, "Douglas and La Pointe are a pair. La Pointe has been a first hand for twenty years, and none of us can understand how he has gotten by. He's not too good a papermaker, and he certainly is poor with the men. It shows in the crew, too. The men get discouraged and don't care. Instead of working together, they all pull against each other."

"What do you mean?" Murray inquired.

"Well," MacSweeney said, "for instance, when they see something wrong, if it is not their particular responsibility, they don't say anything about it. And when there's a break, they don't work together. They don't jump so fast to catch it, either."

Murray asked about Teddy, who had taken the fourth hand's place, and MacSweeney grinned. "It's not definite yet," he replied. "He used to be our fifth hand. He's a nice kid and could handle the work, but he didn't really want the promotion because he didn't want to work under

Douglas. Finally, he took it when the personnel man promised him he could come back to this shift if he couldn't get along with Douglas."

MacSweeney's comments caught Murray's interest, and he became alert for the opinions of the management group regarding this crew. Dave Nichols, for instance, approached Murray a day or so later, while La Pointe's crew was operating No. 9 machine, and remarked that he had been having trouble with this crew. To locate the bottleneck, he said, he had spent his "loafing time" around No. 9 for a couple of weeks. In this time, it had become clear to him that the root of the difficulty was the fourth hand, who did not seem to Nichols to be doing his work. Consequently, Nichols had sent the man to work in the beater rooms, where there was a necessary minimum of work to do and he would not hold anyone up if he did no more than that.

Paul Blanchard, in the course of a conversation with Murray, said there was some feeling that La Pointe was not good enough to take the higher speed on the new machine. Production records, however, indicated that he had held his own over a period of time. "It is true," Blanchard said, "that he doesn't like the speed, and maybe he doesn't make as good quality as some of the others, but he always makes just about good enough paper to get by. When he gets the machine set, he is afraid to make any changes for fear he will get into difficulties. The others are always trying to do a little better, and they know more about their machines; but it doesn't show up in the records."

On another occasion, John Graham, the production manager, commented:

La Pointe should never have been put on No. 9 in the first place. The speed of the machine scares him. As soon as he gets things set, he doesn't dare make a change, no matter what goes wrong. In general, that system works pretty well, so that his unsatisfactory work does not show up too much in the production records. He knows how to keep out of trouble. Still, when something goes wrong on the wet end of the machine, the only thing he can think of is to grab a hose and start washing down the screen. That, of course, has to be done, since if you don't wash it down quick enough, you can get into a lot of trouble. Still, there are a lot of other things to be done. We will never get that crew right until we move him. I know he ought to be moved, and I think Dave Nichols knows it. However, some of the other foremen don't know it yet. They will find out in a while, and then we can move him. We will have to put him over on the other side of the river on one of the slower machines. He may not like it very much, and the foremen will not like it. But sooner or later, everyone will agree that he will have to be moved, and then we will be able to do it.

"You did move one of his hands, didn't you?" Murray asked.

"Yes," Graham answered. "He was a big awkward boy who I don't think will ever make a hand. His father wanted him on the machines, so we put him on. But he's an awkward boy, always getting in his own way. Sooner or later, he'll get hurt."

7. MARSHALL COMPANY (D)

Joe Murray, a member of the Harvard Business School faculty, who was studying the Marshall Company paper mill, had been on hand when paper machine No. 9 started up for the first time since its rebuilding, and he had spent considerable time each day observing its operation.[1] In July, 1947, four weeks after No. 9 had started up, Murray heard from Paul Blanchard, the assistant production manager, that the machine was running into trouble. Among other things the new winding equipment ordered for the machine had not arrived; and the old equipment, which was obsolete, kept getting out of adjustment and lagging behind the output of the machine. The crew was having difficulties keeping proper tension on the new calender stacks. The gates, or "slices," which controlled the flow of pulp to the wire, were giving them some kind of trouble.

After talking to Blanchard, Murray went out to the machine to see if he could learn more from Dave Nichols and the men about the present outbreak of trouble.

Murray found Jack Walsh, the foreman of No. 9 machine, sitting by himself by the dry end of the machine. Walsh appeared to be staring at the floor. A dial over his head registered the present machine speed: 600 feet per minute.

> Joe Murray: How well does she run at 600?
> Walsh: Oh, the machine is running O.K., but we're having trouble with the winders. It's all we can do to keep up.
> Murray: How about the slices—are they giving you any trouble?
> Walsh: Yeah.
> Murray: Any ideas what to do about it?
> Walsh: I don't know. Maybe we won't be able to do anything about it. You see the stock coming out from under the slices? It's supposed to flow out flat, but you see those places where it keeps bubbling up in spurts? That makes the paper thicker in some places than others and causes all kinds of trouble. I've never seen anything like it before. There's no way you can set the slices so the stock will flow like it should.
> These slices are part of the new headbox. It's built for high-speed

---

[2] See Marshall Company (B) and (C).

667

operation, and I don't know how it's going to work out. Maybe it'll work all right when we get the machine running about 750, but I don't know. We could try out some ideas now that might fix it; but every time we change anything at the headbox, it changes the paper formation, and that throws the winders all off, so we haven't been able to do much. As far as I'm concerned, I wish we had the old machinery back again. Well, I guess I'll go have a look at No. 14.

After Walsh left, Murray wondered how this difficulty would work out. He knew that Walsh was one of the youngest foremen; he had been foreman for only about a year and had not been in charge of a rebuilt machine before, nor had he ever worked on one. On the other hand, Walsh's supervisor, Nichols, had had a great deal of experience and know-how; and Walsh, like the men, had great respect for Nichols. Nichols had watched Walsh's progress from fifth to first hand on the paper machines and "brought him along" to be foreman.

Murray recalled what Walsh had told him about the way the men handled their own technical problems on the machines. If they ran into difficulties, Walsh said, they tried to fix things up themselves; if they failed, they called him in. Walsh believed that he helped the men sometimes because of his own know-how, sometimes because he brought in a fresh point of view, and sometimes because he was in a position to take responsibility for the execution of an idea they had figured out by themselves.

From what some of the other "bosses" told Murray, he realized that the relationship between Walsh and his men was not accidental. A man did not get much specific training. The other hands and the bosses expected a new man to learn the job from working on it along with the rest of the crew. Once a new man learned his first job, he could stay in it as long as he wanted to. If he wanted to move ahead, it was up to him to watch what was going on, to take the initiative, and to keep asking questions. When the older hands and bosses saw that a new man was the kind that would "jump in there quick" and take hold of things, they would start keeping an eye on him and "bring him along." Nichols, for instance, said that he got a lot of fun out of working with the younger men and watching them grow. In five or six years, he said, you could see a great difference in a man, not just in his ability on the machine, but in his whole personality. During the past year, he had been bringing the young men along to replace first hands and foremen who were getting promotions or retiring, and more such vacancies were still opening up.

The reasons the bosses gave for not providing specific training were that each machine was different, that each crew did things in a different way, that they all "learned something new every day" about their jobs, and especially that they wanted the men to learn to do what they were most interested in doing.

Murray also recalled that on the day when machine No. 9 was starting up, Nichols had explained how he planned to get up production on it. During the first day the machine speed built up to 390 feet per minute.

> DAVE NICHOLS: It seems funny to me working on a machine that's running so slow. I've just finished starting up No. 1 and No. 2, and they're running twice as fast as this one—about 720 to 760 feet per minute. Working on this one throws you all off balance. We'll get the machine broken in after three or four weeks so she'll carry the load all right, but it'll take three or four months before we can get it up to top speed.
>
> It'll take that long to train the men. It's too early to give them instructions yet. I have to see how it runs. I learn as I go along; then I teach the men. Up to 500 feet per minute, things will probably go pretty smooth. But around 500 feet, I expect we'll run into trouble. Well, I'll speed the machine up till the trouble starts, then slack off and figure out what to do about it—and then speed it up some more. At the same time that I'm putting new things on the machine to make it run better, I'll be explaining to the men what to do with them.

On another occasion, Nichols told Murray that he had started working in paper mills when he was 14 and had finished high school while working.

> NICHOLS: In those days, you didn't need a college education like you do now. I came to Marshall when I was 27, and they made me superintendent of five machines. I used to keep everything to myself; when I saw something that ought to be done, I just used to do it. The important thing was that I could do it, not that other people could be trained to do it right. So long as I had the information in my head, everything seemed all right to me. My experience was all my own, and I wouldn't share it with anyone. Then, during the middle 1930's, I had a lot of trouble in my family. Mr. Brewster helped me a lot during that period; and somehow, I got to looking at things another way. I started to think that it was better to help other people, and it has gotten to be a lot of fun watching them grow. When you keep everything to yourself, what have you got when you are gone? When you train someone, he goes right on working for a long while.

In looking to the future, Nichols told Murray that he would like to work at his present job for three or four years more and then continue in some sort of advisory capacity.

NICHOLS: I can't take the responsibility as well as I used to; and in a little while, I would like to turn it over to someone else. Changes are going on all the time in the industry, and you've got to keep up with them if you are going to keep on doing a good job. When machine coating came in, that was a whole new set of problems. We put the coating units on No. 1 and No. 2 and speeded them up, you know. They will produce better than 760 feet per minute. I started them up, and they went well.

We broke in Phil Hathaway to take charge of them. He was trained in the research department and knows a lot about paper. He's a good boy and is coming along well. Right now, I am training him to take over from me. On machines No. 1 and No. 2, I'm not giving them any orders at all. When I think something ought to be done, I tell Phil, and he talks it out with the foremen. Of course, I talk to all the men from time to time myself, but that is a little different. I'm just helping them out where I can. Phil has all the responsibility on those machines. When we convert machines No. 11 and No. 14 to machine coating, I'll put him over there, too. He'll do well.

While Murray was thinking about some of these earlier conversations, Nichols appeared. After a few minutes' conversation, Murray asked: "How about the trouble on the slices?"

Nichols smiled. "Oh, I'm going to put something on to fix that!" He explained in detail how he was going to improve the flow of pulp after it left the slices by putting a spreader bar across the wire a few inches from the slices.

When he had finished, Murray asked: "Does Walsh know about your plans for the spreader bar?"

At this, Nichols grinned broadly. "No, I haven't told him yet. He's got enough to think about now, and there's no use in his trying to look too far ahead."

Murray asked: "Do the crew ever get very discouraged when they speed up the machine and find themselves in trouble?"

"Oh, yes, the younger men get more discouraged than the older men do. The older men are more used to it."

Before leaving, Nichols remarked to Murray that he had told John Graham about his plans for the spreader bar. "Mr. Graham just nodded, as he usually does, but he didn't say anything about it."

8. MARSHALL COMPANY (E)

FOLLOWING ITS entry into the field of specialty papers in the early 1930's, the Marshall Company accepted orders for various items in rapidly increasing numbers. The specialty items were those papers, either plain or coated, which the customers of the Marshall Company further processed to make a finished product. Stock for carbon paper and envelopes were typical of the items which the company produced. The company had entered this field to utilize certain of its paper machines which were too old to produce high-speed commercial printing paper efficiently. Although these machines were "not worth a nickel on the books," according to Austin Brewster, the paper they produced brought a higher profit margin than did many of the standard commercial grades.

The mill made these specialty papers largely according to customers' individual specifications. The sales department, soon after the line was initiated, requested that someone be assigned to handle the production and quality problems that had developed around these specialized orders. Brewster selected for the job Paul Blanchard, who had come to the company upon graduation from a large engineering school and during his three years at the mill had acquired some experience with customers' problems. Brewster assigned Blanchard to work under Will Sawyer, who was responsible for making certain that all the plain paper sold by the company was up to the customers' specifications. Blanchard continued in this work for about ten years, until Sawyer died suddenly in 1943. Blanchard then dropped the supervision of the specialty papers to take over Sawyer's work. Following the precedent set by Sawyer, he reported on his new work directly to John Graham, the production manager, and had full responsibility for the quality standards of the plain paper shipped out of the mill. He could and did hold up any order that did not seem suitable.

Joe Murray, a member of the Harvard Business School faculty, who was studying the operation of the mill in the summer of 1947, held several discussions with Blanchard to learn more about the growth of the specialty group. He had become particularly interested in its relations with the rest of the organization. According to Blanchard, at the time when he took over the plain papers (both standard grades and specialty items), the work he had been doing on specialty papers was largely absorbed by Ned Kenyon, George Duffy, and later Louis Rathbun, with help from Harry Chase in the paper machine department and Tom Sullivan in the coating department. These men constituted a loosely organized specialty department which worked closely with the research department and with each of the operating departments on these specialty grades. They knew more about the requirements on certain of these papers than anyone else in the mill.

When Murray asked Blanchard about the background of some of these men, he found that Kenyon was a college graduate and senior member of this specialty group. He had been trained in the coating department and was well liked there. He remained much interested in the technical problems of coating papers. The coated specialty papers came under his supervision, and his work on them brought him into close contact with Sullivan in the coating department.

Duffy had been trained at Topsfield, a small branch mill of the Marshall Company, where he had gone to work when he graduated from high school. For some years the Topsfield mill had made a very thin tissue paper to be used as "body stock" by customers who manufactured carbon paper. About 1935 the company decided to make paper of this type at the Marshall mill and brought Duffy down to help with the change. Blanchard said that everyone felt Duffy worked out so well that they kept him on to follow all orders for this type of paper.

Rathbun was a comparatively new man in the department and acted largely as a handy man for Kenyon, doing any sort of odd job that Kenyon might want done. Blanchard, in talking to Murray about Rathbun, said that "they found him working as a laborer mixing dyes in the coating department." Rathbun believed that this job gave him severe headaches, and he had to stay out of work for several days at a time.

> PAUL BLANCHARD: Rathbun finally went to see the Baptist deacon about it a few months ago. The deacon spoke to Mr. Brewster, who said he would like to see Rathbun—you know, his door is always open to the men. When Rathbun went in to see Mr. Brewster, he took his wife and child along with him. Mr. Brewster got quite a chuckle out of that. Rathbun just wanted to see if he could get some other kind of work. I don't think he had any idea that he would be put in the front office. However, Mr. Brewster liked his looks. When he got out his record, he found that he was a college graduate. So he called me up at home—I had just gone home to lunch. He told me about Rathbun and asked me if I could come down and talk to him. I said: "Sure. I

haven't started lunch yet. I'll be right down." Guess I talked to him for an hour or so, and the upshot of it was that we put him to work here in the specialty department. He's been working in the coating department following runs we're interested in. Of course, the fumes are pretty bad around some of the runs, and I asked him if he thought it would bother him. He said he didn't know but he would like to try. It doesn't seem to be doing him any harm. He hasn't been out since he has been up here.

Chase originally came to work for the Marshall Company shortly after Blanchard. He had worked with Blanchard on No. 16 paper machine, which the company used at that time to treat papers with certain dyes. He continued to do this type of work; and eventually, when the company built up these orders sufficiently to justify using machine No. 16 for this purpose, he was put in complete charge of it. Since there were never enough orders to keep this machine running full time, Chase also worked as an assistant foreman on paper machines Nos. 5, 6, 7, and 8. He had worked closely for a long time on these machines and was thoroughly familiar with them.

Blanchard continued his talk with Murray.

BLANCHARD: During the war the specialty line grew so large that the sales department asked to have me assigned back to the specialty job; so, some time during 1945, I took it on in addition to my regular work with the plain papers. Mr. Brewster speaks of me as the assistant production manager, but my job really is in between manufacturing and sales. I get all the complaints. Whenever anything goes wrong with a product, I hear about it—that is, on the specialty grades, both plain and coated, and all other plain papers. Perhaps I'm supposed to have something to do with the standard coated papers; but in actual practice, I have nothing to do with them. The men who work on the plain papers come to me with their problems. On the other hand, Mr. Prout—he is superintendent of the coating department—talks directly to Mr. Graham. I have nothing to do with it.

As far as the specialty papers are concerned, Ned Kenyon does practically all of the detailed work. He talks directly with the salesmen and with the customers when it is necessary. Many of these papers involve the research department, and Kenyon works closely with them. He works out all the details he can handle; and when he gets stuck, he comes to me. In dealing with the sales office, I usually take only the situations where there is some policy decision involved. Once a month, Dunn, the salesman for these specialty papers, comes to the mill. We get together with Kenyon and Pete Fraser of the research department for one or two evenings sessions. I keep a record of our general conclusions in this little black book. In meetings of this sort, we can keep the manufacturing problems and the customer requirements clearly in front of us.

Mr. Brewster was talking to me about this department the other day. We had hoped Kenyon would be able to take over the specialty department. In many ways, he does. Much of the work deals with coated papers, which interest him; but he gets so interested in a problem that he drives it into the ground and tends to neglect other problems which are more important to the company but not so interesting to him. In many ways, he has the attitude of a research worker. Still, he is a hard worker; he has worked every night this week, for example, and all of his work is useful. He has an unusually good mind, one that I admire very much. We have been in many tough spots that we couldn't have gotten out of without his help.

At that point in the conversation the telephone rang, and Blanchard talked for a few minutes with Brad Dunn regarding the shipping date of a coated specialty paper scheduled to be delivered during that week. Since this paper was not on the schedule for the week, Dunn wanted to know when to expect it. Blanchard said he would look into the matter and call him back. As he hung up, he said to Murray: "I guess he called me because he couldn't get hold of anyone else. He probably tried to reach Kenyon and couldn't find him." Blanchard then made several calls around the mill and found that the order was being held up because of a shortage of a particular dye that was necessary. This dye was expected during the week, and the paper would probably be run the following week. He called Dunn and gave him this information.

He had hardly finished this call when the director of research, Herbert Parkhurst, called to discuss a coating problem in connection with a run of specialty paper which had gone through the mill a few days before. Blanchard and Kenyon had spent most of the previous afternoon working with the research department on this problem but had arrived at no conclusion. They had decided, after they left the research department, to make some experimental runs in the mill in order to find a solution for their problem. Now, however, Parkhurst apparently felt that some further discussion might be profitable. Blanchard finally agreed that he would find Kenyon and that they would both come over right away to see what could be worked out.

Several days later, Murray came into Blanchard's office.

JOE MURRAY: Paul, I was interested in the talk we had about the specialty department the other day. Would this be a good time to continue it?

BLANCHARD: Sure.

MURRAY: Mr. Brewster has told me several times that one of your most important needs at the moment is to find someone to "back up Paul." We've discussed Kenyon briefly. Now, what about George Duffy? How does he fit in?

BLANCHARD: Well, I think he's a good man—in fact, a very good man, although I don't think Austin Brewster agrees with me. We've had quite a few discussions about him, first and last. Austin feels that his outlook is not right for a management position. I'm not so sure. He came down here from Topsfield, you know, when we started making tissue. He was on night inspection up there at the time. He is very good on the technical problems of No. 6, the machine we've used for tissues ever since he came. He's worked hard and built himself up to a position where the men now come to him with their problems. He works a lot with Mr. Fletcher, who, as you know, is the final authority on all plain papers, and he's getting a good knowledge of papermaking. He works hard and gets along well with the men, but he has trouble getting things done—getting his ideas across.

MURRAY: You mean he has difficulty expressing himself to the customers and the men above him? Does he have any experience in that sort of thing?

BLANCHARD: No, I suppose he really hasn't much experience. He came up the hard way, after all. He didn't go to college, and he has worked most of his time here in this mill. He drives so hard that he often upsets people. But he's doing a fine job in the mill. He's worked with me for a long while, several years longer than Kenyon. He reports directly to me on No. 6. He works only on plain papers, anyway, and Ned Kenyon isn't much interested in them. In theory, Duffy has authority only over the quality of the thin paper made from No. 6; but because the men come to him with all types of problems on this machine, he is practically the foreman of it. The men ask him about mechanical or production matters on No. 6, and he tells them what to do. Then he tells Dave Nichols, the superintendent of the paper machines, what he has done. I've often heard Dave say that he doesn't have to worry about No. 6. That's George's problem!

MURRAY: How does Harry Chase fit into this picture?

BLANCHARD: Well, he's been working on the dye papers ever since he came to the mill, just after he graduated from high school. As you know, he's in charge of No. 16, where all that kind of work is done. He knows more about those papers than anyone else in the mill. The problems on No. 16 are very different from those on the other paper machines. If we put one of the foremen in charge of it—say, Jackie Walsh—it would keep him too busy. Although the machine is located in the basement on this side of the river right under the other machines that Walsh follows, it would still keep him out of the way too much. Chase is a good man. He's a top-grade mechanic and can tell at once when things are going wrong with the machine. He deals with the men well—you know, not rough-handed—but he takes no nonsense from them. They always know where they stand with him. When we are running No. 16, we keep Harry Chase pretty busy, but he still manages to get some time to help out on the paper machines on the other side of the river. He has worked with the crews over there a long time and knows them well. He really has two jobs; we built them up to keep him busy where his skills are particularly useful. On the dye papers, he reports directly to me; and on his assistant foreman's work, he reports to one of Dave Nichols' foremen.

MURRAY: I see him around the front office more than any of the other foremen, even when you're running dye papers.

BLANCHARD: Yes, that's right. He gets up into the office whenever he can. He expected to have Ned Kenyon's job and was very disappointed when he did not get it. They still do not get along together at all well in the mill, although they see a lot of each other outside. Harry would like to have a desk somewhere up here near my office, but he really doesn't need one. We have given him drawer room here in one desk or another where he can keep some of his papers, but that doesn't seem to help. We have set up a perfectly good office for him down by No. 16 at the far end, but he doesn't like to use it any more than he can help. He likes to deal directly with the salesmen and the customers on the quality, production, and scheduling problems of the dye papers; and on the whole, I'm glad to have him do it. We put in a telephone down in his office so that he can take care of this without leaving his machine. Still, he doesn't seem to like it very much.

We've often thought that it would be a good idea to organize a specialty division with the necessary production equipment all in one place. No. 16 is more like a coating machine than a paper machine; and in some ways, it ought to be in the coating department. On the other hand, if we put it in the coating department, it will be like the buffing machine that's there now, an orphan. It will not get the supervision that is necessary. We've thought of having a dye machine, a calender, a coating machine, and a winder all in the same place, to be used only on specialty orders. We don't want to build a new building; that would cost too much. The only place we have now big enough is in the old wood room in the pulp mill. We could fix that up so that it'll hold the equipment, and it has a railroad siding that'll be handy for bringing in supplies and shipping paper. On the other hand, it's too far away from everything else. All the body stock will have to be trucked outside; that'll be difficult, particularly in winter, and will be sure to damage some paper. Perhaps the most serious problem is that it will be too far away from the coating and calendering and we won't be able to use the experience of that department.

Later that day, Murray discussed with Brewster the salary payroll of the mill. Brewster said that he had selected out of this payroll a group of men that he "kept his eye on." He called this group his "personal payroll"; and the main thing he considered, when deciding to put a man on this payroll, was whether or not he would continue to grow. Murray asked whether Kenyon and Duffy were on this payroll.

AUSTIN BREWSTER: Kenyon is on it. He's a brilliant chemist and is doing excellent work on special problems, particularly in connection with coated papers. He isn't broad enough in his point of view on management problems. He has too many outside interests—too many things that have nothing to do with the company—that's his trouble.

Duffy is in a different situation. Blanchard is very anxious to have him put on this personal payroll, and my judgment on this may be wrong. I'm holding him back for one reason. During the trouble with the union organizers at Topsfield in the early stages of the war, when I was away from the mill a good deal, I asked him to work as night inspector there, and his answer was: "I don't want to be a scab." That was a foolish thing to say to me. I know that he had a brother who was sort of a leader of the employees' group at Topsfield and that he was brought up in the town. Still, I don't get his reasoning. It would have been different if I'd been asking him to take a union man's job. It all showed me that he hasn't grown up and isn't management caliber. He may grow up to become a night inspector along with Carlson and Kimball, but I don't think he will amount to much more than that. Paul Blanchard argues with me about it and thinks I'm too hard on Duffy—maybe I am. Paul says that he does good work.

9. MARSHALL COMPANY (F)

IN ADDITION to its leadership in specialty items during the past fifteen years, the Marshall Company, over a period of thirty years, had led the paper industry in the development of standard grades with established specifications on which its customers could rely. The company, together with six paper merchants who handled its products, formed an association to set these standard grades. The association organized three committees: an advisory committee to consider trade customs, a grading committee to study customer trends and new uses for papers, and one on merchandising to pass on all advertising. In effect, since the association based its decisions on customer requirements, they set the standard for the paper mill.

Joe Murray, a member of the Harvard Business School faculty, who was studying the operation of the Marshall Company's paper mill, found that the management gave increasing attention to the problems involved in producing specialty items and standard grades of quality satisfactory to its customers. After learning something about the connection of Paul Blanchard, the assistant production manager, with the specialty papers, Murray became interested in relating Blanchard's work to that of Fletcher, who was concerned with the quality control of the standard grades of plain papers.

Murray heard that Fletcher spent a couple of hours each morning in the control room, looking at samples of paper produced on the machines during the preceding night, checking the results of tests on the samples, and discussing with various people what should be done about the problems that cropped up. No one at the mill except Austin Brewster himself had tried to define Fletcher's position to Murray. Brewster had said that Fletcher was the "chief inspector," but had also said that he often thought that Fletcher and Dave Nichols should be "rolled into one."

Murray knew that Fletcher's routine included an early morning round of the machines, an hour or two in the control room, further visits to the machines and to the calendering office, the finishing department, and the beater rooms. During these trips, he passed on information, looked for trouble, and discussed ways of handling it. If a machine crew saw a huge red-penciled arrow pointing at one of the specifications on the production order form or saw a heavy red line under a substandard test report on the machine data sheet by their machine, they would say: "He's been around again." One day, fifteen years ago, Fletcher carried a pedometer with him and discovered that he had walked twelve miles through the mill. Since then, the development of the control room, the addition of three inspectors, and the increasing consciousness of quality control problems throughout the mill had made it possible for Fletcher himself to do a great deal less of the "leg work."

On a particular morning early in July, Murray found Fletcher in the control room at 8:30 A.M. At 9:00 o'clock, Blanchard came in and began looking at samples with Fletcher and talking them over.

The work of Blanchard and Fletcher was complicated in July, 1947, by continual shortages of papermaking materials and limitations in production facilities. It was frequently necessary to ration output to customers, who were often willing to take paper even though it did not meet their stated specifications and who seldom returned it without good reason. The management, however, anticipated that in the near future, as output caught up to demand throughout the industry, the customers would become increasingly particular about what they would accept.

Blanchard's contacts in the mill included daily rounds of the control room, paper mill, calendering, coating, and finishing. During these rounds, he discussed customer complaints and other problems with Fletcher and his inspectors, with the quality control men, with the foremen, and directly with the men. For example, if a customer returned some defective paper, he would bring a sample back to the machine crew responsible for it, talk it over with them, and try to figure out what had happened and how to prevent it from happening again. "Sometimes, the men admit they're at fault," Blanchard said. "Sometimes, they put the blame right back on management; and sometimes, they figure out new ways of licking a problem we hadn't thought of before."

After Blanchard and Fletcher had talked over the samples for a while, one in particular caught their attention. This was a sample of book paper currently in production on machine No. 11. No. 11 was one of the older machines; it was used for quantity output of plain paper and of body stock for coated paper. Production costs on this machine tended to run higher than on some of the other machines. Like the others, it had acquired over the years certain characteristics of its own that created difficulties in controlling the quality of the paper.

Decisions as to what papers should run on machine No. 11 took place in the scheduling office under the direct supervision of Mr. Elcott, who reported to John Graham. Elcott's knowledge of the machines and of the paper scheduled on them was so thorough that he could wake to a telephone call at 3:00 A.M. and tell a worried foreman who had run out of work or who was faced with a machine breakdown what to do about it.

The customer's specifications for the book paper included a maximum bulk limit, that is, a maximum thickness for the paper. The paper had consistently exceeded this limit on the current order and on several previous ones, all of which had been run on No. 11. Blanchard and Fletcher discussed various ways of reducing the bulk. One possibility was to beat the fiber longer before it went to the paper machines. This would break down the fiber, but it would also result in greater hydration of the pulp. The paper machine was adjusted to handle pulp of the present degree of hydration. If wetter pulp entered the machine, it would still be moist when it arrived at the dry end. There was no way to increase the heat in the dryer rolls; the only alternative would be to slow down the machine so that the pulp would be exposed to the dryers for a longer time.

Fletcher suggested slowing the speed of the machine by 100 feet per minute.

PAUL BLANCHARD: Can you imagine prevailing on anyone out there in the papermaking department to slow the machine down?

FLETCHER: It wouldn't be easy.

BLANCHARD: Maybe we can lick this by heavier calendering on the paper machines.

FLETCHER: I was out by the machine yesterday, and we tried that. But we started getting calender cuts in the paper, so we had to give it up. Those stacks at the machine won't take the heavier calendering.

BLANCHARD: I guess we'll have to send it down to the supercalendering department. I don't know whether it will work or not. This is the third order of this kind of paper we've sent down there. We might as well mark the order for calendering in the first place. Mr. Goodwin will know what to do about it if anybody does.

FLETCHER: Have you heard any more from the sales office about it?

BLANCHARD: Yes, I got a call yesterday asking if we couldn't do something to end the trouble for good. We'll try to get by with calendering; but if I hear direct from the customer on it, we're going to have to do something more. On each order, we've had to notify them in advance that we're not meeting their bulk specifications. I think they've been squashing the paper to make it fit inside the book covers. There's no telling how long they'll be willing to keep that up."

JOE MURRAY: If supercalendering can't handle it, what could you do about it?

BLANCHARD: Well, we could change the furnish. We're short on cellate pulp, but it certainly cuts down the fiber thickness. That's one answer.

FLETCHER: That would be easy enough to do. I could speak to my inspectors, or the beater engineers, or Jack Dugan, who's in charge of the furnish specifications, and any one of them could make the change. But we couldn't do that. We've already promised more paper requiring cellate pulp than we can make with the cellate we have on hand plus what's been promised us, and I doubt if there'll be any more available for months. What about slowing down the machine—any chance?

BLANCHARD: That would be a tough one to put through. The men like this paper now; they can earn a good bonus on it. They'd howl if we cut down their output. Besides, Dave Nichols is already behind on the tonnage figure Mr. Brewster wants for this month. Dave would feel pretty bad if he had to take another slowdown. Even if we asked him, he would probably talk us out of it.

FLETCHER: No. 11 itself might be the cause of the trouble. This order could be run on No. 14.

BLANCHARD: Any change like that would certainly have to go through the front office. I've got another order running on No. 14 right now. The sales office is kicking about the price, and the only way we could cut the cost would be to shift it to another machine; but Elcott has already made the decision about that. If we wanted to get a change, we'd have to talk to Graham. Then it would be up to him.

MURRAY: What are the chances of your asking the customer to put up with it the way it is?

BLANCHARD: Not when it's a standard paper like this. Kenyon is out in Buffalo now to see if a customer can't adapt his machines to handle some heavy-bulk specialty paper we're sending him. That's a new item, and it looks as if it might be easier to make some modification of the customer's equipment than to change the paper. But when we've got a standard paper like this, we should be able to put it out according to specifications.

FLETCHER: Well, we're not going to do anything about it now, anyway.

Fletcher left the control room to go down to the mill, and Blanchard went back to his office.

10. MARSHALL COMPANY (G)

JOE MURRAY, a member of the Harvard Business School faculty, who was making a study of the Marshall Paper Company, dropped into the office of Paul Blanchard, the assistant production manager, one morning and sat down. He had previously discussed with Blanchard in some detail Blanchard's relations with the specialty group and with the men who worked in the production office and in the papermaking department.[1]

Blanchard began the conversation casually.

> PAUL BLANCHARD: Morning, Joe. I had an interesting thing happen to me a minute ago. I just finished talking to Mr. Prout on the phone about that wax-coated paper we are running. Ned Kenyon had been having some trouble with it; and when he got stuck, he finally came in to see me. We went over the situation carefully and decided what must be done. I called Mr. Prout and told him our conclusions. He just flatly refused to do it.

In July, 1947, the demand for papers of all kinds heavily exceeded the supply of materials and papermaking facilities. The Marshall Company sales and production personnel frequently found it necessary to ask customers to accept paper that differed from established specifications. They were making every effort, however, to meet customer requirements in coated papers as well as other types.

Many of the high-quality papers produced by the mill, in addition to certain of the specialty papers, were coated papers. The coating department was one of the major divisions of the mill. Mr. Prout had worked in the coating and calendering department for many years while his father had been its superintendent, and had succeeded to the position when his father retired. He reported directly to John Graham. Austin Brewster considered Prout a "technically excellent man." Murray heard that Prout felt that his department was an empire separate from the rest of the mill.

Blanchard's supervisory work on the specialty papers, plain and coated, occupied a major portion of his time and took him into most of the departments of the mill. The remainder of his supervisory work

---

[1] See Marshall Company (E) and (F).

dealt largely with the quality of the standard plain papers. On this work, he dealt with the papermaking department, which was under the supervision of Dave Nichols, and with the finishing department, which was headed by Frank Goodwin. On the supervision of the coated specialty papers, however, he dealt with Prout, who was responsible to Graham for production and quality of all coated papers.

BLANCHARD: I usually can get things done with Frank Goodwin in the finishing department. He trained me right. Over a long period of time, he taught me to be careful in the way I deal with him. I never got into any real trouble with him; but every once in a while, at first, he would call me up and say: "Paul, what was that business you were talking about to So-and-so this afternoon?" After I'd explained and we had come to a conclusion, he'd make some comment such as: "It would have been easier to have talked to me in the first place." For a long time now, I've always gone to him first on anything I thought ought to be done. If for any reason he is away, of course I don't hesitate to talk to Hank Crawford in the plain paper section of the finishing department, or to Allen on a coated specialty paper. I'm always careful, however, to ask them to talk to Frank about the problem when he gets back.

When I go down through the mill, naturally I see things that ought to be changed, or the men tell me about things that need improvement. I generally talk to Crawford or even to Phillips or McColl in the finishing department about things there; and in one way or another, they seem to get done. I don't know exactly what happens. I suppose they go to Frank and say something like: "I was talking to Paul Blanchard the other day, and such and such seemed like a good idea. What do you think?" Discussing a problem and leaving the conclusion for them to act upon seems to work pretty well with the men who are about my own age. With the older men, it doesn't seem to work so well.

JOE MURRAY: How about men like Bill Phinney, superintendent of the pulp mill? He's about your age, isn't he?

BLANCHARD: Well, I don't see much of him, anyway. He deals directly with Mr. Brewster or Mr. Graham. My work doesn't take me into the pulp mill very much. Once in a while, something comes up, and I go over to see him; but that isn't often. I want to see him now on that run of dirty pulp we had the other night. We ran 80 tons of paper, as you know, on machines No. 11 and No. 14 before we stopped the run. It seems ridiculous that the people in the pulp mill would try to save 16 to 18 tons of pulp and let us spoil 80 tons of paper. If they had let us know in advance, perhaps we could have made some kind of paper where the dirt did not matter so much. The pulp mill had storage room for that much pulp, and they could have held it for a little while so that we could have had some choice of what kind of paper to use it in. You know, we could have used it in one-side coated paper, where it would have been covered up, or in paper for bottle and can labels, where the print would hide the dirt. Coming unexpectedly over the week end, as it did, it upset the night men. They are not as intimately acquainted with customer requirements as the day men and did not know exactly what ought to be done. Selling that paper to the jobbers may not be too serious a problem. We'll still make a profit on it, although a smaller one than we would have made on the original order. The worst thing is that we are behind in our allotments on that order. We can't tell the customer that we just can't make good enough paper to ship to him. We have to tell him that we are behind on our schedules; we will be, too. All the other orders will get upset.

I see Phinney on that sort of thing. I talk to him from time to time on things that affect the quality of the paper, but I don't see him regularly in the course of my ordinary work. John Graham has probably talked to Phinney about that load of dirt already, but I wouldn't expect John to talk to me about it. He would expect me to see Phinney myself to find out what it was all about and to see what can be done to stop its happening again.

Mr. Prout's department is different. I work with them all the time. I go through there every day, as I go through the paper mill and the finishing department. Naturally, I see things, and the men talk to me. I remember when I was going through the calendering department the other day. One of the rolls of paper—they weigh about two thousand pounds, you know—was propped up on the bench with a stick. It might have been kicked loose or jarred out and caused a serious accident. I talked to the man who was handling the paper and told him how dangerous it was. He told me a lot about how hard it was to handle the rolls there now, since the benches were getting worn out, and things like that. I went in to see Mr. Prout after that and discussed the situation with him, but I don't think much happened. I have no idea what he did about that particular roll or the man who was working on it. I imagine that the condition of the benches was just a temporary thing, while he was waiting for the maintenance department to get around to fixing it.

Sometimes, I don't have any luck in dealing with Mr. Prout. Often, I can ask him to do things in a certain way and explain the reasons, and he will do it. Sometimes, I can't get anywhere with him. When you came in, I had just asked him to have the machine running the light tissue shut down until we had finished running the paper that required the wax finish. I explained to him how we had tried to run them both together and couldn't make it work. He merely said to me, "I will not shut down that machine," and hung up. This is a situation where I will have to work out something with him. Both the tissue and the wax-finish paper are specialty papers, and at the present time the quality of neither of them is good enough to sell. He's running them on those two machines that have the joint temperature control, and they just won't work for those runs. If we get the temperature high enough to handle the wax on one of the machines, it's too high for that very thin paper on the other machine, and it comes through brittle. We've tried all the combinations we can think of, and there seems to be nothing we can do to run them both at once. The other machines that will take these orders are all tied up, so we have to run them on these machines.

MURRAY: What are you going to do now?

BLANCHARD: Well, I guess I had better go down and talk it over with Mr. Prout. We will have to work out something.

11. LEWIS EQUIPMENT COMPANY

When William Conrad, a casewriter from the Harvard Business School, approached Samuel Coates, the plant manager at Lewis Equipment Company, about case possibilities, he found that Coates did have a number of concerns that sounded like good case leads. Coates explained that, even though he had been promoted to his present assignment several months earlier, he did not feel that he had as yet made nearly as

Exhibit 1

LEWIS EQUIPMENT COMPANY
Partial Organization Chart

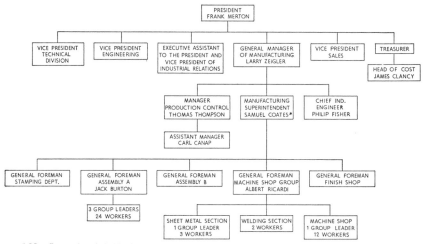

* Mr. Coates had left his former position as general foreman of the stamping department about a year earlier.

many improvements in the plant's operations as he believed were possible. In particular, Coates expressed concern about his general foremen (see Exhibit 1 for a partial organization chart of the company).

Sam went on to explain that he personally was under considerable pressure from his superiors to improve factory performance. He did not believe that these demands were entirely reasonable, but he believed he could make progress in meeting them if only he could find a way to get better co-ordination among his foremen. Sam also wanted his foremen to spend more of their time and interest in helping their own people overcome the daily problems on the factory floor. He believed his foremen were often too distracted to attend to the practical issues of training and encouraging their employees in getting their work done properly and on time. He wanted his foremen to feel responsible for all aspects of their unit and to fight for the things they felt were necessary to make their unit effective. Sam reported that he was having difficulty in getting his foremen thinking and working along these lines. Starting with this lead, William Conrad decided to spend some time with two of the foremen involved to learn more about the situation.

Company Background

The Lewis Equipment Company had been started some fifteen years earlier as a science-based company producing an increasing line of equipment and instruments that were used primarily in the oil industry. After a period of early financial success and rapid growth, the company had, in recent years, experienced severe competition and had been operating at a loss for about two years. At this time the company employed approximately 900 people, of which a considerable number were engineers and scientists. The factory operated on a job order basis, and most of the products were produced to customer specifications. These customer requirements were highly technical in nature and subject to frequent change. In addition the Technical and Engineering Divisions designed new products that were periodically added to the product line.

Assembly Department A

The first department that Conrad chose to study was Assembly Department A under the general foremanship of Jack Burton. Most of the workers in the department were women. The individual jobs were relatively simple in nature, but careful work was necessary to insure proper quality, and both manual dexterity and experience were required to develop speed of assembly. During their first conversation Jack explained about the nature of his work and his problems.

> BURTON: I have one main final assembly line that makes up twelve different types of equipment that are each produced two to six times a year. There are ten people in this production line along with a group leader. I also have a subassembly line that makes small quantities of a variety of components and also finishes some assemblies that are produced only once or twice a year. Then I have the wire and harness line—these are the harnesses and cables used in the finished assemblies.
>
> We're having a lot of trouble with the specifications. The trouble is that we are not given enough time to work out the problems in specifications

when they come to us. I have to accept what the engineers give me as the bible, even though there are plenty of errors from the engineers. All the control around here is really in the engineering department. The final test is also done by the engineers, but there is a logic in this because we could develop our own slipshod technique if we did not have the engineers for final tests.

I get a monthly schedule in rough-draft form from production control that tells me what to do and when to do it. It keeps the material flowing. I usually get the report on the first of each month, which I don't like, because if I knew in advance what the work would be like for the ensuing months I could go around to the paint foreman, etc., and put pressure on him to get the specific materials that I need for a crash program, so I would be better off.

I get a weekly direct labor utilization report made out by accounting. The accounting department makes this report up from the time cards and tells me what percentage of productivity resulted from our past weekly efforts. My yearly percentage of productivity to date is 62 per cent, officially, but this note on the side of the sheet shows that actually I should be at 64 per cent productivity. Only a small amount of the jobs are actually timed. The standards on about 90 per cent of the jobs are estimated. Management is interested in improving the per cent of productivity over last year's productivity. For instance we are now at 62 per cent while last year this department was at a 45 per cent productivity. But that improvement isn't much help, because the selling price and the budget are based on the standard times so that no matter how high the productivity is, if it is anything lower than 100 per cent, they always complain.

We would show an even better percentage productivity figure if the rework hours were counted in the proper place. For example, last January we had 21 per cent rework. On rework we have to eat it. If a late engineering spec change causes rework, we have to eat it, as far as the productivity figures go.

I think they are hiding their heads in the sand. They don't want to know the true cost picture. If they cross-charged rework costs to the department that caused the trouble, it would be waving a red flag in their faces and showing where the real problem lies.

The Direct Labor Utilization Report

Burton's frequent reference to the direct labor utilization report prompted Conrad to look into this subject. He learned that this particular control system had been initiated by Mr. Merton, the company president, shortly after he had arrived at the company some three years previously. This system, designed to alert management to possible problem areas and to assist in product and inventory control, encompassed all of the company's manufacturing and assembly activities and a somewhat smaller proportion of the remaining hourly paid labor force. Mr. Merton had made every attempt to have all of the manufacturing jobs and assembly operations rated, but with frequent design modifications requested by customers and the frequent introduction of new products, this goal had never quite been achieved. Currently, some 70 per cent of the direct labor force in the manufacturing division were working on rated jobs.

Generally the control system was not unlike progressive cost accounting procedures found in other medium-sized firms working on a job order basis. It was primarily aimed at controlling manufacturing labor costs by comparing the total actual time expended in manufacturing work to the accumulated standard times for each part or assembly produced. These standard times for manufacturing the necessary individual parts and for their assembly were determined by industrial engineering.

The cost accounting department distributed weekly on Friday afternoon, a direct labor utilization report for each department covered by the system along with a summary for the total factory organization and the total company. (See Exhibit 2 for a guide to the method of calculation of the various items.) The two most significant measures upon which subordinate organizations were evaluated were known as the productivity and efficiency ratings. Of these two ratings, the productivity figure was the more frequently quoted and discussed rating. Conrad asked James Clancy, the head of cost accounting, what the significance was of these weekly reports. The latter commented as follows:

> CLANCY: The reports are of some significance since the president looks at the figures every week. He usually gets the productivity and efficiency for total company and total manufacturing and plots them on a big chart in his office, which goes back several years. Sometimes he asks for reports on individual departments but he never looks at them for more than ten minutes. I would say Mr. Zeigler[1] better be interested in them, since he knows Merton is going to talk to him every week manufacturing's performance doesn't look good. . . . A lot of the managers say that the system is a bunch of rubbish—Mr. Zeigler always says that he doesn't believe in the system. But I know they're concerned because Merton believes in it. You watch them on Friday pacing up and down, waiting to see what the results are. Their actions show that they are interested in it.

The total factory productivity and efficiency percentages were currently averaging approximately 69 per cent and 79 per cent respectively which were slight increases over the previous two years. Exhibit 3 charts

---

[1] Mr. Zeigler was the general manager of manufacturing.

the productivity and efficiency percentages for the factory by months for the two preceding years. The company percentages followed closely the total factory figures, owing to the fact that of the total company hours available, 75 per cent were made up of hours contributed by the factory. Exhibit 4 is a sample of the actual reports that were distributed on a weekly basis to the managers and foremen concerned.

Exhibit 2

LEWIS EQUIPMENT COMPANY

SAMPLE DIRECT LABOR UTILIZATION REPORT WITH GUIDE TO METHOD
OF CALCULATION

1. Total hours available = The total hours recorded on the time cards of the employees in the department concerned during the reporting period.

2. Hours used on indirect labor = % of group leader's time spent on supervising × 8-hour day × Number of working plus inspector's and days in reporting period clerical help's time

3. Hours available for direct labor = #1 minus #2

4. Hours direct labor on nonrated jobs = Total hours expended on jobs that industrial engineering hasn't rated and/or on special jobs requested by other departments.

5. Hours variance = Hours expended due to "Acts of God" (e.g., machine breakdowns, power failures, snow storms) plus total rework hours.*

6. Hours direct labor on rated jobs = #3 minus (#4 plus #5)

7. Standard hours produced = Standard hours allowed for each × Jobs completed in reporting period

8. % Efficiency on rated jobs = #7 divided by #6.

9. % Total productivity = #7 plus #4 divided by #1.

10. Rework*
    a) Responsible
    b) Not responsible

* Work hours expended on rework were broken down into two classifications: (a) the unacceptable workmanship of the particular organization being measured; (b) the rework occasioned by subsequent faulty work in other departments or by revisions in product design made by engineering, necessitating a rework of the job.
  Mention was usually made at the bottom of the Utilization Report of the absolute amounts of rework completed during the reporting period.

Conrad also secured direct evidence of Mr. Zeigler's concern with the productivity records. At the end of the first quarter of the current year, when labor utilization percentages were dropping in successive weeks, Mr. Zeigler sent the following note to his subordinates:

> Please write up your suggestions on how we are to salvage this situation. Remember, last month's productivity was only 69 per cent. By Tuesday I will expect concrete courses of action from each of you, if you are to meet or beat budget.

Conrad learned that Mr. Zeigler had sent similar notes on other occasions.

Fortified with this information, Conrad went back to observing activities in Assembly Department A.

The Pump Episode

On one of his early trips to the assembly department, Jack Burton started telling Conrad of a problem he was having:

BURTON: A little while ago my group leader of the subassembly group brought to my attention a problem concerning this pump unit. He

Exhibit 3

LEWIS EQUIPMENT COMPANY

TOTAL FACTORY LABOR "EFFICIENCY" AND "PRODUCTIVITY"

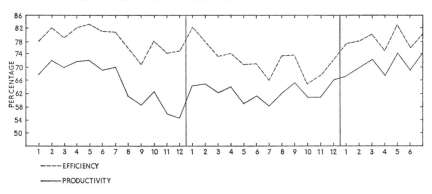

was asking me how we could put the units together and be sure they would pass final test. I noticed that there might be a chance of having some brass filings get in the critical parts if we were not careful. My group leader dug up the assembly specs which the engineers had drawn up in order to put this critical subassembly together. It called for cleaning the parts twice so that there would be positive assurance of a positive test. Then the group leader saw that the industrial engineers had not allowed enough time for the double cleaning. My group leader actually timed how long it took him to make the double cleaning, and it was considerably over the allotted time. I had the group leader figure the correct amount it would take so that we could resubmit it and get the actual time put down that we were spending on this cleaning operation.

Later in the afternoon when the casewriter was talking to Burton, Phil Fisher the head of the industrial engineering department, came up and raised the topic of the standard allowed time on the cleaning operation.

FISHER: What's wrong on this pump assembly operation?

BURTON: Come over here and look at this. Our cleaning operation on the pump assembly is taking more time than you people have allowed. (*Hands him the engineering assembly sheet which describes the dual cleaning operation.*)

Exhibit 4

LEWIS EQUIPMENT COMPANY

DIRECT LABOR UTILIZATION REPORT
TOTAL MACHINE SHOP GROUP
Including the Sheet Metal and Welding Shops

	Week Ending 6/4	Week Ending 6/11	Week Ending 6/12	Week Ending 6/25	Week Ending 7/2	Total Month Ending 7/2
1. Total hours available.............	565	892	946	800	812	4015
2. Hours used on indirect labor.......	59	86	85	90	89	409
3. Hours available for direct labor....	506	806	861	710	723	3606
4. Hours direct labor on nonrated jobs.	8	26	37	44	17	132
5. Hours variance...................	18	19	13	16	5	71
6. Hours direct labor on rated jobs....	480	761	811	650	701	3403
7. Standard hours produced..........	303	388	508	484	266	1949
8. % Efficiency on rated jobs (Standard hours produced/hours on rated jobs 7/6)...........................	58	51	63	74	38	57
9. % Total productivity (Standard hours + nonstandard hours/hours available 7 + 4/1)...............	55	46	58	66	35	52
Rework.....................						
a) Responsible..............	0	0	0	0	0	0
b) Not responsible...........	18	19	13	16	5	71

FISHER (*after reading the sheet*):   I can't understand why they have duplicate cleaning operations on this. I don't think it's needed. Look, they've got sixteen operations for this part. Look, the three sections to this assembly procedure shows that part A and C are almost the same thing. They're exactly alike.

BURTON: I've got to have those chips out of there to get these pumps past final assembly test. We go by the engineering specifications. Look, this is the engineering assembly S. O. P.[2] It says that we should have two cleaning operations.

FISHER: There's not such a thing as an engineering S. O. P. concerning assembly. I'm going up and see about this. I'm going to see if we can't get

---

[2] Standard operating procedure.

one of the duplicate operations for cleaning taken out of the specifications. We've got an ultrasonic cleaner that will do this job perfectly and eliminate one of these operations. That's what we've got the cleaner for anyway, to do jobs like this. This is ridiculous having so many operations. We'll be spending more time cleaning it than it takes to make it. How are we going to make any money doing this? (*Fisher leaves the room.*)

BURTON (*to casewriter*):   He's worried about the cost of this—claiming that we will never be able to make a profit on the product if we have to have so many operations. Look at him worried about something like this. That's the chief engineer's job. The chief engineer is the one to worry about whether or not we can make a profit using so many operations with such designs. It's up to the chief engineer to determine whether we can sell a product and make a profit. It's not up to Phil Fisher. (*Jack Burton leaves the room and the casewriter talks to Phil Fisher who is coming into Burton's office as the latter leaves.*)

FISHER (*to casewriter*):   Boy, I just can't understand it. If I were to have seen that specification sheet with that many operations on it, I would have blown my top. Some engineer started on this and because he didn't know what he was doing, he just kept applying more operations on operations. I know that if I was a foreman, I wouldn't allow that specification to come into my department without saying anything about it. How is the company going to make any money anyway? (*Jack Burton comes back into his office.*)

FISHER: I want to try and clean a couple of pumps, using just one operation. I've got an idea how we can cut this down.

BURTON: Oh no you're not. I want to first check and see what final test has to say about the ones we've already done using two cleaning operations. I'm not going to have you trying to clean them with only one operation when maybe they aren't getting a positive test with two. (*Burton goes out and talks to the final test engineer and returns.*)

BURTON (*to Fisher*):   The test engineer said that the one we cleaned using the double operation didn't test positively. I'm not going to have you try to make a single operation out of it when we can't even get it with a double. I'm way behind on rework anyway, and I can't afford the time messing around with it.

A little later on in the afternoon the casewriter had a chance to talk to Jack Burton further about the pump-cleaning incident.

BURTON (*to casewriter*):   You know what Phil Fisher tried to do? He got my group leader behind my back and asked him to make up two complete units so he could try to test them, using only one cleaning operation. My group leader said definitely no. I'd already warned the group leader of what Phil might do, and I told him not to play his game. It's this kind of thing that he does behind my back that really makes me mad. This is no isolated incident. This happens every day around here with him. He's always going off on a different set of directions. He tells me every once in a while that I'm not co-operating with him. I don't know why I have to keep shuffling my people around to try out his ideas when I am so far behind on my work. If they want to test some parts and make a better operation, they can do it themselves. They can set it up. I'm not going to have them disrupting my operation.

A little while later Fisher approached Burton.

FISHER: Hey, Jack. Come on in the test room. I want to show you what we're doing. (*The group moves to the test room.*) Look, we have a valve on the pump in the ultrasonic cleaner. Using this device, we could eliminate the operation "C" (*pointing to the engineering specifications*).
BURTON: I don't care what you do. I just want a final result!
FISHER: I just wanted to show you what we were doing to keep you up to date. This way we can be sure that the top isn't scarred when we put it in the tester.
BURTON (caustically):   I don't care if there's any scars on the top!
FISHER: I thought you said it had to pass final test with a good visual inspection?
BURTON: It's the fingerprints and the filings inside the pump that cause the trouble. I'm not interested in the outward appearance. It goes in a shield anyway.
FISHER: Oh. It goes in a shield? I didn't know that.

In a later interview with the casewriter, Fisher had a chance to explain some of his motives and methods in running the industrial engineering department.

FISHER: This pump-cleaning operation is the type of thing that Jack Burton should be doing and working on. That's the foreman's job. Jack's a good man but he doesn't have enough work to do. When Burton and I get together, it's rather rough between us. He's firm in his opinion and I'm firm in mine.

I guess some people consider me the most hated man in the firm, but I'm rather proud of that position if we can get out of our present rut. I just don't have enough men in the industrial engineering department to do any real big work so I have to rely on the foremen doing the job. What I have to do is to create a big stink or something so that we get some reaction from these people. We raise the commotion in the department and let the foremen take over and do the improvements from there. I think we're on the verge of a breakthrough here if we can get these foremen up using a stopwatch and watching these people and seeing if they're using the correct procedures. Why, on this pump-cleaning operation—sure, we're spending. We've got two of our men spending two hours of their time this afternoon in order that we can save a half hour when we finally go to assembly. But if this works out, we'll save the company a lot of money. You've got to spend a dollar in order to make $3.00.

Later, Jack Burton told the casewriter some of his views on Philip Fisher.

> BURTON: Phil Fisher isn't held in very high esteem because when he came in to the company a little less than a year ago he had too much initiative and tried to do too many things. He got so many projects going that he hasn't had time to finish them up.
>
> I really don't know what the industrial engineers do. It's all I can do to compose myself when I have to talk about them. I get so mad when I think about all their activities. Fisher has them doing so many projects that they don't have time to do the things they're really supposed to be doing. Take, for instance, the harness board that I showed you earlier this morning. They're supposed to be making those up for us. The boards take about four hours to make up so that we can begin assembly. We're having to make up our own boards, eight hours of nonproductive time that we get charged with. The last run-through, we had to clear the boards that we already made several weeks before. It took one hour to clear them and then four hours of nonproductive time to build new ones. This is the type of job that they should be doing. They should be working on giving us better standards, too. The standards are way off because they are based on methods that haven't been worked out yet. That makes the productivity report an unfair basis for measuring our work. That's my big gripe with industrial engineering.

Final Assembly Shutdown

When William Conrad arrived at the plant on the following day, he found that the main final assembly line had been temporarily shut down. This was necessary because production scheduling was unable to supply some front plates that were essential. The required plates had just been started into the paint shop that morning.

Burton commented:

> This shutdown is not unusual because we always have this. It's typical. Tom Thompson[3] works his production schedule from a predicted percentage of productivity figure that Zeigler gives him. I don't know where they get the figure. I know that recently they were talking about an 85 per cent productivity. I don't know where they got that. I think it was something about fixing up the line so it would be more efficient, but it certainly has never reached that level of productivity. That 85 per cent figure means

---

[3] Production control manager.

purchasing has to hurry up and buy some more parts and materials. Then someone gets blamed for high inventories and it swings way over the other way.

The Machine Shop

Knowing that Sam Coates was also particularly concerned about the machine stop, Conrad decided to spend a few days observing this department and it's foreman, Albert Ricardi. The machine shop did a wide variety of machining operations on job lots of parts needed for subsequent assembly.

In one of their early conversations Ricardi explained:

> When I took over this shop last year it was rapidly moving backwards. I took over and started instituting some changes. We've made some real progress, but it doesn't show in the figures. Accounting has been cutting us into bits. The standards being used are not real standards. They're guesses—pulled out of the air. Then we get hit with the productivity report and we're bums. All they're interested in is making us look bad. I have to spend about 97 per cent of my time just coddling all the people who come down here from other departments.

The casewriter came in early the following Monday morning and was present when Tom Thompson, the production control supervisor for the manufacturing division, came into Ricardi's office.

THOMPSON: Al, we really need this job. There's only one operation left on it, and it has to be done. Al, I know you're in a bind, but we need this by today. Is there anything you can do?

RICARDI: We're really shorthanded today. Well, I could see what we could do about putting it in the process.

THOMPSON: I've talked to Brown over in the model shop, and he said he could do it for me, that is, if it's all right with you.

RICARDI: No. We don't get any credit on it that way. We've started the job, and I want to finish it.

THOMPSON: Well, Al, I understand how you feel about it, and I know it will disrupt your operation.

RICARDI: Well, we'll see what we can do about it, but I'm not guaranteeing anything. Maybe we can get it out this afternoon. (*Thompson leaves.*)

CONRAD: Well, Al, how do you feel on this blue Monday?

RICARDI: Not so good. All my good workers and good machinists are out, and I don't know what I'm going to do. My inspector is out, and I'm really going to be running around like a chicken with his head cut off. I guess when your luck runs out, it really goes all at once. Saturday we were running around and found that the drill press operator had drilled the counterbore shallow on those plates we were doing. We had to run eighty-four of those pieces over again. You don't have to be a machinist to see that the men around here leave a lot to be desired. And then there's Tom Thompson coming down here. If they would leave us alone, we would get ahead and get something running and we wouldn't have all these rush jobs. Every time they send in and ask us to do something of a rush nature, that cuts out our general efficiency, and we just can't get ahead. That's why I ignored Thompson. When the men quit a job in the middle of it, they get confused or forget and make mistakes. It takes them time to get started again. Here's Thompson asking me to do a rush job. I just can't afford to do it.

Scheduling Problems

Several days later Conrad was walking through the shop with Ricardi when he commented on a pile of finished parts.

CONRAD: These castings really look nice, Al. I think Archie did a pretty good job on them.

RICARDI: Yes, they look nice all right, there is no doubt about that. But we have another lot of fifty more coming along right now. I just got the order in today.

CONRAD: What? I thought Archie just finished up this lot.

RICARDI: Yes, I know. They should all have been done at the same time. If we had had the order of fifty that we got today, it would have been a complete gift. As it is now, we will have to set up the machines again and run the whole batch through. They really don't know how much it is costing them. That is what is wrong with this company. They are afraid to ask how much something costs. When someone asks them or they try to price a product, they use the standard hours, but the standard hours aren't near what we actually spend on making the product. They don't allow us any time for setups or making fixtures or for any unforeseen events. Those are the main times that are involved. I asked the accounting department one day how much it really cost to make a product and they gave me the computations from the standard hours, I told them that they were no good. They were left without any answer.

Machine Shop and Production Control

In the course of a number of conversations with Sam Coates, Conrad learned that Coates was well aware of the same signs of trouble in the assembly department and the machine shop that Conrad had seen. For instance, Coates told Conrad of a recent talk he had had with Ricardi.

COATES: Just today I happened to mention the production control group to Ricardi and he about exploded. He started pacing up and down. He said that Carl Canap, the assistant production control manager, was personally out for him. I was shocked by the vehemence. When he calmed down I asked him, "Al, what have I been saying to you!" He stopped. "You are running the shop, not Sam Coates or Larry Zeigler or production control. Now why do you feel threatened? Don't you realize that you have forgotten more machine shop operations and the scheduling of machine shop work than Carl Canap will ever learn." I told him that he had to assert himself in a positive way. I told him that he was running the shop and no one else.

Mr. Coates told the casewriter that since this conversation he was attempting to remedy the conflict between Ricardi and Carl Canap by having the latter's boss, Tom Thompson, temporarily work with Ricardi instead of Mr. Canap. Sam continued, "If Tom can charm Al so that they work well together, then, later, when Al deals with Canap, he'll let all the little things that have been bothering him go by. Just for Al to be with Thompson will help out a lot in smoothing over the relationship between Al and Carl."

In the morning of the day following the Ricardi-Coates conversation, Conrad observed Tom Thompson talking to Ricardi about scheduling problems and procedures. Carl Canap had not made an appearance. Later in the day, Coates and Ricardi were sitting in the former's office, when Ricardi's assistant came in and stated that Carl Canap had just requested that the machine shop stop production of an item that was only partially completed and substitute a "rush job" which used the same machine. Ricardi immediately commented to Coates.

RICARDI: See, Sam, this is the type of thing that I have been talking about. We lose all our efficiency by breaking down in the middle of an operation.

COATES: Al, what have I been telling you for the last week and a half? You don't stop an order in the middle of production. You clear out the job before you start another.

RICARDI (*after a long pause*):   What do I do?

COATES: Al, you're the foreman, not Carl Canap. You're the foreman of this shop, not anyone else.

RICARDI (*turning to face the assistant*):   Don't do anything.

Approximately fifteen minutes later Coates and Ricardi were interrupted in their conversation by Carl Canap, who burst through the doorway and with an angered tone of voice questioned Mr. Coates.

CANAP: Sam, I understand you and Al won't allow that rush job to be substituted. Is that true?

COATES: Don't look at me, Carl. Al is the foreman of this outfit, you talk to him.

CANAP: What about that, Al?

RICARDI (*pause*):   That's right.

CANAP: Do you realize you are hurting the company, losing sales, losing money? What is this company coming to if we can't rearrange the schedule a little just because somebody wants to get a little extra credit on the weekly report. Do you realize what this means?

COATES (*angrily*):   Listen here, Carl, Al is right. We're not going to switch, and henceforth you'll not be stopping production in the middle of any operation. This is my decision, and I want you to stick by it.

CANAP (*walking out of the office*):   If that's the way you want it, that's the way it will be.

Sam Coates' Views

Some few days later Sam Coates was talking to the casewriter about the general situation:

COATES: Higher management has become so concerned with the figures that they forget about what we're actually producing, what's finished, and what's good quality. The figures get divorced from what they stand for. But if you're going to have the system, you have to play along with it. I'm sure there are a lot of details about the figures that my foremen and particularly Al are overlooking. In fact, I think he's making himself look poor. His desk is in such a disarray and things come so fast that he just gives up and says, "Oh, to hell with it!" Al has got to learn that he can't work on a bunch of long and hard jobs at the same time and expect to get a good productivity rating. He's got to get his work finished up by Saturday so he can get credit for it. He's not making the most of what he's got down there.

12. EMPIRE GLASS COMPANY

IN THE FALL of 1963, a Harvard Business School case researcher visited the glass container plant of Empire Glass Company in French City, Canada. He was interested in studying the way a control system is perceived and used by plant personnel in a multiplant company and how the system was related to the other aspects of plant operations. Empire Glass Company had developed, in the years following World War II, a control system for use by its plants which was considered by some accountants to be quite sophisticated. Within its division of Empire, the French City plant was a preferred site for production management trainees because, according to a division training executive:

> The French City chaps look at the controls as tools. They show trainees that they really work. The French-Canadian atmosphere is good too. In a French-Canadian family everything is open and aboveboard. There are no secrets. The trainees can ask anyone anything and the friendliness and company parties give him a feel for good employee relations.

Products, Technology and Markets

Empire Glass Company, in 1963, operated a number of plants in Canada. The principal products of the French City plant were glass jars and bottles. Of these, "packers' ware" constituted the largest group, including jars for products like tomato catsup, mayonnaise, jams and jellies, honey, and soluble coffee. Milk bottles, beer bottles, and soft-drink bottles were also produced in large quantities. A great variety of shapes and sizes of containers for wines and liquors, drugs, cosmetics, and chemicals were produced in smaller quantities.

Most of the thousands of different products, varying in size, shape, color, and decoration were produced to order. Typical lead times between the customer's order and shipment from the plant were two to three weeks in 1963, reduced from five and a half weeks to six weeks in the early 1950's, according to French City plant executives.

The principal raw materials for container glass are sand, soda ash, and lime, which are melted in batches in furnaces or "tanks." Forming is done by automatic or semiautomatic machines, which fill molds with molten glass and then blow it into shape. The "ware" then goes through an automatic annealing oven or lehr where it cools slowly under carefully controlled conditions to avoid the stresses that would be set up in rapid cooling. If the glass is to be coated on the exterior to increase its resistance to abrasion and scratches, this coating—often a silicone film —is applied in the lehr.

Quality inspection is critical. If the "melt" in the furnace is not completely free from bubbles and "stones" (unmelted ingredients or pieces of refractory material) or if the fabricating machinery is slightly out of adjustment or molds are worn, rejection can be very high. Although a number of machines are used in the inspection process, including electric eyes, much of the inspection is still visual and is performed mostly by women.

Any decorating (application of trade-mark or other design by silk screen methods) is then added and inspected. Packing in corrugated containers (or wooden cases for some bottles) then follows.

Although glassmaking is one of the oldest arts and bottles and jars have been machine-molded at relatively high speeds for over half a century, the French City plant had spent substantial sums each year for modernizing its equipment. These improvements had substantially increased the speed of operation and had reduced visual inspection and manual handling of glassware. However, according to a general foreman, a production worker of the 1940's could return in 1963 and not feel entirely out of place.

No hand blowing was done in the plant and, contrary to the early days of the industry, most of the jobs were relatively unskilled and highly repetitive. They gave the worker little control over method or pace. The mold makers, who made and repaired the molds, and the machine repairmen and those who made the equipment setup changes between different products were considered to possess the highest level of skill.

Wages were high, perhaps the highest paid in French City. However, the rumble of the machinery, the hiss of compressed air in the molding operation plus the roar of fuel in the furnaces made the plant extremely noisy, and the furnaces and molten glass gave off a very great amount of heat. Production employees had belonged to two national unions for many years, and bargaining was done on a national basis. Output standards were established for all jobs, but no bonus was paid for exceeding standard.

The French City plant to some extent shipped its products throughout Canada, although transportation costs limited its market primarily to Eastern Canada. While some of the customers were large and bought in huge quantities, many were relatively small.

The Plant Organization

James Hunt, plant manager, had been manager of the French City plant since January, 1961. Prior to that he had been assistant plant manager. He had risen from an hourly worker through foreman up to plant manufacturing engineer in the maintenance end of the business. He presented to the researcher the appearance of self-assurance and intimate, firsthand knowledge of operations and events within the plant. He was seldom without a cigar clutched in his teeth, commonly at a rakish upward tilt.

As plant manager, Hunt had no responsibility for sales or research and development activities. In fact, both Hunt and the district sales manager in his area had separate executives to whom they reported in the division headquarters, and it was in the superior of these executives that responsibility for both sales and production first came together.

At the case researcher's first meeting with Hunt, he welcomed him to the plant with the comment: "Everything here is open to you. We think we have a pretty good plant here, but we want you to see for yourself."

In response to the researcher's indication of interest in the interrelationships of the people in plant management, Hunt went to a cabinet in his office and from among a number of manuals prepared by corporate staff in British City, pulled out a large, loose-leaf volume labeled "Position Analysis Manual" and handed it to the researcher. There, for each person from assistant foreman up to plant manager, he found six to ten pages reproduced from typewritten sheets which described the individuals' responsibilities and duties. Hunt said:

> You will see that frequently two managers with different job titles are assigned responsibility for the same task. [He implied that it was up to them to work out their own pattern of mutual support and co-operation.] However, I don't have to adhere strictly to the description. I may end up asking a lot more of the man at certain times and under certain conditions than is ever put down on paper.
>
> In effect, the staff[1] runs the plant. We delegate to the various staff department heads the authority to implement decisions within the framework of our budget planning. This method of handling responsibility means that staff members have to be prepared to substantiate their decisions. At the same time, it gives them a greater sense of participation in and responsibility for plant income. We endeavor to carry this principle

---

[1] The personnel reporting directly to Hunt. The organization chart (Exhibit 1), which included a photograph of each individual was widely distributed. An enlarged version, under glass, was mounted on a wall of the lobby at the main entrance where it could be seen by all plant personnel and visitors.

into the operating and service departments. The foreman is given responsibility and encouraged to act as though he were operating a business of his own. He is held responsible for all results generated in his department and is fully aware of how any decisions of his affect plant income.

As our division personnel counsel and assist the plant staff, so do the plant staff counsel and assist the department foreman. Regular visits are made to the plant by our division manager and members of his staff. The principal contact is through the division manager of manufacturing and

Exhibit 1

EMPIRE GLASS COMPANY

FRENCH CITY PLANT, MARCH 1, 1963

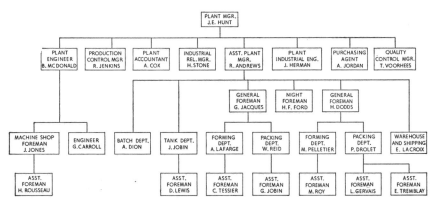

his staff; the manager of industrial engineering, the manager of production engineering and the manager of quality control. [There was no division staff officer in production control.]

However, the onus is on the plant to request help or assistance of any kind. We can contact the many resources of Empire Glass Company, usually on an informal basis. That is, we deal with other plant managers directly for information, when manufacturing problems exist, without going through the division office.

Each member of the staff understands that we, as a plant, have committed ourselves through the budget to provide a stated amount of income, and regardless of conditions which develop, this income figure must be maintained. If sales are off and a continuing trend is anticipated, we will reduce expenses wherever possible to retain income. Conversely, if we have a gain in sales volume, we look for the complete conversion of the extra sales at the profit margin rate. However, this is not always possible, especially if the increase in sales comes at a peak time when facilities are already strained.

Assistant plant manager, Robert Andrews, was something of a contrast to Hunt. He was tall and slender, while Hunt was relatively short with a tendency toward overweight. Andrews talked intently but with a reserve which contrasted with Hunt's ebullience. However, Andrews too, had a ready smile. He thought and moved quickly but without giving off as much visible nervous energy as Hunt. He had been promoted from quality control manager to his present position in January, 1961. In talking about his job Andrews said:

> I am responsible for all manufacturing operations within the plant. The operating group reports directly to me, and I also stay in constant contact with the staff departments to assure good communication and expedient handling of some items. During the summer months, which is our busiest period, the plant employs about 500 hourly workers. Approximately 250 work on the day shift, 150 on second, and 100 on third shift. They are supervised by fifteen salaried members of the supervisory staff plus a number of working supervisors who are appointed as activity increases. They usually supervise second- and third-shift operations.
>
> Our foremen have full responsibility for running their departments: quality, conditions of equipment, employee relations, production according to schedule, control of inventory through accurate reporting of spoilage and production, and cost control. The foreman is just as accountable for these in his department as the plant manager is for the entire plant.
>
> We have given the supervisory personnel status. Such things as "the white shirt,"[2] a personal parking spot, an office—these all assist in maintaining the foreman's position of authority in the eyes of his employees. He is no longer the best man with the wrench—he is the man with the best over-all supervisory qualifications.

---

[2] Andrews was referring to a norm that the researcher had already observed while circulating in the plant. The plant manager, the management staff, the foreman, the clerks in the office departments, all wore white shirts with ties but no coat. The union president, who worked at his production job except while handling union affairs, also wore a white shirt but without a tie. The vice president and other production workers wore colored shirts, usually sport shirts.

The force of this practice was observed by the researcher in an exchange between Ray Jenkins, production control manager, and Tom Voorhees, quality control manager, which took place in the main office area of the plant:

JENKINS: Hey Tom, where are you going? Knocking off for the day? Why are you so dressed up? [Voorhees had on a suit, white shirt and tie.]

VOORHEES: No, I've just been in the office all morning. I usually don't stay there so long, but my assistant is kind of a fat fellow and likes the window open, so I put my coat on because it was cool. I just kept it on when I ran down here.

JENKINS: Well, we'll let it pass this time.

RESEARCHER: I take it this is a coats-off organization?

JENKINS: Oh, very definitely. I would never think, for example, of wearing my coat out on the floor of the factory. That would be absolutely out of bounds.

RESEARCHER: Is it just accidental that everyone wears a white shirt, too?

JENKINS: Oh, no, it's a French City plant practice. You wouldn't last five minutes in here with that shirt (pointing to researcher's striped shirt) if you worked for Empire. You'd probably get a comment before you even got to your desk in the morning.

RESEARCHER: Is this requirement written down somewhere?

JENKINS: No, it's just sort of in the air. A new man comes to work here and he gets the message right away—no coat but a white shirt.

Production control manager, Ray Jenkins, was slight of build, moved fast and talked fast. Like James Hunt, he was practically a chain smoker, only he smoked cigarettes and a pipe instead of cigars. Jenkins described his job as follows:

> The production control manager is basically responsible to plan and control plant inventories and production schedules to meet sales requirements consistent with effective and efficient utilization of facilities, materials, and manpower. Our aim is to attain maximum length of run without affecting service and exceeding inventory budgets.
>
> I have a scheduler for each of the major operating departments, plus clerks to service the schedulers and a schedule co-ordinator reporting directly to me. The scheduler works very closely with his department foreman. Although their desks are just outside my office, the schedulers spend a good deal of time in the plant. They are also in frequent telephone contact with the sales offices at least once a week.
>
> Our high-volume food and beverage lines are, generally speaking, manufactured to estimate. We make a monthly manufacturing program, which then is converted to a daily schedule. The lower-volume lines are scheduled formally on a weekly basis with job priority listing made several times a week by the foreman and the scheduler.

Andrew Cox, plant accountant, appeared to be the oldest of the management staff and rather more serene. Cox talked of his job:

> I am responsible directly to the plant manager but functionally to the division controller. My basic function is to develop and supervise an organization for the maintenance of accounting records and the preparation of reports therefrom in accordance with company policies and procedures. My organization is divided into three groups—general accounting, cost accounting, and office services. A few years ago we developed a stenographic pool in office services, and now only the plant manager has a private secretary. Because of the diversity of products, many thousands of individual product costs must be developed and applied by the cost section. The annual proposed sales and income budget, because of its essentially financial nature, is co-ordinated by the plant controller. However, complete responsibilities for the development of departmental budgets is assigned by the plant manager to the responsible operating and staff groups concerned.
>
> We are the auditors who see that every other department is obeying rules and procedures. It is our responsibility to know all that is in the instruction manuals. There are twelve volumes of general instructions and lots of special manuals.

The plant industrial engineer was Joe Herman. The researcher was impressed with the mobility of Herman's face and the high level of activity which he, as well as most of the other members of the management staff, exhibited. Herman stated:

> Industrial engineering in Empire Glass Company is active in the fields of time study, budgetary control, job evaluation, and methods improvement. Our company is on a standard cost system—that is, all our product costs are based on engineered standards, accurately measuring all labor, direct and indirect, and material that is expended in the manufacture of each and every item we make in our plants. All the jobs in the French City plant, up to and including the foreman, have been measured and standards set. Actually, there are company-wide bench marks for most jobs, including the foreman's. For foremen the standard is used as a guide in increasing or reducing the supervisory force. If measurement shows that the quantity of supervisory work is less than 75 per cent of standard, a foreman is taken off. If the workload is heavy and we find 75 per cent of a supervisory job is there, we add a supervisor.
>
> Most of the machinery is just like that in other Empire Glass Company plants. Standards are established wherever the equipment is first used—which may be in the development engineering department in British City. We, of course, may make adjustment for local conditions. However, all our standards are forwarded to division, which checks them against standards in use at other plants.
>
> Industrial engineering spearheads the cost reduction program within the organization. In fact, we should spend three quarters of our time on cost reduction. We have recently made an arrangement with the cost accounting group which is going to eliminate a lot of time this department has been spending in checking to see which standards applied to particular products being manufactured. Now cost accounting will do this work, which is essentially clerical and took time we could otherwise spend on cost reduction work. The budgeted savings this year from methods improvement is in six figures, and we now expect to exceed that by a substantial amount.

Harold Stone, industrial relations manager, was a large, slow-speaking man who wore a small mustache. He had been with Empire Glass Company a long time and had been assistant plant manager of one of its smaller plants before coming to French City. He was proud of the fact that the French City plant had never experienced a strike and that formal written grievances were almost unheard of.

In discussing company training programs which he conducted at the plant, Stone said that all management personnel, including foremen and assistant foremen, had taken the four-day "Communications Course," designed by the Empire corporate staff but conducted at the plant level, often with personnel from other Empire plants participating. The emphasis was on learning how to listen more effectively so as to unblock the flow of information up and down in the organization. A four-day course, "Conference Leadership," had been given to some of the management people, and others were scheduled for its next repetition. Emphasis in this course was on role playing as a conference participant as well as conference leader.

Stone then commented on some of his other responsibilities. Several of them were represented by an impressive display in the manufacturing area near the main entrance, occupying a space about fifty by twenty feet. During the time the researcher was in the plant, the backdrop contained several panels about twelve or fourteen feet high on safety, on a housekeeping contest then underway, and on job security and industrial competition. All slogans and other comments were in both French and English. In the open area in front of the backdrop there were smaller displays, including a five-foot chart on an easel which showed the manufacturing efficiency rating (actual production cost versus standard cost) of the previous month for each of the Empire Glass Company plants and their standing within their division.

Contests between departments were conducted frequently. Prior to the thirteen-week housekeeping contest, there had been a safety contest. Stone declared that in two of the last five years, there had been only one lost-time accident. Absenteeism was so low that statistics were no longer kept on it. Turnover was exceptionally low, which he attributed in part to the high wages and fringe benefits of the plant.

Turning to another aspect of Empire's personnel policy, Stone stated:

> We believe that it is important that the supervisor and the employee understand each other, that they know what the other person thinks about business, profit, importance of satisfying the customer, and any other aspect of business. While a great deal can and is done within the regular business framework, we also believe that rapport between the supervisor and the employee can be improved in the social contacts which exist or can be organized. For this reason we sponsor dances, bowling leagues, golf days, fishing derbies, picnics, baseball leagues, supervision parties, management week ends and many unofficial get-togethers. Over many years we have been convinced that these activities really improve management-labor relations. They also provide a means for union and management to work closely together in organizing and planning these events. These opportunities help provide a mutual respect for the other fellow's point of view.

Some of these events were held in the plant cafeteria, which was another of Stone's responsibilities. The researcher was able to see the elaborate decorations prepared for an employees' children's Christmas party and for a supervisors' party. In addition, all employees, including the plant management, ate their lunches in the plant cafeteria, which was plain and functional except when decorated for a party.

It was Stone's responsibility to maintain the confidential file in connection with Empire's performance appraisal program for salaried employees. Procedures for handling the program were spelled out in one of the corporate manuals. Two forms were completed annually. One called for a rating of the employee by his supervisor, first on his performance of each of his responsibilities outlined in the "Position Analysis Manual" and then on each of twelve general characteristics such as co-operation, initiative, job knowledge, and delegation. In another section the supervisor and the appraised employee were jointly required to indicate what experience, training or self-development would improve performance or prepare for advancement by the employee prior to the next appraisal. The appraisal was to be discussed between the supervisor and the employee; the latter was required to sign the form, and space was given for any comments he might want to make. The second form was not shown to the employee. It called for a rating on over-all performance, an indication of promotability, and a listing of potential replacements. It was used for manpower planning, and after comments by the supervisor of the appraiser, it was forwarded to the division office.

Managerial Practices and Relationships

After becoming acquainted with most of the key executives at the French City plant and with their major responsibilities, the researcher turned his attention to some of their activities and to their relations to each other in performing their duties.

He observed that Hunt and the four staff managers whose offices were closest to his seldom worked alone at their desks (see Exhibits 2 and 3). They were either in the manufacturing area or in each other's offices having impromptu meetings of twos, threes, or fours much of the time. Often a production supervisor or an office staff person would be in the group. The offices of Andrews, Jenkins, Herman, and Cox were identical to each other and similar to Hunt's, except they lacked the carpet, drapes, and polished wood furniture he was provided with, and the upper part of their partitions were entirely of glass. They all contained a conference table and extra chairs.

In addition to these frequent informal meetings, there were a number of regular meetings involving plant management personnel. Most of these were held in a large, well-appointed conference room with a highly polished wooden table seating twenty or more people. The plant manager met monthly with the management staff and also with the production supervisors to discuss performance against the budget. The plant manager, assistant plant manager, and the industrial relations manager also held a monthly meeting with key union representatives. This was informal and the discussion centered on problems of one of the parties or mutual problems which were not current grievances.

Exhibit 2

EMPIRE GLASS COMPANY

INFORMATION ABOUT CERTAIN PERSONNEL

| | | | Approximate Length of Service | | |
| | | | | | |
Name	Position	Approximate Age	French City	EGC	College Education
James Hunt.......	Plant manager	40–45	8	18	None
Robert Andrews...	Assistant plant manager	35	3	8	Agricultural engineering
Andrew Cox......	Plant accountant	50	15	23	None
Ray Jenkins.......	Production control supervisor	45	18	18	None
Harold Stone......	Personnel supervisor	45–50	5	29	None
Joe Herman.......	Plant industrial engineer	30–35	1	10	Engineering
Tom Voorhees....	Quality control supervisor	30	5	5	Engineering in Netherlands
G. E. Jacques.....	General foreman	45–50	25	25	None
Henry Dodds......	General foreman	50	18	18	None
L. G. Adams......	District sales manager	45–50	18	18	None

Exhibit 3

EMPIRE GLASS COMPANY

FRENCH CITY PLANT—DIAGRAM OF OFFICE AREAS

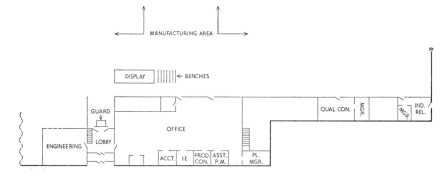

The production control manager chaired a meeting held every Tuesday and Friday morning, attended by the assistant plant manager and both general foremen. Each department foreman and his scheduler appeared briefly to discuss scheduling problems. A plant cost reduction committee was chaired by the plant industrial engineer; the plant manager, assistant manager, the plant engineer, the production control manager, and the general foremen were members. There were other committees involving fewer different interests or meeting less frequently.

Later interviews added to the researcher's understanding not only of the management practices but of the attitudes of the key executives toward their jobs and the requirements of the organization.

James Hunt, Plant Manager

During a discussion of the budget Hunt told the researcher that plant income was the actual sales realization not a transfer price. Therefore income was adversely affected when either sales failed to come up to the forecast on which the budget was based or sales prices were reduced to meet competition. Hunt also informed the researcher that sales managers, too, have their incentives based on making or exceeding the budget and that their forecasts had tended to be quite accurate. Overoptimism on one group of products had usually been offset by underestimation of sales on other products. However, because no adjustment was permitted in budgeted profit when sales income was below forecast, the fact that sales were running 3 per cent below the level budgeted for 1963 was forcing the plant to reduce expenses substantially in order to equal or exceed the profit budgeted for the year.

> RESEARCHER: The budget rather puts you in a straitjacket then.
> HUNT: No, the budget is a guide—a kind of signpost—not a straitjacket.

The researcher then suggested to Hunt that there were probably some accounts in the budget which left some slack for reducing expenses if sales fell below forecast.

> HUNT: No, we never put anything in the budget that is unknown or guessed at. We have to be able to back up every single figure in the budget. We have to budget our costs at standard, assuming that we can operate at standard. We know we won't all the time. There will be errors and failures, but we are never allowed to budget for them.
> RESEARCHER: It seems to me that there must be some give somewhere.
> HUNT: Well, I suppose there are some contentious accounts like overtime and outside storage. We do have arguments with division on those. For example, I might ask for $140,000 in the budget for overtime. The division manager will probably say $130,000—so we compromise at $130,000.
> RESEARCHER: How about cost reduction? You budget a certain amount there, I understand. Do you have the specific projects planned when you prepare the budget?

HUNT: We budget for more than the savings expected from specific projects. We might have $100,000 in specific projects and budget $150,000.

RESEARCHER: I would think this is one place where you might really push for extra cost savings in order to offset an income loss like you've had this year.

HUNT: Yes, this is one of the areas we're pushing hard this year.

RESEARCHER: Can you delay repairs and overhauls to reduce expenses?

HUNT: At the time we make the budget we prepare an overhaul schedule in detail. It establishes the amount of labor and material that we expect to go into the overhaul as well as setting the time—which is cleared with production control so it will be the least inconvenient. Then any change from this schedule must be approved at the division level.

RESEARCHER: I understand you have an incentive for managers based on performance of the plant compared to budget.

HUNT: The bonus is paid on the year's results. It is paid as a percentage of salary to all who are eligible—they are the ones on the organization chart I gave you. There are three parts to it—one part is based on plant income, one on standards improvement or cost cutting, and the third on operating performance. We can make up to 20 per cent by beating our plant income target and 25 per cent on cost reduction and operating efficiency together. But we have to make 90 per cent of our budgeted income figure to participate in any bonus at all.

I think we have the 25 per cent on efficiency and cost reduction pretty well sewn up this year. If we go over our budgeted income, we can get almost 35 per cent bonus.

RESEARCHER: Has the French City plant made a bonus in recent years?

HUNT: We have always made a certain amount—about 10 per cent. In the past the bonus was based more on efficiency than anything else. We're one of the larger plants, and it made it harder for us. The larger plants just don't have the control. We don't know as well what the individual men are doing as in the smaller plants.

While Hunt and the researcher were at lunch early in December, the conversation drifted back to the maintenance operation.

HUNT: We have been holding off work on molds [for shaping the jars and bottles] until next year. Jones [machine-shop foreman] had been planning to wait until the new year to fix up the molds. They were laid aside after the production runs ended in which they were used. The only trouble is, he started his program too early. Now we are going to have to run some more of some of those bottles this year, and he'll have to repair the molds.

I told Jones he knew what had to be done, that I expected him to keep the savings he planned and I didn't want to hear about his troubles. However, I know I will have to go along if he can back up his reasons why he can't save all the money he projected for December.

At another time Hunt discussed with the researcher some of his practices as plant manager:

HUNT: I never look for answers to problems in these *(pointing to manuals in a cabinet in his office)*. If I get a memo that refers specifically to an instruction in a manual, then I look it up. Otherwise I never touch them. I count on my accountant to keep me straight on rules and procedures. He has several shelves full of manuals and he's supposed to know what is in them. I don't look at this [loose-leaf book containing accounting reports] either. I don't look backward, I look forward. When I get information, I act on it right away. Once it goes in the book, I don't look at it except when I'm trying to spread a new budget over the year. Then I use past history.

Nor do I write many memos. When I have something to say I go tell the person or persons right away. I think people read into letters what they want. I guess you could say I follow the head-on approach. Unfortunately, I use the same approach with my superiors, and once in a while I get called down for it.

RESEARCHER: I am interested in knowing which of the things you do you believe could not be delegated to someone else.

HUNT: For one thing, I can't delegate relations with sales. Production control handles individual scheduling problems with salespeople, but the manager has to look at the over-all relationship. There are a lot of things production control can't do. The manager has to make the final decisions. Then there is capital budgeting. Also, the manager must be close to the people. For example, one of our foremen was having some trouble with his men. I suggested that he take them out, and I allotted him some money to do it. He took them bowling and bought them some drinks. He got closer to them and his relationship with them improved a lot. He still has a lot of parties. At the foreman level, I believe you can't get too close to your men. I think maybe a manager can get too close.[2]

Robert Andrews, Assistant Plant Manager

ANDREWS: Well, a budget system like this certainly doesn't leave much for the imagination. Your job is pretty well laid out for you. I suppose we could run a plant this size if this were the whole company without such an elaborate system. But with a big company, if you don't have a budget system that is pretty explicit, you can lose an awful lot of ground.

RESEARCHER: How important to you are the sales estimates?

---
[2] Hunt took a daily tour of the plant and was observed by the researcher to call by name and speak in a folksy manner with many production workers and foremen.

ANDREWS: They affect everybody in the operation. Salespeople can put a lot of blue sky into their estimates because they can't afford to send a pessimistic estimate up to division. But it ends up hurting us. It simply causes inefficiency around here when things don't turn out the way sales predicted. I think we'd almost rather they would hand in pessimistic reports so we could be a little bit more sure where we stand on the production line.

RESEARCHER: When you talk of your duties, I don't hear you say anything about increasing production volume.

ANDREWS: We have standards. So long as we are meeting the standards we are meeting our costs, and we do not worry about increasing production. We don't tell the foreman that he needs to get more goods out the door. We tell him to get rid of the red in his budget. I'm content with a 100 per cent performance. I'd like 105 per cent, but if we want more production, it is up to IE to develop methods change.

RESEARCHER: What, then, are the principal skills you expect of a foreman?

ANDREWS: Communications and use of available control procedures. The foreman is expected to communicate effectively with all plant person-nel, including staff heads. He must be able to convince his employees of the importance of certain aspects of their jobs, discipline or praise them when it is deserved. In all cases he must get his point across as "boss" and yet maintain the spirit of co-operation and teamwork that has marked our operation. Our control procedures are easy to apply. In each department there is an engineered standard for each operation covering labor, mate-rials, and spoilage. Without waiting for a formal statement from account-ing, a foreman can analyze his performance in any area and take corrective action if necessary. Then he receives reports from accounting to assist him in maintaining tight cost control. One is a daily report which records labor and spoilage performance against standard. The monthly report provides a more detailed breakdown of labor costs, materials and supplies used, and spoilage. It also establishes the efficiency figure for the month. This report is discussed at a monthly meeting of all of my supervisors. Gener-ally the plant industrial engineer and a member of the accounting staff are present. Each foreman explains his variances from standard and submits a forecast of his next month's performance.

RESEARCHER: You mentioned communication between the foreman and staff managers. Does the foreman go directly to a staff manager with a problem or through you?

ANDREWS: A foreman may go directly to a staff manager, or more usually one of his assistants, or he may go to his general foreman or myself. And a staff manager may go direct to a foreman. I'm usually brought in on the more important ones.

RESEARCHER: How does the foreman know which ones to bring to you?

ANDREWS: I really don't know how, but they seem to know.

RESEARCHER: Do they keep you sufficiently informed, or bring too much to you?

ANDREWS: Oh, they do pretty well, on the whole. I don't think I ever get too much information, but I do have to get after a foreman occasionally for failing to tell me something he should have.

Production Control

The biweekly production control meetings observed by the researcher lasted about an hour. Jenkins and Andrews sat at the head of the conference table. The two general foremen were also present throughout the meeting, while Hunt frequently dropped in for a time. Each production foreman and the production control scheduler working for his department came into the meeting at a prearranged time, and when their turn came they reported on what products they were currently running and on any problems they were having or which they anticipated. Most of the questions as well as instructions given in the meeting came from Andrews. It was also he who usually dismissed one foreman-scheduler pair and called on the next. Questions from Andrews or Jenkins were seldom clearly addressed to either the foreman or scheduler. They were answered more frequently by the scheduler than the foreman, and often a scheduler would supplement comments made by the foreman. Generally, the schedulers were younger but spoke with more self-assurance than the foremen.

There were frequent references to specific customers, their needs, complaints, and present attitude toward Empire Glass. Both Jenkins and Andrews tended to put instructions and decisions in terms of what was required to satisfy some particular customer or French City plant customers in general.

The researcher was especially interested in a part of a Tuesday production control meeting involving a foreman, "Mo" Pelletier, and the scheduler for his department, Dan Brown. While Dan was making the status report, the researcher observed that Mo was shaking his head in disagreement with Dan, but without saying anything. Dan was telling of his plan to discontinue on Friday the order being processed on a certain line, to shift to another order on Friday, and then return on Tuesday to the product currently being produced.

ANDREWS: I don't think your plan makes much sense. You go off on Friday and then on again Tuesday.

Mo (*to Dan*):   Is this all required before the end of the year? [This was asked with obvious negative emotional feeling and then followed by comments by both Andrews and Jenkins.]

DAN: Mind you—I could call sales again.

JENKINS: I can see the point, Dan. It is sort of nonsensical to change back after so short a run.

MO: This would mean our production would be reduced all week to around 300 instead of 350. You know it takes four hours to make the changeover.

DAN: But the order has been backed up.

ANDREWS: It is backed up only because their [sales] demands are unreasonable.

DAN: They only asked us to do the best we can.

ANDREWS: They always do this. We should never have put this order on in the first place.

MO: If you want to we could. . . . (*Makes a suggestion about how to handle the problem.*)

ANDREWS: Production-wise, this is the best deal (*agreeing with Mo's plan*).

DAN: Let me look at it again.

ANDREWS: Production-wise, this is best; make the changeover on the week end.

JENKINS (*summarizes; then to Dan*):   The whole argument is the lost production you would have.

MO: It'll mean backing up the order only one day.

ANDREWS (*after another matter in Mo's department has been discussed and there is apparently nothing further, Andrews turns to Dan and smiles*):   It's been a pleasure, Dan. (*Dan then returned the smile weakly and got up to go somewhat nervously.*)

As Jenkins and the researcher were leaving the conference room after the meeting, Jenkins commented to the researcher.

JENKINS: Danny got clobbered as you could see. I used to stand up for him, but he just doesn't come up here prepared. He should have the plans worked out with his foreman before they come up.

After another one of the production control meetings, Jenkins again discussed an incident which had occurred in the meeting.

JENKINS: We in production control are the buffer between the sales and operating people. That discussion about the Smith bottle you heard is an example. Andrews is basically concerned with efficiency. He doesn't want to make anything that can't be made to standard. Now those little cracks we're getting mean that if we continue running, our spoilage rate will skyrocket—maybe double or triple what it normally would be. Andrews hates this because it drives his efficiency down. But what he didn't know upstairs was that Jim Hunt had made a personal commitment to the customer to get those 50,000 bottles out today, and he was going to do

it come hell or high water. Andrews just never had a chance when he
started making noises about shutting the line down. So I won and Bob lost
this time, but he's able to be big about it and see the real issue. Where it
really gets tough for him, though, is that by the end of the month this
particular problem will have become lost in the figures. People will have
forgotten that today, November 8, a decision went against Bob Andrews.
All they will notice is that according to the accounting reports, Andrews
had bad efficiency for the month of November.

To avoid looking bad he has to find another operation where there is
some slack and produce more efficiently. That's the only way he can protect himself, but it puts a lot of pressure on him. Bob and I are usually
able to work these things out fairly well. We know that the problem is
more or less built into our jobs.

In discussing his job Jenkins frequently commented on how he
thought a decision or problem would affect someone else in the plant.

JENKINS: If all you had to do was manage the nuts and bolts of production scheduling and not worry about the customer or how people were
going to react, this would be the easiest job in the whole plant. You could
just sit down with a paper and pencil and lay it out the best way. But because the customer is so important and because you've got to look ahead
to how people are going to react to a given kind of schedule, it makes the
whole job tremendously complicated. It isn't easy!

Andrew Cox, Plant Accountant

COX: We want the budget to be realistic; but we also want it to be
something of a target for our management and operating personnel. At
the French City plant our goal over the years has been to present budgets
which reflects improvement in the per cent return of gross plant income
to gross plant sales as well as return on employed capital. We have been
reasonably successful in this despite constantly rising labor and material
costs.

The budget is a plan to insure the success of the company. We put a lot
of stress on competition within the company and against other companies
in our field. We here at French City want to do as well as any other plant
in Empire Glass. . . . The essence of the present control system was developed fifteen years ago. There were a lot of gripes and criticism when it
was introduced. The big difference between then and now is that now the
people on the floor use the reports as a tool. . . . We've done a lot of
training since then. It took maybe ten years to get the job done.

RESEARCHER: Have there been changes in the bonus plan over the
years?

COX: Yes, at one time the bonus plan was based on departmental
results—on departmental efficiency. Under this there was a tendency for

the departments to work at cross-purposes, to compete rather than co-operate with each other. For the last seven or eight years, the emphasis has been on the plant, not the department. The latest plan is geared not only to the attainment of budgeted cost goals but also the attainment of budgeted income. This is consistent with the attention we are placing on sales. I think the company was disturbed by what they sensed was a belief that those at the plant level can't do much about sales. Now we are trying to get the idea across that if we make better jars and give better service, we will sell more.

RESEARCHER: I assume there must be some accounts in the budget where you leave yourself some room to maneuver.

COX: Well, in this company there is very little opportunity to play footsy with the figures.

Guillaume Jacques, General Foreman

Jacques was completely bilingual, and he felt his French background was an advantage in dealing with the workers, an estimated 90 per cent of whom were French Canadians. In describing his job he stated that he worked closely with both the assistant plant manager and the production control manager, but more with the latter. He said the job of general foreman was to regulate the troubles of the department and compared it to the relationship of a father and his children.

RESEARCHER: Are the standards and the budget important in your work?

JACQUES: Yes, very important. Most of the time they ask you not only to meet your budget but to do better, saving such and such amount of money. The assistant foreman has to check constantly, each production line each hour, to be sure they are close to standard.

RESEARCHER: Can you keep the employee satisfied as well as meet the budget requirements?

JACQUES: Yes, you've got to make the worker understand the importance of keeping the budget. I get them in the office and explain that if we don't meet the budget we'll have to cut down somewhere else. It is mathematical. I explain all this to them—they have given me a budget to meet, I need them for this, they need me to give them work. We work like a team. I try to understand them.

RESEARCHER: Do you feel under tension in your work?

JACQUES: Sure I work under tension, but don't all supervisors? You try to go along with the temperament of the men as much as possible. Myself, I ask the men to go out to have a beer with me, to go to a party. It relaxes them from our preoccupations. Right now, for example, there is this party with the foremen coming up. At these gatherings it is strictly against the rules to talk about work. These things are necessary.

Jacques commented on the advances in technology and reduction in the number of employees needed. He said that he felt management had done a good job with the union in persuading the workers that cost cutting, although it meant reducing the number of people on the floor, actually increases job security in the long run.

Henry Dodds, General Foreman

RESEARCHER: Do you and the foremen participate in establishing the budget?

DODDS: I'm responsible for preparing the budgets for my department, and the foreman participates in my area because I ask him for his thoughts. We have to make a budget for each production department.

RESEARCHER: Does the foreman get a copy of the budget?

DODDS: Yes, each foreman has a copy of the budget for his department. It's prepared by the industrial engineers and the accounting department from our work sheets.

RESEARCHER: Does the production worker see the budget?

DODDS: He doesn't see the budget. He has the machine operating standard; if he meets this he is doing his share. The standard is set so that if he works the machine at full capacity, he achieves 110 per cent of standard.

RESEARCHER: Since you don't have wage incentives, is there any problem in getting the employees to produce up to standard?

DODDS: Well, there is usually some needling when a man is down below standard. He's asked, "Why don't you get to be part of the crew?" It doesn't hurt anything. . . . You only get a good day's work out of people if they are happy. We strive to keep our people happy so they'll produce the standard and make the budget. We try to familiarize them with what is expected of them. We have targets set for us. The budget is reasonable, but it is not simple to attain. By explaining our problems to the workers we find it easier to reach the budget.

Dodds emphasized that an understanding of plant problems and objectives on the part of the foremen was also important. He told of a current program to try to fill the need for a certain type of cutting machine in one plant area by releasing several similar machines from another area for conversion to accomplish the new purpose.

DODDS: Because the foremen understood the program, they will cooperate to clear the machines of work and make them available.

RESEARCHER: Do you have situations where a foreman thinks a standard is too high and the worker cannot make it?

DODDS: We haven't run into an instance of that in eight years. The industrial engineer goes over the standard with the foreman and he has an opportunity to question it before it is approved by management. Usually they explain the standard to the operator, and they always tell the operator what the industrial engineer is doing.

Interviews with Foremen and Production Workers

Foremen and production workers who were interviewed were all very much aware of the budget, and workers often explained behavior of foremen in terms of the requirements of the budget. Most of the foremen and many of the workers accepted the necessity of keying their activities to the work standards and the budget. One notable exception was a foreman of many years' service who said:

> We have a meeting once a month upstairs. They talk to us about budgets, quality, etc. That's all on the surface; that's a lot of bull. It looks good. It has to look good but it is all bull. For example, the other day [a foreman] had a meeting with the workers to talk about quality. After that an employee brought to his attention a defect in some products. He answered, "Send it out anyway." And they had just finished talking to us about quality.

Although they accepted the necessity of standards and budgets, many foremen and workers expressed feelings of pressure from superiors and from the control system. In contrast were the comments of one of the younger and more ambitious foremen—a French Canadian.

> What I like about this department is that I am in charge. I can do anything I like as long as I meet up with the budget. I can have that machine moved—send it over there—as long as I have good reasons to justify it. The department, that's me. I do all the planning and I'm responsible for results. I'm perfectly free in the use of my time (*gives examples of his different arrival times during the past week and mentions the fact that he came in twice on Saturday and once on Sunday for short periods).* . . . One thing I like here is that we don't get swelled heads about the positions we hold. Each man here—foreman, manager, and so on—is an employee of the company. We each have a job to do. You can talk freely with any of the staff heads.

Most of the foremen were bilingual French Canadians. Some expressed dislike of the troublesome problems they felt were inherent in a job directing the work of others. One declared he would not want the manager's job for this reason, "although he is well paid for it."

No negative statements by foremen about the plant manager or the management staff were heard by the researcher. However, one expressed a desire to return to hourly work. Another felt that the foremen needed a union.

Foremen tended to view the production worker as irresponsible and interested, insofar as his job is concerned, only in his pay check and quitting time. One foreman expressed himself as follows, "We do all the work; they do nothing." Even an officer of the union commented:

> They don't give a damn about the standards. They work nonchalantly, and they are very happy when their work slows up. If the foreman is obliged to stop the line for two minutes, everyone goes to the toilet. There are some workers who do their work conscientiously, but this is not the case with the majority.

When speaking of their work, several of the production workers expressed feelings of pressure, although others declared they were accustomed to their work and it did not bother them. One said:

> Everyone is obsessed with meeting the standards—the machine adjuster, the foreman, the assistant foreman. They all get on my nerves.

One old-timer clearly differentiated the company, which he considered benevolent, from his foremen:

> I'm not talking about the company. I'm talking about the foremen. I can understand that these men are under tension as well as we are. They have meetings every week. I don't know what they talk about up there. . . . The foremen have their standards to live up to. They're nervous. They don't even have a union like us. So if things go bad, well, that's all. . . . They make us nervous with all this. But there's a way with people. We don't say to a man, "Do this, do that." If we said, "Would you do this?" it is not the same thing. You know a guy like myself who has been here for thirty-five years knows a few tricks. If I am mad against the foreman, I could do a few little things to the machine to prevent it from keeping up with the standards and no one would know.

Another said:

> I'd prefer working for a dollar an hour less and have a job that is less tiring. It is not really hard, but you have to work fast. . . . Our nerves are on edge here. . . . The worst ones aren't the foremen but the schedulers. It is never the fault of the machines but always the operator. . . . They are always on us. But they are good people here just the same. They replace us when we are tired or want to go to the toilet. The foremen could be much worse.

Those who complained about their foremen, however, tended to contrast the manager and the management staff, as did one worker, who said, "They're people—polite people. They speak to you properly."

Although a number of workers expressed sentiments similar to those quoted above, most workers conveyed to the researcher a feeling of over-all satisfaction with their jobs. Typical was the comment of the worker who said, "Truly, it is a good company, and it pays well." In a recent Harvard research study of a number of jobs in twelve plants in several different industries in the United States and Canada, the French City plant workers who were included ranked highest of the twelve plants in job satisfaction.

In Pursuit of Budgeted Goals

The researcher was particularly interested in a series of events he observed which related to a special meeting of the entire French City plant management held in November. On his first visit to the plant, James Hunt and several of the staff managers had mentioned to him the fact that sales for the year had fallen below expectations and that their bonus was in jeopardy as a result.

One day in early November the researcher noticed an unusual amount of activity in the accounting section. Hunt came into the area frequently, and he and Cox from time to time would huddle with one of the accountants over some figures. In the afternoon the researcher observed several management staff members saunter by the plant accountant's office, one of them two or three times, without the purposeful air they usually had when walking in the office. The researcher learned from Cox that the extra activity was due to the fact that the report on the October results was to be issued that day.

At one point in the afternoon, while the researcher was in Cox's office for a prearranged interview, Hunt walked in and sat down but said nothing. After a few minutes he started out the door.

Cox: Jim, did you want to see me about something?
HUNT: I'm waiting for your story (*referring to the report of October results*).

Hunt then strolled about the accounting area for a time and then left.

A week later Hunt scheduled a joint meeting of the management staff and the line organization to go over the October results. This was a departure from the usual practice of having the groups in separate meetings. Prior to the meeting Hunt discussed with the researcher what he hoped to accomplish in the meeting.

HUNT: The meeting this afternoon is simply to get things straightened out. Those figures we got last week showed that some of the accounts did what they were expected to do, some did more, and some did a good deal less. The thing we have to do now is kick those accounts in the pants that are not making the savings they planned to make. What we've been doing is raising the expected savings as the time gets shorter. It may be easy to save 10 per cent on your budget when you've got six months; but with only six weeks, it is an entirely different matter. The thing to do now is to get everybody together and excited about the possibility of doing it. We know how it can be done. Those decisions have already been made. It's not unattainable, even though I realize we are asking an awful lot from these men. You see we are in a position now where just a few thousand dollars one way or the other can make as much as 10 per cent difference in the amount of bonus the men get. There is some real money on the line. It can come either from a sales increase or an expense decrease, but the big chunk has to come out of an expense decrease.

RESEARCHER: Do you expect some wrangles this afternoon about who is right and who is wrong?

HUNT: No, we never fight about the budget. It is simply a tool. All we want to know is what is going on. Then we can get to work and fix it. There are never any disagreements about the budget itself. Our purpose this afternoon is to pinpoint those areas where savings can be made, where there is a little bit of slack, and then get to work and pick up the slack.

RESEARCHER: Am I right that any time there is a departure from budgeted expense or budgeted sales, you and the other managers immediately begin to look for other plant accounts where the losses can be made up?

HUNT: Yes, that is an automatic decision or else we'll give the department that has been losing money a certain period of time to make it up. Also, any time anybody has a gain, I tell them I expect them to maintain that gain.

The researcher also talked to Bob Andrews concerning the methods used to pick up the projected savings.

ANDREWS: When you have lost money in one sector you have to look around for something else that you can "milk" to make up the difference.

RESEARCHER: Do you ever ask for volunteers?

ANDREWS: No, we do the "milking." Those guys just have to do what we say. How much we can save pretty much depends on how hard the man in the corner office wants to push on the thing. I mean if we really wanted to save money we probably could do it, but it would take a tremendous effort on everybody's part and Jim would really have to crack the whip.

Special Line and Staff Meeting

The meeting was held in the conference room at 4:00 P.M. Hunt and Cox sat at the far end of the table, facing the door, with an easel bearing a flip chart near them. The chart listed the projected savings in budgeted expense for November and December, account by account. The group of about thirty arranged themselves at the table so that, with only a couple of exceptions, the management staff personnel and general foremen sat closest to Hunt and Cox and the foremen and assistant foremen sat toward the foot of the table.

Hunt opened the meeting one or two minutes after four and declared that performance against budget for October would first be reviewed, followed by discussion of the November and December projections. He stated rather emphatically that he was "disappointed" in the October performance. Although money had been saved, it represented good performance in some areas but rather poor performance in others. The gains made in the areas where performance had been good must be maintained and the weak areas brought up, Hunt declared.

He then turned the meeting over to Cox who reviewed the October results, reading from the report which everyone had in front of him. Where performance was not good, he called on the individual responsible for that area to explain. The essence of the typical explanation was that the original budgeted figure was unrealistic and that the actual amount expended was as low as it could possibly be under the circumstances. Hunt frequently broke into the explanation with a comment like, "Well, that is not good enough" or, "Can you possibly do better for the rest of the year?" or "I hope we have that straightened out now." When he sat down, the person giving the explanation was invariably thanked by Cox.

Following this part of the meeting, Cox, followed by Jenkins, commented on the sales outlook for the remainder of the year. They indicated that for the two months as a whole sales were expected to be about on budget. After asking for questions and getting one from a foreman, Hunt said:

> Well now, are there any more questions? Ask them now if you have them. Everybody sees where we stand on the bonus, I assume. Right?

Hunt then referred to the chart on plant expense savings and began to discuss it, saying:

> The problem now is time. We keep compressing the time and raising the gain [the projected savings for the year had been raised $32,000 above what had been projected in October]. You can only do that so long. Time is running out, fellows. We've got to get on the stick.

Several times Hunt demanded better upward communication on problems as they came up. He gave an example from the previous month and declared:

This sort of thing is absolutely inexcusable. We simply cannot have such a thing happen again. We've got to know ahead of time when these mix-ups are going to occur so that we can allow for and correct them.

As Cox was covering projections for November, account by account, the following exchange took place when he came to manufacturing efficiency:

COX: Now we have come to you, Bob. I see you're getting a little bit more optimistic on what you think you can do.

ANDREWS: Yes, the boss keeps telling me I'm just an old pessimist and I don't have any faith in my people. I'm still a pessimist, but we are doing tremendously. I think it's terrific, fellows (*pointing to a line graph*). I don't know whether we can get off the top of this chart or not, but at the rate this actual performance line is climbing, we might make it. All I can say is, keep up the good work . . . . I guess I'm an optimistic pessimist.

The following comments were made during the discussion of projected savings for December in the equipment maintenance account.

COX: Where in the world are you fellows going to save $8,000 more than you originally said you would save?

McDONALD: [A noncommittal response.]

JONES: I'd just like to say at this point to the group that it would be a big help if you guys would take it easy on your machines. That's where we are going to save an extra $8,000—simply by only coming down to fix the stuff that won't run. You're really going to have to make it go as best you can. That's the only way we can possibly save the kind of money we have to save. You have been going along pretty well, but all I've got to say is I hope you can keep it up and not push those machines too hard.

Although Jones spoke with sincerity, the researcher noted that a number of sly smiles and pokes in the ribs were exchanged by foremen at the end of the table nearest the door.

Hunt concluded the meeting at about 5:30 P.M., still chewing on his cigar.

HUNT: There are just a couple of things I want to say before we break up. First, we've got to stop making stupid errors in shipping. Joe [foreman of shipping], you've absolutely *got* to get after those people to straighten them out. Second, I think it should be clear, fellows, that we can't break any more promises. Sales is our bread and butter. If we don't get those orders out in time, we'll have no one but ourselves to blame for missing our budget. So I just hope it is clear that production control is running the show for the rest of the year. Third, the big push is on *now!* We sit around here expecting these problems to solve themselves, but they don't! It ought to be clear to all of you that no problem gets solved until it's spotted. Damn it, I just don't want any more dewy-eyed estimates about performance for the rest of the year. If something is going sour we want to hear about it. And there's no reason for not hearing about it! (*Pounds the table, then voice falls and a smile begins to form.*) It can mean a nice penny in your pocket if you can keep up the good work.

That's all I've got to say. Thank you very much.

Interview with Ray Jenkins

The room cleared immediately, but the researcher engaged Ray Jenkins in further conversation in his office:

RESEARCHER: You got a nice little boost there at the end of the meeting.

JENKINS: No, I'm afraid that little bit of advice there at the end won't make a great deal of difference in the way things work out. I mean that; not that I don't appreciate that sort of thing. It's just that it won't make any difference. As I was telling you before, you have to play off sales against production. It's built into the job. When I attend a meeting like that one upstairs and I see all those production people with their assistants and see the other staff managers with their assistants, and I hear fellows refer to corporate policy that dictates and supports their action at the plant level, I suddenly realize that I'm all alone up there. I can't sit down and fire off a letter to my boss at the division level like the rest of these guys can do. I haven't got any authority at all. It is all based strictly on my own guts and strength. Now Bob is a wonderful guy, I like him and I have a lot of respect for him, but it just so happens that 80 per cent of the time he and I disagree. He knows it and I know it; I mean it's nothing we run away from, we just find ourselves on opposite sides of the question and I'm dependent upon his tact and good judgment to keep from starting a war.

Boy, it can get you down—it really can after awhile, and I've been at it for—God—twenty years. But in production control you've just got to accept it—you're an outcast. They tell you you're cold, that you're inhuman, that you're a bastard, that you don't care about anything except your schedule. And what are you going to say? You're just going to have to swallow it because basically you haven't got the authority to back up the things you know need to be done. Four nights out of five I am like this at the end of the day—just completely drained out—and it comes from having to fight my way through to try to get the plant running as smoothly as I can.

And Andrews up there in that meeting. He stands up with his chart and he compliments everybody about how well they are doing on efficiency. You know, he says, "Keep up the good work," and all that sort of stuff. I just sat there—shaking my head. I was so dazed you know, I mean I kept saying to myself, "What's he doing? What's he saying? What's so great about this?" You know, if I could have, I'd have stood up and I'd have said, "Somebody go down to my files in production control and pick out any five customer orders at random—and letters—and bring them back up here and read them—at random, pick any five." You know what they would show? Do you know how many broken promises and how many missed delivery dates and how many slightly off-standard items we've been pushing out the door here? I mean, what is an efficient operation? Why the stress on operating efficiency? That's why I just couldn't figure out why in the world Andrews was getting as much mileage out of his efficiency performance as he was. Look at all the things we sacrifice to get that efficiency. But what could I do?

Interview with District Sales Manager

Having heard how Jenkins felt about the pressures of the budget on sales, the researcher visited the district sales manager, L. G. Adams, and discussed the impact of the plant budget on the sales department with him.

ADAMS: That's probably my biggest problem on this job, getting the boys here to see that if they really want to serve the customer, they can't hold their own budget up as a shining standard all the time. The budget comes to dominate people's thinking and influence all their actions. I'm afraid even my salesmen have swallowed the production line whole. They can understand the budget so well they can't understand their customers. And the French City plant boys are getting more and more local in their thinking with this budget. They're not thinking about what the customer needs today or may need tomorrow; they just think about their God-damned budget.

If the customer will not take account of your shortcomings, and if you can't take account of the customer's shortcomings, the two of you will eventually end up at each other's throats. That's what this budget system has built into it. Suppose, for example, you want to give a customer a break. Say he has originally planned for a two-week delivery date, but he phones you and says he really has problems and if you possibly could he would like about four days knocked off that delivery date. So I go trotting over to the plant, and I say, "Can we get it four days sooner?" Those guys go out of their minds, and they start hollering about the budget and how everything is planned just right and how I'm stirring them up.

RESEARCHER: It is probably hard to do this very frequently.

ADAMS: That's for sure! You can't go running to them all the time but only when you really need something in the worst way. You can't let those plant guys see your strategy you know. I want to tell you, it is taking an awful lot out of a guy's life around here when he has to do everything by the numbers.

The researcher learned after the first of the year that the report being sent by Hunt to division would show, despite the fact that sales had fallen about 3 per cent below budget, that profits for 1963 had exceeded the amount budgeted and that operating efficiency and cost reduction had both exceeded the budget by a comfortable margin. This enabled the managers and supervisors at the French City plant to attain the salary bonuses for which they had been striving.

13. HIGGINS EQUIPMENT COMPANY (A)

IN THE SUMMER of 1960, executives of the Higgins Equipment Company were concerned about the effectiveness of their executive committee. John Howard, Higgins' president, was disappointed that he had not been able to get other executives involved in these meetings. Other executives complained that the meetings dealt with minor matters and were usually inconclusive.

Company History

The Higgins Equipment Company was founded near Los Angeles, California, in 1920 by John Higgins to manufacture electrical testing equipment. "Jack" Higgins started the small firm to produce several devices he had invented while he was an engineering faculty member at the University of California. His selection of employees was based on all-around mechanical skill, ingenuity and industry. From the start, Jack Higgins and his employees developed close and informal working relationships.

One of the original employees recalled the early days:

> I can remember during my first years here coming in early and sitting at my desk with my full attention on my work and never on the clock, for a full eight hours or more. Talking was not allowed. Singing or whistling was cause for dismissal. And anyone who came to work improperly dressed was sent home. There was no fooling; we were here to work. This all seems like it was impossibly strict now, but somehow you didn't mind it, because Jack Higgins was right there beside you working harder than any one of us.

Another employee explained it this way:

> Jack Higgins had us doing all kinds of jobs that we knew nothing about, but we learned fast. I didn't know anything about soldering or sheet metal work, but pretty soon I felt pretty proud of the job I could do. Then, when he bought the plating equipment I was put in charge of that. Jack gave you the feeling you could handle anything. After a little while he added personnel work to my duties. There was no end to it. No one worried about job overlap in those days because everyone did everything.
>
> Jack believed that there shouldn't be distinctions between anyone in the company—not on the grounds of function, job level, or anything else. That's why all of us, Jack included, stayed on the time clock and why there was so little difference between the highest and lowest salary.

During the first decade of its existence, Higgins was primarily a production shop, depending on the technical skills of Jack Higgins and his associates to attract customers. In 1930, however, Tom Rawson (executive vice president in 1960), who had joined the company in the late 1920's, persuaded Jack Higgins to expand the company's sales activities. Until this time the company had relied on direct-mail advertising, but increased competition convinced Rawson that new sales had to come from direct customer contact in the field. Rawson became Higgins' first field salesman. At about this same time, John Howard (president in 1960) joined the company as an engineer. For the first year with the company he worked on the development of a new testing device, making several major advances in design. However, the new equipment was slow to gain market acceptance, and Howard got Jack Higgins' consent to join Tom Rawson in the field and thereafter split his time between sales and research. The early sales efforts of Howard and Rawson were the beginning of the company's nationwide direct sales force which in 1960 intensively marketed the testing instrument line.

Sales activity expanded rapidly until the beginning of World War II. During the prewar period, the company's testing instruments evolved from simple electrical devices to more complex electronic ones requiring increased design sophistication. With each increment of money and enthusiasm which was being injected into Higgins development and sales efforts, the production department receded further from its initial position of dominance in company affairs.

In 1942, John Howard succeeded Jack Higgins as company president. There was a continuing but not expanding market for the company's testing instruments during the war. Howard and other members of Higgins management, in a desire to continue company growth, decided to use the organization's newly acquired competence in electronics to manufacture radio equipment for the government. This decision brought about a rapid increase in the size of manufacturing facilities. Before the war, Higgins had relied successfully on the use of informal, home-grown production methods, many of which had been developed by Jack Higgins and his early associates. The management emphasis on all-around technical skills, ingenuity, industry, and close personal relationships had continued unabated through the company's development. The rapid expansion caused by the war, however, brought to the company a group of trained and experienced production specialists who were foreign to the Higgins "family" spirit. The advent of this new type of manager and employee, plus the continual crises caused by a new product line and the extraordinary pressures for output associated with wartime contracts, created personal tensions and a certain degree of operating chaos in the heretofore intimate and conservatively managed company. While sales volume grew to an all-time high, profit margins shrunk.

At the end of the war, John Howard, fearing that prewar informality in operating procedures was responsible for the wartime confusion, promoted one of the newly hired production specialists, Jerry Browne, to the post of production manager, with instructions to "bring order out of chaos." Browne immediately hired specialists in methods analysis and production scheduling and control as his lieutenants. While the new production team did not fit easily into the informal and relatively intimate atmosphere shared by the long-service employees of other departments, it forged a cohesive production department and won a reputation for highly systematic production methods and procedures. These changes resulted in higher productivity and lower costs, and John Howard, though not entirely comfortable with members of the new production regime, was generally satisfied with the results.

For several years after the war, Higgins management abandoned the war-stimulated radio product line in favor of an all-out effort to revitalize the test equipment line. Finally, in 1949, Roger Sloane, director of research, convinced John Howard and Tom Rawson that Higgins had a capability for successfully developing and producing radio products. Ralph Johnson (sales vice president in 1960), who had recently joined the Higgins sales department, supported Sloane, contending that the radio market had great potential. Initial steps in entering the commercial radio equipment market were taken slowly, with Johnson personally selling Higgins equipment to large customers. Gradually, however, Johnson selected a network of independent, technically qualified manufacturers' representatives who aggressively promoted and distributed the radio line. The testing equipment line, which was sold to an entirely different type of customer, continued to be marketed by the company's own sales force.

From 1949 to 1960 the company grew rapidly, the number of employees increasing from slightly over 100 to more than 600. In spite of this growth, John Howard attempted to maintain much of the family spirit of the prewar Higgins organization. All employees continued to be paid on a straight salary basis plus a share of profits. A chapel was established on the company's premises for the meditation of employees. Employees were encouraged to speak to John Howard personally about their problems. The researcher was repeatedly told by employees, particularly older ones, how valuable the egalitarian and informal atmosphere established by the founder and continued by his successor was to them.

One older employee explained his feelings:

> The thing that stands out for me most is the warm personal relationship that has always existed between management and employees. The pattern was set by Jack Higgins through his profit-sharing plan, and Mr. Howard has carried it out thoroughly since he took over, with a very personal feeling. Because the company has been so fair and proper to me, I have felt a tremendous loyalty toward it. Of course, now we're too big and things are changing. This is very upsetting to Mr. Howard, because he cannot go out and find out everybody's first name and find out all about their problems.

Almost all the old-timers specifically credited Howard for the loyalty they felt:

> Mr. Howard *is* the Higgins Equipment Company. If he hadn't come along, I doubt that I could have stuck it out. But now my whole life is in this company.

Mr. Howard also felt strongly about maintaining the family feeling:

> We're a company with a personality, a heart. I tell the new people it will take a year before they understand the philosophy of the company, the co-operation, self-sacrifice, decency, honesty—until they really feel they are one of us. By that time, I tell them, they'll have "Higginsitis," a kind of disease. And, after ten years, the only way we could get rid of them would be to shoot them.

Company Situation in 1960

In the summer of 1960, several Higgins executives were concerned about the quality and speed of decisions which had been made on a number of important issues confronting the company over the past several years. Although sales volume was increasing, profits had fallen from the prior year's level. Some credited increased competition in both product lines for a less profitable mix of sales in 1960. Others said that because the company's product line had been expanding in recent years, it was more difficult for it to maintain high-volume, low-unit-cost production schedules and still keep the size of parts inventories to levels consistent with the company's financial position. In addition, there had been an increasing number of disputes between research and engineering personnel, on the one hand, and production personnel on the other, about problems related to the design and timeliness of new products. Similarly, there had been frequent differences of opinion between production and sales personnel about matters relating to equitable production scheduling decisions.

The company had recently received a series of detailed complaints from its manufacturers' representatives, whose sales of radio equipment accounted for well over 50 per cent of company dollar volume. Their complaints emphasized the company's failure to consult representatives about the choice and design of new products, the difficulty representatives had in keeping abreast of product development as it progressed, and particularly, the accusation that Higgins management was either complacent or naïve about this portion of the product line.

Although individual managers recognized that these problems were generally the result of the company's rapid growth, there was disagreement about underlying causes and methods of remedy. A sales executive, for example, outlined his thinking about differences between sales and production:

> The thing that really fouls up the schedule is how far behind we get in the introduction of new products. For example, we planned to have an important new machine in production four months ago, but it's still tied up in design. It isn't customer unpredictability that hurts us so much, it's the engineering problems.

Production executives had a different view:

> Mr. Howard wants to know why we are always rushing at the end of the month to get out the goods and meet our schedule when we've got such a huge backlog of orders. The trouble is we often don't have the orders in hand until the middle of the month. The salespeople talk about all these millions of dollars worth of orders in our backlog without mentioning that most of it isn't scheduled for shipment for months yet. It gives a false impression.

.   .   .   .

> When you don't have the working capital, you're depending on getting out one month's sales to buy the next month's materials. If we could carry a much bigger finished goods inventory, I could schedule production a lot more economically. As it is now, we have to try to produce whatever orders come in this month. We're making every product at once, so it means an awful lot of short runs.

Roger Sloane, director of research, explained some of the difficulties this way:

> I used to be able to spend a lot of time at the bench working on product designs. That was before we got into the radio field. I was very much in favor of that move, but I never realized how it was going to pull me away from the work I like best.

When engineering was small, we used to get involved in the whole thing right from development on through into production. There was just Anton [a mechanical engineer], Howard, and myself, and almost no paper work. Anton knew everyone in the company, and he'd work out the methods with the production people. I worked closely with the foreman of electrical assembly. It was free and easy, and we always had plenty of time left over to work at the bench. But now things are larger and more complex and the old methods have broken down.

Of course, some of the men feel that Howard could help by staying out of research, but they forget the great knowledge he has about test equipment customers' desires. He knows more about this than anybody in the company. He does have some difficulty in keeping up with all the new advances because of his other duties, but he has a tremendous ability to visualize an approach to solving mechanical problems, as evidenced by all the contributions he has made to the testing devices over the past twenty years.

Another executive saw the problem as being of a more fundamental nature:

Mr. Howard says that sales and R&D are his departments, and Rawson is supposed to be in charge of production and accounting. The result is that neither of them feels any responsibility for pulling things together.

Tom Rawson believed that many of the problems centered around his position in the organization:

The executive vice president is supposed to do what the president asks him to do. He is supposed to have an open desk and be available for whatever the president wants. The trouble is, there shouldn't be a certain portion of the company right under the president's personal control. He should be the czar over all. Of course, my problem is with the engineers. They know they don't work for me, so when Howard is out, they say, "Oh well, Howard will be back later, so we won't pay any attention to Rawson." This obviously weakens my position. I've spoken to Howard about this and told him that an executive vice president ought to be a watchdog out front for everything. The production boys ask me to do something, and I can't do it. It creates bad feeling between production and engineering and production and sales—this sort of special attention they get from Howard.

John Howard explained his thinking about his position in the organization:

My primary job is to relate the company to its customers. I am still very important in maintaining our relations with important customers. Of course, I have done a lot of work with research in the past, and I still am associated with them. I have a cubicle down there so I can go down, but I just don't have time with all the pressures on me. It has gotten so that with the new complex electronic equipment I have a hard time keeping abreast of things. [The casewriter noticed that the research cubicle with Mr. Howard's name on it was actually occupied by two junior engineers who were performing experiments on a new piece of equipment.]

While certain executives were concerned with these particular problems, there was a feeling among some members of management that the real problem was that they had not been able to work together effec-

Exhibit 1

HIGGINS EQUIPMENT COMPANY (A) *

ORGANIZATION CHART—1960

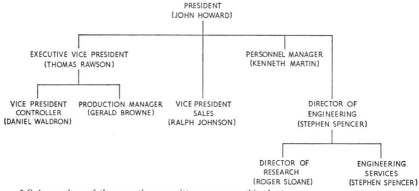

* Only members of the executive committee appear on this chart.

tively to deal with these other issues. In an attempt to improve their co-ordinative effectiveness, the controller had proposed in 1958 that an executive committee be established. The president concurred and regular meetings had been held since early 1959. (The position of its members and their background are outlined in Exhibits 1 and 2, respectively.)

Exhibit 2

HIGGINS EQUIPMENT COMPANY (A)

John Howard—president, 61 years old, liberal arts graduate of an Ivy League college, joined company in 1928 in an engineering capacity. Worked exclusively on development for over a year and then split his time between development and field sales work on testing instruments until he became asssitant to the president in 1938. Became president, 1942.

Thomas Rawson—executive vice president, 63 years, master electrician, joined the company in 1927 as a traveling representative to collect debts from customers. In 1930 became company's first salesman and built up testing instrument sales force. In 1938 was made treasurer, but continued selling. In 1942 was appointed executive vice president with direct responsibility for financial matters and production. Rawson and Howard, between them, owned sufficient Higgins stock to command practical control of the company.

Ralph Johnson—vice president of sales, 50 years old, Bachelor's degree in engineering, joined the company in 1947 as a salesman, was influential in establishment of radio product line and did early selling himself. In 1948 he was made sales manager, but continued to devote much of his attention to development of force of manufacturers representatives. He was appointed vice president—sales in 1954. His background, personality, and function made him a natural protege of Mr. Howard.

Gerald Browne—production manager, 62 years old, trade school graduate, joined Higgins in 1945, promoted to production manager within months of his discovery and report of widespread irregularities in management behavior in production and accounting departments. Reorganized production department, and brought a new cadre of production "specialists" to the company.

Stephen Spencer—director of engineering, 45 years old, Master's degree in engineering, joined company in early 1960 as director of engineering replacing John Haverstick. After two years of academic research, he joined a large industrial firm. Rose to director of engineering in a division of another large company before joining Higgins company.

Daniel Waldron—vice president and controller, 48 years old, joined company in 1931, while he was attending business college. Performed several jobs involving production scheduling, accounting, and cost accounting. Left Higgins for three years, 1942–1945. When he returned he was named controller, but also handled all personnel matters. He was appointed vice president in 1954.

Roger Sloane—director of research, 47 years old, joined Higgins in 1936 in research areas. Was instrumental in major innovations in testing devices and in design and development of radio line. Appointed director of research in 1942. While the director of engineering had administrative responsibility for research personnel, Sloane was responsible for all technical research matters. Sloane owned a substantial minority portion of Higgins stock.

Kenneth Martin—personnel director, 33 years old, joined company in 1955 as personnel director after several years experience in this area with a national manufacturing concern.

Executive Committee Meetings

The executive committee usually met biweekly on Monday afternoons in John Howard's office. One typical meeting was held during January, 1960. The other members of the committee had gathered and were listening to Tom Rawson tell several jokes, when John Howard returned from lunch. Howard interrupted Rawson.

HOWARD [president]:   I have no formal agenda today, but Tom [Rawson] has some important things on his mind.

After this introduction, Rawson began a discussion of the type of label to be put on a new piece of equipment being introduced into the line. Waldron, Spencer, and Howard began to discuss the relative costs of the two proposed types of labels. Johnson interrupted, agreeing with Howard that the difference in cost between the two labels was not as important as appearance.

JOHNSON [sales]:   I never worry too much about the costs on these items. After all we are trying to put out a "Cadillac" product and to worry about a few cents doesn't seem important.

SPENCER [engineering]:   I agree, let's put out the best-looking product.

HOWARD [president]:   That's it, we are trying to put out "the Cadillac," and we should make sure that our product looks like it. Now what's being done on your cost reduction program?

MARTIN [personnel]:   We have gotten 550 suggestions contributed . . . but. . . .

HOWARD [president]:   What I was really wondering about is why there are so many lights burning around here at night.

BROWNE [production]:   That's not our fault. The new guard we've got just doesn't know enough to turn them off. We have to get him to take care of it. The maintenance people can't do anything about it.

HOWARD [president]:   I think we should transfer the responsibility to the maintenance people and let them worry about the lights.

SLOANE [research]:   The trouble over in engineering is that the circuits are arranged so that we can't turn on a few lights without turning on the whole group.

Rawson and Spencer confirmed that it was impossible to turn on only a few lights. Howard shifted the topic.

HOWARD [president]:   Those guards are unreliable mentally anyway. They are just old duffers who can't be counted on. We will have to do something about it. Now, Tom, you better bring on the "hot" topic.

RAWSON [executive v.p.]:   Well, we have been receiving several complaints about the ventilation in various departments. One of these has gotten as far as the State Industrial Relations Commission, so I think we will have to do something.

The discussion focused on these complaints for several minutes with Browne and Waldron explaining the nature of the complaints. Howard finally suggested that they retain the services of a heating engineer to see what improvements could be made in ventilation, to which Browne replied:

BROWNE [production]:   Those fellows don't do any work—just engineering.

HOWARD [president]:   Have your people look up with a smile instead of a scowl, and we won't have so much difficulty with this stuff. It is all part of the same pattern. We need more high-class, high-caliber men with the Higgins spirit. We don't have the same type of person that we used to have.

RAWSON [executive v.p.]:   I don't think our difficulty is just the people. It seems to me what we have to do is put a limit on our expenditures, so all of you fellows will back me up and stick to them. We've got to be more concerned about details of how money is spent.

Howard then suggested that Ralph Johnson report on several conventions he had just attended. Discussion centered on these for several minutes, after which Howard reported on a recent trip he and Rawson had made to New York with a group of other business executives to visit the United Nations. The conversation then drifted into a discussion of world and local political issues, until Howard interrupted:

HOWARD [president]:   Dan [Waldron], do you have anything you want to vent your spleen on?

WALDRON [controller]:   Is the information going to be available from engineering on the new model on the tenth as scheduled?

Roger Sloane assured Waldron that they were doing their best to get things ready on time. Steve Spencer added that he thought it would be ready. There was a brief lull, which Ken Martin broke:

MARTIN [personnel]:   I would like to get this question of a floating holiday straightened out for next year, in case someone wants the day after New Year's Day as his day off.

HOWARD [president]:   The thing to do on that is to sell the employee on it and then take your vote. I don't think we need to discuss it here. Say, Roger [Sloane], you haven't said a word all afternoon.

SLOANE [research]:   I did want to talk a bit about this new device we are going to build for the Navy. We've got to get down and make some decisions about prices and product design. I'm also concerned about its effect on production schedules. If we get the contract, it will be a big one and something that calls for careful planning.

HOWARD [president]:   That's something that will have to be worked out, but I don't think it should tie up the whole group. Why don't you work it out with the others later. . . . If that's all we've got, we'll meet again two weeks from today—unless something big comes up sooner.

Another meeting, one similar to the several executive committee meetings the casewriter attended, was held in March of 1960. The same members were in attendance in John Howard's office when he opened the meeting:

HOWARD [president]:   One item I want to raise is what Jane Drake's responsibilities should be in regard to public relations.[1] She wants us to define what we want her to do in this area. I originally thought we might ask her to define her limits and capabilities for us first, but she felt we should outline the area of her responsibility first, and I think she is probably right. I guess management should define the job for her. Now what I thought I might do is put together a little pamphlet for her outlining what public relations should accomplish and what she should do.

RAWSON [executive v.p.]:   That sounds like an excellent idea to me. Why don't you go ahead and take care of that. You know better than any of us what her capabilities are.

JOHNSON [sales]:   I agree. That seems like a good way to get it started.

HOWARD [president]:   O.K. I'll do that. That's all I have then.

Tom Rawson then made several suggestions about ideas that might be covered in the proposed pamphlet, stressing the importance of handling visitors and incoming telephone calls properly. Howard replied:

HOWARD [president]:   I always answer my own phone, and if I can't help the person I reroute the call myself. Many of them are customers, and I think we have to treat them with much concern and consideration.

RAWSON [executive v.p.]:   Let's drop that one for now. You'll go to work with Miss Drake on that?

HOWARD [president]:   What does anyone else want to talk about? (*Pause.*) Say Dan [Waldron], I was very pleased to see that our costs and performance records looked so good. Some of our expenses are down below standard now. That's what we have to continue to do. I like to hear good news like that.

RAWSON [executive v.p.]:   Tomorrow at 9:30 we are going to hold a pricing meeting on our new transmission equipment. Do you [Howard] want to come?

HOWARD [president]:   I don't really see any point in it, unless I can be of some help. (*Pause.*) I won't be in until 10:00. Why don't we hold the meeting then. I don't know if I can be of much help, but I would like to know what's going on. This is an important matter to me too. I know we will have to raise the price over the old stuff, but I don't know how much.

WALDRON [controller] (*to Rawson*):   Can I talk a little bit about scheduling?

HOWARD [president]:   I would rather start it at a higher price and drop the price later, than start at a lower price and have to raise it.

---

[1] Jane Drake was Mr. Howard's personal assistant who had recently been placed in charge of public relations.

JOHNSON [sales]:   Competition already has similar equipment on the market, and their prices must be met.

HOWARD [president]:   Well, this is a luxury item to the user, and we should sell it that way.

WALDRON [controller]:   Well, I'd like to move on to the question of scheduling for the third quarter.

JOHNSON [sales]:   Jerry [Browne] and I have worked out the schedule for the third quarter at 2.6 million in radio equipment.

WALDRON [controller]:   We can't physically make that much in the third quarter, because we have two weeks when the plant will be shut because of vacations. You know that would be the highest in our history in that line. Production is now spread over so many items with short runs been slow in finishing the design on some of the new components, and our that the problem is to decide what we should cut back on. Engineering has preproduction runs are all behind schedule. One thing we could do is buy parts for these items, but I am reluctant to do that until the preproduction runs have proved out the item. We can't do that and minimize our investment in inventory, which I feel is essential.

BROWNE [production]:   One cause for the difficulty is that we haven't dropped any items from the line in such a long time. We are trying to make too many things in a plant our size.

HOWARD [president]:   I've heard of companies which diversified themselves right out of business. Maybe we need some drastic measures to cut down the number of lines.

Ralph Johnson argued against this view, pointing out that the items were necessary to meet competition. Roger Sloane supported his position. Jerry Browne indicated his belief that part of the difficulty was due to shortcomings in engineering.

BROWNE [production]:   It's like Dan [Waldron] says. They [engineering] have gotten behind on the design work, and our preproduction runs are consequently behind. Either we reduce some of the items or we have to get them caught up so we can handle it all in the plant.

John Howard intervened again to make several general observations about the unfavorable experiences of other companies when they overextended the scope of their product lines.

BROWNE [production]:   We're meeting the schedule right on the nose except for these new products. They are what is causing the trouble.

SLOANE [research]:   I still think we should consider the possibilities of subcontracting. This might be a good idea if we don't have the space, time, and manpower ourselves.

Rawson, Howard, and Spencer agreed with this suggestion, but Waldron objected.

WALDRON [controller]:   With our financial situation we can't afford to increase the size of our inventories. The competitive situation is such that we have to be able to have a wide number of short production runs.

JOHNSON [sales]:   That's right, we can't maintain the competitive position of our line or prices unless we have this capability.

SLOANE [research]:   Why don't we consider the possibility of subcontracting some of the standard parts like amplifiers that we can get long runs on.

RAWSON [executive v.p.]:   Well, making it here is the cheapest, and we are already worrying about price increases.

SPENCER [engineering]:   That brings us right around again to the need for a price change. I think we should try and make a moderate price increase.

HOWARD [president]:   That's inevitable anyway, but we have to re-evaluate the whole thing.

RAWSON [executive v.p.]:   One thing we could do is think about relocating the stock room and giving more space to assembly.

WALDRON [controller]:   Well, Jerry [Browne] has already been working out some ideas on that, but that takes time. We have to get something done for the next quarter.

BROWNE [production]:   One other place we get into trouble is with purchasing. They don't purchase the parts and the shortage holds up the line.

HOWARD [president]:   It's almost 12:30. Let's break up for lunch.

Rawson and Waldron continued to argue for several minutes. Finally, Howard got up to leave, although the price-cost issue was felt by the others to remain unresolved. Several men left the room arguing with Howard that it was necessary to come to some decision.

About the time of the above meeting, several members of management expressed the feeling that the executive committee had not appreciably increased the effectiveness of management decisions. They were concerned about how to improve the committee's performance.

Daniel Waldron, controller, expressed these views:

> We had reached the point two years ago when doing things collectively didn't work as well as it used to. We had to think in terms of an organization chart and responsibility fixed in certain people. The organization chart has been my responsibility, and the creation of the executive committee was my idea. But neither of these has fully materialized, because top management must make the organization click. The rest of us can't operate much differently until the top people see a need to do so.
>
> I had hoped the executive committee meetings would help us find a way to make future plans in conjunction with the managers of the various

departments. It hasn't worked out that way yet, because Mr. Howard doesn't really see the need for it. He uses the meetings as a place to pass on routine information and think over everyday problems. It's understandable. After all, Mr. Howard is used to working step by step with specific individuals. He's been very successful in those relationships. Why should he have to change his whole mode of operations just because someone like me suggests it?

I am faced with a conflict—on the one hand I feel responsible and loyal to Mr. Howard and Mr. Rawson, and on the other I feel that they don't want to do what has to be done and it's up to me to do it. They will resent it if I do what they should be doing, and I'll be uncomfortable if I intrude. I don't know what to do except to go very slowly. You must be patient while management and others in the organization learn new ways of behaving. I've got to be patient with Howard and his use of the committee, for instance.

Steve Spencer, director of engineering, expressed a similar view:

The real problems rarely come up in the executive committee meetings. Those meetings have been concerned with trivia. There's hope that they may become more important now that we're trying to jack ourselves up. The squeeze on profits plus the comments of the manufacturers' representatives have made us more aware of the need for change.

The company is organized so informally that we can only fight fires. We have a great need for a co-ordinating mechanism, but the people don't want to lose the personal feeling of being involved in everything.

Tom Rawson, executive vice president, was also critical of the executive committee's effectiveness:

I don't get much out of the committee meetings. I think that's just passing information without making decisions. Nothing gets jelled. We lose a lot of time if we don't come to a decision. I think things ought to be buttoned up after an hour. This is Howard's failing. He postpones decisions, and then he forgets what has been said, and this costs money.

John Howard, however, expressed a different view about the usefulness of the executive committee and particularly his role in it:

I feel that I can't make snap judgments in the committee or with an individual. This sort of thing is too indicative of one-man rule. The people would just shut up then. I've got to think about it first. I always go to the executive committee for solving problems. I try to train them there, and I rely on them for help. I rarely disagree with a solution they come up with.

Of course, we all worry that when the old school is gone we may not be able to hold on to the spirit of the company. I preach at Dan [Waldron] and Ralph [Johnson] all the time and try to imbue them with the Higgins spirit, so they will carry on, and I do the same with the executive committee and with Ken Martin. This is what I mean by training. One of my most important jobs is to train the young people to my way of thinking. I do this in the executive committee by sharing responsibility. I believe in multiple management. There can't be a one-man firm.

14. HIGGINS EQUIPMENT COMPANY (B)

IN EARLY 1960, the president of the Higgins Equipment Company, John Howard, confided to researchers that he was distressed by company personality problems and by their effects on his organization. Of major recent concern had been the director of engineering's behavior and its effect on relations between the two sections of the engineering department and between both of them and sales and production. The only solution to this problem, the president explained, was to ask Haverstick, the engineering director, to leave, a resolution made all the more difficult by virtue of the man's having been with Higgins for only a year. President Howard said:

> Personalities of Haverstick's type, this conflict type, bother one personally. I dislike strife and I'm always trying to smooth it out. Now Stephen Spencer, the man we have chosen as Haverstick's successor, is peace loving. He's the opposite to what Haverstick was. I'm sure output could be increased by 5 to 10 per cent with better co-operation. Haverstick was arrogant and too young. He was trying to tell people in other departments how to run their affairs without having a clean house himself. I find so far that I can turn to Steve who is very co-operative and very able. I think we'll be able to give him a bonus this year.

About a year later, just as the researchers were concluding their study, Steve Spencer was also discharged. Steve, it was said, "lacked qualifications." Sales and production had been upset by what they saw as a "lack of direction" in engineering. R&D, a subdivision of engineering, felt it was not getting proper technical assistance. New product developments continued to fall behind schedule, while development and expected product costs proved unpredictable.

Company History

The Higgins Equipment Company manufactured a line of electrical testing and radio equipment for industrial and scientific customers. While the vast majority of dollar sales were composed of standard, assembly-line products, an increasing number of orders called for unique specifications, from a particular color of paint to an entirely untried basic design. Historically, the company has passed through three growth stages. Between 1917 and 1927 occurred the "production phase" in which the founder successfully constructed his own prototypes, personally supervised production and arranged for the sale of his products. The period 1927 to 1947 saw an accelerating emphasis on sales. Finally, 1947–1960 was an era of explosive growth. R&D became the spearhead of expansion. It was shortly before this last period that Howard became president. (See Higgins Equipment Company (A) for further development of company history.)

Department Heads

The organization chart (see Exhibit 1) shows Stephen Spencer to be

Exhibit 1

HIGGINS EQUIPMENT COMPANY (B)

ORGANIZATION CHART—1960

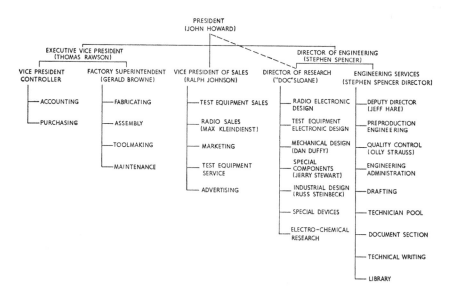

both head of the entire engineering department and of the staff section, engineering services. Engineering services was the result of the growth of auxiliary services which accompanied the enlargement of R&D staff and activities. Originally all of these services had been performed by R&D men or by their personal assistants. In effect, there had never been a decision to establish an engineering services section. It had simply emerged as R&D men freed themselves of what they considered to be details.

The sales department was headed by Ralph Johnson, a vice president and heir apparent to the presidency of the company upon Howard's retirement which was scheduled for 1963. Sales administration problems had been greatly compounded by the addition of the radio line, which required new demands of distribution, sales personnel with entirely new technical and sales skills and, thus, actual sales organization. Growth of the department had never quite caught up with the rapidity of expansion which entry into the radio field brought about.

The production department was headed by Gerald Browne who had the title of factory superintendent. While sales and engineering both reported directly to the president, the production and control departments reported to the executive vice president, Thomas Rawson. Because Rawson was relatively inexperienced in both of these areas and because of the dynamic personality of Howard, the production and control departments were not as forcefully represented in top management deliberations as were sales and engineering. The production department was particularly sensitive about this inbalance, despite its deep affection for Rawson.

See Exhibit 2 for personal background data on the central figures in this case.

Exhibit 2

HIGGINS EQUIPMENT COMPANY (B)

Jeff Hare—deputy director of engineering services, 34 years old, Bachelor's degree in Engineering, brought to Higgins in 1960 by Stephen Spencer as his assistant. The deputy's job, as such, had not previously existed, although Hare took on some duties previously performed by a newly retired member of the department. Previously worked as engineering assistant in an engineering graduate school. Then 11 years experience with Spencer's previous employer as junior and senior development engineer.

Preproduction engineer, 39 years old, technical high school graduate, joined Higgins in 1951. Experienced senior mechanical draftsman—designer and technician. Assumed the newly created post of preproduction engineer in 1954, supervising two engineering school trainees and working closely with the drafting department in fitting into a metal package the separate electronic and mechanical units of Higgins' products.

Olly Strauss—quality control, 38 years old, high school graduate, joined Higgins in 1949, and worked for eight years on final assembly and test of equipment before taking over the newly integrated quality control operation. Previous work as a technician in a large engineering school.

Engineering administrator, 34 years old, undergraduate degree in business administration, joined Higgins in 1955. Experience in engineering scheduling and budgets. First man to fill the office of engineering administrator. With two clerks and a secretary he assembled the data necessary to develop time schedules and cost estimates for development projects. Administered these aspects of projects in progress.

Drafting foreman, 44 years old, technical high school graduate, in charge of fifteen draftsmen, many capable of mechanical design and electronic detail

Exhibit 2* (*Continued*)

drafting. Many years experience as senior designer and section manager in drafting department of a large electronics firm.

Technician pool foreman, 36 years old, with Higgins for 17 years, 10 as assembler and assistant foreman in production, 7 as technician and pool manager in engineering. Administered affairs of and participated in working supervision of 50 technicians working as R&D assistants, pilot-run assemblers and special devices production force (the latter section run by R&D engineers for the production of nonstandard orders).

Document section manager, 43 years old, high school graduate, long experience as production and engineering clerk and section supervisor. Joined Higgins in 1956 as engineering change-order clerk. Promoted in 1958 to manage a ten-man group responsible for collecting data for and publishing parts lists, blueprints, change orders, and the other large volumes of paper which passed between R&D and production.

Technical writing supervisor, 40 years old, liberal arts graduate, many years experience as technical writer and supervisor. Came to Higgins in 1954 as supervisor of twelve men and women who wrote and illustrated instructional and promotional material for Higgins' products.

Librarian, 50 years old with a great deal of experience in public and school libraries, more recently in industrial libraries. Within a budget, he subscribed to technical journals, purchased books, and collected public data upon the request of R&D personnel.

* For the background of other key personnel see Higgins (A), Exhibit 2.

Roger Sloane (Doc)

In spite of occasional and sometimes frequent friction between department and subdepartment heads, there was one man who never became involved in these disputes. "Doc" Sloane, head of R&D, enjoyed universal admiration among Higgins employees and officers. "Of course, everyone loves Doc," explained the president. "If you took a vote, I know he'd be the most popular man in the company." The president's interest in Doc's work had personal overtones. He explained, "I started out in development work before devoting myself to sales. I like to think I can still contribute in both arenas. (The researchers noticed that the president's name plate hung on a cubicle door in the R&D department.) I have always taken pride in the immaculate housing of our equipment and in its high quality, but why is there so much friction in getting out designs into production? A designer I trust asked me this the other day. 'Why should we work so hard when they deliberately foul things up?' We've got good men in R&D but something happens between their efforts and the end product to create problems for us."

Doc always appeared unhurried, contemplative, and candid in his approach to people and problems. His manner of dress and appearance gave the impression of a janitor rather than the most highly educated and renowned electronic designer at Higgins. He described his feelings about his job as follows: "We are a long way from being a research group in the usual sense of the word. There is no kidding ourselves we are anything but a bunch of Rube Goldbergs. But that is where the biggest kick comes from solving development problems, dreaming up new ways to do things. That's why I so look forward to the special contracts we get involved in. We accept them not for the revenue they represent but for the subsidized basic development work for standard products which they let us do. I like administration the least. The most important thing in the relationships between people is mutual respect, not organizational procedures. Anyway, administrative work takes away from development time." Doc felt that production was resistant. "There are power interests in production which resist change. But you know I'm not a fighting guy. I suppose if I were I might go in there and push my weight around a little. In my view the company's future rests squarely on development engineering. Either we've got it there or we haven't. This is John Howard's conception, too."

It was Doc's suggestion in 1954 that the company re-enter the radio field, which it had briefly been in during World War II, as well as maintain its position in the test equipment market. This proved a highly profitable venture, both in terms of sales and in terms of technical challenge. "Although," Doc said ruefully, "it took me further from my own bench."

R&D under Doc Sloane

The researchers found evidence to indicate that R&D had high morale and the capacity to accomplish among its interdependent subunits tasks free from the overlay of personal resentment and political intrigue. There seemed to be a close complementarity between the goals of this department and over-all company goals. Central values expressed by members included personal learning, development, and independence. They also felt proud of personal contacts with technically oriented customers, which became increasingly necessary as Higgins' products became more technically specialized and sophisticated. Doc, himself, worked as a part-time sales engineer, consulting with customer engineers.

Sociometric data[1] indicated that the R&D section consisted of three major social groups. These groupings correlated well with measures of individual competence and to some extent with education, experience,

---

[1] Elicited by questions concerning friendship choices and through observations of work and nonwork interactions.

and age. The researchers called these three groups the "Scientists," the "Would-be Scientists," and "the Youngsters." Below is a schematic presentation of what the researchers interpreted from their observations and interviews each group was giving to and receiving from each of the others.

Engineering Services under Steve Spencer

The other section of the engineering department, engineering services, was supposed to provide ancillary services to R&D and to conduct liaison between R&D and other Higgins departments. Top management described the functions of engineering services as, "establishing and

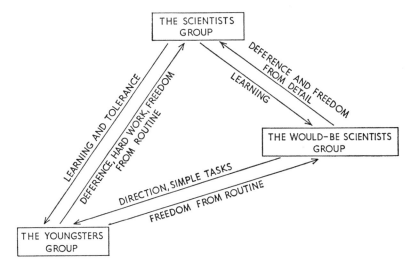

maintaining co-operation with other departments, providing service to development engineers, and freeing more valuable men (R&D designers) from essential activities which are diversions from and beneath their main competence." The background and experience of primary engineering services and other key personnel are shown in Exhibit 2.

Sociometric measures revealed that engineering services was not a cohesive group. Many of its members were located in other departments. Its quality control personnel were hardly noticeable in the midst of production's assembly operation. Its technicians, assigned to R&D's development engineers, worked primarily in R&D cubicles or the area devoted to production of special devices. Generally, the remaining engineering services offices were assigned to widespread leftover spaces between elements of R&D.

Among the main functions of engineering services were drafting and provision of technicians from a central pool. Other major functions included: engineering administration which scheduled and expedited engineering projects; the document section which compiled parts lists and published engineering orders; preproduction engineering, composed of several technicians who pulled together into mechanically compatible packages R&D's individual components; and finally, quality control which inspected incoming parts and materials, in process subassemblies, and finished instruments against predetermined standards.

Researches compared the interaction patterns *prescribed* (i.e. how people were supposed to behave) for engineering services personnel in their work relationship with R&D and production people with the *actual* patterns of interaction which they observed (see Exhibit 3).

Exhibit 3

HIGGINS EQUIPMENT COMPANY (B)

(*a*) PRESCRIBED INTERACTION-INFLUENCE PATTERNS*

R&D–ENGINEERING SERVICES

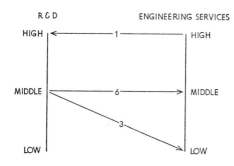

ENGINEERING SERVICES–PRODUCTION

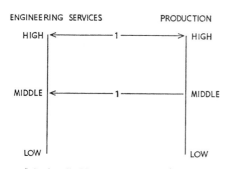

* As described by top management, in response to the question, "Who is supposed to communicate with whom and whose opinion, if either should dominate?" The vertical lines represent an array of department members, broken into three groups according to job rank, as indicated by the title, pay, and responsibilities. Arrows indicate interacting pairs of men. Numbers affixed to arrows represent the number of pairs in interaction. Double-ended arrows indicate a mutual influence, while single-ended arrows depict one-way influence between two men. The interaction recorded in this exhibit refers to personal contact rather than that which may also have occurred through the routine, nonpersonal, interdepartmental flow of paper.

Exhibit 3 (Continued)

(*b*) OBSERVED INTERACTION-INFLUENCE PATTERNS†

R&D-ENGINEERING SERVICES

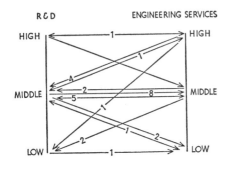

DATA:

TOTAL INTERACTORS:
21(55 % OF TOTAL POPULATION)

R&D INTERACTORS:
12(60% OF R&D POPULATION)

ENGINEERING SERVICES INTERACTORS:
9(55 % OF ENGINEERING
SERVICES POPULATION)

ENGINEERING SERVICES-PRODUCTION

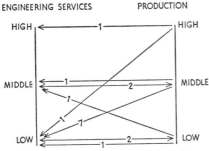

DATA:

TOTAL INTERACTORS:
20(43% OF TOTAL POPULATION)

ENGINEERING SERVICES INTERACTORS:
7(41% OF ENGINEERING
SERVICES POPULATION)

PRODUCTION INTERACTORS:
13(46 % OF PRODUCTION POPULATION)

† The researchers developed the chart of observed interaction influence by prolonged observation. Each interaction was recorded and a judgment made concerning the balance of influence between the individuals involved, on the basis of whose point of view tended to dominate most frequently. For example, far more often than not, when Browne was in discussion with Spencer concerning such matters as a production-originated engineering change order, Browne's opinion would carry the day. Or where Spencer and Sloane discussed such things as the budget for a new project, their ideas tended to merge and the decisions emanating from their deliberations tended to reflect the opinions of both men.

Steve Spencer, when asked about his job, gave the following description:

My role in the company has never really been defined for me. It is complicated by Doc's unique position. In a nebulous way, he works through me and I through him. But he is not the least bit interested in the routines of administration. My relationship with him and his people is somewhat ambiguous. He is highly regarded in this company, and I have a great deal of affection and respect for him myself. But I can't count on him for any responsibility in scheduling projects, checking budgets or what-have-you. In some senses, I'm in charge of R&D and in others I'm not.

My biggest problem is getting acceptance from the people I work with. I've moved slowly rather than risk antagonism. I saw what happened to Haverstick, and I want to avoid that. But although his precipitate action had won over a few of the younger R&D men, he certainly didn't have the department's backing. Of course, it was the resentment of other departments which eventually caused his discharge. People have been slow accepting me here. There's nothing really overt, but I get a negative reaction to my ideas.

Browne [production head] is hard to get along with. Before I came and after Haverstick left, there were six months intervening when no one was really doing any scheduling. No work loads were figured, and unrealistic promises were made about releases. This puts us in an awkward position. We've been scheduling way beyond our capacity to manufacture or engineer.

I wish I could be more involved in the technical side. That's been my training, and it's a lot of fun. But in our setup, the technical side is the least necessary for me to be involved in.

Steve went on to explain that:

Certain people within R&D, for instance Russ Steinbeck, head of the radio electronic design section, understand scheduling well and meet project deadlines, but this is not generally true of the rest of the R&D department, especially the mechanical engineers who won't commit themselves. Most of the complaints come from sales and production department heads because items are going to production before they are fully developed, under pressure from sales to get out the unit, and this snags the whole process. Somehow, engineering services should be able to interview and resolve these complaints, but I haven't made much headway so far.

Salespeople were often observed taking their problems directly to designers, while production frequently threw designs back at R&D, claiming they could not be produced and demanding the prompt attention of particular design engineers. The latter were frequently observed in conference with production supervisors on the assembly floor.

Steve was asked where he sought help:

I should be able to go to Howard, but he's too busy most of the time and he's only really interested in the electrical test equipment line. Howard sees himself as head of engineering but I have to take the initiative. Doc isn't interested in planning and there are problems the front office just doesn't understand. Jeff Hare [Steve's deputy director] is a big help to me. He's here to help take the load off the development engineers [in R&D], but they tend to feel they're losing something when one of us tries to help. They feel it's a reflection on them to have someone take over what they've been doing. They seem to want to carry a project right through the final stages, particularly the mechanical boys. On the other hand, production people see themselves as methods and preproduction people and they want to get their hands on the product at an early stage.

Consequently, engineering services people are used below their capacity to contribute and our department is denied functions it should be performing. There's not as much use made of engineering services as there could be.

Steve Spencer's technician foreman added his comments:

Production picks out the engineer who'll be the "bum of the month." They pick on every little detail instead of using their heads and making the minor changes that have to be made. The fifteen-to-twenty-year men shouldn't have to prove their ability any more, but they spend four hours defending themselves and four hours getting the job done. I have no one to go to when I need help. Steve Spencer is afraid. I'm trying to help him but he can't help me at this time. I'm responsible for fifty people and I've got to support them.

Jeff Hare, whom Steve had brought with him to the company as an assistant, gave another view of the situation:

I try to get our people in preproduction to take responsibility, but they're not used to it, and people in other departments don't usually see them as best qualified to solve the problem.

Production always says it is drafting that is making the errors. Well, that isn't fair because all engineering and R&D are involved, not just the last ones to handle the material. But I haven't made much headway in changing that point of view. There's a real barrier for a newcomer here. Gaining people's confidence is hard. [Hare resigned from Higgins six months after coming to the company, stating, "There just isn't a job for me here."]

Another of Spencer's subordinates gave his view:

If Doc gets a new product idea you can't argue. But he's too optimistic. He judges that others can do what he does—but there's only one Doc Sloane. We've had 900 production change orders this year—they changed 2,500 drawings. If I were in Steve's shoes I'd put my foot down on all this new development. I'd look at the reworking we're doing and get production set up the way I wanted it. Haverstick was fired when he was doing a good job. He was getting some system in the company's operations. Of course, it hurt some people. But, there is no denying that Doc is the most important person in the company. What gets overlooked is that Howard is a close second, not just politically but in terms of what he contributes technically and in customer relations.

This subordinate explained that he sometimes went out into the production department but that Browne, the production head, resented this. Men in production said that Haverstick had failed to show respect for old-timers and was always meddling in other departments' business. This was why he had been fired, they contended.

Olly Strauss was in charge of quality control. He commented:

> I am now much more concerned with administration and less with work. It is one of the evils you get into. There is tremendous detail in this job. I listen to everyone's opinion. Everybody is important. There shouldn't be distinctions—distinctions between people. I'm not sure whether Steve has to be a fireball like Haverstick. I think the real question is whether Spencer is getting the job done. I know my job is essential. I want to supply service to the more talented men and give them information so they can do their jobs better.

R&D's Views of Engineering Services

Said Dan Duffy of the mechanical design department:

> In olden days I really enjoyed the work—and the people I worked with. But now there's a lot of irritation. I get my satisfaction from a good design and from finding solutions to troublesome problems. But it's not as satisfying as it used to be. I don't like someone breathing down my neck. You can be hurried into jeopardizing the design.

Russ Steinbeck, head of the radio electronic design section, was another designer with definite views:

> Production engineering is almost nonexistent in this company. Very little is done by the preproduction section in engineering services. Steve Spencer has been trying to get preproduction into the picture, but he won't succeed because you can't start from such an ambiguous position. There have been three directors of engineering in six years. Steve can't hold his own against the others in the company. Haverstick was too aggressive. Perhaps no amount of tact would have succeeded.

Jerry Stewart was head of special components in the R&D department. Like the rest of the department he valued bench work. But he complained of engineering services:

> The services don't do things we want them to do. They tell us what they're going to do. I should probably go to Steve, but I don't get any decisions there. I know I should go through Steve, but this holds things up, so I often go direct.

Views of the Sales Department

The researchers talked to representatives of the sales department, first its head, Ralph Johnson. Ralph explained that his reps made promises to customers, only to find the equipment months late in development. He was persistent in trying to get design engineers to conventions so that they could know the customer's point of view. "We shouldn't have to be after the engineers all the time. They should be able to see what problems they create for the company without our telling them." Ralph described himself as "a moderator—a man who settled disputes."

Max Kleindienst was head of radio sales under Johnson. He explained to the researchers that a great number of decisions concerning sales were made by top management. Sales was understaffed, he thought, and had never really been able to get on top of the job.

> We have grown further and further away from engineering. The director of engineering does not pass on the information that we give him. We need better relationships with R&D. It is very difficult for us to talk to customers without technical help. We need each other. The whole of engineering is now too isolated from the outside world. The morale of engineering [services] is very low. They're in a bad spot—they're not well organized.
>
> People don't take much to outsiders here. Much of this is because the expectation is built up by top management that jobs will be filled from the bottom. So it's really tough when an outsider like me comes in.

Views of the Production Department

The researchers paid a call on the production department and its head, Gerald Browne. Gerry said he believed in having a self-contained department. "There shouldn't be a lot of other people breathing down your neck." Gerry and his lieutenants universally expressed their preference for "getting new products into production, establishing procedures for getting standard products into the line, then spending our time doping out new methods and processes for getting our job done better."

One of Gerry's rules was that "I never talk to the underling of a department head. I always talk to the head himself. I always go down the line." He objected to final quality control (engineering services) being separated from his department. He felt it should be a continuation of assembly. "Olly Strauss's superiors don't understand Olly's problems. He'd rather work for me; he's told me that many times."

Purchasing should also have been under production, according to Gerry. Only a few days before he had thrown his storeroom master key on the board-room table in front of the president. "Here, I don't want it any more. I've been accused of fouling up inventory control!"

Gerry later explained his feelings about engineering:

> The trouble with engineering is that they are tolerance crazy. They want everything to a millionth of an inch. I'm the only one in the

company who's had any experience with actually machining things to a millionth of an inch. We make sure that the things that engineers say on their drawing actually have to be that way and whether they're obtainable from the kind of raw material we buy.

Engineering services "just didn't check drawings properly," Gerry explained. Gerry spent a considerable proportion of his time going over new product drawings, personally returning those which he found to be in error.

So finally they have to listen to us. Changes have to be made because they didn't listen to us in the first place. Engineering services says we've got to keep our hands off quality control. But, then, something like this happens: Doc comes in here one day, with a sour look on his face, saying there was some burnt wire on the equipment sent to an electronic show. I said, "You just look here. We didn't make that equipment; your technicians did!"

Gerry recounted his pleasure in doing things which engineering had said were impossible. "But I never tell them how we did it. They ought to be as smart as we are out here in production. Of course, the thing that really gets them is that I don't even have a degree."

In the course of their work, the researchers learned that when the men presently in charge of production took control after World War II, they did so as the result of a management turnover occasioned by discovery of illegalities committed by previous production men during the war. Prior to that time, production had controlled purchasing, stock control, and final quality control (where final assembly of products in such cabinets was accomplished). Because of the wartime events, management decided on a check-and-balance system of organization and removed these three departments from production jurisdiction. The new production managers felt they had been unjustly penalized by this reorganization, particularly since they had uncovered the behavior which was detrimental to the company in the first place.

The researchers also talked to Tom Rawson, age 65, executive vice president of the company. Tom had direct responsibility for Higgins' production department.

There shouldn't really be a dividing of departments among top management in the company. The president should be czar over all. The production boys ask me to do something for them, and I really can't do it. It creates bad feeling between engineering and production, this special attention that they [R&D] get from Howard. But then Howard likes to dabble in design. Browne feels that production is treated like a poor relation.

As the researchers were concluding their field work at the Higgins Equipment Company, they found an opportunity to discuss the engineering department and its problems with the president, John Howard. He reflected on what he termed "the unhappy necessity of letting Steve Spencer go."

I can't understand why we have such poor luck with engineering heads. The man in there before Haverstick was technically well qualified. He'd been a good designer for us before we promoted him to be the first head of engineering. But he took to drinking heavily, and we had to relieve him of the responsibility. Then Haverstick seemed so promising. They say he is doing well in his new job at the —— company. But they operate much differently from the way we do. Then, Steve Spencer—he seemed to have all the qualifications we needed. And he certainly was a gentleman. But he never could get things done. Apparently he couldn't gain the respect of the design boys. So, here we are, looking for a new man. I'm beginning to wonder whether we'll ever find him.

Concepts and Research Findings

1. "CLASSICAL" ORGANIZATION THEORY

THE FOLLOWING historical survey of the traditional conceptions of organizational behavior is taken from the second chapter of *Organizations*, by James G. March and Herbert A. Simon.[1]

The authors distinguish two facets of the tradition: Taylor's[2] "scientific management" and Urwick's[3] and others' theories of departmentalization.

1. Scientific Management

Taylor saw the primary organizational problem to be that of analyzing the relation between human characteristics and the purposive aspects of organizations. "The goal was to use the rather inefficient human organism—by specifying a detailed program of behavior—that would transform a general-purpose mechanism, such as a person, into a more efficient special purpose mechanism."

The data relevant to solving the problem thus posed were largely restricted to the physiological; and Taylor's group quite naturally, therefore, focused on that relatively narrow range of tasks found on the production floor or in clerical departments. These tasks were highly repetitive, did not require complex problem-solving activity, and were susceptible to direct observation, simple description, and straightforward categorization and measurement. In this milieu worked the time-study man, whose aim was "to define the task as to restrict considerably the behavioral alternatives with which the worker is faced." Job method choices were restricted both by the detail of the description and by the time standard set for performance.

Scientific management theorists, then, were concerned with the development and optimum operation of "man-machine systems." The dimensions along which their theory and procedures developed were the capacity, speed, durability, and cost of the composite mechanism. The inherent limits within which the mechanism must work, according to the theory, were the subject of considerable investigation. Speed was

---

[1] New York: John Wiley & Sons, Inc., 1958.

[2] See F. W. Taylor, *Scientific Management* (New York: Harper & Bros., 1947), or *The Principles of Scientific Management* (New York: Harper & Bros., 1911).

[3] See L. Urwick, *The Elements of Administration* (New York: Harper & Bros., 1944).

a primary focus of research toward which the Gilbreths and many others devoted their efforts. The attempts in this respect to develop standard-unit (therblig, etc.) systems are undoubtedly known to the reader.

Fatigue, a prime component of the durability dimension, was the basis for considerable study during the 1920's by Elton Mayo and others. Their findings led to the development of conceptual structures whose dimensions were sufficiently different from those of the scientific management group as to create an entirely new school of thought.[4]

The units of the cost dimension were money and time. Wage rates were stipulated to be competitive and sufficient to motivate the worker to produce at an optimum rate. March and Simon point to three areas of question which cast doubt on the simple relationship of monetary reward and productivity posited by scientific management theory: "(a) that wage payments represent only one (but perhaps the major single one) of a number of rewards in the system; (b) that the utilities associated with wages may be discontinuous—reflecting some notion of satisfactory wages—and hence may not be at all linearly (or even monotonically) related to wage payments; (c) that these utilities change through time and with shifts in aspirations, so that the impact of wage incentives is not stable."[5]

The propositions of physiological organization theory can be summarized as follows: Find the best way of performing a job, provide the worker with an incentive to use the best way at a good pace, and use specialized experts to set the conditions within which the worker is to perform.

2. Theories of Departmentalization

Under this heading, March and Simon discuss a second, overlapping development which they call "administrative management theory." It shares with scientific management "a preoccupation with the simpler neuro-physical properties of humans and the simpler kinds of tasks that are handled in organizations." They point out, however, that this second group of theorists carry their analysis well beyond the limits set by Taylor and his followers.

The general problem addressed is how, given a statement of organization purpose, the unit tasks necessary to achieve that purpose can be

---

[4] Elton Mayo, *The Human Problems of an Industrial Civilization* (New York: Macmillan Co., 1933; Boston: Division of Research, Harvard Business School, 1946); F. J. Roethlisberger and W. J. Dickson, *Management and the Worker* (Cambridge: Harvard University Press, 1939).

[5] March and Simon, *op. cit.,* p. 19.

identified. Once identified, how can these unit tasks be grouped into jobs, jobs into administrative units, and administrative units into top management departments at minimum cost? The basis for understanding this theory, the authors point out, is "to recognize that the total set of tasks is regarded as given in advance."

The departmentalists have attempted so to assign activities that a minimum number of task groups are formed consistent with man-days available. The difficulty of optimizing this efficiency lies in the fact that departmentalization along the lines of purpose may conflict with ideal task groupings based on process specialization. For example, the rationale behind the formation of a marketing department may constrain against the efficient use of stenographers across department boundaries.

Finally, March and Simon note the tendency in administrative management theory to view an organization member as an inert instrument performing an assigned task. Personnel characteristics are, furthermore, seen as "givens" rather than variables. "[The] grand theories of organizational structure have largely ignored factors associated with individual behavior and particularly its motivational bases."

3. Consequences of These Theories

In order to highlight the consequences of these models of organization (called by these authors and others the "machine model"), March and Simon, in the third chapter of their book, describe how three sociologists view the machine model in operation; one of these will be described briefly here.

Robert K. Merton.[6]   Merton proposed that the top hierarchy imposes a demand for control on the organization in the form of increased emphasis on the reliability of behavior, i.e., representing a need for accountability and predictability of behavior. Control is sought by institution of standard operating procedures and by ensuring that procedures are followed.

The consequences, as Merton sees them, are a reduction in personalized relationships (organization members are viewed not as individuals but as possessors of positions), an increase in the internalization of rules (procedures take on the positive values initially accruing to the goals they were designed to achieve), and a narrowing of the range within which decisions are made (categories for thinking through a problem are decreased). In turn and as a result, behavior becomes more rigid,

---

[6] See, among other writings of Merton, *Social Theory and Social Structure* (2d ed.; Glencoe, Ill.: Free Press, 1957). In these writings, Merton draws heavily on the work of Max Weber, which was concerned primarily with government bureaucracies.

an intense *esprit de corps* develops, and a propensity to defend organization members from outside attack is increased.

The net result within the organization is a high degree of reliability, maximized defensibility of behavior, and a reduced effectiveness in dealing with extraorganization individuals and groups (e.g., customers). Since part of the system is maintained by these techniques, there is a continuing pressure to reinforce the same techniques. Even customer dissatisfaction and resultant complaints serve to redouble efforts to maintain control. The system is circular. March and Simon reproduce the diagram shown in Exhibit 1 as a summary of this system.

Exhibit 1

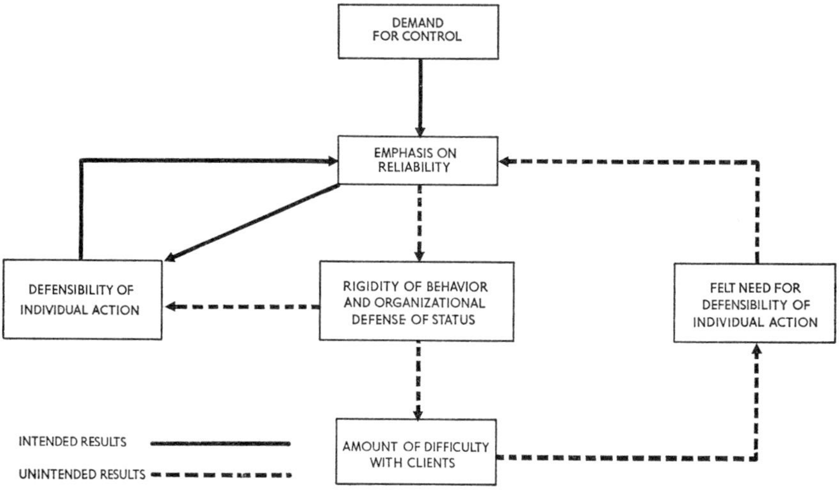

2. STAFF-LINE RELATIONSHIPS*

Douglas McGregor

CONVENTIONAL ORGANIZATION theory deals with the staff-line relationship in terms of the principle of authority, naturally. The central chain of command is that of operations; other functions provide services and advice to the line. They cannot be given authority (except within their own functions) because to do so would violate the principle of unity of command: that any individual must have only one boss. There can, of course, be more than one line function (sales, for example), so long as there is sufficient independence that the principle of unity of command is not violated.

A second relevant principle is that authority must equal responsibility. Since the line requires certain services in fulfilling its responsibilities, it must have authority over them.

These principles may be given formal recognition in organization charts and position descriptions, but one would never deduce them from study of the realities of organizational life! Every member of lower and middle line management is subject to influences from staff groups which are psychologically indistinguishable from the authority exercised by his line superiors.

> Such influences are not limited to people above the manager in the hierarchy either. A clerk in accounting may disallow an expense item in the budget of a general manager; a proposed salary increase initiated by a plant superintendent may require approval by a clerk in the personnel department. The fact that these staff people are following procedures formally approved by the line does not alter the psychological nature of the influence involved or the reactions to it.

In the textbooks on organization one finds elaborate circumlocutions designed to reconcile such inconsistencies. However, euphemistic terms like "coordination," "the authority of knowledge," and "acting in the name of" do not hide the fact that the conventional staff-line distinction in terms of authority is an illusion. The industrial organization is an elaborate complex of interdependent relationships, and interde-

* Excerpts from Douglas McGregor, *The Human Side of Enterprise* (New York: McGraw-Hill Book Co., Inc., 1960), chap. xi. Reprinted by permission of author and publisher.

pendence means that each party can affect the ability of the other to achieve his goals and satisfy his needs. So long as the basic managerial strategy is one of direction and control, authoritative forms of influence exercised by staff groups will creep into the relationship no matter what the logical principles require. The struggle for power in a setting where goal achievement is based on acquiring it will not be eliminated by recourse to logic.

The climate of line-staff relationships in industry today does not often reflect the quality of mutual confidence. . . . Quite typically, line managers regard staff groups as a "burden" rather than as a source of help. They see them as preoccupied with their narrow specialties to the point where they are unconcerned about the welfare of the business as a whole. They look on staff advice as generally impractical, usually hemmed in by overly standardized and bureaucratic procedures. As one line manager who was working out some difficult problems in union-management relations put it: "I keep away from the staff. They'd help me to death."

Staff groups, on the other hand, frequently have a jaundiced view of the line. They perceive line managers as exclusively concerned with maintaining their authority and independence, lacking in appreciation of the professional qualifications and accomplishments of staff groups, basically resistant to change and improvement.

These attitudes are often covered over by a quantity of humorous kidding, the hostility in which is barely concealed. There are exceptions, of course, but by and large staff-line relationships are far from ideal. In private conversation with either group, a casual comment about the other is often sufficient to start a torrent of deprecatory comment interspersed with "see if you can top this" illustrations. A term which frequently comes to mind is "scapegoating."

The Line Utilizes the Staff

There are many causal factors behind this rather unsatisfactory state of affairs. One of the most important is related, I believe, to line management's growing appreciation of the inadequacy of authority as the exclusive means of managerial control. However, the appreciation is at the level of practice rather than theory, and this is the source of much difficulty.

Too much reliance on authority produces counterforces among subordinates. Even the manager who is committed to the assumptions of Theory X[1] becomes aware of this. Among the alternatives which have

---

[1] McGregor elsewhere defines "Theory X" as a theory of human behavior based on the following three key assumptions: (1) The average human being has an inherent dis-

been offered as solutions to this problem is that of delegation. This principle, as ordinarily presented, emphasizes such ideas as "putting decisions near the point of action," controlling subordinates "through policy," giving "general rather than detailed supervision," and allowing subordinates "the freedom to make mistakes."

The upper-level manager who holds to Theory X can usually accept the idea of delegation, but when he puts it into action he is faced with a loss of the control on which his whole conception of management is based. He is helpless before the possibility that poor decisions may be made; productivity may drop, things may get out of hand. Since he lacks genuine confidence in his subordinates, these fears are real.

Fortunately, as he usually discovers, there is a way out of the dilemma. He can delegate and yet keep control. He need not rely on authority in the direct sense *if he can assign to someone else* the responsibility (1) for making sure his subordinates stay within policy limits and (2) for collecting and providing him with data which will enable him to know what is happening in time to step in before serious trouble arises.

Accordingly, he begins to use staff groups such as accounting, personnel, and engineering to develop and administer a system of managerial controls. When he adopts a policy, he assigns to the appropriate staff the responsibility for working out the necessary procedures and making sure they are followed. (After all, he has made the essential decision; let the specialists work out the details. Moreover, he can't spend his time worrying about whether specific procedures are followed; his concerns are with policy and with results. Let the staff "coordinate" the implementation).

As a manager it is his responsibility to know what goes on. He can't abdicate, even if he delegates. If he can get daily reports on certain crucial aspects of the operation, and weekly and monthly reports on other aspects, he will be able with very little expenditure of time (and without breathing down anybody's neck in the old authoritarian way) to delegate without losing his ability to direct and control.

As a further refinement, he discovers the principle of "management by exception." It is not necessary to study a lot of detailed reports of the activities of his subordinates. The staff can do this for him, and prepare reports which point up only those things which are out of line and therefore require his attention. He may even go one step further and assign to the staff the task of investigating the "variances" and correcting them —reporting to him only those they are unable to handle themselves.

Now things are in good shape. He no longer exercises close, direct authority over his subordinates. He has delegated to them. He directs

like of work and will avoid it if he can. (2) Because of this human characteristic of dislike of work, most people must be coerced, controlled, directed, threatened with punishment to get them to put forth adequate effort toward the achievement of organizational objectives. (3) The average human being prefers to be directed, wishes to avoid responsibility, has relatively little ambition, wants security above all.

by means of policy; the decisions are made at the point of actions; his subordinates have the freedom to make mistakes. There is no risk involved because he has a group of staff specialists who keep a detailed eye on every important aspect of the operations. He can concern himself with major problems, with formulating policy, with the more important aspects of management, because things are "under control." If anything is not as it should be, either the staff will see that it is corrected or notify him so that he can take care of it before serious difficulties arise.

A nice situation—or a travesty? It depends on your theoretical assumptions. There are textbooks, articles, and consulting firms which will provide help in setting up this kind of a managerial strategy, complete with control charts and colored signals. Of course, it will be necessary to reckon with some consequences. The staff have now become policemen, exercising by proxy the direct authority which was "relinquished" by the line. Countermeasures of a familiar kind will appear, but they will be directed toward the staff, and, because the staff is neither particularly feared nor respected, the countermeasures may be even more effective than if they were directed at line management. There is a fair amount of research evidence indicating that middle and lower management groups tend to develop protective mechanisms which, although more elaborate and considerably more costly to the organization, are psychologically identical to those developed by workers to defeat the administration of individual incentive plans.

A large and successful manufacturing company discovered recently, after changing the management of a major division, what company top management described as "appalling" evidence of fudging of production and quality data, misreporting of costs, and ignoring of preventive maintenance which had been going on for years. The relevant headquarters staff groups, and even the division top staff people, were completely unaware of the situation until a new line management uncovered it.

The costs will not be trivial: subordinate managers will quickly develop their own independent data-gathering mechanisms (utilizing clerical time) to ensure that they will know at least as much as the staff about what is going on. Many man-hours will be consumed by the staff in tracking down variances which have already been discovered and corrected at the source. Ingenious methods for defeating staff control procedures will be developed, and the staff will be kept busy developing new ones to compensate for these. Antagonisms between line and staff will prevent the kind of collaboration that is essential for achieving organizational objectives. (Examples like those . . . of the employees who "followed the blueprint" with glee when they knew that doing so would result in an unsatisfactory product will be multiplied many times over at various managerial levels). Those controls which the superior indicates by his actions are important to him will be carefully watched by subordinates; others will be ignored.

If such costs as these are worth the gains, this form of "delegation and control" will work after a fashion. Human beings are surprisingly adaptable. Basically, however, there are few managerial practices which produce as many negative consequences for the organization as this one of assigning control responsibilities to the staff. Whether my analysis of the reasons for it is correct or not, the practice (in varying degrees and forms) is widespread.

I believe these phenomena are responsible to a large degree for the "accordion effect" often noted in large companies. First, a big movement toward decentralization takes place. A few years later, after the consequences described above have taken their toll, top management decides that things have gotten out of hand, and there is a general tightening up in the direction of centralization. The inability to control a large, complex organization centrally leads after a while to a new attempt at decentralization. There are indications that this cycle has also occurred within Soviet industry, although the surface manifestations have been different.

The logic behind the strategy of control outlined above is so subtly persuasive that it is difficult to argue against it: Every manager is responsible for results within that portion of the organization which is under his supervision. He is held accountable by those above him. Obviously he cannot fulfill this responsibility unless (1) he knows what is going on within the unit, and (2) he is able to do something about things that go wrong.

This logic is unassailable if one accepts the assumptions of Theory X: that most people have to be made to do what is necessary for the success of the organization, that they will not voluntarily accept responsibility, that they are limited in capacity. Management by direction and control inevitably results in strategies similar to the one we have been examining.

3. TWO CONCEPTS OF AUTHORITY *

Walter B. Miller

WHEN EUROPEAN traders, soldiers, and missionaries first began to move into the western Great Lakes region around 1650, they found in the area that is now Wisconsin, Illinois, and Indiana, a group of Central Algonkian tribes. Eight of these tribes spoke slightly divergent dialects of a single language, Central Algonkian. They were approximately the same size and showed considerable similarity in religion, social organization, cultural traditions, and general way of life. These eight tribes were the Potowatami, Sac, Menomini, Fox, Mascoutin, Kickapoo, Miami and Illinois.

The Central Algonkians were village-dwelling Indians, each tribe averaging about 3,000 people. Although some agriculture was practiced, hunting was the primary subsistence activity, and hunting and warfare the focal interests of tribal members. Politically, each tribe was an autonomous and independent sovereignty, maintaining both hostile and friendly relationships with neighboring tribes in a shifting pattern of intertribal wars and alliances. The Central Algonkians had developed effective modes of exploiting their physical environment and maintaining a satisfactory social and ecological balance. They were extremely skillful hunters and, as the incoming Europeans soon learned, equally effective fighters.

But these same Europeans were struck by what appeared to them a most remarkable phenomenon: The Central Algonkians seemed to carry out their subsistence, religious, administrative, and military activities in the virtual absence of any sort of recognizable authority! Traders, soldiers, and missionaries alike were impressed by this. One of the first Europeans to contact the central tribes was Nicholas Perrot, a French fur trader and coureur de bois. He recorded these impressions around 1680:

> Subordination is not a maxim among these savages, the savage does not know what it is to obey. . . . It is more necessary to entreat him than to command him. . . . The father does not venture to exercise authority

* Reprinted by permission of author and publisher from *American Anthropologist*, Vol. LVII, No. 2 (April, 1955), pp. 271–89.

over his son, nor does the chief dare give commands to his soldier. . . . [If] anyone is stubborn in regard to some proposed movement, it is necessary to flatter him in order to dissuade him, otherwise he will go further in his opposition. . . .

Similar impressions were recorded by Jonathan Carver, one of the first Englishmen to explore the Central area. He wrote, about 1770:

Although [the Indians have both military and civil chiefs], yet [they] are sensible of neither civil nor military subordination. As every one of them entertains a very high opinion of his consequence, and is extremely tenacious of his liberty, all injunctions that carry with them the appearance of a command are instantly rejected with scorn. On this account it is seldom their leaders are so indiscrete as to give out orders in a peremptory style. . . . [There] is no visible form of government; they allow of no such distinction as [that between] magistrate and subject, everyone appearing to enjoy an independence that cannot be controlled.

It is apparent from these reactions that the Europeans saw in the Central Algonkian situation, not a system for coordinating collective action that was different from their own, but rather the absence of any kind of regulatory system. Carver's impression that "there is no visible form of government" is echoed again and again by Europeans who contacted the Central tribesmen. Such perceptions and evaluations were evidently influenced in large part by what the Europeans were accustomed to.

A Contemporary European Type of Authority Relationship

[At the time the Europeans first contacted the Central Algonkian tribes, the Europeans were accustomed to a society in which highly concentrated authority was exercised by certain role incumbents. For example,] the amount of authority exercised by the sixth-century English Lord, the sixteenth-century Jesuit Superior, and the seventeenth-century French King [would] appear extreme to most present-day Europeans. However, in present-day European societies there are numerous role-relationships that share, in less extreme form, certain characteristics of these earlier prototypes. Setting aside contemporary role-relationships such as the Fuhrer-citizen relationship of Nazi Germany or the Commissar-comrade relationship of Soviet Russia, Europeans are familiar with numerous less spectacular role-relationships that entail the exercise of authority, and which they accept as a normal and necessary part of life. Some of these are master-servant, officer–enlisted man, boss-employee, teacher-pupil, parent-child, foreman-worker, pastor-parishioner, orchestra leader–sideman, coach–team member, director-cast member, captain–crew member, doctor-patient, chief–staff member.

It would seldom occur to the average European to question the validity of such relationships. The amount of authority they involve is not seen as excessive but as normal and right. Europeans accept the fact that the functioning of their factories, hospitals, churches, and other organized institutions depends on the authority exercised through these role-relationships and others like them. But a member of sixteenth-century Algonkian society would regard such authority as oppressive and intolerable. Although collective action was successfully coordinated in the political, economic, military, and religious spheres, it would be difficult to point to a single role-relationship in Algonkian society that was essentially analogous to the European type of authority relationship. . . .

In the European cultural tradition a rather remarkable phenomenon can be noted: authority, or "power," is conceptually equated with height or elevation. It is conceived as originating in some elevated locus, and as passing down to lower levels. This metaphorical way of thinking about authority is closely tied in with European religious conceptions, many of which utilize the notion that power originates in a supernatural being or group of beings located in the heavens, or some elevated location. Central Algonkian religion places its deities at the four corners of the universe, and on the same plane as humans.

This way of conceptualizing authority is so well integrated into European culture that it is difficult to deal with authority in any other way. The equation of authority with altitude is firmly built into European linguistic systems; the terms *super*ior, *infer*ior, and *super*ordinate, *sub*ordinate, have been key terms in this discussion. A man with considerable authority is said to be in a *top* position, *high*-ranking way *up* there, one with little authority is on the *bottom,* in a *lowly* position, *down* and out. We speak of the *haute*-monde and the *under*world, of *over*lord and *under*ling, of *upper* and *lower* classes. . . .

[Another] mode of conceptualizing authority is pointed up by comparison with that of the Central Algonkians. While the Central Algonkian conceives of authority as the resultant of ongoing interaction between individuals, the European tends to reify authority—to picture it as a substance, generally a liquidlike substance. We speak of the "flow" of authority, of "going through channels," of the "fountain-head" of authority. As a substance, authority can be quantified, and thus we speak of a great deal of authority, little authority, no authority.

The "table of organization" chart, used so widely to represent organizational structure, utilizes these metaphorical conventions whereby authority is reified, quantified, elevated, and pictured as flowing downward. A number of boxes, representing offices or authority agencies, are placed on different vertical levels and joined to one another by lines or arrows. The "locus," or loci, of power is placed at the top; agencies with "less" authority are put at lower levels; arrows denote the "flow" of authority from one box to another; each box can serve as an area or passage through which authority can be transmitted from one place to another. . . .

The vertical authority relationship is a fundamental building block of European society. Without it the phenomenon of "ranked" authority —where given individuals are permanently empowered to direct others —would be impossible, and ranked authority is an indispensable feature of European organizational systems.

A society where authority is conceptualized in a different way would have to organize collective activity according to different principles. Following sections will describe how [one of the best known of the Central Algonkian tribes, the Fox Indians,] conceived of authority and organized collective action. . . .

Gods and Men in Fox Society

One way to gain insight into the way that authority was conceived and organized in Fox society is to look at the Fox system of religion. The pantheon of any society can be seen as a projective system, whereby the essential features of the social organization of the projecting society are attributed to a group of supernatural beings, whose relations reflect those existing among the people themselves. . . .

The basic concept of Fox religion is manitu. . . . Manitu is a kind of generalized essence of supernatural power. . . . A significant characteristic of manitu power is that it is never possessed permanently by any being or group of beings; it is always held conditionally. It is lost, gained, lost again—its possession being measured by quality of performance in a particular area of activity. To succeed means that manitu power is possessed; to fail means that it is lost. . . .

Fox cosmology presents a picture of scores of powerful manitus jockeying with one another in a constant and unending struggle for temporary superiority. Each is potentially able to vanquish the other—for conquest depends, not on possessing an intrinsically superior amount of power, but rather on how carefully, or shrewdly, or skillfully each antagonist utilizes the resources he possesses in any particular encounter.

. . . But it is important to note the *results* of these combats. The combats serve merely to establish a temporary prestige advantage for the winner. The loser is subject to feelings of shame at having been outwitted. He is never subjugated by virtue of his defeat. Conquest does not in any way grant to the victor the prerogative to direct or control the future actions of the vanquished. No permanent relationship of superordination-subordination is instituted as the result of demonstrated possession of superior power, because the vanquished always has direct access to an unlimited store of manitu power, by use of which he may, and often does, defeat his adversary in the next encounter. Thus there can be no stable, vertical hierarchy of gods who derive permanent power from superiors. . . .

In Fox society, each individual is related directly to the source of supernatural power, and each has his own individual deity. At the onset of adolescence, each Fox male goes out into the forest where he fasts for four days and four nights. During the course of this fast he has a vision of a powerful manitu—an animal, bird, manitu-human, or natural object. The boy is told by the manitu that henceforth he will be under his protection, and that he will control the particular power possessed by the manitu. In the course of the visitation the manitu instructs the boy in acceptable ethical and moral behavior. This "instruction" is given not in the form of rigid commands or interdictions, but rather as advice. . . .

But the grant of manitu power and supernatural guardianship is not outright; the manitu needs the services of the boy as much as the boy needs his. In exchange for supernatural power, the boy agrees to present to the manitu periodic gifts of tobacco, which the manitu craves but can get only from humans, and to adhere to his guardian's ethical precepts in order to please him. The boy-manitu relationship is couched in terms of mutual obligations, not in terms of a one-way power flow. If the boy neglects his obligations, the manitu may withdraw his support; if the boy fails in some important undertaking, this evidence that the manitu has not done his part entitles the boy to seek a new protector. . . .

The Fox Concept of Power

The relations between gods, and between gods and men, as they are depicted in Fox religious mythology, are based on Fox ideals of right and proper interpersonal relations. The myths are direct products of such ideals, and since in myths the actions of men and manitus are not restricted by the limitations of finite reality, the behavior therein exemplifies these ideals in their purest form.

Manitu power represents to the Fox a vital and absorbing aspect of interpersonal relations—the ability to control, automatically and magically, the actions of others. Its characteristics, as they emerge from a consideration of relations within the Fox pantheon, can be described in the abstract.

Power is universally available and unlimited; it does not have a unitary locus; it is everywhere and equally available to all.

The possession of power is temporary and contingent; it is not a quality permanently possessed by any being; but can be gained and lost, possession being demonstrated by successful performance in specific situations.

Demonstrated power does not grant to its possessor the subsequent right to direct the actions of any other being.

Power is not hierarchical; since its possession is temporary and contingent, fixed and varying amounts of power are not distributed among a group of beings arranged in a stable hierarchy.

The control of power is dangerous; powerful beings are to be feared, not adored or admired.

Thus even in its purest conceptualized form, "manitu power," the ability to control others, emerges as substantially different from the European concept of vertical authority. The concept of manitu served as a fundamental precept governing concrete day-to-day behavior in Fox life. As a guide to interpersonal relations it had this implication: it is both dangerous and immoral for one individual to exercise any substantial control over others. As a personal attitude it was manifested as an intense and deep-rooted resentment of anything perceived as an attempt to control one's actions.

The next sections will show how these ideals worked out in practice: how authority was organized, how activity was coordinated, and how individuals related themselves to authority.

The Organization of Authority in Fox Society

A number of formalized agencies in Fox society operated to bring about the coordination of collective action. Such agencies were limited in number, and highly circumscribed in the amount and kinds of authority exercised. Three formalized positions of authority (authority-roles), and one formal group which functioned to implement collective action (authority organ) will be described.

The nominally paramount authority-role was that of village chief. The role was a permanent one, in that it was held by the same man over an extended period of time. Incumbency was determined by hereditary factors, each village chief being selected from the same lineage group—the Bear totemic group. The functions of the village chief did not involve any directive authority. On the contrary, the role-definition called for mild, nonaggressive, noninitiative behavior. The Fox name for this role was "peace chief," or sometimes "kindly chief." The village chief acted to symbolize peaceful and harmonious intergroup relations, nonaggressive behavior, and the unity of the village group. The closest his role functions came to permitting direction was that he was expected to act as arbiter and peacemaker in the event of dissension in council meetings.

The role of war leader involved a modicum of directive authority. During a war expedition the war leader was authorized to size up the situation and suggest desirable action. But this authority was limited in two ways. First, no one was obligated to accept the direction of the war leader if he didn't want to. Any warrior in the tribe who was granted manitu power in a vision could lead a war party, but war party membership was entirely voluntary, and members could leave at any time during a war expedition if they were not satisfied with the way things were going. No war-party leader would be imprudent enough to issue direct commands. The incumbent of the war-chief role, by far the most "powerful" authority role in Fox society, communicated his directives in the form of suggestions as to desirable action which war-party members could act on or not, as they saw fit.

Second, incumbency of the war-chief role was strictly limited in duration. The authority prerogatives of the war leader, circumscribed as they were, were confined to the duration of the war expedition itself. At its termination, the war leader, who had been invested for a few days with this dangerous amount of authority, was not permitted to re-enter the village until he had participated in a ceremonial wherein his temporary authority was vividly and symbolically revoked. . . . Comparing the roles of village chief and war chief, we see that where even a small amount of directive authority was associated with the role, tenure was strictly limited; where tenure was extended the amount of authority was strictly limited.

The role of ceremony leader similarly involved very little authority. The ceremony leader was a man who had committed to memory one or more of the many religious rituals which played so important a part in Fox life. He put people through the paces of a given religious ceremony, signaling beginnings and endings of a preset sequence of traditionally prescribed ritual episodes. His functions did not include formulation or initiation of religious activity; he did not serve to mediate the relationship between man and manitu; and, like the war chief, his authority functions were limited to the duration of the ritual itself and did not extend beyond the area of ceremonial activity.

The village council served as the tribal decision-making agency in matters involving collective welfare or concerted action. The council was composed of the headmen of each of the extended family groupings that composed the tribe, plus any other man who demonstrated ability in council affairs. The amount of influence exerted by any councilman depended on his own personal capability and not on the status of the totemic group he represented. The village chief served as the presiding officer of the council, but had no more influence by virtue of his position than any other member; in fact, he was expected to participate only minimally in council discussions.

The mechanism whereby the adherence of the people to council decisions was obtained was the unanimous decision. . . . No course of action was agreed on by the council unless all members were in accord with the final decision. Since each Fox was represented in the council by a member of his own family group, and since considerable and extended intratribal discussion preceded all matters involving the collectivity, a concluded council decision had taken into account, and in some way accommodated to, the wishes of everyone involved in the execution of a given enterprise. Thus the act of decision-making itself insured the tribal validation of the decision. If there was any considerable opposition to a course of action involving full tribal participation, such a course could not be adopted, since this would make impossible the necessary unanimous decision; there was no necessity to force dissidents to participate in a policy of which they did not approve. The line between the people and the council was thinly drawn; all were welcome to attend and participate in council sessions; if a matter were of sufficient import, a formal meeting of the whole tribe was called. The whole decision-making mechanism was characterized by extreme reluctance to permit decisions as to action to be concluded by any group smaller than the participating group itself.

The Coordination of Collective Action

Since authority roles were so weakly invested with the right to direct, how, in fact, was action coordinated? Even today an observer of Fox society is struck by the fact that organized activity appears to proceed in the absence of any visible authority. A Fox taking part in a fairly large and complex organized enterprise (200–300 people) conducted each year was asked how he knew so well what to do without being told. His answer was "I just do the same as I did last year."

This answer furnishes a key to understanding the Fox method of co-ordinating collective action. Just as each individual related himself directly to the source of supernatural power, each individual participating in organized activity related himself directly to the body of procedural rules governing that activity. He was free to select and execute appropriate modes of action; his access to procedural rules was not mediated through another person who transmitted these rules to him.

It seems obvious that this system would hardly be adequate to insure success in a modern military landing operation, the construction of a skyscraper, or the production of a moving picture. Why, then, did it work in Fox society? In the first place, the *range* of activities involving coordinated action was quite limited. Only about five of six such activities (the war party, religious ceremonial, council meeting, some group games) were frequently recurrent; the total number of recurrent collective activities did not exceed ten or twelve. Second, the *size* of the group participating in such activities was limited. The war party consisted of about five to fifteen men; the religious ceremony involved fifteen to forty participants. Only very infrequently were larger groups involved in a coordinated enterprise. Third, since the rate of social change in Fox society was slow, the procedure of such activities was familiar to all participants. They had observed or taken part in them since early childhood; each knew his own part and how it fitted in with the parts of others; the activities changed little from year to year. Fourth, the "division of labor" in Fox society was neither complex nor ramified. There were few real specialists, no secret or esoteric groups of craftsmen; in important coordinated activities such as ceremonials and council meetings, the whole range of the population—all age groups and both sexes —was customarily participant.

Thus it was possible for each participant in a collective activity to "control" the plan of action that governed its conduct. He was familiar with the procedural directives specifying the part he was to play and was able to act out these directives without being told what to do. It was as if the action plan for each activity were "built into" each participant. In activities such as the ceremonial, where a person in a position of authority presided over the proceedings, he exercised only "nominal" authority functions, such as signaling the beginnings and endings of set episodes, or recalling the proper sequence of events. . . .

Authority and the Individual

Fox subsistence economy was based on tracking and killing wild game, mostly by individual hunters. Success in hunting expeditions required that individuals spend long periods in complete solitude, traverse many miles of difficult wilderness, undergo extended hardship and deprivation, and exercise considerable initiative and ingenuity to contend with animal quarry which could resort to many devices to outwit a pursuer. Such a subsistence system put a premium on qualities of individual initiative, self-dependence, forbearance, and the capacity to size up a situation and act on one's estimate.

To early European observers the Fox individual appeared unusually haughty, self-contained, and quick to resent anything he perceived as limiting his right to independent action. . . . But what the Europeans perceived as resentment of authority could be described more accurately as resentment of authorities. Just as the Fox related himself directly to supernatural power, and to the procedural rules governing collective action, so he deemed it his inviolable right to respond directly to the rules governing general behavior. The intensity of Fox resentment of external direction was matched by an equally intense conformity to internalized cultural directives. The Fox individual was highly moral; he felt individually responsible for knowing and acting in accordance with the regulations of his society. An order was an insult; it implied that he was inadequate in his knowledge and performance of traditional rules of correct behavior.

4. TWO VIEWS OF JAPANESE INDUSTRIAL ORGANIZATION

The Japanese Factory[1]

JAPAN's experience with industrialization provides a useful indication of the range of organizational adaptations and adjustments possible or necessary in introducing a technology which is the product of one kind of culture into another culture. There is an urgent need for a further understanding of the outcomes of the introduction of modern industrial technology into cultures markedly different from our own. The book is an attempt, on the basis of limited observation, to set out the broad outlines of the organization of the Japanese factory.

In Japan, loyalty to the group and an interchange of responsibilities—a system of shared obligation—take the place of a primary reliance on a relationship between the worker and the firm. The firm will not discharge an employee even temporarily except in the most extreme circumstances. He will not quit the firm for industrial employment elsewhere. This applies to all levels of the organization. The labor departure rate of Japanese factory employees is generally between 2 and 3 per cent per year. Thus there is very little flexibility of the work force within the Japanese system.

The selection of personnel in a Japanese factory is related more closely to education than to any other consideration. Recruitment directly from schools into the company is to all intents and purposes the *only* way in which men enter the firms. When young Japanese businessmen are asked what they would do if offered a better position at more pay in another firm, the general reaction is blank silence, a result of the fact that such an eventuality is so improbable—both the offer of another position and the possibility of accepting were it offered—that there is no response.

There are two broad categories of employees in a firm, the KOIN and SHOKUIN. The first are wage-earners and the second are salaried employees. Japanese companies prefer to hire KOIN with "stable natures." This means young men just out of middle school (aged 14 or 15) who are the sons of farmers, living in rural areas, and strongly desirous of finding urban, factory employment. The KOIN will remain in the plant

---

[1] Adapted from James G. Abegglen, *The Japanese Factory* (Glencoe, Ill., Free Press, 1958).

for which they are hired for the remainder of their careers. There are two subgroups among the SHOKUIN. Those persons who are high school graduates and occupy lower level positions are distinguished from those who are college graduates occupying higher positions and eligible for the topmost rank. Firms will not hire high school graduates as KOIN, nor can individuals in the organization rise past the limits set upon them by their education. SHOKUIN are selected by a firm from "approved" schools; this means, at the college level, for example, that only graduates from a small number of top-rated universities will be considered. Once hired, the SHOKUIN are transferred from factory to factory as needed, and are assigned out of the main offices. In this system, once the worker has been selected, the company practically speaking foregoes the right to find the worker incompetent. He was selected for qualities of background, personality, and general ability that may not in fact make him a competent employee. Should the firm find him useless, it does not dismiss him but may only move him from job to job within the general category of his employment status until he is placed in a harmless and perhaps not useful position. In any event, once admitted into employment, employees of Japanese firms will not be fired on grounds of lack of ability.

The entire salary of a Japanese employee is largely based on his educational status on entering the company and the length of time he has served. In addition he is paid allowances based on the size of his family, his attendance record, and his job rank. This last salary item is the only one that is related closely to the nature of the work performed. It is not at all difficult to find situations where workers doing identical work at an identical pace receive markedly different salaries, or where a skilled workman is paid at a rate below that of a sweeper or doorman. Motivation for work output rests in large part on loyalty and group identification. The Japanese employee is part of a very personal system in which his total functioning as a person is seen as management's responsibility and in which his group membership transcends his individual privileges and responsibilities. For example, a particular problem arose in a metals-processing firm in Shikokn. The workers' wives are grouped together in a financial co-operative. Each member contributed a sum of money to a fund from which members could withdraw, in turn, substantial sums for the purchase of durable household goods and other items. Some wives, eager to purchase a washing machine or radio, withdrew funds ill-advisedly from the group bank. When several of the workers' wives were unable to make the requested repayment to the group fund, the other members turned to the personnel department of the company for recovery of the money. When called to the office, one of the husbands found his monthly paycheck reduced and his family budget reviewed. He then received some general advice on the financial management of his affairs. The important point to note is that wives, workers, and company were right to assume that the company, although it had no direct concern in the matter, would act in the situation and, further, that all parties concerned would accept the company's intervention.

To obtain a perspective on the underlying nature of the social organization of the large Japanese factory, it is useful to look briefly at a small factory where one finds its analogue and paradigm. The silk factory of Mr. Watanabe will serve as an example; one which is slightly larger than average and has 30 looms and 19 employees. The workers in the factory are essentially an extension of the Watanabe family. The 15 women employees are young girls, aged 15 to 21 years. They are from farm homes in the surrounding villages, and their employment has been arranged between Mr. Watanabe and their parents. They live in a wing of the family house, their food is prepared jointly with that of the family, and special holidays and occasions are enjoyed by the entire group, both family and workers. Mr. Watanabe acts in fact *in loco parentis*. He provides care, advice, and counsel for his workers; and finally—no small part of his duties as factory owner—arranges or assists in the arrangement of their marriages. The girls enter the plant immediately after middle school graduation, serve a three-year apprenticeship, and then, usually after two additional years of work, marry. The niceties of labor laws governing wages, hours, unionization, and similar factors do not penetrate the shop with any regularity. The hours are governed by work demands and extend to well over 60 hours each week. The wages are low indeed, and consist largely of the food, lodging, and clothing, and care provided as one would provide for a large and slightly improvident group of relatives. Relations are close and warm, and the girls have a most intimate knowledge of each other. There is little leisure, and the Sunday holiday is spent largely in small domestic tasks. The world is a most confined one, seldom extending beyond the factory compound. This interval in the workers' lives, the five or seven years between school and marriage, is part of the accepted scheme of things for these girls, an interval in which they are cared for and in which they work in a fashion not at all inconsistent with their backgrounds.

While the size of the organization of a large factory precludes the intimate knowledge of and interaction with superiors that is the central force in the operation of the small workshops, two types of relation which parallel the system of the small shop may be seen in the large firm. The first is the strong tie between the company and the worker described earlier, the lifetime commitment of worker and firm to each other, and the elaborate system of extramonetary obligations and rewards that have been developed in the large plant. The second is the intrafirm relationship developed in the clique system at the management level (those who went to the same university, for example) and in the apprentice-teacher and worker-foreman relationship in the factory itself. The formal organization of the factory is elaborated in a wide range and considerable number of formal positions. Formal rank and title in the hierarchy are well defined, but the authority and responsibility of ranks are not. Partly in consequence, the decision-making function is exercised by groups of persons, but responsibility for the decisions is not assigned to individuals. When a man must spend his entire career in one factory or company, it is important that his prestige and reputation and his relations with others retain their integrity. The decision-making system is admirably adapted to this end.

From the observations of this study it would appear that, although the technology of modern industry was introduced into Japan, the factory organization at the same time developed consistent with the historical customs and attitudes of the Japanese and with the social system as it existed prior to the introduction of modern industry. Thus, looking beyond the modern equipment and the formal organization, the systems of relationships are more nearly similar to those which seem to have characterized an earlier Japan and which now characterize the nonindustrial areas of Japan than they are similar to the factory organization of the West. But selective adaptation should not be remarkable; it would be much more remarkable if any people were able in one fell swoop to put off their past, their training, and habits of mind and don successfully and permanently totally new social paraphernalia. This study indicates that efforts to change the economy of other nations in the direction of industrialization might better be concerned with an identification of basic elements of the preindustrial social system and with the introduction of new technologies and financial systems in the context of the older relationships, than with making these nations over in the image derived from Western experience.

Management Organization and Decision Making[2]

Before I arrived in Japan, I had done enough reading to expect a society that was ceremonious and hierarchical, and I indeed found one. The Japanese have preserved in this hurried modern world the respect

[2] Excerpted from Stanley S. Miller, "Management by *Omikoshi*—Traditional Features of Modern Business in Japan," *Management International,* Vol. 3, No. 1 (1963).

for seniors and deference to elders that seems to come from a more gracious age than ours. With all this emphasis on rank and authority, I had also expected to find a line-of-command system of decision making, moving down from senior to junior like a military organization. But I found nothing of the sort. Instead of an authoritative line of responsibility, there seemed at first to be no locus of responsibility at all in the Japanese organization. This is a result of group decision making, a very old and deep-seated practice in Japan.

Rather than enjoying the stimulus of debate, Japanese rather tend to seek the harmony of agreement. This is true even in the rhythms of ordinary conversation, which seems designed to result in a series of gratifying responses such as *"Ah so, des ne,"* or *"Honto des yo,"* where an American conversation might be more apt to include, "No, I don't think so."

In a business meeting, this means that the group does not like to take action without general endorsement. The principal parties are usually sought out privately beforehand to sound out their positions so that the meetings themselves can avoid embarrassing arguments. Strongly held minority positions can hold up a project for months because of the unwillingness of the leaders to be accused of "tyranny of the majority." Furthermore, even when group consensus is achieved, it may not be a clear-cut commitment to carry out the project to its conclusion, but merely an endorsement to go along one stage further to see what will happen.

The Japanese organization is hierarchical rather than democratic, in the sense that various kinds of stratification impose clearly marked vertical barriers. For example, university graduates become managers; high school graduates do not. But within the upper layer, there is a high degree of participation in the councils of the business, even by the junior men. They may wait a long time before obtaining official authority, but they can voice their opinions because the system calls for maximum participation in a new project.

Americans who find paternalism oppressive should keep this in mind. A Japanese executive once asked me what was the main difference between business organization in our two countries. While I was thinking, his assistant, who had studied in America, said: "In Japan we emphasize human relations; in America they are profit-minded." I was dumbfounded by this response, because I had considered myself as an exponent of the freedom of human action in a rather materialistic and stratified Japanese society. The young Japanese meant it as a compliment to the United States. He meant: "We base our decisions on friendship, to protect each other; in America they analyze return on investment."

Decisions based on friendship can develop into management by cliques, and this has not been absent from either Japan's business or its political history. In business, decisions that would be considered in America to be the responsibility of one department are usually shared by other departments. For example in the *ringiseido* system, one group submits a plan of action in the form of a report that goes the rounds of all the executives for approval, and the president may well add his own seal if enough support has already been obtained, so there are apt to be a lot of private dinner parties to sound out prior approval on other projects. In politics, prewar Japanese history was dominated by inner-groups who rotated official responsibility among themselves. Like the old merchant monopolies and *zaibatsu* management, they fought off outsiders who tried to enter their councils. For example, statesmen from Satsuma and Choshu, the two powerful clans who led the Restoration of 1868, dominated political decisions in Japan from 1881 until well into the twentieth century and brought along their own proteges despite mounting pressure from outsiders.

A large management organization based on voting cliques and without clearly defined centers of responsibility can develop a sense of mystery as to its future moves. It may attain objectives, but it will be difficult to evaluate its position at any one time.

In discussing this situation at a management seminar, one very able executive described the traditional organization in Japan as "Management by *Omikoshi*." The *omikoshi* is the portable shrine taken out in the streets on festivals. Two long poles are strapped in parallel to its base, and it is carried on the shoulders of perhaps a dozen men. The fun of it is to carry the shrine, shout *"washoi, washoi"* in unison, and push your weight against the weight of the other pole carriers. The *omikoshi* makes headway, but in an enjoyable rollicking motion from side to side, and sometimes turns completely around before it can sway forward again.

Another executive at the seminar pointed out that the *omikoshi* did in fact have a leader, since there is a man up ahead encouraging the group to move forward. However, in my observation of neighborhood festivals in Tokyo, I have noted that the linkage between the leader and the team was more ceremonial than operational, and that some of the carriers occasionally lifted their feet off the ground and hung on for the ride.

5. THE INFLUENCE OF TECHNICAL CHANGE ON ORGANIZATION STRUCTURE

OVER A PERIOD of several years careful field studies were made of a number of plants in Great Britain: a rayon manufacturer, a large engineering concern, a number of Scottish firms in various fields that were all interested in entering the electronics field, and eight English firms previously established in different segments of the electronics industry.[1] The researchers "hoped to be able to observe how management systems changed in accordance with changes in the technical and commercial tasks of the firm, especially the substantial changes in the rate of technical advance."[2]

The Scottish firms under study expected to enter the electronics area by recruiting technical people, setting up laboratory groups, and securing development contracts from the government.

Most of the Scottish firms failed to realize their expectations. In half the cases, laboratory groups were disbanded or disrupted by the resignation of their leaders. Others were converted into test departments, "troubleshooting" teams, or production departments. Common to all predicaments was, first, the determined effort from the outset to keep the laboratory group as separate as possible from the rest of the organization; second, the appearance of conflicts for power, and over the privileged status of laboratory engineers; and third, the conversion of management problems into terms of personalities—to treat difficulties as really caused by the ignorance, stupidity or obstructiveness of the other side. These failures were interpreted by us as an inability to adapt the management system to the form appropriate to conditions of more rapid technical and commercial change.

There seemed to be two divergent systems of management practice. Neither was fully and consistently applied in any firm, although there was a clear division between those managements which adhered generally to the one, and those which followed the other. Neither system was openly and consciously employed as an instrument of policy, although many beliefs and empirical methods associated with one or the other were expressed. One system, to which we gave the name "mechanistic," appeared to be appropriate to an enterprise operating under relatively stable

---

[1] Tom Burns and G. M. Stalker, *The Management of Innovation* (London: Tavistock Publications, 1961).

[2] *Ibid.*, p. 4.

conditions. The other, "organic," appeared to be required for conditions of change. In terms of "ideal types" their principal characteristics are briefly these:

In mechanistic systems the problems and tasks facing the concern as a whole are broken down into specialisms. Each individual pursues his task as something distinct from the real tasks of the concern as a whole, as if it were the subject of a sub-contract. "Somebody at the top" is responsible for seeing to its relevance. The technical methods, duties, and powers attached to each functional role are precisely defined. Interaction within management tends to be vertical, i.e., between superior and subordinate. Operations and working behaviour are governed by instructions and decisions issued by superiors. This command hierarchy is maintained by the implicit assumption that all knowledge about the situation of the firm and its tasks is, or should be, available only to the head of the firm. Management, often visualized as the complex hierarchy familiar in organization charts, operates a simple control system, with information flowing up through a succession of amplifiers.

Organic systems are adapted to unstable conditions, when problems and requirements for action arise which cannot be broken down and distributed among specialist roles within a clearly defined hierarchy. Individuals have to perform their special tasks in the light of their knowledge of the tasks of the firm as a whole. Jobs lose much of their formal definition in terms of methods, duties, and powers, which have to be redefined continually by interaction with others participating in a task. Interaction runs laterally as much as vertically. Communication between people of different ranks tends to resemble lateral consultation rather than vertical command. Omniscience can no longer be imputed to the head of the concern.

The central problem of the Scottish study appeared to be why the working organization of a concern did not change its system from "mechanistic" to "organic" as its circumstances changed with entry into new commercial and technical fields. The answer which suggested itself was that every single person in a firm not only is (*a*) a member of a working organization, but also (*b*) a member of a group with sectional interests in conflict with those of other groups, and (*c*) one individual among many to whom the rank they occupy and the prestige attaching to them are matters of deep concern. Looked at in another way, any firm contains not only a working organization but a political system and a status structure. In the case of the firms we studied, the existing political system and status structure were threatened by the advent of a new laboratory group. Especially, the technical information available to the newcomers, which was a valuable business resource, was used or regarded as an instrument for political control; and laboratory engineers claimed, or were regarded as claiming, elite status within the organization.

Neither political or status preoccupations operated overtly, or even consciously; they gave rise to intricate manoeuvres and countermoves, all of them expressed through decisions, or discussions about decisions, concerning the internal structure and the policies of the firm. Since political and status conflicts only came into the open in terms of the working organization, that organization became adjusted to serving the ends of the political and status system of the concern rather than its own.

The individual manager became absorbed in conflicts over power and status because they presented him with interests and problems more immediately important to him and more easily comprehended than those raised by the new organizational milieu and its unlimited liabilities. For increases in the rate of technical and commercial change meant more problems, more unfamiliar information, a wider range of work relationships, and heavier mental and emotional commitments. Many found it impossible to accept such conditions for their occupational lives. To keep their commitments limited meant either gaining more control over their personal situation or claiming exemption because of special conditions attached to their status. These purposes involved manoeuvres which persistently ran counter to the development of an organic system, and raised issues which could only be resolved by a reversion to a mechanistic system.

The Scottish study developed eventually into two complementary accounts of the ways in which the adaptation of management systems to conditions of change was impeded or thwarted. In one set of terms, the failure to adapt was attributed to the strength of former political and status structures. In other terms, the failure was seen as the consequence of an implicit resistance among individual members of concerns to the growth of commitments in their occupational existence at the expense of the rest of their lives.[3]

The Scottish study was followed by the study of the eight English electronics firms. These studies "concentrated on two topics: the management difficulties which seemed peculiar to firms engaged in rapid technical progress, and the particular problem of getting laboratory groups on the one hand (research—development—design) to work effectively with production and sales groups on the other."[4]

The eight English firms were not only much larger but much more committed to electronics development and manufacture than were the firms of the Scottish study, which were in the earliest stages of their careers in electronics. The situations available for study were more complicated; they were also more intimately related to the commercial and industrial destinies of the firms and to the lives of the people in them.

---

[3] *Ibid.,* pp. 4–7.

[4] *Ibid.,* pp. 7–8.

There was, for example, much more variety in the kind of group within the firm affected by an acceleration in the rate of technical change, and in the responses to change made by different firms. In firms which operated consciously on organic lines, changes from any direction were regarded as what they manifestly were—circumstances which affected every part of the firm and everybody's job, in some way. Organizational changes, additional tasks, and growth in any particular direction tended to be seen as the concerted response of the firm to a new situation; although debate and conflict were present, they were manifestly present and could be treated as part of the new situation to be reckoned with. In firms which operated according to mechanistic principles, the response to change was usually to create a new group, or to reconstitute the existing structure, or to expand an existing group which would be largely responsible for meeting the new situation, and so "not disrupt the existing organization."

This latter response, which in the Scottish firms characteristically led to the segregation of the new development team from the rest of management, was now visible in the way some firms dealt with big changes in market conditions. A Head Office sales department, or a new sales forecasting and market study group, might be created. Management might be reconstructed on product division lines, so as to extend the control of sales over the activities of the firm. Engineers might be recruited from development laboratories, or directorships offered to men of outstanding reputation from other firms. More significantly still, a new technical departure might be made the province of a newly created laboratory group independent of the laboratory concerned with the obsolescent techniques. In such cases, the confinement to prescribed section of its organization of the total response of the firm to change meant that for the rest of the firm the challenge of the new situation became instead a threat offered by the "new men" to the power, standing and career prospects they had hitherto enjoyed. This was especially the case with development engineers. Previously the element in every firm which had been identified with expansion and innovating change, they now saw their leading role passing—in part—to sales. The development-production conflicts typical of the Scottish study were overshadowed in the English firms by sales-development conflicts, by the resistance of the professional innovators to an innovating change.

Political conflict appeared to be clearly related to the particularism which was fostered by the separating out of the tasks of the firm according to specialist functions. Given a mechanistic system, changes of all kinds, including expansion, continually threw up new institutions within the firm which were intended to carry the whole of a new defined task and which themselves engendered political problems.

The conceptions of mechanistic and organic management have also proved useful in analysing the arrangements made inside firms for passing work through from the earliest stages of development to final manufacture. The tendency is to regard the whole process as an articulated series of separate specialist functions made for the creation of "hand-over" frontiers between departments and for language barriers; it also went with a predilection for tethering functionaries to their posts. The need for communications beyond the formal transmission of instructions and drawings led to the appointment of liaison specialists—interpreters whose job was to move across the linguistic and functional frontiers and to act as intermediaries between the people "getting on with the job." Organic systems recognized the supreme importance of common languages and of each functionary's being able to seek out and interpret for himself the information he needed. The fewer distinguishable stages, the fewer interpreters and intermediaries, the more effectively were designs passed through the system.

Many of the insights generated by the English study were suggested in the first place by the distinctive response made by different concerns to a major change in market conditions as against techniques, as was the case with the firms in the Scottish study. The decline in government work and the increased emphasis on selling in the so-called "commercial market" affected all concerns in the same way, although to a different extent. The first observable distinction was between the firms which saw that a sales function had been discharged by the laboratory engineer working on government development contracts, and that a similar role was equally necessary with commercial users, and those which overlooked this sales function in connexion with defence ministries and regarded market exploration and development as the province of salesmen. There were a number of aspects of this difference. Some concerns had always been wary of committing themselves too heavily to government work; others had allowed themselves to become educated into commercial unfitness by too complete a dependence on defence contracts. In general, it could be said that the first kind of firm tended to regard the market as a source of design ideas which the firm then attempted to realize, the second kind as a sink into which should be poured applications of techniques developed within the firm. Successful manufacturers of domestic radio and television receivers offered the most striking demonstration of the first principle. So much so, that in these firms not only the management system but the way in which individuals' jobs were defined, and the code of conduct prevailing in the concern, seemed to be generated by constant preoccupation with the market on the part of every member of management.[5]

The researchers were also interested in the impact of "organic" management systems on the individual:

Organic systems are those which are best adapted to conditions of change. By common consent, such conditions are at present affecting a widening

---

[5] *Ibid.,* pp. 8–11.

sector of industrial and occupational life. The code of conduct characteristic of organic systems—those better fitted to survive and grow in changing conditions—comprehends more eventualities than that necessary in concerns under stable conditions. More information and considerations enter decisions, the limits of feasible action are set more widely.

The extension of the boundaries of feasible action and pertinent consideration makes for a fuller implication of the individual in his occupational role. As the pace of change, especially technical change, accelerates, and as the organic systems better equipped to survive under these conditions also expand, the occupational activities of the individual assume greater and greater importance within his life. This is in keeping with the commonly observed tendency for occupational status to assume an increasingly dominant influence over the location of individuals in British society. But it also denotes a greater subjection of the intellectual, emotional and moral content of the individual's life to the ends presented by the working organizations of the society in which he exists.

Developing a system of organized industrial activity capable of surviving under the competitive pressures of technical progress, therefore, is paid for by the increased constraint on the individual's existence. In Freudian terms, men's conduct becomes increasingly "alienated," "work for a system they do not control, which operates as an independent power to which individuals must submit." Such submission is all the more absolute when it is made voluntarily, even enthusiastically.[6]

----

[6] *Ibid.,* p. 11.

6. THE SEARS ROEBUCK STUDY

THE PERSONNEL department of the Sears Roebuck Company has for many years been conducting research in the field of employee attitudes and morale.[1] In the course of the study, organization structure appeared to be so important an influence of attitude and morale that a comparative study was made between the structure of intermediate-size department stores and attendant conditions found within those stores.

Stores of this size, it was found, could be grouped into two distinct structure patterns. In the first the researchers found a store manager, an assistant manager who shared the duties of his superior, and thirty-two department managers. In the second type of store were a store manager, five or six second-level managers, and four to six department managers reporting to each of the second-level managers. In effect, then, Type I stores had two levels of authority above the salesman; Type II stores had three.

The researchers found that cost and profit figures for the two types of stores showed that Type I had a significantly more effective structure than Type II. Of equal importance, Type I stores produced more than their share of promotable personnel, while Type II produced less than their share.

In the follow-up interviews with the managers of the stores studied, some differences in attitude were discovered. Store Manager I talked optimistically about his subordinates and their capacities. He demonstrated pride in their success. Store Manager II spoke, on the other hand, of the difficulty he encountered in finding conscientious people to work for him. He was wont to place on the government or the educational system the blame for spoiling young people. Said Worthy: "These managers often seemed to expect the worst of their people and generally found their fears justified. They found that people had to be watched, that their work had to be checked closely—otherwise no telling what might happen."[2]

Because the personnel researchers at Sears were curious about which came first, the personality of the manager or the structure, they exam-

---

[1] For a summary statement on the interim results of this program, see James C. Worthy, "Organizational Structure and Employee Morale," *American Sociological Review*, Vol. XV, No. 2 (April, 1950).

[2] See William Foote Whyte, *Modern Methods in Social Research* (Washington, D.C.: Office of Naval Research, 1952).

ined several cases of cross-structure manager transfers. Type I managers were found to modify Type II structures until their new store assignment became identified in structure from the one they had left. Type II managers, similarly, reformed their new assignments to conform to the previous situation.

Worthy was concerned that his findings meant that only changes in personality could effect any significant change in organization structure. However, he felt such was not the case, as indicated in this quotation by him:

> Fortunately, there appears to be an alternative; or, rather, there appears to be another factor at work as a determinant of organization structure which is relatively independent of the character and personality of the key people in it. This is the generally accepted body of organization principles developed under the aegis of scientific management: the principles of the functional organization, the limited span of control, etc. Many businessmen have set up their organizations along these lines, not so much because that is the way they might have done it if left to follow their own instincts but because these are the accepted ways of how an organization *should* be set up. Many of these men, if given an alternative theory of organization, could readily adapt to it. It is for this reason that the development of a more adequate system of principles is of such vital importance.[3]

---

[3] William Foote Whyte, *Man and Organization* (Homewood, Ill.: Richard D. Irwin, Inc., 1959), pp. 15–16.

7. EXPERIMENTS IN STRUCTURAL DESIGN[1]

IN RECENT YEARS a considerable number of experiments have been conducted in an effort to throw light upon the relation between organizational structure and task performance. Many of these experiments have started on the premise that organizational structure is in effect a communications network, with information, instructions, and commands flowing in prescribed channels. A variety of networks have been tested experimentally: the wheel (all information from the "spokes" clearing through the man at the hub and in some instances activities being directed by him); the closed chain or circle (each performer exchanging information with a performer on his right and left around a circle); the each-to-all network; and so on. Such networks have been

---

[1] This summary of research findings owes much to a literature review prepared by D. J. Hall and included in his "Tentative Proposal for and Experimental Study of Work Group Structure and Behavior," unpublished, 1963. The principal sources used in the review follow:

Bernard M. Bass, "Experimenting with Simulated Manufacturing Organizations," *ONR Technical Report,* Vol. 27 (1961).

Alex Bavelas, "Communication Patterns in Task-Oriented Groups," *Acoustical Society of America Journal,* Vol. 22 (1950), pp. 725–30.

Rocco Carzo, Jr., "Some Effects of Organization Structure and Group Effectiveness," *Administrative Science Quarterly,* Vol. 7, No. 4 (March, 1963), pp. 393–424.

Robert L. Chapman, *et al.,* "The System Research Laboratory's Air Defense Experiments," *Management Science,* Vol. 5 (1959), p. 250.

Arthur M. Cohen, "Changing Small-Group Communication Networks," *Administrative Science Quarterly,* Vol. 6, No. 4 (March, 1962), pp. 443–62.

Murray Glanzer and Robert Glaser, "Techniques for the Study of Group Structure and Behavior: Empirical Studies of the Effects of Structure in Small Groups," *Psychology Bulletin,* Vol. 58 (1961), pp. 1–27.

Harold Guetzkow and Herbert A. Simon, "The Impact of Certain Communication Nets upon Organization and Performance in Task-Oriented Groups," *Management Science,* Vol. 1 (1955), pp. 233–50.

G. A. Heise and G. A. Miller, "Problem Solving by Small Groups Using Various Communication Nets," *Journal of Abnormal and Social Psychology,* Vol. 46, pp. 327–35.

Harold J. Leavitt, "Some Effects of Certain Communication Patterns on Group Performance," in E. E. Maccoby, T. M. Newcomb, and E. L. Hartley, *Readings in Social Psychology* (3 ed.; New York: Holt 1958).

Josiah Macy, Jr., Lee S. Christie, and R. Duncan Luce, "Coding Noise in Task-Oriented Groups," *Journal of Abnormal and Social Psychology,* Vol. 48 (1953), p. 401.

Harold Pepinsky, *et al.,* "Team Productivity and Contradiction of Management Policy Commitments," *Journal of Applied Psychology,* Vol. 43 (1959), p. 264.

Pauline Pepinsky, *et al.,* "The Effects of Task Complexity and Time Pressure Upon Team Productivity," *Journal of Applied Psychology,* Vol. 44 (1960), p. 34.

M. E. Shaw and G. H. Rothschild, "Some Effects of Prolonged Experience in Communication Nets," *Journal of Applied Psychology,* Vol. 48 (1956), pp. 281–86.

M. E. Shaw, "Some Effects of Problem Complexity upon Problem Efficiency in Different Communication Nets," *Journal of Experimental Psychology,* Vol. 48 (1954), pp. 211–17.

tested with tasks ranging from very simple to relatively complex, with data collected on quantity, quality, and speed of output, together with the effect on the satisfactions derived by the participants under different arrangements.

It is much too soon to reach firm conclusions; the data are not always significant and sometimes seem to reveal contradictory results. Properly evaluated, however, they suggest certain tendencies which may be summarized very tentatively as follows:

1. The effect of the structural design depends partly upon the nature of the task (whether simple or complex, repetitious or varying, and so on).
2. For simple, prescribed tasks the wheel structure (i.e., a centralized communication structure) is efficient, even with an unpopular man at the center. Peripheral group members (the "spokes") were relatively dissatisfied with their jobs, but this did not impair their performance. (This finding contradicts some popular views about structure and morale.)
3. For more complex tasks the circle or each-to-all structures seem to be superior in results and satisfactions.
4. The circle network seemed to facilitate the quick adaptation of the work group to sudden and confusing changes in task.
5. Highly structured groups have difficulty in performing in an environment which is subject to sudden and unpredictable change.
6. Repetition in any type of network leads to improvement in task performance.
7. Groups persist with an inefficient problem-solving system, once they see that it at least enables them to reach a solution.
8. A group tends to develop a "tradition" or pattern of behavior in the course of its work, even when unstructured, and this pattern tends to persist. That is, the group will often apply past experience in a new situation whether it is appropriate or not.
9. A group rapidly changes its structure when the task becomes too complex for it, and short cuts are found when task pressures on the existing structure become too great.

8. MANAGEMENT BY INTEGRATION AND SELF-CONTROL*

Arthur H. Kuriloff

INTRODUCTION

I PROPOSE to tell you about an experiment in management by integration and self-control which has been going on for two and one-half years in my company, Non-Linear Systems, Inc. We develop, manufacture, and sell precision instruments used in measuring the basic electrical quantities of voltage, resistance, and ratios of these quantities. Necessarily, therefore, we are strongly oriented toward the engineering approach.

Most of our top management are professional engineers with many years of experience. Over the years we have seen many spectacular engineering achievements. We have come to understand that no matter what the apparent difficulty of the technical problem, if enough time and money are available, the problem can very likely be solved. And so I suppose, after many years of engineering practice, technical achievement began to pall. Consciously or not, we sought new worlds to conquer. Our opportunities came as, in time, we moved from the practice of engineering to its management.

As we began to study the many areas of management, we came to see the need for new ways, better ways of managing for the accomplishment of the technical task. Early in our study we discovered that an engineering degree did not give us the license to manage an enterprise. Being engineers by training, however, we thought that we ought to approach the general problems of management on some kind of rational basis.

We found that there is at the disposal of the inquiring mind today a growing and comprehensive literature, the result of forty years of investigation by skilled and competent researchers in the problems of the manufacturing and business enterprise. This data covers a multitude of the aspects of organization. Many facets of human effort involved in the business or manufacturing enterprise have been searched out over the years. The literature is scattered over a broad spectrum of research

---

* Arthur H. Kuriloff is vice president of Non-Linear Systems, Inc., of Del Mar, California. This article is reproduced by permission from the proceedings of the 15th Annual Meeting of the Industrial Engineering Institute at the University of California.

activity. Contributions come from many fields—sociology, psychology, business management, industrial engineering, human relations, general semantics, anthropology. We became intrigued by the possibilities of applying this data to our business. We decided then to enter into an experiment to see if we could reorder and restructure our enterprise on the basis of this research. Our experiment lay in what we may now call the general field of management.

How does one go about managing an enterprise? There is no single subject that I know of which may be labeled management just as there is no single subject called engineering one can study. If we consider current management theory, we find a number of different schools. Each is at odds with the others, each defends its own position, each claims that the others have major deficiencies. In a recent article, Harold Koontz of UCLA, outlines the major schools of management theory. Briefly stated these are:

1. *The Management Process School.* This group concerns itself primarily with management as a *process* of getting things done through and with people operating in organized groups. Management theory is regarded as a way of organizing experience so that practice can be improved through research, testing, and teaching of fundamentals involved in the management process.

2. *The Empirical School.* This approach identifies management as a *study of experience.* By studying cases in which management techniques of various kinds were tried, by examining successes and failures, it is felt that one can develop the abilities to deal with the problems of management.

3. *The Human Behavior School.* This school believes that the essence of good management lies in understanding *how people behave and interact in groups.* Using the psychologist's clinical eye, the proponents vary from those who see the human behavioral aspects of management as a portion of the management job to those who see it as the total job.

4. *The Social System School.* This group views management as an intact *social system* based on cultural interrelationships. They develop from a sociological approach the theory of management based on co-operation of systems involving persons able and willing to communicate with each other and act toward the accomplishment of a conscious, common purpose.

5. *The Decision Theory School.* This school believes that the essence of management lies in *making decisions.* It therefore concentrates on decision making as the central core of management theory. As an apparent outgrowth of economic theory it uses the tools of the economics theorists to develop its theses, expanding these to include the whole spectrum of management activity.

6. *The Mathematical School.*   The theoretical development of this approach to management theory is an expansion of the *methods of operations research.* Heavily emphasized are the establishment of mathematical models and processes. By use of these techniques, practitioners believe they can develop the best of the possible choices in the solution of any management problem.

From the consideration of the various possibilities I have briefly outlined, it became apparent to us that we were indeed entangled in a prickly thicket of management theory. We resolved, therefore, to hack a path through the thorns by relying on our training in the engineering approach. Just as the engineer draws on the particular discipline he requires to solve an element of a problem, we determined to use whatever tool, from whatever discipline seemed appropriate, to try to solve the particular management problem in which we were engaged. If an engineer wishes to design a cantilever beam, he uses theory from mechanics and the strength of materials. If he wishes to determine the voltages and resistances in an electrical network, he uses circuit theory. So, we concluded, we must do with our management problems.

We would take what we could from the several schools of management theory. But we would not limit ourselves to these. We would employ management process theory, or psychology, or group behavior theory, or industrial engineering, or whatever field of study or discipline seemed indicated to solve our problems. But first we had to acquire insight into the totality of our fundamental problem, that is, the nature of the enterprise and its organization.

The Hierarchy of the Enterprise

We ultimately determined that there were four levels of abstraction with which we had to contend in organizing and managing our enterprise.

The Total Enterprise.   We concluded that the whole of the enterprise must be treated as an element of society. We had to define our business, its goals, and objectives. We had to consider the nature of its responsibility to the social structure of which it is part. We had to assure to the best of our ability its capacity to survive.

The Organization of the Enterprise.   We had to define the organizational relationships within the enterprise; the formal structure, departmentation, and departmental interrelationships had to be determined.

The Nature and Organization of the Departments.   The way in which the departments were to be structured, the groups of people within the departments, and the nature of their internal operations were problems which we had to solve.

The Utilization of the Individual. We had to consider the most desirable ways of employing the individual worker. We had to explore, test, and define ways in which his relationship to the group and to other workers could be ordered for maximum total effectiveness.

These four categories mark what I term the organizational hierarchy. Many disciplines must be tapped to find appropriate answers for the multiplicity of problems in each. To see how we approach our experiment at each of these levels of abstraction in the hierarchy, we should probably most properly reverse the order of the hierarchy and consider first the problems of the individual.

The Individual

Every business operates on the basis of some kind of philosophy. This philosophy is seldom overtly expressed, if indeed it is considered consciously by management at all. Nevertheless, it can be shown that the organization of any business enterprise stems directly from the philosophy of those who run it.

The business enterprise is a *group of people* banded together for the sake of an economic purpose. It is clear that the organizational structure and operational style must stem from management's view of the people who form the organization. The philosophical assumptions management makes about the behavior and nature of its people determine these patterns directly.

The covert traditional philosophy says that the employee is a pair of "hands." In fact, when industrial organizations hire people, they very often talk about hiring "hands." These hands are considered homogeneous and interchangeable. They may be substituted readily for one another on the production line. Since production line tasks are usually cut down to a minimum number of small repetitive motions, no great skills are required. The tasks may be learned by the new worker with negligible training.

In addition, the average hand is thought to be really not very bright and essentially unmodifiable. He is inherently lazy, will shun work whenever possible, lacks sound judgment, is shortsighted and prone to error. On top of all this, he is probably a little dishonest. He must be watched closely if he is to give an honest measure of work for a day's pay. To sum up all these statements, we may say that he cannot be trusted. Therefore, the pattern and operational style of the organization are structured to detect and correct error. The kind of organization that results is very common in our conventional enterprise. It is often called the "accounting" model, displaying a complex pyramidal network of authority relationships with many layers of organization. The attendant difficulties in communication, the distortions in content, as directives and information flow up and down the communication ladder are well known to all of us.

On the other hand, what kind of organization emerges if management views the individual in a different fashion? Suppose we were to say that people are not "hands"; they are individual human beings. Each has a discrete and different complement of traits and talents. Suppose we assume that people are not lazy; work is a normal part of the business of living. Suppose we say that people are capable of being trained; their skills may be enlarged by adequate and proper coaching. They can do a bigger and better job if we make it possible for them to do so, if we assume that training is a major part of management's job. In addition, suppose we say that people are fundamentally honest; they can be trusted. We can tolerate error as a normal part of human endeavor so long as it remains within reasonable bounds. We can accept a mistake providing it isn't repeated. If we make these assumptions then we can organize our enterprise completely differently. We find then that we do not need time clocks to assure the worker is doing a full day's work. We can eliminate many layers of authority in the organization structure. We can improve our communications by shortening and paralleling the channels. We can adopt something closely resembling the organizational structure we are trying in our experiment at Non-Linear Systems, Inc.

If you will examine the diagram (see Exhibit 1) of our basic organization you will see how the organizational pattern at Non-Linear Systems looks. In it you will find a group of eight men in the top block called the Executive Council. This is the executive management of the company. It is concerned with the establishment of goals, the definition of the business, and over-all strategic planning. The next level, that of departments, involves those functions requiring day-to-day operations. The managers of these departments are concerned with tactical operations. They do the planning needed for day-by-day work, for procurement, for manufacturing, for sales, for collecting the monies for sales, for recording personnel data, for maintaining the plant, and so on.

Significant in our experimental approach to management is the way individuals are organized into working groups. We use the group method in every department in our company. Groups range in size from three to nine people. As an instance of how the group works, we might look at our engineering operation. The engineering group is known as a project team. It is under the management of a project manager. He is a

Exhibit 1

NON-LINEAR SYSTEMS, INC.
ORGANIZATIONAL CHART

BOARD OF DIRECTORS

EXECUTIVE COUNCIL
PRESIDENT AND VICE PRESIDENT (8)

Establishes operating policies. Plans, directs,
coordinates and controls the business as a whole.
Vice Presidents function virtually as "Assistant"
Presidents in one or more of the following areas
as required: Employee Attitude, Performance
and Development – Innovation and Development –
Market Standing – Physical and Financial
Resources – Productivity – Profitability –
Public Responsibility – Quality Assurance.

DEPARTMENTAL MANAGEMENT

ENGINEERING

Designs and develops company
products. Prepares supporting
engineering information for the
use of other departments within
the company, as well as the
customers.

MANAGERS OF PROJECT TEAMS (12)

Manager	Printed Circuitry
Manager	Plant Facilities
Manager	Materials
Manager	Instrument Assembly
Manager	Personnel Services
Manager	Quality Assurance/Control
Manager	Industrial Engineering
Manager	Instrument Assembly
Manager	Fabrication
Manager	Systems
Manager	Components
Manager	Southeast Region
Manager	Northeast Region
Manager	North Central Region
Manager	Sales Promotion
Manager	Southwest Region
Manager	Service
Manager	South Central Region
Manager	Distribution
Manager	Northwest Region

PRODUCTION

Provides services necessary to make
available personnel, material and
physical facilities for the fabrication
and manufacture of components, and
for the assembly of such components
together with purchased parts into
completed instruments and systems
ready for shipment.

SALES

Obtains and fills sales orders.
Invoices customers and collects
receivables. Furnishes customers
with factory services, maintenance,
training, and technical information.
Collects marketing data, prepares
national advertising and new
product releases.

highly skilled, competent, experienced electronic engineer. He has working with him in the minimum size group of three, a product designer and an electronic technician. Each project group works in its own rooms; sometimes two, sometimes three rooms. The project manager occupies a private office. His product designer has a private office and his technician works in a development laboratory next to the other two rooms. When a new product is started, the project manager receives from the Executive Council a specification for the instrument. The specification consists of a small sketch plus inputs, outputs, and tolerances. There may be some explanatory notes. An indication of the approximate sales price of the instrument tells the project manager how much he can spend for parts in the production instrument. He studies the specification and comes back with his recommendations. After consultation with the Executive Council, the changes that seem reasonable or desirable are made in the specification. The manager is told to go ahead with his work. He may now proceed in his individual fashion with the development of the instrument. He can buy any item he needs without countersignature so long as the amount does not exceed $2,500. He develops the instrument. In time he comes up with an engineering prototype. His product designer and his technician have worked closely with him through all phases of the job.

When the prototype is ready, the Executive Council examines it. If we find that it meets its specifications and looks satisfactory generally, we proceed into production. If there are deficiencies, we may ask that further development work be done. When we consider the item ready for production, we assign one or two people from an instrument assembly department to help build several prototypes. This is usually done in the project manager's quarters. We use the prototypes for sales, reserving one for a production model. Meanwhile the project manager and his little group have produced the necessary drawings and technical data needed for production.

We believe that the project manager should develop the original instrument, help build the production prototypes, consult with the people in our assembly department who must put it together, stay cognizant of technical and production problems throughout the active life of the instrument. The project manager has authority in technical matters as long as the instrument is made. No one may make a change in the design without his approval.

Now let us look at an instrument assembly department as an example of how a manufacturing group works. The average group in instrument assembly has seven people. One of the seven is an expert electronic technician. He has had years of experience and is extremely competent technically. He is known as an assistant assembly department manager. The group itself is made up of all kinds of people. When we made the switch from our old assembly lines two and one-half years ago to the present group method, we did not fire anyone. We simply reorganized the available people into groups of seven each.

Each group in the instrument assembly department is self-contained. By this I mean they do the whole job. They put complete instruments together from kits of parts, electrical components and hardware. They place components on the etched circuit boards, do the soldering, fabricate harnessing. They build up the hardware from the pieces delivered with the kits and assemble the total instrument. They then run the machines in, calibrate them, troubleshoot and repair if necessary. When they get all through, they sign the quality assurance tag on the instrument and place it in its shipping box.

There is no formal planning. The members of the group decide who will do what by mutual consent and decision. They know each other's strengths and weaknesses and will generally do a far better job of planning when left alone than if directed by some kind of authority.

There are some very interesting things happening in these groups. The capabilities of the people have been developed in two and one-half years to the point where they were able to write their own instructions for procedure in assembly. They write their own troubleshooting instructions. They help each other; they help members of other groups; they help write the service manuals we require for each instrument. They have acquired the skills and knowledge to build half a dozen or so different kinds of instruments in each group. By the way, as a company we manufacture over forty different kinds of standard instruments. It is very interesting to walk through the rooms where these groups are operating. You will see some groups building several different kinds of instruments, for example. They seem able to adjust readily and to accommodate to changes from one kind of an instrument to another with no apparent disorganization. It seems very clear to us that the experiment is showing markedly improved performance of the people in the instrument assembly groups since the change in the organization of two and one-half years ago. In fact, production figures now show performance 30% better than any time in the company's history.

I said that there is no formal planning in the procedures in these departments. By that I mean we do not have a formal planning office in our company. The planning done within the groups result from the groups' ideas of what should be done and when things should be done

However, the total work of the instrument assembly departments must be planned from week to week. We accomplish this kind of planning by what we call our reservoir system of operation. The Executive Council establishes maximum and minimum quantities for each kind of instrument we build. We change the mix from time to time as conditions in the sales areas change. Now all the instrument assembly managers have to do to find what kinds of instruments to build next is to count the number of instruments in each stack in the storeroom, check against maximum and minimum quantities, and thus determine what instruments to stop and start building during the next few weeks. Additional data comes from weekly meetings of the instrument assembly department managers with managers of several other departments. Among these are representatives from the materials department, which is responsible for buying parts and components, and the distribution department which has inputs from the sales regions all over the country. The managers thus receive some notion of what sales prospects are for the next few weeks and even months. The instrument assembly department managers use this data in making calculated decisions to adjust their product mix.

The reservoir concept as I have described it for instrument assembly represents an idea we are experimenting with throughout the whole company. We believe that it is possible to develop reservoirs in all areas of operation in the company. These reservoirs produce what might be called feedback in a servosystem. Operations of the department are adjusted in accordance with the command signals of feedback from the reservoirs. For example, in our components department which makes precision wire wound resistors, stepping switch assemblies, and cable harnesses, a reservoir system similar to that in instrument assembly becomes readily workable. In the distribution department the reservoir consists of backlog of orders as yet unfilled. In the sales regions we have an idea that the reservoir concept can be developed in terms of potential for making sales and for creating new customers.

The Departmental System

We should now look at the structure of organization delineated by the department system shown in the organizational chart. One must ask the question when setting up the structure of an enterprise: What is the logical sequence or process by which to get from idea through development, production, sales, collection of receipts for sales, and to perform all the necessary other functions to keep the enterprise running? That is what we did in considering the structure of our departmental relationships. We tried to organize our company by the logical flow of process in getting from idea through development, sales, and collection of receipts.

We therefore set up our organization as shown on the chart, starting with development of the product in the project teams. Each department to the right represents the next logical step in the total process. The significant point in this is: We have at our command a very simple straightforward procedure to accommodate growth. All we have to do is duplicate departments. For example, we have twelve project teams shown in engineering. We have two instrument assembly departments. If it becomes necessary for the purpose of our continued growth to add engineering strength, all we have to do is create one, two, three, or as many new project teams as required. If we need more productive capacity for the assembly of instruments, we merely parallel the two departments we have with one, two, three, or four more. We can do this in the other departments as required.

It is our opinion that the total department should be kept small, certainly not over fifty people. In this way we find that our strength of management is concentrated in depth in the performance of the job. We do not have to spread our management thin. We concentrate it so that its power is felt through every detail of the operation. We are able to sweep out the cobwebs from the dusty corners. We think this is a very effective way to use people; we think this is very efficient in total performance. We think we have discovered a simple key toward the perfection of our own operations as we aim to future growth.

The Total Enterprise

The last level of abstraction in the organization of our company might be called the total enterprise. This consists of the whole organization as it is indicated on the chart. As I mentioned before, the Executive Council is comprised of eight members. In addition to the president, who is chief officer of the Executive Council, we have a vice president for each of the eight areas in which objectives must be set and accomplishments measured in any kind of business enterprise.

The Executive Council is a strategic operating group. It plans for the long-range growth and accomplishment of the company. It sets the product line strategy. It establishes the policies governing the operation of the company and the departments. It initiates action in the eight areas of management, for example, innovation: the creation of customers, the creation of new ideas for new products, the creation of new ways of doing things in our company. We believe that the activities in these eight areas thread through the whole fabric of our operation. We do not compartmentalize the efforts of our vice presidents by rigid proscription. Each of the vice presidents works from what might be termed anchor points within his general area of operation. It is apparent that there will be times when there are overlaps in the functions of these executives. Therefore, we prefer to use the term anchor points to describe the key points from which each man operates. When there are problems of overlap, the vice presidents resolve the situation between themselves.

The departmental organization which I have previously described reports to the Executive Council in terms of functions. For example, problems having to do with capital investment are referred to the Vice President, Physical and Financial Resources; problems having to do with setting of prices go to the Vice President, Profitability, and so on.

We are oftentimes asked, "What will you do when you grow? Is your present organizational pattern good enough to carry you as you get larger?" Or sometimes we are asked, "How large can you grow before the present organization becomes ineffective?" We must truthfully say that we do not know the answers to these questions yet. We think that the present form of organization will be operable until we grow to two or three times our present size, that is, until the number of people in the company total somewhere between six and twelve hundred. At that time we expect that we shall grow by federal decentralization. This is growth in the fashion of the *amoeba proteus.* It puts out a little element which enlarges, carrying with it a portion of the nucleus of the parent cell. The element then separates from its parent. It continues to grow by itself and finally reproduces its parent in size. In other words, there become two entities similar to the original one. So we hope it will be with our company. When we reach the point of division we will probably split off on the basis of a somewhat different product line. We will very likely establish our division in some other geographical area. This division of the company will be set up in the same way as at Del Mar. That is, it will have its Executive Council and its departmental organization. The two divisions then will report through their Executive Councils to a central council, one added step in the hierarchy. We are, of course, in the realm of considerable speculation. We do not know just how our plans will eventuate, but we expect to apply the same approach in the solution of these future problems as we have in trying to solve the ones with which we now live daily.

We have now briefly considered some of the ideas in what we call management by integration and self-control. The central core of ideas in this kind of management demands that the individual know what part he plays in the achievement of company goals. A management approach based on trust provides the permissive atmosphere in which he can set his own objectives, initiate and carry through the appropriate activities required to achieve these objectives. The resources of the individual are more fully employed in this activity. His abilities are used and improved by training. He becomes a better human being and a better citizen. The enterprise begins to pay off its debt to society.

Conclusion

In concluding my remarks, it might be fruitful to consider briefly some of the philosophical implications of my thesis. Each economic enterprise is an organ of society. In the words of Professor Theodore J. Kreps, of Stanford University, "The economic enterprise is a way of life. It is not simply a segment of the community co-operating or competing with other segments, such as labor, consumers, or farmers. It is the community getting its daily bread. Its goals, its ethics, its welfare are inseparable from the goals and aspirations and welfare of the community."

The enterprise is therefore permitted to operate freely and openly under the mandate of the public. It may freely innovate new directions for growth, method, and scope of operation so long as it stays within the legal bounds which derive from the public consensus. So long as the enterprise does not violate the ultimate formulations of what society considers good it is free to pursue its future as it sees fit. In turn, it owes to the society which fosters it, obligations which it must honor. If it fails to honor its debts, it will ultimately perish under the remorseless pressure of social opinion.

Since the enterprise is the fundamental wealth-producing agent in our society, it must number among its foremost tasks that of survival. To survive, it must produce economic and social good. Its future, to be secure, must rest on a foundation of production for maximum utility. Only in this way can the markets it creates endure. Its operations must be fundamentally ethical; in conduct and act, its behavior must be ethical.

The enterprise in the same sense as man may be considered a time-binding entity. To endure under the public consensus, it must transmit social good through time. It must evolve by developing more socially valuable characteristics. Ultimately the value of its social contributions must devolve on its consideration and treatment of the smallest component of both its own structure and that of society—the individual.

We believe that the future of our economic and political society depends explicitly on the way in which we view and treat the individual.

If we provide the kind of milieu in our industries such as that possible in managing by integration and self-control, if we encourage the intellectual growth of our individual workers, if we tap the latent resources of their minds, we cannot help but improve our industrial enterprise itself. We increase the capabilities of our people for becoming better citizens. We make the best social contributions in meeting the obligations of our enterprise to our community, city, state, nation, indeed the community of man.

References:

Those who wish to refer to the sources of many of the ideas we are using in our experiment in management will find the references here listed extremely useful.

DRUCKER, PETER F. *The Practice of Management.* New York: Harper & Bros., 1954.

MCGREGOR, DOUGLAS. *The Human Side of Enterprise.* New York: McGraw-Hill, 1960.

HAIRE, MASON. *Psychology in Management.* New York: McGraw-Hill, 1956.

LIKERT, RENSIS. *New Patterns of Management,* New York: McGraw-Hill, 1961.

BERLE, ADOLF A., JR. *Power Without Property,* New York: Harcourt, Brace Co., 1959.

KOONTZ, HAROLD. *The Management Theory Jungle.* Graduate School of Business Administration, U.C.L.A. Division of Research, Reprint No. 9–1962.

SECTION VII

Organizational Change

Introduction

THE CONCEPT of the administrator as a change agent has been implicit in many of the other sections of this book, particularly in Section IV, where we considered problems of taking remedial action from a supervisor's position. We address it explicitly now in this, the concluding section, partly because we believe the capacity to diagnose the need for change, implement change, and predict the consequences of change is the ultimate skill of the administrator, and partly because the action orientation of the change agent role is one which cannot be completely explored in a course such as this.

This chapter, therefore, may be regarded as a bridge between the basic purposes of this course—knowledge about organizational behavior and diagnostic skill training—and other kinds of training which focus more on the development of individual insight, membership and leadership skills, and the internalization of learning and experience around the change agent role.

It is clear that change is inevitable in any organization. Some of these changes are forced on the organization by pressures from without (competition, shifts in market patterns, significant technological breakthroughs, etc.), while others are planned by people in the organization as a means of maintaining the health of the company or business in a dynamic society. While the former are often regarded by company people as challenges to be met, the latter are more often perceived as upsetting to the stability and equilibrium of individuals, groups, or the entire company and are resisted by those who see in the changes a threat to accustomed and comfortable ways of thinking and behaving.

Of what do we speak when we consider planned change in an organizational setting? How do the problems of taking action to implement change in the total organization differ from those of taking action in the sense of diagnosing problems observed in simpler systems such as the small group, as we did in Section IV?

The readings and cases in this section will help to make the differences more clear. Essentially, problems of change in the total organization are similar to, but more complex than, problems of change involving the individual or the small group. There are more variables to be studied and understood, and the consequences of action are less predictable.

The cases and readings selected for this section clearly reflect the fact that change comes up in many different forms in organizations and goes through multiple stages in being carried out. This fact is reflected in the sense that each case and each reading in the section is unique—it is difficult to generalize about them. It can be said that the first four cases present different perspectives on the change process. Alpha Company (A) and (B) show a department manager attempting to carry off a significant change in a production plant—and failing. We can learn much from an analysis of his failure. Given the benefit of hindsight, could we plan a change program that would have been successful? The Dan Weber case looks at the rapid change in a dynamic industry from a point of view of a young engineer planning his own career. Do we see how he could gain the perspective that would equip him to work with, rather than against, some needed change forces in his company? The Supra Oil Company case jumps to a top management group, considering a structural change in the marketing area of a large oil company. Is the thinking behind this recommended change sound?

As we move into these change cases, a number of difficult issues inevitably arise, and the readings are selected to be of some help in handling these issues. A particularly troublesome question is—change for what? What are appropriate criteria to guide the planning of change? Dalton's article (Reading 1) addresses this issue. Changes often develop resistance, and the next three readings report some research findings concerning the nature and causes of the resistance that people can make to the introduction of change. These readings link well with the two sequential cases (The Yoker Company and Tidewater Manufacturing Company) that permit us to test our ability to predict responses to change efforts.

It is often helpful to recognize that deliberate change efforts usually emphasize either modifications in organization structure and procedures (as in Supra Oil) or educational and training efforts (as seen in Alpha). Reading 5 reports a systematic large-scale change experiment that emphasized structural and procedural change. Reading 6 reports another large-scale change that placed emphasis on educational intervention. These two readings taken together represent a sample of the increasing literature of systematic research on organizational change. The subsequent reading by Benne (7) pulls together much of the conceptual work which has been done to date specifically involving the stages of change and the role of the administration as an agent of change.

The Benne reading provides a good framework of ideas to bring to bear on the remaining cases in this section. Randley Stores (A) and (B) describe an entire organization moving through the entire sequence of change from original diagnosis to planning and implementation. We can see that new problems emerge as the first round of change is completed, and we can join in assessing the results and planning further change efforts. Denver Transportation Company and Dallas Chemical Corporation are also cases that present change programs in midstream. Further change is clearly needed in these situations and we can use all of our diagnostic skill in developing plans for such further change. The final reading by James E. Richard offers a highly personal account of the experience of a company president in carrying out a change program in his company. It seems to end this volume on an open-ended note; the challenge to managers of using their intelligence and skill in guiding useful change in organizations is a never-ending one.

Cases

1. ALPHA COMPANY (A)

IN LATE JULY, Arthur Adams, a case researcher at the Harvard Business School, learned from John Crofts, divisional director of personnel of the Alpha Company, that the division had recently received approval from the company's executive committee to go out of business on Delta powders, part of the Delta line of materials. Delta was one of the departments of the Gamma Division of the company, which had nation-wide production and distribution facilities in the field of chemicals for both industrial and commercial customers.

The type of material which constituted the Delta line was first pro-duced in the United States shortly before World War I. During World War II and immediately afterwards, there was a large increase in de-mand and production was expanded. There were two temporary declines in production during postwar recessions, and in each case production later improved to approximately full capacity of the facilities at Gamma. The variations in sales had corresponded with those of the major com-petitors' in the Delta product line; in recent years, the Alpha Company had held about one sixth of the national market in the Delta products field. Starting late in the prior year, a decline in sales had led to some cutbacks in production.

The Delta line comprised two major product groups. One of these was "liquids," approximately two thirds of which was sold directly to customers; the other third was used as a raw material in the production of the second group, the powders. Powder was sold in bags and drums to industrial customers, who used it for a variety of purposes. There was a large variety of powder formulations, each designed to meet technical specifications determined by customers' needs.

The Delta powders and liquids production facilities at Gamma oc-cupied a large five-story building. It was one of the largest buildings in physical size at the Gamma plant and was located farthest from the central offices of the company. At peak production about 200 employees worked in the Delta building. This was slightly less than 10 per cent of the work force at the Gamma plant. Of the workers in the Delta building, about one half were in powders, one quarter in liquids, and the rest in duties such as shipping and cleaning, which served both products.

In the course of his interviews at the plant, Adams learned of certain actions taken by management in relation to the Delta powder line during the preceding six months. In April, the operating superintendent of Delta liquids, Joseph Sienna, was shifted to become operating superintendent for powders in order to improve production. Shortly after he came to this position, Sienna rearranged the organization of foremen to give closer control over the production of each shift. He also held meetings with each of the three shifts of workers to improve their work attitudes. In May, one of the three units which produced powders was rebuilt at a cost of about $150,000 to produce formulations with new quality characteristics. Late in July, it was decided that the powder operations would be discontinued because of lack of profitability in a very competitive market.

Before he talked to the workers, Arthur Adams talked with Scott Bennett, the manufacturing superintendent in the Delta area. Bennett told him:

> We did not have a very good attitude in powders, and I think this attitude made quite a bit of difference. If everybody had had a piece in the outcome of this department—not an impersonal thing like being a stockholder, but if they really were concerned about getting out the production and trying to keep the conversion costs to a minimum—we might have been able to lop off one half of the conversion costs.
>
> In the liquid area, on the other hand, there's been enough prestige, pride, and know-how built up over the years so that it is a very easily managed group of people. It would be really nice to know what makes the difference between powders and liquids. I've managed both. It's possible that I helped shape the attitudes, with Sienna in particular, of the liquids group. I attribute the development there to Sienna. That's why he was brought here to powder, to dispel some of the antimanagement feelings and morale. He was making maneuvers in this direction in group meetings, but it was not favorably received. He talked like he did to the liquids department crew. He was accused by some of propaganda. The men respect him, but they don't conform to what he wants. The attitudes are too ingrained.

The Production Process

The process for producing Delta powders involved mixing certain raw materials; bonding these materials together through heat and pressure by passing them through revolving rolls; cooling, cutting, and grinding the blended mass into a powdered state; blending these powders to meet the customers' technical specifications; and packaging the resultant blend. The processing was done in batches, each of which usually took from three to four hours to complete. A batch ran through one of three independent units. A unit was a combination of interconnected machinery, the various elements of which were located on the several floors of the Delta building. Some of these elements served as storage points; thus, the equipment between two storage points could be

Exhibit 1

ALPHA COMPANY (A)

Operator	*Process*
Batchmaker and process helper (for all three units)	Mixing
	Charging
	↓
Roll operator	Rolling
	Cutting
	↓
Lead operator	Grinding
	Batch blending
	Storage
	↓
Blending operator and process helper	Final blending
	Packing out

shut down, if a "plug-up" occurred in one element, while the equipment before and after the storage points continued to operate.

The equipment responsibilities of the various operators roughly coincided with the grouping of machinery elements between storage points. Although each operator's equipment was located on two or more floors of the building, its large size and extended layout made it impossible in most cases for an operator at one work station to see or hear an operator at another. The various pieces of equipment required differing degrees of mental attention and of physical effort for operating, regulating, and guarding against difficulties, which occurred at various points in the process. Some of the latter could be corrected quickly, some required continuous close attention during the run of a batch, and some required that the unit be shut down and one or more of its elements cleaned laboriously.

Fire hazards existed at almost all points in the process; various control systems and automatic equipment shutoffs had been installed at different points in the process. In addition, there were numerous safety operating regulations designed to guard against the fire hazards. A large amount of dust, more at some points than at others, was generated in the operations of the process. The dust affected both the working conditions of the men and the fire hazards.

Job Arrangements

Each unit was operated by four men directly assigned to it (a "unit crew") and by two others who did the "batchmaking" for all three units. These jobs are described in Appendix A in descending order of pay.

The process sequence and each operator's corresponding position according to his machine responsibility are listed in Exhibit 1.

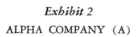

Exhibit 2

ALPHA COMPANY (A)

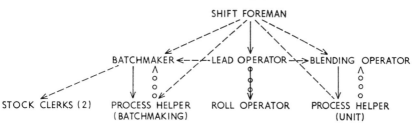

KEY:

⟶ RELATIVELY FREQUENT SUPERVISION AND DIRECTION.
---⟶ RELATIVELY INFREQUENT SUPERVISION AND DIRECTION.
○ ○ ○> HELPING.
⊕—⊕—⊕> SUPERVISION AND HELPING.

Exhibit 2 summarizes the major required interactions among the job positions.

The Union

The workers of the Gamma plant were the members of a local authorized international union. The workers in the Delta area elected a shop steward for each shift and a member of the plant-wide grievance committee. The three men serving in these posts at the time of this case worked in the powders area, though they represented the workers in both liquids and powders.

Pay

The Gamma plant union contract called for fifteen pay grades, with an average differential of four cents between grades. The grades and corresponding pay levels of the major jobs above were as follows:

Position	Grade	Hourly Pay
Lead operator	12	$2.45
Batchmaker	11	2.42
Blending operator	9	2.34
Roll operator	8	2.30
Process helper	6	2.22

The differences in the hourly job grade levels were based on the points they received in a scale made up of ten factors. The latter, together with the points used in weighting them, were as follows: Experience 0–20 points, Initiative 0–15, Physical Effort 0–12, Working Conditions 0–12, Education 0–10, Mental Effort 0–9, Visual Attention 0–6, Responsibility for Materials and Equipment 0–6, Responsibility for Records and Reports 0–5, and Unavoidable Hazards 0–5.

Work Hours, Lunch, Smoking, etc.

A workday consisted of an eight-hour shift, with two ten-minute breaks. The breaks were normally taken during two half-hour intervals prescribed by management for each set of shift hours. A few years previously, the Delta powders management had agreed with the union that a worker who had a short period free of work could take a smoke period in addition to these breaks, if he obtained permission from the shift foreman.

A man was expected to eat his workday meal either while on his work station or during his ten-minute breaks. Smoking was absolutely prohibited throughout the plant grounds and buildings except in authorized areas. For Delta powders, the authorized area was a sizable smoking room on the first floor of the building.

Job Assignments

Any position that became available for a few weeks or longer was filled through a "bidding" system. After the job opening was posted on the area bulletin board, any man could bid; the selection from among those bidding was based upon prior experience in the vacant position and area seniority. Failing any bids from within an area, the bidding became plant-wide.

Reassignments caused by a decline in the number of jobs were handled according to area seniority. The man with the lowest area seniority in a given job category was removed from that job; he could then "bump" any man in the entire plant in a job of the same or lower grade who had less seniority.

As a result of both bidding and bumping, a change in the job assignment for one man could affect men on several other crews on the same or other shifts. For example, if one crew was disbanded, the lead operator of that crew might replace a lead operator on another crew, who, in turn, might bump a blending operator on his own crew, who, in his turn, might bump a process helper on a different shift, and so on.

Temporary Work Assignments—Upgrading

In addition to the more permanent job reassignments described above, there was a variety of occasions when management wished to have a work assignment filled for a short period of time (an hour to a week or two). In such cases, a foreman could ask a man working at a lower-grade-level job if he would "upgrade" to fill the other job temporarily, and for which work he would be paid at the higher-grade rate. If no man was willing to upgrade and the work was urgent, the alternative was to ask a man working in the same job category to work another shift at overtime pay rates.

At the time of the research, about forty men were assigned to the Delta powder production area. Since men with lower seniority had been transferred following the recent cutbacks, those remaining had high seniority. Three quarters had over eight years' seniority in the area; a few had worked in powders since the early 1930's. About a quarter of the men were of French-Canadian extraction; a quarter were Negroes; almost a quarter had generally Yankee-Anglo-Saxon names; and the rest were of Polish, Irish, or other ethnic background. About a quarter of the men had finished high school, the rest stopping at earlier grade levels. About 30 per cent were in their late thirties and about the same proportion in their forties; most of the rest were below thirty-five years of age.

Interview with Sienna

In April, Joseph Sienna became operating superintendent of the powders section "in an effort to improve production efficiency in the area." Sienna was forty-one years old; had a Bachelor's degree in engineering and had recently completed his work for a Master's degree in business administration; and had spent almost all of his eight years with Alpha in the Delta liquids area. Following are comments obtained from Sienna in an interview:

> I'd better first say that I've been the operating superindendent here only the last three months. I came from liquids upstairs to whip this into shape. I'd got things going well there, and I came here to get the people working together as a group and get things straightened out. They felt my knowledge of the materials and experience of administration from up there would be useful here to build a good team.
>
> To get this place on its feet, I'd do what's on this list I made up shortly

after I came here. Let's see. There was the problem of getting the hourly people going, creating an organization, giving leadership, getting the hourly people to feel they were contributing something by coming here—not just putting in their eight hours, but getting a feeling of accomplishment. As a result of that, production would have gone up. Then there was maintenance, control of costs, inventory, and basic research.

I tried to follow through on this. The first thing I did was get all the hourly men on each shift and have a meeting in the smoking room. I did it with all three shifts within twenty-four hours of the time I had come in. I spoke an hour and a half to some of the shifts. I talked to them about boom times, what it was like then and what happened at the end of a boom—how the big squeeze comes along. Then I worked up to the point of where they could help. I told them what management was doing. Then I asked, "Does Alpha continue to make Delta powders or does this go out of business?" I asked that question three months ago, three months before the decision! I took up the stockholders, what they get and what they should get. Then the loss of jobs and how that affected them. Then I went into what the men could do, and then the need for co-operation.

First, they could increase safety practice; pay more attention to safety; eliminate abuses; do a day's work for a day's wage. This was an obligation according to the contract; after all, Alpha didn't shortchange them on payday. They could stop careless operations and shortcuts, such as in discharging materials, using off-grade stuff, and some others I named. Keep the equipment running, each carry his own load, not have someone carry him. This is downright stealing, if they didn't do a fair day's work.

I talked about the various kinds of people who disrupt the works. There was the "fair-weather man"—just works hard when things are going well; the "chronic griper"—always complaining; "the pretender"—they got a charge out of this when I talked about the guy who tried so hard pretending that he's working that he's more tired at the end of the day than the rest; "the agitator"—the guy who can't stand to see any harmony; "the horseplay artist"—all he can do all day long is play jokes on others; and "the conscientious worker"—these are fairly much in the majority, fortunately for us. Then I went into absenteeism, lateness, and those things. I even dug into the Bible a bit. You know that story about the talents. I told them if we do not exercise our talents, we'll have to answer for it. Then the need for a team approach. Then I summarized, saying that labor always seems to think that the more they produce the less jobs they will have. But I reversed that thinking; or at least I told them that in powders, the higher the production rates, the cheaper the costs, and the better the quality, then the bigger the percentage of the market we could get and the more that sales could sell. I told them that each man was really responsible for his own job security; no one could do it for him.

It took an hour and a half. I told them beforehand that this wasn't going to be an opportunity for them to speak, to air their complaints, and so on. It would have taken eight hours to get through everybody's questions. I told them that they'd have all the time they wanted later on to complain, suggest, ask questions, and so on. I had a meeting with each shift about a month later. I've forgotten all the things they wanted. They were quite constructive in all the comments. To put it in one sentence, people felt that no one seemed to care. This justified my appraisal that they didn't have the proper quality of leadership.

It was funny—I made the *Record,* the union paper. Usually one page discusses what's happening in several areas in the plant, but this time the whole thing was devoted to what happened in this area.[1] Their impression of what I said was just the opposite of what I really said.

You know, that article wasn't the expression of the rank and file. They don't go along with it. There are a few agitators who have control. I don't know why the others aren't able to do something. A lot of fellows came up to me and apologized and said they had nothing to do with the writing of it.

Then I tried with crew huddles. They had worked upstairs in liquids. I've been trying to write a paper on them; the training director wants me to, and says he will get it published, but I never have time. They're not an original idea with me; I'd read about them in some journal—about getting the people together, then having them talk over their problems. I'd always talked with the men up there about their children, and so on. They liked me, or they seemed to. So about five years ago I started the crew huddles about once a month. I'd point out things that were wrong and then see what the reaction was. I figured I knew enough so that I could control the meeting. We left out all the union-management gripes and

---

[1] The following are excerpts from the article in the union paper which Sienna showed Adams: "Within a twenty-four-hour period all Delta powder operations were shut down for a total of almost five hours so that a high-ranking member of Delta supervision could be absolutely assured of having a full audience on all shifts. The objective apparently was to make us think as 'one' in matters concerning economics, job security, labor, management, government, or anything else that might reflect directly or indirectly on Delta operations.

"The philosophies, theories, and principles we should embrace . . . sounded very similar to the ideas being put forth by big business through such channels as . . . the N. A. M."

'This wheel with the life and death message wasn't exactly unfair, though, because he admitted that some of us might have our own opinions. However, rather than chance someone asking embarrassing questions, he served notice that there would be no customary question and answer period. These tactics were very much resented. We have learned what we have by our own experience."

". . . We wonder about the so-called facts we are told. . . . He said that if we could 'produce cheaper' we would be in a better competitive position to 'sell cheaper.' "

"Another wheel in a similar capacity had something different to say at a prior meeting about these same facts. . . . He stated . . . we weren't big enough to survive a price war."

". . . After such a meeting as this, some people feel brainwashed, while still others feel the speaker is the victim of the very hogwash he is trying to sell—at least the latter would make him sincere."

talked man to man. The men found they could really sound off on their gripes. And they really got interested in the operation. We'd been able to work out things pretty well. They almost used to say we'd been able to negotiate our own contract. If we'd discipline a man or want something a certain way, sometimes the steward (the union steward who represented the workers in both powders and liquids) would try to get involved, but the men would tell him to mind his own business. And if one guy was out of line, the other fellows would use the old Army routine to get him back in line—give him a bad time 'til he did. Sometimes the guys here called the men upstairs in liquids "Koreans," saying all they wanted was food, clothing, and money and they were happy.

But there was a difference down here. There was a closed-mindedness and an unwillingness to learn new things, with a few exceptions. So I saw a long, hard road to be able to open enough minds. This included the foremen.

There wasn't enough time. But I did have a couple of fellows come talk with me. I had some converts. I had four converts in sixty men from two meetings. At that rate—or the rate would have increased as there were more converts—then it would have taken a year's time so we could operate like we did upstairs. The guys would get to know me. Since if they'd trust me and know me, then they'd come along. They'd know I'm not two-faced. No matter where people work, they're the same. If you prove yourself to them, you'll get them with you. There's a wealth of brain power in the lower ranks; it's just not tapped yet.

I'm too high in the department to do this personally with the men. And I don't have time to train others. If the top executive set up an organization to do just this, expanded the training department, and hand-picked those people prone to do this kind of thinking in *real* personnel relations and had them try and give the religion to every supervisor in the plant, then you'd see something.

I changed the organization completely. I did this the first thing, but I forgot to mention it to you. We had had three foremen, two of them each in charge of different units, and the third, just taking care of all personnel matters. We also had three building foremen who were on shifts; these men knew a little, so they could deal with some of the problems but not enough. I tried to train them, but they were mostly old-timers. When the hourly personnel were transferred from one unit to another, sometimes they'd come under a different foreman and would play one foreman against another. So I changed the organization. I decided there would be one foreman on each shift and the men would have to answer to him for their production rates, their time, and all that. And there would still be the building foreman who would work alongside.

Well, the production rates started to rise. Then we had to shut down one unit; they spent $150,000 on that so they could take on more kinds of business. But that hadn't really gotten going before we were told we were going out of business.

But there were always things that were interfering, things that had to be done, of course. That may seem contradictory to you. But I could see this was a long haul, with a lot of high pressure to get things done. All we were doing was fighting fires; I could see that improvements would be so slow that I'd almost go out of my mind trying to get them. I was used to upstairs where I had smooth clockwork. Here the guts of the clock were out. I accepted it as a challenge. If I could make things mesh as I had done elsewhere, make things work better, then I would have satisfaction.

As things went along, I had doubts. I don't think I give up easily. I've been reprimanded for never giving up and sticking with things too long. I'm a die-hard in a way. But under these conditions it was difficult to motivate—to keep them pumped up, all gassed up. They'd seem to run out of gas after a few days. It was quite a job. The two supervisors were good, but they needed training, everyone needed training. The foreman, rather than lead, had to be led by the nose, just like I had to lead the hourly men. I promoted the one foreman with any gumption to general foreman.

When business goes downhill, decisions to spend money go up to high levels, even to the president of the company. Everyone is breathing down our necks. We make no decisions. For example, I'm supposed to get the inventory immediately into line; I have to drop everything and get the information. I was like a man on a yo-yo. What do you call that thing that moves on the stage—oh yeah, a marionette. I was a marionette. I was completely at their beck and call. I was tied down and couldn't get at any problems. I felt like a robot. I knew what I was doing would eventually show results, but it hadn't started showing on the horizon yet. I had to soul-search daily to keep from blowing apart. My frustration was high and accomplishment was low. I put out my maximum effort—worked nights, but felt I had done nothing. If those guys had only left me alone. I had a sense of claustrophobia. Daily, I was trying to figure out which problem should be done first.

The best way to explain it is that topside was in a state of panic, and this was coming on down and pushing through. I had to depanicize the whole thing, be a buffer and keep the pressure off those who reported to me.

The days were lost. Three months now, it sure is lost. But there's one thing I did gain, that's self-control. I decided I wasn't going to get any ulcers. No matter how strongly they wanted something right away, I'd promise them, and then I would just see what could be done. I'd go home at night and forget. Usually I could—sometimes I'd wake up in a sweat. But I could shut it off pretty well. And I had to help keep those below, those in the soup, from feeling it.

Appendix A

ALPHA COMPANY

SUMMARIZED JOB DESCRIPTIONS, DELTA POWDERS UNIT CREW

The *lead operator* (*a*) co-ordinated and was partly responsible for directing the work of the whole unit; and (*b*) directly tended certain elements of the unit's machinery spread over three floors. Most of the machinery operated automatically but required periodic checking, unless operating difficulties were experienced. In this case almost continuous observation might be necessary. Tending the equipment meant operating mechanical or electrical controls and reading and interpreting process indicators and gauges. The lead operator also periodically packed out certain intermediate by-product materials, an activity which was dusty and involved manual movement of heavy drums. In addition, at specified points in a batch, the lead operator took samples of material to the laboratory for testing. The job required a relatively high amount of technical knowledge, working knowledge of the other operators' jobs, and a great deal of movement throughout the whole unit. It offered some freedom for planning work activities, at least as long as the unit was operating satisfactorily.

The *batchmaker* charged the raw materials into each unit separately. The job required only minor technical knowledge, but accurate work was very important. It involved frequent and heavy physical labor and was relatively dirty. The batchmaker directed the activities of the process helper and of two stock clerks, who moved materials on lift trucks. He had some flexibility in timing his activities, although this decreased when all three units were operating.

The *blending operator* operated equipment to make the final blend of powders, and other equipment to pack the blend into shipping containers. The job required a moderate amount of technical knowledge, which was used infrequently. It also required heavy physical labor, including a large amount of lifting and moving heavy containers, and was relatively dirty. The blending operator directed the activities of a process helper. The blending operator's work was practically independent of the rest of the unit; a blending operator might even work on an otherwise shutdown unit. Hence, he had a large amount of flexibility in timing his activities.

The *roll operator* operated and tended the rolls and certain other pieces of equipment. Proper operation of the rolls required a fairly high degree of technical skill and judgment and constant alertness. On some batches it required almost continuous but moderate physical activity; on others, only continuous observation was necessary for long periods of time. The roll operator had charge of a number of controls and valves and watched numerous gauges and indicator lights as well as the process taking place in the rolls. He adjusted his machines in various ways, shoveled spilled-over material back into them, and used a wooden prod to keep sticky material going through the rolls. At the end of each batch, he emptied a dust collector located in a different area of the unit from his rolls; in this he was assisted by the lead operator.

The roll operator's work station was dusty, hot, and noisy. The rolls had to be tended on a practically continous basis while they were operating. Unless relieved by another man, the roll operator shut down his equipment when he left his immediate work area. Hence, he had little flexibility in timing his activities while the rolls were operating, though he did have some during a shutdown.

The *batchmaking process helper* assisted the batchmaker. The work required practically no technical knowledge but heavy physical labor under relatively dusty conditions. The helper's activities were directed by the batchmaker. The former was subject to other work requested by the foreman.

The *unit process helper* assisted the blending operator mainly in the packing-out process. The work was otherwise similar to the batchmaking process helper's.

2. ALPHA COMPANY (B)

During his study of the Delta powders workers, Adams tried to describe the social structure of the work group. He drew his conclusions from the observations he made of the workers' behavior at work and in the smoking room and from data from interviews he held with them.

He observed very few interactions occurring around the work itself; however, he did observe persisting interaction and seating patterns in the smoking room, both during smoking breaks and at other times during the shifts. These observations were confirmed by a description of how the men sat, given to him by one of the union representatives. On the basis of this data, Adams drew the following rough conclusions about the membership pattern and social structure of the powders work group.

About half of the powders workers appeared to be members of a "regular" group. They sat at the most favorable location in the smoking room, most often engaged in conversation while there, and stayed longer than the other workers, sometimes up to an hour at a time. The regular group included some area mechanics, but none of the liquids workers. The three union officials appeared to be high-ranking regulars. The majority in the regular group were of French-Canadian extraction, but there were also some of Irish, Polish, or Italian background. A much smaller subgroup was made up wholly of Negroes.

The men in liquids had about as much seniority as those in powders, but they were slightly older, a few more men being in their late forties and a few less under thirty-five. Looking at other aspects of the group in liquids and powders, two other differences struck Adams. First, the ethnic group that formed the regulars in powders—French-Canadian, Polish, Irish, and Italian—were in the minority in liquids. Secondly, there were also differences in the backgrounds of the people in the higher-paid jobs. In powders, of the fourteen men having high-graded jobs, nine had the regulars' ethnic backgrounds and one was a Negro. In liquids, by contrast, of the nine high-graded jobs, five were filled by Negroes and none was filled by a member of the regulars' ethnic groups.

The Values of the Work Group

When Adams reviewed his interview data, he concluded that the men's beliefs about their work, their behavior, and their supervision could be stated as follows:

1. A man's work should be clearly delineated and not subject to change.
2. A man should have some freedom to determine his own actions on the job.
3. The men should stick together as a group.

The men felt that it was important that they be left to do their regular work without frequent interruptions, after being given any necessary specific instructions for the orders in process. They disliked close checking and frequent instructions from their supervisors on what to do.

The men's values about group cohesiveness were expressed in a number of ways. They felt, for example, that the whole group should "gang up" on a foreman who tried to crack down on an individual or on the group as a whole. They felt that each worker should produce at about the same level of production to prevent any supervisory comment to one man about his production rate. They felt that disputes between the men should be handled within the group first and that no man should act as an informer to management. Also, they felt that no man should "act like a supervisor" over another.

Attitudes about Delta Powders as a Place to Work

The men said that the powders workers formed a pretty good "family," so that outsiders were not welcome; that most of the men liked to work there; and that many wanted to return to powders, if they were transferred elsewhere following temporary cutbacks. The men noted that workers "down at the other end," thought of powders as a poor place to work, dirty and hazardous; but they said that conditions had improved, and they spoke almost with pride about how tough, dirty, and hazardous powders had once been. They said that all the men got along pretty well, regardless of racial differences; and that workers and supervisors enjoyed many joint outside activities, such as athletics and parties.

The regulars noted that the powders group stuck together against management actions; a union steward described the group as "sort of a clique" over which the stewards had good control. Several of the men described instances of horseplay and caustic remarks against those who did not produce at about the same level. One union steward, after describing the men's concept of the "right level" of production, spoke of an instance when the men working on one unit had decided to race to see how much production they could turn out. Production during the race was 50 per cent above normal.

Men's Attitudes about Their Jobs

Some of the younger regulars who expressed aspirations for bettering themselves considered all of the hourly jobs in powders as routine and monotonous. Nevertheless, they and the other regulars, as well as many of the other workers, agreed that some jobs were more desirable than others.

The men had mixed feelings about the lead operator's job. For though it was considered the most interesting, had the most responsibility, and was capable of giving a feeling of accomplishing something, the men felt that the lead operator's authority to make decisions about the work had been steadily lessened, while the responsibility for errors and the physical labor remained. In addition, the lead operator's relationship with the rest of the men raised a problem; although the men said that a lead operator could do a good job only if the other operators did their work well, they expressed dislike for a few lead operators who, the men said, "just gave orders." They were particularly critical of any lead operator's concerning himself with the behavior of a worker on a crew other than his own.

The batchmakers said their job offered free time between batch-charging operations and that it was well paid, but that it involved a good deal of heavy physical labor. The regulars liked the blending operator's job, because it was independent from the rest of the unit, thus allowing the operator to "take a break" without affecting production. They also liked its relative freedom from direction by either the lead operator or the foreman. The blending operators spoke of their job as well paid; those interviewed seemed to find it particularly important that they themselves made it a good job, "since we all stay at about the same level of production."

All of the men interviewed, except one, disliked the roll operator's job. They disliked just watching machinery and standing in one place, where it was hot, dusty, humid, sticky, and dark. One man said that it was just a "mule job." The regulars intensely disliked the process helper assignment, partly because it was just physical labor, and partly because the process helper was always subject to being called off by the foreman to do other, often dirty work.

Almost all the men spoke of the difficulty of adjusting to a new crew, of having to make friends, learning how to talk with them, knowing what to say, and learning whom you can joke with. They spoke of the crews "sticking together." The union officials said that whenever reassignments were made, there were "more complaints than you can shake a stick at. You can bet the assignments seem unfair to the men. There is always someone who is dissatisfied. It is a question of leaving a crew. They hate to leave the people they are accustomed to work with. We have to sit down and explain to them why it is the way it is."

The Men's View on Upgrading

Adams talked with the three union officials, Gagnon, Allard, and McNally, about upgrading:

ALLARD: Upgrading trouble runs in spurts. They'll ask one guy, and he'll refuse. Then they'll ask the others, and it becomes a big issue. It all turns back to overtime. Like when the company is cutting back and tries to tighten up on costs. Instead of asking an operator to stay on with overtime, they'll try to get someone to upgrade. If one guy does upgrade, he's blackballed. The guys who upgrade are even the very ones who want overtime the most. One of the fellows the other week was about to upgrade for a few lousy cents an hour. But he finally told his boss that the guys were mad and he wouldn't take the higher job. So they had to organize two twelve-hour shifts to cover the higher-level job assignment.

This upgrading problem has happened more times than I can keep track of. It comes in spurts. It may happen several times a shift. It has happened a good hundred times or more in the last couple of years.

The union doesn't play any part in this. The contract stipulates that we can't make an issue of it, if a man upgrades willingly. So the union is sort of out of this question. It doesn't like to get involved in overtime.

GAGNON: Delta powders is sort of a clique. The men stick together. This is the hardest shell for management to crack in the plant. I guess it was partly because there was such a small number of people and so the stewards had better control than over a large group. In a small group the men won't cut each other's throat. Like, for example, on taking a higher-level job, if it will hurt someone else's overtime, they won't hurt each other.

McNALLY: I felt I had to have the support of my people and upgrading was one of the main questions here. When we had bull sessions, we could see a definite attempt to try to break up the coalition, always trying to convert someone to upgrading. Sometimes they did this in a group meeting, sometimes individually, with maybe five or six foremen talking to one individual. It was almost made into a personal thing as a favor to the foreman.

A lot of fellows were violently opposed to upgrading. The individual compares himself to the whole corporation, which is begging him to do something for just this little bit of difference in money. This is a legal right he can exercise, and he can make more money if the group sticks together on this. Of course, some fellows are willing to go up as a matter of protection; they can get in a unique position with a foreman, who can't pick on them if they get in a scrape or something.

The Men's Views of Sienna's Reorganization

Two of the union officials, Gagnon and McNally, commented in the course of their interviews at some length about the moves that Joseph

Sienna made starting in April, after he had been brought into powders as operating superintendent:

> GAGNON: You know, Sienna was given the powders area to himself for a while. He had the sole responsibility and all the foremen reported to him. There were a lot of changes, a lot of changing around. There were hard feelings among some of the supervisors themselves. Like if I worked for you and then a couple of weeks later, it turned out you were under me, there would be resentment. Well, that's what happened here.
>
> There was resentment at the worker level. All the crews laid low for a while. The men can tell just what the supervisors do and where they are. They know in a few minutes what they are up to.
>
> Then there was a meeting a while back. We got one story that if we got out more production, we could sell cheaper than the competition; but then we also heard that we couldn't undercut them on the selling price, because they could cut underneath us. So we had both arguments; one contradicted the other. So we didn't think there was any truth behind it, but that it was just a way of trying to get us to raise production, so they could make more profit. It would have been all right if he had used just one argument. You see, Sienna came from liquids, and he had liquids all sewed up. Up there, the guys will do just as management says. They won't answer back, and they'll do something if management just drops a hint. But in powders, a lot of guys run by the job description. They'll do a few favors, but they won't do more than that.
>
> I guess Sienna figured he could just move things around. We felt the management guys hadn't been doing their job, so he was brought in to straighten things out. At the time we heard him, we thought it was a lot of malarkey.
>
> He told us all kinds of things—like he described different kinds of workers. There were lazy guys and there were people who would do this and people who would do that, and then he asked what categories we would fit in. The guys resented this. They had no chance to answer; he wasn't looking for an answer. There was no question period. Oh, about a month later there was, but by then the guys had forgotten the questions they were going to ask.
>
> The men resented it. The union, you know, wrote an article in the union paper. And Sienna didn't like that article. As a matter of fact, a little later on he said the article hurt.

Later in the interview, Gagnon was talking about job duties:

> GAGNON: You know, some of the job descriptions overlap, like those for the blending operator and process helper. Well, recently Sienna wanted the process helpers to do some of the blending operators' work. We almost got a sitdown strike out of it.
>
> Sienna said that just because the company was wrong in the past, there

was no reason they had to keep on being wrong in the future. According to the job specifications, a process helper can dump the material provided it is not for shipment—for example, if it is for rework or something like that. If it is for shipment and has been inspected and weighted up, then the blending operator is the one to do it. In this case the material was O.K. for shipment but there was no blending operator around, so they decided the helper should do it, since his job description says he can dump material. In the eight years I've been here, I've never seen a process helper dump stuff alone. This is the kind of thing that caused resentment at his being in the job.

This kind of thing could affect your job. Suppose I had to go home at 12:00 instead of 3:00. Well, if there was stuff to dump, he'd want to let the helper do it alone and not call in a blending operator for three hours overtime. After eight years of the way it has been, you can't just change it around. It's not just the guys in that case, but others will feel the same thing will happen. There were rumors around that they were going to take the process helpers away and the blending operator was going to work alone. The men figured this was a start in the direction of getting one man to do it. If one guy could do it for three hours, then he could do it for eight.

McNally talked as follows on some of the same subjects as Gagnon:

McNALLY: When I came here, I was impressed with the personal relationships under the old Delta superintendent. They were good, especially for a big company. After the safety meetings, they used to explain some of the facts and figures of how they were competing. But they never said we were in this position of having to go out of business. The big pitch was to increase production. They'd go through their economic theories until they came out with an answer. After years of the same story, you get the idea this is just a routine to get more work out of us. Then they came out with the announcement. Perhaps they would rather go out of business than disclose the actual figures of the company. In a place like this, where there's a union, you can't expect a guy like Joe Sienna to call us in and discuss this without any real figures. We'd consider ourselves damn fools to take his word for it.

You see, there's been a big change in the hiring requirements here. They've got workers with more education, and I don't think supervision fully changed with this. People here grew more and more to think for themselves, like on economics and politics. So when the supervisors come down to the smoking room, we have our own thoughts about those kinds of things. At least for someone of my kind, if a guy comes down with a smooth personnel relations job, I just think he's trying to con me, so I buck back. They did a lot of things designed consciously or unconsciously to get the sympathy of the workers for the company.

Before Sienna came in here this wasn't just one big happy family, but we got along most of the time. In the past two years there's only been one really serious grievance. We don't holler unless there's lots of ground. Of course, it also indicates the company is not pushing us too far. But when Sienna came in, there was trouble right off the bat. He came from a small department where he was quite close to the people and had these crew huddles; and he used to keep the liquids area quite separate from powders. For years there had been no grievance up there and very few disciplinary incidents. He told me this. I heard from a foreman that Sienna thinks of himself as a whiz in personnel relations, but he is really very inexperienced, very opinionated. He was told by someone that he might have tough sledding when he came in here; but he thought he could get along anywhere he went.

This may sound like we were lining up the guns for him. No, we weren't. We gave him consideration. He may have meant well, but he gave us a real good personnel relations job. He gave us all this economics and politics and even threw in some religion to convince us. When he was through, we could feel ourselves insulted. He didn't allow any questions or want any criticism publicly. Myself and all the shop stewards felt that he tried to make a big play for the men. We felt that if we didn't make a move to counteract it, it would look as if we agreed with him. The result on this was that there was a grievance not too long after it. Later, I saw Porter [department superintendent] on that grievance and when he asked me what I thought of the talk that Sienna gave, I told him we didn't like it. Sienna tried to set up meetings to redo what he had done—I think this was actually Porter's idea. But he avoided getting into discussions of what he had said before. I asked him a question of what he had said at a foremen meeting, but he avoided me and said he wanted to talk with me in private.

He called me in to hear me, but he talked. I felt him out. I told him as far as grievances go, we could have good relations just by settling them. He agreed, but added, "Whenever it is good for the company." All grievances can't be settled that way. Most of these guys are probably pretty good chemical engineers, but they fail on personnel relations.

The Men's Views of the Decision to Go Out of Business

Almost all of the workers interviewed expressed surprise and regret that powders was going out of business. It was described as "kind of a shock" and "like being hit on the head." Gagnon, a shop steward said, "It's hard to believe that we're going out of business. We thought it was just a move to get more production out of us." Several of the men said that they had worked there many years and "it was kind of home" to them.

Five regulars and three others voluntarily gave Adams statements on inadequacies in the Delta powders situation that they thought were related to management failures; i.e., failures to make proper expenditures on equipment or material, to plan production more efficiently, or to cut out supervisory "dead weight." One of the men who had very little contact with the other employees said that the whole problem was the hourly men's fault. Four regulars made statements which implied directly or indirectly that the men had not produced as much as they might have and that the fault for this lay with improper supervisory and management actions. Allard, one of the shop stewards, made the following statement:

ALLARD: In my opinion it was wholly due to supervision not using the right judgment. The shift foremen would let the men get away with murder in order to get out the production. If a foreman would tell a guy to do something or say not to take too long smoke breaks, it would get so the hourly people would stop putting out production. So the foreman, rather than being put in the spot where he had less production than the other foreman, would close his eyes to things that shouldn't have been gotten away with. So when people got into the habit of getting away with a little, they'd want more, and it would get out of hand. One guy gets away with it, then another. For example, on getting permission for extra smoke breaks, each time the foreman would mention it to me, I'd talk to the men. But I couldn't ask them just by myself. They'd be under the impression I was a company man. I couldn't stick my neck out. The only kind of shop steward they want is a fighting, aggressive steward. I once told Lou [Gagnon] that there were a lot of guys out of line on his crew, yet he never stuck his neck out. He was afraid of a few individuals on his crew who might give him the business.

This goes back quite a while ago. This department was one of the hardest to work in. It had tough supervision and a lot of bad grievances. So supervision must have been told to get better relations. Once it got freer, the union and the shop stewards got stronger and stronger. You know, I really don't understand why some guys never work.

McNally, the union grievance representative, spoke as follows:

McNALLY: I don't think the shutdown was necessary. The management knew we had the potential to produce a hell of a lot more than we were doing. I knew what the potential was here. Could have doubled the production if we had made the effort. It's only natural to ask why the guys weren't doing it. Well, there are different shift arrangements. When you're on five days and then off two, the only advantage is eight cents per hour night differential. But when you're on six days and off two you get time and a half for Saturday and double on Sunday. Maybe $15 or $20 a week. Of course, it was strictly selfish on the part of the people to see they kept on six and two. When the other manufacturing superintendent was here, back about four years ago, he tried to get at the problem. His idea was that there wouldn't be any more back and forth between six and two and five and two. He would try to keep it at a level amount; and after he said that, we actually did stay on six and two until the recession slack off. He was attempting to make the fellows seem secure.

If the company could have built confidence among the people and stewards, the fights about deviations from the contract in order to get more production or better satisfaction for a customer wouldn't have existed. Now the general belief among the men is not to give in on anything that isn't in the contract. After the management has got something for a while, they think it's theirs. If they would agree to cut them out later on, then they could ask for other advantages and get them. I'm not saying they shouldn't have the advantages they have legally, but if they built trust and confidence—then they would get dollars-and-cents results. The men don't have trust in management. Even though that's a two-way street, they're the only ones who can initiate anything. The union can't. If a shop steward thought that something could be done, but his people didn't have the same confidence in it, he'd be sticking his neck out.

3. DAN WEBER

In November, 1963, Mr. Dan Weber, assistant chief of operations research in the research and development department of the Aircraft Propulsion Division, was concerned about the positions of himself and his operations research group in the departmental organization. Divisional management had just made an announcement that a complete reorganization of the R&D department would occur at the end of the calendar year. No details of the change were made available at the time of the announcement.

In the seven years since coming with the R&D department, Mr. Weber had already been involved in two major reorganizations. In this same period he had advanced from the usual starting position of engineering draftsman to his current assignment as assistant chief of the OR group. Mr. Weber took pride in the fact that while he had been in the OR group it had expanded from a two-man group to its current staff of fifteen engineers.

Yet, this accomplishment had not left Mr. Weber without concerns for his own career advancement and for the OR group's future role in the R&D department. One of these concerns, he told the casewriter, was that the upper echelons of departmental management did not yet comprehend the full significance and potential usefulness of OR techniques for the programming and planning of departmental activities. At the same time he expressed concern as to his own career strategy. Should he stay with OR work and the satisfactions it provided, in view of the fact that the traditional internal routes to top positions in departmental management and higher were through project management and design engineering? On the other hand, he believed that the OR operations had potential utility for the Aircraft Propulsion Division which, if recognized and realized, could also bring him significant promotions. In the context of the upcoming reorganization, Mr. Weber was giving serious consideration to the resolution of these concerns.

Background

The Aircraft Propulsion Division, a division of a large, widely diversified corporation, had experienced severe cutbacks in its government contracts for both production and R&D business following the end of the Korean conflict. Lagging somewhat behind other jet engine pro-

Exhibit 1

THE AIRCRAFT PROPULSION DIVISION
NATIONAL EXPENDITURES FOR AIR DEFENSE AND SALES,
1951 THROUGH 1962
(In Millions of Dollars)

Year	National Expenditures (Year Ended 6-30)				Per Cent of Total			Aircraft Propulsion Division (1942–1949 = 100)
	Aircraft	Missiles	Space	Total	Aircraft	Missiles	Space	
1962	$6,449	$3,523	$1,300	$11,272	55%	32%	13%	$221
1961	5,898	2,972	744	9,614	61	31	8	229
1960	6,670	3,500	401	10,571	63	33	4	194
1959	7,658	3,339	145	11,132	69	30	1	179
1958	8,448	2,737	89	11,274	75	24	1	197
1957	7,978	2,095	76	10,149	78	21	1	312
1956	7,146	1,168	71	8,385	85	14	1	493
1955	8,037	718	74	8,829	91	8	1	243
1954	8,335	504	....	8,839	94	6	..	291
1953	7,417	295	....	7,712	96	4	..	370
1952	4,888	169	....	5,057	97	3	..	368
1951	2,412	21	....	2,433	99	1	..	113

SOURCE: *Statistical Abstract of the United States.*

ducers, the top management of the Aircraft Propulsion Division had taken two steps to reorient its R&D department; in 1957, a four-year program for increasing research facilities had been undertaken with a budget of $40 million, and early in the same year, the R&D department had been completely reorganized. The pure projects system had been discarded in the reorganization in favor of a systems engineering approach. Management explained the change as follows:

> In the emerging aerospace age, the wide variety of devices and components that must be co-ordinated into the development of advanced, high-performance weapons systems requires a new R&D approach, a new vision. The "systems approach" is an answer to this need; it provides the technical viewpoint to integrate the many and diverse components into a smoothly functioning whole.

Under the systems approach the unit of management changed from specific R&D projects to the more specialized systems areas wherein similar component systems for several projects could be grouped. Before the change a project manager had direct responsibility for everyone working on a given project, such as the development work for a lightweight gas turbine suitable for powering helicopters and subsonic airbreathing missiles. Under the new structure the project manager was eliminated and the direct responsibility for the engineers was divided among systems managers according to the particular type of system on which each engineer was working. Continuing the above example, the development of the lightweight gas turbine would be staffed by some engineers reporting to the chief of the design group, some to the chief of the metallurgy group, some to the chief of the thermodynamics group, and so on.

These early actions in the Aircraft Propulsion Division were specific cases of a more widespread industry response to the changing nature of air power as a component of national defense. Overshadowed by the expediency of the production effort for the Korean conflict, the rapidly increasing technology of electronics, rocketry, nuclear power, and space travel opened possibilities of radically different propulsion systems for aerospace weapons and reconnaisance vehicles. These developments plus the likelihood of jet-propelled commercial airliners before the end of the 1950's commenced a reorientation in the aircraft engine industry toward the probable future requirements for survival in the emerging aerospace industry. Exhibit 1 indicates the magnitude and swiftness of the change in government spending from conventional aircraft to missiles and space vehicles.

For the Aircraft Propulsion Division the task of shifting emphasis to the aerospace orientation was formidable. For fifteen years, the division had been one of the leading developers and producers of jet engines for military fighters and bombers. One of the first to begin volume production of jet engines, the division had achieved an industry-wide reputation for development of improved designs enabling more favorable thrust-weight ratios. Post-World War II and the Korean conflict were periods of volume production for the division's highly successful engines. In 1956, the division had received approval for production of a high-thrust jet engine to power a new advanced supersonic all-weather fighter.

Despite the assurance of a minimum five-year production run on this latest power plant and subsequently modified versions, management had realized that the future of jet engines for the defense market would be limited. The demonstrated advances in rocketry and the possibilities of nuclear power for aircraft propulsion were signaling an inevitable revolution in propulsion for military airpower. Rocket-powered missiles and space vehicles would shortly present feasible alternatives to the interception, bombing, and surveillance functions of conventional military aircraft.

The significance of the impending change was that the new engines were not an evolution of the gas turbine but were based on radically different design principles. Whereas before, the power plant was a separate and interchangeable component within the total aircraft system, in the new era, aerospace vehicles basically would be "nonair-breathing" rocket engines upon which would be mounted a nose cone containing a war head and/or electronic guidance and surveillance devices. The change promised to be of considerable more complexity for the industry than had been the change from piston engines to jet engines.

But the Aircraft Propulsion Division had more direct evidence of change than the above. The 1956 cancellation of a development contract in the division for a new design gas turbine engine capable of extremely high altitude performance sharpened the realization of the alternatives presented by rocket power. As part of a development package for an advanced high-altitude reconnaisance plane, the entire project had been canceled when an analysis of comparable lead times indicated that an alternative missile system would make the aircraft obsolete shortly after planned production would have begun. The division had spent over $65 million on this project and had strongly anticipated eventual production. Only about two thirds of this expenditure had been covered by government contract. The 1957 reorganization followed shortly thereafter.

1957 Reorganization

Mr. Weber had been working in a development project for a light-weight gas turbine engine about three months prior to the reorganization of 1957. During this time he was an engineering draftsman in the design area of the project. Working with him under the supervision of Mr. Frank Mintz were seven other engineering draftsmen. In the reorganization Mr. Mintz was assigned to take over and restaff the operations research group. Two years earlier the OR group had been initiated when two mathematicians had been hired by the department for that purpose. These men were unfamiliar with the problems endemic to the R&D department, and the applications of OR had been few. Both of the men had resigned shortly before the reorganization was effected. Mr. Mintz chose Mr. Weber to join him in the OR group and decided that initially the two of them would comprise the group. Neither of the men had any background in OR, although both were familiar with some of the recent developments in the field. The two of them formulated the initial activities of the group by reading books and visiting an OR operation at a nearby aircraft company. Mr. Mintz had been with the division for ten years and was familiar with both the methods of operation and the problems of co-ordination of the R&D department. Mr. Weber had majored in aeronautical engineering as an undergraduate and obtained a masters in mathematics before coming to the division directly out of college.

At the departmental management level, several major changes were made in the reorganization (see Exhibits 2 and 3). Mr. Edward Lovio, previously in command of the entire department as vice president for engineering, became vice president for research and development. The number of engineers under his command was reduced from 2,500 to 150. Mr. Lovio had come to the company during World War II and had become well recognized throughout the gas turbine industry as an outstanding designer. He was given credit for the successful engines developed at the close of World War II and during the Korean conflict, and he was generally considered to be the chief engine designer in the Aircraft Propulsion Division.

Mr. J. Escalona, formerly chief of the development group, was promoted to the position of manager of engineering assembly. In the reorganization the production department took over the responsibility for engineering assembly and Mr. Escalona reported to the vice president for production after the change. Mr. Escalona had been primarily concerned with the development of the high-thrust jet engine that was just beginning production. Engineering assembly was charged with the responsibility of providing all engineering services needed in connection with actual engine production and had employed 2,000 of the R&D department's 2,500 professional personnel. Mr. Escalona replaced Mr. Martin Haag who was retiring from the company at this time. Mr. Haag had advanced to his former position in a manner similar to Escalona's move. In 1949, when a highly modified version of the principal jet

Exhibit 2

THE AIRCRAFT PROPULSION DIVISION
R&D DEPARTMENT (PARTIAL)
(Prior to 1957)

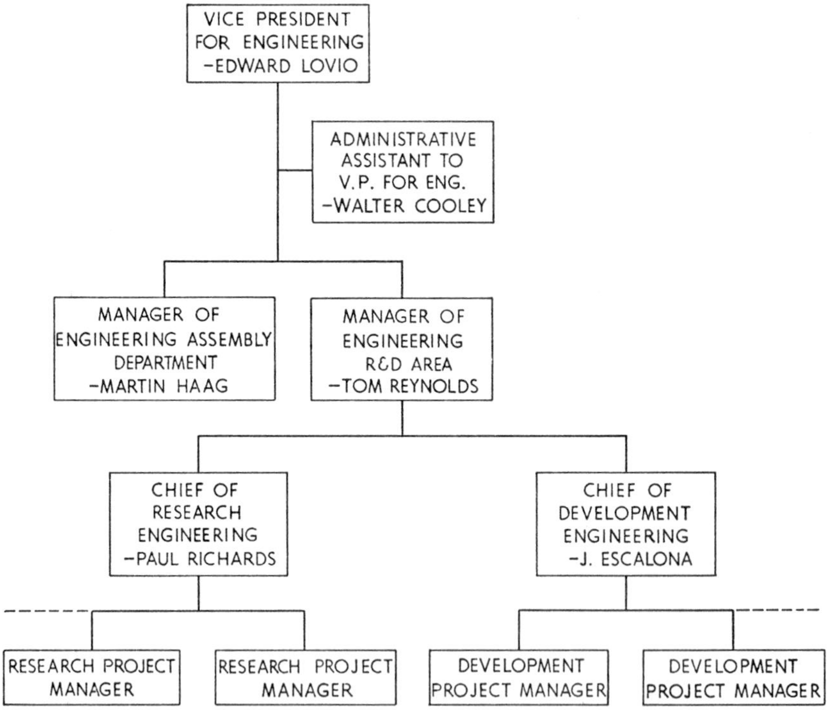

engine then in production was phased from development into production, Mr. Haag, who had had chief responsibility for its development, was promoted to head engineering assembly.

Under Mr. Lovio the R&D function was divided into two sections. A small scientific research staff was established under the leadership of William Ballard. Staffed with ten engineers and scientists, the staff was to work on any problems which the vice president for R&D, Mr. Lovio, deemed important. The second subdivision was the R&D area. Mr. Tom

Reynolds remained as manager, and reporting to him as chief of the research engineering section was Mr. Paul Richards.

With the phasing of the high-thrust engine out of development and into production and with the cancellation of the high-altitude jet engine development contract, the R&D department was left without any sponsored development contracts. Approximately 400 of the previous 500 engineers employed in the R&D area were in development projects, the

Exhibit 3

THE AIRCRAFT PROPULSION DIVISION
R&D DEPARTMENT (PARTIAL)
(1957–1959)

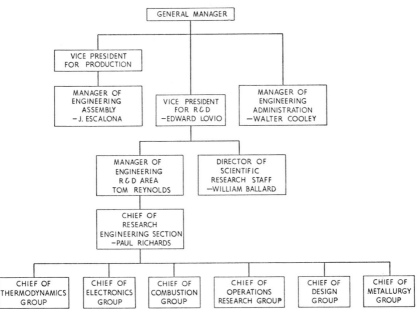

remaining 100 in research. Fifty of those development engineers were transferred to engineering assembly pending the start-up of volume production on the high-thrust engine. Another 50 were transferred to the research engineering section, and the remaining 300 were laid off. The 150 engineers in the research engineering section were reorganized into systems groups as follows: thermodynamics, electronics, combustion, design, metallurgy, and OR (see Exhibit 3).

Mr. Weber interpreted the 1957 reorganization and subsequent events as follows:

> If you wanted to come up with the first big blow—this was really a big blow to Ed Lovio. The major amount of manpower was taken away from

him. He is one of the original engineers of the division and very well respected in the industry. He considers the past successes of the division as his successes, as his engines. I would say there is a major portion of truth to this; but whenever you have a large organization, there are many, many people who have actually contributed to the design. It becomes a fine line of distinction as to whose design it really is at that point. Probably back in World War II our first production jet engine was his design. The modified versions produced during the Korean conflict are a little more hazy; and the current production engine becomes even more hazy. My impression is that he would have liked to go out in a blaze of glory with some basically new engine design. He has stayed on waiting for the division to get a new major contract of this type. I've been with the division for about seven years, and the R&D department still hasn't come up with such a contract. You could almost see the pressure building up—getting near retirement, he wanted this one last success.

The scientific research staff was sort of a window dressing. It had ten people or so to start with. The major effort of this whole R&D department went down through a chain of three people: Lovio, Reynolds, and Richards. There were many conflicts between these three men in that each was trying to run the entire 150-man section independently of the others. Each of them prior to this reorganization had several major areas of responsibility. Then, they were left with only 150 engineers between them, and the getting of new business was looming all the more important. If you were at the bottom as I was, you got a lot of conflicting directions. One day one would come in and say to do this; later another would come in and say to do that; and so back and forth, each one trying to somehow get the project moving in a good direction.

After a while more business started to come in, and they resolved the problem after a fashion. The chief of research engineering, Mr. Richards was interested in missiles, so he worried about a project to develop cases for the rocket engine of a surface-to-surface guided missile. Dr. Reynolds was interested in getting into the guidance area, so he worried about a nose-cone development contract we had obtained. And Mr. Lovio worried after the few jet engine projects in a vague sort of way.

As business picked up in 1957, the problems of co-ordination between various systems groups became of concern to Mr. Richards; he assigned a group of technical writers to the OR group to improve communications and co-ordination in the development of research proposals for government contracts. Mr. Weber described this phase in the development of the OR group in the following way:

> After the reorganization there were no formal project managers or anything like this in the new organization. It turned out that OR was doing a lot of the lower level co-ordination unofficially. We were assigned

a number of technical writers, who prepared proposals for contracts. There are a lot of sections that have to be prepared: aerodynamics, structures, electronic systems, etc. Many different pieces of information came into this proposal from group chiefs responsible for the specific areas, and often you would find a lot of inconsistencies. For example, someone would say that the design was this and someone else would say it was that; and in the end we were actually resolving the technical differences that had not shown up until the proposal had got to the point at which each section had to put it down on paper and submit it as part of the whole proposal.

We are actually doing a lot of the in-between co-ordination and getting the project divisions clarified. At first all the groups were relatively small, and we were in a one-room type of thing. The whole outfit was about 150 engineers; so we all knew each other.

Changes in R&D Resources

The Aircraft Propulsion Division in 1958 revised upward its planned expansion of R&D facilities. Under the revision $56 million would be expended by 1963 with an increased emphasis on electronic and metallurgical research. The core of this latter expenditure was to be the construction of an $18 million research center for basic studies in aerospace and materials science.

Adjustments in personnel during this same time period also reflected the reorientation. Both additions and reductions were made to the R&D staff between 1957 and 1959. The shrinkage was concentrated among those engineers with backgrounds principally in gas turbine design. At the same time the department was hiring for the new research facilities which were under construction. This recruitment focused on engineers and scientists trained in the basic sciences or the developing space technology.

1959 Reorganization

By the middle of 1959, the R&D department had grown to 250 engineers and scientists. Several projects were underway, and poor co-ordination increasingly delayed completions of projects beyond scheduled dates. It was in this context that the general manager of the Aircraft Propulsion Division announced another reorganization of the R&D department (see Exhibit 4) that also involved some higher management shifts (see Exhibit 5). The 1959 reorganization involved five important steps as follows:

1. The functions of R&D and engineering administration were centralized under the position of a vice president for engineering. To fill this

position the division hired a retired Air Force general who had spent 25 years in logistics work. This man, Mr. Raymond Montgomery, was unfamiliar with aeronautical engineering and Mr. Richards was placed as assistant to the vice president for engineering.

2. Mr. Lovio remained as vice president for R&D but was given the additional position of research advisor to the general manager of the division.

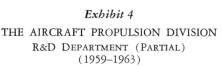

Exhibit 4

THE AIRCRAFT PROPULSION DIVISION
R&D DEPARTMENT (PARTIAL)
(1959–1963)

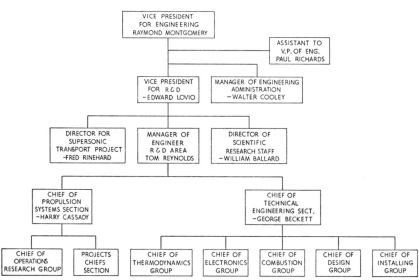

3. At this time an additional section was formed reporting to Mr. Lovio, the supersonic transport project, directed by Mr. Fred Rinehart. Mr. Rinehart had been recently hired from an aircraft firm. This section was to bring together the various R&D activities that had been going on toward the development of an advanced turbojet engine to power a supersonic transport which might be produced by the late 1960's. Rinehart's project was to have high priority since it appeared by late 1958 that the division was not going to obtain a significant share of the jet engine market for commercial airliners as the airlines changed from piston engines to gas turbines in the immediate future.

4. The R&D department under Mr. Reynolds was reorganized to include a section of project chiefs to co-ordinate the various engineering activities needed on particular contracts. These project chiefs along with

the OR group now reported to the manager of propulsion systems, Mr. Harry Cassady. The other systems groups reported to the manager of technical engineering, Mr. George Beckett. Both Mr. Cassady and Mr. Beckett were formerly group chiefs.

5. A systems planning committee was organized within the R&D department. This committee was to meet weekly with the primary tasks of: (1) recommending to the executive committee of the division those

Exhibit 5

THE AIRCRAFT PROPULSION DIVISION
"DIVISION-LEVEL" MANAGEMENT (PARTIAL)
(1959–1963)

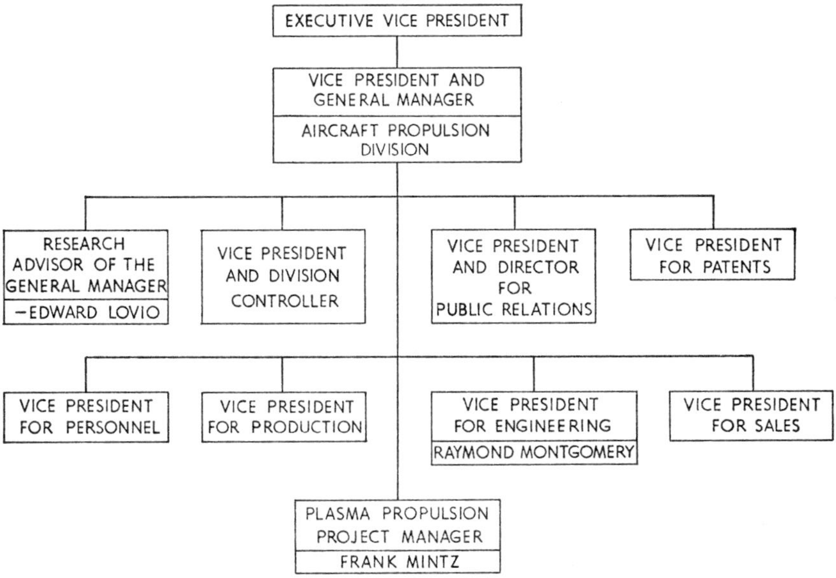

projects which should be undertaken by the R&D department, (2) determining the levels of effort to be expended on each of these proposals, and (3) selecting those projects upon which the R&D department should enter bid proposals to government agents. The vice president for engineering was committee chairman, and his assistant, Mr. Richards, was secretary. The regular membership also consisted of the vice president for R&D, the manager of R&D, the manager of engineering assembly, and two members from the sales department. Other members of the R&D department, the production department and the sales department could attend upon invitation of a regular member.

Mr. Weber had the following comments to make about the 1959 reorganization:

There was some interesting running around during the 1959 reorganization. Paul Richards ran out from under Mr. Lovio and Dr. Reynolds and started working directly with the new vice president for engineering. Mr. Richards pretty much initiated it himself. He and Mr. Lovio had often gotten into arguments in departmental meetings—so much so that it got to be an open antagonism. Richards felt that Lovio was old-fashioned in his approach and often told him so in project review meetings. So Richards pretty much ran out from under Lovio. Yet it was sort of a mutual type of thing. General Montgomery had very little, if any, engineering background. He was brought in as a manager rather than as an engineer; and initially he didn't understand the R&D department. Being where he was in a new organization, he was trying to figure out what was going on; and he needed someone to lean on.

Following the reorganization, Paul Richards was a pretty high-status individual. He had a lot to say about the R&D activities. Many of the communications that came from the general went through Richards. If he said something, people jumped because they figured it was coming from the general. But after the first year or so, there was a gradual erosion of the implied authority of Mr. Richards. Just now he has little influence or status. People are more likely to find out if communications have come from him or from the general before going ahead. Richards is a good administrator and engineer. He gave Frank Mintz the authority and encouragement to reorganize the OR group back in 1957. But, General Montgomery just didn't know whom to trust after a while. The general is a nontechnical man himself and he had gotten conflicting opinions from Richards and Lovio as well as from some of the others. Then, too, Montgomery has been under increasing pressure from the top for the last two years. Although business had been increasing, no major projects promising of volume production have been secured.

There had been some rather rash promises made to the executive committee of the division by Ed Lovio as to what new business an increased effort in R&D would bring. With only a few years left to run on the current production engines, top management is worrying what they're going to do with a huge assembly plant of over three million square feet of floor space with nothing to assemble. In one sense, this whole thing was sold before General Montgomery ever arrived. He is the innocent victim.

Shortly after the 1959 reorganization, Mr. Mintz was given the responsibility of being a project chief in addition to his duties as chief of the OR group. Unlike the typical project chief assignment Mintz's project reported directly to the general manager of the division. Mintz was to co-ordinate not only engineering but also sales and production planning activities related to his particular project. With the increased responsibilities of his promotion, Mintz devoted less attention to the OR group. In late 1963, Mr. Weber expressed the following:

About 80 to 90 per cent of the time Mintz is over in his project job. Actually, for about the last three years, I have been running the OR group or really doing his job, although he's had the title. I've had pretty much of a free hand in operating and running the area, and working directly with the project chiefs and group chiefs. With Mintz being in the job by title but not having direct contact with the work, we lose a certain amount of "ear" at the management level. He's not up on everything that's going on in the OR group; he couldn't be when he's doing another full-time job. Being one level lower, I don't have a direct line to the management level when certain problems come up where we should be represented. He may be at some of the meetings, but he's not cognizant of some of the work we've done. And in one sense management will say the area is being represented and they want it represented; but he's not really capable of representing it at this time. This really presents a problem. I think that the use of OR would have progressed a little faster if the situation weren't as hazy as it has been for these three years.

Activities in the OR Group

Following the 1959 reorganization, the separation of co-ordinating activities from OR and the promotion of Mintz to his additional duties allowed Mr. Weber to redirect the activities of the OR group. He described the post-1959 activities as follows:

We've primarily worked on the analysis of propulsion systems. Our OR activities have involved systems analysis rather than business analysis. We have helped in the definition phase of a project—the directions it should go and things like that. In the main this is a type of analysis they need in order to develop new weapon systems. We can analyze a given propulsion system and determine the various capacities and limitations that are inherent in the integrated system. Mr. Cassady, manager of propulsion systems, has been the principal user and has shown the principal interest. His interest is confined mainly to turbojet systems. Another area that has shown an interest has been the sales department. Several people, particularly the director of advanced engine sales, has worked closely with us in that a lot of the studies that we do are sales-oriented, such as an attempt to show one of our power plants as superior to someone else's under a range of probable conditions.

In addition to the system analysis function, another area for OR is in showing that the concepts that R&D are coming up with are good ones for the long-run development of the entire division as against an alternative approach to R&D. Essentially this involves problems flowing from the other direction—from top management. We've got several pressing problems of this type in the R&D department. One is the choice of projects and then the allocation of the resources of the division to the chosen projects. These two are related, of course, and I think we can be of some help on these. But the attitude here toward resource allocation and advanced planning using OR techniques has been less than favorable. I still envision this as an R&D department problem and as an R&D department task. Primarily it's R&D work and the systems planning committee's primary task is essentially this. An example of this kind of application would be when there are a lot of proposals or requests for proposals from the various military services or NASA and there has to be an evaluation and decision as to which should be bid. It's done on a hit-and-miss basis now; we could develop some logical criteria for selection, assign relative values to each proposal, and analyze various combinations of potential projects as alternative programs for the department.

Finally, I see a third function for a continuing OR group. This would be the generation and improvement of OR techniques themselves within the group. We stumble across both the needs and potential of new techniques as we make applications in various areas. Unfortunately we haven't gotten to this point with our group yet.

One thing we've always found—when we get a request for work, it is not usually a clearly defined request. We spend a lot of time trying to decide just what the problem is. Definition has always been one of our major concerns. In terms of the final approach to the problem, we generally determine this and seldom are refused by the manager requesting the work. This definition phase also gives us an "in" to generate additional applications. I would say that 50 per cent of the work that we do is generated within our group. We see a need and tell the chief what we can do; he agrees and off we'll go and do it.

For the most part we have not been too much involved in co-ordination of the type we did with the publications responsibility when we had the technical writers. However, on occasion, because of our way of thinking of problems from the broad systems viewpoint, we end up working for a project chief. Like the project chiefs we had to work with the various group chiefs to get our work done. Co-operation has to be there. I've worked with most of the fellows long enough and know them well enough, and they know what we're doing well enough that co-operation hasn't been a major problem. We've worked most closely with the growing electronics guidance area. Lovio's suspicion of OR has caused some friction in our work with the design group, but my having worked with them when I first came to Western allows me to have a pretty good relationship with most of the people in that area. Of course, you can't be pushy with them; I've done many jobs for them and helped them out so that when I need something we usually work it out together.

When you consider the three functions that OR can fill in the Division—systems analysis, planning and project selection, and development of OR techniques—I guess the question is where within the organization we can most effectively perform the task. One possible place that OR could be located would be as a staff operation to the vice president for engineering, like the position that Paul Richards has as assistant. We have worked on some problems with General Montgomery which have filtered down to us through Mr. Richards. On the other hand, there are advantages of doing the systems analysis type of work—being down in the R&D organization gives us close working relationships with a direct line to the technical groups on whom we depend for information and mutual problems. If we tried to split off part of the group to go as a staff operation with the rest staying where we are now, we probably would lose the balance of talents that we now have.

We have many different kinds of people working in the OR group, ranging from mathematicians to economists. I don't want to divide the men into a substructure because each one's particular talent may be needed on any given problem. Most of them have worked with me now for several years and identify me as their section head. It's been small enough that they know that I am aware of what they are doing. I perform two functions—one is arbitration among the fellows, the other is to assign the men to the specific problems. On certain jobs where the scope is broad or unusual, I'll call a general meeting to discuss that job and in essence to get the benefit of the various talents in the group. Considering the value of these talents, it just doesn't seem feasible to split the group into separate operations.

On the other hand, as the group gets larger, more and more of my time goes to administration. There are a million administrative problems in this kind of operation. This is one thing that I don't like about the job—I'm getting farther away from the technical side. I really don't have time to get into an OR problem. In one sense I do stay involved—most of the fellows like to use me as a sounding board for their approach to various problems, and the blackboard in my office sees a lot of use. I try to provide time for them, but it's getting to be a problem of keeping track of each activity. In addition to this I have to make visits to various government agencies to explain our analyses and to make presentations at the various meetings here. Then I have the meetings of the Operations Research Society to attend several times each year.

The Systems Planning Committee Meeting

In October, 1963, Mr. Weber was asked to attend a regular meeting of the systems planning committee. He later described this experience as follows:

We had a meeting of the systems planning committee where General Montgomery, Mr. Lovio, Harry Cassady, myself, and about three representatives of the sales department were present. We were discussing whether to start up a new project on a particular type of power plant, and if we did, what procedure we would use. I had some ideas which I expressed on how to go about it. I got shot at by Mr. Lovio in a general sort of way—not on the ideas but on the area of OR in general. He had used it as a scapegoat in many cases, always as an excuse for the government not letting more development contracts. "Too much studying being done and not enough doing," he would say. We have had a few discussions on this privately and also some openly before. He took this meeting as one of the times he was going to shoot me down. Well, it ended up with everyone talking at once. I happened to be sitting next to General Montgomery, so I started telling him my ideas on what should be done. He was sitting and listening while the others were talking in small groups.

I was more than a little annoyed at the actions in this meeting. Being the junior man of the whole group by several levels, I was upset that none of my superiors had even attempted in any way or shape to defend the area of OR. I felt that if they call you into a meeting for something like this they want your opinion—that's what you are there for. You're not there just to sit around and listen. Otherwise they wouldn't want you in the meeting. At least one of them could have defended the general area of OR. I don't think they necessarily had to agree with my specific approach to the problem, but I think they shouldn't have let me get shot at in the general area of OR.

I addressed this feeling to Mr. Mintz and Mr. Cassady after the meeting. We were in Mr. Mintz's office, and I told them that the support for me should have come from Dr. Reynolds in that he was at a high enough level to mean something and I was in the meeting because of him. About the time I was telling this to Mintz and Cassady, in walked Dr. Reynolds. Mr. Cassady said something like, "Dan felt like he didn't get any support today and that you're not in favor of OR!" Dr. Reynolds replied, "Oh yes, I am. Yes, I am; you know it, Dan!" I felt like asking, "When?"

Apparently Reynolds later talked with Mr. Lovio because a day or two later he came by and apologized to me, saying that there was nothing personal in what he had said at the time. I had not taken it personally as much as a matter of needing support for the area and not having any reasonable success in getting it. There in an open meeting with General Montgomery and especially an outside influence, the sales department, we were having an inside fight. Maybe that's why I didn't get any support— no one wanted to have an inside fight at that time.

Anticipated 1963 Reorganization

The events surrounding the meeting described above were still on Mr. Weber's mind when he was informed of the impending reorganization. He commented to the casewriter at the time:

All this poses an interesting question for me. Should I shoot for top management or not? Where does one want to go? I think I could be happy staying in the OR type of work. I like the work; I like the challenge; and the headaches are relatively few compared with departmental management. The difference in compensation is not that great. It's probably more than double what I am getting now; but if I were chief, my potential salary wouldn't be far under that of departmental management. Of course, there is a great difference between what a departmental manager makes and what the divisional general manager is paid. Then you're talking over $100,000 a year, and I wouldn't be adverse to that position or salary.

I would like to see the area of OR move up. Sometime in the future I think it could become a division-level activity. Although this would not be top management nor top salary, it would certainly be considered an advancement in terms of prestige or status. The status of the OR operation depends on the stature of the person running it. If he is valuable to the operation and they know it, the man and OR will get divisional-level rather than departmental-level position. The corporation will be forced to do this in order to hold on to the fellow. This is how I look at it from a practical viewpoint.

I go to meetings of the OR Society and invariably the discussion gets around to "how to sell OR." I have always been convinced that you do not really have to sell OR; if you do a good job, it will sell itself. We follow the idea that if people are not feeding us problems, we ask ourselves: "What are the significant problems the Department is facing?" Then we attack them and put out what we've done. Once that someone sees that an OR approach can be useful to them, they're going to ask for more. I don't mean to sound like we can solve all of the division's problems with OR, but I do definitely think we have a valuable contribution to make.

Exhibit 6

THE AIRCRAFT PROPULSION DIVISION
R&D DEPARTMENT
AGES AND SENIORITY OF MANAGEMENT
(Partial Listing)

	Age*	Seniority*
Edward Lovio	65	20
Martin Haag	63†	14†
Raymond Montgomery	61	4
Walter Cooley	58	20
William Ballard	52	16
Tom Reynolds	48	18
Paul Richards	45	16
George Beckett	43	16
Harry Cassady	43	13
J. Escalona	41	14
Frank Mintz	39	16
Fred Rinehart	38	4
Dan Weber	34	7

* As of 1963.
† At time of his retirement in 1956.

4. *SUPRA OIL COMPANY*

JOHN NICHOLS, a university research worker, had a talk with Mr. Bennett[1] about the headquarters sales organization of the Supra Oil Company, one of the larger integrated oil companies in the country. Excerpts from the conversation follow:

NICHOLS: You mentioned that you're planning to make some organizational changes here at headquarters. I wonder if you could tell me something about that.

BENNETT: Well, sure I will. I don't want to take too much credit for this thing, but it sort of got started because in the last couple of years I've been doing some beefing around here about the fact that I was being kept terribly busy with a lot of the operating details of the sales organization. You can see what I mean by looking at the organization chart we have been working under. (*Mr. Bennett produced a chart from his desk drawer and indicated all the people that were currently reporting to him.*) [See Exhibit 1 for a copy of this chart.]

You can see that with all these people looking to me for leadership I am not in a position to give them the right kind of guidance that I think they should have on their jobs. I just couldn't take the time. It didn't work too badly some time ago, but since I've been made a member of the board of directors, those activities have taken more of my time. What with being on additional committees and things of that kind, I just couldn't give seventeen headquarters' division managers the amount of help and attention that they really need. I think one of the things that they miss is that they're not in close enough touch with me or anybody else higher up the line so that we can be in a good position to appraise their work. We hear about it from some of the field people when they are doing a lousy job, but we don't hear much about it if they're doing a good job. Occasionally a field man will report that he is getting a lot of help from some staff outfit here, but that's rather rare. So we don't have a very good basis for appraising the good things that they do. So we started talking about what might be done to straighten this out.

Our plans are taking pretty definite shape now. Let me show you what we have in mind. (*Mr. Bennett sketched on a pad of paper a diagram to indicate the planned organizational changes.*) [See Exhibit 2.] You see, we will have two regional managers instead of three. We'll be making one of the present regional managers the manager of the headquarters sales divisions. Those are the divisions that specialize in promoting and selling

---

[1] Mr. Bennett was assistant general manager of sales.

our different specialty products. Then we'll set up a new job for Wingate, who has been acting as an administrative assistant here at headquarters. He'll take charge of a good number of headquarters sales staff divisions that were reporting directly to me. Those are staff divisions like price analysis and advertising. We will also give each of the two remaining regional managers an assistant manager. Those will be new positions too.

Exhibit 1

SUPRA OIL COMPANY

PARTIAL ORGANIZATION CHART OF THE SALES DEPARTMENT

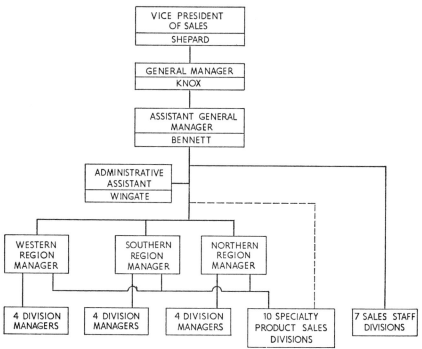

NICHOLS: How did you get these plans started?

BENNETT: I raised it with Shepard [vice president of sales] quite a while back.

NICHOLS: Would you say that was maybe six months ago?

BENNETT: I think it probably was six months ago. Shepard's first reaction was unfavorable. You see, I expected him to feel that way because he was the one that had the most to do with setting up our current organizational plan. But I approached him on it two or three times and complained a little bit and kept raising the question, and finally he said, "Well, I'm going to be leaving here pretty soon. You people have got to live with the organization. If you think it would work better some other way, I certainly won't object to your changing it." Well, that sort of thing gave me the green light, so then I went ahead and raised the question with Mr. Weld [president]. That is, Mr. Knox [general sales manager] and I did. The first time we went to him we talked about it just verbally in general terms. He said he thought it sounded like a pretty good idea and asked that we come back with two or three alternative ways of doing the thing in very specific terms. We talked to him once since then and, as a

Exhibit 2

SUPRA OIL COMPANY

PROPOSED ORGANIZATION CHART OF THE SALES DEPARTMENT

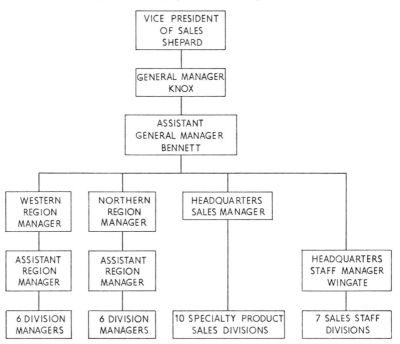

matter of fact, I'm going to see him this afternoon to see if he'll give us a final O.K. to go ahead with these plans.

NICHOLS: If you get his approval, what would you predict—that it might be another month before the change actually takes place?

BENNETT: Well, I would say so. I think if we've got this thing going in a month that we will be doing pretty well. I'm going to want to talk to my regional managers and then the headquarters divisional managers about this, but they should buy it all right. I think it will be a fairly simple job to sell it to them. You see, they will in effect be getting more chance to have access to their boss. I think it will work out much better, and they will see the point to it.

NICHOLS: You say that you are making one less region and making the third regional manager the head of—I guess you are calling him the headquarters sales manager. Are all three of those jobs going to continue to be on an equal level?

BENNETT: Yes, they will, but actually this job of headquarters sales manager will be sort of a training position for somebody to step into my job here as assistant general sales manager. That's what we have in mind. I think it will be a good assignment for training for my job. Then too, we're going to be able to open up a couple of new positions here, the assistant regional managers. I think that is going to be very useful from a management development standpoint. You see, one of our problems is that a number of the top executives here are all about the same age. You see, Knox and myself and the three regional managers are all about the same age, and then the heads of a lot of our headquarters divisions here are men of about our age who—well, they won't retire immediately, but they don't have a terribly long time to go. So we can't look to too many of those people to be our successors here at headquarters. We want to bring in some people from the field who will step in here as assistant regional managers in training for the job of regional managers.

NICHOLS: I take it then that you will be picking the people for those jobs from your field division men on the basis of talent and ability rather than on the basis of seniority.

BENNETT: Yes, that's right, we're going to pay very little attention to seniority in picking them. As a matter of fact, the two people we have in mind are two of our newest division managers, but they are both very able people. We think this will give us a chance to give them a good training for future development here.

This change that we are proposing, however, will not drastically change anybody's status here at headquarters, and I don't think it is going to cause us much trouble to put it in. You see, nobody will be jumped over the head of anybody else ahead of them in the management line. We think it's going to help a lot to have an assistant regional manager in here because that means that both he and the regional manager will be able to spend more time out with the field organization. One will be able to cover matters here at headquarters while the other is gone.

NICHOLS: Does that mean that your field people will be getting more top-level supervision as a result of this change?

BENNETT: Well, in a sense that's true of course, but it won't be taking any authority or responsibility from the field people. We just feel that they will be in closer personal contact with the people here at headquarters. We think it is very necessary that we do more of that. You see, if our regional managers and assistant managers can get out in the field and meet with the people, they will have a better basis for appraising different people that come along, and they can make sure we get the best people in the jobs that open up. Sometimes it's pretty hard to tell here at headquarters just who some of the best people are out in the field. You see, some division may have a job open up, and they will have a candidate for that job whom they will recommend highly for the promotion. That may be all well and good, but we want to know whether or not there may be a better man in some other division whom we aren't hearing about who might be shifted over for that promotion. You can't blame the division people for that sort of thing because they will have their favorite candidate and will of course be recommending him. We've made a few mistakes along the way because of this sort of thing, and if we have more personal contact we will be able to do a better job of it.

NICHOLS: Will this mean that you will be able to spend more time in the field?

BENNETT: Yes, I do hope that it will mean that. I want to do that very much. I think I ought to get out in the field more to keep in touch with what's going on in the market. It's really pretty hard to keep in touch with things while you are spending your time here at headquarters. You know, I want to get out and talk to people and see what they are talking about and see what kind of problems they are up against.

NICHOLS: I've heard several comments on this business of getting a feel for the market by getting out in the field. I take it that is quite a different process from keeping in touch with the market on what you might call a statistical basis?

BENNETT: Well, yes, it is. You see, I can look at the reports here in the office, and I may see that some district or some division is not doing too well at all on the basis of the figures in comparison with the competition. But I don't know just what the story is behind those figures. On a personal basis I could probably begin to get some answers to it. It could be any one of a number of things. I might go out there and find that it's a temporary situation because the competition is in effect going out and buying the business away from us, or I might find out that our people are not being very smart or aggressive about promoting our products, or I might find out that they do not know some of the facilities that we have available that would help them compete for the business. You see, one way we can compete for the business is the fact that this company has available some pretty good capital resources, and, if we don't have good outlets in a given district, we're often in a position to offer to put up some capital to get some better outlets. That way we can do a better job of competing for the business, and sometimes the local people don't know that those possibilities exist, or perhaps they're a little reticent about putting up proposals. Or even if they do put up proposals, if we haven't been out in the field to see for ourselves what's going on, we probably don't do as good a job of appraising the proposals they do put up.

NICHOLS: In other words, the figures tell you that maybe something ought to be checked into, but you've got to go out and talk to people to find out what is really going on?

BENNETT: Yes, that's right. You have to take a personal look. You can find out a lot faster than you can by correspondence just what is going on and what can be done about it.

NICHOLS: Won't this reorganization mean that some of the people both here and in the field will have new bosses now?

BENNETT: Yes, that's right, but it's not too drastic a change. You see, we used to have only two regional managers some time ago. I guess we shifted off that system some four or five years ago. When I was out in the field as manager of a division, I was reporting into the northern regional manager, who was Mr. Shepard at that time. Then I was brought in here as his assistant for the whole region. It was about that time that we set up this business of having three regions and I was named one of the regional managers, and at that time Mr. Shepard became general manager.

NICHOLS: Well, it sounds as if that previous move might have been motivated somewhat as a desire to develop people and perhaps give you a chance to take over a regional managership before you might otherwise have had a chance to.

BENNETT: Yes, I think that's right. At that time that move was the way we could open things up for further management development, and now we are sort of doing it the other way around. Everybody knows that the arrangement we are now proposing may well be changed again in a few more years.

We like to change the organization around a little bit like this from time to time just to let people know that we are not going to be static about things. Of course, we want to do it in a way so that some of our senior people do not get bypassed or jumped over by some of the younger ones because that not only bothers the individual but it also hurts morale further down in the organization. You see, when some of the people further down see some of that sort of thing happening, they are apt to conclude that it might happen to them some day, and it's pretty discouraging to them. The way we are doing it now we can bring up some younger people without jumping over anybody's head who is senior.

I think an organization change of this kind is also useful in that it indicates to some of our younger people that they need not feel discouraged if they are in a position where someone is above them in line who shows no signs of being promoted on up. This situation might make a person feel that he is being blocked from future promotion by his boss. But he is encouraged when he sees an occasional organizational shift of this kind because it makes him realize that things can happen in the future that might shift the organization around to a point where he can be sprung loose for a move on up even though his boss may not be promotable.

NICHOLS: Then I take it that one of the predominant thoughts in this whole reorganization was one of management development?

BENNETT: Oh, that's certainly true. That was one of the prime reasons we're proposing this, because we think it will help us develop our managers and this gives us a way of doing it without upsetting the organization too much.

That afternoon Mr. Bennett kept the appointment with Mr. Weld that was mentioned in the conversation above. Upon entering Mr. Weld's office, Mr. Bennett handed Mr. Weld a copy of the revised sales organization chart.

BENNETT: Here's the final version of our reorganizational plans. Do you think it is all right to go ahead on this?

5. THE YOKER COMPANY

Part 1[1]

THE YOKER COMPANY was a small, family-owned company located in a large Spanish city, engaged in the manufacture and installation of central heating systems for private houses or institutional buildings. The company had been in the same business for thirty years.

Company headquarters were located in a two-story building. The manufacturing shop was on the first floor. Seventeen semiskilled and four skilled workers, supervised by a foreman, prepared all the boilers and radiators needed for installations. On the second floor, three clerks, one accountant, and a draftsman handled all the administrative work. The company had two salesmen. Four highly skilled workers were in charge of installation work.

The company was managed by a former draftsman who had been with the company for twenty-five years. Mr. Yoker, the owner, was occupied with his interests in other companies and did not have time to spend in this organization.

The manufacturing process of building boilers and radiators was very simple. Workers had been doing the job for years and knew all the problems related to it. The major operation in building a traditional boiler was to put together several steel plates, which were, in general, prepared by outside concerns. Some of the plates had to be modified before assembly, but on the whole the job did not require much skill. As contrasted to other companies in the boiler industry, the Yoker Company manufactured a line of "traditional design" boilers, and, therefore, the skill requirements in this shop were relatively low. Because of the simplicity of design, employees of the Yoker Company did not have the skills required for employment with most other companies in the industry.

Production had been stable for many years. The customers of the company were mainly schools, institutions, and religious orders. The company was well known among them, and little sales effort was needed.

Workers in the shop had been working together for a long time. All

---

of them were almost the same age and had similar regional origins. The differences in skills were minimal, and wages were almost identical. Even the foreman was considered as another worker. Workers felt that the work was dull and monotonous, but steady.

The base wage earned by these workers was 10 per cent lower than wages paid by other companies in the industry. However, constant availability of overtime work made it possible for them to earn an additional 30 per cent. The shop had been working overtime consistently for the past four years, even though at times sales did not require it. (In the country in which the Yoker Company was located, it was illegal to fire or lay off employees. Thus, most managements paid low base wages, kept employment to a minimum, and manipulated overtime in conformity with fluctuations in sales.) A further source of income was available for these workers in maintenance work performed on boilers sold by the Yoker Company to large institutions. The company had no formal responsibility for maintenance, but workers often privately engaged to perform such functions. This work added another 10 per cent to their wages, making the total above their base pay 40 per cent.

The manager scheduled the work of the shop. The workers considered the manager to be a good man who kept out of shop problems so long as they were able to meet the schedule. Workers liked this "independence." The foreman indicated they could keep their independence so long as they worked to management's expectations. Workers were very close to each other, a strong group having grown up among them. The main norms of the group were: (a) to produce on schedule; (b) to help each other. If a worker had to leave the shop before quitting time, others would do his job for him.

A change took place when Mr. Yoker retired from his other occupations. As he had a great deal of spare time, he decided to spend a few hours a day in his company. After some days of observation, he decided to introduce a new line of boilers with a different design and to increase the productivity of the workshop by introducing tighter controls on the workers.

Shortly thereafter a new control system was introduced by which every worker had to record the job done every day. Moreover, every worker had to sign in on arrival and sign out at the end of the working day.

Meanwhile, Mr. Yoker started working on the development of the new boiler. In essence, the new boiler operated on the same principles as the old ones, with the addition of an electric fan to accelerate the heating process. The calculation of the proper characteristics of the electric fan for each model of boiler required extensive experimentation with measurements of temperature, intensity, fan speeds, air volumes, etc. Two months later, the new boiler was in an experimental stage, and Mr. Yoker began the construction of experimental models. Mr. Yoker often discussed with the workers possible ideas which could be incorporated in the new models.

PREDICTIONS

THE YOKER COMPANY

PART 1

From what I know of the company's operation and the changes introduced by Mr. Yoker described in Part I, I would predict that:

a) Productivity of workers would be (high) (standard) (below standard). Explain the reasons for your prediction.

b) Workers would be (highly) (moderately) (dis-) satisfied with their job. Explain why.

c) Relations between Mr. Yoker and the workers would be (cordial) (neutral) (strained). Explain why.

THE YOKER COMPANY

Part 2

FOLLOWING the introduction of the new working regulations—job cards, signing in and out, and generally tighter controls on shop activity—production began to decrease rapidly. Workers would often purposely delay an assembly, pretending ignorance of what was to be done next. Although more accurate records of time spent on each job were now available, the level of productivity had dropped significantly.

As time went on, Mr. Yoker often consulted the workers for their ideas, and gradually workers became interested in the new process. The level of skill required in manufacturing went up, and soon the fans were being manufactured in the shop. This was a major jump in the complexity of work performed by the "semiskilled" workers. The electric motors to drive the fans, and some ball bearings were purchased outside, but the delicate assembly and fitting and finishing of the fan assembly were done in the shop.

Productivity started to go up again. The foreman commented that the workers were very proud to be performing such difficult and interesting tasks.

Gradually, the procedures of checking in and out were removed, although the job cards for work done by each operator were still in use. Worker morale seemed to be quite high.

POSTPREDICTION ANALYSIS

Refer to your predictions at the end of Part 1. How closely do they match the information above? Do inaccuracies in your predictions reflect inadequate analysis? If so, explain the analytical failure. If not, what additional information would you have needed in Part 1 to improve your predictive accuracy and how would you have used that information?

6. TIDEWATER MANUFACTURING COMPANY

Part 1[1]

TIDEWATER MANUFACTURING COMPANY was a work-clothing factory owned entirely by the G. C. Carter Company, a large well-established firm having several other diverse subsidiaries. It was located in the same southern city as Carter Company, in an old two-story, brick structure on a residential street in a once proud but presently decaying neighborhood. Tidewater had begun operations during the Great Depression. Its equipment, mode of operation, and product patterns had remained largely unchanged since its founding.

Manufacturing operations were divided between the factory's two floors. The back half of the first floor (the front was occupied by a grocery store) was used for the storage of uncut material, flat shirt boxes, miscellaneous supplies, and finished goods. Here, also, the material was cut to pattern by the cutter and his helper. The latter tied the various cut pieces into bundles and hauled them upstairs on a dumb-waiter. The female employees of Tidewater, referred to as the "Ladies," sewed the pieces into shirts and trousers upstairs.

The Ladies worked in difficult surroundings. The air was choked with cloth dust and the otherwise unoccupied areas of the worn wooden floors were covered with bundles and bundle bands. In the winter, two gas burners kept the room comfortably warm, but the room temperature frequently went over $100°$ F. in the summer.

The work layout of the second floor is shown in Exhibit 1. On the four long tables were mounted about eighty belt-driven sewing machines. Most of the machines had been modified to perform specific operations and were set up with special attachments and permanent jigs. At her regular position on a line, a Lady normally performed only one of the twenty or so operations in the sewing of a shirt or pair of trousers. To start work, she picked up a small bundle of pieces from the floor, say to the left on her chair, placed the bundle on the table to the left of her machine, restacking the bundle on the table to her right as she performed her operation on each piece. When she had finished a bundle,

---

[1] This is a prediction case. You should answer the questions at the end of Part 1 before continuing on to Part 2.

she retied it with a band of scrap cloth and tossed it to the floor near the chair of the next Lady.

There were few personnel transfers between tables, although occasionally a Lady would catch up with the preceding operator, and either offer to help the operators next to her, or, if they refused to "divide stacks," she would move for a few minutes to any vacant position on her line. If there were no vacancies, she waited for the preceding operator to

Exhibit 1

TIDEWATER MANUFACTURING COMPANY
SEWING ROOM LAYOUT
(Second Floor)

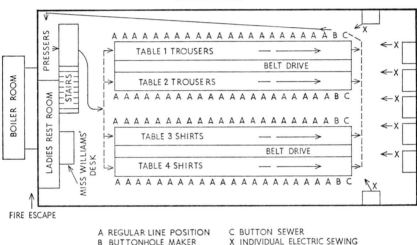

A REGULAR LINE POSITION   C BUTTON SEWER
B BUTTONHOLE MAKER   X INDIVIDUAL ELECTRIC SEWING
←— DIRECTION OF WORK FLOW   MACHINES FOR COLLARS,
                                 WAISTBANDS, CUFFS AND POCKETS

finish a bundle. Time was seldom lost because of productivity imbalances between Ladies.

However, although the overhead belt drive seldom failed, the old belt-driven machines broke down frequently. When a breakdown occurred, the Lady affected moved to any vacant position, regardless of line. Several machines often became inoperative simultaneously. When, as sometimes happened, there were more machines out of order than there were absences, vacancies were filled in descending order of seniority. Those without a work station performed menial tasks at the legal minimum wage rate.

Seven of the more senior Ladies made collars, waistbands, cuffs, and pockets at very old electric sewing machines located along the walls. These seven Ladies and the buttonhole maker and button sewer, who sat at the last two positions of each line, were the most skilled, the fastest and the highest-pay-rated workers. Their fifteen positions were highly regarded and sought by the other operators.

The Ladies were paid on piecework count. Rates for each operation had been established soon after Tidewater initially commenced production by bargaining between the Ladies and management of the parent company. Some adjustments had been necessary in the beginning, but the present pattern was at least twenty years old. Proportionate changes in rates were made by the Carter management as the profits of a style changed.

Since the factory had no management of its own, the cutter and his helper worked independently, while the Ladies were supervised by Miss Williams, who was Tidewater's most senior employee. She sat near the head of the stairs where she could survey the work area and see anyone entering or leaving the room. In the morning she checked the timecards to see that everyone had punched in; if anyone had not, she determined why and made a note in her daily diary. She then commenced her job of inspecting, repairing, and counting finished goods before they were pressed. (The pressers boxed the shirts and bundled the trousers.)

She also entered in the diary her count of finished garments by stock number and then itemized the day's production by operation for each employee. Since it was not practical for Miss Williams to count the individual operations performed, she accepted the tally each Lady made of the number of bundles she had completed during the day. The forelady's pay was based on the total number of garments produced. There had never been enough discrepancy between reports and actual total production to warrant questioning the adequacy of the accounting system.

Miss Williams signaled the Ladies when to take their two fifteen-minute breaks and half-hour lunch period by ringing a bell. The Ladies were not allowed to chat during "work-time." Infraction of this rule was tantamount to dismissal. The Ladies accepted this dictum as a rule for their own safety. Miss Williams had once talked to the operator next to her while sewing buttonholes. After ten years, she still displayed the semblance of a buttonhole in her right thumb. Her accident caused the rule to be established.

However, the Ladies did not heed Miss Williams' pleas to keep the workroom neat, except on Friday. During the week, the sewing area was cluttered with bundles, parts of bundles, and bands. The Ladies refused to clean up. They explained, "We get paid for what we sew, not what we sweep." However, they worked together on their Friday afternoon break to put the room in order.

The Ladies ranged in age from the middle thirties to the late fifties. They were either married or widowed. The married Ladies contributed significantly to their family's income, their husbands being low-paid workers in the nearby shipyards or docks. Although few of them had finished high school, they frequently expressed the desire to have their children graduate from high school and even college. Most of the Ladies had worked for Tidewater for five to twenty years. There were no dominant religious or ethnic affiliations in the group. However, all were Caucasian.

The Ladies walked to work in small groups whose composition was largely determined geographically. They did not associate much in other ways, however, devoting most of their nonwork time to their families.

The president of Carter's, Mr. G. C. Carter, and the general manager, Mr. T. O. Cartwright, visited the factory every Friday, bringing the weekly pay envelopes for the forelady to distribute. The two men inspected the premises while the Ladies worked, but they did not talk to the Ladies at that time. After the inspection tour, the men discussed with Miss Williams any sewing room problems that may have existed. Mr. Cartwright posted the current area production and pay rates for clothing workers on the bulletin board with any other information concerning other local clothing factories. The two men next went downstairs to talk with the cutter and his helper.

Mr. Carter, who was very elderly, then seated himself to wait for the Ladies to come downstairs on their way home. As they left, he exchanged pleasantries with each one and listened with courteous attention to her complaints and suggestions. The Ladies complained most about the temperature of the room, the limited restroom facilities, and the mechanical faults of the old sewing machines. They expressed great interest in the productivity and pay rates that Mr. Cartwright posted, although they were not interested in general trade news.

Since the end of World War II, many of Tidewater's local competitors had replaced their old equipment with fast, electric sewing machines. Tidewater had steadfastly retained its old equipment. However, in 1950, Carter management became increasingly aware that frequent machine breakdowns were rapidly reducing the profitability of Tidewater's operations and the company's ability to compete on price. Machine breakdowns tended to imbalance a line, form a bottleneck, reduce productivity, and frustrate the Ladies. Furthermore, in the "line" method, the Ladies spent a relatively large portion of their time tying and untying small bundles and in changing operations. Historically, the Ladies had produced more and had consequently earned more than the area average. However, the growing number of machine breakdowns was reducing their output and earnings.

Tidewater had always carried a large material inventory. Cloth was purchased whenever market prices were low, regardless of immediate needs. But, feeling that the straight line lent itself to short runs, the parent company carried a relatively small inventory of finished goods. Production delays had been occurring so often in recent years, however, that Carter's was frequently out of sizes and was forced to delay portions of customers' orders. Customers had begun to complain about Carter's degenerating service. They also complained that the Tidewater line was out of style and was becoming hard to sell.

In 1950, to respond to these complaints, Carter management commissioned an agent to buy and lease eighty secondhand electric sewing machines. They used these two methods of procurement to minimize investment and allow for expansion or contraction of Tidewater's machine capacity. They knew the Ladies would need some time to become accustomed to different machines, but believed that over-all productivity would improve in time. They did not know what proficiency the Ladies would ultimately achieve, however. Each electric machine was mounted on a table of its own, which would accommodate larger bundles than those presently in use, thus making possible a reduction in the time spent in tying and untying. The newer machines were expected to have fewer breakdowns. They were to be delivered in June, 1950.

As a second step in reducing customer dissatisfaction, Carter commissioned a prominent firm to design and deliver a set of new patterns by July 1, 1950. After much informal discussion among those at Carter's who dealt with the factory, it was decided that newer machines and patterns were all that was needed to restore Tidewater's former high level of production and profits.

During the first two week ends in June, overhead electric outlets were installed. In late June, the agent commissioned to procure the machines notified Carter's that he was ready to deliver. After the Ladies had gone home on Friday, a junk dealer's crew and men from Carter's removed the old machines, tables, and belt-driven mechanisms. On Saturday the new machines were delivered.

PREDICTIONS

TIDEWATER MANUFACTURING COMPANY

PART 1

From what I know of the company's operation and the change to be introduced by Mr. Carter described in Part 1, I would predict that:

a) Productivity of workers would be (high) (standard) (below standard). Explain the reasons for your predictions.

b) Workers would be (highly) (moderately) (dissatisfied) with their job. Explain why.

c) Relations between the workers and members of management would be (cordial) (neutral) (strained). Explain why.

TIDEWATER MANUFACTURING COMPANY

Part 2

WHEN THE LADIES returned to work on Monday, they were surprised by the extent of change wrought by the electric machine installation. The individual tables of the machines took up considerably more room than the four old tables had occupied. Sewing machines were crowded helter-skelter right to the stair landing.

No previous machine assignments had been made. Each Lady slowly chose her machine. Simultaneous choice of one machine by two or more Ladies was settled by coin-tossing. The Ladies made a few attempts to move the machines into straight-line order. However, it quickly became obvious that there was not enough room to maneuver the machines, so most were left where they had been initially placed.

Soon the Ladies began to search for the unfinished bundles they had been working on on Friday. Finished goods, bundles of pieces, and loose pieces had been mixed together during the move. Disagreements among several Ladies over partially finished bundles were settled by the Ladies sharing similar bundles equally.

When the Ladies commenced sewing, they found that the machines not only sewed much faster than the belt-driven ones but also responded much more quickly to the foot control pedals. Moreover, most of the machines were multipurpose and did not have the special sewing attachments and jigs which had previously aided the Ladies in sewing accurately. As a result, they made numerous mistakes which had to be ripped out and sewn over.

Within a week after the arrival of the electric machines, pieces cut to the new patterns also reached the Ladies. These pieces had more curved edges and required more darts[2] than similar pieces cut to the old patterns. These changes made sewing more tedious for the Ladies.

Each Lady still performed one operation on a bundle. However, some Ladies were catching on to the new machines faster than others and were continually running out of work. Because the machines were placed randomly to accommodate their individual tables, few Ladies sat side by

---

[2] A dart is a means of tapering the shape of a garment at a place which cannot be shaped economically by altering the pattern. It requires careful folding and sewing of a long triangle perpendicularly to the edge of the piece of cloth.

side. This seating arrangement made "dividing stacks" impractical. In order to obtain more work after she had run out, an adept worker had to move bundles or change positions; most Ladies preferred to move to vacant machines. The pattern of vacant positions was changing daily because of an abnormally large number of absences. Consequently, some Ladies frequently moved from one "line" to another. These moves often disrupted the bundle-passing sequences of the lines which were complicated by the randomly positioned machines.

The Korean war, which began in June, 1950, caused the demand for Tidewater's products nearly to double. Part of this demand surge was created by the award of a small government contract for naval officers' uniforms. For the first time, some of the Ladies were requested to work overtime in order to meet production schedules. Since the Ladies prepared evening meals for their families, they consented to work overtime grudgingly.

The scheduling clerk, Mr. B. W. Otis, a young, inexperienced Carter employee, began scheduling very short runs to supply the parent company with sizes that were sold out. He also visited the factory often to urge the Ladies to work faster. The Ladies responded to his efforts by cursing and sticking out their tongues.

Government inspectors also visited the factory sporadically to check the quality of the naval uniforms. The Ladies complained to Mr. Carter that the inspectors were "old maids and snoops."

Carter management was concerned that productivity had dropped about 15 per cent below that anticipated and showed little signs of improving. They also recognized the growing dissatisfaction of the Ladies. They felt that some changes would have to be made.

POSTPREDICTION ANALYSIS

Refer to your predictions at the end of Part 1. How closely do they match the information above? Do inaccuracies in your predictions reflect inadequate analysis? If so, explain the analytical failure. If not, what additional information would you have needed in Part 1 to improve your predictive accuracy and how would you have used that information?

TIDEWATER MANUFACTURING COMPANY

Part 3

THE CARTER COMPANY management took three steps to increase the productivity and morale of the Ladies. First, the scheduling clerk was authorized to increase the size of each run so that the entire plant would work on the same style for as much as a few weeks at a time. This change would enable most of the Ladies to repeat the same operation for several days. They had been changing operations every few hours under the short-run conditions. Through this repetition, Carter management believed that the Ladies would gain proficiency and confidence in the electric machines and, thus, would increase their productivity.

Secondly, Mr. Otis instructed the cutter's helper to tie similar pieces together in large bundles so that the Ladies would need to do less tying and untying.

Finally, Mr. Carter, Mr. Cartwright, and Mr. Otis—the three men concerned with Tidewater's problems—reduced the number of visits they had been making to the factory since the electric machines were installed. They believed their frequent presence distracted the Ladies and made some of them nervous. Therefore, Mr. Carter and Mr. Cartwright began visiting each Friday as before, and Mr. Otis was on hand only at the start of each run.

PREDICTIONS

TIDEWATER MANUFACTURING COMPANY

PART 3

From what I know of the company's operation and the change to be introduced by Mr. Carter described in Part 3, I would predict that:

a) Productivity of workers would be (high) (standard) (below standard). Explain the reasons for your predictions.

b) Workers would be (highly) (moderately) (dissatisfied) with their job. Explain why.

c) Relations between the workers and members of management would be (cordial) (neutral) (strained). Explain why.

TIDEWATER MANUFACTURING COMPANY

Part 4

THE SHIFT to longer production runs at Tidewater Manufacturing Company caused the Carter Company to "back order" a large amount of work clothing initially, but the demand stemming from the Korean war was so large that very few sales were lost. Longer runs did permit the Ladies to gain familiarity with the machine capabilities and, hence, to work faster at their operations. Soon absences dropped to the "pre-electric" level.

In order to provide a sufficient number of pieces for the longer-run orders, the cutter and his helper began cutting stacks having many more layers of cloth. They found this method of cutting saved a great deal of time and, thus, enabled them to keep farther ahead of the Ladies.

With most of them working at a fairly uniform rate and with the larger backlog of bundles, the Ladies ran out of work less often. However, the number of vacant positions decreased with decreasing absences; so on those fewer occasions when a Lady caught up, she had little choice but to go on to another operation on the stack she had just finished. The Ladies soon found that they could perform up to five operations on a bundle without seriously disrupting a bundle-passing sequence.

By the end of 1950, the Ladies had mastered the electric machines and were meeting all production schedules without overtime. During the summer of 1951, Carter management decided not to hire replacements and to return borrowed or leased machines as Ladies left Tidewater. In this way they hoped to balance the increasing productivity with an anticipated return of the working demand to normal levels.

In June, 1952, there were fewer than fifty Ladies at Tidewater. They performed from one to five operations on their bundles. However, they now stacked bundles around their chairs, as well as on their individual tables, and moved finished bundles only once or twice a week. The new work flow was called a "bundle system."

Although fewer than fifty machines remained, floor space was still limited. The ever-increasing lot sizes resulted in more and more bundles being stacked around the operators' chairs. The machines had been moved until they were located more according to their size and shape than according to their part in the sewing process. However, machines of the same type tended to be grouped together.

The Ladies' new complaint concerned the sequence in which goods were scheduled. The Ladies could sew chambray and drill items very rapidly, but denim and heavy twill goods slowed them down. More important from the Ladies' point of view was that changing from very heavy to light material, or vice versa, necessitated changing machine needles and tension adjustments. Moreover, heavy material sometimes caused needles to break. Yet, Mr. Otis scheduled lots without regard to the weight of the material but according to the parent company's needs. The Ladies said that if he had to work as hard as they did, he would be more considerate. They also said that he should visit the factory more often so that he could see how much trouble he caused.

Mr. Carter and Mr. Cartwright continued to visit the factory on Friday afternoons. The general manager also continued to post the current production and pay rates for clothing workers in the area on the bulletin board.

The Ladies were still interested in the productivity and pay rates of other clothing factories, but they were particularly proud of their own productivity, which was now 150 to 175 per cent of the local average. Frequently, informal competitions got started among the operators with the loser buying soft drinks for the winner. The Ladies were also pleased with their take-home pay, which was again considerably more than the local average.

The management of the parent company was pleased with the profits the factory yielded. The work-clothing business was extremely competitive, and many factories had closed in recent years. Some of the financially stronger factories had replaced post-World War II machines with ultrahigh-speed ones in order to increase productivity sufficiently to lower their prices to meet renewed foreign competition. Despite Tidewater's older equipment, its high-quality workmanship and moderate prices had built a stable consumer demand in the surrounding area.

POSTPREDICTION ANALYSIS

Refer to your predictions at the end of Part 3. How closely do they match the information above? Do inaccuracies in your predictions reflect inadequate analysis? If so, explain the analytical failure. If not, what additional information would you have needed in Part 3 to improve your predictive accuracy and how would you have used that information?

7. RANDLEY STORES, INC. (A)*

Part 1

RANDLEY STORES, Inc., was in 1957 an expanding chain of over seventy-five supermarket stores in and around a large eastern metropolitan area. Although a few older and smaller grocery stores remained in the chain, most stores were large and modern with complete grocery, meat, and produce departments. Since the early 1950's the company had been building six to ten stores a year, many in new suburban shopping centers.

In 1954 and 1955, Randley top management had concluded that the chain should be decentralized. Formerly, each store had three separate departmental managers, each of whom was closely supervised by a different headquarters representative. Final decisions as to new equipment, merchandise displays, promotions, demotions, hiring and discharge of permanent employees, etc., were made almost entirely by these representatives. Management agreed that this kind of centralization had been adequate during the early stages of the organization. New stores, however, were being built, (a) further and further away from headquarters, (b) to handle a much larger variety of merchandise, and (c) for minimum volumes of $2,000,000 a year.

Because of these factors, management, in the spring of 1956, announced an organizational change that would create a new position in the stores, that of store manager.

These men were to be picked from among the ranks, given a two-month training program in which they were to spend time in each of the three departments in a variety of stores, and placed in new stores as they were built. It was the hope of top management, although fully aware that it would not be easy, to begin then to shift a substantial amount of responsibility from headquarters to the store level. Moreover, management thought the change should introduce a unity into the store personnel, who had hitherto kept to their own departments, thereby adding to the payroll expense of the stores by not moving tem-

* This case was produced as a by-product of a research study that is more fully reported in Paul R. Lawrence, *The Changing of Organizational Behavior Patterns* (Boston: Division of Research, Harvard Business School, 1958).

porarily to a department needing assistance for a brief time. In general, in the words of one executive: "We want some day to have real administrators running our stores, not just errand boys."

Some six months after the change was announced, a researcher from the Harvard Business School asked to observe some of the store situations in which these organizational shifts were occurring.

After only a short period, it became clear to the researcher that he could easily observe the ways individuals were responding to the change by watching the interactions between district managers and store managers and the way in which district managers talked about these interactions. (See Exhibit 1 for a chart of the formal relationships.) The

Exhibit 1

RANDLEY STORES, INC. (A)

PARTIAL ORGANIZATIONAL CHART, AFTER REORGANIZATION IN 1956

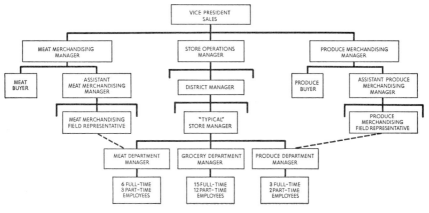

Source: Researcher's reconstruction.

store manager was being asked to assume more over-all administrative authority in his stores; and it was the district manager's job, according to the formal organizational change, to see to it that the store managers eventually behaved according to the new organizational expectations.

This case, then, focuses on two district managers—DM1 and DM2—as they talked with their subordinates and as they talked with the researcher. For purposes of comparison the two district managers picked were those closest together in certain external respects. Both were long-service employees of the company. They were in their fifties. They had for some time been the district managers of two of the largest and most important districts in the company. They had grown accustomed through the years to performing their duty in a way that was compatible with the traditional organizational patterns. Each had a reputation in the business as an expert in the field. Both were regarded by top management as high in quality of task performance.

Part 2 of this case includes selections from conversations the district managers had with the researcher, in which they talked about their beliefs about themselves and their behavior in the organization, and about their attitudes toward subordinates, superiors, and the reorganization. Part 3 includes excerpts from conversations these men had with various store managers in their respective districts. In addition, it includes comments that two store managers made to the researcher about the district managers. Part 4 shows some quantitative data the researcher collected on the kinds of things these men discussed with their store managers and the ways in which they discussed them.

RANDLEY STORES, INC. (A)

Part 2

THE RESEARCHER talked with and observed the district managers over a period of several weeks and in a variety of contexts. The following statements were culled from these conversations and classified under "statements indicating a district manager's beliefs about himself as a district manager," "statements indicating a district manager's attitude toward subordinates," "statements indicating a district manager's attitude toward superiors," and, finally, "statements indicating a district manager's attitude toward the reorganization."

District Manager 1: Beliefs about Himself as a District Manager

One thing I've done lately is stop worrying about being fired. It happened mostly last summer when I was sick. I had a lot of time to think. I decided that it wasn't worth while worrying about things like that, and that I might as well go ahead and do what I was going to do and stop worrying about it. I also decided I was going to speak up more when I disagreed about something. So, I go ahead and say what I want to say, and I'm perfectly willing to take what follows. I don't think I'm going to get fired because, actually, I think I'm doing a pretty good job as a district manager. . . .

I'm the sort of person who is pretty critical of himself; and so, when I think I'm doing reasonably well, that must mean that my bosses think I'm doing pretty well. . . .

I don't think any of us should be too proud to use the good ideas that somebody else has. . . .

The important thing is to teach yourself the new tricks first, and then you might have a chance to teach someone else. . . .

I've always been known as a maverick in this organization.

DM1: Attitudes toward Subordinates

My notion of a good supervisor is one who doesn't talk any more than his subordinates do. Of course, you've got to do some of the talking to explain to them the kinds of things they ought to know about what the company wants them to do; but you have also got to give them plenty of chance to talk about their problems and the things they have on their minds, or you are not going to get very far. . . .

873

I'm interested in my store managers' opinions; and of course, I want them to know what mine are. . . .

I won't do the same thing every time I go into a store; if I did, I would blow my brains out after a while because this job would be so dull. Of course, I don't do things the way I used to a few years ago. Even in the stores without store managers, I've been letting the department managers handle more matters, like working out displays, than I used to, more than I imagine some of the other district managers do. Besides, how the hell am I going to develop my men if I don't let them do things like that? . . .

I believe that if a store manager can come up with his own answer to a problem, it is going to be the best answer in almost every case. It may not agree exactly with the way I would do it; but unless he is really wrong, you ought to go ahead and let him do it in his own way, and he'll be better off. That is the only way you can teach him to take the initiative on these matters. . . .

I believe in giving my men suggestions instead of giving them hell! . . .

He's a very good meat manager, but you have to be kind of careful how you talk to him because he is apt to take criticism in a rather childish way. He's likely to get sensitive and feel hurt if you criticize the way he runs his counter. That is why I step to one side to speak to him about his dirty floor. I've learned to handle him all right, and he does a very good job. . . .

You know, you can't expect perfection out of people, and different people work differently. They can't all be as fast as some. . . .

As far as I'm concerned, the number one part of a store manager's job is that he has to have administrative ability. He's got to get people to do the job—that is the best definition of administration I know of. . . .

I let the store manager know where he stands. At regular times, I sit down with the fellow, and we work out a written report evaluating his performance and trying to improve it. It is done with the man right there because it isn't going to do him any good if we just file a report in the head office. Sometimes, these sessions are pretty frank and a little tough on the fellow; but as far as I am concerned, he has to know his shortcomings and straighten them out.

DM1: Attitudes toward Superiors

The people who run this business make some mistakes, but they are really decent people. I don't hesitate to disagree with (the vice president of sales) on something or other, and you can really discuss things with him. He's hard-working, too. Of course, after we have discussed things, he has to decide what he is going to do; and if he says we are going to do something, I'll do the best I can to make it work. . . .

A couple of things came up recently that I think the district managers should have been consulted on by top managers. On one item, I was so upset I got hold of my boss on the spot. It was a matter that affected the people in our stores, and the district managers should have been consulted before the decision was made. We are closer to the situation; and I think, actually, most of the top men would be glad to get our opinion. They just didn't bother to ask us. . . .

This is a very friendly company, and I don't know anyone in the company who is afraid to speak up to anybody else. It has always been like that since I can remember, and I think it stems largely from the top. . . .

It is the same as in any organization you get into; there is always a certain amount of politics in it, and you have to expect that. . . .

I worked for (Mr. Z) for many years, and I never did agree with his ideas about how to run things. I always did things somewhat differently then he would have. We grew to respect each other in spite of that.

DM1: Attitudes toward Reorganization

The store manager is my representative in the stores. . . .

This store manager program is still pretty new . . . , but I think it is already showing that it is paying for itself. We can add the store manager's salary to our store payroll and still have a better over-all performance in that store. He can give us a lot of valuable supervision there. . . .

I have to keep watching myself in working consistently through the store manager. Every once in a while, I slip back into the habit of speaking to whoever happens to be handy when I see something I don't like, but you really lose the effectiveness of what you are trying to do if you do that. Sometimes, I have to remind other people, too, that come into the store, to deal with the store manager.

District Manager 2: Beliefs about Himself as a District Manager

(Mr. X) is the best store manager in the whole chain. I never saw a guy who is so much like me in the way he acts in a store. He sometimes is tough on the people, but he really gets the work done. For my money, he is the best. . . .

I like a supervisor who is really the boss, really running things, a take-charge guy. . . .

I was the one who started the first big self-service store in the chain. In that store, we started a great many of the ideas that have since come into common use in the company. . . .

I think the first thing you are here for is to make some money for the company. In order to do that, you have to go out and get a volume of business. You've got to be selling things, and selling them in a way that doesn't run your costs up too much. To do that, you have to keep your shelves filled up with good merchandise, properly presented. These are the fundamentals. If you do those things right, it will show up in the figures. . . .

I'm getting paid to have good merchandising ideas. Anybody who is a district manager has to be interested in merchandise and selling merchandise; and in doing this, you have to work with people to get them to understand this stuff so they can do it themselves. . . .

I never give the store one figure on sales projections and the office another. The reason is that I simply can't lie. That is my biggest weakness. I'm not a diplomat. If I've got something on my mind, I just spill it. I can't fight it. When I get something on my mind, I want to get it done today and not put it off. I suppose I carry that to such an extent that it is a fault of mine. . . .

We've got too much heart in this company. We're just not business-like.

DM2: Attitudes toward Subordinates

You really have to train store managers to look after those details, and I have to follow up to make sure it is done. You see, I've written out complete notes about everything I talked to this store manager about today, so there is no excuse for his not doing something about these matters. Then I'll check these notes with him when I come back. You have to spend a lot of time with some of these fellows, explaining these things to them. . . .

I find, in my own experience, that I can work much better with the people under me who've learned to accept my criticisms, even welcome them, instead of those who seem to be fighting them. . . .

(To store department heads.) I want each of you fellows to know that the store manager is constantly getting demands from above on how to do things. When he comes to you with something, it is not just personal; he is getting orders from the district people to do things, and he has to follow through on them. . . .

You saw that I had to go down and go all over with that store manager again what I want done on the drug counter. Now, I've done all that before, and I've gone into all those details before. He told me once before it couldn't work out there, and I showed him how to make it work; and then, today, we have to go right back through the whole thing all over again. Now, that is not the way you should have to treat the manager. I shouldn't have to spell things out that way for him. If I had (Store Manager X) here, I would just say to him: "Put the drug counter up there," and that would have been the end of it. It would have been done. Now, that is my idea of a good store manager.

DM2: Attitudes toward Superiors

I may argue about something ahead of time; but once the decision is made, right or wrong, I will carry it out. . . .

This is the first time I've found out what this new system is all about. Can you imagine that! They ought to tell us about these things if people are going to come in and put them into our store.

I used to be pretty outspoken, and that was part of the thing that got me in trouble. I was known as the great dissenter, but I've stopped all of that now. . . .

In this business, you can't do anything right. It gets you, one way or the other. . . .

People at headquarters always accuse me of not being patient enough to work out the problems that come along with new changes in the organization. I don't think they practice what they preach. . . .

No one in the front office is much interested in my opinions.

DM2: Attitudes toward Reorganization

I'm one of the few people who doesn't like this new setup. I thought the old way was much better. I had a team with my two assistant district managers operating in my territory that you just couldn't beat. . . .

I'm one of the few guys in the business who thinks this whole inventory control theory simply won't work. . . .

I'm perfectly willing to live with the way things are. You sort of have to learn to do that, you know. I wasn't too happy when this country was being run by Democratic presidents, but I lived through it, and there is something to be said for the things they did. It is the same way in this company. They have some reasons for what they are doing. I just don't happen to think it is right, but I'm perfectly willing to live with it.

RANDLEY STORES, INC. (A)

Part 3

THE RESEARCHER observed a number of interactions between the two district managers and some of their store managers. A few of these interactions are presented in Part 3 so that a comparison can be made between this aspect of the district managers' behavior with the other data in this case.

District Manager 1

DISTRICT MANAGER 1: Do you want to place an order for some new display steps with a formica top? Here is the story on them, and this is what it would cost you to order them.

STORE MANAGER: Let's see what that would figure out to be. It sounds like it would run to $400 or $500.

DM1: Well, how many two- or three-tier displays do you have now?

SM: I've got three of the three-tier and two of the two-tier; so you see, it would be a lot of money. I can't see spending that much.

DM1: That is what I feel, too; that is an awful lot of money. You've got to sell a lot of merchandise to make $500. O.K., so much for that. Have you figured out how much the wage rate changes are going to affect your weekly payroll?

SM: I don't think it is going to be very much.

DM1: Well, I think you had better figure it out. You don't realize how much it is going to be. It turns out to be more in some of these stores than they think. It can easily be $100 a week.

SM: I don't think so. Last week, we had a man out, but we also had some overtime; and you see, the figures didn't go up at all. I think it ought to go up at the most about $50.

DM1: Well, maybe that's right. You may be that lucky, but I thought you might want to figure that out. Let's go on to something else.

. . . .

On one occasion, District Manager 1 and the store manager were having a discussion when the grocery department manager took the researcher aside and pointed out that as far as he was concerned, his store room was the nicest looking in the whole chain—the cleanest and the

878

one with the least inventory. He told the researcher that the inventory was down to less than two times weekly sales and that they were not on the new inventory control system that the company was slowly instituting "or anything else." He told the researcher: "It is all done by memory," and pointed to his forehead. When they rejoined the others, District Manager 1 was talking about inventory handling.

DM1: Well, I think you fellows have a point; but when our methods consultant sends in a report that we should mark merchandise when it goes on the selling floor and not in the basement, I've got to listen to him, even though that does require a whole new system, because I'm not a technician and I don't know about these things. My only point is—I say, let's not close our minds to this thing, because when a fellow like that comes up with a recommendation, I think we've got to consider it.

GROCERY MANAGER: What about the payroll in those stores? Is it the same?

DM1: Yes, it is. It doesn't cost any more the other way; as a matter of fact, it costs a little bit less, and they cut down the inventory.

SM: Well, our problem here is that our shipment from the headquarters warehouse comes in on Thursday. Everybody in the store is on the selling floor, waiting on customers, and you can't concentrate on the storage area. You simply couldn't handle a demand marking system here, because our part-timers come in on Thursday at 3:00 o'clock, and they are here for three hours. Well, if those fellows had to mark merchandise, they simply wouldn't be able to get in on the shelves by 6 o'clock; they just couldn't do it.

DM1: Well, I can certainly see that, and it is obvious that every store is not the same. But you fellows don't have the new shelf allocation system here; and when you do get that system, you can go through a whole week on all but a very few items by just putting them up once. That is all part of the new inventory control system that is going in. Your shelves won't look as good—I know that, I won't argue that fact. The shelves and your display counters and tables may look very poor, and I don't like it. But it will cost you a lot less to put out merchandise on Monday, Tuesday, and Wednesday than on Thursday, Friday, and Saturday, when your whole selling area is packed with people. I think you are completely right, that when you don't have the shelf allocation system, you can't go to demand marking. You've certainly done a tremendous job in this store, and I have no complaint about it.

GM: Well, yes; it is all guesswork, though.

DM1: That is right. We've found, in the other stores, that you can cut your labor 'way down if you're on the shelf allocation system, no matter how good guesses you have made in the past about the kind of stuff you need and when you need it.

SM: Well, when they put us over on that shelf system, I'll consider it.

DM1: Well, you're right. I think that is the time to consider it. You have certainly done a hell of a job here, and I think it is tremendous.

GM: Well, it's not just me; it's guys here like Bobbie (*points to a young fellow who is opening a carton*).

District Manager 2

A researcher and District Manager 2 entered a store one day, when the latter walked immediately up to the store manager.

DM2: Boy, it is hot in here! What's going on?

SM: Yeah; sure, it is hot. I just went down and turned off the heating system.

DM2: It certainly is too hot. Just what are you doing about it?

SM: Well, this happened once before, and it got too hot. You see, the thermostat is hooked up so it is tied in with the outside weather, and it works that way. There was something that didn't work right about it, so I got the repair people out here to look it over, and they said they got it all fixed.

DM2: What are you doing about it now?

SM: Well, I turned the heat off, and I called the office.

DM2: Can you adjust the thermostat you've got?

SM: No, it is all locked up. You've got to get the maintenance people out here, and they are coming out.

DM2: Boy, it's just too hot in here; it's too hot.

SM: For Christ's sake, of course it is too hot. What do you think I've got my coat off for? Even in my shirt, it is too hot.

DM2: Well, what can I do for you on this thing? Can I give you any help until you get it squared away?

SM: No, I don't think there is anything you can do. We are doing what we can. I've got the heat turned off now, so it should cool off.

.   .   .   .

On one occasion the researcher observed the opening day of a new store. During the morning the only interactions between District Manager 2 and his new store manager were as follows:

DM2: You'd better keep an eye on the front entrance where they are passing out carriages and keep the flow in and out going steadily.

The store manager nodded and for the next four hours remained at that task almost continuously.

At one point during the morning the opening surge fell off somewhat, and the store manager went out to the back room for a cup of coffee, where he met District Manager 2.

SM: Say we have some awfully slow people on the cash registers out there.

DM2:   I don't think so. Four out of your seven people are experienced, aren't they?

SM: Yes.

DM2:   Well, that's about as good as you can expect on an opening day with four good people in there.

SM: Well, yes, that is right.

.   .   .   .

District Manager 2 told another store manager once to get some merchandise out of the employees' lunchroom. When the store manager carried it out and set it in the hall, District Manager 2 then told him to take it down to the store office and put it there.

SM: Well, the trouble is, the office is too full to put it in.

DM2:   What have you got down there?

SM: Some cases of cash register tapes.

DM2:   Well, that shouldn't be. The thing for you to do is to move that tape out of there, and then you can put this merchandise down there.

SM: O.K.

After discussing some further points with this store manager, District Manager 2 continued:

DM2:   What I suggest for you to do is to get yourself a notebook, just like this one I carry, to keep notes on things I'm telling you—to write down now. Then you will have them in one place and be able to keep track of them. It is sort of a little date book. Well, I guess that's all I've got. Any questions?

SM: No.

.   .   .   .

The researcher talked to the various store managers who worked for District Managers 1 and 2. The following comments from two such store managers seemed particularly interesting.

SM (who worked for DM1):   Yes, I've really got a good deal here in this store, because I've got good boys, and we work together pretty well. . . . There are a lot of little things that go together to make a good store. . . . The district manager has to be on your side. He can't be doing things that will keep you from moving in as boss, but there's a lot more to it besides that. You've got to have good personalities in the store on a department head level and on the store manager level; and if your district manager is going to criticize somebody or pay somebody a compliment, he should have you along, and maybe he could mention it was the store manager's idea. So, if you get all these things working together, and they are really all just little things, you're going to have a good store.

. . . .

SM (who worked for DM2): You know, DM2 really goes by the book on things like special displays and does things the way the company wants, and that's the way they have to be done here. He really sticks by the book; and that's the way it should be because, of course, if you go by the book, you're going to keep out of trouble. Now, I know there are a lot of district managers who wink at stuff like that because they realize a fellow has a few cases of junk that he wants to move, and island wings are usually a good way to do it. I know that Charlie has a hell of a lot of stuff down there in the back room that he'd like to clean out; but gee, if I ever let him start putting up carriages of merchandise around the store, he'd have those carriages all over the place. You know, they don't stay in one place, either. You put a carriage down there by that drug table that has a few items on it, and you come back in a half hour and some damned little kid has pushed it 'way over there to the coke machine. And you just can't have stuff like that. Of course, it's the same sort of thing in any job. You have to figure out what kind of a fellow your boss is and play the game his way. You figure out how your boss wants it done, and that's how you do it.

RANDLEY STORES, INC. (A)

Part 4

THE RESEARCHER wished to check the feel he had concerning the differences he saw in the behavior of District Manager 1 and District Manager 2, as well as some of the similarities. Consequently, he designed a simple method of recording interactions he observed between the two district managers and their various store managers. In this way, he recorded who talked; the length of each separate speech; the category of speech (i.e., asking a question, supplying information, giving an opinion, giving directions or suggestions); the type of topic involved (discussion of people, merchandise, record systems, physical plant, and small talk); and finally, who initiated new topics.

As for the kinds of topics that were classified, such questions as: "Is Joe doing a good job?" "What would you think of transferring Mary?" "Is Bill still asking for more money?" "Why did you assign that work to John?" etc., were considered as "discussion of people." Under "mer-

Exhibit 2

DISTRICT MANAGER–STORE MANAGER INTERACTION ANAYLSIS, BY
CLASSIFICATION OF SPEECH AND TOPICS

Category	DM1	SM	DM2	SM
Average per cent of talking time....................	58	42	75	25
Average per cent of talking time asking questions........	9	4	9	2
Average per cent of talking time giving information.....	17	23	26	17
Average per cent of talking time giving opinions........	17	10	12	4
Average per cent of talking time giving suggestions/directions..	15	5	28	2
Average per cent of new topics initiated................	77	23	86	14
Average per cent of total talking time of both DM and SM spent on people....................................	48		11	
Average per cent of total talking time of both DM and SM spent on merchandise............................	16		32	
Average per cent of total talking time of both DM and SM, record systems.....................................	22		47	
Average per cent of total talking time of both DM and SM, physical plant.......................................	7		10	
Average per cent of total talking time of both DM and SM spent on small talk.................................	7		0.5	

chandise" fell communications about the amount, kind, handling, and explaining of merchandise. Under "record systems" came all discussions of payroll records, procedures for scheduling people, sales figures, etc. Under "physical plants" were included discussion of store maintenance, housekeeping, new equipment, etc. "Small talk" was all joking, "kidding," and talk not related to business.

The results are shown in Exhibit 2. In this exhibit the record of District Manager 1 covered 227 minutes, of which 157 minutes occurred during early days of the week and 70 minutes late in the week. There were 1,115 separate comments, recorded on nine separate store visits with three different store managers.

The record of District Manager 2 covered 456 minutes, of which 293 were early and 173 late in the week. The separate comments, numbering 2,092, were recorded on four separate store visits with three different store managers.

8. RANDLEY STORES, INC. (B)

RANDLEY STORES, Inc., was in 1957 an expanding chain of over seventy-five supermarkets in and around a large eastern metropolitan area. Almost all of these stores were large and modern, with complete grocery, meat, and produce departments. For a number of years the company had been building six to ten large stores a year, many in new suburban shopping centers.

In 1954 and 1955, Randley top management had concluded that the chain should be reorganized by decentralizing the direction of the stores. Formerly, each store had three separate departmental managers (for grocery, meat, and produce), each of whom was given direct and detailed supervision by a district manager or by his two assistant district managers (one for meat and one for produce). Final decisions as to new equipment, merchandise displays, promotions, demotions, work assignments, much of the merchandise ordering, etc., were made almost entirely by one of this team of three district supervisors. Each district manager and his assistants supervised about ten to twelve stores. This form of centralized supervision had been adequate in the past; but as new stores were added that were much larger, carried a greater variety of merchandise, and were further from headquarters, management became increasingly convinced that each store needed a well-trained, over-all store manager. Therefore, in the spring of 1956, management announced an organizational change that would create the position of store manager in each supermarket. It was the hope of top management, although fully aware it would not be easy, that a substantial amount of responsibility and decision making could be shifted from headquarters and district management to these men. In the words of one executive: "We want some day to have real administrators running our stores, not just errand boys."[1]

As one part of this reorganization, management decided to shift the assistant district managers (ADM's) from the line job of directly supervising the meat and produce departments for their line boss, the district manager, to a staff job as product merchandisers advising and consulting with the perishable department managers in the stores while

---

[1] See Randley Stores, Inc. (A) for a more complete description of the store manager aspects of the reorganization.

reporting to the merchandise managers of meat and produce at head-quarters. This shift in formal organization, job function, formal authority, title, and reporting superior affected a group of about eighteen men. The way the formal organization chart changed is indicated in Exhibit 1 (page 871).

Management was well aware that it would be difficult for these men to make an effective transition into their new organizational roles. Many of them were older, long-service employees. Furthermore, their new superiors, the merchandise managers, were senior company executives who would be accustomed to giving orders and pushing their subordinates to achieve a high sales volume and quick turnover on the perishable items. However, top management, and especially the vice president of sales (46, 24),[2] was convinced that this move was necessary to build up the proper role for the store manager without losing the merchandising know-how of the old assistant district managers. The store operations manager (38, 16) also stated that one of his big jobs with his district managers and store managers was getting them to work together with the product merchandisers in such a way as to develop the merchandising ability of the store managers as well as to insure good merchandising in the perishable departments.

> STORE OPERATIONS MANAGER: I want the product merchandiser to be a technical adviser to the store manager. And this is a two-way deal because the store manager is the product merchandiser's agent for follow-up of the merchandiser's ideas. What I'd like to see in the stores between these two groups is to have the merchandisers talk over their problems with the store managers. I'd like to have them kick around merchandising problems. Now, the product merchandiser might come into the store in the morning, look it over, talk with the store manager, and say: "It seems to me that this case should be set up a little earlier. I'm in here at 9:30, and there are a lot of people starting to shop, and the case isn't finished yet"; and he could say that he's discussed this with the men in the department, tell the store manager that he doesn't know quite what it takes in this particular store to get going earlier, but that this seems to him to be a useful thing to do. And he could either work this out with the store manager right there or keep him informed of it as he goes along. And this can be done; I'm sure it can.

Some six months after the organizational changes were announced, a researcher asked to observe some of the store situations in which these shifts were occurring. In making his observations, one of the topics that

---

[2] These numbers indicate the age and years of service with Randley Stores, Inc, for the individual involved.

interested the researcher was the evolving relationship between the men in the newly created positions of product merchandiser and store manager, as well as the others—such as store department managers, district managers, and merchandise managers—who were involved. As part of his work the researcher spent a considerable amount of time in a new store at Antioch just before and after its opening. The following series of events center around the produce department in the new store.

Around 12:30 P.M. on the day before the opening of the new store, the researcher saw the new manager of the store's produce department standing in front of his empty display tables. The researcher asked him when his people were going to start putting up the produce and how long it took to set up a stand of this size.

PRODUCE MANAGER (46, 11): Well, we're waiting for the bosses to come out and tell us how to do it. You know, the produce merchandise manager (55, 29) and his assistant (39, 20) have to set everything up on one of these openings. We're just waiting until they get here, and then we'll all go to work. It'll be up, though.

Three weeks later, around 8:00 in the morning, the researcher and the newly appointed store manager (48, 23) at Antioch were exchanging pleasantries when the store manager interrupted:

STORE MANAGER: Gee, the produce merchandisers were in yesterday. You should have been here. They really raised hell. Of course, I can't blame them too much because our men didn't use too good judgment in the fruit department. You know, you are supposed to alternate green vegetables with the yellow ones, then the red ones, and so on; and then, when they found out that they were backed up on lemons and limes— I guess they had about eight cases of lemons and three cases of limes— they really went through the roof. It's a funny thing about those guys, though. They never ask; they just start raising hell.

Around 8:20 the researcher noticed the produce department manager putting up his produce. In the back room the No. 2 man and No. 3 man in the fruit department were busily wrapping produce. Since the researcher had never met these men, he explained to them that he was interested in seeing how this store got set up and some of the problems of running a supermarket.

NO. 3: Talk about business problems—you just stick around here a little while, and you'll see plenty of problems (*laughs*).
NO. 2: Yeah, we've got problems around here. You should have been around here yesterday if you wanted to see some real problems.

RESEARCHER: What was that?

NO. 2:   Oh, some of the bosses landed on me in here. They were really working me over. My head was bobbing back and forth so fast that I didn't know what was going on.

RESEARCHER: What was the trouble?

NO. 2:   Well, a lot of things. They thought we weren't doing the job right. Principally, they were mad about the fact that we had some inventory piled up back here. I don't know what they think I'm supposed to do about this thing. They sent me in here to help out the produce manager, you know. He's an awfully nice guy, but he hasn't had much experience in these bigger stores. I'm supposed to be backing him up and helping him do this right. Well, what am I supposed to do? Do they expect me to squeal on my boss? I didn't fill out that order last week. About all I could do was take it.

RESEARCHER: Was this the assistant produce merchandise manager who was in here?

NO. 2:   Yeah, that's who it was—he and the produce merchandiser (44, 21) for the Antioch store. The assistant produce merchandise manager kept saying: "I'm not supposed to talk to you about these things, but . . . ," and then he'd let me have another one. And he kept saying: "I've worked in a store; I know you can do this." Well, he may have worked in a store, but I'm sure he's forgotten how hard it is to estimate what your sales are going to be just two weeks after you've opened a new store in a new town. How do we know just what's going to sell? Why, for the first two weeks around here, we couldn't get enough potatoes and onions to keep the shelves loaded up, they were selling so fast. So we ordered a good slug of them, and now we've got them backed up. This isn't a problem that is too serious. There is nothing in here that will spoil. We'll get it all unloaded by next Saturday. We just won't send in a big order this week, and we'll get it all out of the way. But they don't like that. They hate to see the inventory, so they jump on us for it. So you can see what we were up against. You stick around, and you'll see some more today. I think the produce merchandiser is going to be back.

RESEARCHER: How do you figure that?

NO. 2:   Well, he must have been catching it yesterday. So he's got to dish it out to somebody. I think he'll come in today. I tipped off the produce manager as soon as we got in today to expect him around. It was the produce manager's day off yesterday, and I had to catch it all.

About 9:40 the researcher saw the No. 2 man out in front having a cup of coffee.

NO. 2 (*in a whisper*):   You should have been around a few minutes ago. Things are already happening.

RESEARCHER: What's the story?

The No. 2 man put his finger up to his lips and walked on into the store. The researcher followed him and saw the produce merchandiser at the tables rearranging the fruit and vegetables. The produce department manager was following behind him. There was no talk going on. The produce merchandiser was rearranging all the produce on the display table. A second later the produce department manager walked up and started rearranging the same boxes, trying to line them up perhaps even a little neater. The produce merchandiser said nothing during the next ten minutes except at one point, when he said: "Tell your boys not to put these price tags on the baskets," and the produce department manager nodded.

The researcher walked up after a while and introduced himself to the produce merchandiser and told him a little bit about who he was.

RESEARCHER: Looks like you have some problems here.

PM: You leave this place alone for one day and everything goes to hell. (*He turns away after this comment.*)

Later, in a conversation with the store manager, the researcher learned that the store's district manager (DM2; 55, 33) had been in the store on the previous day at the same time as the assistant produce merchandise manager.

RESEARCHER: What did DM2 do when those head office guys were chewing out the fruit department?

SM: Oh, he agreed with them all along. I guess it did look pretty sloppy over there.

RESEARCHER: Well, then DM2 joined in with them. I thought the merchandisers were supposed to come to you if they had any problems and not raise hell with the men in the stores.

SM: Well, it all depends on the guy. It's different under each one of them. Each DM is different, too. Actually, you know, this was a pretty drastic change for these old ADM's. They've had complete charge of their own departments for twenty years. Now, this store manager program is a pretty big change, and I don't think they've gotten used to it yet. Also, I don't think they've gotten together with the DM's and ADM's and the store managers, off in some hotel room some place, and really spelled out to everybody how this new program is supposed to work, and particularly how these ADM's are supposed to behave in the store now that we have changed over to this program. It's a pretty big change for those guys to get used to, and it's not written down any place how we're all supposed to act under this new deal.

A lot of fellows told me, when I was on my training program, that the store managers are supposed to let go of that, but what are you going to do when these guys come in and start raising hell?

I remember, on the training program, when I was with a store manager, he went into his fruit department in the morning and asked to see some guy, one of the clerks, and the fellows told him he wasn't there any more. The store manager said: "What do you mean, he isn't here any more?" And the fellow said the produce merchandiser transferred him last night. He was supposed to report to this other store in the morning. And the store manager said: "Temporarily?" And the other guy said: "No, permanently." We went back to the manager's office, and he was really pretty upset about it, because he figured: "My God, how's the store manager's program coming along if I don't even know what's going on in my own store?" And he said it made him look like a chump to everybody and tore down the whole store manager's program in the eyes of the fruit department.

But I don't know; those guys did have a point yesterday. Those watermelons looked pretty sloppy, and I certainly don't know how many watermelons are supposed to be cut at the beginning of the week. I figure the fruit man should know those things, or he wouldn't be a fruit man. All I can do is look at the department through the eyes of the customer, as they told us in the training program; and if things look O.K. to me, that's all I can do about it. But then, these fruit guys come in here and tear everything apart.

RESEARCHER: Have you ever talked to them about it?

SM: No, I've never talked to them about it. Maybe it's good to have these outside guys prodding the fruit people now and again. After all, the guys in the fruit department see me every day, and I don't know the details of this fruit business. But I couldn't go up to the produce ADM and say: "Look here, you guys; if you've got any trouble, bring it to me; I'm the store manager here." They'd go to DM2, and he'd think I had a swelled head or something with my new title.

I don't know; it's not too bad, though. As long as things run fairly smooth and that productivity figure is high and we're making a profit, that's all I can ask for. It'll just take time, I guess, and we'll have to sweat it out. But I know it's tough for those guys to change, just like it was tough for me to change from being a grocery manager to being a store manager. After all, I was in the grocery business twenty-three years as manager, and they must feel sort of the same way about it. I don't know what's in the company's mind; you never know. Maybe they'll do away some day with ADM's; you don't know.

. . . .

About the same time the researcher learned of another incident that involved conflict between the produce executives and the store executives—in this instance centering around the produce merchandise manager and another district manager, DM1 (48, 22). This instance also gave the researcher a chance to observe the store operations manager handling such a conflict between two important groups. District Manager 1 introduced the subject during a conversation with the store operations manager in one of the stores.

DISTRICT MANAGER 1:   I suppose you had a lot of fireworks in your merchandise meeting yesterday at headquarters.

SOM: No, not particularly.

DM1:   I thought you would have heard a lot from the produce merchandise manager.

SOM: I heard a lot from PMM afterward about some of the troubles you have been giving his stomach.

DM1 (*with strong feeling*):   Well, that's nothing compared with what he's been doing to us. You know, PMM dug into an issue here that, for once, I don't intend to give an inch on. I think I'm right on this, and I don't intend to back down.

SOM (*to researcher*):   Maybe you'd like a little background on this issue.

RESEARCHER: Well, I heard some mention of it in last Monday's meeting.

SOM: That's correct, you heard a little bit about it; but let me tell you more about the history of this thing. We first got interested in prepackaging produce back—I think it was during the war, isn't that right?

DM1:   Yes, around then. I think it was in 1944.

SOM: You see, the old practice in the produce business was to sell by the unit. You know, a dozen oranges, etc. The best way of measuring most kinds of produce is by weight. For a number of years now, we have been trying to set up some basis for selling most of our produce by weight. Many of the other chains in this part of the country haven't picked it up, though, and that has put us in a little bit of an awkward position. We've had a long history of switching from one thing to another, trying to find the best answer to this whole question. For a while, we put our scales right next to our cash registers and had our cashiers weigh the fresh produce as we sold it. Then we experimented with having scales out in the produce department and having a clerk there weigh the produce for the customer before he comes around to the checkout station. More recently, DM1, in some of his stores, has been turning completely to the prepackaging of fresh produce and not using the scales at all on the selling floor.

DM1:   And I think it's working out, too. Of course, in anything new of this kind, we're going to run into some problems; but if we make up our minds to make this system work, I'm sure we can.

SOM: The current problem with PMM is partly this prepackaging thing, with some other issues thrown in. As I got the impression from talking to him, he ran into a number of situations while he was out looking around at some stores of DM1's on Wednesday that were an odd combination of circumstances. Partly, they reflected matters of bad judgment on the part of some of our people in the stores; but of course, the whole combination of events sparked PMM into blaming prepackaging for the whole problem, and he got very upset. This isn't the first time PMM has got upset, and he really gets upset. I'm sure it's true that he couldn't eat a thing for lunch on Wednesday because what he saw bothered him so.

DM1: He wasn't the only one that was bothered.

SOM: Well, that's true; but you know, PMM is sort of an artist about his work. He thinks almost constantly about trying to get the best possible kind of produce into his stores to be sold. He also has worked very closely with most of the men who are handling produce in our stores. He thinks of them as his boys, and he's trained a lot of them. When he sees something going on he doesn't think is right, he takes it as a personal reflection on him. I think he's got two or three comments in his whole barrage of statements that he had to say about what happened Wednesday—two or three things that have some logic to them.

He mentioned one thing that is a potential problem in prepackaging. It's not a good argument for dropping the prepackaging, but it's an argument for something we've got to be careful about, or we will get into trouble. He pointed to the fact that when you have to prepackage your produce, this tempts the store to prepackage some of it the day before, to have it ready to set out the first thing in the morning, to get started fast when the store opens. He said if they start prepackaging too much of it the night before, it's going to come out in worse shape than it would if they had put it up fresh on the day they were going to sell it. I think he's got something of a point there.

Of course, we have given our people instructions that they are to prepackage only a minimum amount the night before so that most of it will be freshly packed the next day. If they are not rushed the night before, there is always a temptation to package too much and save the rush the next morning.

DM1: Well, that's all right, but it just wasn't true that that's what he ran into on Wednesday. I am willing to admit that the store he went into Wednesday morning wasn't in very good shape, but it was the day right after a holiday. He was dealing with a fruit man who likes to put all the stuff away when he closes down for holidays, so he didn't have everything in very good shape when PMM went in there Wednesday morning. But he hadn't prepackaged a lot of that stuff before—it had just gone out that morning.

SOM: Well, in his mind, there was too much prepackaging the night before.

DM1:   But it really wasn't so.

SOM: Well, I think that's right; but you know PMM—he could have talked our produce man into agreeing with him.

DM1:   Well, that's true. I know that department manager would probably say, "Yeah, yeah," to PMM, just to get rid of him and save the argument.

RESEARCHER: When PMM sees something that bothers him, I take it he just starts talking to the nearest person.

SOM: Oh, he sure does. You ought to hear him; he really blows up. He goes at it full force. (*He mimicks some of PMM's swearwords.*)

DM1:   The worst part of this is that it was his own assistant merchandise manager who gave us the idea of going to complete prepackaging in the stores. It really saved us a lot of money. One thing PMM saw that he was upset about was that we were selling some junk peppers for the price of a higher quality pepper. He was right on that; that was a mistake. But the mistake was made in the warehouse; they sent us junk peppers when we ordered high-quality peppers; and they charged us for the high-quality peppers, too. I'll admit that my produce men should have noticed that, but we didn't make the initial mistake.

But PMM has no right to upset my people by his explosions, to say nothing of me. He was trying to put me right back in the hospital.

At this point, Produce Merchandiser 1 (39, 19), who covered most of the stores of District Manager 1, walked up and joined the conversation.

SOM: We were just talking about the stores that PMM visited on Wednesday and got all upset about. (*DM1 walks across the store to take care of some other business; SOM turns to researcher.*) PM1 here is right in the middle of this whole problem.

PRODUCE MERCHANDISER 1:   You're certainly right—I'm in the middle.

SOM: You see, he works for PMM's organization, but he has to get along with all the people in the stores.

DM1 (*coming across the floor*):   Take a bite of this pear.

PM1:   No, thanks.

DM1:   Isn't that an awful-looking pear? We've got a whole bunch of these out in the back room.

PM1:   That's nothing. We've got an awful lot more down in the warehouse. We'll be spending a long time getting rid of those. We've been trying to do it in small baskets and then in individuals and then in big baskets, and we can't sell them any way.

DM1:   You were saying that PMM is an artist and really a terrific buyer. You know, I could make a few comments about his buying.

SOM: Just hold that. That's not the issue here.

PM1:   You know, PMM got all upset because he didn't find things the way he wanted them when he came into one of our stores, but he got there at 11:00 o'clock on the day after a holiday and was surprised that things weren't in good shape. I don't know what he expects at that time of day. Of course, they weren't in good shape. He went out and came back at 1:30, and everything was all right by then. He just hit a store where our produce manager was really conscientious and put all his produce away for the holiday. That meant it took him longer to get it out on the shelves when he started out on a Wednesday.

DM1:   Well, I think we should have had another man in that store that morning, and that was my fault. But those mistakes happen once in a while, and PMM's got to expect that. Besides, if we let him have his own way, he'd have so many people in the produce department that it would run our payroll all out of control. Another thing is that he thinks that all the produce men ought to get up at 2:00 o'clock in the morning and start to work setting up their merchandise. He doesn't realize that these people are working on hours these days.

PM1:   You know, that's absolutely right. During Easter week, I was out with him at 6:30 one morning lining up some plants to sell in our flower shops. He told me at 6:30 to call up the Highland Park store and speak to them about the plants. I started to go to the telephone to put in the call, and I suddenly realized that nobody would be at the store at that time in the morning. I went back and told him that. He thought I ought to call, anyway. He couldn't really get it through his head that people wouldn't be working at that hour of the day. He knows it, but he just won't accept it. He had me going out placing phone calls to that store at 6:45, 7:00, 7:15, 7:30, right on down to almost 8:00 o'clock, when we finally got somebody.

SOM: That's certainly true; he knows that we are on hours now, but he does find it awfully hard to accept. But I think we have a couple of things to do now in order to smooth over this present problem with PMM. I picked up a couple of ideas from him, out of all the rash of things he is upset about, that have a certain validity to them; and I think we ought to do something about them. As I get it, one thing we can do is to leave our scales on the produce floor instead of taking them out of there and putting them in the back room. I think we could use them out there just for those few instances when we have to get started fast some morning on an emergency basis. Instead of stopping to prepackage some items then, we could just dump a few things out loose in the bin and sell them in bulk.

DM1:   Well, that makes a lot of sense; I can accept that, all right. That's no problem; we can do that. As a matter of fact, the only reason we took the scales into the back room is that we thought we might use the space for something else. But that isn't important.

PM1:   Yeah, that's right. I think that's a good idea. We can bring the scales out and have them there for those special times.

DM1:   I want to make sure that everybody understands, though, that they'll just use the scales that way during an emergency period; and as fast as possible, we're to get on a prepackage basis on all items, so we can stop having a man look after the scales.

PM1:   That's right; we'll just use the scales for emergencies.

SOM: And there's one other thing I think we ought to remind our people of, and that is that we don't want to use the scales as a catchall. A lot of stuff can get littered in there and make a real eyesore. We've got to keep the scales cleaned.

PM1:   Sure, we'll take care of that, too.

SOM: The second thing we could do is to lean over backwards to try to get our produce people to understand that they are not to prepackage any more than the bare minimum to get them started the next morning. That is, they're not to prepackage too much stuff the night before that will be a little bit less than fresh when they put it out to sell the next morning. They could get into some sloppy habits on that. I think PMM is right. It's something we can take care of, though, if we check up on them, give them close supervision, and train them right to do this job.

PM1:   That's all right; I will make that clear to them.

DM1:   Sure, that kind of thing could be abused. We'll have to watch that.

SOM: Well, I think if we really lean over backwards on this thing for the time being, and try to make sure we don't get into those sloppy habits, we'll be a lot better off. And of course, that will help the situation with PMM.

DM1:   Then you want no other changes?

SOM: No, aside from those things, I think we ought to run just the same. And I want you to tell your men it's better not to take orders from anyone but you as the district manager or, of course, the store manager.

DM1:   Well, good. I'm glad to hear you say that.

SOM: There's no reason you can't have them say that, very politely, to anybody who starts trying to give them instructions.

DM1:   Oh, that's right. I always tell them to be very polite about it but nevertheless to make it clear that they aren't in a position to take instructions from anyone but me or the store manager.

PM1:   Well, that's fine. I think that's all right.

. . . .

A few days later, the store operations manager told the researcher that he was going to discuss the relationship between the product merchandisers and the district managers at the next district managers' supervisory meeting. The researcher attended this meeting; and toward the end of the biweekly meeting, the store operations manager raised the topic.

> SOM: Now, I want to raise the general subject we're going to spend the rest of the morning on, and I do hope we'll be able to clear out of here by 12:00. That is the question of how it's working out with you district managers under the new setup for your special product merchandisers in meat and produce. DM2, I think you're the one that asked that we have a discussion of this topic? Why don't you start in and tell us what you have in mind?

In the discussion that followed, District Manager 2 reported that he seemed to be getting somewhat slower action on the problems the product merchandisers should be solving. District Manager 1 reported that after working through some initial problems, the new arrangement had been going very well. The rest of the district managers were either mildly positive or noncommittal about their experience.

At about this time the vice president of sales entered the meeting and sat quietly near one end of the table.[3] After a few minutes of general discussion a district manager trainee who was attending the meeting spoke up.

> DISTRICT MANAGER TRAINEE: One of the things I've run into going around with some of these product merchandisers is that it seems to me they're having a lot of trouble convincing some of the department heads in the stores to give them space to handle the merchandise they want to sell. For instance, I was going around with a man trying to get space for a "special" on roses a week ago, and it was really pathetic to watch his struggles to get the space.
>
> DM1:   Now, hold on there. I don't think he had such a tough time.
>
> VICE PRESIDENT OF SALES: Well, I'm glad to hear he did have a tough time. I'd much rather hear that people are fighting for space than apathetic about it. I like to see some of that fighting going on in the organization over who is going to have the space. It's only when that stops that I begin to worry about it.
>
> DM3:   I think it's a good thing, too. They're getting the space they need, but it's a good thing that they have to argue with some of our store people in order to get it.
>
> VPS: That's right. The final decision as to who should have the space should rest with you district managers and, in turn, the store peo-

---

[3] The vice president of sales often came to these meetings late, so that committee members would have "plenty of time to warm up" without his presence.

ple. The merchandise people have to convince you that they are going to be using their space to maximize your sales and profits.

DM2: Well, I'm glad this has come up because, you know, that's what really bothers me about this whole merchandiser thing. I was really bothered about that fellow canceling our date to travel around with me simply because his merchandise manager happened to get the bright idea that he'd like to travel with him that day, and I was just wondering who really ought to have priority on that kind of thing.

DM5: The first man who made the appointment ought to govern.

VPS: Didn't your product merchandiser tell his merchandise manager that he had a prior date with you?

DM2: No, that's what bothered me. He didn't even tell him. He just agreed to go with him, and then called me back and told me he couldn't go with me.

VPS: That just isn't right. That's plain discourtesy. There's no excuse for that. You really can't blame that on the merchandise manager. I think you ought to tell the merchandiser what you think of that.

DM1: Well, let me mention something that happened to me. I'll have to bring personalities in on this thing, but it's all just between us here in the room. I ran into PMM in one of my stores a while back, and he was hopping mad because he discovered for the first time when he walked in that store that we were prepackaging some of our produce and preweighing it prior to putting it in the racks. He thought it was terrible, and he told me he wanted it changed right there. I told him that the whole program had been cleared with his assistant and that I thought it made a lot of sense and was working out very well. Well, you know, PMM can be pretty strong when he talks about these things. He wanted me to change it right on the spot. I didn't do it. I showed him what we were doing and talked about it; and I think probably a week from now, he's going to be convinced that we've got the right answer to the thing. But he sort of acted as if he could tell us how to do that kind of thing in the store.

VPS: I want to make myself perfectly clear on this issue—and I can speak on this because I'm in an organizational position to make it stick. Those merchandise managers and the merchandisers under them are a service function to the district managers and to the store managers. The final decisions as to what goes on in the store are up to you men. If they start to dictate or think they can dictate what goes on in the store, it's up to you to resist their intrusion. Otherwise, we're going to get all mixed up. And if there's any question about it, you know where I stand on this matter. And I intend to make it stick. I think, in 99 per cent of the instances where there is an intrusion of this sort, you people ought to be able to handle it yourself on an informal basis with the man involved. But you should feel perfectly free to force the issue on up, if you have to, to get it settled.

SOM: I told the group earlier that in some of these instances, where there's a problem on coverage, I could handle these things on an informal basis if they do get into trouble of this kind. (*To the men.*) Sometimes, if you let me know about it, I can handle it without really causing a lot of trouble; and in other cases, I think probably it would be better if you could handle it yourself through a direct contact with the merchandise manager concerned.

VPS: I can just imagine what happened to PMM on that thing. I bet he came back here and really bawled out his assistant for not telling him that he had O.K.'d that change in the store and to make sure it wouldn't happen again. What that thing with PMM amounted to was a slip-up in communication between him and his own assistant. If I know PMM, that won't happen any more; and as you say, he'll probably be all for that plan as soon as he has time to think about it.

SOM: Well, I see it's after 12:00, and I think we've about squeezed this topic dry. Why don't we call it quits at this point?

.   .   .   .

About two months later, the store operations manager called on the vice president of sales with the suggestion that he hold a meeting with the product merchandisers to spell out clearly the merchandisers' position in the organization since the January 1 organizational change. The store operations manager had received several reports from his district managers that the merchandisers were not happy with their present position as they saw it. Their old positions as assistant district managers had been recognized to be a steppingstone to a district manager's job; and now, they feared they were in a dead-end assignment. Moreover, in the change, some of the merchandisers had been given a number of the smaller stores to handle which, since they were older and not very profitable, were less desirable assignments than the large supermarkets.

In thinking over the store operations manager's request for a meeting, the vice president of sales reviewed his own ideas on the purposes and goals of the organizational change as it related to the product merchandisers. It was his conviction that the product merchandisers must assist the store managers not only in helping them to run their stores, but in helping them develop merchandising ability.

VPS: We are double-talkers as far as our stores are concerned. We tell the manager: "You've got to have a complete line"; and then the next day, we come in and say: "You're heavy on inventory." We tell him he's got to give the customer good service; and then we come in and tell him to keep the payroll down. We tell him he's got to have a snappy-looking fruit department; and then we come in and tell him that he's too heavy on perishable items.

The vice president of sales realized that this sounded contradictory, but he felt that there was a "razor's edge" in the middle that he had to achieve—a fine balance between good operation and successful merchandising. In order to do this, he had as a goal the "marriage" of the merchandising and operating functions.

When the organizational change was initiated, he had realized there would be a potential conflict between the store manager, who had overall responsibility for a given store, and the product merchandiser, who was concerned with his limited area. He predicted the conflict, and he also knew that it would be one of his big jobs during the year to deal with it satisfactorily.

The idea of a specific meeting with the product merchandisers had not occurred to the vice president of sales; and he wondered whether or not such a meeting should be held, what it might accomplish, and what might go on at such a meeting in order to accomplish its purpose.

9. DENVER TRANSPORTATION COMPANY

BILL HALL had just entered his office when the telephone buzzed, and he picked up the receiver:

GEORGE WILLIS: Bill, this is George Willis, Mountain Air Lines. You boys have fouled up again. The crew on 326 this morning were kept waiting an hour for a car to take them to their hotel, and the captain's mad as hell. If you can't prevent this, we're going to have to make other arrangements.

BILL HALL: I'm awfully sorry, George. I'll look into it right away. We'll give you good service. We're working on improvements in airport dispatching right now.

The conversation ended shortly afterwards.

Complaints such as this were of great concern to Hall. One year ago, he had been brought in as operations manager for Denver Transportation Company, with instructions to improve its service, and he was not at all satisfied with his progress. He had done everything within his knowledge to improve operational procedures and planning, to train and increase supervision, to "firm up" supervisory responsibilities, and to better communication facilities (see Exhibit 1). Further, he had secured sufficient additional drivers and equipment to handle the rapidly increasing airport and tourist business. For the most part, Hall's activities were well received by drivers, supervisors, and dispatchers. Still, complaints came in: The buses were late; they were overcrowded; the wrong type of limousine was sent. The complaints were being caused by errors in judgment and planning on the part of supervisors and dispatchers, and Hall did not know what to do about it.

Denver Transportation Company, known as DTC, was founded in 1926 to provide transportation for air-line passengers and crews to and from the Denver airport. It had grown by adding sight-seeing buses, chauffeur-driven limousines, taxis, and "U-Drive" cars, as well as airport buses as the airport and tourist business expanded. After World War II, there was a mushrooming of tourist trade and considerable

Exhibit 1

MAJOR STEPS TAKEN BY BILL HALL TO IMPROVE SUPERVISORY
AND DISPATCHING EFFECTIVENESS, 1955–56

1. Worked personally with each supervisor and dispatcher, "firming up" his authority, responsibilities, and functions.
2. Had weekly meetings attended by supervisors, dispatchers, and the sales manager to iron out problems and to plan ahead.
3. Discussed complaints with the dispatcher and/or supervisor involved, trying to get at the cause and to help the man prevent making the error again.
4. Added one man to the dispatcher force and increased airport supervision by one. Warner added to dispatching, Smith and Goodhue to airport supervision—Smith to replace Bemis, who retired, and Goodhue as additional help.
5. Assisted in the training of the new supervisors.
6. Established an automatic telephone exchange for DTC, which enabled dispatchers and supervisors to contact drivers at taxi stands, terminals, hotels, the airport, etc., by dialing a local number rather than going through the old DTC switchboard. The same dial service allowed the driver to contact his supervisor or dispatcher directly as well.
7. Constructed a magnetic dispatch board for the purpose of spotting the location of each DTC vehicle and pointing up which were busy and which were available for hire. This replaced a clumsy pegboard which had been used for the same purpose.
8. Improved the forms used in the operations department. A major improvement was the establishment of one form with carbons to transmit orders from sales to supervisors to dispatchers to drivers. This replaced several separate forms and the chance of errors in time, date, place, etc., in transcribing.
9. Developed a chart allowing the airport supervisor and dispatchers to keep track of all arrivals and departures on one master sheet, rather than separate sheets for each air line.

growth in general business and federal government operations in this city, and DTC's business expanded vigorously. Its 1940 fleet of 16 buses, 45 taxis, 11 chauffeur-driven Cadillacs and crew cars, and 41 "U-Drive" cars had increased threefold by 1956; and the passenger-miles operated[1] had increased even more.

DTC's business came from three sources:

1. From individuals who decided on their own to take a DTC bus, taxi, or limousine.
2. From various agencies that sold tickets for airport-to-hotel transportation and for sight-seeing; this would include travel agents, hotel desks, and air-line tour departments.
3. From organizations that contracted with DTC for transportation services; this included transporting air-line crews to and from the airport in special cars and many charter bus assignments ordered by air lines and others.

Management considered the latter two sources to be the most important. These organizations demanded top service from a ground transportation firm because their customers blamed them, not DTC, for poor ground transportation.

---

[1] Number of passengers carried times miles traveled.

In airport and sight-seeing activities, DTC had the bulk of the Denver business prior to World War II. With the great expansion in the area after the war, competition moved in. DTC was not only unable to develop fast enough to hold all of the new business; but in addition, its service had deteriorated to the point where in recent years, some customers were being held mostly by promises and personal friendships of DTC management.

The owners of DTC were intent on maintaining leadership control of the Denver transportation activities in which they were engaged.

Exhibit 2

DENVER TRANSPORTATION COMPANY

ORGANIZATION CHART, 1956

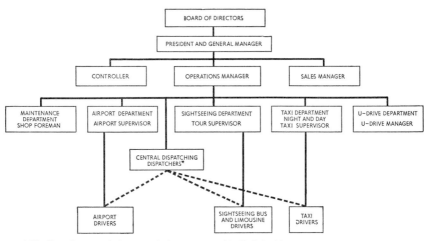

* The dispatchers were in frequent telephone contact with all of the drivers.

They had recently secured capital for additional equipment; and it was up to Hall, the operations manager, to obtain drivers, to put the new equipment to optimum use, and to give the kind of service that would satisfy the air lines, hotels, and travel agents. The airport, taxi, and sight-seeing departments were all receiving complaints; and Hall realized that something would have to be done to correct the poor judgment and planning exhibited by the supervisors and dispatchers involved. Exhibit 2 shows the 1956 organization chart of the operations departments. Exhibit 3 represents a page from the company's operations manual, indicating the duties of various supervisors and dispatchers. Exhibit 4 lists the 1956 supervisory and dispatching employees and their backgrounds.

Management had always believed in seniority and in promoting men

Exhibit 3

DENVER TRANSPORTATION COMPANY

Functions of Supervisors and Dispatchers, 1956

AIRPORT SUPERVISORS:

1. Direct movements of air-line passengers and crews to and from the airport by bus, taxi, or crew car.
2. Keep in close touch with air lines as to passenger load, times of arrival and departure, special flights, and related information.
3. Inform central dispatching as to flight times and the number and types of vehicles needed.
4. Answer questions of passengers, assist in the loading of buses, and record the passengers per bus for control purposes.
5. Train airport drivers.

TOUR SUPERVISOR:

1. Schedule sight-seeing buses and limousines according to presold tickets and anticipated cash business.
2. Co-ordinate large movements and clear them with the police department, hotel doormen, and other interested parties.
3. Inform central dispatching as to the times of tours and the types of vehicles needed.
4. Train sight-seeing bus and limousine drivers.

TAXI SUPERVISORS:

1. Schedule maximum taxi coverage for peak hours and for special downtown events.
2. Inform central dispatching of such schedules.
3. Spot-check DTC taxis on the road.
4. Train taxi drivers.

DISPATCHERS:

1. Supply vehicles at the times ordered by supervisors.
2. Take telephone orders for and dispatch taxis.
3. Take telephone orders for buses and limousines and supply them after clearing with the supervisor involved.
4. Handle all customer calls at night when the sales office is closed. If people call about sight-seeing tours, try to sell them on going by DTC.

Exhibit 4

DENVER TRANSPORTATION COMPANY

Operations Personnel, 1956

Name	Position	Age	Years of Service	Previous Employment	Education
Abbott	"U-Drive" manager	42	10	Mechanic	11th grade
Candis	Dispatcher	28	8	Miner	12th grade
Goodhue	Assistant airport supervisor	35	5	Accountant	College
Hall	Operations manager	45	1	Traffic manager	College
Hayman	Tour supervisor	49	16	Bus driver	7th grade
Jacobs	Assistant airport supervisor	40	11	Farm hand	10th grade
Johnson	Night taxi supervisor	56	20	Truck driver	6th grade
Kelly	Airport supervisor	51	18	Carpenter	9th grade
Matola	Dispatcher	36	6	Taxi driver	10th grade
Pollock	Dispatcher	30	6	Clerk	12th grade
Roscoe	Assistant airport supervisor	38	12	Miner	7th grade
Smith	Assistant airport supervisor	44	5	Mechanic	9th grade
Sontag	Day taxi supervisor	55	23	Taxi driver	5th grade
Trigger	Dispatcher	33	4	Clerk	11th grade
Warner, T.	Dispatcher	27	6	United States Army	12th grade
Warner, R.	Dispatcher	34	10	Truck driver	11th grade

up through the ranks for dispatching and supervisory jobs; the position of operations manager was the only exception to this policy. New men were started as taxi drivers, moved up to airport drivers, then to sight-seeing bus or limousine drivers, and finally to dispatching or supervisory jobs. The drivers and dispatchers were members of the Teamsters' Union, and management's seniority and promotion policy was spelled out in the contract:

SECTION 5. *Seniority.* In the event of any layoff of employees, employees with the least amount of seniority shall be laid off first. In the event of any rehiring of employees, the employee with the most seniority shall be rehired first.

In making promotions, if there is no material difference between qualifications of applicants, the one having the greater length of continuous service will be selected. If there is a material difference between the qualifications of the applicants, the best-qualified applicant will be selected; however, he shall be on a probationary period for six (6) months.

In 1940, DTC had been able to secure plenty of young men who were willing to start out as taxi drivers. Furthermore, dispatching and supervisory jobs were simpler then, and so management's promotion policy worked well. In 1956, Hall was having considerable difficulty in employing taxi drivers who had the ability to progress in the company. There were, in fact, plenty of taxi drivers available; but they were not men who possessed the characteristics that would enable them to be good sight-seeing drivers, dispatchers, or supervisors.

Taxi drivers received a guaranteed salary of $225 per month or 40 per cent of gross revenue produced, whichever was greater. Since anyone who owned an automobile could start a taxi firm by paying a small business license fee and firms were unrestricted as to the number of cabs they might license, competition was keen. For several years the DTC taxi department had represented little more than a break-even operation for the company. Taxi competition held down the number of trips available to a DTC driver; as a result, his salary and tips were low. This, coupled with the lack of prestige involved in "operating a hack" and the availability of good jobs in the community, did not serve to encourage able young men to become taxi drivers. Recently, Hall had suggested to the president that the taxi department be eliminated, for it caused a good deal of the dispatching load and was relatively unprofitable. The president, however, felt strongly that a taxi department was necessary to give twenty-four-hour service to the hotels and airports, for the many independent taxi operators only worked during the peak hours, and the air lines, hotels, and others relied on DTC for service at odd hours.

Hall could find plenty of men who would like to drive a sight-seeing bus or limousine. Here, the pay was good, the tips were high, and there was a certain amount of prestige. These jobs required men with good appearance, manners, and personality. On the sight-seeing buses the drivers had to speak well over a microphone, know their tours thoroughly, be able to handle groups of people skillfully, and be entertaining. Some of the tours lasted for six or eight hours. To keep thirty people interested for this length of time required a personable driver-conductor.

Though to a lesser degree, Hall would also be able to find good men to start out in airport bus work. The pay was good, and the job was only one step removed from a sight-seeing assignment. In fact, since airport buses were used for sight-seeing work on occasions when the airport was not very active and the sight-seeing load was heavy, it was necessary for the day shift airport drivers to be able to handle the shorter sight-seeing tours. With the company policy of promoting airport drivers to sight-seeing jobs, a good percentage of the men reaching the airport driver level had to have the characteristics necessary to make good sight-seeing drivers. The turnover rate among taxi drivers was 38 per cent a year; among airport drivers, 15 per cent a year; and among sight-seeing bus and limousine drivers, 6 per cent a year.

As DTC's operations expanded, the job of dispatcher or supervisor became increasingly more complex. Airport supervisors who used to keep the schedules of plane arrivals, DTC equipment available, and other such information in their heads now had to resort to scheduling on paper and long-range planning. Better co-ordination had to be maintained with central dispatchers. Dispatchers who in the past were able to get by when sending a sight-seeing bus a little late to a hotel to pick up a load of people now found these errors were compounded when two or three buses were called for and a hundred or more people were kept waiting. Sometimes, when the dispatching loads got heavy, the dispatchers would neglect to give taxi and bus drivers sufficient information about a particular assignment. Hall knew that in following up the Mountain Air Lines complaint at the beginning of the case, he would get an answer such as this:

> AIRPORT SUPERVISOR: I was really busy then; three planes had just arrived, and the buses were filling up. Central dispatch told me the crew car was on its way, and I thought it would be right along.
>
> HALL (*to himself*):   This man should have found out when the crew

car left downtown and exactly when the dispatcher thought it would arrive at the airport. He has instructions to send the crew in taxicabs at our expense if a crew car isn't available. He just doesn't use his head The rest of the supervisors aren't any better, except Tom.[2] He's certainly improved the scheduling on the late airport shift, but the men don't seem to like him yet.

Hall had studied the drivers carefully and felt that the current supervisors and dispatchers were the best available among the work force. Some of the sight-seeing drivers were more intelligent than their supervisors and dispatchers, but they lacked any desire to assume supervisory responsibility. They were extroverts and thoroughly enjoyed guiding tourists. Several of them had been supervisors or dispatchers at one time or another and had been transferred back to driving because they did poorly or because they disliked the job and requested the transfer. Many of the sight-seeing and airport drivers felt fully qualified to be supervisors; and even though some did not want supervisory jobs, Hall thought they seemed resentful when Tom Goodhue, a DTC accountant, was given the position of assistant airport supervisor.

In Hall's judgment, DTC drivers, especially the old-timers, were very loyal to the company, and high morale was evident. For many years the company had maintained benefits such as one week's paid vacation, life and hospitalization insurance on a joint employee-employer contribution basis, and a no-interest loan policy. When bus drivers became too old to handle a big bus, they were given limousine assignments or work on one of the company's several commercial parking lots. Company parties for drivers and their wives or girl friends were held several times a year and were thoroughly enjoyed by the workers. The small executive force of the company knew all the drivers by their first names and maintained a genuine "open-door" policy.

On their own initiative, the sight-seeing drivers had formed a small cowboy band which played at company parties. When big tourist groups were going on eight-hour sight-seeing tours, they were supplied with box lunches, and the cowboy band played for them during the lunch period. This made a big hit with the tourists and was a strong selling point for DTC with travel agents. The band had made up a vocal number entitled "Sight-see with DTC," which they played often at gatherings. The company planned to use this song for promotional purposes.

The Teamsters' Union had moved in seven years ago through the or-

---

[2] Tom Goodhue was an accountant who had been transferred to operations two months ago because of developing eye trouble.

ganizing help of several DTC taxi drivers. Management believed that the union was voted in at the NLRB election only because of the large number of relatively new taxi drivers in the total driving force. Quite a few of the old-timers came to management and asked whether they should join the union. Management encouraged them to join on the grounds that they wanted men on their side within the union rank and file. Unionizing had improved the relations between DTC drivers and the employees of many of DTC's customers such as the hotels (doormen), railroads, and air lines. Furthermore, when DTC was asked to handle conventions (which were very profitable), it chartered buses from the local transit system and trucks to carry luggage from a moving company. Since all of these firms were teamster-organized, their drivers used to resist working with DTC (since it was nonunion), and many difficulties resulted.

In the seven years in which the Teamsters Union had been bargaining agents for DTC workers, it had been unsuccessful in increasing wages except partially to cover cost-of-living rises; and these small increases were offered by management independently. No changes had been made in worker fringe benefits, and management felt that the DTC old-timers were responsible for the lack of union aggressiveness. Hall realized that any activities on the part of management that reduced driver morale could very well increase the union's strength with DTC drivers. Furthermore, as the work force grew larger and, as a result, less familiar with management, Hall was afraid of a corresponding increase in union power. He feared this especially because large wage and/or fringe benefit increases would work a real hardship on DTC. For a service firm, wages are the main item of expense, and rates are pretty well set by what the customer considers "fair." Any increase in rates could discourage people from sight-seeing and/or increase competition.

There were several reasons on the part of management for establishing the policy of promoting men through the ranks; the most often cited were:

1. Management felt that able and senior workers should be rewarded.
2. Management felt that a man who had experience in all of the operations would make a better supervisor or dispatcher.

In regard to the latter reason the president felt that a supervisor could better understand the drivers and their problems after having been a driver himself. He thought it would be difficult to absorb the many details of a supervisory job without having had driving experience. The same applied to dispatching, for drivers and customers would ask a dispatcher a multitude of questions involving train and flight departures, street and building locations, rates for trips between two points by taxi, sight-seeing tour information and rates, and airport bus schedules and rates. Further, it was believed that a supervisor or dispatcher employed from the outside would have difficulty in getting the co-operation of the drivers. On the other hand, Hall pointed out that in two months, Tom Goodhue had learned the airport job and was already outperforming the old supervisors in duties such as planning and scheduling. Hall realized, however, that Goodhue had not as yet secured the full co-operation of the drivers and that it would not be wise to put him in full charge of an airport shift until he did.

10. DALLAS CHEMICAL CORPORATION[1]

IN THE SPRING of 1959, Dr. Caldwell, the director of research at Dallas Chemical Corporation, called a meeting of laboratory management to discuss the problem of formal recognition of scientists who stayed in research work. Attending the meeting were the personnel manager, Mr. Keats, and the two laboratory directors, Dr. Faulkner and Dr. Maughan. Six months before, Dallas' research division had initiated a "technical ladder of advancement" for those scientists who chose to remain in direct scientific work rather than assume research management positions. The purpose of this meeting was to analyze the effects of this technical ladder and arrive at some decisions on future action in this area.

The research laboratories of the Dallas Chemical Corporation were a separate entity and maintained only loose ties with any of the other corporate divisions. They had been located in a small university town for the past fifteen years, and much of the academic atmosphere pervaded the laboratories. No development work or engineering was done by the professional staff of 400 persons; they were strictly basic researchers in all areas of Dallas' interests.

Dr. Caldwell opened the meeting by reviewing the events leading up to the company's initiation of the technical ladder of advancement.

DR. CALDWELL: Let me briefly review the events which led up to our decision last year to initiate a technical ladder. Our interest, as you may recall, was stimulated about a year and a half ago by both internal and external forces. You may recall the loss of several highly regarded individuals to other companies for reasons that appeared to be better positions and increased status. At the same time there appeared in the literature several articles pertaining to various methods of rewarding technical personnel. At that time Mr. Keats made a study of the procedures and policies used by several other laboratories comparable in size and work scope, and he presented a plan to our research council for the adoption of the title of Fellow of the Technical Staff. This was to be the only step in the ladder and was to be the highest status our technical men could obtain. Six months ago we made a public announcement of this position plus the appointment of eight of our best scientists as "fellows." These men are, as you are well aware, outstanding in their fields and also our most senior

[1] This case was made possible by a grant from the Industrial Research Institute.

men. Now that six months have passed, I would like to hear from you any reactions of your own or your men concerning the position plus your recommendations for the next step to be taken.

MR. KEATS: Since I made the original study at the time we adopted the Fellow title, I have been doing a lot of thinking and talking with outsiders on this action. When I first presented our plans to the research council I rationalized this move on the basis of having a desire to show to everyone associated with these labs that management wants to reward those men who have contributed to the company's benefit over the years. The other reason was a desire to remove the lack-of-a-title stimulus which drives some of our good men out of research. Let me explain this last one in more detail. For years we have done our best to give the researchers whatever they wanted within reason. One very selfish reason we have done this was because the researcher who saw a difference between his present job and a job in management or a research job at another company would be much more prone to leave for this reason. One of the areas in which these differences occur is the title and status of the job. Before this dual ladder was conceived, this was one area in which research was particularly weak. Ours is a management-oriented society where a man's position depends upon his title. When I say this was our weak area, I mean we were losing men to other labs and to nonresearch work when everything but the title was the same. Thus our introduction of the technical ladder was our first attempt at correcting the title problem.

DR. FAULKNER: Six months ago, when this idea was originally presented, I agreed with you, but from reactions to the dual ladder in my lab I conclude that this is not practical at Dallas research. Let me show you where these arguments fail when applied to our research staff. In my lab, recognition of men is primarily through the work they are doing and the articles they have published. Management cannot confer prestige and recognition; it can only hope to recognize formally this "position" of these men who have done well in their profession. In fact our first action of conferring the title of Fellow on those eight outstanding men was primarily for the purpose of borrowing some of their prestige for the title. This earned recognition which I am speaking of pertains only to the laboratory and the scientists as a professional group. Certainly this title has an effect, but upon whom? Obviously upon the people who cannot recognize a man for what he has done but only for the title he wears. This comprises most of the rest of the corporation plus the outside world, the man's family and friends. Perhaps this is the group we want to please, but I think not. What does it matter what they think of you? This is hollow prestige—praise for a title not for the man or his accomplishments. As for removing the title difference which might motivate good researchers out of science, I doubt that this is important; the good researcher has such a strong motivation to contribute that the quest for a title is a comparatively weak force.

DR. MAUGHAN: Without appearing to be a fool I would like to agree with both you and Keats. I think you are both correct but that you are talking about different people. Perhaps we have diagnosed the problem correctly but treated the wrong patient. By that I mean that the eight men who have received the titles were the last ones to need them. They had recognition, money, honors and whatever else was needed. The Fellow title was only frosting. However, there *is* a group which is drastically affected by management's attitude toward titles and that is the younger men; these are the ones who have not yet received formal recognition and who are most prone to leave the lab because of their poor status. At this point I want to disagree with Dr. Faulkner on the importance of being recognized outside the professional group. Many of these men have families and friends who are important and are interested in how they are doing, and to these people "how they are doing" is equated with their title. The older men, their wives and families, have learned to live with their position, but to the young men, it is doubly hard, for they see their friends in business and the universities climbing the various ladders and they have no signs of progress to show. As a generalization I also think that the younger generation is more title-conscious. To state my position fully, I think that the need for a title provides a motivational force of varying intensity for the individual, but on the whole stronger in our younger and less well-recognized colleagues. I think that the pressure from the outside can be strong enough in some cases to veer a good researcher from strictly scientific work in our labs to other labs or nonscientific work. As an aside I think that the size of the lab has grown to the point where a man may no longer be recognized for his accomplishments alone as all of our Fellows were. It now may take the formal approval of the lab management before a man is recognized for his work, even within the lab.

MR. KEATS: If we accept your hypothesis of the value of the title being dependent upon the position of the man receiving it, this would tie in nicely with the results which I have observed. For one thing the results have been very negligible; no one is either very pleased or displeased. Most of the staff are waiting to see if any other titles are introduced and who will be recognized in the next few years. By giving more men recognition and recognizing the younger men, management will make a real contribution to their position both within and outside the labs.

DR. FAULKNER: Yes, and it is these younger men who may be hurt the most by this system of giving titles. We haven't mentioned any of the ill effects of this "ladder." My men have commented that one of the big advantages to our lab is its democracy, and they are worried that formal titles would result in a stratification detrimental to communication. One or two of them left labs just because of this; for example, they don't like to see all the senior scientists eating together and they dislike the loss of first-name intimacy. Many also fear that the granting of titles will produce a harmful competition for titles which could endanger the co-operation and communication between our scientists. One of our big selling points in recruiting men has been this lack of competition, which created a different atmosphere than at many labs. The final thing that I think we should consider is what the effect of not receiving a title is. How will it affect the performance of the man who doesn't get the title, both the mediocre one who doesn't rate one and the good man whom we misjudge? I realize that the first step has been taken and we can't turn back, but I certainly think we should go slow in the future, first comparing the advantages that have been mentioned against the liabilities of each new step.

MR. KEATS: I have to agree with most of your points, but the problem is what can be done about this reaction? How can we even measure it? To your list of problems with the technical ladder I would like to add one more. A major complaint is that we give the men a title only and no other rewards such as a bonus, a raise, or many of the little trappings they expect with high management positions. It is difficult to tell the younger men that the Fellows have been on the same financial level as members of the laboratory management for years. I have tried to point out that it is our policy to pay a man equally for his contribution whether he is in a research management position or actual scientific work. Most of the younger men don't believe this, and it is impossible to prove this with our policy of salary secrecy. As far as the trappings of the position go, you all recognize that our policy has been to minimize the trappings in the entire laboratory. We have no private parking lots or dining rooms, and researchers obtain space, service personnel, and equipment only when they can show a need. This puts us in a definite bind as compared to other labs, or even some product divisions of our own company, in which salary increases and all sorts of little trappings are included in a promotion or new title.

DR. CALDWELL: As I have been sitting here listening to the arguments both pro and con for this technical ladder it strikes me that we are involved in a problem much more complex than originally anticipated. If we accept the hypothesis of Dr. Maughan that the real effects of this title business are felt most strongly in the middle echelons, then we can concede that our first efforts have been negligible because they were misdirected. These top men had all the recognition they needed; the Fellow title was frosting on the cake. However, these first efforts were not entirely wasted for two reasons: first, we had a definite desire and duty to recognize these men for their contribution to Dallas' research; secondly, this move has acquainted the entire technical staff with the knowledge that management wants to recognize them formally and their time will come. As I see it we are now progressing to more reactive material—those men who have not been widely recognized. Selection of these men will be much more controversial. The reactions here to our actions should be much more substantial, and we need to give careful thought and planning to the situation to make sure that reaction is favorable. As to the problem of not providing any physical rewards with the title, I think much of this may be solved by my explaining our salary policy of not associating a raise with a promotion but publicizing the fact that the top salary barriers have been removed for this group of men.

Specifically what I would like to see come out of this meeting is a decision as to what our next step should be, naming more Fellows or initiating a new position for younger men or both. This entire problem has suddenly been exposed as an iceberg with the most dangerous part hidden. I do not think it appropriate or possible to arrive at a decision immediately. Let's meet again next week at this time. That will give you some time to sound out the men in your groups. I hope by next week we can detail a course of action on this subject.

Concepts and Research Findings

1. CRITERIA FOR PLANNING ORGANIZATIONAL CHANGE

Gene W. Dalton

THE ADMINISTRATORS MUST, more or less frequently, make a commitment to introduce an important change into the organization or segment of the organization he is concerned with. As students of business administration, you have been asked to make such a commitment to a change proposal in regard to the cases you have studied. This process is not new, but it is particularly highlighted by the cases in this section that emphasize change.

When we begin to discuss and assess recommended changes and action proposals, however, we find ourselves immediately faced with a normative problem. What is our purpose in recommending the actions we propose? What ends do we seek to attain? Against what criteria shall we measure the outcomes? These questions are neither naïve nor are their answers obvious. Every person involved in planning organizational changes must address these questions in some way. Part of the complexity of the problem arises from the fact that any behavioral act and its consequences can fruitfully be examined and evaluated from a number of different viewpoints. One way of bringing some of the viewpoints into focus is to examine the event or proposal in terms of its functional or dysfunctional effects for different operating systems. In this paper we shall examine three types of relevant operating systems—the total organization, the small face-to-face work group, and the individual. We will be considering the factors which work to maintain the effective operation of these systems, as well as some of the problems and possibilities for facilitating their growth and development. We shall examine each of these systems separately, but first let us make note of some general tendencies and potentialities of human behavioral systems.

Maintenance and Growth

Investigators from a variety of disciplines have reported the tendency for human behavioral systems to *maintain* and *preserve* themselves. Given sufficiently effective mechanisms within a system and a sufficiently favorable environment, the system will tend to maintain a steady state or a *moving equilibrium.* When parts of the system are pulled out of balance, or when some of its essential operations are blocked or threatened, the system *reacts* and mobilizes to restore the system to its prior balance. This *"homeostatic tendency"* was first noted and explicated by students of biological systems, but has also come to be an essential conceptual tool for those trying to understand the behavior of social systems.

Another characteristic of individuals, groups, and organizations which is sometimes overlooked by those who focus on the reactive tendencies of human systems is the potential which these systems have to *grow* and *develop.* Human systems have in common the *potential for increasing internal complexity* and for expanding their capacity to influence their environment. They can "learn" from their transactions with their environment and thus increase their capacity to act on their environment—to become *proactive* as well as reactive. That all such systems do not grow and develop does not deny the existence of this potential. Rather it points to the fact that growth takes place only when certain factors are present and under certain favoring circumstances.

We shall not try to draw a falsely concrete demarcation between maintenance and growth, between reaction and proaction.[1] An action or a series of acts may have both reactive and proactive elements. It is often difficult to distinguish between maintenance and growth. Without trying to draw any artificial distinctions, let us keep in mind these two general characteristics of human behavioral systems as we examine separately each of the three systems listed in the second paragraph of this paper.

The Total Organization

For an organization to maintain itself and function effectively, it must have a number of different well-understood sets of activities. It must have a production system—a set of activities for producing goods, services, or ideas which the organization seeks to provide for its environment. Ideally, the best technological knowledge would be used in designing these activities. It must have a marketing and distribution system, which again would ideally use the best available knowledge in promoting and distributing the product. It must have a product designing system to create technically practical and commercially useful prod-

---

[1] For a more detailed description of reactive and proactive tendencies in organizational systems, see J. V. Clark, "A Healthy Organization," *California Management Review,* Vol. 4, No. 4 (Summer, 1962), pp. 16–30.

ucts. To bind these required activities together, it must have a communication-decision system. Ideally, necessary choices and decisions would be made for the organization by the individual most expert on the issue involved. A set of rewards and punishments (financial and nonfinancial) is also needed. Ideally, the rewards would be highly valued by the members of the organization and would be administered in such a way as to reinforce those activities which contribute to organizational purpose and extinguish those activities which do not. Finally, a set of sentiments are needed which function to insure the full contribution of those who work in the organization. Ideally, the dominant sentiment would be unswerving loyalty to the purpose of the organization. When any of the elements described above are completely inoperative in an organization, the system will have difficulty maintaining itself and will tend to disintegrate or go through a series of convulsive reorganizations or both.

We also noted that human systems have the potential to grow and complicate as well as maintain themselves. Full achievement of organizational purpose is impossible without such growth. (We defined growth as an increasing capacity to cope with the environment rather than in terms of increasing size.) Where this potential is not realized, we find organizations which tend to become primarily defensive and inflexible in their strategies and highly vulnerable to environmental shifts.

What are the features of an organization which tends to realize this potential? These are more difficult to state. Less is known about organizational growth than about organizational maintenance, but at least three features appear to be necessary. First there has to be a system for gathering information from the outside—for sensing and anticipating customer needs and ways of filling them. In effect, they must be "open-ended" rather than "closed" systems. However, new information, ideas, and technology are not useful unless the organization has a second feature—a built-in set of procedures for changing itself and a set of attitudes which tolerate and facilitate change. The Scottish firms studied by Burns and Stalker,[2] which brought in a new electronic technology but were unable to incorporate the change into the *existing* organizational framework, were finally unable to utilize the new technology. Third, some mechanisms and attitudes have to be developed and maintained which facilitate the confrontation of and integration of divergent ideas.[3]

As we have described a model of an organization oriented entirely

---

[2] T. Burns and G. M. Stalker, *The Management of Innovation* (Chicago: Quadrangle Books, 1962).

[3] M. P. Follett, *Dynamic Administration* (New York: Harper & Bros., 1940), pp. 30–49.

toward the achievement of organizational purpose, the reader may have begun to share some of William Whyte's concern about the rise of the "organization man."[4] Nevertheless, we need to be reminded, occasionally, of the obvious fact that the achievements of large-scale healthy organizations constitute an essential ingredient in modern civilized life. If our business organizations did not do a reasonable job of achieving their purpose, we would not have the material means to sustain our complex society.

The limits of this model lie in the fact that it takes into account only one system—the organization itself. Our purpose in this paper is to explore some of the other systems which must also be taken into account in building a model for a healthy organization.

The Work Group

One of the richest of man's experiences derives from working together with others to achieve a common end. In almost every known culture, men have been known to seek out these experiences. In our own society, an expanding body of literature[5] attests to the fact that people in larger organizations tend to form small, informal work groups even in circumstances where their formation would appear to be difficult and unlikely. These groups provide their members an opportunity for social exchange, for gaining esteem and emotional support. These groups spontaneously develop a system of interactions and activities and develop norms which influence the behavior of their members.

For an organization to be most functional at this level, the members would have to have a set of activities in which they could jointly engage and have the opportunity to interact around these activities. From these minimal conditions, a system of activities and interactions will tend to emerge and provide its members with the satisfactions of membership. The organization need not provide the detailed procedures, only the conditions.

The question may be posed as to why an organizational planner should take this dimension into account. If these systems tend to form spontaneously and maintain themselves, why should they be planned for? Moreover, is it not true that they have often been known to work at

---

[4] William H. Whyte, Jr., *The Organization Man* (New York: Simon and Schuster, Inc., 1956).

[5] P. M. Blau, *The Dynamics of Bureaucracy* (Chicago: University of Chicago Press, 1955); G. Homans, *The Human Group* (New York: Harcourt Brace & Co., 1950); G. F. F. Lombard, *Behavior in a Selling Group* (Boston: Harvard Business School, Division of Research, 1955); A. Zaleznik, *Worker Satisfaction and Development* (Boston: Harvard Business School, Division of Research, 1956); A. Zaleznik *et al., The Motivation, Productivity and Satisfaction of Workers: A Prediction Study* (Boston: Harvard Business School, Division of Research, 1958).

cross-purposes to organizational goals? The answer to this latter question is, of course, in the affirmative. In fact, a large part of organizational planning in the past has sought to prevent the formation of such groups. These efforts to isolate individual activity and to prevent joint efforts have proved enlightening. When isolation is successful, investigators have often found high employee dissatisfaction, and high turnover.[6] More frequently, however, groups have formed around a set of collusive relationships (i.e., rate restriction) or purely social activities (i.e., betting pools, collections, horseplay, etc.). The primary question is often not whether a group will form and provide some social satisfactions for its members, but whether these satisfactions will be derived from relationships built around task accomplishment or whether the time and energy invested in obtaining these satisfactions are drained off into nontask-related and ritualistic activities.

Are groups to be taken into account, however, only because they are a necessary evil? What about the potential capacity for the small group to complicate and exert an increasingly effective and positive influence in the organization? We are aware of the contribution of the highly effective paper-machine crews in the Marshall Company. Barnes[7] reports the development of a highly creative engineering group which was given relatively great freedom to develop its own work patterns. Clark[8] reports a work group which spent a year meeting in the members' homes to design a whole new methods handling system in their department. For most of this time their work was unknown to management.

This potential is too often unrealized, however. Many, if not most, work groups in American industry could be described as "frozen" groups. Let us examine the way this term was used by Zaleznik, Christensen, and Roethlisberger, to describe industrial work groups they had observed carefully. They described the characteristics of these work groups as follows:

1. These groups have few, if any, ways of relating themselves in a positive fashion to the organizational settings in which they live. They seem to be able to develop only in one direction, i.e., in the direction of maintaining their values in an environment which seems to be indifferent to them.
2. Their regular members and leaders have little opportunity to exer-

---

[6] E. Mayo, *The Human Problems of an Industrial Civilization* (New York: Viking Press, 1960); C. R. Walker, and R. H. Guest, *The Man on the Assembly Line* (Cambridge, Mass.: Harvard University Press, 1952).

[7] L. B. Barnes, *Organizational Systems and Engineering Groups* (Boston: Harvard Business School, Division of Research, 1960).

[8] Clark, *op. cit.*

cise their influence, leadership, and responsibilities except in the direction of maintaining the group's social life and organization. Excluded from participation in the setting, planning, and implementation of production goals, they devote most of their energies to the maintenance of production norms.

3. But even the internal developments of their social life become merely endless one-level elaborations of existing values that stay at constant levels of sameness—same routine activities, same routine conversational topics, same patterns of "on-the-line" output, same collective beliefs, same "gripes," same problems and the same resolution of them.

4. Thus these groups offer few opportunities for the self-development of their members. If the individual in such a group identifies with the regular social subgroups, he is bound by their norms, values, and limited aspirations. In terms of self-development the price paid for regular membership is high. But also high are the costs of nonconformity. The deviants and isolates incur not only the penalties of social isolation but the penalties of social antagonisms as well. They become the butt of jokes and the victims of horseplay. In this situation their chances to influence change in others or in themselves are limited. Thus under both circumstances the opportunities for doing new things, for developing new ways for doing them, for assuming increased personal responsibility, and for personal self-development are seriously limited.

To such groups that have lost their organizational health, i.e., that are incapable of development except in the lopsided way we have described, we shall give the name "frozen." Such groups appear in many businesses at different organizational levels but, as many studies have shown, they flourish at the work level. The social pathology they manifest is one of incomplete growth and development. Although they can and do develop along one dimension, this very internal dead-level elaboration prevents and works against their external development.[9]

Guidelines for "unfreezing" such groups or for preventing their crystallization are not fully defined. Still, you have two points from which to begin your analysis. First you can examine some of the conditions of "frozenness" and explore how each might be altered. Second, you have your own experiences in groups from which you might be able to draw.

The Individual

We turn now to the individual. The individual comes to the organization to satisfy a number of complex needs. We are forced to oversimplify

---

[9] Zaleznik *et al., op. cit.*, pp. 390–91.

in describing these, but we might begin by stating that the individual seeks from the organization the means with which to provide economically for himself and his family. This, however, is only a beginning. He has needs for safety and security. We have mentioned the social needs which he brings with him to the organization. He also has needs to maintain some level of self-esteem and a sense of personal accomplishment. He seeks, not always successfully, to achieve some kind of esteem in the eyes of others. When these needs listed here are frustrated, we often find patterns of high turnover of personnel, or militant unionism, or both. Ideally, for an organization to be functional at this level, it would be so designed so as to fulfill each of these needs for the contributing members of the organization.

It would also provide something more. It would provide those conditions which would facilitate individual growth and development. There is a great deal of ferment and controversy among psychologists concerning the nature and the determinants of individual growth. Allport,[10] Rogers,[11] and Bronfenbrenner[12] postulate a persistent *tendency* among individuals in the direction of growth, increased capacity, and self-determination. Robert White[13] has gathered considerable research evidence to support his theory of a universal human *need* for increased competence. Maslow[14] describes a need for what he calls "self-actualization." Argyris[15] goes so far as to make organizations responsible for much of the neurosis of our time by frustrating the needs of the individual for growth and self-determination.

We need not enter into the controversy. There *is* general agreement that the individual has the *potential* capacity to learn, complicate, and take greater responsibility for his own behavior. For an organization to be fully functional along this dimension, it must provide conditions which facilitate individual growth. What are these conditions? Again there is a wide range of formulations among those interested in individual growth, but a few ideas tend to be held in common. First, there is sufficient opportunity and encouragement to take self-determined action and take responsibility for this action. Second, the environment is suffi-

---

[10] G. Allport, "The Open System in Personality Theory," in *Personality and Social Encounter* (Boston: Beacon Press, 1960).

[11] C. Rogers, *On Becoming a Person* (Cambridge, Mass.: Riverside Press, 1961).

[12] U. Bronfenbrenner, "Toward an Integrated Theory of Personality," in Robert R. Blake and Glenn Ramsey, *Perception* (New York: Ronald Press, 1951).

[13] Robert White, "Motivation Reconsidered, The Concept of Competence," *Nebraska Symposium on Motivation,* 1960.

[14] A. H. Maslow, *Motivation and Personality* (New York: Harper & Bros., 1954).

[15] Chris Argyris, *Personality and Organization* (New York: Harper & Row, 1957).

ciently supportive so that taking such action is not seen as too dangerous, and third, the individual is able to obtain clear-cut and valid feedback regarding the consequences of this action.

A Multifunctional Approach to Analysis and Planning

Our examination of these three levels of behavioral systems points up two things. First, the human values represented in each level are both real and important. Second, and perhaps more significant, it provides us with a scheme which will help us in explaining and even predicting problems in organizations where behavior is functional at only one of these levels. It provides us with a multifunctional approach to the evaluation of behavior and behavioral change in organizations. Using this approach, we are led to examine an act or a proposal in terms of its function for each system and in terms of its probable effect on the system's reactive tendencies and its potential for growth. Let us try out our scheme by examining three instances of behavior in organizations which tend to be aimed at achievement at only one or two of these levels.

Perhaps the movement which is, in the mind of many persons, most closely identified with the first level, achievement of organizational purpose, is the scientific management movement. Frederick W. Taylor, one of the founders and leading exponents of scientific management described an incident showing how he went about trying to change organizational behavior.[16] Taylor himself stated that he was trying to effect change at two levels, "to secure the maximum prosperity for the employer, coupled with the maximum prosperity for each employee." Taylor found a gang loading on the average of about $12\frac{1}{2}$ tons of pig iron per man per day. He estimated that each man ought to be able to handle forty-eight tons per day instead. Following his own "inflexible rule to talk and deal with only one man at a time," Taylor sought out a Pennsylvania Dutchman named Schmidt and spoke to him as follows:

"Schmidt, are you a high-priced man?"

"Vell, I don't know vat you mean."

"Oh yes, you do. What I want to know is whether you are a high-priced man or not."

"Vell, I don't know vat you mean."

"Oh, come now, you answer my questions. What I want to find out is whether you are a high-priced man or one of these cheap fellows here. What I want to find out is whether you want to earn $1.85 a day or

---

[16] F. W. Taylor, *The Principles of Scientific Management* (New York: Harper & Bros., 1911).

whether you are satisfied with $1.15, just the same as all those cheap fellows are getting."

"Did I vant $1.85 a day? Vas dot a high-priced man? Vell, yes, I vas a high-priced man. . . ."

"Well, if you are a high-priced man, you will do exactly as this man tells you tomorrow, from morning till night. When he tells you to pick up a pig and walk, you pick it up and you walk, and when he tells you to sit down and rest, you sit down. You do that right straight through the day. And what's more, no back talk. Now a high-priced man does just what he's told to do, and no back talk. Do you understand that? When this man tells you to walk, you walk; when he tells you to sit down, you sit down, and you don't talk back to him. Now you come on to work here tomorrow morning and I'll know before night whether you are really a high-priced man or not. . . ."[17]

Taylor reports that indeed Schmidt did do exactly as he was told. He moved forty-seven tons and earned $1.85 per day. Immediately, Schmidt's earning *did* rise and the profits for the company *increased*. But when we examine this change from a multifunctional point of view, other factors are brought into focus. If Taylor's approach is taken with each member of the firm, what effect does it have on individual learning and growth? If individual growth is blocked, what effect will this have on organizational growth? What kinds of response might we expect from the work groups affected? How might the groups act to protect and maintain themselves? How would defensive group action affect the profitability of the firm?

Let us turn to another example. In the case, Work Group Ownership of an Improved Tool,[18] we find an instance of strong group development. Two workers having developed a new high-speed tool bit, shared it only with the members of their work group, keeping it hidden from management. The members of the group were able to "peg production" and still earn incentive earnings. With their extra time, they applied greater care and workmanship to their other products. They established a reputation for accuracy and low spoilage. At the group level, we find high functionality. We find cohesion, loyalty, and co-operation around a task. The group was not only maintaining itself but was becoming more capable of dealing with its environment. Individual members were being rewarded by the group not only for conformity but for creativeness and skill. But the company, which was planning to set up a new

---

[17] *Ibid.*

[18] See page 405.

plant unit making the same product, was deprived of the benefit of the innovation.

To fill out our triad, we turn to a poignant account of a utopian society, the Fruitlands experiment, made famous by the skillful pen of Louisa May Alcott.[19] Here was an organization, created to maximize individual growth. However, the features which we described earlier as essential for the maintenance of an organization were never developed. Hence, Fruitlands failed as a productive organization and thus became dysfunctional at all three levels.

Before we leave our examination of changes which were functional at only one or two levels and their consequences, let us also take the time factor into account. A change which is functional at only one level may appear to be successful because its dysfunctional effects at other levels are not immediately apparent. Likert[20] points to an unrecognized dysfunctionality in a number of cost-reduction drives and crash programs for immediate productivity increases. Research indicated that pressure drives for increased production in a well-established organization yielded substantial and immediate increases in productivity. Hidden, however, was the fact that these gains came through a "liquidation of human assets." Hostilities increased, there was a greater reliance upon authority, loyalties declined, motivation to restrict production began to increase and eventually turnover increased. The liquidation of these assets was not reflected in standard organizational measures of profit and loss for several quarters. Yet eventually even these measures came to show that the cost to the organization had been much higher than the initial savings.

When we begin to raise into question such "good" things as cost reduction and drives for greater productivity, we must underscore a point which may have already become apparent to the reader. We should be forewarned when we try to take a multifunctional approach to organizational analysis and planning that a certain amount of "tough-mindedness" will be required. We may have to re-examine some of our most cherished beliefs. Old friends such as "management prerogatives," "span of control," "good human relations," "line-staff," etc., will have to prove themselves again. Some of our pet antipathies toward organiza-

---

[19] L. M. Alcott, "Transcendental Wild Oats," from *Silver Pitchers,* 1876. Reprinted in *The Transcendentalist Revolt Against Materialism,* G. F. Whicher, ed. (Boston: D.C. Heath & Co., 1949).

[20] R. Likert, *New Patterns of Management* (New York: McGraw Hill Book Co., Inc., 1961), pp. 61–76. Also see R. Likert and S. Seashore, "Making Cost Control Work," *Harvard Business Review,* November–December, 1963.

tions, groups, and individuals will have to be recognized and corrected for. All of us, including the writer, have our hobbyhorses, which we like to ride. But if we are in earnest about seeking multifunctionality, we cannot take sides with the organization, the group, or the individual. Instead we shall be forced to face up to their interdependence.

Let us now turn to the idea of synthesis. We have seen how a recognition of the interdependence of the parts of an organization complicates our view of organizational change. Because the actions of any part of the organization affect all other parts, our analysis of the consequences of any behavior must take into account a number of things at once. Yet the very interconnectedness of the parts of the organization and the overlapping of the systems we have mentioned raise the possibility of reducing this complexity through a process of *synthesis*. Some procedures, norms, practices, and rules tend to be functional at all three levels *at once*. They do several pieces of work simultaneously. The needs of the organization, the group, and the individual are all addressed by a single act. Thus a real economy is achieved.

To illustrate such a synthesis, we shall return to the Marshall Company. We shall examine the norms and mechanisms related to training, learning, and promotion. We watched Nichols both training and being trained as he helped to start up Machine No. 9. Graham stood in the background and watched. Nichols reported that:

> "Graham doesn't say much to me when I'm starting up a machine. Later on, he will tell me things he thought might have been improved—even some of the little things. But now, he won't bother me."

We read how Nichols allowed the second hand to try to thread the paper on the thread rolls till it became fairly clear that he was temporarily "in over his head" and needed help. Next, we noted that the "second hand" allowed the "third hand" to try out the "second hand's" tasks, *if he showed an interest*. The "second hand" describes what he was doing as follows:

> "You really just learn by doing. You master your own job, and then you watch the next fellow working, and do as much as you can. Of course, some of the guys think if you do your own job and then stop, that's what you get paid for. But you don't learn anything that way."
>
> "Isn't there any feeling that you cut in on someone else's job by learning it?" Murray asked.
>
> "Oh, no. You can do as much as you know how," Bolton said. "A good man will keep you busy answering his questions; and when he does that,

you bring him along. Of course, the thing is, you've gotta keep learning so you know more than the other guys." Bolton paused and seemed for several seconds to be thinking intently. "There's one fellow," he said, hesitantly. "He's no good. He came over from the other side of the river during the war and worked up to be second hand. Now, guys are coming back from the service who know more than he does. Men under him are better than he is, but he gives orders and pretends to know more than anyone else. No one likes him."

The same procedure worked at all levels in the organization. Dudley, talking about people at the management level, informed the researcher that a man is allowed to take on as much responsibility as he thinks he can handle. He promotes himself. He is not pushed. But he *is* held responsible for his performance. He can get help and coaching when he wants it, but it isn't pushed on him. If he is able to handle the new responsibility, his reputation and influence increase and he can take on more responsibility. If he tries to move beyond his capacity, he loses reputation and influence.

What kind of synthesis do we observe? Along the individual dimension, an employee is allowed to seek security at the level he finds comfortable. He isn't pushed or punished for staying there. But he also has the opportunity to learn, grow, and test himself. The group activities and norms are built around the helping, teaching exchange. Douglas was being ostracized for giving orders rather than learning, and teaching. Trying to move too fast without learning the skills involved was similarly punished. Social satisfactions were derived from the exchange of knowledge and skill for esteem. The learner was obligated to ask for help, the person with greater knowledge was obligated to help. The organization was served well by an effective placement-training system, an effective reward system (taking responsibility, high performance, teaching, and learning were rewarded), and a set of attitudes which stressed organizational loyalty and fostered change.

A more dramatic synthesis is illustrated in the British Coal Industries case.[21] The workers on one shift (the fillers) were dependent on the workers on a prior shift with little interaction and no control over the men in the prior shift. In their dependent isolation, the fillers were often depressed and outraged. To protect themselves, they formed collusive small groups, leaving the old, ill, and helpless without support. Secrecy, mistrust, and mutual scapegoating prevailed. Absenteeism was high, productivity was low, and the miners were leaving the coal fields.

Finally, an organizational innovation was discovered at one mine and

---

[21] P. R. Lawrence et. al., *Organizational Behavior and Administration* (Homewood, Ill.: Irwin-Dorsey, 1961) p. 107.

applied to others. Under the new composite system, instead of one shift doing all the cutting and another shift doing all the filling, each shift took up the work where the group from the previous shift left off. When they completed that phase, they redeployed to the next task. Moreover, all the men from the three shifts were formed into a single self-selected composite group. The members were given the responsibility for distributing the task and shifts among themselves. Control over the interaction between men on different parts of the cycle was now in the hands of the cycle group.

Partly because the new pattern followed an earlier tradition and partly because the new pattern met the needs of the men in the situation, the new pattern produced significant changes. Individual isolation and victimization dropped. Absenteeism declined. The composite group developed a sense of mutual responsibility and the amount of unnecessary work created by one shift for another by careless work or from technical breakdowns dropped from 25 per cent to 5 per cent of the men's time. Less supervision was required and productivity was 17 per cent greater. Thus improvement along all three dimensions was synthesized in one change.

The illustrations from the Marshall and British Coal cases, as reported here, do not reflect the painful difficulty or the drain on time involved in working out this synthesis. They are in no way meant to minimize the difficulty of finding multifunctional solutions to organizational problems. On the contrary, they are cited to illustrate some of the kinds of creative solutions to problems which we shall be seeking in the coming weeks.

The Legitimacy of Organizational Planning

Having gotten more deeply into the criteria for planning and instituting organizational change, a number of readers may have come face-to-face with an uneasy feeling about the legitimacy of planning at all. Isn't this manipulation? Instead of leaving this as an uneasy feeling, let us confront it. In fact, we are all constantly engaged in the process of influencing those around us, though we may not admit it. As long as we keep this process intuitive and the criteria implicit, the question of manipulation does not seem to arise. But when we try to state explicit criteria, questions concerning Machiavellianism and manipulation immediately appear. We tend to feel no concern about introducing a new budgetary control system until we explicitly take into account how it will change behavior. Yet attempts to influence others when we do not consciously consider our effect are more likely to be detrimental than open conscious planning. There is nothing humanistically wrong with planning per se. It is planning without knowledge or awareness which is humanistically wrong, to say nothing of inefficient.

The problem of excessive conformity in our society, if there is one, is not fostered by organizational planning per se, but by the kinds of models used. The reader may take issue with the organizational model presented here, but not with the process of conscious planning. This paper has advocated a multifunctional planning model which addresses simultaneously the needs of the organization, the work group, and the individual. It provides one model which we may find useful. But whether this exact scheme is personally useful to each reader is secondary. More important is that each of us adopts some point of view large enough to include the other points of view which exist in any situation.

2. RESISTANCE TO CHANGE*

Paul R. Lawrence

RECENTLY, WHILE making some research observations in a factory manufacturing electronic products, a colleague and I had an opportunity to observe a number of incidents that for us threw new light on this matter of resistance to change.[1] One incident was particularly illuminating:

> We were observing the work of one of the industrial engineers and a production operator who had been assigned to work with the engineer on assembling and testing an experimental product that the engineer was developing. The engineer and the operator were in almost constant daily contact in their work. It was a common occurrence for the engineer to suggest an idea for some modification in a part of the new product; he would then discuss his idea with the operator and ask her to try out the change to see how it worked. It was also a common occurrence for the operator to get an idea as she assembled parts and to pass this idea on to the engineer, who would then consider it and, on occasion, ask the operator to try out the idea and see if it proved useful.
>
> A typical exchange between these two people might run somewhat as follows:
>
> ENGINEER: I got to thinking last night about that difficulty we've been having on assembling the x part in the last few days. It occurred to me that we might get around that trouble if we washed the part in a cleaning solution just prior to assembling it.
>
> OPERATOR: Well, that sounds to me like it's worth trying.
>
> ENGINEER: I'll get you some of the right kind of cleaning solution, and why don't you try doing that with about 50 parts and keep track of what happens.
>
> OPERATOR: Sure, I'll keep track of it and let you know how it works.

With this episode in mind, let us take a look at a second episode involving the same production operator. One day we noticed another en-

* Excerpts from the article "How to Deal With Resistance to Change," *Harvard Business Review*, May–June, 1954. Reprinted by permission.

[1] For a complete report of the study, see Harriet O. Ronken and Paul R. Lawrence, *Administering Changes: A Case Study of Human Relations in a Factory* (Boston: Division of Research, Harvard Business School, 1952).

gineer approaching the production operator. We knew that this particular engineer had had no previous contact with the production operator. He had been asked to take a look at one specific problem on the new product because of his special technical qualifications. He had decided to make a change in one of the parts of the product to eliminate the problem, and he had prepared some of these parts using his new method. Here is what happened:

> He walked up to the production operator with the new parts in his hand and indicated to her by a gesture that he wanted her to try assembling some units using his new part. The operator picked up one of the parts and proceeded to assemble it. We noticed that she did not handle the part with her usual care. After she had assembled the product, she tested it and it failed to pass inspection. She turned to the new engineer and, with a triumphant air, said, "It doesn't work."
>
> The new engineer indicated that she should try another part. She did so, and again it did not work. She then proceeded to assemble units using all of the new parts that were available. She handled each of them in an unusually rough manner. None of them worked. Again she turned to the engineer and said that the new parts did not work.
>
> The engineer left, and later the operator, with evident satisfaction, commented to the original industrial engineer that the new engineer's idea was just no good.

Social Change

What can we learn from these episodes? To begin, it will be useful for our purposes to think of change as having both a technical and a social aspect. The *technical* aspect of the change is the making of a measurable modification in the physical routines of the job. The *social* aspect of the change refers to the way those affected by it think it will alter their established relationships in the organization.

We can clarify this distinction by referring to the two foregoing episodes. In both of them, the technical aspects of the changes introduced were virtually identical: the operator was asked to use a slightly changed part in assembling the finished product. By contrast, the social aspects of the changes were quite different.

In the first episode, the interaction between the industrial engineer and the operator tended to sustain the give-and-take kind of relationship that these two people were accustomed to. The operator was used to being treated as a person with some valuable skills and knowledge and some sense of responsibility about her work; when the engineer approached her with his idea, she felt she was being dealt with in the usual way. But, in the second episode, the new engineer was introducing not only a technical change but also a change in the operator's customary way of relating herself to others in the organization. By his brusque manner and by his lack of any explanation, he led the operator to fear that her usual work relationships were being changed. And she just did not like the new way she was being treated.

The results of these two episodes were quite different also. In the first episode there were no symptoms of resistance to change, a very good chance that the experimental change would determine fairly whether a cleaning solution would improve product quality, and a willingness on the part of the operator to accept future changes when the industrial engineer suggested them. In the second episode, however, there were signs of resistance to change (the operator's careless handling of parts and her satisfaction in their failure to work), failure to prove whether the modified part was an improvement or not, and indications that the operator would resist any further changes by the engineer. We might summarize the two contrasting patterns of human behavior in the two episodes in graphic form; see Exhibit 1.

It is apparent from these two patterns that the variable that determines the result is the *social* aspect of the change. In other words, the operator did not resist the technical change as such but rather the accompanying change in her human relationships.

Exhibit 1

TWO CONTRASTING PATTERNS OF HUMAN BEHAVIOR

	Change		
	Technical Aspect	*Social Aspect*	*Results*
Episode 1	Clean part prior to assembly	Sustaining the customary work relationship of operator	1. No resistance 2. Useful technical result 3. Readiness for more change
Episode 2	Use new part in assembly	Threatening the customary work relationship of operator	1. Signs of resistance 2. No useful technical result 3. Lack of readiness for more change

3. PARTICIPATION IN DECISION MAKING AND WORK GROUP PRODUCTIVITY

AN EXPERIMENT was conducted in a clothing factory to test the effects of participative methods of introducing job changes on productivity.[1] In this factory, job changes occurred frequently and nearly always were accompanied by a sharp drop in productivity. The researchers set up four experimental groups to test their hypothesis that participation in planning and carrying out the change would make a significant difference in people's acceptance of the change. In each of these four groups the proposed change modified the established work procedure to about the same degree; all the groups were paid on a modified piece-rate method.

Group 1, the control or "no participation" group, went through the usual factory routine. The production department modified the job, and a new piece rate was set. The small group of operators was called into a meeting, where they were told that competition necessitated a job change. The change was explained in detail, as was the new piece rate. Questions were answered, and the group was then directed to resume work using the new method.

Group 2, the "participation through representation" group, was handled differently. Before any changes took place, a group meeting was held, and the need for a change was presented as dramatically as possible. Management then presented a plan to set up the new methods and new piece rate. This plan was essentially the same as the usual one except that a few representatives of the group were elected to help management work out the new method and the new rate.

Groups 3 and 4, the "total participation" groups, were both handled in the same way. All the operators met with management, and the need for cost reduction was presented. A general agreement was reached that some savings could be effected. The groups then discussed how existing work methods could be improved and unnecessary operations eliminated. When the new work methods were agreed on, all the operators were trained in the new methods, and all were observed by the time-study men for purposes of establishing a new piece rate on the job.

Exhibit 1 presents the productivity data for the groups.

---

[1] Lester Coch and J. R. P. French, Jr., "Overcoming Resistance to Change," *Human Relations,* Vol. I, No. 4 (1948). Reprinted in D. Cartwright and A. Zander (eds.), *Group Dynamics* (Evanston, Ill.: Row Peterson Co., 1953), pp. 257–79.

Exhibit 1

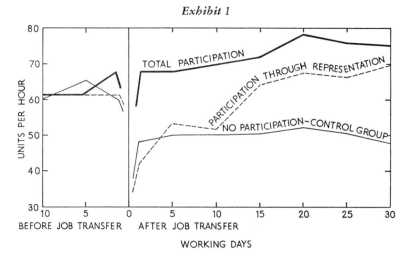

In addition to these results, the researchers reported that in Group 1, "resistance developed almost immediately after the change. Marked expressions of aggression against management occurred, such as conflict with the methods engineer, . . . hostility toward the supervisor, deliberate restriction of production, and lack of cooperation with the supervisor. There were 17% quits in the first 40 days. Grievances were filed about piece rates; but when the rate was checked, it was found to be a little 'loose.' " In contrast, in Groups 3 and 4, there were no signs of hostility toward the staff or toward the supervisors, and there were no "quits" during the experimental period.

4. THE EFFECT OF GROUP DECISION ON SUBSEQUENT BEHAVIOR

Experiments on Changing Food Habits

During World War II the government was interested in encouraging the consumption of certain nourishing foods for which there was relatively low demand. The Food Habits Committee of the National Research Council sponsored a series of experiments to determine the most effective methods of persuading consumers to change their family diet. These experiments have been widely cited as showing the superiority of group discussion to lectures or individual persuasion as a method of influencing behavior. Decisions to use certain foods were more likely to be followed by those who reached a "group decision" than by those exposed to other influence techniques.[1]

In the first experiment, three groups of Red Cross volunteers (13 to 17 members) were given a persuasive lecture on the advantages of serving beef hearts, sweetbreads, and kidneys, as well as advice on how to overcome resistance to such foods. Three similar groups participated in a discussion led by an experienced group worker; in general, the same points were brought out as had been covered by the lecture. Both discussion and lecture groups were asked how many had previously served any of these meats and, at the end of the meeting, to indicate by a show of hands whether they were now willing to serve one of them during the following week. Discussion group members were also told that they would later be asked whether they had made any change in their family diets, whereas those who attended the lectures were not given this information. The follow-up (after one week) disclosed that 32 per cent of the discussion group members, compared with only 3 per cent of those who heard the lecture, had served one of the meats which they had never served before.

In a subsequent experiment the groups consisted of six to nine housewives who were neighbors but not accustomed to meeting together. This time the same person conducted both lectures and discussions. She was not highly trained as a discussion leader. The desired change was an

---

[1] Kurt Lewin, "Studies in Group Decision," in D. Cartwright and A. Zander (eds.), *Group Dynamics* (Evanston, Ill.: Row Peterson Co., 1953), pp. 287–301; and "Group Decision and Social Change," in Newcomb and Hartley (eds.), *Readings in Social Psychology* (1947), pp. 330–44.

increased consumption of fresh and evaporated milk. Between 15 and 30 per cent of those who attended lectures reported an increase in their family's milk consumption after two and four weeks, whereas from 45 to 50 per cent of the group decision housewives reported a similar change. The results were almost the same after four weeks as after two weeks, although at the two-week follow-up, neither population was told that a later check would be made.

In a third experiment, group decision was found more effective than *individual* instruction in persuading mothers to feed their newly born babies cod liver oil and orange juice. When a nutritionist gave each mother 20–25 minutes of individual instruction, approximately 20 per cent of the mothers followed the nutritionist's advice on cod liver oil and 40 per cent on orange juice after two weeks, and 55 per cent of them followed it on both foods after four weeks. However, when groups of six mothers reached a decision (after instruction and discussion), some 45 per cent of them followed this decision in regard to cod liver oil and 85 per cent in regard to orange juice after two weeks. After four weeks the corresponding percentages had increased to 88 per cent and 100 per cent.

Taken as a whole, this series of experiments showed that while there was more resistance to some changes in food habits than to others, such changes were much more likely when a group discussed and decided to make the change than when the arguments in favor of the change were presented by lecture or individual instruction. The principal reason seemed to be the greater involvement aroused by the group decision method.

A Similar Experiment in Industry

In subsequent years, similar results were reported in a variety of field settings. One such replication of the earlier experiments was conducted among 29 supervisors of 395 workers in a large manufacturing plant.[2] The desired change was for supervisors to submit less biased performance ratings of their workers. (The supervisors tended to overrate workers in the higher job grades and to underrate those in the lower grades.) The supervisors were randomly divided into three groups, one of which was a control group which received no instruction prior to submitting its ratings.

The leader of the discussion group "introduced the problem by showing a graph of the previous rating and raised the question why it was that the highly skilled workers were consistently rated higher in per-

---

[2] Jacob Levine and John Butler, "Lecture vs. Group Decision in Changing Behavior," in Cartwright and Zander, *op. cit.*, pp. 280–86.

formance than the less skilled. From that point on, the leader merely acted as moderator, and avoided injecting himself into the discussion."[3] After 90 minutes' discussion the group unanimously decided henceforth to ignore job grades when rating individual performance. The lecture group also attended a 90-minute session which opened with "a detailed lecture on the technique and theory of employee performance rating." The errors in the previous ratings were explained, and the supervisors were told that they were supposed to rate only individual performance and not the difficulty of the job. "After the lecture, questions were encouraged and asked by the raters. Complete answers were given."[4]

The subsequent performance ratings by supervisors who had reached a group decision showed a significant change in the desired direction; there was less tendency to overrate workers in the higher labor grades. However, no significant change was recorded in the rating procedure followed by supervisors in either the control or the lecture groups. These findings were interpreted as a confirmation of Lewin's results "in demonstrating the greater effectiveness of group decision over the lecture method of training."

A Test of the Separate Elements Involved in Group Decision

In the original group decision experiments, no distinction was possible between several different aspects of the experimental procedure which might have explained the outcome. An ingenious recent experiment[5] has systematically "addressed the problem of breaking down the operation of group decision used by Lewin and his coworkers into several separately meaningful factors, which could be individually assessed for their probable contribution to the Lewinian results."[6]

The experiment was designed to analyze separately the effects on subsequent action of four major variables:

1. Participating in a *group discussion*
2. Reaching a *decision* regarding future action
3. Indicating public *commitment* to act
4. The degree of *group consensus* regarding intention to act

The subjects for the experiment were students in a beginning course in psychology at the University of Michigan. They were exposed to various methods of persuading them to volunteer to serve in psychological and sociological experiments. Their willingness to serve was deter-

---

[3] *Ibid.,* p. 282.

[4] *Ibid.,* p. 283.

[5] Edith B. Bennett, "Discussion, Decision, Commitment, and Consensus in 'Group Decision,'" *Human Relations,* Vol. VIII, No. 3 (1955).

[6] *Ibid.,* p. 252.

mined by whether or not they subsequently presented themselves as volunteers, so that the results did not have to depend solely upon differences in verbal reports of action.

Thirty-six matched groups of eight to sixteen students were formed, three of which were assigned to each of 12 "experimental treatments." The 12 experimental variations were formed by combining three types of "influence attempt" (discussion, lecture, and control) with four "decision and commitment" variations (no decision, anonymous decision, partially anonymous decision, and public commitment). The procedures followed in each of the 12 treatments were carefully specified and described in the report. Every effort was made to insure the success of the experimental manipulations, and the results were accurately measured and tested for significance. The conclusions were summarized as follows:

1. Group discussion, as an influence technique, was *not* found to be a more effective inducement to action than a lecture or no influence attempt at all.
2. The factor of decision regarding a future action *was* found to be effective in raising the probability that such action would be executed.
3. A decision indicated by a public commitment was *not* found to be more effective in assuring the execution of the decision than one indicated less publicly or anonymously.
4. A high degree of actual or perceived group consensus regarding intention to act *was* found to raise the probability that individual members of the group would execute the action above the probability of action by members of groups characterized by a low degree of consensus.

Two of the variables, group discussion as an influence technique and public commitment, were thus found to be inessential to the reproduction of previously obtained results.

It was further shown that the combination of the other variables—the process of making a decision and the degree to which group consensus is obtained and perceived—was alone capable of generating differences as large as those reported in the classic experiments of Lewin and his co-workers.[7]

In concluding her report, the author pointed to the need to avoid some of the overgeneralizations that have been drawn from the dramatic results of previous experiments, and to define more carefully in the future what is involved in the group decision process.

---

[7] *Ibid.,* p. 271.

5. AN EXPERIMENTAL CHANGE OF DECISION LEVELS AND EFFECTS ON PRODUCTIVITY AND SATISFACTION

OVER A period of two years an extensive experiment in large-scale organizational change was conducted by the Human Relations Program, Survey Research Center, at the University of Michigan.[1] The study was designed to test two hypotheses: that an increased role in the decision-making processes for rank-and-file groups (1) increases their satisfaction (and vice versa) and (2) increases their productivity (and vice versa). The experiment was conducted in four parallel divisions engaged in routine clerical work in a nonunionized industrial organization. The rank-and-file employees were women, mostly young and unmarried, with high school education.

In the "autonomy" program the supervisors in two divisions were trained to delegate more decision making to lower echelons. In the "hierarchically controlled" program, authority was given to higher line officials to increase their role in running the divisions, and increased power was given to staff groups to institute change. These people were also trained to perform these new roles. Before-and-after measurements by attitude surveys of employees indicated that they clearly perceived that the decision-making processes in both programs had, in fact, changed in the designed manner.

The results of the experiment on different measures of satisfaction and on productivity (direct labor costs per volume of work) are summarized in Exhibit 1.

The researchers also studied employee turnover data during the experiment and found that of the nine employees who left for other jobs because of dissatisfaction, all but one were in the hierarchically controlled program. In exit interviews, 23 of the total number of girls who left for all reasons made unfavorable comments about pressure, work standards, etc.; and 19 of these were in the hierarchically controlled program.

In both programs the work volume was fixed so that the productivity index could be improved only by reductions in the size of the work force.

---

[1] For a brief description of the study, see Nancy Morse and Everett Reimer, "The Experimental Change of a Major Organizational Variable," *Journal of Abnormal and Social Psychology,* Vol. 52, No. 1 (January, 1956), pp. 120–29.

Exhibit 1

Effect of Change Programs on:	Experimental Groups	Mean before	Mean after	Difference
Perceived opportunities for self-actualization and growth	Autonomy program	2.43	2.57	+.14*
	Hierarchically controlled program	2.37	2.24	−.13*
Satisfaction with relations with immediate supervisor	Autonomy program	3.71	3.80	+.09
	Hierarchically controlled program	3.64	3.48	−.16
Satisfaction with relations with assistant manager	Autonomy program	3.71	3.86	+.15*
	Hierarchically controlled program	3.64	3.28	−.36†
Satisfaction with relations with manager	Autonomy program	3.93	4.15	+.22†
	Hierarchically controlled program	3.50	3.01	−.49†
Satisfaction with supervisor as representative of employees	Autonomy program	3.48	3.74	+.26†
	Hierarchically controlled program	3.59	3.43	−.16
Satisfaction with assistant manager as representative of employees	Autonomy program	3.43	3.75	+.32†
	Hierarchically controlled program	3.15	2.86	−.29
Satifsaction with manager as representative of employees	Autonomy program	3.79	4.17	+.38†
	Hierarchically controlled program	2.92	2.52	−.40†
Satisfaction with company	Autonomy program	4.01	4.18	+.17*
	Hierarchically controlled program	4.15	3.88	−.27†
Satisfaction with job	Autonomy program	3.16	3.19	+.03
	Hierarchically controlled program	3.13	3.00	−.13*
		Mean Control Period	Mean Experimental Period	Difference (Per Cent)
Productivity index for year control period and year experimental period	Autonomy program	48.6%	58.6%*	10.0†
	Hierarchically controlled program	48.5%	62.6%*	+14.1†

* Significant at the 5 per cent level, one-tailed t-test for paired data.
† Significant at the 1 per cent level

6. A STUDY OF ORGANIZATION DEVELOPMENT*

Robert R. Blake and Jane S. Mouton; Louis B. Barnes and
Larry E. Greiner

THIS ARTICLE describes how behavioral science concepts of team learning form a link between individual learning and total organization development. The link is important because it suggests some answers to a long-standing problem in industry: how to test and demonstrate the large-scale usefulness of human relations research and teaching. . . . The large-scale program in organization development described in this article may be a major step forward. It was regarded as highly successful both by the businessmen involved and by outside observers; the results *were* measured.

New to most executives in concept and design, the program makes use of a "Managerial Grid" approach to more effective work relationships. The Grid helps to give businessmen a language system for describing their current managerial preferences. It also involves classroom materials and an educational program for designing more productive problem-solving relationships. Even more important, the program is meant to be taught and applied by line managers over a time span involving six overlapping phases.[1] . . .

The evaluation took place in a large plant (about 4,000 employees), which was part of a very large multiplant company. The parent company will be called "Piedmont" and the relevant plant unit "Sigma," for purposes of disguise. . . . Among Sigma's 4,000 employees were some 800 managers and technical staff personnel. These managers and staff personnel were all exposed to a Managerial Grid training program beginning late in 1962. At the request of the research manager in Piedmont's employee relations department, an evaluation study was designed shortly thereafter to follow up the effects of that program. The study included questionnaires, interviews, observations, and a combining

---

* Excerpts from the article "Breakthrough in Organization Development" *Harvard Business Review,* Nov.–Dec., 1964. Reprinted by permission.

[1] Dr. Blake's and Dr. Mouton's work went into the earlier design stages of the Managerial Grid concepts and teaching materials.

of company records in order to separate program effects from nonprogram effects.[2] . . .

Managerial Grid

The Managerial Grid identifies five theories of managerial behavior, based on two key variables found in organizations. One variable reflects concern for production or output; the other variable, concern for people. In this instance the term "concern for" refers to the degree of concern, not the actual results. That is, it does *not* represent real production or the extent to which human relationship needs are actually met. It *does* indicate managerial concern for production and/or people and for how these influence each other.

These two variables and some of their possible combinations are shown in Exhibit 1. The horizontal axis indicates concern for production, and the vertical axis indicates concern for people. Each is expressed on a scale ranging from 1, which represents minimal concern, to 9, which represents maximal concern.

Briefly, the lower left corner of the Grid diagram in Exhibit 1 shows a 1,1 style. This represents minimal concern for production and minimal concern for people. The 1,9 style in the upper left corner depicts maximal concern for people but minimal concern for production. The 9,1 style in the lower right corner portrays maximal concern for production and minimal concern for human relationships. The 9,9 style in the upper right-hand corner represents maximal concern for both human relationships and production. The 5,5 style in the center of the diagram is "middle of the road" in both areas of concern.

Once managers have studied the classroom material accompanying the Grid [Phase # 1], it is possible for them to revise practices and procedures so as to work toward a 9,9 organizational climate [later Phases]. These efforts use an educational program as the core, in contrast to more conventional ways of getting better organizational results (e.g., changing organizational structure, leadership replacement, tightened accounting controls, or simple pressuring for more output). . . .

In some respects, the program sounds simple, and yet any manager recognizes the difficulties involved in influencing a large organizational unit toward changes in values and performance. Such was the challenge

---

[2] The actual program, carried out by the Sigma plant's line management with minimal help from Blake and Mouton, was independently evaluated by Dr. Barnes and Mr. Greiner. In this sense, Barnes and Greiner are the independent auditors of a program originally designed by Blake and Mouton.

Exhibit 1

THE MANAGERIAL GRID

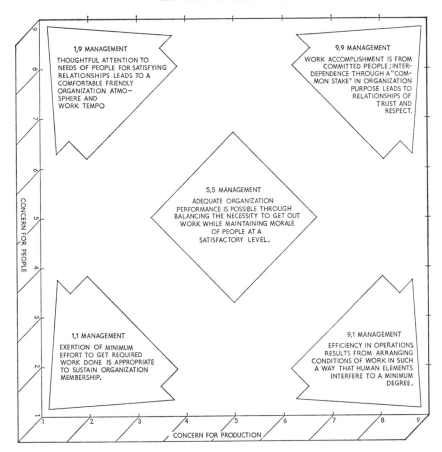

1,9 MANAGEMENT

THOUGHTFUL ATTENTION TO NEEDS OF PEOPLE FOR SATISFYING RELATIONSHIPS LEADS TO A COMFORTABLE FRIENDLY ORGANIZATION ATMO- SPHERE AND WORK TEMPO

9,9 MANAGEMENT

WORK ACCOMPLISHMENT IS FROM COMMITTED PEOPLE; INTER- DEPENDENCE THROUGH A "COM- MON STAKE" IN ORGANIZATION PURPOSE LEADS TO RELATIONSHIPS OF TRUST AND RESPECT.

5,5 MANAGEMENT

ADEQUATE ORGANIZATION PERFORMANCE IS POSSIBLE THROUGH BALANCING THE NECESSITY TO GET OUT WORK WHILE MAINTAINING MORALE OF PEOPLE AT A SATISFACTORY LEVEL.

1,1 MANAGEMENT

EXERTION OF MINIMUM EFFORT TO GET REQUIRED WORK DONE IS APPROPRIATE TO SUSTAIN ORGANIZATION MEMBERSHIP.

9,1 MANAGEMENT

EFFICIENCY IN OPERATIONS RESULTS FROM ARRANGING CONDITIONS OF WORK IN SUCH A WAY THAT HUMAN ELEMENTS INTERFERE TO A MINIMUM DEGREE.

CONCERN FOR PEOPLE

CONCERN FOR PRODUCTION

facing the Sigma management in 1962. The rest of this article describes how Sigma faced that challenge with the help of the Grid program.

Evaluation Goals

This part describes the early findings and conclusions of a research study which evaluated the Sigma plant's program in organization development. The evaluation was suggested by the research manager in Piedmont's employee relations department. Those responsible for the program at the Sigma plant gave the idea immediate support. A research design was presented to the Sigma management and accepted. On-site field work began in June 1963 and ended in November 1963.

The evaluation of this large-scale organization development program seemed important for a number of reasons:

. . . Corporate managements have had trouble in transferring behavioral science concepts into organizational action. The Sigma program represented a deliberate effort to move these concepts from the classroom into the mainstream of organization life.

The Sigma program was run by *line* managers. Even Phase #1, which introduced Managerial Grid concepts, was directed by rotating pairs of line managers. Staff experts and outside consultants played peripheral roles only. Typically, programs of this kind and scope involve considerable outside guidance and/or teaching.

Any management development program which focuses on self-introspection and self-other relationships runs some risk of psychiatric disturbances. The question was whether the Managerial Grid program at Sigma was able to avoid such problems by using exercises involving managerial styles rather than depending on the deeper exploration of personal characteristics. Altogether about 800 managers and technical men experienced Phase #1 at Sigma. These men were of varying ages and educational backgrounds. They came from all areas and levels of the organization.

The program at Sigma sought collective group changes, not just individual changes in attitudes and behavior. Most management development programs treat the individual as the learning unit. The six phases of the Grid program were explicitly aimed at group and cross-group shifts in attitudes and behavior.

Consequently, a "successful" program at Sigma might have important implications for business and the behavioral sciences alike. Sigma's experience might help answer the following questions implied in the above reasons for an outside evaluation:

> Can a program based on behavioral science concepts be translated into meaningful organization action?
> Can management take primary responsibility for such a program?
> Can important attitude and behavior changes be accomplished without their being psychologically threatening?
> Can a change of focus from the individual to the group aid collective learning and behavior change?

Measurement Problems. Given the possibility of Sigma's running a "successful" program, how were we to determine whether it was *really* successful? How was organization development to be adequately identified and measured? Such questions involve major issues in behavioral science methodology, and the answers are complex.

Put bluntly, there is no really satisfactory way of identifying and measuring organizational change and development. Too many variables are beyond control and cannot be isolated. An investigator never knows when "extraneous" factors are just as responsible for an important finding as are the "key" factors identified in his research.

Yet this complexity provides no excuse for not attempting to evaluate such programs. The important thing is to approach the project with some qualms and to apply caution. On this basis, we hope to show how different "measures" of Sigma's program furnish enough evidence for readers to piece together what happened before and during the program. These measures include productivity and profit indexes, results of opinion and attitude surveys from members of management, and evidence of behavioral changes taken from interviews and conversations.

Exhibit 2

RELEVANT OPERATING FIGURES, 1960–1963

	1960*	1961	1962	1963
Gross revenue	100	101.6	98.2	106.6
Raw material costs	100	98.8	97.2	103.2
Noncontrollable operating costs	100	97.5	101.8	104.6
Controllable operating costs	100	95.0	94.1	86.2
Net profits before taxes	100	229.0	118.0	266.0
Number of employees	100	95.5	94.1	79.5
Total production units	100	98.5	98.2	102.2

* 1960 used as a base year, since it was the first year that Sigma's records could be compared with post-merger years. . . .

None of these indexes is satisfactory by itself, and even when used jointly, they require cautious application. Each finding can only be treated as a piece in the over-all puzzle. It is the consistency and direction of the many different findings which lead us to believe that something important was happening at the Sigma plant. . . .

Significant Changes

Phase #1 of Sigma's organization development program began in November 1962 with 40 managers participating in a one-week Managerial Grid Seminar. This phase continued until the summer of 1963, by which time 800 managers and technical men had completed it. Meanwhile, the earlier participants began to embark on later phases of the organization development program. . . .

Productivity and Profits. There were significant increases in productivity and profits during 1963, when the organization development program was in effect. Exhibit 2 indicates that total production rose somewhat (with fewer employees), and profits more than doubled. . . .

Exhibit 3

PRODUCTIVITY AND CONTROLLABLE COSTS, 1960–1963

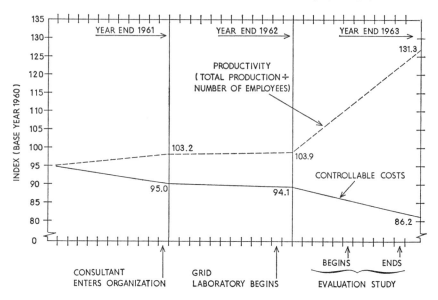

Exhibit 3 shows how these productivity and controllable cost measures for 1963 compared with previous years. (Productivity, in this case,
is represented by dividing the number of employees for each year into
the number of total production units.) The only really comparable year
in terms of profit increase, according to Exhibit 2, was 1961. However,
the profit increase in 1961 was due more to factors outside of the Sigma
management's control than in 1963. Exhibit 3 shows that the 1961
increase in productivity and decrease in controllable costs were very
small compared with 1963. Most impressive, Exhibit 3 shows that the
productivity index per employee increased from a high in 1962 of 103.9
to a new high of 131.3 in 1963 without the aid of substantial invest-
ments in plant and equipment. . . .

Practices and Behavior. Because the research was begun after the
beginning of Sigma's organization development program, we have only
a few accurate indexes of changes in practices and behavior. However,
the ones available are important indicators of the changes taking place
in the plant. They include:

> Increased frequency of meetings.
> Changing criteria for management appraisals.
> Increased transfers within the plant and to other parts of the organiza-
> tion. . . .

Attitudes and Values. The anonymous survey questionnaires asked each manager to report on his views of organizational relationships during the fall of 1963 as compared with a year earlier. Exhibit 4 shows that improvements had occurred in boss-subordinate relationships, within departments, and between work groups. Perceived improvement was highest in intergroup and interdepartmental relationships, although impressively high in the other areas too. Improvement was again seen as higher in administrative-line than in technical-staff areas. . . .

Exhibit 4

CHANGES IN WORKING RELATIONSHIPS, 1962–1963

PER CENT OF MANAGER RESPONDENTS REPORTING IMPROVEMENT IN:

	THE WAY THEY WORK TO-GETHER WITH THEIR BOSS	THE WAY THEIR WORK GROUPS WORK TOGETHER	THE WAY THEIR WORK GROUP WORKS WITH OTHER GROUPS
A. OVER-ALL IMPROVEMENT (N=598)	49%	55%	61%
B. DEPARTMENTAL IMPROVEMENT			
MOST IMPROVEMENT			
ADMINISTRATIVE SERVICES (N=67)	59%	68%	65%
PLASTICS (N=106)	55%	60%	68%
LEAST IMPROVEMENT			
RESEARCH AND DEVELOPMENT (N=43)	36%	41%	59%
ENGINEERING (N=90)	37%	35%	55%

Some Underlying Factors

The material discussed so far suggests that Sigma's program made an important contribution to; (*a*) productivity and profits, (*b*) changes in practices and behavior, and (*c*) at least some changes in attitudes and values among managers.

Although the underlying motivation may have existed long before this program, Sigma's program seemed to provide the specific vehicles for mobilizing and directing managerial energy. Perhaps other programs or methods would have worked just as well, though, as already stated, Sigma and other Piedmont plants had earnestly engaged in a number of them without comparable results in the past. In addition, the "hands-off" policy of the new headquarters group had not gained widespread improvement at Sigma any more than the more directive line taken by the previous headquarters group had. Furthermore, the plant manager's early managerial toughness had gained resistance as well as slow results.

Therefore, what were the causal factors in and around the organization development program that permitted it to make a contribution to Sigma's improved position? To examine these (and to gain even further understanding of the program's influence), we turn our attention next to a review of evidence and opinion that describes the underlying factors which seem crucial to Sigma's program and its contributions.

Headquarters Role. Earlier, we described the events which led Piedmont to exert pressures on the Sigma plant management for improved performance. In some respects, the pressures may have been overly subtle. Sigma's management did not fully appreciate just how important certain issues were to headquarters until these issues emerged in open discussion. This occurred for the first time during the three-day meeting suggested by Blake. As a result of this meeting, headquarters personnel became the source of help they sought to be, rather than the ambiguous threat they had been. At the same time, headquarters left implementation, including the organization development program, in the hands of the Sigma plant management.

The results of this new relationship seemed to satisfy headquarters management. The verdict late in 1963 was that Sigma had made considerable progress and that headquarters-plant relationships had improved. After the first year of Sigma's program, Piedmont's management expressed strong pleasure and partial surprise at Sigma's improved position.

Consultants' Contribution. At this point the work and reputation of Blake and Mouton provided the specific departure point for an organization development effort. Their prior design of the Grid Seminar and their six-phase concept of organization development represented a significant contribution, even though they themselves spent little time at the plant.

Plant Manager's Support. An early and especially important factor was the support and subsequent involvement of the plant manager. His enthusiasm became a strong stimulus and model for the rest of the plant. He remained in the middle of the program rather than on the outside where he might have guided the effort with impersonal mechanisms. More important, he made some significant modifications in his own behavior.

These changes in the plant manager's behavior could not be called major personality changes. Instead, they seemed to reflect changes in his concept of working with others on management problems. Most of the changes were consistent with behavior he had long practiced within the organization. He had a reputation for being a creator and advocate of new projects. He had always disliked being second to others. He had a profound respect for science and extended some of this respect to the behavioral sciences. Finally, he had always explained and shown his ideas to others before implementing them. During the program, the plant manager found that although the ground rules of management relationships had changed, none of them violated his basic beliefs. One of his top subordinates made the following comments:

> He has certainly taken a hard look at the way he runs his business and is trying to change. I think he is trying to involve more people and is more considerate of others. It is not so much a change, though, as it is a recognition that others once misunderstood him. I think he found that others saw him as intolerant because of his enthusiasm. I've always seen him as a pretty strong "9,9," but no one else seemed to recognize it. He has a real strong "9,1" backup theory though. I think his experience in the Managerial Grid session made him stop and think; being a real intelligent man, he's made a change. He has learned to listen and to be more patient. Also, we have learned to talk better and insist on having a say. It's a two-way street.

Top-Management Involvement. The Sigma top-management group became involved at an early date in discussions of the program. More important, they chose to become involved not only as students in the Phase #1 training but as rotating instructors for two-week periods. Our material shows this group to be among the key supporters of the program and instrumental in the follow-up projects.

Moreover, the teaching-learning role provided further evidence of the program's impact. Using questionnaire data, we derived "most improved" and "least improved" categories from weighted scores taken from subordinates' ratings of superiors' improvement. As many as 16 of the 22 "instructors" were among the 87 "most improved" bosses as evaluated by their own managerial subordinates. Only one "instructor" was included in the 35 "least improved" superiors.

This finding suggests that being an instructor in Phase #1 served to reinforce a man's understanding of 9,9 principles as well as to aid his on-the-job practice.

The 9,9 commitment of this group had apparently been strengthened by their early success in reducing manpower under delicate community and union conditions. When 9,9 problem-solving methods helped them to accomplish the difficult manpower reduction task, the top-management group became strong supporters of the organization development program.

Considering their involvement and support, what did this group look like in action? Were they now a collection of 9,9 supermen? Had each made significant changes in his behavior? These questions are important, and the answers are "no." Instead, the top-management group had agreed collectively (and continued to reinforce) a set of 9,9 ground rules among themselves. The balance was precarious, however. Two or three key individuals seemed to be most highly respected as 9,9 interpreters and proponents. Several others were "take-charge" and "task-oriented" members who still demonstrated respect for the 9,9 ground rules. Still others helped to formulate issues in nonthreatening ways. The tie that bound the group together was its shared commitment to 9,9 concepts and practices. As long as this tie held, the members seemed to feel that they could continue their pacesetting role within the organization. . . .

Learning Readiness. The factors identified above did seem to influence men at or near the top of Sigma's organization. But these factors were not sufficient to explain the diverse attitudes found among the managers. There were less-evident forces which affected each manager in the plan. One of these was the attitude of some managers which made them more ready than others to learn in the Phase #1 training and thereafter. The data suggest that on-the-job "improvement" ratings corresponded with a boss's self-evaluation *before* Phase #1 training, and his team's evaluation of him *during* Phase #1 training. (These two evaluations were done with the assistance of Grid teaching material made available to us.)

An analysis of this material shows that:

Technical managers and staff tended to rate themselves as less 9,9 *before* Phase #1 than their colleagues did *during* Phase #1 training. In other words, technical men tended to be "overrewarded" by their colleagues.

Administrative managers tended to rate themselves as more 9,9 *before* Phase #1 than their colleagues did *during* Phase #1 training. In other words, administrative men were "underrewarded" by their colleagues.

In other words, it is the administrative managers, "underrewarded" by their teams, who showed more improvement than technical managers, who were "overrewarded." Why? One explanation is that administrative managers, rating themselves as 9,9 to begin with, were given an incentive to improve by the sobering comments of their Seminar teammates. Technical managers, who tended not to see themselves as 9,9 to begin with, were given little incentive to improve because their teams told them they were "better" than they thought they were.

Reinforced Efforts. The final factor underlying the plant changes at Sigma occurred after Phase #1 training. This involved the extent to which boss and colleagues reinforced a manager's efforts to change his behavior. To show the importance of this reinforcement, we can examine its presence among the "most improved" and the "least improved" managers (according to their subordinates' weighted ratings).

Exhibit 5 shows that 77% of the 87 "most improved" managers had bosses who were also "most improved." This suggests that a man's superior is a major force in his learning and improvement, until we note that 55% of the 35 "least improved" managers *also* had bosses who were "most improved." Apparently the boss's improvement wasn't the most important reinforcing agent, although it does seem to have exerted some influence.

Exhibit 5 also shows that colleague reinforcement may have been a more important key than boss reinforcement. Of the "most improved" managers, 92% worked in settings where "most improved" colleagues outnumbered "least improved," while only 26% of the "least improved" managers worked in similar settings.

A closer analysis of these 26% "least improved" managers in "most improved" groups shows they were outnumbered by "most improved" colleagues by only a 2.55 to 1 ratio. In contrast, the 92% "most im-

Exhibit 5

RELATIONSHIP BETWEEN MANAGER IMPROVEMENT AND SUPERIOR-COLLEAGUE SUPPORT*

	Superior also rated among "most improved"	Setting where "most improved" colleagues outnumbered "least improved" colleagues
Managers rated as "most improved" (N = 87)	77%	92%
Managers rated as "least improved" (N = 35)	55%	26%

* Evaluations by subordinates.

proved" managers worked in settings were "most" outnumbered "least" by a ratio of 3.41 to .33. This suggests that the chances for manager improvement in the eyes of subordinates were greatest when a manager worked with larger numbers of others who also sought improvement. Or put another way, possibly one "least improved" cynic was enough to dampen his fellows' enthusiasm and therefore their chances of being among the "most improved." This possibility is supported by the fact that 60% of the "most improved" managers worked in settings where there were *no* "least improved" colleagues to disillusion the 9,9 atmosphere being built.

These data suggest that Phase #1, the plant manager, and a man's boss all played secondary roles when it came to making the lessons of

Phase #1 "stick." The most important reinforcers were a manager's own colleagues who either encouraged and supported, or discouraged, his improvement efforts.

Conclusion

We can return now to the reasons for studying the Sigma program which were given at the start of Part II. To begin with, we wish to know whether the program had been successful in transferring behavioral science concepts into organizational action. Now, after reviewing the program and its consequences, even a conservative answer to this question would seem to be "yes." The program had become a part of day-to-day managerial activities at Sigma. Both in opinion and behavior, most managers endorsed the work patterns presented in the Phase #1 Grid Seminar.

A second reason for studying the Sigma program was the unusual teaching-learning role adopted by line management. The evidence shows that not only did senior line managers take the key "instructor" roles during Phase #1, but they later stood out as among the "most improved" managers in the eyes of their subordinates. It seems likely that the "instructor" roles helped to reinforce their attempted 9,9 behavior back on the job.

With regard to psychiatric difficulties, which was another concern in studying the Sigma program, there was, to the best of our knowledge, no evidence of any such issue among the 800 men who participated in the program. This suggests that the Phase #1 Grid training was relatively "safe" in this company setting because of its emphasis on managerial styles rather than on personal introspection.

The final reason given for studying the Sigma program involved the question of groups as units of learning versus individuals. As we have seen, learning (improvement in the eyes of subordinates) was greatest when supported strongly by colleague values and norms. Where this reinforcement was weak or not present, managers were far more likely to be evaluated as among the "least improved" by their own subordinates. Consequently, colleague groups apparently were crucial in helping individual learning become organization development.

The chances are fairly strong that this crucial factor has been missing in countless would-be organization development programs—including previous efforts within Sigma and Piedmont. In all of these cases, the supporting groundwork of shared values was most likely neglected or made too abstract to be implemented.

Management Implications. The lessons from this study also involve a number of implications for businessmen. Initially, it *does* appear that behavioral science and human relations education can assist with large-scale organization development under certain conditions. These conditions, as suggested by our data, include:

Demanding but tolerant headquarters.

An enthusiastic and involved top-manager and senior management group.

Educational strategy that effectively and continuously builds team problem solving and mutual support into work-related issues.

An organization whose work requires some interdependent effort and common values.

This study suggests that managerial and team effectiveness *can* be taught by managers with outside assistance. Furthermore, it appears that this type of educational strategy can help to make significant contributions to organizational effectiveness. This in itself seems to be an important lesson for management to recognize and use in its future efforts to build stronger organizations.

7. CHANGES IN INSTITUTIONS AND THE ROLE OF THE CHANGE AGENT

Kenneth D. Benne

1. A Way of Analyzing Change in Institutionalized Behavior[1]

Over time, no institution or organization is exempt from change. In our century a student returning ten, or even five, years after graduation to the school which he had attended, probably finds changes not only in pupil, teacher, and administrative personnel but in teaching practice, pupil-teacher relationships, administrator-teacher relationships, methods of enforcing discipline, official definition of the behaviors which constitute discipline problems, etc. And the same will probably be true for an executive returning to the industry or business where he once worked, the nurse returning to her old hospital, the social worker to his or her agency, etc.

It is relatively easy thus to identify changes in institutionalized patterns of behavior after they have occurred. It is quite a different matter, and a more difficult one, to analyze changes while they are going on. It is an even more difficult task to predict potential changes before they happen and to influence significantly the direction and tempo of processes of change while they are under way. Yet, more and more, the "management function" in organizations requires this sort of conscious provision of impending changes and deliberate efforts to shape these changes according to some criteria of worse or better, of retrogression or progress. The deliberate planning of change has become part of the responsibility of "management" in all contemporary institutions, whether the task of the institution is defined in terms of health, education, social welfare, industrial production, propagation of religious doctrine, or practice of whatnot—in hospitals, schools, social agencies, factories, churches, etc.

Whatever other equipment "managers" require in analyzing change potentialities and in planning and directing change in institutional settings, they need some conceptual scheme for thinking about change. This need for a conceptual scheme stems from the confusing variety of specific behaviors, feelings, and attitudes which accompany any actual

---

[1] Part 1 has been adapted from a statement by Kenneth Benne and Max Birnbaum proposed for use in the Boston University Summer Workshop in the Improvement of Human Relations.

process of change and which appear as "data" and "symptoms" for the "manager" who confronts a particular situation requiring change.

One useful scheme for thinking about change has been proposed by Kurt Lewin. Lewin looked upon a level or phase of behavior within an institutional setting not as a static "habit" or "custom" but as a dynamic balance of forces working in opposite directions within the social-psychological space of the institution. Take, for example, the production level of work teams in a factory. This level fluctuates within small limits around x units of production per day. Why does this patterned level persist through time? Because, Lewin states, the forces tending to raise the level of production are equal to the forces tending to depress it. Among the forces tending to raise the level of production might be: (a) the various pressures of supervisors on the work team to produce more, (b) the desire of at least some team members to attract favorable attention from supervisors in order to get ahead individually, (c) the desire of team members to earn more under the incentive plan of the plant, etc. Such forces Lewin called "driving forces." Among the forces tending to lower the level of production may be: (z) a group standard in the work team against "rate busting" or "eager beavering" by individual workers, (y) resistance by the team members toward accepting training and supervision from managements, (x) feelings by workers that the product they are producing is not very important, etc. Such forces are "restraining forces." The balance between these sets of forces which determines the established level of production Lewin called a "quasi-stationary equilibrium." We may diagram this equilibrium as shown in Exhibit 1.

Exhibit 1

FORCE FIELD DIAGRAM

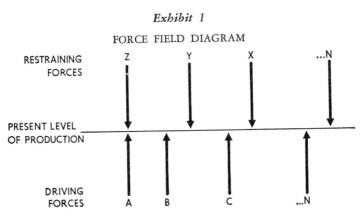

According to Lewin, this same type of thinking about patterns of institutionalized behavior applies not only to levels of production in industry but to such various equilibriums as levels of discrimination in communities, democratic or autocratic ways of working in organizations, supervisor-teacher relationships in school systems, working relationships among levels of a hospital or other organization, etc.

According to this way of looking at patterned behavior, how does change in it take place? Change occurs when an imbalance occurs between the sum of restraining forces and the sum of driving forces. Such imbalance unfreezes the pattern and the level changes until the opposing forces are again brought into equilibrium. An imbalance may occur through (1) a change in the magnitude of any force, (2) a change in the direction of a force, or (3) the addition of a new force. Let us look at examples, relevant to our original illustration, of each of these ways of unfreezing a situation.

1. Suppose that the members of the work team join a new union. The union, in pressing for shifts in over-all wage policy, increases the suspicion of workers toward the motives of management, including supervisors. This may tend to increase restraining force y. The equilibrium will be unfrozen, and the level of production will move down, unless increases in driving forces also occur. In this case, as the level of production falls, supervisors will tend to increase their pressures toward greater production—driving force a will tend to increase. This release of increased counterforce will tend to bring the system into balance again somewhere near the previous level. But the increase in magnitude of these opposed forces may increase the tension and stress under which people work, even though the level of production does not go down very much. The situation, under such conditions, becomes more psychologically explosive, less stable and predictable, less amenable to rational control.

2. A war situation demanding more and more of the product which the work team is producing may convert restraining force y—a feeling that they are not producing anything important—into a feeling that they are doing important work and that they are not working hard enough, provided they are committed to the war effort. The level of production will almost certainly rise as the direction of force y is reversed, to bring the behavior pattern back into a state of equilibrium at a new level of production.

3. Suppose a new driving force, d, is added in the shape of a supervisor who wins the trust and respect of the working team. The new force is motivation on the part of the working team to make the well-liked supervisor look good in relation to his colleagues and superiors—at least to keep him from looking bad. This force may operate to offset in part a generally unfavorable attitude toward management. Or the work team, through participation in setting its own standards of production may significantly reduce restraining force z.

These examples suggest that change, according to this view, takes the form of unfreezing an existing equilibrium, movement toward a new equilibrium, and refreezing of the new achieved equilibrium. Planned change must manipulate situational forces to accomplish unfreezing, to direct the movement in generally desirable directions, and to rearrange the situations so that the system does not backslide to its old level but maintains the new change.

This discussion also suggests that there are three major strategies for achieving change in any given pattern of behavior: (1) increase the driving forces, (2) decrease the restraining forces, and (3) a combination of the two. In general, if strategy *a* is adopted, the tendency is to increase the tension level in the system, since restraining forces are not reduced and may be correspondingly increased under pressure to change. A higher tension level means more instability and unpredictability in the situation and the likelihood of irrational rather than rational responses to the change attempt.

Everyone knows that a change in an organization is often followed by a reaction toward the old pattern after the pressures toward change are relaxed. A hospital or school system, after a survey, puts into effect some of the survey recommendations for improvements under pressure from the board and/or superintendent. When they relax their vigilance, the old patterns creep back in. This raises the problem of how to maintain a desirable change once accomplished, how to refreeze the institutional pattern at a new level. Some examples of ways backsliding may occur are appropriate here. Those affected by the change may not have participated enough in planning to have fully internalized the change which those in authority are seeking to induce. When the pressure of authority is relaxed, there is no pressure from those lower down to maintain the change. Again, the change in a part of the institution may not have been accompanied by enough co-relative changes in overlapping parts of the system to maintain the temporary change in the part, etc.

2. The Change Agent

As change has become more and more a normal expectation in contemporary societies, under the impact of such developments as scientific research, technological development, and intercultural mixing, roles have developed in the society with the expected functions of stimulating, guiding, and stabilizing changes in certain ranges of behavior. Trainer, supervisor, therapist, social worker, manager, community organizer, consultants of various sorts suggest themselves as examples of such social roles. And older roles like those of teacher, rabbi, priest, and preacher have come to incorporate responsibilities for planned change into their more traditional job descriptions.

The name "change agent" may be applied to all of these roles where the person filling the role has as part of his work the stimulation, guidance, and stabilization of changed behavior, whether the social unit which serves as "client system" to the change agent is a person, a small group, an organization, a local community, or some larger social system. The emphasis of the change agent is upon planned or deliberate intervention into the processes of change under way in and around the client system to influence the direction, tempo, and quality of the change which takes place.

Up to now, the change agent has been identified with various professional roles, but laymen and volunteers also may and do function as change agents. In fact, processes of change in voluntary associations and in communities in America are just as often, if not more often, "engineered" by laymen and volunteers rather than professionals.

And the change agent may be a group or team, rather than an individual. As a matter of fact, with increasing specialization of knowledge and skills in our society, the services of a change agent team are more often required in complex processes of rehabilitation or reform than the helping effects of an individual change agent acting alone.

3. Phases in the Process of Planned Change

When we look at change process from the standpoint of the knowledges, sensitivities, and skills required by a change agent, the simple change sequence of unfreezing, movement, and refreezing can be usefully expanded into a more complex set of phases. Eight phases are recognized here.[2]

1. *Diagnosis of the Problem of the Client System.* What is the trouble and what seems to be causing the trouble?
2. *Assessment of the Motivation and Capacity of the Client System to Change Itself.* What are the readinesses and resistances to various possibilities of change within the client system?
3. *Assessment of the Motivations and Resources of the Change Agent.* Why does the change agent want to help the client, and what are

---

[2] This analysis draws on the analysis of change agent skills made by the National Training Laboratory staff in the report of its 1947 laboratory session and upon R. Lippitt, J. Watson, and B. Westley in their book, *The Dynamics of Planned Change* (New York: Harcourt, Brace & Co., Inc., 1958).

the practical, ethical, psychological, sociological, and other limits of his ability to give help to a particular client system?

4. *Selecting Appropriate Change Objectives and Targets.* Of all the possibilities of change, which are most important and within the power of the client to accomplish; and which is, all things considered, the best first step to take in an experimental attempt to change?

5. *Choosing the Appropriate Type of Helping Role.* Shall the change agent mediate or counsel? Demonstrate or encourage? Represent some wider reality to the client system or support the client in its or his peculiar view of reality?

6. *Establishing and Maintaining a Working Relationship with the Client System.* How to get a mutually acceptable and commonly understood picture of the responsibilities of the change agent and of the client in the client's efforts to solve its (or his) own problem.

7. *Termination (or New Continuity) of Helping Relationship.* When and how does the change agent pull out and leave the client on his own?

8. *Choosing Appropriate Specific Behaviors and Techniques for Giving Help.*

These are phases, not chronological steps or stages, of a helping process. Phases 1, 2, and 3, for example, may come up again and again for reconsideration during a process of consultation, supervision, or training. And so with all the others, except perhaps Phase 7, the termination of the relationship.

4. Importance of the Diagnostic Phases of Helping with Change

The first three phases of helping with change are diagnostic phases. They involve assessment of the state of the client system with respect to its stresses and strains (actual or potential problems), its motivation and power to reduce these stresses and strains (what aspects of the client system can and should be exposed or unfrozen), the motivations and capacities of the change agent (what his or its own stresses and strains are, what he wishes to accomplish through a helping relation with this client, what his limitations and resources are relative to this client and this client's needs). And what about the compatibility or incompatibility of change agent and client motivations, expectations, and value systems?

To accomplish an adequate diagnosis, data are needed. Some of these data are observations of present state; others are observations about how the client responds to probing and interaction relative to change possibilities; still others are feelings, hunches, and aspiration. These data must be amassed by change agent and client; but they must also be sorted, interpreted, and evaluated into a decision about whether to establish a change relationship and if so, where and how to begin in the process of changing.

There are arts of such diagnosis which can be developed only through evaluated practice and experience. But there are concepts and ideas which may help to guide the processes of data collection and interpretation. The scheme of force field analysis already presented is useful at this point. Only a few illustrations can be given here of this usefulness. Change in behavior can occur only if the balance of forces affecting a given behavior can be disturbed or upset. Points of stress between opposing forces are thus potential starting points in change. But which of the points of strain are at present so "full of dynamite" that the client cannot talk or think about them rationally? And which, while presenting difficulties, can be openly faced, probed, and dealt with by the client system? The most stressful points in the client system are thus not necessarily the best starting points for change. Which points of stress, if handled adequately, would open up others to examination and resolution? Which are dead ends?

How accessible to manipulation are various important factors affecting the present pattern of behavior which may be located during the diagnosis? Accessible to the client group and accessible to the change agent? This is a question both of the position and status of the change agent and client relative to forces which might be manipulated in bringing about change and of the abilities and competences of both to provide the resources required by the problem.

These questions suggest the kinds of queries which a change agent might well put to himself as he examines and probes a change situation, and which he attempts to help the client ask and answer in the course of defining the problems on which constructive efforts are to be concentrated.

One additional comment on Phase 3 may be useful in conclusion. Why should the change agent be aware of his own motivations in seeking to help a client? First, because a realistic and mutually acceptable relationship between change agent and client is hard to achieve if the change agent is "kidding" himself about his motivations in offering or providing help. The danger to such a relationship is not so much the fact that the change agent has personal needs which he seeks to satisfy in helping others—this is always true—but that, being unaware of or denying these needs, he cannot realize and build the trust and confidence in his integrity on the part of the client which an adequate helping relationship requires. Second, a change agent cannot achieve "objectivity" in his own assessment of a client's situation or in supporting efforts by the client system to achieve "objectivity" toward its own plight if his perceptions are clouded and distorted by personal motivations and needs of which he is unaware. Awareness of his own motivations is an important prerequisite to a change agent's stimulation of similar awareness in a client.

8. A PRESIDENT'S EXPERIENCE WITH DEMOCRATIC MANAGEMENT*

James E. Richard

THE THEME proposed for my remarks today is the idea of "democracy applied in industry." My first thought was to object somewhat to this use of the word "democracy." However, my second thought was to welcome it as giving me an opportunity to make a point.

I believe that businessmen can validly object to the term "democracy in industry." In a country where private ownership of capital is the legal and practicing tradition, it can be misleading to speak of applying democracy in industry. In the political sense, we think of democracy as being a method of representation, in which the power of control ultimately rests in the hands of the electorate. Now can employees control? Of course, if stockholders happened to be employed in the company, some measure of control would rest with the employees. But if not, and if stockholders are to protect their equity, it surely seems to follow that it is *not* their function to put ultimate control into the hands of employees, who do not have ownership responsibilities.

In this sense of ultimate power of control, the view might well be defended that we have the very opposite of democratic conditions in business. Because we hold *being* democratic a value, we tend to overlook this very real, built-in limit upon democratic processes in business.

A Dilemma for Managers

With this clarification, I go on to my major point. Today we *are* concerned with 20th century man's need to find and express himself as a particular individual in an increasingly organized and impersonal society. Ours is predominantly an industrial society, dominated by the fact of organization. So we feel an urgent need to solve the problem of the individual person in his conflict with the constrictions of formal structure.

This results in a true dilemma for managers. On the one hand, we have the force for logic, order, and control, and on the other, the need for the freely responsive, the creative, and the impulse for change.

---

* James E. Richard is president of the Red Jacket Manufacturing Co. of Davenport, Iowa. This paper appeared as No. 18 of a series of occasional papers published by the A. G. Bush Library of Management, Organization, and Industrial Relations, University of Chicago. Reprinted by permission.

In industry, the most immediate necessity is for logical planning, doing, and controlling. The realities of the market place demand competitively effective planning and control as a naked necessity for survival. But in a larger sense, we need the productivity and creativity of people more than ever before. There is the real question of whether our traditional practices of organization are not serving to limit and defeat the very quality of human creativity to which we aspire.

There certainly is a compelling need for logic and order, for standardization and conformity to standards. These methods have made industry exceedingly productive. And yet our ideas of organizational structure, job simplification, incentives, and employee relations, as well as our control systems, require, and tend to develop, submissive, dependent performance. Sometimes active or passive revolt is generated. More often an appalling measure of unhealthy dullness is the result.

Besides the practical management difficulties we experience, our sense of ethical and social concern is deeply distressed by the problem of the individual subordinated to the organization. I assume that it is *not* simple acquiescent, conforming, or apathetic performance we would like to see, but a lively interest and sense of excellence.

It would be absurd to deplore organization as "bad" since it is a necessity. And yet we are faced with the problem of reconciling the pressures for logic, system, order, and control with the irrepressible needs for latitude, self-expression, personal identity, and creativity.

Early Experiments

In our company some years ago, we became interested in this problem, and we set out to try some experiments. From experience and by trial and error, we discovered some things that worked for us. And perhaps more important, by making mistakes we found some things that didn't work.

Our first experiment was to try to develop something in the nature of "participation" or "communication" from the bottom up. We created what we called "forums," which we held regularly on paid company time. These were conducted by top management or staff men, and we talked about company matters. We explained programs, invited comments and questions, and dealt with some controversial shop questions. We also wrote informational letters to the employees. We had open houses for the families, and the executives went out into the plant and encouraged workers to express their views. We worked hard at all this. And we did have considerable success in helping the men and women in the plant to get more representation of their needs and interests. But we unwittingly put the foremen and much of the management in a tough spot.

It seems easy to see now, looking back, but it wasn't so easy to see then. While we were *helping* the men and women in the shop, we were putting great *pressure* on the foremen and management. This hadn't been our intention. In our eager desire to alleviate our sense that workers were so completely at the bottom, we came up with an undesirable result.

Here I might make an observation. In this matter of manipulating people, of which we, as managers, are so frequently accused, I have noticed that much of our manipulation is unconscious and unintentional. This, of course, doesn't excuse it and perhaps makes it worse. But we sometimes achieve a freer situation in one place only at the expense of someone somewhere else. This is why we need to keep trying to find better ways of becoming aware of the consequences of our management actions or inactions. The true results are not always easy to foresee and not always what we hoped for.

Focussing on Supervision

Our next step was to take a much keener look at the predicament of supervision, of the foremen and staff men running the plant. We realized more than we had what a difficult situation the shop foreman is in, with the pressures from the top, the controls, the limiting circumstances in which he has to work, the production schedules, and the costs he has to stick to. And yet countering these, he has the pressures from the men with all their needs and interests. His task of trying to bring together in some kind of effective way the interests and needs of the men and women in the shop with the objectives of management is considerable.

Our efforts to work things from the bottom up, with their mixture of success and undesirable consequences, made it clear that in providing a freer atmosphere for people in the organization, there is a very considerable distance from the point of being concerned about this problem to the point of taking action on it. We saw, for one thing, that to install a "participation system" or a "communication system" of one kind or another is just as bad, perhaps even worse, than installing arbitrary, top-down pressure. To insist that people participate when there may be built-in factors that make participation contrived can be manipulative, and not even as straightforward as autocratic methods.

We developed an hypothesis that went something like this. The more centralized and dominant the leadership pattern of an organization, the more rigid the organizational structure. The more rigid the organizational structure, the more imposing must be the control. When dominance and rigidity are enforced, acquiescence is required. Acquiescence spawns dependence. To the degree that people are required to be dependent, their freedom to apply ingenuity and creativity to their work is reduced. Therefore, a centralized, dominant, controlling leadership and organizational pattern tends to reduce the usefulness of employees as living, thinking, creative people.

When we recognized our bottoms-up effort for what it was, we drew back from the unnatural interference of top management's going directly to the bottom of the organization. Instead we tried to provide a freer, less controlling situation for supervision. We attempted to put as much of the decision-making, policy-making, and actual operating responsibility as we possibly could into the hands of the foremen and staff group.

The traditional role of the superintendent was radically altered. He concentrated on placing as much authority as he possibly could into the hands of supervision, as much as they could and would take. A really extensive use of consultative, collaborative practices was developed. This process, in fact, developed very far in the course of three or four years. The superintendent became so successful at it that he actually became more a part of the group than a controlling authority over it. Much of what would have been traditional controlling authority was successfully distributed to the group itself.

Our Positive Results

The positive effects of this were remarkable and richly rewarding. The foremen and staff men changed from passive, dependent, and acquiescent men to men who were effective, self-starting, responsible, and deeply involved. They shifted their anxious upward focus to a much more responsible attitude toward each other and toward the men and women in the plant. They developed some interesting methods of organizing themselves. They utilized the superintendent's office, which was a large working conference room, to handle their agenda in a unique way. They used a large chart pad on his wall, and maintained a completely open and accessible agenda, of which they as a group kept control.

They had previously been fed to the gills with the management literature about the conference leader—how he shuts up the noisy, brings out the reticent, and plays the whole thing like a gifted maestro. (I'll never forget the $700 we spent once for a set of little blue books, complete with conference leader's guide, and diagrams on how to arrange the chairs.) Actually, one of the best ways I know for one man to run the show is for him to seize the agenda and clutch it jealously to his breast, unfolding it, scrap by scrap. So when we say that our factory supervision as a group took over control of their own agenda we're describing an unusual process. It is not a simple process. But when understood and done well, it can be a most efficient method.

In most cases in an operating group, there is a live agenda. But knowing what it truly is, who has it, and what allotment of time and treatment it should have takes real attention. Without claiming this to be universally true, I feel a group can draw up an agenda much more wisely than a single person.

In the course of time, this development among our plant supervisory group became extremely mature. And when the day came for the superintendent to leave his job for another, some unusual methods seemed called for to replace him. After some perplexity, this matter was resolved by the group members themselves selecting—in this case from among themselves—the man to succeed the department superintendent. That was about four years ago. The group still remains effectively intact, and more than ever it effectively utilizes its methods of collaboration and self-control.

Some Problems

However, all did not end without problems for us. The first-felt ramifications were with our executive management. This whole development carried threatening implications for them. It raised such questions as: "Can managers really give up control? Should they give up control? Do people *want* more leeway? Should they have it? Will they really take it? Can they be trusted? Are they competent?" Many of these questions were answered by the responsible and disciplined performance of the foremen and the factory management staff. But some more gnawing questions were present for executives. "Isn't the manager paid more because he knows more or contributes more? Can a manager *afford* to give up control? How will he get ahead if he can't demonstrate some superiority of contribution or knowledge?"

In addition, there was the fact that some men get real satisfaction from manipulating, controlling, and guiding people. For some men there is challenge and excitement in the game of company politics. This game is looked upon as the way to get ahead. And to some, business is business, and people are paid to perform—everything else is nonsense. Sentiments like this are very common. And the whole traditional program of management rewards and status is constructed to reinforce this set of attitudes and motivations. Ours was no exception.

Thus, our well-intentioned interest in the improvement of our factory management group was welcome to them, who had nothing to lose and everything to gain, but far from welcome to the higher executive men. Some of the executives had arrived at their positions by virtue of years of energetic and intelligent response to a top-centered set of leadership values. These values were quite different from the values that seemed implicit in the position taken by the plant superintendent. (This is not to say that they did not *agree* with some of the objectives and benefits of the process.)

We tackled these natural questions. We worked on them, talked about them, and thought about them. This led us to a further question, "How can the bottling up of ideas and energy be overcome?" Granted the price paid by persons pitted against each other; granted the cost when men climb over each other in self-centered aspirations; granted also the deadly pressure of boredom, disinterest, cynicism. But *must* an executive and a natural leader become a faceless quantity and reduce himself in the interests of greater expressiveness for a lot of other people?

Freeing the Manager

We worked on all of these questions. We conceived that a primary function of leadership in an organization is to provide the conditions under which people can have the maximum freedom to be responsible, interdependent, and self-controlled. Instead of acting in such a way as to reduce this freedom, the manager should have the prime responsibility for the over-all vitality and health of the organization, and should be rewarded accordingly. We felt that the traditionally prime function of motivating, goading, and controlling might become a secondary function, and might conceivably, in a free organization, even disappear. We felt that if a manager did not have to be the sole judge, the evaluator, the prime controller of people in the organization, these functions might eventually be provided for in other ways. This might then free him to be creative *with* the organization rather than *for* it.

For a long time, these notions were purely hypothetical. It did seem that there might be some significant differences between the circumstances of the higher executive group and the foreman-level supervisory group. One expression of this was a tendency among the executives to be more reserved in their inter-personal relations. Perhaps they felt more responsibility for harmony. At any rate, the foremen seemed more capable of hot and direct dispute with each other. On the executive level, there was a great deal of politeness but sometimes a rather surprising lack of real exchange.

To some of the executives, the foremen seemed to be going through an undue amount of talk, and things often seemed disorganized and chaotic. Conversely, to the foremen it seemed that upper executives weren't leveling with each other, were competing, and under the surface were pulling against each other. We began to learn that some men find anything but a surface relationship very difficult. Dealing with strong feelings seems painful to them.

One natural way of dealing with these problems is the use of authority from above, or of corridor manipulations against cohorts and those below. For men of this bent, being in a situation where personal effectiveness may depend upon a high degree of exchange with others can be terribly difficult. In fact, this was so important that over a number of years the make-up of our management organization gradually changed. Managerial capacity for more than a surface relationship began to be important. With the retirement of some of the older men who were accustomed to a more inhibited way of working with each other, young men came in who had a greater capacity for informal directness. Gradually throughout the management, there developed the capacity for group processes based on a sense of informality and open exchange.

Developing Group Action

We grew a long way from the days of the conference leader guide, and more and more dropped controlling and restrictive techniques. We also learned how to differ constructively. We began to discover that there are different kinds of groups and group relationships, with different purposes and circumstances. At one early point, we moved to the other extreme, and went to the totally unstructured group. I smile now to remember some of the hours we spent trying to discover what we were meeting about when we first became acquainted with group-centered methods. I believe some of the older men who retired from the company about then still believe we spend most of our time in a room together trying to figure out why we are there and what to do.

However, out of all this came a very strong feeling that we liked informality. We gradually began not to want formal organization nor many, if any, permanent committees. Instead we began to depend upon the initiative of individuals or combinations of individuals to form groups as problems arose, to include any one who had an interest in the problem, and to disband whenever the problem was solved.

We found that the main requisite for this kind of natural responsiveness to situations was a climate in which people felt really involved, responsible, and interested, and where men felt self-confident, secure, and open. This kind of atmosphere really works when it exists, but much organizational growth must take place before the condition exists. Creating such an atmosphere takes time, and we found that it must mushroom slowly throughout the organization. It probably began at the top.

We became less and less inclined to try to "teach" development to people. We came to feel that when "taught," personal growth and development are somewhat like an old-fashioned mustard-plaster. It sometimes sticks to the skin and keeps in some heat, but it doesn't have any effect on the inside.

Organizational Changes

We began to depend more and more on face-to-face experience and on living together. We began to stake out responsibilities for each other, but we didn't like formal or rigidly described functions. We came to feel that functions are really quite clearly discernible on a commonsense basis, and that the important thing is to develop skill at recognizing and handling areas of overlapping interests together. About the only place anything resembling an organization chart concerns us now is when some of us get together over a problem and need to set up the running plays and signals. We scarcely ever get into any of the old wrangles about whose right and responsibility it is to carry the ball. We simply have the occasional question of who does have the ball and who is blocking.

Thus we feel that we have evolved an over-all management that functions in some significantly different ways from our pattern of years ago. Our management really does extend from president to foreman, and we have made some real efforts to shift the emphasis of power. Operating control has been significantly diffused from a few to many. The positive results have clearly been to relieve men of a cog-like feeling and a sense of dependency. Direct, open, straightforward relationships have become natural. Interestingly enough these include the capacity for open, direct differences, sometimes hot and heavy. We try to specialize in bringing differences into the open so that we can work them through. I believe we have developed a more mature capacity for simple live-and-let-live, based on a fundamental interest in deeper relationships.

The relevant point, to me, is that this is not a system. It is, in fact, the opposite of logically conceived and constructed organization. It is a *process* of direct, living relationships which cannot be synthesized but must be grown from the distinctively human joys and pains of life.

Difficulties and Drawbacks

Accompanying our present stage of organization are some difficulties too. Reduction of centralized power and control frustrates some of the company's outside connections. Some customers, suppliers, and members of the public need to have simple points of contact which are dependable and quickly responsive. For instance, there was the letter from the marketing man of a major supplier, who wrote, "I have lost my point of contact; please tell me if I am taking my problem to the right place in your organization." And there was the salesman of another, large, aggressive supplier who was indignant, seemed to feel almost cheated, that he couldn't play purchasing, engineering, and sales off against each other, and that his divisional manager's effort to go "higher" was unfruitful. For in our company, purchasing, engineering, and marketing have close ties.

A second kind of problem is long-range planning. In the early stages of planning, we have not found a way to be very inclusive. Planning to some degree seems a special function of a few who have fewer operating responsibilities, and this tends to force structure into the organization.

Third, there is the fact that many people in the organization are deeply accustomed to a controlling, directing atmosphere. There are those who actually do need the concrete structure of organization in order to function. I'll never forget the day the switchboard operator exploded, "What this place needs is a Boss!" But much more serious were the several instances of men in management who were unable to handle themselves without stern control, or who misinterpreted warmth and personal concern from cohorts. As we attempted to reduce the lines of controlling authority and put men more on their own, some transferred their dependence to cohorts for discipline or control. We have had some unhappy experiences which seem to have demonstrated that this kind of atmosphere really requires a pretty mature capacity for contribution and self-control. It can throw dependent persons into conflict.

And, finally, there is the very complicated but relevant question,

"Can this approach extend beyond management? If so, how?" Granted that throughout management, a broad latitude of freedom and individual responsibility can be developed and people learn how to function on an inter-dependent basis, what becomes of the people further down in the organization? As things traditionally stand, people are narrowly limited by the work processes and by systems at the worker and clerical levels. Can order and control be relaxed further downward?

We are on the edge of these questions now. We shall probably keep trying. We find it reassuring to look backward and see that we have come, according to our lights, some way forward, despite several rather startling mistakes.

Summary

In summary, I observe that to refer to "democracy" in industry can be a misnomer. The total business situation is exceedingly complex, and subject to many pressures and limitations. There are many real and practical limits in business which force us to discard perfectly good value-questions as being ill-advised or inapplicable at our present state of knowledge.

However, I believe it is practical and relevant to attempt a conceptual framework from which to derive practical applications in daily management and I believe that it is pertinent and sound for us, as managers, to concern ourselves with man's eternal struggle within himself to be free and yet to be ordered. I believe it is of special importance for us in management to attempt to rescue talented individuals from the lowered aspirations, the boredom, and the habits of mediocrity so often induced by life in an organization. I believe we should become painfully aware that we have established organizational settings in which order, harmony, and predictability have been given more emphasis than individual achievement and excellence. I believe that business management must continue to try to develop a process of life that strives for meaning and purpose, having as our goal the climate which permits every person to serve the values that have nurtured him, with the freedom of the mature and the responsible.

Question-and-Answer Period

Q. *How long have you been working at this orbit?*
A. I think about six years.
Q. *How have you done financially?*
A. We're making money. We're moderately profitable. It's a good question. I think that we have not done this at the expense of

hard-headed business. But I'm not sure that one can say that this method helps you make more money, nor that it's done at the expense of the balance sheet.

Q. *Your place in the field hasn't changed materially?*

A. No, but we have great hopes for our place in the field.

Q. *How do you resolve basic problems between two members of this management?*

A. I think the simple answer is that we try to talk it out.

Q. *Is there any final say-so? Does somebody step in and say, "Joe, we're going to do it this way"? And Joe has to buckle down?*

A. Sure. I'll get academic for a minute and say that I think Mary Parker Follett said a very wise thing, I guess twenty or thirty years ago: that there are three basic ways to resolve human conflict. One is by dominance, in which somebody loses and somebody wins. The second is by negotiation, in which somebody gives a little and gains a little and somebody else also gives a little and gains a little. Finally, there's resolution by integration, in which nobody loses, and everybody comes out better together. We shoot for integration, if we can, recognizing this to be an ideal. We recognize that sometimes negotiation is necessary, and sometimes dominance. Sometimes we have to pinpoint who's in charge so he can make a decision.

But commenting on this further, I personally took an interest one time in this question, and Bob Burns led me to a part of The University of Chicago called the Counseling Center where they were concerned with counseling and psychotherapy. We took a great interest in the process of counseling. Actually there are several processes of counseling. We were interested in the client-centered school. This is where there is lots of emphasis on listening of a particularly unevaluative kind. We practiced and worked, and made some horrible errors in attempting to listen. But out of this came a kind of operating notion which we have been able to adapt and use for ourselves, and it's the thought that when a person is in conflict with himself, or when two persons are in conflict with each other, another presence, of a noninterfering but really interested kind, can be helpful.

Q. *Does this give some release to the manipulative instincts of your higher level management when they're called on to resolve these differences by this client-centered counselling?*

A. I don't know if I follow you.

Q. *Suppose you have some feeling of conflict or loss on the part of your managers. Now when they get to be expert counselors and are called upon to resolve differences, doesn't this give them a release, to be able to exercise their manipulative skills?*

A. I don't want to get out on a limb here, and suggest that we all become psychotherapists or that anybody in business become a psychotherapist. But I do make the point that there are some things we can learn from this process. The people in our place aren't trying to counsel each other in a deep sense. I think it's more relevant to say that we use an awareness of some of the things pertaining to counseling. For example, that disharmony is permissible, that a good old straightforward battle can be a healthy thing.

We found more ways of not using political indirections on each other. We gradually became more comfortable dealing with what had previously seemed taboo questions. The old habit was that if a fellow came up to you and said something critical, you tended to hear him say you were a drip. And frequently that's the way he said it. And then gradually we learned how to take emotion for granted, and accept it, and deal with it. A man can say he disagrees with you without your feeling he is labeling you a drip. But this is a long way around in responding to your question. I think that greater capacity for what I call deeper-than-skin-surface relationships can remove the necessity amoung us for manipulation. We learn how to express our strong feelings directly and how not to be upset by strong feelings in other persons.

Q. *What about the selection of personnel?*

A. This question is a very real problem. An organization that develops in this way becomes very closely knit, with a constructive capacity to deal with disharmony as well as harmony. So it's hard finding someone to walk into this atmosphere who's unused to the business of squaring off. It's hard to find the man who's developed a tolerance for direct contact. I'm inherently suspicious of projective testing and that kind of thing. For selection I don't know at the moment of tests that can tell me, in a way I can believe, how a man's going to be in action.

In finding persons for our management organization, we've done a lot of inquiring. We've looked into the possibility of appealing to social scientists for help, and to a number of psychologists who work on this kind of thing. To date, we've ended up doing it ourselves. Aware that we could be making a botch of it, we try to describe to a candidate what we're doing. We try to understand him as best we can in a number of direct interviews, and then we just take a chance. We've made some mistakes, and we've found some fellows that have worked out very well.

We've been doing the hiring together. I have friends who say this is a hell of a process. They say you compound all the errors of everybody. But I think our batting average has been good on making a very careful scrutiny of the man and having the whole organization meet him to try to figure out whether they like him and think he's competent. I think our successes have been greater than our failures.

There's the problem of selection and appraisal of new men, and then there's the problem of performance evaluation in the organization. That's another story, but I don't want to hold you all up.

Q. *Does anyone want him to go ahead and talk about it? I think he should.*

A. Well, all right. We've fired men. We've downgraded men. We've upgraded men. And we've transplanted men and reshaped functions. We've pulled some real boners. But by and large, I think we've found some effective methods.

Now this is a sophisticated process, and I'm not trying to tell myself or anyone else that it isn't. In industry we're so accustomed to not admitting that feelings are a fact. Yet feelings are as much a fact as the mixture we put in our iron. When you reach the stage where you have the capacity to accept plain, ordinary feeling and to deal with it, then you get at a lot of things that used to cause problems. Whenever it's possible to recognize that human facts are just as clearly relevant in a work situation as accountants' facts and engineers' facts, and whenever (this will be a great day) the engineers and the accountants begin to admit this too, then you reach the stage where you can really accomplish something. In such an atmosphere if a man isn't doing a job, you can talk about the fact and he can talk about it. To the extent that people in an organization can become really expressive about what they're trying to do, what they think and see and feel, performance appraisal can become a two-way integrating process rather than a top-down evaluation.

Q. *I wonder if you could tell us the effect these patterns of management have had on union-management relations?*

A. Well, we don't have a union. We haven't had one since 1947. We had the Farm Equipment Workers C.I.O. at the time and had a bad strike.

Q. *I presume they've tried to organize since? Have your methods helped withstand unionization?*

A. I don't think they have. I don't know. I'd like to say that I sure hope this line of inquiry doesn't start management thinking about it because it may appear that here's the way to keep the union off. I don't know if it does or not. But I don't think it matters whether it does or not, because I think, as Dr. Ohmann said, the union surely has a place. And one of the reasons that it's got as much place as it has is that management hasn't been in that place. Conceivably we might be able to bring this kind of give-and-take

I've been discussing into the shop and get rid of the piecework system and the methods card. If we ever arrived at the point where men in the shop have a chance to do some of the planning and get their brains to work on some of the problems, this might eliminate the need for a rigidly structured union. But I'm not so sure that management can or should ever try to assume the function of doing everything.

Indexes

Index to Cases

Al Ruskin 18
Allied Food Company 377
Alpha Company (A) 810
Alpha Company (B) 822
American Magnolite Company 482
American Radiatronics Corporation 345
Anderson Manufacturing and Development Company 211
Arthur Walton 229

Battleship "Y" 328
Beacon Publishing Company 32
Belmont-White Company 549
Ben Reed 238
Betty Randall 73

Case of the Changing Cage 124
Claremont Instrument Company 415
Cleveland Junior Chamber of Commerce 263
Crown Fastener Company, The 411

Dallas Chemical Corporation 909
Dan Weber 831
Dashman Company 16
Daycomb Company 30
Denver Transportation Company 900

Electronics Stock Control Group, The, Parts 1–5 320
Empire Glass Company 700
Excellent Insurance Company (A) 245
Excellent Insurance Company (B) 252
Excelsior Bakeries, Inc. 65

Fort Worth Pharmaceutical and Chemical Corporation 528

Gillen Radio Corporation 259
Gordon Company, The 623
Grayson Company 552

Haig Chemical Company 503
Hampton Shipyard, The 631
Harkness Machinery Company (A) 10
Harkness Machinery Company (B) 15
Higgins Equipment Company (A) 728
Higgins Equipment Company (B) 743

Jim McFee (A) 25
Jim McFee (B) 29

Kilkenny Lumber Company 144

Lewis Equipment Company 686

Markham Instrument Company 114
Marshall Company (A) 640
Marshall Company (B) 650
Marshall Company (C) 660
Marshall Company (D) 667
Marshall Company (E) 671
Marshall Company (F) 678
Marshall Company (G) 682
Maynard Aircraft 140
Merrill Manufacturing Company, Parts 1–5 388
Metropolitan Steel Company 51

Norse Electronics (A) 241
Norse Electronics (B) 243

Perkins Component Company 541

Randley Stores, Inc. (A) 870
Randley Stores, Inc. (B) 885

Slade Company, The 76
Stiles Corporation, The 383
Superior Slate Quarry 132
Supra Oil Company 848

Thermophysics Research Group, The, Parts 1–2 523
Tidewater Manufacturing Company, Parts 1–4 859
Times-Herald 89
Twin City Trust Company 610

United Diesel 473

Walt Rogers 255
White Company, The 151
Work Group Ownership of an Improved Tool 405

Yoker Company, The, Parts 1–2 855

Index to Concepts and Research Findings

Bank Wiring Observation Room, The 175

Changes in Institutions and the Role of the Change Agent 952
"Classical" Organization Theory 757
Comparative Effectiveness of Groups and Individuals in Solving Problems,
The 202
Conceptual Scheme for Describing Work Group Behavior, A 154
Conditions Influencing the Effect of Leadership Style on Group Perform-
ance 427
Conveyor Work, Interaction Potential, and Worker Satisfaction . . . 184
Criteria for Planning Organizational Change 914

Defenses and the Need to Know 266
Diagnosing Interdepartmental Conflict 582

Effect of Group Decision on Subsequent Behavior, The 933
Engineering Supervisors in the Middle 439
Experimental Change of Decision Levels and Effects on Productivity and
Satisfaction 937
Experimental Reorganizations in an Indian Textile Plant 196
Experiments in Structural Design 790

First Line Supervisors, Upward Influence, and Work Group Satisfaction . 430
Foreman: Master and Victim of Double Talk, The 434
Functional Point of View, The 41

Group Cohesiveness, Anxiety, and Productivity 193
Group Membership, Satisfaction, and Productivity 187

Influence of Technical Change on Organization Structure, The . . . 782

Management by Integration and Self-Control 792
Modes of Resolving Role Conflict 305
Motivation in Work Groups: A Tentative View 451
Motivation, Role Behavior, and Development 302

Need Hierarchy: A Theory of Motivation, The 446